encyclopedia of
religious freedom

ROUTLEDGE ENCYCLOPEDIAS OF RELIGION AND SOCIETY

David Levinson, *Series Editor*

The Encyclopedia of Millennialism and Millennial Movements

Richard A. Landes, *Editor*

The Encyclopedia of African and African-American Religions

Stephen D. Glazier, *Editor*

The Encyclopedia of Fundamentalism

Brenda E. Brasher, *Editor*

The Encyclopedia of Religious Freedom

Catharine Cookson, *Editor*

encyclopedia of
religious freedom

Catharine Cookson, Editor

Religion & Society
A Berkshire Reference Work

ROUTLEDGE
New York   London

Published in 2003 by

Routledge
29 West 35th Street
New York, NY 10001
www.routledge-ny.com

Published in Great Britain by Routledge
11 New Fetter Lane
London EC4P 4EE
www.routledge.uk.co
A Berkshire Reference Work

Routledge is an imprint of Taylor & Francis Group

10 9 8 7 6 5 4 3 2 1

Library of Congress Catalog-in-Publication Data
Encyclopedia of religious freedom / Catharine Cookson, editor.
        p. cm. – (Routledge encyclopedias of religion and society)
    "A Berkshire Reference work".
    Includes bibliographical references and index.
    ISBN 0-415-94181-4 (hardcover: alk paper)
    1. Freedom of religion–Encyclopedias. 2. Religion–
Encyclopedias.
    I. Cookson, Catharine. II. Series.
    BV741.E47 2003
    323.44′2′03—dc21
                                2003005354

Contents

Editorial Advisory Board

List of Entries

List of Entries

Introduction

Religion is a human conundrum: We have both loved and hated in the name of God, have both waged peace and inflicted torture. Governments throughout the ages have feared religion's disorderly and disparate energies, and its voice for the oppressed of every society. Yet societal law and good order depend upon the discipline and virtue of its citizenry, traits fostered by the world's religions.

The *Encyclopedia of Religious Freedom* introduces readers to the myriad interstices of religion and the state. The United States' experience with religious freedom is a main focus, but the *Encyclopedia of Religious Freedom* breaks new ground by offering insights and coverage that cross global regions and historical epochs. As the fourth volume in the *Religions and Society* series, this work is neither an encyclopedia of religions nor a legal handbook. Nor do we limit the discussion of religious freedom to the often arcane fine points of constitutional law. We also explore lived realities: Pressures on religious exercise and freedom of conscience come from the public and the press as well as the police.

This volume is being published at a time in human history when religious freedom is again a major issue and much in the news. Our articles on government support of religion, religion and public education, minority rights, and religious freedom in Islamic nations provide important historical, political, and social context for major current discussions.

Like the other volumes in the series, the *Encyclopedia of Religious Freedom* is aimed at a general audience. It reflects the efforts of scholars from around the world and from a variety of disciplines, including (but not limited to) law, religious studies, history, philosophy, theology, and political science. The authors have provided the most up-to-date information on the topics they cover; the language of the articles is clear and accessible, and references at the end of each article give readers the opportunity to pursue the topic in more depth. Volume 5 in the *Religion and Society* series, entitled *Religion and War,* is a companion volume to this volume.

Coverage

The 140 articles in this volume cover seven major elements of religious freedom: key concepts, U.S. history, world history, world religions, major issues, minority groups and their rights, and key documents.

Key Concepts

These articles cover theories, paradigms, and more general theoretical concepts or philosophical issues significant to the history, problems, and promise of religious freedom. They provide the basic introduction to the topics in the encyclopedia, with specific illustrations or applications covered in other articles. Included in this category are articles on:

Children and Religious Freedom in the United States
Civil Religion
Establishment, Equal Treatment
Establishment, Separation of Church and State
Free Exercise Clause
Free Speech Clause

Freedom of Conscience
Heresy
Human Rights
Natural Law
New Religious Movements
Outsiderhood and American Protestantism
Pluralism and Religious Identity in Lawmaking
Religion and Politics
Religion in the Courtroom
Religious Nationalism
Religious Tolerance
Sacred Space and Conflict
Secularism and Modernity
State Churches
Utilitarianism and J. S. Mill
Women, Religious Freedom, and Human Rights

U.S. History

The articles directly relevant to U.S. history cover events, concepts, eras, disputes, persecutions, ideological differences, and so forth, and the influence these have had on the realization of the ideal of religious freedom in the United States. Included here are articles on:

Constitution, Founding Era of the
French Colonies in North America
Great Awakenings and the Antebellum Period
Immigration
Law Enforcement and Religious Groups
Maryland: Colonial to Early Republic
New England: Colonial to Early Republic
New York: Colonial to Early Republic
Pennsylvania: Colonial to Early Republic
Pledge of Allegiance
Slavery
South, U.S.: Colonial to Early Republic
Spanish Colonies in North America

World History

These articles focus on religious freedom in particular periods, eras, nations, and empires and cover topics such as policies, laws, de facto treatment of minority religious groups and key individuals, documents, institutions, and events. Included are articles on:

Africa
Augustine on Religious Coercion

Balkans, East Europe, and Russia
British Empire
Byzantine Empire
Canada, Australia, New Zealand
China, Communist
China, Imperial
Church and State in Modern Europe
Convivencia
England, Early Modern
England, Victorian
English Civil War
French Revolution
Germany and Prussia
Inquisition
Islamic Empire, Medieval
Israel
Japan
Jihad
Leiden
Middle East
Pakistan
Reformation, Early Modern Europe
Roman Empire
South Africa
South America
Spanish Empire
Tibet
Turkey
United Kingdom
Witch-Hunts

World Religions

Articles on world religions focus on the religion's stand or stands on freedom of religion or conscience and on the relationship between the religion and governments, noting competing views within the tradition, and the current situation. The articles mention resources (scriptures, writings of theologians, doctrine, traditions, practices) within the religion that support respect for religious freedom and those that tend to support religious persecution, with historical incidences of both. Included are articles on:

Baha'i
Buddhism
Confucianism
Hinduism
Islam
Jainism

Judaism
Orthodox Christianity
Roman Catholicism
Shintoism
Sikhism

Major Issues

Issue articles delve into specific issues of religious freedom in the United States and explain the context and basics of the controversy in an even-handed manner, covering all sides of the issue, and mentioning key cases, individuals, and groups involved. Articles cover:

Brainwashing
Chaplains: Military and Legislative
Conscientious Objection and Pacifism
Creationism
Drugs in Religious Worship
Fundamentalistic Religion and Politics
Government Funding of Religious Organizations
Political Attitudes and Religiosity
Preservation of Faith Commitments
Prisons
Religion and Protest
Religion and Public Education
Religious Displays on Public Property
Religious Terrorist Groups
Religious Test Oaths
Sabbatarians
School Prayer and Discrimination
Spiritual Healing
Zoning

Minority Groups and Their Rights

The articles on minority groups explain points of collision between particular minority religious groups and the majority's social boundaries and societal laws (and points where the law has had, successfully or unsuccessfully, to defend group members from vigilante violence), placing these collisions in historical and religiocultural contexts. A one-volume encyclopedia cannot offer comprehensive coverage of all minority groups, so we have selected a representative sample of groups that have had an impact on law and on history:

Baptist Dissenters in Virginia
Cathars

Christian Science
Coptic Christians
Falun Gong
Family, The
Individualist Religions
Jehovah's Witnesses: Global
Jehovah's Witnesses: United States
Jews in Europe
Jews in the United States
Millennialist Groups
Mormons
Native American Church
Nineteenth-Century U.S. Utopian Communities
Peace Churches
Pentecostalism
Radical Religious Groups: African-American
Radical Religious Groups: White
Rastifari and Religious Freedom
Roman Catholics: Colonial to Nineteenth Century
Scientology
Unification Church
Waldensians

Key Documents

Several articles cover particular documents relevant to the history, problems, and promise of religious freedom. The articles explain the contents of the document, trace its development, and discuss its influence in the history of religious freedom:

Code Noir
Confederate Constitution and Religion
CSCE Vienna Document
English Test Oaths and Toleration Acts
European Convention on Human Rights
Fourteenth Amendment
Letter on Toleration
U.N. Declaration on Discrimination
Universal Declaration of Human Rights
Vatican II
Virginia Declaration of Rights
Virginia Statute for Religious Freedom
Williamsburg Charter

Acknowledgements

My passion is to work at the excruciating juncture where conscience and law collide, and the general editorship of this encyclopedia was a delight and a labor of love. I learned so much from the authors, and am eternally grateful to the coeditors, Derek Davis and Satvinder Juss, for their generous time and their expertise, and to David Levinson, Elizabeth Eno, and the general editing team at Berkshire Publishing for their trust and their tireless efforts. I took on this project a few weeks before I learned that I had to undergo extensive treatments for cancer, and these good folks were there through it all with both encouragement and elbow grease when my energy flagged. Thank you.

Catharine Cookson

Africa

Africa is a vast continent in which most of the world's religions are represented, and the state of religious freedom there varies not only from country to country but often from one region to another within a country.

North Africa is predominantly Muslim while sub-Saharan Africa is largely Christian—with significant exceptions. In North Africa the Coptic Church has long been part of Egyptian and Ethiopian culture. Similarly, for centuries Islam has been part of the culture of coastal peoples of eastern Africa, such as the Malinke, Hausa, Songhai, and Bornu peoples, and is continuing its expansion southward in western Africa. In addition to these Sudanic peoples, Islam has had success among the peoples of the Guinea Coast, including the Yoruba in Nigeria and the Temne in Sierra Leone (there has also been conversion to Christianity, Roman Catholicism in particular, along the Guinea Coast).

Islam and Christianity are about evenly balanced, with approximately 25 percent of the population practicing each. The other 50 percent comprises mainly adherents of traditional religions, with a few adherents of Hinduism, Judaism, Buddhism, and other religions.

These traditional religions share some basic features. All acknowledge a distant creator god beyond human understanding or control. Instead of directly approaching the high god with their petitions, adherents of traditional religions appeal to spirits associated with everyday life, including nature gods, various totemic gods, ancestors.

Christianity came to North Africa in the first century CE, reaching Egypt and Ethiopia even before Rome. In the fourth century, St. Augustine of Hippo, himself African, helped spread the religion across North Africa. Christianity came to sub-Saharan Africa only in the late fifteenth century, and there were African clergy by the sixteenth century. Many Christians along the West Coast trace their family's adherence to Christianity to these early days.

Islam arrived in sub-Saharan Africa in the seventh century CE when Arab armies swept across North and sub-Saharan Africa. Almoravids from the kingdom of Ghana swept into Spain where their descendants remained until the Reconquista (the last Muslim stronghold in Spain fell in 1492). Islamic advances continued in sub-Saharan Africa as rulers of the Sudanic kingdoms of Ghana, Mali, Songhai, Kanem Bornu, and the Hausa States became Muslim.

After its introduction, Islam mostly spread peacefully by way of Muslim traders. Growing European influence, however, prompted Holy War (jihad) that spread Islam and led resistance to European colonization. Islam continues to spread in Africa, claiming about 146 million adherents—roughly 25 percent of the population. Though the main Muslim strongholds are Egypt, Nigeria, Algeria, Sudan, and Morocco, there are also Muslims in Malawi, Zambia, and Mozambique.

Religious Competition and Freedom

In countries with little religious strife, such as Ghana, Christians and Muslims tend to settle their differences relatively peacefully. Other areas, such as the Casamance region of Senegal, have seen apparent Christian–Muslim clashes that are actually more ethnic than religious. However, in Nigeria and Sudan there is overt hostility between Christians and Muslims. It is important to distinguish ethnic clashes with a religious cast from outright religious conflict.

Nigeria

Nigeria provides a clear example of religious conflict. Its population of 103.4 million people is 50 percent Muslim, 40 percent Christian, and 9 percent "traditionalist"; members of other religions make up the remaining 1 percent of the population. About 12 million of the Christians are Catholic, the rest being distributed among various Protestant denominations. Charismatic and evangelical churches have recently grown greatly in membership.

In Nigeria, most Muslims are in the north while most Christians are in the south. Though there are significant numbers of Christians in the north and Muslims in the south, the major opposition is between northerners and southerners. The Islamic north is a patchwork of Sufi brotherhoods and Sudanese associations that tend to oppose one another.

Nigeria is a federal state, so central government has only limited power to regulate internal state matters. Although Nigeria is constitutionally secular, it does belong to the Organization of the Islamic Conference. Islam enjoys privileged treatment by the government and is the de facto official religion of most northern states. A number of northern states have imposed Islamic shari'a law, and attacks on Christians have increased. Rioting in November 2002 stemming from the Miss World pageant caused the deaths of over 200 people, most of them Christians. The violence broke out several days after a reporter in Lagos—now under a *fatwa*, or death sentence— wrote that the Prophet would not have opposed the contest.

Kaduna, the capital city of northern Nigeria's Kaduna state, saw Muslim–Christians clashes over the imposition of shari'a. According to the Nigerian Bible Society, about 875 Christians were killed and 800 churches were burned or demolished in Kaduna in religious conflicts in 2001. In spite of the many deaths, the Kaduna state government still plans on fully implementing Islamic law.

On 15 February 2001, a shari'a bill was signed into law in the state of Bauchi. Muslim legislators said that "only the Muslim *ummah* [community] will be affected by the Islamic law." However, the Christian Association of Nigeria claims that in other northern Nigerian states that have adopted it, shari'a has been applied to Christians as well in matters such as family law and disputes between Christians and Muslims.

The Christian community has repeatedly asked the Nigerian government to address the shari'a issue, since it is detrimental to the peaceful coexistence of the various religions in the country. Christians insist that the introduction of shari'a in most northern states is aimed at the gradual Islamization of the whole country.

There is a greater degree of tolerance in the southern part of the country. It is possible, for example, for a Muslim to convert to Christianity in the South— something that is impossible in the north.

The campaign by northern Nigerian states to establish Islamic law has brought new Muslim– Christian conflicts to a country already plagued by religious, ethnic, economic, and political strife. With a population evenly divided between Christians and Muslims, the desire for Islamic law in the predominantly Muslim north threatens to dash any hope of national unity.

Senegal

There are about 12 million people in Senegal, 92 percent of whom adhere to Islam, 6 percent to traditional African religions, and 2 percent to Christianity. Since 1984, the Diola tribe of the Casamance region, composed mainly of Christians who wished to have their own independent state, have been involved in bloody clashes with other tribes represented in the state of Senegal.

In spite of these apparently Christian–Muslim clashes, the conflict should more properly be regarded as ethnic in origin. Senegal has prided itself on its secular government and freedom of worship. In the north being Muslim is a matter of national identity; in the south, however, Islam is a sign of colonization by northern tribes. While the various ethnic groups generally follow their own Islamic traditions, Muslim brotherhoods cross tribal lines providing some common ground.

Though the large colony of mainly Shi'ite Syro-Lebanese strongly support the Islamist movement, only a few people—considered extremist by most Senegalese—are demanding a formally Islamic state. Islamists resent the rejection of the shari'a by the state; they further resent the inclusion of Muslim schools within the public school system.

Sudan

Sudan has a population of 36 million people, 70 percent of whom adhere to Islam, 25 percent to traditional religions, and 5 percent to Christianity. Most Muslims are found in the north of the country, while the Christians are mainly in the south and in the city of Khartoum. While Sudan officially espouses freedom of worship, Islam is effectively the state religion, the government having stated that Islam must inform the country's laws, policies, and institutions.

International agencies have accused Sudan of abducting Christian and animist children and raising them as Muslims. The government has also taken children into the military for forced religious indoctrination and participation in Sudan's civil war. Prisoners taken in this war, which pits the Arab and Islamic north against the "rebel" Christian and animist south, have been forced to adopt Islam and have even been sold into slavery. As of 2002, over 2 million Christians and animists had died in the civil war.

The Sudanese government forbids Christian communities to build permanent churches. Conversion may only be one-way: non-Muslims may convert to Islam, but the 1991 Criminal Act makes Muslim conversion to another religion punishable by death. Christians have been arrested for their beliefs and activities, and while Muslims may preach to Christians and animists, Christians are forbidden to seek converts. Foreign missionaries and religious organizations have experienced many administrative roadblocks, such as delayed processing of work permits and residence visas.

All abandoned children are regarded as Muslim and open to adoption only by Muslims. This policy applies even when the children are known animists or Christians. Non-Muslims are allowed to adopt non-Muslim children only, but Muslims may adopt any child. Conversion is sought in every walk of life. In prisons the government supports Islamic organizations that entice non-Muslim inmates to convert. Islamic non-governmental organizations also withhold food and other essentials from needy people in war zones unless they become Muslims. All children in refugee camps are required to study the Qur'an; in contrast, rebel-controlled areas offer complete freedom of worship.

The Larger Context

Freedom of religion and conscience is fundamental to political and other freedoms. The United Nations has recognized this by placing religious freedom in its constitution, and all member states have agreed to grant such freedom to all their populations. Though both Nigeria and Sudan, for example, guarantee religious freedom to their people, in practice, both have not lived up to their guarantees; Sudan, moreover, violates the U.N.-guaranteed right to change one's religion.

The majority of countries in Africa, however, tend to be tolerant of religious differences. Ghana, for example, is a model of amity, where differences are generally settled peacefully. Senegal with its vast majority of Muslims is tolerant of both its Christians and adherents to traditional religions.

Frank A. Salamone

See also British Empire; Coptic Christians; Islam; Rastifari and Religious Freedom; Slavery; South Africa

Further Reading

Abubakar, A. (1989). *Africa and the challenge of development: Acquiescence and dependency versus freedom and development*. New York: Praeger Publishers.

Aid to the Church in Need, Italy. (1998) *Religious freedom in the majority Islamic countries, 1998 report*. Retrieved December 17, 2002, from http://www.alleanzacattolica.org/acs/acs_english/acs_index.htm

Anderson, G. N. (1999). *Sudan in crisis: The failure of democracy*. Gainesville: University Press of Florida.

Bell, H. (1999). *Frontiers of medicine in the Anglo-Egyptian Sudan, 1899–1940*. Oxford, UK: Oxford University.

Cowen, D. V. (1961). *Foundations of freedom, with special reference to Southern Africa*. Cape Town, South Africa: Oxford University Press.

Creevey, L., & Callaway, B. (1994). *The heritage of Islam: Women, religion, and politics in West Africa*. Boulder, CO: Lynne Rienner.

Karp, I., & Bird, C. S. (Eds.). (1980). *Explorations in African systems of thought*. Bloomington: Indiana University Press.

Lewis, P. (Ed.). (1998). *Africa : Dilemmas of development and change*. Boulder, CO: Westview Press.

Welch, C. E. (1995). *Protecting human rights in Africa: Roles and strategies of non-governmental organizations*. Philadelphia: University of Pennsylvania Press.

Wright, S. (1998). *Nigeria: Struggle for stability and status*. Boulder, CO: Westview Press.

Asia *See* Baha'i; Buddhism; China, Communist; China, Imperial; Confucianism; Daoism; Falun Gong; Hinduism; India; Islam; Islamic Empire, Medieval; Israel; Jainism; Japan; Jihad; Judaism; Middle East; Pakistan; Shintoism; Sikhism; Tibet; Turkey; Unification Church

Augustine on Religious Coercion

The reasoning of St. Augustine (or Augustine of Hippo, 354–430 CE) on religious coercion is important. Since his views supplied theological justification for the Inquisition, Augustine influenced religious freedom and persecution in Europe long after his death. As well, he forcefully argued that law should encode the rights of truth over those of error.

The Donatist Controversy

Augustine's focus vis-à-vis coercion was the Donatist church, although his views are implied in his arguments concerning the Manichaean heretics and the pagans. The Donatists emerged primarily in North Africa after the persecutions inflicted by Emperor Diocletian between 303 and 305 CE. Donatists held that clergy who had surrendered Christian scriptures to Roman authorities when ordered to had sinned, thereby forfeiting the legitimacy of their ordination; these clergy, therefore, could no longer perform valid sacraments. The Donatist faction cut itself off from churches that disagreed with it on the implications of this sin.

Most churches held that the sin of surrendering sacred books was insufficiently serious to disqualify clergy from further sacred functions. Although several councils of bishops confirmed the majority opinion, roughly half the North African churches upheld the Donatist position over the fourth and early fifth centuries.

Augustine's Engagement with Religious Coercion

Augustine first considered the issue of religious coercion, or more precisely, government coercion of religious practice, in the early 390s CE. Earlier, in the mid 380s, he had made outstanding political connections in Rome and Milan, and positioned himself for a major governmental position. He relinquished this career in 386, and was baptized a Roman Catholic at Easter of 387 by Bishop Ambrose of Milan. He was later ordained Roman Catholic priest after three years of semi-retirement in rural North Africa.

As a relatively recent Christian convert and a new clergyman, Augustine first argued against using coercive force in religious matters. He argued that genuine faith must be freely chosen: while coercion might shape practice, it could not change hearts.

In a letter to Vincentius, Augustine later admitted reversing this position: "The Donatists are much too active, and it seems to me it would be advisable for them to be restrained and corrected by the powers established by God [e.g., the Roman Empire; see Romans 13:1]. For we now rejoice over the correction of many who hold to Catholic unity, defend it so sincerely, and are so happy over their freedom from their former error. . . . However, a strange force of habit makes some of them think that they cannot be changed for the better except under the influence of this fear, and then they turn their anxious minds to consider truth" (Augustine 1953, 56–57).

Augustine changed his thinking on coercion under the pressures of office after becoming a bishop in the Roman tradition (397 CE) and as he developed his theology. As a bishop, he was a civic as well as spiritual leader and was responsible for the well-being of his clergy. Augustine faced a rival Donatist bishop in Hippo, and the conflict led to unsuccessful plots against his life and the targeting of certain priests in his diocese.

Augustine the teacher as depicted by Benozzo Gozzoli in one of a series of seventeen frescoes in the Church of Saint Augustine at San Gimagnano, completed in 1465.
COURTESY HUNGARIAN ACADEMY OF SCIENCES.

Augustine's theology also moved toward a doctrine of coercion during his first ten years in the clergy. In Book 8 of his *Confessions*, written between 397 and 401 CE, he describes how habits of behavior had kept him from committing himself fully to Christianity in his years of secular success in Milan. His analysis of the influence of habit corresponded fairly closely to Aristotle's, which was widely understood by the educated of the day, and implied that behavior must sometimes change for truth to be comprehended.

Moreover, passages from the Old Testament could be read fairly straightforwardly to endorse use of physical force to bring a person to truth. The New Testament also supported his arguments, for example, in Luke 14:23 (KJV). In this parable, the host of a banquet spurned by the invited guests, tells his servants to "compel them to come in." Hence, if the Donatists were to ignore God's invitation by persuasion to join the Catholic majority, then government should "compel them to come in." Who could expect Donatists to abandon their habitual allegiance if they never came to hear mainstream Catholic preachers?

Further key concepts, such as the conclusion that God (not human virtue in the clergy) guaranteed valid rituals, and the interpretation of Christian charity as requiring us to bring our neighbors to the joy of the truth we hold, supported the position that the truth of the majority churches must overcome "erroneous" religious practice.

In 405, even before Augustine's arguments were presented to him, the Emperor promulgated a law repressing Donatist religious practice. Moreover, Augustine vainly urged an admirer, a governor in the region, to forgo capital punishment of the Donatists. So despite his political skills and background, Augustine's influence on contemporary practice appears to have been slight.

Augustine's views are instructive in part because of their complexity. Even today, his reasoning reminds us that opposition to religious freedom can be deeply embedded in social contingencies, civic responsibilities, and elaborations of widely held lines of thought.

Sandra Lee Dixon

Further Reading

Augustine. (1951). *Letters, Vol. I.* (W. Parsons, Trans.). New York: Fathers of the Church.

Augustine. (1953). *Letters, Vol. II.* (W. Parsons, Trans.). New York: Fathers of the Church.

Augustine. (1979). Writings against the Manichaeans and against the Donatists. In P. Schaff (Series Ed.), *A Select Library of the Nicene and Post-Nicene Fathers of the Christian Church, Vol. 4.* Grand Rapids, MI: W. B. Eerdmans Publishing Co.

Augustine. (1991). *Confessions.* (H. Chadwick, Trans.). Oxford, UK: Oxford University Press.

Bonner, G. (1963). *St. Augustine of Hippo: Life and controversies.* Philadelphia: Westminster Press.

Brown, P. (1963). Religious coercion in the later Roman Empire: The case of North Africa. *History, 48,* 283–305.

Brown, P. (1964). St. Augustine's attitude to religious coercion. *Journal of Roman studies, 54,* 107–116.

Brown, P. (1967). *Augustine of Hippo: A biography.* Berkeley and Los Angeles: University of California Press.

Fitzgerald, A. D. (Gen. Ed.). (1999). *Augustine through the ages: An encyclopedia.* Grand Rapids, MI: W. B. Eerdmans Publishing Co.

Frend, W. H. C. (1952). *Donatist church: A movement of protest in Roman North Africa.* Oxford: Oxford University Press.

Baha'i

The Baha'i perspective on protecting the right of freedom of religion and conscience flows from core Baha'i principles and beliefs. The Baha'i faith teaches that all religions come from one God or "Unknowable Essence," who is beyond the full understanding of human beings. Baha'is believe that God reveals himself to humanity through divine teachers or messengers (such as Moses, Christ, and Muhammad) in ways that are suited to human capacity. These manifestations of God reveal both eternal spiritual truths and impermanent social laws and practices suited to the time in which they appear. The Baha'i faith was founded in 1853 in Persia (today, Iran) by Baha'u'llah (1817–1892), whose title means "the glory of God." "Baha'i" is Arabic for "follower of the glory." Baha'u'llah was exiled and imprisoned for most of his life because of the faith he proclaimed. He taught that all people are equal in the sight of God, that all religions are one, and that the world is entering an era in which the oneness of humanity will eventually be recognized and fully established. Baha'is recognize Baha'u'llah as the manifestation of God for this age.

Since there is no clergy in the Baha'i faith, nor other individuals vested with religious authority, there can be no competing authoritative interpretations of Baha'i teachings on freedom of religion or other subjects. Authority resides primarily in the Baha'i scriptures and secondarily in a system of elected institutions. Each Baha'i community (that is, all the Baha'is residing in a certain town, county, or city) elects annually a nine-member local assembly that is responsible for supporting and governing the Baha'i life of the community. National assemblies are elected annually in some 180 countries. The international governing body (elected every five years) is the Universal House of Justice, whose seat is in Haifa, Israel, close to Baha'u'llah's burial place, a site of pilgrimage for Baha'is.

In 2002, the Baha'i faith had about 5 million adherents worldwide, representing a wide range of social and economic classes within their own societies and more than 2,100 ethnic, racial, and tribal groups (Statistics 2001, 313). It is the second most geographically widespread religion in the world. This scope and diversity within its membership, along with its universal founding principles, give the Baha'i community a perspective on protecting religious freedom that is based on its global experience. But Baha'is have also been the object of persecution in some parts of the world, and have relied on international human rights mechanisms and other means to address these situations.

Freedom of Religion in Baha'i Teachings and Practice

In addition to recognizing the divine origins of all of the world's major religions, a basic Baha'i teaching is that every individual has the right and the responsibility to search out spiritual truth for herself or himself ('Abdu'l-Baha 1982, 291). One consequence of this principle is that children raised in Baha'i families, although growing up with a Baha'i identity, will often make their own declaration of faith at a time they choose. Another consequence is that Baha'is are

Baha'i shrine and terraces on Mt. Carmel, in Haifa, Israel. COURTESY OF BAHA'I WORLD NEWS SERVICE.

enjoined to teach their faith to others in ways that respect the other person's degree of interest and freedom of conscience.

While upholding the principle of freedom of belief, a central goal of Baha'i life is to eliminate prejudice and to promote unity and peace among all people, regardless of race, ethnicity, language, age, sex, culture, economic or educational class, religion, or any other difference. Thus, the Baha'i view is that while individuals are free to choose their own belief system, they are not free to discriminate against or oppress others, whether as a result of religious precepts or otherwise. In April 2002, the Universal House of Justice addressed a lengthy letter on this subject to the world's religious leaders, which has been delivered by Baha'i assemblies to leaders of congregations and religious groups at the national and local levels around the world (The Universal House of Justice 2002).

The letter from the Universal House of Justice observed that while great progress is being made in overcoming prejudice based on race, gender, and nationality, religious prejudice remains firmly entrenched. The House of Justice wrote, "[t]he greater part of organized religion stands paralyzed at the threshold of the future, gripped in those very dogmas and claims of privileged access to truth that have been responsible for creating some of the most bitter conflicts dividing the earth's inhabitants" (Universal House of Justice 2002, para. 10). It urged "renunciation of all those claims to exclusivity or finality that, in winding their roots around the life of the spirit, have been the greatest single factor in suffocating impulses to unity and in promoting hatred and violence"(The Universal House of Justice 2002, para. 16). It concluded by affirming continued cooperation and the commitment of the Baha'i community to interfaith discourse but with the conviction that such activities, if they are to be effective, must honestly address the question of the oneness of religion.

In the Baha'i view, enjoying the right of religious freedom implies the responsibility to use that freedom for the well-being of all humanity. This requires overcoming all animosities and prejudices, creating orderly structures for protecting rights and promoting social justice, and ultimately basing all relationships on the recognition that humanity is one family. Baha'is believe not only that "unity in diversity" is the goal for humanity but that unity is necessary in order to overcome all the ills of our time. Baha'u'llah wrote, "The well-being of mankind, its peace and security, are unattainable unless and until its unity is firmly established" (Shoghi Effendi 1974, 203). This can be achieved only if individuals and communities exercise their freedom with a sense of responsibility for the good of all.

Although Baha'is associate closely with other organizations working for human rights and peace, they do not become involved in partisan politics. Baha'i teachings require that Baha'is be obedient to the established government where they live and that they work for change and justice through legal means.

Persecution of Baha'is

Baha'is have been persecuted sporadically since the founding of the Baha'i faith, generally in Muslim countries and most severely in Iran. The Muslim belief that Muhammad is "the seal of the prophets" (that is, the last prophet) conflicts with Baha'u'llah's teaching that divine revelation is continuous. (Baha'is understand "seal of the prophets" to refer to the end of an era and not the end of revelation.) Therefore, in Muslim countries the Baha'i faith has often been regarded by governments and Islamic religious officials as a heretical sect of Islam rather than as an independent world religion. In addition, charges of immorality against Baha'is are based on the fact that, in accordance with the Baha'i principle of the equality of women and men, there is no segregation of the sexes at Baha'i gatherings and men and women participate equally in community life.

In Iran, although the Baha'is are the largest religious minority in the country (approximately 300,000 members), the Baha'i faith is not a "recognized" religious minority under the Iranian constitution and so does not benefit from any legal protections (Martin 1993, 253). Since 1979, more than two hundred Baha'is in Iran have been killed and thousands jailed. Since 1983, the Iranian Baha'i community has been denied the right to assemble and the right to maintain its administrative institutions. Baha'is have been entirely barred from higher education and from public employment, their property has been confiscated, and arrests and detentions continue.

National governments and the United Nations have protested the treatment of Baha'is in Iran. Since 1982, the U.S. Congress has adopted eight resolutions condemning Iran's treatment of Baha'is. The United Nations General Assembly has adopted annual resolutions condemning Iran's actions as human rights abuses and calling for the emancipation of the Iranian Baha'i community. Since 2000, Iranian government officials have made statements suggesting that the Baha'is will gain some legal protections, but as of the end of 2002 there has been little change. In the meantime, the Baha'i community of Iran is establishing an alternative system to provide higher education to its young people and is doing what it can to protect and support those who are harassed and detained and their families.

Martha L. Schweitz

Further Reading

'Abdu'l-Baha. (1982). *The promulgation of universal peace.* Wilmette, IL: Baha'i Publishing Trust.

Afshari, R. (2001). *Human rights in Iran: The abuse of cultural relativism.* Philadelphia: University of Pennsylvania Press.

The Baha'is of the United States. (2001). *Welcome to the Baha'i faith.* Retrieved December 5, 2002, from http://www.us.bahai.org

Farhoumand-Sims, C. (2001). The universal declaration of human rights, cultural relativism and the persecution of the Baha'is in Iran. In Tahirih Tahririha-Danesh (Ed.). *Baha'i-inspired perspectives on human rights* (pp. 64–89). E-book: Juxta Publishing. http://www.juxta.com

Hatcher, W., & Martin, J. D. (1984). *The Baha'i faith: The emerging global religion.* San Francisco: Harper & Row.

Martin, J. D. (1993). The case of the Baha'i minority in Iran. In *The Baha'i world 1992–93* (pp. 247–271). Haifa, Israel: Baha'i World Centre.

Shoghi Effendi. (1974). *The world order of Baha'u'llah.* Wilmette, IL: Baha'i Publishing Trust.

Statistics. (2001). In *The Baha'i world 1999–2000* (p. 313). Haifa, Israel: Baha'i World Centre.

The Universal House of Justice. (1985). *The promise of world peace.* Retrieved December 5, 2002, http://www.bahai.org/article-1-7-2-1.html

The Universal House of Justice. (2002). *Letter to the world's religious leaders.* Retrieved December 5, 2002, from http://www.bahai.org/article-1-1-0-1.html

Balkans, East Europe, and Russia

The Balkans include the countries of former Yugoslavia as well as Greece, Albania, Bulgaria, and Romania. Since the break-up of the Soviet Union, "East Europe" has been used to designate the western republics of the former USSR, apart from Russia.

Slavs have formed the predominant ethnic element in this area since the sixth century, pushing to the coast the Illyrians (ancestors of the Albanians) and the Greeks and isolating the Latin-speaking population (today's Romanians). The ninth-century Magyar (Hungarian) invasions and post-fourteenth-century Turkish settlement add to the ethnic diversity of the area, while Russia's expansion incorporated many different nationalities.

The region is dominated by Orthodox Christianity, which spread across the area in two main waves. The first was the preaching of Christianity in the communities of the Roman Empire (Asia Minor, today's Greece, and the Adriatic coastline, first to fourth centuries CE)—the regions consolidated into the East Roman/Byzantine Empire, centered at Constantinople. The second was the conversion of the Slavs, which occurred from the ninth to the eleventh centuries and was facilitated by the missionary work of Cyril and Methodius, who translated the Scriptures into the vernacular. Orthodoxy (Orthodox Christianity) is considered the national religion in Serbia, Montenegro, Romania, Bulgaria, Ukraine, Moldova, and Belarus. It is recognized as having played a special role in the Russian Federation, is considered one of the three traditional religions of Albania and Bosnia, and is the state religion of Greece. According to the principles of *symphonia,* which can be defined as harmony, church-state relations were historically characterized by a close alliance between a national church and a centralizing monarchy by the early Middle Ages, the northwestern Balkans (Slovenia, Croatia, and Hungary) fell into the Roman Catholic orbit, and Catholicism also played a role in those areas controlled by the Polish and Hapsburg monarchies. Judaism in the area dates back to Roman times and was augmented by the conversion of the Khazars (a people living around the northern portion of the Caspian Sea) in the eighth century CE, and the arrival of Jews expelled from Western Europe during the fifteenth and sixteenth centuries. Protestantism spread in the sixteenth century among Hungarians and Germans in Transylvania, and farther east by German settlers in the Ukraine in the eighteenth century. Small Protestant communities also were formed at the end of the nineteenth century, especially as a result of American proselytizing. Islam was spread by merchants among the Turkic populations along the Volga River (today's Tatars and Bashkirs) in the ninth century, and was introduced to the Balkans by the Ottomans. Islam is the predominant religion in Albania and Bosnia. Russia's southward and eastward expansion brought additional Islamic and Buddhist populations under its sway.

The Balkans

Medieval Balkan legislation—such as the decrees of the councils of Preslav (918) and Trnovo (1211) in

RUSSIAN LAW ON RELIGIOUS FREEDOM

On 1 October 1997 the Russian Federation promulgated a new law on religious freedom. The opening paragraph of the new law indicates that citizens will have more religious freedom but also reaffirms the special status of Russian Orthodoxy.

ON FREEDOM OF CONSCIENCE AND RELIGIOUS ASSOCIATIONS
The Federation Assembly of the Russian federation,

- affirming the right of each person to freedom of conscience and freedom of religious profession, as well as to equality before the law irrespective of religious affiliation and convictions;
- assuming that the Russian federation is a secular state;
- recognizing the special role of Orthodoxy in the history of Russia and in the establishment and development of its spirituality and culture;
- respecting Christianity, Islam, Buddhism, Judaism, and other religions, constituting an integral part of the historical heritage of the peoples of Russia;
- considering it important to cooperate in the achievement of mutual understanding, toleration, and respect in matters of freedom of conscience and freedom of religious profession;
- adopts the present federal law.

Source: *The 1997 Russian Law on Religion.*
Retrieved May 15, 2002, from http://www.ripnet.org/law/ruslaw.htm

Bulgaria, and Zica (1221) in Serbia—proscribed pagan practices and deemed the dissemination of heresy a capital offense. In theory, all subjects were to be members of the state church; in practice, the need of medieval rulers for the skills and services of those who practiced other faiths led to the extension of limited toleration. Thus, in the Code of Serbian Emperor Stefan Dushan (1349), heretics were to be expelled (Article 10) and it was forbidden to proselytize among the Orthodox (Article 8); however, Article 160 extended protection to the emperor's guests (such as German Catholic miners) to practice their own faith and be represented by members of their faith in legal matters (Article 153).

The 1082 Treaty between the Byzantine Empire and Venice allowed Italian merchants to have Roman Catholic churches in Constantinople; similar treaties with Muslim powers (such as with Sultan Bayezid at the end of the fourteenth century) allowed for the construction of mosques. In the regulations promulgated by the Demetrius Chomatianos, archbishop of Ohrid (in today's Macedonia), religious minorities were allowed to have houses of prayer in their assigned districts within the city.

Beginning in 1354, the Ottoman Turks extended their dominion over the Balkans (Constantinople, capital of the Byzantine Empire, fell in 1453). While motivated by the desire to spread Islam, the Ottomans also extended toleration to "People of the Book" (Christians and Jews).

The Ottomans divided the population of the Balkans based on their religious affiliation rather than by ethnicity or religion (the millet system). Each community was governed by its own laws, and religious leaders were civil officials under the Ottoman state (*ethnarchs*). As an Islamic empire, members of the Muslim millet were the most privileged, and so, in some areas of the Balkans, large numbers of the local population converted, which augmented Muslim Turks who settled in the region. While the non-Muslim population suffered legal disabilities (including limits on political and economic freedom, and most notoriously, being subject to the *devshirme*, the "tribute of children," which called for children to be taken from their homes at an early age to be raised as Ottoman Muslims), the Ottomans respected the internal autonomy of each community and made no attempt to interfere in matters of faith and dogma.

This practice contrasted with the Catholic powers, notably the Hapsburg monarchy in Austria, who warred with the Ottomans for supremacy in the region.

Military necessity persuaded governments to consider broadening the right to religious liberty. Under increased threat from the Ottoman Empire, the Hapsburg monarchy was forced to extend religious freedom for Protestant Hungarians and Orthodox Serbs to secure their loyalty. As a result of these guarantees, in 1690 thousands of Serbian Orthodox led by their Patriarch Arsenius left Ottoman-controlled territory to settle in a new frontier zone (*krajina*) under Austrian rule. Ultimately, Emperor Joseph II extended full toleration to Jews, Protestants, and Orthodox in 1781.

As Ottoman power waned, there was growing pressure on the Turks to grant more rights to their Christian populations. In 1774, the treaty of Kuchuk Kainardji gave Russia the right to make representations to the Ottoman sultan on behalf of Eastern Christians. Following the Crimean War, Western powers encouraged the Ottoman government to proclaim full legal equality between Muslims and Christians (the *Hatti-Humayoun* of 16 February 1856). Ottoman traditionalists, however, resisted calls for reform and liberal concessions were ultimately withdrawn.

Beginning with the Greek revolt against Ottoman rule in 1821, the Balkan nationalities moved to free themselves from imperial domination and create nation-states. As Balkan nations achieved independence, the traditional religion (whether Orthodoxy or Roman Catholicism) was established as a state church. Provisions for religious freedom were usually understood in communal terms (permitting ethnic minorities the right of free exercise of their own faith) and were counterbalanced by strict restrictions on proselytizing. This pattern has been preserved in the Greek constitution into the twenty-first century. Another defining characteristic was the intrusive role of the state in regulating religious activity (especially through registration requirements) in order to organize, own property, and engage in public activity. The regime adopted by the Romanian Grand National Assembly in 1948, including provisions for withdrawing recognition from religious groups, reflected standard Balkan practices. The Communist regimes that came to power after World War II preserved such arrangements (other than disestablishing state churches and curtailing religious education in schools), and with some modifications, they remain in force today.

The use of religion to determine ethnicity (a process accelerated by the creation of a distinct Bulgarian Exarchate in 1870 to differentiate Bulgarian-speaking Orthodox from their Greek and Romanian coreligionists) became more pronounced. One famous example was the provisions for the exchange of populations between Greece and Turkey (Lausanne, 1923), whereby Greek-speaking Muslims were reclassified as Turks, while Turcophone Christians (*karamanlilar*) were defined as Greeks. Among the South Slavs, religion served to differentiate Croats (Catholics), Bosniaks (Muslims), and Serbs (Orthodox Christians) and religious differences were brought to the fore during the civil wars of the 1990s.

Russia and East Europe

When Prince Vladimir of Kiev converted to Christianity (988 CE), East Europe moved into the Byzantine orbit. Paganism was proscribed and in some cases forcibly eradicated; the *Novgorod Chronicle* records the execution of shamans in Kiev as late as 1277. Heresy was also a prosecutable offense, although Metropolitan Photius (in office 1408–1431) urged that heretics be separated from the community, but not tortured or killed. In Russia, groups like the *strigolniki* (who rejected the sacraments of the official church), the Judaizers, and the Old Believers (who split with the official church in disputes over church ritual and reform) often faced severe civil penalties. A particularly harsh example was a 1685 decree by the regent Sophia that prescribed death for heretics or schismatics.

Foreigners, however, had the right to live in their own districts and freely practice their religion, provided that they sought no converts, a practice confirmed by the 1229 treaty between the city of Novgorod and the Hanseatic league. Religious toleration was later extended to Catholic and Protestant Europeans and Muslim Tatars who entered into Russian service, of which Peter the Great's 1702 decree is a leading example. Yet, this toleration was always precarious; the Testament of Patriarch Joachim (1690) advocated the expulsion of all heretics and infidels from Russia.

After the Mongol invasions of the thirteenth century, the lands that today form the Ukraine and Belarus were absorbed into the Polish-Lithuanian Commonwealth. Seeking religious uniformity, the

Polish kings promoted Catholicism, though a solution eventually was sought in the creation of the Uniate (Eastern-Rite Catholic) Church at the council of Brest-Litovsk (1596). Orthodox could retain their rituals and customs as long as they acknowledged the Pope of Rome as their leader. Polish persecution of Orthodox who refused to join the Uniate Church precipitated the Cossack uprising in 1648. After these lands came under the Russian Empire, the Russian government in 1839 and 1875 forcibly dissolved the Uniate Church and sought to reunify it with the Orthodox Church.

The 1649 Law Code forbade Russian Orthodox to leave their church and mandated the death penalty for non-Orthodox peoples engaged in proselytizing. State policy fluctuated between trying to convert non-Orthodox populations and extending toleration for the sake of civil peace. A major issue arose as to whether those converted to Orthodoxy by force (and their descendants) had the right to leave the Orthodox Church. Such matters were only settled when the Decree on Religious Toleration (17 April 1905) superseded earlier legislation and gave all residents of the Russian Empire the right to freely choose (or abandon) any religion.

The Russian Revolution (1917) brought a virulently antireligious government to power, which, as Vladimir Lenin noted, "must combat religion" (Lenin 1963, 406). By the decree of 23 January 1918, all religious bodies were deprived of their standing as legal entities and were stripped of the right to own property or engage in educational activity. The separation of church and state (January 1918) was followed by a major attack designed to destroy religion as a public institution. Between 1918 and 1939, tens of thousands of clergy were executed and over 90 percent of all houses of worship were closed or destroyed. Soviet legislation on religion (adopted in 1929 and revised in 1975) permitted worship only; no charities or educational activities were allowed.

World War II demonstrated the mobilizing power of religion, especially Orthodoxy, and so the modus vivendi proposed by Josef Stalin (a highly circumscribed existence for the major traditional religions provided they pledged absolute loyalty to the state, coupled with massive repression against sectarians and dissidents) became standard operating procedure in all Communist regimes, with the exception of a renewed assault on religion launched by Nikita Khrushchev (USSR premier 1958–1962) that was emulated in several other Communist states.

The Post-Communist Legacy

The Communist desire to separate the church from society has produced overwhelmingly secular societies, where only a small percentage of the population is religiously active. Nevertheless, religion retained a great deal of legitimacy as a link to the nation's pre-Communist culture and history. As Communist regimes collapsed, restrictions on religion were lifted. In Russia, Soviet decrees were annulled by the 25 October 1990 law on religion. However, the influx of foreign missionaries and the growth of nontraditional religions in the region led to a backlash; a new Russian law (passed 26 September 1997) placed restrictions on the ability of religious groups having less than fifteen years' presence in the country to organize, own property, and engage in missionary work.

With the exception of Greece, there are no state churches in the region, yet the traditional faiths often have a recognized status because of their importance in the national culture. Social attitudes continue to link ethnic identity with nominal membership in a specific religion (e.g., Greek with Orthodox, or Turk with Islam). While all the constitutions provide for freedom of religion, social attitudes still foster discrimination against members of minority faiths, particularly at the local level.

Nikolas K. Gvosdev

See also Orthodox Christianity

Further Reading

Castellan, G. (1992). *History of the Balkans from Mohammed the Conqueror to Stalin*. Translated by Nicholas Bradley. Boulder, CO: East European Monographs.

Dvornik, F. (1974). *The making of Central and Eastern Europe*. Gulf Breeze, FL: Academic International Press.

Geraci, R., & Khodarkovsky, M. (Eds.). (2001). *Of religion and empire: Missions, conversion, and tolerance in Tsarist Russia*. Ithaca, NY: Cornell University Press.

Gvosdev, N. K. (2001). *An examination of church-state relations in the Byzantine and Russian empires with an emphasis on ideology and models of action*. Lewiston, NY: Edwin Mellen Press.

Hawkesworth, C., et al. (2001). *Religious quest and national identity in the Balkans*. New York: Palgrave.

Lenin, V. I. (1963). Proletary, No. 45. In *Collected works: Vol. 15* (pp. 406). Moscow: Progress Publishers.

Muller, A. W. (1973). *Historical antecedents of the Petrine ecclesiastical reform.* Seattle: University of Washington (Ph.D. Dissertation).

Obolensky, D. (1982). *The Byzantine inheritance of Eastern Europe.* London: Variorum Reprints.

Pospielovsky, D. (1984). *The Russian Church under the Soviet regime, 1917–1982.* Crestwood, NY: St. Vladimir's Seminary Press.

Ramet, P. (1987) *Cross and commissar: The politics of religion in Eastern Europe and the USSR.* Bloomington: Indiana University Press.

Witte, J., Jr., & Bourdeaux, M. (Eds.). (1999). *Proselytism and orthodoxy in Russia: The new war for souls.* Maryknoll, NY: Orbis Books.

Baptist Dissenters in Virginia

In Colonial Virginia the law permitted only one church—the Anglican Church or the Church of England. Others including the Presbyterians, the Quakers, and the Baptists sometimes were tolerated and sometimes persecuted. The Baptists felt that toleration implied a favor granted by men while religious liberty was a right already given by God. They wanted full religious freedom for all persons to believe, or not to believe, according to the dictates of their own conscience.

The first Baptist minister to gather a church in Virginia was Robert Norden, who arrived in the colony about 1714. He soon found that he was no freer to preach unhindered in Virginia than he had been in England. He was required to register and was designated by the court as "an Anabaptist preacher." He was told where he could preach and a local residence was approved for meetings. In some counties Baptist dissenters were not permitted to hold meetings behind locked doors or under the cover of darkness.

Baptists sometimes shared a common meeting-house with other denominations. Because the law did not recognize them, Baptists often held their meetings in private homes, arbors, groves, and barns. In some communities the Baptists were persecuted with acts of violence while in others they were tolerated. In some localities, overly zealous authorities arrested Baptist ministers for "preaching with no authority" or teaching and preaching "contrary to

the laws." In many places the Baptists were despised and "viewed by men in power as beneath their notice" (Semple 1810, 14).

In general the Baptists of Colonial Virginia were composed of the common folk. They included small farmers, shopkeepers, and laborers. Occasionally they attracted a few members of the establishment. Their worship style, their simple gospel story, and perhaps their polity with its democratic form of church government also appealed to African-Americans who joined in large numbers.

In Colonial Virginia there were three streams of Baptists: the Generals, the Regulars, and the Separates. Most of their distinctions were based upon subtle differences in doctrine. Some were social distinctions. In time, the Generals gave way to the other two parties. The differences in the two groups illustrate the diversity that always existed among Baptists. In general, the Regulars were the better-educated townsfolk who appreciated the value of education and expected a carefully crafted sermon from the minister. The Separates, given more to emotional displays in their religion, were the country folk who felt the minister should be open for heavenly inspiration. The two groups also differed on the necessity for a written confession of faith. The Regulars favored a statement of beliefs while the Separates were suspicious of anything that smacked of limiting freedom of belief. However, the two parties worked closely in their common pursuit of securing religious liberty. In 1787 a formal union was effected.

The Baptists in Virginia initially began with small numbers but began to grow despite persecution and perhaps even because of opposition from the establishment. The evangelical nature of the Baptists along with their enthusiastic worship style, effective itinerant preachers, and use of popular hymn singing aided in the attraction of large crowds. Spiritual revivals also swept across the landscape. In 1771 a Separate Baptist meeting attracted upward of 5,000 people to rural Orange County. In counties where imprisoned Baptist ministers preached from the jail windows it was reported that great crowds gathered to hear the preachers. "By the time of the Revolution it is estimated that [the Baptists in Virginia] counted 10,000 members, which doubled by 1790" (Gewehr 1930, 106).

The Baptists of Virginia maintained a vigilant campaign to secure religious liberty. They held to a broad and all-inclusive concept of "equal Liberty and

BAPTIST DISSENTERS, THOMAS JEFFERSON, AND THE SEPARATION OF CHURCH AND STATE

The following letter was sent by President Thomas Jefferson to the Danbury (Connecticut) Baptist Association in 1802 in response to their letter of 7 October 1801 in which they stated their concerns about religious liberty. Jefferson's letter is considered a major document in the battle for religious freedom because of his use of the phrase "a wall of separation between Church & State."

To messers. Nehemiah Dodge, Ephraim Robbins, & Stephen S. Nelson, a committee of the Danbury Baptist association in the state of Connecticut.

Gentlemen

The affectionate sentiments of esteem and approbation which you are so good as to express towards me, on behalf of the Danbury Baptist association, give me the highest satisfaction. My duties dictate a faithful and zealous pursuit of the interests of my constituents, & in proportion as they are persuaded of my fidelity to those duties, the discharge of them becomes more and more pleasing.

Believing with you that religion is a matter which lies solely between Man & his God, that he owes account to none other for his faith or his worship, that the legitimate powers of government reach actions only, & not opinions, I contemplate with sovereign reverence that act of the whole American people which declared that their legislature should "make no law respecting an establishment of religion, or prohibiting the free exercise thereof," thus building a wall of separation between Church & State. Adhering to this expression of the supreme will of the nation in behalf of the rights of conscience, I shall see with sincere satisfaction the progress of those sentiments which tend to restore to man all his natural rights, convinced he has no natural right in opposition to his social duties.

I reciprocate your kind prayers for the protection & blessing of the common father and creator of man, and tender you for yourselves & your religious association, assurances of my high respect & esteem.

Th. Jefferson

Jan. 1, 1802.
Source: *Church & State* 55 (January 2002): 13.
Washington, DC: Americans United for Separation of Church and State.

Impartial Justice." They referred to "liberty of conscience" as "dearer to us than property and life." Although they were fast becoming the largest religious society in Virginia, the Baptists insisted that religious freedom be for all. John Leland, the Baptist minister and effective spokesman for religious liberty, declared that "all should be equally free, Jews, Turks, Pagans and Christians" (Greene 1845, 118). Baptists also practiced a voluntary religion, which was free from all sources of possible coercion including the government, churchly officers, and even parents.

The Baptists of Virginia helped secure religious freedom for all Americans to enjoy. They accomplished their mission by enduring persecution, petitioning the authorities, and influencing the founding fathers.

Persecution of the Baptist Dissenters

The first arrests of the Baptists in Virginia occurred in Fredericksburg in 1768 when five men were led to jail; along the way they sang a hymn, "Broad is the road that leads to death," which forever after was identified with the Baptist dissenters of Virginia. Crowds listened to their jail-window preaching and they even influenced the Anglican priest of the parish, who offered security if they posted bond. They remained in jail for forty-three days.

The imprisonments spread across Eastern Virginia. In Orange four Baptists were "charged as vagrant and itinerant persons and for assembling themselves unlawfully under the denomination of Anabaptists and for teaching and preaching schismatic doctrines." Among the prisoners in Orange was Elijah Craig, who preached from jail until he was "confined to the inner dungeon."

The most widely known of the imprisonments was the confinement of James Ireland, a young preacher who was arrested while praying and was imprisoned for six months in Culpeper. While in jail, he was subject to several attempts on his life. The slaves who gathered to hear his jail preaching were caught by patrollers and were stripped and beaten for listening to the Baptist preacher.

John Waller had been on the grand jury to try the case of a Baptist preacher, Lewis Craig of Spotsylvania. He later dated his conversion to the influence of Craig's courthouse testimony. Waller became a noted evangelist and, in time, was placed in four different jails for a total of 113 days. Among the jails was the flea-infested prison at Urbanna in Middlesex County. He was offered his freedom if he would agree to preach no more and leave the county; and in a letter to the judge, he stated that he could not sign such a statement "for fear of sinning against God." In Caroline County he was given twenty-one lashes with a horsewhip for preaching and an eyewitness account recorded that after the public whipping he mounted the stage and "preached with a great deal of liberty," declaring that he "had scarcely felt the stripes for the love of God."

In Chesterfield County, seven ministers were imprisoned. Local tradition holds that a wall was built around the jail to keep the crowds from hearing the preachers, but they would wave a handkerchief on a pole and the crowds knew to come closer to hear the preaching. The wealthiest man in the county befriended the preachers and brought them food and water and even opened his barn to be used as a Baptist meetinghouse.

In Fairfax County, Jeremiah Moore was imprisoned perhaps three different times for preaching the gospel. In Culpeper, Nathaniel Saunders and William McClannahan were arrested on a warrant charging that they were encouraging sedition by preaching against the laws of Great Britain. In Accomack on Virginia's Eastern Shore, Elijah Baker was imprisoned for preaching and was even kidnapped with the instructions to the ship captain to take him outside of American waters and get rid of him. His imprisonment in 1778 was the last of the jailings: "These imprisonments of more than 30 individuals in the jails of nine counties so far from arresting the Baptist movement had accelerated it by arousing sympathy for the prisoners, by kindling interest in their message and by awakening understanding and appreciation of their insistence on unrestrained exercise of freedom of belief in religion and liberty to preach the Gospel to every creature" (Ryland 1955, 84).

Petitions for Religious Liberty

During the course of the imprisonments, Baptists began to appeal directly to the House of Burgesses in Williamsburg, seeking relief from their various grievances in the form of petitions or "memorials." These were carefully and even eloquently worded documents, which borrowed heavily from the language of the Enlightenment. Often they reflected the sentiments of a large body but were authored by an individual. They carried the signatures of varying numbers from a few individuals to ten thousand persons: "It was through these petitions that the Baptists enlisted the support of the majority of the people and were able to penetrate the walls of opposition set up by the established order. The people at the grassroots level could participate in this form of protest and put pressure on the governing authorities" (Moore 1986, 1227).

Beginning in 1770, the Baptists attempted to persuade the House of Burgesses in matters that affected them. The earliest attempt was to protest the requirement for ministers to bear arms and attend drills, which interfered with their ministerial duties. In 1772 a petition from Baptists in Amelia called for "liberty of conscience."

"At a meeting of the Separate Baptists held on August 12, 1775, at Dupuy's Meeting House in Powhatan County, the first organized action in Virginia for religious freedom and the separation of church and state was taken" (Moore 1986, 1228). "It was therefore resolved at this session, to circulate petitions to the Virginia Convention or General Assembly, throughout the state, in order to obtain signatures. The prayer of these was, that the church establishment should be abolished, and religion left to stand on its own merits: And, that all religious societies should be protected in the peaceable enjoyment of their own religious principles, and modes of worship" (Semple 1810, 62).

Most of the Baptist-originated petitions came from the grassroots rather than a formal meeting. They were circulated widely and non-Baptists were invited to sign: "The Baptist petitions were remarkable for their consistency in opposing every threat to religious liberty. These petitions do not contain any self-seeking or preferential treatment. Nor at any time did Baptists favor any form of assessment to support their churches and ministers. For this reason Baptists won the favor of Jefferson and Madison for their consistent stand" (Moore 1986, 1229).

Among the many petitions were appeals to recognize the marriages performed by all clergy. Established church ministers had been the only ones recognized by the Virginia government for performing marriages.

In 1785 a general assessment bill would have benefited all religious societies with monies from the government. The Presbyterians gave some support to the proposed bill and the Baptists registered the only consistent opposition to the bill.

The petitions of the Baptist dissenters gave a collective voice for proponents of religious freedom. The mammoth petition with the ten thousand signatures, in part, stated:

> Equal Liberty! That invaluable blessing: which though it be the birth right of every good Member of the State has been what your Petitioners have been Deprived of, in that, by Taxation their property hath been wrested from them. . . . Your Petitioners therefore having long groaned under the Burden of an Ecclesiastical Establishment beg leave to move your Honourable House that this as well as every other Yoke may be broken and that the Oppressed may go free: that so every religious Denomination being on a Level, Animosities may cease, and that Christian Forbearance, Love and Charity, may be practised towards each other, while the Legislature interferes only to support them in their just Rights and equal privileges. (Eckenrode 1910, 48)

Influencing the Founding Fathers

The persecutions of the Baptists and the peaceable and lawful petitioning for proper redress did not escape the attention of the key leaders of Virginia and the new Republic. Thomas Jefferson's Baptist neighbors in Albemarle County impressed him. He even sat on his camp stool to hear outdoor Baptist preaching in Charlottesville. He recognized the Baptist church meetings with their congregational decision making as the purest form of democracy.

James Madison shared the Baptist aversion toward mere toleration. When the General Assessment Bill was proposed, Madison was aware of the Baptist opposition to any religious society, including theirs, benefiting from the public treasury. A Baptist statement emphasized "that should the legislature assume the right of taxing the people for the support of the gospel it will be destructive to religious liberty."

Thomas Jefferson's "Act for Establishing Religious Freedom" and even James Madison's First Amendment to the U.S. Constitution were influenced, directly or indirectly, by the acts observed by the two founders including the opposition by Virginia Baptists to all forms of religious tyranny. In March 1788 John Leland, the Baptist minister, most likely met with James Madison and convinced him to add religious liberty in an amendment to the Constitution.

The founding fathers heard the Baptists. Upon his election as president, George Washington wrote the General Committee of the United Baptist Churches in Virginia (Ryland 1955, 137): "I recollect with satisfaction, that the religious society of which you are members, have been throughout America, uniformly, and almost unanimously, the firm friends to civil liberty. No one would be more zealous than myself to establish effectual barriers against the horrors of spiritual tyranny, and every species of religious persecution."

Fred Anderson

Further Reading

Alley, R. E. (1973). *A history of Baptists in Virginia*. Richmond: Virginia Baptist General Board.

Eckenrode, H. J. (1910). *Separation of church and state in Virginia*. Richmond: Virginia State Library.

Estep, W. R. (1990). *Revolution within the revolution: The first amendment in historical context, 1612–1789*. Grand Rapids, MI: W. B. Eerdmans Publishing Co.

Gewehr, W. M. (1930). *The great awakening in Virginia, 1740–1790*. Durham, NC: Duke University Press.

Greene, L. F. (1845). *The writings of the late Elder John Leland*. New York: G. W. Wood.

Isaac, R. (1982). *The transformation of Virginia, 1740–1790*. Chapel Hill, NC: University of North Carolina Press.

James, C. F. (1899). *Documentary history of the struggle for religious liberty in Virginia*. Lynchburg, VA: J. P. Bell Co.

Little, L. P. (1938). *Imprisoned preachers and religious liberty in Virginia*. Lynchburg: J. P. Bell Co.

Moore, J. S. (1986). Virginia Baptist petitions for religious liberty, 1770–1798, in *Virginia Baptist register, 25*, 1225–1239. Richmond: Virginia Baptist Historical Society.

Ryland, G. (1955). *The Baptists of Virginia, 1699–1926*. Richmond: Virginia Baptist Board of Missions and Education.

Semple, R. B. (1810). *History of the Baptists in Virginia*. Richmond, VA: John O'Lynch, Printing.

Brainwashing

The concept of brainwashing (alternatively referred to by terms such as mind control, coercive persuasion, thought reform) comes originally from a Chinese term (*szu hsiang kai tsao*), which refers to sociopolitical attitude correction translated in English as "to cleanse [or wash clean] thoughts." In the United States, the term *brainwashing* was coined in 1953 by CIA-connected journalist Evan Hunter. Hunter and his successors used the term literally to refer to a psychotechnology developed by Communist regimes in the Soviet Union and China that was allegedly capable of subverting the free will. The term attained religious significance in the early 1970s with the appearance of a large number of new religious movements (NRMs). Opponents of these groups formed a countermovement, the Anticult Movement (ACM), to combat the groups themselves as well as individual affiliations with them. The ACM drew upon the post-Korean War brainwashing literature as evidence that affiliations with the NRMs were not in fact legitimate religious conversions but rather the product of brainwashing by NRM leaders. Brainwashing has been used in other cases since and it has been claimed that individuals engaged in deviant behavior was a result of mental coercion. Patty Hearst unsuccessfully mounted a brainwash-ing defense, and most recently some defenders of John Walker Lindh, the so-called American Taliban, have argued that he was brainwashed. The brainwashing issue has raised religious liberty issues because brainwashing is usually associated with minority or controversial religious groups and essentially serves as the basis for distinguishing between legitimate and illegitimate religion expression.

Historical Development

There has been conflict over new religious groups throughout American history despite the image of America as a land of religious freedom. The first amendment to the Bill of Rights asserts that states and the government can neither create a state church nor interfere with religious practice. However, this amendment represented a political compromise intended to allow the competing jealous sects and churches of the time to coexist peacefully. The historical reality is that there often has been intense opposition to religious newcomers. In the nineteenth century, for example, there were organized campaigns against both Catholics and Mormons due to allegations of extreme influence over adherents that resemble contemporary brainwashing claims. Other new religions that followed (Jehovah's Witnesses, Seventh-Day Adventists, and Christian Scientists) also have been opposed as cults by conservative Christian organizations. The most recent cohort of NRMs includes controversial groups such as the Unification Church (Moonies), International Society for Krishna Consciousness (Hare Krishnas), Children of God (renamed The Family), and Church of Scientology, all of which have generated comparable opposition from conservative Christian organizations. What distinguishes the current controversy from prior episodes is that opposition to NRMs is being orchestrated largely by the secular ACM, which alleges that NRMs gain and retain members through brainwashing, while religious opposition alleges spiritual deception.

The Contemporary Anticult Movement, Brainwashing, and Deprogramming

The current controversy over NRMs began in the early 1970s with the appearance of a diverse array of NRMs that attracted adherents as the 1960s countercultural protest movement waned. The ACM formed

UNITED STATES V. FISHMAN (1990)

In this landmark case, the United States District Court rejected the use of "brainwashing" testimony. Part of the court's reasoning is provided below.

To the extent understood by the Court, the controversy surrounding the proffered testimony stems from the fact that psychologists and sociologists are limited to investigating the range of observable responses to environmental stimuli. Coercion is a feature of the external environment; its effect or degree must be inferred from the constricted range of behavior most people exhibit in that environment. Similarly, free will is ineffable and not susceptible to direct observation or measurement. To borrow an example from one of the amici briefs discussed above, when a seemingly fit but harmless beggar asks for money, some people are inclined to give money and others are not. But when a mugger holds a knife at a victim's throat and asks for money, most people give it. Mugging accompanied with the threat of physical force is quite coercive, while begging ordinarily is not. The Court finds general acceptance within the scientific community (and elsewhere) that armed mugging is sufficiently coercive to overcome an average person's free will. But the proffered testimony in this case relates to coercive persuasion without the use or threat of physical force. The subject of the testimony is thus similar to a harmless beggar's attempt to coerce money from a stranger. There is no consensus within the scientific community regarding whether the deprivation of free will occurs in these circumstances, nor is there a consensus on how to measure this deprivation.

Source: United States, Plaintiff, v. Stephen Fishman, Defendant No. CR-88-0616-DLJ. United States District Court for the Northern District of California 743 F. Supp. 713. Filed. Jehovah's Witnesses United. Retrieved May 15, 2002, from http://www.jehovah.to/freedom/fishman.htm

almost immediately to oppose groups they designated as "cults," a term intended to distinguish such groups from legitimate religious groups. The basis of the distinction is that cults are groups that putatively engage in "destructive" practices that subvert individual autonomy, voluntarism, and self-directedness. In its initial form ACM ideology asserted that rapidly growing cults were unprecedented in their organization, tactics, and destructiveness. The most significant distinguishing characteristic attributed to cults was the use of a potent psychotechnology (brainwashing) that could rapidly alter individual beliefs and behaviors as well as create long-term emotional damage. Unscrupulous gurus were ultimately responsible for developing these techniques to exploit innocent followers for their own pleasure, power and profit, with innocent and vulnerable youth as the primary targets. The rapid growth in size, wealth, and power of cults posed an ever greater threat to society. It was in this context that the ACM began developing countermeasures—forcibly extricating individuals affiliated with NRMs and seeking legal sanctions against the organizations themselves. Early ACM organizations developed the practice of deprogramming, which involved abducting, confining, and confronting NRM members about their affiliations. The practice quickly mushroomed in the 1970s, and there were probably several thousand such deprogramming practices over the next ten to fifteen years.

As the ACM developed, it sought legal auspices for combating brainwashing. Since opposition quickly developed to physical abduction and confinement of NRM members by deprogrammers, the ACM turned to court-ordered conservatorships that granted family members legal control over aging, mentally incompetent relatives. For a time this tactic was successful. However, NRMs soon began contesting conservatorships. In a pivotal case, *Katz v. Superior Court* (1977), a California judge granted legal custody of five adult members of the Unification Church to their parents. That decision, however, was reversed on appeal, and the conservatorship strategy quickly disintegrated.

Later the ACM developed a new initiative that involved bringing civil suits against NRMs, typically contending that brainwashing involved the intentional infliction of emotional distress. This tactic also succeeded for a time, but ultimately was unsuccessful when courts refused to accept brainwashing testimony from ACM expert witnesses. There were several significant court cases. In *Robin George v. ISKCON* (1983), former member Robin George sued Hare Krishna, and in *Molko and Leal v. Holy Spirit Association* (1983), two former Unification Church members sued that church. Brainwashing testimony was central to both cases. In the Molko and Leal case, the testimony of ACM experts was rejected by the trial court, and an appeals court concluded that the expert opinions in the case lacked scientific basis. In the George case the mind control–related charges were dismissed by a Los Angeles court after several appeals, and the suit was finally settled in 1993. In 1989, a federal case, *U.S. v. Fishman*, involved a claim by a defendant that his crimes were the product of the debilitating influence of his membership in a cult. The judge ruled against allowing mind control testimony in the trial on the basis that it did not possess scientific standing.

Ultimately the ACM was severely weakened by the demise of its largest and most visible organization, the Cult Awareness Network (CAN). The mother of Jason Scott, an adult member of the Life Tabernacle Church, a branch of the United Pentecostal Church International, believed her son had been brainwashed and obtained a referral to a deprogrammer from CAN. When the coercive deprogramming effort failed, Scott brought legal charges against CAN and the deprogrammer. The judgment in the case bankrupted CAN, and the organization closed in 1996.

While brainwashing theory has not fared well in U.S. legal and political forums, it has had a recent impact in Europe. A number of European governments proposed action against NRMs in the wake of the 1994 murder/suicides by the Solar Temple in Switzerland and Canada. American ACM officials consulted with European governmental officials, who made ACM brainwashing theory a key component of reports and legislation. In 1998, France established a new office, the Mission Interministérielle de Lutte Contre les Sectes (The Interministerial Commission to Make War on the Sects) to monitor "mental manipulation" (a parallel to brainwashing).

The Debate Over Brainwashing

The brainwashing explanation for NRM affiliations has been vigorously debated since the 1970s. Most social scientists who have studied NRMs have explained NRM affiliations as conversions, but they often describe conversion and the conversion process in quite different terms. For example, the concept of conversion has been used to refer to all of the following concepts: the adoption of a new symbolic identity and mode of discourse; a strengthening of one set of social network ties and a corresponding weakening of ties with another network; role playing by converts rather than experiencing a dramatic personal transformation, and a process of gradual drift rather than sudden personal change. Several scholars assert that there is no single conversion phenomenon; rather, there are a number of different kinds of conversion in which the dynamics may be very different. Most of these scholars distinguish between limited and more pervasive personal transformation, and they tend to argue that whatever transformation does occur is a product of both individual and group initiative.

A minority of social scientists and mental health professionals, many of which are connected with the ACM, have continued to propound brainwashing theories. As in the case of conversion, there is no single brainwashing theory; however, ACM-connected scholars have developed a multiplicity of theories. In these theories contemporary brainwashing is variously conceptualized as a trauma that undermines normal cognitive functioning, a process that attacks one's core sense of being, a relational disorder in which individuals become involved in inappropriate types of social relationships, and as a process that consists of creating high exit costs for NRM affiliates such that separation from the group becomes extremely difficult. The diverse formulations specify an array of means by which cultic brainwashing is accomplished. These include hypnosis, dietary changes and restrictions, limitations on sleep, continuous indoctrination, intense social pressure, a totalistic environment, and isolation from outside contact and sources of information. In sum, there is no definitive statement of either conversion or brainwashing that has received unanimous support.

A number of specific arguments have been made in the debate among advocates and opponents. The pivotal issues are whether there is a distinctive brainwashing process that can be distinguished from other social influence processes, whether the process termed brainwashing is effective in changing and controlling behavior, and whether formal or informal social intervention is justified.

- Advocates contend that there is a distinctive brainwashing process that is reflected in the various recruitment and socialization practices employed by NRMs. Opponents claim that NRMs are ideologically and organizationally diverse and that it is implausible that a diverse array of movements with few connections to one another would have discovered and implemented parallel practices at exactly the same historical moment.
- Advocates argue that contemporary brainwashing constitutes a psychotechnology that builds on the devastating Communist brainwashing practices of the Cold War era. Opponents counter that Communist brainwashing programs were in fact a failure as only about a dozen of the three thousand POWs held in Korea and China refused repatriation. Advocates and opponents concur that POW camps and NRMs differ significantly in that physical coercion was present in the former but is not in the latter. However, advocates argue that psychological coercion functions comparably in cultic brainwashing, while opponents contend there is no evidence to support that position.
- Advocates assert that brainwashing by cults is extraordinarily effective and difficult to resist. Opponents respond that only a tiny proportion of those individuals NRMs seek to recruit actually affiliate, defection rates are extremely high, and the groups that triggered the brainwashing debate achieved their only real recruitment success for a brief time during the 1970s. Scholars on both sides acknowledge that some individuals have difficulty separating themselves from movements with which they affiliated, particularly if commitment is intense, social bonds are strong, or leadership and control practices are manipulative.
- Advocates maintain that cultic brainwashing reduces and is destructive to individual autonomy, voluntarism, and self-directedness. For evidence they rely on accounts provided by former members who express regret about their movement experiences and are likely to report engaging in actions that they in retrospect regard as self-destructive. Opponents reply that affiliates with NRMs often are unsatisfied with their lives and join movements as an act of independence and self-assertion. For evidence they rely more heavily on accounts provided by current members and former members who report positive experiences during their NRM affiliations. There is agreement on both sides of the debate that the vast majority of individuals who affiliate with NRMs do not find what they seek since most disaffiliate, usually after a very short time.
- Advocates report high rates of psychological trauma among former NRM members that they attribute in part to destructive brainwashing practices. Opponents respond that ACM coercive deprogramming and exit counseling practices produce some of the trauma advocates report and that reliance on hostile former members' biases substantiates research findings. Both camps agree that some NRM members have been victimized by manipulative and exploitative practices. It is the extensiveness and representativeness of such practices that is at issue.

The Future

Brainwashing is a claim that has been made throughout American history in situations of intense political and religious conflict. The controversy surrounding NRMs is the most recent chapter, and there is reason to expect that the brainwashing debate will continue in some form. As individual autonomy, voluntarism, and self-directedness continue to become more central to societal functioning, any group that strongly embeds individuals is likely to be deemed detrimental to individual well-being and therefore illegitimate. Indeed, concern has been expressed on these very grounds about Opus Dei within the Catholic tradition, some Orthodox Jewish groups within the Judaic tradition, and shepherding and discipleship groups in the Protestant tradition. It is therefore probable that allegations of "undue" or "excessive" influence will be raised by groups with an interest in distinguishing between legitimate and illegitimate religious expression. Such disputes are likely to constitute a new testing ground for the limits of religious liberty.

David G. Bromley

See also Family, The; New Religious Movements; Unification Church

Further Reading

Bromley, D. G. (1988). Deprogramming as a mode of exit from new religious movements: The case of the unificationist movement. In D. G. Bromley (Ed.), *Falling from the faith* (pp. 166–184). Newbury Park: Sage.

Bromley, D. G., & Richardson, J. T. (Eds.). (1983). *The brainwashing/deprogramming controversy*. Lewiston, NY: Edwin Mellen Press.

Bromley, D. G., & Robbins, T. (1992). The role of government in regulating new and unconventional religions. In James Wood (Ed.), *Governmental monitoring of religion* (pp. 101–137). Waco, TX: Baylor University Press.

Bromley, D. G., & Shupe, A. (1979). Just a few years seem like a lifetime: A role theory approach to participation in religious movements. *Research in Social Movements, Conflicts and Change 2*, 159–185.

Bunker, G., & Bitton, D. (1975). Mesmerism and Mormonism. *BYU Studies, 15*, 146–170.

Conway, F., & Siegelman, J. (1982, January). Information disease: Have the cults created a new mental illness? *Science Digest*, 86–92.

Davis, D. B. (1960). Some themes of counter-subversion: An analysis of anti-Masonic, anti-Catholic, and anti-Mormon literature. *The Mississippi Valley Historical Review. 47*, 205–224.

Davis, D. H. (Ed.). (2000). *Religious liberty in northern Europe in the twenty-first century*. Waco, TX: Baylor University (J. M. Dawson Institute of Church-State Studies).

Hunter, E. (1953). *Brainwashing in Red China: The calculated destruction of men's minds*. New York: Vanguard.

Lifton, R. J. (1963). *Thought reform and the psychology of totalism*. New York: W. W. Norton.

Lofland, J., & Skonovd, N. (1981). Conversion motifs. *Journal for the Scientific Study of Religion, 20*, 373–385.

Lofland J., & Stark, R. (1965). Becoming a world-saver: A theory of religious conversion. *American Sociological Review, 30*, 862–874.

Long, T., & Hadden, J. K. (1983). Religious conversion and the concept of socialization: Integrating the brainwashing and drift models. *Journal for the Scientific Study of Religion, 22*, 1–14.

Melton, J. G. (Ed.). (1990). *The evangelical anti-cult movement: Christian counter-cult literature*. New York: Garland.

Ofshe, R., & Singer, M. (1986). Attacks on peripheral versus central elements of self and the impact of thought reforming techniques. *The Cultic Studies Journal, 3*, 3–24.

Saliba, J. A. (1990). *Social science and the cults: An annotated bibliography*. New York: Garland.

Shupe, A., & Bromley, D. G. (1980). *The new vigilantes*. Beverly Hills, CA: Sage.

Sirkin, M., & Wynne, L. (1990). Cult involvement as relational disorder. *Psychiatric Annals, 20*, 199–203.

Snow, D., & Machalek, R. (1984). The sociology of conversion. *Annual Review of Sociology, 10*, 167–190.

Zablocki, B. (1998). Exit cost analysis: A new approach to the scientific study of brainwashing. *Nova Religio, 1*, 216–249.

Zablocki, B., & Robbins, T. (Eds.). (2001). *Misunderstanding cults*. Toronto: University of Toronto Press.

Brethren *See* Conscientious Objection and Pacifism; Peace Churches

British Empire

The British Empire, a product of an expansionist trading island, evolved from the seventeenth century and lasted until the late twentieth century. Britain itself was the product of the Norman Conquest from the eleventh century onward that swallowed up England and Wales, and less successfully Ireland and southern parts of Scotland. Eventually the whole British Isles was incorporated into one United Kingdom (1801), which lasted until Ireland left (1921), leaving Northern Ireland with the other three countries as part of a smaller United Kingdom. Effectively what is meant by Britain is the United Kingdom, and one of the greatest unifying factors in this union has been its common Protestant heritage (excluding southern Ireland), against what was seen as a Catholic continental threat. Probably equally important for unity was the concern for international trade. The economies of all four countries became dominated by trading merchants who wanted access to world trade markets. To trade they wanted military security from native and European threats and secure colonies or plantations in which to develop that trade. This made a large British state more economically and

RELIGION AND EDUCATION IN COLONIAL UGANDA

Missionary work to convert colonized peoples to Protestantism was an important component of the British Empire. The following text describes how schools started by both Protestant and Catholic missionaries in Uganda helped create a new social order that favored people who were educated.

Religion and education were inextricably linked. The Church Missionary Society, for example, had stressed education as the moral basis of the Christian presence in Uganda. The White Fathers and the Mill Hill missions also recognized how important education would be, both to the missions and to the country. Catholics and Protestants vied with one another to produce the more effective educational programs. King's College, Budo, and Gayaza High School, for boys and girls respectively, were the main Protestant secondary schools. Kisubi or St. Mary's was established by the Catholics. As well, "the Protectorate authorities welcomed students at all levels of education since it was only they who could fit into the increasingly complex pattern of modern administration. So there began to emerge a new class, an aristocracy of education which in time tended to usurp the positions of importance formerly occupied by the men who had led the religious factions in war and had won their place in a peaceful land by their strength of character, by their experience and by their powerful following."

Education, then, became one important point of entry into positions of power and prestige.

David E. Apter

Source: *The Political Kingdom in Uganda: A Study in Bureaucratic Nationalism*, 2nd ed. (Princeton, NJ: Princeton University Press, 1967), 129.

militarily beneficial and politically desirable. Trade was regarded as religiously sanctioned and of divine purpose for the Protestant merchants who dominated it. And Britain became increasingly dominated by merchant traders whose Whig politics and classical liberal economics gradually began to establish themselves as a cultural norm and combined with their religious beliefs.

From the mid–sixteenth century on the English began to pride themselves as free born and chosen by God, something they intimately associated with their Protestantism. Around this core the other parts of the union quickly began to muster and associate. The veracity of this was believed to be shown in Britain's increasing wealth and power as it emerged from being a group of insignificant offshore islands to a world economic, colonial, military, naval, and trading power by the mid–eighteenth century. This strongly reinforced a belief in divine mission and Protestant principles, which during the eighteenth century increasingly became entangled with ideas of economics wherein wealth and material success came to be seen as signs of divine approval (most

famously reflected in the works of Weber and Tawney). However, religion had always been closely associated with ideas of social order and political ideals: in preindustrial society religion was also effectively culture. Consequently as British religion and trade spread so too did the sociopolitical ideals and concepts of Protestant culture. This is most clearly seen in Britain's first great colony (America), which was almost entirely a planted colony (excluding the indigenous native population) stemming from the early seventeenth century but which by the eighteenth century had a population largely born in America and a flourishing economy. Most of the population was derived from nonconformist Protestant sects, particularly under the influence of Ulster and Scots Presbyterians. These colonists, as a result of their Calvinist beliefs, at odds with the Anglican religion dominant in Britain, developed radical political ideas of equality, individualism, self-government, and autonomy that led to their eventual breakaway in the American war of independence. At the time, the war was regarded as about religious freedom as much as political freedom, the one being derived from the other and both conflated in economic ideals of free trade.

Nineteenth-Century British Empire

After the loss of the American colonies the British Empire re-formed around its trade links with the Caribbean, India, and increasingly also with Africa, and throughout the nineteenth century it additionally established new settler colonies in Canada, Australia, New Zealand, and South Africa. Outside of the settler colonies the empire was almost a by-product of trade, with the British being drawn in to help maintain order and security amongst native populations and eventually ending up ruling large native populations, usually with their own indigenous religion and culture. This posed different imperial problems to the settler colonies, which were effectively simply transplants of Britain. Settler colonies could easily proceed to self-government in Britain's own image, applying the religious and cultural principles of Britain by simple transplant. They became predominantly Protestant and applied Protestant principles of individual freedom, salvation, and civic responsibility. Such settler colonies evoked the same political and legal ideals as Britain and by the beginning of the twentieth century they had reached the status of autonomy and even regarded themselves as part of the British Imperial project.

The "native" colonies (colonies in which the colonists were only a small group of white elite) posed different problems. By the terms of nineteenth-century Protestant values most were seen as either backward or degenerate peoples, unenlightened by Christian (invariably implying Protestant) learning. This led to a movement amongst increasingly evangelical Christians to go out and save "ignorant" natives. Here, again, religion and politics were entirely conflated since religious salvation was intimately interwoven into ideas of civilization and "civilizing" the natives; that is, inculcating political ideals of social and political behavior that would assist the natives in finding their true salvation. Salvation in Protestant opinion was an individual affair that could be determined in this life, or at least its signs identified. Once again, trade, politics, "civilization," and religion all found common cause in a mutually sustaining manner. A set of common values of civilization and political ideals based on the moral authority of the same religious culture greatly enhanced the prospects of increased trade amongst those sharing that culture and made policing the empire a simpler and less taxing task. This in turn was justified by ideas of religious correctness that interpreted, according to Protestant values, the very success of the empire as a sign of God's approval and divine grace. Through the empire lay salvation, and it was the mightiest empire of its time. Thus men were inspired by a religious ideal of the empire; it was going about God's work.

Not every imperialist may have been inspired by such religious motives, but many were, especially the missionaries and many of the more famous imperial military commanders. An image of soldiers going off to fight imperial wars with a sword in one hand and a Bible in the other was quite common. However, many administrators had grave reservations since they regarded attempts at overt religious conversion as politically destabilizing. Proselytizing missionaries could disrupt stable and contented communities with new ideas and values; they could undermine local authority and political systems and power relationships that helped to maintain stable and peaceful relationships within a colony. Much of the empire was maintained as much by local willingness to cooperate and indigenous local princes' and chiefs' preference for British rule in return for British support for their positions as by overt force. Consequently, many Christian missionaries were regarded by colonial administrators as quite dangerous, since they upset local political calculations.

The situation varied within the empire. In Africa the indigenous populations were looked on as ignorant savages almost completely lacking in any culture and thus in need of "civilizing" en masse. Meanwhile, in Asia, particularly India, where extensive and ancient civilizations and sophisticated religions already existed, the colonial attitude changed to one of regarding native religion/culture as degenerate and in need of reform. Either way the tasks involved became popularized as the "white man's burden," to save the "ignorant" and "degenerate" from themselves. However, while Christianity took at least a nominal hold in many of Britain's African and Caribbean colonies, it made little direct impact in Asia, where most native people remained attached to their traditional religions.

But the real force of religious influence probably lay not so much in overt missionary zeal as in the religiously grounded cultural and religious ideas implicit in colonial government. Ideas such as "good" government, "efficient" administration, and legal concepts of freedom of conscience and thought, free expression, individual rights and responsibilities, and the rule of law were introduced into many colonial territories for the first time. All of these had their roots in early Protestant theology, which stressed the importance of individuals finding their own salvation in a free and autonomous manner and in an open way. Freedom to question and criticize in an open religious and political market was central to Protestant theology and formed the basis for democratic government and pluralist societies. The right to scrutinize one's rulers and call them to account was another derivative of a Protestant theology that stressed individual accountability before God. This was aided by schools and formal education as they were introduced, very often the work of missionaries, where the cultural and political ideals translated from Christianity were imbued into the educated sectors of the native population, even where they remained loyal to their traditional religions.

Twentieth-Century Empire

The very ideals that inspired empire now began to work against it, particularly after World Wars I and II, when the invincibility and thus divine sanction of imperial rule was severely dented. However, the greatest threat to the imperial venture lay in the very ideas and ideals the imperialists themselves planted. As imperialists strove to save native populations and individuals, they implanted the ideals of individual and collective salvation (particularly the idea of a nation-state) that led to a desire among the colonized to seek their own salvation without the hindrance of colonial rule. Also, an educated native elite began to apply concepts of scrutiny, accountability, and freedom to seek one's own salvation against the colonial power that introduced such notions. Consequently, independence movements emerged first in the Asian colonies and later in the Caribbean and then African colonies using the very ideas of imperialism against empire. All aspired, at least in rhetoric, to concepts of nation-statehood and democratic self-rule that descended directly from Protestant theology, especially as that theology evolved in nineteenth-century evangelical movements. Adding to this, but less overt, was the introduction of science and the ideas of scientific government and economics. Science was strongly rooted in the Enlightenment of the eighteenth century, which stressed the idea of the seeking of scientific laws as the pursuit of and understanding of God's laws. For Protestants in particular, science was a religious vocation that once again stressed ideas of openness, debate, critical analysis, and independent judgment applied as much in politics and religion as in natural science.

Meanwhile, the white dominions (colonies that became predominantly white settler populations, such as Canada or Australia) have maintained a steady commitment to Protestant political ideals in both practice and theory, with (until recently) the exception of South Africa. But even now South Africa has become a democratic society in line with the ideals of the Commonwealth, which replaced the empire as a voluntary association of former colonies. And the religiopolitical ideals of modern democracy, freedom of the individual, and individual rights and property rights are at least nominally adhered to.

The British Empire became a major exporter of Protestant ideas of religious freedom. The ideas may have taken hold more strongly in the predominantly white settler colonies, but even in the native colonies, the ideal of religious freedom is at least aspired to. Meanwhile, the United States, another colonial offspring of Britain, has probably become the most powerful contemporary champion of such ideals with the demise of British imperialism as its own "neo-imperialism" continues to uphold the same values of religious freedom that it brought from Britain.

James Dingley

Further Reading

Canny, N. (1998). *The Oxford history of the British empire.* Oxford, UK: Oxford University Press.

Colley, L. (1994). *Britons.* London: Verso.

Lawrence, J. (2001). *The rise and fall of the British empire.* London: Abacus.

McManners, J. (Ed.). (1993). *The Oxford history of Christianity.* Oxford, UK: Oxford University Press.

Porter, R. (2000). *Enlightenment.* London: Penguin.

Tawney, R. (1938). *Religion and the rise of capitalism.* London: Peregrine.

Turner, B. (1993). *Citizenship and social theory.* London: Sage.

van der Veer, P., & Lehmann, H. (1999). *Nation and religion.* Princeton, NJ: Princeton University Press.

Weber, M. (1976). *The Protestant ethic and the spirit of capitalism.* London: Allen and Unwin.

Buddhism

Buddhism is a rich and culturally diverse set of beliefs and practices that revolve around the teachings of the historical Buddha, who first articulated his message of salvation in the sixth century BCE. Since the formation of the earliest Buddhist communities in India, this religious view and way of life has been constantly changing as it continues to spread and take hold of new values and customs. There remains, however, great similarity between the practices of the various geographically and historically disparate Buddhist societies and cultures.

As with all major world religions, there is no single and definitive definition of Buddhism; it needs to be examined and understood within the contexts of the cultures where it took root. Buddhism continues to grow, exponentially, especially in East Asia, Southeast Asia, Central Asia, Central Mongolia, and the West, as it offers believers alternative approaches to ecology and society.

The Buddha's Life

Traditional accounts of the Buddha's life and teachings have been widely disseminated through various media, including art and architecture, song and dance, and ritual and scripture. Most of these accounts are didactic, and include the following narrative. The Buddha was miraculously born as a warrior-caste prince in a northern-Indian Himalayan kingdom. Astrologers predicted that the prince, named Siddhartha Gautama, would one day be either a great king or a great religious teacher. His father the king, not wanting to loose his son to the religious life, shielded him from the world's suffering. He kept him inside a palace fortress surrounded by all kinds of pleasant diversions: including beautiful women, delectable food, sports, and the finest arts and literature. The king believed that if his son became dissatisfied with the world he would ponder over life's perplexities, and embark on a religious quest. As a young man, Prince Siddhartha married a beautiful princess, and had a son. At twenty-nine, he left the palace, on the first of what are known as the four famous chariot rides. On his first ride he saw an old person, and was told by his charioteer that this was not the only old person in the world, but that everyone ages. On the second tour he saw a sick person, and on the third he saw a corpse. On the fourth trip he saw an austerely religious yogi who had embarked on a life of renunciation and self-denial in search of release from pain. At that moment Prince Siddhartha decided to oppose his father's wishes and follow the religious path. He left for a homeless life in search of liberation from the world of suffering.

Siddhartha Gautama studied many yogic disciplines ranging from techniques for entering mystical states to severe bodily chastisement, and concluded that self-mortification would not solve the problems of birth, sickness, aging, and death. At the age of thirty-four, he sat in meditation under a tree all night long. After fending off attacks by Mara (the world of illusion) and his army, he awakened with the dawn to a new and transcendent state of wisdom and enlightenment (nirvana) that allowed him to become the Buddha.

During his lifetime, Buddha's teachings spread throughout northern India, neighboring kingdoms, and beyond. He broke all of the boundaries of caste as his men and women disciples included kings, priests, merchants, farmers, outcastes, yogi mendicants, robbers, and thieves. He taught a widening circle of lay followers, as well as a core religious community of nuns and monks (*Sangha*) responsible for spreading his message.

Statue of Buddha at the Yun Gang Rock Cave, in Yun Gang, Hennan, China in 1986. COURTESY OF JINGHAO ZHOU.

His personality is traditionally described as one of dignity, affability, wisdom, and kindness. He possessed a majesty that awed kings, while his compassionate heart allowed him to comfort the sick and downtrodden. Ever mindful and calm, the Buddha directly faced all kinds of adversity and danger with composure and wisdom. The Buddha died at age eighty, in the home of a benefactor who inadvertently served him a meal made with poisonous mushrooms. Even dying, the Buddha remained calm and consoled this friend, thanking him for a meal that allowed him to enter into nirvana's eternal bliss.

Buddhist Shrines and Teachings

It is said that Buddha instructed his followers to cremate his body and distribute his ashes among the various groups of his followers, who were to enshrine them in stupas (relic mounds). These sites have become places of pilgrimage for Buddhists, as they represent places where Buddha was present. Early texts and archaeological records are replete with records of worship at stupas connected with key places in Buddha's life, such as the sites of his birth, enlightenment, first teaching, and death. However, stupas are also found in sacred places that predate Buddhism.

By the seventh century, the practice of enshrining the sacred relics of the Buddha is no longer evident in the archaeological record. It was replaced by the practice of enshrining small tablets engraved with a four-line verse believed to be the culmination of Buddha's teaching: "The Tathagata has explained the cause of all things that arise from that cause. The great renunciate has also explained their cessation." (*Renunciate* is the standard term used to refer to Buddha as the great renouncer of worldly or materialistic desires.) Although the exact meaning of this pithy statement has been widely debated, it is said to hold the essence of the four noble truths taught by the Buddha during his lifetime.

The Four Noble Truths

The first truth is that life is marked by suffering, an agonized bondage to the meaningless cycles of birth and death, amidst a transitory flux that is momentary, impermanent, and without essential being. The second truth is that the principal cause of this condition is a profound ignorance of the illusory nature of the phenomenal world. This ignorance engenders uncontrollable desires and endless cravings for transient entities, and the mistaken attribution of ultimate worth to finite forms that come into being only to decay and dissolve. The third truth is that the elimination of ignorance of the illusory nature of the phenomenal world and the extirpation of endless desires will break the causal sequence and so bring about final salvation. The fourth truth is that for the yogi to achieve liberation he or she must follow the Eightfold Path, an integral combination of ethical and meditative methods that together purify one's motivations and mind. This practice leads to the attainment of complete enlightenment and nirvana—the release from suffering.

The Dharma and the Eightfold Path

The term *dharma* means religion for Buddhists. It refers to the totality of the Buddha's teachings, which can be summarized in the Eightfold path: "right views, intention, speech, action, livelihood, effort, mindfulness, and concentration," which are sometimes further reduced to wisdom, morality, and meditation. "Right views and intentions" signify the commitment to the Buddha's dharma. The general characteristics of the dharma have been summarized in an ancient formulaic prayer which is chanted repeatedly in the sutras and which is used liturgically. "The dharma is well taught; it belongs to the Lord; not to any other teacher; its results, when it is put into practice, are visible in this very life; it is timeless; it invites the enquirer to come and see personally what it is like; it is progressive; leading from lower to higher states of existence, and it is to be understood by the wise each one for himself." (Sangharakshita 1993, 8)

The content of the dharma consists of various doctrines and teachings. These teachings are not theoretically speculative, but are anchored in the real-life experiences of the Buddha. They derive from an organic view of the world that sees humans as being intimately part of and interconnected with nature.

New Buddhist Currents

Today, many Buddhists are actively engaged in movements that call for world peace and the ecological replenishment of the planet. Their actively nonviolent involvements coincide with Buddha's this-worldly teachings. Cultural tolerance, religious pluralism, and practical concern for greater equity, justice, and peace are common themes in these movements.

Consider for example, the Dharmmayietra, an annual peace walk in Cambodia that began with the repatriation of refugees from the Thai border camps during the U.N.-monitored transition to democracy in 1992 (Poethig 2002, 19). There are numerous other examples. As part of their training, Thai monks participate in village self-help projects in rural areas. Many of them remain in rural communities long after graduation, as they have become immersed in the social, cultural, political, environmental, and ecological aspects of sustainable rural development. For example, Pongsak, the abbot of Wat Palad near the Chang Mai border in northern Thailand, has continued to work with villagers to reforest and irrigate rapidly desertifying land in the face of obstacles such as police raids (Batchelor & Brown 1992, Ch. 8). The Buddhist Sarvodaya movement that emerged in 1958 in Sri Lanka is another example that involves students interested in getting in touch with their roots by learning from farmers. The approach was so successful that today this movement comprises a network of over 4,000 villages operating health programs, educational programs, agricultural projects, and small-scale industries. One remarkable achievement of this movement is that it helped rejuvenate Sri Lanka's ancient and elaborate irrigation system, originally built around temple communities that were overseen by monks.

Buddhism continues to take many forms in many places as it adapts and changes in accordance with local contexts and in relation to global processes. While some Buddhists consciously decide to retreat from the human world in an effort to escape from suffering, others, sometimes at great risk to themselves, get involved in pro-people and pro-ecology movements. Buddhism of this latter sort is best understood as a living process that moves across religious and political boundaries, intersecting with an ecumenical array of international humanitarian groups.

Kathleen Nadeau

See also China, Communist; China, Imperial; Individualist Religions; Japan; Tibet

Further Reading

Batchelor, M., & Brown, K. (Eds.). (1992). *Buddhism and ecology*. London: Cassell.

Sangharakshita (1993). *A survey of Buddhism through the ages, its doctrines and methods through the ages*. Glasgow, UK: Windhorse Publications.

Poethig, K. (2002). Movable peace: Engaging the transnational in Cambodia's Dharmmayietra. *The journal of the scientific study of religion, 41*(1), 19–28.

Byzantine Empire

The Byzantine Empire is a term used in European scholarship, from the seventeenth century onwards, to describe the affairs of the Roman Empire in the Eastern Provinces from the sixth century of the Christian era to its final collapse, usually dated to 1453, when Ottoman armies overran the capital, Constantinople (now Istanbul). The Byzantines described themselves simply as *Romaioi* (Romans) and saw in their own history a direct continuation of the culture and polity of the ancient Roman Empire. There were, however, some significant changes, for the term "Byzantine culture" signifies above all else how the Roman Empire had become Christian and Greek-speaking.

Constantine: "Equal to the Apostles"

The starting point, at least symbolically, should be drawn much earlier than the sixth century (the age of the greatest of the East-Roman emperors—Justinian [483–565]), and ought rather to be the time of Constantine I (reigned 306–337), who through a bitter civil war in the early fourth century emerged as the

The Hagia Sophia in Istanbul. At the crossroads of Christianity and Islam, it was a church, then a mosque, and now a museum. COURTESY OF JOHN A. MCGUCKIN.

undisputed ruler of a vastly extended Roman world that had for a long time been suffering the unsettling effects of a succession of short-lived military emperors. Constantine saw in the ascendant Christian movement a powerful potential ally, and gave the church legal protection at the beginning of his reign and increasing benefits and concessions in the course of his long and stable rule.

After Constantine, Christianity emerged as the single dominant Mediterranean religion. When he founded a new capital for the empire of Rome (causing the city of Rome to enter into many years of comparative obscurity), Constantine made a fresh start, and selected a strategic site between Europe and Asia. The city of Constantinople, named after him, was begun in 324 and dedicated in 330. Within the following century it would become the greatest city in the ancient world. In the eleven hundred years of Byzantium that were to follow, Christian Greek culture gave Roman imperial affairs a new ethos and a new philosophy, often producing results that were both remarkable and admirable. The Byzantine Empire, as a distinctive form of Roman imperium, thus extended from 330 to 1453. It continues to live on, of course, as a dominant cultural and historical foundation for Greece, for most of the Slavic countries, and for the remainder of eastern Europe, such as the Latin-speaking tribes of Wallachia, Romania, as well as in its direct religious embodiment in the Eastern Orthodox churches, ranging from Moscow to Ethiopia. All Byzantine culture can be said to turn around two polarities: first, the legal and social presuppositions of the internationalized form of late antique Roman civilization; and second, how the former were reexamined in the light of Christian religious axioms.

European Scholarly Prejudices

The scholars of the Enlightenment, far from being fully aware of the pertinent facts and in possession of few of the texts (since most things Byzantine had slid into obscurity with the fifteenth-century Ottoman conquest and the bitter suppression of the Greek schools), passed a singularly harsh judgment on the Byzantine achievement, one that became almost a commonplace of history textbooks until the middle of the twentieth century. From that time onward, with a renaissance of scholarly work in the area, a fuller appreciation of matters has emerged to expose the levels of imperialist bias that had been operating in the way earlier Western writers had denigrated Byzantium as being a "rigid," "hieratic," "totalitarian" society, generally hostile to personal freedoms and always ready to suppress religious dissonance.

The picture of unrelievedly depressed horizons, what one British Byzantinist once called "a gloomy and intolerant despotism under the dead hand of orthodoxy" (Mango 1969–1970, 9), was much exaggerated. Even so, our contemporary understanding of how the Byzantine culture approached issues of personal, religious, and intellectual freedom needs some careful exegesis; for like most medieval societies, the Byzantines understood the function of the body politic was to achieve consensus and *symphonia,* not to protect all individuals and shelter their right to free expression.

The Significance of Roman Law

The condition of the empire's radical religious dissidents, such as Jews, was limited. The Jewish community was required to live in a separate part of the capital, and from that segregationary practice, as copied by the great Byzantine colony of Venice, the term *ghetto* first entered into Western history. But the rights of Jewish citizens, though not so extensive as those of Christians, were protected under law in all matters relating to security of person and goods, and the force of Roman law in that regard was generally applied.

Roman law underwent its greatest and most systematic revision under the Christian emperor Justinian in the sixth century, a codification that had immense influence on the establishment of Roman case law as a standard in later European societies. The law enshrined the empire as constitutionally Christian. The first duty of the emperor was to command the military and civil arms of governance in order to guarantee the security of the Christian borders against all "infidel" foes. His second duty was to establish within the Christian borders a harmony of faith, by constant cooperation with the church and its leaders.

Under the terms of ancient Roman philosophy of law, the emperor was the *Nomos Empsychos,* himself the source and origin of law. As such, he could not be tried by law. The church insisted, however, that he was nonetheless subject to the law's own source and origin—the will of God as manifested in the charter of Christ's gospel. This gave the church much control over imperial behavior and established a complex web of restrictions to hinder the development of political absolutism. It was axiomatic, for example, that the Christian emperor continued the role and status of the ancient kings of Israel. He was called the New David and was seen to be a type of the God-favored messiah-king, whose righteous battles in defense of the territory of the Christians would be favored by the same God who once brought the Israelites into the possession of the Promised Land. The Byzantines, accordingly, called themselves the New Israel, and this biblically based theocratic view explains much of their social and religious legislation. Non-Christians were tolerated more liberally than Christians who dissented from the canons of Orthodoxy as they were progressively established at the great councils of the church.

From 325 when Constantine held the first Ecumenical Council at Nicaea, to 781 when the Seventh Council was held, essential aspects of the international Christian polity were established by worldwide synods of bishops, whose judgments were then given status of Roman law, comparable to senatorial decrees once validated by the emperor. Significant parts of the Christian world, particularly Armenia, Syria, Egypt, and Ethiopia, reacted negatively to the judgments enshrined there about the person of Christ, and though they were supposedly condemned by the official Church (the mainstream Greek and Latin churches) and their leaders were technically forbidden from occupying episcopal offices in the various cities, it was abundantly clear that local attitudes were the primary force in carrying the orthodoxy of the day.

Despotism and Its Limitations

Official state persecutions aimed at establishing internal orthodoxy were always few and far between, and rarely had much long-term success. Almost all Byzantine theorists found the violent enforcement of religious belief profoundly distasteful. Measures of intolerance that can be cited, such as Emperor Theodosius's (347–395) closing of the ancient schools of (pagan) philosophy in 391, were symbolic endings of pre-Christian cultural institutions that had already been in terminal decline for some time. Theodosius's determination to suppress "paganism" showed itself in several permissive measures for local (Christian) populations who wished to dispossess the old pagan temples, and nowhere was this more actively pursued than in the Egyptian countryside, which saw

many ancient cult centers overthrown and (smaller) Christian churches established in their place. While this can indeed be regarded as an example of imperial despotism in the service of establishing a new religion, it also needs to be contextualized in the light of how the old religion's temples were vastly powerful landowners, and burdensome sources of taxation, which locals were only too glad to be rid of. Christianity's rise to power shows the imperial authorities were as much following in the wake of popular religious and political movements as creating them.

Again, in 390, when Theodosius applied a traditional imperial punishment to the city of Thessalonica for a riotous murder of one of his officials by sending in troops to decimate the crowds, Bishop Ambrose of Milan delivered to him a public rebuke, and formally cut him off from communion in the body of Christians. It was a dramatic sign that indicated the church would no longer allow arbitrary acts of supreme power to pass unchallenged. Theodosius was forced to do public penance. For the first time in Roman history a supreme ruler had been openly compelled to acknowledge the demands of a higher code of law—ethical imperatives deriving from religion and common humanity. Henceforth Byzantine rulers knew only too well that the church validated their power only if they maintained the terms of the gospel charter—only, that is, if they served to fulfill the function of the "righteous king" (as described in the Psalms and the biblical books of the Kings), whose primary duties were the protection of the widow and orphan. If rulers failed, and despotically applied principles the church abhorred (and by and large the church reflected general opinion throughout these centuries), they had forfeited the right to rule.

Byzantium never adopted a formal dynastic principle, seeing the imperial office as a divine charism. For this reason, although the church confirmed the legal code's description of the ruler as the Supreme Autocrat of the Romans, the great number of Emperors whose policies were frustrated by local resistance, and the very large number who ended their days violently after short and controversial reigns, all give testimony to the fact that there was a very large gap indeed between autocratic theory and political and social reality.

The long Byzantine centuries, in fact, gave rise to a generally peaceful and creative culture where slavery increasingly waned, and agriculture and the arts were encouraged. Things were far better, of course, for the inner core of imperial citizens, those who inhabited the great cities of the Byzantine world: Constantinople, Antioch, Rome, Thessalonica, and Alexandria. The free expression of their rights in daily life was generally higher than that of lower classes, because they had recourse much more easily to the legal courts and a range of offices that many a peasant serf would have had difficulty in accessing. In such cases, they had an advocate in the *Episcopos*, the local bishop who was required to be the "father of the poor" and the defender of the rights of the downtrodden. Many bishops, particularly those of the provinces, have left a valiant record of calls for the protection of the poor. Theirs was a moral voice that carried even to the great capital centers and was instrumental in founding a system of public philanthropy (major sites, with endowment, devoted to the care of the sick, the orphans, and the elderly) that was not to be emulated until late modernity.

Byzantium, then, was indeed a totalist society. But like all eras of Rome, certainly the pre-Christian Roman ages, the lack of democratic vote by no means meant that the populace was powerless; the old adage was taken seriously: *vox populi vox Dei* ("the voice of the people is the voice of God"). Street violence and insurrection were powerful means the masses had to change and direct policy. The imperial court and army were usually careful to be finely attuned to those sentiments. The overall conclusion has to be that while Byzantium advocated an absolutist vision of a closed society (one Orthodox faith, one God, one empire), the reality was always more complex and more flexible. When Emperor Justinian issued legal condemnations and suppressions of those who rejected his Council of 553, for example, his wife, Theodora, was simultaneously actively funding those selfsame dissidents, something that cannot but be seen as a typically Byzantine compromise.

Orthodoxy and Heterodoxy

The dominant official views on single-state orthodoxy in Byzantium also had a practical effect of making people intensely aware of the multitude of different religious debates that took place. These were too numerous to list here in their entirety, but a few examples will suffice. Through the fourth century the Arian crisis divided Byzantine society over basic issues of the divine (or nondivine) status of Jesus Christ; the eighth and ninth centuries were similarly wracked over the question whether sacred images were permissible (Judaism and Islam had taken a highly negative view, which Byzantium would reverse); and from the eleventh to the fourteenth centuries deep divisions occurred over the status of relations with the Western Catholic church. In all of these times of bitter disputes, Byzantine writers and thinkers expressed themselves readily and freely. If their positions differed from the official view, and they gained a following, they were usually exiled to a provincial town. If their opposition was bitter and long-sustained they were sometimes punished more savagely for having "offended the imperial majesty"; but usually, the dissidents continued to write from obscurity, and much of the surviving body of Byzantine literature could rightly be described as variously "apologetic."

The existence of a large body of mobile monk-theologians in the Christian East afforded Byzantine society a vibrant subset of celibate and poor scholars who could express robust differences of opinion, without having to fear for their careers or their family security. The social status of the "holy man" was profoundly rooted in the pride the local regions took in their ascetics and teachers. As a result, even when state orthodoxy was being prosecuted, the Byzantine world more or less kept faith with the underlying principle of its formal methodology for recognizing what orthodox doctrine was. For the Byzantines always insisted that to be a central element of the faith of the universal church, an opinion or teaching had to command the assent of the whole body. This, of course, was not something that could be mechanically applied, and was generally a retrospective canon of judgment, but it was proven over and over again to be effective in the long term: for many an emperor's attempt to establish state orthodoxy foundered on the rocks of popular disapproval.

Byzantine Philosophies of Personhood and Freedom

The many attempts over the different centuries to establish a state consensus on the person and status of Jesus (known as christological orthodoxy) had been a cause of many factions in Byzantium, but strangely enough it was also the stimulus for perhaps the greatest contribution of the Byzantines to the theory of freedom. In the course of the centuries between 325 and 781 philosophers and theologians labored to create a technical vocabulary of "personhood." It was developed, first and foremost, to speak of the divine Son of God, but soon, of course, included high-level discussions of the nature of humanity and of human personhood, which the Son of God was believed to have assumed at his incarnation. The Byzantines elevated several key terms for personhood (*psyche, hypostasis, physis, persona,* and *prosopon*), and for the first time in the history of ancient philosophy, they distinguished them closely. Ancient Hellenistic thought had not, strictly speaking, evolved much beyond the old understanding of an individual as a legal entity that was capable of possession. So ancient thought understood a person as the thing that "possessed" a body and so on. The deficiencies of this schema, now exposed in a highly important philosophical and religious domain, led the Byzantines to redefine "person" as a charismatic entity called to communion with the divine, a spiritual force of ultimate worth and of inalienable equality with all other persons regardless of the differences in social status that were marked materially in common society. The individual person was defined as supremely a moral agent, self-determinant and creative (*autoexousios* as the important eighth-century theologian John of Damascus put it). This could be called a quasimystical view of the dignity, rights, and equality of all persons. It was moved by the Byzantine christological debates to center stage of philosophical and religious consciousness, and thus became, perhaps, one of the greatest contributions to the philosophy of freedom and personhood in the history of western thought.

John A. McGuckin

See also Orthodox Christianity

Further Reading

Browning, R. (1980). *The Byzantine empire.* London: Weidenfeld & Nicolson.

Byron, R. (1987). *The Byzantine achievement.* London & New York: Routledge & Kegan Paul. (Originally published 1929)

Cavallo, G. (1997). *The Byzantines.* Chicago & London: Chicago University Press.

Constantelos, D. (1968). *Byzantine philanthropy and social welfare.* New Brunswick, NJ: Rutgers University Press.

Davis, L. D. (1987). *The first seven ecumenical councils.* Wilmington, DE: Michael Glazier Publishers.

Geanokoplos, D. J. (1984). *Byzantium: Church society and civilisation through contemporary eyes.* Chicago & London: Chicago University Press.

Hackel, S. (2001). *The Byzantine saint.* New York: St. Vladimir's Seminary Press.

Hussey, J. M. (1986). *The Orthodox church in the Byzantine empire.* Oxford, UK: Clarendon Press.

Kazhdan, A. P. (Ed.) (1991). *The Oxford dictionary of Byzantium.* Oxford, UK: Oxford University Press.

Mango, C. (1969–1970). *A Memoir of Romilly Jenkins.* Washington, DC: Dumbarton Oaks Publications.

Mango, C. (1980). *Byzantium: The empire of new Rome.* London: Weidenfeld & Nicolson.

McGuckin, J. A. (2001). *Standing in God's holy fire: The tradition of Byzantium.* New York & London: Orbis & Darton Longman & Todd.

Meyendorff, J. (1974). *Byzantine theology.* New York: Fordham University Press.

Runciman, S. (1990). *Byzantine style and civilization.* London: Penguin Books.

Treadgold, W. (1997). *A history of the Byzantine state and society.* Stanford, CA: Stanford University Press.

Canada, Australia, New Zealand

Canada, Australia, and New Zealand share some similarities in their traditions: British colonization has left a legacy of the common law, Judeo-Christianity, and the conventions of parliamentary democracy. So too have these countries been challenged by the relationship between their indigenous peoples and Anglo-Saxon arrivals. High levels of migration for all three countries during the latter half of the twentieth century ensured cosmopolitan lifestyles and the steady weaving of new beliefs and traditions into the fabric of society.

Despite all three countries registering an increasing number of non-Christian religious believers, the reality remains that Christianity—mainly Roman Catholic and Anglican—continues to dominate despite a recent decline in its following. In part this is because of the British legacy and Christian thread that is marbled through the common law and system of parliamentary democracy. While these countries share a robust rule of law and varying (but generally strong) protections of religious freedom, the reality is that a non-Christian believer is more likely to suffer discrimination than a mainstream Christian believer. It would be misleading, however, to suggest that violations of freedom of religion are systemic or widespread in any of these comparatively tolerant societies.

Canada

Canada has an overwhelmingly Christian population, mostly Roman Catholic (46 percent) and Protestant (36 percent). Self-described atheists make up 12.5 percent of the Canadian population. Members of other religions include Jews (1.2 percent), Muslims (0.9 percent), Buddhists (0.6 percent), Hindus (0.6 percent), and Sikhs (0.6 percent). Jehovah's Witnesses, Scientology, new religious movements, and indigenous beliefs constitute 10.3 percent of the population.

Historical Background on Indigenous Peoples in Canada

Canadian indigenous peoples have traditionally led their lives within the framework of a complex spirituality in which human beings are interrelated and form part of a harmonious, balanced universe. European settlers, however, sent native children to notorious residential schools, a practice that persisted until the latter part of the twentieth century. At these schools, native children were forbidden to speak their own language and their religious and cultural beliefs were often the subject of ridicule.

Freedom of Religion and Belief in Canadian Law

There is no established or state-sponsored religion or church and religious law is not imposed by civil authority. The Canadian Constitution of 1867 provides that provincial legislatures may not discriminate in their lawmaking function on the basis of a school's denomination. Protection of freedom of religion, however, is found in the Charter of Rights and Freedoms. Section 2 of the charter, "Fundamental

Freedoms," declares that:

> Everyone has the following fundamental freedoms:
> (a) freedom of conscience and religion;
> (b) freedom of thought, belief, opinion and expression, including freedom of the press and other media of communication;
> (c) freedom of peaceful assembly; and
> (d) freedom of association.

Further, section 15 declares that every individual is equal before and under the law and has the right to the equal protection and equal benefit of the law without discrimination based on religion.

Canada has an independent statutory body—the Canadian Human Rights Commission—that handles complaints from citizens who feel their right to freedom of religion has been violated. Under the Canadian Human Rights Act 1977, the Canadian Human Rights Commission is mandated to protect citizens from a range of entities discriminating against them on the basis of their religion. The various provinces and territories of Canada also have laws prohibiting certain forms of discrimination on the basis of religion.

In practice, the peoples of Canada enjoy a generally unrestricted practice of religion, although like most societies, Canada is not without blemish. The B'nai Brith Canada League for Human Rights received 280 reports of anti-Semitic incidents in 2000: an increase of 5 percent from the previous year. In May 2001, a Muslim chaplain filed suit in the Federal Court against an Ontario provincial judge who had ejected him from the courtroom in 1993 for wearing a Muslim cap. The chaplain's initial complaints filed with the provincial and federal human rights commissions were dismissed because the law provides for immunity from human rights laws for judges.

Canada's conservative Christian organizations, such as the Evangelical Fellowship of Canada (EFC) and the Canada Family Action Coalition have also been lobbying members of parliament to resist increasing legal recognition of same-sex relationships. In July 2002, a decision of the Ontario Divisional Court found that the opposite-sex nature of marriage in the current common law, which states that marriage is "the union of one man and one woman," violated the section 15 equality provision of the *Canadian Charter of Rights and Freedoms*. The gov-

ernment of Canada has appealed the decision and the EFC was granted leave to intervene in that appeal. Similar tensions exist in the debate concerning a bill to outlaw hate literature (Bill C-415), which conservative Christian groups argue may be wide enough in ambit to allow the Bible itself to be considered "hate literature." These open and emotive debates will continue to test Canadian society's ability to manage the relationship between its conservative religious constituents, the Canadian Human Rights Commission, and the government.

Australia

In the last one hundred years, the complexion of Australia's religious face has changed. In 1901, Christians represented 95.9 percent of the Australian population, with four major religious denominations accounting for 87.1 percent of the population. These were the Church of England (39.7 percent), Roman Catholic (22.7 percent), Wesleyan and other Methodists (13.4 percent), and Presbyterian (11.3 percent).

According to the Australian Bureau of Statistics, *2001 Census*, in 2001, Christians represented 68.0 percent of the population, with the two major denominations, Anglican and Catholic, accounting for 46.5 percent of the population. Buddhism accounted for 1.9 percent of the population and Islam for 1.5 percent. In 2001, around a quarter (25.3 percent) of the population stated they had "no religion" or chose not to answer the question. New religious movements in Australia number in the several hundred. Most have their origins overseas and range in size from small and exclusive groups to organizations with thousands of members.

Historical Background on Indigenous Peoples in Australia

Australian indigenous peoples view religion, culture, law, society, economy, and the land as inextricably linked. Aboriginal creation theory conceives that nature and culture were formed simultaneously by totemic spirits. Like their Canadian counterparts, Aborigines become the subject of assimilationist policies designed for their "best interests." For example, between the 1940s and the 1960s, thousands of mixed-race Aboriginal children were forcibly removed from their parents and given to adoptive white families.

Freedom of Religion and Belief in Australian Law

The Australian legal system purports to treat Australia's many different religious communities equally. There is no established or state-sponsored religion or church and religious law is not imposed by civil authority. The Federal Constitution in section 116 provides limited protection to freedom of religion: "[T]he Commonwealth shall not make any law for establishing any religion, or for imposing any religious observance, or for prohibiting the free exercise of any religion, and no religious test shall be required as a qualification for any office or public trust under the Commonwealth."

The constitution falls short of guaranteeing a personal right to freedom of religion and belief but it does restrict the Federal Parliament from legislating in a manner that prohibits the free exercise of religion. Australia's highest court—the High Court—has interpreted this provision broadly, noting: "[T]he guarantees in s. 116 of the Constitution would lose their character as a bastion of freedom if religion were so defined as to exclude from its ambit minority religions out of the main streams of religious thought" (*Church of the New Faith v. Commissioner for Payroll Tax [Vic.]*, 1983).

This interpretation of the constitution is consistent with the modern trend of Australian judges implying fundamental freedoms into the constitution in accordance with international treaties signed by Australia. In addition to the limited constitutional protection, Australia also provides protection in some other pieces of federal legislation. The federal Racial Hatred Act allows citizens to complain about racially offensive or abusive behavior.

The Australian Human Rights and Equal Opportunity Commission (HREOC)—an independent federal statutory authority—handles complaints from citizens who believe that their rights of religious freedom under international law have been violated. The commission can also recommend to the Australian Parliament that certain legislation limiting freedom of religion should be amended to promote compliance with international law. In addition to protections at the federal level, most Australian states and territories also provide that discrimination on the ground of religion is unlawful.

While the combined layers of federal and state legislation afford a high degree of protection of freedom of religion or belief, there is still some evidence of discrimination against non-Christian religious believers. The HREOC notes in its 1998 report on freedom of religion in Australia: "Despite the legal protections that apply in different jurisdictions, many Australians suffer discrimination on the basis of religious belief or non-belief, including members of both mainstream and non-mainstream religions and those of no religious persuasion."

This statement reflects the contemporary position in Australia that despite being an officially secular society, history and convention have left a distinctly Christian footprint on Australian civic life. Because of this some discrimination against non-Christian religious believers still occurs.

New Zealand

New Zealand is a predominantly Christian society although it is increasingly becoming religiously diverse. According to the 1996 census, approximately 60.6 percent of citizens identified themselves as Christian or as affiliated members of individual Christian denominations with less than 3 percent affiliated with non-Christian religions. Anglican, Roman Catholic, Presbyterian, and Methodist churches have all experienced a decline in their numbers while the number of New Zealand Buddhists and Muslims doubled between 1991 and 1996 and the number of Hindus increased by approximately 50 percent (although they each still constitute less than 1 percent of the population). By 1996, over one-fourth of the New Zealand population indicated no religious affiliation, up 33 percent from the census five years earlier. Anglicans, however, remained by far the largest religious denomination, accounting for 18 percent of the population in 1996.

Historical Background on Indigenous Peoples in New Zealand

The Maori, New Zealand's indigenous population, originally had a complex pantheon of gods and traditional beliefs that governed all aspects of life. Although a minority of the Maori still follow traditional beliefs, the overwhelming majority are Christian. While the Maori were never subjected to assimilationist policies like the Canadian and Australian indigenous peoples, an aggressive program conducted by European missionaries converted significant numbers of Maori to Christianity.

Freedom of Religion and Belief in New Zealand Law

There is no established or state-sponsored religion or church and religious law is not imposed by civil authority. New Zealand does not have a written constitution. The highest legislative authority dealing with religious freedom is the New Zealand Bill of Rights Act 1990. Section 13 of that act reads: "Everyone has the right to freedom of thought, conscience, religion, and belief, including the right to adopt and hold opinions without interference." In addition, section 15 reads: "Every person has the right to manifest that person's religion or belief in worship, observance, practice, or teaching, either individually or in community with others, and either in public or in private."

A special protection of minority religious rights is provided in section 20. Part II of the New Zealand Human Rights Act 1993 prohibits discrimination on the ground of religion or belief within the areas of employment, accommodation, education, and goods and services: limited exceptions exist for employment by religious bodies.

The Human Rights Commission of New Zealand—an independent statutory authority—is empowered by the Human Rights Act 1993 to handle complaints by citizens who feel that they have been unlawfully discriminated against on ground of their religious beliefs. Citizens can also assert their rights under the Bill of Rights Act 1990 and the Human Rights Act 1993 in the courts.

The growing number of non-Christian communities in New Zealand have called for the government to take into account the increasingly diverse religious makeup regarding holiday flexibility, and the government has responded by removing some constraints on trade associated with the Christian faith. The Human Rights Commission presented an educational seminar on religious freedom in the year 2000–2001.

Alice Tay and Hamish Redd

Further Reading

Ahdar., R., & Stenhouse, J. (Eds). (2001). *God and government: The New Zealand experience.* Dunedin, New Zealand: University of Otago Press.

Australian Bureau of Statistics. (2001). *2001 Census.* Retrieved September 5, 2002, from http://www.abs.gov.au

Canadian Department of Justice. (2001). *Freedom of religion.* Retrieved September 5, 2002, from http://canada.justice.gc.ca/en/justice2000/librel.html

Human Rights and Equal Opportunity Commission. (1998). Article 18—Freedom of religion and belief. Retrieved September 5, 2002, from: http://www.humanrights.gov.au/human_rights/religion/index.html

Naylor, A., & Sidoti, C. (1994). Leap of faith: Religious freedom in Australia. In A. Tay & C. Leung (Eds.), *Australian law and legal thinking in the 1990s* (pp. 422–443). Sydney, Australia: University of Sydney.

New Zealand Human Rights Commission. (2001). *Annual report 2001.* Retrieved September 5, 2002, from http://www.hrc.co.nz/org/pubs/orderform.htm

The Oslo Coalition on Freedom of Religion or Belief. (2000). *Freedom of religion or belief country report: Canada.* Retrieved September 5, 2002, from http://www.hri.ca/partners/forob/e/instruments/northamerica/canada.htm

U.S. Department of State. (2001). *International religious freedom report.* Retrieved September 5, 2002, from http://www.state.gov/g/drl/rls/irf/2001/5677.htm

Court Case

Church of the New Faith v. Commissioner for Payroll Tax (Vic.), 154 CLR 120 (1983).

Cathars

The Cathars are the most famous heretics of the Middle Ages, the vivid paradigms of religious dissent from the Catholic Church to which all other medieval heretics are compared and by which they are understood. It is generally assumed that the Cathars first appeared in the middle of the twelfth century and that they adopted their stark dualist beliefs (good God, bad God, benign spirit, evil matter) from heretical Bogomil missionaries journeying from the Balkans to western Europe. In less than a half century the Cathars had immigrated far and wide from the Mediterranean to the North Sea until, around 1200, they established an elaborate "Church" with systematic doctrines, a holy ascetic elite, and corresponding affiliations in Languedoc, northern Italy, Catalonia, England, northern France, and the Rhineland. This epic narrative reaches its tragic crescendo in the bloody violence of the Albigensian Crusade (a crusade conducted by the Catholic Church against the Cathars from 1208 to 1229) in southern France and, thereafter, the relentless persecutions of Cathars (from 1233) during the Inquisition until Catharism disappears, for all intents and purposes, sometime in the early fourteenth century.

Intriguingly, very few men and women were actually called "Cathars" in the Middle Ages. Certainly some heretics went by this name in the Rhineland and in northern Italy, but much more frequently they were known by a variety of names like "Manichaeans," "Arians," "Publicani," "Paterini," "Albigenses," and "good men." It is only in the last century that Cathar, for instance, has absorbed the more regional designation of Albigensian for the heretics of southern France and so become the term of choice amongst scholars. Yet, in making the Cathars such coherent and concrete figures, in classifying certain individuals and their thoughts as similar to each other, in joining dissenting dots until a pervasive heretical "Church" appears, the specificity of what heresy meant is lost in a kind of cultural determinism; in that if there were no Cathars, then something intrinsic to the Middle Ages must have produced them, no matter the evidence to the contrary. This social fatalism, implicit in so much research on heresy, effectively predestines the Middle Ages to be full of dissent, obsessed with the marginal and, as a consequence, gripped with an immutable need to persecute.

All this has the interesting effect of causing scholars to emphasize the writings of Catholic intellectuals, especially Italian inquisitors and former heretics, who present an image of Catharism (and so heresy) as doctrinally coherent and international. This image is in stark contrast to the testimonies collected by inquisitors, especially in southern France, where thousands of men and women confess to a heresy that was quite malleable in belief, not always opposed to the Catholic Church, and distinctly localized.

An even more fascinating aspect of this tendency to search for the meaning of a heresy only through the articulation of its ideas is that, somewhat ironically, this was how inquisitors themselves came to understand heterodoxy by the beginning of the fourteenth century. This intellectualization of heresy, which affected not only those who persecuted but also those who deliberately chose to resist the church, necessitates more wariness than is usually given in the general interpretation of Catharism outlined at the beginning.

Mark Gregory Pegg

See also Heresy; Inquisition

Further Reading

Barber, M. (2000). *The Cathars: Dualist heretics in Languedoc in the High Middle Ages.* Harlow, UK: Longman.

Lambert, M. (1998). *The Cathars.* Oxford, UK: Blackwell.

Pegg, M. G. (2001). *The corruption of angels: The Great Inquisition of 1245–1246.* Princeton, NJ: Princeton University Press.

Chaplains: Military and Legislative

A chaplain is generally considered to be a clergyperson assigned to a special ministry such as military, hospital, prison, legislature, or royal household. The title itself can be traced back to the early days of the Christian church in Europe and referred to clergy who were assigned to a specific chapel, e.g., the Queen's chapel. In the modern era chaplains are assigned to posts where there are specialized needs or problems, or for which specialized training is required. Many nations have chaplaincy services but this article will focus on the United States. Chaplains range from volunteers (many police and fire department chaplains fall into this category) to part time to full career paths. Volunteer chaplains and those in the private sector, such as hospital settings, do not pose free exercise or establishment problems, so will not be discussed in this article. Legislative and military chaplains, on the other hand, do raise substantial constitutional questions.

Legislative Chaplains

Since the earliest days of the United States' legislative branches, both the U. S. Senate and the House of Representatives have had full-time, paid chaplains.

U. S. Senate

When the first Senate convened in New York City in April 1789, one of its first orders of business was to appoint a committee to select a chaplain. The committee selected Samuel Provoost, an Episcopal bishop. The bishop served in a part-time capacity but since that time the position has evolved into a full-time career and the chaplain is considered one of the officers of the Senate. Every session of the Senate for over two hundred years has been opened with a prayer by the chaplain. In addition the chaplain serves as spiritual advisor and counselor for the senators and their families and staffs (currently more than 6,000 persons). Most chaplains also lead Bible study groups and prayer breakfasts. Dr. Lloyd John Ogilvie, the sixty-first chaplain of the Senate, was

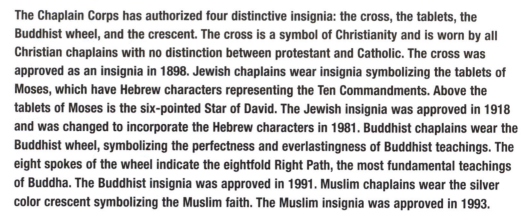

The Chaplain Corps has authorized four distinctive insignia: the cross, the tablets, the Buddhist wheel, and the crescent. The cross is a symbol of Christianity and is worn by all Christian chaplains with no distinction between protestant and Catholic. The cross was approved as an insignia in 1898. Jewish chaplains wear insignia symbolizing the tablets of Moses, which have Hebrew characters representing the Ten Commandments. Above the tablets of Moses is the six-pointed Star of David. The Jewish insignia was approved in 1918 and was changed to incorporate the Hebrew characters in 1981. Buddhist chaplains wear the Buddhist wheel, symbolizing the perfectness and everlastingness of Buddhist teachings. The eight spokes of the wheel indicate the eightfold Right Path, the most fundamental teachings of Buddha. The Buddhist insignia was approved in 1991. Muslim chaplains wear the silver color crescent symbolizing the Muslim faith. The Muslim insignia was approved in 1993.

Lawrence P. Crocker

Source: *The Army Officers Guide, 47th ed.* (Mechanicsburg, PA: Stackpole Books, 1996), 622.

elected in 1995. He stated that "I see my role as Chaplain to be an intercessor, trusted prayer partner, and faithful counselor to the Senators as they seek to know God and discover His will in the monumental responsibilities entrusted to them."

House of Representatives

On 9 April 1789, the House of Representatives appointed its own committee to select a House chaplain. A chaplain was selected on May 1. In September a law was passed by both houses to provide salaries for these chaplains. For most of the nation's history legislative chaplaincies have not been controversial. However, in 2000 a controversy broke out when the Republican House leadership rejected a Roman Catholic applicant in favor of a Protestant minister. The House had never had a Catholic chaplain despite the fact that a quarter of the nation and a slightly larger percentage of the House profess to be Catholics. Amidst charges of anti-Catholicism on the part of House leaders, the Protestant applicant withdrew and a priest was appointed. Aside from a Catholic appointed for one year in 1832 in the Senate, this is the only Catholic to serve as chaplain. No Jews, Muslims, Jehovah's Witnesses, or other non-mainstream ministers have served.

State Practices

Individual states vary widely in their use of legislative chaplains. Some states such as Kentucky invite local clergy from a variety of denominations to open legislative sessions but do not pay them. Other states have full-time, paid chaplains. There seems to be no common pattern.

Constitutional Issues

The most serious challenge to the constitutionality of legislative chaplains came in *Marsh v. Chambers* (1983), when a Nebraska legislator sued the state arguing that paying chaplains is clearly a violation of the establishment clause of the First Amendment to the U.S. Constitution. The Nebraska legislature had hired a Presbyterian minister and employed him for sixteen years by the time of the suit. A District Court held that having a chaplain was not a violation, but paying him was. The Court of Appeals held that both having and paying a chaplain were clearly unconstitutional under each provision of the *Lemon v. Kurtzman* (1971) test, which requires that legislative actions (a) have a secular legislative purpose, (b) neither advance nor inhibit religion, and (c) do not entail excessive entanglement. The Supreme Court reversed, declaring paid chaplaincies to be constitutional. Arguing for the Court, Chief Justice Burger simply ignored the *Lemon* precedent and wrote that "in light of the unambiguous and unbroken history of more than 200 years, there can be no doubt that the practice of opening legislative sessions with prayer has become part of the fabric of our society. To invoke divine guidance on a public body entrusted with making the laws is not, in these circumstances, an establishment of religion or a step toward establishment; it is simply a tolerable acknowledgement of beliefs widely held among the people of this country." *Marsh* remains the law to date.

Military Chaplains

Religious ministers accompanied immigrants to North America since the first settlement in 1609. Distinctions between settlers and soldiers were often vague, since citizens took up arms regularly against the native population. Chaplains were regularly paid to accompany military expeditions. During the Revolutionary War the Continental Congress provided for chaplains in the army, to be paid the salary of a captain. Military chaplains were so taken for granted that the founders who drafted the First Amendment apparently did not see any constitutional difficulties with paying chaplains out of federal funds. Indeed, in 1792 Congress reorganized and expanded the armed forces, and made provisions for chaplains to be paid fifty dollars a month, equivalent to that of an infantry major. One of the members of the House of Representatives who voted for the position and the pay was James Madison, who drafted the First Amendment. Madison later expressed some doubts about the wisdom of having chaplains, except possibly in the navy. But then he added, "The chance of a devout officer might be of as much worth to religion as the service of an ordinary chaplain." The problems with a zealous commanding officer promoting the cause of religion (presumably his own) among the troops under his command apparently did not occur to Mr. Madison. Both the Union and the Confederacy employed chaplains during the Civil War. In 1899 Congress institutionalized the military chaplaincy by requiring individual chaplains to receive the endorsement of their parent church bodies.

The chaplaincy is a well-established institution in all branches of the armed forces. While chaplains are volunteers, they must be nominated and endorsed by some recognized religious agency and accepted by the appropriate military command. They enter at the rank of captain and are evaluated in much the same manner as other officers. If they are passed over for promotion or lose their agency endorsement they must leave the service.

Constitutional Issues

The constitutionality of the military chaplaincy has never been seriously challenged even though it is a clear case of government paying clergy of many different denominations precisely to perform religious functions, including conducting rituals. The reason is that soldiers put in a military environment are taken out of their normal work and living situations and put in a command and control environment in which it would be difficult or impossible to pursue normal religious practices. (The same argument can be made for chaplains in prison and government hospitals.) Therefore, lest soldiers be deprived of their religious liberty, they are provided opportunities within the military to attend religious services and have religious counselors. Occasional lawsuits have been filed either to declare military chaplains an unconstitutional establishment of religion or at least to argue that denominations, not the government, should pay their salaries. The courts, including the Supreme Court, have dismissed these suits for lack of standing or on the basis of a necessary deference to military judgments.

Paul J. Weber

See also Establishment, Separation of Church and State

Further Reading

Abercrombie, C. L., III. (1977). *The military chaplaincy.* Beverly Hills, CA: Sage.

Greenwood, C. L. (1974). The constitutionality of the military chaplaincy: An historical study. *The Chaplain, 41,* 23.

Weber, P. J. (1980). The First Amendment and the military chaplaincy: The process of reform. *Journal of Church and State, 22,* 459.

Court Cases

Lemon v. Kurtzman, 403 U.S. 602 (1971).

Marsh v. Chambers, 463 U.S. 783 (1983).

Children and Freedom of Religion in the United States

When legal and religious obligations collide, one is bound to be compromised. The stakes are compounded when the conflict involves children, as parental duties may clash with the state obligation to safeguard incompetents, including minors (assumed under the legal doctrine of *parens patriae*, giving the sovereign guardianship over persons under disability; see *Black's Law Dictionary*). More specifically, parents' religious values (including their conception of beneficence) and family autonomy directly clash with the state's conception of beneficence. There is the further consideration of the extent to which a child has a personal right to the free exercise of religion.

Legal Protections, Legal Responsibilities

Although not specified in the Bill of Rights, parental interest in the care, custody, and control of a child in the United States is "perhaps the oldest of the fundamental liberty interests" recognized by the U.S. Supreme Court. The Rehnquist Court reaffirmed this right in *Troxel v. Granville* (2000), citing the 1923 case of *Meyer v. Nebraska*, in which the liberties protected by the Due Process Clause of the Fourteenth Amendment were found to include "the right of parents to 'establish a home and bring up children' and 'to control the education of their own.'" The 1925 case, *Pierce v. Society of Sisters*, had also reinforced the importance of family autonomy, noting that "the child is not the mere creature of the State; those who nurture him and direct his destiny have the right, coupled with the high duty, to recognize and prepare him for additional obligations." In *Pierce*, the Court overturned a general requirement that all children attend public schools, and allowed parents to send their children instead to educationally equivalent, privately funded secular or religious schools that met the state's basic interests and strictures.

State flexibility respecting education has been more the exception than the rule, and statutory obligations normally trump parents' religious freedom and parental rights of control. In *Prince v. Massachusetts* (1944), the United States Supreme Court upheld the criminal conviction of a Jehovah's Witness under child labor laws for permitting her nine-year-old ward to sell religious literature with her on public sidewalks. The record in *Prince* showed that the girl considered herself a devout Jehovah's Witness and had "begged" to be allowed to help distribute the literature; her aunt was with her, supervising the entire time. If the literature had been given away instead of offered for sale the law would not have applied.

In light of the child's assertion that her street evangelizing was a central religious obligation and vital to her worship, its prohibition as "child labor" effectively barred her from practicing her religion until the age of eighteen. The United States Supreme Court, which a year earlier had held that the street evangelism of the Jehovah's Witnesses was central to their religion, deferred to the state in overruling both the guardian's and the child's express wishes that the child fulfill her religious obligations. In *Prince*, however, the Court found that use of child labor in selling papers on the streets was a harm that the state had a vital interest in preventing, based upon its *parens patriae* power to protect the health, safety, and welfare of the child. The Court justified overriding religious and parental liberties in an often-quoted paragraph:

> Parents may be free to become martyrs themselves. But it does not follow they are free, in identical circumstances, to make martyrs of their children before they have reached the age of full and legal discretion when they can make that choice for themselves. (*Prince v. Massachusetts* 1944, 170)

Note the inflammatory use of "martyrs" in describing this case. Yet, as pointed out by Justice Murphy, the lone dissenter, no evidence supported the Court's decision:

> To the extent that they [i.e., "the crippling effects of child employment . . . in public places"] flow from participation in ordinary commercial activities, these harms are irrelevant to this case. And the bare possibility that such harms might emanate from distribution of religious literature is not, standing alone, sufficient justification for restricting freedom of conscience and religion. . . . The evils must be grave, immediate, substantial. . . . Yet there is not the slightest indication in this record, or in sources subject to judicial notice, that children engaged in distributing literature pursuant to their religious beliefs have been or are likely to be subject to any of the harmful "diverse influences of the street." . . . Moreover, Jehovah's Witness children invariably make their distributions in groups subject at all times to adult or parental control, as was done in this case. The dangers are thus exceedingly remote, to say the least. And the fact that the zealous exercise of the right to propagandize the community may result in violent or disorderly situations difficult for children to face is no excuse for prohibiting the exercise of that right. (*Prince v. Massachusetts* 1944, 170)

If the latter was indeed the sentiment that fueled the decision in *Prince v. Massachusetts*, it amounts to protecting children from the disdain of the majority for believing in an unpopular religion.

Thus parents who practice a religion that is outside the mainstream may have their ability and right to raise their children in their faith curtailed by the sensibilities and judgments of the legislative majority. The only requirements for a law to be constitutional under the free exercise clause are that the law target behavior and not a religion, and be generally applicable to all citizens who engage in the proscribed behavior. The religious freedom of parents and children is subject to well-meaning state oversight under statutes or administrative regulations that deem the behavior to be a threat to the health, safety, or welfare of the child. This paternalistic oversight is often warranted: A parent who believes that God wants the child to starve, or believes that physical or mental torture of a child is a religious obligation, must be stopped. Tragedy of another kind may occur, however, where *Prince v. Massachusetts* is used to justify government intervention when the actual harm to the health and safety of a child is nebulous. It should also be noted that secular society regularly tolerates, if not encourages, risky *secular* behavior: witness the numerous injuries children and adolescents suffer as a result of football, hockey, gymnastics, and the licensing of 16-year-olds to drive.

Conceptual Frameworks

Courts have ruled that a child should be protected by the state from certain of the parents' religious practices until the child is old enough to choose a religion for itself. What the state is in essence requiring is that parents, and, indeed, the entire church community, somehow suspend a portion of their conceptual framework when raising their children. But life cannot be compartmentalized, and conceptual frameworks cannot be manipulated in such a manner. A child is a bundle of complexities and not an isolated, miniature, autonomous self. A child learns and is raised only within the context of a community. In religious freedom cases, the community often means the family and the larger religious community to which the family belongs. As philosopher Charles Taylor notes, "A self can never be described without reference to those who surround it" (Taylor 1989, 35). Indeed, the court has the entire process of instilling moral and spiritual values reversed. A child needs a

moral/religious framework as it starts in life, a framework that the child can later build upon, renovate, or even reject. But where the state forbids the parents to raise their child within their religious framework, what religion or structure does the state offer to replace it? And if the parents simply exclude the child from a core practice of an otherwise integrated religious framework, the result is a child who develops an internally contradictory conceptual structure/framework. The child is disoriented at best, and "base-less" at worst. As Taylor explains,

> Later, I may innovate. I may develop an original way of understanding myself and human life, at least one that is in sharp disagreement with my family and background. But the innovation can only take place from the base in our common language. Even as the most independent adult, there are moments when I cannot clarify what I feel until I talk about it with certain special partner(s) who know me, or have wisdom, or with whom I have an affinity. This incapacity is a mere shadow of the one the child experiences. For him, everything would be confusion, there would be no language of discernment at all, without the conversations which fix this language for him. (Taylor 1989, 35–36)

A practice that is fundamental to the structural framework of a religious community is obligatory, and differs from a strongly held belief, which may be subject to persuasion from dominant religious and secular frameworks. Rather, the practice and its underlying belief are crucial components of the basic identity and framework of the involved families and their community.

Concomitantly, the forces opposing a particular religious practice often operate within a scientific and/or secular framework that assumes religion to be superstitious and illogical. Laws grounded in social scientific and scientific disciplines, on the other hand, are assumed to be objective and impartial, and thus to work benevolently in the best interests of the child. Such opposing assumptions and worldviews make the dialogue needed to resolve any conflict exceedingly difficult.

Examples

To preserve the integrity of their faith and prevent the chaos that abandoning a core religious practice would cause, religious groups lobby state and federal legislatures for changes in or exemptions from laws that interfere with their religious freedom. Sacramental wine given to children at Catholic, Lutheran, and Episcopalian services, for example, is not subject to the prohibition against underage drinking of alcoholic beverages. The successful lobbying efforts of home-schoolers for exemptions from requirements to send their children to formal public or private schools are more controversial. Should home-schooled children be taught using the same curricula and educational outcomes assessments as public school children?

Almost as controversial is the application of child abuse laws to parental spanking done with religious motives: When does discipline cross the line into harmful and actionable assault and battery? Religions that practice spiritual and faith healing have obtained legislative assistance in having their healing methods accepted as satisfying requirements in child welfare statutes that parents furnish their children with medical care. These exemptions might not, however, be applied as a defense against manslaughter charges when such faith healing methods were unsuccessful (see *Walker v. Superior Court* 1988). Parents involved in contentious child custody disputes continue to play the religion card against spouses with unconventional religious beliefs and practices.

As pertains to education, children's religious freedom rights must be balanced against the school's need to preserve order and an educational atmosphere. A steadily growing consensus is emerging, built on the paradigm of neutrality. If a secular club can use school grounds and communication facilities, then a student religious organization must also be permitted access. If an assignment is open-ended (such as, "write an essay on any topic" or "write a book report on any book"), then essays and reports of a religious nature must be accepted along with secular ones.

The Future

As the religious diversity of the U.S population increases and as local, state, and federal governments continue efforts to make conditions safer for children, the frequency of conflicts between civil and religious obligations will also mount. Society owes children protection from violent and abusive parents, but the issues surrounding the intersection of chil-

dren, parents, religious duties, and the law are not all so clear cut. As federal courts turn away from a strict scrutiny of government action and policy in religious freedom claims, will legislators and administrators be open to considering exceptions from statutes and regulations for minority religious practices? Will state courts become fair and open forums for considering the clash between law and conscience? Will prosecutors become more amenable to exercising prosecutorial discretion, and pursue only truly harmful cases while dropping the more nebulous instances where laws are violated out of religious, not criminal, intent?

Catharine Cookson

See also Religion and Public Education

Further Reading

Cookson, C. (2001). *Regulating religion: The courts and the free exercise clause.* New York: Oxford University Press.

Coons, J. E. (1996). The religious rights of children. In J. Witte & J. D. van der Vyver (Eds.), *Religious human rights in global perspective* (pp. 157–174). Dordrecht, Netherlands: Kluwer Law International.

King, M., & Piper, C. (1991). *How the law thinks about children.* Brookfield, VT: Gower.

Peters, S. F. (2000). *Judging Jehovah's witnesses: Religious persecution and the dawn of the rights revolution.* Lawrence: University Press of Kansas.

Taylor, C. (1989). *Sources of the self: The making of the modern identity.* Cambridge, MA: Harvard University Press.

Wald, M. (1975). State intervention on behalf of "neglected" children: a search for realistic standards. *Stanford Law Review, 27*, 985.

Court Cases

Meyer v. Nebraska, 262 U.S. 390 (1923).
People v. Pierson, 176 N.Y. 201, 68 N.E. 243 (1903).
Pierce v. Society of Sisters, 268 U.S. 510 (1925).
Prince v. Massachusetts, 321 U.S. 175 (1944).
Regina v. Wagstaffe, 10 Cox Crim. Cas. 530 (Cent. Crim. Ct. 1868).
Troxel v. Granville, 530 U.S. 57 (2000).
Walker v. Superior Court, 47 Cal.3d 112, 253 Cal. Rptr. 1 (1988).
Wisconsin v. Yoder, 406 U.S. 205 (1972).

China, Communist

China is the largest country in eastern Asia and the fourth largest country in the world. It is bounded by thirteen countries: Russia and North Korea in the east; Russia and Mongolia in the north; Kazakhstan, Kyrgyzstan, Tajikistan, Afghanistan, Pakistan, and India in the west; and Nepal, India, Bhutan, Laos, and Vietnam in the south. Chinese civilization began with the Xia dynasty, dated from 2100 to 1520 BCE. Chinese history roughly went through three periods or stages: Imperial China (1700 BCE–1911 CE), Republic of China (1912–1949), and Communist China (1949–present). The last Chinese emperor was overthrown by the nationalist revolution of 1911. After civil wars between the Nationalist Party and the Communist Party between 1946 and 1949, the Communist Party defeated the Nationalist Party and established the People's Republic of China on 1 October 1949. At the beginning of the twenty-first century, China had 1.3 billion people and covered 9,561,000 square kilometers (3,692,000 square miles).

Religious Demographics

China's religious heritage is made up of the *san jiao* (three traditions): Confucianism, Daoism, and Buddhism. According to official Chinese reports, in the early 2000, there were over 100 million religious believers in China, but most professed faith in one of these three traditions. China had about 13,000 Buddhist temples and 200,000 Buddhist monks and nuns, and over 1,500 Daoist temples and more than 25,000 Daoist priests and nuns. China is also a country with a diversity of religious beliefs. Islam and Catholicism were introduced into China in the seventh century, and Protestantism came to China in the nineteenth century. As of 2003, there were 18 million Muslims and 30,000 mosques; 4 million Catholics, 4,000 clergy, and more than 4,600 churches; and 10 million Protestants, more than 18,000 clergy, and more than 12,000 churches.

The Chinese government has paid special attention to ethnic religious beliefs, and the law protects the rights of indigenous ethnics to freedom of religions and their cultural heritages. The Law of the People's Republic of China on National Regional Autonomy stipulates: "Organs of self-government in ethnic regional autonomous areas protect the right to freedom of religious belief of the citizens of all ethnic groups." Since the reform movement initiated by Deng Xiaoping in 1978 to modernize China, the Lamaist Buddhist and Islamic faiths have become more vigorous in Xinjiang and Tibet. The Chinese government reports that since 1980 it has invested about 200 million yuan for the maintenance and reconstruction of religious places in Tibet, including Potala Palace—the residence of the Dalai Lama—and the Jokhang, Tashilhunpo, and Samye monasteries. (As such religious places are often tourist attractions, the investment also yielded economic benefits to the Chinese.) There are currently more than 23,000 mosques with 29,000 clergymen in the Xinjiang Uygur Autonomous Region, and over 1,700 places for Buddhist activities with 46,000 resident monks and nuns in Tibet. Although it is difficult to evaluate precisely the situation of religious freedom in Tibet, a report from the U.S. Department of State's Bureau of Democracy, Human Rights, and Labor (4 March 2002) contends that the Chinese government strictly controls access to and information about Tibet.

Chinese Religions and the Communist Party of China

The Communist Party of China is a ruling party. The party's ultimate goal is the creation of a Communist social system. In order to fulfill its ultimate goal, according to the Constitution of China and the Communist Party of China, the party takes Marxism-Leninism and Mao Zedong's thought as its guide to action. Atheism is a central tenet of Marxism. Based on Marxism, God did not create man, but man created God to escape the misery of this world and to reach so-called supernatural beings in heaven. Religion was a negative feeling of the ruled class, which was the reflection of their miserable life in capitalist society. The ruling class used religion to anesthetize the people to maintain the capitalist system. At this point, religion is the opiate of the people. Therefore, the abolition of religion and the abolition of the capitalist system are the same process. The party requires its 64 million members to believe in Marxist atheism, and to educate the masses of various ethnic groups with the Marxist perspective on religion.

When the party put Marxism into religious practice, it inevitably resulted in serious consequences. After the party came to power in 1949, the Chinese government began to carry out a policy that monitored

REGULATIONS GOVERNING THE RELIGIOUS ACTIVITIES OF FOREIGN NATIONALS WITHIN CHINA

Decree No. 144 of the State Council
signed by Premier Li Peng, 31 January 1994

Article 1. This regulation is formulated in conformity with the Constitution in order to protect the freedom of religious belief of foreign nationals in China and to safeguard the public interest.

Article 2. The People's Republic of China respects the religious freedom of foreign nationals in China and protects friendly visits, cultural and scholarly exchanges and other such religious activities between foreign nationals and religious circles in China.

Article 3. Foreign nationals may participate in religious activities in religious venues in China, including monasteries, temples, mosques and churches; and, at the invitation of a religious body at or above the provincial, autonomous region or municipality level, may discuss the scriptures and preach.

Article 4. Foreign nationals may hold religious activities for other foreign nationals at venues recognized by the Religious Affairs Bureaus of the People's Government at or above the county level.

Article 5. Foreign nationals in China may request Chinese clergy to perform religious rites such as baptisms, marriages, funerals, and Taoist and Buddhist rituals.

Article 6. When foreign nationals enter China, they may carry printed materials, audio and visual materials and other religious items for their own use; if these are brought in quantities which exceed those for personal use, such items will be dealt with according to the relevant Chinese customs regulations.

Religious publications and religious audio and visual materials whose content is harmful to the public interest are forbidden.

Article 7. Foreign nationals recruiting students within China for overseas religious studies or who come to China to study or teach in Chinese religious educational institutions are subject to the relevant Chinese regulations.

Article 8. Foreign nationals who engage in religious activities in China must respect Chinese laws and regulations. They are not permitted to establish religious organizations, liaison offices, and venues for religious activities or run religious schools and institutes within China; they are not allowed to recruit believers among the Chinese citizenry, appoint clergy or undertake other evangelistic activities.

Article 9. The Bureaus of Religious Affairs at or above the county level or other offices concerned should act to dissuade and put a stop to religious activities of foreign nationals which violate this regulation. If the violation constitutes an immigration offence or a matter of public security, the public security organs will dispense penalties according to the law; if the violation constitutes a crime, the judiciary will investigate to determine where criminal responsibility lies.

Article 10. This regulation will be applied to the religious activities of foreign nationals within China.

Article 11. The religious activities in mainland China of Chinese citizens residing overseas, or residents of Taiwan, Hong Kong and Macao will be subject to this regulation.

Article 12. Interpretation of this regulation will lie with the Religious Affairs Bureau of the State Council.

Article 13. This regulation takes effect from the date of issue.

Source: Amity News Service.
Regulations Governing the Religious Activity of
Foreign Nationals within China.
Retrieved November 26, 2002, from
www.amityfoundation.org/ANS/Religious%20Laws/reg1.htm

Roman Catholic Church in Shanghai, 1998. COURTESY OF JINGHAO ZHOU.

and regulated all religions, cutting Chinese religious organizations off from foreign countries. In 1950, the first Chinese Christian Conference drafted the *Christian Manifesto: The Direction of Endeavor for Chinese Christianity in the Construction of New China,* which launched the Three-Self Movement. The movement was based on the Three-Self Principles—self-administration, self-support, and self-propagation—originally introduced by Christian missionaries in the mid-1800s. These principles stress that the church must be organized by Chinese Christians themselves, not by foreigners, and that Christians must support the new socialist China. Many religious believers do not see the Three-Self Movement as being based on Christianity. Rather, they see it as evidence of the government plotting actively against all religions. During the ten years of the Cultural Revolution from 1966 to 1976 in China, all religions were denounced, all religious believers were persecuted, all religious meeting places were closed, all religious activities were prohibited, and all church properties were confiscated.

After the Cultural Revolution, the Chinese government made good efforts to restore freedom of religious belief and reopened sites for religious activities. The news and reports on religious activities, including the celebration of religious festivals such as Christmas, Corban, and the birthday of Buddha, are regularly published in the official press. Since the 1990s, China began to join international religious groups and activities, such as the World Council of Churches, the Fifth World Conference on Religion and Peace, and World Catholic Youth Day. The associations of Buddhism, Daoism, and Islam have also developed international exchanges. By contrast, Catholicism developed more slowly than Protestantism and other faiths, because two unresolved issues—Vatican recognition of Taiwan and the consecration of bishops—continued to complicate the issues facing the church. Due to the fact that the pope publicly recognized in 2001 the errors committed by the church in China, it is expected that the relationship between the Vatican and China will improve in the future.

Religious Freedom in China

Under the constitution of China, including the versions of 1954, 1975, 1978, and 1982, the Chinese people have the right to enjoy religious freedom. Every version of the constitution protects freedom of speech, assembly, association, procession and demonstration, and religion. Article 88 in the Constitution of 1954 stated that "citizens of the People's Republic of China enjoy freedom of religious belief." Article 28 in the Constitution of 1975 stated that citizens "have the freedom to practice a religion, the freedom to not practice a religion and to propagate atheism." Article 36 in the Constitution of 1982 stated that "Citizens of the PRC enjoy freedom of religious belief. No organ of state, mass organization, or person is allowed to force any citizen to believe or not to believe in religion." The main difference between the Constitution of 1982 and the Constitution of 1978 on religion is the elimination of the phrase "freedom not to believe in religion and to propagate atheism." It is also worth noting that only five religions are protected under the Constitution of China: Buddhism, Daoism, Islam, and Protestant and Catholic Christianity.

To control Chinese religions, the Chinese government makes distinctions between normal and abnormal religious activities. According to the Chinese government, abnormal religious activities are usually conducted by "a small number of people, actuated by some abnormal purposes, who conduct religious activities in an excessively frequent and long manner" (Kolodner 1994, 470). To prohibit abnormal religious activities, the Fifth National People's Congress (NPC) adopted the Criminal Law in 1979. Article 147 reads, "A state functionary who unlawfully deprives others of their freedom of religious beliefs or violates the customs and habits of minority nationalities to a serious extent, will be sentenced to detention or imprisonment for not more than two years." Article 99 states, "Those organizing and utilizing feudal superstitious beliefs and secret societies or sects to carry out counter-revolutionary activities will be sentenced to a fixed-term imprisonment of not less than five years." Although the NPC passed the law recently to delete the term "counter-revolutionary" in the criminal law, the party has applied this term in practice, e.g., the party makes distinctions between Falun Gong and normal religious activities and regards Falun Gong as counter-revolutionary. Since 1999, the campaign against Falun Gong has been intensified. According to a report released by the U.S. Department of State's Bureau of Democracy, Human Rights, and Labor (4 March 2002), approximately 100 Falun Gong adherents have died in jails.

The Characteristics of Religious Practice in Communist China

Unlike democratic countries, Communist China has party organs and a hierarchy of state to manage religions. The state control of religion is the basic characteristic of Chinese politics under the Communist regime. The party/state controls Chinese religions, first of all, through official Chinese ideology—Marxism-Maoism-Dengism. Second, the state controls religions through religious policy, which is made by the party and is above the law in Communist China. Third, all schools, colleges, and universities educate students by Marxism, Communism, and atheism. Fourth, the associations of different religions, as liaisons between religions and the government, put religious policy in practice. The Religious Affairs Bureau, as an agency of the government, is the mediator between religious organizations and the party; the United Front Office represents the party to make religious policy; and the Public Security Bureau forces all religious groups and believers to implement party policy.

Generally, religious policies are implemented by the Religious Affairs Bureau, which has a national office to direct the provincial and municipal bureaus, which in turn direct the city and county level bureaus. Under the Religious Affairs Bureau, party policy is implemented by the major religious organizations, including the Buddhist Association of China, the China Daoist Association, the China Islamic Association, the Three-Self Patriotic Movement Committee of Protestant Churches of China, the China Christian Council, and the China Catholic Patriotic Association. The Religious Affairs Bureau is directed by the United Front Office, a party branch, and cooperates closely with the local Public Security Bureau, which is responsible for enforcing religious policies. If religious believers and organizations violate party policies, the Public Security Bureau punishes them according to the criminal law.

Religious Policies

The most important document regarding religious policy to be published after the Cultural Revolution was Document 19, issued by the central committee of the Chinese Communist Party on 31 March 1982 and published in the official journal *Red Flag* on 16 June 1982. In Document 19 the party summed up the historical experience of the party regarding the religious questions since the founding of the People's Republic of China, promoted a moderate religious policy, and called for restoration and administration of churches, temples, and other religious buildings. At the same time, the document also declared that religion must not interfere with politics, education, or marriage and family life, and reaffirmed that the government prohibited criminal and counterrevolutionary activities under the cover of religion.

Regulations Governing Venues for Religious Activities—Decree No. 145 and Regulations Governing the Religious Activities of Foreign Nationals within China, issued by Premier Li Peng in January 1994, are the most important regulations for religious organizations and believers to follow as of 2003. Registration is the key for the Chinese government to control religions. According to the Decree 145, registration is required for the establishment of a venue for religious activities. The registration is based on the "three-fix" policy: patriotic association, a fixed meeting point, and activities confined to a specific geographic area. The regulation reinstates that venues for religious activities shall not be controlled by persons or organizations outside China. Without the government's permission, the land, mountains, forests, or buildings cannot be used for religious purposes; donations from persons and organizations outside China cannot be accepted; and religious articles, art works, and publications cannot be published. If violation of the stipulations of this regulation constitutes an act in violation of public security, the public security organs shall mete out penalties in accordance with the relevant regulations of the PRC Public Security Administration Penal Code; if the violation constitutes a criminal act, the judiciary shall undertake an investigation to determine criminal responsibility.

Regarding foreigners' religious activities in China, according to Regulations Governing the Religious Activities of Foreign Nationals within China, foreign nationals may participate in religious activities in religious venues in China, including monasteries, temples, mosques, and churches, which are recognized by the Religious Affairs Bureaus of the People's Government at or above the county level. They may invite Chinese clerical personnel to conduct such religious rituals as baptisms, weddings, funerals, and prayer meetings. However, they are not permitted to establish religious organizations, liaison offices, or venues for religious activities or run religious schools and institutes within China. They are not allowed to recruit believers among the Chinese citizenry, or to appoint clergy or undertake other evangelistic activities. When foreign nationals enter China, they may carry printed materials, audio and visual materials, and other religious items for their own use, but if these are brought in quantities that exceed those for personal use, such items will be dealt with according to the relevant Chinese customs regulations.

Jinghao Zhou

See also China, Imperial; Tibet

Further Reading

Barrett, D. B. (Ed.). (1982). *World Christian encyclopedia.* New York: Oxford University Press.

Boyle, K., & Sheen, J. (1997). *Freedom of religion and belief.* New York: Routledge.

Bush, R. C., Jr. (1970). *Religion in Communist China.* New York: Abingdon Press.

Ching, J. (1993). *Chinese religions.* Maryknoll, NY: Orbis Books.

Eliade, M. (Ed.). (1979). *The encyclopedia of religion* (Vol. 8). New York: Macmillan Publishing Company.

Kolodner, Eric. (1994). Religious rights in China: A comparison of international human rights law and Chinese domestic legislation. *Human Rights Quarterly, 16,* 470.

MacInnis, D. D. (1989). *Religion in China today: Policy and practice.* Maryknoll, NY: Orbis Books.

van der Vyver, J. D., & Witte, J., Jr. (Eds.). (1997). *Religious human rights in global perspective: Legal perspectives.* The Hague, Netherlands: Martinus Nijhoff Publishers.

Van Housten, R. (Ed.). (1988). *Wise as serpents, harmless as doves.* Pasadena, CA: William Carey Library.

U.S. Department of State; Bureau of Democracy, Human Rights, and Labor. (4 March 2002). Country reports on human rights practices, 2001: China. Retrieved October 29, 2002, from http://www.state.gov/g/drl/rls/hrrpt/2001/eap/8289.htm

China, Imperial

"Imperial China" refers to the period of Chinese history from ancient times to the day when the last Chinese emperor was overthrown in 1911. During this period of time, Chinese traditional religions along with imported religions constituted part of Chinese culture and the Chinese way of life. It is known that in imperial China there were at least seven religions, including ancestral religion, witchcraft, Confucianism, Daoism, Buddhism, Christianity, and Islam.

Traditional Chinese Religions

China's religious heritage is made up of three religious traditions—Buddhism, Daoism, and Confucianism. The three Chinese traditional religions have assimilated into each other and developed peacefully together.

Confucius (551 BCE–479 BCE) was the first great teacher and thinker in Chinese history. His sayings were recorded by his disciples and reflected in the four Confucian works: *The Analects of Confucius, The Great Learning, The Doctrine of the Mean,* and *Mencius.* Confucius taught the principles of benevolence, loyalty, righteousness, propriety, and knowledge, and dealt with five relationships—between ruler and subject, between father and son, between husband and wife, between elder brother and younger brother, and between friend and friend. Confucianism went through two epochs in imperial China. The first epoch was the period from the Confucian time to the Tang dynasty (618–907 CE) and was characterized as traditional Confucianism. In the Song dynasty (960–1279) Confucianism entered into the second epoch, characterized as neo-Confucianism (*li xue*). Neo-Confucianism assimilated Buddhist cosmology, modified its theoretical system, and made Confucian ethics and political theory more metaphysical. The most significant neo-Confucian scholars, such as WangYangmin, Zhu Xi, Cheng Hao, and Cheng Yi, introduced important new interpretations of Confucian theory.

Confucianism has served both secular and religious functions throughout history. Some scholars refuse to call Confucianism a religion, because Confucius did not perform miracles and discuss death and the existence of gods, and because Confucianism does not have religious texts, systematic rituals, and formal organizations. As a matter of fact, the *Analects* records Confucius's prayers, fasting, and regular attendance of worship services. Confucius discusses God using the term *shang-di* ("heavenly god" or "ancestors") and heaven using the term *tian*. Confucius as a sage was worshipped by the vast majority of Chinese people in imperial China. *Wen miao*, Confucian temples, were established everywhere, using identical designs. In a Confucian temple, religious rituals were held twice a year, in mid-spring and mid-autumn, worshipping the ancestors of Confucius, however these ritual services were not convened by priests, but by state officials and Confucian scholars.

Daoism (or Taoism) was originally derived from several sources, some dating back as far as the fourth century BCE including, witchcraft, yin-yang theory, ghost ideas, the theory of Chinese medicine, and the religious ideas of Laozi (c. sixth century BCE). Daoists synthesized these sources and formed a unique religious system, which was reflected in the Daoist canon, comprising about 1,120 volumes. Daoism is a salvation religion that guides its believers beyond this transitory life to a happy eternity. Daoism associates human weakness and sickness with sin and tries to heal such ills with the confession of sin, forgiveness, and the ritual practices of prayer and penance. Beginning with the Han dynasty (206 BCE–220 CE), Daoists practiced techniques concerning immortality, because they believed that what was buried in the tomb was not one's true body but only a resemblance. Daoism in its beginning was associated with Chinese peasant rebellions, but in the third century CE it shifted its emphasis from a realistic world to the transcendental values of nihilism. Like Buddhism, Daoism has no central authority, but organizes districts presided over by *dao shi,* Daoist priests, who lives in Daoist temples and can marry and have children.

Buddhism began its difficult journey in China in the first century BCE, arriving via the Silk Road from India. At its inception, Buddhism was treated as a foreign religion, yet it gradually became the Chinese way of life when its concepts were conveyed to the Chinese mind by using Daoist terms. Because Buddhists at the beginning traveled only to the cities to attract rich people, officials, and scholars, Buddhist temples were built only in the urban areas at that time. Through the translation of scriptures and Buddhist teachings, Buddhism opened the way of Buddhahood to Chinese believers. In the fourth century CE, Buddhism penetrated into the highest social and economic circles. Then wealthy Buddhists began founding Buddhist temples, supplying the monks with necessities, and paying for the translation of Buddhist texts. Some Buddhist scholars became advisors for the imperial court in official decision-making. In this way, Buddhist influence on Chinese society became increasingly strong, but at the same time, Buddhist monks were charged with sedition, laziness, immorality, and opposing Confucian tradition by Chinese officials as well as the general public who were influenced by the Confucian tradition. However, Buddhism in China continued to develop and spread rapidly among the populace. Buddhism in China reached maturity during the Tang dynasty and reached its peak at the beginning of the Song dynasty. Several schools of Buddhism, such as the School of Pure Land, the School of Three Treatises, the Garland School, and the Mere Ideation School, strongly influenced the development of Chinese Buddhism. Chinese Buddhism began declining during the Song dynasty. The four most important factors contributing to this decline were the moral corruption of high-level clergy; the institution of civil service examinations that forced Chinese scholars to seek office through a study of the Confucian classics; diminishing support of Buddhism from India, the country of its origin; and the introduction of Western culture.

Christianity and Islam in Imperial China

Beginning with the seventh century, Western religions found a footing in China. The Persian Bishop Nestorian Alopen (d. c. 451) was the first Christian missionary to China, beginning the Nestorian mission in 635 CE in Ch'ang-an (present-day Xi'an), the capital city of the Tang. The Tang dynasty was the most glorious dynasty in Chinese history, and the emperor Tang Tai Zong (r. 627–649) was relatively open-minded. After Nestorian died, he received an honor from Emperor Tang Tai Zong, and in 781 CE, the Nestorian monument was erected outside Ch'ang-an. Although there was considerable collaboration between Buddhists and Nestorians, the Nestorians had little impact on Chinese society.

The second wave of the Christian mission was the Franciscan mission, a Roman Catholic missionary movement of short duration. Giovanni da Montecorvino (1247–1328), the first Catholic missionary and a zealous monk, arrived in China from Italy in 1292 during the Yuan dynasty (1279–1368), which was a great empire that adopted a tolerant religious policy. Giovanni da Montecorvino, together with other Catholic missionaries, was allowed to build churches and to baptize Chinese believers, but the

Catholic mission did not have much influence on China until Jesuit missionaries came to China in 1583 during the Ming dynasty (1368–1644).

The Chinese government in the beginning of the Ming dynasty closed its doors to foreigners and only permitted them to establish churches in Macao, but Matteo Ricci (1552–1610) finally opened the way to develop Christian mission on the mainland. Ricci, who was originally from Italy but ordained in Goa, India, developed Christian mission in new ways, making friends with local peoples, learning Chinese culture and tradition, and applying the concepts of heaven and *shang di* to his mission. Thus, the Christian missionary movement in the sixteenth century represented by Ricci gradually extended its influence and was relatively successful.

Christian missionaries did not make much progress in China until China was defeated in the first Opium War (1840–1842), which led to the opening up of five treaty ports to Western countries in 1842 and to the fourth wave of Christian mission. Soon thereafter, large numbers of Christian missionaries were flowing to China, signifying a new era for the Christian missionary movement in China. However, Christianity was still regarded as a foreign religion and was only tolerated by the Chinese government. The Taiping Rebellion in the middle of the nineteenth century and the Boxer Uprising in the beginning of twentieth century reflected the hostilities of the Chinese toward Christianity.

Although Christian missionaries worked in China for centuries, they were not so successful in converting the Chinese people. The response to the Christian faith in China was always minimal, and the church never constituted more than 1 percent of the national population. Why? Theologically, the central Christian doctrines, such as creation, sin, and incarnation, contradict traditional Chinese culture. Politically, the contacts between China and Western Christians before the nineteenth century were mutually beneficial, but Christians were supported by gun ships and protected by unequal treaties in the nineteenth century. Consequently, the Chinese people had little sympathy for Christianity. Culturally, some Western missionaries had a tendency to criticize Chinese culture. Some Western missionaries even understood that destroying the traditional Chinese culture was the first task of Christian mission in China. Theoretically, the Chinese people, especially the Chinese intellectuals, had difficulty accepting European-centered methodology.

In the seventh century CE, Islam came to China from Southeast Asia. Unlike Christian missionaries, the Muslims came to China as immigrants or traders, who set up their families and continued their Muslim faith. Thus Muslims in China gradually assimilated into the Chinese culture and society and became isolated from the rest of the Islamic world. The development of Islam in China was a slow process, and Muslims did not build their own religious temples until the Song dynasty. Due to moderate religious policy, there was a large Muslim infiltration in the Yuan dynasty, especially in western provinces of Gangsu, Sichuan, and Yunnan. The Muslim population continued to increase throughout the Ming and the Qing (1644–1912 CE) dynasties. It is estimated that there were about 15 million Chinese Muslims by the end of imperial China.

The Characteristics of Chinese Religions

The word "religion" did not have an equivalent term in China until the Chinese people created the word *zong-jiao* in the late nineteenth century. *Zong* refers to clan, tribe, and ancestor; *jiao* refers to teaching. When the Chinese people put the words *zong* and *jiao* together for the equivalent of "religion," they were reinforcing the Chinese understanding of the role of ancestral religion. The basic content of the ancestral religion in imperial China is to worship ancestors as well as the land, clouds, sun, moon, mountains, rivers, and spirits. The ancestral religion classified four types of gods: heavenly god, earthly god, human spirit, and material god. Correspondingly, there are four types of worship: heaven worship, land worship, ancestor worship, and grain worship. However, according to archaeological evidence, including grave offerings and inscriptions on oracle bones and in bronze sacrificial vessels, Chinese religion derived from ancestor worship. The Chinese people believed that *shang-di* were still alive in heaven after their death, and had authority to bring harm or good fortune to their descendants. Thus sacrifices became a basic religious ritual to worship *shang-di* in ancient times. The ancestral rituals began taking form during the Zhou dynasty (1045–256 BCE) *I Ching* is a classic text from that time which codified ancestral religion for the first time. Some important concepts, such as "mandate of heaven" and "son of heaven," were employed to justify social order and religious rituals. Based on these concepts, no one was allowed to establish oneself on the throne unless she or he had been chosen by heaven or *shang-di*; the emperor's power as a representative of divine power on earth is the sole power. In imperial China, there would have been no meaningful distinction between divine power and political power. Although Chinese ancestral religion was seriously attacked in the Warring States period (770–221 BCE), the Han dynasty and the following dynasties basically followed religious codes written in the Zhou dynasty.

The traditional ancestral religion had a profound impact on Chinese society for over two thousand years. First, it deeply influenced all religions in China. The traditional Chinese ancestral religion has more adherents than any other religious faith and was an important unifying force for the fifty-six nations in China. In imperial China, almost every city had its *cheng wang miao* (temple of the city-god); every village has its *tu di miao* (temple of the village-god); and every Chinese home had a religious shrine for ancestor worship. For most of the Chinese people, including both the nobility and common people, ancestor worship was first, and the belief in other religions was second. Therefore, the traditional ancestral religion actually became an established religion and dominated other religions, though it did not have a formal religious structure. Other religions were not permitted to contradict the ancestral religion in ideas, moral code, belief, or rites.

Second, the ancestral religion impacted the daily life of the Chinese nation. Compared with other types of religions, the ancestral religion was easier to develop among common Chinese people by religious rites, prayer, festivals, and ceremony. Ethically, the ancestral religion maintained human moral behavior and social order through ancestor worship; economically, the ancestral religion, through grain worship, land worship, and nature worship, sanctified the process of agricultural production and the natural environment.

Third, the ancestral religion impacted Chinese culture. Confucianism was the mainstream of Chinese culture. Confucianism had a profound influence on Chinese society because the central principles of Confucianism preserved traditional Chinese familial values. Filial piety is not merely an ethical value, but has a "religious resonance." In the later imperial China of the Ming and the Qing dynasties, ancestor worship was more popular and was completely dispersed into every family as one of the basic familial functions. The core of Confucianism was actually extending ancestral religion to Chinese culture.

Fourth, the ancestral religion impacted Chinese politics. The development of ancestor worship in China went hand-in-hand with the evolution of the dynastic political system. Important sacrificial rites were national events, and were presided over by the king or emperor, thereby indicating that the king's power was endowed by heavenly power. Ancestral religion maintained the king's power through the rite of heaven worship. The combination of ancestor worship and the dynastic political system produced the teaching of loyalty and filial piety.

Another characteristic of Chinese religions in imperial China was that the central government controlled religions from the national level to local levels by using ideology and coercive forces, not only over Daoism and Buddhism, but later over Islam and Christianity. Beginning with the Zhou dynasty, all local officials were appointed by the central government. The so-called local government was administered by a single magistrate assigned by the central government, who was assisted by his staff and managed all local matters. The Chinese government in the Zhou dynasty already codified ancestral religion. The Qin dynasty (221–206 BCE),—which divided China into provinces and counties, governed by centrally appointed governors and magistrates—revised the Zhou dynasty's codes and established *li bu* (the Ministry of Rites) to manage religious affairs. The Qin dynasty lasted only twenty-one years; its fall was attributed to the fact that it was ruled through military force, and without religious principles. Drawing a lesson from the demise of the Qin dynasty, Dong Zhongshu, a Confucian scholar and chief minister, suggested that the emperor Han Wu Di (140–86 BCE), the first emperor of the Han dynasty, espouse only Confucianism and abolish all other schools of thought in order to establish a benevolent government. After the Han dynasty, adherents of Daoism and Buddhism gradually gained ground and even participated in politics. Under this circumstance, in the Tang dynasty, the Chinese government carried out a new religious policy of laying equal stress on the three religions. After Islam and Christianity came into China in the seventh century CE, the central government extended its reach to regulating foreign religions, but Christianity in China was relatively independent because of Western military and political power. Since the Yuan dynasty took over Tibet, the Chinese government has exercised sovereign rights over Tibet and asserted the right to appoint religious leaders. The Qing dynasty established a special department to deal with Tibet's religious affairs and established a special religious policy for Tibet, which grants more religious freedom to the Tibetan people than to the Han Chinese, who make up about 95 percent of the Chinese population.

Jinghao Zhou

See also Buddhism; China, Communist; Confucianism; Daoism

Further Reading

Ching, J. (1993). *Chinese religions*. Maryknoll, NY: Orbis Books.

Eliade, M. (Ed.). (1979). *The encyclopedia of religion* (Vol. 8). New York: Macmillan.

MacInnis, D. E. (1989). *Religion in China today: Policy and practice*. Maryknoll, NY: Orbis Books.

Smith, D. H. (1968). *Chinese religions*. New York: Holt, Rinehart and Winston.

Thompson, L. G. (1979). *Chinese religion: An introduction*. Belmont, CA: Wadsworth.

Christian Science

Christian Science, the popular name for the First Church of Christ, Scientist, was born out of the practical application of divine principles of spiritual healing as discerned through the prayers and experience of the church's founder, Mary Baker Eddy (1821–1910). In 1875 Eddy, a lifelong New Englander, published the first edition of the foundational scripture (used together with the Bible) for Christian Scientists: *Science and Health with Key to the Scriptures*. By 1895, Christian Science was centrally organized around the "Mother Church" in Boston, Massachusetts, and by 1926, the census figures showed a growing membership of over 200,000, up from 85,717 members in 1906. Christian Science branch churches are nonhierarchical: There are no ordained ministers; lay leaders are elected. Readers who help conduct services are elected from among the membership for three-year terms, and men and women have equal status.

The Christian Science worldview is that of the Western world turned inside out. The Western normative world construct regards "matter," that is, that which is perceived through the five senses, as the locus of all cause and effect. According to that worldview, achieving a material effect upon the physical world requires the use of the material, mechanical forces of the outer world. Christian Science, however, sees the spiritual or mental realm of Principle as the locus of all cause and effect in the material realm. Thus, it is Principle that is truly real, and the appearance of causation, of effective power, in the physical or material plane is an illusion. The material world is "illusion" not because it does not exist, but because the spiritual (Divine Principle) is the ultimate source of power over the material and can correct all error (including sin, sickness, and disease).

Christian Science and Spiritual Healing

In the theology of Christian Science, God does not dispense health and healing at his inscrutable whim, nor does God expect an unthinking, unquestioning faith. Rather, the Christian Science God is one of Principle: unchanging, constant, all-powerful, and all-loving. This Principle acknowledges and produces only health; sickness or disease are violations of the Principle, and thus the Principle is not responsible for the existence of these errors. One must therefore attune one's life and thought back to Divine Principle in order to achieve a healing of the error. Christian Scientists often refer to the principles of mathematics as an analogy to Divine Principle: If one adds two plus three and gets a total of six, the fault does not lie with the principle of addition.

The comparison to mathematical principles is also helpful in explaining the freedom of the Christian Scientist in spiritual healing matters. Christian Scientists are not required by the Church to refrain from using medical doctors to treat illnesses; the Church respects the autonomy of each individual's spiritual choice. But the lack of ecclesiastical consequences does not mean that conventional Western medicine is compatible with Christian Science spirituality. A person, by way of analogy, is equally free to apply the principles of mathematics incorrectly and arrive at the wrong answer. But if a person wishes to arrive at a correct and useful answer or result, he or she will correctly apply the principle. And once a person has demonstrated to him- or herself the usefulness of applying the principle correctly, while still certainly free to apply it incorrectly or even to abandon it, why would anyone want to do so?

Christian Scientists are Christian Scientists precisely because they have proven the principles to their own satisfaction through empirical demonstra-

CHRISTIAN SCIENCE ON THE NATURE OF ILLNESS

For Christian Scientists, illness is an error, in the sense that it is not part of humanity's true nature. Like a mathematical error, it must be corrected.

Christian Science healing is in fact one way of worshipping God. It is an integral part of a deeply felt and closely reasoned view of ultimate reality. This very fact sometimes causes its use of the words "real" and "unreal" to be misunderstood. For when Christian Scientists speak of illness as unreal, they do not mean that humanly it is to be ignored. They mean rather that it is no part of man's true, essential being but comes from a mortal misconception of being, without validity, necessity, or legitimacy. Like a mathematical error which has no substance or principle to support it, sickness is not to be ignored but to be consciously wiped out by a correct understanding of the divine Principle of being. This is the metaphysical basis of Christian Science practice.

Source: Christian Science Publishing Society,
A Century of Christian Science Healing.
(Boston: Christian Science Publishing Society, 1966), 241.

tions. Christian Scientists believe in the principles not because God, the Bible, Mary Baker Eddy, or the church told them to, but because applying those principles has helped them heal aspects of their own life. Written and verbal testimonials of healings are an important part of Christian Science ritual and practice: Every Wednesday, for example, members of local branch churches across the country gather to exchange witnessing testimony of the outworkings of

divine order in every aspect of their lives. Church publications dating from the founding of Christian Science contain written testimony of various sorts of healings. And although it is popular and convenient to dismiss such testimonials as either the consequence of the illness having been psychosomatic or imagined to begin with, a fair examination of the testimonies belies a quick dismissal.

All Christian Scientists practice their religion, but there are also people known as "practitioners," who provide expert spiritual healing help on a professional basis. The Church emphasizes that this is a religious vocation: "the practitioner's diagnosis is neither medical nor psychological ... but spiritual." (Christian Science Publishing Society 1966, 140). The practitioner is a layperson, not a member of the clergy (there are no clergy in Christian Science).

Christian Science and Religious Freedom

Christian Science theology and healing practices challenge the conventionalities of two major societal institutions in the United States: the medical establishment and the Protestant establishment. Thus, it should come as no surprise that from the beginning, Christian Scientists have had to struggle to maintain their religious freedom. Mainstream Protestant Christianity at the end of the nineteenth century was

The Christian Science Church, Boston, Massachusetts, c. 1900–1920. COURTESY OF LIBRARY OF CONGRESS, PRINTS AND PHOTOGRAPHS DIVISION, DETROIT PUBLISHING COMPANY COLLECTION.

CHRISTIAN SCIENCE TESTIMONIALS

The testimonials of those who have been healed through Christian Science indicate that the conditions being treated were real, and the recoveries remarkable.

The range of conditions healed [as reported in over 7,100 testimonials published from 1969 to 1988] included congenital, degenerative, infectious, neurological, and other disorders, some considered terminal or incurable. These testimonies included over 2,400 healings of children. More than 600 of these involved medically-diagnosed conditions, life-threatening as well as less serious, including spinal meningitis (in several cases after antibiotics failed to help), pneumonia and double-pneumonia, diabetes, food poisoning, heart disorders, loss of eyesight from chemical burns, pleurisy, stomach obstruction, epilepsy, goiter, leukemia, malaria, mastoiditis, polio, rheumatic fever, and ruptured appendix.

Source: D. N. Williams, Viewpoint:
Christian Science and the Care of Children: Constitutional Issues.
Church and State, 9 (1989): 19–20,

reeling from the effect of the forces of modernity: science, biblical criticism, urbanization, and industrialization. Added to these problems was the external challenge posed by successful new religious groups such as Christian Science. This was a time when the cultural hegemony of mainstream Protestant groups began to weaken.

In addition to creating furor by its intrusion into territory once dominated by the mainstream Protestant churches, Christian Science also trampled upon territory staked out by conventional Western medicine in general and by the American Medical Association in particular. Allopathic medicine (medicine that cures by applying counteractive rather than complementary remedies to problems; the term is generally used for the interventionist, combative approach to illness and disorder that has come to characterize the medical mainstream) had by this time assumed the mantle of an orthodoxy, defining itself as sole possessor of healing arts, and used the legal and political arena (with impressive but by no means total success) as a means of insisting on its orthodoxy and the consequent illegitimacy of all other healing methods. Thus, Christian Science practitioners were prosecuted for practicing medicine without a license. These prosecutions, plus the flurry of criminal prosecutions of parents who used faith or spiritual healing methods in the early decades of the twentieth century, caused Christian Scientists to lobby state legislatures across the country, successfully obtaining express statutory exemptions for spiritual healing.

By far the most controversial aspect of Christian Science is parents' use of spiritual healing methods on their children. Statutory provisions accepting religiously based methods of healing as sufficient medical care under child neglect laws have not protected Christian Science parents from manslaughter and other criminal charges when spiritual healing methods fail and the child dies. Two such well-publicized cases are the California case of *Walker v. Superior Court*, in which a mother was convicted of manslaughter in the death from meningitis of her four-year-old daughter, and *Commonwealth v. David R. Twitchell*, in which the parents were convicted of involuntary manslaughter in the death from peritonitis of their two-and- a-half-year-old son. (The latter conviction was reversed on a technicality.) Former Christian Scientists write scathingly of the terrible psychological and physical effects that Christian Science has had on children. Caroline Fraser's book, *God's Perfect Child*, is an example of the genre; a *Kirkus Review* (posted on the amazon.com website for Fraser's book) deemed the book "a one-sided expose" and "incendiary" but also concluded that the questions the book raise with regard to religious freedom and children's rights were legitimate.

The appropriate treatment of Christian Science parents whose child does not achieve healing raises an excruciatingly difficult religious-freedom issue. On the one hand, parents whose children engage in risky, secular pursuits such as football, gymnastics, and driving a car are normally not legally sanctioned when their children are injured or killed by these pursuits. Parents whose children suffer and die while under medical care do not have to also suffer legal ramifications. In contrast, Christian Science parents raise their children under a strict liability standard: If something goes wrong, they are criminally responsible.

There have been movements to remove spiritual healing from protection under child neglect statutes, under the rationale that government must protect children from parents' religious practices that the state feels promote martyrdom, until the child is old enough to choose a religion for itself. The practical difficulties with this position have simply not been addressed, however: What the state is in essence requiring is that parents, and, indeed, the entire religious community, somehow suspend a portion of their framework when raising and otherwise dealing with their children.

Spiritual healing is the heart and soul of the Christian Science religious framework. Christian Scientists and supporters argue that if parents are required to exclude their child from this fundamental practice of an otherwise integrated religious framework, the result will be a child who is disoriented at best, and "base-less" at worst. Of course, critics of Christian Science would respond that at least the child lives to be an adult if the state intervenes.

Mark Twain wrote scathingly of Christian Science. Even so, he understood the mind-set of the religiously faithful parent better than anyone else engaged in the debate, both then and now:

I have received several letters (two from educated and ostensibly intelligent persons), which contained, in substance, this protest: "I don't object to men and women chancing their lives with these people, but it is a burning shame that the law should allow them to trust their helpless little children in their deadly hands." Isn't it touching? Isn't it deep? Isn't it modest? It is as if the person said: "I know that to a parent his child is the core of his

heart, the apple of his eye, a possession so dear, so precious that he will trust its life in no hands but those which he believes, with all his soul, to be the very best and the very safest, but it is a burning shame that the law does not require him to come to *me* to ask what kind of healer I will allow him to call." The public is merely a multiplied "me." (Twain 1986, 39)

Prosecutors and judges would do well to ponder Twain's insight before they bring the criminal-justice system to bear on grieving parents who were doing "the very best" for their children. Civil intervention to force medical care upon a child may very well be the best course of action when the child's life is at stake, but even here the government must proceed with respect for the different framework and value system of the family, and in a way that is least intrusive.

Catharine Cookson

See also Spiritual Healing

Further Reading

Ahlstrom, S. E. (1972). *A religious history of the American people.* New Haven, CT: Yale University Press.

Batten, M. P., DesAutels, P., & May, L. (1999). *Praying for a cure: Medical ethics in conflict with religious freedom.* Lanham, MD: Rowman & Littlefield.

Christian Science Publishing Society. (1966). *A century of Christian Science healing.* Boston: author.

Christian Science Publishing Society. (1989). *Freedom and responsibility: Christian Science healing for children.* Boston: author.

Christian Science Publishing Society. (1990). *Christian Science: A sourcebook of contemporary materials.* Boston: author.

Cookson, C. (2001). *Regulating religion: The courts and the free exercise clause.* New York: Oxford University Press.

Eddy, M. B. (1994). *Science and health with key to the scriptures.* Boston: First Church of Christ, Scientist.

Fraser, C. (1999). *God's perfect child: Living and dying in the Christian Science church.* New York: Metropolitan Books.

John, D. (1962). *The Christian Science way of life.* Englewood Cliffs, NJ: Prentice Hall.

Monopoli, P. A. (1991). Allocating the costs of parental free exercise: Striking a new balance between sincere religious belief and a child's right to medical treatment. *Pepperdine Law Review, 18,* 319.

Schoepflin, R. B. (2002). *Christian Science on trial: Religious healing in America.* Baltimore: Johns Hopkins University Press.

Taylor, C. (1989). *Sources of the self: The making of the modern identity.* Cambridge, MA: Harvard University Press.

Twain, M. (1986). *Christian Science.* New York: Harper. (Original work published 1907).

Whittenbury, E. K. (1990). *Walker v. Superior Court*: Religious convictions may bring felony convictions. *Pacific Law Journal, 21,* 1069.

Williams, D. N. (1989). Viewpoint: Christian Science and the care of children: Constitutional issues. *Church and State, 9,* 19–20.

Court Cases

Commonwealth v. David R. Twitchell, 416 Mass. 114, 617 N.E.2d 609 (1993).

People v. Pierson, 176 N.Y. 201, 68N.E. 243 (1903).

Prince v. Massachusetts, 321 U.S. 158 (1944).

Regina v. Wagstaffe, 10 Cox Crim. Cas. 530 (Cent. Crim. Ct. 1868).

Walker v. Superior Court, 47 Cal. 3d 112, 253 Cal. Rptr. 1 (1988).

Church and State in Modern Europe

Relations between church and state determine the scope of religious freedom and equality, primarily of religious groups and secondarily of their followers. Church–state relations in contemporary Europe range from systems characterized by institutional unity of the state with one or more creeds, to systems characterized by institutional separation of the state from any creeds. (The first type of system is subject to many variations, while the second can be divided into several subsystems.) Systems of institutional separation, however, generally prevail.

Characteristics Common to All Systems

Common characteristics shared by all systems of church–state relations include: a) The public practice of religion, except in certain countries, is not an exclusive right of state churches, recognized religious communities, or registered religious organizations, by virtue of special laws relating to creeds or of general statutes concerning private corporations; b) European countries have not, like the United States, devised a legal definition of religion compatible with international standards. As a result, they generally inadequately protect the freedom of *new* creeds.

Systems of Institutional Unity

Systems of institutional unity inherently do not secure equality between religious communities; they do, however, guarantee the autonomy of non-state creeds. The exception is Greece, which only partly guarantees such autonomy, as statutes do not fully protect the religious freedom of minority creeds. Norway goes further, institutionally protecting the "religious" freedom of those who hold no religious beliefs. Denmark has a procedure for recognizing creeds, related to the attachment of legal consequences to religious marriages. Greece inappropriately attaches a similar procedure to the granting of permits for churches or places of worship. Iceland associates the recognition of religious organizations with their registration. The United Kingdom accepts a theistic definition of religion.

Finland, Sweden, and the United Kingdom offer legislative guarantees of relative ecclesiastical autonomy for their state churches, while Denmark and Greece guarantee ecclesiastical self-administration. State churches may be organized as either public law corporations (Denmark, Finland, Greece) or private law corporations (Sweden, the United Kingdom). On the other hand, non-state churches are organized as private law corporations.

Systems of Institutional Separation

The systems of institutional separation between church and state found in continental Europe comprise: a) subsystems of a Catholic established church; b) subsystems of special recognition of one or more creeds, which may disguise an established church or churches; c) subsystems of a multi-denominational state; and d) subsystems of positive state secularity.

Subsystems of a Catholic Established Church

Subsystems of a Catholic established church prevail in Liechtenstein, Monaco, and Malta, and the principal effect is the autonomy of both the Catholic Church and other creeds. The constitution of

THE CONTINUING TIES OF CHURCH AND STATE

Although in most nations in modern Europe the trend has been toward a separation of church and state, this is not the case everywhere. One region where religion and national identity remain closely linked is the Balkans. The following description of Serbia in the 1950s remains true today.

The real significance of the Serbian Orthodox faith and the local church is found in part in the ceremonial observances at home and also in the complete identity of faith and nationality. The Church played a most important role in maintaining a national consciousness during the hundreds of years of Turkish rule, as was brought out in Chapter 2. Serbia has been relatively homogeneous, and to say that a person is a Serb also implies that he is a member of the Orthodox faith. During the existence of Serbia, as an independent state and later, after the formation of the Kingdom of Yugoslavia, the Orthodox religion remained in effect the official Church of Serbia. The peasants have always identified themselves as closely with the Church as with the State.

Until 1863 there was no church in Orasac, and the villagers attended the one in Bukovik. Under the leadership of their first priest, who was himself born in Orasac, an attempt was made to enlist the support of people from Kopljare and Orasac villages to help build a local church. There was great difficulty deciding on a site, because the people of Orasac wanted it built in the center of the village while those from Kopljare wanted it in their village. A compromise of sorts was reached when it was decided that the church would be built in Orasac and the priest would move his residence to Kopljare (it was later moved back to Orasac). Construction was started in 1868 and was completed in 1870, the peasants themselves supplying most of the funds and labor. Until 1950 all the priests in the Orasac-Kopljare parish were born in villages in the Jasenca region, providing a further bond between the villagers and their church.

Joel M. Halpern

Source: *A Serbian Village*.
(New York: Columbia University Press, 1958), 233.

Malta, however, makes Roman Catholic values an evaluative basis of its legal order, and a significant consequence of this is the state prohibition of divorce.

Subsystems of Special Recognition

Subsystems of special recognition, under the influence of Orthodox culture that has insufficiently assimilated human rights principles, may enshrine the basis for exclusive privileged treatment of an established church or churches. Special recognition of one or more creeds is accomplished by the constitution (in Bulgaria, F.Y.R.O.M. [Macedonia], and Moldova), by law (in Russia), or in practice as a result of government policy (in Belarus and Romania). However, the principles of equality of religious organizations (in Belarus, Russia, and F.Y.R.O.M.), of separation of state and creeds (in Bulgaria, Russia, and F.Y.R.O.M.), and of autonomy of religious organizations (in F.Y.R.O.M. and Moldova) are constitutionally safeguarded. Furthermore, the Russian Constitution guarantees the secular character of the state and the non-establishment of religion. The Moldavian constitution also enshrines the principles of state cooperation with recognized creeds and the potential regulation of their relations through conventions.

Bulgaria, F.Y.R.O.M., Russia, and Moldova recognize their Orthodox churches. At a secondary level, Russia recognizes its other traditional religions, namely, other Christian sects, Islam, Buddhism, and Judaism. Bulgaria, based on a law of Communist origin, and Moldova, by virtue of a new law, continue to attach the recognition of creeds to registration with the government (as of 2002, Moldova was preparing a draft law concerning creeds). The new law of F.Y.R.O.M. on religious organizations has largely been declared unconstitutional by its Constitutional Court, since it reflects the totalitarian ideology of the previous regime. Russia, despite its constitutional system of positive secularity, has enacted a new law that discriminates in favor of traditional creeds, particularly the Russian Orthodox Church, through unequal treatment of religious associations and onerous preconditions for their registration. Belarus has implemented a policy favoring the Russian Orthodox Church. And in Romania, the committee that grants permits for the construction of houses of worship, even of non-Orthodox creeds, includes two Orthodox Church representatives.

Registration of religious organizations with the government is mandatory in Belarus, Bulgaria, F.Y.R.O.M. (whose Constitutional Court has, however, repealed this), Romania, and Moldova. Successive Bulgarian governments have intervened in the internal affairs of the Orthodox Church and the Muslim community without respecting their autonomy. Moldova, for political reasons, recognizes and registers only the Orthodox Church of Moldova, subject to the Russian Orthodox Church, while refusing to recognize or register the Bessarabian Orthodox Church, subject to the Orthodox Church of Romania, or the Church of the True Orthodox-Moldova, subject to the Russian Overseas Orthodox Church. It does not recognize these latter two churches because it considers them to be schismatic in relation to the former, whereas it should recognize them as divergent religious communities in the context of democratic religious pluralism. In Romania, by virtue of a law dating from Communist times, registration is linked to the recognition of religious organizations by the government.

Subsystems of a Multi-denominational State

Subsystems of multi-denominational states may expressly recognize one or more religions at a constitutional level (in Cyprus, Italy, Spain, Poland, and Lithuania) or at a general legislative level (in Israel), or may not recognize them at all. In such subsystems, church–state relations are regulated by legislation or conventions. Agreements these states have with the Holy See fall within international law, while all other ecclesiastical conventions are in the domain of domestic public law.

The countries where these subsystems apply generally accept the principles of church–state separation, of the state's multi-denominational nature, of graduated equality through the differentiation of the legal regimes of the various creeds, of the benevolent neutrality of the state, and of church autonomy. Belgium, moreover, institutionally protects the religious freedom of those who hold no religious beliefs. The graduated equality of religious groups is predicated on the idea that differential treatment does not constitute religious discrimination, if it is based on objective and reasonable grounds in each case and refers only to social and not religious differences. However, under Portugal's religious freedom law of 2000, the privileges granted to the Catholic Church in the 1940 Concordat were extended to other registered religious communities in the interests of religious freedom. There is a distinction between registered (by virtue of a law or statute relating to associations) and non-registered religious organizations. Austria, the Czech Republic, Hungary, Italy, Latvia, Lithuania, Poland, Portugal, the Slovak Republic, Slovenia, Spain, and Ukraine have laws for the registration of creeds. This distinction is found in virtually all countries having these subsystems. Its consequences are not limited to the right of association of religious groups, but are related to the concession of religious rights and privileges.

A second distinction arises from the establishment of multi-tiered structures for the legal regimes of religious communities. Such multi-tiered structures are based on the legal character of public or private law (in Germany), official recognition (in Austria or Belgium), and the historic (in Hungary) or traditional character (in Latvia) of particular churches or religious communities. The draft law in Yugoslavia is also grounded on the criterion of traditional character.

In a recent law, Austria introduced the regime of "registered religious confessional communities," intermediate between the recognized and non-recognized religious communities. The Czech Republic and Latvia have patterned their regimes after the Austrian model.

Official recognition of religious communities in Austria, Belgium, and Lithuania is established by law. This is incongruous with the equality of creeds, because some creeds have no right to official recognition, despite meeting the requirements prescribed by law (Austria, Lithuania) or developed through administrative and legislative practice (in

Belgium). Similarly unequal access to enhanced religious freedom exists in other countries as well, by means of selective agreements between the government and religious communities (in Italy, Portugal, Spain, and Poland). In contrast, Germany provides for the right of religious organizations to acquire the status of public law corporations.

This multi-tiered structure is further grounded on agreements between certain states and the Holy See and on conventions signed by their governments and particular religious communities. Thus, Germany has a Concordat with the Holy See, as well as ecclesiastical conventions with the Evangelical Lutheran Church and with other religious communities enjoying the status of public law corporations. Hungary has signed international agreements with the Holy See, and agreements with its three other historic churches. Italy has a Treaty with the Holy See and eight agreements with minority creeds that possess legal status by virtue of a special law. Spain has international agreements with the Holy See and three agreements with minority creeds that are "deeply rooted" in Spanish society. Croatia, Israel, Lithuania, Poland, Portugal, and the Slovak Republic all have international agreements with the Holy See. Luxembourg and Slovenia have agreements at a national level with the Catholic Church.

Subsystems of Positive State Secularity

Systems of positive state secularity generally accept the principles of church–state separation, the benevolent neutrality and positive secularity (or laicity) of the state, the non-recognition of any religion, and the autonomy of creeds. The Constitution of Albania mandates that the relations between the state and religious communities be regulated by legal agreement. In Estonia, religious organizations have at their disposal only the status of private law corporations by virtue of general statutes relating to associations and special legislation concerning religious communities. Under these systems, countries either adjust their laws to the organizational structures of all creeds (in Netherlands) or of the main creed in their society (in France, relative to the Catholic Church), or prescribe only the common form of association for their religious organizations (in Ireland).

However, in Alsace and Lorraine in France, the general, statewide system of church–state relations does not apply. Here, local law effectively maintains a multi-denominational state that officially recognizes four religious communities. In this district, the Concordat between Napoleon Bonaparte and the Holy See is still in force.

Turkey represents a special case of secular state. This country does not adhere to tenets characteristic of positive state secularity, because it imposes on its Muslim population a Sunni version of Islam and does not accommodate other Muslim communities or the principle of the autonomy of creeds. In effect, it fully administers Muslim religious affairs. It insufficiently respects the autonomy of two of the three religious minorities that are recognized by the Treaty of Lausanne, and does not recognize the autonomy of any other religious minority.

Appropriate Government Policy for the Future

European governments are bound by international law to enact and implement genuine equality among all religious communities. They are thus urged seriously to consider the religious freedom and equality of new creeds.

Kyriakos N. Kyriazopoulos

See also Balkans, East Europe, and Russia; Germany and Prussia; Turkey; United Kingdom

Further Reading

Boyle, K., & Sheen, J. (Eds.). (1997). *Freedom of religion and belief: A world report*. London: Routledge.

Clark, E. A. (1996). Church-State in the Czech Republic: Past turmoil and present transformation. *Brigham Young University Law Review*, 1019–1086.

Davie, G. (2000). *Religion in modern Europe: A memory mutates*. Oxford, UK: Oxford University Press.

De Jong, C. D. (2000). *The freedom of thought, conscience and religion or belief in the United Nations (1946–1992)*. Antwerp, Netherlands: Intersentia.

Durham, W. C., Jr., & Homer, L. B. (1998). Russia's 1997 law on freedom of conscience and religious associations: An analytical appraisal. *Emory International Law Review, 12*(1), 101–246.

European Consortium for Church-State Research (Ed.). (1994). The legal status of religious minorities in the countries of the European Union. *Proceedings of the European Consortium for Church and State Research, Thessaloniki, Greece, 1993*.

European Consortium for Church-State Research (Ed.) (1999). New religious movements and the law in the European Union, *Proceedings of the European Consortium for Church and State Research, Lisbon, Portugal, 1997.*

Evans, C. (2001). *Freedom of religion under the European convention on human rights.* Oxford, UK: Oxford University Press.

Garlicki, L. L. (2001). Perspectives on freedom of conscience and religion in the jurisprudence of constitutional courts. *Brigham Young University Law Review, 2001*(2), 467–509.

Minnerath, R. (1998). The position of the Catholic Church regarding concordats from a doctrinal and pragmatic perspective. *Catholic University Law Review, 47,* 467–476.

Platvoet, J. G., & Molendijk, A. L. (Eds.). (1999). *The pragmatics of defining religion: Contexts, concepts & contests.* Leiden, Netherlands : Brill.

Robbers, G. (Ed.). (1996). *State and church in the European Union.* Baden-Baden, Germany: Nomos Verlagsgesellschaft, in conjunction with the European Consortium for State and Church Research.

Ruebner, R., Martin, M. L., & Gasey, C. H. (1993). Religion and the law in the commonwealth of independent states and the Baltic Nations. *Touro Journal of Transnational Law, 4,* 103–148.

Stahnke, T., & Martin, J. P. (Eds.). (1998). *Religion and human rights: Basic documents, Center for the Study of Human Rights.* New York: Columbia University Press.

Torfs, R. (1996). Church and state in France, Belgium, and the Netherlands: Unexpected similarities and hidden differences. *Brigham Young University Law Review,* 945–971.

Van der Vyver, J. D., & Witte, J., Jr. (Eds.). (1996). *Religious human rights in global perspective: Legal perspectives.* The Hague, Netherlands: Martinus Nijhoff Publishers.

Civil Religion

Civil religion is a set of common beliefs, values, and rituals that invest a political state with transcendent significance. Civil religion usually includes a shared sense of history and destiny; an understanding of national endeavor as universally meaningful; a sense of chosenness; a collective, unifying force; and rituals and beliefs that reinforce commonality over sectarian differences.

The phenomenon of civil religion has ranged widely over both time and space, marking public life in places as distant geographically and temporally as the ancient Greek and Roman city-states and Japan in the decades prior to World War II. In each instance, public rituals sanctified the ruling government's activities and served to cement citizens together in a common civic identity.

The concept's modern currency originated with the French philosopher Jean-Jacques Rousseau (1712–1778). Recalling the devastation caused by Europe's wars of religion, Rousseau in *The Social Contract* (1762) argued that a political state required a civil religion to secure the unity of its people. His civil religion stood apart from Christianity and contained few creedal basics: God exists; there is a life to come in which virtuous behavior will be rewarded and bad deeds punished. The government had not only the right but the duty to enforce this civil religion; all other beliefs were to remain matters of private opinion and could be held only insofar as they did not conflict with the civil religion. In Rousseau's conception, sectarian religious intolerance was disallowed as destructive to the harmony of the state; those who violated this injunction would be either banished or executed.

During the French Revolution, Jacobin leaders attempted to establish and rigorously enforce a civil religion similar to Rousseau's ideal model. They tried to replace Christianity with a religion of the Supreme Being, one which celebrated the Revolution with new rites, festivals, and public art. In 1793 the revolutionaries signaled how completely they wished to de-Christianize the country by introducing a new calendar, one which marked time not from the birth of Christ but from the new government's genesis a year earlier.

While this French model sought—and soon failed—to replace traditional religion with a religion of the republic, many contemporary scholars have sought to distinguish such historical incarnations of church-state union from modern civil religion. Today the term more accurately describes a set of beliefs and practices that are intimately related to, but nevertheless distinct from, both church and state.

The Renewal of Interest in Civil Religion

In a seminal 1967 essay, the sociologist Robert N. Bellah announced that "there actually exists alongside of and rather clearly differentiated from the churches an elaborate and well-institutionalized civil religion in America" (Bellah 1967, 1). He defined civil religion as "an understanding of the American experience in the light of ultimate and universal reality" (18). Such a faith both legitimates the nation's political authorities and endows its purposes with transcendent meaning. While overlapping with Christianity, Bellah contended, it did not represent a specific, sectarian religion. Instead, by invoking values such as liberty, equality, justice, and religious tolerance, the U.S. civil religion "borrowed selectively from the religious tradition in such a way that the average American saw no conflict between the two" (13).

The God of civil religion takes an active, special interest in the United States' endeavors but, Bellah insisted, the civil religion was not equivalent to nation worship. In fact, its transcendent dimension enabled the civil religion to stand in judgment over national endeavors; indeed, that was sometimes its most significant function. Though eight years later, in *The Broken Covenant*, he criticized the U.S. civil religion as "an empty and broken shell" (Bellah 1992 [1975], 142), Bellah nevertheless maintained that it represented a healthy aspect of U.S. public life that deserved attention, maintenance, and reinvigoration.

Civil Religion in the United States

Bellah's essay sparked ongoing cross-disciplinary debates about civil religion's contents, forms, functions, and meanings. Though multiple conversations have discussed civil religion in countries as diverse as Canada and South Africa, the most vigorous conversations have addressed civil religion in the United States.

A conception of U.S. civil religion predated the nation's founding. In his 1749 pamphlet *Proposals Relating to the Education of Youth in Pensilvania*, Benjamin Franklin wrote of "the necessity of Publick Religion," a generalized moral and religious sensibility that could counteract "the mischiefs of superstition" among the people. In his *Autobiography*, Franklin indicated that civil religion should include "the essentials of every religion." overlapping tenets that transcended denominational particularities. Thomas Jefferson, stated in the Declaration of Independence (1776) that all people "are endowed by their Creator with certain inalienable rights." Without some sense that those rights came from God, Jefferson held, those rights—and therefore the republic—might be jeopardized. In his 1796 Farewell Address, George Washington affirmed that "Of all the dispositions and habits which lead to political prosperity, Religion and Morality are indispensable supports." He and other founders, including John Adams, believed that the nation's survival depended upon a virtuous citizenry, and virtue's best guarantor was religion. Though a diversity of religious denominations existed, they believed that what religious people held in common was enough to ensure that citizens would be up to the moral task of maintaining their newly minted democratic republic.

Presidents as Priests

As with most religions, the U.S. civil religion has clergy, sacred texts, common rituals, and a sacred historical narrative. Presidents have customarily acted as "priests of the public religion" (Marty 1987, 61). Since Washington, they have called for national days of prayer and thanksgiving and have frequently invoked God in their public speeches. Presidents have also found themselves "officiating" at public "services" in times of national crisis. For example, Abraham Lincoln often interpreted the nation's Civil War in light of God's providential plan. He believed that the will of the people was the surest clue to the will of God, but resisted identifying the nation's purposes with that of the divine. In his Second Inaugural Address (4 March 1865), he noted that both the North and the South "read the same Bible, and pray to the same God; and each invokes His aid against the other. . . . The prayers of both could not be answered; that of neither has been answered fully. The Almighty has His own purposes." Upon his assassination six weeks later, on Good Friday, Lincoln became for many a Christ figure, someone sacrificed on behalf of a sinful people in order that the nation might be redeemed.

Through radio and television, U.S. presidents have had more opportunities to serve as priests to the republic. After the space shuttle *Challenger* exploded in 1986, Ronald Reagan spoke in a nationally televised memorial service of how the astronauts had "stirred the soul of our nation." He concluded that "We can find consolation only in faith, for we know in our hearts that you who flew so high and so proud now make your home beyond the stars, safe in God's promise of eternal life." Such remarks by these "priests" often become part of civil religion's canon, taking their place alongside other sacred texts such as the Declaration of Independence, the Constitution, and the Gettysburg Address.

The Bible as Sacred Text in U.S. Civil Religion

Perhaps the most important sacred text in the U.S. civil religion has been the Bible. Bellah noted that "behind the civil religion at every point lie Biblical archetypes" (1967, 18). The eighteenth-century minister and theologian Jonathan Edwards (1703–1758) delivered a sermon entitled "The Latter-day Glory Is Probably to Begin in America." Like the original Puritans, he thought that God had carved out a special providential role for the American colonies. In 1777 Nicholas Street, a Connecticut minister, interpreted the war with Britain as God's judgment upon the disobedient colonies: Like children in need of discipline, the disobedient colonists should "kiss the rod" of Great Britain and accept the purifying punishment they so richly deserved. Nineteenth-century Protestants similarly interpreted the Civil War as God's punishment of his chosen people who, like the Israelites in the Bible, had not conformed sufficiently to God's will. African-American Protestants inverted that same theme, interpreting their own experiences of slavery as those of a captive people under Pharaoh, with deliverance soon to be theirs.

Despite the Bible's obvious Christian particularity, civil religion has customarily remained vague enough so that most religious citizens could hear in it echoes of their own beliefs. The historian Sidney Mead argued that by the late nineteenth century, a separate "religion of the Republic" had come to exist alongside but distinct from denominational religion. Civil religion had replaced sectarian religions in fulfilling citizens' needs for social cohesion, individual meaning, and a sense of connectedness to something transcendent.

Civil Religion's Nondenominational Character

Most sacred symbols in the United States' civil religion are poured from this nondenominational mold. The nation's coins declare "In God We Trust," while its bills display the Great Seal, which boasts "Annuit Coeptis," meaning "God has favored our undertaking." From 1954 to 2002, schoolchildren declared in the Pledge of Allegiance that the United States was "one nation, under God." The U.S. Supreme Court begins its sessions with the plea, "God save this honorable Court." Avoiding specificity, these examples all reinforce civil religion by affirming the nation's special relationship with the divine.

Commemorations of the nation's trials and ideals, from Independence Day celebrations to Memorial Day to Thanksgiving, often take on a civil-religious hue. Other holidays celebrate the nation's saints and martyrs: Washington, Lincoln, John F. Kennedy, Martin Luther King Jr. Certain geographical locations have become sacred ground: Arlington Cemetery and the Tomb of the Unknown Soldier, the Gettysburg battlefield, the Vietnam Veterans Memorial. These places and ceremonies all form part of the nation's sacred narrative, one in which all citizens can share.

The Future of Civil Religion

The problem of civil religion is one posed uniquely and acutely by a religiously plural nation with no established church. In such a circumstance, as in the United States, civil religion can become an informal establishment, one which offers "both an invitation and exclusion" (Eisenach 2000, 6) by unofficially defining the boundaries of full citizenship. In the nineteenth century, when white Protestants dominated U.S. public culture, moral consensus was easily reached. However, as Catholics, Jews, African-American Protestants, and eventually Muslims, Hindus, and Buddhists all emerged as full participants in civic life during the twentieth century, the nature of that informal establishment became more and more contested.

Part of the problem stems from competing conceptions of civil religion. Is civil religion properly understood as a prescriptive phenomenon or a descriptive one? Those following Rousseau suggest that a civil religion is necessary for social cohesion—it is something to which people must assent to become full citizens. Others, following the sociologist Émile Durkheim (1858–1917), may understand civil religion as a collective representation that inevitably emerges from an already united people. This moral consensus does not provide commonality; it is instead the expression or reflection of it.

The tensions inherent in civil religion could be seen in the National Prayer Service held on 14 September 2001, three days after terrorist attacks on New York City and Washington, D.C. It wedded faith and nation in typical fashion: with political leaders gathered together, military colors processed into the sanctuary ahead of the Christian cross. The program included two classic hymns from the U.S. civil religion: a soloist sang "America, the Beautiful" and the congregation joined in "The Battle Hymn of the

Republic." As they sang the last verse, echoes of the nineteenth-century, pan-Protestant version of civil religion resounded strongly.

But the service also wrestled with the meaning of civil religion amid radical religious pluralism. Though the people sang "A Mighty Fortress Is Our God," written by the very Protestant reformer Martin Luther, planners omitted the verse that refers directly to "Christ Jesus" as "the right man on our side" who "must win the battle." Most significantly, the ceremony visibly broadened the U.S. civil religion as a Muslim imam joined Catholic, Protestant, and Jewish clerics in praying and reading sacred scriptures.

This service suggested powerfully the possibilities and limitations of civil religion in the new millennium. The more diverse a people, the more generalized its civil religion must become to retain its potency. However, as its boundaries expand to accommodate religious pluralism, civil religion may become so diluted as to retain little substantive content. Though scholarly debate seems presently exhausted, the question of civil religion—linked as it is to questions of national unity and identity—will continue to play an important role in future conversations.

R. Jonathan Moore

See also French Revolution; Pledge of Allegiance

Further Reading

Bellah, R. N. (1967, Winter). Civil religion in America. *Daedalus, 96,* 1–21.

Bellah, R. N. (1992). *The broken covenant: American civil religion in a time of trial* (2nd ed.). Chicago: University of Chicago Press. (Original work published 1975).

Bellah, R. N., & Hammond, P. E. (1980). *Varieties of civil religion.* New York: Harper & Row.

Casanova, J. (1994). *Public religions in the modern world.* Chicago: University of Chicago Press.

Cherry, C. (Ed.). (1998). *God's new Israel: Religious interpretations of American destiny* (Rev. ed.). Chapel Hill: University of North Carolina Press. (Original work published 1971).

Davis, D. (1997, Summer). Law, morals, and civil religion in America. *Journal of Church and State, 39,* 411–425.

Dewey, J. (1934). *A common faith.* New Haven, CT: Yale University Press.

Durkheim, É. ([1912] 1995). *The elementary forms of religious life* (K. E. Fields, Trans.). New York: The Free Press.

Eisenach, E. J. (2000). *The next religious establishment: National identity and political theology in post-Protestant America.* Lanham, MD: Rowman & Littlefield.

Herberg, W. (1960). *Protestant, Catholic, Jew: An essay in American religious sociology* (Rev. ed.). New York: Anchor Books. (Original work published 1955)

Marty, M. E. (1987). *Religion and republic: The American circumstance.* Boston: Beacon Press.

Marty, M. E. (1997). *The one and the many: America's struggle for the common good.* Cambridge, MA: Harvard University Press.

Mathisen, J. A. (1989). Twenty years after Bellah: Whatever happened to American civil religion? *Sociological Analysis, 50*(2), 129–146.

Mead, S. E. (1975). *The nation with the soul of a church.* New York: Harper & Row.

Nisbet, R. (1987). Civil religion. In M. Eliade (Ed.), *The encyclopedia of religion* (pp. 524–527). New York: Macmillan.

Parsons, G. (2002). *Perspectives on civil religion.* Aldershot, UK: Ashgate.

Pierard, R., & Linder, R. (1988). *Civil religion and the American presidency.* Grand Rapids, MI: W. B. Eerdmans Publishing Co.

Richey, R. E., & Jones, D. G. (Eds.). (1974). *American civil religion.* New York: Harper & Row.

Rousseau, J.-J. (1762) *The social contract.* Retrieved December 18, 2002 from http://www.constitution.org/jjr/socon.htm

Tocqueville, A. de (1988). *Democracy in America.* New York: HarperPerennial. (Original work published 1848)

Wilson, J. F. (1979). *Public religion in American culture.* Philadelphia: Temple University Press.

Code Noir

The introduction of African slaves into the colonies of the French Caribbean in the mid-seventeenth century necessitated the creation of new laws to regulate slavery and to define the responsibilities of slave owners in French colonial society. The sixty articles of the Code Noir ("Black Code"), promulgated as a royal edict by King Louis XIV in 1685, represented the culmination of this legislative task. Issued during a period of escalating Catholic absolutism in France,

SELECTIONS ON RELIGION FROM THE CODE NOIR

I.

We wish and intend that the edict by the late King of glorious memory our very honored lord and father of 23 April 1615 be enforced in our islands, by this we charge all our officers to evict from our Islands all the Jews who have established their residence there, to whom, as to the declared enemies of the Christian name, we order to have left within three months from the day of the publication of these present [edicts], or face confiscation of body and property.

II.

All the slaves who will be in our Islands will be baptized and instructed in the Catholic, Apostolic, and Roman religion. We charge the planters who will buy newly arrived *negres* to inform the Governor and Intendant of the said islands within a week at the latest or face a discretionary fine, these [officials] will give the necessary orders to have them instructed and baptized within an appropriate time.

III.

We forbid any public exercise of any religion other than the Catholic, Apostolic, and Roman; we wish that the offenders be punished as rebels and disobedient to our orders. We prohibit all congregations for this end, which we declare "conventicules," illicit and seditious, subject to the same penalty which will be levied even against masters who allow or tolerate them among their slaves.

IV.

No overseers will be given charge of *negres* who do not profess the Catholic, Apostolic, and Roman religion, on pain of confiscation of the said *negres* from the masters who had given this charge to them and of discretionary punishment of the overseers who accepted the said charge.

V.

We forbid our subjects of the so-called reformed religion to disturb or prevent our other subjects, even their slaves, from the free exercise of the Catholic, Apostolic, and Roman religion, on pain of exemplary punishment.

VI.

We charge all our subjects, whatever their status and condition, to observe Sundays and holidays that are kept by our subjects of the Catholic, Apostolic, and Roman religion. We forbid them to work or to make their slaves work on these days from the hour of midnight until the other midnight, either in agriculture, the manufacture of sugar or all other works, on pain of fine and discretionary punishment of the masters and confiscation of the sugar, and of the said slaves who will be caught by our officers in their work.

VII.

Equally we forbid the holding of *negre* markets and all other markets the said days on similar pains, including confiscation of the merchandise that will be found then at the market and discretionary fine against the merchants.

VIII.

We declare our subjects who are not of the Catholic, Apostolic, and Roman religion incapable in the future of contracting a valid marriage. We declare bastards the children born of such unions which we desire to be held and considered, we hold and we consider to be truly concubinage.

Source: "Code Noir" (1685). Retrieved May 6, 2002, from http://www.vancouver.wsu.edu/fac/peabody/codenoir.htm

the Code not only provided rules for the administration of slavery but also sought to unify the colonies by establishing the Catholic Church and prohibiting all competing religious forms.

The initial Code was largely composed by the royal minister Jean-Baptiste Colbert at the request of both civil authorities and Jesuit missionaries in the Caribbean. The latter resented the presence of Jewish and Huguenot (French Protestant) slave owners, but Colbert had been reluctant to do anything that might constrain their economic contributions to the colonies. Eighteen days after Colbert's death in 1683, however, Louis acceded to Jesuit demands and banished Jews from the Caribbean colonies. Two years later, when the Code appeared, its very first article reiterated this decree and extended to the colonies Louis XIII's 1615 edict expelling all Jews from French soil. Although Huguenots were not forced into exile by the Code, the third article explicitly proscribed the public practice of any religion other than Catholicism, and the fourth article ordered the confiscation of all slaves held by non-Catholics. These provisions had the effect of increasing Huguenot emigration to nearby British colonies.

Although the Code did not specifically forbid the practice of traditional African religions, it did so implicitly by its attention to the religious lives of the slaves. Most provisions simply restated sporadic policies that had been developing since the 1660s, but the Code attempted to systematize what might be termed a Catholic ethic of slavery. Slave owners were enjoined to catechize their slaves and to have them baptized, and baptized slaves were permitted burial in consecrated ground. No labor was allowed on Sundays and other feast days of the church. Owners were to allow Catholic marriages for their slaves and could not force them into marriages against their will. Minimal standards of care were mandated, and families (including children under fourteen) could not be sold into separation. The Code was also specified the conditions for manumission and accorded freed slaves "the same rights, privileges and immunities" of freeborn citizens. Such seemingly enlightened provisions were militated against, however, by the Code's harsh punitive regulations and by lack of enforcement. The Code was officially abrogated in 1848 with the abolition of slavery in France.

Although some provisions of the Code were adopted locally in Canada, the Code itself was never promulgated there due to a relative lack of slavery. In 1724, however, a revised Code was issued for Louisiana by Louis XV. Adopted and adapted by the subsequent Spanish colonial government, some vestiges of the Code continued to influence racial policies there even after the Louisiana Purchase of 1803.

Rodger Payne

See also French Colonies in North America

Further Reading

Allain, M. (1980). Slave policies in French Louisiana. *Louisiana History, 21*, 127–38.

Breathett, G. (1988). Catholicism and the Code Noir in Haiti. *Journal of Negro History, 73*, 1–11.

Ingersoll, T. N. (1995). Slave codes and judicial practice in New Orleans, 1718–1807. *Law and History Review, 13*, 23–62.

Palmer, V. V. (1995). The origins and authors of the *Code Noir. Louisiana Law Review, 56*, 363–90.

Sala-Molins, L. (1987). *Le Code Noir, ou le calvarie de Canaan.* Paris: Presses Universitaires de France.

Confederate Constitution and Religion

Evangelical religious ideology, along with much clerical support, helped spur the secession of seven slaveholding states from the United States between December 1860 and February 1861. This religious underpinning of the Confederate States of America appeared in the constitution they adopted 11 March 1861. Many of the words of the Constitution of the Confederate States of America were lifted verbatim from the Constitution of the United States, but two important exceptions reveal how the religious views of the framers of the Confederate Constitution differed from those of the framers of the United States Constitution.

First, Confederate leaders preferred to make direct reference to the biblical God in their constitution. The preamble of the Confederate Constitution calls upon "the favor and guidance of Almighty God," which reflects a widely held belief among Southern leaders that the writers of the United States Constitution had tended toward Deism, which had resulted in ungodly ideas, practices, and attitudes in the northern states from which Confederates

THE BIBLICAL BASIS FOR SLAVERY

Among slaveholders in the American South, as well as elsewhere, one source of support for slavery was God's will as set forth in the Bible. The passages below from the King James Version (KJV) are ones frequently invoked in support of slavery, but they have also been interpreted by opponents of slavery as calling for the rejection of slavery. In the KJV, the word *servant* has been used in place of *slave*.

Colossians 3:22–24

Servants, obey in all things your masters according to the flesh; not with eyeservice, as menpleasers; but in singleness of heart, fearing God:

And whatsoever ye do, do it heartily, as to the Lord, and not unto men;

Knowing that of the Lord ye shall receive the reward of the inheritance: for ye serve the Lord Christ.

Colossians 4:1

Masters, give unto your servants that which is just and equal; knowing that ye also have a Master in heaven.

Ephesians 6:5–8

Servants, be obedient to them that are your masters according to the flesh, with fear and trembling, in singleness of your heart, as unto Christ;

Not with eyeservice, as menpleasers; but as the servants of Christ, doing the will of God from the heart;

With good will doing service, as to the Lord, and not to men:

Knowing that whatsoever good thing any man doeth, the same shall he receive of the Lord, whether he be bond or free.

And, ye masters, do the same things unto them, forbearing threatening: knowing that your Master also is in heaven; neither is there respect of persons with him.

wished to be removed. Foremost among these was abolitionism.

Second, the Confederate Constitution contained the words *slave* or *slavery* ten times, a conscious rejection of the ambivalence about the rectitude of slavery and the future of its practice that the framers had expressed by referring to slaves as "other persons" in the Constitution of the United States. A half century of religious wrangling over religion and slavery among white southerners resulted in a common understanding that slavery enjoyed biblical support.

Confederate framers incorporated the substance of the first twelve amendments to the United States Constitution into the text of the Confederate Constitution. Foremost among these was the limiting language of the First Amendment preventing Congress from effecting "an establishment of reli-

gion, or prohibiting the free exercise thereof," which became part of Article I, Section 8, clause 12 of the Confederate Constitution.

This use of the First Amendment's establishment and free exercise clauses revealed the hegemony of hyper-Protestant religious values in a region whose political values scorned the exercise of central governing authority. Southern religious denominations and churches agreed on the central tenets of religion regarding slavery and gender roles; hence, there was no need to prescribe religious beliefs.

The Confederate Constitution also strongly endorsed the idea of state rights. Thus major constitutional debates regarding slavery and morality occurred in the southern state legislatures, where discussion of recognizing slave marriages and repealing the laws banning slave literacy continued throughout the Civil War in hopes of winning divine favor

A Prayer
for the Southern Cause.

O LORD, Our Heavenly Father, high and mighty King of kings and Lord of Lords—who dost from Thy throne behold all the dwellers on earth, and reignest with power supreme and uncontrolled over all kingdoms, empires, and governments—look down in mercy, we beseech Thee, on these "Confederate States," who have fled to Thee from the rod of the oppressor, and thrown themselves on Thy gracious protection, desiring to be henceforth dependent only on Thee. To Thee they have appealed for the righteousness of "their cause." To Thee do they now look up for that countenance and support which Thou alone canst give. Take them, therefore, Heavenly Father, under Thy nurturing care ; give them wisdom in council and valor in the field ; defeat the malicious designs of our cruel adversaries ; convince the North of the "unrighteousness of their cause;" and, if they still persist in their sanguinary purposes, oh! let the voice of Thine own unerring justice, sounding in their hearts, constrain them to drop their weapons of war from their unnerved hands, in the day of battle.

Be Thou present, O God of wisdom, and direct the councils of that honorable assembly ; enable them to settle things on the best and surest foundation,—that the scene of blood may be speedily closed.—that order, harmony, and peace may be effectually restored,—and truth and justice, religion and piety, prevail and flourish among Thy people.

Preserve the health of their bodies and the vigor of their minds ; shower down upon them and the millions they represent such temporal blessings as Thou seest expedient for them in this world ; and crown them with everlasting glory in the world to come.

All this we ask in the name and through the merits of Jesus Christ, Thy Son and our Savior. Amen.

Prayer for the Confederacy. COURTESY OF LIBRARY OF CONGRESS, AMERICAN SONG SHEETS, SERIES 1, VOLUME 7.

by bringing the practice of slavery more in line with the white southern understanding of biblical requirements.

The Confederate Constitution also banned the international slave trade, in part to enhance the possibility of the nascent Confederacy's winning diplomatic recognition. But southern denominations and church leaders had condemned the international slave trade as a godless barbarism, so the pragmatic motives of the framers ran consistent with the beliefs of most southerners.

The Confederate Constitution reflected not only the political beliefs and aspirations of southern leaders, but also the moral and religious sentiments of large segments of the population.

Edward R. Crowther

Further Reading

Faust, D. G. (1988). *The creation of Confederate nationalism.* Baton Rouge: Louisiana State University Press.

Rable, G. C. (1994). *The Confederate Republic: A revolution against politics.* Chapel Hill: University of North Carolina Press.

Silver, J. W. (1964). *Confederate morale and church propaganda.* Gloucester, MA: Peter Smith.

Snay, M. N. (1993). *Gospel of disunion: Religion and separatism in the antebellum South.* Cambridge, UK: Cambridge University Press.

Thomas, E. M. (1979). *The confederate nation: 1861–1865.* New York: Harper & Row.

Confucianism

The English term *Confucianism* encompasses a complex set of religious, philosophical, educational, political, and social teachings and practices that form the bases of the cultural traditions of the Chinese, Koreans, Vietnamese, and Japanese. Although primarily identified with China where it began, the Confucian Way has spread throughout East Asia and now is found wherever the peoples of the East Asian Diaspora live. There has been a great debate in Euro-American and East Asian intellectual circles as to whether or not Confucianism can be called a religion. Some scholars hold that Confucianism is better understood as a philosophy of life, whereas others maintain that there is a strong religious element to the Confucian tradition. A brief review of the history

of the Confucian tradition will be useful before addressing the particular qualities of its religious dimensions.

History

The term *Confucianism* makes semantic sense because members of the Confucian Way have always recognized the pivotal role of Kongzi (Latinized as Confucius; 551–479 BCE) or Master Kong in the founding of the tradition. Kongzi has been given pride of place as the first great teacher of the tradition even though he himself rejected the notion that he was teaching something new. Rather, Kongzi believed that he was a historian and teacher reviving the essential teachings of the great sage kings of the previous ruling dynasties of China. The most revered titles of Master Kong are "First Teacher" and "Teacher of the Ten Thousand Generations."

The followers of Master Kong were renowned for their skill as masters of the rituals and historical traditions of the sage kings. One of the common Chinese terms for these Confucian ritual masters was *ju*, which now simply means scholars who have mastered the profound learning of the Confucian tradition. The term was expanded later to *julin* or "forest of Confucians." Throughout the centuries, Confucian scholars honored the teachings of Kongzi and the classical masters of the tradition by preserving the teachings of the Confucian Way and by applying these teachings creatively to new historical circumstances.

Traditional Confucians hold, without much current scholarly support, that Master Kong was either the author or the editor of the essential teachings of the tradition. Beginning with an essential core of five classical texts, Confucians have defined membership in the Confucian Way by commitment to the study and living interpretation of these works. Over the centuries the list was expanded until it reached a final count of thirteen classics in the Song dynasty (960–1279 CE). The expansion did not mean that new texts were written between the life of Master Kong and the Song dynasty; rather, already existing ancient texts were simply added to the canon until the list was completed at thirteen. The Song canonical texts include great divination and wisdom books such as the *Yijing* (*Classic of Changes*); the works attributed to the great early masters such as Confucius and Mengzi (Mencius; c. 371–c. 289 BCE); books of history, poetry, ritual, and even an early dic-

MULTIPLE RELIGIOUS BELIEFS IN EAST ASIA

The following ethnographic descriptions of religion in the South Korean village of Sam Jong Dong in 1952 show how many people in rural communities in East Asia draw on the beliefs of Buddhism, Confucianism, folk religions, and other religions in managing their daily lives.

Hence a villager often is a Buddhist, yet, orients much of his life according to Confucian ethics. Even a zealous Christian who is urged to sever all relationships with other religious organizations and philosophies may not thrust aside all Buddhist and Confucian belief and ritual. One encounters, in other words, a unique religious synthesis by Koreans of religious and ethical values. Most Koreans are committed to ancestor worship and the sense of propriety as formalized in Confucianism. They usually accept the Buddhist definition of the hereafter as well as the potency of the Buddhist deities. Simultaneously they retain a less sophisticated but a deeply rooted belief in spirits, and associate them with animate and inanimate phenomena.

One informant said that no member of his family was Buddhist. Yet he soon volunteered the information that his wife attended services at the local Buddhist temple at least once a month except for February, August, and December.

It is a widely held belief among the villagers that every religion has the same fundamental good, namely the salvation of the human being. Except among the Christians, there is no thought that a superior deity would be offended if one worshipped another god, for many Koreans find it difficult to understand the competition and even hostility. . . .

A Korean who has not demonstrated in his life any particular interest in Buddhism or Christianity may upon his death bed ask for the aid of Buddha or Christ. The family of such an individual often will arrange for a Buddhist ceremony to assist his entry into paradise. Buddhism remains to most villagers a rejection of the present world, and individual search for eternal salvation.

February and December are considered "bad months" and linked with possible misfortune. August, and often June, are thought of as being reserved for older people to participate in religious or social activities. A fortune teller had advised the same informant that his infant son be registered at the local Buddhist temple with suitable donations of rice and money. This was done.

Eugene I. Knez

Source: *Sam Jong Dong: A South Korean Village.*
(Ann Arbor, University Microfilms, 1960), 118–119.

---

tionary. To study and to seek to embody the vision of these texts and their commentaries defined the Confucian tradition in East Asia through the long centuries.

The Confucian Way has gone through many developments over the last 2,550 years. Moreover, it has spread from its home in China to Korea, Japan, and Vietnam, becoming a vast complex of international philosophic and religious traditions. Along with its geographical expansion across East Asia, the Confucian Way has undergone a series of cultural transformations over the centuries.

These transformations—as they relate to the subject of religious freedom—can be divided into four main historic periods: (1) the classical period of the founding masters (551–221 BCE), which encompassed the lives of Master Kong and classical followers such as Mencius (Mengzi), Xunzi (c. 310–211 BCE), and the Han (206 BCE–220 CE) scholars, editors, and commentators on the classical canon; (2) the middle era from the Wei-Jin period (220–420 CE) to the end of the Tang dynasty and the founding of the Song dynasty (960), which introduced dialogue with revived Daoist movements and with Buddhism; (3) the Song-Yuan-Ming revival and the Qing debates (960–1839), which represented the second great epoch of Confucian thought; and (4) the modern encounter with the West (1839–present), which has faced massive challenges to the whole of the traditional East Asian social, philosophic, and religious world order.

The classical period is hallowed as the founding era of the Confucian Way. The long middle era, enduring for seven and a half centuries, is important because of the rise of organized Daoist sects and the arrival of Buddhism in China and the rest of East Asia. This is often known as the Buddhist era of Chinese religious history. Although Confucianism and Daoism continued as vital traditions, they functioned in constant interaction with the diverse and active Buddhist schools of thought and practice.

The even longer period from the founding of the Song dynasty (960) to the fall of the Qing dynasty in 1911 is the second great epoch of Confucian thought. For almost a millennium Confucianism reasserted itself as the foundation of family life and continued and expanded its dominance of civil society. The famed examination system that was used to recruit officials for the dynastic governments from the Song through the Qing dynasties was based entirely on the teachings of the Confucian Way. The modern period is marked by the first Opium War (1839) and the ongoing confrontation of Confucian East Asia with the imperial outreach of the Euro-American empires.

Religious Dimensions

Scholars of East Asian religious history agree in general that Confucianism, while not an organized religion in the sense of the Jewish, Christian, and Islamic traditions of West Asia, does have a strong religious dimension. If the history of Confucianism is to be understood correctly the religious dimension of the Confucian tradition must be acknowledged and analyzed. The modern Confucian scholar Mou Zongsan (1909–1995) argued that Confucianism has a vertical and horizontal dimension to its teachings. The vertical aspect, of conforming oneself to the mandate of heaven, is the religious dimension of the Confucian Way. The vertical or transcendent goal of the Confucian teaching is how to become a sage, a perfected human being, to live in harmony with the Dao

of the mandate of heaven. The Song dynasty scholars often defined this element as the search "to get the Way [Dao] for oneself in service to others." The sage is the person who perfectly understands and embodies the highest of Confucian virtues, *jen* (humaneness).

Along with the vertical dimension, Mou went on to argue that all the great philosophic and religious traditions of the world also have a horizontal dimension. The horizontal path is that of ethical conduct. Confucianism has always stressed the cultivation of ethical virtues as the basis of human flourishing. Moreover, Confucians have always recognized that human beings are essentially social creatures and that there is an intimate connection between the perfections of the search for the transforming Dao and the practice of ethical life in the secular world. Theories of social organization, including the role of practitioners of religions and their freedoms, are always linked to the question of moral cultivation.

Confucians always held that the role of good government was the promotion of human flourishing. The basis for such judgments was the recognition of the dignity of all persons. One of the most famous axioms of Confucian thought was that all human beings have the potential for becoming sages. Some radical Confucians in the late Ming period (1560s–1640s) even taught that you could find sages in the streets if you took true Confucian teachings to the common people. Moreover, the Confucians believed that it was cultivated talent that makes a person worthy, not the accidents of birth. The doctrines of the essential humanity of all persons include women. Of course, Confucians understood that this was an ideal hope for the future, or perhaps a pious memory about the rule of the sage kings of the ancient past. Nonetheless, Confucians taught that every woman and man was endowed by *tian* (heaven) with a human nature that could manifest the seeds of ethical perfection. The task of the Confucian Way was to help cultivate this moral human nature in service to humane social institutions. The ability to cultivate different religious teachings was part of the human search for moral perfection.

Confucianism and Religious Freedom

Although current notions of religious freedom have their origins in Western debates about human rights, Confucians have also thought a great deal about the notion and praxis of religious freedom. From a Confucian viewpoint, the question can be divided into three parts. These are the questions of the freedom of belief or conscience, the freedom of ritual, and the freedom of social organization. For the most part, Confucians have allowed for people to believe what they will. Confucians were never as concerned about belief or dogma as they were with the public actions of religious communities—in this they differ greatly from many forms of Christian theology. Of course, this does not mean that Confucians would approve of every set of religious beliefs. Confucians clearly believed that some belief systems were better than others. Confucians were also rather tolerant about the rituals or personal practices of other religions as long as these practices preserved social harmony and good order. It was in the area of social organization and the public expression of belief that Confucians were willing to circumscribe the practices based on religious convictions. For instance, Confucians from the classical period on outlawed human sacrifice as simply beyond the pale of proper human conduct. They also wanted to make sure that religious movements did not intrude into the affairs of government beyond promoting charity and ethics.

Confucians, because of their long association with Daoists and Buddhists, were often both tolerant and respectful of the religious convictions and practices of other religious communities. Once the Chinese state was convinced that a new religion was not going to harm individuals or the social order of the country, it was often willing to grant edicts of official toleration. For instance, such an edict was promulgated in the Tang dynasty (618–907 CE) and again in 1692 during the Qing dynasty (1644–1912) allowing for the full practice of the Christian tradition in China. Moreover, many Confucians believed that they could also practice other religions while maintaining their status as Confucian scholars. In the Ming period (1368–1644) there was even a movement proclaiming the unity of the three great religions of China, namely that Confucianism, Daoism and Buddhism were one in their essential ethical teachings.

One of the essential features of the Confucian tradition was its focus on the role of rituals in personal and public life. In terms of the practice of ritual, women and men shared full participation although the roles were differentiated between the sexes. Traditional Confucianism was always a patriarchal

system and the public role of women, especially in community ceremonies, declined from the twelfth century. However, Confucians always maintained that women were fully human persons and just as capable as men of achieving the comprehensiveness of moral self-cultivation. Moreover, especially from the Ming dynasty on, many Confucian families provided their daughters with fine classical educations. The reason for this was the consistent Confucian commitment to education. The family was the first school for all children and it made eminent sense to educate the girls and boys in the basics of the Confucian Way.

Confucians from the very beginning of the tradition served the state as devoted civil servants. Confucians passionately believed that one of the main duties of the state was to keep a careful eye on the activities of China's diverse religious world. At some point in its long history China has been the home of all the major religions of the world. While it is true that Confucians, Daoists, and Buddhists represent the largest religious movements, there have been Jews, Hindus, Christians, and Muslims residing in China as well. Today there is still a large Muslim community made up of both Han Chinese and minority nationalities as well as a flourishing and growing Christian community plus revived Buddhist and Daoist traditions.

The Chinese government's approach to religious freedom has always been informed by a strong historical memory. Any educated Chinese person remembers that there were a number of great religious rebellions at the end of the Han dynasty (206 BCE–220 CE) that contributed to the decline and fall of the first great Chinese empire. Because of this experience, the Chinese state has always maintained vigilance about the rise of sectarian religious movements. And although relatively rare, the Chinese state has mounted great persecutions of religions over the centuries. The most famous of these was in the ninth century CE against the Buddhist community. However, it is interesting to note that it was Daoist advisors rather than Confucian ministers who urged the emperor to persecute the Buddhists.

The preferred approach of the Chinese state was to encourage religious movements to play a positive role within the larger community. Often the Chinese state would even seek to play the role of patron of the various recognized religions of China. The Confucian bureaucracy always kept a careful eye on religious groups and parceled out both rewards and punishments when deemed necessary to preserve social order and harmonious community relations. For example, Confucians approved of Buddhist attempts to provide relief to people during times of famine or flood.

Confucians often had very positive views of other religions such as Daoism, Buddhism, Christianity, Judaism, and Islam and the modern Chinese government recognizes all of them, including Confucianism. The People's Republic of China has recently also become more tolerant of various forms of folk or popular religion, though it is always more wary of these popular religions than of the five great world religions it formally recognizes.

The Confucian view of the relative merits of the other religions is complex. One common position is that Confucianism is the true teaching of the sages, and hence demands education, intelligence, and commitment on the part of anyone who wants to be considered part of the Confucian Way. In short, Confucians believe that they are part of a scholarly elite that not everyone is lucky enough to join. Other religions provide various levels of self-cultivation and provide services and solace to the wider public unable to join in the Confucian Way. However, some Confucians have taken a much more positive view of the other religions. As long as the Confucian scholars do not see any basic conflict between Confucian ethics and the fundamental ethics of the other traditions, then many Confucians have engaged in a positive dialogue with believers in other religions over the centuries.

Confucians as philosophers have always argued that the Confucian Way is predicated on the search for the true teachings and practices of the ancient sages, aided by reading the approved commentaries of later Confucian scholars. If a tradition like Buddhism, Daoism, or even Christianity can help in this arduous process, then it is perfectly acceptable from the Confucian perspective for someone to take an active part in another religion. There was always a demand for freedom of study and debate within the Confucian Way. There was a general consensus on the outlines of the Confucian way as defined by the classical canonical texts, but there was concurrently a rigorous debate about how to interpret the texts for thousands of years. When powerful emperors tried to tamper with the canonical texts, the Confucian community demanded that the texts remain as they were, even when such declarations ended in death for the protesting Confucian minister. Even an emperor could not force a Confucian to give up the freedom of conscience.

Modern Confucians have reaffirmed the classical insights of their tradition concerning religious freedom as part of their engagement with contemporary discussions of human rights regimes. Confucians have linked their reflections on religious freedom as one of the essential human rights with a ringing affirmation of the need for democratic institutions. Moreover, they take a great deal of pride in the fact that, for the most part, Confucian-influenced cultures have been remarkable tolerant of the diversity of human religious traditions throughout the East Asian region.

John Berthrong

See also China, Imperial

Further Reading

Bauer, J. R., & Bell, D. A. (Eds.). (1999). *The East Asian challenge for human rights.* Cambridge, UK: Cambridge University Press.

Berthrong, J. H. (1998). *Transformations of the Confucian way.* Boulder, CO: Westview Press.

Berthrong, J. H., & Berthrong, E. N. (2000). *Confucianism: A short introduction.* Oxford, UK: Oneworld Publications.

Cass, V. (1999). *Dangerous women: Warriors, grannies, and geishas of the Ming.* Blue Ridge Summit, PA: Rowman & Littlefield Publishers.

Cua, A. S. (1998). *Moral vision and tradition: Essays in Chinese ethics.* Washington, DC: Catholic University of America Press.

Davis, M. C. (Ed.). (1995). *Human rights and Chinese values.* Hong Kong, China: Oxford University Press.

de Bary, W. T. (1983). *The liberal tradition in China.* New York: Columbia University Press.

de Bary, W. T. (1998). *Asian values and human rights: A Confucian communitarian perspective.* Cambridge, MA: Harvard University Press.

de Bary, W. T., Bloom, I., & Lufrano, R. (Eds.). (1999–2000). *Sources of Chinese tradition.* 2 vols. 2d ed. New York: Columbia University Press.

de Bary, W. T., & Tu, W. (Eds.). (1997). *Confucianism and human rights.* New York: Columbia University Press.

Fewsmith, J. (2001). *China since Tiananmen: The politics of transition.* Cambridge, UK: Cambridge University Press.

Hall, D. L., & Ames, R. T. (1999). *Democracy of the dead: Dewey, Confucius, and the hope for democracy in China.* Chicago, IL: Open Court.

Hansen, V. (2000). *The open empire: A history of China to 1600*. New York: W. W. Norton.

Ko, D. (1994). *Teachers of the inner chambers: Women and culture in seventeenth-century China*. Stanford, CA.: Stanford University Press.

Rozman, G. (Ed.). (1991). *The East Asian region: Confucian heritage and its modern adaptation*. Princeton, NJ: Princeton University Press.

Tu, W. (1989). *Centrality and commonality: An essay on Confucian religiousness*. Albany: State University of New York Press.

Tu, W. (1993). *Way, learning, and politics: Essays on the Confucian intellectual*. Albany: State University of New York Press.

Yang, C. K. (1967). *Religion in Chinese society*. Berkeley: University of California Press.

Yao, X. (2000). *An introduction to Confucianism*. Cambridge, UK: Cambridge University Press.

Conscientious Objection and Pacifism

Although the terms *conscientious objection* and *pacifism* are frequently used interchangeably, they are overlapping but not synonymous concepts. A conscientious objector is a person who objects to his or her own participation in war because of religious, ethical, or moral beliefs. A pacifist is a person who opposes any form of violence.

Conscientious objectors can be hunters, police officers, or even—as one of the more famous conscientious objectors, Muhammad Ali, was—professional boxers. A conscientious objector may object only to his or her own participation in war rather than to war itself. But conscientious objectors cannot object to participation in war merely because they do not want to die. The objection must be based on a more sweeping concept: For most, the objection is that they believe that God does not want them to participate in any worldly thing such as temporal governments. The United States' legal definition of conscientious objection has an additional element: The objection must be to all wars. Selective objection (objection to particular wars) is not a recognized status in any country at this time.

Conscientious objection is as ancient as the book of Psalms and the beginnings of Buddhism. But the first Christians were also conscientious objectors. Many Roman soldiers, once converted to Christianity, refused to fight and found their way to sainthood through martyrdom.

The Beginnings of Conscientious Objection in the United States

Many of the first Europeans who came to the New World did so to escape forced military service. These were mainly members of what are viewed today as the historical peace churches: the Society of Friends (Quakers), Mennonites, and Church of the Brethren. Even as they settled in the colonies, they exasperated their neighbors by following the principle of non-resistance even in the face of Indian attacks. Because of this, many of the first objectors were whipped and required to pay stiff fines for refusing to join militias. But by the 1700s they were generally tolerated, and most colonies had laws exempting "men of tender conscience" from military service.

But the American Revolution swept that tolerance away, and many conscientious objectors were viewed as traitors. Those who would not fight were required to pay an annual fee for this privilege. If they would not or could not pay this fee, their lands and property were seized, and in a few cases they were dragged to militia units and had muskets tied to their bodies.

The framers of the U.S. Constitution talked about including protection for conscientious objectors in the Bill of Rights. The Second Amendment as originally proposed included language recognizing the rights of conscientious objectors. This language was struck in exchange for a promise that the Congress's first action would be to create a statutory right of conscientious objection. But that law was never passed.

Henry David Thoreau (1817–1862) was one of the most influential thinkers who argued for conscientious objection on ethical reasons. A New England writer and naturalist, he maintained in his essay "Civil Disobedience" (1849) that it is an individual's duty to society to resist immoral laws.

The U.S. Civil War

The next time the issue really arose in the United States was during the Civil War. Once again conscientious objectors were viewed as traitors and cowards (especially considering that many of them had been staunch abolitionists), and fines and even jail awaited them for refusing to fight.

The Civil War brought the first national draft in the history of the country. When the Enrollment Act was passed in 1863, mass protests occurred including draft riots in New York City. The law made no provision for conscientious objectors, but the draftee did have the option of paying a fine for a substitute. Most peace groups objected to paying fines. Resistance was so strong that in 1864 Congress said that members of peace churches could serve in hospitals or work for freed slaves instead of fighting. But many objected to alternative service that was under military control. There were an estimated 1,500 conscientious objectors during the Civil War.

The Civil War also saw brutal treatment of conscientious objectors. Many were tied spread-eagled to the ground for hours and kept in the guardhouse without food for days. One Quaker was sentenced to death by a firing squad. As the guns were pointed at him he echoed the words of Jesus: "Father, forgive them, for they know not what they do." The soldiers refused to shoot him and the officer later revoked the death sentence.

The World Wars

Just before World War I, pacifism was a philosophy supported by much of the U.S. public. Jeanette Rankin, the first woman elected to Congress, nearly ruined her political career by voting against America's declaration of war. While many groups remained faithful to their opposition to war, many others felt that at that point war was unavoidable. The Selective Service Act provided a narrowly defined exemption for conscientious objectors from established peace churches, who were allowed instead to perform noncombatant service in the military. Members of peace churches had a chance to be recognized as conscientious objectors, but that was not an option for mainstream Protestant churches or for Catholics. The Hutterites, a pacifist denomination who lived communally, were persecuted terribly for their stance, which was to refuse even noncombatant service in the military.

Many individuals and groups resisted draft registration and the subsequent draft, including the Industrial Workers of the World (IWW or Wobblies). Those who did register and were drafted found themselves in military camps under military direction. Although some objectors were granted farm furloughs or were assigned to relief service in France, more than five hundred objectors spent time in military prisons. Their ill treatment included repeated intense beatings, being hung from the ceiling by their thumbs, and confinement without food or water. There were 86 jail terms of more than 24 years, 142 life sentences, and 17 sentences of execution. Even more objectors died from the harsh treatment they suffered in jail.

In the late 1930s war was again on the horizon and conscientious objectors sought a different course. Efforts of Quakers, Mennonites, Brethren, and Methodists resulted in a new system. In August 1940, Congress voted in the first peacetime draft in the history of the United States, but with it they provided an exemption for men who "by reason of religious training or belief" objected to participation in war. But the exemption allowed only for alternative service: Instead of serving in the military for two years for pay and benefits, they were to serve a selected government or civilian employer for room and board. On 2 October 1940, the very groups that had lobbied for this difference gathered to form the National Service Board for Religious Objectors to oversee the alternative service.

But after the Japanese preemptive attack on Pearl Harbor in 1941, objectors who met the requirements of the act were viewed with hostility—even though 75,000 men filed for objector status. Jeanette Rankin was driven from office for her historic vote against World War II. Those who were recognized as objectors were sent to Civilian Public Service (CPS) camps, which were frequently remnants of the Depression-era Civilian Conservation Corp (CCC) camps, at the demand of President Franklin Roosevelt, who wanted the "cowards" out of sight so they would not infect others.

Selective objectors and absolutists (those who refused to cooperate in the slightest manner with conscription) were almost always denied objector status and faced jail if they refused to fight. Many others with automatic draft exemptions, such as ministers, refused even to register and willingly faced jail. Altogether there were 15,758 convictions for draft law violations throughout the war period.

Many absolutists objected on principle to the Civilian Public Service camps, which although primarily run by the historic peace churches, were under government authority. While the work was technically noncombatant, many perceived it as part of the war effort.

Life in CPS camps was rigid and in some ways oppressive, involving long hours of grueling physical labor. Over 11,950 conscientious objectors fought fires, planted trees, built dams and roads, dug ditches, and filled other needs. If the government had paid the workers wages that were equivalent to those it paid its soldiers, it would have paid out over $18 million. But the law stipulated that only room and board, not wages, were to be given, regardless of whether the objector had dependents—a policy Selective Service admitted was designed to discourage people from becoming conscientious objectors.

There were many in the camps who resisted by doing little or nothing or by doing their work poorly. Others felt the best way to witness to their beliefs was by serving cheerfully and well. Both groups had enough time on their hands to talk and argue and learn. From this constant discussion among young men with the passion of conviction came both unrest and reform. Work stoppages arose both as resistance and to press for reforms in the system.

One of the first reforms conscientious objectors sought was more meaningful service. After much pressure, different opportunities were opened, including working as orderlies in mental hospitals. At that time, most mental hospitals were not much more than warehouses of neglect and maltreatment. The conscientious objectors began by swearing that they would not mistreat or harm any patient, no matter how violent. They ended by exposing in state after state horrible abuse. Eventually conscientious objectors' testimony before congress led to reform. The National Mental Health Foundation was also established by objectors.

Another opening was as volunteers for medical experiments. These experiments on human subjects would never be allowed today, but during the war young men agreed to be starved, dosed with DDT, and given hepatitis. Although much valuable information came from these experiments (including the "Quaker gruel" that was first used for Holocaust victims and continues in use in famine relief), the cost was high. The health of some volunteers was compromised for the rest of their lives, and some volunteers died.

Absolutists in prison also pressed for societal reform: They went on strike to demand that black and white objectors, as well as other prisoners, be permitted to eat together. They went on strike for better jail conditions and fair treatment. One prison warden was reported to say to an objector on a hunger strike that he looked forward to the war ending and the objectors being released so that he could once again have a prison full of murderers and rapists—prisoners he could at least understand.

During World War II some conscientious objectors served as noncombatant members of the military. Although something of a similar nature occurred during the Civil War in the placement of objectors in military hospitals, noncombatant members of the military in World War II worked side by side with other soldiers—just without a weapon. Many of these objectors were on the front lines, and many received Purple Hearts for being wounded in the line of duty. One even received a Congressional Medal of Honor for brave service. Objectors were also among the many who first opened the doors of Auschwitz and Dachau. Through agencies such as the American Friends Service Committee (AFSC), objectors helped bring relief to war-torn Europe even as it was gradually being freed by the armed forces.

Postwar Reforms

All the talk and arguing and working in difficult places and times built a camaraderie among conscientious objectors that led many of them to greater things. Reforms in mental institutions and prisons continued. One conscientious objector, Bayard Rustin, went on to work with Martin Luther King Jr., and is credited with introducing the young King to nonviolent tactics. Another, David Dellinger, went on to be a leader in the movement against the Vietnam War and is best remembered as one of the Chicago Seven who were prosecuted for disrupting the 1970 Democratic Convention.

The peacetime draft that had been established on the eve of World War II remained in place even after the war's end. Nevertheless, from 1948 to 1952, objectors were exempted completely from service. In 1952, in response to the increased need for troops in the Korean War, conscription law again required objectors to either perform alternative service or noncombatant duty. General Hershey, who had been influential in the establishment of the CPS camps during World War II, went on record saying that he would never make the mistake of having objectors all work together again. Selective Service and draft boards began to make individual alternative service assignments. They did, however, now offer minimal pay.

Meanwhile, pressure to expand the definition of conscientious objector to include nonreligious objectors was increasing. Congress expanded the definition ever so slightly, such that those with a belief in a "Supreme Being" could, if they desired, qualify as conscientious objectors.

The Vietnam War

The Vietnam War drew a conscientious "no" not only from religious pacifists and political liberals, but from mainstream U.S. youth, minorities, and disadvantaged groups—and even from some within the military. Many went beyond acquiring CO status and alternative service: Some did not register; others burned their draft cards. Still others fled to Canada or became (until it was no longer allowed) perpetual students, as university students were exempt from the service. Antiwar leaders included longtime pacifists such as Jeanette Rankin and members of the peace churches. Other leaders included Benjamin Spock, who was the author of a well-known book on baby and child development; the brothers Phil and Daniel Berrigan, who were Catholic priests; and civil-rights leaders Julian Bond and Martin Luther King Jr., who was assassinated on the eve of a planned march in Washington against the Vietnam War.

At the beginning of the Vietnam War, a young man named Dan Seeger applied for conscientious objector status but refused to claim belief in a Supreme Being. The Supreme Court eventually decided in 1965 that requiring a belief in a Supreme Being was too close to establishment of religion by the state. A second case challenged the requirement that a conscientious objector be religious. Again the Supreme Court agreed, and the word *religious* was struck. A conscientious stand against warfare no longer was tied to religion.

The Vietnam War also saw an increase in selective objectors—those who, while not objecting to fighting in wars in principle, objected to fighting in the Vietnam War. Since selective objectors had no legal status, they either had to become draft dodgers, fleeing to Canada or elsewhere to avoid the draft, or they had to lie to receive status as conscientious objectors. Many chose instead to go to prison for their beliefs.

By 1972 more registrants were claiming conscientious-objector status than were being inducted in the military. The draft ended in 1973. At the same time conscientious objection began to expand its boundaries to include those who argued that war was wrong because of the environmental destruction it caused and those who objected because of the likelihood that war would lead to nuclear holocaust.

Military tax resistance became the most common outlet for witnessing one's conscientious objection.

By May 1991, during the Persian Gulf War (1990–1991) as many as two thousand military personnel had applied for discharge as conscientious objectors. Many chose jail sentences and punitive discharges rather than participate in the war, when faced with obstacles to their rightful discharge. Since then, more than a hundred service members sought a conscientious-objection (fully honorable) discharge each year until September 2001. Since then, the number of service members seeking conscientious-objection status has actually increased, especially in the light of threatened war with Iraq.

Many conscientious objectors are also pacifists or become pacifists after time. A pacifist rejects, to the best of his or her ability, all violence. They reject any killing, whether it be the death penalty, war, or self-defense. Some reject abortion on the same basis. Beyond refusing to kill, they also refuse to fight. Although the popular image of a pacifist is of a person who simply takes whatever abuse may be heaped upon him or her, the reality is different and often extremely confrontational, as any student of the civil-rights movement's nonviolent tactics is aware. Pacifists often are vegetarians (refusing to eat animals) and even vegans (refusing to eat animal products—for example, milk or honey). Some might say that the ultimate extension of peaceful coexistence encompasses not only all people, but all animal species as well.

J. E. McNeill

Further Reading

Ackerman, P., & Duvall, J. (2000). *A force more powerful: A center of nonviolent conflict*. New York: St. Martins Press.

Bell, J., & Angell, N. (1972). *Reminiscence of war resisters in World War I*. New York: Garland.

Early, F. H. (1997). *A world without war: How U.S. feminists and pacifists resisted World War I*. Syracuse, NY: Syracuse University Press.

Eller, C. (1991). *Conscientious objectors and the Second World War: Moral and religious arguments in support of pacifism*. New York: Praeger.

Gioglio, G. (1993). *Days of decision: An oral history of COs in the military during the Vietnam War*. Trenton, NJ: Broke Rifle Press.

Hallock, D. (1998). *Hell, healing and resistance: Veterans speak*. Farmington, PA: The Plow Publishing House.

Moskos, C. C., & Chambers, J. W., II, (Eds.). (1993). *The new conscientious objection: The secularization of objection to military service.* New York: Oxford University Press.

Sareyan, A. (1994). *The turning point: How men of conscience brought about major change in the care of America's mentally ill.* Washington, DC: The American Psychiatric Press.

Zuses, R. (Ed.). (2001). *Words of conscience: Religious statements on conscientious objection.* Washington, DC: Center on Conscience & War.

Constitution, Founding Era of the

The first sixteen words of the First Amendment to the U.S. Constitution provide that "Congress shall make no law respecting an establishment of religion, or prohibiting the free exercise thereof." The first ten words are commonly called the establishment clause, the last six the free exercise clause; together they are frequently referred to as the religion clauses. The religion clauses express two purposes: to prohibit the establishment of religion, and to guarantee the free exercise of religion. In the words of one authority, the clauses express "a tradition of freedom *of* religious exercise and a tradition of freedom *from* religious exercise."

The precise meaning of the religion clauses is elusive. Surviving records of the founding period, especially of the debates of the framers in formal session and of the states' ratification proceedings, inadequately treat the subject. The uncertainty regarding the framers' intent can be seen in a brief review of the proceedings that produced the Constitution's provisions on religion.

The Constitutional Convention

The religion clauses grew out of the concern of the states that the Constitution of 1787 paid little attention to the subject of religion. In contrast to the Declaration of Independence, the Constitution contained no references to God. Its only reference to religion was the prohibition against religious tests for federal officeholders, contained in Article VI, clause 3: "No religious test shall ever be required as a qualification to any office or public trust under the United States." Only Roger Sherman of Connecticut disapproved of the provision, not because he disagreed with its purpose and effect, but because he thought including the provision in the Constitution was "unnecessary, the prevailing liberality being a sufficient security against such tests."

Church–State scholar James E. Wood Jr. has noted that this provision "precluded the possibility of any church–state union or the establishment of a state church." This is an important recognition. In the absence of the provision, Congress might have had the power to compel subscription to a particular church, to Protestantism, to Christianity, or to any other religion, in order to hold office. Instead, the provision rendered one's religion irrelevant to one's capacity to serve the country officially.

No further discussions on the subject of religion occurred at the Constitutional Convention. The framers believed that the national government should have very little to do with religion, and that religious matters were best left to the states. Congress was thus powerless, even in the absence of the First Amendment, to enact laws aiding religion.

Convention delegates rejected a proposal from George Mason of Virginia to include a bill of rights in the Constitution. The almost uniform belief of the delegates was that any bill of rights would be superfluous. The new federal government possessed only limited powers delegated to it by the states; no power had been granted it to legislate on any subjects that might be included in a bill of rights. It would be the states, though, fearful of a national government that would arrogate power unto itself, which would insist upon specific protections for individual freedoms, including religious liberty.

Ratification Controversy

From late 1787 until 1789, the proposed Constitution was considered by the various state ratifying conventions. A strong anti-federalist element developed quickly; it opposed ratification, fearing that the new document's centralizing tendencies would crush the rights of states and individuals. For many of the states, the only solution to this problem was to mandate the inclusion of a bill of rights in the Constitution. Indeed, six of the thirteen states—Massachusetts, New Hampshire, North Carolina, New York, Rhode Island, and Virginia—accompanied their instruments of ratification with a list of recommended amendments that would secure various personal liberties, such as "rights of conscience," "liberty of the press," and "trial by jury."

Thomas Jefferson (1743–1826), third President of the United States, pictured in an engraving (c. 1901) from a painting by Rembrandt Peale. COURTESY OF LIBRARY OF CONGRESS, PRINTS AND PHOTOGRAPHS DIVISION.

It is clear from the amendments proposed that no state favored the establishment of religion by Congress. But what was the meaning of an "establishment" that was to be beyond the federal exercise of power? Did it mean that only a national church, sect, or denomination was not to be established? Or did it mean more—the prohibition of support for any church, sect, or denomination, or even for religion in general? The evidence does not permit conclusive generalization as to what was meant by "an establishment of religion." It is apparent that the states wanted to reserve jurisdiction over religion for themselves (indeed, many maintained establishments of religion) and felt that the federal government was not to meddle in religious matters. Whether or not Congress was to be prohibited from offering any type of nondiscriminatory financial support to churches, however, or even to promote religion in general, is not entirely clear from an examination of the debates of the state ratifying conventions.

The First Congress and the Emergence of the Religion Clauses

James Madison had been among those who argued that a bill of rights was unnecessary, insisting that the national government had no power to infringe upon individual rights. He soon came to appreciate the honest fears of the delegates to the state conventions, however, who insisted upon a clear prohibition of federal infringement on the rights of conscience as well as other individual liberties. Largely on the basis of his assurances to secure before the First Congress the kinds of amendments that the states wanted, a majority of the states ratified the Constitution.

After the Constitution was ratified, Madison offered a number of proposed amendments to the First Congress to allay the apprehension of many of the states. On 8 June 1789, at the opening of the First Congress, Representative Madison proposed, among others, the following amendment: "The civil rights of none shall be abridged on account of religious belief, nor shall any national religion be established, nor shall the full and equal rights of conscience in any manner or in any respect be infringed."

Anti-separationists claim that the word "national" proves Madison intended nothing more than a prohibition against the preference of one religion over another. Yet a number of facts suggest that Madison might have opposed more than just the establishment of a national church. Madison had led a 1785 fight in the Virginia legislature against a bill calling for a general tax assessment for the support of not one, but of all Christian denominations. In his renowned "Memorial and Remonstrance," Madison repeatedly referred to the assessment bill as an "establishment of religion." After retiring from the presidency, Madison in 1817 expressed his disapproval of tax-supported chaplains for Congress and the armed services, and of presidential proclamations of days of thanksgiving.

Significantly, he described these as "establishments" and "the establishment of national religion." All of this makes it difficult to know conclusively what Madison meant when he submitted his proposed amendment prohibiting the "establishment" of a "national religion." He may have been signifying not that the federal government had no business preferring one church or religion over others, but that national action on behalf of any or all churches or religions was outside the purview of permissible government action.

Madison's proposed amendment was referred to a specially formed select committee. The committee changed the wording of the proposal several times, but eventually settled on the following: "No religion shall be established by law, nor shall the equal rights of conscience be infringed." Debate on the Select Committee's proposed amendment opened on 15 August 1789. Peter Sylvester, a lawyer from New York, feared that the clause "might be thought to have a tendency to abolish religion altogether." Perhaps Sylvester was concerned that the proposed amendment would prohibit nondiscriminatory governmental aid to any forms of religion. Sylvester might also have thought that the proposed amendment would be construed by Americans as a congressional outlawing of religion altogether; if that was the essence of his thinking, he was not concerned with the issue of governmental aid to religion, but with the much larger issue of the very survival of religion.

The House, acting as a committee of the whole, passed a revised amendment proposal: "Congress shall make no laws touching religion, or infringing the rights of conscience." Five days later, on 20 August 1789, Fisher Ames of Massachusetts moved that the amendment read: "Congress shall make no law establishing religion, or to prevent the free exercise thereof, or to infringe the rights of conscience." Without debate, this proposal was adopted by the necessary two-thirds of the House. The amendment as submitted to the Senate, however, reflected a stylistic change that gave it the following reading: "Congress shall make no law establishing religion, or prohibiting the free exercise thereof, nor shall the rights of conscience be infringed."

The Ames amendment must have provoked controversy in the Senate, since several alternative versions were suggested in its place. The first new Senate version read: "Congress shall make no law establishing one religious sect or society in preference to others, nor shall the rights of conscience be infringed." After further debate, the Senate rejected two alternative wordings. First, it rejected language providing: "Congress shall not make any law, infringing the rights of conscience, or establishing any Religious Sect or Society." Second, it rejected language providing: "Congress shall make no law establishing any particular denomination of religion in preference to another, or prohibiting free exercise thereof, nor shall the rights of conscience be infringed."

Considerable disagreement exists among church–state scholars as to what these Senate drafts mean. For example, Douglas Laycock argues that all three drafts favored the "no preference" viewpoint, meaning that Congress could provide support to religion, provided it was nondiscriminatory. Yet all of these drafts were rejected, seemingly because the Senate wanted a wording favoring a broad interpretation of the establishment clause, one apparently in which little or no government aid would be provided to religion. Laycock (1985–1986, 880) comments: "At the very least, these three drafts show that if the First Congress intended to forbid only preferential establishments, its failure to do so explicitly was not for want of acceptable wording. The Senate had before it three very clear and felicitous ways of making the point." Gerard Bradley, however, holding to a narrower interpretation, suggests that the rejected versions all were aimed at prohibiting a national church, indicating, despite the fact that all three versions were rejected, the dominant idea among the Senators—no national church.

On 3 September 1789, the Senate adopted a draft that treated religion more generically: "Congress shall make no law establishing religion, or prohibiting the free exercise thereof." Six days later, the Senate again changed its mind and adopted, as its final form of the amendment: "Congress shall make no law establishing articles of faith or a mode of worship, or prohibiting the free exercise of religion." Like the three defeated motions, however, this has the unmistakable meaning of prohibiting acts that prefer one church or sect over others—clearly a narrow intent.

The Senate version of the amendment was then sent to the House, which rejected it. Perhaps this action indicates that the House was not satisfied with merely a ban on the preference of one church or sect over another; they had, it seems, a broader intent.

A House–Senate joint conference committee was then created to resolve the disagreement over the religion amendment. A compromise amendment was eventually agreed upon on 25 September 1789 and passed by both branches: "Congress shall make no law respecting an establishment of religion, or prohibiting the free exercise thereof." The religion clauses, comprising merely sixteen words, had been approved.

The First Amendment, with eleven other amendments, was submitted to the thirteen state legislatures for ratification. By June 1790, the necessary nine states had approved all ten amendments comprising the Constitution's Bill of Rights.

The Search for Meaning

The foregoing sketch of the historic development that eventually produced the religion clauses of the First Amendment indicates a lack of clarity in the framers' intentions. Many questions loom: What is an "establishment"? What is a law "respecting" an establishment of religion? What is meant by "religion" or the "free exercise thereof"? Moreover, extrapolation from the meaning of such terms is frustrated by the paucity of records of the debates in Congress and the state ratifying conventions. One writer has said that the "men who wrote the Constitution wrote under great duress and heightened pressure; they developed the document in a politically charged environment and were subject to compromise and negotiation." Indeed, the clauses reflect the disagreements of the framers, but the final compromise seems to favor a broader interpretation advocating little government support of religion; the more narrow interpretation favoring non-preferentialism was closely considered, but rejected.

The Movement for Religious Liberty

Because the framers' intentions are fraught with ambiguity, since the "original intent" is not monolithic, it is preferable to think of the founding era as a period of transition within a larger movement toward religious liberty that began in the 1630s and climaxed in the 1830s. This movement had three primary components: the disestablishment movement, the movement to end religious tests for holding public office, and the movement to decriminalize religious behavior.

Disestablishment

The disestablishment movement began in the 1630s when Roger Williams challenged the Congregational establishment in Massachusetts and began a new colony (Rhode Island) based on nonestablishment and religious freedom for all. Most colonies, however, followed the traditional practice of "establishing" one or more churches, that is, giving them monetary and other benefits that other churches did not receive. But Pennsylvania and Delaware joined Rhode Island in refusing to establish churches. The disestablishment movement languished until the Independence movement in the 1770s.

By the time the Constitutional Convention was convened in 1787, seven of the original thirteen states had altogether abandoned governmental support of religion. In all of those states, government support of any church or churches was considered contrary to the basic principles of religious liberty. The delegates understood at that time, to be sure, that a diversity of tightly guarded establishments still existed in the colonies, and that the legal status of those establishments lay outside of their authority. The remaining six of the original thirteen states—Massachusetts, Connecticut, New Hampshire, South Carolina, Georgia, and Maryland—were eventually convinced likewise on this point, but it was not until 1833 that Massachusetts, the final holdout, disestablished the Congregational Church.

Religious Tests

The movement for religious liberty in the founding era was also characterized by the gradual disappearance of religious tests for holding public office. Following Old World practices, all of the thirteen original colonies required an attestation of religious belief or affiliation as a prerequisite for holding public office. These oaths were viewed as instruments of social control, given the traditional view that citizens were only trustworthy as civil servants if they were willing to affirm their allegiance to basic religious tenets. All of the colonial oaths went beyond requiring only a belief in God, often mandating a belief in the Trinity, the Scriptures, or in some cases, a commitment to Protestantism.

In the eight years following Independence, eleven of the thirteen original states adopted new constitutions. As indicated, many states ended their religious establishments, but most continued to require religious oaths for civil officeholders. Only Connecticut and Rhode Island failed to adopt new constitutions, but the constitutions of both states required officeholders to be Protestants.

Of the new state constitutions adopted prior to the Philadelphia Convention of 1787, only the Virginia and New York constitutions declined to require religious oaths of civil servants. Nevertheless, the "no religious test" clause of the federal Constitution became a model that many of the states chose to adopt. Before the turn of the century, the states of Georgia (1789), South Carolina (1790), Delaware (1792), Vermont (1783), and Tennessee (1796) either prohibited or removed their constitutions' religious tests. Moreover, as a newly admitted state, Kentucky, in its 1792 constitution, opted not to require a religious test of civil officeholders. Although many other states retained their religious tests well into the nineteenth and even the twentieth centuries, most of them have since repealed them.

Decriminalization of Religious Behavior

From colonial times, it was typical for legislatures to enact statutes that criminalized certain types of religious behavior. For example, in early Massachusetts the crime of blasphemy might be punished by imprisonment, whipping, or having a hole bored through one's tongue. In Maryland, even into the eighteenth century, Catholics could not participate in mass or proselytize. There was even a statute in Maryland that required Catholic parents to forfeit certain property to a child who was willing to convert from Catholicism. In Virginia, taking God's name in vain was punishable by death. Gradually, especially after the Constitution was adopted, such statutes were seen as unconducive to religious liberty and began to disappear.

Implications

Examination of the 200-year movement for religious liberty in America (1630s to 1830s), reveals that the movement was still under development in the years where the original intent (1774–1791) is typically sought. The framing of the Constitution and First Amendment provide the basic outline of what the framers intended with regard to the desired relationship between religion and government in America. However, discerning the latent *effects* and *outcomes* of an inchoate "original intent" requires looking beyond the founding era. It is there that, regarding disestablishment, elimination of religious test bans, and the decriminalization of religion, a maturer notion of religious liberty and more fully developed manifestations of the framers' "original intent" are found.

Derek Davis

See also Establishment, Separation of Church and State; Free Exercise Clause, Religious Test Oaths

Further Reading

Ball, H. (1987). The convergence of constitutional law and politics in the Reagan administration: The exhumation of the "jurisprudence of original intention" doctrine. *Cumberland Law Review, 17* (Summer), 877–90.

Bradley, G. V. (1987). *Church–state relationships in America*. Westport, CT: Greenwood Press.

Dreisbach, D. L. (1996). The Constitution's forgotten religion clause: Reflections on the article vi religious test ban. *Journal of Church and State, 38* (Spring), 261–95.

Fleet, E. (Ed.). (1946). Madison's detached memoranda. *William and Mary Quarterly, 3*, 554–59.

Gales, J. (Ed.). (1834). *Annals of the Congress of the United States*. Washington, DC: Gales and Seaton.

Kurland, P., & Lerner, R. (1987). *The founders' Constitution*. Chicago: University of Chicago Press.

Laycock, D. (1985–1986). Nonpreferential aid to religion: A false claim about original intent. *William and Mary Law Review, 27* (Special Issue, 1985–1986), 875–923.

DePauw, L. G. (Ed.). (1971). *Documentary History of the First Federal Congress of the United States of America* (Vols. 1–3). Baltimore: Johns Hopkins Press.

Madison, J. (1966). *Notes of debates in the Federal Convention of 1787* (A. Koch, Ed.). Athens: Ohio University Press.

Rutland, R. A. (Ed.). (1976). *The papers of James Madison*. Charlottesville: University of Virginia Press.

Stokes, A. P. (1950). *Church and state in the United States*. New York: Harper and Brothers.

Van Patten, J. (1983). In the end is the beginning: An inquiry into the meaning of the religion clauses. *St. Louis University Law Journal, 27* (February), 1–95.

Wilson, J. F. (1990). Religion under the state constitutions, 1776–1800. *Journal of Church and State, 32* (Autumn), 764–73.

Wood, J. E., Jr. (1987). No religious test shall ever be required: Reflections on the bicentennial of the U.S. Constitution. *Journal of Church and State, 29* (Spring), 199–208.

Zollman, C. (1991). Religious liberty in the American law. *Michigan Law Review, 17*, 355–373.

Convivencia

The coexistence of the three faiths of Judaism, Christianity, and Islam in the Iberian Peninsula, or *convivencia*, existed from approximately the eighth to the fifteenth centuries CE. This system of religious toleration produced a rich, dynamic culture unique in world history.

Background

Philologist and literary historian Américo Castro first used the term *convivencia* in the book, *España y su historia* (1948), where he argued that the coexistence of these three "castes" was the central feature defining the history of Spain and the "makeup" of the modern Spaniard. Aspects of Castro's work have been refuted, but he did provide a conceptual framework for approaching the history of this pluralistic society.

Convivencia must be understood within the context of a newly conquered territory. The Muslim armies swept over approximately two-thirds of the Iberian Peninsula in 711 CE, subdued native populations, and brought them under military and political domination. The theoretical and juridical underpinnings for the phenomenon we call *convivencia* had emerged upon the death of Muhammad, when Muslim armies had begun making extensive conquests to the east and west of the Islamic heartland, and developed a system for handling newly conquered peoples. Using Qur'anic law and the principles of the *hadith*, Muslim rulers identified Jews and Christians as protected peoples (*dhimmi*), subject to the laws of the *dhimma* or covenant. These "Peoples of the Book" had received a revealed scripture Muslims recognized as divinely inspired, so they could not be killed with impunity, as could pagans or polytheists, but must be tolerated.

Legal measures were prescribed for dealing with the *dhimmi*, including the so-called Pact of Umar (seventh century) and the documents of taxation for unbelievers. These imposed obligations on non-Muslims, such as: not to build any new, or repair any old, monasteries or churches; not to teach the Qur'an to their children; not to manifest their religion publicly nor convert anyone to it; not to display crosses or [Christian or Jewish] books in the roads or markets of Muslims; to show respect toward Muslims, rising from their seats when Muslims wished to sit; to give board and lodging for three days to all Muslims who passed their way; to wear identifying marks, such as the yellow girdle called a *zunnar*, yellow patches or marks on headgear and cloaks, and specified saddlery. The pacts specified that the *dhimmi* were subject solely to the authority of Islam, and anyone who spoke improperly of Muhammad would forfeit the protection of the covenant. All free adult males were ordered to pay the *jizya* or poll tax, in addition to a land tax, in exchange for protection. Non-Muslim merchants were also required to pay the Muslims one-tenth of their merchandise, if they traveled on business. These measures were maintained largely to protect the dominant Muslim faith from corruption, and the strictest limitations were those associated with religious or philosophical concerns. Non-Muslims were second-class citizens who, if they kept their places, were tolerated by the Muslim government. Muslims did not want Christians to draw positive attention to Christianity, which could produce converts (for which there is evidence), and so ringing church bells was also prohibited. In market places, however, interaction between the three religious groups was both frequent and somewhat freer.

Convivencia and Acculturation

In the Iberian Peninsula, despite the strictures of *dhimma*, there was considerable formal and informal acculturation. Tolerant and learned Muslim rulers, notably Abd-al-Rahman III (ruled 912–961) brought religious scholars, scientists, poets, and artists of all three faiths from the far reaches of the empire to enrich the activities of his courts. The tenth and early eleventh centuries, in fact, are considered the Golden Age of the Jews in Spain because of the intense educational and cultural interaction in which these *dhimmi* participated. The career of Hasdai ibn Shaprut, personal physician to the caliph, patron of the Jewish community in Córdoba, and benefactor of great Jewish Talmudic academies as far away as Mesopotamia, exemplified the international character of this cosmopolitan, learned world. Jewish, Christian, and Muslim translators preserved Greek and Roman classics and disseminated modern learning from east to west. Formal acculturation continued under Christian rulers whose realms were extending farther down the peninsula as a result of the *Reconquista* (the reconquest of formerly Christian territory from the Muslims), after the eleventh century. Most notable among these was Alfonso X (r. 1252–1284), whose school of translators produced

works on a wide range of topics, from theology to falconry. In this latter phase of *convivencia*, when the covenant was not so much religious as political (with Christians being dominant), long-term aspects of informal acculturation also became evident. Language, food, dress, and music are just some examples of considerable informal acculturation during this period.

Decline of *Convivencia*

The peaceful coexistence of the three cultures was remarkably successful for several centuries. The system worked best when there was a strong central power, such as the Caliphate of Córdoba (ending 1031). There were several phases of intolerance within this period, as demonstrated by the massacres of Christians in Córdoba in the ninth century, or the persecution of both Christians and Jews by the Almoravids and Almohads (fanatical Muslim groups) in the eleventh and twelfth centuries. But permanent decline in *convivencia* followed the Christian crusades to the Holy Land, which had both long-term and far-reaching effects in Iberia. Once the Iberian Peninsula became the western front of the crusade against Islam, peaceful coexistence became increasingly difficult. Owing partly to foreign clerical influence in al-Andalus, and partly to the determination of Christian kings to combine political and religious ideologies to unify and expand their territories, the unique experiment we call *convivencia* came to a bitter end. The expulsion of both Muslims and Jews from Christian Spain beginning in the late fifteenth century was the final chapter of this religious and social phenomenon.

Rowena Hernández Múzquiz

Further Reading

Burns, R. I. (Ed.). (1990). *Emperor of culture: Alfonso X the learned of Castile and his thirteenth-century renaissance.* Philadelphia: University of Pennsylvania Press.

Chejne, A. G. (1974). *Muslim Spain: Its history and culture.* Minneapolis: University of Minnesota Press.

Colbert, E. P. (1962). *The martyrs of Córdoba.* Washington, DC: Catholic University Press.

Collins, R. (1995). *Early medieval Spain: Unity in diversity, 400–1000* (2nd ed.). New York: St. Martin's Press.

Constable, O. R. (Ed.). (1997). *Medieval Iberia: Readings from Christian, Muslim, and Jewish sources.* Philadelphia: University of Pennsylvania Press.

Glick, T. F. (1979). *Islamic and Christian Spain in the early middle ages*. Princeton, NJ: Princeton University.

Harvey, L. P. (1990). *Islamic Spain: 1250–1500*. Chicago: University of Chicago Press.

Hillgarth, J. N. (1976). *The Spanish kingdoms: 1250–1516*. Oxford, UK: Clarendon.

Lewis, B. (Ed.). (1974). *Islam from the prophet Muhammad to the capture of Constantinople*. Oxford, UK: Oxford University Press.

Mann, V. B., Glick, T. F., and Dodds, J. D. (Eds.). (1992). *Convivencia: Jews, Muslims, and Christians in medieval Spain*. New York: George Braziller.

Mendocal, M. R. (2002). *The ornament of the world: How Muslims, Jews, and Christians created a culture of tolerance in medieval Spain*. Boston: Little, Brown & Company.

Nirenberg, D. (1996). *Communities of violence: Persecution of minorities in the middle ages*. Princeton, NJ: Princeton University.

O'Callaghan, J. F. (1975). *A history of medieval Spain*. Ithaca, NY: Cornell University Press.

Wasserstein, D. J. (1985). *The rise and fall of the party-kings: Politics and society in Islamic Spain, 1002–1086*. Princeton, NJ: Princeton University Press.

Wolf, K. B. (1988). *Christian martyrs in Muslim Spain*. Cambridge, UK: Cambridge University Press.

Coptic Christians

The Coptic Church is the Christian Church in Egypt. The word *Copt* is an English word taken from the Arabic word *Gibt* or *Gypt*. After their conquest of Egypt in 641 CE, the Arabs called the indigenous population of Egypt "Gypts." The word *Copt* or *Coptic* simply means Egyptian. However, since the Muslim population of Egypt calls themselves Arabs, the word refers to Egyptian Christians.

History

Throughout the Coptic Church's history it has been the church of a minority group in Egypt and has been persecuted periodically. St. Mark the Evangelist reportedly founded the first Coptic Church in the first century and became the first bishop of Alexandria. However, according to tradition, even before the ministry of Jesus, many Egyptians accepted him as the Savior. This is attributed to the stories in the Gospel of Matthew that put the holy family in Egypt during their flight from King Herod, who died in 4 BCE. There are many legends about miracles attributed to the Christ child in the Nile delta and the valley of the Nile.

Until the Council of Chalcedon in 451 CE, the Coptic Church was a part of the Roman Catholic Church. During the council, the Copts opposed the majority of the council on the nature of Christ, saying that he was both human and divine in union. After this, the Coptic Church became an autonomous entity in Egypt. The bishop at Alexandria therefore became both the Patriarch of the See of St. Mark and the Pope of Alexandria. The current Pope of Alexandria is Pope Shenuda III, who was called after the death of Pope Cyril VI in 1971.

The Copts have always been a minority group in Egypt and have had many points of collision with the majority's social boundaries and societal laws. Like Christians in other parts of the Roman Empire, the Coptic Christians were persecuted by their Roman conquerors, which ended during the time of Constantine I in in the early fourth century CE. Certain Roman emperors felt more strongly than others that unity and peace were dependent on religious conformity. Thus, they required all in the Roman Empire to worship the emperor as god. All those refusing to conform to Roman worship were considered to be atheists and therefore treasonous. This type of persecution was sporadic; it depended on the emperor's wishes at the time. Emperors who specifically targeted Coptic Christians were Septimus Severus in 202 CE, Decius (emperor of Egypt) from 249–251 CE, and Diocletian in the Great Persecution of 303–305 CE. Constantine I ordered a halt to the Roman persecution of Christians in 313 CE and sought to bring about peace. He moved the capital from Rome to Byzantium (renamed Constantinople) and began the Byzantine reign, which ended for Egypt in 619 CE with the conquest of the Persians.

The Coptic Christians were also persecuted by their Roman Catholic counterparts at least once in history. Cyrus Al-Muqawqas, the bishop of Rome from 631–642 CE, wanted to unify the Copts with the Roman Catholic Church. Toward that end, he passed the Ecthesis Edict, forbidding Coptic Churches from referring to Christ using the term *energies*, which was in their traditional liturgy. Many Copts were seized for disobeying the edict and tortured. The patriarch's brother Mina was tortured and drowned. Cyrus enacted these edicts in order to bring the Coptic minority back into the Roman Catholic Church, but he was unsuccessful.

VICTIMS OF TORTURE BY EGYPTIAN POLICE IN THE VILLAGE OF EL-KOSHEH

The following is the first page of a list of 1,014 Coptic Christians tortured in August and September 1998 by Egyptian police. The list was obtained by Freedom House's Center for Religious Freedom and is posted on their website, www.Freedomhouse.org.

#	Victim's Name	Age	Date Arrested	Date Released	Type of Torture
1	Boktor Abul-Yamin Mikhail	55	8/16/98	9/17/98	Electric shock, suspended by wrists from the ceiling while blindfolded
2	Mikhail Boktor Abul-Yamin	29	8/18/98	9/17/98	Electric shock, suspended by wrists from the ceiling while blindfolded
3	Al-Amir Boktor Abul-Yamin	19	8/18/98	9/17/98	Electric shock, suspended by wrists from the ceiling while blindfolded
4	Elaine Aziz Saleeb	45	8/16/98	8/21/98	Electric shock, beaten with hands and whip
5	Hania Boktor Abul-Yamin	15	8/18/98	8/21/98	Electric shock, beaten with hands and whip
6	Amora Boktor Abul-Yamin	12	8/18/98	8/22/98	Electric shock, beaten with hands and whip
7	Romani Boktor Abul-Yamin	10	8/18/98	8/21/98	Electric shock, suspended by legs from ceiling fan
8	Mikhail Melik Mikhail	53	8/16/98	9/18/98	Electric shock, beaten with whip while blindfolded
9	Nasra Mikhail Melik	17	8/16/98	8/19/98	Electric shock and beaten with whip
10	Abdu Mikhail Melik	23	8/16/98	9/22/98	Electric shock, suspended by wrists from ceiling and nose broken
11	Mirziqa Mikhail Melik	14	8/16/98	8/21/98	Electric shock and beaten with whip

(cont.)

VICTIMS OF TORTURE BY EGYPTIAN POLICE IN THE VILLAGE OF EL-KOSHEH (cont.)

12	Hanan Mikhail Melik	29	8/15/98	8/15/98	Electric shock and suspended by wrists from ceiling while blindfolded
13	Rasmiya Guirguis Zaki	47	8/18/98	8/19/98	Electric shock and beaten with hands and whip
14	Ghattas Sergious Boulous	59	8/17/98	8/21/98	Electric shock, beaten, and suspended by wrists from ceiling
15	Saleeb Sergious Boulous	54	8/18/98	8/21/98	Electric shock, beaten, and suspended by wrists from ceiling
16	Deryas Sergious Boulous	52	8/15/98	8/17/98	Electric shock, beaten, and suspended by wrists from ceiling
17	Nayer Ghattas Sergious	25	8/19/98	8/21/98	Electric shock, beaten, and suspended by wrists from ceiling
18	Talasoun Ghattas Sergious	30	8/22/98	8/233/98	Electric shock and beaten with whip
19	Atiyat Ghattas Sergious	28	8/19/98	8/20/98	Beaten with hands and whip
20	Morris Shukrallah Morcus	35	8/20/98	8/23/98	Electric shock, suspended by wrists from ceiling while blindfolded
21	Gamal Morris Shukrallah	18 Months	8/19/98	8/20/98	Dashed to the floor and beaten with whip
22	Samira Ghattas Sergious	28	8/21/98	8/21/98	Beaten with hands
23	Sana'a Ghattas Sergious	19	8/21/98	8/21/98	Beaten with hands
24	Nahid Ghattas Sergious	14	8/21/98	8/21/98	Beaten with hands
25	Waniyssa Y'waqim Louka	49	8/24/98	8/24/98	Punched in the face and beaten
26	Sabri Shukrallah Morcus	25	8/19/98	8/27/98	Electric shock and hanging from ceiling while blindfolded

27	Nagi Amin Morcus	25	8/19/98	8/27/98	Electric shock and hanging from ceiling while blindfolded
28	Saad Selim Morcus	34	8/19/98	8/29/98	Electric shock and hanging from ceiling while blindfolded
29	Helmy Youhana Luka	65	8/17/98	8/19/98	Electric shock, beaten with hands and whip
30	Atyyah al-Abed Luka	72	8/19/98	8/21/98	Electric shock, beaten with hands and whip
31	Makram al-Abed Luka	67	8/17/98	8/19/98	Electric shock, beaten with hands and whip
32	Yacoub Georgeious Luka	54	8/15/98	8/16/98	Electric shock, beaten with hands and whip
33	Ni'mat Ghoubryal al-Abed	25	8/15/98	8/17/98	Beaten with hands and whip
34	Guirguis Nasseif Halim	25	8/19/98	8/21/98	Electric shock, beaten with hands and whip
35	Thabet abul-Yamin Mikhail	59	8/20/98	8/29/98	Electric shock and beaten with whip
36	Jawad Thabet abul-Yamin	18	8/20/98	8/23/98	Electric shock and beaten with whip
37	Shawqi Habib Shenouda	52	8/16/98	8/25/98	Electric shock and beaten with hands and whip
38	Mansour Shawqi Habib	26	8/19/98	8/26/98	Electric shock, beaten with whip, and suspended by wrists from ceiling
39	Safa'a Shahdy Fikri	22	8/26/98	8/27/98	Beaten with whip
40	Adel Tamer Arsan	40	8/16/98	8/21/98	Electric shock and suspended by wrists from ceiling

In 642 CE, the Muslims conquered Egypt; Islam became the majority religion and Islamic law was promulgated. Although Muslim law as a rule respects Christians as "people of the book," the Muslim majority in Egypt has periodically persecuted the Coptic Christian minority. During the rule of 'Abd Allah ibn 'Abd al-Malik from 705–730 CE, Copts were excessively taxed, tattooed, imprisoned, flogged, and sometimes murdered for their beliefs. The tattoos were a mark to distinguish the Copts as a minority group in the area; they were usually in the shape of a cross. Many later caliphs used the tattoo and required special dress or badges to identify the Copts. Required clothing was usually all-black attire with blue or black turbans. Sometimes, as during the rule of Caliph Salah al-Din in 1283 CE, Copts were forbidden to ride horses in order to demean them. Instead, they were required to ride donkeys, which were shorter and ensured that their Muslim conquerors could physically look down on them. Sometimes, as during the rule of Sultan al-Ashraf Khalil in 1293 CE, Copts were dismissed from public service jobs for a time.

Many times during these persecutions, Coptic churches were looted and sometimes destroyed. The relics and many of the sacred objects of the church were taken from the congregation in these lootings. In one round of these raids during the Mamluk Dynasty in 1320, Coptic churches were stormed and destroyed by the Muslim government. In this case, the Copts retaliated by setting many fires in Cairo. Due to the uprising, the government put the Covenant of Umar in place, reaffirming the minority status of the Copts. The Coptic Church has existed in this minority situation since that time.

Current Status

The tattoos that had historically been used to persecute Copts have become a badge of faith for modern-day adherents. The tattoo is worn usually on the inside of the right wrist. Modern Copts often think of the tattoo as a permanent reminder of vows made to God, and sometimes as a protective mark against evil. Not all Copts are tattooed, however. There has been a decline in the practice of tattooing, either due to their minority status or the mark's sometimes superstitious use.

In the modern world, the Coptic Church represents approximately 10 percent of Egypt's population. The Church has recently attempted to reconcile some of the rifts between it and other religious groups. Pope Shenuda III met with Pope Paul VI in 1973 in order to repair the distance between the churches. They signed the confession of their common Christological faith at that time. Shenuda has also met with other Orthodox churches and Protestant churches in order to open the lines of communication between the churches. There are now Coptic churches in the United States, Canada, Australia, and Europe. In addition, there is the independent Coptic Church in Ethiopia, which is a daughter church of the Egyptian Coptic Church.

The current Coptic Church in Egypt remains under Muslim rule. In 1981, a misunderstanding with President Anwar al-Sadat culminated in the exile of Pope Shenuda III to the Monastery of Saint Bishoi. Along with the pope's exile, eight bishops and twenty-four priests were imprisoned, as well as many other church members. The exile lasted until 1985, when President Hosni Mubarak revoked President Sadat's earlier decree. The pope has continued to work at improving relations with the Islamic majority in Egypt. Shenuda, however, refuses to have the Coptic Church identified as a Christian minority, insisting that they are Egyptians and part of Egypt.

Over the last three decades of the twentieth century, Egyptian Islam has slowly been overshadowed by Wahhabism—a stricter, more literal interpretation, largely practiced in Saudi Arabia. This type of Islam is less tolerant of other faiths, and there has recently been more of a strain between the Muslims and Coptic Christians in Egypt. In April 1999, a human rights report entitled *Egypt's Endangered Christians* was released by Freedom House's Center for Religious Freedom. The report detailed recent police brutality and terrorist acts against the Coptic Christians. While they are able to practice their faith, they do so in a climate of fear. Many Copts in Egypt have led protests against the felt discrimination by the government. A group of over 10,000 Coptic Christians in Sydney, Australia, led a protest in support of the Egyptian Copts in 1999.

Dawn L. Hutchinson

See also Africa; Byzantine Empire

Further Reading

Atiya, A. S. (Ed.). (1991). *The Coptic encyclopedia*. New York: Macmillan.

Center for Religious Freedom. (1999). *Egypt's endangered Christians*. Washington, DC: Freedom House.

Frend, W. H. C. (1984). *The rise of Christianity*. Philadelphia: Fortress Press.

Meinardus, O. F. A. (1999). *Two thousand years of Coptic Christianity*. Cairo, Egypt: American University in Cairo Press.

Creationism

Surveys suggest that the majority of religious Americans find the biological theory of evolution controversial and that their views on the topic vary considerably (Scott 1997). There is also considerable evidence that many Americans believe that the creation story in the Book of Genesis is the true account of how humans came into being. Some of these views are linked to religious beliefs—but not all. In no modern nation have creationists been so active and so successful as in the United States. Antievolutionist sentiments are growing elsewhere, but usually—as among Turkish Muslims—as a result of a strong religious bias. In the United States, Protestant Fundamentalists are those most likely to find the evolutionary theory to be inconsistent with religious beliefs, but not every opponent of evolution is a Fundamentalist. In the last decades of the twentieth century, Fundamentalists campaigned against the theory of evolution by promoting creationism as an alternative and by attempting to prohibit or limit the teaching of evolution in the public schools. They also actively promoted the teaching of creationism, in a variety of forms, in public schools and made it a part of the science curriculum in home schooling and private religious schools.

Evolution

Evolution has been defined by evolution advocate Eugenie Scott (1997, 225) as: "Change through time has occurred and the present is different from the past." Most people now equate evolution with biological evolution: "Living things descend with modification from ancestors through the process of natural selection" (Scott 1997, 265). The theory of evolution by natural selection was proposed by Charles Darwin (1809–1882) and Alfred Russel Wallace (1823–1913). Both sought to account for the rise and extinction of all species on the basis of variation, which, they argued, can be found within all species. The environment (nature) selects from preexisting variation and over time causes species to change and become better adapted to their respective environments. Darwin and Wallace contended that as species modify to changing environments, they eventually diverge so much from the original species that they themselves become separate, new species. Thus, "natural selection" accounts for both the origin and extinction of species and operates to make each species as well adapted to its particular environment as possible. According to Darwin and Wallace, evolutionary change has no particular direction because adaptive traits do not always arise when they are needed and most, if not all, species eventually face extinction.

Creationists reject evolution and believe, instead, that the universe and all life forms came into existence by the direct acts of a creator who is external and independent of the natural universe. The debate between creationists and evolutionists centers on five basic issues: 1) Is the universe divinely created or did it come to existence without the intervention of supernatural forces? 2) Is the earth thousands of years old or billions of years old? 3) Does life begin out of nothing or is it the result of chemical processes? 4) Can one species become another or is there only modification within the species? 5) Did humans evolve from other life forms? (Eve & Harrold 1991, 3).

With but few exceptions, Darwin's 1859 book *Origin of Species* was well received among clergy, and James R. Moore (1979, 92) concludes that by the end of the nineteenth century most leading Christian thinkers in both Great Britain and the United States had come to terms with Darwin's theory of natural selection. By the end of the nineteenth century the educational establishment in the United States had incorporated Darwin's ideas. In 1895, for example, the National Education Association advocated including the theory of evolution in high-school textbooks.

Antievolution and Creationism

Organized opposition to the theory of evolution in the United States roughly corresponds to the emergence of Fundamentalism as a religious and political movement (c.1909–1912). Evolutionary theory was only a secondary target of Fundamentalists. Their primary objective was to force out what they saw as "modernism" and "liberalism" from mainline Protestant denominations. It has been argued that Fundamentalists were opposed to evolution and evolutionary theory largely because the liberal

DEBATE

UNDER AUSPICES OF

TEMPLE JUDEA MEN'S CLUB

CLARENCE DARROW
Rabbi SOLOMON GOLDMAN

"IS RELIGION NECESSARY"

AT

ORCHESTRA HALL

MONDAY EVENING, MAY 18, 1931

AT 8:15

MAIL ORDERS NOW TO ORCHESTRA HALL

TICKETS ON SALE AT BOX OFFICE AFTER MAY 8TH

Or . . . Tickets may now be secured at office of
H. B. Ritman, President, Temple Judea Men's Club,
33 N. La Salle Street, Room 2227—Phone Randolph 6752
And . . . At Temple Judea, 1227 Independence Boulevard
Phone Crawford 0685

A poster from 1931, announcing a debate featuring Clarence Darrow, the defense attorney in the 1925 Scopes Trial.
COURTESY OF THE SPECIAL COLLECTIONS DEPARTMENT, UNIVERSITY OF IOWA LIBRARIES.

denominations seemed to support it. Whatever their reasons for opposing evolution, Fundamentalist groups lacked the necessary funding to bring the issue to a focus, and they did not gain much public attention until after World War II.

The Scopes "Monkey Trial"

The most famous battle between evolutionists and antievolutionists took place in Dayton, Tennessee. In January 1925 the Tennessee House of Representatives passed a bill making it unlawful for state-supported schools to teach any theory denying the divine Creation as taught by the Bible. Violation of this law was a misdemeanor and the punishment a fine of from $100 to $500. In May, John Thomas Scopes, a high-school science teacher in Dayton, at the instigation of the American Civil Liberties Union (ACLU), agreed to test the constitutionality of the law. The ACLU provided Scopes with legal counsel, including the eminent Chicago attorney Clarence Darrow. Three-time presidential candidate William Jennings Bryan joined the prosecution team. The trial lasted eight days, from 10 to 18 July. On the seventh day of the trial, Bryan submitted to a lengthy examination by Darrow in which Bryan affirmed his belief in Old Testament miracles (e.g., that Joshua commanded the Earth to stand still) and his acceptance of the Genesis account of Creation. The outcome of the trail was never in doubt because Scopes's defense attorneys had already admitted that Scopes had taught the forbidden theory. He was convicted after less than ten minutes of jury deliberation, and fined $100. William Jennings Bryan died just five days later. The Scopes trial was one of the most highly publicized legal battles in American history, and in many respects rivals the coverage given to the O. J. Simpson murder trial in 1995 (Numbers 1998, 77).

The Battle in the Schools

Of the various religious freedom and public education issues in the United States, the debate over the teaching of evolution and/or creationism has drawn a fair share of media attention. The battle began in the second decade of the twentieth century and continues in the twenty-first century.

Between 1922 and 1929, forty-six state legislatures considered bills that would have made it illegal to teach evolution. Only three states actually passed such bills—Tennessee, Mississippi, and Arkansas—although Oklahoma prohibited the use of textbooks that promoted evolution, and Florida condemned the teaching of evolution as "improper and subversive"; however, the teaching of evolution science was never illegal in Florida.

After the Soviet Union launched *Sputnik* in 1957, the federal and state governments invested heavily in science education in the public schools. Texts which taught evolution came into general use and were widely distributed, and evolution was taught as the "keystone" of modern biology (Numbers 1998). Those who objected to evolution and the teaching of it remained active during this period, but received less media attention than in the past.

During the 1970s, resistance to the teaching of evolution stiffened and groups like the Creation Research Society, the Institute for Creation Research, and the Creation Science Research Center tried to ban the teaching of evolution or sought to have both evolution and creationism taught as equally plausible theories. Although antievolutionists cite so-called scientific problems of evolution in their case against the teaching of evolution, Scott (1997, 263) argues that their real concern is the threat to religion, and especially to Fundamentalist Christianity, caused by the evolutionary model. Biblical literalists (whether Christians, Jews, or Muslims) fear that if their children learn evolution, they will cease to believe in God and, therefore, will not experience salvation.

During the 1980s, bills promoting equal time for the teaching of evolution and creation science were introduced in twenty-six state legislatures, but only the bills introduced in Arkansas and Louisiana became law. The Arkansas bill became the focus of much media attention. It was challenged by proponents and opponents of both creationism and evolution. Many opponents of the bill—including leaders of the Methodist Church, the Roman Catholic Church, the Episcopal Church, the African Methodist Episcopal Church, the Presbyterian Church, and Reform Jews—were not Fundamentalists. A number of Southern Baptist ministers and Rev. Bill McLean, the lead plaintiff, clearly would have placed themselves in the Fundamentalist camp. In 1982, Arkansas's equal time law was declared unconstitutional in Federal District Court, but the failure of the Arkansas bill did little to halt efforts to pass equal time legislation elsewhere. Unlike the Arkansas bill, the Louisiana law was never challenged in the state courts. It remained on the books until 1987, when the U.S. Supreme Court decided that equal time laws like

Louisiana's violated the clause establishing separation of church and state because such laws serve a religious, not a scientific, purpose (*Edwards v. Aguillard* 1987). Despite the Supreme Court ruling, the battle continues at the state level as in the past. In 1969, the California Board of Education issued guidelines for its public-school biology courses. The board recommended equal time for the Genesis account of Creation. Proposals for equal time gained renewed attention following an influential 1978 article by Wendell Bird published in the *Review*. Bird's article posed a legal justification for the teaching of creation science whenever evolution science was taught in the public schools and gave additional credence to the doctrine of equal time. In 1999, the Kansas School Board voted 6 to 4 to downplay the importance of evolution in its statewide curriculum standards. The most hotly contested local election in 2000 was the Republican primary for a seat on the Kansas State Board of Education in which conservative Linda Holloway, who had voted for the new standards, raised more than $90,000 in campaign contributions. Moderate Republican Sue Gamble, who said she wanted to reverse the new standards, raised over $36,000. By comparison, a typical candidate for a seat on the Kansas School Board spends less than $2000. Gamble—the moderate—won the election.

The battle also is increasingly focused in the school textbook industry. One state, Texas, plays the central role in deciding which textbooks will be used in classrooms across the nation. This is because Texas children and adolescents constitute about 13 percent of the U.S. school population, making Texas the primary market for textbook publishers. In addition, the textbooks are approved in Texas by a state board, which tends to be politically and socially conservative. To gain acceptance in Texas, publishers have been willing to rewrite text to downplay the role of evolution or to present evolution in a way that does not conflict with creationism. In some cases, these books are then published across the United States, in other cases different versions are prepared for different markets.

The battle also continues on the local level, as increasing numbers of U.S. parents choose to educate their children at home or in private schools that teach creationism. Creationists have developed variations of creation theory that accounts for evidence of evolution in the geological record and might also be more acceptable to the courts and to public officials. They believe these theories should be taught alongside the evolutionary theory. For example, a Dallas-based creationist organization, the Foundation for Thought and Ethics, has sponsored an antievolutionist supplemental biology textbook entitled *Of Pandas and People*. The text does not explicitly mention God or Creation, but tacitly argues for an "intelligent design" of life forms and the abrupt appearance of new species.

While creationism and antievolutionism are often linked with Fundamentalism, it should be noted that not all creationists are Fundamentalists and comparatively few Fundamentalists would call themselves creationists. Many creationist organizations—like the American Scientific Affiliation, the Creation Research Society, and the Institute for Creation Research—were founded by well-established scientists and scholars, and most of the leadership within these organizations have earned Ph.D.s in the biological sciences, physics, and/or engineering. Fundamentalists have little influence in these organizations.

Stephen D. Glazier

See also Religion and Public Education

Further Reading

Bird, W. (1978). Freedom of Religion and Science Instruction in Public Schools. *The Yale Law Journal, 87*, 513–70.

Eve, R. A., & Harrold, F. B. (1991). *The creationist movement in modern America*. Boston: Twayne Publishers.

Eve, R. A., & Harrold, F. B. (1994). Who are the creationists? *Population Review 38*, 65–76.

Gould, S. J. (1983). *Hen's teeth and horses' toes: Further reflection in natural history*. New York: W. W. Norton.

Harrold, F. B., & Eve, R. A. (Eds.). (1995). *Cult archaeology and creationism: Understanding pseudo-scientific beliefs about the past*. Iowa City: University of Iowa Press.

Hayward, J. L. (1998) *The creation/evolution controversy: An annotated bibliography*. Lanham, MD: Scarecrow Press.

Larson, E. J. (1997) *Summer for the gods: The Scopes trial and America's continuing debate over science and religion*. New York: Basic Books.

Moore, J. R. (1979) *The post-Darwinian controversies: A study of the Protestant struggle to come to terms with Darwin in Great Britain and America*. New York: Cambridge University Press.

Numbers, R. L. (1992) *The creationists: The evolution of scientific creationism*. New York: Alfred A. Knopf.

Numbers, R. L. (1998) *Darwin comes to America*. Cambridge, MA: Harvard University Press.

Scott, E. C. (1997) Anti-evolution and creationism in the United States. *Annual Review of Anthropology 26,* 263–89.

Toumey, C. (1994) *God's own scientists: Creationists in a secular world.* New Brunswick, NJ: Rutgers University Press.

Webb, G. K. (1994) *The evolution controversy in America.* Lexington: University of Kentucky Press.

Court Case

Edwards v. Aguillard, 482 U.S. 578 (1987).

CSCE Vienna Document

The Concluding Document of the Vienna Meeting (1986) of the Representatives of the Participating States of the Conference on Security and Co-operation in Europe (CSCE) is commonly known as the "Vienna Document." This document summarizes the third major follow-up meeting in the Helsinki Process launched by the signing of the Helsinki Final Act in 1975. Negotiated between 4 November 1986 and 19 January 1989 in the new atmosphere created by perestroika and glasnost in the USSR, the Vienna Document marked a major transition in the Helsinki Process, especially with regard to human rights. It signaled a shift from Cold War tensions concerning human rights to increased cooperation, and established a "human dimension mechanism" for supervision of CSCE human rights commitments (Bloed 1990, 21–24). This began the transition from the non-institutionalized Conference for Security and Co-operation in Europe (CSCE) to the present Organization for Security and Co-operation in Europe (OSCE—renamed 1994), which includes human rights monitoring institutions such as the Office for Democratic Institutions and Human Rights (ODIHR).

CSCE and OSCE commitments such as those formulated in the Vienna Document are generally adopted by consensus at OSCE Summits or Ministerial meetings. These commitments build on each other and constitute an ever-expanding corpus of human rights norms. For example, the commitments on freedom of religion and belief in the Vienna Document have been repeatedly reaffirmed and clarified (ODIHR 2001, 39–41). While OSCE commitments are not legally binding treaty obligations, they are politically binding (Bloed 1993, 22–25, ODIHR 2001,

xv–xvi) on the fifty-five participating OSCE states (the United States, Canada, and the nations of Western Europe and the former Communist bloc).

The fact that OSCE commitments are not legally binding has facilitated the adoption of norms more concrete than those typically encountered in other international human rights instruments. Principles 16 and 17 of the Vienna Document constitute a detailed set of commitments to abandon many of the specific forms of religious oppression that had characterized the Communist era. Thus, Principle 16 commits participating OSCE states to: "eliminate discrimination against individuals or communities, on grounds of religion or belief"; "foster a climate of mutual tolerance and respect"; recognize the legal entity status of law-abiding groups seeking incorporation or registration; respect the autonomy of religious communities; respect rights to obtain religious education at all levels; protect the rights of parents to raise their children in line with their convictions; and protect the rights to acquire, produce, possess, use, and disseminate publications and other items relevant to the practice and transmission of religion or belief. Principle 17 emphasizes that limitations on freedom of religion or belief are permitted only on the narrow grounds recognized by international law. The specificity of these commitments makes the Vienna Document one of the strongest statements of the meaning of the fundamental right to freedom of religion or belief at the international level.

W. Cole Durham Jr.

Further Reading

Bloed, A. (1990). *From Helsinki to Vienna: Basic documents of the Helsinki process.* Dordrecht, Netherlands: Martinus Nijhoff Publishers.

Bloed, A. (1993). *The conference on security and co-operation in Europe: Analysis and basic documents, 1972–1993.* Dordrecht, Netherlands: Kluwer Academic Publishers.

Fry, J. (1993). *The Helsinki process: Negotiating security and cooperation in Europe.* Washington, DC: National Defense University Press.

ODIHR/OSCE (2001). *OSCE human dimension commitments: A reference guide.* Warsaw, Poland: OSCE Office of Democratic Institutions and Human Rights.

Sneek, T. J. W. (1994). The CSCE in the New Europe: From process to regional arrangement. *Indiana International Law and Comparative Law Review, 5,* 1–73.

D

Daoism

There are a variety of perspectives and practices within Daoism (or, in older romanization, Taoism) concerning the meaning and attainment of religious freedom. Yet the fundamental Daoist perspective is that the quality of religious freedom one has depends on a harmonious relationship with the *Dao* ("Way" or "Path")—Daoism's Ultimate Reality.

When considering the meaning and manifestation of religious freedom in relationship to the Chinese phenomenon of Daoism, there are three preliminary points to keep in mind. First, one should consider what Daoism is. The term *Daoism*, although problematic to define, is commonly used today by scholars and practitioners of Daoism to refer to a) specific beliefs and practices associated with particular lineages (sects or schools) and b) an expansive corpus of literature (the Daoist Canon) originating from Chinese culture. Second, Daoism is a historically enduring religious tradition that contains continuities (defining features) in the midst of numerous discontinuities (variation in beliefs and practices due to historical and sociocultural changes). While the ineffable *Dao* is the main referent for Daoists' Ultimate Reality, how one individual or group of Daoists speculates about the *Dao* or cultivates the *Dao* can vary widely over time and space. The same consideration applies to ideas and manifestations of religious freedom within Daoism. Third, investigating ideas about and manifestations of religious freedom with respect to Daoism is tantamount to asking questions about the nature of humanity in relation to the entire cosmos. Asking what religious freedom means for a Daoist is to ask specifically "What does it mean for a human being to be truly free?" The answer inevitably involves an investigation into the nature of the *Dao* and humanity's relationship with the *Dao*. Western notions of religious freedom related to individual and group rights are relevant, especially with respect to the modern period from the nineteenth century to the present. Nevertheless, the goal in Daoism regarding religious freedom is to be one with the *Dao*.

Enduring Beliefs

The Chinese texts that record many of the enduring notions about the nature of the *Dao* and what harmony with the *Dao* looks like in human living include the *Daodejing* (translated as *The Way and Its Power*) and the *Zhuangzi* (*Master Zhuang*). Written between the fourth and third centuries BCE, the *Daodejing* describes the *Dao* as the ineffable, nameless origin of all things. The hidden mystery of the *Dao* is manifested through the phenomena and processes of the natural world, which include human beings and their activities. Like water, which has the ability to cut through hard surfaces over time, the *Dao* overcomes the hard by virtue of being soft, overcomes the strong by virtue of being weak. These traits imply the principle virtues of the *Dao* and the central teaching of the *Daodejing*; namely, nonaction (*wuwei*) and natural or spontaneous self-becoming (*ziran*). Human beings, both male and female, have the potential of embodying these same virtues in their daily lives. The *Daodejing* points to the archetype of the sage ruler as an example of a person who is in harmony with the *Dao*. The sage ruler governs according to the principle

DAOISM AND BUDDHISM IN CHINA

In China, a popular belief is that Daoism is the religion of life and Buddhism the religion of death. The actual situation is considerably more complicated as indicated by this description of religious life in Taipei, Taiwan, in the 1960s.

A correlation between Buddhism and death services and Taoism with services for the living appears natural. Buddhist priests are famous for their funeral services, their bone pagodas and tablet halls, and their salvation festivals for the lonely ghosts. Also as a result of the kinds of services which are offered in their temples, Buddhist temples are believed to be polluted by the influence of death. Likewise, most community temples whatever their designation are identified with Taoism both by the people and by many of the scholars whom I have quoted. These temples must be carefully guarded from any contact by the dead, because their gods epitomize the yang life-giving force in the world. This correlation only holds so long as community temples are identified with Taoism, and services for the dead are restricted to Buddhists.

However, there is no exact correlation between community temples and Taoism, for as I shall show, Buddhists also frequently participate in services in community temples. In addition not all Taoist priests are restricted from offering funeral services, so there is, in fact, no basis for the exclusive identification of Buddhists with death and Taoists with life. This does not mean that there is no division of priests into life-and-death-oriented specialists, but merely indicates that such a division is not absolutely congruent with the sectarian division between Buddhism and Taoism.

Nevertheless the assumption that such an association does exist is found in the folk belief and expressed in the popular saying that "Taoists do not offer the ('flaming mouth') service for feeding the hungry ghosts, and Buddhist monks do not offer the li-tou service." This saying is evidence that in the folk view there is identification of Buddhism and Taoism with death and life parameters of the religion.

The performance of the priests of different religions together on some occasions in the same temples came as a great surprise to the researcher, accustomed as he was to thinking of different religions as being distinctive and mutually exclusive. It also sensitized me to the inadequacy of our conceptual categories of "Buddhist" and "Taoist" in dealing with Taiwanese folk religion, where apparently these terms carry a different connotation from ours. I wondered if it was possible to formulate an explanation or model of religion which would account for the fact that both kinds of priests sometimes performed in the same temples at the same times as well as accounting for the popular association of Taoism with life ceremonies and Buddhism with death services.

Philip C. Baity

Source: *Religion in a Chinese Town,*
Asian Folklore and Social Life Monographs, 64.
(Taipei, Taiwan: Chinese Association for Folklore, 1975),
164–165, 170.

of nonaction. The sage ruler is unobtrusive in the affairs of human society. In this manner "[g]overnment," suggests the scholar Ellen Chen, "blends so well with the natural environment that its actions are indistinguishable from those of nature" (Chen 1989, 97–98). By exhibiting an acute knowledge of self in relation to the natural world, the enlightened sage ruler is free from the tendency to grasp power and rule by force. The sage ruler guides society toward spontaneous transformation. The sage ruler also exemplifies the nature of true human freedom, which is living in harmony with self, others, and the environment—all of which are characteristics of the *Dao*.

The *Zhuangzi*, an extravagantly written metaphysical text dating between the fourth and third centuries BCE echoes the *Daodejing* on the topic of true freedom. Through a literary style that mixes fantastic imagery and tales, humor, and paradoxical language, the *Zhuangzi* "jolts the mind into awareness of a truth outside the pale of ordinary logic" (Watson 1964, 5). In the *Zhuangzi* the perfected person, an archetype similar to the sage ruler of the *Daodejing*, knows the Way of Heaven (*tiandao*; synonymous with the *Dao*) and humanity's place within nature. Consequently, the perfected person is free to wander, not being limited by desires for recognition. As the sinologist Victor Mair explains, "Only the [perfected person] can attain unbounded freedom by being oblivious to achievement and fame, by not distinguishing between self and other, and by entering a realm of creative unconventionality" (Kohn 2000, 42). Moral axioms, philosophical musings, the realities of life and death, none of these preoccupy the thoughts of the perfected person in the *Zhuangzi*. As the story of Master Zhuang's response to his wife's death indicates, there is a time for mourning and a time for forgetting (moving on). Responding to a colleague's bewilderment at his seeming lack of emotion over his wife's death, Master Zhuang pointed out that his behavior mirrored the normal course of nature. His wife's movement from prebirth to life and then to death, which followed a path similar to that of the seasons, was no different than Master Zhuang's movement from sadness to acceptance. The examples of Master Zhuang and other perfected persons in the *Zhuangzi* stress that human freedom is intimately connected to one's harmonious relationship with nature (which is to say, one's knowledge of and union with the *Dao*).

The lessons of the *Daodejing* and the *Zhuangzi* have endured over the centuries in Chinese culture, inspiring both Daoists and non-Daoists (for example, Confucian literati and Buddhist masters) in their teaching and practice. Practitioners and thinkers in the Daoist tradition might all agree that human freedom (intellectual, emotional, physical, and spiritual) is synonymous with living in harmony with the *Dao*, but how that harmonious relationship is articulated and cultivated varies considerably.

Means of Cultivating the *Dao*

From the *Daodejing* and the *Zhuangzi* there are indications of which techniques to use in order to cultivate a harmonious union with the *Dao*. Among them are the yogic practices of controlled breathing, physical stretching, and deep concentration. Drawn from older traditions in China, these practices were available to both elite and common, male and female devotees. Their influence on Daoism has been visible for centuries. The techniques were designed to perpetuate a long and healthy life, a sign of one's merging with the *Dao*, by bringing one's mind and body in balance with the dynamic processes of *qi* (primordial energy). During the Han dynasty (206 BCE–220 CE) interests in achieving longevity began to coincide with the pursuit of immortality, a physical and mental state of freedom that transcended temporal and spatial boundaries. According to Daoist metaphysics, those who achieved the status of immortals embodied the characteristics of the sages and uniquely exemplified the meaning of "returning to the origin," which Daoism scholar Isabelle Robinet expresses as a "moment when movement and stillness are mingled, when everything perpetually produces everything and regenerates and reorganizes itself" (Robinet 1997, 16). As Daoist communities developed and became more institutionalized around a priesthood (*daoshi*; third to fifth century CE), they absorbed many of the diverse beliefs and techniques of the Han concerning the cultivation of longevity and immortality.

As the various ritual and alchemical texts of the Daoist canon indicate, there are numerous ways to cultivate the life of an immortal. Who will successfully travel the path to immortality and what technique is most successful in achieving immortality is highly unpredictable. Thus in the Chinese legends and fables about immortals one learns that "[p]easants, beggars, merchants, officials, and empresses have become immortals" (Kohn 2000, 109). Even a "stroke of luck" could be the only factor involved in one's transcendence (109). Nonetheless, for the majority of male and female *daoshi* in traditional and contemporary Daoism, achieving immortality, and consequently a reunification with the *Dao*, is wrought by practicing inner and outer alchemy, performing community rituals for the living and the dead, and living an exemplary moral life.

Sociopolitical Contexts

From the beginning of Daoism's institutionalization in the second century CE to the end of China's imperial age (1911), Daoist hermitages, temples, and monasteries experienced sociopolitical freedom when the patronage of the imperial family was intact. During periods in which the imperial government supported Daoism, emperors often built Daoist altars, commissioned Daoist rituals to validate their rule, financially supported Daoist clergy, published Daoist texts, and gave Daoist leaders political power over other religious groups. During the Tang dynasty (618–907), for example, Emperor Xuanzong (685–762) was so enthralled by Daoist teachings and practices that "he gave [D]aoism the status of an official teaching by establishing [D]aoist schools and official examinations on [D]aoist texts, whose study could thenceforth open the door to official appointment" (Robinet, 186). On the other hand, when Daoists lacked close ties to the central government, imperial proscriptions limited Daoist practices, controlled the number of priestly and monastic ordinations, and in some cases caused destruction of entire sets of published Daoist texts.

During the latter part of the Qing dynasty (1644–1912) and until the Communist 1949 victory in China's civil war, Daoist institutions experienced a growth in lay participation, due in part to a decrease in monastic and priestly ordinations. Deemed superstitious and morally corrupt by government officials, local elites, and intellectuals, Daoist priests lost much of the moral authority they had previously enjoyed in the community and became increasingly isolated from the public. They ventured into the public arena from their monasteries and temple compounds primarily when called upon to perform ritual services for individuals and groups. The modernization of Chinese society during this period also contributed to a large number of Daoist, as well as Buddhist, properties being confiscated by local and central governmental authorities. These kinds of social, political, and economic pressures, along with the disruptive effects of World War II, caused many Daoist leaders to migrate from major urban areas in the north (such as Beijing and Shanghai), to other parts of China in the south (such as Guangdong and the British colony of Hong Kong), and establish new centers of Daoist learning.

After 1949, the quantity and quality of freedom that Daoists have experienced has depended on their country of residence. Daoists in Hong Kong, Taiwan, and in other countries where the Chinese diaspora exists, have been relatively free to practice their rituals and manage their temples and centers of learning. Before the modernization policies of Deng Xiaoping in 1979, Daoist leaders in China were severely limited in their efforts to run their institutions and organize large community rituals, as was the case for all religious traditions officially recognized by the central government. During China's Cultural Revolution (1966–1976), religion in China experienced one of its worst setbacks. Many properties owned by religious institutions were destroyed, and religious practice was limited or simply forbidden. Since 1979, however, Daoist monasteries that were destroyed during the dark times of the 1960s and 1970s have been either partially or fully reconstructed. Likewise, Daoist community rituals and other temple activities that are not deemed superstitious by the Religious Affairs Bureau are prevalent throughout China. The study of Daoism at universities and the quality of education for new clergy and monastics has increased as well.

Implications

Contemporary Daoist believers understand the meaning and implications of religious freedom from a modern, Western political standpoint; Daoists want to practice their rituals and assemble freely in an environment that is not oppressive, just like other religious believers. To this end Daoists work with local and national governments and collaborate with representatives of other traditions. Contemporary Daoists also understand "religious freedom" from the perspective of a specific belief system that is conditioned by Chinese culture. In the context of a plurality of beliefs, practices, and techniques, Daoist adepts generally agree that true lasting freedom for self and society is dependent upon one's harmonious relationship with the *Dao*.

Geoff Foy

See also China, Communist; China, Imperial

Further Reading

Chen, E. (1989). *The Tao Te Ching: A new translation with commentary*. New York: Paragon House.

Dean, K. (1995). *Taoist ritual and popular cults of southeast China*. Princeton, NJ: Princeton University Press.

Ho, K. M., & O'Brien, J. (Eds. & Trans.). (1990). *The eight immortals of Taoism: Legends and fables of popular Taoism*. New York: Meridian.

Kirkland, R. (1997). The historical contours of Taoism in China: Thoughts on issues of classification and terminology. *Journal of Chinese Religions*, 25, 57–82.

Kohn, L. (Ed.). (2000). *Daoism handbook.* Leiden, Netherlands: Brill.

Robinet, I. (1997). *Taoism: Growth of a religion* (P. Brooks, Trans.). Stanford, CA.: Stanford University Press.

Saso, M. (1990). *Blue dragon, white tiger: Taoist rites of passage.* Washington, DC: The Taoist Center.

Shipper, K. (1993). *The Taoist body* (K. C. Duval, Trans.). Berkeley and Los Angeles: University of California Press.

Tsui, B. P. M. (1991). *Taoist tradition and change: The story of the Complete Perfection sect in Hong Kong.* Hong Kong: Christian Study Centre on Chinese Religion and Culture.

Watson, B. (Trans.). (1964). *Chuang Tzu: Basic writings.* New York: Columbia University Press.

Drugs in Religious Worship

The use of drugs in religious worship has been controversial for thousands of years. Because there are few religions that use drugs or provide information about the drugs themselves, society has been reluctant to accept drugs as appropriate for religious use. Consequently, the practice of using drugs in religious worship continues to raise the question of what kinds of practices are protected by religious freedom principle.

Psychotropic Drugs

Psychotropic drugs are substances that cause a psychological change. There are three kinds of psychotropic drugs: psychic sedatives, including narcotics, barbituates, and tranquilizers; psychic stimulants that change one's mood; and psychic deviators or hallucinogens including LSD, psilocybin, mescaline, and harmine. Hallucinogens are not physically addictive, unlike the psychic sedatives. Typically most drug-using religions use a hallucinogen to induce a "religious experience." Shamanism, an ancient practice all over the world, employs the use of a shaman or specialist in hallucinatory substances to cure patients, curse an enemy, tell the future, or manipulate the supernatural entities. Shamans use hallucinogens to communicate with the supernatural realm and unlock resources within themselves.

Aum Shinrikyo, a religious group in Japan, produces LSD, mescaline, methamphetamine, PCP, and sodium thiopental for religious experiences. Shoko Asahara, the leader of Aum Shinrikyo, is considered the guru or source of enlightenment. Followers believe that chemical experiences are derivative of the energy or spiritual power of Asahara. The hallucinogens are used to expand the consciousness of participants and increase their energy or spiritual power.

LSD

LSD is a popular hallucinogenic that when taken can cause an experience of awe, depth, bewilderment, or revelation, which is often viewed as religious. Many scholars contend that the taking of LSD does not constitute a religious practice. However, if religion is thought of as an expanding of the consciousness or discovery of the energy within, then the practice of LSD can be considered to have deep religious overtones. Much like the concept of nirvana in Hinduism or Zen in Buddhism, LSD is used to experience ecstasy and revelation through an altered state of consciousness.

Peyote

Peyote is the most familiar hallucinogen used in religious worship and was used by Native Americans as early as the sixteenth century. Unfortunately there is little knowledge about the drug and what it actually does. The earliest practices of ingesting peyote were usually forbidden by law. Many questions surround the use of peyote. For example, how closely does the drug-induced state resemble a religious one? Can a distinction be made between drug-induced experiences and religious experiences? Does peyote ingestion duplicate a religious experience and thereby generate a theology of its own?

In Native American culture peyote is used as a symbol and a sacrament. Native Americans attribute many qualities to peyote, such as healing and teaching. The sacrament of peyote ingestion parallels the Christian practice of communion. The participants ingest peyote as a symbol of God's love physically inside of them. They see the cactus buttons as divine because God endowed them with his love and compassion. The drug is used to simulate a deep religious experience that draws the individual closer to God or nature. Native Americans believe that by ingesting peyote the individual develops compassion and love for others because God's love now rests inside of them. The Native American Church is now a nationwide organization that helps protect the peyote ritual.

Peyote comes from a small cactus, the *Lophophora williamsii*, found primarily in the Rio Grande valley of Texas and in northern Mexico. It is ingested by either chewing the buttons or drinking tea or water with peyote dissolved in it. Alhough peyote is listed as a narcotic or intoxicant in U.S. law, there is no scientific proof that peyote use for ritual purposes is injurious or causes any harm to the body. It does not produce any of the effects of narcotics or intoxicants (impairment of muscle coordination, loss of self-control, sleep or hangover, or addiction). Peyote more closely resembles hallucinogens. The active ingredient, mescaline (closely related to adrenaline), can cause various hallucinations depending on the particular user. Peyote was prohibited before there was an investigation of its effects. There are diverse justifications for the prohibition of peyote. Many historians believe it was banned originally because it was being used as a medicine instead of resorting to common Western practices. Many Native Americans use peyote as a last resort, while some with serious illness use it in conjunction with Western medicine. However, many Western doctors know little or nothing about peyote and its effects on the body thereby making it a suspicious drug.

Legal Aspects of Drug Use in Religion

Native Americans have struggled against law and varying prohibitions against their sacred ritual. For hundreds of years, the Native Americans have practiced a religion involving peyote. Despite this long history, many states enacted laws preventing Native Americans from using peyote. In *George L. Whitehorn Jr. v. Oklahoma* (1977) the Oklahoma State Court found a viable state interest in controlling substances, thereby making peyote users register as church members in order to possess or use peyote. This was a problem for Native American peyote users because their churches did not keep accurate records, if any at all. Then in *Employment Division, Department of Human Resources of Oregon v. Smith* (1990), the Supreme Court upheld Oregon's denial of employee benefits to Alfred Smith and Galen Black for using

peyote in a Native American church ceremony. Numerous scholars viewed the decision as a setback to religious freedom. Many states, including Oregon, subsequently changed their laws to allow the sacramental use of peyote by Native Americans. *Smith* is the most widely recognized case involving the use of peyote for religious sacrament in which religious freedom was inhibited in favor of greater social control. In U.S. law, the 1990 Supreme Court decision illustrates the difficult balance between religious freedom and other state interests such as fighting the war on drugs. In 1994 Congress enacted *The American Indian Religious Freedom Act Amendments* (1994) allowing the sacramental use of peyote by Native Americans in their religious worship. This act permits Native Americans to engage in peyote ceremonies without penalty of law. Previously the laws about legalization of peyote varied from state to state. Now, there is one uniform law that allows Native Americans to practice peyote sacraments without restriction.

Research Directions

Despite many research attempts there are vast deficiencies in the knowledge of the effects of drug use on brain activity. The consequences and dangers of using drugs in religious worship remain a mystery and use remains vulnerable to restriction. The Native American usage of peyote has made considerable strides in gaining legal authorization. As the definition of religion expands, the meaning of the free exercise of religion may well expand also to include new practices and beliefs.

Sara Mya Patterson

Further Reading

The American Indian religious freedom act, U.S. Code, Title 42, Chapter 21. Sub. 1, sec. 1996a (1994).

Clark, W. H. (1969). *Chemical ecstasy: Psychedelic drugs and religion*. New York: Sheed and Ward.

Dobkin de Rios, M. (1984). *Hallucinogens: Cross-cultural perspectives*. Albuquerque: University of New Mexico Press.

Forte, R. (1997). *Entheogens and the future of religion*. San Francisco: Council on Spiritual Practices.

Harner, M. J. (Ed.). (1973). *Hallucinogens and Shamanism*. New York: Oxford University Press.

Huxley, A. (1990). *The doors of perception; and, heaven and hell*. New York: Harper and Row.

Kaplan, D. E., & Marshall, A. (1996). *The cult at the end of the world: The terrifying story of the Aum doomsday cult, from the subways of Tokyo to the nuclear arsenals of Russia*. New York: Crown Publishers.

Pahnke, W. N., & Richards, W. A. (1996, 1996). Implications of LSD and experimental mysticism. *Journal of Religion and Health 3*, 175–208.

Slotkin, J. S. (1975). *The peyote religion: A study in Indian-white relations*. New York: Octagon Books.

Smith, H. (2000). *Cleansing the doors of perception: The religious significance of entheogenic plants and chemicals*. New York: Penguin Putnam.

Steinmetz, P. B., S. J. (1990). *Pipe, Bible and peyote: Among the Oglala Lakota: A study in religious identity*. Knoxville: University of Tennessee Press.

Zaehner, R. C. (1972). *Zen, drugs and mysticism*. New York: Vintage Books.

Court Cases

Employment Division, Department of Human Resources of Oregon v. Smith, 494 U.S. 872 (1990).

George L. Whitehorn Jr. v. Oklahoma, Okl.Cr. 561 P.2d 539 (1977).

E

England, Early Modern

Religious freedom as it is understood in the twenty-first century did not exist at the start of the early modern period in Britain. Religious freedom is now thought of in terms of the right to believe and practice any religion, or to not profess any religious beliefs at all, in the absence of any state-supported religion established and enforced by law. By contrast, when the Wars of the Roses came to a close with the victory of Henry Tudor (reigned 1485–1509) over Richard III (reigned 1483–1485) in August 1485, the rulers of every nation in Europe still acknowledged the supreme authority of the Church of Rome in all matters touched by religion, and saw supporting and enforcing conformity to that spiritual authority as one of the primary duties of the secular state. Yet, by the end of the early modern period in the first decades of the eighteenth century demands for tolerance of nonconformist religious beliefs and for the separation of church and state had become focal issues of British (and British-American) constitutional discourse. The rights of religious freedom we enjoy today developed from foundations laid in early modern Britain.

The Reformation and Henry VIII's Break with Rome

Although earlier English monarchs had periodically asserted the right to control or influence church affairs that they saw as within their secular realm, these episodes never seriously threatened the power of the papacy to determine the content of religious belief. Whether one looks at the infamous battle of wills between Henry II (reigned 1154–1189) and Thomas Becket over the clergy's immunity from criminal prosecution in the royal courts, the various taxation squabbles in the reigns of Edward I (reigned 1272–1307), Edward II (reigned 1307–1327), and Edward III (reigned 1327–1377), or other examples, they can all be seen as instances of secular rulers defending their own civil powers and royal coffers against intrusions by the church. Popes and kings might have disagreed over the precise location of the boundaries between secular and spiritual authorities, but not over whether they were indeed two separate spheres of authority over the subjects of the realm.

Indeed, at the start of the Reformation Henry VIII (reigned 1509–1547) would be titled "Defender of the Faith" by Pope Leo X for his 1521 rebuttal of Martin Luther, the *Assertio Septem Sacramentorum*, which the king had dedicated to the pope. When Thomas More had cautioned Henry VIII that his chapter on papal authority gave too much authority to the pope, the king had responded, "We are so much bounden unto the See of Rome that we cannot do too much honor unto it" (Solt 1990, 12). A mere six years later, in 1527, Henry VIII would try to convince the pope to annul his marriage to his queen, Catherine of Aragon, so he could marry his mistress, Anne Boleyn. The eventual refusal by Pope Clement VII to annul the marriage in 1533 would lead Henry VIII to embrace just enough of the Reformation to break with Rome and establish a Protestant Church of England with the king as its official head.

CONFISCATION OF THE LESSER MONASTERIES, 1536

In this act, King Henry VIII confiscated monasteries whose congregations numbered less than twelve, citing instances of the presence of sin and irreverence. However, the lands belonging to these monasteries were also an irresistible economic opportunity for the king; in succeeding years, he managed to gain control of larger religious establishments as well, selling the land to private investors.

An act whereby all religious houses of monks, canons, and nuns which may not dispend . . . above the clear yearly value of two hundred pounds are given to the king's highness his heirs and successors for ever. Forasmuch as manifest sin, vicious carnal and abominable living, is daily used and committed amongst the little and small abbeys, priories, and other religious houses of monks, canons, and nuns, where the congregation of such religious persons is under the number of twelve persons, whereby the governors of such religious houses and their convent spoil destroy consume and utterly waste, as well their churches monasteries priories principal houses farms granges lands tenements and hereditaments, as the ornaments of their churches and their goods and chattels, to the high displeasure of almighty God, slander of good religion and to the great infamy of the king's highness and the realm if redress should not be had thereof; and albeit that many continual visitations have been heretofore had by the space of two hundred years and more, for an honest and charitable reformation of such unthrifty carnal and abominable living, yet nevertheless little or none amendment is hitherto had, but their vicious living shamelessly increaseth and augmenteth, and by a cursed custom so rooted and infested that a great multitude of the religious persons in such small houses do rather choose to rove abroad in apostasy than to conform them to the observation of good religion; so that without such small houses be utterly suppressed and the religious persons therein committed to great and honorable monasteries of religion in this realm, where they may be compelled to live religiously for reformation of their lives, there can else be no reformation in this behalf.

Stephen B. Baxter, ed.

Source: *Basic Documents of English History.*
(Boston: Houghton Mifflin Company, 1968), 67.

The assumption of the royal supremacy by Henry VIII and the establishment of the Church of England was already under way in 1533 through parliamentary statutes forbidding any appeals of ecclesiastical cases except those involving heresy to the "Bishop of Rome," forbidding the paying of any papal dues or taxes, and giving the king a role in the drafting of canon law. Although these acts of Parliament had identified "the supreme head of the Church of England" as the king, the 1534 Act of Supremacy specifically identified the king as "the only supreme head in earth of the Church of England," and broadened the spiritual authority of the crown to cases of heresy, effectively fusing the spiritual offense of heresy with the civil crime of treason.

While Henry VIII made no claim to exercise the priestly powers of ministering to the members of the church by performing marriages, celebrating Mass, or other functions that touched the personal relationship of his subjects to God, through his claim to the powers of ecclesiastical administration Henry asserted the crown's right to appoint church officials and to define the structure and doctrine of the church. Within the year, the first martyrs would be executed or imprisoned for heretical treason, and the dissolution of the monasteries would begin the final transfer of the remaining monastic wealth that once flowed to Rome to the royal treasury. The Henrician Reformation would eventually stabilize around the various Declarations of Faith issued from 1536 to 1543.

The instability of the Tudor royal succession would, however, combine with the new royal supremacy to create many more martyrs and much more religious discord before the end of the Tudor era at the close of the sixteenth century. The reigns of Henry VIII's children would see the official Protestant doctrine of the Church of England redrafted multiple times by statute, convocations of clergy, and royal injunctions under Edward VI (reigned 1547–1553) and Elizabeth I (reigned 1558–1603). In between their reigns Mary (reigned 1553–1558) would restore Catholicism. Although Mary abandoned the title of Supreme Head of the English Church, she retained most of the power that went with it, especially the right to punish heresy as treason. Mary would become known as "Bloody Mary" for her zealous persecution of Protestant heretics. Almost three hundred were burned at the stake during her short reign, three times as many as in the previous 150 years. Even though nonconforming Protestants and Catholics were persecuted and executed during the reigns of Henry VIII, "Bloody Mary" in particular would serve as a rallying cry for anti-Catholic movements for generations to come.

The Elizabethan Settlement, the Early Puritans, and "Popish Plots"

The form of Protestantism Elizabeth I established by 1563 was a doctrinal compromise that would become known as the *via media* between the pseudo-Catholicism of her father and the more extreme Protestantism of Edward V's reign. The very real threat posed by the Catholic doctrine that allowed the pope to depose heretical monarchs by giving papal authority to rebellions and invasions limited the Elizabethan via media to Protestant subjects. In practice, however, all subjects who refused to conform to the authority of the Church of England would be considered dangerous recusants. The early Puritans would come to be seen as almost as great a threat as the Catholics. Both groups of recusants opposed the control of religion by the state, and many of the most vocal also advocated some degree of church influence or control over the civil realm. These increasingly vocal Puritan recusants and Catholic plots to dethrone Elizabeth were dealt with through the Oath of Supremacy, the law of treason, the Act of Uniformity, and the Bond of Association.

The loyalty oath had been enacted as part of the 1559 Act of Supremacy, which required all clergy and state officials to swear "true faith and allegiance" to the only "supreme governor" of the realm, Queen Elizabeth. Later statutes would extend the requirement to cover every official from the highest to the lowest rank, including, among others, schoolmasters and those holding university degrees. A refusal to take the oath, or attempts to equivocate its meaning, could, and often did, lead to charges of treason, especially as the penalties for refusal were increased over the years. Most charges of treason were brought before the High Court of Commission, rather than the common law courts, and used an "oath ex officio," which required the accused to swear to testify completely and truthfully before being told what crime they were being charged with. Very few brought before this court would escape punishment, which could include heavy fines, forfeiture of property, imprisonment, execution, or a combination of some or all of these.

The 1563 Act of Uniformity required every subject to attend church every Sunday and on holy days. Cumulative civil fines and forfeitures punished nonattendance. The Bond of Association was a voluntary group of nobility and gentry pledged to make certain that every public official conformed to the state church and was truly loyal to the Queen. By the end of the Tudor era church and state were united and indivisible. The early Puritan Separatists are notable for insisting on a strict separation of church and state under such a regime despite the likely penalties they would suffer.

The Stuarts and the Wars of the Three Kingdoms

Hoping to build on the Elizabethan Settlement, Scotland's James VI attempted his own failed via media with Catholicism upon succeeding to the English throne in 1603 as James I (reigned 1603–1625). Any chance at success was destroyed as a result of the abortive Catholic Gunpowder Plot to blow up the Parliament along with all its members, the king and queen, his council, and his heir at its opening session in November 1605. A host of anti-Catholic measures followed, including an Oath of Allegiance that Catholic recusants had to take in addition to the Oath of Supremacy. The additional oath required a pledge of "faith and true allegiance" to James as the "lawful and rightful King" (1606 Oath of Allegiance, in Jones

1999, 272) and a denial of the pope's power to depose the king or destabilize the realm. James had also made a partially successful attempt to include Puritan recusants in his reforms of the Church of England at the Hampton Court Conference in 1603 that led to the Canons of 1604. The measure of dignity this provided to them encouraged some, but not all, recusant Puritans to conform. James also made several failed attempts to "reform" the Presbyterian Scottish Kirk along Anglican lines.

These efforts by James VI and I were characterized by his strong belief in the divine right theory of monarchy, under which the laws of the realm and doctrines of the church should obediently conform themselves to the monarch's inclinations. When his reforms were spurned by the English and Scottish Parliaments, James would attempt to implement them through his royal prerogative power. Although such absolutist actions by royal decree were invariably incomplete and created political unrest, James's heir, Charles I (reigned 1625–1649), would rely upon the royal prerogative even more than his father. The attempts by Charles I at imposing tolerance toward Catholics and Anglican-style reforms of the Scottish Kirk undoubtedly contributed to his being deposed and executed for treason by the English House of Commons in 1649.

During the Interregnum from 1649 to 1660 England was ruled by the Puritan Commonwealth and then Protectorate of Oliver Cromwell and his successors. Although the monarchy was gone, church and state were, if anything, more united than before. The Oath of Supremacy was restyled as an Engagement of Loyalty to the Commonwealth required of all officials of church and state. Cromwell would use military force to seize control of Scotland, which had not approved the execution of Charles I, subsequently raising his son Charles to the Scots throne, and Ireland. In Ireland, this led to the imposition of an Anglican-style state church throughout the whole island for the first time in the history of English colonization of Catholic Ireland. The Protectorate would not long survive the death of Oliver Cromwell in 1658, and in 1660 the Stuart line was restored to the throne in the person of Charles II.

The Restoration and the Glorious Revolution

The experiments in tolerance of the restored Stuarts, Charles II (reigned 1660–1685) and James II (reigned 1685–1688), would be accompanied by further attempts to impose by royal decrees and military force an Anglican-style episcopate church structure in Presbyterian Scotland, as well as additional statutory loyalty oaths in the three kingdoms. Test Acts would be also be enacted in the 1670s in England and 1681 in Scotland to enforce the new oaths of nonresistance, loyalty, and conformity to the Anglican faith that had been enacted in the 1660s. "Transportation to the colonies" was added to the repertoire of punishments for refusing to take the oath. Those recusants forced to leave their country for their conscience would join those in the British-American colonies who had voluntarily settled there to pursue their own ideas of religious freedom. In the colonies some would unify church and state more tightly than in Britain. Other settlements in the colonies would be founded on Separatist principles, some of which would advocate genuine tolerance of differing religious beliefs.

The Quakers, who refused as a matter of conscience to take any oath, were specified as dangerous nonconformists as early as 1662 in the statute that added transportation as a penalty for nonconformity. Although Catholics initially showed a surprising willingness to take the new loyalty oaths, the Test Acts' requirement of conformity to the established Anglican Church prohibited them from holding any public office until they were finally repealed in the mid-1800s. The oaths and tests of religious conformity quickly came to be directed primarily against otherwise loyal Catholics and those Puritan sects that opposed the absolutist policies of the restored Stuarts. The imposition of oaths and religious tests in Scotland would ultimately lead to the "killing times" of 1684–1688, during which one hundred dissenters were imprisoned, transported, or executed. The resulting diversity of political and religious dissenters meant that debates over religious freedom would not lack voices on either side of the Atlantic.

When the Catholic James II reneged on his promise not to impose tolerance for Catholics on his kingdoms by issuing the Declaration of Indulgence in 1687, it led to widespread passive disobedience and an invitation by some of the most influential members of Parliament to the Dutch Protestant William of Orange (reigned 1689–1702) to take the throne with James's Protestant daughter Mary as his co-sovereign queen (reigned 1689–1694). The Glorious

Revolution Settlements of 1688 and 1689 resulted in the English Bill of Rights, the Scottish Claim of Right, and Acts of Parliament in both England and Scotland granting limited tolerance for dissenting Protestants. The attempt by James II to retake the throne through a Catholic uprising in Ireland led to the military pacification of Ireland by William III and destroyed any hopes for limited tolerance of any sort being extended to Catholics in the three kingdoms.

The eighteenth century would see a continuing mix of limited tolerance and state-established religions in the three kingdoms—Anglicanism in England and Ireland, and Presbyterianism in Scotland. Although the people living in Britain and Ireland in the early modern period clearly did not enjoy the same rights to religious freedom as we now do in the twenty-first century, the struggles that they endured and the debates they engaged in set the stage for the development of those religious freedoms we now cherish. The last of the laws against religious recusancy in Britain and Ireland would be abolished by the mid-nineteenth century. Major advances in religious freedom occurred in America with the Test Clause (prohibiting the use of oaths or other religious tests to limit access to positions in the federal government) and the First Amendment (prohibiting the establishment of a national religion and guaranteeing the right to freely exercise one's religion) to the U.S. Constitution. Similar constitutional clauses would be included in some, but not all, of the American states by the end of the eighteenth century. The addition of the Fourteenth Amendment in 1868 provided the foundation for eventually applying the guarantees of religious freedom in the U.S. Constitution to the several states in the twentieth century.

Erin Rahne Kidwell

See also English Civil War; English Test Oaths and Toleration Acts

Further Reading

Buckley, G. T. (1965). *Atheism in the English Renaissance.* New York: Russell & Russell.

Charlton, K. (1999). *Women, religion, and education in early modern England.* New York: Routledge.

Coffey, J. (1997). *Politics, Religion and the British Revolutions: The mind of Samuel Rutherford.* Cambridge, UK: Cambridge University Press.

Cressy, D., & Ferrelli, L. A. (Eds.). (1996). *Religion and society in early modern England: A sourcebook.* New York: Routledge.

Guibbory, A. (1998). *Ceremony and community from Herbert to Milton: Literature, religion, and cultural conflict in seventeenth-century England.* Cambridge, UK: Cambridge University Press.

Hamilton, D. B., & Strier, R. (Eds.). (1996). *Religion, literature, and politics in post-Reformation England, 1540–1688.* Cambridge, UK: Cambridge University Press.

Hill, C. (1990). *A nation of change and novelty: Radical politics, religion, and literature in seventeenth-century England.* London: Routledge.

Jones, D. M. (1999). *Conscience and allegiance in seventeenth-century England: The political significance of oaths and engagements.* Rochester, NY: University of Rochester Press.

Kendall, R. (1986). *The drama of dissent: The radical poetics of nonconformity, 1380–1590.* Chapel Hill: University of North Carolina Press.

King, J. N. (1982). *English Reformation literature: The Tudor origins of the Protestant tradition.* Princeton, NJ: Princeton University Press.

McCeachern, C., & Shuger, D. (Eds.). (1997). *Religion and culture in Renaissance England.* Cambridge, UK: Cambridge University Press.

McCullough, P. E. (1998). *Sermons at court: Politics and religion in Elizabethan and Jacobean preaching.* Cambridge, UK: Cambridge University Press.

Patterson, W. B. (1997). *King James VI and I and the reunion of Christendom.* Cambridge, UK: Cambridge University Press.

Questier, M. C. (1996). *Conversion, politics, and religion in England, 1580–1625.* Cambridge, UK: Cambridge University Press.

Schochet, G. J., Brobeck, C., & Tatspaugh, P. E. (Eds.). (1990). *Religion, resistance, and civil war: Papers presented at the Folger Institute Seminar "Political thought in early modern England, 1600–1660."* Washington, DC: Folger Institute, Folger Shakespeare Library.

Solt, L. F. (1990). *Church and state in early modern England.* New York: Oxford University Press.

Sommerville, C. J. (1992). *The secularization of early modern England: From religious culture to religious faith.* New York: Oxford University Press.

Todd, M. (Ed.). (1995). *Reformation to revolution: Politics and religion in early modern England.* New York: Routledge.

Whiting, R. (1989). *The blind devotion of the people: Popular religion and the English Reformation*. Cambridge, UK: Cambridge University Press.

England, Victorian

Religious freedom was restricted in numerous ways in Victorian England (1837–1901) due to state commitment to the Church of England. This church, often referred to as "Anglican," is a Protestant Christian denomination with Episcopalian church government (based on the role of bishops). Nevertheless, the ideal that the law would bolster the Church of England and restrict the rights of adherents of other denominations or faiths or of unbelievers was dramatically eroded in the nineteenth century, making the Victorian age one of major advances in religious freedom for all.

In nineteenth-century England, four major groups were discriminated against due to their religious beliefs: Protestants outside the state church (often called Nonconformists or Dissenters), Roman Catholics, Jews, and unbelievers. Unbelief has innumerable variations, and the Victorians used a range of labels for people in this category, including infidels, freethinkers, secularists, agnostics, and atheists.

Nonconformists ranged across a spectrum of denominations, some more acceptable and others less so from an Anglican perspective. Wesleyan Methodism had the greatest affinity to the state church, and was the largest religious body outside it. It arose from within Anglicanism during the eighteenth-century Evangelical revival, a movement that stressed a personal conversion experience. Next came other varieties of Methodism (generally offshoots from Wesleyanism). Thereafter came other Protestant denominations committed to orthodoxy in doctrine, the largest of which were the Congregationalists (whose church government was based on the autonomy of local congregations) and the Baptists (who rejected infant baptism in favor of believers' baptism). The Quakers, or the Religious Society of Friends, held beliefs and practices that set them markedly apart from the rest of English Protestantism: they refused to swear any kind of oath—even to testify in a court of law; they were pacifists; and they adopted distinctive styles of dress and speech. The Unitarians were the Protestant group of some note and political influence that was farthest from the rest doctrinally. Unitarians denied the basic orthodox beliefs in the Trinity and the deity of Jesus Christ.

The Rights of Protestant Nonconformists

Nonconformists were by far the largest and most organized politically of the four major disadvantaged groups. Moreover, as concessions to any of the four groups strengthened the cases of the others, the campaigns of Dissenters were a major engine of change that produced greater religious freedom for all. This is particularly true as Victorian Nonconformists based their claims on the general principle of religious equality for all before the law, and thus supported legislative changes addressing the situations of other discriminated-against groups.

Dissenters won a major victory in the decade before the Victorian era when the Test and Corporation Acts were repealed in 1828. These acts had prohibited Nonconformists from holding a wide range of civic offices, including being members of Parliament (MPs). These exclusions did not function in practice, however, as an annual Indemnity Act was also passed relieving Dissenters from the force of those laws. Nevertheless, Nonconformists resented the inferiority implied and the insecurity generated by always being on probation and having their civil rights presented as a temporary privilege. In the eighteenth century, a political pressure group, the Dissenting Deputies, was founded to agitate for change, and in the Victorian era it moved on to focus on other grievances. A more militant organization, the British Anti-State Church Association (later renamed the Liberation Society), was founded in 1844. Beginning with the 1847 General Election, the Dissenting community also strove to have some of their own, who would advocate greater religious freedom, elected to Parliament, a strategy that produced a harvest of Nonconformist MPs in the second half of the nineteenth century.

External pressure on Parliament and representation from within produced a string of legislative successes for Dissenters in the Victorian age. A chief goal of Nonconformists was to end mandatory church rates—a tax that forced them to support Anglican worship financially. Dissenters objected to being coerced into aiding religious practices to which many of them objected on theological grounds, and they resented the double burden of needing to give money to support their own religious community as well as aiding someone else's. After numerous bills failed to pass into law over a couple of decades,

CATHOLIC EMANCIPATION ACT, 1829

This act is significant in English history as it emancipated Catholics, meaning that they could now sit in Parliament and hold public office. It did not mean, however, that they enjoyed full religious freedom, and discrimination continued.

An act for the relief of his majesty's Roman Catholic subjects.

Whereas by various acts of parliament certain restraints and disabilities are imposed on the Roman Catholic subjects of his majesty, to which other subjects of his majesty are not liable; and whereas it is expedient that such restraints and disabilities shall be from henceforth discontinued; and whereas by various acts certain oaths and certain declarations . . . are or may be required to be taken . . . as qualifications for sitting and voting in parliament, and for the enjoyment of certain offices, franchises, and civil rights: be it enacted . . . that from and after the commencement of this act all such parts of the said acts as required the said declarations . . . be and the same are (save as hereinafter provided and expected) hereby repealed.

And be it enacted that from and after the commencement of this act it shall be lawful for any person professing the Roman Catholic religion, being a peer, or who shall after the commencement of this act be returned as a member of the house of commons, to sit and vote in either house of parliament respectively, being in all other respects duly qualified to sit and vote therein. . . .

And be it further enacted, that it shall be lawful for persons professing the Roman Catholic religion to vote at elections of members to serve in parliament. . . .

And it be further enacted, that no person in holy orders in the church of Rome shall be capable of being elected to serve in parliament as a member of the house of commons. . . .

And be it enacted, that it shall be lawful for any of his majesty's subjects professing the Roman Catholic religion to hold, exercise, and enjoy all civil and military offices and places of trust or profit under his majesty, his heirs or successors, and to exercise any other franchise or civil right, except . . . to hold or exercise the office of guardians and justices of the United Kingdom, or of regent . . . nor . . . of lord high chancellor, lord keeper or lord commissioner of the great seal . . . or the office of lord lieutenant, or lord deputy, or other chief governor or governors of Ireland. . . .

Stephen B. Baxter, ed.

Source: *Basic Documents of English History*.
(Boston: Houghton Mifflin, 1968), 215.

abolition of compulsory church rates was finally achieved in 1868.

Another Dissenting goal was ending the Anglican monopoly on marriages and burials. The main victory in terms of marriages came in 1836, the year before Victoria's accession, when administration of Dissenting weddings was transferred to the Guardians of the Poor. (Hitherto an Anglican clergyman, church building, and liturgy had been essential to a legal marriage.) Dissenters were annoyed by the implied degradation, and in 1856 succeeded in having this responsibility transferred to the Registrar's Office. Burials were a thornier grievance that was addressed piecemeal throughout the Victorian era. In the early nineteenth century, the only burial grounds available to the vast majority of the population were in parish churchyards, and the Church of England demanded that one of their own clergymen perform all burials there using the Anglican rite. A series of acts of Parliament in the mid-Victorian period permitted the creation of non-denominational cemeteries in urban areas. The crucial victory, however, was won in 1880 when legislation passed that allowed Nonconformists to officiate at burials in parish

REMOVAL OF JEWISH DISABILITIES, 1858

This act of Parliament allowed Jews to sit in Parliament as it exempted them from saying the phrase "and make this declaration upon the true faith of a Christian" from the oath taken by members of Parliament.

An act to provide for the relief of her majesty's subjects professing the Jewish religion.

Be it enacted . . . as follows: Where it shall appear to either house of parliament that a person professing the Jewish religion, otherwise entitled to sit and vote in such house, is prevented from so sitting and voting by his conscientious objection to take the oath which by an act passed or to be passed in the present session of parliament has been or may be substituted for the oaths of allegiance, supremacy, and abjuration in the form therein required, such house, if it think fit, may resolve that thenceforth any person professing the Jewish religion, in taking the said oath to entitle him to sit and vote as aforesaid, may omit the words "and I make this declaration upon the true faith of a Christian", and so long as such resolution shall continue in force the said oath, when taken and subscribed by any person professing the Jewish religion . . . may be modified accordingly. . . . Nothing herein contained shall extend or be construed to extend to enable any person or persons professing the Jewish religion to hold or exercise the office of Guardians and Justices of the United Kingdom, or Regent of the United Kingdom, . . . or of lord high chancellor, lord keeper or lord commissioner of the great seal of Great Britain or Ireland, or the office of lord lieutenant or deputy or other chief governor of governors of Ireland, or her majesty's high commissioner to the general assembly of the church of Scotland. . . .

Stephen B. Baxter, ed.

Source: *Basic Documents of English History*.
(Boston: Houghton Mifflin, 1968), 224.

churchyards, replacing the Anglican service with their own.

Another area of discrimination against Dissenters was the requirement that one must affirm the Thirty-Nine Articles (the principal statement of Anglican doctrine) to receive a degree from Cambridge University or to begin studying at Oxford. As these were England's only two universities at the start of the nineteenth century, this restriction thwarted the advance of Dissenters in numerous professions, and hampered their attainment of learning more generally. Again, change came in stages. In 1854, Dissenters won the right to obtain bachelor's degrees (except in divinity) at Oxford. In 1856, Cambridge followed suit, allowing master's degrees as well. The Universities Tests Act of 1871 removed all religious tests from, not only degrees at Oxford and Cambridge, but also positions as fellows, tutors, or professors (excepting those that were inherently reli-

gious, such as professorships in divinity). Dissenters made great advances in the area of religious freedom in the Victorian period, but their ultimate goal, the disestablishment of the Church of England, was not obtained.

The Rights of Roman Catholics

The hatred of Roman Catholicism that many English Protestants possessed, and which led to an anti-popery riot in late eighteenth-century London in which hundreds died, is an essential backdrop for understanding campaigns to expand religious freedom for Catholics. Restrictions on Catholics were significantly greater than on Dissenters. The English Catholic community was small, but the rights of Catholics became a major political issue in the early nineteenth century as a result of the Act of Union in 1800, a measure that merged the Irish and British Parliaments into a single

Parliament in London. The massive Catholic population of Ireland began demanding its rights. In 1823, the Catholic Association was founded to organize this impulse. Events seemed to be escalating toward violence, and matters came to a head when the Irish leader Daniel O'Connell (1775–1847) was elected to Parliament in 1828. Catholics had been hitherto barred from serving as MPs, but this situation was widely considered untenable, and Catholic emancipation was achieved in 1829—a decade before the start of the Victorian era. Thereafter, English as well as Irish Catholics could become MPs.

The peak of anti-Catholicism in Victorian England came in 1850 and 1851, in response to Pope Pius IX's decision to normalize the structure of the Catholic Church in England, including appointing bishops with territorial titles. The most senior English Catholic leader would henceforth be the archbishop of "Westminster"—the district of London where the Houses of Parliament were and thus a word that was virtually synonymous with the British government. This move was dubbed the "Papal Aggression," and English Protestants raised an uproar over it, arguing that it was a question of national sovereignty as the pope was deemed a foreign ruler. This agitation culminated in the Ecclesiastical Titles Act of 1851, which prohibited the use of territorial titles by Catholics. The Catholic community simply ignored it; it was never enforced and was repealed in 1871.

The British government supported Catholicism in some ways during the Victorian era, most notably by an annual grant to help to fund the training of Catholic priests at Maynooth College in Ireland, and by allowing Catholic priests to serve as prison and military chaplains. Nevertheless, at the end of the Victorian era numerous anti-Catholic laws were still in force, such as restrictions on Catholic processions.

The Rights of Jews

The Jewish population of Victorian Britain was small, totaling approximately 35,000 in 1850. The fight for Jewish emancipation came to the fore when Baron Lionel de Nathan de Rothschild (1808–1879) was elected to Parliament as a member for the City of London in 1847. Rothschild was an eminent leader of one of Europe's great wealthy families but, as a Jew, the required Christian oath prohibited him from serving as an MP. A long parliamentary campaign ensued during which many Anglicans in Parliament, including most bishops in the House of Lords,

opposed admission of Jews. Opposition was usually on the general grounds that the legislature ought to be Christian, but the debate was not devoid of rankly anti-Semitic remarks. The Seventh Earl of Shaftesbury (1801–1885)—then an MP under his earlier title of Lord Ashley—is considered a great humanitarian and the most prominent Evangelical Anglican layman of the Victorian age. Nevertheless, he opposed Jewish emancipation forcefully, betraying establishment protectionism at its baldest when he told the House of Commons: "Some years ago they stood out for a Protestant Parliament. They were perfectly right in doing so, but they were beaten. They now stood out for a Christian Parliament. They would next have to stand out for a white Parliament; and perhaps they would have a final struggle for a male Parliament" (Larsen 1999, 127).

Nonconformists, however, strongly supported Jewish emancipation; it was finally achieved in 1859, and Baron Rothschild and two other Jews took their seats in the House of Commons on 6 June 1859.

The Rights of Atheists

The number of people in Victorian England identifiable as atheists is very small. Unbelievers' rights were championed by the National Secular Society, founded in 1866, but even at its height it had no more than 4,000 members. Although religion meant little to some Victorians in practice, few were so committed to unbelief as, for example, to refuse to swear a Christian oath in a court of law. However, the conscientious few who did object had a serious grievance. They were sometimes unable to obtain judicial justice, because although their cases hung on their own testimony, they were not allowed to give evidence. Such discrimination against unbelievers was ended by the Evidence Amendments Acts of 1869 and 1870.

As with the Roman Catholic and Jewish communities, the right of atheists to become MPs came to the fore through one of their own being elected to Parliament. Charles Bradlaugh (1833–1891), founder of the National Secular Society and vocal opponent of Christianity, was elected MP for Northampton in 1880. This led to a protracted parliamentary struggle that ended victorious when Bradlaugh took his seat in the Commons in 1886. Throughout the Victorian era the religious freedom of atheists, skeptics, and other unbelievers was limited by blasphemy laws, which always held out the possibility of prosecution if what unbelievers wrote or said against religion was deemed too offensive.

Religious freedom expanded tremendously in England in the Victorian era, but some forms of religious discrimination persisted, as did the privileging of the Church of England as the establishment religion of the land.

Timothy Larsen

See also British Empire

Further Reading

Addison, W. G. (1944). *Religious equality in modern England, 1714–1914*. London: SPCK.

Larsen, T. (1999). *Friends of religious equality: Nonconformist politics in mid-Victorian England*. Woodbridge, UK: Boydell.

Norman, E. R. (1984). *The English Catholic Church in the nineteenth century*. Oxford, UK: Clarendon.

Royle, E. (1974). *Victorian infidels: The origins of the British secularist movement, 1791–1866*. Manchester, UK: Manchester University Press.

Royle, E. (1980). *Radicals, secularists and republicans: Popular freethought in Britain, 1866–1915*. Manchester, UK: Manchester University Press.

Salbstein, M. C. N. (1982). *The emancipation of the Jews in Britain: The question of the admission of the Jews to Parliament, 1828–1860*. London: Associated University Press.

Wolffe, J. (1991). *The Protestant crusade in Great Britain, 1829–1860*. Oxford, UK: Clarendon Press.

English Civil War

The revolutions and war in seventeenth-century England were crucial for the development of all civil and political rights in the English-speaking world. It is difficult to separate out a discussion of religious liberty from its place in this story, a story that begins with the Puritans.

Background

Puritanism developed in the second half of the sixteenth century during Queen Elizabeth I's reign (1558–1603). When Elizabeth's Catholic, elder half sister, Queen Mary was in power (1553–1558), many Protestants fled England to avoid Mary's reinstatement of Catholicism. Some went to Geneva and studied under John Calvin (1509–1564) and other preachers there. They returned during Elizabeth's reign with a desire to reform England along Calvinist lines. Dissatisfied with Elizabeth's *via media*, or middle way between Protestantism and Catholicism, they sought greater reform of the Church of England (Anglican Church), seeking to purify it of all Roman Catholic elements, and hence the name Puritans.

By the time of Elizabeth's death, Puritans constituted a strong religious minority with a political vision essentially shaped by Calvinism as manifest in Geneva. Puritan Calvinists had already succeeded in taking Scotland in the 1560s, running Mary Queen of Scots out of her own land and placing her young son James VI on the throne. At Elizabeth's death, James became king of England and Scotland, taking the title James I in the latter. Puritans erroneously believed this would be their chance for further reform in England.

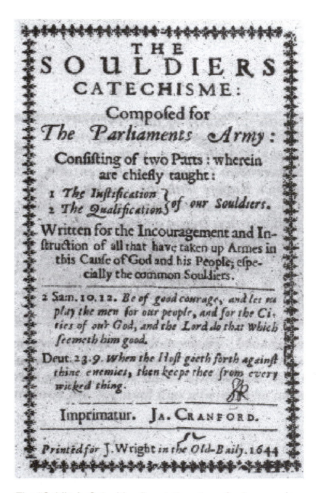

The "Soldier's Catechism", a delineation of rules, regulations and procedures for Cromwell's New Model Army.
COURTESY EASYWEB.EASYNET.CO.UK/~CROSSBY.

SELECTION FROM *INSTRUMENT OF GOVERNMENT* (1653)

XXXV. That the Christian religion, as contained in the Scriptures, be held forth and recommended as the public profession of these nations; and that, as soon as may be, a provision, less subject to scruple and contention, and more certain than the present, be made for the encouragement and maintenance of able and painful teachers, for the instructing the people, and for discovery and confutation of error, hereby, and whatever is contrary to sound doctrine; and until such provision be made, the present maintenance shall not be taken away or impeached.

XXXVI. That to the public profession held forth none shall be compelled by penalties or otherwise; but that endeavours be used to win them by sound doctrine and the example of a good conversation.

XXXVII. That such as profess faith in God by Jesus Christ (though differing in judgment from the doctrine, worship or discipline publicly held forth) shall not be restrained from, but shall be protected in, the profession of the faith and exercise of their religion; so as they abuse not this liberty to the civil injury of others and to the actual disturbance of the public peace on their parts: provided this liberty be not extended to Popery or Prelacy, nor to such as, under the profession of Christ, hold forth and practise licentiousness.

Samuel R. Gardiner (1906)

Source: *The Constitutional Documents
of the Puritan Revolution 1625–1660*, 405–417.

At the Hampton Court Conference of 1604, Puritan leaders gained an audience with James, but were disappointed to learn that he had no intention of supporting a Puritan program, regarding it as a threat to his leadership of the Church of England and to his status as king. He allegedly told the Puritans, "No bishop, no king," instructing them to "conform [to the Church of England] or I will harry you out of the land." Puritans did not conform, but redoubled their efforts to win seats in Parliament, hoping someday to have the power to reform their country.

At the other end of the religio-political spectrum, Catholics also sought reform, desiring that England return to Roman Catholicism. The first attempted revolution of the seventeenth century in England occurred when a Catholic party led by Guy Fawkes attempted to place explosives beneath the Parliament building, hoping to blow up the new king and the Parliament. Authorities learned of and foiled this "Gunpowder Plot" (1604–1605), and Fawkes and his accomplices were executed. To this day many English observe Guy Fawkes Day, when children are given an effigy of Guy Fawkes to throw into a bonfire.

While Catholics continued hoping for rapprochement with Rome, especially late in the century under King James II, Puritans became the major dissenters and eventually led the English Civil War (1642–1649). Charles I, who succeeded James in 1625, had a penchant for alienating Parliament, ignoring Englishmen's historic rights to suit his purposes. However, he often needed Parliament to raise money, primarily used to finance efforts to keep the Protestant Scots under control and force them to conform to the Anglican Church. He dissolved Parliament in 1630, and by 1640 he was again short of funds to pay his army. When he called Parliament back into session that year, events began to spiral out of his control. Parliament now contained many Puritans, other more radical Protestants (including Independents, Separatists, and Baptists), and members of the middle class.

When the "Long Parliament" of 1641 began ignoring the king and asserting its own control, one of its first acts was to pursue William Laud, the archbishop of Canterbury. Laud had led Charles's program to enforce conformity with the Church of

113

THE PERSECUTION OF A FRIAR

The following account from the day book of an English country gentleman decries the fate of a Catholic friar who had been persecuted in England.

15 October, 1724, died in confinement, at the age of seventy-four, Paul Atkinson, a Franciscan friar. He was a native of Yorkshire, and had been infamously betrayed by his female servant, for a reward of 100*l*., under the penal statute of William III against Romish priests. He was condemned to perpetual imprisonment, in Hurst Castle, in the Isle of Wight; and lived there with cheerful composure, beloved and respected by the governor, and the whole neighborhood, as an unfortunate, amiable man. He had been allowed the liberty of occasionally walking abroad, till some wretched bigots complained of the humane indulgence, and then he voluntarily retired to his poor lodging, that he might give no offence nor occasion blame to his kind keeper; he never again left the castle, nor would he permit any application to be made for a mitigation of his doom. Upon his death, in prison, his remains were removed to Winchester, and interred in the cemetery of St. James's, the burial place of many Roman Catholics.

Friar Atkinson is still remembered, and tears have flowed from protestant eyes, for his and fate. It has been presumed that had George I and queen Caroline been fully acquainted with his situation, and his meek demeanor, his prison doors would have been set open. Their majesties were both friends to toleration; and the queen in particular frequently entrusted the duchess of Norfolk with sums of money, for distribution among sufferers of the Roman Catholic communion.

William Hone

Source: *The Year Book of Daily Recreation and Information.*
(London: William Tegg, 1832), 1194.

England. He carried out measures to suppress Puritan preaching, and Puritans suspected erroneously that Laud was a secret Catholic. He was arrested, placed in the Tower of London, and executed in 1645. Meanwhile, Parliament and the country itself split and the Civil War commenced in August 1642. The war was not strictly about religion, and the term "Puritan Revolution" overstates the case. Still, the Parliamentarian side was under heavy Puritan influence, especially when Oliver Cromwell (1599–1658) became its army leader.

Cromwell's Leadership

Cromwell probably converted to Puritanism in the early 1630s, and came to view all of life through the prism of his faith. His New Model Army fought with religious zeal, often praying and singing hymns before battle. They were highly disciplined, with high morale and a deep sense of purpose. As well as Puritans, other religious radicals also sided with Parliament as they recognized that religious tolerance could be won through war. Cromwell believed in religious tolerance as a matter of principle, not just as an expedient measure to gain support for the Parliamentarian side. Various religious radicals supported Cromwell's ejection of bishops from the House of Lords, and his Root and Branch bill, which proposed eliminating bishops altogether from the Church of England. The troops enthusiastically destroyed images and stained glass windows in churches as part of an attempt to eradicate vestiges of Catholicism from the Anglican Church. They were fighting for a godly cause, they believed, and they won. King Charles was captured, tried by Parliament, and executed in 1649. There followed a Commonwealth (1649–1653), where Parliament governed without a monarch.

Cromwell was the leading figure in Parliament, and over time the Commonwealth gave way to the

Protectorate (1653–1660), with Cromwell as Lord Protector. While he had virtually dictatorial powers, he set out to rule in accordance with the Instrument of Government adopted in December 1653. Although liberty of conscience was a fundamental principal of the Instrument, this was not freedom of conscience as understood today. Cromwell did not believe that people had the right to believe whatever they wished and to live in libertine fashion. Rather, he believed that Puritanism should be the law of the land and that there should be a national church, though others should be tolerated. Essentially, Cromwell and his regime would tolerate all Protestants except Quakers, so long as they behaved themselves as Christians; even Catholics were largely left alone. During both the Commonwealth and Protectorate, Cromwell's brand of Puritan toleration ruled. Sectarian dissenters such as Baptists, Independents, and Separatists were given legal right to worship freely. Cromwell also instituted laws aimed at making the nation more godly and moral. Countryside recreations such as horse racing, bear baiting, and cockfighting were all circumscribed. In the cities, theaters were tightly regulated and in some cases closed, as were alehouses. This was an attempt to create a godly commonwealth—modeled after Calvin's Geneva a century earlier—something Puritans in New England had been constructing since 1630.

On Cromwell's death in 1658, his son Richard succeeded as Lord Protector. He was not as skilled as his father, and the nation suffered instability and disunity. England was also isolated diplomatically as the monarchies of Europe were wary of the Parliamentarian and Cromwell regimes, especially given that the Puritans had executed their king. In the 1650s, more and more English citizens came to long for the stability they believed only a monarchy could bring. Richard Cromwell could not hold things together as his father had, and the Restoration of the Monarchy came in 1660 with King Charles I's son taking the throne as Charles II.

After the Restoration, religious toleration became a political football, kicked this way and that by the king and Parliament. Parliament was often bent on reestablishing religious conformity and so set out to persecute the sects. Parliament passed the Conventicle Act of 1664 against the king's wishes. This law required that all worship services involving more than five people use the Anglican Book of Common Prayer, which had been revised in ways offensive to Puritans. The Five Mile Act of 1665 made it illegal for a non-Anglican minister to come within five miles of city or town or teach in a school unless he promised not to advocate change in church or state. In 1672, attempting to help Catholics and win the loyalty of dissenters, Charles issued a Declaration of Indulgence permitting public worship for both groups. Parliament quashed the Declaration and instead passed a Test Act requiring that all civil and military officers take an oath of allegiance and receive the Lord's Supper according to the Anglican Church. Baptists and others who had enjoyed toleration under Cromwell's regime were again fined and imprisoned, author John Bunyan (1628–1688) being a prime example. Likewise, Jeremy Taylor (1613–1667) and other Anglicans who denounced Parliament's refusal to tolerate dissenters experienced similar persecution.

The Glorious Revolution

Charles's successor, his brother James II (1685–1689), was openly Catholic and more brazen in attempting to offer religious toleration in return for loyalty. He issued another Declaration of Indulgence, opposition to which led in part to the Glorious Revolution. The Glorious Revolution of 1688 is arguably the most important event in English political history and almost as significant for American history as well. Emerging from a contest for power between king and Parliament, it also had strong religious overtones as most in Parliament were offended by James's Catholicism. His heir and daughter, Mary, was Protestant, as was her husband, William of Orange of the Netherlands. When James's wife produced a son, and the king placed him in line for the throne ahead of Mary, it appeared that England might have a Catholic monarch indefinitely. This was unacceptable to Parliament, which invited William and Mary to come from Holland to replace James as joint monarchs. James fled and attempted to raise an army, but after a minor skirmish his forces disbanded and he surrendered. Parliament had faced down a king with hardly a shot fired. This Glorious Revolution, as it was called, signified that in England Parliament was supreme over the monarch.

The Glorious Revolution was a triumph for individual rights, solidifying an English system of historic rights in the making since the *Magna Carta* of 1215. One such right was that of religious tolerance. In 1689, Parliament passed the Act of Toleration that kept the Anglican Church as the established church of the realm, but stipulated that dissenting sects and denominations of Christians were to be tolerated. They still suffered some disadvantages and were taxed to support the Anglican Church, but the persecutions of Laud and the Restoration Parliament were ended. The English Civil War had broken the monopoly of the national church, and the Act recognized that religious pluralism was in England to stay. With Anglicans, Catholics, Puritans, Baptists, Quakers, and smaller groups that eventually died out, it became increasingly difficult to force all to conform to a single theology or form of worship. John Locke's odyssey in the area of religious tolerance is indicative of how such pluralism necessitates tolerance.

Locke was reared in a staunchly Puritan home and seriously considered becoming a minister. During the early years of the Restoration, he wrote that while individuals could believe anything they wanted, for the sake of public order they should all conform outwardly to a single style of worship, that of the Church of England. He feared chaos if all worshiped as they pleased. After seven years of Charles II's reign, however, Locke observed that attempts to coerce religious minorities in matters of worship turned them against the state, leading to the possibility of revolt. Whereas Locke had originally believed that pluralism would lead to chaos, by 1667 he believed the opposite—that the threat of instability and chaos was exacerbated by forced conformity in matters of religion. After twenty more years of reflection he authored his famous *Letter on Toleration* (1689) in which he argued that the state had no business attempting to govern individual conscience concerning religion. Locke also wrote his famous *Two Treatises of Government*, which outlined the liberal theory of government and served as a philosophical justification for the Glorious Revolution.

According to Locke's liberal theory, natural individual rights included the right to believe and act on that belief without state interference. Thus began the modern notion of religious liberty. Locke's theory advocated tolerance, not full religious liberty: for the sake of public order, England was right to have a national church, but dissenters would be tolerated as well. Moreover, Locke held out two exceptions to his general theory of toleration. First, atheists need not be tolerated because they presumably lacked the moral foundation necessary in a sound body politic. Second, religious groups that held allegiance to a foreign political power need not be tolerated as they too threatened political stability. In this latter category were Catholics and Muslims, the former because of their allegiance to the pope, the latter because of their presumed fidelity to the Sultan of the Ottoman Empire.

On the issue of religious liberty, the course of Locke's own life paralleled the English experience. Raised under Puritan influences, he observed the revolutionary spirit animating seventeenth-century England as well as the burgeoning of religious pluralism. He simply worked out theoretically what his country lived out existentially. There was nothing inevitable in these developments, but rather a fascinating convergence of forces and events, made possible largely by the Protestant Reformation of the preceding century. These forces brought England to the verge of a modern understanding of religious liberty.

Barry Hankins

See also English Test Oaths and Toleration Acts; Letter on Toleration

Further Reading

Dunn, J. (1984). *Locke*. New York: Oxford University Press.

Hill, C. (1958). *Puritanism and revolution: Studies in the interpretation of the 17th century*. New York: Schocken Books.

Hill, C. (1970). *God's Englishman: Oliver Cromwell and the English revolution*. New York: Dial Press.

Latourette, K. S. (1953). *A history of Christianity* (Vol. 2). San Francisco: Harper and Row.

English Test Oaths and Toleration Acts

The imposition of test oaths was one way the post-Reformation British government attempted to enforce conformity to the Church of England. Intended to create a confessional state in Britain, test oaths were primarily directed against Catholic recusants, but many other dissenters who refused to swear the oaths (especially Quakers) were also persecuted. Although Catholics remained legally restricted until the nineteenth century, most Protestant nonconformists were granted some religious freedom with the passage of the Toleration Act of 1689.

Queen Elizabeth I (1533–1603) introduced the Oath of Supremacy in 1559. All holders of political office had to acknowledge the monarch as the "supreme governor" of the Church of England—an assertion of ecclesiastical supremacy that Catholics could not accept. Elizabeth's successor, James I (1566–1625), added an Oath of Allegiance in 1606 following the abortive "Gunpowder Plot" of the previous year. This oath targeted papal temporal power, specifically the pope's claim to possess the authority to depose monarchs and release their subjects from obedience. Although some English Catholics were willing to concede this, Pope Paul V forbade Catholics to swear the oath, fueling English Protestant suspicions that Catholicism encouraged political disloyalty and rebellion.

With Dissenters in charge of government during the Interregnum (1649–1660), the oaths were suspended, but they returned with the restoration of the monarchy in 1660. The new king, Charles II (1630–1685), had Catholic sympathies and proposed to institute broad religious toleration when he assumed the crown. The "Cavalier Parliament," however, instead passed the laws collectively known as the Clarendon Code (1661–1665) that entrenched the Church of England and severely penalized all religious nonconformity. In 1672, Charles again attempted to introduce a measure of religious liberty in his "Declaration of Indulgence," but Parliament responded with the first Test Act (1673). This reinstated the test oaths and further demanded disavowal of the doctrine of transubstantiation and public reception of communion according to the rites of the Established Church. A second Test Act reiterated these requirements in 1678, extending them to members of the House of Lords, following rumors of the "Popish Plot" against the king in favor of his Catholic brother.

The death of Charles brought his brother to the throne as King James II (1633–1701). In 1687 and 1688, James issued his own Declarations of Indulgence hoping to gain the political support of Protestant nonconformists as well as Catholics. When the birth of a male heir threatened to assure a Catholic succession, James's opponents turned to William of Orange, Charles's grandson and James's son-in-law, to launch an invasion and secure the nation to Protestantism. As a result of this "Glorious Revolution," James fled to France and William and his wife, Mary, became joint monarchs. To form a consensus supporting this de facto revolution, the Act of Toleration (1689) exempted most Protestant nonconformists from attending Anglican services and permitted the formation of separate congregations, but Catholics, Jews, and Unitarians had to

await the ultimate repeal of the Test Acts in 1828 to achieve their own religious liberties.

Rodger Payne

See also English Civil War

Further Reading

Greaves, R. L. (1990). *Enemies under his feet: Radicals and nonconformists in Britain, 1664–1677.* Stanford, CA: Stanford University Press.

Grell, O. P., Israel, J. I., & Tyacke, N. (1991). *From persecution to toleration: The glorious revolution and religion in England.* Oxford, UK: Clarendon Press.

Jordan, W. K. (1932–1940). *The development of religious toleration in England* (Vols. 1–4). Cambridge, MA: Harvard University Press.

Kenyon, J. P. (1986). *The Stuart constitution, 1603–1688* (2nd ed). Cambridge, UK: Cambridge University Press.

Miller, J. (1973). *Popery and politics in England, 1660–1688.* Cambridge, UK: Cambridge University Press.

Spurr, J. (1989). The Church of England, comprehension, and the Toleration Act of 1689. *English historical review, 104,* 927–946.

Establishment, Equal Treatment

Equal treatment is an approach to interpreting the establishment clause in the First Amendment of the U.S. Constitution. Equal treatment says that government ought to treat religiously based educational, health, and social service programs no better and no worse than similar or parallel secular programs. It is also sometimes referred to as substantive or positive neutrality, or simply neutrality, since its supporters argue that it is the only way for government to be truly neutral on matters of religion. It has increasingly been used by the U.S. Supreme Court in applying the establishment clause to instances where government has offered certain benefits or support to religiously based providers of services to the public. The equal treatment principle says that for government to offer recognition or benefits to secular groups and to deny them to faith-based groups of the same type due solely to their religious character is to discriminate against religion.

Michael McConnell has described the basic concept of equal treatment with these words: When

FEDERAL GOVERNMENT SUPPORT FOR FAITH-BASED COMMUNITY INITIATIVES

This announcement about faith-based initiatives appeared in 7 July 2002 edition of the *Federal Register*, the government's daily publication of rules and notices pertaining to federal agencies. Federal support for these programs is made possible through the court's equal treatment interpretation of the establishment clause.

DEPARTMENT OF HEALTH AND HUMAN SERVICES

Office of Community Services

[Program Announcement No. 2002-14]

Compassion Capital Fund Demonstration Program

AGENCY: The Office of Community Services (OCS), Administration for Children and Families (ACF), Department of Health and Human Services (HHS).

ACTION: Announcement of the request for competitive applications and the availability of federal funding to organizations to provide technical assistance to help faith-based and community-based organizations.

SUMMARY: This announcement, together with other steps that HHS is taking, lays a foundation for expanding the role in social services of faith-based and other community-serving groups, building capacity and knowledge among these organizations to better meet the needs of the poor and low-income families and individuals, and encouraging the replication of effective programs. The program announced here will provide Compassion Capital funds to organizations (herein referred to as "intermediary organizations") that have demonstrated an ability to assist faith- and community-based organizations, particularly smaller organizations, in a variety of areas, including, but not limited to, their efforts to effectively operate and manage their programs, access funding from varied sources, develop and train staff, expand the types and reach of social services programs in their communities, or replicate promising models or programs. (Throughout this document "social services" be taken to include promotion, treatment, and prevention services related to primary health care, substance abuse treatment, mental health treatment, HIV/AIDS and related aspects of public health services directed to low-income families and individuals.) In addition, recipients of awards under this announcement will issue awards or sub-awards for start-up and operational costs to qualified faith- and community-based organizations to expand or replicate promising or best practices in targeted areas.

The Administration for Children and Families (ACF) is the agency designated to issue initial awards under the Fund. However, the work supported through such awards is expected to address a broad array of services and programs and to complement related activities in other parts of HHS and other federal departments. The Compassion Capital Fund will help further the President's goals and objectives regarding faith- and community-based organizations and will enhance work being supported by multiple federal agencies. ACF estimates that the funds available under this announcement will support 15-25 cooperative agreements with intermediary organizations. The Federal government plans to work in partnership with others who have similar goals and interests in strengthening organizations operating closest to those most in need.

Therefore, ACF seeks applicants who can share in the cost of the activities described in this announcement. Applicants are expected to provide at least 50 percent of the amount of Federal funds requested (i.e., one-third of the proposed total budget).

Source: *Federal Register* 67 (7 June 2002), 39561–39570.
Retrieved September 27, 2002
from: http://www.access.gpo.gov/su_docs/aces/aces140.html

speech reflecting a secular viewpoint is permitted, then speech reflecting a religious viewpoint is permitted, on the same basis. And vice versa. When the government provides benefits to private programs and activities—whether charitable endeavor, health care, education, or art—there should be no discrimination or exclusion on the basis of religious expression, character, or motivation (McConnell 1998, 32).

Equal treatment stands in contrast to a strict separation, no-aid-to-religion approach to interpreting the establishment clause. That approach says no government funds may go to support religion in any form. Otherwise, the government may be taxing a person of one religion to support another religion. This, supporters of no-aid-to-religion say, is a gross injustice and a violation of the establishment clause.

History of Equal Treatment

The seeds of the equal treatment principle can be found already in the landmark *Everson v. Board of Education* case decided by the Supreme Court in 1947. In it the court's rhetoric strongly supported the strict separation, no-aid-to-religion position, but then turned around and approved government-paid bus transportation for students in religiously based schools. It declared: "State power is no more to be used so as to handicap religions than it is to favor them" (*Everson v. Board of Education* 1947, 18).

Equal treatment received its first clear articulation, however, in a 1981 case dealing with a Christian student group at the University of Missouri at Kansas City. It had been denied the use of campus facilities that all other student groups had been granted. The Supreme Court ruled that this policy of the university violated the students' free speech rights and that allowing them to use campus facilities would not violate the establishment clause of the Constitution. The Supreme Court, quoting from the Court of Appeals, noted that allowing the students to meet on campus "'would no more commit the University ... to religious goals' than it is 'now committed to the goals of the Students for a Democratic Society, the Young Socialist Alliance,' or any other group eligible to use its facilities" (*Widmar v. Vincent* 1981, 174).

Since 1981 the Supreme Court has applied equal treatment reasoning in finding constitutional the use of a public school auditorium by a church for the showing of Christian films on child rearing, the use of public high school facilities for religious clubs meeting during non–school hours, the display of a cross by a private group on a state capitol grounds, the placement of public school teachers in religiously based schools to teach remedial classes, and the use of vouchers given to parents to fund their children's education, including in faith-based schools. It is not an exaggeration to say, as Jeffrey Rosen has written: "The Supreme Court is on the verge of replacing the principle of strict separation with a very different constitutional principle that demands equal treatment for religion" (Rosen 2000, 42–43).

In what is probably the clearest example of the Supreme Court applying the equal treatment principle, in 1995 the court considered a case arising out of the University of Virginia. The university had a policy of subsidizing a host of student publications, representing a wide spectrum of viewpoints, but turned down a Christian student publication for funding because of a policy of not funding religious publications. In a close 5-4 vote the court held that if the university subsidized student publications representing a wide range of viewpoints, it could not exclude a religious student publication. Justice Anthony Kennedy, writing for the court majority, used neutrality rather than equal treatment terminology, but clearly upheld the equal treatment principle: "We have held that the guarantee of neutrality is respected, not offended, when the government, following neutral criteria and evenhanded policies, extends benefits to recipients whose ideologies and viewpoints, including religious ones, are broad and diverse" (*Rosenberger v. Rector* 1995, 839).

Similarly, two years later Justice Sandra Day O'Connor clearly articulated the equal treatment principle when she wrote that there is no incentive to advance religion "where the aid is allocated on the basis of neutral, secular criteria that neither favor nor disfavor religion, and is made available to both religious and secular beneficiaries on a nondiscriminatory basis" (*Agostini v. Felton* 1997, 231).

Congress and the presidency have also been moving in the equal treatment direction in recent years. In 1996 Congress added a provision to the welfare reform bill then moving through Congress that is based on equal treatment principles. It is termed charitable choice and seeks to assure that faith-based groups are able to compete on an equal basis with secular groups for contracts and grants to provide social services. Since then similar provisions were added to three other acts of Congress. President George W. Bush created an Office of Faith-Based and Community Initiatives in the White House and gave it a mandate to level the playing field so that faith-based groups could compete equally with secular groups for government contracts to provide social services. These actions are clearly based on the fundamental concept found in the principle of equal treatment: justice is done and no constitutional violation occurs when government does not exclude faith-based groups from government contracts and grants, but treats them equally with secular groups—no better and no worse.

At this time no one can predict whether or not the Supreme Court and the political branches of government will fully accept the equal treatment principle over the no-aid, strict separation principle. Equal treatment has been gaining in strength over the past twenty years, but the issue is far from settled. Advocacy groups such as the American Civil Liberties Union and Americans United for Separation of Church and State continue to oppose it. President Bush's faith-based initiative ran into strong opposition in Congress and elsewhere. No one can say whether the Supreme Court will further embrace equal treatment and neutrality, or will pull back from it and move to strengthen the no-aid, strict separation principle. Two principles are contending for dominance on the Court, and it is risky to predict which one will ultimately prevail.

The Rationale in Support of Equal Treatment

The supporters of the equal treatment principle argue that they take a middle position between two extremes, both of which they reject. One of these positions believes that public life should be clothed in religious or even Christian ceremonies and symbols. It insists that the United States is still fundamentally a Christian nation and that when the government recognizes this fact by way of ceremonies such as teacher-led school prayer or favoring religious organizations, it is only recognizing who we are as a people. The extreme opposite position argues that the public realm should be a religion-free realm. Public life should be devoid of all religious ceremonies and symbols, and government funds should only go to thoroughly secular educational and social service organizations, never to those with a religious base or orientation. To do otherwise is to align government in support of certain religious faiths or of religion in general.

The equal treatment, neutrality position rejects both of these options. It argues there is a huge difference between government itself engaging in prayers or other religious ceremonies, and government treating religious organizations and citizens on the same basis as secular organizations and citizens. When government itself engages in promoting religion or in favoring religious organizations over their secular counterparts it is tilting in favor of religion. This is neither just nor necessary. It is not just because the religious among us would be favored over the nonreligious; it is not necessary because genuine religion does not need the support of government to flourish.

But equal treatment also rejects the second option of the public sphere needing to be a religion-free zone. It argues that a secularized public realm is no more neutral than a religious public realm. Here one comes to the heart of the rationale for the equal treatment position and why its adherents reject the no-aid, strict separation position. No-aid, strict separation implicitly assumes, they argue, that a secularized public realm is a neutral realm. But equal treatment advocates argue an area of life that has been sanitized of all religious references does not occupy an area of neutrality between religions and secularism, it *is* secularism.

The end result for which equal treatment calls is neither a religiously clothed public realm nor a secularized public realm, but—as McConnell has put it—"a pluralistic public sphere in which every viewpoint and worldview is free to participate and 'to flourish according to the zeal of it adherents and the appeal of its dogma,' to borrow the words of Justice William O. Douglas in *Zorach v. Clauson*" (McConnell 1998, 36).

Advocates of equal treatment also point out that government today is active in supporting, promoting, providing, and subsidizing a whole range of educational, health, and social services. Government provides or subsidizes education from preschool through the postdoctoral level. It funds health care, homeless shelters, welfare-to-work programs, drug and alcohol rehabilitation programs, spouse abuse shelters, AIDS prevention efforts, and much more. It is hard to think of any area of society and its needs where government is not involved in some way. In all of these fields government itself, secular nonprofit organizations, and faith-based organizations—all three—are actively providing these services.

The supporters of the equal treatment interpretation of the establishment clause argue that in this situation, if government would run its own secular programs and would help subsidize private secular programs, but would deny all help to the religious programs that were providing virtually the exact same services, government would be discriminating against religion. Government would no longer be neutral between religion and nonbelief. If the religion clauses of the First Amendment mean anything at all, they argue, they mean that government ought not to favor any one religion over any other religion, nor ought it to favor religion over secular views of life nor secular views of life over religion.

The Impact of Equal Treatment

One thing on which the advocates of equal treatment and of no-aid agree is that the outcome of the debate will be very consequential for public policy and American society more broadly. If the equal treatment, neutrality position prevails, public policy options such as vouchers for K–12 education, more

government funds going to religious higher education, and more governmental financial support for faith-based social service programs would all be constitutional and their adoption or rejection would be decided by the normal policy-making process, not ruled off the table by the courts.

Supporters of equal treatment believe this will lead to a renewed level of religious freedom for persons of all faiths and of none, as faith-based programs and activities are no longer put in a disadvantaged position, as compared to their government-run and secular counterparts. They also believe the poor and needy of our society will receive better options for educating their children and overcoming such social ills as poverty, homelessness, and unemployment. Advocates of the no-aid, strict separation position fear public educational, health, and social services will deteriorate as available funds are stretched further; religion itself will be corrupted by the influence of government; and religious freedom will be compromised.

Stephen V. Monsma

See also Establishment, Separation of Church and State

Further Reading

Gedicks, F. M. (1995). *The rhetoric of church and state.* Durham, NC: Duke University Press.

McConnell, M. (1998). Equal Treatment and Religious Discrimination. In S. V. Monsma & J. C. Soper (Eds.), *Equal treatment of religion in a pluralistic society* (pp. 30–54). Grand Rapids, MI: W. B. Eerdmans Publishing Co.

Monsma, S. V. (Ed.). (2002). *Church-state relations in crisis: Debating neutrality.* Lanham, MD: Rowman & Littlefield.

Monsma, S. V., & Soper, J. C. (Eds.). (1998). *Equal treatment of religion in a pluralistic society.* Grand Rapids, MI: W. B. Eerdmans Publishing Co.

Reichley, A. J. (1985). *Religion in American public life.* Washington, DC: Brookings.

Rosen, J. (2000, January 30). Is nothing secular? *The New York Times magazine,* 40–45.

Court Cases

Agostini v. Felton, 521 U.S. 203 (1997).

Everson v. Board of Education, 330 U.S. 1 (1947).

Rosenberger v. Rector, 515 U.S. 819 (1995).

Widmar v. Vincent 454 U.S. 263 (1981).

Establishment, Separation of Church and State

Establishment refers to the union between government and religion. An established religion is a government-sanctioned faith. The opening words of the First Amendment to the U. S. Constitution provide that: "Congress shall make no law respecting an establishment of religion. . . ." Americans largely agree that this language prohibits a government-sponsored church in the United States, but debate what, if any, laws may be made "respecting" religion. In particular, Americans disagree as to whether the separation of church and state is a legitimate First Amendment doctrine and, if it is, what "separation" entails. The debate confirms that intermixing politics and religion is controversial.

Early American Establishments of Religion

Many of the Europeans who left their countries of origin to settle in the American Colonies came seeking a place to practice their faith. Their diversity of beliefs, and the variety of circumstances they found in America, resulted in a range of practices. Although established religions existed until well past the founding of the United States (1776, Declaration of Independence), the particular details of these government-sponsored faiths varied. Thomas J. Curry, a student of early American church–state relations, notes the "ambiguities of 'establishment' in the colonies" (Curry 1986, 105).

From 1620, when New England was first settled, establishment in America differed from establishment in Europe. In England and on the Continent, establishment was exclusive and monolithic. Establishment meant the legal union of a single denomination with the state, as in, for example, the Anglican Church in England, the Presbyterian Church in Scotland, the Roman Catholic Church in Spain and Italy, and the Lutheran Church in Sweden. In such countries, the established church was privileged, enjoying advantages such as designation as the official national creed, having its clergy solely authorized to perform rites and offer sacraments, being supported by tax revenues, and having attendance at its services made mandatory. Establishment in America took several other forms. "The American experience, always remarkably diverse, comprehended exclusive establishments,

dual establishments, and general or multiple establishments" (Levy 1994, 11). These variations can be grouped geographically.

In Virginia, the Carolinas, Maryland, and Georgia, the Church of England (Protestant Episcopal Church) was the established religion. Though establishment in these five colonies most closely resembled the European form, the resemblance was not complete. The 1776 Virginia Declaration of Rights, for example, while not ending establishment, proclaimed that "all men are equally entitled to the free exercise of religion" (Article 16), and the Virginia Assembly adopted a law that same year exempting "dissenters from the church established by law" from being taxed for its support. Rhode Island, Pennsylvania, Delaware, and New Jersey never established any religion. Still, Pennsylvania, Delaware, and New Jersey required candidates for public office to swear religious oaths, "as a means of excluding atheists and enemies of civilized society" (Curry 1986, 133).

In each of the remaining four states—New York, Massachusetts, Connecticut, and New Hampshire—diversity of history and belief led establishment to take unique, local forms. For example, New York's initial state religion, the Dutch Reformed Church (Calvinist), was disestablished when England supplanted the Netherlands as the governing authority. The "Duke's Laws" of 1664 (named after James, duke of York, brother of King Charles II of England, to whom Charles II granted the Dutch Colony) required each township in New York to support a Protestant church, electing to a pastorate a minister preferred by local residents. Over the next seventy years, this system of multiple local establishments evolved into a system where several religions could be established within a single township where different faiths existed. A system of dual establishments existed in Massachusetts where a struggle between Anglicans and Congregationalists resulted in a 1727 exemption—"An Act for the Ease of such as soberly dissent"—that relieved Anglicans from facing jail if they did not pay for Congregationalist churches and ministers.

The "wall of separation" imagery that has come to figure prominently in modern-day American debates over establishment was first used at this time by Roger Williams (1604?–1683). Williams, a dissenting, crusading minister who was expelled from Massachusetts in 1636 and who eventually participated in founding Rhode Island, warned in 1644: "[when Christians] have opened a gap in the hedge

SELECTION FROM THE DUKE OF YORK'S LAWS, 1665–1675

Church

Whereas the publique Worship of God is much discredited for want of painful & able Ministers to Instruct the people in the true Religion and for want of Convenient places Capable to receive any Number of Assembly of people in a decent manner for Celebrating Gods holy Ordinances These ensueing Lawes are to be observed in every parish (Viz.)

1. That in each Parish within this Government a church be built in the most Convenient part thereof, Capable to receive and accommodate two Hundred Persons.

2. That For the making and proportioning the Leview and Assessments for building and repairing the Churches, Provision for the poor, maintenance for the Minister; as well as for the more orderly managing of all Parochiall affairs in other Cases exprest, Eight of the most able Men of each Parish be by the Major part of the Householders of the said Parish Chosen to be Overseers out of which Number the Constable and the aforesaid Eight Overseers shall yearly make choice of two of the said number, to be Church wardens and in case of the Death of any of the said Overseers and Church wardens; or his or their departure out of the parish The said Constable and Overseers shall make Choice of another to Supply his Room.

3. Every Overseer is to take the Oath of Allegiance at the time of his Admittance into his office in the Presence of the Minister Overseers and Constable of the parish, besides the Oath of his Office.

4. To prevent Scandalous and Ignorant pretenders to the Ministry from intruding themselves as Teachers; No Minister shall be Admitted to Officiate, within the Government but such as shall produce Testimonials to the Governour, that he hath Received Ordination either from some Protestant Bishop, or Minister within some part of his Majesties Dominions or the Dominions of any foreign Prince of the Reformed Religion, upon which Testimony the Governour shall induce the said Minister into the parish that shall make presentation of him, as duely Elected by the Major part of the Inhabitants [the word "freeholders" here occurs in Roslyn copy] housholders.

5. That the Minister of every Parish shall Preach constantly every Sunday, and shall also pray for the Kinge, Queene, Duke of Yorke, and the Royall family. And every person affronting or disturbing any Congregation on the Lords Day and on such publique days of fast and Thanksgiving as are appointed to be observed. After the presentments thereof by the Church wardens to the Sessions and due Conviction thereof he shall be punished by fine or Imprisonment according to the merit and Nature of the offence, And every Minister shall also Publiquely Administer the Sacrament of the Lord's Supper once every Year at the lleast in his Parish Church not denying the private benifit thereof to Persons that for want of health shall require the same in their houses, under the penalty of Loss of preferment unless the Minister be restrained in point of Conscience.

6. No Minister shall refuse the Sacrament of Baptism to the Children of Christian parents when they shall be tendered under penalty of loss of preferment.

7. Ministers are to Marry Persons after Legal publication of Sufficient Lycence.

8. Legal publication shall be so esteemed when the persons to be Married are three Several Days asked in the Church, or have a Special Licence.

9. Sundays are not to be prophaned by Travellers Labourers or vicious Persons.

(cont.)

SELECTION FROM THE DUKE OF YORK'S LAWS, 1665–1675 (cont.)

10. That no Congregations shall be disturbed in their private meetings in the time of prayer preaching or other divine Service Nor shall any person be molested fined or Imprisoned for differing in Judgment in matters of Religion who profess Christianity.

11. No Person of Scandalous or vicious Life, shall be Admitted to the holy Sacrament, who hath not given Satisfaction therein to the Minister.

Source: "Excerpts from the Duke of York's Laws, 1665–1675."
Retrieved November 6, 2002, from:
http://www.lihistory.com/vault/hs320b1v.htm

or wall of separation between the garden of the Church and the wilderness of the world, God hath ever broke down the wall itself, removed the candlesticks, etc., and made his garden a wilderness, as at this day."

Religion in the Declaration of Independence, the Constitution, and the Bill of Rights

The Declaration of Independence (1776) contains four theistic references: "nature's God" and "creator" in the first two paragraphs, and "supreme judge of the world" and "divine providence" in the concluding paragraphs. By contrast, the delegates to the Philadelphia Convention who drafted the U.S. Constitution hardly considered religion at all. South Carolina delegate Charles Pinckney's proposal that "no religious test or qualification shall ever be annexed to any oath of office under the authority of the U.S." was adopted, then revised by the Committee on Style, as Article VI of the Constitution. Other than this provision banning religious test oaths, the 1787 Constitution of the United States makes no mention of God or religion.

Ratification of the Philadelphia Constitution was debated in the states between September 1787 and September 1788. Many of those opposed to ratifying the work of the Philadelphia Convention agreed with Virginian George Mason's wish that the new constitution "had been prefaced with a Bill of Rights." Nevertheless, just which specific rights ought to be included in such a listing was not made clear during the constitutional ratification debates.

Vague allusions to religious liberty, and a general assumption that the new national government would have no authority to legislate regarding religion, provided few precise guidelines with which to define church–state relations. The meaning of "establishment" was rendered no more definitive by the four-month (June–September 1789) congressional debate of Representative James Madison's proposed amendment during the First Congress, or by the state ratification debates that followed congressional adoption of the establishment clause. Consequently, the ten short words that became part of the U.S. Constitution in 1791 as part of the First Amendment—"Congress shall make no law respecting an establishment of religion"—are the point of departure for controversies over church–state relations, not the end of them. Thomas Jefferson's assertion, in his 1802 letter to the Connecticut Committee of the Danbury Baptist Association, that the First Amendment's religion clauses built "a wall of separation between Church and State" only added fuel to these controversies.

Struggling to Define "Establishment"

The establishment clause, like the rest of the Bill of Rights, originally applied only to the national government. Its explicit language states that "Congress shall make no law. . . ." It was not until 1947, when the U.S. Supreme Court in *Everson v. Board of Education*, interpreted the Fourteenth Amendment (1868) due process clause as "incorporating" (i.e., including) the establishment clause, thereby apply-

THE FIRST AMENDMENT TO THE U.S. CONSTITUTION

Congress shall make no law respecting an establishment of religion, or prohibiting the free exercise thereof; or abridging the freedom of speech, or of the press; or the right of the people peaceably to assemble, and to petition the Government for a redress of grievances.

ing it to the states, that the Court increasingly chose to become involved in church–state controversies, most of which arise in states and localities. Prior to *Everson*, the Court had upheld congressional appropriations to a Roman Catholic hospital for indigent care (*Bradfield v. Roberts* 1899), and to Roman Catholic schools that held tribal funds in trust to pay tuition for Sioux Indian children (*Quick Bear v. Leupp* 1908).

Between *Everson* and the Court's decision in *Lemon v. Kurtzman* (1971), the justices struggled to interpret the establishment clause coherently and to devise logical criteria that could be applied consistently to a variety of controversies. There were seven major establishment clause cases from 1947 to 1968. The prevailing pattern was that the Court, under Chief Justices Vinson and Warren, was more inclined to accommodate modest public aid to religious schools and religious education than to tolerate prayer or creationism in public schools, where the justices required strict separation. In general, the Warren Court adopted a "purpose and effect" test (*School District of Abington Township v. Schempp* 1963), even if the justices did not always employ that test to arrive at predictable outcomes.

Then, in 1971, assembling elements from two decades of precedent created in establishment clause decisions, the U.S. Supreme Court under Chief Justice Burger adopted a three-pronged test in *Lemon v. Kurtzman*: "First, the statute must have a secular legislative purpose; second, its principal or primary effect must be one that neither advances nor inhibits religion; finally, the statute must not foster 'an excessive entanglement with religion.'"

Many observers, including several Supreme Court Justices, consider the Court's establishment clause jurisprudence to be a failure. The *Lemon* test is faulted for providing no standard at all. It was made too pliable, hence adaptable to a range of specific circum-

stances, and too susceptible to manipulation by shifting coalitions of justices. The consequence is that its application has been "serpentine" (Foster and Leeson 1998 II: 56–59).

Fundamentally, the Court's failure is rooted in a dilemma. On the one hand, as Justice Wiley B. Rutledge wrote in *Everson*: "No provision of the Constitution is more closely tied to or given content by its generating history than the religious clause of the First Amendment." On the other hand, "[t]he specific historical record, rather than disclosing a coherent 'intent of the Framers,' suggests that those who influenced the framing of the First Amendment were animated by several distinct and sometimes conflicting goals" (Choper 1986, IV: 1650).

Present-Day Controversies

Twenty-two years after *Lemon*, concurring in *Lamb's Chapel v. Center Moriches Union Free School District* (1993), Justice Scalia complained "like some ghoul in a late-night horror movie that repeatedly sits up after being repeatedly killed and buried, *Lemon* stalks our establishment clause jurisprudence once again...." The Court has not abandoned its discredited *Lemon* doctrine because the justices have found the doctrine's very ambiguities convenient in the absence of any alternative standard on which a majority of them can agree.

Since 1992 (*Lee v. Weisman*), the Court has disposed of establishment clause controversies via shifting coalitions among the justices marshaled in the context of four categories of church–state controversy: government aid to parochial schools by such means as vouchers, various aspects of religion in public schools (e.g., evolution v. creationism), public holiday displays containing religious symbols (such as crèches), and prayer in public schools. In these shifting coalitions the justices have tended to array themselves between two poles: accommodation of religion and strict separation. The difference between these two poles can be illustrated in terms of Roger Williams's and Thomas Jefferson's shared imagery of a "wall of separation." Justices embracing accommodation either reject the metaphor per se, or find no constitutional problems reconciling the "garden of the Church" with "the wilderness of the world." In contrast, justices espousing strict separation seek to buttress the constitutional wall and are wary of any statutory breaches.

While espousing freedom of religion, the United States has historically been a nation whose culture and power structures have been Protestant dominated. Thus a story from the Christian Gospels might usefully illustrate the complex relationship between religion and the state. The Pharisees, Judaic priests described in the Gospels as among Christ's opponents, sought to "entangle" him in a verbal trap, by asking: "Tell us, then, what you think. Is it lawful to pay taxes to Caesar, or not?" Aware that his answer could put him in jeopardy by seeming either impious or treasonous, Christ asked to be shown a coin bearing Caesar's likeness and replied: "Render . . . to Caesar the things which are Caesar's, and to God the things that are God's" (Matt. 22:15–22; KJV; see also Luke 19–26). Although quite likely as aware as Christ was of the verbal trap, neither the justices of the Supreme Court nor the American people have found it easy to implement the principle that Christ so eloquently articulated.

James C. Foster

See also Establishment, Equal Treatment

Further Reading

Berns, W. (1977). Religion and the founding principle. In R. Horwitz (Ed.), *The moral foundations of the American republic*. Charlottesville: University Press of Virginia.

Choper, J. H. (1986). Separation of church and state. In L. Levy, K. Karst, & D. Mahoney (Eds.), *Encyclopedia of the American Constitution* (Vols. 1–4). New York: Macmillan.

Choper, J. H. (1995). *Securing religious liberty: Principles for judicial interpretation of the religion clauses.* Chicago: University of Chicago Press.

Corwin, E. S. (1949). The Supreme Court as national school board. *Law and Contemporary Problems, 14,* 3–22.

Curry, T. J. (1986). *The first freedoms: Church and state in America to the passage of the First Amendment.* New York: Oxford University Press.

Dackson, W. (1999). Richard Hooker and American religious liberty. *Journal of Church and State, 41,* 117.

Dreisbach, D. L. (1997). Sowing useful truths and principles: The Danbury Baptists, Thomas Jefferson, and the wall of separation. *Journal of Church and State, 39*(3), 455–501.

Foster, J. C., & Leeson, S. M. (1998). *Constitutional law: Cases in context* (Vol. 2, pp. 40–114). Upper Saddle River, NJ: Prentice Hall.

Gianella, D. A. (1967). Religious liberty, nonestablishment, and doctrinal development. *Harvard Law Review, 80,* 1381–1431.

Gianella, D. A. (1971). Lemon and Tilton: The bitter and the sweet of church-state entanglement. *Supreme Court Review, 147,* 192.

Howe, M. D. (1965). *The garden and the wilderness: Religion and government in American constitutional history.* Chicago: University of Chicago Press.

Kurland, P. B. (1962). *Religion and the law of church and state and the Supreme Court.* Chicago: Aldine.

Levy, L. (1994). *The establishment clause: Religion and the First Amendment* (2nd rev. ed.). Chapel Hill: University of North Carolina Press.

Pfeffer, L. (1951). Church and state: Something less than separation. *University of Chicago Law Review, 19,* 101.

Smith, R. (1993). Conscience, coercion, and the establishment of religion: The beginning of the end to the wandering of a wayward judiciary? *Case Western Law Review, 43,* 917.

Straughan, G. (2002, October). *The Supreme Court, religious liberty, and parochial schools: From bus transportation to school vouchers.* Paper presented to the Annual Meeting of the Pacific Northwest Political Science Association, Bellevue, WA.

Van Alstyne, W. W. (1963) Constitutional separation of church and state: The quest for a coherent position. *American Political Science Review, 57,* 865.

Court Cases

Bradfield v. Roberts, 175 U.S. 291 (1899).

Everson v. Board of Education, 330 U.S. 1 (1947).

Lamb's Chapel v. Center Moriches Union Free School District, 508 U.S. 384 (1993).

Lee v. Weisman, 505 U.S. 577 (1992).

Lemon v. Kurtzman, 403 U.S. 602 (1971).

Quick Bear v. Leupp, 210 U.S. 50 (1908).

School District of Abington Township v. Schempp, 374 U.S. 203 (1963).

European Convention on Human Rights

The European Convention on Human Rights (1950) protects the right to religious freedom. Article 9 sets out the right in two parts. The first section guarantees "freedom of thought, conscience and religion." It is clear from this that the right is not confined to religion. In fact, as worded, the Convention treats freedom of religion as a derivative of freedom of thought and conscience. As such, the right is as relevant to atheists and agnostics as it is to followers of a given religion. The right militates against the imposition of religion on any person: Every person has the right to "change his religion or belief either alone or in community with others" and to be able "to manifest his religion or belief, in worship, teaching, practice and observance." This right is drawn almost verbatim from Article 18 of the Universal Declaration of Human Rights (1947).

The second section of Article 9 then restricts the first part by permitting the state to make such restrictions "as are prescribed by law and are necessary in a democratic society." These limitations have to be "in the interest of public safety, for the protection of public order, health or morals, or for the protection of the rights and freedoms of others." It is noteworthy that the 1947 Declaration did not restrict the right in any way, although other international human-rights instruments of the postwar period have.

The preamble to the Convention describes the rights specified therein as "fundamental freedoms which are the foundation of justice and peace in the world." Indeed, rights pertaining to freedom of conscience, such as to believe or not to believe, are the oldest of the internationally recognized human rights, going back at least to the Peace of Westphalia of 1648. The international community has had the longest experience of these rights. The preamble to the Convention suggests that under the European Convention rights of conscience are truly fundamental and subject to limitations only in extreme cases.

The Council of Europe is the most advanced international body working for the protection of human rights in the world today. It has the best enforcement machinery. There is an individual right to petition to the European Court of Human Rights in Strasbourg, where the European Convention is applied. Applications used to be made first to the European Commission of Human Rights, which would find the case admissible before forwarding it to the European Court. The procedure is first to determine whether a specific right stipulated in the Convention has been abridged by a government, then to consider whether the challenged governmental action is justifiable under the circumstances. If no specific right is shown to have been abridged, the case is dismissed.

European institutions have been diffident in matters of religious discrimination up to the last decade of the twentieth century. No doubt this is in part because many of Europe's wars in previous centuries were religious. Newly emerging democratic institutions in Europe after World War II were more concerned with promoting secular rights. Since its inception in 1955, the European Commission has received more than twenty thousand petitions involving rights of conscience. In only forty-five cases has the Commission published decisions in which an Article 9 challenge was raised, and in only five of those cases did the court rule the challenge admissible. The European Commission has declared every petition brought by a conscientious objector to be inadmissible, whether protesting against military conscription, corporal punishment in state schools, or compulsory insurance taxes. Of the five cases the Court ruled to be admissible, three were later found not to present Article 9 violations. Of the remaining two cases, only in one did the Court find there to be a violation of Article 9. That case was *Kokkinakis v. Greece* (1993). It was the first European Court decision to consider freedom-of-conscience rights under Article 9, the first to have found a governmental breach of such rights, and the first decision to offer a detailed critique of the limitations that a state may impose upon such rights. The decision paved the way for other cases to be considered by the Court.

Kokkinakis was a Jehovah's Witness who was prosecuted and convicted in 1986 under a Greek law against proselytizing. He had already been arrested more than sixty times for proselytizing in Greece and had spent more than five and half years in jail. The

Court's ruling upholding his rights is in some ways the finest exposition of the legal and philosophical basis of religious-rights law. It held that freedom of thought, conscience, and religion were fundamental to a democratic society, important for believers, but also for atheists, agnostics, and those who are uninterested in religion. Further, it held that pluralism itself depended on those freedoms. The Court's statement reconciled religious faith with democratic value. The implication of the statement is that the rights of religious believers can be truly protected only when atheists have the right not to believe, and vice versa. Religionists and secularists ignore this at their peril.

Satvinder S. Juss

Further Reading

Council of Europe. (1950). European Convention of Human Rights. Retrieved December 26, 2002, from http://www.hri.org/docs/ECHR50.html#Convention

Harris, D. J., Boyle, M., & Warbrick, C. (1995). *Law of the European convention on human rights*. London: Butterworths.

Janis, M., Kay, R., & Bradley, A. (1995). *European human rights law, texts and materials*. Oxford, UK: Clarendon Press.

Court Case

Kokkinakis v. Greece, 260-A Eur. Ct. H.R. (ser. A) 18, 36 (June 24, 1993).

Falun Gong

Li Hongzhi (b.1951), a provincial army clerk, introduced Falun Gong to the People's Republic of China (PRC) with a speaking tour in 1992 and the publication in 1994 of his book, *China Falun Gong*. Falun Gong combines elements of Buddhism and Daoism with the traditional Chinese exercise tradition known as *Qi Gong*. *Qi Gong*, like acupuncture, is rooted in the indigenous Chinese idea that the human body consists of energy, or *qi*, which affects both physical and spiritual health. While the *Qi Gong* tradition claims a 7,000-year history in China, it was officially banned by the PRC during the Cultural Revolution until it was legalized in 1979, when it was determined to be a traditional physical exercise devoid of spiritual values. *Qi Gong* practice traditionally required years to master the slow, stylized movements thought to increase the quality of energy flowing through the body thereby improving both health and longevity. Li Hongzhi claims that his Falun Gong practice effectively circumvents the traditional long training and results in immediate and profound results that include supernatural capabilities as well as improved physical health.

Li Hongzhi first introduced Falun Gong to commoners but eventually the grassroots movement began to attract members of the Communist Party and high-ranking government officials. The group grew phenomenally throughout the 1990s, eventually drawing positive attention and endorsement from the state-controlled media. Then, on 25 April 1999, with absolutely no advance notice, over ten thousand Falun Gong practitioners encircled Zhongnan Hai, the home of PRC leadership in Beijing, in silent peaceful protest. The protesters wanted to file a complaint about a recent article in a state-sponsored magazine that contained a slanderous attack on Falun Gong. Ten years after the Tiananmen Square protest the PRC leadership was shocked that a massive protest could have been organized without having attracted the attention of its intelligence service.

A few months later, on 22 July 1999, the State Council officially banned Falun Gong, labeling it an "evil cult." This was followed by legislation banning "evil cults" passed by the Standing Committee of the National People's Congress on 30 October 1999. In the months that followed, several other official government actions were taken in an effort to exert social control over the Falun Gong spiritual movement and to garner support in the international arena. Falun Gong practitioners insist they have no political motivations and despite the penalty of imprisonment in labor camps, have continued to publicly protest for an end to the ban. Intense international publicity campaigns have been waged, with Falun Gong citing widespread human rights violations and the PRC insisting that Falun Gong is an evil cult with political aspirations. Because of the tight control of the press in the PRC, independent confirmation has been difficult to establish. International human rights organizations have verified that thousands of people have been sent to labor camps and estimates of deaths range from dozens to two hundred.

Craig Burgdoff

Further Reading

Edelman, B., & Richardson, J. T. (2002). Falun Gong and the law: Development of legal social control in China. *Nova religio: The Journal of Alternative and Emergent Religions 5*(2), 213–224.

Li, H. (1999). *China Falun Gong.* New York: Universe Publishing Company.

Lowe, S. (2001). China and new religious movements. *Nova religio: The Journal of Alternative and Emergent Religions, 4*(2), 213–224.

Schechter, D. (2000). *Falun Gong's challenge to China: Spiritual practice or "evil cult"?* New York: Akashic Books.

Yang, J.-M. (1997). *The root of Chinese qigong: Secrets for health, longevity, and enlightenment.* Roslindale, MA: YMAA Publication Center.

Family, The

The Family is a contemporary religious group that grew out of the 1960s Jesus Movement. Originally named the Children of God, the movement was founded by Moses David Berg (Father David) in 1968. Berg led the movement until his death in 1994. At present the Family is active in over one hundred nations. A total of just under ten thousand full-time Family members live in "homes" of no more than a few dozen members each. The movement also claims about three thousand affiliated members who do not reside in homes and another thirty thousand sympathetic supporters of its ministry. Well over half of the movement membership currently is second-generation young adults.

History

Moses David Berg was born David Brandt Berg in 1919 to a family of evangelists and became a minister in the Christian and Missionary Alliance denomination in 1948. In 1944 he married Jane Miller, and the couple bore four children. He clashed with denominational leaders over his advocacy of racial integration and redistribution of wealth and in 1951 was relieved of pastoral duties. Until 1968 Berg worked as an independent evangelist. He and his children then formed an evangelistic team and ran a coffeehouse in Huntington Beach, California, that ministered to disaffected youth. His apocalyptic message rejecting a corrupt world and its churches ("Churchianity") produced a flow of youthful converts. When opposition to his ministry mounted from families of converts, the group moved several times. At this juncture Berg also announced the end of his marriage and a new relationship with Maria, a young disciple. In 1970 Berg moved to Europe, and by the end of 1971 most of the membership had left America. Berg lived in seclusion for the remainder of his life, communicating with his followers through written messages.

Beliefs and Organization

Family theology draws heavily on the Fundamentalist Christian tradition. Traditional precepts include belief in the Trinity, virgin birth, salvation through faith, and the Bible as God's inspired Word. Theologically The Family is unconventional in its assertions that Father David is the End Times prophet and that spiritual revelations are an ongoing source of God's guidance. Socially the movement is

Moses David Berg (1919–1994), the Founder of The Family. COURTESY OF THE FAMILY AND DAVID G. BROMLEY.

distinguished by its communal lifestyle and its rejection of the secular world, conventional churches, and a materialistic lifestyle. The most controversial aspect of The Family was the movement's belief that sharing and demonstrating the power of God's love is the highest divine priority and the implementation of that precept by sharing sexual love inside and outside of the movement. This tenet is based on the biblical verse in Matthew, "Follow me, and I will make you fishers of men." This evolved into "flirty fishing," in which sexuality was used to recruit members. The practice spread through the movement after 1978 and was accompanied by a general sexual libertarianism that in some cases involved sexual relationships between adults and teens or younger children. These practices were ended in 1987 as a result of opposition inside and outside the movement and the AIDS epidemic.

The Family is communal and has experienced a number of reorganizations in an effort to create an organizational structure that produced a balance of integration and independence, autonomy and discipline. Berg developed the "Mo Letters" as a means of communicating spiritual messages to his disciples, guiding his followers, and administering the movement. Following Berg's death, Maria assumed movement leadership; the following year she married Peter Amsterdam, a longtime Berg disciple. The movement retains its distance from conventional society through endogamous marriage, homeschooling of children, renting homes rather than owning property, financing itself largely through donations from sympathetic outsiders ("provisioning") and sale of literature, and allocating members' time to evangelistic activity.

Controversies

The Family has been embroiled in controversy through its history. Conservative Christians assail The Family on theological grounds, particularly over Berg's standing within the movement as the End Times prophet, his prophetic revelations, and his legitimation of sexual sharing. Secular opposition to the movement has centered on its recruiting and sexual practices. Organized resistance to the movement quickly escalated in the early 1970s on the part of families who contested conversions of their offspring. These families banded together to create the first anticult organization, Free Our Children from the Children of God (FREECOG). There was a wave of physical abduction and "deprogramming" of members who anti-cultists contended had been subjected to cultic brainwashing ("programming"). Deprogrammings dwindled as most members migrated to Europe, and anti-cultists began targeting other groups.

The most serious legal problems for the movement occurred in the 1990s and resulted from the period of sexual experimentation prior to 1987. Movement apostates influenced governments in a number of countries to take action against Family members. In 1990 a Family home in Barcelona, Spain, was raided and two dozen children were held by authorities for almost one year. In the court hearing The Family was exonerated, and the presiding judge characterized government actions as resembling the Inquisition. A year later police and social workers entered Family homes in Melbourne and Sydney, Australia, and took children into custody. The children were released and no charges were filed in either case. There were armed police raids on homes in Lyon and Marseilles, France, in 1993. Again, no charges were filed at the conclusion of those investigations. In September 1993, homes in Buenos Aires, Argentina, were raided by heavily armed police. Adults and over one hundred children were taken into custody. After extensive physical and psychological examinations of the children, charges were dismissed.

The pivotal legal case occurred in England in 1993 when the grandmother of a Family member sought legal custody of her grandson. The judge in the case thoroughly investigated Family beliefs and activities based on allegations of sexual abuse. Although the judge awarded the mother custody over the grandmother, he also required an open admission by Family leaders that some of its earlier policies and practices had been harmful to children. The Family also was required to attribute these harmful elements of its lifestyle to Berg and his teachings. The Family followed up on the court decision by creating a "Ministry of Reconciliation" through which it acknowledged past abuses and sought to reestablish relationships with disaffected former members.

David G. Bromley

See also Brainwashing

Further Reading

Bainbridge, W. S. (2002). *The endtime Family*. Albany: State University of New York Press.

Chancellor, J. (2000). *Life in the Family*. Syracuse, NY: University of Syracuse Press.

Davis, D. (1984). *The children of God*. Grand Rapids, MI: Zondervan.

Lewis, J. R., & Melton, J. G. (Eds.). (1994). *Sex, slander, and salvation*. Stanford, CA: Center for Academic Publication.

Melton, J. G. (2001). *The Family/the Children of God*. Salt Lake City, UT: Signature Books.

Van Zandt, D. (1991). *Living with the Children of God*. Princeton, NJ: Princeton University Press.

First Amendment *See* Establishment, Equal Treatment; Establishment, Separation of Church and State; Free Exercise Clause; Free Speech Clause

Fourteenth Amendment

When the Constitution was written and ratified in the late eighteenth century, it was clear that the establishment clause and free exercise clause, in fact all of the Bill of Rights, applied only to the federal government and not to the states. Thus the states were free to legislate on religious matters, have their own religious tests for holding public office, and favor or disfavor various religions within their borders. Given that the original thirteen states entered the federal union with some nervousness, jealously guarding their accustomed autonomy, no other arrangement was possible. All of this changed, however, in 1868 with the passage of the Fourteenth Amendment.

Incorporation

Section One of the Fourteenth Amendment, in pertinent part, provides: "No State shall make or enforce any law which shall abridge the privileges and immunities of citizens of the United States; nor shall any State deprive any person of life, liberty, or property, without due process of law; nor deny to any person within its jurisdiction the equal protection of the laws."

The Supreme Court, in a series of cases decided in the twentieth century, held that most, though not all, of the Bill of Rights is binding on the states as a result of the Fourteenth Amendment. This process of "selec-

tive incorporation" began in 1925, in *Gitlow v. New York*, when the Supreme Court recognized that the free speech and press guarantees of the First Amendment are "fundamental rights and liberties protected by the due process clause of the Fourteenth Amendment from impairment by the states." In its ruling, however, the court offered no significant historical analysis of either the First Amendment or the Fourteenth Amendment, or their relationship to each other.

The religion clauses of the First Amendment were subsequently embraced by the Supreme Court's incorporation doctrine. In *Cantwell v. Connecticut* (1940), the court invalidated a Connecticut statute requiring a license to be obtained before religious groups could solicit funds door-to-door. The Court's basis for the holding was that the free exercise clause is applicable to the states: "The fundamental concept of liberty embodied in the [Fourteenth] Amendment embraces the liberties guaranteed by the First Amendment." The *Cantwell* case was monumental in its effects. Because the free exercise clause was now binding on the states, it would usher in a new era of federal court jurisdiction over religion in America. As in *Gitlow*, however, the court offered no analysis of why the incorporation doctrine was applicable.

Seven years later, in *Everson v. Board of Education* (1947) the court extended the incorporation principle to the establishment clause, again without providing a historical or legal rationale for applying the doctrine. Later that year, however, Justice Hugo Black, in a dissenting opinion in *Adamson v. California* (1947), gave an extended exposition of the history of the Fourteenth Amendment, concluding that one of the chief objects of the Fourteenth Amendment "was to make the Bill of Rights applicable to the states," thereby casting the protective net of the first eight amendments around persons who were threatened by state action. To support his position, Justice Black appended a thirty-three-page summary of the congressional debates leading to the ratification of the amendment in 1868, quoting chiefly the speeches of its primary author, Republican Representative John Bingham of Ohio. Although the Court majority rejected Black's view that the Fourteenth Amendment incorporates all of the first eight of the Bill of Rights, it reaffirmed its allegiance to "selective incorporation." The Court majority, affirming past decisions, understandably did not root its decision in the intentions of the framers of the Fourteenth Amendment, but rather in the principles of "justice" and "ordered liberty." In other words, as Justice Benjamin Cardozo

SELECTION FROM LETTER FROM JAMES MADISON TO THOMAS JEFFERSON, 6 SEPTEMBER 1787.

The Convention consists now as it has generally done of Eleven States. There has been no intermission of its Sessions since a house was formed; except an interval of about ten days allowed a Committee appointed to detail the general propositions agreed on in the House. The term of its dissolution cannot be more than one or two weeks distant. A Govermt. will probably be submitted to the people of the states consisting of a President cloathed with executive power, a Senate chosen by the Legislatures: and another house chosen by the people of the states jointly possessing the legislative power and a regular judiciary establishment. The mode of constituting the executive is among the few points not yet finally settled. The Senate will consist of two members from each state and appointed sexennially: The other, of members appointed biennially by the people of the states in proportion to their number. The Legislative power will extend to taxation trade and sundry other general matters. The powers of Congress will be distributed according to their nature among the several departments. The States will be restricted from paper money and in a few other instances. These are the outlines. The extent of them may perhaps surprize you. I hazard an opinion nevertheless that the plan should it be adopted will neither effectually answer its national object nor prevent the local mischiefs which every where excite disgusts agst the state governments. The grounds of this opinion will be the subject of a future letter.

Julian P. Boyd, ed.

Source: "Madison to Jefferson, 6 September 1787."
The Papers of Thomas Jefferson, vol. 24.
(Princeton, NJ: Princeton University Press, 1950–1973) 102.

had stated it in an earlier case (*Palko v. Connecticut* [1925]), certain portions of the Bill of Rights had been absorbed in the Fourteenth Amendment on the basis "that neither liberty nor justice would exist if they were sacrificed."

Whether the Bill of Rights applied as much to the states as to the federal government was a question that could arise only because of the existence of the Fourteenth Amendment. Before its ratification in 1868, there was nothing in the Constitution that could prevent a state from executing religious heretics, from refusing to grant a criminal defendant a trial by jury, or from conducting a frivolous search of one's home. The Bill of Rights was originally added to the Constitution to appease popular fears by restricting the powers of the new federal government; it was not intended to apply to the states. This understanding was clearly affirmed in *Barron v. Baltimore* (1833), where Chief Justice John Marshall held: "Had Congress engaged in the extraordinary occupation of improving the Constitutions of the several states by affording the people additional protection for the exercise of power by their own governments in matters which concerned themselves alone, they would have declared this purpose in plain and intelligible language."

Thus, any restraints on the states derived from state constitutions and common law practices, not from the U.S. Constitution. The point of Justice Black's historical analysis in Adamson was that the first section of the Fourteenth Amendment transformed that situation by embracing the Bill of Rights, thereby nationalizing its requirements: What the national government could not do, the various states could not do.

But is this really what the framers of the Fourteenth Amendment intended? This remains an open and heavily debated question. Although dozens of books and hundreds of articles have been written

James Madison (1751–1836), Fourth President of the United States, by David Edwin in Philadelphia between 1809 and 1817. COURTESY OF LIBRARY OF CONGRESS, PRINTS AND PHOTOGRAPHS DIVISION.

on the subject, scholars still line up on both sides of the debate. From one side, it is reasonable to hold that the Fourteenth Amendment's framers intended to overrule *Barron v. Baltimore* and make the Bill of Rights applicable to the states. After all, John Bingham, who authored Section 1 of the amendment, repeatedly said that the amendment would overrule the *Barron* case. Indeed, Bingham said this no less than thirteen times

in one day during House arguments. Bingham's testimony is the most compelling evidence for incorporation, but clearly there were other leading figures in the House and Senate who shared the same view, and many of the day's leading newspapers and magazines reported a similar understanding.

This view comports with the plain meaning of the words of the amendment as well as the broader historical context. The southern states, before and during the Civil War, had violated most all of the Bill of Rights in their maintenance of slavery. The whole idea of the Fourteenth Amendment was to end the abuse of blacks, to be achieved by requiring that blacks, as well as all other persons, were entitled to the most fundamental catalog of rights and freedoms: the Bill of Rights. This is the broader historical context.

But from another side this view can be challenged. Many of the members of the Thirty-Ninth Congress expressed views that were contrary to Bingham's. Senator Lyman Trumbull, chairman of the Senate Judiciary Committee, held that "the great fundamental rights set forth in this Bill [are] the right to acquire property, the right to come and go at pleasure, the right to enforce rights in the courts, and to make contracts," rights that are not specifically named in the Bill of Rights. And indeed the Supreme Court adopted the view (until *Gitlow* in 1925) that the Fourteenth Amendment was intended to protect a very limited category of rights.

Thus the problem does not offer a simple solution. The original intentions of the framers of the Fourteenth Amendment, much like the original intent of so many provisions of the Constitution, are often elusive, to say the least. When the constitutional text is unclear, most experts would agree that the task of judges and scholars is to determine, as best they can, how the people of the states who ratified the document understood the text. Nevertheless, in the case of the Fourteenth Amendment, this task is an especially difficult one because, as Supreme Court Justice John Harlan noted in a dissenting opinion in *Reynolds v. Sims* (1964): "Reports of the debates in the state legislature on the ratification of the Fourteenth Amendment are not generally available." Indeed, a complete record of the ratification proceedings is available from only one state, Pennsylvania.

So, left without clarity of what either the Thirty-Ninth Congress or the state ratifying conventions meant, where do we turn? If we examine the broader historical context, we discover considerable evidence that the Fourteenth Amendment was a conscious attempt to "complete" a Constitution that had been "incomplete" from the beginning.

"Completing" the Constitution

The Supreme Court's decision to make the Bill of Rights binding on the states makes sense if examined from the perspective of the "Father of the Constitution," James Madison. As is well known, Madison was the architect of the main outlines and chief principles of the Constitution. The Convention of 1787 did not accept everything he proposed, and he accepted his rejected ideas gracefully. But while many of Madison's ideas were preserved in the Constitution, he was particularly concerned about one missing element: the failure of the Constitution to grant Congress a power to veto any law made by a state. As a student of history, Madison believed that all previous federal unions had failed because the member states tended to encroach on the powers of the central government or on the power of the other member states. He contended that a veto power would allow the Congress, acting as a caring agent of all member states, to review all state legislation. He failed in his efforts to convince his colleagues of the wisdom of this provision, however. Without this element, he informed his friend Thomas Jefferson by letter, the Union would not last very long. Presciently, Madison saw the states regularly oppressing minorities, and felt the veto power would enable Congress to promote justice and stability within the states, ultimately protecting the states from themselves.

True to Madison's fears, the Union did not last long. The Civil War is perhaps the best evidence that Madison had properly diagnosed the Constitution's main weakness: its inability to control the states. The southern states had abused the rights of the slave minority, denying them all manner of rights, even the status of citizens, an atrocity sanctioned by the *Dred Scott* case in 1857. Pure and simple, black people had no rights that whites were legally obligated to respect.

These abuses were the result of an incomplete Constitution. For Madison, a congressional veto power over state legislation was to supply a way in which that principle was to be made effective in the states. Congress would have the ability, to be exercised only if necessary, to force the states to respect the basic rights of all persons to life, liberty, and the pursuit of happiness as provided in the Declaration of Independence—rights believed to be embodied in the Bill of Rights. It should also be noted that, after the Constitution was adopted by the states, in proposing the First Amendment at the First Congress Madison urged its extension to the states (i.e., incorporation) because "the State governments are as liable to attack these invaluable privileges as the General Government is, and therefore ought to be cautiously guarded against" (*Annals of Congress* 1834, 441). This proposal, however, like his proposal for a

135

congressional veto power over state legislation, failed, since the majority of his colleagues believed that they should "leave the State Governments to themselves" (*Annals of Congress* 1834, 755). His "incorporation" proposal comes much closer to matching the Thirty-Ninth Congress's remedy for limiting the states' power, although for Madison it was probably less vital than a congressional veto power over state legislation.

Seen in this broader perspective, the Fourteenth Amendment's framers were seeking merely to complete the Constitution along the lines envisioned by Madison. The mechanism was not quite the same—making binding on the states the Bill of Rights rather than simply giving to Congress a veto power over state enactments—but the result was essentially the same: the states must respect the basic rights of all human beings. *Barron v. Baltimore* perpetuated the incompleteness of the Constitution; the Fourteenth Amendment completed it.

Religious Liberty Implications

Religious liberty in the United States is closely linked to the incorporation of the establishment and free exercise clauses, thus making them binding on the states. While state and local governments are not to be automatically distrusted in the advancement of religious liberty, time has proven that parochial attitudes often develop that are insensitive to the religious conscience of some citizens. Our system does not eliminate state sovereignty on all matters of religion, but on the major questions, such as the right of public school teachers to lead their classes in prayer or the right to display religious symbols on government property, good policy dictates that the Supreme Court establish and uphold uniform laws that are binding on all Americans. In so doing the court helps Americans to live out the motto, E Pluribus Unum (Out of Many, One), which accords with the intent of the framers of the Fourteenth Amendment, whose paramount goal was a united citizenry whose common and equal rights would be respected.

Derek H. Davis

Further Reading

Annals of Congress (1834). (Vol. 1). Washington, DC: Gales and Seaton.

Berger, R. (1989). *The Fourteenth Amendment and the Bill of Rights*. Norman: University of Oklahoma Press.

Berger, R. (1987). *Government by Judiciary: The Transformation of the Fourteenth Amendment* (2nd ed.). Indianapolis, IN: Liberty Fund, Inc.

Bickel, A. (1982). *The Least Dangerous Branch*. Indianapolis, IN: Bobbs-Merrill.

Bork, R. H. (1986, February). Original intent and the Constitution. *Humanities 7*, 26–38.

Boyd, J. P. (Ed.). (1950–1973). *The Papers of Thomas Jefferson*. Princeton, NJ: Princeton University Press.

Brennan, W. J. (1986). The Constitution of the United States: Contemporary ratification. *South Texas Law Review 27*, 433–435.

Curtis, M. K. (1986). *No state shall abridge: The 14th Amendment and the Bill of Rights*. Durham, NC: Duke University Press.

Ely, J. H. (1980.) *Democracy and distrust: A theory of judicial review*. Cambridge, MA: Harvard University Press.

Farrand, M. (1966). *The Records of the Federal Convention of 1787*. New Haven, CT: Yale University Press.

Nelson, W. E. (1988). *The Fourteenth Amendment: From political principle to judicial doctrine*. Cambridge, MA: Harvard University Press.

Zuckert, M. P. (1992, Spring). Completing the Constitution: The Fourteenth Amendment and Constitutional rights. *Publius: The Journal of Federalism 22*, 76–88.

Court Cases

Adamson v. California, 332 U.S. 46 (1947).

Barron v. Baltimore, 32 U.S. 243 (1833).

Cantwell v. Connecticut, 310 U.S. 296 (1940).

Dred Scott v. Sandford, 60 U.S. 393 (1857).

Everson v. Board of Education, 330 U.S. 1 (1947).

Gitlow v. New York, 268 U.S. 652 (1925).

Palko v. Connecticut, 302 U.S. 319 (1925).

Reynolds v. Sims, 377 U.S. 533 (1964).

Free Exercise Clause

The free exercise clause of the First Amendment of the U.S. constitution states that "Congress shall make no law . . . prohibiting the free exercise [of religion]." As the reference to Congress makes clear, this clause—like the First Amendment generally—was originally designed to constrain the federal government alone. Since the 1940s, however, the Supreme Court has extended the free exercise clause to state governments as well (including their local subdivisions, such as cities and counties). According to the Court, the Fourteenth Amendment's due-process clause ("No State shall . . . deprive any person of life, liberty, or property, without due process of law"), which was adopted after the Civil War, was intended to accomplish this result.

Freedom of Belief and Profession

The Supreme Court has consistently held that freedom of religious *belief* is absolutely protected by the free exercise clause and that this protection extends to disbelief as well. Thus, the government is categorically precluded from mandating, prohibiting, or regulating religious or irreligious beliefs as such. In *Torcaso v. Watkins* (1961), for example, the Supreme Court invalidated a religious oath requirement for state office holders, thereby reading the free exercise clause to mirror Article 6 of the original Constitution, which explicitly bans such religious tests, but only for federal offices. "[N]either a State nor the Federal Government," wrote the Court, "can constitutionally force a person 'to profess a belief or disbelief in any religion.'" As *Torcaso* suggests, the free exercise clause protects not only the right to hold religious or irreligious beliefs, but also the right to state them publicly or, conversely, to refuse to do so.

Needless to say, religious liberty would be impoverished if it did not protect religious belief, religious disbelief, and the profession or denial of either. Yet freedom of belief, however fundamental, is rarely an issue as a practical matter, and the First Amendment independently protects freedom of speech, including religious and irreligious speech. As a result, the free exercise clause would be largely redundant if it did no more than protect religious and irreligious belief and speech. Even so, the Supreme Court in early cases suggested that the clause indeed does nothing more and that, in particular, it provides no protection for religious conduct (other than speech). Thus, in *Reynolds v. United States* (1879), the Court held that the free exercise clause did not protect the Mormon practice of polygamy. "Laws are made for the government of actions," the Court wrote, "and while they cannot interfere with mere religious belief and opinions, they may with practices," lest "every citizen . . . become a law unto himself." According to *Reynolds*, citizens have the right to *believe* in a religious practice such as polygamy, and they have the freedom to express their opinion through speech. Yet they are not free to act on their belief by actually engaging in the religious conduct.

Freedom of Religious Conduct

In later cases, the Supreme Court rejected the narrow approach of *Reynolds* and interpreted the free exercise clause to protect religious conduct (including not only affirmative acts, but also religiously motivated abstentions), thereby granting individuals the freedom not only to decide what they *should* do religiously, but also to do it. To qualify as the exercise of religion within the scope of the clause, the conduct must, at a minimum, be sincerely motivated by religious beliefs. Curiously enough, however, the Supreme Court has never provided a definitive constitutional definition of the beliefs that qualify as religious for this purpose. Such beliefs at least include beliefs derived from conventional, theistic religion, such as a Biblically informed commitment to the Sabbath. Although the Court's doctrine is unclear, religious beliefs may also include a broader set of moral convictions, including, for example, nontheistic but conscientious objection to military service. In any event, the claimant must be sincere in two respects: He or she must sincerely accept the religious belief as true or genuine and, in addition, it must be that belief—and not secular self-interest, for example—that actually motivates the conduct in question.

The Supreme Court has never suggested that the protection of religious exercise in the form of conduct is absolute, and for good reason; imagine, for example, the act of religiously motivated human sacrifice. Instead, the Court has indicated that the regulation of religious conduct is presumptively unconstitutional, at least in certain circumstances, making it invalid unless it serves an important governmental interest. The Court sometimes has stated that "substantial burdens" on the exercise of religion trigger "strict scrutiny," a strong form of presumptive invalidity that permits a law to survive only if it is "necessary" to serve a "compelling" governmental interest. Whatever the precise nature of the Court's analysis, it involves a balancing of competing interests, weighing the presumptively protected, religious-liberty interest of individuals against the government's interest in controlling their behavior.

Prior to *Employment Division v. Smith* (1990), the Supreme Court's free exercise doctrine protected religious conduct not only from laws that targeted religious conduct for discriminatory treatment, but also

137

from nondiscriminatory, neutral laws of general applicability. If the government could not justify the application of a nondiscriminatory law to religious conduct, an exemption from the law was constitutionally required. This analysis extended not only to laws that directly burdened religious conduct by making it illegal, but also to laws that imposed more indirect burdens, burdens that discouraged religious conduct by making it difficult or costly.

In *Sherbert v. Verner* (1963), for instance, South Carolina law made unemployment compensation available only to those who would accept Saturday employment. The Court granted a free-exercise exemption to a Saturday Sabbatarian, ruling that the Saturday work condition could not be applied to her. The Court noted that the burden that the law imposed on the Sabbatarian might properly be described as indirect; it did not make her religious practice illegal. But the law nonetheless exerted "unmistakable" pressure on the exercise of religion by forcing the Sabbatarian "to choose between following the precepts of her religion and forfeiting benefits, on the one hand, and abandoning one of the precepts of her religion in order to accept work, on the other hand." The state argued that it had a compelling interest in avoiding fraudulent religious claims, but the Court ruled that the state's argument did not justify precluding all claims for religious exemptions, including those that were undeniably sincere.

In *Wisconsin v. Yoder* (1972), the Court addressed a generally applicable, compulsory-education law that, as applied, imposed a direct burden on religious conduct. The Wisconsin law required parents to send their children to school until the age of sixteeen. Old Order Amish, however, could not follow the law after their children completed elementary school (eighth grade) without abandoning a religious obligation: protecting their children from the worldly influences of high school. As the Court noted, the law's impact on the Amish parents' religious exercise was "not only severe, but inescapable," because it "affirmatively compell[ed] them, under threat of criminal sanction, to perform acts undeniably at odds with fundamental tenets of their religious beliefs." As in *Sherbert*, the Court invoked a form of strict scrutiny, stating that "only those interests of the highest order and those not otherwise served can overbalance legitimate claims to the free exercise of religion." The Court recognized Wisconsin's strong interest in education, but it found that requiring Amish teenagers to attend one or two years of high

school would do little to serve that interest, especially since the Amish community itself provided an alternative form of education, including informal vocational training. Accordingly, the Court ruled that the Amish were entitled to an exemption from the law.

Throughout the 1970s and 1980s, the Supreme Court continued to apply the doctrinal approach of *Sherbert* and *Yoder*, although the Court's rejection of various free exercise claims suggested that the "strict scrutiny" standard of review was not as strongly protective as its language implied. In *United States v. Lee* (1982), for instance, the Court rejected an exemption sought by the Amish from the payment of social-security taxes, finding that the government's interest in a uniform tax system should prevail—even though the Amish had their own support system and were not claiming any social-security benefits. In addition, the Court adopted explicit exceptions to strict scrutiny for military and prison regulations, and it ruled that the free exercise clause did not limit the government's internal operations, including its use of government land, even if those operations had an adverse effect on religious practices, such as the use by Native Americans of sacred sites. Outside these exceptional areas, however, the Court continued to endorse a relatively demanding standard of review, and, indeed, it specifically reaffirmed *Sherbert* in several comparable cases, the last of them, as of 2003, decided in 1989.

The Limited Protection of Religious Conduct after 1990

Employment Division v. Smith (1990) marked a dramatic and controversial turn in judicial doctrine. In *Smith*, the Court was asked to recognize a free-exercise exemption for the sacramental use of an otherwise illegal drug, peyote, by members of the Native American Church. Not only did the Court refuse to do so, but, on a 5-to-4 vote, it also declined to apply the analysis that *Sherbert* and *Yoder* appeared to require. Although the Court purported to distinguish and preserve its particular holdings in those and similar cases, it renounced their doctrinal underpinnings. Thus, the Court declared that nondiscriminatory laws affecting religious conduct do not implicate the free exercise clause, do not require any type of special constitutional justification, and do not require religious exemptions. Quoting its century-old opinion in *Reynolds*, the Court suggested in *Smith* that to grant a religious exemption would be to permit the religious believer, "by virtue of his beliefs, 'to become a law unto himself.'" The Court especially objected to the prospect of balancing religious claims against competing state interests in a wide variety of possible contexts, a task for which, according to the Court, judges are not well suited.

Although more complex interpretations of the Court's doctrine are possible, *Smith* essentially reduced the free exercise clause to a prohibition on deliberate discrimination against religion. Accordingly, a burden on religious conduct no longer triggers presumptive constitutional protection unless the burden results from a law that targets that conduct for unequal treatment. At least as to conduct, the clause no longer protects religious freedom or voluntarism as an independent value. Instead, it ensures a type of formal religious equality. Indeed, under *Smith*, the free exercise clause is analogous to the Fourteenth Amendment's equal protection clause, which also guards against purposeful discrimination based on impermissible criteria.

Needless to say, *Smith* dramatically reduced the significance of the free exercise clause, because laws that purposefully discriminate against religion are rare. As became clear in *Church of the Lukumi Babalu Aye, Inc. v. City of Hialeah* (1993), however, such laws are not nonexistent. In *Lukumi*, the Supreme Court invalidated a series of ordinances that had been adopted by the City of Hialeah, Florida, in a transparent attempt to stop the establishment and spread of the Santeria religion, which practices animal sacrifice as a principal form of devotion. The ordinances effectively outlawed Santeria animal sacrifice even as they left other animal killings unaffected. "At a minimum," the Court wrote in *Lukumi*, "the protections of the Free Exercise Clause pertain if the law at issue discriminates against some or all religious beliefs or regulates or prohibits conduct because it is undertaken for religious reasons." Unlike, for example, a general ban on animal killing (which, under *Smith*, would raise no free exercise issue), the Hialeah ordinances specifically targeted Santeria religious exercise. As a result, they triggered presumptive constitutional protection requiring "the most rigorous of scrutiny," and they could not survive that review. More generally, the Court made it clear that laws discriminating against religious conduct are almost invariably unconstitutional.

Notwithstanding *Lukumi*, the Supreme Court's contemporary free exercise doctrine, focusing on discriminatory laws, offers far less protection than the doctrine that prevailed before *Smith*. Critics have urged state courts to follow pre-*Smith* doctrine as a matter of state constitutional law, and they also have pressed for legislative action, both in Congress and in the states, to adopt the pre-*Smith* approach in religious-liberty statutes. These efforts have had some success, but they raise constitutional issues of their own. Critics also hope that the Supreme Court someday will reconsider the doctrine of *Smith*, but there is no reason to believe that any major doctrinal change is in the offing.

Daniel O. Conkle

Further Reading

Choper, J. H. (1995). *Securing religious liberty: Principles for judicial interpretation of the religion clauses.* Chicago: University of Chicago Press.

Cookson, C. (2001). *Regulating religion: The courts and the free exercise clause.* New York: Oxford University Press.

Epps, G. (2001). *To an unknown God: Religious freedom on trial.* New York: St. Martin's Press.

Evans, B. N. (1997). *Interpreting the free exercise of religion: The constitution and American pluralism.* Chapel Hill: University of North Carolina Press.

McConnell, M. W. (1990). The origins and historical understanding of free exercise of religion. *Harvard Law Review, 103*(7), 1409–1517.

Noonan, J. T., Jr. (1998). *The lustre of our country: The American experience of religious freedom.* Berkeley and Los Angeles: University of California Press.

Smith, S. D. (1995). *Foreordained failure: The quest for a constitutional principle of religious freedom.* New York: Oxford University Press.

Witte, J., Jr. (2000). *Religion and the American constitutional experiment: Essential rights and liberties.* Boulder, CO: Westview Press.

Court Cases

Church of the Lukumi Babalu Aye, Inc. v. City of Hialeah, 508 U.S. 520 (1993).

Employment Division v. Smith, 494 U.S. 872 (1990).

Reynolds v. United States, 98 U.S. 145 (1879).

Sherbert v. Verner, 374 U.S. 398 (1963).

Torcaso v. Watkins, 367 U.S. 488 (1961).

United States v. Lee, 455 U.S. 252 (1982).

Wisconsin v. Yoder, 406 U.S. 205 (1972).

Free Speech Clause

It is hardly surprising that the First Amendment's guarantee of freedom of speech and press clearly encompasses religious expression. After all, a substantially larger share of what was spoken and written in colonial times dealt with religious matters than would be true in modern times. Preparing future members of the clergy was a primary mission not only of many private colleges, but even of those that were funded by the states; Thomas Jefferson's University of Virginia, founded in 1819, departed from that pattern and became the first purely secular institution with no divinity or theology program. Thus it would have been startling if the framers had created an explicit safeguard for "speech" in the Bill of Rights without intending to confer full protection on religious as well as secular speech.

Religious Speech and the Supreme Court

It was not until 1940, however, that the status of religious speech received any attention from the courts. Several Jehovah's Witnesses, members of the Cantwell family, had antagonized many citizens of New Haven, Connecticut, in the late 1930s with their strident attacks on Catholicism and other traditional faiths, and were charged with breach of the peace and incitement. Although the state courts saw ample evidence to sustain such charges, the Supreme Court unanimously reversed the convictions, in *Cantwell v. Connecticut* (1940). The Justices relied chiefly on the free exercise clause of the First Amendment, which for the first time in this case they held binding on the states through the due process clause of the Fourteenth Amendment. Yet the analysis the court applied to overturn these convictions seemed equally applicable to free speech claims, with which the Justices were more familiar: "[W]e find only an effort," wrote Justice Roberts, "to persuade a willing listener to buy a book or contribute money in the interest of what Cantwell . . . conceived to be true religion."

While the Cantwell case would undoubtedly have come out just as it did without any reliance on the free exercise clause, it offers the earliest evidence of the often parallel and mutually reinforcing roles of freedom of expression on one hand and religious liberty on the other. In that sense, proselytizers and other religious speakers, like the Cantwells, seem to enjoy a dual constitutional status, and in many such early cases that is indeed the situation. In recent years, however, the once seemingly simple and concordant relationship between speech and religion has become vastly more complex. It is no longer possible to know with certainty whether religious speech enjoys the same level of constitutional protection as secular expression, or greater or lesser protection. The answer depends heavily on the circumstances.

In the late 1980s a group of students at the University of Missouri–Kansas City wanted to

A religious gathering in Nashville, Tennessee, in 1936. *Ben Shahn*, COURTESY OF LIBRARY OF CONGRESS, PRINTS AND PHOTOGRAPHS DIVISION, FSA-OWI COLLECTION.

use campus meeting rooms for religious events. The administration refused their request because of the religious nature of the group and its program; Missouri is one of several states (including California and Washington) whose constitutions demand a greater separation of government and religion than the federal establishment clause requires. Implementing that principle, the university as a matter of policy denied use of its facilities even by on-campus religious groups. The students went to court and, after a rocky road through the federal system, got a resounding vindication in the U.S. Supreme Court (*Cantwell v. Connecticut* 1940).The Justices, ruling in favor of the student religious group's free speech claim, found that the university had created a "public forum" in its campus facilities and, once having done so, could not constitutionally exclude one subject matter or viewpoint—i.e., religion—from that forum. Religious groups had as clearly protected an expressive interest in equal access to those public facilities as did any secular organization. One justice recognized there might be legitimate concerns about abuse of such a right—recurrent and aggressive proselytizing, for example—but insisted the administration could meet any such need without categorically barring religious activities.

A decade and a half later the high court revisited the issue in a subtler and more difficult form. The University of Virginia, recalling Mr. Jefferson's secular sense of its mission, barred the use of mandatory student fee funds for support of religious (as well as partisan political) publications. A student religious group submitted a printer's bill for one issue of an avowedly Christian journal called *Wide Awake*. The administration refused to pay the bill, and the students went to federal court. A district judge sustained the university's position, finding that concern about breaching the "wall of separation" amply justified the denial of funds. The court of appeals went even further, holding that if funding had been provided for such a journal the university would have violated the First Amendment's Establishment Clause. The students then sought and obtained Supreme Court review.

The Justices were sharply split, but by a bare majority they held in the students' favor on free speech grounds. In *Rosenberger v. Rector and Board of Visitors* (1995) the majority ruled that the university's funding policy effectively singled out certain speech for disadvantageous treatment solely on the basis of its subject matter or content. Though there was legitimate concern that giving public funds to religious

journals could create establishment problems—the four dissenting justices agreed with the lower courts that it inevitably would—the majority found any such concern to have been "trumped" by the need for government to be evenhanded in its treatment of all messages.

The issue posed by the Rosenberger case is strikingly narrow. On one hand, everyone agreed that a state university could not constitutionally make a direct money grant to a student religious organization for any purpose. On the other hand, the university's desktop publishing equipment in the student union was clearly available to all groups; it would have been unthinkable—and patently unconstitutional—for access to be denied solely on the basis of a journal's subject matter. It was only the narrow issue of paying the printer's bill for *Wide Awake* that posed a problem. Yet the problem it did pose split the Supreme Court justices as sharply as any constitutional issue in recent years.

Not long after the Rosenberger case came down, a very different sort of religious speech issue was on its way to the high court. For most high schools in Texas, Friday-night football games generated almost religious fervor. In some communities a student would deliver a religious message, even a prayer, just before the game began. Though audience participation was nominally optional, some students felt that such a message carried effective endorsement by the school, and thus carried a coercive quality.

Eventually one such student sued the Santa Fe, Texas, school district, arguing that such a practice violated the establishment clause of the First Amendment. Strong support could be found for such a claim in several earlier cases. In 1990, the high court had held that public schools could not empower clergy to deliver benedictions and invocations at graduation ceremonies, since those who wished not to pray were "subtly coerced" by the very nature of the event and its importance to them and their families (*Lee v. Weisman* 1992). That ruling left open a host of difficult issues, which are still working their way through the courts—most notably whether an individual student valedictorian might include a religious message in her otherwise secular remarks.

Returning to Friday night football in Texas, the justices ruled decisively in June 2000 that the arrangement used in Santa Fe did indeed violate the establishment clause, as the objecting students had argued (*Santa Fe Independent School District v. Doe* 2000). Not only those students who had to listen—

the teams, bands, ushers, and many others—but even those attending simply as spectators could not constitutionally be enlisted in such an unmistakably religious moment at an extremely significant public event. It was not only the importance of the event itself, but also the way in which the student speaker was chosen, and the school administration's role in that selection process, that moved the majority to place Friday-night football prayers in the same constitutional category as Saturday- or Sunday-morning graduation invocations.

This time the roles of the constitutional safeguards were effectively the reverse of those in *Rosenberger*. There free speech seemed resoundingly to have trumped religious freedom. Now the free speech claim appeared to be the loser; indeed, the three dissenting justices in the Santa Fe case argued that the majority had improperly equated private student speech (clearly protected under the First Amendment, in their view) with government speech (which they agreed ought not be used to convey a religious message). The contrast between these two major Supreme Court decisions highlights the extreme uncertainty of a relationship—between free speech and religious freedom—which seemed so clear and simple a half century ago. Religious speech is, of course, First Amendment speech quite as much as expression on other subjects. Government may not discriminate against a particular speaker or a message simply because the subject is religion. Yet religious messages may at times be different, and if they may properly be attributed to government, or if the circumstances of their utterance impose coercive pressure upon reluctant listeners, then an otherwise dispositive free speech claim may yield to a concern for religious liberty and neutrality.

Other Instances of Religious Speech

Several other intriguing situations involving religious speech have made their way through the lower courts, but have not yet reached (and in fact probably will not reach) the Supreme Court. Occasionally a parishioner will take umbrage at a personally derogatory or accusatory statement made by a member of the clergy, and may seek legal redress. If the statement occurred in a sermon, or in an official church or temple publication, the clergy defendant may seek to persuade the court that ordinary secular principles of libel law cannot comfortably be applied to such a case. The court would, in other words, effectively need to probe principles of religious law in order to determine whether, in context, an accusation is defamatory. If the case arises between members of the clergy, one of whom feels unfairly accused by another, the risk of going beyond ordinary secular legal principles is magnified. For a century and a quarter, the Supreme Court has made clear that civil courts should avoid deciding such matters, and should leave religious disputes for the most part to religious institutions. In some such cases, therefore, courts have abstained from pursuing libel claims that would be fair game under virtually any other conditions.

A quite different problem may arise if a member of a religious community has been "shunned" by neighbors and co-worshipers. Several suits have been brought by Amish persons, for whom such a severe sanction means not only ostracism, but effectively forecloses commercial and economic ties as well, and may imperil a family's livelihood. Courts have divided, not surprisingly, in the few such reported cases. Some courts have felt that civil judges ought not to interfere in so centrally religious a sanction, while others have focused instead on the secular consequences of a status that may indeed have deeply religious roots and implications.

In yet another set of split decisions, civil courts a decade or so ago wrestled with issues of "deprogramming" or liberation of young people who had come under the spell of a cult. Here again the split in results is understandable. For some courts, the arguably religious nature of the cult or community poses no insuperable barrier to the intervention of a civil judge, or the issuance of the kind of order that would release any person unwillingly held captive by another. Yet there have been cult cases in which civil judges have felt constrained by the doctrinal and quasi-theological implications of any inquiry into the relationship between cult and member, even before reaching the question of remedies.

Finally, the whole issue of civil litigation against clergy and religious bodies was vastly complicated by the crisis of the spring and summer of 2002 within the Roman Catholic Church. While most such issues do not centrally implicate speech or expression, some of the earlier cases had sought to fashion and apply a doctrine of "clergy malpractice" against what was claimed to have been negligent or even venal pastoral counseling. In such cases, long before the current crisis, courts were sharply torn between concern for aggrieved victims who sought legal redress on one hand, and on the other hand the hazards of fashioning a judicial standard of "appropriate counseling," which might diverge sharply from the church's tradition and policy. Recent events have made civil courts understandably more receptive to such claims for relief, and less deferential than they would have been even a year earlier to pleas by religious bodies for abstention and self-determination.

What seemed a clear and simple answer when the Cantwells railed at Catholics on the streets of New Haven has now become bewilderingly complex and uncertain. Perhaps the most that can be said with confidence is that both the free exercise clause and the free speech clause do indeed protect religious expression, just as the framers of the Bill of Rights surely intended. That there are times and situations when freedom of expression and religious neutrality are not in perfect harmony seems an inevitable result of the evolution of both major elements of the Bill of Rights. Jefferson and Madison might, indeed, well have warned later generations of such difficulties.

Robert M. O'Neil

See also Establishment, Equal Treatment; Establishment, Separation of Church and State; Fourteenth Amendment; Jehovah's Witnesses: United States

Further Reading

Choper, J. H. (1995). *Securing religious liberty: Principles for judicial interpretation of the religion clauses.* Chicago: University of Chicago Press.

Cordes, M. W. (2000, Summer). Politics, religion, and the first amendment. *DePaul Law Review, 50,* 111.

Dreisbach, D. L. (1986). *Real threat and mere shadow: Religious liberty and the First Amendment.* Wheaton, IL: Crossway Books.

Laycock, D. (1986). Equal access and moments of silence: The equal status of religious speech by private speakers. *Northwestern Law Review, 81,* 1.

McCarthy, M. (2001). Preserving the establishment clause: One step forward and two steps back. *Brigham Young Education and Law Journal, 271.*

Miller, W. (1986). *The first liberty: Religion and the First Amendment.* New York: Knopf.

Court Cases

Cantwell v. Connecticut, 310 U.S. 296 (1940).
Lee v. Weisman, 505 U.S. 577 (1992).
Rosenberger v. Rector and Board of Visitors, 515 U.S. 819 (1995).
Santa Fe Independent School Dist. v. Doe, 530 U.S. 271 (2000).

Freedom of Conscience

The mythology of religion in the United States begins long before its independence, with the image of Puritans leaving England in search of greater freedom to worship not as they chose, but as their consciences required. This notion of a person (or community of people) feeling forced to choose between the laws of society and what he or she understands to be a mandate from God is at the heart of the notion of freedom of conscience. The *Oxford English Dictionary* defines conscience as "inward knowledge" and a "consciousness of right and wrong." It notes that "opinions as to the nature, function, and authority of conscience are widely divergent, varying from the conception of the mere exercise of the ordinary judgement on moral questions, to that of an infallible guide of conduct, a sort of deity within us."

In the United States the notion of conscience took on specifically more theistic dimensions and initially was directly related to concepts of religion. In the same year that the Declaration of Independence was penned in Philadelphia, the Virginia Declaration of Rights (ratified on 12 June 1776) defined religion as "the duty which we owe to our Creator and the manner of discharging it" and declared that "all men are equally entitled to the free exercise of religion, according to the dictates of conscience" (Article 16). As sociologist of religion Phillip Hammond concludes, "probably most Americans at the time [of the ratification of the U.S. Constitution], including those who wrote and voted on the First Amendment, imagined most 'consciences' to be Christian and saw the 'free exercise' provision as a guarantee that people could express their Christianity in whatever manner they wanted" (Hammond 1998, 39).

Freedom of Conscience in the Early Republic

What would become the First Amendment to the U.S. Constitution began as a statement protecting individual conscience. Even before the Constitution was ratified, delegates at the various state conventions were making suggestions about the language they would want inserted into a bill of rights to be appended to it. For example, in late June 1788 citizens from New Hampshire suggested the following: "Congress shall make no laws touching religion, or to infringe the rights of conscience" (quoted in Witte 2000, 64). Within two months, Virginia, New York, North Carolina, and Rhode Island had proposed similar amendments.

When Congress debated amendments to the Constitution (between early June and late September, 1789), the language of conscience was prominent among the proposals. On 8 June James Madison (1751–1836) proposed two religion amendments to the House of Representatives: "The civil rights of none shall be abridged on account of religious belief or worship, nor shall any national religion be established, nor shall the full and equal rights of conscience be in any manner, or any pretext infringed" and "No state shall violate the equal rights of conscience, or the freedom of the press, or the trial by jury in criminal cases" (quoted in Witte 2000, 65).

When the House passed on to the Senate its version of a Bill of Rights in late August, the text still retained the notion of conscience: "Congress shall make no law establishing religion, or prohibiting the free exercise thereof, nor shall the rights of conscience be infringed" (quoted in Witte 2000, 71).

The Senate removed the language of conscience, and on 24 September 1789, the committee of House and Senate members appointed to iron out the differences finally agreed upon what was to become the First Amendment: "Congress shall make no law respecting an establishment of religion, or prohibiting the free exercise thereof."

Freedom of Conscience and the States

The fact that Congress had removed specific mention of conscience from the U.S. Constitution did not adversely affect the states and their decision to retain such a notion in their own state constitutions. As historian John K. Wilson notes, ten of the states had had colonial charters that mentioned religion, and all ten contained guarantees for liberty of conscience. After the American Revolution, "every substantial state constitution written during the period 1776–1800 (and there were nineteen) includes a protection of religious freedom" (Wilson 1990, 761). Many were similar to that found in the North Carolina constitution: "That all men have a natural and unalienable

right to worship Almighty God according to the dictates of their own consciences ... all persons shall be at liberty to exercise their own mode of worship" (Constitution of North Carolina 1777: Declaration of Rights, Article XIX; Constitution, Article XXXIV).

However, such rhetoric was often misleading. As Wilson describes it, rights in these early states were often limited in some way: to Christians (in Delaware before 1792, and in New Hampshire), Protestants (in New Jersey and Vermont), Christians and Jews (in South Carolina), or believers in God (in Pennsylvania). In addition, elected officials were often required to swear oaths that, by virtue of containing specifically Protestant or even generally Christian statements of faith, excluded a variety of religious believers.

Although the situation improved over the course of the nineteenth century, the record for protecting freedom of religious conscience is rather dismal. In the 1845 *Permoli v. First Municipality of New Orleans* decision, the U.S. Supreme Court had strictly interpreted the U.S. Constitution to apply the First Amendment religious-liberty protections only to congressional action, thereby leaving most questions involving religious rights to the states to resolve. Consequently, as the political scientist Frank Way describes it, in the early years of the century, state courts around the country regularly ruled against those who violated community (meaning primarily Protestant) standards of religious behavior. They criminalized blasphemy while permitting Sabbath closing restrictions, and prayer and Bible reading in public schools, thereby limiting deviance from well-established practice. Things did not improve until the end of the century, when immigration and a natural increase in religious diversity made a single religious position difficult to maintain.

Freedom of Conscience and the U.S. Supreme Court

On the federal level, in its early years the U.S. Supreme Court ruled several times on matters that involved the rights of conscience, but its record was not particularly encouraging for those who felt compelled to perform some activity because they believed God required it of them. One of the earliest cases involving a religious believer being refused the right to exercise his freedom of conscience was also one of the most important, for it established the standards by which many of the cases since then have

SELECTION FROM *EMPLOYMENT DIVISION, DEPARTMENT OF HUMAN RESOURCES OF OREGON, ET AL. V. SMITH ET AL.* SUPREME COURT OF THE UNITED STATES 494 U.S. 872.

Our decisions reveal that the latter reading is the correct one. We have never held that an individual's religious beliefs excuse him from compliance with an otherwise valid law prohibiting conduct that the State is free to regulate. . . . The mere possession of religious convictions which contradict the relevant concerns of a political society does not relieve the citizen from the discharge of political responsibilities. We first had occasion to assert that principle in *Reynolds* v. *United States*, 98 U.S. 145 (1879), where we rejected the claim that criminal laws against polygamy could not be constitutionally applied to those whose religion commanded the practice. "Laws," we said, "are made for the government of actions, and while they cannot interfere with mere religious belief and opinions, they may with practices. . . . Can a man excuse his practices to the contrary because of his religious belief? To permit this would be to make the professed doctrines of religious belief superior to the law of the land, and in effect to permit every citizen to become a law unto himself. . . ."

been decided. In the 1879 *Reynolds v. United States* decision, the Supreme Court ruled that a Mormon man could believe whatever he wished, but he could not act on those beliefs—in this case, the belief in plural marriage (polygamy). The Court cited Thomas Jefferson's Act for Establishing Religious Freedom (passed in Virginia in 1786), which said that although government could not control the minds of its citizens, for the purposes of civic order, it had a duty to control their actions. In the eyes of the justices on the Court, the Mormon practice of plural marriage was not only contrary to basic Christian principles, it was a threat to society as well.

The distinction between one's beliefs and one's actions enabled the Court to approach cases involving claims for freedom of conscience with greater direction. With the ability to separate action from belief, the Supreme Court could justify limitations on actions it considered threatening. In *United States v. Macintosh* (1931), and again in *Hamilton v. Regents of the University of California* (1934), the Court ruled against men raising conscientious religious objections to participating in military training or duty. It would not be until 1940, when the Supreme Court—under the authority of the Fourteenth Amendment—applied the First Amendment to state as well as federal action—that the rights of individual religious conscience would be more successfully protected. Several important decisions illustrate the evolution of the protection of these rights. The first, *Cantwell v. Connecticut* (1940), involved Jehovah's Witnesses who

were charged with disturbing the peace and soliciting without a license when they preached on a city street corner. The Supreme Court ruled that the Jehovah's Witnesses could not be required to get the approval of a municipal official, who might deny them a license to preach just because he did not like what they had to say. The Jehovah's Witnesses, who preached because they felt God required it of them, had the right to preach as their consciences required.

In *West Virginia State Board of Education v. Barnette* (1943), the Supreme Court ruled that Jehovah's Witness students had the right to abstain from participating in the school's morning flag salute ceremony. Three years earlier, in *Minersville School District v. Gobitis*, the Supreme Court had ruled that, for the sake of national unity, schools had the right to punish students who did not participate in the same ritual, regardless of the religious objections raised by the Jehovah's Witness students and their parents. In 1943, in what many regard as a reversal of *Gobitis*, the Supreme Court reasoned that national unity and patriotism could not be coerced successfully, and that the Jehovah's Witness schoolchildren had a constitutionally protected right not to participate. In effect, the decision protected not their right to free speech, but their right to silence in the face of government expectations.

Just one year later, in *United States v. Ballard*, a case involving claims of mail fraud, the Supreme Court ruled that the content of a person's religious beliefs was not subject to the approval of the legal system. The Court was faced with an appeal over jury instructions in a case involving a man who, with several family members, claimed to be able to heal people through the mail. In the original case, the jury was instructed to disregard the seemingly strange beliefs expressed by the three people involved. These instructions were challenged, and eventually the Supreme Court decided that, while the actions of those involved in the case could be subject to scrutiny, their beliefs could not be. As the Court noted in its decision, "Men may believe what they cannot prove" (*United States v. Ballard* [1944]).

Based on these precedents, by the early 1960s the Supreme Court was expanding its understanding of what was eligible for protection in cases involving claims of religious conscience. In the 1961 *Torcaso v. Watkins* decision, which involved an atheist man who was not allowed to take a state government job because he would not take an oath that contained a statement of belief in God, the Supreme Court ruled that the protection of the rights of conscience was not necessarily limited to those claiming a belief in a deity. Two years later, in *Sherbert v. Verner*, the Court rejected the "action versus belief" doctrine it had established in the *Reynolds* decision: It ruled that a Seventh-day Adventist woman who refused to work on her Sabbath (and as a result was fired and denied unemployment benefits) could not be forced to choose to act or not act on her beliefs. Her actions were required by conscience because of her beliefs. By the end of the 1960s, the Court had expanded its understanding of the rights of conscience even further, ruling in *United States v. Seeger* (1965) and *Welsh v. United States* (1970) that men could be classified as conscientious objectors and thus excused from military service even if they lacked traditional religious training or a traditional belief in God.

Freedom of Conscience in the Supreme Court Today

Regardless of the trajectory of these few important cases, it would be inaccurate to say that the Supreme Court always ruled in favor of the protection of freedom of conscience. For example, in 1961 the Court ruled in *Braunfeld v. Brown* that observant Jewish merchants were still required to obey Sunday closing laws even if it created a financial burden due to the religious prohibition of working on Saturday, the Jewish Sabbath. Ten years later, the court's decision in *Gillette v. United States*, that a man could not claim

conscientious-objector status even if he believed that the Vietnam War was unjust based on his interpretation of Catholic doctrine, seemed to contradict *Seeger* and *Welsh*. In 1977, in a decision that limited its ruling in *Sherbert*, the Court decided in *Trans World Airlines v. Hardison* case that employers could avoid responsibility for firing workers who raised religious objections if they made a reasonable effort to accommodate those objections. In the 1986 *Goldman v. Weinberger* decision, the Supreme Court ruled that an observant Jewish officer who violated the military dress code by wearing a skullcap—which is required for Orthodox Jewish men—could be disciplined. That same year, the Court ruled in *Bowen v. Roy* that, regardless of the religious objections raised by her parents, a child could be assigned a Social Security number by the federal government. A year later, in 1987, the Court ruled in *O'Lone v. Estate of Shabazz* that prison officials did not have to accommodate all the demands of prisoners seeking religious exemptions.

The most significant recent ruling, as of 2001, in the line of decisions on freedom of conscience is the 1990 decision in *Oregon Employment Division v. Smith*. The case involved two members of the Native American Church who were fired for using peyote (a cactus derivative with hallucinogenic properties that the church considers to be a sacramental substance) and subsequently denied unemployment benefits. First, the Court concluded that in its history it had never permitted religious claims to overrule generally applicable laws if the religious activity in question was illegal. Second, in any case not involving claims for unemployment benefits, the religious claim had always been coupled with some other claim for constitutional protection (like a claim for the protection of the right to free speech). Third, the Court noted that as long as the law was enacted by a duly empowered democratic institution (like a state legislature) and was generally applicable, the only recourse a religious community might have would be through the democratic process.

The significance of this decision cannot be underestimated. It returned the "action versus belief" distinction first articulated in the *Reynolds* decision; religious believers were once again in the position of being told that they might believe what they wished, but that limitations on how they act based on those religious beliefs could be established by the legislature. The protections of the *Sherbert* decision—including the requirement that legislatures prove a compelling need to limit actions based on religious conscience, as well as the requirement that they prove that there was no other less restrictive alternative to that limitation—were removed by *Oregon Employment Division v. Smith*. After the *Smith* decision, legislatures need only pass laws that are generally applicable, even if those laws have the effect of limiting the ability of a particular religious community to act on its beliefs.

Congress attempted to reverse the impact of the *Smith* decision with the Religious Freedom Restoration Act, which it passed in 1993. This act sought to return the standards of religious freedom to those established in the *Sherbert* decision. However, the Supreme Court ruled in 1997 that Congress had overstepped its authority, and reaffirmed the limits it had established in *Smith*. As of 2003, the limits on the protection of religious freedom, and therefore the limits on freedom of conscience, are dictated by the Court's statement in the *Smith* decision.

The Future of Freedom of Conscience?

It is possible that the future of freedom of conscience will not rest on the Court's rulings on religion. In 1990 and 1995, the Court ruled in favor of greater religious freedoms by citing the free-speech aspects of the religious claims in question. The scholar Phillip Hammond has identified other areas of the law—particularly cases involving abortion, euthanasia, and gay rights—as potential areas from which greater freedoms of conscience are to emerge. His argument—that religion is the language of conscience, and not the opposite—turns on its head the traditional view of conscience as rooted in religious worldviews, and makes possible the expansion of freedom of conscience into areas not necessarily limited to religion.

Eric Michael Mazur

See also Free Exercise Clause; Jehovah's Witnesses: United States; Virginia Declaration of Rights

Further Reading

Constitution of North Carolina (1776). Retrieved November 15, 2002, from the Avalon Law Project at http://www.yale.edu/lawweb/avalon/states/nc07.htm#b1

Flowers, R. B. (1994). *That godless court? Supreme Court decisions on church-state relationships*. Louisville, KY: Westminster John Knox Press.

Hammond, P. E. (1998). *With liberty for all: Freedom of religion in the United States*. Louisville, KY: Westminster John Knox Press.

Handy, R. T. (1984). *A Christian America: Protestant hopes and historical realities* (2nd ed.). New York: Oxford University Press.

Way, H. F. (1987). Death of the Christian nation: The judiciary and church-state relations. *Journal of Church and State, 29*(3), 509–529.

Wilson, J. K. (1990). Religion under state constitutions, 1776–1800. *Journal of Church and State, 32*(4), 753–773.

Witte, J. Jr. (2000). *Religion and the American constitutional experiment: Essential rights and liberties*. Boulder, CO: Westview Press.

Court Cases

Bowen v. Roy, 476 U.S. 693 (1986).

Braunfeld v. Brown, 366 U.S. 599 (1961).

Cantwell v. Connecticut, 310 U.S. 296 (1940).

Employment Division v. Smith, 494 U.S. 872 (1990).

Gillette v. United States, 401 U.S. 437 (1971).

Goldman v. Weinberger, 475 U.S. 503 (1986).

Hamilton v. Regents of the University of California, 293 U.S. 245 (1934).

Minersville School District v. Gobitis, 310 U.S. 586 (1940).

O'Lone v. Estate of Shabazz, 482 U.S. 342 (1987).

Permoli v. First Municipality of New Orleans, 44 U.S. 589 (1845).

Reynolds v. United States, 98 U.S. 145 (1879).

Sherbert v. Verner, 374 U.S. 398 (1963).

Torcaso v. Watkins, 367 U.S. 488 (1961).

Trans World Airlines v. Hardison, 432 U.S. 63 (1977).

United States v. Ballard, 322 U.S. 78 (1944).

United States v. Macintosh, 283 U.S. 605 (1931).

United States v. Seeger, 380 U.S. 163 (1965).

Welsh v. United States, 398 U.S. 333 (1970).

West Virginia State Board of Education v. Barnette, 319 U.S. 624 (1943).

French Colonies in North America

At its height in the mid-eighteenth century, the French colonial empire in North America stretched in a great arc from the Gulf of St. Lawrence to the Great Lakes, down the Mississippi River to the Gulf of Mexico and out into the islands of the Lesser Antilles. As was the

SELECTION FROM THE QUEBEC ACT, 1774

The Quebec Act of 1774 played a major role in keeping French Canada loyal to England. However, when many English Protestants settled there after the American Revolution, the Act of 1791 limited French liberties and ultimately produced the French/British conflicts in Canada. The following paragraphs pertain to religious freedoms granted to the French Roman Catholics.

"V. And, for the more perfect Security and Ease of the Minds of the Inhabitants of the said Province," it is hereby declared, That his Majesty's Subjects, professing the Religion of the Church of Rome of and in the said Province of Quebec. may have, hold, and enjoy, the free Exercise of the Religion of the Church of Rome, subject to the King's Supremacy, declared and established by an Act, made in the first Year of the Reign of Queen Elizabeth, over all the Dominions and Countries which then did, or thereafter should belong, to the Imperial Crown of this Realm; and that the Clergy of the said Church may hold, receive, and enjoy, their accustomed Dues and Rights, with respect to such Persons only as shall profess the said Religion.

"VI. Provided nevertheless, That it shall be lawful for his Majesty. his Heirs or Successors, to make such Provision out of the rest of the said accustomed Dues and Rights, for the Encouragement of the Protestant Religion, and for the Maintenance and Support of a Protestant Clergy within the said Province, as he or they shall. from Time to Time think necessary and expedient.

"VII Provided always. and be it enacted, That no Person professing the Religion of the Church of Rome, and residing in the said Province, shall be obliged to take the Oath required by the said Statute passed in the first Year of the Reign of Queen Elizabeth, or any other Oaths substituted by any other Act in the Place thereof; but that every such Person who, by the said Statute, is required to take the Oath therein mentioned, shall be obliged, and is hereby required, to take and subscribe the following Oath before the Governor, or such other Person in such Court of Record as his Majesty shall appoint, who are hereby authorized to administer the same; *videlicet*,

"I A.B. do sincerely promise and swear, That I will be faithful, and bear true Allegiance to his Majesty King George, and him will defend to the utmost of my Power, against all traitorous Conspiracies, and Attempts whatsoever, which shall be made against his Person, Crown, and Dignity; and I will do my utmost Endeavor to disclose and make known to his Majesty, his Heirs and Successors, all Treasons, and traitorous Conspiracies, and Attempts, which I shall know to be against him, or any of them; and all this I do swear without any Equivocation, mental Evasion, or secret Reservation, and renouncing all Pardons and Dispensations from any Power or Person whomsoever to the contrary. So help me GOD."

And every such Person, who shall neglect or refuse to take the said Oath before mentioned, shall incur and be liable to the same Penalties, Forfeitures, Disabilities, and Incapacities, as he would have incurred and been liable to for neglecting or refusing to take the Oath required by the said Statute passed in the first Year of the Reign of Queen Elizabeth.

"VIII. And be it further enacted by the Authority aforesaid, That all his Majesty's Canadian Subjects within the Province of Quebec. the religious orders and Communities only excepted. may also hold and enjoy their Property and Possessions, together with all Customs and Usages relative thereto, and all other their Civil Rights, in as large, ample, and beneficial Manner. IS if the said Proclamation, Commissions, Ordinances, and other Acts and Instruments. had not been made, and as may consist with their Allegiance to his Majesty, and Subjection to the Crown and Parliament of Great Britain; and that in all Matters of Controversy, relative to Property and Civil Rights, Resort shall be had to the Laws of Canada, as the Rule for the Decision of the same; and all Causes that shall hereafter be instituted in any of the Courts of Justice, to be appointed within and for the said Province by his Majesty, his Heirs and Successors. shall, with respect to such Property and Rights, be determined agreeably to the said Laws and Customs of Canada, until they shall be varied or altered by any Ordinances that shall. from Time to Time, be passed in the said Province by the Governor, Lieutenant Governor, or Commander in Chief, for the Time being, by and with the Advice and Consent of the Legislative Council of the same, to be appointed in Manner herein-after mentioned.

Source: *Statutes at Large*, xxx, 550.
14 George III, c. 83 (UK).

case with other European colonial powers, France used civil legislation to enforce the religious conformity of the colonists, and justified its occupation of this vast territory in part by promoting the evangelization of its native peoples. Thus issues of religious establishment and the toleration of dissent were caught up in the larger problems of political unity, nationalist competition, and colonial exploitation.

The First Colonies

French claims to an American empire originated with the explorations of Jacques Cartier (1491–1557), who attempted to establish a colony on the banks of the St. Lawrence River in the early 1540s. Two deadly winters there quelled colonial aspirations for a while, but the cause was renewed by Gaspard de Coligny (1519–1572), King Henry II's (1519–1559) chief minister and a Huguenot (French Calvinist), who was driven in part by his desire to establish a sanctuary for his coreligionists. Efforts to found Huguenot colonies in Brazil (1555–1560) and Florida (1564–1565), however, foundered on Portuguese and Spanish hostility toward encroachment by French "heretics" into areas they had previously claimed. Following the destruction of these colonies, the French turned their attention again toward the less inviting regions surrounding the Gulf of St. Lawrence.

During this period of false starts, France itself was convulsed by dynastic rivalries and religious conflicts between Protestants and Catholics. With the infamous St. Bartholomew's Day Massacre of 24 August 1572, a royally sanctioned war of extermination began against the Huguenots. Coligny was killed and the country was plunged into a religious civil war. When Henry of Navarre (Henry IV, 1553–1610) finally secured the throne by converting to Catholicism in 1589, he brought a temporary end to the religious strife by issuing the Edict of Nantes (1598), which granted religious toleration to the Huguenots. Thus, even as an officially Catholic France again turned its attention to American colonization in the early seventeenth century, Huguenot explorers and merchants remained instrumental in the foundation and settlement of the first permanent colonies.

The colony of Acadia (Nova Scotia) was founded in 1604 by the Huguenot Pierre du Gua Sieur de Monts (c. 1568–c. 1630) and his associate Samuel de Champlain (c. 1567–1635), a devout Catholic. The principal settlement of the colony, Port Royal, had both a Huguenot minister and Catholic priest in residence, but this attempt at ecclesiastical balance was short-lived. Enthused by the potential for native conversions, the Society of Jesus (Jesuits) became a financial partner in the colony in 1610. With the Huguenot officials and colonists interested primarily in trade, the Jesuits were able to dominate the religious life of the colony until the British destroyed Port Royal in 1613.

In 1608, de Monts founded the colony of Quebec and placed it under the administration of the capable Champlain. Champlain invited Récollet friars (an order of French Franciscans) to open missions for the conversion of the local Algonkian people. The economic power in the colony, however, was in the hands of Huguenot traders and merchants who looked askance at Catholic missionary activities. When the Récollet mission proved ineffectual, the Jesuits arrived in 1625 and quickly commandeered the evangelization

THE JESUITS AND THE IROQUOIS

The following material collected by anthropologist Anthony Wallace from the *Jesuit Relations* (the writings of Jesuit missionaries in North America) provides some insight into the nature of Jesuit efforts with Native North Americans.

When the black-robed Jesuit fathers began the preaching of the gospel to the Seneca nation in the year 1668, they quickly found that the Seneca were rigidly attached to Iroquoian religious traditions. Particularly obstinate were they in looking to their dreams for guidance in all the important affairs of life.

"The Iroquois have, properly speaking, only a single Divinity," wrote Father Fremin "—the dream. To it they render their submission, and follow all its orders with the utmost exactness. The Tsoanontouens [Seneca] are more attached to this superstition than any of the others; their religion in this respect becomes even a matter of scruple; whatever it be that they think they have done in their dreams, they believe themselves absolutely obliged to execute at the earliest moment. The other nations content themselves with observing those of their dreams which are the most important; but this people, which has the reputation of living more religiously than its neighbors, would think itself guilty of a great crime if it failed in its observance of a single dream. The people think only of that, they talk about nothing else, and all their cabins are filled with their dreams. They spare no pains, no industry, to show their attachment thereto, and their folly in this particular goes to such an excess as would be hard to imagine. He who has dreamed during the night that he was bathing, runs immediately, as soon as he rises, all naked, to several cabins, in each of which he has a kettleful of water thrown over his body, however cold the weather may be. Another who has dreamed that he was taken prisoner and burned alive, has himself bound and burned like a captive on the next day, being persuaded that by thus satisfying his dream, this fidelity will avert from him the pain and infamy of captivity and death,—which, according to what he has learned from his Divinity, he is otherwise bound to suffer among his enemies. Some have been known to go as far as Quebec, travelling a hundred and fifty leagues, for the sake of getting a dog, that they had dreamed of buying there . . ."

Father Fremin and his colleagues were appalled: Some Seneca might, any night, dream of their deaths! "What peril we are in every day," he continued, "among people who will murder us in cold blood if they have dreamed of doing so; and how slight needs to be a offense that a Barbarian has received from someone, to enable his heated imagination to represent to him in a dream that he takes revenge on the offender." It is small wonder that the Jesuits early attempted to disabuse the Seneca of their confidence in dreams, propounding various subtle questions, such as, "Does the soul leave the body during sleep?" and "Can infants in the womb dream?" either affirmative or negative answers to which would involve the recognition (according to the Jesuits) of logical contradictions in native theory.

But Jesuit logic did not discourage Seneca faith. The Quaker missionaries who reached the Seneca 130 years later found in them much the same "superstitious" respect to dreams that their unsuccessful predecessors had discovered. "They are superstitious in the extreme, with respect to dreams, and witchcraft," wrote Halliday Jackson, "and councils are often called, on the most trifling occurrences of this nature. . . ."

Anthony F. C. Wallace

Source: *The Death and Rebirth of the Seneca*.
(New York: Vintage Books, 1972), 59–60.

efforts. Huguenot officials refused to ship supplies for the Jesuits into the colony, however, and the society appealed to the crown for relief. The king responded by suppressing all non-Catholic religions in Quebec, extending this ban to Acadia in 1629.

This de facto establishment of Catholicism was further legitimized with the formation of the Company of New France (also known as the Company of One Hundred Associates) by Cardinal Richelieu in 1627. Richelieu (1585–1642) was the chief minister of King Louis XIII (1601–1643) and a staunch opponent of Protestantism who maintained that the colonies in North America should be not only outposts of French civilization, but of French Catholicism as well. Thus, the company's charter excluded all non-Catholics from Quebec and banned their further immigration, although these policies were never consistently enforced.

Religious life in the Quebec under Richelieu's company reflected two powerful yet contradictory forces in French Catholicism during the seventeenth century. On the one hand, Catholicism had become an expression of French nationalism, and Catholicism there was flavored accordingly by nationalistic sentiments. A concept of ecclesiastical autonomy from Rome—termed "Gallicanism" after the ancient Roman name of the region of France (Gaul)—had in fact been partially sanctioned by the pope in the Concordat of Bologna in 1516. Thus Richelieu's policies in Quebec were an attempt to unify the colony under a banner of joint religious and nationalist unity while at the same time ensuring that religious affairs remained under the control of the state.

On the other hand, Catholicism in France had been profoundly affected by both the Catholic and Counter Reformations of the sixteenth century. Influenced by the universalizing and centralizing reforms of the Council of Trent (1545–1563), and by emerging forms of spirituality that exalted austerity, duty, and even martyrdom, French Catholicism had entered into what Robert Choquette termed "an age of missionaries, mystics and martyrs"(Lippy et al. 1992, 148). Champlain's invitation to the Récollets to open missions illustrated this aggressive and reformed Catholicism, but it was the Jesuits who came to embody its spirit in New France.

The Jesuits in New France

From the beginning, French colonization had expected that native peoples would be swiftly con- verted to the Catholic religion and thereby incorporated into the structure of French society. Initial efforts, however, were disappointing, and the Récollet mission in Quebec was largely ineffective when the Algonkian subjects demonstrated little enthusiasm for either conversion or "Frenchification."

The Jesuits arrived in 1625 to assist the mission effort. From 1629 to 1632 Quebec had to be abandoned due to its conquest by the British, but with the return of the French in 1632 the Jesuits gained complete control of the missions. In 1634, they opened a mission among the sedentary Hurons of Georgian Bay, and for the next sixteen years, the Huron mission would be the proving ground for Jesuit attitudes toward native conversions.

Most Europeans regarded Native American religions as inferior to Christianity, even demonic. Efforts to evangelize the native peoples ranged from indifference among the English colonists to the ruthless suppression of Pueblo religions by Franciscan friars in Spanish New Mexico. Jesuit missionary ideology, influenced by recent successes in Asia, attempted to affirm religious commonalities and to minimize the introduction of nonessential cultural elements into evangelistic efforts. The Superior of the Mission, Jean de Brébeuf (1593–1649), instructed his missionaries to live as Hurons among the Hurons, and so the annual reports filed by the missionaries— collectively titled the *Jesuit Relations*—are filled with ethnographic information about native religions and cultures. Published in France from 1632 to 1673, the *Relations* proved to be valuable tools for propaganda and recruitment, and also helped to promulgate the Jesuit ideal of creating in Quebec a Christian utopia. Ironically, Jesuit successes among the Hurons aided the rapid disintegration of their culture and their virtual destruction by the Iroquois in 1650. Brébeuf and others gained the martyrdom they had sought.

In Quebec itself, support of papal supremacy (ultramontanism) and the independence of the Society of Jesus from local ecclesiastical control placed the Jesuits at odds with government officials. In 1663, the charter for the Company of New France was revoked and colonial affairs were placed under the jurisdiction of the newly formed Company of the West, which was backed by the crown and directed by Louis XIV's (1638–1715) chief minister Jean-Baptiste Colbert (1619–1683). By bringing under its control the educational and social welfare agencies of the religious orders in Quebec, the royal government further Gallicanized the Church of New France and essentially made the church an arm of the state. As the need for regular ecclesiastical administration grew, the appointment of a bishop became a contest between ultramontanist and Gallican factions. A compromise candidate, François-Xavier de Montmorency Laval (1623–1708), became Vicar Apostolic in 1658 and the first Bishop of Quebec in 1674, but increasing Gallicanism eventually pushed the Jesuits west out of Quebec.

The French Caribbean

Competition with England had led France to establish a colony on the Caribbean island of Saint-Christophe (later St. Kitts) in 1625. Other colonies were subsequently founded on Martinique, Guadeloupe, St. Domingue (Haiti), and several smaller islands. As in Quebec during this period, these colonies were administrated by trading companies organized by Richelieu and therefore ostensibly Catholic. Huguenot merchants, not banned here as they were in Quebec, continued to immigrate to the French colonies of the Caribbean, as did many Jews who were fleeing the Portuguese capture of the Dutch colony in Recife, Brazil, in 1654. Under Colbert's administration, economic development was preferred over religious conformity, and government officials thus ignored the presence of these religious dissenters. In 1671, Colbert even secured royal sanction for Jews to settle in the islands and to have their rights of conscience respected so long as they did not cause scandal to Catholics.

The decimation of the native population by earlier Spanish explorations meant that there would be no missions on the order of those of New France, but the introduction of African slavery in 1639 brought new questions about religious conversions. Royal decrees mandated that slaves be catechized and baptized into the Catholic faith, but missionaries complained that Jewish and Huguenot slave owners ignored this directive. Thus, in 1683, only eighteen days after the death of Colbert, King Louis XIV banished all Jews from the colonies in response to Jesuit demands. Two years later, this ban was restated in the Code Noir, a royal edict primarily designed to regulate the practice of slavery in the Caribbean but also aimed at strengthening the establishment of the Catholic Church and unifying religious life there. Continuing this policy of Catholic absolutism, Louis officially revoked the Edict of Nantes a few months later, but then attempted to resettle Huguenots escaping from France in the Caribbean. This unsuccessful and contradictory project ended in 1689, by which time most Huguenots had found refuge in nearby British colonies.

Louisiana

In New France, the Jesuits had transferred their missionary activities into the region surrounding the Great Lakes and the Upper Mississippi Valley (Illinois). In 1672, while seeking a passage to the Pacific, Louis Jolliet (164–1700) and the Jesuit priest Jacques Marquette (1637–1675) discovered the route to the Mississippi River, and missions and trading posts were soon established along its banks. In 1682, René-Robert Cavelier de La Salle (1643–1687) sailed the river to its mouth and laid claim to the Lower Mississippi Valley, which he named Louisiana in honor of King Louis XIV. Not until 1699, however, were the French able to establish a permanent settlement there (on Biloxi Bay). New Orleans was founded in 1718 and four years later it became the capital of Louisiana.

Established during the reign of the devoutly Catholic Louis XIV, there was never any question but that Louisiana would be closed to all non-Catholics. But the ideal of religious conformity clashed with practical considerations. Swamps, epidemics, and miserable weather made Louisiana an undesirable place to settle. In an effort to make the colony prosperous, the crown granted in 1717 a twenty-five-year trade monopoly to the resurrected Company of the West (later the Company of the Indies) headed by the Scottish financier John Law (1671–1729). The charter of the company placed the colony under the authority of the bishop of Quebec and charged colonists to catechize Native Americans and slaves and to construct churches, but so desperate was Louisiana for colonists that government officials looked the other way when Law—himself a Protestant—settled German Protestants upriver from New Orleans. An attempt to unify religious life in the colony came in 1724 when a revision of the Code Noir was promulgated there that mimicked the original code by ordering the expulsion of the Jews (a symbolic act since there were few if any Jews there) and requiring masters to oversee the conversion of their slaves to Catholicism. Sporadic enforcement of the latter led to a large Catholicized African Creole population but also permitted the importation of syncretistic Afro-Caribbean religions such as voodoo.

The End of the French Colonies

Continued wars between England and France eventually led to the dismemberment of France's colonial empire. The Treaty of Utrecht, which ended the War of the Spanish Succession in 1713, ceded Acadia and surrounding areas to the British. The British tolerated the Catholic faith of the Acadians, but efforts to impose an oath of allegiance to the British crown were unsuccessful in part because religious liberty for Catholics was not guaranteed. Finally, in 1755, the British governor demanded that the Acadians swear an oath or face exile. Thousands fled to other French colonies or were forcibly deported by the British; many of these eventually resettled in Spanish-held Louisiana to become the Cajuns. The government of Nova Scotia immediately passed legislation to outlaw Catholicism in the colony, to expel or imprison any priests, and to disenfranchise any remaining Catholics.

The expulsion of the Acadians coincided with the beginning of the Seven Years' War, which ended in 1760 with the British conquest of New France and some of the Caribbean colonies. Faced with governing a population of some 65,000 Catholics, the British government ultimately granted Catholics religious freedom in the Quebec Act of 1774. Louisiana had been secretly ceded to Spain in 1762 in order to keep it out of British Protestant hands. Briefly returned to France, it was finally sold to the United States in 1803. The Catholic majority in Quebec, south Louisiana, and on some islands of the Caribbean remains as the legacy of the French colonial enterprise in North America.

Rodger Payne

See also Code Noir

Further Reading

Brasseaux, C. A. (1986). The moral climate of French colonial Louisiana, 1699–1763. *Louisiana History, 27,* 27–41.

Eccles, W. J. (1987). The role of the church in New France. In Eccles, W. J. (Ed.), *Essays on New France* (pp. 26–37). New York: Oxford University Press.

Eccles, W. J. (1998). *The French in North America, 1500–1783* (Rev. ed.) East Lansing: Michigan State University Press.

Ellis, J. T. (1965). *Catholics in colonial America.* Baltimore: Helicon.

Jaenen, C. J. (1976). *The role of the church in New France.* Toronto, Canada: McGraw-Hill Ryerson.

Lippy, C. H., Choquette, R., & and Poole, S. (1992). *Christianity comes to the Americas, 1492–1776.* New York: Paragon House.

O'Neill, C. E. (1966). *Church and state in French Colonial Louisiana: Policy and politics to 1732.* New Haven, CT: Yale University Press.

French Revolution

The French Revolution is difficult to date. And yet the dates one assigns to it are critically important to a consideration of its impact on religious freedom. Exactly when the Revolution began and when it ended depend markedly on what one believes the revolutionaries wanted to accomplish, and what one sees as the results of their struggle. If the conflict was primarily born of the challenge to the absolute monarchy—an effort to modernize an essentially medieval institution in light of utilitarian principles of government—then the Revolution began in 1789, with the formation of a National Assembly whose members expected, at the very least, to share power with a transformed monarchy. And it ended in 1793, with the execution of Louis XVI, the hapless inheritor of at least one century of brewing hostility and democratic yearnings. This narrowest of time frames might be defended despite the nominal restoration of the monarchy in 1815, given the vastly diminished role of the last of the Bourbon kings, the short-lived nature of their return to power, and the complicating influence of the new Napoleonic elite.

If, on the other hand, one considers the Revolution as a more complex transformation of French (or even European) society and, to some degree, culture, one would choose a much broader time period. This is especially true if one tries to assess the impact of this Enlightenment-inspired struggle on the topic of religious freedom and religious toleration. Here one must look at the entirety of the eighteenth century, if not also the scientific revolution that preceded it; and one might rightly include the career and influence of Napoleon Bonaparte, who rose to power by virtue of opportunities born of the Revolution, and who extended some of the rationalist principles of that movement to the far corners of Europe, albeit ironically through military conquest and virtual dictatorship. In this sense, the revolution-

SELECTION FROM THE *DECLARATION OF THE RIGHTS OF MAN AND OF THE CITIZEN*

Approved by the National Assembly of France, 26 August 1789

The representatives of the French people, organized as a National Assembly, believing that the ignorance, neglect, or contempt of the rights of man are the sole cause of public calamities and of the corruption of governments, have determined to set forth in a solemn declaration the natural, unalienable, and sacred rights of man, in order that this declaration, being constantly before all the members of the Social body, shall remind them continually of their rights and duties; in order that the acts of the legislative power, as well as those of the executive power, may be compared at any moment with the objects and purposes of all political institutions and may thus be more respected, and, lastly, in order that the grievances of the citizens, based hereafter upon simple and incontestable principles, shall tend to the maintenance of the constitution and redound to the happiness of all. Therefore the National Assembly recognizes and proclaims, in the presence and under the auspices of the Supreme Being, the following rights of man and of the citizen:

Articles:

1. Men are born and remain free and equal in rights. Social distinctions may be founded only upon the general good.
2. The aim of all political association is the preservation of the natural and imprescriptible rights of man. These rights are liberty, property, security, and resistance to oppression.
3. The principle of all sovereignty resides essentially in the nation. No body nor individual may exercise any authority which does not proceed directly from the nation.
4. Liberty consists in the freedom to do everything which injures no one else; hence the exercise of the natural rights of each man has no limits except those which assure to the other members of the society the enjoyment of the same rights. These limits can only be determined by law.
5. Law can only prohibit such actions as are hurtful to society. Nothing may be prevented which is not forbidden by law, and no one may be forced to do anything not provided for by law.
6. Law is the expression of the general will. Every citizen has a right to participate personally, or through his representative, in its foundation. It must be the same for all, whether it protects or punishes. All citizens, being equal in the eyes of the law, are equally eligible to all dignities and to all public positions and occupations, according to their abilities, and without distinction except that of their virtues and talents.
10. No one shall be disquieted on account of his opinions, including his religious views, provided their manifestation does not disturb the public order established by law.

Source: *Declaration of the Rights of Man and of the Citizen.*
Retrieved November 6, 2002,
from: http://www.civnet.org/resources/document/historic/french.htm

---

ary movement began perhaps with the publication of the *Encyclopedia* in 1751 (Diderot 1965), and ended with the fall of Bonaparte in 1815.

For our purposes this broader view is warranted. The Revolution was, of course, an attempt to change the structure of French government. In this it was ultimately successful. Beyond this, however, the leading lights of revolutionary thought also sought to dismantle the entire matrix of traditional institutions that characterized the so-called ancien régime—

specifically, the medieval church and state, whose power and legitimacy were still so intimately commingled. And they sought to establish a new, more rational and utilitarian concept of social and political organization for France, and beyond. It is this more profound purpose of the Revolution that accounts for its germinal importance to revolutions around the globe ever since the newly formed National Assembly drafted the Declaration of the Rights of Man and Citizen in August of 1789 (Kishlansky 2001).

In terms of religious freedom, the impact of this movement is mixed. Religious minority groups represented in France at the time (specifically Protestants and Jews), and even nonbelievers, certainly gained civil rights in the course of the Revolution (though in the case of Jews in France that freedom was late, hard-won, and in many respects costly). And the rhetoric of religious toleration was spread to much of Europe through Napoleon's application of this revolutionary principle. But the Revolution also imposed a concept of a secular religion, advanced in opposition to traditional Christianity, which was arguably just as restrictive as earlier efforts to enforce Catholic orthodoxy. In sum, the Revolution was most successful at promoting civic freedom *from* religion, and to some degree freedom *of* religion. It was somewhat less successful at establishing a thoroughgoing freedom of thought.

From Enlightenment to Revolution

Strapped for cash and facing economic collapse, the government of Louis XVI reluctantly called the traditional advisory body, the Estates General, into session in the spring of 1789. But against the background of the successful American Revolution, and even more so the ideas of Locke, Hobbes, and assorted other political theorists of the seventeenth and early eighteenth centuries, the monarchy could hardly contain and manage the proceedings. Fairly quickly, a new educated elite emerged from the so-called "Third Estate"—those not of the traditional noble or clerical classes—inspired by the notion born of the Enlightenment that men not only could reorganize their world for the better, but also that these human efforts were the only means of achieving progress. God, who ruled the medieval world, was now merely a watchmaker—at most a creator—who, after that initial act, now left the affairs of men, and the fulfillment of their potential, in their own hands. Consequently, what basis in nature could there be for

hereditary monarchs, the privileges of a feudal aristocracy, or the domination of a restrictive church?

Representatives of the Third Estate, along with some sympathetic members of the First and Second Estates, broke away from the Estates General, recast themselves as a National Assembly, and set about the work (in some cases unforeseen) of reorganizing the principles on which French society rested. Also during that turbulent summer of 1789, shopkeepers and artisans in Paris, fearful of the building political crisis, stormed the royal prison called the Bastille on 14 July 1789. Such popular insurrections became a hallmark of the Revolution, and proved that the aspirations of the lower classes would demand a place in the struggle alongside the constitutional challenges of the bourgeoisie.

The Assembly, meanwhile, drafted an ideological blueprint for its movement—the Declaration of the Rights of Man and of the Citizen of 27 August 1789, which included a statement of support for religious freedom and freedom of thought in general; their successor assembly put the church under the thumb of the emerging revolutionary state with its Civil Constitution of the Clergy (July 1790); and they generally set themselves on a collision course with Louis XVI and the rigid feudal caste system that supported his monarchy and which had dominated French life since just after the death of Charlemagne in 814 CE.

The Radical Phase

The king, in part out of a sense of obligation to the Catholic Church, vacillated or resisted, tried to flee Paris incognito, and sought aid to foment counter-revolution from monarchial relatives elsewhere in Europe. For these efforts, he and his particularly maladroit queen, Marie Antoinette, lost their heads on the guillotine. In other countries of Europe, fearful monarchs began to see the demise of their own legitimacy in this French political movement, and raised armies against the new French government. And even republican Americans feared the most violent possibilities of this assault on traditional privilege for the propertied.

With the execution of Louis XVI on 21 January 1793 and the advent of war with much of the rest of Europe, the more moderate voices of the movement began to still themselves or leave the country. The threat posed by war led to a retreat from civil liberties and freedom of speech. And divisions within the revolutionary movement itself brought paranoia and retaliation. Two of the leading lights of the Revolution, Georges-Jacques Danton (1759–1794) and Maximilien Robespierre (1758–1794) lost their heads during the radical phase known as the Reign of Terror, the latter in part for his ruthless political trial and execution of the former. In all some 25,000 French men and women were executed for antirevolutionary actions or speech between January 1793 and late summer of 1794, despite the original principles of freedom and due process espoused in the movement's foundation documents. Under military threat from abroad the Revolution is said to have begun to "eat its own children," and surely many principled participants began to perceive this as so. The common people, meanwhile, continued to suffer under the adverse economic conditions that they had believed the Revolution would ameliorate. Wartime privations only exacerbated their plight, and a general conscription of men to fight in the revolutionary army in August of 1793 (the first such drafting of a citizen army in the history of Europe) brought predictable grumbling along with its modern nationalizing effect. Internal counterrevolutionary movements sprang up and though ultimately suppressed, left many with a sense of chaos.

De-Christianization

Between the execution of the king and the downfall of Robespierre in July 1794, the governing revolutionary assembly, now called the National Convention and influenced increasingly by Parisians looking for more radical reform, had adopted a general program meant to purge French society of what were deemed outmoded medieval superstitions and institutions. Part of this was an extended program of "de-Christianization." Included in these efforts were reforming the yearly dating system (replacing the Christian calculation with one stemming from the founding of the French Republic) and changing the names of months to reflect natural features such as the seasons and climate. Notre Dame Cathedral was declared the "Temple of Reason," and efforts were made to close churches and harass dissenting clergy members in the provinces. These efforts, including the prosecution of priests who had refused to take the oath of loyalty to the state required by the Civil Constitution (nearly 50 percent of French priests became refractory clergy by resisting the oath), were

unpopular in many areas of the country. And in the long term, these attempts to uproot the Christianity that had been a feature of French life since the conversion of Clovis in 496 failed.

Napoleon Bonaparte and the Export of the Revolution

From this reality sprang the career of Napoleon Bonaparte, a Corsican-born army officer, whose rise to prominence through sheer military acumen would not have been possible under the old regime. Increasingly dependent on the military to maintain its legitimacy, the revolutionary government embraced and then fell to Bonaparte, who claimed to be a true son of the Revolution and an ardent supporter of its ideals of liberty, equality, and fraternity. His ascent to Consul for Life and then Emperor of the French and his brutal march across Europe and eventual military defeat and exile are well documented. However, early in his rise to national prominence, he extended the religious principles of the early French Revolution by finally granting full civil rights and status as citizens to France's Jews. While French Protestants' rights had been made clear by the Declaration of the Rights of Man, the Jews' position had remained precarious, and the revolutionaries had proven themselves highly uncomfortable with the thought of following the promise of that document to the point of embracing Jewish Frenchmen. Under Napoleon, however, and after the calling of a council of Jewish notables to establish that Judaism would not prevent its adherents from being good citizens and (not incidentally) good soldiers, civil rights were proclaimed in France for the members of Europe's oldest minority. And with Napoleon's later military victories, this "emancipation" of the Jews was established elsewhere in the empire, providing a modern foundation for the dismantling of medieval Europe's tradition of anti-Semitism.

Its insufficiency in this regard, however, was made abundantly clear in the travesty of the Dreyfus Affair of the nineteenth century, and even more horrifically by the Holocaust of the twentieth. In devastating irony, the application of the Enlightenment's diminished role for the Christian church may have neutralized Christian protection at least of Jewish life, while failing to eradicate the ideological residue of long years of Christian denigration and discrimination against Jews. The French Revolution, moreover, assumed and encouraged French Jewish assimilation, and stoked a growing literature denouncing those Jews who clung to a distinctive appearance, diet, or mode of life, even if such distinctiveness derived from religious requirements. The Enlightenment writer Voltaire, whose concept of a "natural religion" had underlain revolutionary deism, had even blamed the Jews for spawning Christianity, so that to the extent to which he rejected Christianity as "superstitious," he held the Jews responsible!

Implications

By any measure, the French Revolution irrevocably changed the form of French government, and also the concept behind it. Gone were the absolute monarchs, their feudal nobility, and their landowning church and cardinal ministers. Gone too were the ideas that these kings were somehow sacred and that they ruled by virtue of a divine right. Government itself was no longer sacred or immutable. In some respects religion, or at least the institutionalized church, had also lost its sacrality, or at least its invulnerability.

It is in this last area, as well as in its invention of a language of revolution and political freedom, that the French Revolution had its greatest impact. Generally this boded well for religious freedom for those minorities most represented in France at the end of the eighteenth century. The ideals of the Enlightenment, with regard to religious toleration, were made concrete and practicable. Protestants and Jews benefited in obvious ways.

But the Revolution had its limits. Politically, it did not democratize government as thoroughly as some of its most ardent voices had hoped. In terms of religion it was not without its own oppressive triumphalism, and even its most tolerant ideology often proved weak in the face of profound religious intolerance. Its effects were felt, then, in the very short term; and one may hope that the freedoms espoused will be continually realized, perhaps, in the very long term. In the middle period, however, its legacy—perhaps like all legacies—has been put to use in complex, imperfect, and unforeseen ways by the heirs.

Patricia Behre Miskimin

See also Civil Religion; Letter on Toleration

Further Reading

Cobb, R. (1970). *The police and the people: French popular protest 1789–1820*. New York: Oxford University Press.

Cobb, R. (1987). *The people's armies*. New Haven, CT: Yale University Press.

Cobban, A. (1964). *The social interpretation of the French Revolution*. Cambridge, UK: Cambridge University Press.

Diderot, D. (1965). *Encyclopedia: Selections* (N. S. Hoyt, Trans.). London, MacMillan.

Doyle, W. (1980). *Origins of the French Revolution*. London: Oxford University Press.

Furet, F. (1992). *Revolutionary France, 1770–1880*. Oxford, UK: Blackwell.

Godechot, J. (1965). *La prise de la Bastille: 14 juillet 1789* [The storming of the Bastille: 14 July 1789]. Paris: Gallimard.

Jordan, D. (1985). *The revolutionary career of Maximilien Robespierre*. New York: Free Press.

Kishlansky, M. A. (Ed.). (2001). *Sources of the West* (4th ed.) (pp. 114–115). New York: Longman.

Lefebvre, G. (1970). *The French Revolution*. New York: Columbia University Press.

Lefebvre, G. (1990). *Napoleon*. New York: Columbia University Press.

Michelet, J. (1967). *History of the French Revolution*. Chicago: University of Chicago Press.

Palmer, R. (1941). *Twelve who ruled: The committee of public safety during the terror*. Princeton, NJ: Princeton University Press.

Palmer, R. (1959–1964). *The age of the democratic revolution: A political history of Europe and America, 1760–1800*. Princeton, NJ: Princeton University Press.

Soboul, A. (1979). *The Parisian sans-culottes and the French Revolution*. London: Greenwood.

Friends, Society of *See* Conscientious Objection and Pacifism; Peace Churches

Fundamentalistic Religion and Politics

Fundamentalists claim to be advancing the cause of religious freedom through their political activism, but opponents say that Fundamentalistic politics

157

EQUAL ACCESS ACT OF 1984; SEC. 4071.
DENIAL OF EQUAL ACCESS PROHIBITED

(a) Restriction of limited open forum on basis of religious, political, philosophical, or other speech content prohibited

It shall be unlawful for any public secondary school which receives Federal financial assistance and which has a limited open forum to deny equal access or a fair opportunity to, or discriminate against, any students who wish to conduct a meeting within that limited open forum on the basis of the religious, political, philosophical, or other content of the speech at such meetings.

(b) "Limited open forum" defined

A public secondary school has a limited open forum whenever such school grants an offering to or opportunity for one or more noncurriculum related student groups to meet on school premises during noninstructional time.

(c) Fair opportunity criteria

Schools shall be deemed to offer a fair opportunity to students who wish to conduct a meeting within its limited open forum if such school uniformly provides that —

(1) the meeting is voluntary and student-initiated;
(2) there is no sponsorship of the meeting by the school, the government, or its agents or employees;
(3) employees or agents of the school or government are present at religious meetings only in a nonparticipatory capacity;
(4) the meeting does not materially and substantially interfere with the orderly conduct of educational activities within the school; and
(5) nonschool persons may not direct, conduct, control, or regularly attend activities of student groups.

(d) Construction of subchapter with respect to certain rights

Nothing in this subchapter shall be construed to authorize the United States or any State or political subdivision thereof —

(1) to influence the form or content of any prayer or other religious activity;
(2) to require any person to participate in prayer or other religious activity;
(3) to expend public funds beyond the incidental cost of providing the space for student-initiated meetings;
(4) to compel any school agent or employee to attend a school meeting if the content of the speech at the meeting is contrary to the beliefs of the agent or employee;
(5) to sanction meetings that are otherwise unlawful;
(6) to limit the rights of groups of students which are not of a specified numerical size; or
(7) to abridge the constitutional rights of any person.

(e) Federal financial assistance to schools unaffected

Notwithstanding the availability of any other remedy under the Constitution or the laws of the United States, nothing in this subchapter shall be construed to authorize the United States to deny or withhold Federal financial assistance to any school.

(f) Authority of schools with respect to order, discipline, well-being, and attendance concerns

Nothing in this subchapter shall be construed to limit the authority of the school, its agents or employees, to maintain order and discipline on school premises, to protect the well-being of students and faculty, and to assure that attendance of students at meetings is voluntary

Source: Legal Information Institute, US Code Collection.
Retrieved July 29, 2002 from: http://www4.law.cornell.edu

undermines the separation of church and state. American Christian Fundamentalism emerged in the early twentieth century in reaction to liberal Protestantism, and Fundamentalists began politicizing their worldview in the 1920s. Fundamentalist Protestants—between 10 and 25 percent of the American population—are a subgroup of Evangelicals who are millenarian and believe that the Bible is inerrant and must be interpreted literally. Their political involvement usually focuses on opposition to social forces they believe threaten their way of life or the country's morality. George Marsden, a leading historian of American Fundamentalism, defines it as a militantly antimodernist Christian movement, "opposed [to] both modernism in theology and the cultural changes that modernism endorsed" (Marsden 1980, 4). Marsden indicates that while, by the 1960s, "most of this new evangelical sub-culture repudiated 'Fundamentalist' as too exclusivist in implication, 'Fundamentalistic' remains a useful adjective to describe many of its most conspicuous and controversial traits" (Marsden 1980, 195). In this article, "Fundamentalist" refers to this broader description of Fundamentalistic traits.

After experiencing setbacks in their antievolution campaign following the 1925 Scopes trial, most Fundamentalists retreated from politics, only re-emerging as a national political force in the late 1970s with the advent of the Christian Right. The Christian Right did not attract the support of all Fundamentalists, but throughout the late twentieth century served as a powerful interest group for Republican Fundamentalists who favored a conservative social agenda including support for school prayer and the rights of private Christian schools, as well as opposition to abortion, feminism, and gay rights.

Separation of Church and State

Organizations such as the American Civil Liberties Union and People For the American Way claimed that Fundamentalists' political causes threatened the religious liberties of non-Christians by imposing a theocratic moral agenda on them, and in some cases, the courts agreed. The Supreme Court declared that Fundamentalist-supported legislation opposing teaching evolution in public schools violated the First Amendment's establishment clause, which says that "Congress shall make no law respecting an establishment of religion." The Supreme Court ruled against public school prayer on similar grounds in *Engel v. Vitale* (1962). Religious conservatives were unable to win approval for other forms of school prayer in *Wallace v. Jaffree* (1985), *Lee v. Weisman* (1992), or *Santa Fe Independent School District v. Doe* (2000), and in 1984, they failed to pass a constitutional amendment supporting voluntary school prayer. Christian Right leaders such as Jerry Falwell and Tim LaHaye said that the Supreme Court had misinterpreted the establishment clause by imposing a stricter separation of church and state than the Constitution required.

Some defenders of religious freedom criticized Fundamentalists' interpretation of the First Amendment as historically and legally inaccurate, and they expressed alarm when Religious Right leaders said that those who do not adhere to the Judeo-Christian tradition are not qualified to hold public

159

office, or that America is a "Christian nation" that must return to its traditional religious heritage.

Claims of Religious Discrimination

Fundamentalists have responded that they, not their opponents, are defenders of religious liberty, and have frequently used the rhetoric of religious freedom to promote their cause. Pat Robertson, a presidential candidate in 1988, claimed his opponents discriminated against his religious beliefs when they questioned whether being a televangelist made him unfit for the presidency. Fundamentalists also exploited the issue of religious freedom in arguing that the promotion of "secular humanism" in public schools violated the establishment clause; district courts, however, rejected that argument.

Fundamentalists often based their legal arguments against religious discrimination on the First Amendment clause that prevents Congress from "prohibiting the free exercise" of religion, but they did not always succeed in court. The Supreme Court ruled in *Bob Jones University v. United States* (1983) that Fundamentalists could not use the free exercise clause to protect the tax exemption status of private Christian schools that practiced racial discrimination for religious reasons. In the 1990s and the early twenty-first century, Fundamentalists attempted to use the First Amendment to defend the right of organizations and individuals to discriminate on the basis of sexual orientation because of their religious convictions.

In spite of Fundamentalists' distrust of the Supreme Court, legal organizations associated with the Religious Right, including the Rutherford Institute and the American Center for Law and Justice, won several cases for clients who claimed that they had experienced religious discrimination. District courts upheld the right of non-accredited, private, Christian schools to operate for religious reasons, and the Supreme Court affirmed the right of children to pray silently in public schools. In *Widmar v. Vincent* (1981) and *Rosenberger v. University of Virginia* (1995), the Supreme Court declared that state universities violated the liberties of campus Christian organizations when they denied them equal access to funds and meeting space. In *Harris v. McRae* (1980), the Supreme Court upheld the Fundamentalist-supported Hyde Amendment that restricted Medicaid funding for abortion, and ruled that this legislation did not violate the First Amendment's establishment clause, even if it echoed religious doctrine.

Fundamentalists have also won recognition of their right to freedom of religious speech. The Supreme Court ruled in *Board of Airport Commissioners v. Jews for Jesus* (1987) that airports could not prohibit evangelizing organizations from distributing literature in public areas. In 1975, when a group of California professors filed Petition 2493 with the Federal Communications Commission (FCC) to freeze licenses for religious stations, a massive protest from Fundamentalists convinced the FCC to deny the petition. The Religious Right also successfully lobbied for the Equal Access Act (1984), which prohibited schools from discriminating against religious and political student groups that wanted to use their facilities, and the Religious Freedom Restoration Act (1993), which restricted the grounds on which courts could rule against a defendant's claim to religious freedom. The Supreme Court later declared the Religious Freedom Restoration Act unconstitutional as applied to state laws and regulations (the Act still applies to federal law).

Fundamentalists have used political influence to further their own religious liberty, but some claim the Christian Right has disregarded the First Amendment in its attempt to impose its values on the rest of America. At the beginning of the twenty-first century, Fundamentalists and their opponents continue to debate issues of religious freedom in Congress and the courts, with the outcome still uncertain.

Daniel K. Williams

See also Creationism; Establishment, Equal Treatment; Establishment, Separation of Church and State

Further Reading

Chidester, D. (1988). *Patterns of power: Religion and politics in American culture.* Englewood Cliffs, NJ: Prentice Hall.

Diamond, S. (1998). *Not by politics alone: The enduring influence of the Christian Right.* New York: Guilford.

Durham, M. (2000). *The Christian Right, the Far Right and the boundaries of American conservatism.* Manchester, UK: Manchester University.

Hunter, J. D. (1991). *Culture wars: The struggle to define America.* New York: Basic Books.

Larson, E. J. (1989). *Trial and error: The American controversy over creation and evolution.* New York: Oxford University Press.

Lienesch, M. (1993). *Redeeming America: Piety and politics in the New Christian Right.* Chapel Hill: University of North Carolina Press.

Marsden, G. M. (1980). *Fundamentalism and American culture: The shaping of twentieth-century Evangelicalism, 1870–1925.* New York: Oxford University Press.

Martin, W. L. (1996). *With God on our side: The rise of the Religious Right in America.* New York: Broadway Books.

Provenzo, E. F., Jr. (1990). *Religious fundamentalism and American education: The battle for the public schools.* Albany: State University of New York Press.

Ravitch, F. S. (1999). *School prayer and discrimination: The civil rights of religious minorities and dissenters.* Boston: Northeastern University.

Wald, K. D. (1987). *Religion and politics in the United States.* New York: St. Martin's Press.

Watson, J. (1999). *The Christian Coalition: Dreams of restoration, demands for recognition.* New York: St. Martin's Press.

Court Cases

Board of Airport Commissioners v. Jews for Jesus, 482 U.S. 569 (1987).

Bob Jones University v. United States, 461 U.S. 574 (1983).

Engel v. Vitale, 370 U.S. 421 (1962).

Edwards v. Aguillard, 482 U.S. 578 (1987).

Epperson v. Arkansas, 393 U.S. 97 (1968).

Harris v. McRae, 448 U.S. 297 (1980).

Lee v. Weisman, 505 U.S. 577 (1992).

Rosenberger v. University of Virginia, 515 U.S. 819 (1995).

Santa Fe Independent School District v. Doe, 530 U.S. 290 (2000).

Wallace v. Jaffree, 472 U.S. 38 (1985).

Widmar v. Vincent, 454 U.S. 263 (1981).

G

Germany and Prussia

The German nation, or "second" German Empire, has existed only since 1870/1871. The roots of the Central European territory now occupied by Germany go back to the year 911 and the East Franconian Empire. This first Germanic empire was consolidated by Otto I (reigned 936–973) who, when crowned Emperor, took on both the leadership of the Christian West and the protection of the Roman Church. The Ottonian "empire" was a confederation of clerical and secular principalities each having sovereign powers. From 1125 on, the Empire was not always hereditary, as the princes sometimes elected one of their peers to be king. This territory, called the Holy Roman Empire of the German Nation since the fifteenth century, also included northern Italy and Burgundy. Between 1056 and 1500, serious political disputes arose between the emperors and popes, and at times one side or the other had the advantage. (By contrast, the young French nation entered the European stage in 1254 as a great power; at times, a second pope reigned next to the first, in Avignon, France.) The princes were eventually ascendant in Central Europe, weakening the imperial center. The royal house of Hapsburg-Austria achieved supremacy in the Empire in 1438 and managed to keep the imperial crown until 1806.

Schisms from Roman Catholicism and the Development of Various Denominations

With the exception of John Wycliffe's (c. 1330–1384) and Jan Hus's (1372–1415) followers, all early schisms from the Roman Church were successfully countered. The moderate Hussites (Utraquists) gained special status in Bohemia, and from 1485 on this region had Utraquist as well as Roman Catholic churches. Martin Luther's (1483–1546) Reformation caused a denominational schism from Roman Catholicism in Central Europe, a schism that was formalized at the Imperial Parliament (*Reichstag*) of Augsburg in 1555.

Starting from the cities of Strasbourg (Martin Bucer), Zurich (Huldrych Zwingli), and Geneva (John Calvin), a second type of Reformation developed. Denominational and political alliances between the resulting "Reformed" Protestantism and Lutheranism failed. The Religious Peace of Augsburg of 1555 only related to a peace between the Roman Catholics and the Lutherans; the Reformed (mainly Calvinist) and the radical wing of the Reformation (Anabaptists and others) were expressly excluded. Adherents of other faiths received the right to leave the country, retaining their possessions, and being redeemed from serfdom. The empire lost its universal religious significance, but remained a "Holy Empire" as long as the emperor was a Catholic and Protector of the existing imperial Church.

The Treaty of Westphalia of 1648

The Thirty Years' War (1618–1648) resulted from unresolved problems of faith and power in the Empire. The Treaty of Westphalia of 1648, concluded in Münster and Osnabrück, reestablished religious peace and extended it to the Reformed churches as well ("sects" such as Anabaptists were excluded from this treaty). The minority of Protestant states organized themselves into the Corpus Evangelicorum in the Imperial Parliament. After 1697, the ascendant power of Kurbrandenburg (Brandenburg-Prussia) and the electoral prince of Brandenburg assumed leadership of the Corpus. Questions of denominational relevance were not determined by majority decisions; rather the empire made a commitment to mediate. All imperial states retained the *ius reformandi*—the right to reformation—in their territories, but the forced conversion of subjects when a ruler joined another denomination was discontinued. The "norm year" 1624 became the reference point for assigning territories to particular denominations, a rule that had the effect of protecting minorities. As well as the official religion, most territories allowed private services or at least home worship for other denominations. The empire had developed into a confederation of over 350 sovereign territories that retained the right to form alliances with foreign countries; the power of the emperor was based on the Hapsburg imperium.

Gradual Collapse of Religious Polemics and Prussia's Rise to Power

Since Brandenburg-Prussia was divided not only by geography, but by denomination (Calvinists, Lutherans, and Catholics in the Duchy of Cleve), it supported religious tolerance as a requirement of state. This territory developed into a politically sovereign, mercantile state based on military power and administration. Friedrich Wilhelm I (reigned 1640–1688), influenced by Calvinism and the early Enlightenment, subordinated church to state interests, and integrated ecclesiastical into state administration. Between 1662 and 1664 he ordered the Lutheran and Reformed Churches to cease aiming polemics at each other. With his Jews Edict (*Judenedikt*) of 1671, he extended tolerance to the Jewish minority, which, along with the Huguenots, contributed to the prosperity of the country. The Huguenots (who fled France and had been received in the country since the Edict of Potsdam in 1685) were granted full religious freedom with the right to hold public office, schooling in French, and their own ministers. In 1701 Prince Elector Friedrich III (reigned 1688–1713) acquired the royal title of King Friedrich I. Friedrich Wilhelm II (reigned 1713–1740) continued his father's policy of unification, receiving refugees from Salisbury in Austria in 1732, settling them in depopulated areas of East Prussia. With added lands won by war and military campaigns,

Prussia raised itself to the rank of a major European power. This lead to polarization within the German empire between mainly Protestant Prussia and Catholic Hapsburg.

Religious Tolerance under Benevolent Despotism

The changed state–church relationship was based on the doctrine of natural right of territorialism. By this doctrine, a country's ruler exercised authority over its official church affiliation, ensuring order and tolerance among the various religious groups. An individual's inner religious conviction was a private matter, but formal religious practice was not. The state had the responsibility to ensure peace and prosperity for all, protecting freedom of conscience and promoting general moral norms. The state defined itself as a secular social contract between authorities and subjects in the form of a legislative body. This development followed on the concept that all humans shared individual human rights—especially human dignity, which in principle included the equality of all people and a certain range of freedoms. In Germany, Immanuel Kant's (1724–1804) ethics and jurisprudence were formative of the idea of a state under the rule of law.

The Codification of Prussian General Law (*Allgemeines Landrecht für die Preussischen Staaten*) of 1794

The earliest manifestation of these ideas in Germany emerged in Prussia. The enlightened Friedrich II (reigned 1740–1786) was tolerant in religious matters if it was good for the polity and did not infringe on state interests. He thus sponsored construction of the Catholic St. Hedwig's Cathedral in Berlin (1747–1773) and tolerated the Jesuits, since this was advantageous for Catholic schools. The legal position of Jewish communities was guaranteed in 1750. Churches were considered as religious communities important for the education of the people, the task of which was to raise levels of general morality for the sake of the state.

In jurisprudence, this policy found expression in the Prussian General Law (*Allgemeines Landrecht für die Preussischen Staaten*) initiated by Friedrich II and enacted in 1794. According to it, "every church association [was] obliged to teach its members reverence for the Godhead, obedience of the laws, loyalty towards the state and good moral views of their fellow citizens." The General Law distinguished between church and spiritual associations: the former received "the rights of privileged corporations"; the latter were only "tolerated." Thus the freedom of religion, faith, and conscience, guaranteed for all for the first time, was ordered hierarchically. Members of an unprivileged religion had to accept limitations to their religious freedom: they could not, for example, ring bells to call for service, or perform ceremonies outside their meeting place.

The End of the Holy Roman Empire of the German Nation

The tolerant jurisprudence of the Hapsburg monarchy under Joseph II (reigned 1765–1790), who also aimed to establish a national Catholic church in Austria, was not as far-reaching as the Prussian General Law. Joseph's Patent of Tolerance of 1781 did not even grant Protestants a status as tolerated religious communities, as Prussia had to religious minorities. After the French Revolution, the concept of secularization (enshrined in the *Reichdeputationshauptschluss* law of 1803) eliminated the clerical principalities and bishoprics which had existed since the Middle Ages. In 1806, Franz II (reigning as Franz I, Emperor of Austria, 1804–1835) renounced the imperial crown and declared the end of the Holy Roman Empire of the German Nation.

Equal Civil Rights for the Churches and the Combat of "Sects"

Religious matters, except for the emancipation of the Jews, played no official role in the German Federation (*Deutscher Bund*), founded in 1815. Since each of the approximately forty German states usually included more than one denomination, a fundamental constitutional principle of the Federation was equality. Religious tolerance and civil equality now became real for the privileged denominations, while individual states retained their rights to supervision and control. Many believers saw a violation of religious freedom in the state-sponsored Union of Lutheran and Reformed Churches, and in states such as Prussia, this Union led Lutheran communities to separate from the state church. The churches only gained constitutional autonomy with the Frankfurt (Imperial) Constitution (*Frankfurter Reichsverfassung*)

of 1849. Paragraph 147 of this reads: "Every religious community orders and administers its own matters independently, but remains subject to general state law. The state grants no privileges to any religious community; furthermore, there is no state church. New religious communities may constitute themselves; a recognition of their profession by the state is not necessary." But these regulations only took effect many years later, in some places only after the 1918 Revolution. The old and new Free Churches (Mennonites, Methodists, and Baptists) were the subject of strong polemics even after 1849, and people were warned of the "dangers of sectarianism." To thwart the "English-American kind of sects," mainline churches discriminated against the Free Churches until the civil registry office was introduced: Baptist children could not receive given names since they were not baptized, and there were compulsory baptisms and troubles with marriage matters. Since churchyards were mostly owned by state churches, deceased members of Free Churches were buried in the part of the churchyard reserved for suicides.

Kulturkampf and Civilian Status Legislation in the Empire

When the Northern German Federation (*Norddeutscher Bund*) of 1869 was founded, all member states were granted the right to religious freedom: "All still-persisting limitations of civil and civic rights deriving from the differences of religious denominations, are hereby annulled. Especially, the right to take part in the communal and country assembly and to hold a public office, shall not depend on an individual's religious denomination." This federal law was integrated into the Constitution of the "Second" German Empire, of January 1871. Furthermore, this "small German" (*kleindeutsch*, i.e., without Austria) empire led by Prussia relinquished any religious basis. It was not meant to be Protestant, but "modern" and neutral regarding religion. Perhaps because of this, struggle ensued between the liberal state and Catholicism in its religious, political, and social manifestations. This conflict—*Kulturkampf*—led to a juridical separation of church and state and to the restraint of church presence in public life. Civil status legislation and the introduction of state monitoring of schools ended the effective participation of the churches in civil legislation. In 1874 the state enacted a Law on Leaving the Churches: a person intending to leave a church simply made a declaration in local court, and his or her civic duties toward the church ceased at the end of the year.

Weimar Republic Constitution of 1919: "Limping Separation" of State and Church

Even in the nineteenth century, state authority over the church had noticeably relaxed, as evidenced by the development of church constitutions and legislative bodies. However, not until the revolution of 1918 was the power of sovereign princes over the church removed. The Constitution of the Weimar Republic established that there was no state church, and also prohibited churches from exercising state-like powers. Other regulations of state–church law, though, restricted the principle of separation of church and state. Traditional elements of the relationship between church and state continued in the new republican era. The state assured the churches that their status under public law would remain unchanged. Nominally, all religious and ideological associations were granted equal opportunity to acquire the same legal status as the established churches; but in fact, the old hierarchy of religious associations was maintained. As well, the Weimar government and certain state governments did not want completely to relinquish state authority over the church and tried to retain elements of state control with legislation. During the Weimar Republic period, concordats and church treaties formed the relationship that enabled larger religious associations to remain "social powers of order." This concept of a "limping separation" (coined by German jurist Ulrich Stutz) of state and church, existing since 1919, is based on the assumption that the majority belongs to a mainline church.

Waves of Church Leaving and Combat Against "Sects"

Under these new circumstances, every religious and secular community was initially able to act with a great degree of freedom. But both mainline churches (established Protestants—i.e., Lutherans, Reformed, United—and Catholics) were indignant about their rivals. Protestantism especially suffered, and waves of people repeatedly left the mainline churches: between 1919 and 1932, an average of 191,868 members per year left mainline Protestant

churches. In 1922, the Apologetische Centrale organization was founded in Berlin-Spandau by Protestant churches to fight the alleged threat from both religious and secular worldview communities. In 1931 the Weimar President issued the Decree for the Combating of Political Disturbances that empowered the state to act against new denominations such as Jehovah's Witnesses. This decree could be applied when "a religious association under public law, its institutions, customs or items of religious worship are insulted or maliciously brought into contempt."

During the Third Reich, both mainline and Free churches were under considerable political pressure. National Socialist anti-clerical propaganda triggered new waves of church-leaving from 1937 on. Yet the Apologetische Centrale initially supported the gestapo when it persecuted small "sects." Unlike members of the mainline churches, adherents of small denominations as well as Jews were targeted and exterminated on a large scale.

Church and State in the Federal Republic of Germany

Due to political compromise, regulations from the Weimar Constitution (1919) concerning state policy towards the church were incorporated into Article 140 of the Constitution of the Federal Republic of Germany (1949). Accordingly, the Protestant and Catholic mainline churches, along with other religious associations, can be granted corporate status, thereby receiving public legal rights normally granted only to the state. These include the rights to: raise taxes from members of the association, make their own laws, create new sub-organizations with a public legal status such as institutions and foundations, establish contractual relationships of a public legal nature between employer and employee, and place members in radio and television monitoring bodies. According to the Constitution it is not difficult to obtain corporate status. A religious association merely has to "guarantee permanency by their constitution and by the number of their adherents." Today there are more than two dozen such "acknowledged religious associations." While the state would prefer a more restricted use of corporate rights, there has been a tendency to enlarge the privileges of religious associations that already have corporate status.

The Western occupying powers (the United States, Great Britain, and France) were satisfied with this uninterrupted continuity "from Weimar to Bonn" (the title of a 1970 essay by historian Golo Mann). They awarded the mainline churches the status of having been resistance organizations during the Third Reich, and saw them as public educators. The Anglo-American nations saw the re-education, re-Christianization, and democratization of the German people as closely linked.

The Hierarchy of Denominations and Worldview Communities in Contemporary Germany

While German citizens have increasingly abandoned mainline churches, these churches, in cooperation with the state, have been trying to preserve the hierarchical ranking of denominations established when the state had authority over the church. On top, there are the Protestant and Catholic mainline churches; beneath these are the Free churches that in the 1920s were still considered "sects," including Baptists, Methodists, and Quakers. Other groups are ranked below the Free churches because they—for example Seventh-day Adventists—support special doctrines with partially "sectarian" features. Other "sects" are ranked below these groups, including the New Apostolic Church, Jehovah's Witnesses, and Christian Science. Ranked below these are esoteric and new-Gnostic ideologies, and movements such as Rudolf Steiner's Anthroposophy. On the second-last level of the scale come missionary Eastern religions, new religions, and so-called youth cults, including Transcendental Meditation and Hare Krishna. "Psycho-organizations" like Scientology and others stand at the bottom of the ranking.

Measures Taken by State and Mainline Churches to Limit Religious Pluralism

This hierarchy considerably qualifies the freedom of religion guaranteed in the Constitution of the Federal Republic of Germany, since there are "churches and others." Churches are closer to the state not only because they have the legal status of "corporation[s] under public law." They are also regarded as experts in religious matters, and church commissioners for sect issues became members of the Enquete Commission on So-called Sects and Psycho-groups, appointed by the German Federal Parliament in 1996.

After two years the Commission published a final report containing research and expert opinions showing that new religious and ideological movements harbor no more danger than other social groups (such as sports teams or community associations), and that any misuse of freedom can be dealt with by existing legal means. The majority of Commission members, however, recommended legislative action contradicting the actual findings of the Commission. They suggested changing tax and association laws, tightening the paragraph on usury, giving state support to private counseling centers, and passing a law on life-counseling services. The Federal Administrative Office is to gather and dispense relevant information, and the Commission's activity could be continued under the auspices of a federal foundation.

A number of these suggestions have been acted on, and in November 2001 the so-called religious privilege (*Religionsprivileg*) was eliminated from the law on associations. Now religious communities that have not received corporate status, but only have the status of associations, can be forbidden by the state. Jehovah's Witnesses have struggled since the early 1990s to gain public-law status, and the Church of Scientology has been monitored by federal and state secret services. At the end of June 2002, the Constitutional Court answered the constitutional appeal made by the Osho movement: "The basic right to religious and worldview liberty as established in article 4, paragraphs 1 and 2 of the Fundamental Law offers no reservation against the state and its organs dealing publicly—even in a critical manner—with the communities protected by this law. This look at them must, though, preserve the law of religious and worldview neutrality of the state and must therefore be cast with caution. Defamation, discrimination or a wrong representation of a religious or worldview community are therefore prohibited to the state."

Gerhard Besier

Further Reading

Besier, G. (1998/2000). *Kirche, politik und gesellschaft im 19. und 20. Jahrhundert* (Church, politics, and society in the nineteenth and twentieth centuries). Munich, Germany: Oldenbourg.

Johnston, A. (1996). *The Protestant Reformation in Europe* (6th ed.). London: Longman.

McLeod, H. (2000): *Secularisation in Western Europe, 1848–1914*, Basingstoke, UK: Macmillan.

Robbers, G. (Ed.). (1995). *Staat und Kirche in der Europäischen Union* (State and church in the European Union). Baden-Baden, Germany: Nomos.

Saine, Thomas P. (1997): *The problem of being modern, or the German pursuit of enlightenment from Leibniz to the French Revolution*, Detroit, MI: Wayne State University Press.

Government Funding of Religious Organizations

The battle over government funding of religious organizations is fundamentally a battle over the meaning of the First Amendment clause of the United States Constitution that mandates, "Congress shall make no law respecting an establishment of religion." One interpretation favors a narrow, limited establishment clause that does not prevent the government from funding essentially religious institutions when it is in the state's best interests to do so. Furthermore, this argument draws upon a notion of equality: religious institutions should be treated equally along with secular ones. An opposite interpretation deems religion to be in a special, inalienable, category and denies the very existence of governmental power either to fund/support, or to oppress, religion and religious ministries.

The modern debate over governmental power versus freedom from government coercion in matters of religion is at least as old as the debates between Patrick Henry and James Madison in the Commonwealth of Virginia. On the one hand, Christian dissenters (including Virginia Baptist John Leland, and New Englanders Roger Williams and Isaac Backus) championed a "two-kingdoms," separation of church and state approach whose core principle is that government has no power to act in matters of religion. Laws that prohibit as well as support religion are null and void, void ab initio. Freedom of religious conscience is retained as an inalienable right—meaning, that the state does not and cannot possess the power to support or inhibit religion, even if the majority of the people want the government to have this power. The government had no authority over religion, and so had created serious civil disorder by using coerced public tax monies to support religious ministries and worship.

On the other hand, Patrick Henry and others reasoned that since religion was necessary to make citizens virtuous, religion was thus necessary to civil order, and, therefore, government support of religion was vital to civil order. To fill what he perceived to be a dangerous void left when Virginia disestablished the Anglican Church, in 1784 Henry introduced a bill to provide for teachers of the Christian religion. The bill was what we would today call "non-preferentialist" in that it did not prefer one Christian sect over another. In fact, under this bill no Christian's (the bill is not clear with respect to non-Christians) tax monies went to the support of the religious institution of another: The bill exacted a tax that went only to the church of one's choice. Henry premised the bill in terms of religion's usefulness to government. He argued the need for religious authority to guide citizens' consciences as well as a fear of the spread of anarchy from an immoral, unvirtuous citizenry.

Madison (in his 1785 *Memorial and Remonstrance*) and a groundswell of Christian dissenters in Virginia wrote petitions opposing this bill. They, too, believed that religion was the basis of a virtuous citizenry necessary for the Republic to flourish. But they maintained that government had no authority or jurisdiction in matters of religion, that individual freedom of conscience prevented government from exacting tax monies to support religious ministries, and that state support of religion was corrupting and useless. Henry lost this round, and Madison, seizing the moment, quickly introduced a bill Jefferson had written back in 1777. The Virginia Congress passed this bill and on 16 January 1786, it became the Statute of Virginia for Religious Freedom. The key part of the statute reads, "No man shall be compelled to ... support any religious worship, place, or ministry whatsoever. . . ."

To move the debate to the federal level: By the time of the First United States Congress in 1789, momentum was broadening protection for religious freedom from the narrow notion of "tolerance" to the more expansive protection of the "free exercise" of religion. Early leaders in crafting democratic alternatives to British rule moved as well to a more radical idea: the abolition of government establishments of religion. Antiestablishment was a concept first advanced in the colonies by Roger Williams in Rhode Island. As we have seen, champions of this radical change included Virginians James Madison and Thomas Jefferson. Jefferson, ambassador to France, was in Paris for the five most critical years in the creation of the new nation. Via the post he engaged in a lengthy conversation with Madison, which included Jefferson's insistence upon a bill of rights. Persuaded of the need, Madison shepherded the First Amendment to the new Constitution through the Congress in 1789. That passage prohibited federal laws respecting an establishment of religion, but was mute on state laws. Representative James Madison sought, unsuccessfully, to correct that condition. On 17 August 1789 he supported an amendment that would have read: "No state shall infringe the equal rights of conscience, nor the freedom of speech, or of the press, nor of the right of trial by jury in criminal cases." Madison went on to argue that "this is the most valuable amendment on the whole list." While Madison failed in his efforts to have the First Amendment apply to state laws, the fact remains that the First Amendment as passed and ratified bars the federal government from taking such actions that establish religion or prohibit its free exercise. It was left to later generations to consider the implications of the First Amendment for financial involvement between the entities of state and church.

Developments in the Twentieth Century

While the states had addressed religious freedom in their individual state constitutions (varying from separation to establishment), de facto state and local Protestant domination remained the norm throughout the nineteenth century. The flood of Roman Catholic immigrants by the middle of that century set in motion events that would slowly erode the Protestant domination. After the Civil War, the U.S. Congress sought to impose uniform civil rights protections on the states. To that end, it had passed the Fourteenth Amendment: "No state shall make or enforce any law which shall abridge the privileges and immunities of citizens of the United States; nor shall deprive any citizen of life, liberty or property, without due process of law; nor deny to any person within its jurisdiction the equal protection of the laws." Still, it wasn't until the mid-twentieth century that the U.S. Supreme Court would act to ensure that Bill of Rights protections were enforced against the states.

Change came suddenly with the decision in *Cantwell v. Connecticut* in 1940, which set forth the proposition that the Fourteenth Amendment applied the First Amendment to state laws. Writing for the court, Justice Owen J. Roberts stated that the free exercise clause "embraces two concepts—freedom to believe and freedom to act. The first is absolute but, in the nature of things, the second cannot be."

Seven years later all nine justices endorsed a reading of the establishment clause of the First Amendment that essentially barred both federal and state actions that would allow public funds to be allotted to religious institutions. In the 1947 *Everson v. Board of Education* all nine justices rejected public funding of religious schools, while five of them argued that New Jersey's funding of public school transportation was constitutional as a child benefit. In some ways this was the same argument advanced by Justice Roberts.

In 1971 an explicit blueprint was spelled out concerning the reach of the establishment clause in *Lemon v. Kurtzman*. Chief Justice Warren Burger delivered the majority opinion: "Every analysis in this area must begin with consideration of the cumulative criteria developed by the Court over many years. Three such tests may be gleaned from our cases. First, the statute must have a secular legislative purpose; second, its principal or primary effect must be one that neither advances nor inhibits religion; finally, the statute must not foster 'an excessive government entanglement with religion.'"

Judicial and scholarly objections to *Lemon* have been frequent since 1971. Much of the heat in this debate has been centered for thirty years on the same theme that first emerged in 1947: Does the establishment clause prohibit government funding of religious institutions? The most recent United States Supreme Court decision, *Zelman v. Simmons Harris*, rendered on 27 June 2002, continues that debate. In a 5 to 4 decision the Court held that a voucher program established by the Cleveland City School District is constitutional. Analysis of the court's opinion makes clear that the majority endorsed some forms of government funding of religious educational institutions. The four-member court minority saw the matter otherwise. Many scholars, as well, considered the decision to be a significant victory for proponents of greater involvement of the government in religious schools. However, as this article was prepared no clear picture had emerged as to the future implications of this single decision. For that reason, this analysis will assess the subject without speculating further on the implications of *Zelman*.

Faith-Based Initiatives

A second front emerged in the last decade of the twentieth century when Senator John Ashcroft began to add language to numerous congressional bills that would provide for what he defined as "charitable choice"—which invited charities (both secular and religious) to provide welfare services. In 1996 he inserted language into President Bill Clinton's welfare reform bill that would allow states to make contracts with houses of worship "without impairing the religious character of such [religious] organizations." In spite of strong opposition from groups such as Americans United and People For the American Way, Senator Ashcroft's advocacy proved effective and by the time of the election of President George W. Bush in 2000 charitable choice was well established.

A new label emerged in 2001 by the direction of the new administration. An office in the White House called "Faith-Based Initiatives" was established under the direction of Bush advisor Karl Rove. Failing to get additional legislation through Congress that would further extend "charitable choice," on 12 December 2002, President George W. Bush signed Executive Orders (EO) that sought to change existing law in two significant ways: (1) "A faith-based organization that applies for or participates in a social service program supported with Federal financial assistance [that is, tax monies required from all Americans, of all faiths and none] may retain its independence and may continue to carry out its mission, including the definition, development, practice, and expression of its religious beliefs, provided that it does not use direct Federal financial assistance to support any inherently religious activities, such as worship, religious instruction, or proselytization." President Bush's justification for providing public tax dollars to support sectarian religious social service ministries is that to preclude them would be "unfair treatment." Then, (2) he gave these religious groups a special exemption, lifting civil rights protections enacted in 1965 by President Lyndon Johnson's Executive Order 11246. That EO provided that federal contractors (that is, private organizations receiving federal funds) "will not discriminate against any employee or applicant for employment because of . . . religion. . . ." Under the new EO this protection "shall not apply to a Government contractor or sub-contractor that is a religious corporation, association, educational institution, or society, with respect to the employment of individuals of a particular religion to perform . . . its activities."

Because of their special status under the Constitution, religious groups traditionally have been exempted from civil rights laws that otherwise protect against religious discrimination. The difference now is that religious discrimination in hiring is supported with public tax dollars.

Religious social service groups like Catholic Charities have for decades received federal funds. In order to meet establishment clause concerns, however, the religious group had to set up a separate organization, keep separate accounts, and ensure that worship and proselytizing did not commingle with its tax-funded social services. Now, commingling of secular and sectarian is encouraged, and all that is required is that the sectarian part of the ministry be done with church money.

President George W. Bush's faith-based organizations initiative raises many difficult questions. The need and desire of evangelical churches to retain their distinctive Christian character in their social ministry is understandable and indeed compelling. This fusion transforms "social service" into a true Christian ministry. But how can the churches claim, on the one hand, that they cannot shed their religious character in order to provide these services and yet, on the other hand, that government funding of these religious ministries is not government funding of religion? Explaining the issue in constitutional terms, it appears that some churches want the establishment clause bar lowered to allow equal treatment, but then at the same time want the special privileges that are accorded to religion when religious freedom is regarded as an inalienable right. Additionally: Will "equal treatment" of religion translate in practice to equal treatment of all religions? Can Wiccan covens with excellent child care programs and services realistically expect to receive funding? By dint of public relations, political power, and evangelizing, will the religious organizations that are the most affluent among us stand to collect the lion's share of the tax dollars?

Some who support government funding of religious social services argue that a close and cooperative relationship between religion (usually meaning Christianity) and the state is necessary to fulfill America's divine destiny and even speak in terms of a "Christian America." Most who support the faith-based initiatives argue that government support of religious social services is necessary to promote the general welfare and solve intractable social problems. Those who oppose government funding hark back to the original debate between James Madison and Patrick Henry, and maintain with Madison and Thomas Jefferson that no one, through tax dollars, should be compelled to support any religion or religious ministry whatsoever.

Catharine Cookson

Further Reading

Alley, R. S. (Ed.). (1999). *The Constitution and religion.* Amherst, NY: Prometheus Books.

Bush, G. W. (2002, December 12). *Executive Order: Equal Protection of the Laws for Faith-based and Community Organizations.* Retrieved January 21, 2003 from: http://www.whitehouse.gov/news/releases/2002/12/20021212-6.html

Davis, D., & Hankins, B. (Eds.). (1999). *Welfare reform and faith-based organizations.* Waco, TX: J. M. Dawson Institute of Church-State Studies.

Hudson, W. S., & Corrigan, J. (1990). *Religion in America* (5th ed.). New York: Macmillan.

McLoughlin, W. (1991). *Soul liberty: The Baptists' struggle in New England, 1630–1833.* Providence, RI: Brown University Press.

Roundtable on Religion and Social Welfare Policy. (2002, December 20). *Updates on Actions and Activities by the Bush Administration to Expand the Faith-Based Initiative.* Retrieved January 21, 2003, from http://www.religionandsocialpolicy.org/news/article.cfm?id=299

Walsh, A. (Ed.). (2001). *Can charitable choice work? Covering religion's impact on urban affairs and social services.* Hartford, CT: The Leonard E. Greenberg Center for the Study of Religion in Public Life, Trinity College.

Court Cases

Cantwell v. Connecticut, 310 U.S. 296 (1940).

Everson v. Board of Education of Ewing Township, 330 U.S. 1 (1947).

Lemon v. Kurtzman, 403 U.S. 602(1971).

Zelman v. Simmons Harris, U.S.S.Ct. docket no. 00-1751 (2002).

Great Awakenings and the Antebellum Period

The years preceding the U.S. Civil War saw the increasing democratization of Protestant America as well as the birth of new religious denominations that responded to concerns about rapid social and political changes. Outpourings of religious enthusiasm swept the country from 1800 onward, with the population experiencing renewed religious fervor that constituted a social movement and solidified the centrality of churches in the U.S. imagination. The mainstream Protestant denominations attempted to negotiate the public role that religion would play in a nation that had separated church and state, while the populist impulses of the new republic made the individual centrally important in matters of both salvation and political reform.

The social changes experienced differed according to geography and denomination. The white,

Revivalist Charles Grandison Finney (1792–1875).
COURTESY OF HTTP://XROADS.VIRGINIA.EDU.

southern experience of religious awakening was essentially socially conservative and individualized. The Baptists and Methodists overwhelmingly predominated in the area, and camp meetings for the purpose of evangelizing would attract thousands. With the population sparsely distributed over rural landscapes, camp meetings provided a primary form of social interaction, particularly for women. Christian reform for white southerners focused on internal morality, and despite some of the preachers' personal reservations about slavery, tended to uphold it as a God-sanctioned institution. However, enslaved blacks also felt the reverberations of the religious enthusiasm, but, for many, Christian ideals entailed the end of the institution of slavery.

In the North, as industrialization and westward expansion made the population more mobile, religious creativity peaked during times of social flux; this religious enthusiasm resulted in a series of religious revivals along the Erie Canal and the western borders from around 1820 to 1850. New Englanders, concerned that excesses in emotion and preachers' informality would hamper the cause of Christianity, attempted to curtail the new styles of exhortation but failed to convince the new generations to abandon their ways. Later, primarily in the 1830s, the canal area and western frontier hosted a burgeoning drive toward utopian communities that experimented with social roles even as they attempted to retain many of the older communal and economic structures they saw being threatened in this period. Some of those utopian communities pushed the limits of religious freedom, giving courts the opportunity to decide where the line was drawn between social governance and freedom of religion.

Individualism and Awakening

The antebellum period saw the ideals of democracy erode the remains of Calvinist Puritanism, with the notions of individual responsibility for conversion and the universal possibility of salvation replacing ideas of predestination and exclusivity. According to Calvinist tenets, the salvation of souls is predetermined before birth; the individual had no control over his or her religious fate. The concept of a predetermined "elect" group of the saved ran counter to the democratic impulses of the epoch. The ideals of self-rule and the equality of all in God's eyes came up against religious teachings about the all-powerful nature of God and his ultimate determination of the

fate of souls. The new social atmosphere required theological compromises on what role grace, and specifically the actions of the Holy Ghost, had in determining one's salvation. The most influential of these posited that while the Holy Ghost alone could effect salvation, the individual must keenly desire it in order to open himself or herself to that possibility. While the Methodists had always upheld the possibility of universal salvation, the Baptists and Presbyterians largely had adopted the new theological stance by 1820. The spike in religious activity brought about by the new measures contributed to a period of awakening, or an intense expression of religiosity that significantly altered people's lived experience of society.

Reform and Limitations

One of the most lasting and important hallmarks of the epoch was the proliferation of benevolent societies, voluntary organizations composed largely of women. The pervasive optimism of the period had led many to believe that the millennium, the thousand-year reign of Christ on Earth, was a tangible goal that would be completed when the full Christianization of the United States could be accomplished. The progressive ethos of this form of millennialism continued in social-reform movements, with many of the faithful believing that society could be perfected by human hands, and that its perfection would in turn usher in Christ's reign. Sabbatarians attempted to enforce Sundays as legally regulated days off, hoping to counter capitalism's excesses with Christian virtues, but encountered resistance both from those arguing for freedom of trade and of religion.

The temperance movement, founded in 1808 and in full bloom by the 1830s, was among the most important and longest-lived of the reforms, seeking to eradicate the use of hard alcohol—or sometimes all alcohol—as well as caffeine and tobacco. Association with a church, and frequently often temperance, was an unspoken requirement for many employment opportunities, a fact that infringed on workers' religious freedom.

Like all the great reform movements of the period, the abolition movement began with Christian logic and rhetoric. While the Quakers had been firmly opposed to slavery even before the American Revolution, the new democracy pressed the question of what constituted equality and for whom. The Presbyterians denounced slavery in 1818, but like many who were morally opposed to the institution, saw no practical way to end it without God's intervention. The prevalence of racism in the North and South alike made blacks so unwelcome in society that their existence only in strictly controlled conditions such as slavery often seemed the better option to many whites. And for many slaveholders, the institution itself was the means by which to Christianize the pagan Africans. William Lloyd Garrison (1805–1879), the founder of the abolition movement, "revived the Revolutionary generation's notion of slavery as a national sin but turned it into *the* national sin, substituting slavery for intemperance as the bellwether of America's fidelity to its covenant with God" (Abzug 1994, 135). By casting the argument in Christian evangelical terms, Garrison posited that freedom was a religious, rather than strictly political, matter. David Walker 1785–1830), a free black who did not subscribe to Garrison's policy of nonviolence, urged slaves to revolt and envisioned an apocalyptic race war that would obliterate the United States with the aid of God. Over time, however, abolition and other reform movements came to be championed in the political arena, and the decline of the awakenings was due in large part to the fact that where before those reforms had been seen as spiritual matters, now they were being seen as urgently political ones.

The antebellum period also saw a wave of anti-Catholic sentiment, expressed most strongly during the riots of the 1830s. Revivalist preachers in New England, most notably the Reverend Lyman Beecher (1775–1863), aroused anti-Catholic feelings during sermons that incited a group of Protestants to attack homes of Irish Catholics in Boston and to stone them for three days in 1829. Four years later, a group of Irish seeking reprisal beat a Protestant to death, resulting in much of the Irish section of Boston being sacked and burned. Culminating in the 1834 burning of an Ursuline convent in Charlestown, Massachusetts, anti-Catholic sentiment was fostered by sensationalist journalism and supported by nativist feelings that Catholicism was in direct opposition to the ideals of democracy. The acquittal of all the men responsible for the convent burning testifies to the ongoing conflict in the period between a desire to protect religious freedom and fear that Catholics' supposed dedication to the pope and church in Rome was antithetical to American values.

Utopian Reactions

For the North and West, the tumultuous changes in the antebellum era centered on the increasingly industrialized and capitalist economy, the mobility of the younger generation in these conditions, and the changing pattern of gender and familial relations with the birth of a middle class. In tandem with these, the far-reaching ideals of republicanism that influenced Protestant Christianity left many feeling uprooted and in search of new answers. Several utopian communities flourished during the period in the 1790s. These communities tried to come to terms with the social upheaval by implementing new religious and communitarian values. The groups were admixtures of unusual, and often incendiary, social experimentation and conservative drives toward precapitalist economic and communal structures. In their most extreme forms, they challenged the boundaries of religious freedom because their appeal to a higher law than the civil law of the land was implicitly an attack on the state.

The Shakers

The Shakers were among the utopian communities that thrived during this era. In 1774, their founder, Mother Ann Lee (1736–1784), moved her small group of followers to the American colonies from England. Ann Lee had received visions that convinced her that carnality was the root of worldly evil. She implemented strict celibacy among her followers, advocating love for the entire community as a higher goal than the selfish love of exclusive erotic attractions and familial ties. She embraced pacifism, abolished individual ownership of property, and focused on the benefits of honest labor, telling her followers to put their "hands to work and their hearts to God," (Foster 1984, 28). At her death in 1784, the Shakers remained a small group centered in New England and New York. By 1830, however, their numbers had soared to around four thousand, and, by the end of the antebellum period, to six thousand in more than sixty communities from New England to Indiana.

The Shakers already threatened normative social mores by denying the primacy of the family, and the lawsuits against them implicitly or explicitly called the extent of religious freedom into question. One of the most famous cases took place in New York in 1817, when Eunice Chapman attempted to obtain a divorce from her Shaker husband and custody of their children. The proposed law would have declared all Shakers "civilly dead," an act that would have overturned the prevailing norm of the husband retaining custody of the children. While the court granted Eunice Chapman a divorce, it did not embrace such far-reaching measures as civic disenfranchisement on the grounds of religious choice.

The Oneida Community

The Oneida Community encountered similar legislative difficulties, and like the Shakers, the courts in the main found in favor of the utopians. Founded by John Humphrey Noyes (1811–1886), the community flourished in upstate New York in the years 1848–1880. Believing that the millennium had arrived as Jesus predicted during the lives of the apostles, Noyes implemented the conditions of perfection as he understood them. This included communal living and equal love for all members rather than exclusive attachments. Unlike the Shakers, however, the Oneidans understood equality of love to include a sexual component, and practiced group marriage among members. In 1848, Noyes argued that the Oneidans' sexual arrangements were decreed by God and the Bible, and were therefore protected under the U.S. Constitution's provisions for freedom of conscience and religion. Although there was no resulting court case, Noyes inadvertently brought unwanted attention to his community that made it a subject of social censure.

Like the Shakers, the Oneidans' iconoclastic sexual behavior drew legal interest toward them, and in 1851 the Oneida County district attorney Samuel Garvin, in the course of investigating an assault and battery charge, brought nine community members before the grand jury and asked them explicit questions about their sexual practices. The assault case was settled out of court after locals signed a petition attesting to the Oneidans' good character, but Garvin continued to try to prosecute the community until a second petition boasting many local dignitaries was circulated. Group marriage was suspended for five months during the investigation, but the overall legal effect on the community was negligible.

Implications

The democratization of Protestant Christianity during the antebellum period reflected the anti-aristocratic ethos of the new republic even as it opened the way for an ever-increasing number of voices to be heard in the religious arena. Imbued with a new egalitarianism,

Protestants began to experiment with new doctrines, resulting in splintering theologies and the undermining of the hegemony of the major denominations. While by and large religious freedom was upheld in the most extreme cases of experimentation, like those of the utopian movements, the cost for these victories was often a sense of security in an increasingly multiple and idiosyncratic religious environment.

Cathy Gutierrez

See also Slavery

Further Reading

Abzug, R. H. (1994). *Cosmos crumbling: American reform and the religious imagination.* New York: Oxford University Press.

Barkun, M. (1974). *Disaster and the millennium.* New Haven, CT: Yale University Press.

Boyer, P. (1992). *When time shall be no more: Prophecy belief in modern American culture.* Cambridge, MA: Belknap Press.

Cross, W. (1950). *The burned-over district: The social and intellectual history of enthusiastic religion in western New York, 1800–1850.* New York: Harper & Row Publishers.

Foster, L. (1984). *Religion and sexuality: The Shakers, the Mormons, and the Oneida Community.* Urbana: University of Illinois Press.

Handy, R. T. (1971). *A Christian America: Protestant hopes and historical realities.* New York: Oxford University Press.

Hatch, N. O. (1989). *The democratization of American Christianity.* New Haven, CT: Yale University Press.

Johnson, P. E. (1978). *A shopkeeper's millennium: Society and revivals in Rochester, New York, 1815–1837.* New York: Hill and Wang.

Klaw, S. (1993). *Without sin: The life and death of the Oneida community.* New York: Penguin Press.

McLoughlin, W. G. (1978). *Revivals, awakenings, and reform: An essay on religion and social change in America, 1607–1977.* Chicago: University of Chicago Press.

Mathews, D. G. (1969). The Second Great Awakening as an organizing process, 1780–1830: An hypothesis. *American Quarterly, 21*(1), 23–43.

Ryan, M. P. (1981). *Cradle of the middle class: The family in Oneida County, New York, 1790–1865.* New York: Cambridge University Press.

Weisbrod, C. (1980). *The boundaries of utopia.* New York: Pantheon Books.

Heresy

Systems of religion that require that the faithful adhere to strict standards of belief and worship generally produce a concomitant idea of heresy (broadly defined as beliefs that are in opposition to religious dogma). The terminology of heresy originated in the Judeo-Christian tradition, deriving from the Greek word *hairesis*, which means both "deliberate choice" and "sect." The word is employed by Josephus to describe several sects widespread in Judea, and is applied to St. Paul in Acts 24:5 and Acts 28:22 by Roman authorities.

Definitions and Interpretations

In its earliest usages, "heresy" seems to have neutral connotations. Philosophical schools as well as religious movements were characterized by the word without any evident derogatory meaning. Only one pejorative use of *hairesis* is found in Christian scripture, according to which "sects (*haireseis*) of perdition" are introduced by "false teachers" (in 2 Peter 2:1).

One can define heresy either narrowly or broadly. Broadly conceived, the concept of heresy goes along with any religion that attempts to codify its doctrines in an orthodox manner, excluding those who refuse to profess a core set of teachings yet claim to adhere to the faith. The formulation of orthodoxy thus logically entails the possibility of heresy and a concern for its appearance and dissemination.

According to this broad definition of heresy, many religions can be said to embrace heresiography.

In Judaism, the tradition of "false prophets" seems to imply a standard of orthodox faith against which to judge deviations. Evidence suggests recurrent attempts throughout Jewish history to enunciate the minimum standards for salvation, whether in the case of the Mishnah (in the first or second centuries CE) or Moses Maimonides (in the late twelfth century). A host of words denigrating Jews who challenged rabbinical authority were introduced into Hebrew, especially after the destruction of the Temple in 70 CE.

Islam likewise evinced concern about the fragmentation of its central tenets. While often, and correctly, characterized as a religion of law and practice rather than theology and belief, the heresiographical impulse may be found in many writings by Muslim thinkers and in statements of Islamic creed. Some scholars of Islam propose that the distinction between "law" and "faith" that supposedly renders Islam's orientation less doctrinal than other creeds requires reevaluation, on the grounds that widespread polemics regarding *shari'a*—Islamic law—involved significant theological argument as well. Islamic tradition also evolved a set of terms, such as *bid'a* and *Kufr*, that conveyed the principal elements of the concept of heresy. Indeed, modern Arabic has taken over from European languages the words *hartaqua* and *hartaqi*, connoting "heresy" and "heretic" respectively. Even non-monotheistic, non-Abrahamic religions can contain a heresiographical dimension. Some Confucian and Neo-Confucian movements attempted to standardize their salient religious teachings and thereby to condemn dissenting views. The Ch'eng-Chu school of Neo-Confucianism, for instance, the authorized belief

FOURTH LATERAN COUNCIL (1215): CANON 3—*ON HERESY*

We excommunicate and anathematize every heresy raising itself up against this holy, orthodox and catholic faith which we have expounded above. We condemn all heretics, whatever names they may go under. They have different faces indeed but their tails are tied together inasmuch as they are alike in their pride. Let those condemned be handed over to the secular authorities present, or to their bailiffs, for due punishment. Clerics are first to be degraded from their orders. The goods of the condemned are to be confiscated, if they are lay persons, and if clerics they are to be applied to the churches from which they received their stipends. Those who are only found suspect of heresy are to be struck with the sword of anathema, unless they prove their innocence by an appropriate purgation, having regard to the reasons for suspicion and the character of the person. Let such persons be avoided by all until they have made adequate satisfaction. If they persist in the excommunication for a year, they are to be condemned as heretics. Let secular authorities, whatever offices they may be discharging, be advised and urged and if necessary be compelled by ecclesiastical censure, if they wish to be reputed and held to be faithful, to take publicly an oath for the defense of the faith to the effect that they will seek, in so far as they can, to expel from the lands subject to their jurisdiction all heretics designated by the church in good faith. Thus whenever anyone is promoted to spiritual or temporal authority, he shall be obliged to confirm this article with an oath. If however a temporal lord, required and instructed by the church, neglects to cleanse his territory of this heretical filth, he shall be bound with the bond of excommunication by the metropolitan and other bishops of the province. If he refuses to give satisfaction within a year, this shall be reported to the supreme pontiff so that he may then declare his vassals absolved from their fealty to him and make the land available for occupation by Catholics so that these may, after they have expelled the heretics, possess it unopposed and preserve it in the purity of the faith—saving the right of the suzerain provided that he makes no difficulty in the matter and puts no impediment in the way. The same law is to be observed no less as regards those who do not have a suzerain.

---

system of the Chinese imperial administration from c. 1300 until c. 1900, persistently strove to define its creed in an orthodox manner and condemn deviation. Just as in Western and Middle Eastern religions, Confucian and Neo-Confucian authors formulated a language of heresiography to describe the relation between the "correct Way" and the "strange shoots" of deviation.

Christian Interpretations

Early Christianity was as broadly heresiographical as the religions previously mentioned, although more systematically. Beginning after c. 150 CE, Christian apologists, acting on St. Paul's attacks on religious diversity among alleged followers of Jesus, condemned the heretical tendencies of numerous Christian sects. As it developed from St. Justin and Irenaeus in the second century, through Tertullian and Hippolytus of Rome in the third, and culminating in Epiphanius in the fourth, extensive antiheretical classification and criticism became a hallmark of Christian polemic, accompanying the construction of unitary Christian doctrine. While early Christianity may have been the most systematic major religion in specifying its core teachings, it followed a pattern common to other creeds.

Yet, in a second, narrower sense, the concept of heresy is particularly connected with Christian tradition, insofar as heretical "error" is seen to necessitate correction and punishment with both temporal and spiritual consequences. Heresy was singled out by Christians as especially dangerous, different in kind from apostasy and other forms of infidelity. It thus demanded stronger persecution and extirpation than other modes of unbelief.

Catholics who take the cross and gird themselves up for the expulsion of heretics shall enjoy the same indulgence, and be strengthened by the same holy privilege, as is granted to those who go to the aid of the Holy Land. Moreover, we determine to subject to excommunication believers who receive, defend or support heretics. We strictly ordain that if any such person, after he has been designated as excommunicated, refuses to render satisfaction within a year, then by the law itself he shall be branded as infamous and not be admitted to public offices or councils or to elect others to the same or to give testimony. He shall be intestable, that is he shall not have the freedom to make a will nor shall succeed to an inheritance. Moreover nobody shall be compelled to answer to him on any business whatever, but he may be compelled to answer to them. If he is a judge sentences pronounced by him shall have no force and cases may not be brought before him; if an advocate, he may not be allowed to defend anyone; if a notary, documents drawn up by him shall be worthless and condemned along with their condemned author; and in similar matters we order the same to be observed. If however he is a cleric, let him be deposed from every office and benefice, so that the greater the fault the greater be the punishment. If any refuse to avoid such persons after they have been pointed out by the church, let them be punished with the sentence of excommunication until they make suitable satisfaction. Clerics should not, of course, give the sacraments of the church to such pestilent people nor give them a Christian burial nor accept alms or offerings from them; if they do, let them be deprived of their office and not restored to it without a special indulgence of the apostolic see. Similarly with regulars, let them be punished with losing their privileges in the diocese in which they presume to commit such excesses.

Source: H. J. Schroeder, trans.
The Disciplinary Decrees of the Ecumenical Council.
(St. Louis: B. Herder Book Co., 1937), 242–243.

What made heresy special was the fact that heretics had been admitted, through baptism and other sacraments, into the unified soul—the communion—of the Christian church. Heterodoxy was particularly horrific because its followers maintained not only that they were Christians, but that their version of Christianity was truer and more pure than the orthodox one. Heresy was therefore a disease of the soul that was extremely contagious if not quickly treated; preventing its spread to other believers justified even the use of violence against those who persisted in upholding it. And Christianity, with its universalistic ambitions, found the temporal resources to enforce its spiritual vision in a way that other religions were unable or unprepared to pursue. In the study of religious freedom, this strict understanding of heresy, that came to typify Christian orthodoxy in the late Roman imperial period, sets Christianity apart from world religions that subscribed to a broader understanding of heresy.

The first several centuries of Christian history, scholars have noted, witnessed many more heretical movements than any other religion of that or other times. Such quantitative data, while illustrative, do not fully capture the character of the historical evolution of the place of heresy within Christianity. The perseverance of longstanding heterodox views and the appearance and spread of new ones, in the period following the official integration of the Christian church into the Roman Empire, suggests that the content of Christianity, as opposed to its general form, had been ineffectively disseminated to late classical society. The Bishop of Hippo, and eventual saint, Augustine, expressed frustration with the heresies that he fought—a testament to the widespread and deep roots of Christian diversity. Some scholars have suggested that the range of beliefs considered heretical grew along with the confidence of a Christian church supported by the political mandate of the empire. But it also seems that the imposition of orthodoxy encouraged the spontaneous emergence of innovative expressions of heretical sentiment.

St. Augustine ultimately concluded that patient fraternal correction—his original remedy for heresy—had to be supplemented with physical compulsion and even execution. Persecution became an approved treatment for the contagion, yet the ability of ecclesiastical officials to impose coercive penalties declined with the erosion of a centralized imperial regime. Until the eleventh century, evidence for heresy among European Christians is so sketchy as to preclude sustained conclusions. Even the widely held view that new Christian heresies began to crop up with alarming frequency after about 1100 has been effectively countered. That church and secular authorities began to uncover and exterminate heresy during the High Middle Ages may instead reflect the increased theological zeal of consolidating political and ecclesiastical institutions, resulting in the "persecuting society" posited by R. I. Moore (1987). The weight of attempts to repress heresies and heretics is proportional to the rigor of efforts to define orthodoxy and establish uniformity.

The Fourth Lateran Council of 1215, which proscribed a range of heresies and other forms of religious and moral non-conformity, represents in many ways the peak of the persecuting impulse during the Latin Middle Ages. The Council propounded a series of decrees that amounted to a comprehensive standard for inclusion in and exclusion from the community of Christian believers. Those who asserted membership, whether through baptism or other sacraments, yet refused to obey their clerical superiors in matters of creed and conduct, were subject to excommunication and related temporal penalties (imprisonment, confiscation of property, and corporal and capital punishment). The canon law that formed the backbone of institutional ecclesiastical development in the twelfth century stipulated a fixed legal procedure, *inquisitio*, to address reputed crimes of flagrant heresy.

Ironically, the stimulus for the decrees of the Fourth Lateran Council was yet another round of demands for clerical renewal. These demands arose from the persistent belief among the laity and some high-minded churchmen that the clergy had become corrupt and were leading astray the souls in their

charge. The persistence of heresy in Christian Europe may thus be intimately linked with a reforming sentiment that remained wholly orthodox and reflected an acceptable measure of religious zeal. Both the popular heresies that the church struggled to suppress (such as Catharism) and the more elite heresies (centered in the schools) whose advocates courted the censure of ecclesiastical authorities (such as the Spiritual wing of the Franciscan order) tended to direct their outrage into criticizing clerical corruption and calling for renewed moral and spiritual purity.

Yet the impression that authorities in medieval Christian society were uniformly persecuting in the treatment of heretics is misleading. Widespread anticlericalism fostered sympathy toward and protection of heretics by secular officials who were not themselves heretics, as was the case with the Cathars in thirteenth-century Orvieto. Powerful European rulers regularly sheltered accused heretics amongst the intelligentsia and employed them as counselors and polemicists in their causes against popes and the ecclesiastical hierarchy generally. A highly educated scholastic author such as Marsiglio of Padua (himself accused of heresy) in the early fourteenth century was able to argue that the excommunication of heretics should not entail temporal penalties like the denial of civil rights and freedoms—a position echoed by early modern proponents of toleration and liberty of conscience. In sum, resistance to the strict imposition of orthodoxy remained a feature of Latin Christianity throughout the Middle Ages.

In the wake of the Reformation, with the shattering of confessional and institutional unity, "heresy" increasingly acquired an unfocussed meaning as a general term of religious derision. Christians of differing affiliations cited heresy in accusing each other—Catholics against Protestants, and Protestants against one another and Catholics—so that eventually the epithet "heretical" came to denote nearly any form of apostasy or infidelity. In effect, the meaning of heresy in Western society was transformed from a narrowly technical one referring to obdurate dissent from orthodox authority, into an off-handed charge levied against anyone expressing a belief different from one's own.

Enlightenment thinkers made past heretics into heroic figures who struggled to realize religious toleration and humanistic values. A body of literature that recounted "histories of heresy" formed a mainstay of modern defenses of tolerance. John Stuart Mill in *On Liberty* held up heterodox movements of the Middle Ages as bearers of truths whose suppression slowed human progress. Some recent historians of heretical ideas barely conceal their admiration for the independence of mind expressed in the dissenting outlooks they study. Such apparent anachronisms retain the earlier sense of horror with which heresy was viewed by the orthodox, but they revalue heretical doctrines as expressions of personal or communal autonomy and refusals to submit to arbitrary power.

Cary J. Nederman

See also Augustine on Religious Coercion; Cathars; Inquisition

Further Reading

Henderson, J. B. (1998). *The construction of orthodoxy and heresy: Neo-Confucian, Islamic, Jewish, and Early Christian Patterns*. Albany: State University of New York Press.

Lambert, M. D. (1977). *Medieval heresy*. London: Edward Arnold.

Lansing, C. (1998). *Power and purity: Cathar heresy in medieval Italy*. Oxford, UK: Oxford University Press.

Laursen, J. C. (2002). *Histories of heresy in early modern Europe: For, against, and beyond persecution and toleration*. New York: Palgrave.

Lund, R. D. (Ed.). (1995). *The margins of orthodoxy: Heterodox writing and cultural response, 1660–1750*. Cambridge, UK: Cambridge University Press.

Moore, R. I. (1977). *The origins of European dissent*. London: Penguin.

Moore, R. I. (1987). *The formation of a persecuting society*. Oxford, UK: Blackwell.

Nederman, C. J. (2000). *Worlds of difference: European discourses of religious toleration, c. 1100–c.1550*. University Park: Pennsylvania State University Press.

Peters, E. (Ed.). (1980). *Heresy and authority in the middle ages*. Philadelphia: University of Pennsylvania Press.

Vaneigem, R. (1994). *The movement of the free spirit* (R. Cherry & I. Patterson, Trans.). New York: Zone Books.

Vodola, E. (1986). *Excommunication in the middle ages*. Berkeley: University of California Press.

Hinduism

India is one of the most socially and religiously complex nations in the world, and its primary religion, Hinduism, is one of the most complex of the world's religions. This dual complexity means that any discussion of religious freedom in Hinduism is subject to multiple interpretations.

The two largest religions in India are Hinduism (81 percent of the population) and Islam (12 percent), followed by Christianity (2.3 percent) Sikhism (2 percent), and Jainism. There is also a growing Buddhist population of about 5 million, a small but influential Parsi (Zoroastrian) community, tribal peoples who maintain their indigenous religions, and numerous new religious movements. There are also large Indian diaspora populations in the United Kingdom, the United States, Sri Lanka, and Canada and significant indigenous Hindu populations in Indonesia and Thailand. Nepal, like India, has a majority Hindu population and defines itself as a Hindu state.

Hindus and Muslims live throughout India, although Jammu and Kashmir is the only state with a Muslim majority. Uttar Pradesh, Bihar, Maharashtra, West Bengal, Andhra Pradesh, and Kerala have large Muslim populations. Christians are concentrated in the northeast and south, and Punjab, in the northwest, has a majority Sikh population. The three small Jewish communities have now mostly relocated to Israel.

Religious Freedom and Toleration in the Past

Hinduism emerged about 1500 BCE in the Indus Valley in what is now Pakistan and then spread south and east across what is now India. It is often pointed out that Hinduism differs from other world religions such as Christianity and Islam in that it has no single founder, no single set of beliefs and rituals shared by all followers, and no central organization. It has sometimes been described as a religion of a million gods, because it seems that each village in India has some gods and rituals that are unique to it. This multiplicity of belief and the overarching belief in the major deities of Brahma, Siva, and Vishnu has led some experts to classify Hinduism as a polytheistic religion. Today, however, experts are comfortable treating it as a monotheistic religion because all the deities can be considered manifestations of Brahma, the ultimate divine ground of the universe (of which the Brahma mentioned above is just one).

There are two sides in the debate over whether or not Hinduism is a tolerant religion. Some argue that

Hinduism has long been among the most tolerant of religions, and that any intolerance that has emerged recently is the result of efforts by others, such as Muslims and Christians, to convert Hindus. Others see the reverse, characterizing the Hinduism of the past as basically intolerant and arguing that tolerance appeared only quite recently with the emergence of modern India as a secular nation since 1948.

The argument for tolerance rests on the core belief in Hinduism that Hinduism accepts worship of God in any form and is therefore, by definition, accepting of all other religions that worship God. In essence, whatever from worship may take, the worshipper is worshipping Brahma. For this reason, Hindus do not seek convert from other religions and see no reason for Hindus to convert to other religions. Also offered in support of Hinduism as a tolerant religion is the diversity in Hinduism itself; the emergence of other major religions in India (Buddhism, Jainism, and Sikhism); the acceptance in India of Christians, Jews, Zoroastrians, and Tibetan Buddhists persecuted elsewhere; and the separation of church and state within Hinduism itself, with one caste category (Brahman) responsible for religion and another (Kshatriya) for the affairs of state.

Proponents of the view that Hinduism has not been an especially tolerant religion take a different view of history. They point out that a martial tradition is associated with the rise and spread of Hinduism, with considerable conflict among rival Hindu groups and with outsiders such as the Greeks and the Kushans. They also note that Hindus have often viewed other religions as inferior, and that this mind-set persists in twenty-first century Hindu nationalism. And, while it true that Hinduism has been a seedbed for new religions such as Buddhism and Sikhism, repression of those same religions has also occurred. They point to the case of Buddhism, which was eventually driven from India. Also, the presence of reform movements implies the existence of problems to spark the reforms, and the reform movements, like the new religions, often met with repression.

Religious Freedom and Toleration since Independence

India's constitution established India in 1948 as a secular nation with considerable religious freedom. However, the government does have the right to interfere in the activities of religious groups that it deems disruptive to the political and social order. Using that authority, the government has upon occasion arrested Muslims and banned Muslim organizations, and state governments have attempted to control the building of non-Hindu houses of worship. The power of the states is significant in religious affairs, as much legal authority resides with the states, making it difficult to uniformly enforce federal laws concerning religious freedom.

Religious freedom is enhanced through the accommodation of personal-status laws that allow different religious communities to use their own religious laws to govern matters such as marriage, divorce, adoption, and inheritance. Some of the personal-status laws have been criticized by human-rights advocates as harmful to women (for example, Muslim laws governing divorce, which favor men), and Hindu nationalists view these laws as discriminating against Hindus.

The law allows people to evangelize for their religion but prohibits public criticism of other religions. Since the 1960s, the government has refused to grant special visas to foreign missionaries (usually Christians) and has expelled some who stayed after their tourist visas expired. The label *missionary* (as in missionary schools or missionary hospitals) is now viewed by some as negative and suggestive of foreign corruption of Indian society. In fact, most Christian institutions are run by Indian Christians, not outsiders. The National Commission for Minorities and the National Human Rights Commission investigate charges of discrimination but can make only recommendations to local and state governments.

Critics of government policy charge that in the broad sense and in its application in some states, it allows or even supports a process of "saffronization" (after the saffron robes of some Hindu clerics) that seeks to make India a Hindu nation, with Muslims and Christians treated as second-class citizens and Buddhism, Jainism, and Sikhism treated as branches of Hinduism. This policy is most pronounced in states such as Orissa and Gujarat, whose ruling political parties espouse a philosophy of Hindu nationalism.

To many observers, Hindu nationalism, which has been a potent political issue since the 1980s, is the key force in religious relations in India today. Many experts argue that it is the basic cause of conflicts between Hindus and Muslims, Hindus and Christians, and Hindus and Sikhs. Violence between Hindus and Muslims, the most common and deadly form of religious violence in India, is commonly labeled "communal violence" or "communal riots" and has been going on for over a hundred years.

Hindu Nationalism

Hindu nationalism first emerged as a political movement in 1875 with the founding of the Arya Samaj (Society of Aryans) by the reformer Dayanand Saraswati (1824–1883). It was followed by the Hindu Mahasabha (Hindu General Assembly) in 1915 and, most importantly, the Rashtriya Svayamsevak Sangh (National Volunteer Union, or RSS) in 1925. RSS has formed the core of the Hindu nationalist movement since its founding and has produced several major political organizations, including the Bharatiya Janata Party (Indian People's Party or BJP), the Vishva Hindu Parishad (All-Hindu Council) and the Bajrang Dal (Bajrangs's Troop). Together they form the *sangh parivar* (the Sanskrit term for the RSS family) and share the goal of creating a Hindu India.

In 1923 the ideology of *Hindutva* ("Hindu-ness") was set forth by the Hindu scholar and nationalist V. D. Savarkar (1883–1966) in his booklet *Hindutva*, and later expanded upon by M. S. Golwalkar (1906–1973), also a devout Hindu. Savarkar linked India and Hinduism by defining a Hindu as someone who both views India as his or her homeland as well as the holy land. Thus, by definition Muslims, Christians, and others are outsiders, as their religious loyalty lies outside India.

In the 1980s the BJP emerged as a major national political party, and in 1998 it formed the core of the national coalition government. The party is also powerful in several states, although nationalist ideology is stronger in state party units in the north than in the south, where party units are more tolerant of ethnic minorities and other religions.

Ideologically, Hindu nationalists believe that Hindutva is the national ethos of India and that unity among all Hindus is created by a shared homeland, shared ancestry, and shared culture. For political purposes, the BJP has restated this ideology in the slogan: "One nation, one people, and one culture." Hindu nationalists also reject some elements of Western culture and stress the need to create unity among Hindus and to combat Western and Muslim influences.

Critics of the Hindu nationalism agenda suggest that it is based on a selective interpretation of Hindu history and beliefs, corrupts Hinduism for political purposes, favors high-caste Hindus, seeks to destroy the cultural and religious heterogeneity that has long been a defining feature of Indian society, and has created hostility among India's religious communities.

Hindu-Muslim Relations

Conflict between Hindus and Muslims in India dates to the tenth century, when Muslims began the incursions into India that eventually led to the establishment of the Mughal Empire (1526–1857). Relations between Hindus and Muslims were generally peaceful; the degree of religious freedom afforded Hindus varied with the ruler. Akbar (1542–1605) was known for his tolerance and is considered one of the greatest of the Mughal emperors; his great-grandson Aurangzeb (1618–1707) grew increasingly intolerant during the course of his reign. An event of particular significance for later Hindu-Muslim relations took place in 1025, when Muslims destroyed the Hindu Somanth Temple in Gujarat, a primary place of worship for Hindu Brahmans. Hindu nationalists in the twenty-first century continue to cite this event as a sign of Muslim hostility toward Hindus, and competing claims for ownership of sacred places is often a precipitator of violence between Hindus and Muslims.

Hindu-Muslim violence became more frequent in the late 1800s. India was at the time part of the British Empire, and the Government of India Act of 1909 politicized religious identity. The Act, which was an attempt at political reform, institutionalized "communal representation," with Hindus and Muslims voting in separate elections for parties representing each religious community. The goal was to provide representative government in which Muslims were not always outvoted by the majority Hindus. The reforms ultimately turned the Indian National Congress (INC) into a political party representing Hindu positions. The Muslim League, established in 1906, worked for decades with the INC for Indian independence and Muslim-Hindu unity in a free India, but separated from the INC in 1940 because of that party's Hindu nationalism. From then on, it called for the establishment of a separate state on the subcontinent for Muslims.

Pakistan became an independent nation on 14 August 1947 and India on 15 August. Independence was followed by a massive migration of Hindus from Pakistan to India and Muslims from India to Pakistan. The migration, which involved some 14 million people, was hardly peaceful, and about 1.5 million died in the turmoil. The partition failed to solve the Hindu-Muslim problem in India, and conflict has continued since 1947 over issues such as access to political power, minority rights, Indian identity, and control of sacred sites. The situation in India has not been improved by three border wars between India and Pakistan and the ongoing conflict in Kashmir, which has a Muslim majority but is ruled by India. Muslims in India both resent being viewed as disloyal to India and fear religious repression by Hindu nationalists.

Hindu-Muslim violence was a regular feature of Indian life during the 1990s, often occurring as a cycle of violence with violent acts attributed to one community being avenged by the other. A key focus of violence is the status of the Babri Masjid, a mosque in Ayodhya in northern India. Hindus believe that the mosque was built on an ancient Hindu site that is the birthplace of the Hindu god Rama. In 1986 a court opened the mosque to Hindus, which angered Muslims, who restrict non-Muslim access to their sacred sites. Violent protests by both groups raged for several years, and in December 1992 the mosque was destroyed. Widespread rioting throughout India followed, with some 2,200 people killed. A government investigation blamed Hindu nationalist political parties for the destruction, supporting Muslim claims that the state and local government officials failed to prevent or punish anti-Muslim actions.

The most recent major events include the Muslim firebombing of a train carrying Hindu worshippers in February 2002 in Gujarat. That event led to two months of rioting and left over a thousand people dead. Other violence included a September 2002 attack on a Hindu temple and a Hindu revenge killing and the continuing fighting in Kashmir among separatists supported by Pakistan, the Indian army, and local groups.

Christians in India

According to tradition, Christians first arrived in India in the first century CE when St. Thomas established Syrian Christian communities in Kerala. Historical evidence shows a continual Syrian Christian population in India since the sixth century CE. Roman Catholicism arrived with the Portuguese in 1498, and during the period of British rule

Protestant missionaries became active. In 2003 there were about 25 million Christians in India, concentrated in the south and northeast. During the period of British rule (c. 1850–1947), missionaries and churches were important forces in social change, playing a role in education, legal, and social reforms. Missionary activity also stimulated Hindu and Buddhist reform movements.

One of the most difficult issues is the relationship between Christians and the government. After much debate, Catholics and Protestants supported the independence movement and the establishment of a secular state, believing that a secular state would guarantee religious freedom. After independence new Protestant churches were established in southern India, northern India, and Pakistan; there were new converts and closer Protestant and Catholic ties.

Christians charge that the rise of the BJP and the emergence of Hindu nationalism have been accompanied by repression of Christianity and assaults on Christians and their institutions. These attacks became especially frequent in the late 1990s and early 2000s. For example, the website Persecuted for Christ in India lists seventy-nine attacks in 1997 and 1998. These include beatings, harassment of Christians, disruption of Christian services, the murder of church officials, and the rape of nuns. Many of the attacks have been in Gujarat, and Christians claim that the government at worst encourages and supports the attacks and at best does nothing to prevent them or to punish the perpetrators. Public pronouncements by some BJP officials indicate that Christians are seen by some Hindu nationalists as foreigners whose allegiance is to an authority outside India. In addition, human-rights organizations note that Christian missionaries have been active and successful in converting Hindu untouchables (Dalits), who remain poor and disadvantaged, to Christianity, and that that activity is seen as a threat by some Hindu nationalists. Some untouchable communities view Christianity, Islam, and Buddhism as the means to economic and political freedom in India.

Implications

Limitations on religious freedom and conflict between religious groups, especially Hindus and Muslims, have implications that go far beyond the nature of the social order and community relations in India. The Hindu-Muslim conflict in India and Kashmir is one piece of a larger conflict between Hindu India and Muslim Pakistan, two nations with nuclear weapons. Many people in both nations, in other nations in the region, and around the world fear that the Hindu-Muslim conflict can easily escalate into war, with the possibility of a regional nuclear holocaust. This means that controlling Hindu-Muslim violence is a major challenge for India and involves resolving the Kashmir issue and lessening hostility with Pakistan.

David Levinson

See also Jainism, Sikhism

Further Reading

Allchin, F. R., et al. (1995). *The archaeology of early historic South Asia: The emergence of cities and states.* New York: Cambridge University Press.

Chaudhuri, N. C. (1996). *Hinduism: A religion to live by.* Delhi, India: Oxford University Press.

Das, V. (1992). *Mirrors of violence: Communities, riots and survivors in South Asia.* Delhi, India: Oxford University Press.

Golwalkar, M. S. (1947). *We, or our nationhood defined.* Nagpur, India: Bharat Prakashan.

Hansen, T. B. (1999). *The saffron wave: Democracy and Hindu nationalism in modern India.* Princeton, NJ: Princeton University Press.

Oddie, G. A. (1979). *Social protest in India: British Protestant missionaries and social reforms.* Delhi, India: Manohar.

Oddie, G. A. (1991). *Religion in South Asia: Religious conversion and revival movements in South Asia in medieval and modern times* (2nd rev. and enlarged ed.). Delhi, India: Manohar.

Olivelle, P. (1999). *Dharmasutras: The law codes of ancient India.* New York: Oxford University Press.

Pandey, G. (Ed.). (1993). *Hindus and others: The question of identity in India today.* New Delhi, India: Viking Penguin.

Savarkar, V. D. (1989). *Hindutva: Who is a Hindu?* (Reprint ed.). Mumbai, India: S. S. Savarkar. (Original work published 1923)

U.S. Department of State. (2002). *International religious freedom report 2002.* Washington, DC: Bureau of Democracy, Human Rights, and Labor, U.S. Department of State.

Van der Veer, P. (1994). *Religious nationalism: Hindus and Muslims in India.* Berkeley and Los Angeles: University of California Press.

Varshney, A. (2002). *Ethnic conflict and civic life: Hindus and Muslims in India.* New Haven, CT: Yale University Press.

Human Rights

The topic of religion and human rights is a critically important one, given the history of violence, persecution, and other forms of injustice that have taken place in the name of religion. This article focuses on the aspects of human rights that are most pertinent to religious freedom and on some of the ways in which religion and human rights come into conflict.

Defining Human Rights and Religious Freedom

The term *human rights* is generally agreed to have grown out of the Western liberal tradition, being first expressly articulated in the eighteenth century in documents such as the U.S. Declaration of Independence (1776) and the French Declaration of the Rights of Man (1789) but with older roots in the natural-law and natural-rights traditions of political philosophy. Today human rights is taken to signify justified moral and legal claims to the protection of certain fundamental interests. Human rights are understood in international law to be universal; that is, persons are entitled to human rights simply by virtue of being human and not because of their particular citizenship, ethnicity, religion, gender, or other specific attributes.

However, there are a number of philosophical theories—including legal positivism and cultural relativism—that contend that human rights are in some ways historically relative and politically contingent upon a particular nation's recognition of them. In recent years, a number of critics of international human rights, including Western postmodern and feminist scholars and leaders of Asian nations, have criticized the currently accepted concept of human rights as being culturally biased in favor of Western, liberal nations and gender biased in favor of the men primarily responsible for drafting the documents that articulate the concept. In opposition, defenders of international human rights have pointed out

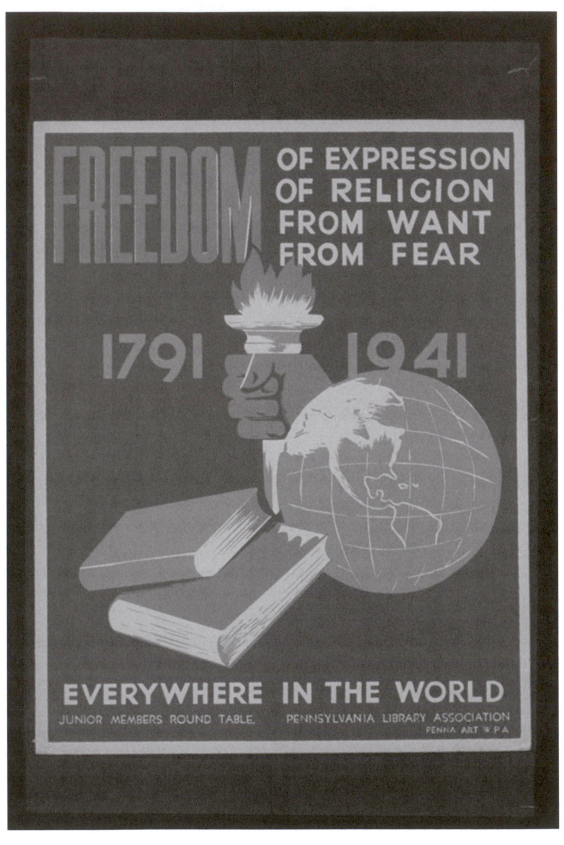

A Pennsylvania Library Association Poster promoting President Franklin Delano Roosevelt's Four Freedoms, c. 1936–1941. COURTESY OF LIBRARY OF CONGRESS WORK PROJECTS ADMINISTRATION POSTER COLLECTION.

that members of many non-Western nations actively participated in the drafting of the international human-rights system, and that, regardless of their historical development, many non-Western nations now embrace international human rights.

The terms *religion* and *religious freedom* are not specifically defined in the United Nations' human-rights documents. These terms appear in connection with freedom of belief and conscience, both of which are broad enough to encompass many views that are not specifically religious. In addition, strictly speaking, freedom of religion encompasses freedom *from* religion, that is, the right to be free from coercion or forced attempts to compel religious belief.

Some of the most frequent violations of religious human rights around the world include violations of the right to choose one's religion (or no religion), the right to change one's religion, the right to worship in public and private, and the right not to be discriminated against on religious grounds. Other violations include acts of intolerance, persecution, jailing, and even murder; failure to protect the rights to freedom of thought, conscience, and religion or belief; failure to protect the rights to manifest beliefs, or to conscientious objection, or to dispose of religious property; and failure to protect against the desecration of sacred sites, including religious sanctuaries and cemeteries.

Overview of the International Human-Rights Protections for Religion

The current formulation of human rights at the international level is contained in several United Nations documents: the Universal Declaration of Human Rights (UDHR; 1948), the International Covenants on Civil and Political Rights (ICCPR; 1966), and the International Covenant on Social and Economic and Cultural Rights (ICSECR; 1966). Together these three documents are often referred to as the "international bill of rights." They are supplemented by a number of other treaties and conventions covering the human rights of specific groups (women, children, indigenous peoples, racial and religious minorities, and so forth).

The founders of the United Nations recognized that the right to the exercise of religious beliefs is fundamental to personhood and basic human freedom; therefore in drafting the UDHR they explicitly included freedom of religion along with freedom of thought and conscience as a basic human right.

However, as Natan Lerner, a scholar in international law, notes: "It has been rightly asserted that the subject of religious human rights was shunned and neglected more than any other similar subject, perhaps as a consequence of the generally acknowledged fact that no topic has divided humankind more" (Lerner 2000, 11).

Several provisions in the UDHR pertain to religious human rights, but the most pertinent is Article 18, which states: "Everyone has the right to freedom of thought, conscience and religion; this right includes freedom to change his religion or belief, and freedom, either alone or in community with others and in public or private, to manifest his religion or belief in teaching, practice, worship and observance."

Of the United Nations' member nations in 1948, forty-eight signed the Declaration and eight abstained. Being a Declaration rather than a binding treaty, however, no enforcement mechanisms for protecting the religious (or other) rights specified in the UDHR existed until 1966, when the two covenants were adopted (those treaties were ratified in 1976).

Before discussing the covenants, however, another interim development should be mentioned. In 1956, Arcot Krishnaswami from India was appointed by the U.N. Subcommission on Prevention of Discrimination and Protection of Minorities to study rights pertaining to religion and belief, and to draw up a program of action to eradicate religious discrimination. Krishnaswami's study encompassed eighty-two countries. His report, issued in 1959, concluded that the collective aspect of the freedom to manifest religion or belief was especially important, as it was more prone to legal problems, including interference by the state. Many of the principles of religious human rights articulated in the Krishnaswami study have been incorporated in the U.N. Declaration on the Elimination of All Forms of Intolerance and Discrimination Based on Religion or Belief (1981), discussed below. Krishnaswami's study is also significant as the first specific step taken by the U.N. to redress neglect of religious human rights in the international community.

In 1966, the two main human-rights treaties of the U.N., the ICCPR and the ICESCR, were adopted by U.N. resolution. Article 18 of the UDHR was very influential in the drafting of the two treaties. The ICCPR is the only U.N. human-rights treaty with articles on religion and belief that contains measures of implementation. Its Article 18, like Article 18 of the UDHR, guarantees that neither governments nor individuals can interfere with a person's thoughts or beliefs as long as those beliefs are not manifested in actions, behavior, or conduct: It protects the right of everyone to freedom of thought, conscience, and belief, including the right to have or adopt a religion or belief of one's own choice. Articles 18 and 27 of the ICCPR protect the right of ethnic minorities to maintain their language, culture, and religion, which involves the control of sacred sites, skeletal remains, burial artifacts, and other items of religious and cultural significance. Article 20 of the ICCPR is also important to religious human rights, as it specifies in Section 2 that "Any advocacy of national, racial or religious hatred that constitutes incitement to discrimination, hostility or violence shall be prohibited by law." As of 2002, 148 states had ratified or acceded to the ICCPR.

The ICESCR also refers to religious rights, although less directly. Article 13, Section 1 cites the necessity of ensuring "understanding, tolerance, and friendship among all . . . religious groups." Article 13, Section 3, refers to the liberty of parents to ensure the religious and moral education of their children in conformity with their own convictions, and Article 2, Section 2 forbids all forms of discrimination, including discrimination based on religion. Unlike the ICCPR, however, the implementation system of the ICESCR has not been effective in contributing to the dialogue on religious rights and violations of those rights.

Despite the UDHR and the two covenants, freedom of religion and of belief were relatively neglected in the overall human-rights regime until the 1980s, as they have been in international relations more generally. However, in the past two decades, more than 150 major new national and international statutes and constitutional provisions on religious rights have been issued. In 1981, after years of intensive lobbying and complicated negotiations, came the landmark Declaration on Intolerance.

Articles 1 and 6 of the Declaration provide a catalog of the rights that meet minimum universal standards for religious human rights. Although this catalog is broad, it is not complete. Article 1 generally follows the model of Article 18 of the ICCPR; it distinguishes between three fundamental freedoms (thought, conscience, and religion), which are universally protected, and their external manifestation (in worship, observance, practice, and teaching), which may be limited as prescribed by law in order to protect public safety, order, health, morals, or the fundamental rights of others.

Article 6 of the Declaration includes a detailed description of the rights that fall within an accepted minimum standard, including the freedom to teach a religion or belief in a location suited to that purpose. In other words, it covers to the right to proselytize, which the international-law scholar Johan van der Vyver claims "is perhaps the most controversial aspect of religious freedom" (van der Vyver 1996, 128). This right to proselytize is closely linked to the disputed right to change or leave one's religion.

Also notable is Article 6's recognition of collective and group rights as well as individual ones. As Lerner notes, this represents significant progress over previous international-law agreements, "especially as it anticipates the needs of religious communities or congregations, which are necessary in order to establish and maintain places of worship and religious institutions, appoint religious leaders, and establish federations" (Lerner 2000, 25).

Nonetheless, the Declaration is deficient in its protection against religious discrimination and intolerance. Like the UDHR, since it takes the form of a declaration rather than a covenant or other binding agreement, the Declaration on Intolerance is not legally enforceable. However, as an official U.N. document, it has some force as international law, and signatory nations are expected to adhere to its terms to the extent that it is considered to embody rules of customary international law.

In addition to these main documents relating to religion, the U.N. Declaration on the Rights of Persons Belonging to National or Ethnic, Religious, and Linguistic Minorities (1992) protects religious minorities. Article 1 requests states to take measures to protect the existence and identity of religious minorities. Article 2 grants persons belonging to minority groups the right to profess and practice their religions and to participate in religious life. This document represents some progress over the ICCPR in the protection of religious minorities.

In addition, the Geneva Conventions of 1949 contain provisions prohibiting any adverse distinctions based on religion or faith, and they urge respect for people's religious convictions and practices. The UNESCO Convention against Discrimination in Education (1960) allows separate education systems for religious purposes provided certain conditions are met (such as that participation is optional and conforms to authorized standards, and that no one is compelled to receive religious instruction inconsistent with his or her personal convictions). The Declaration on the Rights of the Child and the Convention on the Rights of the Child (1989) also address religion and education as they affect the interests of the child. The U.N. Convention on the Protection of the Rights of Migrant Workers and Their Families (1990) contains provisions guaranteeing the religious rights of migrant workers.

Many regional and national laws also provide protections for religious human rights. For example, the United States passed the International Religious Freedom Act in 1998. Religious human rights in Europe are governed by several legal agreements, especially the 1950 European Convention for the Protection of Human Rights and Fundamental Freedoms, and monitoring bodies, including the Council of Europe, the Organization for Security and Cooperation in Europe (OSCE), and the European Union.

Some Problem Areas in the Field of Human Rights and Religion

Only a few of the most significant problems in the field of human rights and religion can be mentioned here. First, while there has been considerable agreement among member nations of the U.N. regarding the content of religious freedoms in international law, disputes remain, mostly concerning the interpretation of the requirements of these international standards. The more serious problem is the open repudiation in practice of norms that the majority of states in the United Nations have accepted in binding international agreements.

A second major problem is the tension or conflict between religious rights and other human rights. The UDHR and other international human-rights documents protect the freedom of religious exercise alongside other basic rights, including the right to participate in government, to freedom of speech, of movement, to travel, and so on. However, in some instances, protecting the right to religious freedom may impair or infringe upon the ability of the state to protect other human rights. The Convention on the Elimination of All Forms of Discrimination Against Women (1979) contains certain protections for women's human rights that clash with the practices of some religious traditions. Several states sub-

mitted reservations about the clauses that they perceived to conflict with their religious traditions when they ratified that Convention.

In cases of tension or conflict, which rights should be given priority? Among those who have argued that religious freedom should be regarded as more special than other human rights are Elizabeth Odio Benito, the former U.N. Special Rapporteur of the Subcommission on Prevention of Discrimination and Protection of Minorities, and David Little, former director of the Religion, Nationalism, and Intolerance project at the United States Institute of Peace.

Such views may lead to a privileging of religious rights, even when they conflict with the protection of other rights. It needs to be remembered that while the world's religions have been among the staunchest defenders of human rights, religious groups have also at times been the most egregious violators of human rights. This has been especially true for women's rights. Women's rights to equality under state and international human-rights law frequently clash with the rights of religious collectivities to self-determination. The repressive religiously based laws of the Taliban are well known, but there are many other examples. In her 1999 essay "Religion and Human Rights," for example, Martha Nussbaum, feminist philosopher and law professor at the University of Chicago, describes violations of women's human rights in the name of religion in Pakistan, Bangladesh, India, Iran, Israel, and the United States.

The possibilities for tension or conflict between religious rights and other human rights raises the question of the ultimate compatibility of the multiple sets of rights. Those who reject the importance of human rights come from diverse, sometimes mutually antagonistic, sources. Indeed, as religious studies scholar Sumner Twiss observes, "There is unquestionably a widespread perception that universal human rights are in significant tension with religious, moral, and cultural diversity in the world" (Twiss and Grelle 2000, 158). Some fundamentalist religious groups view international human rights as part of the secular ethos that they reject in favor of their own views of absolute truth. In addition, as noted earlier, some non-Western governments reject international human rights because they were written in developed nations with insufficient attention given to the distinctive needs and interests of the developing world.

On the other hand, scholars who believe that the compatibilities between multiple types of rights are more compelling than the differences, such as the legal historian and law and religion specialist John Witte, find a basis for human-rights principles in ancient religious belief and practice itself. Such scholars tend to view religion as a positive resource for peace and human-rights implementation.

A third seemingly intractable problem involving religion and human rights concerns balancing the rights of people to proselytize on behalf of their religion, and the rights of others, especially communities, and in particular communities of minority peoples in danger of cultural extinction, to be free of such activities, which may lead to conversions and changes of religion that are considered to be damaging. Since the drafting of the UDHR, some states' representatives have argued against the right to change one's religion. In recent years, conflicts have arisen in Central and Eastern Europe and Africa between indigenous churches and foreign religions promoting their missionary agenda. For example, as Witte describes: "In the war for souls in Russia . . . two absolute principles of human rights have come into direct conflict: The foreign religion's free exercise right to share and expand its faith versus the indigenous religion's liberty-of-conscience right to be left alone in its own territory" (Lerner 2000, 80). These issues have not been resolved and, according to Lerner, will probably significantly complicate any attempt to consider a draft convention on religious rights.

One aspect of this problem is the tension between individual and group rights. The tension is felt, for example, in countries that recognize religious laws as binding public or civil law, such as India and several Islamic countries. Although a particular religious law (prohibiting divorce, for example) may protect the interests of the collective by helping preserve the collective's religious identity and way of life, the law may very well infringe upon the religious beliefs or conscience of individual members of that collective.

In sum, religious rights and other human rights are in tension in a number of ways. Some tensions have been satisfactorily resolved over the years since the U.N. has begun to address them, while others may never be completely resolved, but only provisionally and partially settled through uneasy compromises that deal with particular conflicts and nations at particular times.

Lucinda Joy Peach

See also Universal Declaration of Human Rights

Further Reading

An-Na'im, A. A. (1992). Toward a cross-cultural approach to defining international standards of human rights. In An-Na'im, A. A. (Ed.), *Human rights in cross-cultural perspectives: A quest for consensus* (pp. 19–43). Philadelphia: University of Pennsylvania Press.

Bloom, I., Martin, J. P., & Proudfoot, W. L. (Eds.). (1996). *Religious diversity and human rights.* New York: Columbia University Press.

Boyle, K., & Sheen, J. (Eds.). (1997). *Freedom of religion and belief: A world report.* New York: Routledge.

Hackett, R. I. J., Silk, M., & Hoover, D. (Eds.). (2000). *Religious persecution as a U.S. policy issue.* Hartford, CT: Center for the Study of Religion in Public Life.

Howland, C. (Ed.). (1999). *Religious fundamentalisms and women's human rights.* New York: St. Martins Press.

Lerner, N. (2000). *Religion, beliefs, and international human rights.* Maryknoll, NY: Orbis Books.

Little, D. (2000). Does the human right to freedom of conscience, religion, and belief have special status? *Brigham Young University Law Review, 3,* 603–610.

Nussbaum, M. C. (1999). *Sex and social justice.* New York: Oxford University Press.

Nussbaum, M. C. (2000). *Women and human development: The capabilities approach.* New York: Cambridge University Press.

Office of the High Commissioner for Human Rights. (1966). *International covenant on civil and political rights.* Retrieved October 9, 2002, from http://www.unhchr.ch/html/menu3/b/a_ccpr.htm

Office of the High Commissioner for Human Rights. (1966). *International covenant on economic, social and cultural rights.* Retrieved October 9, 2002, from http://www.unhchr.ch/html/menu3/b/a_cescr.htm

Okin, S. M. (1997). Is multiculturalism bad for women? *Boston Review* 22(4). Retrieved October 9, 2002, from http://bostonreview.mit.edu/BR22.5/okin.html

Stahnke, T., & Martin, J. P. (Eds.). (1998). *Religion and human rights: Basic documents.* New York: Columbia University Press.

Swidler, L. (Ed.). (1986). *Religious liberty and human rights in nations and in religions.* Philadelphia: Ecumenical Press, and New York: Hippocrene Books.

Traer, R. (1991). *Faith in human rights: Support in religious traditions for a global struggle.* Washington, DC: Georgetown University Press.

Twiss, S. B., & Grelle, B. (Eds.). (2000). *Explorations in global ethics: Comparative religious ethics and inter-religious dialogue*. Boulder, CO: Westview Press.

United Nations (1998). *Human Rights Today: A United Nations Priority*. Retrieved October 9, 2002, from http://www.un.org/rightsHRToday/

United States Department of State, Bureau of Democracy, Human Rights and Labor. (2002). Religious Freedom. Retrieved October 9, 2002, from http://www. state gov/www/global/human_rights/drl_religion. html

United Nations General Assembly (1948). Universal Declaration of Human Rights. Retrieved October 9, 2002, from http://www.un.org/Overview/rights. html

Van der Vyver, J., & Witte, Jr., J. (Eds.). (1996). *Religious human rights in global perspective: Religious perspectives*. The Hague, Netherlands: Martinus Nijhoff Publishers.

Immigration: United States

For each new wave of immigrants that entered the United States, religion has been a crucial basis for building community, reconstructing identity, and adapting to a new and unfamiliar land. For these reasons, immigration continues to shape and reshape the American religious landscape, influencing where and how people worship and to whom they pray.

In early colonial America, most colonies were founded for essentially economic and political reasons. The first American colony, Jamestown, was founded in 1607 by second- and third-generation English sons seeking fame and fortune; likewise, the state of Georgia was founded as a defensive buffer against the Spanish-controlled Florida to the south. Some colonies, however, were established with strong religious intentions. In 1620 and the decades thereafter, the Pilgrims from England settled in the New England colonies in search of a new religious community where they could freely practice their faith. Following the Pilgrims, waves of English colonists, many of them Puritans, also settled in New England. At the heart of their settlement lay the determination to create a "New Jerusalem" devoted to God, a model society free of the Old World's corruption and oppression. With such foundations, religion permeated New England culture and was evident in the names people had, the books they read, and even their form of government, which originally granted citizenship only to church members.

Other colonies also had religious foundations. In the early 1630s, the Calverts, well connected to the rulers of England who were at the time Catholic, founded Maryland largely for English Catholics. Because most of the settlers in Maryland were Protestants, however, the Catholics in Maryland had to practice their faith cautiously. This led the Calverts to issue the Act Concerning Religion in 1649, which ensured that all Christians who accepted the Trinity (Catholics, Anglicans, and moderate Protestant dissenters) had the right to profess and practice their religion freely. The official toleration of these Christian groups and the local control of churches helped Maryland to emerge as a colony with a multidenominational Christian community.

Diverse Christian immigrants could also be found in other colonies. In the late 1600s, the Society of Friends (Quakers) flocked to Pennsylvania fleeing religious persecution in England. Land-hungry German Lutherans and Scots-Irish Presbyterians also joined the Quakers and by the eve of the American Revolution, Pennsylvania boasted more than two hundred Lutheran and German Reformed churches. During the late 1600s and the early 1700s, the Amish and the Mennonites (two offshoots of the Anabaptists) also sought refuge in Pennsylvania, followed by other "radical" Protestant sects like the Moravians in the late eighteenth century.

The settlement of these different Christian groups in the New World challenged the traditional belief in a single established church for the state. The new conditions of life in America simplified religious rituals and increased lay leadership and many immigrants wanted simply to be left alone to practice their religion as they saw fit. And some immigrated precisely because they wanted to break away from the church-state system. These factors along with evangelical revivals like the First and the Second Great Awakenings of the 1700s (and early 1800s) helped to shape the denominational character of religion in America and moved the colonies closer to disfavoring an established church and denying all state-related privileges to any particular religious group. Although unintentional at first, religious pluralism, in both theory and practice, eventually became the law of the land.

Following the independence of the American colonies from England in 1776 and the subsequent drafting of the U.S. Constitution, one of the rights that the U.S. Constitution safeguarded was freedom of religion. As Amendment 1 of the Bill of Rights states, "Congress shall make no law respecting an establishment of religion, or prohibiting the free exercise thereof. . . ." (Amendments to the U.S. Constitution, Bill of Rights, 1791). The separation of church and state in the United States gives individuals the freedom and choice to practice and support religious affiliation or nonaffiliation. Since the framing of the Constitution, various waves of immigrants entered the United States. The immigrants that entered between the mid-1800s and the 1920s and the most recent wave of post-1965 immigrants have had a notable impact on American religion.

1850s–1920s

From the middle of the nineteenth century to the turn of the twentieth century, immigrants from Ireland, Germany, Italy, Poland, Russia, and the other southern and eastern parts of Europe arrived in the United States. This new wave of mostly Southern and Eastern European immigrants brought Catholicism and Judaism onto the greater American religious landscape. There were some non-European immigrants among the roughly 27 million immigrants that arrived during this time, but the majority of the immigrants (about 80 percent) were from European nations.

Driven by potato famines in their country, the Irish Catholics immigrated to the United States in large numbers in the 1840s, and many Jewish immigrants from Germany followed a few decades later. More Catholics and Jews filled the country at the close of the nineteenth century and the beginning of the twentieth century from Southern and Eastern European nations. By 1920, the Catholic population,

consisting of some twenty-eight different ethnic groups, numbered about 17 million. In 1840, the Jewish population made up less than 1 percent of the U.S. population (15,000); by 1920, however, they made up more than 3 percent of the U.S. population (over 3 million). The influx of these new immigrants was not met favorably by the descendents of the earlier Protestant European settlers; there were anti-Catholic and anti-Jewish sentiments and violence. This kind of hostility, however, diminished during World War II as immigration halted and the children and grandchildren of the new immigrants gradually achieved socioeconomic mobility and assimilated into U.S. society.

The new wave of European immigrants further increased the denominational character of the American Christian community. In 1800, there were about thirty major denominations; by 1900, the numbers increased to more than two hundred. This increase can be attributed to immigration along with the related sectarianism, sectionalism, and revivalism among the different Protestant Christian groups. At a broader level, however, the new wave of Catholic and Jewish immigrants reshaped the United States into a Judeo-Christian nation that included Protestantism as well as Catholicism and Judaism as its major religions. This led some immigration scholars to predict that the generation of European immigrants would lose their distinct ethnic identities and adopt broader religious identities as Protestants, Catholics, or Jews. America was characterized as a "three religion country" or a "triple-melting pot" with different ethnic groups melting into these three broad religious communities. This picture of America, however, has changed with the latest wave of post-1965 immigration.

1965 to the Present

Until the 1960s, the majority of the immigrants traced their roots to European nations (not counting African-Americans), with only a small presence of immigrants from Asian and Latin American countries. This changed in the 1960s with revised U.S. immigration policy. International and domestic pressures with war raging in Vietnam and Civil Rights movements escalating at home, along with a shortage of professionals in the U.S. labor market, pushed Congress to enact new, more egalitarian immigration policies (in contrast to discriminatory acts like the

Chinese Exclusion Act of 1882). This led to the passage of the Hart-Cellar Act in 1965, which abolished the national origins quota system and established an annual limit of 170,000 visas for immigrants from countries in the eastern hemisphere. The new immigration act made it easier for American citizens to bring their relatives to the United States and gave preferences to individuals who possessed job skills that were in short supply. Since the law went into effect in 1968, immigration from various non-European nations, namely from Asia and Latin American countries, has sharply increased. At least 80 percent of the approximately 12 million newcomers who entered the United States in the 1970s and 1980s came from Asia or Latin America, with a smaller percentage of those from Middle Eastern, Caribbean, and African countries.

Some of the new non-European post-1965 immigrants practice two of the three Judeo-Christian religions, either Protestant Christianity or Catholicism. A few participate in the available mainstream Protestant or Catholic churches, but most participate in separate immigrant congregations due to language and cultural barriers. In 1988, there were approximately 2,018 Korean American churches, and in 1994 there were about 700 Chinese Protestant churches in the United States. In the mid-1990s, there were about 3,500 Catholic parishes where mass was celebrated in Spanish. The arrival of the new wave of non-European Christian immigrants breathed new life into aging mainline Protestant denominations and Catholic parishes and made the American Christian community even more ethnically and culturally diverse.

Among the new immigrants, Protestant and Catholics also include those who were not formerly Christian but converted to or adopted the Protestant or Catholic religion upon settling in the United States. Because Christianity is still the dominant American religion, converting to Christianity renders immigrants "less foreign" and facilitates their overall integration into the larger society. For example, highly educated and professional Chinese Americans convert to Christianity as part of their Americanization process and Southeast Asian refugees find that converting to Christianity helps them to gain greater access to social services and support from the local churches and charities. Additionally, simply having more choices of religion in the United States can increase conversion rates.

Among post-1965 immigrants, there are also immigrants who bring religions that are foreign to the Judeo-Christian tradition like Islam, Hinduism, and Buddhism. For example, the majority of immigrants from Pakistan and various Middle Eastern countries continue to practice Islamic religions in the United States; Asian Indian immigrants continue to practice Hinduism as well as other diverse religions like Islam, Sikhism, and Zorastrianism. Many Chinese, Vietnamese, Cambodian, and Korean immigrants practice Buddhism. In the early 1990s, researchers counted between 1,000 and 1,200 mosques and other Islamic centers and about 1,500 to 2,000 Buddhist temples and meditation centers in the United States. There are also a variety of informal religious organizations that meet through small house churches or seasonal festivities.

With the latest wave of immigrants, the United States' religious market has become even more diverse. One of the consequences of this is that native born Americans, not just immigrants, have more choices in their religion. A formerly Christian or nonreligious European American can become a Buddhist; an African-American Baptist can convert to Islam. With the availability of various different religions and religious organizations, Americans can also mix and blend a number of religions together to create their own personalized religions. The array of religions that the new wave of non-European immigrants has brought enables the greater American population to have more choices in their religious beliefs and practices and renders the picture of a "three religion" America out of date.

These changes in religion, however, would not have been possible without the freedom of religion guaranteed by the U.S. Constitution. Religious tolerance, which has been made a necessity with the coexistence of diverse religious groups since colonial America, has enabled the United States to house multiple different religions and adapt itself to the vast changes that have occurred through the immigration of new religious groups.

America's tolerance for religious diversity helps immigrants and their subsequent generations to retain and reshape their religions. Although religion often fueled tensions among the different ethnic and racial groups, being religious, whatever the religion, was not inconsistent with being American. Scholars of contemporary immigrants' religious participation also testify to the unique character of America's religious freedom that continues to make religion so pivotal for immigrants.

The freedom of religion that immigrants enjoy in the United States enables them to maintain and even revive their religions in the new land, which helps to make America one of the most religiously diverse nations in the world. In addition, the United States is also one of the most "religious" countries in the Western world. Some scholars argue that the constant flow of immigrants with their diverse religions continuously invigorates America's religious market, which increases Americans' overall religious participation. Immigrants who arrive as Christians or who later convert to Christianity can revive preexisting Christian communities. Immigrants who bring non-Christian religions can provide others with more options in their religious participation. And because immigrating itself is said to be a theologizing experience that heightens religiosity, a country with a high percentage of immigrants such as the United States is more religious.

On the other hand there are those who argue that the immigration of diverse religious groups actually secularizes America. The number of alternative worldviews that different immigrant religious groups introduce makes it difficult for any single religious group, particularly those that are monotheistic, to claim their religion as the "one true" religion; an individual's faith in a particular religious worldview is thus challenged and made uncertain within a highly pluralized religious market. This argument, however, should be tempered with the fact that religious pluralism has existed since colonial America without significantly dampening American's religious spirit. Moreover, it should be noted that this debate can change based on how one measures religion or religious participation (for example, by church attendance or belief in one God or many "gods"). While the debate continues, the inexorable relationship between immigration and religion continues to shape and color the American religious landscape.

Rebecca Y. Kim

See also Buddhism; Fourteenth Amendment; French Colonies in North America; Great Awakenings and Antebellum Period; Hinduism; Islam; Maryland: Colonial to Early Republic; New England: Colonial to Early Republic; Pennsylvania: Colonial to Early Republic; Sikhism; Spanish Colonies in North America

Further Reading

Dolan, J. P. (1975). *The immigrant church.* Baltimore: Johns Hopkins University Press.

Ebaugh, H. R., & Chafetz, J. S. (Eds.). (2000). *Religion and the new immigrants.* Walnut Creek, CA: Altamira Press.

Greeley, A. M. (1972). *The denominational society.* Glenview, IL: Scott, Foresman.

Herberg, W. (1955). *Protestant, Catholic, Jew.* Garden City, NY: Doubleday.

Joselit, J. W. (2001). *Immigration and American religion.* Oxford, UK: Oxford University Press.

Warner, S. R., & Wittner, J. G. (1998). *Gatherings in diaspora.* Philadelphia: Temple University Press.

Williams, R.B. (1988). *Religions of immigrants from India and Pakistan.* New York: Cambridge University Press.

India *See* Hinduism

Individualist Religions

Individualist religions are those in which individuals draw on a variety of sources to create personal beliefs and rituals that may or may not be shared with others. These contrast with group-organized religions with formalized beliefs and traditions; members must accept these and are usually subordinate to religious leaders.

Almost everything we "know" about reality we learn from others, and we uphold this knowledge or "paradigm of reality" through reinforcement from others who share these beliefs. Without such reinforcement, individuals may come to suspect that their beliefs, especially if they run counter to the majority paradigm, are wrong or even insane. Ultimately, individuals may abandon such beliefs in the interest of conformity. Those holding alternate beliefs usually reinforce them through association with others who share them, creating a cognitive minority.

Some have always found that group-organized religions, whether universalist (e.g., Christianity, Islam) or group-organized "new religious movements" (e.g., Unification Church, Children of God), provide neither adequate guidelines for living nor

THE REPRESSION OF SIBERIAN SHAMANISM

The repression of shamanism among the indigenous peoples of Siberia and conversion to Orthodox Christianity was an element of Russian colonization of the region. However, shamanism did not disappear entirely, as indicated by this ethnographic account from the late nineteenth century. Further repression during Soviet rule in the twentieth century almost eradicated shamanism, but it has revived since the demise of the Soviet Union.

In the Yakut district all Yakuts with rare exceptions have been baptized according to the "ancient faith" [Christianity] rite, or were born from parents of that faith. Yet one can hardly be sure that a Yakut, professing the ancient faith, has given up his shamanist creed, or that he does not have recourse to the latter. I have personally known two shamans, one of them in the Yakut's district, the other on the Kytach island on the mouth of the Lena, who were both known as followers of the "ancient faith."

The aborigines seldom have an opportunity to see a priest of the ancient faith. In view of the enormous extension of the parishes, of the scattered settlements, and of the extraordinary difficulties in securing communications, he is hardly in a position to see each member of his faith once a year; and if he visits him in one of the settling-places he may not stay longer than two or three days because he must be through with his travel as long as the paths and roads are practicable. One may safely estimate that eight percent of the aborigines population has never seen a Christian church. His eminency, the former Yakut bishop Dionysius even told me that sometimes priests had died without having communicated, leaving a written confession of sins.

No wonder, therefore, that the aborigines who are considered as Christians and place the image of a saint in the front corner of their tents which is adorned with wax candles nevertheless approach their shamans in order to satisfy their religious needs.

It is difficult to admit that the autochthonous Yakut who is so conservative, in all his customs and convictions and has not changed his manners and way of life during the centuries, should have yielded so easily in his religious belief. If the Yakut professes the Christian faith because the ruling class professes it and would not sanction the election of a delegate in the village community other than orthodox, and because only for Christians there is a chance to get once a decoration (medal) from that white Tsar, who somewhere, very far, lives in a tent of glass, and, sitting on a gigantic tabouret of sugar, sucks sugar unceasingly—if, I repeat, the Yakut poses as a Christian in order to become the boss of those who surround him, such practical considerations do by no means convince him that it is necessary to give up his shamanism and to approach the latter faith as soon as he feels prompted; particularly because he will not find a similar satisfaction in Christian belief.

Just as the autochthonous Yakuts, the Russian merchants of the area use to sacrifice to the spirit of a locality in order to dispose him favorably. Everybody gives what he can afford; some will tear a piece out of their garments, others will pull some hairs from the manes of their horses to fix them on a tree or sign-post, some give money, and he who possesses nothing, at least a stone, a horse skull, a horse hide, or his stick. Such offerings are called delburgja salaka.

Friedrich S. Krauss

Source: *Das Schamanentum der Jakuten* [Yakut Shamanism].
(Wien, Germany: Alfred Holder, 1888), 167–168.
Translated by the Human Relations Area Files.

satisfactory answers to major philosophical and existential questions. They embark on personal quests for meaning and may become part of cognitive minorities, even though their answers derive primarily from *personal* spiritual experiences rather than input from others.

People on such spiritual quests today have the advantage of mass communication. Newspapers, television, specialty bookstores, workshops, and the Internet are all sources of information leading to the creation and reinforcement of such beliefs. Like-minded people need not be nearby; "cognitive minorities" have become "virtual," defying geographical boundaries. This liberation of belief has opened Western society to alternate belief systems, and the number of individualist religions has grown.

Individualist religions contrast with empiricism and materialism that hold that reality is limited to what can be perceived with the five senses or their extensions—spirits, life after death, and the like cannot, by definition, exist. Like group religionists, individualists believe that there is an "alternate" reality wherein lies power, and that people may directly access that power—be it gods, spirits, or non-sentient transcendent "energy." The personal experience of the transcendent is paramount. This provides powerful spiritual help in this world and assurances of survival after death.

"Classic" Individualist Religions

Individualist religions have existed alongside group-organized religions for centuries. These have become prominent at various times and include shamanism, witchcraft, and formal philosophies such as Theosophy, Swedenborgianism, and Spiritualism. "Classic" individualist religions such as the two discussed below have influenced more recent forms.

Spiritualism can be either individualist or quasi-group. Its fundamental beliefs are the human soul's continued existence in the spirit world after death and the ability of the dead to contact the living. Other elements may be added, including the ability to heal psychological and physical illness with the help of spirits.

Although such beliefs are thousands of years old, Spiritualism as a quasi-formalized belief system became popular in the 1850s after Margaretta and Catherine Fox claimed they could contact spirits who responded with a series of knockings. Interest

tapered off, but Spiritualism continues as a cognitive minority in North America and Britain, and in various forms throughout Europe and South America.

Spiritualist "churches" appear occasionally, centered on mediums who can contact the spirit world and conduct healings, but these churches tend to be short-lived. Small groups of friends may meet in "circles" through which spirits are contacted, spirit messages are received, and limited conversations with spirits occur. Individuals supposedly maintain daily contact with personal helping spirits: they need only keep communication lines open to bring spirits into personal consciousness.

Shamanism is not a religion per se, but a complex of ancient methods for dealing with spirits, helping society, and healing that may date back to the Upper Paleolithic. It exists alongside other belief systems or organized religions. Shamans are a bridge between this world and the spirit world. In contrast with mediums, traditional healers, and other religious practitioners, they are unique in that they can, with the help of spirits, journey into the spirit world and return alive. These journeys are undertaken for a number of reasons, including to rescue lost souls, acquire knowledge, and help and heal people. Shamans continue to be found in indigenous societies mainly in North and South America, the Circumpolar Arctic/Sub-Arctic, Siberia, and South and East Asia.

Recent Individualist Religions

Since about the 1960s, individualist seekers form a part of what some call the "mystical movement." They are usually middle class, in their mid-twenties to late sixties and older. Most are well educated, frequently to university level, and though they are successful are searching for existential meaning.

"New Age" is a broad term covering a wide variety of popular mystical interests, including trance channeling, tarot, and astrology. Others that are not part of New Age include neo-paganism, core and neo-shamanism, and the revival of traditional shamanism.

Neo-paganism (paganism) in Europe and North America is a general designation, incorporating wicca (good witchcraft), goddess worship, nature beliefs, and ecological concerns. Although some argue that it is a continuation of ancient paganism, the current revival derives from early- and mid-twentieth-century writers such as Gerald Gardner and Margaret Murray. A premise of neo-paganism is the interconnectedness of all things. The movement is pantheistic or panentheistic and may be polytheistic; nature is alive, and the Divine is inherent in it; everything has a spirit with the potential to communicate with people. Attunement with nature is important. For some the goddess, symbolizing "mother earth," is the primary deity. Rituals are conducted within a sacred circle separating the sacred from the profane; this circle is a microcosm of the interconnected world. Magic, an important element, is based on interconnectedness through which one can theoretically influence other areas of material and nonmaterial reality. Usually magic is performed for benevolent purposes following the old credo "an it harm none, do what you will." Although some elements from core and neo-shamanism may be used, they should be considered entirely separate from neo-paganism.

Core and neo-shamanism have similar origins but evolved different approaches to shamanic spirituality and goals. Popular interest in shamanism, beginning in the 1960s, was enhanced by the writings of two anthropologists. Carlos Castaneda began a series of books about Don Juan, an alleged Yaqui Indian sorcerer. At the same time Michael Harner began to develop and teach core shamanism.

Neo-shamanism is an eclectic, amorphous set of beliefs which can include parts of Harner's system and various shamanic traditions, incorporating assorted rituals and beliefs from various indigenous spiritual systems, input from miscellaneous "shamans" who may or may not be from indigenous societies, and new inventions. Major sources of inspiration are Plains and Pueblo Native American cultures, but there is growing interest in European "shamanism" drawing on reconstructed Celtic and Nordic traditions. People attempt to become "shamans" by practicing assorted rituals, not all of which relate to traditional shamanism.

Core shamanism, created by Harner, is a "purist" approach to shamanism. He recognized that, regardless of idiosyncratic cultural overlays, all forms of shamanism share basic elements that can be adapted to the needs of people today. The method involves learning to journey to the spirit world, usually aided by drumming, to contact and receive aid from spirits. Spirits are the teachers, not Harner. It is dualistic in that humans, "God," and spirits are separate. Nevertheless, it agrees with much of neo-shamanism's and neo-paganism's pantheistic focus.

Religious Freedom and Problems

Religious rights and freedoms are affected not only by political sanctions but also by society's perception of particular belief systems. Ridicule and other forms of condemnation can be just as devastating as political oppression, and have been experienced by traditional systems, such as shamanism, as well as contemporary individualist religions.

Persecution, Ridicule, and the Revitalization of Shamanism

With the encroachment of Western society, universalist religions, and the materialist paradigm, shamanism has been disappearing under the pressure of subtle scorn from Western "modernity," as well as from outright persecution and violence. Shamans are still active in Nepal but in Kathmandu, for example, they are often ridiculed by Westerners and some Nepalese. Tourist hotels put on "dramas" of shamanic rituals that mock shamans. Since Western contact with the New World, Christian missionaries have worked vigorously to overthrow shamans. In 1800s Alaska, Russian Orthodox priests destroyed shamanic paraphernalia and threatened shamans with damnation if they continued practicing their rituals. More recently the former Soviet Union, especially under Stalinism, persecuted and denounced shamans as deceivers, confiscated their property, accused them of medical fraud, and imprisoned them. Since at least the 1980s, attitudes toward shamanism have shifted, and in some places there are attempts to revive traditions. The few surviving shamans in Siberia and elsewhere are attempting to teach the younger generation. Harner's core shamanism practitioners have been invited to help some get in touch with their spiritual powers, and restore shamanic healing and traditions.

Western Individualist Religions: Ridicule, Condemnation, and Concerns

In modern Western society, freedom of belief from overt persecution is legally established, and media attention has usually contributed to acceptance of alternate beliefs. Nevertheless, the real or perceived power of formal group-organized religions or the public can create an oppressive situation for dissenters.

Those who adhere to empiricist/materialist beliefs consider individualist religious beliefs "nonscientific," and patently absurd. Believers are characterized as gullible or out of touch with reality.

Individualist believers who talk with or see spirits are clearly insane—most likely schizophrenic. Magazines such as *Skeptical Inquirer* and conjurers such as James Randi have a goal of debunking of such beliefs.

Social sanctions, including severe criticism, sarcasm, mockery, ridicule, and ostracism can be used to condemn one who holds "deviant" religious beliefs. Many people fear job loss if their employers discover their beliefs. This concern has led some Spiritualists as well as individualist academics in certain fields to hide their beliefs. Academics who research individualist religions or group-organized new religious movements using participant observation methods have also been severely criticized by peers.

There is a concern that important initiators of individualist religions could become tyrants, such as those commonly associated with group-organized new religious movements (e.g., Bhagwan Shree Rajneesh). Because of the individualist nature of the systems, however, it is highly unlikely that individualist religion initiators have either the will or the ability to become oppressive gurus with a subservient following.

Negative attitudes among members of some sectors of universalist religions can also be severe. Between the fourteenth and eighteenth centuries fear of witchcraft led to witch hunts and executions. Today, fear of witchcraft has led to a general condemnation of individualists because it is erroneously thought that they bring the devil and evil into the world. Although individualists claim that spiritual healing comes from God or spirits, some critics maintain it is "in fact" the work of the devil and leads its believers to hell. There is also fear that the individualists are subversive or commit sexual abuses and other moral transgressions.

Core and neo-shamans are accused of stealing indigenous people's beliefs. This is frequently alleged by some Native Americans and the issue is heavily politicized (some also object to neo-shamans entering their sacred areas). In contrast, other Native Americans welcome the interest in their beliefs and traditions, and a few have undertaken to teach beliefs to "outsiders." These beliefs, however, are sometimes invented and geared to the expectations of those on spiritual quests.

Neo-paganism, of course, is opposed by Christians. A more sinister potential, especially in European Celtic and Nordic neo-paganism, is becoming apparent to some researchers. They see close parallels between German forms of "scientific neo-paganism" and rise of fascism between World War I and II and some sectors of European neo-paganism and the new right today.

The Future

Early in the twentieth century Ernst Troeltsch hypothesized that a purely personal spiritual and mystical "secret religion of the educated classes" would evolve, particularly among educated urbanites, based on syncretism, polymorphism, and seeing truth in all religions. Though particular individualist religions may fall from favor, it is likely that individualist quests for meaning and transcendence—Troeltsch's "secret religion"—will increase in importance and have growing influence throughout Western society.

Joan B. Townsend

Further Reading

Adler, M. (1986). *Drawing down the moon: Witches, druids, goddess-worshippers and other pagans in America today* (2nd ed.). Boston: Beacon Press.

Balzer, M. M. (1983). Doctors or deceivers? The Siberian Khanty shaman and Soviet medicine. In L. Romanucci-Ross, D. E. Moerman, L. R. Tancredi (Eds.), *The anthropology of medicine: From culture to method* (pp. 54–76). South Hadley, MA: J. F. Bergin.

Berger, P. (1971). *Rumour of angels: Modern society and the rediscovery of the supernatural.* Baltimore: Penguin.

Brunton, B. (1994). Tuva: Land of eagles. *Shamanism, 7*(1), 3–20.

Castaneda, C. (1968). *The teachings of Don Juan: A Yaqui way of knowledge.* New York: Ballantine Books.

Cookson, C. (1997). Report from the Free Exercise trenches: A case study of religious freedom issues faced by wiccans practicing in the United States. *Journal of Church and State, 39,* 723.

Cross-Cultural Shamanism Network. (1985). *Shaman's drum: A journal of experiential shamanism.* Willits, CA: Cross-Cultural Shamanism Network.

Harner, M. J. (1980). *The way of the shaman.* New York: Harper and Row.

Hoppál, M. J. (2000). *Shaman traditions in transition.* Budapest, Hungary: International Society for Shamanistic Research.

Lady Liberty League: Religious freedom support for wiccans, pagans, and other nature religions. Retrieved

December 5, 2002, from http://www.circlesanctu-ary.org/liberty

Lewis, J. R. (Ed.). (1996). *Magical religion and modern witchcraft*. Albany: State University of New York Press.

Lindquist, G. (1997). *Shamanic performances on the urban scene: Neo-shamanism in contemporary Sweden*. Stockholm Studies in Social Anthropology, no. 39. Stockholm: Gotab.

Luhrmann, T. M. (1989). *Persuasions of the witch's craft: Ritual magic in contemporary England*. Cambridge, MA: Harvard University Press.

Nelson, G. K. (1969). *Spiritualism and society*. London: Routledge and Kegan Paul.

Poewe, K. (1990). Scientific neo-paganism and the extreme right then and today: From Ludendorff's *Gotterkenntnis* to Sigrid Hund's *Europas Eigene Religion*. *Journal of Contemporary Religion, 14*(3), 387–400.

Starhawk [Miriam Simos]. (1989). *The spiral dance: A rebirth of the ancient religion of the great goddess* (2nd ed.). San Francisco: Harper and Row.

Townsend, J. B. (1988). Neo-shamanism and the modern mystical movement. In G. Doore (Ed.), *Shaman's path: Healing, personal growth and empowerment.* (pp. 73–83). Boston: Shambhala.

Townsend, J. B. (1997). Shamanism. In S. Glazier (Ed.), *Anthropology of religion: A handbook* (Chapter 16, pp. 428–469). Westport, CT: Greenwood.

Townsend, J. B. (1999). Core shaman and neopagan leaders of the mystical movement in contemporary society. *Dialogue and Alliance: A Journal of the International Religious Foundation, 13*(1), 100–122.

Townsend, J. B. (2001). Modern non-traditional and invented shamanism. In J. Pentikainen (Ed.), *Shamanhood: Symbolism and epic* (pp. 257–264). Biblioteca shamanistica no. 9. Budapest, Hungary: Akadémiai Kiadó.

Troeltsch, E. (1931). *The social teaching of the Christian churches* (Vol. 2.). (O. Wyon, Trans.). London: George Allen and Unwin.

Inquisition

The Inquisition is usually associated with the Roman Catholic ecclesiastical tribunals, most active in Europe between the thirteenth and seventeenth centuries CE. These courts primarily investigated charges of heresy and other religious dissent. Inquisitors heard evidence against and convicted such offenders, imposing public penances on those who promised to return to orthodoxy. Convicted heretics who refused to renounce their "errors," or who relapsed into dissent, were sentenced to death and turned over to secular authorities for execution.

Historical Background

Because inquisitorial courts employed torture and capital punishment to coerce adherence to Roman Catholic teachings, "The Inquisition" has acquired a reputation as an intolerant, tyrannical, and monolithic institution that suppressed religious freedom in medieval and early modern Europe. Though this view is somewhat correct, the historical context of the Inquisition must be considered. First, there never existed any single, centralized "Inquisition" as popularly believed. Scholars identify three phases of inquisitorial activity: beginning in 1231 all over medieval Europe, in 1478 in Spain, and finally in 1542 in Italy. Each phase consisted of many local inquisitions either convened by bishops in certain regions for specific purposes, or comprising papally or even royally sponsored itinerant courts that convened as required. Second, though inquisitorial courts did use torture to extract confessions, and ordered obdurate heretics burned alive, they were no more arbitrary or cruel in applying these measures than were secular criminal courts of the day. Since the purpose of inquisitorial action was to protect community religious homogeneity and to save wayward souls, these trials usually ended not in burnings but in recantations and public penances designed to demonstrate that Roman Catholic "truth" had triumphed. Beside the carnage of the crusades, witch-hunts, and religious wars committed in the name of Roman and Protestant Christianity in medieval and early modern Europe, the record of inquisitorial killings appears moderate in comparison.

The term *inquisitio* derives from the participle of the Latin verb *inquiro*, to investigate, and was used by first century BCE Romans to denote a search for evidence as part of a legal action. Roman courts were typically managed by a *praetor* or judge, whose duty it was to gather evidence (the "inquisition"), and who was permitted to use torture against "infamed" or heinous criminals if evidence against them was wanting. Christianity began in the Roman Empire, and when it finally became the state religion in the

BERNARD GUI'S *INQUISITOR'S MANUAL*—DEALING WITH THE BEGUINES

The following instructions for dealing with the Beguine sect in southern France in the fourteenth century are a good example of the "inquisitor manuals" used in medieval Europe. Gui's manual was one of the most popular.

1. The following deals with the sect of those commonly called Beguins or Beguines:

   The sect of Beguines, who call themselves "poor brothers" and say they observe and profess the third rule of Saint Francis, sprang up recently in the provinces of Provence and Narbonne. Their erroneous opinions began to be exposed around the year of our Lord 1315, more or less, although they were considered suspect by many even earlier. During the following years, in the provinces of Narbonne, Toulouse and Catalonia, many of them were seized, held in custody and, their errors having been detected, many of both sexes were judged heretical and burned. This occurred from the year of our Lord 1317 on, particularly at Narbonne and Béziers, in the diocese of Agde, at Lodève, around Lunel in the diocese of Maguelonne, at Carcassonne, and at Toulouse (where three foreigners were executed).

4. Concerning the outward signs by which they can be recognized to some extent:

   It should also be recognized that, as Augustine says in *Against Fausus*, "men cannot be bound together in either a true or false religion unless they are joined by common participation in some signs or visible sacraments." Thus the Beguins observe certain special practices of this sort, and display certain modes of behavior in speech and other areas through which they can be recognized by others. Their way of giving or returning a salutation is as follows: When they come to or enter a house or meet one another on a journey or in the street, they say, "Blessed by Jesus Christ," or "blessed be the name of Lord Jesus Christ." Again, when they pray in church or elsewhere they commonly sit hooded and bent over with their faces turned toward the opposite wall or a similar location, and rarely seem to kneel with hands joined as others do. Also, at the midday meal, after the food has been blessed, the Gloria in excelsis Deo is said kneeling by those who know it. At the evening meal those who know it say the Salva, Regina, also kneeling.

6. The following deals with the way Beguins are to be examined and questioned:

   It should be recognized and kept in mind that some of these Beguins have studied and know more than others about the preceding articles, having been more fully instructed or trained in them; for it is their custom to move gradually from bad to worse, conveying their doctrine little by little rather than all at once. Thus in the process of investigation a skillful inquisitor may inquire about all these things, a few, or only one, putting all others aside, as seems expedient to him, in view of the quality or condition of the person being examined and the demands of the inquisitorial office. Thus a list of questions to be asked is presented below, based on the errors they have been found to hold; yet it should not be assumed that every one of them ought to be asked to each and every person being interrogated. Instead, those should be asked which the individual inquisitor considers fitting, so that the manner and style of investigation can be fitted to the specific case at hand. Thus by suitably posed questions and the answers arising from them the truth will more subtly and more easily be discovered, while deceit will more quickly be detected when the interrogated does not respond clearly and properly to the question, seeking to avoid a direct answer by hiding behind a shelter of words. All of these things are learned more fully through experience.

David Burr, trans.

Source: "Inquisitor's Manual." *Medieval Sourcebook*. Retrieved July 24 2002, from http://www.fordham.edu/halsall/source/bernardgui-inq.html

fourth century CE, it retained the inquisitorial trial method along with other Roman institutions.

The leaders of this Christian church, calling themselves "orthodox" or "true believers," faced challenges to their teachings and authority from dissenters they identified as heretics, a term deriving from the Greek *hairesein* (Latin, *haeresis*) meaning "choice." The orthodox party believed that heretics willfully chose doctrines differing from the norm, and so threatened Christendom as "traitors" against God. Armed with the coercive legal power of the Roman state, early Christian leaders began gradually to harass and then prosecute heretics according to imperial laws and the inquisitorial trial process that supported their church. The use of legal inquisitions fell dormant during the centuries following the collapse of Rome around 500 CE, partly because there were few heretics to prosecute during this unstable age, and partly because new Germanic kingdoms replaced older Roman laws with their own *wergeld* and trial by ordeal. When heresy resurfaced as Cathar dualism and Waldensian asceticism in the twelfth century, clerics were surprised and unprepared to deal with what they believed was a revival of ancient heresies.

Pope Innocent III (1198–1216) initially responded to the threat with a policy of *caritas* or "caring persuasion," but these preaching missions and the Franciscan and Dominican friars who staffed them enjoyed little success. The pope then turned in frustration to *potestas*, coercive force, by launching a crusade against the Cathars in southern France in 1209. Since the crusade "successfully" eliminated thousands of Cathar dissidents in the region over the next two decades, Pope Gregory IX (1227–1241) realized that *potestas* was more effective against religious nonconformity, and took steps to codify and legitimize its use by reviving the old Roman inquisition.

In 1231 Pope Gregory issued the bull *Ille humanis generis* authorizing the first papally appointed inquisitor, a German Dominican, to seek out heresy in his region and bring such cases as he found to trial, abjuration (recantation), and penance. The pope quickly issued similar commissions to inquisitors across Europe, advising them to correct religious error "with love" if possible, but authorizing the use of force on unrepentant heretics. Pope Innocent IV (1243–1254) formalized the office of "inquisitor of heretical depravity" in 1243, and sanctioned torture in his 1252 bull *Ad extirpanda* to secure confessions from uncooperative suspects.

Procedures and Functions

Drawing on the old Roman inquisitorial model, in the mid-thirteenth century these itinerant heresy courts began to employ rules of indictment, evidence, conviction, and sentencing that gradually became standardized. When inquisitors first arrived in an area they preached a public sermon demanding local cooperation, and established a grace period during which suspected religious dissidents might freely confess to secure more lenient treatment. The grace period also served as the "inquisition" or evidence-gathering time, when denunciations of alleged offenders were heard from local witnesses, and summonses were prepared to call less-cooperative suspects to trial. To protect the evidentiary process and the accused from false witness, defendants could name their enemies so as to eliminate unreliable testimony, while those who falsely accused were themselves subject to harsh penalties. When suspects appeared before the tribunal they were informed of the charges and asked to respond, but witnesses' names were kept secret to shield them from retaliation.

Accused individuals who confessed their guilt had to abjure their "erroneous" beliefs and swear to name other heretics they might know or suspect. They were then assigned public penances ranging from fasting on bread and water, public humiliation or flogging in the local church, or the wearing of distinctive yellow crosses, to the more severe penances of imprisonment, long-distance pilgrimage, or even exile. Defendants who refused to confess had to be convicted by "full" proofs including either the testimony of two responsible witnesses or a confession extracted under torture. Since "partial" or circumstantial proofs were insufficient to convict, confession was sometimes the only means to prove heresy absolutely. Torture could be applied in such cases, but rules forbade bloodshed, protected children and pregnant women, and insisted on the free repetition of confessions twenty-four hours after torture had ceased. If defendants still refused to confess and abjure after having thus been convicted, or if previously abjured penitents relapsed, they were turned over to local secular authorities for corporeal punishment and confiscation of their property. Most kingdoms in western Europe had criminal laws by the thirteenth century allowing them to execute heretics on behalf of the church, which could not carry out death sentences on its own. Most condemned heretics were treated to a *sermo generalis* announcing their conviction and obstinate heresies, and then usually burned to death publicly to warn would-be offenders. These procedures became fairly regularized over the next few centuries, thanks in part to the appearance of many inquisitorial "how-to" manuals, including those by the Frenchman Bernard Gui (1324) and, most famously, the *Directorium inquisitorium* (1376) of the Aragónese Dominican Nicholas Eymeric.

Although medieval inquisitions were nominally directed by the papacy, they in fact functioned relatively independently. They were often staffed by Dominican or other mendicant friars, who required the local bishop's permission to operate in an area. Bishops established some courts themselves, and so were not directly sanctioned by the pope and did not necessarily employ Dominican inquisitors. Permission to initiate proceedings was often required from the local civil authorities as well, so inquisitorial procedures frequently mirrored those of secular courts in most locations. And, just as torture and capital punishment were standard in medieval secular justice, the violence employed by the inquisitions was not especially cruel or unusual for its day. Because the desired outcome of heresy trials was abjuration and penance—to burn unrepentant dissidents was to admit failure—most modern scholars agree that inquisitions imposed the death penalty far less frequently than has been supposed. As the activity and influence of medieval inquisitions waned in the fifteenth century, however, they did put to death some of their most celebrated victims, including Czech reformer Jan Hus (1415), French heroine Joan of Arc (1431), and Florentine demagogue Fra Girolamo Savonarola (1498).

The Spanish Inquisition

In Spain, medieval inquisitions operated most actively against Cathar heretics in the kingdom of Aragón, despite the fact that much of the Iberian Peninsula had supported a diverse population of Christians, Jews, and Muslims since the early Middle Ages. These peoples had generally lived together in peace for centuries until crop failures, livestock epidemics, and the Black Death ravaged their country in the fourteenth century, causing Christians to search for someone to blame. Jews residing in Christian kingdoms in Spain were particularly harassed, often being lynched or forced to convert to Christianity to atone for the misfortunes they had supposedly wrought. These converts, known officially as *conversos* but pejoratively as *marranos* (pigs), were often publicly devoted to their new faith, but not all *conversos* were enthusiastic Christians and some continued to practice Judaism in secret. Because many former Jews found lucrative employment as royal tax collectors in fifteenth century Castile, anti-Semitic resentment grew among tax-paying Christians who accused *conversos* of being "false" Christians and thus heretics. Intending partly to mollify public anti-Semitism, and partly to help unify their newly joined kingdoms of Aragón and Castile, King Ferdinand (1474–1516) and Queen Isabel (1474–1504) petitioned the pope for permission to initiate inquisitorial proceedings against suspect *conversos* in 1478.

Pope Sixtus IV (1471–1484) complied in November, issuing a bull of institution permitting their "Most Catholic Majesties" to appoint three inquisitors in Spain. By autumn 1480 these Dominicans had begun their work, and by 1482 they were assisted by several more inquisitors, including Tomás de Torquemada, soon named Inquisitor-General for Aragón and Castile. Torquemada was president of the "Council of the Supreme and General Inquisition" or *Suprema*, one of five advisory councils forming the inner core of Spain's royal government. Torquemada's ruthlessness prompted Pope Sixtus to condemn the inquisition's worst abuses in April 1483, but his plea was ignored by Ferdinand, who was determined to direct the inquisition as an instrument of national unification and control. By 1600 the *Suprema* was supervising the activities of fifteen to twenty local inquisitions, each operating independently but following procedures standardized by Torquemada's *Instructiones* handbook issued in 1484.

Inquisitorial tribunals in early modern Spain functioned much as their medieval predecessors had elsewhere in Europe. Two inquisitors typically arrived in an area with their team of legal, financial, and secretarial assistants. They then announced a grace period, accepted confessions, made accusations, and determined guilt based on evidence from secret witnesses; finally, they issued verdicts, penances, and sentences. Property was ordinarily confiscated and held against the possibility of conviction but, contrary to popular belief, the proceeds did not enrich the inquisitors but were used instead to support the accused awaiting trial in prison and to pay court expenses. Torture was also used in Spain to extract confessions, but surviving records indicate that inquisitors made more moderate use of torture than did contemporary secular courts. Death sentences were also relatively infrequent because, like the earlier medieval inquisition, its Spanish counterpart primarily sought abjuration and penance as a public reminder of the righteousness of Roman faith. When death sentences were carried out, the victims were condemned and their offenses recited in an *auto-da-fé* or "act of faith" sermon, after which they were burned alive before an often enthusiastic crowd. Thanks to the vast records left by inquisitorial notaries, it is estimated that fewer than 10,000 died at the hands of the Spanish inquisitions during the 356 years of their existence. This number is horrific, yet it pales beside the conservative estimate of over 100,000 deaths generated by Protestant, Catholic, and civil tribunals during the 300-year span of the European witch-hunt.

Spanish inquisitions at first mostly prosecuted "heretic" *conversos* and some apostate *moriscos* or converted Muslims, but in later years they also investigated Spanish Protestants, deist intellectuals, suspected sorcerers and witches, and even native peoples in the New World. New World inquisitorial courts were established originally on the island of Hispaniola, and later in Mexico City, Lima, and Cartagena, to pursue *conversos* who had fled prosecution in Spain. These inquisitions also eventually tried Native-American "new Christians" who, like apostate *conversos* and *moriscos*, were thought to have returned to their old gods. Joseph Bonaparte suspended inquisitorial operations when he became king of Spain in 1808; the courts were revived in 1813 but were finally dissolved by the new Spanish constitution of 1834.

The Final Inquisitions

The Protestant Reformation inspired the last inquisitorial flurry in sixteenth-century Italy as part of the Roman Catholic Counter-Reformation. Pope Paul III (1534–1549), the first pontiff to take the Lutheran and Calvinist schism with Rome seriously, initiated ecclesiastical reforms designed to win back Protestants. When a final attempt to reconcile Lutheran and Catholic doctrines failed at Regensburg in 1541, the pope issued his bull *Licet ab initio* the following year instituting inquisitorial courts in Italy under the direction of a curial council of inquisitors-general headed by Gian Pietro Cardinal Carafa. Known officially as the "Congregation of the Holy Roman and Universal Inquisition" or simply the "Holy Office," this council oversaw inquisitorial proceedings primarily in Rome and the Papal States, though a few courts functioned in other Italian regions as well. The procedures followed by Roman inquisitors were nearly identical to those of their medieval predecessors, thanks to Nicholas Eymeric's 1376 handbook *Directorium inquisitorium*, which was updated in 1578 for Italian use by Spanish jurist Francisco Peña. The pope also issued an "Index of Prohibited Books and Authors" (1542) to support the Catholic Counter-Reformation and, together with the inquisitorial trials themselves, did much to retard the spread of Protestant teachings throughout the Italian peninsula. The Roman inquisition was the most moderate of all in its sparing use of torture and infrequent recourse to the death penalty, although famous victims such as Giordano Bruno and Galileo Galilei did suffer at its hands. Inquisitions also operated in places such as Venice and Sicily, but in Venice their activities were strictly controlled by the Venetian government, and in Sicily they functioned under the auspices of the Spanish crown and not the papacy. The Roman inquisition fell into disuse by the eighteenth century, was redesignated the "Congregation of the Holy Office" in 1908 by Pope Pius X, and has existed since 1966 as a theological advisory committee of the papal curia with no investigative or coercive powers.

Implications

There is no doubt that the medieval, Spanish, and Roman inquisitions of the Catholic church were intended to suppress religious freedom in various parts of Europe, and employed intimidation, humiliation, torture, and capital punishment to achieve this. While condemning the inquisitions as enemies of religious freedom, students of history are also obligated to re-examine the myth of "The Inquisition" as it has come down into modern times. It is also important to try to understand that inquisitors truly believed they were God's agents, fighting God's battle against Satan to save souls and protect the Christian community. It should also be noted that, unfair and violent as they were, inquisitorial methods were no worse than judicial standards of the day allowed and, in many cases, were more humanely applied than they might have been in less responsible hands. Although the era of inquisitions was a grim one in the religious history of Western Europe, it was also an age from which a great deal can be learned about the need to understand and celebrate religious differences.

Clayton J. Drees

See also Augustine on Religious Coercion; Cathars; Heresy; Roman Catholicism

Further Reading

Ginzburg, C. (1983). *The night battles*. Baltimore: Johns Hopkins University Press.

Kamen, H. (1998). *The Spanish Inquisition*. New Haven, CT: Yale University Press.

Ladurie, E. L. (1978). *Montaillou: Promised land of error*. (B. Bray, Trans.). London: Scolar Press.

Lansing, C. (1998). *Power and purity: Cathar heresy in medieval Italy*. Oxford, UK: Oxford University Press.

Lea, H. C. (1958). *A history of the inquisition of the Middle Ages*. New York: Russell and Russell.

Netanyahu, B. (1995). *The origins of the inquisition in fifteenth century Spain*. New York: Random House.

Peters, E. (1988). *Inquisition*. New York: Free Press/Macmillan.

Rubin, N. (1991). *Isabella of Castile: The first Renaissance queen*. New York: St. Martin's Press.

Islam

Article 18 of the Universal Declaration of Human Rights presented Muslim countries with a serious challenge, because it assumes that the member states of the United Nations are secular in the sense that religion is not the dimension that determines citizenship. This is in contrast to the medieval system, in which adherence to a particular faith, and even to a specific interpretation of it, formed the basis for legitimate membership of the state. People with doubtful loyalty were subjected to the Inquisition in Europe and to the Mihnah (ordeal) in Baghdad. Although today all Muslim countries are more or less secular in their political structure, and although most of them have adopted Western legal systems rather than *shari'a* (Muslim law), nevertheless there are aspects of *shari'a* that remain in force in most of them, and that fact has consequences for religious freedom.

Islamic family law is followed by all Muslim countries with the exception of Turkey and possibly Tunisia. The question of freedom of expression, conscience, and belief is addressed sympathetically in most constitutions but is often violated. The dethronement of *shari'a* from the official state legal system of the Muslim states arrested its development, which has meant that it is less capable of dealing with a changing world and changing social conditions than it might have been. Recent widespread clamor for a return to *shari'a* and popular attachment to its precepts have led governments to refer issues of freedom of religion to the religious authorities. In general, Muslim scholars follow one of the Islamic schools of law. The prevailing schools for Sunni Islam (the majority of the world's Muslims—roughly 90 percent—are Sunni Muslims) are Hanafi, Maliki, Shafi'i and Hanbali. Shi'ite scholars follow the Imami or Zaidi schools. Kharijites (of whom there are only some 500,000; the majority of the world's Muslims who are not Sunnis are Shi'ites) follow the Ebadi school. These schools of law came into being as a result of the work of eminent jurists interpreting Muslim law as enshrined in the Qur'an and the hadith (tradition) of the Prophet Muhammad. The story of religious freedom in Islam begins therefore with the Prophet.

The Qur'an and the Prophetic Tradition: General Principles and Early Application

The Qur'an contains numerous verses emphasizing freedom of religion, such as Surah 2, verse 265: "There shall be no coercion in matters of faith." Tradition says that while in Medina, where he established the first Muslim authority (622 CE), Muhammad signed an agreement with the Jews of the city granting them full rights of citizenship and complete freedom to uphold their beliefs and perform their acts of worship and follow their customs undisturbed.

The Wars of the Prophet

Muhammad's career involved him in conflict primarily with the polytheistic Arab tribes, and especially with his own tribe, the Quraish of Mecca. There was a period of truce between the Prophet and the tribal Arabs, which was broken by the latter. The Muslims mounted an attack on Mecca itself and conquered it in 630 CE, thus destroying the center of resistance to

HATE CRIMES AGAINST MUSLIMS IN THE UNITED STATES AND 9/11

In November 2002, the FBI issued its annual Hate Crime Report, which showed a large increase in the number of hate crimes perpetrated on Muslims or people likely to be identified as Muslims or as being from the Arab Middle East. The number of reported incidents targeting people, institutions, and businesses identified with Islam increased from 28 in 2000 to 481 in 2001. In addition, hate crimes against people because of their ethnicity or national origin of those not Hispanic, not black, and not Asian or American Indian more than quadrupled from 354 in 2000 to 1,501 in 2001. This category includes people of Middle Eastern origin or descent. Most incidents were assaults and intimidation, with three cases of murder and thirty-five cases of arson reported. The FBI figures are an under-reporting of the true figure, as many incidents are not reported to the police. It is believed most of these attacks took place after 11 September 2001 and there have been fewer in 2002. Many Muslims in the United States worry that attacks will increase if war is waged with Iraq.

This increase took place despite efforts by the U.S. government to control anti-Muslim attitudes and activities. The Justice Department opened its Backlash Discrimination Initiative and several dozen perpetrators were prosecuted under state and local laws. The Justice Department also held 250 community forums around the country to prevent violent against Muslims.

Source: FBI Hate Crime Statistics, 2001.
Retrieved December 10, 2002 from http://www.fbi.gov/ucr/01hate.pdf

---

Islam. The Qur'an records some of the campaigns and the directives given to the Prophet with regard to their aims. The ninth Sura of the Qur'an begins with a declaration ending the peaceful coexistence between the Muslims and the polytheists in the very first verse, and in the fifth verse tells the Muslims that "once the sacred months are over slay the polytheists wherever you may come upon them." So Islam was distinctly less tolerant of polytheistic traditional Arab religion than it was of Judaism.

Relationship with the People of the Book

Eventually the Jewish-Muslim relationship soured, and the Jews joined the opposition to the Prophet. Consequently they lost their position as equal citizens and were made to pay *jizya*, a head tax levied on non-Muslims who were "people of the Book"—those whose religions were based on written scripture, such as the Jews, the Christians, and Zoroastrians. Verse 29 of Sura 9 states, "Fight those who have been given scripture but do not believe in God and the Day of Judgment . . . until they pay the tribute."

Muhammad is also reported as saying, "I have been instructed to fight the people until they say

There is no God but Allah." This militant attitude is regarded by some as the last and final statement of Islam regarding other faiths. They perceive Islam as in a perpetual state of war against other religions and claim that those Qur'anic verses calling for peaceful preaching of the faith have been abrogated, as they were only relevant to the period of Muslim weakness and impotence. Others believe that the wars of the Prophet were defensive in nature and that persuasion was his preferred means to conversion.

Notwithstanding the above, we know that the Prophet did not suppress Judaism or Christianity, and he is reported to have instructed that Zoroastrians should be treated as a people of the Book (that is, they should be granted freedom of religion and their able-bodied men should be required to pay *jizya)*.

The Period of the Guided Caliphs (632–661 CE)

The death of Muhammad and the succession of the first caliph, Abu Bakr, occasioned widespread rebellions in Arabia against the authority of Medina. The rebels were labeled apostates. Abu Bakr persuaded his colleagues to declare war against those rebels to bring them back to the fold. In simultaneous and well-planned campaigns the rebels were defeated and Arabia reunified. The action of Abu Bakr against the "apostates," together with statements attributed to the Prophet that "whosoever changes his religion is to be killed" formed the foundation of the rule governing apostasy in Islam. The peoples of the Book were granted their religious freedom provided they paid *jizya,* but the ancient Arab religion continued to be illegitimate and died out.

There are reports of the apostasy of individuals and small groups during the life of the Prophet and during the reign of the second caliph, Omar. In all of them, the responsible officials administered the death penalty without allowing for a period to recant. Omar is reported to have disagreed with the decision and said that had he been present he would have given the apostate time to come back to Islam.

The Successive Dynasties

Thirty years after the death of the Prophet a dynastic system of government became the norm in the world of Islam. The rules concerning the freedom of Muslims to change their religion were formulated by scholars in various parts of the Muslim Empire. The death penalty was generally accepted for both male and female apostates. Ibrahim Al-Nakhi (d. 713 CE) opposed the death sentence and suggested that the apostate should be given unlimited time to recant. His opinion, however, was ignored by the founders of the now established schools of law.

It must be pointed out, however, that Al-Nakhi disputed the death sentence only and not the principle of coercion. Apparently he found no evidence in the Qur'an for such a severe penalty and did not accept as authentic the traditions calling for the death sentence. But he, like all the other jurists of the first Islamic century, called for the Istitabah, that is, inducing the apostate to recant. The method suggested by Caliph Omar, according to reports, was imprisonment.

The Hanifi School in the second Islamic century would suggest such treatment for women. They rejected the death penalty for women on the grounds that it violated the Prophet's instruction not to kill women, and they also reasoned that women posed no danger to the state as they do not normally bear arms. Fighting women, therefore, were to be treated like men. This rationale should have led to an assessment of the wars of Apostasy as being wars to avert a threat to the stability of the state rather than wars to force people to believe. Generally the jurists regarded apostasy to be a danger to the social order. Since the foundation of the state was religion, apostasy was regarded as a betrayal equal to high treason in a secular system. Jurists support the death penalty for apostates to the present day.

Defining Apostasy

The definition of apostasy is crucial to our understanding of the attitude of Muslim jurists to religious freedom. Abu Bakr's wars were waged against rebels who shared the same basic beliefs. Some were Muslims in conviction but they refused to pay the *zakat* (religious tax) to Abu Bakr. They argued that the Qur'an states (Surah 9 verse 103) that the *zakat* was paid to the Prophet as purification and so that he would pray for the donors, and that Abu Bakr had no authority to collect it. Abu Bakr dismissed this argument and treated them as apostates.

The other uprisings were directed at Muhammad's Quraish tribe. Leaders of these tribal revolts claimed to be prophets of equal status to that of Muhammad. Musailamah, the "prophet" of the Banu Hanifah tribe, sought to divide Arabia between his tribe and Quraish. There were also a few cases of individuals converting to other religions. All these instances were listed by historians as cases of apostasy. The jurists came to define apostasy as the renunciation of Islam through conversion to another religion, becoming an atheist, or rejection of well-known parts of *shari'a,* such as the prohibition on the consumption of wine. Failure to treat Islamic texts with respect, insulting God, the Prophet Muhammad, or any of the prophets mentioned in the Qur'an, and holding unacceptable doctrine all also constituted rejection of *shari'a.* This rather broad definition allowed rulers to suppress opposition by labeling its leader an apostate. The doctrine of predestination, supported by the Umayyads, who ruled for close to a century (661–750 CE), was regarded as a fundamental part of the creed. Consequently those who advocated free will were put to death.

The political use of apostasy continued after the fall of the Umayyads and the emergence of the second Islamic dynasty, the Abbasids (750–1258 CE). Under the Abbasids there was a rise in Persian nationalism, led by some of the most brilliant thinkers and poets of the day. The authorities accused them of *zandaqah* (heresy), of professing

Islam while secretly adhering to Zoroastrianism or other ancient Persian religions. It is possible that some Persians did go back to their former faiths, but the presence of some of the most illustrious intellectuals among the accused leads to the suspicion that the accusation was politically motivated. To support this interpretation is the fact that the accused were not allowed to recant and their profession of faith was not accepted: Guilt was established generally by accusation. The jurists at the time supported these severe measures despite their violations of the *shari'a* rules that demand proper evidence and suspend punishment on the confession of faith.

Under the seventh Abbasid caliph, al-Ma'mun (reigned 813–833 CE), the doctrine that the Qur'an was a created text (not an eternal, uncreated text, a theological position held by others and the position that became dominant later in Islam's history) was imposed, and those who did not openly accept it were tortured or even killed. Alongside state intolerance of opposition, the public in all Muslim countries has not generally tolerated those holding minority views. Many scholars suffered mob persecution, sometimes for minor deviations. Tabari (d. 923 CE), the great historian, exegete, and jurist was declared an apostate by the Hanbali jurists of Baghdad. His crime was failure to recognize the founder of their school of law as a jurist. Theologians, philosophers, jurists, and Sufis suffered the fate of being declared apostates, and many books were burned on the altar of their supposed apostasy.

The Modern Age

The conquest of Islamic lands by various European powers occasioned the suspension of the Islamic penal code, though the populace continued to impose its will when the opportunity arose.

Most Muslim states, as mentioned earlier, expressed reservations in connection with Article 18 of the United Nations Declaration of Human Rights. Apostasy is still punishable by death in countries such as Saudi Arabia, Pakistan, and Iran. Apostasy remains illegal in all the other Muslim countries, but is not punishable by death.

The jurists' legacy in relation to this issue was larger than the issue of punishment; it also decreed that the apostate lost all legal rights as a person. He or she would be deprived of property and lose the status of being married. The property, according to most authorities, went to the state. Only a minority

of jurists allowed relatives to acquire the property of the apostate (as if he or she were dead). This has consequences in the present day. In 1986 a university professor in Egypt was declared by the High Court to be an apostate and ordered to be separated from his wife. He and his wife left Egypt and joined the University of Leiden in the Netherlands.

Many people were puzzled by this judgment because the constitution of Egypt supports freedom of expression. More confusing still, the professor continued to declare his allegiance to Islam. Nor was he shown how he deviated from the faith in the eyes of the court. To make matters worse, the venerable and widely respected al-Azhar Mosque (the center of al-Azhar University, a world-renowned center for Islamic studies) in Cairo supported the judgment. Although the professor could have continued to live in Egypt without being molested by the authorities, he worried about the reaction of the general public: In Egypt religious agitators incite assassins to make attempts on the lives in Egypt of condemned writers, novelists, and thinkers. The journalist Faraj Foda was killed and the Nobel laureate Naguib Mahfouz suffered a knife attack; others have to have twenty-four-hour police protection.

The apostasy law applies only to Muslims, but a Dhimmi (non-Muslim living in a Muslim state) is enjoined not to insult the Prophet or Islam. In Pakistan, a young Christian boy was imprisoned after being accused of writing insulting remarks on a wall—this despite the fact that the child was shown to be illiterate. He was sentenced to death, but the appeal court released him in 2002.

The followers of Mirza Ghulam Ahmad (d. 1908), called Ahmadis, are persecuted in Pakistan. They believe their leader to have been a prophet confirming the *shari'a* of the Prophet Muhammad and to be the promised Mahdi ("divinely guided one"; the Messiah). They believe him to have abolished jihad and therefore reject any punishment for apostasy. In 1974 the parliament of Pakistan declared the Ahmadis to be non-Muslims. Many lost their government jobs and their places of worship were no longer to be called mosques. They were denied permission to perform the hajj (the pilgrimage to Mecca that is one of the five pillars of Islamic faith). Their leader was forced to seek refuge in London, where he established his headquarters.

In Sudan under General Jafar Muhammad an-Numeiry, the religious and political leader Mahmud Muhammad Taha was executed for heresy in

1985 when Numeiry introduced *shari'a*. In a bizarre manifestation of support, the Saudi authorities sent a delegation to congratulate the Sudanese on their achievement.

In Iran there is the perennial case of the Baha'is, the followers of Baha Ullah (1817–1892), who founded a new religion and fled Persia in the nineteenth century. Though he himself was an apostate, his followers are born to their creed; nevertheless the authorities in Iran treat them as apostates. They are subjected to persecution (but not executed) for adhering to the Baha'i faith.

New Interpretation of *Shari'a*

The Qur'anic declaration "There shall not be coercion in matters of faith" has been used by apologists to proclaim Islam's commitment to freedom of religion. The apostasy law obviously cannot be reconciled with this principle. Attempts have been made to square the circle. A prominent contemporary preacher, Muhammad al-Ghazali, suggests that one is free to follow any religion until one converts to Islam, upon which one will have consciously abrogated one's freedom. This sophistry does not apply to those who were born Muslim.

A more meaningful examination of the issue came from the leaders of the reform movement, Muhammad Abdu (d. 1905) and his student Rashid Ridha (d. 1936). In their commentary on the Qur'an (*Tafseer Al-Manar*) they argued that the Qur'an guarantees freedom of religion. By far the most elaborate and clear statement on the subject from a religious authority came from eminent sheikh Abd al-Muta'al al-Sa'idi. He published a book in 1955 entitled *Al-Hurriyyah al-Dimiyyah fi al-Islam* (Freedom of Religion in Islam), in which he makes the categorical statement "the apostate has the right to freedom of religion. . . . He should be treated like a person who has never been a Muslim" (al-Sa'idi 2000, 134). This book was republished in the year 2000 in the face of strong opposition from some religious bodies in al-Azhar and elsewhere. This is an indication of the deteriorating state of religious freedom in Egypt and in al-Azhar itself. The author, being confident of his position, included in the second edition articles critical of his position as well as his own rebuttals. The reissuing of this book may indicate that there is a serious move in favor of religious freedom in Muslim learned circles.

Contemporary Islamic movements that have loudly supported the death penalty for apostasy are beginning to have second thoughts. This will involve them in reinterpreting the wars of the Prophet and his Companions as well as the verses of the Qur'an and the texts of the hadith. Leading this trend is Shaikh Ghanoushi, the leader of the Al-Nahda Party of Tunisia. He states that he favors freedom of religion and believes that apostates should be treated like other nonbelievers, and cites several modern religious scholars who support this view. But we must wait for this shift to trickle down to the common people before we can expect there to be sensible academic debate, free from fear, on these important areas of *shari'a*.

M. A. Zaki Badawi

Further Reading

Attas, S. M. N., al- (1985). *Islam, secularism, and the philosophy of the future.* London: Mansell.

Ayoub, M. (1994). Religious freedom and the law of apostasy in Islam. *Islamochristiana* [Journal of the Vatican Secretariat for Non-Christians], *20*, 75–91.

Azzam, S. (Ed.). (1981). *Universal Islamic declaration of human rights.* London: Islamic Council of Europe.

Azzam, S. (Ed.) (1982). *Islam and contemporary society.* London: Longman.

Jundy, A. H., al-. (1992). *Abu Hanifa, the hero of freedom and forgiveness in Islam.* Cairo, Egypt: Dar al-Ma'arif.

Khan, S. (1989). *Freedom of thought and Islam.* Karachi, Pakistan: Royal Book Co.

Sa'idi, A. M., al- (2000). *Al-hurriyyah al-dimiyyah fi al-Islam* [Freedom of religion in Islam] (2nd edition). Cairo, Egypt: Dar Al-Ma'arif.

Shadid, W. A. R., & van Konningsveld, P. S. (1995). *Religious freedom and the position of Islam in Western Europe: Opportunities and obstacles in the acquisition of equal rights.* Kampen, Netherlands: Kok Pharos Publishing House.

Islamic Empire, Medieval

To grasp the extent of religious freedom available under medieval Islam requires an understanding of the early expansion of this faith. Islam's earliest political manifestation was embedded in the clan and tribal affiliations of the Arabian Peninsula, which gradually brought larger territories under Muslim suzerainty. Those who inherited the Prophet Muhammad's authority were called caliphs ("successors"), and they continued to enforce the law articulated by the Prophet and advance the new universal religion. Over time the office of the caliph gradually transformed itself into a royal authority within an imperial polity. The presence or lack of religious freedom, the treatment of minorities, and the kind of religious diversity found in medieval Muslim societies are matters intertwined with the evolution of Muslim political practices.

Abd al-Rahman Ibn Khaldun (1332–1406), the Tunis-born proto-sociologist and historian, pointed out that the Muslim polity had experienced several transitions prior to the development of dynastic rule. Under the Prophet Muhammad the polity was clan based in the city-state of Medina in Arabia. After establishing himself in Medina, Muhammad made Islam the defining characteristic of his polity, distinct from those of his rivals in Mecca and other neighboring territories. Alongside tribal allegiances, religious identity also became crucial in the political organization of the city. This is evident from the social contract Muhammad concluded between the various tribes in a proto-constitutional document known as the "Writing of Medina." It holds persons responsible for fulfilling duties in terms of both tribal allegiance and religious affiliation. The document specifically names the Quraysh, the Meccan tribe, as well as the Aws and Khazraj, the two main tribes of Medina, and sets forth their duties within the compact. It continues, identifying groups by their religious affiliation, and specifying the duties of Muslims and Jews. This clearly indicates that the society of early Medina was multi-religious, with Islam, Judaism, and other Arab religions coexisting with a fair degree of freedom.

The First Four Caliphs

By the time of Muhammad's death in 632, there were already plans to expand the frontiers of the Muslim domain beyond Arabia. The major expansion took place under the rule of the first four successors of Muhammad. Abu Bakr (reigned 632–634), the first caliph, consolidated the ideological and political authority of Islam within Arabia. He subdued Arab Muslim tribes, some of which thought that political allegiance was not part of their conversion to Islam. They demonstrated this by refusing to pay taxes (zakat) to the caliph, not viewing this practice as a universal religious norm. Abu Bakr declared war on these tribes, claiming that as long as they differentiated between prayer—for God—and taxes—for

human authority—he would charge them with apostasy and fight them. The raids on these dissident tribes came to be known as the *ridda* or apostasy wars.

But the charge against these tribes was both controversial and ambiguous. The question foremost in the minds of some Muslims was whether the mere refusal of these tribes to pay *zakat* to the state in itself constituted apostasy. This is the earliest instance where the enforcement of purely religious obligations is viewed as a government responsibility. When the government is mandated to enforce religious obligations, a refusal to perform such an obligation is seen as an affront to its authority constituting a special kind of sedition called *apostasy*. It was Abu Bakr who established the framework within which Islam became both a badge of faith and a sign of political loyalty, even though elements of this can be traced back to the leadership of the Prophet.

This pattern continued under 'Umar I (reigned 634–644), when Muslim expansion continued into Egypt, Palestine, and Persia. The conquests took place under the rubric of *jihad*, where striving in God's cause is an obligation to facilitate the declaration of a universal religion—here meaning monotheism as taught by the Prophet. Though 'Umar maintained a frugal lifestyle, regarding leadership as a holy duty, not everyone saw it this way. On seeing his governor Mu'awiya in Syria dressed in ornate regalia, 'Umar sarcastically asked: "Have you become a Persian king, oh Mu'awiya?" 'Umar wanted to know if his governor thought of himself as a monarch, rather than as a servant of God and the people.

Ibn Khaldun believed that 'Umar was persuaded by Mu'awiya's defense that he was simply following local custom. Mu'awiya claimed he would have had difficulty maintaining authority in a new environment if he did not immerse himself in local political culture and conventions. In contrast, when 'Umar came to take delivery of Jerusalem from its Christian patriarch, the latter was unable to distinguish between 'Umar and his manservant. What distinguished the reign of the first four caliphs from later ones, according to Ibn Khaldun, was that the former took religion seriously and felt restrained by its imperatives. One of the earliest agreements mandating religious freedom was the Covenant of 'Umar with the inhabitants of Jerusalem, guaranteeing the rights of the various religious communities, especially the Christians, after the Muslim conquest of that city.

Under the third caliph, 'Uthman (reigned 644–656), there was both expansion and consolidation of the vast Muslim territories. The centralized tribal political system became unstable because it was unable to deal with the more complex political sub-cultures of the new territories of the Fertile Crescent and Egypt. In the end, 'Uthman fell to political dissent when his disgruntled Egyptian and Iraqi subjects assassinated him. The fourth caliph, 'Ali (reigned 656–661), inherited a shaky realm and quickly moved his capital to Kufa in Iraq, in order to quell dissidence. He had another goal in mind: to keep in check Mu'awiya, his governor in Syria who also aspired to the caliphate. The civil war between the followers of 'Ali and Mu'awiya sowed the seeds for the later sectarian divide that manifested itself between Sunnis and Shi'as. The Shi'as, the partisans of 'Ali, later developed a creed that political leadership was a matter of divine designation, whereas the Sunnis argued that a leader was elected by the will of the community.

Emergence of Imperial Governance

Mu'awiya's (reigned 661–680) ascent to power marked the beginning of dynastic rule and the initial stages of imperial governance. As Mu'awiya was a member of the Umayya tribe, his is known as the Umayyad dynasty, and it ruled Damascus between 661 and 750. The Umayyad rule began to resemble a monarchy, with intergenerational, hereditary succession. This marked a turning point in the understanding of the idea and role of the caliph. During the reign of the first four caliphs, the office of the caliph was marked by its religious function: actively to promote the universal religion of Islam. Political leadership (the caliphate) was a means to a religious end, where religion was the virtue all humanity needed.

Thus religious ends legitimated politics as a necessity, a politics animated by theological reason, not secular reasoning. As part of the political obligation, *jihad* or military struggle became a means to make Islam a universal religion. What is now called "religion" was, in medieval Islam, part of a larger web of social, political, economic, and cultural practices. It goes without saying that each practice is very much a reflex of complex modes of power. To talk of religion as an independent discourse and separate from other practices would be tantamount to doing an injustice to history.

As long as religious motives restrained the exercise of power, the imperial dimension of Muslim governance was somewhat subdued. However, when Muslim caliphs also began to assume royal power and conduct themselves like Byzantine and Persian monarchs, the imperial posture became an obvious and dominant mode of dynastic rule. Furthermore, as the cultural context of Islam's political center shifted first from Arabia to Syria, and then to Baghdad under the Abbasids, political jurisprudence also adapted accordingly. Hence the law increasingly began to reflect the reflexes of imperial power. By the time the Abbasid dynasty (750–1258) succeeded the Umayyads, the office of the caliphate was indistinguishable from that of a monarch. Muslim jurists had no objections to royal authority per se: they were realists and could adapt the rules to changing social conditions. Royal dynastic rule was permissible provided it did not lead to tyranny, excessive luxury, and abuse of resources.

As long as the caliph/monarch fulfilled the duties of the caliphate his rule was legitimate. The principle function of the caliph was to enforce the law, *shari'a*, uphold religion by ensuring that prayers are conducted, engage in the struggle to promote religion (*jihad*), and ensure that juridical standards and ethics research are maintained so that the judiciary and commercial practices conform to the highest standards of justice and equality. In short, the enforcement and maintenance of a comprehensive legal order, akin to a proto–rule-of-law system, was at the center of the caliph's responsibilities.

Social Structure

The medieval Muslim caliphate was a hierarchical society with the male believer at the top of the pyramid and the unbeliever at the base. Women and slaves each had designated roles and were barred from performing certain functions. Equality was always an ideal within a single category, though it was not universally applicable *across* categories and not blind to status and religious distinctions. Jews, Christians, and the little-known Sabeans were designated as "Peoples of the Book," for being communities who were recipients of divine scriptures. They were given a limited autonomy, as "protected people" (*ahl al-dhimma*). Zoroastrians of Persia, and later Hindus of India, were also given the political protection offered to the "People of the Book" by caliphal and juristic authority. Non-Muslims were of course required to pay a specific tax, called *jizya*, in exchange for the protection offered them by the state.

The fortunes of non-Muslim communities fluctuated depending on the will of the monarchical caliphs and the power politics between the Muslim majority and the minority communities. Individual Jews and Christians reached high positions within the bureaucracy and royal courts, often as physicians and scholars. However, as minority communities, there was always a conscious attempt to ensure that they did not surpass Muslims in social status. It is not surprising to learn that from time to time certain legal restraints were placed on the public exhibition of non-Islamic symbols. Some, though not all, Muslim legal schools also favored the believing male above the female, the slave, and the non-Muslim in criminal law.

At times non-Muslims were required to be obviously distinct from Muslims in public and therefore were required to wear different forms of clothing. Freedom of conscience as currently understood did not apply. Non-Muslims could live in Muslim societies subject to certain conditions: they could not insult Islam or any of its symbols, such as the Prophet or the Qur'an, nor could they seek to convert Muslims. Apostasy from Islam to another religion was also forbidden. Each of these offenses was subject to the death penalty. Otherwise, non-Muslims could continue to advance their own institutions and even maintain their own ecclesiastical courts and places of worship.

Internal Division and Diversity

During the early days of Islam, particular theological schools would frequently issue creedal statements delineating formulas of belief and for the observation of religious duties. These creeds gained greater importance, especially in the light of sectarian divisions between rival political and theological ideologies. In addition to the divide between Sunni and Shi'a Islam resulting from early civil war, there were other sectarian cleavages. The Kharijites were rural tribesman who rebelled against what they perceived to be the machinations of urban elites and developed a puritan theology. The Mu'tazilite were rationalist theologians who adopted a good dose of Stoic philosophy in order to convert people to Islam; they also challenged more literalist and fideistic Muslim theologies, especially those espoused by the Hanbalis. Then there were also the rationalist-traditionalist Ash'ari theologians, who defended traditional beliefs by means of rational argument.

The seventh Abbasid caliph, al-Ma'mun (reigned 813–833), was so enamored of Mu'tazilite theology that he made it an official creed, setting in motion a mini inquisition, and thereby alienating the Hanbalis and Asha'aris. Thus a rationalist creed in the hands of political authority resulted in some of the most intolerant displays of religious coercion of the period. The twenty-fifth Abbasid caliph, al-Qadir Billah (reigned 991–1031), later endorsed a formulation that became known as the Qadiri creed. It tried to address the theological issues raised during the reign of al-Ma'mun. The Qadiri creed not only condemned the Mu'tazilite, but also targeted the beliefs of Shi'as and Ash'aris.

While religious diversity was tolerated within limits in medieval Islam, the extent of religious liberty was subject to the exigencies of imperial politics. Empire, says Fowden, "means control without serious competition of an area large enough to pass for 'the world,' the *orbis terranum* or *oikoumene*" (Fowden 1993, 6). The Muslim Empire was no exception, and was one of the most successful world empires of antiquity before it evolved into a more pluralistic and diverse commonwealth. Within that context theologies and religious practices remained largely in tune with the universal aspirations of the imperium.

Ebrahim Moosa

Further Reading

Fowden, G. (1993). *Empire to commonwealth: Consequences of monotheism in late antiquity.* Princeton, NJ: Princeton University Press.

Hodgson, M. G. S. (1977). *The venture of Islam* (3 vols). Chicago: University of Chicago Press.

Khaldun, I. (1967). *The Muqaddimah: An introduction to history* (F. Rosenthal, Trans., N. J. Dawood, Ed.). London: Routledge and Kegan Paul.

Israel

The issue of religious freedom in Israel is complex. Israel is in many ways a modern secular welfare state similar to those of Western Europe, providing a guarantee of basic rights to all religious groups. But at the same time a primary aspect of its identity is that it is the homeland of the Jewish people. Jews represent approximately 80 percent of the population, with Muslims representing approximately 16 percent and a small number of Christians and Druze (a monotheistic religion with its roots in Islam) each representing 2 percent. The interplay of secular and religious principles in a heterogeneous society creates many ambiguities.

At the basic level of religious freedom, Israel is generally considered to be respectful of the rights of the members of all religious groups to practice their own religion. To the extent that religion is a basis for determining certain legal statuses and benefits, however, it seems reasonable to consider those statuses and benefits as part of a discussion of religious freedom.

Religion-Based Differences in Treatment of Individuals

There are really two different ways in which religious differences seem to affect the treatment of individuals in Israel. The first are differences in treatment that arise between different groups of Jews. In Israel, religious authorities make many important decisions that affect a Jewish citizen's civil status. For example, they are authorized to determine whether a conversion to Judaism is legal—a determination that could affect whether an immigrant would be considered to be a Jew and automatically a citizen of Israel under the Right of Return. But in these cases, the only religious authorities allowed to make decisions are rabbis from Orthodox Judaism; rabbis from the more liberal Conservative or Reform movements do not have that power. In addition, this authority of the Orthodox rabbis allows the Orthodox movement to set certain rules for secular (nonreligious) Jews in Israel. This is especially important when one considers that less than 18 percent of the Jewish population is either Orthodox or ultra-Orthodox, while the remainder of Jews either consider themselves "traditional" (they practice many traditions but are not Orthodox) or "secular." In this situation, the state has delegated power to religious authorities who represent fewer than a fifth of the Jews in Israel.

A second way in which religion affects the position of the individual is with regard to some of the benefits provided by the Israeli state. It seems to be the case that many state-funded facilities in predominantly Muslim areas, including schools, are less well funded than similar facilities in Jewish areas.

Israel the Jewish State and Israel the Secular State

In talking about the different treatment of individuals in certain aspects of the operation of the Israeli state, it is important to note that the basis for those differences does not appear to be embedded in the basic principles of the Israeli state, but is policy that is open to change through political action. At the time of the founding of the Israeli state, there was sufficient lack of agreement on how to accommodate the idea of Israel as a Jewish state and as a modern secular state that a constitution was never adopted. Rather, a set of fundamental, or "basic," laws were adopted to establish principles for operation of the state. Governmental practices that affect the distribution of state benefits to members of different religious groups or concerning who makes religious decisions within the Jewish community are not embedded in basic principle, but can be changed by political action. For example, Israel's electoral system has encouraged the formation of many small parties and made it difficult for the major parties to form majorities in the Israeli Knesset (parliament). This has meant that governments of both the Left and the Right are frequently dependent on small religious parties to maintain their majorities. This has given the Orthodox a disproportionately strong voice and allowed them to maintain control of certain religious issues affecting most Jewish Israelis. It has also let them maintain certain benefits of particular importance to the ultra-Orthodox. But it also means that, to the extent that political conflict over these issues continues, they are not necessarily permanent features of Israel.

Juggling the potential contradictions of being both secular and a religious homeland, Israel presents a complex picture on the issue of religious freedom. While respectful of the basic rights of worship for all, the Israeli state does give the Orthodox clergy certain powers over all Jews in the country, regardless of their affiliations, as well as providing benefits unevenly to members of different religious groups.

Nathan H. Schwartz

See also Judaism

Further Reading

Arian, A. (1998). *The second republic: Politics in Israel.* Chatham, NJ: Chatham House Publishers.

Etzioni-Halevy, E. (2002).). *The divided people: Can Israel's breakup be stopped?* Lanham, MD: Lexington Books.

Garfinkle, A. (1997). *Politics and society in modern Israel: Myths and realities* (2nd ed.). Armonk, NY: M. E. Sharpe.

U.S. Department of State (2001, December). *Annual report on international religious freedom, 2001.* Washington, DC: U.S. Government Printing Office.

Jainism

Jains derive their name from the Sanskrit word *jaina*, meaning "victor," as Jain teachers advocated the conquest of bodily desires. Jainism was developed in India by the saint Parsva in the ninth century BCE. It arose as a reaction to the domination of the Brahman caste in Hinduism. Its antecedents lay in the tensions between established orthodoxy and newly emerging reformist sects that rose with the growth of towns, the increase in urban artisans, and the advent of trade and commerce. These changes led to a remarkable burst in religious and philosophical speculation. Wandering ascetics and sophists indulged in unorthodox thinking that ranged from determinism to materialism. Of those independent ascetic movements that were opposed to priestly groups, the most important were Buddhism and Jainism. Both were developed by the princely or warrior castes rather than the priestly (Brahman) caste. But whereas Buddhism made little long-term impact in India, Jainism has left an enduring legacy. The doctrine of vegetarianism and the creed of nonviolence in India is traceable to the Jains.

Mahavira

Although Parsva is considered the mythological founder of an earlier Jain community, historically, it was Mahavira (599–527 BCE) who first gave Jainism its religious and institutional form in the sixth century BCE. Jains believe Mahavira is the twenty-fourth Tirthankara (literally "path-maker," meaning one who has crossed to the shore of realization). The first Tirthankara is said to have lived millions of years ago, and Mahavira succeeded Parsva, who was the twenty-third Tirthankara.

Mahavira was born in Patna, Bihar, in eastern India. Like the Buddha, he was a prince. His name means "great man." According to legend, his mother dreamt that she would have a prophet son. After he was born, his parents, who were already devotees of the Jain faith, determined not to bring any evil into the world, and fasted themselves to death. (Voluntary self-starvation, known as *sallekhana*, is based on Jain rejection of the material world, and is considered a way to liberate the soul from the cycle of transmigration.) At the age of 30 (in 510 BCE), Mahavira, although married and with a family, renounced the world and set out to forge a life of asceticism. He left home and wandered India as a mendicant for thirteen years, seeking enlightenment. His asceticism was so harsh that he relinquished his clothes as reminders of worldly life. When enlightenment came Mahavira understood the place in the world of all living things, their provenance and their end, and he understood the gods, men, and demons. The condition of no living thing was left misunderstood. Mahavira gathered disciples and established an order of monks.

Jainism's Contributions to World Culture

Monks are today central to the existence of Jainism. There are two orders, both of which emphasize austerity, but one is stricter than the other. The Digambaras are "sky clad," or naked in the same way as Mahavira was. The Svetambaras are "white clad": They are allowed three pieces of white cloth as garments. Jain monks take five vows: nonviolent truthfulness, not to steal, rejection of materialism, and chastity. Jainism's three jewels are right faith, right knowledge, and right conduct. Over the centuries, the Jain religion has suffered a decline. Like Buddhism, its chief rival, Jainism is not a missionary religion and therefore has not been associated with the abuses of missionary activity. Jains are respectful of different religions and they discourage religious conversions as they regard all paths to God as being equal. There are only four million Jains left in India today. Yet the impact of Jainism has been disproportionately great in the outside world. This is remarkable for a faith that has disavowed the world.

Fundamental to Jain belief is the desire to preserve all life in the universe. Paradoxically, it is this belief that has led to two important creeds now popular in the secular world. First, there is the doctrine of *ahimsa,* or nonviolence. This is both a socioeconomic and political creed. All life is sacred. If cultivation of the land involves killing insects and pests, then agriculturalists could not be Jains. If craftsman imperil other living creatures, then they, too, should not be Jains. This has meant that Jainism could best be embraced by the trading community. The emphases on frugality in Jainism resonated with the notion of thrift in commercial activity, and trade and commerce became favorite Jain occupations. Jains became known for their financial transactions. Jainism flourished most under royal patronage during the early medieval period. Royal patrons sponsored the building of impressive Jain temples, remarkable array of literary and scholarly works were produced by Jain authors, and Jainism became synonymous with the spread of urban culture.

Politically, the creed of nonviolence manifested itself in India's nonviolent struggle for independence. If it was wrong to harm ants and insects, it was equally wrong to harm people, even people who oppressed others. Mohandas Gandhi used the principle of nonviolence so successfully in his struggle for Indian independence from the British Empire that Nelson Mandela adopted it later in the struggle against apartheid in South Africa.

The second way in which Jain belief in the sacredness of all life has had a major impact on the secular world is in the practice of vegetarianism. Vegetarianism in India spread from the Jains. Indeed, it was the strictness of the Jains regarding preserving life that dictated their practice of nudity: Clothes were forbidden because the folds of clothing might hide insects, which the wearer might then accidentally crush. Acting on the same principle, "the most observant Jains will sweep the ground with a brush—traditionally of peacock feathers—before walking to clear any insect from their path" (Farrington 2000, 86).

Jain Theology

However, the most interesting question in Jainism is that of theology. Theology as practiced in the ancient religions of the East differs from the practice of theology in the Judeo-Christian traditions familiar to the West. Jain teaching was based on the oral tradition and was first recorded in the third century BCE. The final version was not edited until the fifth century CE. The Jain scriptures, called the eleven *Anga*s ("limbs"), record that everything, whether animate or inanimate, has a soul. The purpose of life is to purify the soul. Only the pure soul is released from the body and finds a home in bliss. The soul is burdened by past deeds (karma), and the way to purify the soul—applicable to both men and women—is to live with the Jains as a monk and to take the vow of nonviolence. As in Buddhism, in Jainism the question of a supreme deity was irrelevant, since the focus was on the purification of each soul. According to Acarya Vijay Anandsuri (1837–1896), known as Atmaramji, who was the most important Jain mendicant of the early nineteenth century, Jains do believe in God, but it is God with a difference. For Jains, God is the sum total of all the *jaina*s whose souls have attained enlightenment and liberation. God sits at the top of the universe in the four infinitudes of infinite knowledge, infinite perception, infinite bliss, and infinite power.

In his *Ideals of Jain Tenets*, written in 1884, Atmaramji explained the Jain belief that God did not create the universe, because the universe is eternal. It does not have a beginning. This is consistent with orthodox Indian religious thought, which teaches that God and the universe are separately eternal and uncreated. On the one hand, God is the composite form of all liberated souls, whoever they are and wherever they come from. All beings should be respected equally, hence the strictures of nonviolence. On the other hand, the universe has an awe and a splendor entirely of its own and separate from God. The environment must be respected just as much as the life that lives in it.

Jainism and Religious Freedom

The high point of Jain culture was in the early medieval period when Jains were prominent in the arts, culture, and commerce. In the later medieval period, they were threatened in both northern and southern India when Islamic invasions spread in the north and the Hindu state of Vijayanagar began to dominate in the south. Jainism then lost its royal patronage. The opening of maritime commerce on the west coast of India enabled many Jains to become moneylenders there while others voyaged across the seas to trade and sell their merchandise. Today, there are small flourishing Jain communities in the United States, Canada, and the United Kingdom. Jains demonstrate an exemplary record of a peaceful community that has survived over two millennia without asserting or imposing itself.

Satvinder Singh Juss

See also Hinduism

Further Reading

Farrington, K. (2000). *History of religion* (3rd ed.). London: Chancellor Press, Octopus Publishing Group Ltd.

Larson G. D., & Bhattacharya, R. S. (1987). *Encyclopedia of Indian philosophies.* Princeton, NJ: Princeton University Press.

Lopez, D. S. (1995). *Religions of India in practice.* Princeton, NJ: Princeton University Press.

Keay, J. (2000). *India: A history.* London: HarperCollins Publishers.

Thapar, R. (1966). *A history of India.* Middlesex, UK: Penguin.

Japan

Out of the dormancy of nearly three centuries of self-imposed isolation Japan was thrust into the world community by Commodore Matthew Perry's fleet in 1853. This sudden jolt out of a "peaceful" self-sufficiency precipitated a violent civil war in Japan, bringing the Tokugawa shogunate to its demise and ultimately ending seven hundred years of samurai rule. Government was returned to the emperor and a modern constitutional monarchy was launched in 1868. The government of the Meiji Restoration,

however, did not easily espouse religious freedom. In fact the persecution and in some instances the execution of Christians still continued under the new government.

Though it was the United States and the European powers that forced Japan to open its doors, what had driven it into the prolonged hibernation from the outside world in the sixteenth century was European encroachment that came in the form of Jesuit missionaries. The arrival of Francis Xavier in 1549 ushered in energetic missionary activities, astonishingly converting over three quarters of a million Japanese in a few short decades. This, aided by the knowledge of European colonization of some Southeast Asian nations, was perceived as the threat to the very autonomy of Japan as a nation. European missionaries were expelled, and Japanese clerics and laymen were ordered to abandon their faith on threat of death. The Christian faith went underground and remained in hiding for nearly two and a half centuries, and an untold number of the faithful met a tragic end in persecutions from the late 1500s right up to the mid-1800s. What persuaded the Meiji government to finally abolish the "official" religious persecution and incorporate religious freedom in the new constitution issued in 1889 was external pressure from the countries that had just opened embassies in Japan.

Religious Freedom under the Meiji Constitution

The Meiji Constitution, which was modeled after the German constitution of the time, recognized religious freedom, but with some serious qualifications and only as a privilege granted by the emperor, not a right inherent to the people. Article 28 reads: "Japanese subjects shall, within the limits not prejudicial to peace and order, and not antagonistic to their duties as subjects, enjoy freedom of religious belief." This "qualified" freedom of religion of the Meiji Constitution, which at the same time declares the emperor to be "sacred and inviolable" (Article 3), is a tenuous one at best (*Kodansha Encyclopedia of Japan* 1982, 8).

Japan's newfound membership in the world of nations was seriously handicapped. Many of the early treaties between it and the United States and European nations were flawed and unequal. To seek equality in status the Meiji government adopted a policy aimed at creating a "rich country" with a "strong military" (Fairbank et al. 1978, 153). To

217

provide this policy with ideological backbone the government gave Shinto a special status—not the sectarian Shinto that operates in the personal dimensions of piety, health, and spiritual well-being, but the shrine Shinto whose sphere lies in the public domain of national rites with the emperor at the head of both national lineage and the state. The sectarian Shinto may be "religion," but shrine and state Shinto is not, as the government of the time wished to interpret. It is more than a mere religion; it is the national cult. Thus the establishment of state Shinto is seen not to conflict with the constitutional stipulation of religious freedom. Traditional religions such as Buddhism and newly legalized Christianity as well as the so-called "new religions" such as Tenri-kyo and Konko-kyo enjoy freedom so long as they conform to the national rites.

This is obviously a serious qualifier to the freedom of religion. Even Buddhism, with its long history since introduction from Korea in the sixth century, and which thus had become thoroughly indigenized, had to suffer the same treatment. While Shinto broadly defined had long been the native faith of the Japanese, the majority of the people were professed Buddhists and those who professed to be Shintoists were very few at the time. Indeed, the imperial household had been the ardent sponsor of Buddhism since Prince Shotoku (574–622 CE). Nonetheless, the Meiji government drove Buddhism out of the imperial court in order to make the emperor the exclusively Shinto head of the state. Bringing the divine status of the emperor to the fore was only a short step beyond this development.

Honoring War Dead in a Shinto Shrine

Through wars with Russia and China in the early twentieth century Japan made steady progress along its stated policy of "creating a "rich nation" and a "strong military" (Fairbank et al. 1978, 153). Honoring the war dead for the glory of the nation became the principal means to unite the nation; nationalism and patriotism were heightened to an extreme level. The emperor-centered state Shinto was utilized by the increasingly militaristic government to reinforce its expansionist drive, which ultimately brought Japan into face-to-face confrontation with the United States and its allies in World War II in 1941. Japan's defeat in the war, the subsequent occupation by the allied forces, and the new U.S.-drafted constitution of the postwar government became the

first real turning point in the matter of religious freedom, or so it seemed. The postwar Peace Constitution declared not only the renunciation of military force as the means to promote the national interest, but also demoted the emperor from divine to human status. Shrine Shinto was returned to the ranks of religions. Article 20 of the postwar Peace Constitution states the following: "Freedom of religion is guaranteed to all. No religious organization shall receive privilege from the State, nor exercise any political authority. No person shall be compelled to take part in any religious act, celebration, rite or practice" (*Kodansha Encyclopedia of Japan* 1982, 10). In fact there was no more religious persecution in Japan, at least not by the government. If anything, traditional religions rather suffered public indifference except for Christianity briefly after the war. It was the "new religions" that attracted the faddish interest of the masses in the spiritual vacuum of the postwar era. Religious freedom now yielded to what some called "the free market religious economy of Japan" (Mullins 1998, 22). Yet, a controversy persists as to whether shrine Shinto is not a religion but a national cult, thus deserving official recognition.

Quite apart from the significance and merit of World War II, those who perished in the war were, if not heroes, then sacrifices made to the nation. To their families proper remembrance is only right, if not their glorification. The principal place where some of those who died in the successive wars—Sino-Japanese War (1894–1895); Russo-Japanese War (1904–1905); Second Sino-Japanese War (1937–1945); and World War II (1941–1945)—are enshrined is Yasukuni Shrine in Tokyo, which is unmistakably a Shinto institution. Though it maintained quite a low profile after World War II, some of the leading politicians including prime ministers started paying "official obeisance visits" to it, in part reflecting the grassroots sentiment of the people, many of whom did lose their loved ones in the wars, and in part due to gradual resurgence of nationalistic pressure among conservative political forces. This obviously invited vehement protests from religious groups including Christians, Buddhists, and many new religions. Protesters insist that this symbolic action by governmental officials can be viewed as both serious and ominous: serious because it is tantamount to the government's surreptitious endorsement of shrine Shinto, and thus unconstitutional; ominous because it raises the specter of a renewed militaristic spirit. To those who support the practice of "official obeisance visits," they are simply the equivalent of the laying of a wreath at the tomb of the unknown soldier in other countries, not the outright endorsement of Shinto as religion, nor a reversion to militarism. In recent years, the conservative forces of the Liberal Democratic Party have increasingly favored the practice, making well-publicized and ever more daring "official obeisance visits," even during times of coalition government.

Hiroshi Obayashi

See also Buddhism; Shintoism

Further Reading

Boyle, K., & Sheen, J. (1995). *Freedom of religion and belief.* London and New York: Routledge.

Fairbank, J. K., Reischauer, E. O., & Craig, A. M. (1978). *East Asia: Tradition and transformation.* Boston: Houghton Mifflin.

Fujita, N. S. (1991). *Japan's encounter with Christianity: The Catholic mission in pre-modern Japan.* New York: Paulist Press.

Hardacre, H. (1989). *Shinto and the state, 1868–1988.* Princeton, NJ: Princeton University Press.

Kodansha encyclopedia of Japan (Vol. 2). (1982). Tokyo: Kodansha International.

Mullins, M. (1998). *Christianity made in Japan.* Honolulu: University of Hawaii Press.

Mullins, M., & Young, R. F. (Eds.). (1995). *Perspectives on Christianity in Korea and Japan.* Lewiston, NY: E. Mellen Press.

Murakami, S. (1980). *Japanese religion in the modern century.* Tokyo: Tokyo University Press.

O'Brien, D. M. (1996). *To dream of dreams: Religious freedom and constitutional politics in post war Japan.* Honolulu: University of Hawaii Press.

Jehovah's Witnesses: Global

Jehovah's Witnesses are a Christian group known internationally for their door-to-door ministry. The group, originally known as Bible Students, started as a small Bible study circle in 1870 in Allegheny, Pennsylvania, and has developed into a community of more than 6.1 million active members in 235 lands, with a peak of 15.3 million attending religious services. The Witnesses print and distribute Bibles and Bible literature in more than 300 languages.

Two main characteristics of the Witnesses, their energetic public ministry and strict adherence to their understanding of Bible principles, have been at the center of tensions between the Witnesses and the state, as well as tensions with society in general. The Witnesses' position toward military and political activity and their insistence on their right to communicate their faith publicly have led to numerous legal and social controversies over the definition of freedom of speech, press, assembly, and worship. To a lesser extent, Witnesses have also been involved in litigation involving family and patients' rights.

Establishment and Early Development

Charles Taze Russell (1852–1916) was the founding editor of *Zion's Watch Tower* (now *The Watchtower*), the Witnesses' principal journal. Among those whose writings Russell explored were several Adventist ministers and a former Baptist minister who was a staunch abolitionist and a peace advocate. Although Russell freely acknowledged the positive influence of his association with thinkers of various denominations, the views contained in *Zion's Watch Tower* emerged as the distinctive doctrine and eschatology that to a great extent characterize the body of beliefs presently held by Jehovah's Witnesses.

The Bible Students sought a restoration of original Christian practice and belief, and they held for the inerrancy of the Bible as the inspired word of God. The "great apostasy of Christendom" was a frequent theme of the *Watch Tower.* Russell's early writings were highly critical of large church systems, which, in his view, had abandoned fidelity to the Bible and followed manmade creeds. Bible Student literature denounced doctrines, such as the Trinity, hellfire, and the inherent immortality of the human soul, as nonbiblical, God-dishonoring instruments of social control that instilled morbid fear in worshipers and distanced them from God. Russell also criticized mainstream churches, particularly Catholicism, for their hierarchical divisions and for meddling in politics and war. In 1931 the Bible Students adopted the name Jehovah's Witnesses to more accurately describe their role as evangelizers and to highlight the name of Jehovah.

Caesar's Things and God's

The Witnesses see themselves as subjects of and advocates for the kingdom of God, which they define as a

MAJOR COURT DECISIONS INVOLVING JEHOVAH'S WITNESSES

- Austria: *Hoffmann v. Austria* (1993): European Court of Human Rights (ECHR) ruled that Austria had violated the rights of Ingrid Hoffmann by denying her custody of her two children on the grounds that she was one of Jehovah's Witnesses.
- Bulgaria: *Christian Association Jehovah's Witnesses v. Bulgaria* (1998): The Witnesses took the case to the ECHR after the Bulgarian Supreme Court denied them legal recognition because, among other things, they do not teach the Trinity doctrine. Meetings were disrupted and Witnesses were arrested as a result of the decision. The European Commission of Human Rights recommended a friendly settlement, which gave Jehovah's Witnesses legal recognition. *Stefanov v. Bulgaria* (2001): The ECHR arranged a friendly settlement in which Bulgarian law allows conscientious objectors to perform alternative civilian service.
- Canada: *Saumur v. Quebec (City of)* (1953): Supreme Court of Canada declared unconstitutional a law enacted by the City of Quebec that prohibited Jehovah's Witnesses from distributing religious literature. *Boucher v. The King,* (1951): Supreme Court of Canada ruled that Aimé Boucher should be acquitted of charges of sedition for circulating a pamphlet protesting the mobbing of Witnesses in Catholic Quebec.
- France: *Christian Federation of Jehovah's Witnesses v. France* (application filed with ECHR): The Witnesses are contesting a 60-percent tax on religious offerings, retroactive four years.
- Germany: *Religious Association of Jehovah's Witnesses in Germany v. Berlin Senate* (2000): The Federal Constitutional Court in Karlsruhe ruled that granting religious associations the rights of corporation under public law must not be dependent on the associations' special loyalty to the State. The case was remanded to the Federal Administrative Court to consider whether the religious beliefs and practices of the Witnesses encroach on individual rights regarding membership, childrearing, and medical treatment.
- Greece: *Kokkinakis v. Greece* (1993): ECHR ordered Greece to pay damages and court costs to 84-year-old Minos Kokkinakis, who was arrested more than 60 times for speaking to others about his beliefs as one of Jehovah's Witnesses and for conscientious objection to military service. The court affirmed that Jehovah's Witnesses are a "known religion." *Manoussakis and Others v. Greece* (1996): ECHR overturned the conviction of Titos Manoussakis, who had been sentenced to prison for operating an unauthorized place of worship, even though he had applied for official permission. *Tsirlis and Kouloumpas v. Greece* (1997) and *Georgiadis v. Greece* (1997): ECHR upheld the right of Jehovah's Witnesses to ministerial exemption from military service.
- India: *Bijoe Emmanuel v. State of Kerala* (1986): The Supreme Court of India ruled as unconstitutional the expulsion of Jehovah's Witnesses from school for their conscientious refusal to participate in patriotic ceremonies.
- Japan: *Kobayashi v. Matsumoto* (1996): The Supreme Court of Japan held that the constitutional guarantee of freedom of religion was violated when a Witness student was expelled from school for refusing, on account of conscience, to participate in compulsory martial arts training. *Takeda v. The State* (2000): The Supreme Court of Japan ruled that doctors violated the rights of a patient by administering a blood transfusion without her knowledge or consent.
- Philippines: *May Amolo v. Division Superintendent of Schools of Cebu* (1993): Philippine Supreme Court recognized right of Witness students not to participate in mandatory flag salute.

THE JEHOVAH'S WITNESSES WIN MOSCOW COURT CASE

On 23 February 2001 the Golovinsky Intermunicipal District Court of Moscow issued an important ruling which prevented the government from banning Jehovah's Witnesses groups in Moscow. The court ruling was seen as a crucial test of the 1997 law on religious freedom. The court ruled as follows:

Taking into consideration what has been outlined, the court came to the conclusion that there is no basis for the liquidation and banning of the activity of the religious community of Jehovah's Witnesses in Moscow, since it has not been established that this community in Moscow violates the Constitution of the Russian Federation or laws of the Russian Federation, incites religious discord, coerces to destroy the family, infringes on the individual, the rights, and the freedoms of citizens, inclines [others] to commit suicide or to refuse medical care for individuals who are in a life- or health-threatening condition for religious reasons.

In resolving the question of covering the expenses for the conducted composite expert study, the experts' certificates to cover each of their costs amounting to 19,377.50 rubles, should be accepted. But, considering that four of the experts, without agreement or request to the court, independently raised an additional question for themselves, the court considers it possible to exact the expenses amounting to 16,000 rubles for each expert.

On the basis of the aforementioned, the court, guided by Articles 191 and 197 of the Civil Procedural Code of the Russian Soviet Federated Socialist Republic,

RULED

To deny the application of the Prosecutor of the Northern Administrative District of Moscow to liquidate the Religious Community of Jehovah's Witnesses in the city of Moscow and ban its activity.

To obligate the prosecutor of the Northern Administrative District of Moscow to pay experts Dmitry Alekseyevich Leontyev, Sergei Igorevich Ivanenko, Valeri Pavlovich Belyanin, Marina Mikhailovna Gromyko, and Sergei Andreyevich Nebolsin for the expenses amounting to 16,000 rubles each.

Source: Jehovah's Witnesses in Russia.
Retrieved October 18, 2002, from http:// www.jw-russia.org

real government administered from heaven. Their position in relation to secular governments is analogous to that of an emissary, who may dwell in a foreign land and obey its laws but who avoids involvement in its internal political affairs and maintains primary loyalty to his own government. Citing the paradigm of the early Christians, who abstained from political and military involvement, the Witnesses assume a position of "political neutrality" (cf. John 17:16). They abstain from political activity and military service. Conversely, in line with the directive to "Render therefore unto Caesar the things which are Caesar's"(Matthew 22:21, KJV), the Witnesses believe in scrupulous compliance with government regulations regarding taxation and other civic responsibilities. Based on their reading of Romans 13 and the position of first-century Christians, the Witnesses believe they should obey "Caesar" unless the secular authority orders them to violate divine law. They define this position as "relative subjection."

The principles of relative subjection and political neutrality lie at the heart of the most serious challenges to the Witnesses' freedom of worship. In the decades preceding World War I, the international growth of the Bible Students coincided with the rise of nationalistic movements and the specter of armed conflict in Europe. Increasing demands for overt expressions of loyalty to the nation-state ran counter to the international and fraternal ideals of the Bible Students. Early issues of *Zion's Watch Tower* asserted that according to divine law, even if a Christian were to be drafted, he would not shoot to kill on the battlefield. During World War I, the level of participation among Bible Students generally ranged from noncombatant duty to total conscientious objection.

After Russell's death in 1916, his successor, Joseph F. Rutherford (1869–1942), continued and intensified the critical stance of the Bible Students toward nominal Christian religions. The Bible Students denounced the churches of Christendom as bloodguilty for their part in fomenting and sanctioning World War I. Catholic and Protestant clergy had long regarded the Bible Students as heretical, and intense wartime patriotism during World War I afforded a convenient justification to suppress the Bible Students under the pretense of national security. The widely circulated book *The Finished Mystery* (1917), a posthumous compilation of the writings of C. T. Russell, contained biting criticism, particularly regarding clergy involvement in war. A number of clerics in the United States accused the Bible Students of spreading enemy propaganda and called publicly for the arrest of officers of the Watch Tower Society. Citing *The Finished Mystery*, among other publications, in the spring of 1918 a federal district court convicted Rutherford and seven other directors of the Watch Tower Society under the Espionage Act. Rutherford and six of the seven others were sentenced to four concurrent twenty-year terms and sent to federal prison in Atlanta, Georgia. In the months that followed, Bible Students in the United States and Europe faced mob violence, often instigated by local clergy. Consequently, the organized public preaching activity of the Bible Students came to a virtual standstill. In 1919 an appellate court reversed the convictions of the eight directors, noting the prejudicial character of the trial.

According to the Bible Students' reading of prophetic chronology, the present system had entered into a period called "the last days," during which Christians could expect persecution. In the interwar period, the Bible Students solidified their desire to distance themselves from mainstream Christian denominations and their concept of political neutrality became clearer. The adoption of the name Jehovah's Witnesses crystallized the core identity of the community as it pursued vocal advocacy of God's kingdom with renewed intensity.

The Nazi Era and World War II

By 1933 nearly 59,000 Witnesses were distributing their literature in seventy-eight countries. The disillusioned postwar populace in Germany proved especially receptive, with Witness membership there almost equal to that in the United States. The unabated tension between the Witnesses and dominant churches is evidenced by over 4,000 legal proceedings in 1931 and 1932 involving German Witnesses and their public ministry.

When Adolf Hitler and the National Socialists gained power in 1933, the government almost immediately targeted the Witnesses. The Witnesses were quick to assume that the clergy were behind the charge that Jehovah's Witnesses received financial backing from Jews and Bolsheviks. But the hostility of the Nazi regime itself soon became clear, and the Witnesses found themselves embroiled in a deadly ideological conflict. The Witnesses' doctrine of political neutrality and their supranational worldview placed them squarely in opposition to Nazi ideology. Yet their neutrality also meant that the Witnesses posed no revolutionary threat.

The regime banned meetings, literature, and even membership in the religion. The Witnesses in Germany and around the world responded by denouncing Nazi atrocities as devilish and barbaric. Moreover, Witnesses in Germany continued printing and distributing literature underground and publicized a purported Nazi-Vatican conspiracy. The Nazi regime incarcerated approximately 10,000 Witnesses throughout occupied countries. Some spent years in captivity. About 2,000 Witnesses, male and female, died as a result of torture, privation, and slave labor. The vast majority of Witnesses refused to sign a document renouncing their beliefs and pledging allegiance to the Führer, which would have won them immediate release. The Nazis executed more than 250 Witnesses for their refusal to perform military service. The number of Witness conscientious objectors executed by the regime constitutes the largest number condemned for this reason of any victim group during the Nazi era.

Rather than earning sympathy, Witnesses in Allied lands were attacked as Fascists and Fifth Columnists, agents of Nazism. Again, their refusal to perform military service became a central issue in the banning of the Witnesses or their literature in sixty lands, including the British Empire. Draft boards in the United

States and elsewhere refused to grant Witnesses exemption based on ministerial status. The Witnesses' unwillingness to venerate national symbols also provoked severe popular reactions, including incidents of mob violence. In the United States, Witness children were expelled from school for refusing to salute the flag. Because they would not participate in the political process, the Witnesses chose to protect themselves by vigorously defending their practices in the courts and, according to Anson Phelps Stokes, became "the most frequent litigants among American religious groups in modern times" (Stokes 1950, 542). Between 1935 and 1945, the Witnesses won 32 out of 50 cases in the U.S. Supreme Court, involving compulsory flag salute, selective service, right of assembly, and their public ministry. The court issued several landmark rulings that defined and clarified First and Fourteenth Amendment rights under the U.S. Constitution. Legal scholars point to these cases as the primary catalyst for the strengthening of constitutional protections of religious liberty, as well as freedom of speech, assembly, and press in the United States and subsequently in other countries modeled after American-style democracy. Between 1946 and 1960, the Witnesses argued twelve cases involving military service before the U.S. Supreme Court, half of which were decided in their favor.

The Soviet Era

Especially during the early post–World War II period, Communist-bloc nations targeted Witnesses with varying degrees of severity. About 5,000 Witnesses were imprisoned by the Communist German Democratic Republic during the forty-year ban on their religion, some serving sentences of fifteen years or more. Witness prisoners in Nazi camps had spread their faith among Soviet prisoners and slave laborers, hundreds of whom then returned to the Soviet Union and continued as active Witnesses. The Soviet annexation of territory brought additional Witnesses within Soviet borders. Predictably, the Witness belief in Christian neutrality and their teaching people about a coming kingdom prompted official displeasure. In 1951, some 7,000 Witnesses were deported to labor camps in Siberia. The Soviet government produced propaganda films and pamphlets "unmasking" the Witnesses as CIA spies and agents of American capitalism.

Current Issues

With the breakup of the Soviet Union, the Witnesses initially enjoyed greater freedom of worship in many of the former Communist-bloc countries. More recently, dominant churches in Eastern Europe and Central Asia have attempted to reassert their authority and to use state mechanisms to limit the encroachment of religious minorities on the church's traditional territory. The Witnesses have faced a continuing struggle to achieve or retain legal registration in those lands. With the conclusion of colonial rule and the rise of nationalistic movements in African lands, such as Malawi and Mozambique, the apolitical Witnesses have experienced bans and violent persecution. As the position of conscientious objection has gained recognition in Western Europe, the number of Witnesses imprisoned for refusal to participate in the military has decreased. In July 2000 Taiwan enacted legislation providing for a civilian alternative to military service. In South Korea, where no such provision is made, more than 7,000 Witnesses have been imprisoned.

Since the 1950s numerous cases involving Witnesses have centered on informed consent in medical situations and the patient's right of bodily self-determination. Witnesses readily seek and accept medical treatment; however, in line with a biblical injunction to abstain from blood, Witnesses refuse the transfusion of blood or its major components. Recent advances in nonblood management and surgical techniques have greatly enhanced treatment options. The right of bodily integrity is now well established in the United States but has yet to be secured in many other lands. Witnesses have also been involved in child custody disputes that challenge their parental rights in connection with religious training and child rearing.

The 1990s saw a rise in Western Europe of an active anticult movement, prompting quasi-official inquests and calls for legislation limiting the activities of religious minorities, including Jehovah's Witnesses. The Witnesses continue to use the court systems of various lands to secure the freedom of thought, conscience, and religion.

Jolene Chu

See also Jehovah's Witnesses: United States

Further Reading

Beckford, J. A. (1975). *The trumpet of prophecy: A sociological study of Jehovah's Witnesses*. New York: John Wiley & Sons.

Berger, T. R. (1981). *Fragile freedoms: Human rights and dissent in Canada*. Toronto, Canada: Clark, Irwin & Company Limited.

Besier, G., & Scheuch, E. K. (Eds.). (1999). *Die neuen Inquisitoren: Religionsfreiheit und Glaubensneid* [The new inquisitors: Religious freedom and religious envy]. Zurich, Switzerland: Edition Interfrom.

Canonici, G. (1998). *Les Témoins de Jéhovah face à Hitler* [Jehovah's witnesses in the face of Hitler]. Paris: Éditions Albin Michel.

Chryssides, G. D. (1999). *Exploring new religions*. London: Cassell.

Cole, M. (1955). *Jehovah's Witnesses*. New York: Vantage Press.

Garbe, D. (1994). *Zwischen Widerstand und Martyrium: Die Zeugen Jehovas im "Dritten Reich"* [Between resistance and martyrdom: Jehovah's witnesses in the "Third Reich"]. Munich, Germany: Oldenbourg Verlag.

Helmreich, E. C. (1979). *The German churches under Hitler*. Detroit, MI: Wayne State University Press.

Hesse, H. (Ed.). (2001). *Persecution and resistance of Jehovah's Witnesses during the Nazi-regime, 1933–1945*. Bremen, Germany: Edition Temmen.

Irons, P. (1988). *The courage of their convictions*. New York: The Free Press.

Kaplan, W. (1989). *State and salvation: The Jehovah's Witnesses and their fight for civil rights*. Toronto, Canada: University of Toronto Press.

Kephart, W. M., & Zellner, W. (1998). *Extraordinary groups: An examination of unconventional lifestyles*. New York: St. Martin's Press.

Liebster, S. A. (2000). *Facing the lion: Memoirs of a young girl in Nazi Europe*. New Orleans, LA: Grammaton Press.

Macmillan, A. H. (1957). *Faith on the march*. Englewood Cliffs, NJ: Prentice Hall.

Peoples Pulpit Association. (1917). The finished mystery. *Studies in Scriptures, Vol. VII*. Brooklyn, NY: International Bible Students Association.

Peters, S. F. (2000). *Judging Jehovah's Witnesses: Religious persecution and the dawn of the rights revolution*. Kansas City, KS: University of Kansas Press.

Pfeffer, L. (1953). *Church, state, and freedom*. Boston: The Beacon Press.

Stark, R., & Iannaccone, L. R. (1997). Why the Jehovah's Witnesses grow so rapidly: A theoretical application. *Journal of Contemporary Religion, 12*, 133–157.

Stokes, A. P. (1950). *Church and state in the United States, Vol. 3*. New York: Harper & Brothers.

Watchtower Bible and Tract Society of New York, Inc. (1993). *Jehovah's Witnesses: proclaimers of God's kingdom*. Brooklyn, NY: Watchtower Bible and Tract Society of New York, Inc.

Wilson, B. (1977). Aspects of kinship and the rise of Jehovah's Witnesses in Japan. *Social Compass, 26*, 97–120.

Jehovah's Witnesses: United States

Few religious or secular groups have done more to bolster legal protections for civil liberties than the Jehovah's Witnesses. By litigating hundreds of cases from the 1930s to the present day, the Witnesses have prompted courts at all levels, including the U.S. Supreme Court, to establish or reinforce judicial safeguards shielding a number of core freedoms, including religious liberty. The Witnesses' contributions in this realm have aided all Americans, not merely members of their faith.

Beliefs and Practices

Founded in the 1870s by a former Seventh-day Adventist named Charles Taze Russell, the Jehovah's Witnesses are ardent millenarians; that is, they believe that the temporal world will soon end with a climactic battle between Jehovah God and Satan at Armageddon. After the forces of evil are vanquished in this clash, the Witnesses claim, a kingdom of heaven will exist on Earth for most of those who have remained true to the teachings of the Scriptures. A select group of others will be still more fortunate: they will ascend into heaven and sit at the right hand of God.

Among the Witnesses' more controversial beliefs is their conviction that saluting the American flag amounts to idolatry. Since at least the mid-1930s, members of the faith have refrained from participating in flag-salute exercises because they feel that such ceremonies clearly violate scriptural prohibitions on worshipping any "graven image." As one prominent member of the faith once said, Witnesses believe that saluting the flag is abhorrent because it involves "deification of the flag" (Peters 2000, 34–35).

The Jehovah's Witnesses have come to regard religious proselytizing, not participation in traditional

A GUIDE FOR DEALING WITH WITNESS VISITS

Perhaps the greatest complaint many people have against Jehovah's Witnesses is their door-to-door efforts to convert people of other faiths. While court cases in the United States and other nations have protected this right, the Web is filled with advice from various people and faiths about how to deter these visits or how to cut them short. The following is the introduction from instructions meant for Muslims in Western nations.

A MUSLIM GUIDE TO COUNTERING JEHOVAH'S WITNESSES
The greatest menace to Muslim homes in the West

by Malik Ali

As a Muslim who lives in a Western country, I have come to realise that the greatest harassment comes from a Christian sect that numbers a mere 6–7 million; the Jehovah's Witnesses. The Muslims come across them so often for the very factor that they come knocking on their doors. The group was born in the U.S.A. (Like almost every other cult you might come across) and every weekend they come armed with their contrived New World Translation Bible and their Awake, Watchtower magazines; they'll come pounding on your doors. Yes, the lady and the gentleman who come dressed in business suits. No their [*sic*] not trying to sell you products, but "simply" to destroy your Iman in exchange for their humorous "The world is coming to an end" cult.

Many Muslims are aware of their failed past prophecies; but it's usually your word against theirs. The purpose of this page is to expose these cultist using their own tools. The following are scanned Photostats of the past magazines of Awake and the Watchtower. Articles that these cultists dread if any one was to come across; yet over the past decades they have been handing them out door to door, country to country. The Jehovah's Witnesses view the Islamic faith as satanic, they have written anti-Islamic materials and even travel to Muslim countries to try and witness (their euphemism for convert) to our brethren. Muslims have to understand that Christianity is not a monolithic rock, it comprises of innumerable sects that differ on almost every theological aspect of the Christian faith, and to defend yourselves against it you have to understand the nature of these offspring's [*sic*]. It is pointless arguing with a Jehovah's Witness that the Bible says this and says that. Trying to bring up contradictions, the humanity of Jesus (incidentally, they don't believe Jesus is God, but still acknowledge his divine sonship), etc. Their faith seems to belong in a man made organisation, the Watchtower in New York. They'll vehemently deny this; but ask them where all their magazines, Bibles, commentries [*sic*], religious books and guides are printed. Their [*sic*] are many former Jehovah's Witnesses that have entered the fold of Islam (ironically, it starts from them having visited a Muslim home in order to witness). Although many are trained not to listen, you as a believer can only do your best, and leave the rest to Allah (swt). This page is meant mainly as a defense for Muslims, and not necessarily Dawah to them.

I recommend for Muslims who regularly come into contact with Jehovah's Witnesses, to print out the scanned Photostat articles following from the links below. Trust me, once you've shown them this. They'll give you a pathetic defense and stand their [*sic*] pretending their [*sic*] shocked, and most of them will never come to your houses again. It's difficult for someone to swallow their own past failures that now go against their dogma.

Source: *Jehovah's Witnesses—The Cultic Annoyance to Muslim Homes*
Retrieved June 24, 2002, from: http://www.jamaat.net

Minersville, Pa.
Nov. 5, 1935

Our School Directors
Dear Sirs

I do not salute the flag because I have promised to do the will of God. That means that I must not worship anything out of harmony with God's law. In the twentieth chapter of Exodus it is stated, "Thou shalt not make unto thee any graven image, nor bow down to them nor serve them for I the Lord thy God am a jealous God visiting the iniquity of the fathers upon the children unto the third and fourth generation of them that hate me. I am a true follower of Christ. I do not salute the flag because I do not love my country but I love my country and I love God more and I must obey His commandments.

Your Pupil,
Billy Gobitas

Copy of the letter written by Billy Gobitas to the Minersville, Pennsylvania, school directors, explaining why as a Jehovah's Witness, he had to refuse to salute the American flag.

Sunday-morning church services, as the highest form of worship of their Creator. The Witnesses eagerly spread their faith by publicly distributing tracts, books, and magazines. In the 1930s and 1940s, the Witnesses' fervor as propagandists was well known. They did not canvass small towns so much as they simply overwhelmed them, sometimes descending with as many as 1,000 zealous proselytizers at a time. These canvassers went from door to door and preached in public areas such as town squares.

Campaign in the Courts

The Jehovah's Witnesses' campaign in the courts had its roots in perhaps the worst outbreak of religious persecution seen in the United States in the twentieth century. For several grim years in the early and mid-1940s, vigilantes in nearly every state of the union brutalized members of their faith as they worshiped in public. Targeted largely because they refused to salute the American flag, Witnesses throughout the United States were pummeled in everything from riots involving hundreds of people to scuffles among a handful of men. Witnesses were so widely and viciously abused during the World War II era that the American Civil Liberties Union, among other observers, compared their plight to the persecution of religious minorities in Nazi Germany.

The U.S. Supreme Court's controversial ruling in *Minersville School District v. Gobitis* (a printer's error resulted in the Gobitas name being misspelled in constitutional state law) (1940) helped to ignite some of the worst anti-Witness violence of the period. In an opinion written by Justice Felix Frankfurter, the court denied a claim that the enforcement of a public school district's compulsory flag-salute regulation violated the Witnesses' religious liberty. The perceived anti-Witness tenor of Frankfurter's opinion and the nation's wartime jitters proved to be an incendiary combination for the Witnesses. In the months immediately after the *Gobitis* ruling was handed down, civil liberties groups in all but four states reported anti-Witness rioting.

To make matters even worse for the Jehovah's Witnesses, their persecution was not limited to physical punishment meted out in vigilante attacks. Authorities in dozens of states and communities, for instance, enacted new laws or applied existing ones to suppress their First Amendment freedoms of religion, speech, and assembly. What's more, employers and co-workers often discriminated against Witnesses in their workplaces. Expulsions of Witness pupils from public schools became so widespread that members of the faith in dozens of communities were forced to operate their own makeshift schools. Witness parents were charged with neglect or disorderly conduct following the flag-salute expulsions of their children, and some faced the prospect of sizable prison terms for their alleged crimes. And young Witnesses who registered for the military draft faced rampant discrimination as well.

Buffeted by a gale of intolerance in the early and mid-1940s, the Jehovah's Witnesses proved to be amazingly resilient. Instead of meeting violence and bigotry with lawlessness of their own, the Witnesses pursued judicial recognition of their rights with the same righteous determination that marked their efforts to disseminate the teachings of the Bible. They sought redress by mounting an intense legal counterattack against all forms of religious discrimination. When they were arrested under bogus charges, Witnesses repeatedly asserted stout defenses in court and appealed their convictions. They also sought injunctions that would bar the enforcement of laws that were being used for no other purpose but to suppress their civil liberties.

The Witnesses' legal efforts resulted in hundreds of favorable rulings in municipal, state, and lower federal courts. Led by Hayden Covington, a band of Witness attorneys worked tirelessly in courtrooms throughout the country to combat the manifestations of religious bigotry that were affecting so many members of their faith. Their efforts in cities like Connersville, Indiana, and Harlan, Kentucky, helped to safeguard the Witnesses' civil liberties from a flood tide of persecution.

While their many lower-court victories were significant both practically and symbolically, the Witnesses' most noteworthy accomplishments came before the final arbiter of American constitutional rights, the U.S. Supreme Court. From 1938 to 1946, the high court handed down twenty-three opinions covering a total of thirty-nine Witness-related cases. It was a testament to the Witnesses' far-reaching unpopularity (and perhaps their own contentiousness) that they brought a wide range of disputes before the high court—flag-salute cases, free-speech cases, leafleting-ordinance cases, sedition cases, draft-law cases, tax cases, and even child-labor cases. Among the most significant of these were *West Virginia v. Barnette* (1943), in which the Supreme Court reversed its unfortunate decision in the *Gobitis* flag-salute case,

227

and *Chaplinsky v. New Hampshire* (1942), in which the justices established the "fighting words" doctrine in free-speech cases.

The women, men, and children whose rights lay at the heart of these cases did not always prevail; as the *Gobitas* case showed, they sometimes lost, and with devastating consequences. But the Witness cases from that era nonetheless profoundly affected the evolution of constitutional law by helping to bring minority and individual rights—areas long overlooked by the U.S. Supreme Court—out of the shadows and into the forefront of constitutional jurisprudence. At least one member of the high court acknowledged that the Witnesses' frequent appeals compelled the justices to address matters they had previously overlooked. In 1941, Justice Harlan Fiske Stone wrote, "I think the Jehovah's Witnesses ought to have an endowment in view of the aid which they give in solving the legal problems of civil liberties" (Peters 2000, 186).

Cantwell v. Connecticut and Religious Liberty

For more than half a century, the U.S. Supreme Court's opinion in *Reynolds v. United States* (1878) controlled its religious-liberty jurisprudence. Under the doctrine established by the high court in *Reynolds* (a case that involved the application of a federal anti-polygamy law to Mormons in the Utah Territory), religious beliefs were inviolable, but religious conduct could be subject to state regulation. Reaffirmed by the U.S. Supreme Court in two subsequent cases involving the Mormons and polygamy, it essentially removed religious conduct from the purview of the First Amendment. In many ways straitjacketed by the *Reynolds* precedent, litigants pursuing safeguards for religious conduct were forced to seek shelter under other constitutional protections.

The Jehovah's Witnesses were particularly successful in evading the roadblock of *Reynolds* and gaining judicial protections for their religious conduct. When the members of the U.S. Supreme Court shielded the religious conduct of the Jehovah's Witnesses, they typically cited the protections afforded by the First Amendment to speech, press, and assembly rights. In *Cantwell v. Connecticut* (1940), however, the court more directly addressed a religious liberty claim brought by a Witness.

In 1938, police in New Haven, Connecticut, arrested Witness Newton Cantwell and his sons Jesse and Russell for disturbing the peace and soliciting money for a charitable cause without having first received approval of the state's public welfare council, as was required by law. They were convicted on both charges in local court, and Connecticut's highest court upheld all of their convictions on the permit requirement charge. (It dismissed the disturbing the peace charges against Newton and Russell Cantwell but upheld Jesse's conviction on that count.)

Weary of the obstacle posed by *Reynolds*, attorney Hayden Covington believed that appealing the Cantwells' convictions to the U.S. Supreme Court might prompt an expansion of judicial protections for religious liberty. In two previous cases involving Witness appellants—*Lovell v. Griffin* (1938) and *Schneider v. New Jersey* (1939)—the court had continued its piecemeal incorporation of First Amendment freedoms into the due process clause of the Fourteenth Amendment. The First Amendment applied only to actions by the federal government, but the absorption of some of its protections into the Fourteenth Amendment meant that they now applied to actions by the states as well. Those cases, however, had involved speech and press freedoms; the right to free exercise of religion had not yet been incorporated. Covington urged the court to use *Cantwell* to continue the process of incorporation and bar states from abridging the right to free exercise of religion.

The Supreme Court heeded Covington's request to absorb the free exercise clause into the Fourteenth Amendment. Justice Owen Roberts's majority opinion in *Cantwell v. Connecticut* by no means indicated that the Supreme Court was totally abandoning its reasoning in *Reynolds*. Roberts echoed Chief Justice Waite's opinion in the Mormon polygamy case by writing that the free exercise clause encompassed "two concepts—freedom to believe and freedom to act. The first is absolute, but in the nature of things, the second cannot be." In short, the state might exercise control over some forms of conduct even though they were motivated by an individual's religious beliefs. In the context of the Witnesses' proselytizing, this regulation might involve the nondiscriminatory regulation of the time, place, and manner of their public solicitation (Peters 2000, 184–185).

Cantwell differed from *Reynolds* in the level of scrutiny applied to the actions taken by the state to limit religious conduct. In the Jehovah's Witness case, the Supreme Court viewed the state's regulation under heightened judicial scrutiny. Using this more rigorous standard, the court determined that the application of the permit requirements to the Cantwells' religious conduct represented an unconstitutional infringement on their religious liberty. Although the Connecticut permit law at issue was neutral on its face, Justice Roberts wrote for the Court, it was so broadly drawn that public officials had wide latitude to take actions infringing on religious liberty. He reasoned that a more narrowly drawn law would have not placed "a forbidden burden upon the exercise of liberty protected by the Constitution" (Peters 2000, 184–185).

Cantwell was a watershed for religious liberty. Never before had the Supreme Court recognized constitutional protections for religious conduct. But *Cantwell* did not signal that the justices were enthusiastic about claims made strictly under the free exercise clause. In subsequent Jehovah's Witness cases, the Court seemed willing to strike down generally applicable laws only if they were challenged as infringements of multiple First Amendment freedoms. The court's analysis in these cases typically focused on press and speech issues; religious liberty seemed to take a back seat. Indeed, strict religious liberty claims uniformly failed until *Sherbert v. Verner* (1963), when the U.S. Supreme Court at last reformulated its religious liberty jurisprudence.

The Witnesses' Legacy

A handful of Jehovah's Witness cases reached the U.S. Supreme Court in the late 1940s and early 1950s, but their collective impact on constitutional jurisprudence was relatively modest. A smattering of cases followed in the late twentieth century and early twenty-first century, including, *Watchtower v. Stratton* (2002). In that case, the U.S. Supreme Court struck down on free-speech grounds an Ohio municipality's efforts to regulate the Witnesses' religious proselytizing.

Although it has long been overlooked, the legacy of the Witnesses' efforts in such cases is an important one. Many of the seeds of the "rights revolution" of the 1960s were sown as they repeatedly tested the boundaries of the Bill of Rights during the World War II era. The many cases litigated by the Witnesses were critically important because they forced the Supreme Court to nurture a fledgling body of constitutional jurisprudence. By making it more difficult for states and municipalities to regulate religious

conduct and speech, the law they helped to create benefited members of myriad religious faiths.

Shawn Francis Peters

See also Fourteenth Amendment; Free Exercise Clause; Jehovah's Witnesses: Global

Further Reading

Newton, M. O. (1995). *Armed with the Constitution: Jehovah's Witnesses in Alabama and the U.S. Supreme Court.* Tuscaloosa: University of Alabama Press.

Penton, M. J. (1997). *Apocalypse delayed: The story of Jehovah's Witnesses* (2nd ed.). Toronto, Ontario, Canada: University of Toronto Press.

Peters, S. F. (2000). *Judging Jehovah's Witnesses: Religious persecution and the dawn of the rights revolution.* Lawrence: University Press of Kansas.

Court Cases

Cantwell v. Connecticut, 310 U.S. 296 (1940).

Chaplinsky v. New Hampshire, 315 U.S. 568 (1942).

Lovell v. Griffin, 303 U.S. 444 (1938).

Minersville School District v. Gobitis, 310 U.S. 586 (1940).

Reynolds v. United States, 98 U.S. 145 (1878).

Schneider v. New Jersey, 308 U.S. 147 (1939).

Sherbert v. Verner, 374 U.S. 398 (1963).

Watchtower v. Stratton, 240 F.3d 553 (2002).

West Virginia v. Barnette, 319 U.S. 624 (1943).

Jews in Europe

Jews are known to have lived in Europe since at least the first century of the Common Era. Tens of thousands of Jews lived in Rome at the height of its status as imperial capital, and smaller Jewish communities have left traces in many of the Roman Empire's European provinces.

With a few exceptions, principally the move by Emperor Hadrian (76–138 CE) to suppress Judaism around the time of the Bar Kokhba revolt in the 130s, the Jews of the Roman Empire enjoyed religious freedom. Despite pagan disapproval of monotheism, Roman rulers granted Judaism the status of a "licit religion," giving Jews freedom of worship and exemption from participation in state cultic ceremonies.

JEWISH RELIGIOUS FREEDOM IN HUNGARY

The Jews of Hungary were granted religious freedom in 1867. However, as the following account details, the matter was not so simple, as all expressions of Judaism needed to be considered.

In the 1840's, 1850's, and 1860's, there was great religious strife between Hungarian Jews representing two elements, the Reform and the Orthodox. The Reform groups wanted to introduce certain changes in the religious service that the Orthodox groups opposed—for example, the inclusion of sermons in the synagogue services instead of the traditional interpretations of the Scriptures, with the sermons delivered in Hungarian instead of in Yiddish.

The Reform groups also wanted to remove the reading desk from the middle of the synagogue and give clerical vestments to the rabbi and the cantor. An Orthodox rabbinical convention held in Mihályfalva in 1866 prohibited an observant Jew from entering synagogues where these innovations were being introduced.

The Jews in Hungary were emancipated in 1867. A decree passed by both houses of the Hungarian parliament gave the Jews civil and political rights equal to those held by other Hungarians. King Franz Joseph I was very anxious that the Jews settle their differences and establish autonomous Jewish communities to direct their own religious and cultural affairs. By his decree a General Jewish Congress was called at which both the Reform and Orthodox elements would have their delegations. Out of the total of 200 delegates to the Congress, the Reform element had 132 and the Orthodox element had 88. The major difference between the two groups was the question of the authority of the *Shulhan Aruch*, the Code of Jewish Law.

The Reform group introduced a resolution stating: "If there are a number of Jews in a community who would like to establish a congregation, they must build a synagogue, a cemetery, and a school for children like any other school for children." The Orthodox delegates introduced an amendment adding that: "They must behave in accordance with the laws prescribed in the *Shulhan Aruch*." When this amendment was defeated, the leader of the Orthodox delegates stood up and declared: "Cursed be the man who remains with these sinners." All 88 Orthodox delegates rose and left the Congress hall.

The Reform resolutions were introduced in the Hungarian parliament and were adopted in 1869 as the law of the land, binding all Jews to their acceptance. The Orthodox leadership did not stand still. A delegation of the outstanding rabbis sought an audience with King Franz Joseph I and asked permission to practice the Orthodox Judaism "for which our forefathers were burned." The king promised them complete religious freedom, saying, "If your liberal brethren are not interested in the Torah, I will not force them to observe it, nor will they force upon you its nonobservance." Thus, in 1870 the Hungarian parliament voted that the resolutions of the General Jewish Congress were not specified binding upon the Orthodox Jews and that they might separate and organize themselves in every community and hire rabbis and other religious functionaries according to their own standards.

Solomon Poll

Source: *The Hasidic Community of Williamsburg.*
(New York: The Free Press of Glencoe, Inc., 1962), 12–14.

Jews took advantage of imperial toleration and practiced their religion. At least eleven synagogues and a rabbinic academy served the Jewish community in the city of Rome during the second century. Jews maintained their distinctive traditions, observing their Sabbaths, fast days, and dietary restrictions, despite the scorn expressed by Dio Cassius (c. 150–235) and other leading Roman authors. At times, Romans faddishly adopted selected Jewish rituals, and a smaller number converted to Judaism. Jews proselytized freely and granted converts full-fledged Jewish status.

In 212, the emperor Caracalla (Marcus Aurelius Antoninus, 188–217) extended Roman citizenship to all free inhabitants of the empire, including Jews. While the immediate result of that edict was to make more Jews subject to specific taxes, the gain in their civic status endured for centuries.

Jewish status and religious liberties declined with the Christianization of the Roman Empire in the fourth century and following. From Constantine through the last Western Roman emperors, imperial legislation placed steadily greater restrictions on Jews. The Christian Roman emperors outlawed Jewish missionizing and curtailed Jewish economic activities that could lead to Christians' being subjected to Jewish authority. Fifth-century emperors burdened the Jewish community with new restrictions, prohibiting the construction of new synagogues and abolishing the office of Jewish patriarch.

Nonetheless, as Roman citizens, Jews petitioned imperial authorities for the basic protection of life and property in the face of a rising tide of Christian-inspired mob violence against synagogues. Fourth- and fifth-century records reveal that Jews won a number of judgments, but also that, as the Christianization of the empire proceeded, the synagogue was becoming a target of anti-Jewish zeal.

Jewish religious liberties varied in Byzantium and in the several successor states to the Western Roman Empire. Jews in the European provinces of the Eastern Roman Empire suffered four religious persecutions from the seventh through ninth centuries, exceptions to the general pattern of religious toleration. In Italy, Theodoric (454?–526), king of the Ostrogoths, enforced the privileges enjoyed by Jews in later Roman law, even while remonstrating with the Jews of his kingdom for not converting to Christianity. In seventh-century Visigothic Spain, on the other hand, royal measures against the Jews, including forced conversion and expulsion, set a chilling precedent.

Medieval Scenarios: Under Crescent and Cross

The decline of Jewish security and liberty in late antiquity set the stage for the following centuries. The hallmark of European Jewish history in the Middle Ages was the experience of living under the political and social authority of a rival monotheistic faith community. In both Muslim and Christian states, Jews contended with an officially sanctioned denigration of their faith to subordinate status.

Jews in Muslim-Controlled Europe

While most of the Muslim states in the early Middle Ages were in Asia and Africa, rather than Europe, the Arab invasion of Iberia in 711 brought the Jewish community of Spain into the sphere of Islamic influence. Having suffered under the Visigoths, Jews welcomed and assisted the Muslim invaders. Seeking to control a demographically diverse population, the Muslim rulers of this far outpost of the caliphate were pragmatically tolerant by contemporary standards. Many Jews converted to Islam, but the community, spared coercive conversionist measures, preserved its religious identity.

When, like other provinces of the Arab Caliphate, Al Andalus (Muslim Spain) asserted its independence in the tenth century, its rulers turned to their Jewish subjects for diplomatic services. Jewish courtiers such as Hisdai ibn Shaprut (c. 915–975?) and Samuel ha-Nagid (ibn Nagrela, 993–1055 or 1056) became the leading advisors to their respective caliphs and kings.

Enjoying governmental patronage, these courtiers presided over a growing and self-confident Jewish community. Jewish life in Muslim Spain combined participation in the affairs of the host society with new developments in Jewish learning and culture. For example, the linguistic pride of Muslims in the beauty of the Qur'an's Arabic spurred Andalusian Jews to champion the Hebrew style of their own Bible and to develop their own religious poetry.

While this episode of unparalleled Jewish social prominence and cultural brilliance in Muslim Spain did set the "gold standard" for Jewish accomplishments in medieval society, it was not the lustrous "Golden Age" eulogized by nineteenth-century scholarly apologists. Despite the social and intellectual accomplishments of Iberian Jews under Muslim rule, their status rested on fragile foundations, for theirs was an exceptional case within the Muslim world.

The treatment of Jews in Islam, resting on Qur'anic pronouncements (Sura 9:29) and precedents from the careers of Muhammad and his successors, was part of the Muslim ideology of bringing the world to the worship of the one God at sword's point. As Arab armies spread Islam across the Near East and the Mediterranean in the seventh century, the victorious caliphs elaborated the political subjugation of Jews (and Christians) in conquered lands, imposing on them the *jizya*, a burdensome poll tax, and a host of social and religious restrictions designed to show the superiority of Islam. Jews were to be tolerated in Islam as *dhimmi*, a protected minority whose safety was always contingent on their show of subordination.

Angered at the high status of the Jewish community in Muslim Spain, Muslim preachers and pietists agitated against the prominent Jewish statesmen. In 1066, a Muslim mob assassinated the Granadan courtier Joseph ha-Nagid. The conquest of Muslim Spain by the Almoravids in 1086 further weakened the Jewish community. When a still more zealous dynasty, the Almohads, came to power in 1146, they ended Jewish communal life in Andalusia, closing synagogues and schools and forcibly converting Jews to Islam. Some Jews attempted to practice their faith in secret, while others emigrated to North Africa or Christian Spain.

Jews in Christendom

This latter migration was part of a larger pattern. Jews had been moving into the Christian states of Western Europe since at least the ninth century. The Carolingian emperor Louis the Pious (778–840) invited Jewish merchants to France and Germany to assist in the economic development of his realm, conceding them the right to settle their own disputes within the framework of their religious law. This precedent, repeated in charters granted Jews by temporal and ecclesiastical Christian rulers across Europe for centuries to come, served as a foundation for the religious liberty of Ashkenazic (Northern European) Jewry throughout the medieval centuries and for the impressive development of halakah (Jewish law) in their society. Through rabbinic courts at the local level and intercommunal rabbinic synods, Ashkenazic Jews not only regulated their lives in accordance with religious tradition, but also developed that tradition to respond to the new conditions facing them in the feudalized society of western Christendom.

In general, Jews were welcomed into medieval Christian states when those states were first coalescing. As the national identity of the states became firmer, the alien status of Jews in Christian society became an increasing disability. The Atlantic seaboard states England, France, and Spain grew less hospitable to Jews in the course of their national development, and between 1290 and 1492, monarchs of all three countries expelled their Jews. Meanwhile, rulers in central and eastern Europe invited Jews into their developing countries. The oft-copied charters of Duke Frederick II of Austria and Styria in 1244 and of Duke Boleslav of Poland in 1264 safeguarded the religious liberty of the dukes' Jewish subjects as well as life, property, and especially business opportunities.

Since Jewish communal autonomy rested on grants from political leaders, it was vulnerable to two kinds of disruptions: to breakdowns in authority and to the influence of anti-Jewish lobbying upon the rulers. Both of these developments were all too often reenacted throughout the Middle Ages.

The first of these scenarios includes some of the most infamous examples of medieval violence against Jews: the crusader mobs who massacred the Jewish inhabitants of the Rhineland in 1096 operated in the political vacuum caused by the absence of Germany's Emperor Henry IV (1050–1106), who was then detained fighting an insurrection in Italy. The mass murder of German Jews during 1348–1349 took place against the backdrop of the governmental impotence in the face of the scourge of the Black Death. The large-scale riots against Spanish Jewry in 1391 broke out during an interregnum, always a period of weakness in medieval monarchies.

After suffering these attacks, Jews could petition their rulers for redress. But increasingly, the rulers themselves became adversaries to Jewish liberties and, ultimately, to the continued Jewish presence in Christendom.

Since the fourth century, the views of two church fathers regarding the place of Jews in Christian society, Augustine (354–430) and John Chrysostom (c. 347–407), had contended within Christian thought. Augustine argued that the Jews should be maintained in a degraded state rather than killed, so that they might live to bear witness to the triumph of Christianity. Chrysostom argued on the contrary that Jews should be attacked in their persons and synagogues. Augustinian thought had enjoyed major influence on the development of medieval Christian theology, and in turn, provided a rationale for Christian rulers to tolerate Jews in their societies. In the later Middle Ages, however, Christian antipathy to Jews overwhelmed the more "moderate" position and Christian theologians urged that their states no longer suffer the presence of Jews. This was the religious underpinning of the expulsions of the Jews from state after state.

As Christian society became less tolerant of a Jewish presence, Jewish status became more precarious. Even when they did not expel Jews, Christian rulers curtailed Jewish political and religious liberties and intensified the pressure on Jews to convert to the faith of the majority community. At the Fourth Lateran Council in 1215, Pope Innocent III (1160 or 1161–1216) ordered Jews to wear a distinctive badge, an edict that exposed them to physical assault. A generation later, Pope Gregory IX (before 1170–1241) urged Christian rulers to seize the copies of the Talmud, the most important postbiblical Jewish religious text, on the grounds that the Talmud was the principal obstacle hindering Jews from converting to Christianity. King Louis IX (1214–1271) of France obeyed the papal request, burning the Talmud in 1242 and crippling the religious vitality of French Jewry. In the same year, King James I (1208–1276) of Aragon compelled his Jewish subjects to attend conversionist sermons. Similarly, beginning in 1263, Christian kings ordered Jewish leaders to attend public disputations of religion designed to demonstrate the truth of Christian messianic claims and to lead to conversions. After a series of such disputations in Tortosa, Spain, in 1413–1414, anti-Jewish mob violence destroyed a number of Jewish communities in Aragon, and many Jews converted from fear or demoralization.

Once a community of *conversos* (Jewish-born converts to Christianity) had emerged, a new chapter of infringement upon Jewish religious liberty began. Around 1478, under the guise of prosecuting lapsed conversos, Ferdinand II (1452–1516) and Isabella I (1451–1504), the Catholic monarchs of Castile and Aragon, appointed an Inquisition. Technically, the Inquisition was bound by procedural safeguards, but under the leadership of Tomás de Torquemada (1420–1498), the Grand Inquisitor, it functioned as a secret police, torturing suspects into confessing their adherence to Jewish rituals and then arranging for their executions. Torquemada lobbied the monarchy to expel the professing Jews, on the grounds that they were abetting the attempts of the conversos to return to Judaism. In 1492, the king and queen ordered the expulsion of Spanish Jews. Five years later, the king of Portugal forcibly converted the Jews of his realm, thus ending the 1,500-year Jewish presence in Iberia.

The Early Modern Era

The net result of the anti-Jewish atmosphere of the later Middle Ages was the elimination of Jews from western Europe by 1500. This trend extended to central Europe in the sixteenth century. However, in the two centuries from 1575 to 1775, changes in Western society allowed the Jews to return and to participate in society on a new footing.

The Protestant Reformation and the ensuing Wars of Religion initially damaged Jewish security and liberty in central Europe and unintentionally boosted the Jewish community in Eastern Europe. Martin Luther exceeded most other medieval Christian theologians in the vituperative tone of his anti-Jewish writings. The wave of expulsions of Jews from Germany, which had begun in the fifteenth century, grew far more extensive during the turmoil of Reformation-era conflict, with Luther himself instigating the expulsion of the Jews from Saxony in 1537. Many other Protestant rulers followed suit in the following quarter century. Except for the Jews living in territories controlled by the Holy Roman emperor Charles V (1500–1588), most German Jews fled to Poland, raising its Jewish population dramatically to over 100,000 by 1575. The vitality of Polish Jewish life in the late sixteenth and early seventeenth centuries was one of the high points of Jewish religious civilization in Europe, and the religious creativity of that community enriched the traditional Jewish library with standard works consulted until the present day.

Nonetheless, the long-term effects of the Protestant Reformation advanced European Jewish religious liberty. Decades of bloody stalemate in the wars between Catholics and Protestants inspired European intellectuals to develop theories of religious toleration. The Enlightenment philosophers John Locke (1632–1704) and Montesquieu (Charles-Louis de Secondat, 1689–1755) advanced political theories denying the state any authority to compel the individual's conscience in matters of religion. Originally developed with the diversity of Christians in mind, such theories were gradually, if unevenly, extended to defend the right of the Jew to dissent from the religious majority.

In a secularizing and mercantilist age, such voices of religious toleration, coupled with arguments of the economic and political utility of including Jews in the state, increasingly overcame traditionalist Christian objections. Jews found it possible to enter newly organized states such as the Netherlands, in the 1580s, and to reenter France in the 1590s and England in the 1650s.

The gains in the early modern era were not uniform. The Counter-Reformation Pope Paul IV (1476–1559) and his successors ended the open participation of Jews in Italian society, incarcerating them in ghettos and censoring their religious literature. Many Central European Jewish communities, too, were subject to the enforced segregation of the ghetto and a network of economic disabilities. In 1648, the élan of Polish-Jewry was crushed by the massacre of myriads by the Cossack revolutionary Bohdan Khmelnytsky (c. 1595–1657).

The Modern Era

On the eve of the French Revolution, European Jewry featured a variety of accommodations with its host societies, and some Jews were emerging from the ghetto, but no Jews were full-fledged citizens of their respective states. In the century following the French Revolution, that was to change. Jewish emancipation, and the questions it raised for Jewish religious liberty, would be a hallmark of the modern era.

In 1790, the French Revolutionary National Assembly accorded citizenship to the Sephardic Jews of Bordeaux, a group fully acculturated into French life. It took another year of bitter debate for the Assembly to extend citizenship to the Ashkenazim of eastern France. The delegates only belatedly affirmed that the logic of their revolution trumped their reservations about the cultural distinctiveness and social unpopularity of those Jews.

This episode displays in microcosm much of the dynamic of the European debate over the enfranchisement of Jews. Did Jews merit emancipation unconditionally, or were they obliged to become more like the mainstream? Jewish religious reform movements of the nineteenth century in western and central Europe arose in response to this debate. The reformers had internalized Christian critiques of Judaism and sought to make it more palatable, both to non-Jews and to themselves. In czarist Russia, where state-sponsored restrictions against Jews intensified throughout the nineteenth century and Jewish emancipation was never on the horizon, no Jewish reform movement developed.

After the emancipation of German Jews in 1870, a backlash against the integration of Jews into modern society emerged: anti-Semitism. This movement descended from premodern Christian anti-Judaism and yet differed from it importantly. Whereas anti-Judaism had sought to convert the Jew to Christianity, the new movement claimed the secular, "scientific" basis of racism. Still more insidious than its premodern forerunner, anti-Semitism alleged that the Jew could never regenerate, since the alleged immorality of his character was biological in nature.

European anti-Semitism in the late nineteenth century was most virulent in France, during the scandal over the scapegoating of a Jewish army officer, Alfred Dreyfus (1859–1935), for allegedly having spied against his country. But after the German defeat in World War I and the Great Depression of 1929–1933, Germany became the main source of European anti-Semitism and its voters brought the Nazi leader Adolf Hitler (1889–1945) to power.

Under Hitler, Germany waged a war upon the Jewish people. First, the Nazis eliminated Jews from the German economy and isolated them from society. In 1935, Hitler stripped Jews of German citizenship. In 1938, the Nazis escalated their attacks on Jews and Judaism, destroying hundreds of synagogues during Kristallnacht ("night of broken glass," 9 November 1938) and sending thousands of Jews to concentration camps.

After instigating World War II, the Nazi war against the Jews intensified into a "Holocaust" of mass murder. Nazis segregated Jews into ghettos in Eastern Europe, limiting their food and medical supplies in an attempt to kill the victims. The Nazis also forbade expressions of Jewish religious life in the ghettos. During their 1941 and 1942 invasions of Russia, Nazi execution squads killed over a million Russian Jews. Until their defeat in 1945, the Nazis and their collaborators sent millions of Jews to their deaths in concentration camps, employing a combination of brutal tortures and a fiendishly systematized industrialization of murder. The total number of Jewish victims of Nazism is estimated to be six million.

Most of the half-million Holocaust survivors settled in Israel and the United States. Some who had attempted to return to Poland were killed by Polish anti-Semites. For decades after 1945, central Europe and Poland had small and aging Jewish populations. Soviet Holocaust survivors faced Stalinist-era anti-Semitism and discrimination in employment and educational opportunities. After 1970, when Soviet Jews, in search of personal and religious freedoms, attempted to emigrate, many were jailed for "anti-Soviet agitation."

In the past twenty years, with the liberalization of emigration policies in the Soviet Union and post-Soviet states, Jews have begun to immigrate to Germany, whose postwar constitution prohibits anti-Semitism. Even so, German and Austrian Jews today contend with the resurgence of neo-Nazi sentiments, aggravated by the Arab-Israel conflict, given the dependence of European states upon oil from Arab countries.

British and French Jews, while also facing a rise in anti-Semitism since 2000, have enjoyed the security of living in democratic societies committed to freedom of religion. Their situations most closely parallel not the history of Jewish liberty on their troubled continent, but rather the condition of Jews across the Atlantic Ocean in the United States of America.

Michael Panitz

See also Balkans, East Europe, and Russia; Byzantine Empire; Convivencia; England, Victorian; French Revolution; Germany and Prussia; Heresy; Inquisition; Judaism; Roman Empire

Further Reading

Baer, Y. (1961–1966). *A history of the Jews in Christian Spain* (Vols. 1–2). Philadelphia: JPSA.

Baron, S. W. (1973). *A social and religious history of the Jews* (2nd ed.). New York: Columbia University Press.

Ben Sasson, H. H. (Ed.). (1971). *Jewish society through the ages*. New York: Schocken Books.

Carroll, J. (2001). *Constantine's sword*. Boston: Houghton Mifflin.

Chazan, R. (1980). *Church, state, and Jew in the Middle Ages*. New York: Behrman House.

Davidowicz, L. (1975). *The war against the Jews*. New York: Bantam.

Hertzberg, A. (1968). *The French Enlightenment and the Jews*. Philadelphia: JPSA.

Israel, J. (1989). *European Jewry in the age of mercantilism, 1550–1750*. Oxford, UK: Littman.

Katz, J. (1973). *Out of the ghetto*. Cambridge, MA: Harvard University Press.

Leon, H. (1960). *The Jews of ancient Rome*. Philadelphia: JPSA.

Marcus, J. R. (1973). *The Jew in the medieval world*. New York: Atheneum.

Parkes, J. (1969). *The conflict of the church and the synagogue*. New York: Atheneum.

Pulzer, P. (1964). *The rise of political anti-Semitism in Germany and Austria*. New York: Wiley.

Smallwood, E. M. (1976). *The Jews under Roman rule*. Leiden, Netherlands: E. J. Brill.

Starr, J. (1970). *The Jews in the Byzantine Empire, 641–1204*. New York: Burt Franklin.

Stillman, N. (1979). *The Jews of Arab lands*. Philadelphia: JPSA.

Tal, U. (1975). *Christians and Jews in Germany*. Ithaca, NY: Cornell University Press.

Jews in the United States

The story of religious freedom for Jews in the United States is complex. On the one hand, Jews have enjoyed more freedom, including freedom from persecution, in America than in perhaps any other country except Israel. At the crudest level, American Jews have not suffered the pogroms (or organized attacks against Jews) that have occurred frequently in Europe. On the other hand, for a nation where pronouncements of religious freedom are so often heard and where the First Amendment constitutionalizes the free exercise and official disestablishment of religion, Jews have

Touro Synagogue in Newport, Rhode Island, the oldest Jewish synagogue in the United States in 1971. COURTESY OF LIBRARY OF CONGRESS, PRINTS AND PHOTOGRAPHS DIVISION, HISTORIC AMERICAN BUILDINGS SURVEY OF HISTORIC AMERICAN ENGINEERING RECORD.

confronted throughout American history a perhaps surprising degree of hostility and persecution—that is, anti-Semitism—from governmental actors, religious leaders, and civil society in general.

The Colonial Background

The first group of Jewish colonial settlers arrived in New Netherland (New York) around 1654. Peter Stuyvesant, the director of New Netherland for the Dutch West India Company, did not openly welcome these twenty-three Jewish refugees, fleeing from religious persecution in Brazil. He denounced them as usurious, deceitful, and hateful blasphemers and petitioned the company for permission to banish them. In the end, the Jews were allowed to stay, but they were prohibited from building a synagogue and could practice Judaism only in private. Stuyvesant's attitude presaged what Jews often would encounter in other colonies. A de facto Protestant establishment (an establishment in fact, if not in law) was assumed to exist in most colonies, regardless of whether or not there was an official or governmental establishment.

The Newport, Rhode Island, Jewish settlement, which formed in the late 1670s, is noteworthy. Roger Williams, the founder of Rhode Island, is correctly characterized as tolerating greater religious diversity than the other New England Puritan leaders; freedom of conscience and disestablishment were religious and political cornerstones for Williams. Williams envisioned a "wall of separation" between the "garden" and the "wilderness"—that is, between the spiritual and carnal worlds (Williams 1644, 98). Consequently, Rhode Island provided an exemplary degree of religious liberty for Jews, and Newport became home to one of the largest early Jewish colonial communities. Even so, Williams openly criticized Jews because they "blaspheme" the "true religion" and "stand ... for Satan against Christ" (Jaher 1994, 93–94). Williams hoped that Jews would choose to become Christians, but despite such desires, he would not abide by compelled conversion or persecution, which he deemed unacceptable because "opposite to the Jews conversion to Christ" (Miller 1985, 194).

The Constitutional Framing

If anything, the colonies became even more deeply committed to Protestantism as the eighteenth century progressed. Thus, the Constitution was proposed (in 1787), debated, and ratified in the context of de facto Protestantism. "The vast majority of Americans assumed," according to Thomas Curry, "that theirs was a Christian, i.e. Protestant, country [that would] uphold the commonly agreed on Protestant ethos and morality" (Curry 1986, 219).

The only provision in the proposed Constitution that related directly to religion was article VI, clause 3, which prohibited any religious test or oath for national governmental office. Some anti-federalists, the opponents of the Constitution, feared that this provision would open the door for Jews and other non-Christians to be elected to the presidency or other high office. Future Supreme Court justice James Iredell, one of the leading Federalists (supporters of the proposed Constitution), responded. He acknowledged that article VI, clause 3, would "establish a general religious liberty." Congress would "certainly have no authority to interfere in the establishment of any religion whatsoever." But the purpose was to promote civil peace and order rather than to allow Jews to be elected to high offices. History had proven that religious tests and other persecutions had led to "wars of the most implacable and bloody nature." Iredell candidly relied on the de facto establishment of Protestantism as assurance against electing non-Christians: "[I]t is never to be supposed that the people of America will trust their dearest rights to persons who have no religion at all, or a religion materially different from their own" (Elliot 1836, 192–94).

Ultimately, of course, the states ratified and adopted the Constitution, but only after some Federalist leaders, including James Madison, promised to soon add a Bill of Rights. Despite the occasional expressions of anti-Semitism during the ratification debates and despite the de facto establishment of Protestantism, American Jews (albeit still few in number) welcomed the new Constitution. It placed no official limitations on their political standing; at least under the federal Constitution, Jews were full citizens. Indeed, on 4 July 1788, a parade marched through Philadelphia celebrating the recent adoption of the Constitution. Included in the parade were seventeen clergy, one of whom was a rabbi. In no place outside of America would a rabbi have participated in such an event.

The first Congress, as promised, proposed a Bill of Rights of ten amendments, which the states soon ratified and which then went into effect in 1791. The First Amendment included the antiestablishment and free exercise clauses: "Congress shall make no law respecting an establishment of religion, or prohibiting the free exercise thereof." For the most part, the first amendment merely reaffirmed the preexisting social, religious, and political arrangements; the religion clauses did not alter the de facto establishment of Protestantism. On occasion, then, Congress enacted legislation openly supportive of Protestantism, such as the appointment of Protestant chaplains for the House and the Senate as well as for the army. Moreover, while many Americans opposed having a nationally established church—which would too closely resemble the Church of England—they willingly accepted state and local establishments; several states continued to support officially established churches into the early nineteenth century.

On the whole, then, the framers' generation did not make a principled commitment to accord equal respect and freedom to all religions, non-Christian and Christian alike. Yet, on rare occasions, there were exceptional expressions of openness. Most notably, in 1790, President George Washington sent the following message to the Jewish congregation in Newport, Rhode Island:

> All [in the United States] possess alike liberty of conscience and immunities of citizenship. It is now no more that toleration is spoken of, as if it was by the indulgence of one class of people, that another enjoyed the exercise of their inherent natural rights. For happily the government of the United States, which gives to bigotry no sanction, to persecution no assistance, requires only that they who live under its protection should demean themselves as good citizens, in giving it on all occasions their effectual support. (Schappes 1950, 80)

The Nineteenth and Early Twentieth Centuries

The makeup of the national population began to change during the middle decades of the nineteenth century. Whereas fewer than 5,000 immigrants per year entered the United States in the 1820s, the numbers dramatically increased over the next three decades so that, by the 1850s, more than 280,000 immigrants per year arrived. Jewish immigration nonetheless remained slow. In 1820, fewer than 4,000 Jews lived in this country, and even after an influx of German Jews in the 1830s, Jews numbered only approximately 15,000 in 1840.

Even with such a small Jewish population, anti-Semitism was common. During the early nineteenth century, the most prominent American Jew was Mordecai Noah, who served as the American consul to Tunis from 1813 to 1815. Newspapers constantly referred to Noah with anti-Semitic epithets, such as "Hooked Nose" and "Shylock" (Jaher 1994, 135–36). The secretary of state, James Monroe, finally removed Noah from his post because "the Religion which you profess [is] an obstacle to the exercise of your consular functions" (Johnson 1987, 367). In fact, anti-Semitic attitudes were directly and overtly taught to children. The main tract of the American Sunday School Union was published initially in 1827 as a guide for Bible class teachers and sold 1.6 million copies within seven years. It included numerous examples of traditional anti-Semitism, such as the accusation that Jews killed Jesus. Secular schools also used texts filled with anti-Semitic rhetoric. *The National Pronouncing Speller*, aimed at primary classes and republished seven times by 1874, included a spelling exercise that required students to copy the following: "The selfish Jew, in his splendor, would not give a shekel to the starving shepherd" (Jaher 1994, 207).

This anti-Semitism coexisted with Christian pronouncements of the American commitment to religious freedom. Quite simply, most Americans understood religious liberty from a distinctly Protestant vantage. The clergyman and professor Bela Bates Edwards epitomized this mid-nineteenth-century viewpoint:

> Perfect religious liberty does not imply that government of the country is not a Christian government. The Christian Sabbath is here recognized by the civil authorities in a great variety of forms. Most, if not all, of our constitutions of government proceed on the basis of the truth of the Christian religion. Christianity has been affirmed to be part and parcel of the law of the land. (Handy 1984, 49)

After the Civil War, overt expressions of anti-Semitism actually increased for a variety of reasons, though none was more important than immigration. In the fifty years after the Civil War, 35 million people moved to the United States, including over 2 million Jews, most of whom arrived between 1880 and 1915. American Jews of the late nineteenth century had political equality insofar as they could vote and (at least theoretically) hold public office, but the possibilities for social equality seemed to decrease as the

237

number of Jews in the country grew. Discrimination against Jews in economic affairs was typical. For example, restrictive covenants prohibited the sale of homes to Jews, and insurance companies refused to issue policies to Jews. Jews were routinely excluded from public institutions, such as social clubs, schools and universities, recreational facilities, and even the state militia.

Anti-Semitism continued to grow in the early twentieth century. Throughout the 1920s, Henry Ford published a newspaper, *The Dearborn Independent*, that incessantly attacked Jews with traditional anti-Semitic diatribes, claiming Jews controlled American banking, American agriculture, American journalism, and so on. With this tactic, Ford increased circulation almost tenfold within four years to 700,000 copies per week, only 50,000 less than the best-selling paper in the country. Ford also published an American edition of the notorious *Protocols of the Elders of Zion*. According to the *Protocols*, supposedly written by Jewish "elders," Jews were conspiring to take over the world by controlling capital and the press through hypocrisy, bribery, and fraud. In truth, the *Protocols* apparently had been written for political reasons in the 1890s by an author working for the Russian secret police. Early in the 1930s, public opinion polls suggested that one-third of all Americans thought that Jews had too much power, and one-fifth of Americans wanted to restrict the role of Jews in politics and business. Matters worsened later in the decade: at that point, 41 percent of Americans believed that Jews had too much power; almost one-half of Americans thought that Jews were partly to blame for their own persecution in Europe; and 35–40 percent of Americans would have supported anti-Jewish laws. Anti-Semitism simmered at all levels of American society. Hundreds of thousands of listeners tuned in to Father Charles E. Coughlin's weekly radio shows, which spouted Nazi-like accusations of Jewish world domination, while the educated and the affluent, like Thomas Wolfe and H. L. Mencken, regarded Jews as "beak-nosed Shylocks" and "the most unpleasant race ever heard of" (Sachar 1992, 325).

Even so, Jewish opportunities in America began to expand during the 1930s because of President Franklin Roosevelt and the New Deal. Roosevelt needed talented attorneys to staff his New Deal agencies, yet many elite lawyers were conservative and opposed Roosevelt's social and economic liberalism. Meanwhile, young Jewish attorneys, many of them top graduates, could not find professionally rewarding careers in the private sector because of discrimination at the major law firms. Roosevelt turned to this pool of unemployed or underemployed Jewish attorneys to staff many of his administrative positions; many of Roosevelt's opponents disparagingly referred to the New Deal as the "Jew Deal" (Ginsberg 1993, 113). Regardless of this continuing anti-Semitism, some Jews from Roosevelt's administration were eventually able to enter into the Protestant corporate professional establishment. These Jews had gained important knowledge during their years in governmental service, and, hence, they became extremely valuable sources of expertise for corporate America. Even with their expertise, though, Jews could work for the federal government and then corporate America only if they were willing to become Americanized—that is, Christianized—at least to some significant extent. For a Jew to become a successful American, obvious signs of Jewishness typically had to be washed away in a "kind of cultural bleaching" (Howe 1976, 228). In typical fashion, a partner in a large New York law firm boasted that they had a Jewish attorney who was "devoid of every known quality which we in New York mean when we call a man 'Jewy'" (Auerbach 1976, 186).

After World War II

For diverse reasons, ranging from the Holocaust to the Cold War to changes in immigration policy, overt anti-Semitism became a social faux pas by the late 1950s: anti-Semitism went underground, so to speak, becoming less of the normal and natural experience of daily American life. One survey immediately after World War II revealed that 56 percent of Americans believed that Jews had too much power in the United States. By 1964, the percentage had dropped to 13, and in 1981, 10 percent believed as such. During the 1950s, Jews entered realms of the economy previously closed to them. Jews secured numerous positions at colleges and universities, including the most prestigious institutions, and successfully entered other semiacademic areas, such as publishing. Religious discrimination diminished at law firms and law schools so that, by the 1970s, it was practically eliminated. Jews also made strides in retail businesses, though major corporations continued to discriminate. In particular, with regard to the major corporations, business often was done at elite country clubs, which continued to exclude or limit Jews. In 1966, 665 of 1,152 clubs discriminated against

Jews: 513 barred Jews, and 152 had quotas. Yet, in 1964, the federal government enacted the Civil Rights Act, which prohibited discrimination in employment and in places of public accommodation (such as hotels and restaurants) based on religion (as well as race, color, and national origin).

Despite these advances for American Jews, postwar America experienced waves of Christian religiosity: a period of religious fervor, followed by a declension, followed by a time of fervor, and so forth. The 1950s were a time of fervor. More than once, Congress considered a constitutional amendment that would have declared the nation's commitment to Christianity. The Supreme Court opened its daily sessions with the invocation "God save the United States and this honorable Court"; legislatures at the federal and state levels began daily proceedings with prayers from publicly paid chaplains; and currency was stamped with the national motto "In God We Trust." Bible reading, prayers, and Christmas and Easter celebrations continued as typical activities in the public schools. In fact, during this time, many of these religious and quasireligious (Christian) practices were recast as part of the so-called American civil religion. Some Christian Americans now claimed that matters such as Sunday laws and Christmas celebrations in the public schools were part of a distinctly American civil and therefore secular life.

After World War II, though, Jews and Jewish organizations—especially the American Jewish Committee, the Anti-Defamation League, and the American Jewish Congress—began to press for religious freedom and equality in the courts. These organizations were buoyed by the reduction of overt anti-Semitism in America and spurred by a post-Holocaust sense of urgency. Consequently, the Jewish organizations became involved in almost every major religion-clause case to reach the Supreme Court. In many of these cases, Jews were not the named litigants, yet the Jewish organizations discerned that Jewish interests were at stake. The general position of the Jewish organizations throughout this period was to advocate for the strong separation of church and state: Keeping religion and government separate, it was thought, would help protect Jews from the majoritarian overreaching of Christian democratic majorities.

In this postwar context, the Supreme Court for the first time began to seriously enforce the religion clauses of the First Amendment against the state and federal governments. The court's decisions are best understood by distinguishing the establishment clause cases from the free exercise clause cases. As a general matter, establishment clause claimants assert that the government has promoted religion, either purposefully or otherwise, or that the government has become too entangled or involved with religion. Most free exercise claims arise when the government enacts a generally applicable law that incidentally interferes with the practices or beliefs of some minority religion. The government, for example, might pass laws that prohibit the use of certain drugs, but the members of a religious minority might nonetheless use one of the proscribed drugs as part of their religious rituals (as was the case in *Employment Division v. Smith* [1990] when the state of Oregon prohibited the use of peyote, which was a sacrament in the Native American Church). In such situations, a member of the minority religion typically seeks a free exercise exemption: that is, the free exercise claimant asks the courts to grant an exception from the law so that the religious minority can continue to follow its practices and beliefs.

In many of the establishment clause cases, the court decided favorably to the Jewish position. For instance, *McCollum v. Board of Education*, decided in 1948, involved a challenge to a released-time program where children were released early from their public school classes once each week so that they could attend religious classes, which were held in the public school buildings. Other children, not seeking religious instruction, were not released from their regular classes. Similar released-time programs had, in fact, been adopted in forty-six states. The *McCollum* court, influenced by an amicus curiae brief filed by the Jewish organizations, held that this program violated the establishment clause of the First Amendment, though in a subsequent case, the court upheld a program where the religious instruction was conducted off the public school grounds.

One of the court's most controversial establishment clause decisions was *Engel v. Vitale*, decided in 1962. Reasoning that "a union of government and religion tends to destroy government and to degrade religion" (*Engel v. Vitale*, 1962, 430–31), the court held unconstitutional the daily recitation of a supposedly nondenominational prayer in the public schools. This decision provoked widespread outrage in Christian communities. Local school districts defied the ruling; members of Congress called for a constitutional amendment overturning the decision; and newspapers published editorials and letters condemning the Supreme Court.

While the Jewish organizations have invoked the establishment clause with reasonable success, they have not fared nearly as well when invoking the free exercise clause. For example, two cases decided in 1961 arose from Jewish religious challenges to Sunday closing laws. Among other assertions, the cases involved claims for free exercise exemptions that would have allowed Jewish-owned businesses to remain open on Sundays. Orthodox Jews observe a Saturday Sabbath and thus the Sunday closing laws imposed a severe burden on Jewish-owned businesses, which were forced in effect to remain closed on both Saturdays and Sundays. Even so, the court refused to grant free exercise exemptions in both cases.

Another case is especially disturbing because it revealed the Supreme Court justices' insensitivity to the religious practices of Jews, if not to all religious minorities. In *Goldman v. Weinberger* (1986), an Orthodox Jewish Air Force officer, Simcha Goldman, sought a free exercise exemption so he could wear his yarmulke (skullcap) despite Air Force regulations that sometimes prohibited the wearing of a head covering. The American Jewish Congress argued to the court: "Because petitioner sincerely holds the religious belief that he must keep his head covered at all times, strict enforcement of [the Air Force regulations] forces petitioner—or any other Orthodox Jew—to choose between adhering to his religious beliefs or serving his country in the Air Force. It is 'a cruel choice'" (Brief in *Goldman v. Weinberger*, 1986, 9). Nonetheless, the Supreme Court rejected Goldman's claim. The court mistakenly characterized the wearing of a yarmulke as a matter of mere "personal preference" rather than a centuries-old custom that had attained the status of religious law for Orthodox Jews (*Goldman v. Weinberger*, 1986, 508).

In conclusion, Jews in America have experienced over the years a minimal amount of governmental persecution, especially when compared with that of other countries. Yet, throughout much of American history, partly because of the vitality of Christian culture in this country, Jews have suffered under and been subjected to anti-Semitic attitudes and conduct, to a surprising degree, given the First Amendment's constitutionalization of religious freedom and the separation of church and state.

Stephen M. Feldman

See also Civil Religion; Israel; Jews in Europe; Judaism

Further Reading

Auerbach, J. S. (1976). *Unequal justice: Lawyers and social change in modern America.* New York: Oxford University Press.

Cohen, N. W. (1992). *Jews in Christian America: The pursuit of religious equality.* New York: Oxford University Press.

Curry, T. J. (1986). *The first freedoms: Church and state in America to the passage of the First Amendment.* New York: Oxford University Press.

Dinnerstein, L. (1994). *Antisemitism in America.* New York: Oxford University Press.

Elliot, J. (Ed.). (1836). *The debates in the several state conventions on the adoption of the federal Constitution.* Washington, DC: Printed by and for the editor.

Feldman, S. M. (1997). *Please don't wish me a Merry Christmas: A critical history of the separation of church and state.* New York: New York University Press.

Ginsberg, B. (1993). *The fatal embrace: Jews and the state.* Chicago: University of Chicago Press.

Handy, R. T. (1984). *A Christian America* (2nd ed.). New York: Oxford University Press.

Hertzberg, A. (1989). *The Jews in America.* New York: Simon & Schuster.

Howe, I. (1976). *World of our fathers.* New York: Simon & Schuster.

Ivers, G. (1995). *To build a wall: American Jews and the separation of church and state.* Charlottesville: University Press of Virginia.

Jaher, F. C. (1994). *A scapegoat in the new wilderness: The origins and rise of anti-Semitism in America.* Cambridge, MA: Harvard University Press.

Johnson, P. (1987). *A history of the Jews.* New York: Harper & Row.

Miller, W. L. (1985). *The first liberty: Religion and the American republic.* New York: Paragon House Publishers.

Sachar, H. M. (1992). *A history of the Jews in America.* New York: Vintage Books.

Schappes, M. U. (Ed.). (1950). *A documentary history of the Jews in the United States, 1654–1875.* New York: Citadel Press.

Williams, R. (1953). Mr. Cottons letter lately printed, examined and answered (1644). In P. Miller, *Roger Williams: His contribution to the American tradition* (p. 89). Indianapolis, IN.: Bobbs-Merrill.

Court Cases

Abington School District v. Schempp, 374 U.S. 203 (1963).

Braunfeld v. Brown, 366 U.S. 599 (1961).

Brief of American Jewish Congress on Behalf of Itself, the Synagogue Council of America, and the American Civil Liberties Union as Amici Curiae, Goldman v. Weinberger, 475 U.S. 503 (1986) (No. 84-1097).

Employment Division, Department of Human Resources v. Smith, 494 U.S. 872 (1990).

Engel v. Vitale, 370 U.S. 421 (1962).

Gallagher v. Crown Kosher Super Market of Massachusetts, Inc., 366 U.S. 617 (1961).

Goldman v. Weinberger, 475 U.S. 503 (1986).

McCollum v. Board of Education, 333 U.S. 203 (1948).

Jihad

Usually translated "holy war," jihad is, nonetheless, a concept with numerous shades of meaning, as often contested among Muslims as it is misunderstood in the West. While the idea of a religious battle is often rightly connected with the word, Muslims frequently use jihad to describe any exertion they make on behalf of the faith, quite apart from war. Additionally, it may be used in a completely secular sense, as in a "war on drugs and poverty." It may also be used in a political sense, as in a war of national liberation. Such was the case, for instance, in pre-1948 Palestine in clashes between Arabs and Jews; Arabs appropriated the term to describe their struggle. Thus, while jihad can be used to indicate a war fought for religious reasons, it is important to understand, at the outset, that the term is connotatively rich and historically complex.

According to *A Dictionary of Modern Written Arabic* (Wehr 1979, 168), the root verb from which jihad is taken (*jahada*) means simply "to make an effort, to strive, to endeavor, to take pains." The related noun *jahd* indicates an endeavor or an exertion; and in science, it is the term used for voltage or tension. Within Islam, jihad carries a range of meanings. Islamic scholars speak of a "jihad of the heart," the individual believer's efforts to conform to God's will. In this case, devotion in prayer, fasting during Ramadan, or making the pilgrimage to Mecca may be spoken of as a jihad. "Jihad of the tongue" and "jihad of the pen" are metonymic expressions that describe efforts believers make to propagate Islam through speaking and writing. But there is also a "jihad of the sword," a doctrine that scholars elaborated especially in the classical period of Islam, the Abbasid caliphate, 749–1258 CE. It is this last concept that comports with the idea of a "holy war" and on which this article focuses.

Jihad in the Qu'ran

Pre-Islamic Arabia witnessed intertribal conflict, battles between desert Bedouin clans termed *razzia*. Over time, certain protocols developed to regulate the fighting. The combatants who observed them were regarded as men of honor. Something of that background appears in the Qur'an, but the conflict there involved not clans but the nascent Islamic community and those who opposed or sought to subvert it. Thus, the Qur'an describes the battles as pitting believers who seek to follow God's way (*sabeel Allah*) with unbelievers or polytheists (*mashrikun*).

In the Qur'an, when jihad is used, it generally carries the broad connotation of effort on God's behalf rather than explicit combat. In many verses, the believers are exhorted to give both "their possessions and themselves" in God's cause. "Those who believe, and suffer exile and strive with might and main [*jahada*] in God's cause, with their goods and persons, have the highest rank in the sight of God: they are the people who will achieve [salvation]" (Qur'an 9:20 [Ali translation 1983]; see also 61:11). Such efforts are intended to establish the practice of Islam. "And strive [*jahada*] in His cause as ye ought to strive. ... [E]stablish regular prayer, give regular charity, and hold fast to God! He is your protector" (22:78).

Where physical combat is directly indicated, a different word—*qitaal*—is ordinarily used. *Qittal* indicates "combat, strife, fighting" (Wehr 1979, 870) and it stems from a verbal root meaning "to kill." For instance, the verb occurs in one of the most cited passages on fighting: "But when the forbidden months are past, then fight and slay [*qatala*] the pagans wherever you find them, and seize them, beleaguer them, and lie in wait for them in every stratagem of war" (9:5; cf also 2:190, 193, 217; 4:74, 75; 9:29). Of course, in a number of instances, jihad clearly must be taken, not simply as effort, but as directly indicating combat. For instance, that is the case in 9:81, where the Qur'an describes those who hesitated to join Muhammad in an expedition to Tabuk in northern Arabia to counter a possible Byzantine invasion. They are labeled as those who "hated to strive [*jahada*]" in the cause of God and thus face eternal punishment.

JIHAD: DEFENSE OR AGGRESSION?

Jihad is a complicated concept and one that can and often does mean different things to different people. The following statement, attributed to Osama bin Laden and his associates, is an example of the multiple meanings of the concept of jihad. In the West, this statement is seen as a declaration of war, while to many Muslims it is a statement of defensive jihad, designed to keep the Muslim world free of Western domination.

WORLD ISLAMIC FRONT STATEMENT

23 February 1998

Shaykh Usamah Bin-Muhammad Bin-Ladin
Ayman al-Zawahiri, amir of the Jihad Group in Egypt
Abu-Yasir Rifa'i Ahmad Taha, Egyptian Islamic Group
Shaykh Mir Hamzah, secretary of the Jamiat-ul-Ulema-e-Pakistan
Fazlur Rahman, amir of the Jihad Movement in Bangladesh

Praise be to Allah, who revealed the Book, controls the clouds, defeats factionalism, and says in His Book: "But when the forbidden months are past, then fight and slay the pagans wherever ye find them, seize them, beleaguer them, and lie in wait for them in every stratagem (of war)"; and peace be upon our Prophet, Muhammad Bin-'Abdallah, who said: I have been sent with the sword between my hands to ensure that no one but Allah is worshipped, Allah who put my livelihood under the shadow of my spear and who inflicts humiliation and scorn on those who disobey my orders.

The Arabian Peninsula has never—since Allah made it flat, created its desert, and encircled it with seas—been stormed by any forces like the crusader armies spreading in it like locusts, eating its riches and wiping out its plantations. All this is happening at a time in which nations are attacking Muslims like people fighting over a plate of food. In the light of the grave situation and the lack of support, we and you are obliged to discuss current events, and we should all agree on how to settle the matter.

No one argues today about three facts that are known to everyone; we will list them, in order to remind everyone:

First, for over seven years the United States has been occupying the lands of Islam in the holiest of places, the Arabian Peninsula, plundering its riches, dictating to its rulers, humiliating its people, terrorizing its neighbors, and turning its bases in the Peninsula into a spearhead through which to fight the neighboring Muslim peoples.

If some people have in the past argued about the fact of the occupation, all the people of the Peninsula have now acknowledged it. The best proof of this is the Americans' continuing aggression against the Iraqi people using the Peninsula as a staging post, even though all its rulers are against their territories being used to that end, but they are helpless.

Second, despite the great devastation inflicted on the Iraqi people by the crusader-Zionist alliance, and despite the huge number of those killed, which has exceeded 1 million . . . despite all this, the Americans are once against trying to repeat the horrific massacres, as though they are not content with the protracted blockade imposed after the ferocious war or the fragmentation and devastation.

So here they come to annihilate what is left of this people and to humiliate their Muslim neighbors.

Third, if the Americans' aims behind these wars are religious and economic, the aim is also to serve the Jews' petty state and divert attention from its occupation of Jerusalem and murder of Muslims there. The best proof of this is their eagerness to destroy Iraq, the strongest neighboring Arab state, and their endeavor to fragment all the states of the region such as Iraq, Saudi Arabia, Egypt, and Sudan into paper statelets and through their disunion and weakness to guarantee Israel's survival and the continuation of the brutal crusade occupation of the Peninsula.

All these crimes and sins committed by the Americans are a clear declaration of war on Allah, his messenger, and Muslims. And ulema have throughout Islamic history unanimously agreed that the jihad is an individual duty if the enemy destroys the Muslim countries. This was revealed by Imam Bin-Qadamah in "Al-Mughni," Imam al-Kisa'i in "Al-Bada'i," al-Qurtubi in his interpretation, and the shaykh of al-Islam in his books, where he said: "As for the fighting to repulse [an enemy], it is aimed at defending sanctity and religion, and it is a duty as agreed [by the ulema]. Nothing is more sacred than belief except repulsing an enemy who is attacking religion and life."

On that basis, and in compliance with Allah's order, we issue the following fatwa to all Muslims:

The ruling to kill the Americans and their allies—civilians and military—is an individual duty for every Muslim who can do it in any country in which it is possible to do it, in order to liberate the al-Aqsa Mosque and the holy mosque [Mecca] from their grip, and in order for their armies to move out of all the lands of Islam, defeated and unable to threaten any Muslim. This is in accordance with the words of Almighty Allah, "and fight the pagans all together as they fight you all together," and "fight them until there is no more tumult or oppression, and there prevail justice and faith in Allah."

This is in addition to the words of Almighty Allah: "And why should ye not fight in the cause of Allah and of those who, being weak, are ill-treated (and oppressed)?—women and children, whose cry is: 'Our Lord, rescue us from this town, whose people are oppressors; and raise for us from thee one who will help!'"

We—with Allah's help—call on every Muslim who believes in Allah and wishes to be rewarded to comply with Allah's order to kill the Americans and plunder their money wherever and whenever they find it. We also call on Muslim ulema, leaders, youths, and soldiers to launch the raid on Satan's U.S. troops and the devil's supporters allying with them, and to displace those who are behind them so that they may learn a lesson.

Almighty Allah said: "O ye who believe, give your response to Allah and His Apostle, when He calleth you to that which will give you life. And know that Allah cometh between a man and his heart, and that it is He to whom ye shall all be gathered."

Almighty Allah also says: "O ye who believe, what is the matter with you, that when ye are asked to go forth in the cause of Allah, ye cling so heavily to the earth! Do ye prefer the life of this world to the hereafter? But little is the comfort of this life, as compared with the hereafter. Unless ye go forth, He will punish you with a grievous penalty, and put others in your place; but Him ye would not harm in the least. For Allah hath power over all things."

Almighty Allah also says: "So lose no heart, nor fall into despair. For ye must gain mastery if ye are true in faith."

Source: Federation of American Scientists.
Intelligence Resource Program. Retrieved 25 July 2002, http://www.fas.org

It is important to note that there has been considerable debate among Muslim scholars about the verses that address fighting. Are such verses to be understood as presupposing hostile attack and therefore advocating a *defensive* posture; or do the verses direct unilateral offensive action against unbelievers? An example of a verse that is clearly defensive is 22:39: "To those against whom war is made, permission is given to fight." On the other hand, some verses do not restrict combat to defensive actions only. An example is 9:5, cited in the preceding paragraph.

On balance, the later suras (chapters)—i.e., those that were revealed in Medina—seem to contain references to offensive warfare. These are often called the "sword verses," and religious scholars in the years after Muhammad's death generally regarded them as such. But a fair reading also takes account of the limits they impose. For instance, the second sura, which was revealed in Medina, commands the believers not to "transgress limits" in warfare (2:190) and to "let there be no hostility except to those who practice oppression [*thulm*]" (2:193). Sura eight, also a chapter from Medina, instructs the believers: "But if the enemy inclines toward peace, do thou also incline towards peace, and trust in God" (8:61). The ninth sura, often seen as foremost among those containing sword verses, is direct in commanding warfare: "Fight them, and God will punish them by your hands, cover them with shame, help you to victory over them" (9:14). But it must be noted that the chapter assumes covenant breaking by the enemy. Regardless of how one approaches the Qur'anic verses about jihad generally and fighting specifically, it is important to keep the larger context in view, realizing such verses are historically situated.

Classical Jurisprudence and Jihad

After Muhammad's death in 632 CE, Islam spread very rapidly. Within a decade, the Arab/Islamic armies had taken Egypt and had inflicted heavy losses on the Byzantines and Persians in the areas of present day-Syria and Iraq. Indeed, within a century, Islamic rule reached from Spain to India. Under the early Abbasid caliphate, 749–1258, Islamic scholars developed what has become known as the classical view of jihad. Where the Qur'an had described a battle between belief and unbelief, the clash was yet localized; and the struggles between the nascent Islamic community and its opponents in Mecca and Medina were in view. By the time of the Abbasids, however, the Islamic community was now coterminous with a vast empire. Scholars advanced a general doctrine to describe the preceding two centuries of advance, a doctrine that would now also be relevant to an imperial rule.

In elaborating this more robust doctrine of jihad, Islamic scholars drew on both the Qur'an and the extra-Qur'anic sayings of Muhammad called *hadith*, as well as deliberating the experience of the community. They employed the term jihad to describe that confrontation between *dar al-Islam*, the house of peace, and *dar al-harb*, the house of war. The divide, they reasoned, was categorical. This clash should be seen as perennial enmity, even if there were no actual warfare, one in which there could only be periods of temporary truce. Assuming a single, unified Islamic community, or *ummah*, scholars ascribed responsibility to the caliph for leading in this advance against *dar al-harb*. (For the Shi'a, the imam [religious leader] had the responsibility for leading in jihad.) He would decide when to call for jihad, divinely sanctioned war, in this battle with unbelief; decide when truce should be made; and determine the terms of surrender and the division of booty. Scholars also delineated restrictions on the causes for and proper conduct in jihad, with rough parallels to the West's "just war" doctrine.

On the view of these scholars, the message of Islam was both universal and for all time, for Islam is the "natural religion" of humankind. The aim, however, was not primarily conversions, but recognition of the supremacy of Islam and of Islamic law, the *shari'a*. When war did come, the Islamic army was to offer its adversaries one of three options. A *hadith* of Muhammad, related by Muslim ibn Hajjaj (d. 875 CE), describes the choices:

> When you meet your enemies who are polytheists, invite them to three courses of action. If they respond to any one of these, you also accept it and withhold yourself from doing them any harm. Invite them to (accept) Islam; if they respond to you, accept it from them and desist from fighting.... If they refuse to accept Islam, demand from them the *jizya* (a small poll tax). If they agree to pay, accept it from them and hold off your hands. If they refuse to pay the tax, seek Allah's help and fight them. (Peters 1995, 11)

While other scholars restricted the range of those who might be allowed the option of paying the *jizya*, generally all agreed that there could be a protected status for certain religious minorities, especially the "People of the Book," i.e., Jews and Christians.

Modern Calls for Jihad

Despite the elaboration of the classic doctrine that described a perennial clash between the house of war and the house of peace, calls for jihad grew fewer with the fracturing of the *ummah* into several rival Islamic dynasties and their slow eclipse by Western powers. While the doctrine with its calls for jihad did not disappear, Islam began to live more comfortably in a "world of nation states," a phrase aptly used by Professor James Piscatori in the title of his book, *Islam in a World of Nation-States* (1986). Today, indeed, countries with Islamic majorities are members of organizations like the United Nations, the International Monetary Fund, the World Health Organization, the Arab League, and the Islamic Conference Organization. Such countries operate easily in the international order, recognizing independent national sovereignties, while yet ascribing to a spiritual unity among all Muslims.

But beginning in the late nineteenth century, calls for jihad began once more to surface. Various nationalist movements, as well as government and religious elites, began to draw on the idea. For instance, the charismatic Shaykh Muhammad Ahmad ibn abd Allah (1843–1885) announced himself *mahdi* (literally, "guided one") and led a revolt in the Sudan. His followers in the religious movement swore the following oath of loyalty: "We pledge allegiance to Allah and to his prophet.... We [also] pledge allegiance to thee [i.e., the *mahdi*] in renouncing and abandoning this world and contenting ourselves with what is with Allah.... We pledge allegiance to thee in that we will not flee from the *jihad*." The nationalist Palestine Revolt, 1936–1939, prominently featured a call for jihad against the Zionist "colonizers" and the British mandatory power. A proclamation of the General Command during the revolt reads in part, "The fighters (*mudjahidun*) have sold themselves to Allah. ... They try to get ahead of one another [in hurrying] to the battlefield of jihad and martyrdom. ... We call upon any Moslem and Arab to set out for jihad in the way of Allah ... in defending the holy land" (Peters 1979, 99).

In World War I, the Ottoman government turned to religion to secure supporters for the Central Powers. In November 1914, the Shaykh al-Islam, the highest religious figure in the Ottoman government, issued this *fatwa* (a decision by competent religious authority): "When it occurs that enemies attack the Islamic world ... it [has] become an individual duty for all Muslims in all parts of the world ... to partake in the jihad" (Peters 1979, 56). Interestingly, the *fatwa* stipulated that those outside the Ottoman Empire living under British rule were also commanded to obey the summons to jihad. Sherif Hussein of Mecca, great-grandfather of the late King Hussein of Jordan, issued a counter-call to jihad; and the ulama in Egypt and India were prevailed on to issue *fatwas* to the effect that the people were obliged to obey the British. More recently, Anwar Sadat couched the 1973 war against Israel in terms of jihad, naming the operation to cross into the Sinai "Operation Badr" after an early victory of the Muslims in 623 CE. And, of course, the Persian Gulf War (1990–1991) abounded with competing calls to jihad, with Muslim clerics in Iraq, Saudi Arabia, Jordan, Egypt, and other Islamic countries issuing such appeals.

In the development of what is now sometimes termed "Islamic radicalism" and its emphasis on jihad, perhaps the single most important figure is the Egyptian intellectual, Sayyid Qutb (1906–1966). Qutb, a member of the Muslim Brotherhood put to death by the government for alleged subversive activity, described Egyptian and other Arab societies as *jahiliyya*, a term used to describe the state of ignorance before the advent of Islam. His solution was first to renew lapsed Islamic societies by restoring—as in early Islam—the fusion of *din wa dawla*, religion and state. In an especially memorable phrase, Qutb declared, "Islam has to deliver blows at the political forces that make men the slaves of something that is not Allah" (Peters 1996, 129). Qutb revived the classical terminology of *dar al-harb* and *dar al-Islam*, and he called for action from what he termed "the vanguard," a cadre of faithful who would "initiate this revival of Islam ... and then keep going, marching through the vast ocean of *jahiliyya* which encompasses the entire world" (Qutb 1990, 9). Qutb's works profoundly influenced such groups as the Islamic Jihad in Egypt, the group responsible for assassinating Anwar Sadat; Hamas (the Islamic Resistance Group) in the occupied territories of Israel/Palestine; the Taliban in Afghanistan; and, perhaps most important, Osama bin Laden and the al-Qaeda network, responsible for the attack on the World Trade Center in September 2001.

Ongoing Debate

While the vast majority of Muslims have denounced the violence of Islamic radicals and their calls for expansionist jihad, important questions about jihad and the Islamic community persist. That is especially true after the Persian Gulf War, where individuals and states alike called repeatedly for a holy war, as mentioned previously. To begin, many are deliberating the nature of authority in a faith community of some one billion believers who are spread among nation-states around the globe. Who speaks for such a community? Is his (or her) authority only religious, or could it also be political? Is there a role now for jihad? Who may initiate it? How are calls to Islamic action more generally to be balanced against the demands of citizenship? Yet Muslims have posed such questions for almost one and a half millennia. Within those debates are important resources for deliberation about just war theory, the relationship of the individual and the state, and the nature of civil society. For Islam, above all, is a faith tradition deeply connected to thinking about human dignity and a just social order. As the Qur'an exhorts (39:10), "Say: 'O ye My servants who believe! Fear your Lord. Good is (the reward) for those who do good in this world. Spacious is Allah's earth! Those who patiently persevere will truly receive a reward without measure!'"

Jerry M. Long

See also Islam

Further Reading

Ali, A. Y. (Translation and commentary). (1983). *The holy Quran*. Brentwood, MD: Amana Corporation.

Khadduri, M. (1955). *War and peace in the law of Islam*. Baltimore: Johns Hopkins Press.

Mayer, A. E. (1991). War and peace in the Islamic tradition and international law. In J. Kelsay and J. T. Johnson (Eds.), *Just war and jihad* (pp. 195–226). New York: Greenwood Press.

Peters, R. (1995). Jihad. In John Esposito (Ed.) *The Oxford encyclopedia of the modern Islamic world*: Vol 2. (pp. 369–373). New York: Oxford University Press.

Peters, R. (1996). *Jihad in classical and modern Islam*. Princeton, NJ: Marcus Wiener Publishers.

Piscatori, J. P. (1986). *Islam in a world of nation-states*. New York: Cambridge University Press.

Qutb, S. (1990). *Milestones (Ma'alim fi al-tariq)*. Indianapolis, IN: American Trust Publications.

Wehr, H. (1979). *A dictionary of modern written Arabic*, Wiesbaden, Germany: Otto Harrassowitz.

Judaism

Judaism, the religion of the Jewish people, is founded on the belief in ethical monotheism; that is, that there is only one God, omnipotent and omniscient, creator of the universe, who is just and merciful, and who commands persons to act justly and mercifully; that humanity is made in the image of God. The Jewish people base their origin and religion on the Torah, the Pentateuch or the first five books of the Hebrew Scriptures (Old Testament), wherein Abraham is portrayed as the father of the Jewish people and the founder of their religion.

The Jewish People

Originally known as Hebrews, later as Israelites, the Jewish people and their religion are among the oldest in the world, their beginning going back almost four thousand years. At the beginning of World War II there were 16 million Jews in the world, of whom 6 million perished in the Holocaust. At the end of the twentieth century, the Jewish population was 12 million, of whom 5.7 million are in the United States, 5 million in Israel, 600,000 in France, and 300,000 in Britain.

History

The Bible relates that God entered into a covenant with Abraham, whereby Abraham was promised that he would be the father of a great nation that would take possession of the land known as Canaan (comprising what is now the state of Israel, Palestine, and Jordan), as the Promised Land. Abraham left his birthplace (in what is now Iraq) and migrated to Canaan. His son Isaac lived in Canaan, but Abraham's grandson Jacob (also known as Israel) had to migrate to Egypt, together with his large household of seventy persons, because of a severe famine. In the course of time, the Hebrews became numerous enough to be a separate nation and were enslaved by the Egyptians. God selected one of their people, Moses, to become their leader to emancipate them and lead them to the Promised Land. The exodus from Egypt, at about 1280 BCE, is one of the cen-

SABBATH

The observance of the Sabbath on Saturday and the ritual obligations of the day clearly differentiate Jews from non-Jews, although Jews vary greatly in how, if at all, they mark the Sabbath. The following account by a Hasidic (ultra-Orthodox) Jewish woman in Brooklyn indicates the important the Sabbath holds for some Jews.

"I live from one Shabbos to the next," she said. "I look forward to it all week. We almost always have three or four guests. Sometimes they're neighborhood friends; at other times it's just family, but we're often asked by some official to provide a congenial Shabbos for someone who is traveling or for students who have no other place to go. In the last month we've had people show up from England, Iran, and South Africa; the door is never closed. It's totally unlike what I was used to growing up in Bloomfield Hills. Saturdays were a drag when I was a child. I didn't really understand what the Sabbath was about; no one ever talked about it. We observed it only in a halfhearted way, and neither my two brothers nor my sister and I ever really understood why we were doing any of it. In fact, I hardly understood anything about the deeper levels of Judaism until I became a baalat teshuvah [Hebrew for 'one who has returned']."

Lis Harris

Source: *Holy Days: The World of a Hasidic Family.*
(New York: Summit Books, 1985), 5.

tral events in Jewish history and is celebrated by the holiday Pesah (Passover). Moses died as the people reached the boundary of what was to become their homeland, and Joshua led them to its conquest (at about 1240 BCE).

Moses had led the people through the Sinai wilderness for about forty years. When they came to Mount Sinai, God revealed himself and gave the Israelites the Ten Commandments and made known to Moses the whole of the Torah, which became the written law, and he revealed to Moses also the oral law, that is, the interpretation of the written Torah, and Moses in turn taught both the written and the oral Torah to the people. Thus was born Judaism, and the nation now had a religion. Thus the exodus and the revelation at Sinai became intertwined to constitute the Jews as a nation with Judaism as their religion and the Promised Land as their homeland, their heritage. One nation, one Torah, and one land became inextricably bound together in the national consciousness of the Jewish people.

The conquest of Canaan was not completed until the time of David (c. 1012–972 BCE), who conquered Jerusalem and made it the capital. He was succeeded by his son Solomon, who built the first Temple. Upon his death in 932, ten of the tribes who occupied the north revolted and established the kingdom of Israel, and the two southern tribes remained as the kingdom of Judah. In 722 the kingdom of Israel was conquered by Assyria and its population was exiled and became the lost tribes. In 586 the Babylonians conquered the kingdom of Judah and destroyed the Temple, and the Jews were taken to Babylon. This dispersion came to be known as the first Diaspora. When Persia defeated the Babylonians, Cyrus the Great permitted some Jews to return to their homeland and to build the second Temple, which was completed in 516.

Alexander the Great made the land of Israel part of his empire in 332. In 169 Antiochus, king of Syria, invaded Jerusalem, plundered the Temple, and began to Hellenize the people and to utterly destroy their religion. This led to the revolt of the Maccabeans, the reestablishment of an independent state, and a rededication of the Temple, but in 63 BCE the Romans retook Jerusalem. The Jews rebelled against Rome, and in the year 70 CE the Romans sacked Jerusalem and destroyed the Temple. In the year 135 the Jews were dispersed, and thus began the second Diaspora, which lasted nearly two thousand years, until the establishment of the state of Israel in 1948.

247

The Torah, Written and Oral

The Babylonian exile in the sixth century BCE, the first Diaspora, may be taken to mark the rebirth of the nation into a religious community, the transformation of biblical Judaism into rabbinical Judaism, and the change of loyalty from state and land to Torah. As Jews returned to their homeland from Babylonia and Persia and built the Second Commonwealth, their scholars and rabbis refreshed the teachings of the Torah. Torah became articulated as the oral law. The written Torah could not be interpreted literally. The scholars and rabbis, e.g., held that the provision in the Bible (Exodus 21:23–25, RSV) that the law "life for life, eye for eye, tooth for tooth, hand for hand" (the *lex talionis*), must be interpreted to mean that the wrongdoer should pay money damages to the victim. This understanding of the legal provisions of the written Torah came to be identified with the Pharisees, who had their origin in the second century BCE. They insisted on strict observance of the written Torah but as interpreted by the oral Torah, which included customs and traditions. Pharisaism was democratic in spirit and greatly influenced masses of people. As teachers, they resorted to extensive exegesis of the written Torah. They also emphasized ethical ideals. Orthodox Judaism as we know it today is a continuation of the Pharisaic teaching. The famous Hillel (c. 30 BCE–30 CE) was a leading Pharisee.

The Sadducees opposed Pharisaism. They originated in the third century BCE among the upper and priestly classes that identified themselves by their closeness to the Temple. They accepted only the written Torah, which they interpreted literally. Unlike the Pharisees, they did not believe in immortality and the resurrection, which are not mentioned in the Pentateuch. Since the sect was closely connected with the Temple, they ceased to exist when the Temple was destroyed in 70 CE.

Another sect was that of the Essenes, who lived as a separate, isolated community, mainly in the wilderness of the Dead Sea, from the second century BCE to the end of the first century CE. In the time of Jesus they numbered about 4,000 men, who were mostly celibate and ascetic and lived a communal life. They were organized as a monastic order, had their own rituals, and insisted on maintaining strictest ritual purity. Their religious beliefs were generally those of the Pharisees, but unlike them they did not believe in resurrection and refused to attend services at the Temple. They spent most of their time in study of Torah.

There was also, at the time of Jesus, a small sect known as the Therapeutae, a monastic order who lived on the shore of Lake Mareotis in Egypt. Like the Essenes, they were ascetic and devoted their time to prayer and study of Torah.

Mention may be made also of the Samaritans from Syria, Babylonia, and elsewhere who were settled in Palestine when the Jews were deported in 722 BCE. They believed in the Torah (the Pentateuch) and observed its rituals more strictly than did the Orthodox Jews. They built a temple on Mt. Gerizim. A small remnant of the sect has survived and lives now in Nablus, Palestine, and Jaffa, Israel. In the eighth century CE there arose in Persia a Jewish sect that became known as the Karaites, who, like the Samaritans and the Sadducees, believed in the Torah (Pentateuch) but not in the Pharisaic or rabbinic interpretation; they believed that the Pentateuch must be literally understood and punctiliously observed. A remnant of them has survived and live in Israel as a separate community with a population of 7,000 persons.

The Talmud

The term *Torah* has three meanings: (1) the Pentateuch, the first five books of the Hebrew Scriptures; (2) in addition to the first five books, there are thirty-four additional books in the Hebrew Scriptures (the Old Testament, so that the term Torah in this sense means the thirty-nine books of the Hebrew Bible); (3) Torah in its broadest sense means the Hebrew Bible and the Talmud and the vast literature of interpretation and commentary, including the great body of *responsa* (estimated to comprise some 300,000 written documents).

The Bible states that Moses assembled seventy elders to be associated with him in the governance of Israel (Numbers 11:4–31). The tradition is that this body became, in the time of the Second Temple, the Great Sanhedrin of seventy-one elders. It continued its existence, even after the destruction of the Temple and the dispersion of the Jews, until 425 CE. This body of leading scholars concerned itself with all religious questions.

The Great Sanhedrin, in about the year 100 CE, canonized the books that compose the Hebrew Scriptures, and in the second century it codified the legal and the ethical interpretations of the Bible that are known as the Mishnah. These interpretations had been handed down traditionally by about 150 rabbis (Tannaim). This code has remained the authoritative legal code.

The Mishnah itself needed to be interpreted. The interpretation and commentaries were collected and edited and were called *the Gemara*. The Babylonian Talmud, composed of both the Mishnah and the Gemara, was compiled around 500 CE. The Palestinian or Jerusalem Talmud, a much shorter work, was compiled earlier, around 400 CE. The Babylonian Talmud is considered the more authoritative work. The rabbis who figure in the Gemara are called *Amoraim* (Interpreters). In later centuries eminent scholars published codes of law, the most notable of which are the Mishneh Torah by Maimonides (1135–1204) and the Shulhan Arukh by Rabbi Josef Caro in 1565. Beside the legal rulings, the Babylonian Talmud is a great depository of matter that is biographical, ethical, historical, folkloric, philosophical, theological, astronomical, and even anatomical. Each Talmud is a great depository of the wisdom and ethical and religious thought of the Jewish people that had become part of the remembered tradition from ancient times through the medieval period, a span of some twenty-five centuries.

The Right to Dissent

For a long stretch of years there were deep differences and sharp disputes in the Sanhedrin between two factions, the Pharisees led by Hillel and the Sadducees, whose leader was Shammai (c. 50 BCE–30 CE); the former argued for liberal, reasoned interpretation of biblical law, while the latter stood for the literal, strict interpretation. Generally the majority decided cases in accord with Hillel's opinion; only twenty decisions were made in favor of the position taken by Shammai. The Talmud significantly recorded both the majority and the dissenting opinions. The Talmud relates that once when the two schools were locked in an argument, a heavenly voice cried out: "Both these and those are words of the Living God, but the decision should follow that of the school of Hillel." But, it was asked, if the words of both are words of the Living God, why should only those of Hillel prevail? The answer came: "Because the members of the school of Hillel are amiable of manner and courteous, they teach opinions of both schools, and moreover, they give the opinion of their opponents first" (B. Talmud 13b).

Although the Sadducees did not believe in resurrection, immortality, or the coming of the Messiah, there is no record that they were ever charged with heresy. Nor were the Essenes or any other sectarians tried for heresy. One who denies the oral Torah, or is an Epicurean (*epikores*) or a heretic, may have no portion in the world to come (Maimonides, Mishneh Torah, Laws of Repentance 3:6, 8), i.e., may be punished in the next world, but is not punished in this world.

The story of Elisha ben Avuyah (Aher), who lived at the end of the first century and the beginning of the second century CE as recorded in both Talmuds, relates that this distinguished scholar left the Pharisees and read Greek books, and possibly became a Sadducee and held heretical opinions. He was, it seems, ostracized by his colleagues, but was not tried for his heresies, and his former pupil, the renowned Rabbi Meir, continued to revere Elisha and to respect his teachings. The case of Elisha dramatically confirms the generalization that "courts of justice never attended to cases of heresy; they were left to the judgment of the community" (*Jewish Encyclopedia* 1903, V:353). There were, however, in the codes of law some regulations concerning relations with heretics; e.g., upon his death, relatives of a heretic did not observe the laws of mourning, and priests of the Temple did not accept sacrifices brought by a heretic (*Jewish Encyclopedia* 1903, V:354).

But what about the case of Baruch (Benedict) Spinoza (1632–1677)? He had received an extensive Jewish education in the Hebrew scriptures, Talmud, and the voluminous works of Maimonides on Jewish law and philosophy. His teacher was the famous scholar, Rabbi Saul Morteira, who tried to persuade Spinoza not to express his heretical views publicly. At age 24 he was excommunicated. There is a record of the ban but not of his trial. Apparently, Spinoza had already, before the trial, removed himself from the Jewish community. Scholars believe that the extraordinary action against him was taken in the interests of the safety and welfare of the Jewish community of Amsterdam and not to persecute him for his opinions and beliefs. It is important to think of the ban on Spinoza in the context of Jewish life in Holland at the time. The Jews knew that their life in Amsterdam was a precarious one, that they were not entirely free but were only tolerated, and that Christian society would not treat kindly a person known to be an agnostic or an atheist, whether he be a Jew or a Christian. In fact, Spinoza's *Tractatus*

Theologico-Politicus, published anonymously in 1670, fourteen years after his excommunication, was promptly proscribed by the government.

About twenty-five years before the Spinoza case, the rabbinical court of Amsterdam excommunicated Uriel Acosta, who had published in 1624 a work in which he advocated rationalistic doctrines, attacked rabbinical Judaism and the oral Torah, and urged adoption of the beliefs of the Sadducees.

There are at least two reasons why Jewish history has recorded very few cases of trials for heresy. First, Judaism has no fixed and universally recognized set of dogmas or articles of faith, and no universal authority to formulate and promulgate such a set of beliefs. Individual thinkers have drafted what they called the fundamental principles of Judaism. Philo of Alexandria (20 BCE–50 CE) claimed that there were eight principles essential to Judaism. Hasdai Crescas (1340–1410 C.E.) held that there are three root principles, below which are six fundamental but not indispensable principles, and lastly there are three basic beliefs. Joseph Albo (c. 1380–c. 1444 CE) found only three root principles, from which flow derivative roots, and six beliefs of an inferior order. The prophet Micah (eighth century BCE) summed up (6:8) all that God demands of humanity: "He has showed you, O man, what is good: and what does the lord require of you but to do justice, and to love kindness, and to walk humbly with your God?" The formulation by Maimonides (1135–1204) has received wider and longer recognition than any other, but no universal acceptance. His version of the thirteen principles of faith is included in some editions of the orthodox *Siddur* (prayer book), but there is for it no claim that it is part of liturgy or that it has official standing. In this context, one recalls the incident reported in the Talmud (B.T. Shabat 31a) that when a heathen came before Hillel and asked him to state, while he, the heathen, stood on one leg, what is Judaism, Hillel answered: "What is hateful to you, never do to your fellow man. That is the whole Torah. All the rest is commentary." Hillel's response to the gentile may be taken as representative of Judaism in its emphasis on behavior and action and not on abstract dogmas, articles of faith. Second, the Jewish people never established a central institution authorized to define heresy and to establish procedure to conduct trials and punish heresy. The matter is in the hands of individual rabbis or communities (as in the case of the Amsterdam Jewish community that tried and convicted Uriel Acosta and Baruch Spinoza). An action taken against a heretic was effective only as far as the rabbi's or the community's jurisdiction extended.

The sanction imposed was the ban, of which there were three types: *nezifah* or rebuke, usually imposed for a week; *niddui*, suspension for thirty days; the ultimate sanction, *herem*, or excommunication. Maimonides lists twenty-four offenses for which an offender was liable to be placed under the *niddui*, such as insulting a scholar, contempt of an officer of the court, keeping dangerous animals, none of the offenses of the type we would consider censorship of speech or press (*Encyclopedia Judaica* 1972, 8:351–2). In post-Talmudic law, the *herem* was used to warn against violation of new regulations, to threaten potential offenders. In modern times, *niddui* and *herem* have lost their force. When imposed by ultra-Orthodox rabbis, they may be respected by their followers but are disregarded by all others, and may be said to be ineffective.

In addition to the ban on Spinoza, Jewish history records two other notorious, regrettable uses of the ban. After the death of Maimonides, Northern French rabbis banned study of his *Guide for the Perplexed*, denounced it to the Dominican Order, and made a public bonfire of the book in a public square in Paris in 1233. This action aroused revulsion of feeling and liberal rabbis issued a counterban. The other instance took place in the eighteenth century, when the Hasidic movement aroused much excitement. The movement was essentially a protest against the extensive and almost exclusive study of Talmud and legal codes, to the neglect of sacred writings that might appeal to the emotions. Hasidim in Poland, Russia, and Romania emphasized emotion and fervor in prayer, song, and even dance. Opponents of the movement induced Elijah, Gaon of Vilna (1720–1797), to ban Hasidism in 1777 and again in 1781, but to no avail. Before long, the two camps learned to live together, as if the bans had never been issued.

The Prophets

In ancient Israel people suffered from oppression, poverty, injustices, and wars, and there were no newspapers, no legislative investigations, no investigative journalists. But there were then men who were known as the prophets of Israel. No other nation had prophets—men who fearlessly cried out against wrongdoing, against injustices, against greedy landowners, against kings who committed crimes, against the oppression of innocent people. Sometimes prophets were imprisoned, sometimes they were attacked by mobs, but they were not intimidated and their words have been preserved and made part of the Hebrew Scriptures. Thus Isaiah (eighth century BCE) cried out: "Woe unto them that join house to house, that lay field to field, that there be no room. ..." (Isaiah 5:8). When Ahab, king of Israel (ninth century BCE), and Jezebel, the queen, arranged the murder of Naboth, so that they could take possession of his vineyard, the prophet Elijah appeared before Ahab, and when Ahab saw him he said: "Have you found me, O my enemy?" Elijah accused the king of the murder of Naboth and told him how God would punish him and the queen: "and when Ahab heard these words, he rent his clothes, and put sackcloth upon his flesh, and fasted. ..." (Kings 21:17–29).

The prophets of Israel—Elijah, Amos, Jeremiah, Isaiah, Micah, and the others—are ancestors and precursors of all honest, truth-telling editorial writers, investigative journalists, courageous labor leaders, social reformers, civil libertarians, advocates of human rights. In the ancient world Israel's prophets constituted a unique calling of men who fearlessly responded to God's call.

Pluralism

For centuries the Jewish people, concentrated in European cities, lived separated from the non-Jewish population and maintained uniformity of religious practices and rituals. The emphasis was on orthodoxy (a term not known or used then) and Jewish law. This pattern of life was greatly shaken after the French Revolution (1789) and the Napoleonic Wars (1803–1815), when ideas of liberalism and secular nationalism found their way into the ghettos and shtetls.

There arose in Germany the Reform movement, initiated most notably by Abraham Geiger (1810–1874), which moved away from Jewish law and placed its emphasis on Jewish ethics. The movement was transplanted in the United States as German Jews immigrated after the revolution of 1848. The Reform temples did away with the traditional separation of the sexes, introduced organ music in the services, used the Hebrew language very sparingly, and made other changes. Before the

establishment of the state of Israel, Reform was anti-Zionist. In the late years of the twentieth century, Reform became more traditional, it increased the Hebrew content of its services, appointed women rabbis and cantors, and strongly supported Israel.

The Conservative movement evolved out of the Historical School in nineteenth-century Germany, which was identified with the scholarly work of Leopold Zunz (1794–1886) and Zacharias Frankel (1801–1875). Conservative Judaism developed mostly, like Reform Judaism, in the United States, where the Jewish Theological Seminary ordained most of the Conservative rabbis and trained most of the teachers and cantors for the hundreds of Conservative congregations. Believing in the importance of Jewish law and in the moral purposes of Judaism, the Conservative movement has been seen as standing midway between tradition and modernity, between Orthodoxy and Reform. In its temples men and women sit together and there are women rabbis and cantors. Conservative Judaism holds that growth and development of the Jewish tradition are necessary to meet the exigencies of life, but change must reflect the basic spirit of Jewish law and Jewish ethics.

Orthodox Judaism is divided between the traditionalists who emphasize separatism and minimum contact with the non-Jewish world, as well as strict separation of the sexes in the synagogue and schools, and Modern or Centrist Judaism, which maintains that Torah should be combined with culture, with secular learning. Modern Orthodoxy traces its origin to the work of Samson Raphael Hirsch (1808–1888) of Frankfurt, Germany. Yeshiva University in New York City exemplifies the position of Modern Orthodoxy. All Orthodox synagogues have separate seating for men and women; Modern Orthodox schools teach girls and boys the same curriculum, including classes in Talmud, but the more traditional Orthodox offer a more limited curriculum for girls and have in their synagogues stricter separation of the sexes. There are various shades of traditionalism and modernity among the Orthodox as among the Conservative, Reform, and Reconstructionist branches. There is even a group known as Humanistic Jews that is non-theistic, with its own rabbinical seminary, its own synagogues and rabbis. Judaism is thus, in the widest sense, a pluralistic religion.

While the Conservative and Reform movements are committed to the absolute egalitarianism between the sexes in all respects of life and not only in matters of religious rites and rituals, the Orthodox generally continue to adhere to the principle of separation of the sexes, not only in worship but in other respects as well. Polygamy existed until the eleventh century when Rabbenu Gershom (Gershom ben Judah, 960–1040) banned the practice, and his ruling was accepted as binding by all Jewish communities of Europe; his edict, however, was not extended to Asiatic Jews, who even now are not bound by it. For the latter Jewish communities, the ancient Jewish law provides that men may practice bigamy but women are limited to monogamy. Orthodox Jews adhere to the law that women may not serve as witnesses nor as judges. In the Orthodox marriage ceremony, the man "consecrates" the bride as his wife, but she does not "consecrate" the man. The man initiates a divorce but the wife cannot; if the man is absent and cannot be found, or if he refuses to divorce her, she becomes an "agunah," a bound person. The husband is the sole heir of his wife, but a widow is entitled only to maintenance by his estate as long as she lives.

So, as can be seen from these examples, separation does not mean equality. In the state of Israel, the secular legislature and the courts have effectively made changes in the law that have softened the separation and have advanced egalitarian ideals, and some Modern Orthodox rabbis and scholars in the United States and Europe are striving to emulate the example of Gershom, an early advocate of a philosophy of Jewish human rights.

Milton R. Konvitz

See also Israel; Jews in Europe; Jews in the United States; Middle East

Further Reading

Cohn, H. H. (1971). *Jewish law in ancient and modern Israel*. New York: KTAV Publishing House.

Cohn, H. H. (1984). *Human rights in Jewish law*. New York: KTAV Publishing House.

Cohn, H. H. (2000) "The Law of Religious Dissidents." Jerusalem: *Israel Law Review, 34,* 39–100.

Encyclopedia Judaica (1972). (1st ed, Vols. 1–16). Jerusalem, Israel: Macmillan.

Gordis, R. (2002). The rights of dissent and intellectual liberty. In M. R. Konvitz (Ed.), *Judaism and human rights* (pp. 190–212). New Brunswick, NJ: Transaction Publishers–Rutgers University.

Hamilton, E. (1936). *The prophets of Israel*. New York: W. W. Norton.

Heschel, A. J. (1962). *The prophets*. Philadelphia: Jewish Publication Society.

Jacobs, L. (1964). *Principles of the Jewish faith*. London: Vallentine Mitchell.

Singer, I. (Ed.). (1903). *Jewish Encyclopedia* (1st ed., Vols. 1–12). London and New York: Funk & Wagnalls.

Konvitz, M. R. (1978). *Judaism and the American idea*. Ithaca, NY: Cornell University Press.

Konvitz, M. R. (2002). Judaism and the democratic ideal. In M. R. Konvitz (Ed.), *Judaism and human rights* (pp. 119–139). New Brunswick, NJ: Transaction Publishers–Rutgers University.

Twersky, I. (1972). *A Maimonides reader*. New York: Behrman House.

Law, Disorder, and Religious Freedom

Law is the foundation of civil peace and order, and government exists to maintain and protect that good order. Clashing conceptions of what is necessary for good order lie at the heart of diverse visions of religious freedom. The tension between law and religious freedom might thus be approached through the question, "What is required for civil order to flourish?"

Four Typologies

To resolve the question of what is required for civil order, we must first define the term "order." Within the English/Western tradition, there are four basic typologies for the relationship between religion, order, and the state: the two kingdoms type, the duly ordered relationships type, the levitical type, and the enlightenment type. The four different conceptions of "order" developed under each of these types will help us gain an orientation into the basic questions of religion and the state.

"Two Kingdoms" Typology

The essence of the "two kingdoms" type is that the secular and the sacred are separate kingdoms with distinct powers, jurisdictions, and responsibilities. The laws needed to keep the peace and help society to flourish are concerned only with material issues (actual harm done to specific persons or property) are pragmatic (not perfectionist), and are less comprehensive than laws governing the spiritual realm. The good of civil order requires the secular and the sacred each to exercise the power and authority that belong to it alone. Serious disorder occurs when government regulation strays over into the jurisdiction of the sacred. Tertullian's *Apology* is illuminative of the early Christian paradigm for the proper limits of state authority: "But who has ever suffered harm from our assemblies? [W]e injure nobody, we trouble nobody" (Tertullian c. 200 CE, 47). The state has no legitimate interest in the beliefs and worship of its citizens unless they can be proven harmful to other specific individual members of the community, with concrete and specific evidential proofs brought in a court of law as opposed to philosophical or otherwise tenuous assertions of harm.

The English Dissenters (including Thomas Helwys and Roger Williams) were seventeenth century champions of the two kingdoms type. Helwys wrote, "Let them be heretics, Turks, Jews or whatsoever, it appertains not to the earthly power to punish them in the least measure" (Helwys [1612] 1935, 69). In summary, the two kingdoms type requires that spiritual and material issues be governed by separate religious and civil authorities, and that a respectful questioning of the magistrate's power is required when the matter at issue is one of religion or religious obligation.

Duly Ordered Relationships Typology

In contrast, at the heart of the duly ordered relationships type is the equating of civil order with unquestioning obedience to state authority. This type has its origins in Christian belief: There is no conflict between civil and religious, because all authority ultimately comes from the same source: God. God and civil order both require obedience to the civil authority, and the civil ruler wields God's avenging sword in furtherance of true religion and the *pax deorum*. Otherwise, anarchy reigns. Augustine described "order" as the "arrangement of things equal and unequal in a pattern which assigns to each its proper position" (Augustine [1467] 1984, Book 19, Ch. 13). Augustine noted that for peace to exist, there must be duly ordered, hierarchical obedience of those lower to those higher. The Christian magistrate takes on the role of a surrogate parent, responsible for nourishing the spiritual development of the state wards (i.e., its citizens). God's laws of obedience, of hierarchy, and of obedience to hierarchy created the order necessary for civil peace. The Church of England defended its establishment in terms of the duly ordered relationship type: the parental role of authority (both church and state) to guide members and correct error; the scriptural duty of obedience to authority; and the imperfection of individual judgment, especially judgment that challenges authority. Even after disestablishment in America, the duly ordered relationships type flourished in such doctrines as Patrick Henry's (and Justice Joseph Story's) advocacy of government support of the Christian religion as necessary to promote a virtuous citizenry.

Yet secular and even antireligious governments use the same authoritarian logic and reasoning underlying the duly ordered relationships type to suppress religious freedom. Lip service is paid to the right to freedom of religion, but only insofar as this religious freedom conforms to government-defined needs and requirements. Obedience and governmental perceptions of its needs are the paramount considerations here. There is little consideration of religious freedom as an important limitation on government authority and an inalienable right retained by all persons. There is certainly no conception of a need or requirement to balance government interests against the individual's right to religious freedom.

Levitical Typology

Under the levitical type, order is defined primarily in terms of a sense of purity. Civil disorder is the result of defilement and contamination. To a stronger extent than the duly ordered relationship type, the levitical type compels state-imposed religious conformity and the merging of religious and civil law, because religious tolerance is a serious vice, not a civic virtue. Tolerance invites a contaminating mix that will cause society to sicken and perish. The

Puritans' argument against the Anglican establishment was partly premised in the levitical type: a sense of contamination and defilement from false worship and false religious hierarchy.

Tolerance under the levitical type is a serious threat to the good order of the state for two reasons: First, such defilement invites swift and severe divine/cosmic retribution. A notion of corporate guilt underlies this fear of divine retribution: the sins of the few are visited upon the many. The entire polis becomes accountable for individual sins. Second, spiritual error is as dangerous to civil order as a physical uprising. Such error is not harmless; it corrupts the conscience, the mind, and the soul, thereby affecting citizens' good judgment, common sense, and ability to reason. Such corruption is as dangerous as a plague and as destructive to society as a terrible flood. One example of this type in U.S. law was the argument on the floors of Congress in March and April of 1860 that Mormon polygamy had to be extinguished in the Utah territories because the United States would otherwise face the same destructive wrath of God as did Sodom and Gomorrah.

While the hallmark of the duly ordered relationships type is authoritarianism and rigid obedience, the hallmark of the levitical type is the gut fear of the spread of an evil if it is not utterly contained. (Although not an instance of religious persecution, the fear that led to the banishment of Japanese-Americans to internment camps during World War II can be seen as a levitical type of reaction.) Both types often underlie efforts to suppress minority religions and support the religion of the majority.

Enlightenment Typology

The "enlightenment" type, in contrast, holds that order is achieved by moderation and balance. The essence of this type is an esteem for common sense and reasonableness. True religion, for example, is that which promotes peace, charity, and goodwill among all persons. A state's use of force in furtherance of matters of religion is unreasonable, ineffective, and promotes strife that disturbs the civil peace. The state has no jurisdiction in the areas of religion and religious worship; these are left to one's conscience. Under this type, religion runs into trouble when its dictates are not viewed as "reasonable." Furthermore, religious obligations that tend toward the unusual are less likely to be accorded protection under the enlightenment type as under the two kingdoms type, because the emphasis is not as much on the sacred right to freedom of conscience and the special status of religion, as much as it is on the inherent reasonableness of equal treatment. Locke, for example, noted that since one could freely wash a baby in water at home for nonreligious reasons, one should be equally free to immerse a baby in water for religious reasons.

While reliance upon appeals to God-given reason and common sense are evident from early Christianity, the enlightenment type did not come into its own in theological debates over the scope of state authority until John Locke and William Penn championed its principles during the religious turmoil of seventeenth century England. Thomas Jefferson's beliefs and writings on freedom of religion can be classified comfortably within the enlightenment type, while it is thought that James Madison was influenced by both the enlightenment type (due to the influence of Virginia statesmen like Jefferson) and the two kingdoms type (due to the influence of Baptists Dissenters in Virginia). Madison also came under the influence of the Scottish common sense school from his teacher and mentor, John Witherspoon, at Princeton.

Modern American Cases on Religious Freedom

The two kingdoms type affords the broadest protection to religious freedom. The enlightenment type tends to protect only "reasonable" religious groups but also tends to defend against government's unreasonable use of force against religious freedom. The duly ordered relationships type favors uniform obedience and offers very little, if any, protection to minority religious groups. The levitical type offers the harshest requirements for good order, mandating a strict purity and deeming tolerance as a dangerous sin, not a virtue.

The bewildering array of positions taken by the U.S. Supreme Court on free exercise issues might in part be explained by the persistent influence of these four contradictory ways of defining civil "order" and the relationship between religion and the state. The cleanest example is the pair of cases in the 1940s involving Jehovah's Witnesses' children punished for failing to salute the flag. Justice Frankfurter wrote the opinion for the Court against the children in the first case, *Minersville School District v. Gobitis*, and relied heavily on themes from the duly ordered relationships type: The bedrock of civil order is obedience to authority, and religion owes deference to lawmakers who are charged with determining what is in soci-

ety's best interests. Just a few years later, the Supreme Court reversed itself and overruled the *Gobitis* decision in the case of *West Virginia Board of Education v. Barnette*. While faced with essentially similar facts, the Court instead reasoned that the state itself had violated good order by going beyond its proper realm of authority in compelling conscience (two kingdoms) and, furthermore, the flag salute requirement was unreasonable (enlightenment) because the practical goal of the law (instilling patriotism) could not be gained by the use of force.

Interestingly, the radical narrowing of the free exercise clause protections in the 1990 case of *Employment Div. v. Smith* was justified by a fear of anarchy and need for uniform obedience to legal authority as reflected in the duly ordered relationships type. The *Smith* case eliminated all free exercise exemptions, declaring that the right to religious liberty extends only to legal behavior, and revived the *Gobitis* rationale.

Yet, the influence of the enlightenment type (reasonableness and moderation forbid vendettas) can still be seen in cases where the Court protected non-dominant religious groups from laws targeting (as enacted or as enforced) their religious practices, such as the case of *Church of the Lukumi Babalu Aye v. City of Hialeah* (ritual animal sacrifice found to be targeted by enactors of a general city ordinance).

On the establishment clause aspect of the principle of religious freedom, notions of the common good and good order, equal treatment, and individual religious freedom rights interestingly also come into play in the war over the meaning of the establishment clause. The first question to be asked: "What is necessary for good order?"

One answer invokes the two kingdoms type, maintaining that government has no authority over religious matters and warning that the power to support religion and the power to suppress religion are one and the same. The government, lacking authority in matters of religion, creates serious civil disorder by using coerced, public tax monies to support religion. Laws that prohibit as well as support religion are null and void, void *ab initio*. The freedom of religious conscience is retained as an inalienable right—meaning such power cannot be transferred to the state even by choice and personal consent.

A different answer to the establishment clause question invokes aspects of the duly ordered relationships type, with a bit of the levitical type mixed in. A close and cooperative relationship between Christianity and the state is necessary to fulfill America's calling as the new Chosen Land destined to establish the "kingdom of God in America." There is no conflict between civil and religious, because all authority comes from God. Both government and organized religion have a parental role and thus parental authority to guide citizens and to correct their errors. Government support of religious initiatives is necessary to promote a virtuous citizenry. In the faith-based organizations initiative by President George W. Bush, for example, the guiding vision is of government and churches together curing societal ills assumed to be caused by the poor, the wayward, and the addicted. In the school voucher program, public tax money goes to religious education in order to combat the evils of ignorance (while perhaps promoting religious virtue) in poverty districts with failing school systems.

The notion that government support of religion is necessary for the public good is sometimes accompanied by themes from the levitical type, such as the threat that if Christianity and Christian morals are not promoted and established by the American government, this country will incur the wrath of God. (There were strains of this belief after September 11th, for example.)

The two kingdoms type has been reflected in establishment clause cases striking down government actions such as government-sponsored prayer in public schools (*Engel v. Vitale*, and *Lee v. Weisman*, for example), and the display of a lone Christmas creche in a government building (*Allegheny County v. ACLU*) as unconstitutional establishments of religion. The duly ordered relationships type in turn has been reflected in establishment clause cases such as *McGowan v. Maryland* (upholding Sunday blue laws out of the societal need for a uniform day off), and *Zelman v. Simmons-Harris* (upholding the use of school vouchers in private religious schools). In such establishment clause rulings upholding government support of religion based upon reasoning reflecting the duly ordered relationships type, the rights of religious minorities are often sacrificed to the majority's sense of the common good. Orthodox Jewish merchants must close on Saturday according to their conscience and on Sunday according to the blue laws. All taxpayers are forced to support pervasively religious education by (predominantly) Christian schools under the utilitarian rubric of public necessity combined with the saving technicality that the parents direct the government money to the schools.

Implications

The state's assumption as to what is required to maintain good civil order is a greater influence on the nature of the relationship between government and religion than the mere existence of the words "religious freedom" or "religious tolerance" in their guiding legal documents. This helps to explain why governments whose laws and/or constitutions all pay homage to religious freedom and freedom of conscience may in reality have wildly divergent protocols and protections regarding the extent to which their citizens enjoy a religious freedom that differs from the majoritarian views.

Catharine Cookson

See also Baptist Dissenters in Virginia; Establishment, Equal Treatment; Establishment, Separation of Church and State; European Convention on Human Rights; Free Exercise Clause; Jehovah's Witnesses; Letter on Toleration; New Religious Movements; Religion and Public Education

Further Reading

Augustine (1984). *Concerning the city of god against the pagans* (H. Bettenson, Trans). London: Penguin Books. (Original work published 1467)

Cherry, C. (Ed.). (1998). *God's new Israel: Religious interpretations of American destiny* (Rev. ed). Chapel Hill: University of North Carolina Press.

Cookson, C. (2001). *Regulating religion: The courts and the free exercise clause*. New York: Oxford University Press.

Estep, W. R. (1990). *Revolution within the revolution: The First Amendment in Historical Context, 1612–1789*. Grand Rapids, MI: William B. Eerdmans.

Helwys, T. (1935). *The mistery [sic] of iniquity*. London: Baptist Historical Society. (Original work published 1612)

Kamen, H. (1967). *The rise of toleration*. New York: World University Library.

Niebuhr, H. R. (1988). *The kingdom of god in America*. Middletown, CT: Wesleyan University Press. (Original work published 1937)

Noll, M. A. (2002). *America's God: From Jonathan Edwards to Abraham Lincoln*. New York: Oxford University Press.

Noonan, J. T. (2000). *The lustre of our country: The American experience of religious freedom*. Berkeley: University of California Press.

Tertullian (1989). The apology. In A. Roberts & J. Donaldson (Eds.), *The Ante-Nicene Fathers* (Vol. 3). Grand Rapids, MI: William B. Eerdmans. (Original work by Tertullian written c. 200 CE)

Underhill, E. B. (Ed.). (1846). *Tracts on liberty of conscience and persecution, 1614–1661*. London: J. Hadden.

Court Cases

Allegheny County v. ACLU, 492 U.S. 573 (1989).

Church of the Lukumi Babalu Aye v. City of Hialeah, 508 U.S. 520 (1993).

Employment Div. v. Smith, 494 U.S. 872 (1990).

Engel v. Vitale, 370 U.S. 421 (1962).

Lee v. Weisman, 505 U.S. 577 (1992).

McGowan v. Maryland, 366 U.S. 420 (1961).

Minersville School District v. Gobitis, 310 U.S. 586 (1940).

West Virginia Board of Education v. Barnette, 319 U.S. 624 (1943).

Zelman v. Simmons-Harris, U.S.S.Ct. docket no. 00-1751 (2002).

Law Enforcement and Religious Groups

Both religions and laws attempt to establish an ideal social order and to shape individual predispositions and actions to that ideal. Both also enforce specific sanctions against those who transgress their norms. In U.S. history, interactions between religious groups and the law have played out in legislative bodies, the courts, and sometimes in direct, and occasionally violent, encounters with local police or federal law enforcement agencies. In those diverse encounters each side has endeavored to exert influence over the other. Religious freedom is thus always asserted or exercised in either conflict or consonance with the interests of local, state, or national polities.

The First Amendment

The focal point for considering relations between religious groups and law enforcement is the first amendment to the U. S. Constitution, which stipulates that "Congress shall make no law respecting an establishment of religion, or prohibiting the free exercise thereof." Only in 1940, however, in *Cantwell v. Connecticut*, did the Supreme Court begin to apply the religion clauses of the first amendment to the states, in accordance with the fourteenth amendment. Both the establishment clause and the free exercise clause need to be understood against the backgrounds of official state churches in Europe and the colonial establishments of various Protestant denominations. Further, despite the absence of an established national church, the institutional influence of Protestantism has remained so strong that as late as 1931 in *United States v. Macintosh*, the Supreme Court could still proclaim that "we are a Christian people." That continuing heritage of Protestantism has both explicitly and implicitly shaped how legislatures, courts, and law enforcement agencies understand religion and what they deem to be acceptable forms of religious belief and practice.

Broad governmental interests in maintaining public order, health, and safety, in exercising prerogatives such as taxation, and in providing for the health and education of the citizenry have often been used to challenge specific religious practices or beliefs and have in turn been challenged by them. The historical record of U.S. support for the religious freedom of its citizens is marked by uneven and contentious interpretations and applications of the first amendment, conflict between the law and various religious groups, particularly those towards the margins of the established Protestant denominations, concerted efforts by some religious groups to exercise their religious freedom to influence the law in favor of their own interests, and unsteady compromises between governmental and religious interests. The following examples illustrate the complex dynamics of the relations between religious groups and the law.

The Nineteenth Century

From its origins in the mid-nineteenth century, the new Church of Jesus Christ of Latter-day Saints provoked strong hostility, including violent mob action. Introduced in the early 1840s by the Mormon prophet Joseph Smith, modeled after the practices of the patriarchs in the Hebrew Bible, and made public by Smith's successor Brigham Young in 1852, the Mormon practice of "plural marriage" only exacerbated the anti-Mormonism that had driven the Latter-day Saints across the country from New York to the Great Salt Lake, and inspired the murder of Smith himself in 1844. In 1857, President Buchanan authorized a military expedition designed in part to wipe out the practice of polygamy. At the same time,

SELECTIONS FROM *CHURCH OF THE LUKUMI BABALU AYE V. CITY OF HIALEAH* (91–948), 508 U.S. 520 (1993)

The principle that government may not enact laws that suppress religious belief or practice is so well understood that few violations are recorded in our opinions. Cf. *McDaniel* v. *Paty*, 435 U.S. 618 (1978); *Fowler* v. *Rhode Island*, 345 U.S. 67 (1953). Concerned that this fundamental nonpersecution principle of the First Amendment was implicated here, however, we granted certiorari. 503 U. S. (1992).

Our review confirms that the laws in question were enacted by officials who did not understand, failed to perceive, or chose to ignore the fact that their official actions violated the Nation's essential commitment to religious freedom. The challenged laws had an impermissible object; and in all events the principle of general applicability was violated because the secular ends asserted in defense of the laws were pursued only with respect to conduct motivated by religious beliefs. We invalidate the challenged enactments and reverse the judgment of the Court of Appeals.

The record in this case compels the conclusion that suppression of the central element of the Santeria worship service was the object of the ordinances. First, though use of the words "sacrifice" and "ritual" does not compel a finding of improper targeting of the Santeria religion, the choice of these words is support for our conclusion. There are further respects in which the text of the city council's enactments discloses the improper attempt to target Santeria. Resolution 87-66, adopted June 9, 1987, recited that "residents and citizens of the City of Hialeah have expressed their concern that certain religions may propose to engage in practices which are inconsistent with public morals, peace or safety," and "reiterate[d]" the city's commitment to prohibit "any and all [such] acts of any and all religious groups." No one suggests, and on this record it cannot be maintained, that city officials had in mind a religion other than Santeria.

In sum, the neutrality inquiry leads to one conclusion: The ordinances had as their object the suppression of religion. The pattern we have recited discloses animosity to Santeria adherents and their religious practices; the ordinances by their own terms target this religious exercise; the texts of the ordinances were gerrymandered with care to proscribe religious killings of animals but to exclude almost all secular killings; and the ordinances suppress much more religious conduct than is necessary in order to achieve the legitimate ends asserted in their defense. These ordinances are not neutral, and the court below committed clear error in failing to reach this conclusion.

We conclude, in sum, that each of Hialeah's ordinances pursues the city's governmental interests only against conduct motivated by religious belief. The ordinances "ha[ve] every appearance of a prohibition that society is prepared to impose upon [Santeria worshippers] but not upon itself." *The Florida Star* v. *B. J. F.,* 491 U.S. 524, 542 (1989) (Scalia, J., concurring in part and concurring in judgment). This precise evil is what the requirement of general applicability is designed to prevent.

---

legislative actions culminated in the Supreme Court's 1879 decision that "bigamy" was unconstitutional. In its decision the court distinguished between religious beliefs and religious practices and claimed the right to regulate only the latter. In his 1890 manifesto Wilford Woodruff, then president of the church, declared his intention to abide by the laws of the nation and his pronouncement was accepted as authoritative by the general conference of the church. In 1896 Utah achieved statehood. The conflict over Mormon polygamy resulted in the sacrifice of some religious freedom in order to obtain political self-determination and more peaceful social relations.

The nineteenth century also featured several religiously motivated reform movements in which individuals exercised their religious freedom in attempts to shape behavior throughout the nation. Religious figures were prominent on both sides of the great national debate about slavery. They were also animating forces in the temperance movement, which ultimately bore short-lived fruit with the passage of the eighteenth amendment in 1919, which established Prohibition, only to be repealed by the twenty-first amendment in 1933.

The Twentieth Century

Two incidents involving marginal religious groups stand out in the years leading up to World War II. Acting on their religion's understanding of the prohibition in Exodus 20:3–5 against the worship of graven images, school children who were Jehovah's Witnesses refused to salute the flag, as was required by law in at least thirty states. In multiple legal cases in the early 1940s, the Witnesses' claim to be exercising their religious freedom was rejected and many of their children were expelled from school. The Witnesses' steadfastness provoked what one observer has called the greatest outbreak of religious intolerance in twentieth-century America. Only with the 1943 Supreme Court decision in *West Virginia State Board of Education v. Barnette* was the Witnesses' right not to salute the flag acknowledged.

In 1940 the government began prosecution of Edna Ballard, leader of the "I Am" movement started by her husband Guy, for mail fraud. In a striking departure from the principle of immunity for religious beliefs articulated in the Supreme Court decision in 1879 against polygamy, Ballard was tried specifically because her religious beliefs were asserted to be untrue, and therefore her dissemination of religious materials through the mail constituted fraud. Ballard's conviction on seven counts at the original trial was a crippling blow against the "I Am" movement and served as an ominous threat to other newly formed religious groups. Only in 1954 was the Post Office's fraud order revoked, and by then Ballard's movement could not recover its former vigor.

Contemporary "Cult" Controversies

Similar skirmishes between new religious movements and the law have marked the period since 1970. During that time general suspicions of new groups were successfully exacerbated by a loose coalition of "anticult" moral entrepreneurs and groups. These activists frequently found willing collaborators in the media and in state and national legislatures. In the 1970s several attempts to outlaw marginal religions quickly foundered on lawmakers' inability to distinguish legitimate from illegitimate forms of religion with any degree of persuasiveness. Anticult forces, however, found a much more successful issue in the ways in which newly formed religious groups sought and maintained converts. In its crudest form the anticult position portrayed conversion as the result of "mind control" or "brainwashing"; that argument spawned a coterie of self-identified specialists who styled themselves "deprogrammers." Anxious family members often hired deprogrammers to "rescue" their children from groups of which they did not approve. Very few newly formed religious groups were not touched by the brainwashing/deprogramming controversy; major cases occurred in the Unification Church of Sun Myung Moon, the International Society for Krishna Consciousness, and the Church Universal and Triumphant, among many others. Over time, anticult activists came to adopt a more psychological model that favored "exit counseling" as a means of extricating members from unacceptable religious groups. Anticult efforts were severely damaged, however, by the 1995 a state of Washington district court decision in *Scott v. Ross* that held both Rick Ross and the Cult Awareness Network (CAN) legally culpable in the involuntary deprogramming of a member of a Pentecostal sect. The judgment was upheld on appeal in 1998. Though severely weakened by the *Scott* decision, the anticult coalition continues to advance its argument that religious freedom is denied by "cults," while members of new religions and their partisans assert that anticult activists intend to curtail their religious freedom.

In addition to their recruitment practices, new religious movements also encountered legal inquiries into their child-rearing practices (e.g., the Family/ Children of God, the Branch Davidians), tax-exempt status (the Unification Church, the Church Universal and Triumphant), and forms of healing (Christian Science), among other issues. Many groups became entangled in expensive and long-running legal disputes that threatened their organizational stability.

The cult controversies of the later twentieth century formed the backdrop for the notorious confrontation between agents of the Bureau of Alcohol, Tobacco, and Firearms (BATF) and the Federal Bureau of Investigation (FBI) and members of the Branch Davidian Adventist sect, outside Waco, Texas, in 1993.

Convinced that the Davidians possessed illegal weapons, the BATF executed a thoroughly botched attempt to serve a search and arrest warrant on 28 February 1993. When the Davidians took up arms to defend themselves against what they saw as an attack on their home and church, four BATF agents and six Davidians died in the ensuing conflict. The FBI took control over the scene the next day and conducted negotiations throughout a fifty-one-day siege. The siege ended in a conflagration that claimed the lives of seventy-four Branch Davidians. "Waco" quickly became "proof" for a variety of arguments about religious freedom; anticult activists renewed their charge that cults deprive individuals of their freedom while members of many religious groups sounded alarms about an armed assault against a religious community, no matter what its legal infractions.

Other Contemporary Issues

Although issues related to newly formed religious groups sometimes dominated discussions about religious freedom in the later twentieth century, other themes were prominent as well. Christians who accepted the six-day account of creation in the book of Genesis as historical fact made multiple efforts to legislate the teaching of creationism along with evolution in the public schools. Several cases, including *Lynch v. Donnelly* (1984) in Pawtucket, Rhode Island, addressed the sponsoring of nativity scenes with public funds on public property. In those cases members of a Christian majority often claimed that an antireligious minority was denying their religious freedoms. Also, in 1993, in *Church of the Lukumi Babalu Aye, Inc. v. City of Hialeah*, the Supreme Court declared the city's attempts to legislate against animal sacrifice unconstitutional, thus securing the rights of practitioners of Santeria to conduct central religious rituals.

An array of court decisions in 2002 demonstrated again the complications in applying broad constitutional principles to specific cases. For example, in a decision widely lambasted throughout the country, the Ninth Circuit Court of Appeals declared that the 1954 addition of the phrase "under God" to the Pledge of Allegiance represented an unconstitutional official endorsement of monotheism (*Newdow v. U.S. Congress*, 2002). In Pennsylvania, the state house of representatives voted to reject a proposal to exempt for religious reasons an Amish sect from having to affix the required orange triangles to the rear of their slow-moving buggies (*Commonwealth of Pennsylvania*

v. Jonas Miller, et al., 2002). In Florida, the Department of Highway Safety and Motor Vehicles revoked the license of a Muslim woman who refused to lift her veil so that her face would show on her license (*Sultaana Lakiana Myke Freeman v. State of Florida*, 2002). There is no doubt that cases that feature the conflict between religious visions of the ideal society and similar visions enshrined in law will continue to occupy the nation's courts, particularly as the United States continues to become more religiously diverse.

Outlook

Religious freedom for all U.S. citizens remains more an ideal than a reality. The frequent clashes of legitimate interests of both religious groups and law-making and law-enforcing bodies limit the free exercise of both religion and the prerogatives of the state. In some instances, such as the Church of Jesus Christ of Latter-Day Saints or the Family/Children of God, sustained legal pressures have led religious groups to adapt their beliefs or practices in order to lessen tensions with society. In other instances, such as Unification Church leader Sun Myung Moon's conviction for tax evasion, religious groups have been able to recover from temporary legal setbacks. In still other cases, such as that of the Amish, the extent of religious freedom enjoyed by a group is subject to repeated challenges and adjustments. Since both religious groups and the law are dynamic entities, the nature and limits of religious freedom for any individual or group are continually open to renegotiation. In relation to the law and law enforcement, religious freedom is not a static possession but rather something that can be asserted and rejected, claimed and acknowledged, curtailed or enlarged—all in a series of discrete interactions in specific contexts that, while cognizant of the past, remake the contours of religious freedom each time anew.

Eugene V. Gallagher

See also Brainwashing; Creationism; Fourteenth Amendment; Jehovah's Witnesses: United States; Mormons; Pledge of Allegiance; Religious Display on Public Property; Unification Church

Further Reading

Arrington, L. J., & Bitton, D. (1992). *The Mormon experience: A history of the Latter-Day Saints*. Urbana: University of Illinois Press.

Choper, J. H. (1995). *Securing religious liberty: Principles for judicial interpretation of the religion clauses.* Chicago: University of Chicago Press.

Hall, J., Schuyler, P. D., & Trinh, S. (2000). *Apocalypse observed: Religious movements and violence in North America, Europe, and Japan.* New York: Routledge.

Levy, L. W. (1994). *The establishment clause: Religion and the first amendment.* Chapel Hill: University of North Carolina Press.

Noonan, J. T., Jr. (1998). *The lustre of our country: The American experience of religious freedom.* Berkeley: University of California Press.

Penton, M. J. (1997). *Apocalypse delayed: The story of Jehovah's Witnesses.* Toronto, Ontario, Canada: University of Toronto Press.

Richardson, J. T., & Bromley, D. (Eds.). (1984). *The brainwashing/deprogramming controversy: Sociological, psychological, legal, and historical perspectives.* New York: Edwin Mellen Press.

Robbins, T., Shepherd, W. C., & McBride, J. (1985). *Cults, culture, and the law: Perspectives on new religious movements.* Chico, CA: Scholars Press.

Shepherd, W. C. (1985). *To secure the blessings of liberty: American constitutional law and the new religious movements.* Chico, CA: Scholars Press.

Smith, S. D. (1995). *Foreordained failure: The quest for a constitutional principle of religious freedom.* New York: Oxford University Press.

Sullivan, W. F.(1994). *Paying the words extra: Religious discourse in the Supreme Court of the United States.* Cambridge, MA: Harvard University Press.

Swanson, W. R. (1990). *The Christ child goes to court.* Philadelphia: Temple University Press.

Tabor, J. D., & Gallagher, E. V. (1995). *Why Waco? Cults and the battle for religious freedom in America.* Berkeley: University of California Press.

Wessinger, C. (2000). *How the millennium comes violently: From Jonestown to Heaven's Gate.* New York: Seven Bridges Press.

Court Cases

Cantwell v. Connecticut, 310 U.S. 296 (1940).

Church of the Lukumi Babalu Aye, Inc. v. City of Hialeah, 113 S. Ct. 2217 (1993).

Commonwealth of Pennsylvania v. Jonas Miller, et al., 0624-2002 (2002).

Lynch v. Donnelly, 465 U.S. 668 (1984).

Newdow v. U.S. Congress, 00-16423 (2002).

Scott v. Ross, C94-0079C (1995).

Sultaana Lakiana Myke Freeman v. State of Florida, 48-2002-CA-002828-0 (2002).

United States v. Macintosh, 283 U.S. 605 (1931).

West Virginia State Board of Education v. Barnette, 319 U.S. 624 (1943).

Leiden

During the period 1572 to 1621, a controversy over religious freedom embroiled the city of Leiden, the second largest in the early modern Dutch Republic (c. 1580–1795), the forerunner of the modern-day Kingdom of the Netherlands (1815–). This conflict pitted the city's ruling magistrates (town council) against the leaders of its only officially recognized church, the Reformed (or Calvinist) Church. Since 1572, when Leiden, along with most of the other cities of the province of Holland, successfully rebelled against the rule of Catholic Spain, the magistrates officially declared the Reformed Church the only congregation allowed to worship publicly within the city, and they also outlawed public worship by Roman Catholics, Lutherans, and Mennonites. Similar laws were passed throughout the other towns of Holland, the richest and largest province of the Dutch Republic.

Overview

The consistory (a governing council of preachers and elders) of the Leiden Reformed Church insisted that it be completely autonomous and self-governing and not subject in any way to the authority of the magistracy, even though it depended on the city government to maintain church buildings, pay preachers' salaries, and suppress rival denominations. The magistrates, however, expected that since they had given the Reformed Church exclusive public recognition, in effect making it the city's official church, they would have a say in the Reformed congregation's governance and internal affairs. Mounting tensions broke out into open conflict in 1579, when a radical Calvinist faction in the church leadership insisted that the consistory had the absolute right to select its elders without consulting the magistracy; this faction refused to accept magisterial candidates for elder and, insisting that the freedom of the church had been compromised, schismatically broke away from the rest of the congregation. A year and a half of complicated negotiations, which involved most of the major political leaders of the Republic, was necessary before the schism was healed and the two factions in the church were reconciled. The magistracy and the consistory agreed to a settlement called the Arbitral Accord, which gave the right to nominate elders to the consistory, but granted the magistracy final right of approval. This compromise left bitter feelings on both sides. The Calvinist radicals were especially dissatisfied with the outcome, suspecting that the magistrates were not totally dedicated to the cause of church reform. In particular, they objected to what they saw as magisterial laxity in enforcing laws against Catholics, Lutherans, and Mennonites, all of whom had semisecret congregations within the city. The magistracy maintained that it would prohibit public worship by these groups, but that it refused to impinge on any individual's freedom of conscience. The result was an informal and unofficial toleration of different religious groups within the city, who were left alone as long as they confined their activities to the private sphere. This is turn alarmed the Calvinists, who believed that their church represented the true Christian religion; in particular, they feared that such toleration might lead to the eventual return of the city to Roman Catholicism. Thus the Calvinists wished to preserve the freedom of their own church while denying religious liberty to what they regarded as false and potentially dangerous sects.

Renewed Conflict

These tensions simmered over the next two decades, until a second generation of conflict over religious freedom broke out in the city in the 1600s and 1610s that again resulted in schism in the Reformed Church. The specific point of controversy was a theological conflict between two Leiden University professors, Jacobus Arminius (1560–1609) and Franciscus Gomarus (1563–1641) about the nature of God's grace and salvation. The controversy spread to and divided Reformed congregations throughout the country. The conflict precipitated a national power struggle between Johan van Oldenbarnevelt (1547–1619), the leader of the States (or parliament) of Holland, and Count Maurice of Nassau (1567–1625), the Stadholder (a partial sovereign) of Holland. The supporters of Arminius, or Arminians, sided with Oldenbarnevelt's position that the States, and the cities they represented (like Leiden), were sovereign and not subject to higher authority. Their opponents, the Gomarists, (orthodox Calvinists), supported Maurice's efforts to increase the powers of the Stadholder at the States'

expense. In addition, the Arminians insisted that the Reformed Church be subordinated to magisterial authority, a position naturally supported by the Leiden magistracy. Leiden's Gomarists (who outnumbered the city's Arminians ten to one) saw this as a reprise of the controversies of 1579 to 1580, with the magistracy once again trying to encroach on church liberty. The specific issue of church governance emerged again. In 1614, the magistrates insisted on equal representation of Arminians and Gomarists on the Reformed consistory. For the Gomarists, with their large majority, such an arrangement became increasingly untenable, and by early 1618, they refused to serve with Arminian preachers and elders, effectively splitting the Leiden Reformed Church once again. This time the schism was ended not by negotiation but by outside political intervention. By the autumn of 1618, Maurice of Nassau had secured enough national support to force out the Arminian factions in the town councils of the major cities of the Dutch Republic and replace them with his Gomarist partisans, which he did in Leiden in October 1618. The now Gomarist government of Leiden supported the suppression of Arminians in the city, and the Leiden Reformed congregation was completely in the hands of the Gomarist majority. The government scrapped the Arbitral Accord in 1621 and briefly stepped up legal persecution of Roman Catholics in the city. The era of Leiden's conflicts over religious freedom came to an end.

The controversies about church liberty and religious freedom that troubled Leiden in the decades between 1572 and 1621 afflicted other cities in the Dutch Republic as well, though only in Leiden would they lead to two successive schisms in the Reformed congregation. These conflicts were symptomatic of the larger problem the Dutch Reformed Church had in defining its place and role in the Dutch Republic, a state that regarded itself as Reformed Protestant but, in Calvinist eyes, did not do enough to bring about further reformation in church and society. This ambiguity about the religious identity of the Republic would be a recurring theme in its political and cultural history up to its demise in 1795.

Christine Kooi

Further Reading

Hibben, C. C. (1983). *Gouda in revolt: Particularism and pacifism in the revolt of the Netherlands 1572–1588.* Utrecht, Netherlands: HES.

Hsia, R. P., & Van Nierop, H. (Eds.). (2002). *Calvinism and religious toleration in the Dutch golden age.* Cambridge, UK: Cambridge University Press.

Israel, J. I. (1995). *The Dutch republic: Its rise, greatness and fall, 1477–1806.* Oxford, UK: Clarendon Press.

Kaplan, B. J. (1995). *Calvinists and libertines: Confession and community in Utrecht, 1578–1620.* Oxford, UK: Clarendon Press.

Kooi, C. (2000). *Liberty and religion: Church and state in Leiden's Reformation, 1572–1620.* Leiden, Netherlands: Brill.

Parker, C. H. (1998). *The reformation of community: Social welfare and Calvinist charity in Holland, 1572–1620.* Cambridge, UK: Cambridge University Press.

Parker, G. (1977). *The Dutch revolt.* Ithaca, NY: Cornell University Press.

Pollmann, J. (1999). *Religious choice in the Dutch Republic: The reformation of Arnoldus Buchelius.* Manchester, UK: Manchester University Press.

Schama, S. (1987). *The embarrassment of riches: An interpretation of Dutch culture in the golden age.* New York: Knopf.

Van Deursen, A. T. (1991). *Plain lives in a golden age: Popular culture, religion and society in seventeenth-century Holland.* Cambridge, UK: Cambridge University Press.

Letter on Toleration

John Locke's (1632–1704) *Letter on Toleration* was written in 1685, first published in Latin anonymously in 1689, and translated into English in the same year by William Popple. Although a rather loose translation, Popple's edition is probably the most cited. Locke wrote the *Letter* while in self-imposed exile in the Netherlands, in response to the religious persecutions that were endemic to seventeenth-century Europe.

In the *Letter* Locke advocated a (limited) religious toleration. A central strand of his argument is that as a government cannot compel conscientious religious belief, it is irrational for it to try to do so. Genuine religious conviction, he argued, cannot be compelled through threats or force, the instruments of political power. The most these can produce is dissimulation and an outward observance of religious ritual: to attempt to coerce religious belief is, therefore, to attempt the impossible. This argument about the irrationality of religious persecution, however, is also embedded in broader argument about the proper role of government. This is explained more fully in Locke's *Two Treatises on Government* (1689). The crucial contention is that the role of legitimate political authority is limited to the civil interest of its subjects, to the protection of their lives and property, and does not extend to trying to save their souls. The business of government is to preserve civil order, and only for that purpose is coercion justified. Furthermore, Locke argued, individuals would rightly not risk eternal damnation, and would resist the civil power, if it tried to coerce them into practicing a religion they did not believe.

Locke's case for religious toleration is, however, a limited one. While extending toleration to some non-Christians, two groups are explicitly denied toleration. The first is atheists, on the grounds that since they do not believe in God their word cannot be trusted. The second is Catholics, because they are regarded by Locke as owing their obedience to another temporal authority, the pope. Although undeniably significantly restricting the scope of religious toleration, both exclusions are justified in terms of Locke's arguments because those excluded represent a threat to political authority and civil order.

Locke's arguments did not go unopposed. In particular, his tenacious contemporary critic Jonas Proast was effective enough in arguing that Locke grossly

British philosopher John Locke (1632–1704). COURTESY OF WWW.BRYNMAWR.EDU/ACADS/PSYCH/RWOZNIAK/LOCKE180.GIF.

underestimated the extent to which coercion could encourage true belief that Locke felt compelled to write three further *Letter on Toleration* essays (1690; 1692; the last incomplete on Locke's death in 1704). Despite this criticism, and though much in his position was not new, Locke presented the arguments for religious toleration with such power that the *Letter* played a crucial role in putting the case for religious persecution on the defensive.

John Horton

Further Reading

Horton, J., & Mendus, S. (Eds.). (1991). *John Locke "A Letter Concerning Toleration" in focus.* London: Routledge.

Locke, J. (1823). *Works* (Vols. 1–10). London: Tegg.

Proast, J. (1984). *Letters concerning toleration* (P. A. Schouls, Ed.). New York: Garland.

Vernon, R. (1997). *The career of toleration: John Locke, Jonas Proast, and after.* Montreal, Quebec, Canada: McGill–Queen's University Press.

Maryland: Colonial to Early Republic

Established through the efforts of George Calvert, an English Catholic, the colony of Maryland became the site of the very first experiment in religious toleration in all of British North America. Although increasing religious tensions would eventually end toleration and lead to an established church, Calvert's unique contribution to the development of religious liberty proved to be prescient.

English Anti-Catholicism and the Founding of Maryland

Queen Elizabeth I's policy of the via media (middle way) was an attempt to pacify competing Protestant and Catholic factions and establish a national church in England. It also created two dissenting groups: the strongly Calvinistic Puritans who demanded a more thorough purging of Catholic elements, and the recusants who refused to surrender their traditional Catholicism. To force the religious conformity of the latter, Elizabeth instituted a series of "penal laws" that threatened fines, exile, or even execution for the practice of Catholicism. These laws were extended during the reign of her successor James I in the aftermath of the "Gunpowder Plot" of November 1605, when explosives were discovered beneath the Parliament building and a captured suspect, Guy Fawkes (1570–1606), implicated fellow recusants.

As a privy councillor and secretary of state, George Calvert (1580?–1632), had resigned his political offices, been raised to peerage as the first Lord of Baltimore Manor in Ireland, and converted to Roman Catholicism in the months just prior to James's death in 1625, although the exact chronology of these events is difficult to determine. A vigorous proponent of American colonization, Calvert had already financed a colony in Newfoundland named Avalon (chartered 1623). When he finally migrated to Avalon in 1627, some forty English Catholics accompanied him, undoubtedly to escape the penal laws. A harsh winter there led Calvert to turn his attention further south, but he was refused resettlement in Virginia because of his religion. Returning to England, he sought and obtained a royal grant for lands north of the Potomac River for the colony of Maryland, named after the king's Catholic wife Henrietta Maria.

The charter to establish Maryland as a "propriatary" colony received the great seal on 30 June 1632, but Calvert had died a few weeks earlier and the office of proprietor thus passed to his son Cecilius (1605–1675), the second Lord Baltimore. Using his family's wealth, Cecilius recruited colonists and outfitted two small ships, the *Ark* and the *Dove*, which set sail from London on 22 November 1633. The departing colonists, most of them laborers and indentured servants, took the required oaths of allegiance, but the vessels then stopped briefly at the Isle of Wight where additional passengers boarded—probably Catholics more scrupulous about taking the oaths, which contained anti-Catholic provisions. Among the 150 emigrants were between seventeen and twenty Catholic "gentlemen adventurers" who represented the economic elite of the enterprise, including two priests and a lay member of the Society of Jesus (Jesuits).

Although Protestant colonists were absolutely essential in order to guarantee the financial success

SELECTIONS FROM THE ACT CONCERNING RELIGION (1649)

Forasmuch as in a well governed and Christian Commonwealth matters concerning Religion and the honor of God ought in the first place to be taken into serious consideration and endeavoured to be settled, be it therefore ordered and enacted by the Right Honourable Cecilius Lord Baron of Baltemore absolute Lord and Proprietary of this Province with the advise and consent of this Generall Assembly:

And be it also further enacted by the same authority advise and assent that whatsoever person or persons shall from henceforth uppon any occasion of offence or otherwise in a reproachful manner or Way declare call or denominate any person or persons whatsoever inhabiting, residing, traffiqueing, trading or comerceing within this Province or within any the ports, harbors, creeks or havens to the same belonging an heritick, scismatick, idolator, puritan, independant, Prespiterian popish prest, Jesuite, Jesuited papist, Lutheran, Calvenist, Anabaptist, Brownist, Antinomian, Barrowist, Roundhead, Separatist, or any other name or terme in a reproachfull manner relating to matter of religion shall for every such offence forfeit and loose the somme of tenne shillings sterling or the value thereof to bee levyed on the goods and chattells of every such offender and offenders, the one half thereof to be forfeited and paid unto the person and persons of whom such reproachfull words are or shalbe spoken or uttered, and the other half thereof to the Lord Proprietary and his heires Lords and Proprietaries of this Province. But if such person or persons who shall at any time utter or speake any such reproachfull words or language shall not have goods or chattells sufficient and overt within this Province to be taken to satisfie the penalty aforesaid or that the same bee not otherwise speedily satisfyed, that then the person or persons so offending shall be publically whipped, and shall suffer imprisonment without bail or maineprise [bail] untill he, she or they respectively shall satisfy the party so offended or greived by such reproachfull language by asking him or her respectively forgivenes publically for such his offence before the Magistrate of chief officer or officers of the town or place where such offence shal be given.

And whereas the enforcing of the conscience in matters of religion hath frequently fallen out to be of dangerous consequence in those commonwealthes where it hath been practised, and for the more quiet and peaceable governement of this Province, and the better to preserve mutual love and amity among the inhabitants thereof, be it therefore also by the Lord Proprietary with the advise and consent of this Assembly ordered and enacted (except as in this present Act is before declared and set forth) that no person or persons whatsoever within this Province, or the islands, ports, harbors, creekes, or havens thereunto belonging professing to believe in Jesus Christ, shall from henceforth be any waies troubled, molested or discountenanced for or in respect of his or her religion nor in the free exercise thereof within this Province or the islands thereunto belonging nor any way compelled to the belief or exercise of any other religion against his or her consent, so as they be not unfaithfull to the Lord Proprietary, or molest or conspire against the civil governement established or to be established in this Province under him or his heires. And that all and every person and persons that shall presume contrary to this Act and the true intent and meaning thereof directly or indirectly either in person or estate willfully to wrong disturbe trouble or molest any person whatsoever within this Province professing to beleive in Jesus Christ for or in respect of his or her religion or the free exercise thereof within this Province other than is provided for in this Act that such person or persons so offending, shall be compelled to pay treble damages to the party so wronged or molested, and for every such offence shall also forfeit 20s sterling in money or the value thereof, half thereof for the use of the Lord Proprietary, and his heires Lords and Proprietaries of this Province, and the other half for the use of the party so wronged or molested as

aforesaid, or if the partie so offending as aforesaid shall refuse or be unable to recompense the party so wronged, or to satisfy such fine or forfeiture, then such offender shall be severely punished by public whipping and imprisonment during the pleasure of the Lord Proprietary, or his Lieutenant or chief Governor of this Province for the time being without baile or maineprise.

Source: Religious Freedom Homepage. Retrieved 3 September 2002, from http:// religiousfreedom.lib.virginia.edu/sacred/md

of the colony, there can be little doubt that the Calverts intended Maryland to be a haven for persecuted Catholics as well. Cecilius's father-in-law, Thomas Arundel, had proposed such a sanctuary during the reign of James I, and George Calvert's experience in Avalon underscores his participation in a similar scheme. Moreover, George Calvert's successful negotiations to establish Maryland as a proprietary colony, based specifically on the extensive privileges of the medieval Palatinate of Durham, meant that Maryland was exempt not only from parliamentary oversight but from the penal laws as well. Toleration of religious diversity was thus a practical concern, necessary for the success of the colony. Through his brother and resident governor, Leonard Calvert, Cecilius warned the first colonists that arguments on religion would not be permitted, and Catholics were instructed to worship in private and not to cause scandal to the Protestant majority. Provisory and driven in part by political and financial considerations, Calvert's instructions were nonetheless intended to lay a foundation for a cooperative enterprise rather than a confessional colony.

The charter gave the proprietor "free, full, and absolute power . . . to ordaine, make, and enact . . . any Laws," but also called for the creation of an assembly of freemen to give "advi[c]e assent and approbation" to the proposals of the proprietor (Hall 1910, 104). The initial legislation on religious tolerance in the colony, however, exemplified the implicit tensions between an absent Proprietor (Cecilius never set foot in the colony) and the provincial assembly.

Religious Toleration and Diversity in Colonial Maryland

The colonists disembarked 25 March 1634 at St. Clement's Island, where they held separate Catholic and Protestant worship services. A few days later they moved into an abandoned Indian village on the mainland, which they renamed St. Mary's City. Leonard Calvert summoned the freemen to meet there in 1635, but no records remain of this first Assembly. Apparently, however, the Assembly began to initiate its own laws, leading the Proprietor to respond with a slate of legislative proposals to which he demanded assent. These proposals demanded an oath of allegiance from each colonist "upon the faith of a Christian" and made idolatry and blasphemy capital offenses. In 1638 and 1639, the Assembly met and rejected Calvert's proposals, passing instead a simpler ordinance that made no mention of a Christian oath but instead guaranteed all colonists "their rights and liberties" as prescribed in the Magna Carta. Further, the Assembly asserted in one ungrammatical passage that "Holy Church*es* shall have all *her* rights and liberties" (Brown 1883–present, 1:40, 71, 83; emphasis added). The omissions and ambiguities in the ordinance may have indicated an attempt by the Assembly to guarantee civil rights to all colonists regardless of their religion, or they may have been an attempt to institute traditional immunities for the clergy (Calvert had already clashed with the Jesuits over land distribution), but the lack of supplemental documentation leaves all interpretations tentative and conjectural.

The Protestant government of Virginia immediately protested the founding of Calvert's colony. Minor skirmishes repeatedly occurred, especially over the jurisdiction of Kent Island, where a small colony of Virginians lived. In 1645, with civil war raging in England between Puritan parliamentarians and the monarchy, an anti-royalist named Richard Ingle led the Kent Islanders in an attack on St. Mary's City in a ship named the *Reformation*. Leonard Calvert was forced to flee to Virginia to raise an army while Puritan sympathizers seized control of the government in Maryland. Ingle had the Jesuits and other Catholic leaders taken in chains to England where they could be tried under the penal laws.

As a part of the settlement that allowed the Calverts to regain control of the colony in 1648, Cecilius appointed a Protestant, William Stone, to be the new governor, but obtained from him an oath that he would not discriminate against colonists on the basis of their religion. Calvert also sent the Assembly a bill promoting religious tolerance; the Assembly's amended Act Concerning Religion (1649) officially replaced the informal policies under which Maryland had operated since its founding. By reserving civil liberties to those who professed belief in the Trinity and the deity of Christ, the Act of 1649 was certainly restrictive by contemporary standards, but these provisions represented an attempt to permit the toleration of both Catholics and Protestants on the broadest possible doctrinal basis. Still, the unintentional anti-Semitism in the act led in 1658 to the arrest and conviction of a Jewish physician and businessman, Jacob Lumbrozo, for blasphemy. Found guilty of this capital offense, he was released during a general amnesty after a few days and lived in Maryland without further molestation until his death in 1666.

Religious toleration grew more restrictive as the Puritan influence grew in the colony. By the time of Leonard Calvert's death (1647), Protestants outnumbered Catholics three to one, the result of the arrival of some 300 nonconformists from Virginia who had been invited by Governor Stone to settle along the Severn River. Following the triumph of parliamentarian forces and the execution of Charles I in England, Puritan sympathizers in Maryland established a surrogate government, and in the Battle of the Severn (25 March 1655) defeated a militia led by Stone and overturned the proprietary regime. A Puritan Assembly then repealed the Act of 1649 and in further legislation deprived Catholics of their civil and religious rights. With the surprising support of the "Lord Protector" Oliver Cromwell, Calvert was able after a few years to reassert control. The restoration of the monarchy in 1660 further solidified the proprietary government and the resumption of its policy of toleration.

The Act of 1649, however, had already made Maryland a sanctuary for religious dissent. Itinerant ministers from the Society of Friends (Quakers) appeared in the colony in the mid-1650s and enjoyed remarkable success, even among the Puritans. The Quaker refusal to swear oaths or to bear arms caused

some problems for both the Puritan and proprietary regimes, but in 1668 they were permitted to "affirm" rather than to "swear" in order to hold governmental offices. The 1650s also marked the advent of Presbyterianism into the colony, the result of Scotch-Irish immigration encouraged by Calvert. Similarly, Swedish immigrants brought Lutheranism into the colony, but the Lutheran population remained exceedingly small until Germans began to migrate into western Maryland in the 1740s.

The Protestant Revolution

Despite its professed toleration for religious diversity, the proprietary regime came under fire from Anglicans in the colony who contended that the Calverts deliberately sought to depress Anglican growth. In 1676, the Rev. John Yeo complained to British authorities that religion was in a "deplorable estate" in the colony and in need of an established ministry. Cecilius's son Charles (1637–1715), now the third Lord Baltimore, argued that "Presbiterians, Independents, Anabaptists, and Quakers" as well as Anglicans and Catholics voluntarily supported their own clergy and would be opposed to legislation "which shall compel them to maintain Ministers of a contrary persuasion to themselves" (Brown 1883–present, 5:130, 133). Nevertheless, the Privy Council forced Calvert to establish an Anglican ministry through compulsory taxation, but permitted him the right to present clergy to their benefices.

Anglican opposition to the proprietary regime continued to build, with anti-Catholicism providing further rationale in a region ripe for resistance. Local rebellions began in 1681, stoked by rumors of a Catholic-Indian conspiracy to murder Protestant settlers. Deputies appointed by Calvert to maintain the peace were ineffective, so in 1688 Calvert dispatched William Joseph to be resident governor. Before Joseph could arrive in Maryland, however, the Glorious Revolution overthrew the Catholic King James II and deposed his newborn male heir in favor of the Protestant William of Orange (husband of James's daughter Mary). Joseph's attempts to goad the Assembly into an expression of support for the deposed king and heir led to the formation of the Protestant Association, which seized power in a bloodless revolution in July 1689. The dual monarchy eventually gave tacit approval to the Association government and made royal appointments to key posts in the colony. With the arrival in April of 1692 of Lionel Copley (d. 1693) as the governor, Maryland became a royal colony. The Calverts remained among the principal landholders of the colony, but their proprietary prerogatives and their experiments in religious toleration had ended.

The royal government extended to Maryland the penal laws that barred Catholics from voting, bearing arms, or serving on juries. The imposition of the Test Oath excluded Quakers as well as Catholics from governmental offices. In 1692 the Royal Assembly passed an act establishing the Anglican Church, but a flaw in its language (and that of subsequent acts) prevented royal approval until 1702. William and Mary's own Toleration Act (1689) meant that Protestant dissenters could not be prevented from forming their own congregations and building churches, but the period of Anglican domination was oppressive and drew protests from Quakers and other dissenters.

In 1704 the Assembly passed the Act to Prevent the Growth of Popery, which prohibited public and private displays of the Catholic faith and subjected priests who said Mass to life imprisonment or exile. This repressive act drew a protest from Queen Anne, who objected that private religious practice could not be outlawed. The Catholic gentry responded by constructing private chapels on their estates where circuit-riding Jesuit missionaries administered the sacraments and fostered a quietist family-centered form of Catholic practice.

With his conversion to Anglicanism, Benedict Calvert, the fourth Lord Baltimore (1679–1715), regained the proprietary title in 1715 but with greatly reduced authority. He lived only two months after the restoration and was succeeded by his fifteen-year-old son Charles Calvert (1699–1751) as the fifth Lord Baltimore. The penal laws remained a threat to Catholic life under the last of the Calverts, and an oppressive double taxation was introduced in 1756 that led Charles Carroll of Annapolis, the colony's most prominent Catholic citizen, to consider emigration to French Louisiana. With the defeat of France in the French and Indian War (1763), however, fears of Catholic sedition subsided and restrictions began to ease.

From Colony to State

In the 1770s, evangelical Pietism, represented by German Pietists, Moravians, and especially by the Methodists, entered the colony and attracted a signif-

icant following. With a loss of popular support, the Anglican establishment withered and was finally dismantled with the new state constitution of 1776. Wealthy Catholics cast their lot with the patriot cause and emerged as leading proponents of religious liberty during the Revolution and early national periods. Charles Carroll of Carrollton, son of his Annapolis namesake, was the only Catholic signer of the Declaration of Independence; his cousin John Carroll became the first Catholic bishop of the United States in 1789 and was an important Catholic voice for support of religious liberty and the American religious settlement. Ironically, the new state constitution of 1776 was one of the most repressive of the early national period, levying a tax "for the support of the Christian religion" and mandating "declaration of a belief in the Christian religion" as a requirement for political office. Dedicated individuals such as Solomon Etting, a Jew, and Thomas Kennedy, a Presbyterian and convinced Jeffersonian, finally succeeded in repealing the last of these provisions in 1828. After almost 200 years, the provisional principles first articulated by the Calverts had reached their full expression.

Rodger Payne

See also English Civil War; Immigration

Further Reading

Balmer, R. H. (1986). Church-state issues in the middle colonies from colonization to the mid-eighteenth century. In J. F. Wilson (Ed.), *Church and state in America: A bibliographic guide. The colonial and early national periods* (pp. 1–42). New York: Greenwood Press.

Brewer, J. F. (Ed.). (1985). *Lectures on the history of religious toleration in Maryland.* Baltimore: Loyola College.

Brown, W. H., et al. (1883–present). *Archives of Maryland.* Baltimore: Maryland Historical Society.

Carr, L. G., & Jordan, D. W. (1974). *Maryland's revolution of government, 1689–1692.* Ithaca, NY: Cornell University Press.

Carroll, K. L. (1970). The Quaker opposition to the establishment of a state church in Maryland. *Maryland Historical Magazine, 65,* 149–170.

Ellis, J. T. (1965). *Catholics in colonial America.* Baltimore: Helicon.

Everstine, C. N. (1984). Maryland's Toleration Act: An appraisal. *Maryland Historical Magazine, 79,* 99–116.

Hall, C. C. (Ed.). (1910). *Narratives of early Maryland, 1633–1684.* New York: Charles Scribner's Sons.

Hanley, T. O. (1959). *Their rights and liberties: The beginnings of religious and political freedom in Maryland.* Westminster, MD: Newman Press.

Hanley, T. O. (1971). *The American Revolution and religion: Maryland 1770–1800.* Washington, DC: Catholic University of America Press.

Hennesey, J. (1976). Roman Catholicism: The Maryland tradition. *Thought, 51,* 282–295.

Jordan, D. W. (1982). "God's candle" within government: Quakers and politics in early Maryland. *William and Mary Quarterly,* 3rd series, *39,* 628–654.

Krugler, J. D. (1979). Lord Baltimore, Roman Catholics, and toleration: Religious policy in Maryland during the early Catholic years. *Catholic Historical Review, 65,* 49–75.

Krugler, J. D. (1984). "With promise of liberty in Religion": The Catholic Lords Baltimore and toleration in seventeenth-century Maryland, 1634–1692. *Maryland Historical Magazine, 79,* 20–43.

Rainbolt, J. C. (1975). The struggle to define "religious liberty" in Maryland, 1776–85. *Journal of Church and State, 17,* 443–58.

Mennonites *See* Conscientious Objection and Pacifism; Peace Churches

Middle East

The Arab world in the Middle East is overwhelmingly Islamic. In seventeen of the twenty-one members of the Arab League (excluding Palestine), Muslims constitute 90 percent or more of the population. In nine of these countries, along with Turkey and Iran, 98–99 percent of the inhabitants are Muslim. Only three Arab League members have Muslim majorities that are less than 80 percent (Lebanon, Oman, and the Sudan). In most cases, Islam is the official state religion and the *shari'a* (Islamic law) is formally a major source of legislation, though its implementation varies considerably. Saudi Arabia, the birthplace of Islam, actually claims the Qur'an (the holy book of Islam) as its constitution. Other countries have simply elevated the status of Islam in governance by amending legal documents and constitutions. The dominance of Islam in the Middle East means that religious freedom is determined, to a large extent, by how civil liberties, religion, and faith are understood within the context of Islam.

Like other religions, Islam is subject to multiple interpretations, struggles over meaning, and competing perspectives that influence religious tolerance and pluralism. Some countries hold strict, literal theological positions while others reflect nominal, secular understandings about religious practice and faith. A common observation among scholars of the Middle East is that there often seem to be as many versions of Islam as there are Muslims.

Within this context of interpretive differences, two factors have profoundly shaped religious freedom. First, Islamic movements have emerged to promote *shari'a* principles as a solution to economic underdevelopment, political repression, military impotence, and cultural weakness, which are believed to have been caused by un-Islamic government policies. From this perspective, Islam can rescue society since God rewards the true believers and punishes the unfaithful. In an attempt to assert the hegemony of Islam in society, some Islamic movements have fostered coercive environments that not only erode the freedom of religious minorities, but also infringe upon the rights of Muslims to freely and conscientiously practice Islam.

Governments have also affected the religious environment by trying to control interpretations of Islam. Religion and governance are inextricably linked in the Middle East, unlike in Western liberal democracies where norms of church-state separation predominate. The Prophet Muhammad was both a spiritual and a political leader for the Muslim community (*ummah*), and this model has shaped political systems throughout the region. Governments, however, only propagate and support versions of Islam that enhance their legitimacy and power; they have extended state control over public religious institutions to undermine alternative religious interpretations that might challenge their power, especially those articulated by Islamic movements. The result has been to seriously undermine the right of Muslims to freely practice and interpret Islam without state coercion. The government's reliance on Islam for legitimacy has also adversely affected the rights of religious minorities. The challenge from Islamic movements and governments in the Middle East has impacted a number of religious groups, but the most prominent are the gen-

SAUDI ARABIA AS AN ISLAMIC NATION

The centrality of Islam in Saudi Arabia is both indicated by and established by its constitution, adopted on March 1992 by Royal decree of King Fahd.

Chapter 1 General Principles

Article 1

The Kingdom of Saudi Arabia is a sovereign Arab Islamic state with Islam as its religion; God's Book and the Sunnah of His Prophet, God's prayers and peace be upon him, are its constitution, Arabic is its language and Riyadh is its capital.

Article 2

The state's public holidays are Id al-Fitr and Id al-Adha. Its calendar is the Hegira calendar.

Article 3

The state's flag shall be as follows:

(a) It shall be green.

(b) Its width shall be equal to two-thirds of it's length.

(c) The words *"There is but one God and Mohammed is His Prophet"* shall be inscribed in the center with a drawn sword under it. The statute shall define the rules pertaining to it.

Article 4

The state's emblem shall consist of two crossed swords with a palm tree in the upper space between them. The statute shall define the state's anthem and its medals.

Source: ICL-Saudi Arabia-Constitution. Retrieved 15 May 2002,
from http://www.uni-wuerzburg.de/law/sa00000_.html

---

eral Muslim community, the Shi'a, and Jews and Christians.

The Muslim Community

All regimes in the Middle East depend upon Islam, to some extent, as a basis of legitimacy, a dependence that became increasingly important in the wake of the devastating Arab defeat in the 1967 war with Israel. The humiliating defeat led to societal introspection about the causes of the loss, and various segments of society began to fervently question the legitimacy of Arab rulers. This reflection led many in the Middle East to conclude that a return to a more religious (Islamic) society and political system was necessary to rebuild and strengthen Arab communities, especially in the face of the "Israeli threat."

Governments responded by adopting Islamic rhetoric and policies in an attempt to harness burgeoning religious sentiment in society and undercut the growing support for Islamic movements. Governmental actions were increasingly framed and justified in terms of Islam, and many leaders made certain they were seen in public performing religious duties, such as prayer, alms giving, and the pilgrimage (hajj) to Mecca. Anwar Sadat (1918–1981) of Egypt, for example, called himself the "Believer-President" and was frequently shown on television praying. Other leaders, such as King Hussein (1935–1999) of Jordan and King Hassan (1929–1999) of Morocco touted their genealogical connections to the Quraysh tribe (the tribe of the Prophet Muhammad).

In addition to rhetoric and symbolic gestures, regimes have emasculated the independence of public religious institutions. Mosques, for example, have increasingly come under government control in an effort to ensure that hostile, anti-governmental interpretations of Islam do not find easy access to the public. Preachers are required to get government permission for the Friday sermon (*khutba*); scholars have to receive prior approval before giving religious lessons in the mosques; and prayers at mosques are typically led by state appointed imams (prayer leaders).

Regimes also appoint religious committees and national muftis (Islamic legal experts) to issue fatwas (religious jurisprudential opinions) that support government policy. The Saudi regime, for example, was careful to procure a fatwa from the Council of the Grand Ulama (scholars) before using force at the Ka'ba (the holiest site in Islam) to dislodge an Islamic group that had taken control on 20 November 1979. The regime also made sure to get a fatwa from Abd al-Aziz Bin Baz (1912–1999), the mufti of Saudi Arabia, to legitimate the presence of Western military forces during the Gulf War in 1991. Other examples abound, including Anwar Sadat's use of a fatwa from the Fatwa Committee and Mufti of Egypt in support of the Camp David Accords (1978), which made peace between Egypt and Israel. Government control of the personnel associated with all of these religious institutions has created pro-government religious bureaucracies.

Many other controls have been put in place as well, including the censorship of religious publications and the media, control over Islamic charities and cultural organizations, prohibitions against political parties formed along religious lines, control over the appointment of religious judges (*qadis*), and the formation of Islamic organizations to promote the government's official version of Islam.

These administrative controls have been coupled with forceful repression. Regime concerns about the growing influence of Islamic movements have led to government crackdowns. In Algeria, for example, the military-backed regime cancelled democratic elections in January 1992, after the Islamic Salvation Front Party was poised to take control of Parliament. This prompted a brutal civil war that resulted in more than 150,000 casualties. A similar anti-Islamic movement occurred in Egypt during the 1990s. Violent confrontations between security forces and

the Islamic Group (Gama'a Islamiyya) sparked broad repression under ambiguous terrorism laws that allowed the government to arrest and intern anyone who sowed discord. The more moderate Muslim Brotherhood, which condemns violence and supports elections, was caught in the crackdown and suffered a wave of arrests and massive repression from January 1995 to April 1996. Those arrested included the leaders of professional associations and parliamentary candidates. As in most other countries, the accused were tried in military courts, which provide few legal protections. Repression is often indiscriminate and governments frequently fail to distinguish between violent and nonviolent groups. Although some regimes in the Middle East have exhibited greater tolerance, the overall trend has been toward the political exclusion and repression of any Islamic voice that differs from official Islam.

Pressure for religious conformity has come from Islamic movements as well. In a number of instances, radical religious groups have used coercive tactics in an attempt to enforce their own interpretations of Islamic mores. This includes informal roving gangs of religious enforcers, which police society to ensure religious behavior. In Saudi Arabia, the Committee to Prevent Vice and Promote Virtue receives tacit government approval to monitor society for deviant or un-Islamic behavior, including dating, alcohol consumption, dance parties, or violations of Islamic dress codes, such as not wearing the *hijab* (traditional Muslim head scarf). In several instances, the members of the Committee have burst into private homes to prevent what is perceived to be vice. Although the Saudi case is the most prominent example, self-selected committees also operate in other countries, severely testing religious freedom in society.

The Shi'a

As an important sect of Islam, the religious freedom of Shi'a deserves particular attention. The Shi'a constitute 10–15 percent of the total world Muslim population and tend to be concentrated in the Gulf countries. They believe that the leader of the Muslim community should be a descendent of the Prophet Muhammad's family, through the lineage of the Prophet's cousin and son-in-law Ali (the term Shi'a means "partisans of Ali"). In contrast, the Sunni Muslim majority accepts religious leaders without a genealogical connection to the Prophet.

Although the Shi'a enjoy religious freedom in a few countries such as Lebanon and Iran (they are 89 percent of the population and Shi'ism is the official state religion in the latter country), they have encountered repression elsewhere. This is especially the case in several Gulf countries where Shi'a are either a majority or a sizable segment of society. In Bahrain, for example, where the Shi'a constitute 70 percent of the population, the ruling Khalifa regime has, until recently, limited Shi'a political participation. During the 1990s, this led to massive demonstrations and protests (including a spate of terrorist attacks) that created pressure for greater Shi'a political inclusion and a transition to democracy. Following the death of his father in 1999, Sheikh Hamad bin Isa al-Khalifa opened a dialogue with Shi'a leaders and moved toward greater political freedom.

Shi'a in other Gulf countries have been less fortunate. In Iraq, Saddam Hussein brutally repressed the Shi'a population in the south. Despite their demographic size (58–63 percent of the Iraqi population), the Shi'a have been systematically assaulted by the regime, though the no-fly zone in the southern part of Iraq enforced after the Gulf War provided some limited protection. Shi'a in Saudi Arabia have also experienced repression, though it has not been as harsh (they are only 5 percent of the population but constitute a substantial 33 percent minority in the Eastern Province). Because the official version of Saudi Islam (known in the West as Wahhabism) is strongly opposed to Shi'a theological doctrine, relations between the regime and the Shi'a have been strained. The government does allow Shi'a to have their own mosques, but it has limited public Shi'a religious ceremonies and practices. Shi'a in Saudi Arabia have also been excluded from the government bureaucracy, military, police, and national guard, and have encountered employment discrimination.

Jews and Christians

Islam builds upon the history of both Judaism and Christianity and accepts many Judeo-Christian traditions and beliefs (including the Jewish and Christian prophets). Muslims, however, believe that the earlier Jewish and Christian communities deviated from the message of God, thus requiring the series of revelations that came to the Prophet Muhammad. Because these additional revelations are considered the word of God, Mohammed is seen as the Seal of the Prophets, the recipient of the final and perfect revelation (610–632 CE). Despite many theological differences, the three monotheistic traditions share much in common and Christians and Jews are accorded special status in Islam as People of the Book.

Although this designation has provided some measure of protection for Christians and Jews in the Middle East, there are limitations. For example, under various Islamic empires of the past, Christians and Jews were allowed to practice their religions freely, organize into confessional communities, and own property, as long as they paid a special poll tax (*jaziyya*) to the Muslim authorities. Religious freedom, however, did not translate into political freedom, and Jews and Christians were not allowed to serve in the army or assume positions of direct authority over Muslims, though they often served as advisors to government officials. Under the Ottomans, this arrangement was incorporated into the organization of the empire through the "millet system," which gave civil and religious authority to local confessional community leaders. Christians and Jews were responsible for resolving internal conflicts, paying some taxes collectively, and adjudicating personal status laws, such as those pertaining to marriage, divorce, and inheritance. Some of the norms of the millet system still provide Jews and Christians with a measure of autonomy.

Despite this independence and the legal codification of religious freedom in many Middle Eastern constitutions, Jews and Christians experience considerable limitations for several reasons. First, Jewish and Christian propagation efforts are limited because the conversion of a Muslim to another religion is a serious offense in Islam (the convert is subject to a death sentence in some applications of Islamic law). Most conversions to Judaism and Christianity therefore take place in secret.

Second, the rise of radical Islamic movements has engendered a coercive environment where Jews and Christians feel constrained to openly profess and practice their faith. In Egypt during the 1980s and 1990s, for example, radical gangs affiliated with the Islamic Group physically assaulted participants at a number of Christian events, including weddings. Throughout the same period, the Islamic Group also led attacks against Coptic Christians and their property, particularly in southern Egyptian cities, such as Asyut and Minya. In Algeria in 1996, the Armed Islamic Group kidnapped and beheaded seven French Trappist monks for allegations of proselytizing. Although the vast majority of Islamic groups do not support such violence, the actions of a small section of radicals have created a hostile environment.

Third, in an effort to co-opt the language of Islam to suit regime interests, governments have shown little restraint in limiting the freedom of other religious groups. For example, the Sudanese government has attempted to enforce the *shari'a,* even in Christian and animist communities. It has also used violence against the predominantly non-Muslim south in a civil war that began in 1983 and which has led to an estimated 2 million deaths. In less dramatic repression, the Egyptian government has used ambiguous antiterrorism and incitement laws to crack down on Christian communities and leaders. Christians and Jews are even more constrained in the conservative Gulf countries, where they are almost nonexistent as a minority.

Not all governments are this intolerant. In Jordan, for example, several seats in the Chamber of Deputies (the lower house of Parliament) are reserved for Christians, who have also served in the Senate and other appointed bodies. And since the end of the brutal civil war in Lebanon (1975–1991), Christians, who constitute 30 percent of the population, have actively participated in political life. Yet despite this variance and formal laws that proclaim religious tolerance and freedom, religious minorities in most Middle Eastern countries are operating within a context of intimidation and fear.

Quintan Wiktorowicz

See also Islam; Islamic Empire, Medieval; Israel; Jihad

Further Reading

Bengio, O., & Ben-Dor, G. (Eds.). (1999). *Minorities and the state in the Arab world.* Boulder, CO: Lynne Rienner.

Fuller, G. E., & Francke, R. R. (1999). *The Arab Shia: The forgotten Muslims.* New York: Saint Martin's Press.

Moshe, M. (1999). *Middle Eastern minorities: Between integration and conflict.* Washington, DC: The Washington Institute for Near East Policy.

Nasr, S. V. (2001). *Islamic leviathan: Islam and the making of state power.* Oxford, UK: Oxford University Press.

Wiktorowicz, Q. (2001). *The management of Islamic activism: Salafis, the Muslim brotherhood, and state power in Jordan.* Albany: State University of New York Press.

Millennialist Groups

Millennialists anticipate a transformation of this world that will be, in the widely adopted formulation of religion scholar Norman Cohn, collective, terrestrial, imminent, total, and supernatural. They see human history as moving toward a climax that will totally transform the world as we know it. Millennial groups often have strong moral and political interests. They reflect on what it means to be a good person, what the good society will look like, and how individuals can become worthy of entrance into a new, perfect world. The preaching and proselytizing efforts of millennial groups have elicited reactions ranging from enthusiasm through apathy to antagonism. The freedom of millennialists to express their religious ideas has been often been challenged by those who have vested interests in particular nonmillennial religious messages or who find the proclamation of a transformed social and political order to threaten their own privileges and status. The identification of an imminent end poses a dilemma for millennialists concerning their own roles in the unfolding eschatological scenario. Most often, millennialists conclude that they will have little or no direct role in bringing about the end. Instead, their task will be to spread the word while living lives that will qualify them for salvation when the end does arrive. Some millennialists, however, have become convinced that through their own actions they can experience a foretaste of the transformed conditions of the new world, help bring it about by cooperating with or acting on behalf of supernatural forces, or even force its arrival by taking actions that will trigger the apocalyptic scenario. Such actions have often provoked conflicts with defenders of the status quo. Encounters between millennial groups and their opponents exert pressure on the groups to adapt their beliefs and practices in order to reduce tensions with the surrounding society. How the groups respond to that challenge, balancing fidelity to their millennial visions with strategies for survival, decisively shapes the careers of millennial groups in the United States.

Millennialists devote themselves both to decoding prophetic messages and to discerning the signs of the times, and they typically align the two in a grand picture of history rushing toward its consummation. Even when the knowledge it produces and proclaims is not accepted by the dominant society, millennialism is often a very intellectual phenomenon, given to painstaking textual analysis, thorough examination

THE GHOST DANCE EXPERIENCE

The following is an account of one Pawnee man's experience in the Ghost Dance, a millennial movement among Native Americans in the last half of the nineteenth century.

When I joined in the dance I was filled with some kind of a spirit. I began to tremble and cry. I saw a strange being who wanted to catch me. I ran out of the ring and kept running away from the strange man. When he caught up with me I could see many wonderful things. He told me that if I stopped he would teach me the wonderful things I saw. I would not do this for I wanted to see some of my dead people. I ran until I was exhausted and could go no further and fell down as one dead. I was in a beautiful country where the grass was green. I saw a small pathway which I followed. I came to a clear stream of water and crossed it. Then I came to a cedar tree; on it were feathers of different birds and handkerchiefs of many colors. I took one of red silk and passed on. On a small hill I saw the Child of the Father in the Heavens dressed in purple. He held out his hands so I could see the cuts in them. He did not speak but I knew he wanted me to pass. I went by him and I saw at a distance the village of our dead people. As I neared the village four men came to meet me, each with a pipe in his hand. One of them said. My son, when you return to your people tell them you saw us and that we ask our people for a smoke. We are about to smoke to our people who are still living through the one who is leading us to your land. Go into the village and see your people.' I passed them and went on. Near the village I saw a woman. It was my mother. She embraced me and said. My child, I am glad to see you. We will go where our people are dancing.' So we went on and there in the center of the village our people were dancing the same dance we were dancing. I joined them and men came to me and blew their breaths upon me. I danced a while then one man asked me to tell you that I had seen the dance and that it was all true. He then told me to return, and when I turned round I awoke. I had been lying on the ground for some time. This is the end of what I saw.

Alexander Lesser

Source: *The Pawnee Ghost Dance Hand Game.*
(New York: Columbia University Press, 1933), 63.

of current events, and a determined search for hidden meanings and revealing patterns. Millennial groups often form around someone recognized as an inspired interpreter or creator of sacred texts, such as William Miller in the 1830s and 1840s, Ellen White and Charles Taze Russell in the later nineteenth century, and, more recently, the Rev. Sun Myung Moon and David Koresh, among many others. Millennialist interpretations of history involve the interactions of text, interpreter, and context; and, because only the text remains fixed, millennialism is dynamic and highly adaptable.

The roots of the millennial tradition in the West may go back as far as the Iranian prophet Zoroaster, some 2,500 years ago. In the United States, however, millennialism has been deeply influenced by the biblical tradition, particularly the books of Daniel in the Hebrew Bible and Revelation in the New Testament. But as the United States has become more religiously diverse, forms of millennialism shaped by other religious traditions, including Islam, various Chinese and Indian religions, and many new religious movements, have become more prominent. In addition, many observers have identified hybrid or entirely secular forms of millennialism in political, ecological, and other social movements. Generally, millennialism takes two forms: catastrophic millennialism envisions a thoroughgoing, dramatic, and violent transition to the new order, while progressive millennialism sees incremental movement toward the ideal world.

The Trustee's Office at the Shaker Community in Sabbathday Lake, Maine, the only surviving Shaker community in 2002. COURTESY OF DAVID LEVINSON.

Millennial ideas have consistently had a large audience in the United States, from the time of the first voyages of discovery and European settlements, through the colonial and revolutionary periods, to the nineteenth and twentieth centuries. The present time is no exception.

The Eighteenth and Nineteenth Centuries

The career of Ann Lee, the founder of the United Society of Believers in Christ's Second Appearing, more commonly known as the Shakers, provides an example from early American history of hostile social reactions to a millennial group and the group's resilience. Even before she arrived in America with eight followers in 1774, Ann Lee had been jailed several times in her native England for disrupting church services and enthusiastically proclaiming her sectarian message. In 1780 in New York, Lee and several others were imprisoned under suspicion of sedition. Also, during her itinerant missionary journeys in the early 1780s in Massachusetts, Lee was assaulted several times and accused of witchcraft. Because of their ecstatic practices, celibacy, and millennialist fervor, Lee and the early Shakers were constantly dogged by rumors of intemperance, lewdness, intoxication, and subversion of the public order. After Lee's death in

1784, however, her successor Joseph Meachem fostered standardization of Shaker theology and more formal social organization, which ushered in an era of growth for the Shakers and diminished their tensions with society.

Anticipation of the imminent end of the world was also a focal point of a new religious tradition, the Church of Jesus Christ of Latter-day Saints or Mormons, which began when the fourteen-year-old Joseph Smith experienced a series of visions in 1820. From the start, several features of Mormon millennialism, including Smith's claim to be an inspired prophet, the scriptural status of the Book of Mormon, and the institution of "plural marriage," aroused strong opposition. In 1844 Smith was murdered by a violent mob, a part of the continuing social antagonism that drove the Mormons across the country from their birthplace in New York to the Great Salt Lake basin. The relentless force of negative popular opinion, political maneuvering, and even military actions constrained the ways in which Mormons expressed their millennial dreams and provided the context for their abandonment of plural marriage in 1890. While Mormons did not abandon their expectation of the imminent establishment of God's kingdom, they did modify their behavior in the interim.

John Humphrey Noyes, the founder of the Oneida Community, believed that the kingdom of heaven could be progressively realized on earth among his followers. Like Ann Lee and Joseph Smith, Noyes imagined that the transformed state of humankind would be evident in sexual relations. His particular millennial conviction was that all forms of love, including sexual, would be freely expressed in the holy community. Noyes" advocacy of "complex marriage" became a hallmark of the group that took root in Oneida, New York in 1848. By the mid- to late 1870s external opposition combined with the aging Noyes's diminished ability to lead the community effected the demise of Noyes's millennial experiment.

Late in the nineteenth century a Native American millennial movement provoked a bloody conflict with federal troops. Reacting to repeated defeats in battles with superior U.S. troops, the imposition of Western culture spearheaded by missionaries, the suppression of native religions, the disappearance of the buffalo, and forced confinement to a reservation, members of many tribal groups began to participate in the Ghost Dance movement, inspired by the Paiute prophet Wovoka. Wovoka had prophesied an imminent transformation of the earth that would include the replenishment of natural resources, the return of the buffalo, and the destruction of the white man. Ghost Dancers performed their rituals to induce their ancestors to return and join them in reclaiming the land. Their activities further unsettled already anxious government officials. Ghost Dancers anticipated armed intervention and were assured that special shirts would protect them from soldiers' bullets. Those assurances were proved false on 29 December 1890, when U.S. troops of the 7th Calvary slaughtered more than 150 Miniconjou Sioux at Wounded Knee Creek on the Pine Ridge Reservation in South Dakota in part because officials feared that the Ghost Dance would lead to a widespread Native American uprising.

The Twentieth Century

In the later twentieth century several millennial groups were subjected to harsh efforts at both formal and informal social control. Although books like Hal Lindsey's *The Late Great Planet Earth*, which has sold tens of millions of copies, clearly testified to the wide popularity of millennial ideas in U.S. society, groups subsumed under the antagonistic label "cults" bore the brunt of social opprobrium and repression. A vig-

orous coalition of "anticult" activists subjected millennial groups such as the Rev. Sun Myung Moon's Unification Church, Elizabeth Clare Prophet's Church Universal and Triumphant, the Rev. Jim Jones's People's Temple, and David Koresh's Branch Davidians to intense scrutiny and incited authorities to take action against the groups.

In the case of the People's Temple, external pressures by "concerned relatives" and their supporters culminated in Representative Leo Ryan's fact-finding mission to the church's agricultural mission in Jonestown, Guyana, that triggered his murder and the mass murder/suicide of nearly 1,000 people in November 1978. By then the originally Christian sectarian group had developed an idiosyncratic ideology of "divine socialism" which it was attempting to live out in its isolated encampment in the jungle. A tape of the final moments of the Jonestown community indicates that Jones and at least some of his followers felt betrayed by defectors and besieged by external enemies. They became convinced that it was impossible for them to exercise their religious freedom anywhere in this world. They then sought to cross over into a millennial paradise by an act of "revolutionary suicide."

Although many popular accounts understood the 1993 events at the Branch Davidians' Mount Carmel Center outside of Waco, Texas on the model of Jonestown, it was actually a substantially different situation. The Bible students who accepted David Koresh as a prophet were part of a long-standing sectarian offshoot of the millennialist Seventh-day Adventist church. They conducted their affairs with relatively little outside recognition until the Bureau of Alcohol, Tobacco, and Firearms mounted an ill-advised military raid to serve a search and arrest warrant concerning the possession of illegal weapons. In the ensuing standoff, the FBI's dismissal of Davidian millennial theology as "Bible babble" contributed to the impasse that allowed the final destruction of the community and death of seventy-four people to occur on 19 April 1993.

The widespread association of marginal millennial groups with violence was only reinforced by the suicides of thirty-nine members of Heaven's Gate in 1997 in Rancho Santa Fe, near San Diego, California; the suicides and murders of members of the Order of the Solar Temple in Canada, France, and Europe in 1994, 1995, and 1997; and the deadly release of sarin gas in the Tokyo subway by members of Aum Shinrikyo in 1995. At the close of the twentieth century, the popular expectation that millennial "cults" would turn violent was well entrenched, and it significantly shaped a popular climate that was antipathetic toward such groups.

Also shaping that climate were the actions of several millennialist groups and individuals on the radical right. Although Timothy McVeigh, who was convicted of the 1995 bombing of the Alfred P. Murrah federal building in Oklahoma City, denied any religious motivation, his thinking was deeply nourished by the millennial scenario of *The Turner Diaries*, a novel with religious overtones about the "Second American Revolution" and the paradisiacal new world to which it would give birth. McVeigh also had contacts with subcultures in which images of "Rahowa," a racial holy war, gave shape to a racist and anti-Semitic millennial dream of new white America, often nourished by the distinctive doctrines of Christian Identity churches. Efforts at social control of the radical right occupied organizations like the Southern Poverty Law Center, the Jewish Anti-Defamation League, and some "anticult" organizations, as well as the FBI and other law enforcement agencies. Individuals on the radical right often defended themselves with pleas for free speech and religious freedom.

Several contemporary social movements, including antinuclear activism and the animal liberation movement, have also expressed their concerns in a millennial idiom. For example, the radical environmentalism of groups like Earth First! has sometimes envisioned both a cataclysmic end to the industrialized world order and the growth of a new biocentric world from its ashes. But the use of tactics like "monkey-wrenching" and more violent forms of "ecotage" and "ecoterrorism" by some radical environmentalists to fight back against what they saw as the rape of Mother Earth brought them the attention of both local law enforcement and the FBI and led to the marginalization of their aggressive form of millennialism. Nonetheless, millennialism continues to flourish in the environmental movement and other contemporary social movements.

Implications

Millennialism has always been a significant element in American religious life, even when its proponents have not garnered broad public attention. Because it renders a negative judgment on the status quo and envisions a total transformation of the current order, millennialism has the potential to create

conflict. The specific interactions between millennialists or millennial groups and upholders of the social order can remain on the intellectual level or can escalate into other types of conflict, depending on the specific actors and situations. Strongly hostile reactions can threaten the religious freedom of individuals or millennial groups. But there is nothing inherent in millennial groups that makes them prone to violence or that necessitates repressive actions against them.

Eugene V. Gallagher

See also Great Awakenings and the Antebellum Period; Mormons; Unification Church

Further Reading

Barkun, M. (1974). *Disaster and the millennium*. New Haven, CT: Yale University Press.

Barkun, M. (1986). *Crucible of the millennium: The burned-over district of New York in the 1840s*. Syracuse, NY: Syracuse University Press.

Boyer, P. (1992). *When time shall be no more: Prophecy belief in modern American culture*. Cambridge, MA: Harvard University Press.

Burridge, K. (1969). *New heaven, new earth: A study of millenarian activities*. New York: Schocken Books.

Cohn, N. (1993). *Cosmos, chaos, and the world to come: The ancient roots of apocalyptic faith*. New Haven, CT: Yale University Press.

Hall, J., Schuyler, P. D., & Trinh, S. (2000). *Apocalypse observed: Religious movements and violence in North America, Europe, and Japan*. New York: Routledge.

Kaplan, J. (1997). *Radical religion in America: Millenarian movements from the far right to the children of Noah*. Syracuse: Syracuse University Press.

Kaplan, J. (Ed.). (2002). Millennial violence: Past, present, and future. Special Issue of *Terrorism and Political Violence, 14*(1).

Landes, R. A. (2000). *The encyclopedia of millennialism and millennial movements*. New York: Routledge.

Lee, M. F. (1995). *Earth first! Environmental apocalypse*. Syracuse, NY: Syracuse University Press.

Maaga, M. M. (1998). *Hearing the voices of Jonestown: Putting a human face on an American tragedy*. Syracuse, NY: Syracuse University Press.

Numbers, R., & Butler, J. M. (Eds.). (1987). *The disappointed: Millerism and millenarianism in the nineteenth century*. Bloomington, IN: Indiana University Press.

O'Leary, S. D. (1994). *Arguing the apocalypse: A theory of millennial rhetoric*. New York: Oxford University Press.

Penton, M. J. (1997). *Apocalypse delayed: The story of Jehovah's Witnesses*. Toronto, Canada: University of Toronto Press.

Stein, S. J. (1992). *The Shaker experience in America*. New Haven, CT: Yale University Press.

Stein, S. J. (Ed.). (1999). *The encyclopedia of apocalypticism* (Vol. 3). New York: Continuum.

Tabor, J., & Gallagher, E. V. (1995). *Why Waco? Cults and the battle for religious freedom in America*. Berkeley: University of California Press.

Underwood, G. (1993). *The millenarian world of early Mormonism*. Urbana: University of Illinois Press.

Weber, T. P. (1987). *Living in the shadow of the second coming: American premillennialism, 1875–1982*. New York: Oxford University Press.

Wessinger, C. (2000). *How the millennium comes violently: From Jonestown to Heaven's Gate*. New York: Seven Bridges Press.

Mormons

The experience of the Church of Jesus Christ of Latter-day Saints (referred to as "the Church" or "the LDS Church") brings a unique perspective to the issue of religious freedom. Since its founding in 1830, the Church has known the persecutions of a minority religion as well as the challenges facing a more accepted, thriving church with over 11 million members in more than 160 countries. From its nineteenth-century persecutions, which mark a low point in U.S. protection of religious freedom, to its majority status in certain regions of the United States and its promotion of religious freedom as a core doctrine, the Church's experiences demonstrate the significance of religious freedom to religious expression.

Origins

The Church of Jesus Christ of Latter-day Saints was founded on 6 April 1830 in Fayette, New York, by Joseph Smith Jr. (1805–1844). From its inception, the Church was subject to informal and official opposition lasting approximately sixty years.

The Church was established by Joseph Smith, Jr. who, as a fourteen-year-old boy, sought an answer as to which of the many competing Christian denominations he should join. He testified that he was visited by God the Father and His Son, Jesus Christ, and was instructed to join none of them. Core teachings of the Church include beliefs in Joseph Smith's

The Mormon Temple and Tabernacle in Salt Lake City, c. 1896. COURTESY OF LIBRARY OF CONGRESS, PRINTS AND PHOTOGRAPHS DIVISION, DETROIT PUBLISHING COMPANY COLLECTION.

THE NEGATIVE VIEW OF MORMONISM

In the nineteenth century, Mormonism was an unpopular religion in the United States. This short report, from the *Berkshire Courier* (31 March 1875) in western Massachusetts indicates that plural marriage was one Mormon practice that did not sit well with the general public.

Mormonism Exposed—Mrs. Ann Eliza Young's lecture at town hall on Thursday evening drew a full house. The story of her "life in bondage," as the 19th wife of Brigham Young, was listened to with the most careful attention, and was frequently applauded. Mrs. Young's courageous portrayal of Mormonism will ultimately lead this nation by force of enlightened public sentiment to blot out the foul inequities which Young and his deluded followers are boldly practicing in Utah. Mrs. Young is a fine looking and appearing lady, and made a good impression upon all who heard her or made her acquaintance.

call as a modern-day prophet, the Church as a restoration of the original pure Christianity established by Jesus Christ during his mortal ministry, and the Book of Mormon as a second witness of the divinity of Christ and a translation of records of ancient prophets in the Americas. While some individuals accepted these beliefs, the Church's rejection of traditional Protestantism and its insistence on seemingly incredible divine revelation also attracted many critics.

After facing opposition in New York, Joseph Smith and most early Mormon converts migrated to eastern Ohio, where they established temporary headquarters of the Church in Kirtland in 1831. The influx of Church members with political, social, and religious differences from other Ohio residents raised tensions in the area. In the face of increasing mob attacks from local residents and apostate members, Latter-day Saints left Ohio by mid-July 1838.

Violence in and Expulsion from Missouri

Latter-day Saints also established a second population center in Missouri from 1831 to 1838. When the Latter-day Saints arrived in Jackson County, Missouri, they were met with fear and mistrust by many of the earlier settlers of the region. Many factors, in addition to religious differences, combined to cause this reaction. Latter-day Saints, with strong New England roots, had different cultural expectations than Missouri frontiersmen on issues such as schools, hard drinking, and personal decorum. Church members also often traded and socialized entirely with other Church members, which isolated them and contributed to misunderstandings. Two particularly contentious issues were slavery and relations with Native Americans. Missourians feared that Mormon settlers would tamper with their slaves and sympathize with and ally themselves with Native Americans.

Ultimately, the growing LDS population was seen as a threat to Missourians' political control. "It requires no gift of prophecy," stated a citizens' committee, "to tell that the day is not far distant when the civil government of the county will be in their hands" (Smith 1908, 1:397).

The animosity toward the Saints resulted in vandalism in 1832 and outbreaks of violence starting in 1833. Mobs destroyed homes, whipped or tarred and feathered men, and terrorized women and children. When members gathered to protect themselves from the mobs in November 1833, the county militia negotiated a truce and disarmament. After the Saints disarmed, the militia joined the mob in assaulting Church members, who fled the county in fear.

Mormon settlers moved to northwestern Missouri, where the legislature created Caldwell and Daviess Counties for them in 1836. But LDS growth in these and neighboring counties continued to meet opposition. The grievances and conflicts the Saints had encountered in Jackson County continued, and rumors, mistrust, and false allegations proliferated.

Mob violence also continued. Attempts by Mormon settlers to defend themselves led to exaggerated reports of Mormon-initiated violence that prompted Missouri Governor Boggs on October 27, 1838, to command the Missouri militia that all Latter-day Saints "be exterminated or driven from the state, if necessary for the public good" (LeSueur 1987, 152). A militia general ordered Joseph Smith shot, but he was saved through the selfless courage of a non-Mormon brigadier general who refused to obey the order.

In one of the more brutal attacks on Mormons, the state militia attacked Mormon settlers and their children, three days after the extermination order, at Haun's Mill in Caldwell County, killing seventeen Latter-day Saints and wounding thirteen others.

During their time in Missouri, the Latter-day Saints sought protection from the courts and federal government, but without success. At a time when the ruling Democratic party favored states' rights, Joseph Smith Jr.'s pleas to the Congress and the President fell on deaf ears. President Andrew Jackson refused to intervene in the situation in Missouri, stating that "each state has an unquestionable right to regulate its own internal concerns according to its own pleasure" (Hyman and Wiecek 1982, 15). A few years later, in 1839, President Martin Van Buren also refused to intervene, offering the following explanation: "Your cause is just, but I can do nothing for you. . . . If I take up with you I shall lose the vote of Missouri" (Smith 1908, 4:80).

Exodus to Utah

The persecution of the Latter-day Saints continued after Church members were driven from Missouri to Illinois, where Joseph Smith Jr. and his brother Hyrum Smith (1800–1844) were murdered by a mob in June 1844. Shortly thereafter, Brigham Young (1801–1877), who became the next president of the Church, led thousands of Latter-day Saints on a trek across the plains to modern-day Utah, where Church members hoped they would be free from further persecution. It is estimated that approximately 60,000 Mormon pioneers undertook the migration to Utah by wagon and handcart between 1846 and 1869.

The Latter-day Saints did not escape persecution even after their exodus to Utah. While geographically separated from the violence and mistrust that had characterized their stay in the Midwest, in Utah they faced a new challenge. A large segment of the U.S. population still feared and opposed the Latter-day Saints for a variety of reasons, including the cooperative Utah economy, which was regarded as a threat to capitalism, and especially the practice of polygamy, or plural marriage, by some of the Mormon population.

"That the Mormons were seen as a threat—economically, politically, and religiously—was in a large measure a result of their corporate, organized nature. Individually they might be despised, but scarcely feared. As a group, however, they had to be reckoned with" (Arrington and Bitton 1992, 53).

While Latter-day Saints saw plural marriage as a command from God, the rest of Victorian society was morally offended by the practice. In 1856, John C. Freemont ran for U.S. president on a platform promising to eradicate "the twin relics of barbarism: slavery and polygamy" (Allen and Leonard 1976, 305). James Buchanan, who won the election, also feared to be seen as supporting the Mormons. Responding to false reports of a Mormon rebellion, President Buchanan sent the U.S. Army to occupy the territory of Utah in 1857. The army was recalled three years later at the onset of the Civil War, without having ever militarily engaged the Latter-day Saints.

Legal Opposition from the Federal Government

The Utah territory first applied for statehood in 1849. This and five additional applications for statehood were denied before Utah was finally made a state in 1896. The practice of polygamy by Church members was not only one of the main roadblocks to Utah's admission to the Union, but also led to several pieces of federal anti-LDS legislation from 1849 to 1896.

Congress passed numerous successively harsher pieces of seemingly neutral, generally applicable laws that affected and penalized all Church members. These enactments included the Morrill Anti-Bigamy Act of 1862, which criminalized bigamy in U.S. territories, the Edmunds Act of 1882, which allowed prosecution of bigamous cohabitation and disenfranchised polygamists, and other acts that revoked Utah's grant of the vote to women, abolished spousal immunity in polygamy cases, and, in Idaho, denied civil rights for belief in plural marriage, even among those who did not practice it. More than 1,300 Latter-day Saints were convicted of and served jail time for polygamy-related offenses.

The apex of federal legal persecution of the LDS Church and its members came in 1887 when Congress passed the Edmunds-Tucker Act, which formally dissolved the Corporation of the Church of Jesus Christ of Latter-day Saints and paved the way for federal confiscation of all Church property in excess of $50,000 that was not directly used for religious purposes.

Supreme Court Ruling on Polygamy

In response to a challenge to anti-polygamy legislation, the U.S. Supreme Court issued its first major decision on the free exercise clause of the First Amendment, in *Reynolds v. United States* (1878). The Court, speaking through Chief Justice Waite, held that "Congress was deprived [by the free exercise clause] of all legislative power over mere opinion, but was left free to reach actions which were in violation of social duties or subversive of good order" (*Reynolds v. United States* 1878, 164). By allowing apparently unlimited regulation of actions, even actions required by one's religious beliefs, *Reynolds* set an early precedent of narrow free exercise protections. The Supreme Court expanded its protections to cover religiously motivated action in *Cantwell v. Connecticut* (1940), but appeared to return to the *Reynolds* standard in 1990 in *Employment Division v. Smith* (1990).

Twelve years later, the Supreme Court went a step further in *Davis v. Beason* (1890). *Davis* involved a First Amendment challenge to a statute that conditioned the right to vote on an oath that the would-be voter neither practiced polygamy nor belonged to any group that encouraged or advocated the practice. The statute effectively prohibited any member of the Church from voting. Since only a small fraction of the Church membership practiced polygamy, this law attempted to strike at Church membership more generally.

The United States Supreme Court held that the statute was constitutionally valid. Ignoring the fact that Davis was not himself a polygamist, Justice Field echoed *Reynolds'* findings as to the seriousness of the crime of polygamy. Field said, "Few crimes are more pernicious to the best interests of society and receive more general or more deserved punishment," and therefore no exception could be made under the free exercise clause (*Davis v. Beason* 1890, 341). In 1890, the Supreme Court also upheld the seizure of Church property under the Edmunds-Tucker Act. (*The Late Corporation of the Church of Jesus Christ of Latter-day Saints v. United States* 1890).

After incurring huge debts from being forced to borrow money to cover operating expenses, fight legal battles, and rent property back from the federal government, the LDS Church relented. Wilford Woodruff, then Church president, issued a manifesto in 1890 in which the Church officially abandoned the practice of plural marriage. He described a vision he was given of the devastation that would happen to the Church if the practice were not given up, and encouraged members to abide by the laws that "have been enacted by Congress forbidding plural marriages, which laws have been pronounced constitutional by the court of last resort" (*The Doctrine and Covenants of The Church of Jesus Christ of Latter-day Saints*, Official Declaration 1).

After 1890, public opposition to the LDS Church gradually waned. One significant exception was the debate over the seating of senator-elect and Church leader Reed Smoot from Utah. The Senate held hearings from 1903 to 1907 that focused on LDS Church doctrine, past and present polygamous relationships of Church leaders and members, and Smoot's expected loyalty to the LDS Church hierarchy. Eventually, Senator Smoot was seated and became an influential member of the Senate.

LDS Perspectives on Religious Freedom

LDS doctrine teaches obedience to the laws of the land, yet supports a strong claim for religious freedom for people of all faiths. In 1842, in response to a Chicago newspaper reporter's inquiry about LDS beliefs, Church founder Joseph Smith wrote what would later be canonized as the thirteen Articles of Faith. Two of the Articles of Faith address these aspects of church–state relations. In the Eleventh Article of Faith, members "claim the privilege of worshipping the Almighty God according to the dictates of our [their] own conscience and allow all men the same privilege, let them worship how, where, or what they may" (Smith 1908, 4:541). This claim for religious liberty is tempered by the Twelfth Article of Faith, which reads as follows: "We believe in being subject to kings, presidents, rulers, and magistrates, in obeying, honoring, and sustaining the law" (Smith 1908, 4:541). For this reason, the LDS Church has only expanded beyond the United States when it could do so consistently with the laws of the countries it has sought to enter.

The Church's history of oppression underscores its fundamental commitment to religious freedom. Belief in the importance of religious freedom can be traced back to Joseph Smith Jr., the founder of the LDS Church. He stated:

> If it has been demonstrated that I have been willing to die for a "Mormon," I am bold to declare before heaven that I am just as ready to die in defending

the rights of a Presbyterian, a Baptist, or a good man of any denomination; for the same principle which would trample upon the rights of the Latter-day Saints would trample upon the rights of the Roman Catholics, or of any other denomination who may be unpopular and too weak to defend themselves.

It is the love of liberty which inspires my soul—civil and religious liberty to the whole of the human race. (Smith 1908, 5:498)

In keeping with these beliefs, The Church of Jesus Christ of Latter-day Saints has worked with coalitions of other faiths to promote religious freedom in the United States and throughout the world. For example, the LDS Church was involved in the coalition to create and support the constitutionality of the Religious Freedom Restoration Act and has written amicus briefs in support of other religious freedom issues in the United States Supreme Court. The LDS Church also successfully argued in the United States Supreme Court for the constitutionality of Title VII accommodations for religious employers in the landmark case of *Amos v. Corporation of the Presiding Bishop* (1987).

LDS Views on Religious Tolerance

LDS Church leaders have taught Church members to exercise tolerance and understanding of the religious views of others, particularly when Church members have found themselves to be a majority. As mentioned earlier, the Church's Eleventh Article of Faith articulates the Church's commitment to "allow all men the . . . privilege [to worship God], let them worship how, where or what they may" (Smith 1908, 4:541).

In Nauvoo, Illinois (1839–1846), the first city where Church members formed a majority, religious tolerance was implemented through a Nauvoo City Council ordinance, which provided that "the Catholics, Presbyterians, Methodists, Baptists, Latter Day Saints, Quakers, Episcopals, Universalists, Unitarians, Mohammedans, and all other religious sects and denominations whatever, shall have free toleration, and equal privileges, in this city," and imposed a penalty of up to a 500-dollar fine and six months' imprisonment for the crime of "ridiculing . . . abusing or otherwise depreciating [an]other in consequence of his religion, or of disturbing or interruption any religious meeting within the limits of this city" (Smith 1908, 4:306).

The LDS approach to religious tolerance is based on a theological understanding that focuses on the brotherhood and sisterhood of humanity. In 1978, the First Presidency of the LDS Church, which consists of the Church's president and his two counselors, issued a statement declaring that, "The Church of Jesus Christ of Latter-day Saints gladly teaches and declares the Christian doctrine that all men and women are brothers and sisters . . . as literal spirit children of an Eternal Father. . . . [W]e believe that God has given and will give to all peoples sufficient knowledge to help them on their way to eternal salvation, either in this life or in the life to come" (*Statement of the First Presidency, 15 February 1978*).

Latter-day Saint doctrinal approaches reflect an inclusivist tradition that, while claiming exclusive restored authority from God, recognizes truth and divine inspiration in other religious traditions. The 1978 First Presidency statement affirmed that "great religious leaders of the world" received "a portion of God's light" and that "moral truths were given to [these leaders] by God to enlighten whole nations and to bring a higher level of understanding to individuals" (Statement of the First Presidency, 15 February 1978).

From the LDS belief that all peoples possess truths springs the corresponding emphasis on respecting and building good relations with people of other faiths. Former Church President Howard W. Hunter (1907–1995) said, "[a]s members of the Church of Jesus Christ, we seek to bring all peoples together. We seek to enlarge the circle of love and understanding among all the peoples of the earth. Thus we strive to establish peace and happiness, not only within Christianity but among all mankind" (Hunter 1994, 60). In Utah, one of the few United States states in which there is an absolute LDS Church majority, the Church has cooperated with and given financial and material support to other denominations.

Current Status of the LDS Church

In recent years, LDS demographics have changed dramatically. By 1996, more Church members lived outside the United States than in, only 30 percent of members lived in the western U.S., and less than 20 percent lived in Utah. As these numbers suggest, the LDS Church now faces increasing challenges as a minority religion outside the United States, and is involved in promoting religious freedom worldwide.

While the Church has faced some oppression as a minority faith in totalitarian countries or in countries lacking a stable government, the Church's dramatic history of religious persecution in the United States has not been repeated elsewhere.

Elizabeth A. Sewell

Further Reading

Allen, J. B., & Leonard, G. M. (1976). *The story of the Latter-day Saints*. Salt Lake City, UT: Deseret Book.

Arrington, L. J., & Bitton, D. (1992). *The Mormon experience: A history of the Latter-day Saints* (2nd ed.). Urbana: University of Illinois Press.

Backman, M. V., Jr. (1970). *American religions and the rise of Mormonism*. Salt Lake City, UT: Deseret Book Company.

Bushman, R. L. (1984). *Joseph Smith and the beginnings of Mormonism*. Urbana: University of Illinois Press.

Daynes, K. M. (2001). *More wives than one: The Transformation of the Mormon marriage system*. Urbana: University of Illinois Press.

Durham, W. C., Jr. (2002). The Doctrine of Religious Freedom. In *Brigham Young University 2001–2002 speeches*. Provo, UT: Brigham Young University Publications & Graphics.

Fales, S. L. (1989). *Mormons and Mormonism in United States government documents: A bibliography*. Salt Lake City: University of Utah Press.

Firmage, E. B., & Mangrum, R. C. (1988). *Zion in the courts*. Urbana: University of Illinois Press.

Gaustad, E. S., & Barlow, P. L. (2001). *New historical atlas of religion in America*. New York: Oxford University Press.

Givens, T. (1997). *The viper on the hearth: Mormons, myths, and the construction of heresy*. New York: Oxford University Press.

Gordon, Sarah Barringer. (2002). *The Mormon question: Polygamy and constitutional conflict in nineteenth-century America*. Chapel Hill: University of North Carolina Press.

Hill, M. S. (1989). *Quest for refuge: The Mormon flight from American pluralism*. Salt Lake City, UT: Signature Books.

Hunter, H. W. (1994). *That we might have joy*. Salt Lake City, UT: Deseret Book.

Hyman, H. M., & Wiecek, W. M. (1982). *Equal justice under the law*. New York: Harper & Row.

Jennings, W. A. (1962). *Zion is fled: The expulsion of the Mormons from Jackson County, Missouri*. Unpublished doctoral dissertation, University of Florida.

LeSueur, S. C. (1987). *The 1838 Mormon War in Missouri*. Columbia: University of Missouri Press.

Ludlow, V. H. (Ed.). (1992). *The Encyclopedia of Mormonism* (4 vols.). New York: Macmillian.

Shipps, J. (1998). *Difference and otherness: Mormonism and the American mainstream*. Urbana: University of Illinois Press.

Shipps, J. (1985). *Mormonism: The story of a new religious tradition*. Urbana: University of Illinois Press.

Smith, J. (1908). *History of the church* (7 vols.). Salt Lake City, UT: Deseret News.

Statement of the First Presidency (1978, February 15). Retrieved April 16, 2003, from http://www.byui.edu/Ricks/employee/PECKDD/1978_1st_Pres_Statement.pdf

Court Cases

Amos v. Corporation of the Presiding Bishop, 483 U.S. 327 (1987).

Cantwell v. Connecticut, 310 U.S. 296 (1940).

Davis v. Beason, 133 U.S. 333 (1890).

Employment Division v. Smith, 494 U.S. 872 (1990).

The Late Corporation of the Church of Jesus Christ of Latter-day Saints v. United States, 136 U.S. 1 (1890).

Reynolds v. United States, 98 U.S. 145 (1878).

Native American Church

Native American Church is the name adopted by a constellation of church groups devoted to peyotism, the worship of peyote, a psychotropic plant indigenous to North America. Though relatively few in numbers, peyotists became prominent in the American struggle for religious freedom through their involvement in the landmark U.S. Supreme Court case of *Employment Division, Department of Human Resources v. Smith* (1990).

Peyotism

Archaeologists have documented the use of peyote in the New World as far back as 10,000 years ago. The plant itself, a small, spineless cactus that grows close to the ground, is found mostly in northern Mexico and southern Texas. The "buttons" contain a potent blend of naturally occurring hallucinogens. The taste, however, is bitter and often nauseating, which has limited the popularity of peyote as a recreational drug.

Spanish explorers in Mexico reported seeing peyote worshipers engaged in ecstatic dancing and ritual scarification with knives and hooks. In 1620 the Inquisition banned this "pagan" rite. But peyotism survived, and sometime in the nineteenth century it crossed the Rio Grande and moved into what was then Indian Territory (present-day Oklahoma). By 1890, a new ritual had evolved, which blended aspects of Christian ritual and theology with the music and ritual of the tribes of the Southwest.

A peyote service is usually held in a Plains-style tipi and is supervised by a peyote priest, or "Road Man." The participants gather at sundown to sit all night in the tipi around a ceremonial fire. Participants are offered the chance to eat peyote "buttons" (or drink the sacrament in the form of tea) several times during the night. The rest of the service involves song, prayer, and meditation. Once the sun has risen, the participants leave the tipi, eat breakfast together, and disperse.

Participants describe peyote's effects in subtle terms. The peyote increases concentration and also allows them to ignore the discomfort of sitting cross-legged with no back support for twelve to fifteen hours. Actual hallucinations, or visions, are relatively rare.

Peyotists are urged to be faithful to their spouses, to be self-supporting, and to care for their families. Peyote itself is to be used only in the ritual context, and alcohol in any form, or any kind of illegal drug, is strictly off limits. By 1970, a significant scientific literature had emerged suggesting that peyote religion was a powerful force in helping its adherents maintain sobriety and abstain from drug use.

Attempts at Suppression

No sooner had this new form of peyotism emerged in the 1880s than white missionaries and Indian agents began trying to ban it. In 1918 a group made up of Oklahoma tribes incorporated the Native American Church (NAC), "mother church" of all contemporary peyote sects. Peyote leaders were careful never to challenge authority directly and to keep church matters within the group. Despite this caution, peyotists have been required to defend their

PEYOTE USE IN NORTHERN MEXICO

The following account describes the ritual use of peyote by the Tarahumara Indians of northern Mexico, a region where peyote was used ritually by several Native American groups prior to European conquest. The account also shows how indigenous peyote use in modern times is combined with elements from the Roman Catholicism introduced by the Spanish.

The shaman Habran was continually being called to all parts of the sierra to work his peyote cures. Many people would even come to consult him about minor ailments because his wisdom was respected so highly.

To give a peyote fiesta, in the cure of some sick person, tesguino [corn beer] is made, a cow sacrificed, and lots of food prepared. As in other native fiestas, the dutuburi is danced on a patio that has three crosses. Matachines may also be danced in front of a special cross. At some distance to one side, there is a special patio for the peyote dance (hikuli nawikebo). Two crosses are placed here, one beside the jar containing the peyote, and one for God. Peyote is not dedicated to the four directions but is merely put in front of the two crosses for a time. At this patio for peyote, there is a hole into which one must spit and throw old cigarette butts. One must remove his hat and cross himself on approaching the patio. And one must ask permission to leave it. A quarter of beef is placed here, with all vitals included. The peyotero takes this beef in the end, in payment for his services. A big fire, around which the peyote dancers move, burns all night on the patio.

After dusk, the dancing ceases and everyone present eats a bit of peyote (it is dry and served ground up and mixed with water). Then they drink a little tesguino. All night long they are drunk from the effects of the peyote, although they do not eat it again. If any remains, the special dancers finish it in the morning.

After the eating of the peyote, the shaman rasps with his notched stick for awhile. A circle or hole marked with a cross is made, into which peyote is placed and covered with a bowl, calabash, or small olla. The end of the notched stick is then placed on the overturned container and scraped with another stick. The container gives resonance to the rasping. The rasping sticks are made from wood which grows in the peyote country. On the trips to obtain peyote, one of these sticks is made and brought back. It is considered dangerous to bring back more than one at a time. Only shamans keep them in their possession, since the layman would be in danger of death should he keep one.

Wendell C. Bennett and Robert M. Zingg

Source: *The Tarahumara: An Indian Tribe of Northern Mexico.* (Chicago: The University of Chicago Press, 1935), 293.

---

practice in court and in the legislatures against those who see it as a form of "drug abuse."

In 1926, a Montana court in *State v. Big Sheep* (1926) declined even to consider a religious defense against a charge of peyote possession. And the first federal case, *Native American Church v. Navajo Tribal Council* (1959), held that the First Amendment's free exercise guarantee did not prevent a tribal government from banning peyote possession in an attempt to exclude NAC from its jurisdiction.

But in the famous case of *People v. Woody* (1964), the California Supreme Court invoked religious freedom to dismiss state charges against a group of NAC worshipers arrested at a tipi ceremony. The church also won state legislation exempting its members from drug-use laws in more than half the states, and the federal government issued an administrative rule providing a similar exemption for church members from federal controlled-substance laws, while tightly regulating the harvest and sale of peyote for religious purposes.

The state of Oregon was an exception to the liberalizing trend. *Employment Division, Department of Human Resources v. Smith* (1990) arose in 1983 when Galen W. Black, a white man, was fired as a counselor at a private alcohol and drug abuse agency in Roseburg, Oregon, because he had participated in tipi ceremonies and ingested peyote. The next year, the agency dismissed Alfred Leo Smith Jr., a Klamath Indian, for participation in another tipi ceremony. Even though both men (who were recovering alcoholics) argued that peyotism was an aid to sobriety, the agency insisted that even religious use of peyote violated its philosophy of total abstinence for clients and counseling staff. When Smith and Black applied for unemployment compensation, the state opposed their claims on the grounds that their religious use of peyote had violated state law. Smith and Black, without support from any formal church body, argued that application of the law to them was unconstitutional as a violation of free exercise.

The Oregon state courts held that Smith and Black were protected by the precedent of *Sherbert v. Verner* (1963), which had held that free exercise required "strict scrutiny" of refusals to pay unemployment compensation to claimants whose out-of-work status resulted from religious practice. But when the case reached the United States Supreme Court, the court's majority announced a new rule: when a "neutral, generally applicable" law had the "incidental effect" of burdening a religious practice, the state need not offer any special justification for refusing to exempt believers. The lead opinion, written by Justice Antonin Scalia, dismissed judicial review of individual claims as "a luxury" that a multicultural society could not afford.

The *Smith* decision set off a storm of protest and led to an attempt by Congress to override it through the passage in 1993 of the Religious Freedom Restoration Act (RFRA); the Supreme Court later struck down RFRA in *City of Boerne, Texas v. Flores* (1997). Ironically, the coalition that lobbied for RFRA conspicuously excluded the NAC. The next year, Congress passed the American Indian Religious Freedom Act Amendments of 1994, which bar federal or state prosecution of and denial of public benefits to members of Indian tribes who possess peyote "in connection with the practice of a traditional Indian religion."

The NAC emerged from the *Smith* episode stronger than it had been. Left unsettled were the issues of First Amendment protection for newer peyote sects not connected to the NAC's main branches and the constitutional rights of non–Native American members of NAC congregations. The issue of non–Native American members continues to divide NAC bodies themselves, and the race-specific statutory exemption is of questionable constitutionality.

Garrett Epps

See also Drugs in Religious Worship

Further Reading

American Indian Religious Freedom Act Amendments of 1994, U.S.P.L. 103-344, codified at 42 U.S.C. § 1996a.

Anderson, E. F. (1996). *Peyote: The divine cactus*. Tucson, AZ: University of Arizona Press.

Epps, G. (2001). *To an unknown god: Religious freedom on trial*. New York: St. Martin's Press.

La Barre, W. (1989). *The peyote cult* (5th ed.). Norman, OK: University of Oklahoma Press.

Smith, H., & Snake, R. (1996). *One nation under God: The triumph of the Native American Church*. Santa Fe, NM: Clear Light Publishers.

Stewart, O. C. (1987). *Peyote religion: A history*. Norman, OK: University of Oklahoma Press.

Court Cases

City of Boerne, Texas v. Flores, 521 U.S. 507 (1997).

Employment Division, Department of Human Resources v. Smith, 494 U.S. 872 (1990).

Native American Church v. Navajo Tribal Council, 272 F.2d 131 (1959).

People v. Woody, 61 Cal.2d 716, 40 Cal. Rptr. 69, 394 P.2d 813 (1964).

Sherbert v. Verner, 374 U.S. 398 (1963).

State v. Big Sheep, 75 Mont. 219; 243 P. 1067 (1926).

State v. Soto, 21 Ore. App. 79 (1975).

Natural Law

Natural law can be popularly defined as the moral law written in the minds and hearts of human

A SELECTION FROM THE PLATFORM OF THE NATURAL LAW PARTY OF THE UNITED STATES

NATURAL LAW AND NATIONAL LAW

From the deepest perspective, our national problems have one underlying cause—violation of natural law.

Natural law is the orderly principles—the laws of nature—that govern the functioning of nature everywhere, from atoms to ecosystems to galaxies. Over the past several centuries, modern science has identified many of these laws governing physical, biological, ecological, and social systems. Natural law is inherently "life-supporting": it supports the life and evolution of innumerable species.

Natural law is not a new idea in American government. Our founding fathers believed that the rights of every American citizen to life, liberty, and the pursuit of happiness are based on immutable laws of nature. They felt that, through knowledge of natural law, both science and government would promote the goals of freedom and happiness of the people.

Human behaviors that promote life, liberty, and happiness are in harmony with natural law. When people live in harmony with natural law, they don't make mistakes—they spontaneously uphold higher values, and they enjoy naturally good health and a life free from problems. However, the knowledge of natural law uncovered by modern science—and disseminated through our educational system—has been insufficient to enable citizens to live and act in accord with the laws of nature. Thus, the whole population is constantly violating natural law, causing problems for themselves and their communities.

"Violation of natural law" is action that fails to take natural advantage of the laws of nature, or that stimulates them in ways that cause negative repercussions. Smoking is an example of behavior that runs counter to the natural laws that support good physical health.

Violation of natural law causes stress. Stress has consequences for both mental and physical health; the majority of disease is said to be stress related. Stress causes a complex psychophysiological chain reaction in the human body. Chronic stress leads to an out-of-balance biochemistry that has also been linked with anxiety, fear, anger, impulsive violent behavior, and substance abuse.

Moreover, the combined stress of all the individuals in society builds up and creates a dangerous, criminal atmosphere in the whole community. This epidemic of stress has rent our social fabric and threatens the lives of Americans everywhere.

The government reflects this social disorder. Government is a mirror of the nation. When the country is full of stress and crime, this chaotic atmosphere has a debilitating effect on the performance of government.

To deal with all the problems engendered by social stress, government responds with laws, regulations, and costly social programs designed to protect us from ourselves. Most of the activities of our government—and most of our tax dollars—are spent compensating for the violations of natural law by the population. Laws and costly programs, however, can't solve the problems.

We can have a smaller, more efficient and effective government, one that is capable of solving problems. Such a government would function in alliance with natural law.

Source: The Natural Law Party of the United States of America. Retrieved 3 September 2002, from http:// www.natural-law.org

beings. Though history this basic idea has had three components: (a) there are morally right and wrong actions common to all human beings; (b) each normal person has the capacity to know the difference between right and wrong and make moral decisions about his or her actions; and (c) each person has the human obligation to chose right actions and avoid wrong ones. To follow natural law is to do justice to oneself and others, to affirm the moral reasoning ability that distinguishes humans from other entities, and to achieve the excellence proper to a rational being.

Natural Law among the Greeks and Romans

The concept of natural law has a long history, but was radical when proposed in ancient Greece. It had two implications that undermined traditional theocratic views of government and helped form the foundation of Western civilization; namely, that individuals can and must make moral decisions for themselves independent of either rulers or priests, and that rulers and priests must obey these fundamental laws as does everyone else. No one expressed this better than Sophocles in his tragedy, *Antigone*. King Creon has forbidden anyone to bury the body of Polynices. Antigone rejects this dictate as not a law to be obeyed. "Your law was not made by Zeus," she proclaims defiantly. "Such is not the justice of the gods. Nor did I think that your decrees had such force that a mortal could override the unwritten and unchanging statutes of heaven. For their authority is not of today nor yesterday, but from all time, and no one knows when they were first put into force." Creon kills Antigone for her impertinence but as a result meets his own cruel fate.

Antigone highlights two controversial questions that have dogged the concept of natural law through the centuries. First, where does this natural law come from? Second, what happens if one does not obey it? The Greeks and Romans believed that natural law came from "the gods," but that people could know it by reason. The question remains as to whether commitment to natural law demands belief in God, but even the Christian apostle Paul argued that it does not: gentiles who have not been exposed to Jewish law follow "the law written in their hearts" (Romans 2:15, KJV). Later, the Medieval theologian Thomas Aquinas would similarly argue that while God created all things, humans could nonetheless discover natural law by reason without the aid of faith. In con-

temporary times we might say that natural law is like the origin of the world: one cannot prove whether the world was created by God or by some non-divine "big bang," but we know from experience that it exists. Likewise, whether natural law was created by God or not, we know it exists.

The question as to what happens to people who defy natural law has been as difficult to resolve. The ancients were sure that bad things would follow, whether punishment by the gods or the natural consequences of doing evil. They argued that a person who disobeys natural law is, at the very least, a less developed or whole human being. The great Roman orator Cicero provides the classical answer to both these questions in a passage from *De Republica* that deserves to be quoted at length:

> True law is right reason in agreement with nature, universal, consistent, everlasting, whose nature is to advocate duty and prescription and to deter wrongdoing by prohibition. Its prescriptions and prohibitions are obeyed by good men, but evil men disobey them. It is forbidden by God to alter this law, nor is it permissible to repeal any part of it, and it is impossible to abolish the whole of it. Neither the Senate nor the People can absolve us from obeying this law, and we do not need to look outside ourselves for an expounder or interpreter of this law. There will not be one law at Rome and another at Athens or different laws now and in the future. There is now and will be forever one law, valid for all peoples and all times. And there will be one master and rule for all of us in common—God, who is the author of this law, its promulgator, and its enforcing judge. Whoever does not obey this law is trying to escape himself and to deny his nature as a human being. By this very fact he will suffer the greatest penalties, even if he should somehow escape conventional punishments. (*De Republica*, 3.22–33)

Natural Law and Christianity

The collapse of the Roman Empire and the conversion of Europe to Christianity brought new questions and new scholarship about natural law. One major question concerned the content of natural law; another concerned how this natural law related to Christian ethics, especially the moral norms enumerated in the Bible, most specifically the Ten

Commandments. Thomas Aquinas, the thirteenth century Dominican theologian, proposed in his classic work, *Summa Theologiae* I, II, that there are three levels of content. The first and most basic is simply that "good is to be done and evil avoided" (I.q.94.a.2). This is so fundamental it can be considered commonsensical and self-evident. Even simple persons of good heart can grasp it without proof. The second level of content is more specific, consisting of moral precepts concerned with action "which of itself the natural reason of every person immediately judges must be done or not done" (I.q.100.a.1). Aquinas put the Ten Commandments into this category. Today one would surely add to such a list sanctions against such actions as rape, incest, child molestation, genocide, slavery, and torture. Aquinas does not deny that natural reason can be blinded by passion or cultural accretions, but his argument is that a thoughtful person who gives these actions sufficient consideration will know they are wrong. This is important, as will be seen below.

The third level of natural law content is more sophisticated and concerns actions "which are judged necessary for observance by the more discriminating consideration of reason by those who are wise" (I.q.100.a.1). Aquinas argues that these are "precepts which are found to be in accordance with reason through the careful inquiry of the wise" (I.q.100.a.3). As one might expect, it is the third-level moral precepts that have caused the most controversy and much of the opposition to natural law morality. One controversy has been the Roman Catholic hierarchy's insistence that artificial means of birth control are contrary to natural law. In the United States, Canada, and Europe a large number of theologians, philosophers, and a majority of Catholics disagree with this assessment. Other examples of third-level moralizing might be that environmental protection is a moral responsibility, that nuclear weapons are inherently immoral, that the death penalty is immoral, and that rich nations have economic obligations toward poor nations. Clearly even educated and wise people of good will can disagree on the content of natural law at this level.

If there are levels of and disputes about its content, does this mean natural law changes? And if so, what happens to Cicero's immutable, eternal law of the gods? The answer is that level one never changes—good is to be done and evil avoided; level two can be added to but not taken away from, as people become more aware of evils such as genocide

and rape; and level three develops as circumstances change and moral sensitivity develops. People sometimes do make mistakes when they claim something is required or prohibited by natural law, but disputes over such mistakes have often led to clarifications and new insights.

Natural Law and Conscience

If natural law means that every rational person has the ability to know right from wrong and knows he or she has an obligation to do good and avoid evil, one must consider the concept of conscience. In this context, conscience is the ability to make practical judgments rooted in natural law—but with some qualifications. There are people who cannot properly be said to have a functioning conscience. These would include those too young, senile, and/or mentally incapacitated to make moral decisions. In addition people may have *erroneous consciences*: that is, they may sincerely believe they are doing right but are not. There are also people with *scrupulous consciences* that demand actions of them beyond what reasonable people would consider necessary or prudent. In recognition of the fact that people sometimes reason poorly, Aristotle employed the term "right reason" to describe a proper balance. Today one might more properly think of natural law as a component of emotional intelligence, i.e., a combination of reasoning, intuition, social sensitivity, and common sense.

When conscience functions well in making moral decisions it takes into account a number of factors, such as: (a) the particular circumstances within which one finds oneself having to make a decision, including prevailing civil laws; (b) the enduring, universal values of fairness, self-control, duty, and empathy that are part of one's emotional and intellectual make up—one might call these the innate desire to be just and fair; (c) the wisdom of others, particularly the lessons learned from history, inspirational leaders, our religious heritage, and our culture; (d) the ability to reason through the potential consequences of one's actions, and to acknowledge the power and pull of one's own feelings and passions; and (e) the courage to take the time to reflect and consult others (especially those whose wisdom we value) and a willingness to change our minds and make the right decision at the right time. A person who considers these five factors has done what one should do to make a correct moral decision. Natural law holds that people in similar circumstances should come to the same moral decisions, i.e., there are correct moral decisions and people exercising right reason will come to them. Consciences are not idiosyncratic. One can say that natural law is conscience writ large.

Natural Law and Civil Law

How does natural law fit with the laws of nations and states, i.e., civil law? Natural-law theorists argue that civil laws must conform with natural law or they have no moral claim to obedience. In fact, we may have a moral obligation to disobey unjust laws, and to work for their repeal. On the other hand, natural law itself, based in human consciences that can be clouded by ignorance, passion, cultural norms, and peer pressure, is best supplemented by and applied in written law, including civil law and such statements as the Universal Declaration of Human Rights.

Opponents of Natural Law

Over the centuries the concept of natural law has acquired four categories of opponents: (a) naturalists, both philosophical and scientific: They insist that human beings are simply animals who, like all other creatures, must necessarily obey the laws of nature; there is no separate "free will." They argue that humans are simply more complicated organisms who make more sophisticated decisions than other animals, and that "moral decisions" are simply those actions that assure the survival of individuals or the species. In the current era people might argue that "conscience" is simply a matter of biochemistry. (b) religionists, primarily Protestant: These cast a wary eye on the role of reason in guiding moral decisions, preferring to rely on the expressed will of God as found in the Scriptures. John Calvin in particular argued that the idea of natural law undermined the core of the Christian message, namely that salvation comes only through the saving grace and belief in Jesus Christ. (c) legal positivists: These find natural law too vague and abstract to be of much use, and insist that only laws passed by appropriate legal authorities can be binding. One must also add in the contemporary world, (d) those who object that natural law has become too identified with Roman Catholicism and so conservative in its pronouncements that it has lost credibility.

Contemporary Value of Natural Law

Despite these enemies and objections, some scholars still argue that there is value in reviving the idea of natural law in the twenty-first century. First, there are circumstances in which there simply is nothing else to use as a basis for judging behavior. This is particularly true when evils are committed legally. For example, the effort to exterminate the Jews was done legally in Nazi Germany, yet its leaders were prosecuted at the Nuremberg Trials because they could and should have known they were doing evil. Likewise, segregation in the American South was perfectly legal in the 1960s, yet Martin Luther King used a natural-law argument in his *Letter from the Birmingham Jail* to justify disobeying the law. There will likely be other future circumstances in which people know it is entirely proper to appeal to the moral demands of "a higher law" in opposing published law or customs.

Second, the twenty-first century will see the acceleration of globalization, of the exchange of ideas and goods between people of different religions, languages, cultures, laws, and ethnic backgrounds. If this leads to a world embroiled in religious and cultural conflict, it will be valuable to explore the moral values we have in common. James Q. Wilson has examined a wide variety of cultures and shown that all share the moral sentiments of sympathy (empathy), fairness, self-control, and duty. These may be the basis for dialogue and understanding.

Finally, as scientists explore new biomedical issues such as cloning and genetic manipulation, it is imperative for people, particularly in democratic societies, to realize that they have the ability and duty to make moral as well as medical and political decisions, and that there is a process by which they can do so.

Paul J. Weber

See also Roman Catholicism

Further Reading:

Finnis, J. (1980). *Natural law and natural rights*. Notre Dame, IN: Notre Dame Press.

Finnis, J. (1998). *Aquinas: Social, legal and political thought*. Notre Dame, IN: Notre Dame Press.

George, R. P., & Wolfe, C. (Eds.). (2000). *Natural law and public reason*. Washington, DC: Georgetown University Press.

291

George, R. P. (Ed.). (1998). *Natural law and moral inquiry*. Washington, DC: Georgetown University Press.

McInerny, R. (1998). *Thomas Aquinas: Selected writings*. London: Penguin Books.

McLean, E. B. (2000). *Common truths: New perspectives on natural law*. Wilmington, DL: ISI Books.

Wilson, J. Q. (1993). *The moral sense*. New York: The Free Press.

New England: Colonial to Early Republic

The story of religious liberty in colonial New England is complex. This region on the northeastern seaboard of what would become the United States proved to be a bastion of Protestant religious establishment and enforced religious conformity. Beginning with the first Puritan settlers in 1620s, New Englanders sought to establish a theocratic society based upon biblical law and the rule of the saints. Dissenters faced persecution, banishment, and, occasionally, worse at the hands of the colonial magistrates, but the idea of religious freedom gradually gained a toehold and spread throughout the area. Roger Williams (1603?–1683) established Rhode Island as a haven for religious dissenters fleeing persecution, and various Quakers, Baptists, and Episcopalians arduously and successfully agitated for greater religious freedom. By the time of the Revolutionary War, congregants of most Christian denominations could freely practice their faith throughout New England.

The Puritan Theocracy

Puritan New England has often been called a theocracy. Many commentators have equated theocracy with the rule of a priestly class, but this situation never occurred in colonial New England. Indeed, in 1632 the General Court of Massachusetts Bay, the dominant settlement in New England, passed a law declaring that clergy could not serve in an elected office since such clerical power smacked of "popery." Nevertheless, Puritans were convinced that God *should* rule their land and that he would rule through his saints, i.e., those elected by God for salvation by grace through faith in the atoning work of Christ. Thus, the dominant Puritan colonies of Massachusetts and Connecticut limited the vote to church members.

The Puritans envisioned their "errand in the wilderness" as a positive example to England of how society could be organized along scriptural lines. The state was not an aggregation of individuals but an organic body wherein members entered into a civil covenant obligating them before God to further the establishment of a spiritual community. Notions of individual rights and liberties were circumscribed by the perceived needs of the commonwealth.

Surprisingly, there was a high degree of separation between church and state in the various New England colonies. The idea that the institutional church or clerical class should exercise direct authority in civil affairs seemed a practice most immediately associated with Roman Catholics. But even with this institutional separation, the Puritan state was expected to secure and protect a distinctively Christian commonwealth. The Fundamental Orders of Connecticut (1639) declared that the state must "maintain and preserve the liberty and purity of the Gospel of our Lord Jesus" (Stokes 1950, Vol. 1, 187–188), and when the New England churches met in 1648 to draft a platform of belief, they acknowledged the magistrate's power to enforce religious uniformity and suppress heresy, disobedience, and schism.

The institutional outline for the commonwealths of Massachusetts and Connecticut (New Hampshire and Maine were for much of this time a part of Massachusetts, and Vermont a sparsely populated frontier) was taken from the example of Old Testament Israel. On the shores of the American wilderness, New England Puritans entered into a covenant relationship with God just as Israel had done in the desert wilderness of Sinai. The divine precepts of the Mosaic law were considered by the Puritans to be equally valid in their own day. Thus, one of the first law codes drafted by Massachusetts Bay was simply titled "Moses, His Judicials," and it essentially restored the penal codes of Exodus and Deuteronomy. The code was never fully implemented and later Massachusetts legal codes were not so harsh. The Christian Bible remained, however, the touchstone for determining law and policy across the greatest part of the region.

Puritan political power was entrusted to the elect of God, those "saints" divinely chosen to receive salvation. Ultimate authority of the colony rested in the hands of God, so it made sense that those to whom God had revealed himself in salvation would better discern the will of God. The right to vote was limited

SELECTION FROM *THE BLOUDY TENENT OF PERSECUTION*, BY ROGER WILLIAMS (LONDON, 1644)

In 1635 Roger Williams was banished from the Massachusetts Bay Colony and fled to Rhode Island. In London in 1644 he published his best-known work on freedom, *The Bloudy Tenent of Persecution*, in which he set forth his arguments opposing religious persecution. The following selection is from the Preface.

First, that the blood of so many hundred thousand souls of Protestants and Papists, spilt in the wars of present and former ages, for their respective consciences, is not required nor accepted by Jesus Christ the Prince of Peace.

Secondly, pregnant scriptures and arguments are throughout the work proposed against the doctrine of persecution for cause of conscience.

Thirdly, satisfactory answers are given to scriptures, and objections produced by Mr. Calvin, Beza, Mr. Cotton, and the ministers of the New English churches and others former and later, tending to prove the doctrine of persecution for cause of conscience.

Fourthly, the doctrine of persecution for cause of conscience is proved guilty of all the blood of the souls crying for vengeance under the altar.

Fifthly, all civil states with their officers of justice in their respective constitutions and administrations are proved essentially civil, and therefore not judges, governors, or defenders of the spiritual or Christian state and worship.

Sixthly, it is the will and command of God that (since the coming of his Son the Lord Jesus) a permission of the most paganish, Jewish, Turkish, or antichristian consciences and worships, be granted to all men in all nations and countries; and they are only to be fought against with that sword which is only (in soul matters) able to conquer, to wit, the sword of God's Spirit, the Word of God.

Seventhly, the state of the Land of Israel, the kings and people thereof in peace and war, is proved figurative and ceremonial, and no pattern nor president for any kingdom or civil state in the world to follow.

Eighthly, God requireth not a uniformity of religion to be enacted and enforced in any civil state; which enforced uniformity (sooner or later) is the greatest occasion of civil war, ravishing of conscience, persecution of Christ Jesus in his servants, and of the hypocrisy and destruction of millions of souls.

Ninthly, in holding an enforced uniformity of religion in a civil state, we must necessarily disclaim our desires and hopes of the Jew's conversion to Christ.

Tenthly, an enforced uniformity of religion throughout a nation or civil state, confounds the civil and religious, denies the principles of Christianity and civility, and that Jesus Christ is come in the flesh.

Eleventhly, the permission of other consciences and worships than a state professeth only can (according to God) procure a firm and lasting peace (good assurance being taken according to the wisdom of the civil state for uniformity of civil obedience from all forts).

Twelfthly, lastly, true civility and Christianity may both flourish in a state or kingdom, notwithstanding the permission of divers and contrary consciences, either of Jew or Gentile. . . .

Source: *The Bloudy Tenent of Persecution*. Retrieved 10 December 2002, from: http://www.reformedreader.org/rbb/williams/btp.htm

Roger Williams (1604–1683/84) Statue, Roger Williams Park, Providence, Rhode Island.
COURTESY LIBRARY OF CONGRESS, PRINTS AND PHOTOGRAPHS DIVISION, DETROIT PUBLISHING COMPANY COLLECTION.

to church members who could give an account of the saving work of God in their lives. As restrictive as such a stipulation was, the Puritans expanded the franchise to far more individuals than was done in most other colonies or in their native England.

Puritan Ideas of Freedom and Conscience

The Puritan conception of freedom was substantive and not merely procedural. For the Puritan, freedom and liberty, including religious liberty, did not mean the right to do as one pleased (procedural liberty), but rather, the right to do as one ought, assigning a substantive end towards which liberty was used. Galatians 5:13 (Geneva Bible 1599) rimmed most discussions over the nature of liberty: "For brethren, ye have been called unto liberty; only use not liberty for an occasion to the flesh, but by love serve one another." As late as 1778, an election sermon preached before the Vermont legislature declared, "Liberty consists in a freedom to do that which is right" (Shain 1994, 222).

Puritans advocated liberty of conscience, but in a way that seems excessively narrow to modern Americans. The Westminster Confession (1646) declared, "God alone is the Lord of conscience, and has left it free from the doctrines and commandments of men which are, in any thing, contrary to His Word" (Stokes 1950, Vol. 1, 729). A person's conscience could not be forced to believe that which was contrary to Scripture, but it could be punished for continuing to believe falsehood and doctrinal error. Furthermore, when belief manifested itself in action, it left the realm of conscience and became liable to punishment since it could now threaten civil order.

In his argument with Roger Williams, John Cotton (1585–1652) expressed the common Puritan understanding of freedom of conscience when he declared that differences in unimportant beliefs could be tolerated so long as they did not disturb the civil peace. In more serious cases, a person could be prosecuted for expressing his beliefs when he "erred fundamentally, and obstinately, after just conviction, against the very Principles of Christian religion" (Cotton [1647] 1972, 119–20). If after repeated admonitions from the clergy or other Christians an individual refused to abandon his wrong belief, he would be sinning against his own conscience by denying the self-evident truths of Scripture, and the state could enforce the law of punishment or banishment. Such civil injunctions against wrong belief were not imposed to restore the person to correct belief but to preserve civil order.

Dissenters

The Separatists who first settled Plymouth in 1622 granted a greater degree of toleration to dissent than their more rigorous Puritan neighbors, but Plymouth never became a large colony. (It was forced to merge with Massachusetts Bay in 1643.) Massachusetts, on the other hand, was the intellectual and commercial heart of New England, and the affairs and attitudes of the Massachusetts Bay Puritans proved to be normative for the other Puritan settlements in the area. Rhode Island, established by Roger Williams after his flight from Massachusetts, was an altogether different case, which granted religious freedom to nearly all comers.

The Puritan limits on conscience led to the banishment of Anne Hutchinson (1591–1643) from Massachusetts in 1637. Hutchinson organized Sunday gatherings to review and discuss the sermons of the day. Her stress of God's grace led her to reject outward signs of conversion, and she averred that most Massachusetts ministers had abandoned the gospel of grace for a program emphasizing outward conformity to the moral law. Hutchinson's religious views were perceived as a civil threat, especially since they came at a time of war with the Indians. Furthermore, her teaching on the direct ministry of the Holy Spirit upon an individual challenged the basis of Puritan society. Massachusetts had been founded as a Bible commonwealth and direct revelation bypassed that scriptural foundation of society. Her increasing radicalism led the General Court to banish her from the colony for her antinomian views.

Around the same time, Massachusetts Bay ran into a more serious conflict with one of its ministers named Roger Williams. Williams advocated that the colonial churches break their ties to the Anglican Church and establish pure churches of converted believers. His continued agitation led to his banishment from the colony and he eventually settled among the Narragansett Indians. Eventually he purchased land from them and established the colony of Providence, which in turn merged with the colony of Rhode Island where Hutchinson and her followers had fled. Williams's Providence was established with the explicit hope that it would be a shelter for persons distressed for conscience.

Quakers, Baptists, and Episcopalians also suffered at the hands of the Puritan authorities. By far the most stringent suppression of religious freedom fell upon the Quakers, who were at that time the most radical dissenters in New England. A number of early Quakers flaunted all social conventions, going so far as to march naked through the streets of Boston as a sign of religious protest. In 1658 Quakerism was banned in Massachusetts, and four Quakers, including two women, were eventually hung for their religious beliefs.

Development of Religious Liberty

The severe judgment meted out to the Quakers was one factor that led many New Englanders to reconsider the persecution of religious dissent. Roger Williams became the severest critic of the New England standing order, arguing in his book, *The Bloudy Tenent*, that state coercion of religion did little to further true faith and put civil magistrates into the position where they would "sin grievously against the work of God, and blood of souls" (Williams [1644] 2001, 81). As Williams understood Scripture, the state had no authority over an individual's relationship with God, and the example of Old Testament Israel had been superseded by the teachings of Jesus. Such discontinuity between the Old and New Testament undermined the Scriptural basis framing the entire Puritan project of New England, and many Puritans penned earnest replies to Williams. The ablest defense of the New England Way was by the Reverend John Cotton; his response, *The Bloudy Tenent, Washed and Made White in the Bloude of the Lambe*, argued that even in the New Testament magistrates who did not discern and judge false doctrine brought judgment upon all society. The Old Testament proscriptions against false teaching were of "universal and perpetuall equity to put to death any Apostate seducing Idolater, or Heretick" (Cotton [1647] 1972, 67).

Even as the written debate between Williams and Cotton continued, the lived example of Rhode Island showed that a society with nearly unmitigated toleration could survive and prosper. When Providence and Rhode Island merged in 1663, the royal charter expressly declared that no one "shall be in any wise molested, punished, disquieted, or called in question for any differences of opinion in matters of religion. . . every person and persons [shall] freely and fully have and enjoy his own judgments and consciences in matters of religion"(Stokes 1950, Vol. 1, 205). This was no mere paper liberty. Royal commissioners who visited New England in 1665 reported that in Rhode Island, "They allow liberty of conscience to all who live civilly: they admit of all religions" (Cobb 1902, 436–437).

Locke and the Enlightenment

Throughout the rest of New England, the ideas of John Locke (1632–1704) and the Enlightenment tempered religious intolerance in the early years of the eighteenth century. Locke's ideas, while departing from the biblicism of Puritanism, nevertheless resonated with the Calvinistic concerns of the New Englanders. Locke argued that religious toleration was good because humans were fallible and prone to make mistakes in judgment and legislation. Freedom of conscience, Locke argued, was a natural right that could too easily be taken by an overzealous government. Locke therefore advocated a radical separation of the sacred and the secular in society, relegating religion to an essentially private matter of belief. In return, the state would secure the right for one to believe without defining the content of belief. These

Lockean ideas on liberty found a receptive audience both among the traditional descendants of the early Puritan settlers and the growing numbers of New England dissenters, including the rising class of merchants and intellectuals attracted to Unitarian ideas.

Isaac Backus (1724–1806) and John Leland (1754–1851) were two New England Baptist ministers who used Locke's ideas and writings to agitate for greater religious liberty. Of the two, Backus was more conservative, willing to maintain taxpayer-supported churches and proscriptions against blasphemy and various social sins. Leland, however, marked a return to the absolute conception of soul liberty more akin to the position of Roger Williams, though Leland himself was perhaps more influenced by the liberal ideas of Locke and Thomas Jefferson in coming to this position.

Revival and Revolution

The First Great Awakening that began in the 1730s broke down many of the social barriers against religious dissenters. Divisions within the established churches over the nature of the revival led to a practical disestablishment as the monolithic Puritan religious order fragmented into Old Lights and New Lights, Evangelicals and Proto-Unitarians, Congregationalists and Presbyterians. Furthermore, the focus on inner religious experience that was at the heart of the revivalistic movement cut across denominational lines, allowing the development of a sense of kindred spirit among the various religious bodies of New England.

By the time of the American Revolution (1775–1783), the Puritan idea of a unified holy commonwealth had vanished. Colonial leaders recognized that the American settlements were to be of a different sort. Four of the original thirteen colonies never had any state-established church; all others were increasingly pluralistic. The imperative of war turned public sentiment away from the quest to suppress heterodoxy toward a desire to bring people together in support of the new political order emerging from the conflict with Britain.

Early Republic

During the early republic, most New England states recognized the political and social value of full religious liberty and moved to disestablish their state churches. Connecticut broke all formal ties with an established church in 1818, followed by New Hampshire in 1819 and Massachusetts in 1833. Enlightenment ideas on toleration and liberty came to be accepted as normative by all but the most intransigent sons and daughters of the New England Puritans, and they were few in number and of limited import.

Albert R. Beck

See also Great Awakenings and the Antebellum Period; Letter on Toleration

Further Reading

Carden, A. (1990). *Puritan Christianity in America*. Grand Rapids, MI: Baker Book House.

Cobb, S. (1902). *The rise of religious liberty in America: A history*. New York: Macmillan.

Cotton, J. (1972). *The bloudy tenent, washed and made white in the bloud of the lambe*. New York: Arno Press. (Original work published 1647)

Cotton, J. (1983). *The New England way: John Cotton*. New York: AMS Press.

Field, P. S. (1998). *The crisis of the standing order: Clerical intellectuals and cultural authority in Massachusetts, 1780–1833*. Amherst: University of Massachusetts Press.

Grenz, S. (1983). *Isaac Backus—Puritan and Baptist: His place in history, his thought, and their implication for modern Baptist theology*. Macon, GA: Mercer University Press.

Hall, T. L. (1998). *Roger Williams and religious liberty*. Urbana: University of Illinois Press.

Hamburger, P. (2002). *Separation of church and state*. Cambridge, MA: Harvard University Press.

Hanson, C. P. (1998). *Necessary virtue: The pragmatic origins of religious liberty in New England*. Charlottesville, VA, & London: University Press of Virginia.

McLoughlin, W. G. (1971). *New England dissent, 1630–1833: The Baptists and the separation of church and state*. Cambridge, MA: Harvard University Press.

Miller, P. (1954). *The New England mind: The seventeenth century*. Cambridge, MA: Harvard University Press.

Miller, P. (1956). *Errand in the wilderness*. Cambridge, MA: Belknap Press.

Morgan, E. S. (1963). *Visible saints: The history of a Puritan idea*. New York: New York University Press.

Shain, B. A. (1994). *The myth of American individualism*. Princeton, NJ: Princeton University Press.

Staloff, D. (1998). *The making of an American thinking class: Intellectuals and intelligentsia in Puritan Massachusetts*. New York: Oxford University Press.

Stokes, A. P. (1950). *Church and state in the United States*. (Vols. 1–3). New York: Harper & Brothers.

Vaughan, A. T., & Bremer, F. J. (Eds.). (1977). *Puritan New England: Essays on religion, society, and culture*. New York: St. Martin's Press.

Williams, R. (2001). *The bloudy tenent of persecution for cause of conscience*. Macon, GA: Mercer University Press. (Original work published 1644)

Witte, J., Jr. (1999). A most mild and equitable establishment of religion: John Adams and the Massachusetts experiment. *Journal of church and state, 41*, 213–52.

Zakai, A. (1994). *Theocracy in Massachusetts: Reformation and separation in early Puritan New England*. Lewiston, NY: Mellen University Press.

New Religious Movements

New Religious Movements (NRMs) are often pioneers in testing religious freedom. Such groups challenge the religious status quo and often have beliefs and practices that are new and unfamiliar to the general public, as well as to political leaders and such key people as judges. In sociological terms, NRMs are deviant groups, and as such they test the boundaries of acceptable belief and behavior in societies in which they arise or to which they immigrate. Such boundary-testing problems are exacerbated considerably when NRMs are involved in violence, as has been the case with the Solar Temple, Aum Shinrikyo, Heaven's Gate, and a few other religious groups.

Suppressing NRMs by Labeling Them as Deviant and Dangerous

NRMs face immense definitional problems because they are new and may have practices and beliefs that outsiders do not define as religious. As sociologist Larry Greil has noted, being designated a religion is to partake of a scarce resource, and those groups that have achieved this status do not like sharing that resource with upstart groups wanting to claim this privileged status. Other interest groups in a society may also have reservations about allowing NRMs to be designated true religions. For instance, in the United States there has been well-documented competition between NRMs and branches of psychotherapy for adherents (or patients), and that competition has led some within the therapeutic community to take strong stands against religious experimentation. Some traditional religious organizations have also become involved in efforts to limit the spread of NRMs, in part because NRMs have attracted young people who might otherwise participate in the established religions.

One tactic in the definitional battle is to label NRMs with derogatory, negatively connoted terms, designed to indicate clearly to all that such groups are not "real" religions. For instance, successfully labeling NRMs as "cults" or "sects" has been a quite effective way to exert social control over them. In the United States the term *cult* has been the most used to suggest that a group is a false or fraudulent religion. In Europe the term *sect* carries similar negative connotations, and there has even been some diffusion of the term *cult* from the United States to Europe. Since the terrorist attacks on New York City and Washington, D.C., on 11 September 2001, a widespread climate of fear and concern over terrorists has led some countries to label some NRMs as terrorist groups, as China did with the Falun Gong spiritual movement. Similar efforts have been made to designate Islamic groups in some Western European countries as terrorist organizations. When such labels achieve a hegemonic status, they become very powerful social weapons used to limit the influence and growth of NRMs. Such limitations relate directly to a loss of religious freedom for these groups and their participants.

NRMs have been criticized for how they raise and spend money. Accusations of fraud and misrepresentation abound and have contributed to efforts to limit the fund-raising and proselytizing activities of NRMs in the United States and other countries. In the United States such concerns have led directly to governmental efforts to control NRM methods of handling money, either through attempting local limits on solicitation or through federal efforts to use the tax status of specific NRMs as a way to leverage influence over them.

Accusations of Brainwashing

Another key element in efforts to exert social control over NRMs, and thereby to limit the religious freedom of participants, is to accuse such groups of using brainwashing and mind control to gain and retain participants. When that claim is made, then participation becomes not a matter of religious freedom but one of mental health. These claims, first made in the United States, are plainly part of an ideological arsenal to be used when conflicts arise over the role of NRMs in a society. The fact that the claims are not scientifically defensible is of little moment when battles are being waged for the hearts and minds of those who might choose to participate in NRMs.

Brainwashing accusations and claims of mismanagement of finances are part and parcel of defining NRMs as cults, sects, or even terrorist organizations. According to the normative position concerning NRMs, "real religions" recruit and teach members, whereas cults and sects are accused of using trickery, brainwashing, and mind control to obtain and keep participants. "Real religions" supposedly raise funds in legal and acceptable fashion (usually from their members), while NRMs raise money under false pretenses. "Real religions" are to be afforded the protections for their activities that are found in statutes, constitutions, and international agreements such as the European Convention on Human Rights, whereas cults and sects cannot access such protections, and should, according to some, even be punished for seeking such protections. The notion that NRMs use brainwashing has been diffused around the world, finding applications in a number of societies seeking to exert social control over the activities of NRMs.

Religious Freedom for NRMs in the United States

Contemporary NRMs first came to the attention of the general public and political leaders in the United States in the late 1960s and early 1970s. Since the First Amendment to the U.S. Constitution guarantees freedom of religion, there has been less activity directly regulating religion by governmental bodies, including the Federal government, than occurs in many other societies. However, U.S. federal agencies such as the Internal Revenue Service and the Immigration and Naturalization Service have been pressed into service to help "manage" religious experimentation.

This lack of federal involvement in limiting NRM activities has contributed directly to a number of "self-help" remedies undertaken by citizens who have taken issue with the development and spread of NRMs. These self-help activities have taken three major forms: development of an "anticult" movement (ACM) to combat NRMs mainly through media campaigns and lobbying activities, initiation of "deprogramming" of NRM members, numbering in the thousands, and civil legal actions filed by former members and their relatives against some NRMs. All of these activities have served to limit the religious freedom of NRM participants.

Anti-Cult Movement

The development of so-called anti-cult organizations in the United States has been described in some detail in Anson Shupe and David Bromley's *The New Vigilantes* (1980), and they updated this treatment in the introduction to a 1994 book that examined the anti-cult movement in other societies. This movement has struck a resonant chord with many members of the general public and with political and media leaders. Its message is that many NRMs have engaged in behaviors that are unacceptable, even if not strictly illegal (although there are many claims of illegal activities as well), to ordinary people. The ACM has helped make it seem to the general public that social control over NRMs is justified, despite the fact that those social controls limit the religious freedom of participants. The ACM has also been involved in considerable "mission activity," promoting its views outside the United States.

Deprogramming

The most overt and controversial action sanctioned by the ACM is deprogramming—the kidnapping and incarceration of NRM members for the purposes of getting them to change their minds about their religious affiliation. Thousands of such actions have taken place in the United States over the years, and the practice has spread to other countries in recent decades. This coercive and radical resocialization tactic has sometimes been "successful," and flourished for a number of years, in part because the federal government and most other governmental agencies did not define what was happening as kidnapping. Such actions were defined as "family matters," even though most of those who experienced efforts at deprogramming were of legal age and apparently had made informed decisions about joining an NRM.

Coercive deprogramming fell into disfavor in the late 1970s, after a few adverse court decisions that refused to condone such actions as the kidnapping of adults off the streets. Coercive deprogramming still exists, especially in Japan, but it has been replaced in the United States by so-called exit counseling, which involves NRM participants agreeing to participate in counseling procedures that are not nearly so coercive in nature.

Civil Actions

Freedom of religion for NRM members has also been threatened by civil actions filed by some former members of the NRMs. Although most former members in these high-turnover groups do not think ill of their experience, some do, especially if they came in contact with the ACM. A small minority of former members have filed legal actions against controversial NRMs such as the Unification Church, the Hare Krishna movement, and the Church of Scientology, charging the religions with fraud, misrepresentation, false imprisonment, and intentional affliction of emotional distress. Most of these cases hinged on courts' promotion and acceptance of the view that the participants were in fact brainwashed, a questionable claim, but one that has widespread popular credence. As has been noted, even though brainwashing-based claims are very questionable from a scientific point of view, judges and juries have sometimes yielded to the enticements of such ideas. Some very large awards have been granted at the trial court level in the United States, decisions that, even if overturned or limited at the appeals court level, have had a chilling effect on religious freedom for NRM participants.

Not all such brainwashing-based legal actions by former members have been successful, and there have also been some successful suits against deprogrammings (and parents) that directly challenge the idea that participants in NRMs need to be rescued. But suits by former members against deprogrammers, even when successful, have still required considerable financial resources to fight adequately. Also, in most suits against deprogrammers, the deprogrammers have been successful in claiming that they were simply agents of the parents, and they have used a necessity defense for their actions. (A necessity defense is a claim that the harm done is less than the harm that would ensue if no action was taken.)

NRMs and Religious Freedom Outside the United States

Anti-cult ideas concerning NRMs have spread widely to other countries, sometimes thanks to the direct efforts of U.S.- or European-based organizations. These ideas undergird government efforts in a number of countries to exert control over the spread of NRMs, both indigenous and transplanted.

Western European countries such as the Netherlands, Italy, Denmark, and Sweden have generally not joined in the moral panic about NRMs, whereas neighboring countries such France, Germany, and Belgium have taken strong public stands against them, with France easily being the most virulent in its efforts to exert control and thereby limit the religious freedom of its citizenry. Newly independent states (such as the former Soviet states) have also expended a widespread effort to control NRMs, especially those from the West, and have tried to use NRMs as scapegoats in battles for political control and influence. Other countries in which there have been attempts to limit the activities of NRMs include Argentina, Mexico, Singapore, and Australia.

France has made a major effort to export its ideas and position as one way of defending its own actions in passing a stringent new law concerning minority faiths in France. One report claims that officials of a French governmental agency established to "fight sects" traveled to forty-three countries, including China and a number of newly independent states, in an effort to persuade other countries to adopt France's punitive approach to NRMs and other minority faiths.

Looking toward the Future

Some NRMs have played a role in expanding the boundaries of religious freedom, as when the Jehovah's Witnesses have challenged limitations on their rights to proselytize. However, more often than not, NRMs have not fared very well in legislatures or courts, and indeed, it can be argued that because of their unpopularity in a number of countries, their opponents have been able to enact new strictures on religious freedom. Only time will tell whether contemporary religious movements will gain more religious freedom for themselves and therefore for others.

James T. Richardson

See also Brainwashing; European Convention on Human Rights; Scientology; Unification Church

Further Reading

Ahar, R. (2000). *Law and religion.* Aldershot, UK: Ashgate.

Anthony, D. (1990). Religious movements and brainwashing litigation: Evaluating key testimony. In T. Robbins & D. Anthony (Eds.), *In gods we trust,* (pp. 295–344). New Brunswick, NJ: Transaction Books.

Barker, E. (1995). Twenty years of changes in new religious movements [Special issue]. *Social Compass: International Review of Sociology of Religion,* 42(2).

Borovik, I., & Babinski, G. (1997). *New religious phenomena in central and eastern Europe.* Krakow, Poland: Nomos.

Bromley, D., & Richardson J. T. (1983). *The brainwashing/deprogramming controversy.* New York: Edwin Mellen Press.

CESNUR. (2002). French anti-cult missionaries continue their campaign. Retrieved December 17, 2002, from http://www.cesnur.org/2002.fr_mils.htm

Cote, P. (Ed.). *Frontier religions in public space.* Ottawa, Canada: University of Ottawa Press.

Cote, P., & Richardson, J. (2001). Disciplined litigation, vigilant litigation, and deformation: Dramatic organizational change in Jehovah's Witnesses. *Journal for the Scientific Study of Religion,* 40(1), 11–26.

Davis, D. (Ed.). *Religious liberty in northern Europe in the twenty-first century.* Waco, TX: J. M. Dawson Institute for Church-State Studies, Baylor University.

Davis, D., & Besier, G. (2002). *International perspectives on freedom and equality of religious belief.* Waco, TX: J. M. Dawson Institute of Church-State Studies, Baylor University.

Davis, D., & Hanks, B. (2002). *New religious movements and religious liberty in America.* Waco, TX: Baylor University Press.

Dillon, J., & Richardson J. T. (1994). The "cult" concept: A politics of representation analysis. *SYZYGY: Journal of Alternative Religion and Culture,* 3(3–4), 185–198.

Evans, C. (2001). *Freedom of religion under the European Convention on Human Rights.* Oxford, UK: Oxford University Press.

Ginsburg, G. P., & Richardson, J. T. (1998). "Brainwashing" evidence in light of *Daubert.* In H. Reece (Ed.), *Law and science* (pp. 265–288). Oxford, UK: Oxford University Press.

Greil, L. (1996). Sacred claims: The "cult controversy" as a struggle over the right to the religious label. In L. Carter (Ed.), *The issue of authenticity in the study of religions* (pp. 47–63). Greenwich, CT: JAI Press.

Mullins, M. (2001). The legal and political fallout of the "Aum affair." In R. Kisala, & M Mullins (Eds.), *Religion and social crisis in Japan* (pp. 71–88). London: St. Martins Press.

Pfeifer, J., & Ogloff, J. (1992). Cults and the law [Special issue]. *Behavioral Sciences and the Law,* 10(1).

Richardson, J. T. (1988). *Money and power in the new religions*. New York: Edwin Mellen Press.

Richardson, J. T. (1993). A social psychological critique of 'brainwashing' claims about recruitment to new religions. In J. Hadden & D. Bromley (Eds.), *Handbook of cults and sects in America* (pp. 75–97). Greenwich, CT: JAI Press.

Richardson, J. T. (1996). "Brainwashing" claims and minority religions outside the United States: Cultural diffusion of a questionable legal concept in the legal arena. *Brigham Young University Law Review*, 4, 873–904.

Richardson, J. T. (2003). *Regulating religion: Case studies from around the globe*. New York: Kluwer.

Richardson, J. T., & Introvigne, M. (2001, June). "Brainwashing" theories in European parliamentary and administrative reports on "cults and sects." *Journal for the Scientific Study of Religion*, 40(2), 143–168.

Robbins, T. (2001). New religions in their political, legal, and religious contexts around the world [Special issue]. *Nova Religio: The Journal of Alternative and Emergent Religions*, 4(2).

Robbins, T., & Bromley, D. (1992). Social experimentation and the significance of new religious movements. In M. Lynn & D. Moberg (Eds.), *Research in the social scientific study of religion* (Vol. 4., pp. 1–28). Greenwich, CT: JAI Press.

Shterin, M., & Richardson, J. T. (2000). Effects of the western anti-cult movement on development of laws concerning religion in post-Communist Russia. *Journal of Church and State*, 4(2), 247–272.

Shupe, A., & Bromley, D. (1980). *The new vigilantes: Anti-cultists and the new religions*. Beverly Hills, CA: Sage.

Shupe, A., & Bromley, D. (1994). *Anti-cult movements in cross-cultural perspective*. New York: Garland Press.

Wood, J., & Davis, D. (1993). *The role of government in monitoring and regulating religion in public life*. Waco, TX: J. M. Dawson Institute of Church-State Relations, Baylor University.

New York: Colonial to Early Republic

Throughout its colonial history, New York was a political and cultural leader for what was to become the United States. This was no less true for religious diversity and its accompanying questions of religious freedom. Shortly after 1614, when Dutch colonists established their first settlements along the Hudson River, European settlers representing a variety of religions moved into the colony—a diversity that surpassed that in the other colonies, and that continues today. New York's experiences with religious freedom—and its periodic lack thereof—served as an example for the developing nation.

Dutch Rule, 1614–1664

When the Dutch founded colonies in North America, they did so under the aegis of the Dutch Reformed Church. As the established religion, the Dutch Church enjoyed exclusive dominion over the colony's settlers. This held for New Amsterdam (later Manhattan) as well, although once it began to prosper that settlement attracted the widest variety of colonists. By 1644 the colony of New Netherlands, which stretched from Albany south through New Amsterdam and into parts of present-day New Jersey, housed Catholics, Puritans, Lutherans, and Anabaptists, as well as Dutch Reformed Calvinists. The colonial Dutch government neither sanctioned nor recognized religions other than the Dutch Reformed, but was fairly tolerant in practice.

This tolerance, however, depended on the religion in question. Jews, who represented a small minority in New Amsterdam after their 1654 arrival, received permission from the governor, Peter Stuyvesant (c.1592–1672), to take part in town affairs and to hold religious services in their homes. On the other hand, the larger minority of Lutherans found less freedom to practice their religion. In 1655 they were barred from holding services in their homes, and a Lutheran pastor who arrived in New Amsterdam in 1657 was deported after repeated attempts to minister to the colony's Lutherans. Faced with such limitations on their practice, members of minority religions who did not leave for more tolerant parts generally welcomed the British takeover of 1664.

British Rule, 1664–1683: The First Generation

Minority religious groups still faced discrimination under British rule, but they had more latitude than under the Dutch. Like the Dutch, the British government favored a state church, the Church of England (later Episcopal), but it did not prohibit others from the colony. In 1665 the first British governor, Richard Nicolls (1624–1672) established the "Duke's Laws," which included freedom of religion. He officially recognized Lutheranism in New Amsterdam in 1666;

The Reformed Protestant Dutch Church, Albany, New York, c. 1907. COURTESY OF LIBRARY OF CONGRESS, PRINTS AND PHOTOGRAPHS DIVISION, DETROIT PUBLISHING CO.

Lutherans began erecting a church in 1671; Quakers held meetings by 1681; Jews were conducting services by 1695. Although the Dutch Reformed Church lost official status after the 1664 Dutch surrender to the English, it likewise continued to serve its congregation throughout New York.

Freedom to practice religion, however, did not mean freedom to practice religion without state interference. For instance, although non-Anglican clergy could ply their trade in New York, they needed to be approved by, and served at the pleasure of, the colonial British government. Congregations had to apply to the governor for permission before their clergy could enter the colony, and had to go without clergy until receiving a positive response. Although the state paid only Anglican ministers' salaries, clergy not receiving payment due from their congregations turned to the governor for help, as did congregants not pleased with their clergy. Most non-Anglican congregations, especially those spread across Long Island or the Hudson River, complained that the colonial government would not allow them sufficient clergy. In 1674 Albany's Dutch Reformed complained that the government had assigned them clergy from the wrong denomination: Their new minister had been ordained as an Anglican. Congregants across the colony continued to appeal to the governor for redress of religious wrongs, such as Huntington Puritans complaining of Quakers trespassing their church grounds in 1677, and for religious favors, such as a Jamaica minister requesting an official prayer day for his town in 1678. In another case, Hempstead non-Quakers won approval to prohibit Quaker meetings in their town; they then complained in May 1679 to the current governor, Edmund Andros (1637–1714), that the Quakers were ignoring the injunction.

Quakers struggled with religious freedom more than most during Andros's tenure (1674–80). He allowed them to forego the traditional oath in favor of an "affirmation" when called for jury duty, so they could honor their religious proscription against oath swearing, but prosecuted them for not paying taxes in support of their towns' established (Anglican) ministers and for marrying in Quaker ceremonies, which were not recognized by law. He also fined them for not taking up arms during King Philip's War (1675–76), for holding unapproved meetings, and for protesting their treatment.

Other denominations faired somewhat better. Andros was tolerant of what he perceived to be time-honored religions; his deputy governor, Brockholes, a Catholic, served as acting governor in 1681–83. Yet, popular anti-Catholicism was on the rise in New York in response to a growing Catholic population, and suspicions of Catholics remained high after rumors of the fictitious "popish plot" to overthrow Protestant King Charles II in favor of his Catholic brother, James II, spread from England to the colonies in 1678.

British Rule, 1683–1689: A Catholic Governor and Backlash

Although the "popish plot" was fictitious, James II did succeed his brother to the throne and, beginning in 1683, a Catholic governor, Thomas Dongan (1634–1715), ruled New York. Dongan sailed to New York with an Anglican minister and a Catholic priest, underscoring religious freedom and cooperation. New York Catholics thrived under Dongan's governance, but they also faced rising anti-Catholicism, especially after a Catholic was appointed commandant at Fort Albany, along with governor and deputy governor (still Brockholes) one of the three most powerful positions in colonial New York. Although the prominence of these Catholic men perhaps indicates the degree of religious freedom in the colony, it

also exacerbated Protestant-Catholic tensions, worsened after French Protestant Huguenots thronged to New York in 1685 to escape persecution.

Despite rising tensions, New Yorkers of varying stripes continued to live and work in the town and colony of New York. In 1687, Dongan reported that the town housed Anglicans, Dutch and French Calvinists, Lutherans, Catholics, Jews, and a variety of Quakers, Sabbatarians, Antisabbatarians, Anabaptists, and Independents. Unlike, for instance, Massachusetts, which recognized only one form of religion, the New York government officially tolerated all of them. In practice, however, their freedoms were limited; the Quakers, in particular, continued to suffer legal discrimination. In 1688 after individual pleas went unheeded, united colony Quakers submitted a petition for redress of the wrongs they suffered under Dongan's authority—continuations of those Andros had set in motion—to which they appended a list of items taken from them in payment of fines, and which they demanded returned: sheep, cows, pigs, linens, and household items. Quakers as well as members of other religious minorities continued to request exemption from taxes dedicated to the support of the Church of England.

British Rule, 1689–1691: Leisler's Rebellion

Although most of the complaints lodged against Dongan were similar to those against his predecessors, an increasing number of New Yorkers blamed his Catholicism. A new, Protestant, governor, Francis Nicholson (1655–1728), succeeded Dongan, but rumors spread that he had attended religious services with the Catholic king before setting sail for New York. In 1689, shortly after he took office, a band of disgruntled New Yorkers led by Jacob Leisler (1640–1691) overthrew the appointed government in the lower half of the colony—never quite making it to Albany—and for a time quashed religious freedom in lower New York.

After the coup, Leisler appointed himself lieutenant governor. In February 1689, in one of his first acts, Leisler wrote to civil and military officers throughout the colony, instructing them to detain all Catholics. Leisler also brought suspicion on officials appointed by either Dongan or Andros, claiming that they and others had sent their children to parochial school, donated money to the Catholic Church, or in other ways supported Catholicism and, hence, were untrustworthy.

Leisler held office for less than two years, but in that time he managed to polarize the colony, and particularly the town, of New York. Royally appointed government returned to power in 1691 and hanged Leisler on 16 May 1691. Religious freedom returned to the region, but the rebellion had rent the delicate peace among the colony's religions, and it would not return easily.

British Rule, 1691–1773: Limited Accordance

One of the most severe consequences of the rift was the 1700 State Act, the preamble of which outlawed Catholic clergy, establishing an indefinite prison sentence for those found within the colony, and a sentence of two days in the pillory plus a £200 fine for anyone caught harboring them, an act not repealed until 1784. Since Catholic sacraments require an officiating priest, this ban had the effect of prohibiting much of Catholic practice.

For non-Catholic New Yorkers, however, much of the eighteenth century sustained patterns established during the early decades of British rule. Members of the various religions continued to strain against the government's limitations on religious freedom. Taxes remained their primary complaint. Some complained that they should not have to support Anglican ministers; some argued that their churches should be supported too.

Contested Rule, 1773–1786

The revolutionaries who declared the colonies' independence from Britain in 1773 pledged freedom, but not all colonists were convinced that the religious freedom revolutionaries promised would be greater than what they had from the British, or in the case of Catholics, what they might have under conciliatory British rule. Although Quakers, for instance, often elicited the revolutionaries' antagonism through their refusal as a group to take up arms, late eighteenth-century New Yorkers tended to ignore their religious differences as they made alliances as revolutionaries or Tories. Catholics found themselves in a more complicated situation, however, and struggled the most for religious freedom in revolutionary New York.

When New York representatives met to draft a state constitution in 1776–1777, they agreed that no religion should be supported by the state, and that New Yorkers should have freedom of religion. Yet, they disagreed to whom this freedom should apply. John Jay (1745–1829) argued that the state should retain the power to decide what religious beliefs are against the state's best interests and to censor them; barring this, he proposed an amendment requiring Catholics to pledge allegiance to New York over the pope. The final version of the New York State Constitution, adopted 20 April 1777, included a version of Jay's amendment in the form of a naturalization oath. The religious freedoms granted in this constitution are noteworthy among the early state constitutions. For instance, while Massachusetts's constitution (1780) authorized the legislature to establish a Protestant church, New York's at least nominally provided for the free exercise of religion. Nonetheless, the debate over the extent of these freedoms—and the naturalization oath—reflects the religious tensions that continued to plague New York.

These tensions became more complicated as war tore through the region. Many New York Catholics supported England, perceiving the British as more amenable to their religion. On the other hand, French Catholics sailed to North America to assist the revolutionaries. Some Anglicans, including Jay, promoted revolution, while others emphasized their allegiance to the Church of England and the throne. New York's other religions were similarly divided. Yet, especially in the state's northern and western reaches, many linked Catholics with the British cause.

U.S. Rule, 1786–1813

The revolutionaries' success in the war changed much in the former colonies, but it changed little for New Yorkers' religious freedom. New Yorkers had been pushing the bounds of colonial religious freedom since the 1640s, and the state constitution of 1777 disestablished religion nearly a decade before the U.S. government followed suit.

Nevertheless, New York maintained its naturalization oath through the end of the eighteenth century. In 1801 the state reduced the oath's reach, requiring it only for those Catholics in the government or military. In 1813 the state passed the Act for the Incorporation of Religious Societies, requiring every religious congregation to elect a board of trustees to hold the title to and manage all of the congregation's property, and to set the clergy's salary, in the process imposing one organizational form on all religions in the state.

U.S. Rule after 1813

The early nineteenth century inaugurated many changes for New York. The population adjusted to life under a new government and to social changes. Immigrants poured into the region in greater numbers than before, swelling the ranks of various denominations, especially Catholicism. A range of new religious movements developed in the young republic—many of them in western New York—challenging New Yorkers' religious tolerance. For instance, after Joseph Smith (1805–1844) founded the Church of Jesus Christ of Latter-day Saints in Palmyra, New York in 1830, local antagonism and violence against the fledgling movement's followers led them westward. Yet these changes occurred in a region that had been wrestling with the challenges of religious freedom for two centuries.

Amy E. Lorion

Further Reading

Becker, M. J. (1975). *A history of Catholic life in the diocese of Albany, 1609–1864.* United States Catholic Historical Society Monograph Series No. 31. New York: United States Catholic Historical Society.

Benson, L. (1961). *The concept of Jacksonian democracy: New York as a test case.* Princeton, NJ: Princeton University Press.

Bishop of Buffalo [J. Timon]. (1862). *Missions in western New York, and church history of the diocese of Buffalo.* Buffalo, NY: Catholic Sentinel Print.

Bonomi, P. U. (1971). *A factious people: Politics and society in colonial New York.* New York: Columbia University Press.

Christoph, P. R. (Ed.). (1993). *The Dongan papers: 1683–1688, Part 1. Admiralty court and other records of the administration of New York Governor Thomas Dongan.* Syracuse, NY: Syracuse University Press.

Christoph, P. R. (Ed.). (1996). *The Dongan Papers: 1683–1688 Part 2. Files of the provincial secretary of New York during the administration of Governor Thomas Dongan.* Syracuse, NY: Syracuse University Press.

Christoph, P. R., & Christoph, F. A. (Eds.). (1989). *The Andros papers: Files of the provincial secretary of New York during the administration of Governor Sir Edmund Andros, 1674–1680* (Vols 1–3). Syracuse, NY: Syracuse University Press.

Gilje, P., A., & Pencak, W. (Eds.). (1992). *New York in the age of the constitution, 1775–1800.* London and Toronto, Canada: Associated University Presses.

Goodfriend, J. D. (1992). *Before the melting pot: Society and culture in colonial New York City, 1664–1730.* Princeton, NJ: Princeton University Press.

Hackett, D. G. (1991). *The rude hand of innovation: Religion and social order in Albany, New York, 1652–1836.* New York: Oxford University Press.

Hauptman, L. M. (1999). *Conspiracy of interests: Iroquois dispossession and the rise of New York State.* Syracuse, NY: Syracuse University Press.

O'Callaghan, E. B. (Ed.). (1849). *The documentary history of the state of New-York; Arranged under the direction of the Hon. Christopher Morgan, secretary of state* (Vols 1–4). Albany, NY: Weed, Parsons & Co.

Pointer, R. W. (1988). *Protestant pluralism and the New York experience: A study of eighteenth-century religious diversity.* Bloomington and Indianapolis: Indiana University Press.

Reich, J. R. (1953). *Leisler's rebellion: A study of democracy in New York, 1664–1720.* Chicago: The University of Chicago Press.

Van Laer, A. J. F. (Ed.). (1869–1918). *Early records of the city and county of Albany and county of Rensselaerwyck* (Vols 1–4). Albany: The University of the State of New York.

Nineteenth-Century U.S. Utopian Communities

Utopian communities, also known as intentional communities and communal societies, can be considered as old as the first Hindu ashrams and Buddhist monasteries in the fourth and fifth centuries BCE or the slightly later Essene community in Palestine described in the Dead Sea Scrolls (dating from the third century BCE to second century CE). Mostly, however, they are a more recent phenomenon, associated particularly with the rise of industrialism and the accompanying decline of traditional community life. Utopian communities arise out of a shared conviction that society is seriously, even hopelessly, flawed, and that people can find a better way of life by separating from it and building communities on a different foundation. The foundations have often been expressed in religious terms, but some reformers have believed that religion, at least organized religion, is part of larger society's problem and have built communities based on secular principles.

The First Amendment as a Beacon of Hope for Utopian Communities

The United States has long been an important setting for utopian communities. Historians have viewed the Puritan communities in seventeenth-century Massachusetts as utopian in character; other intentional communities formed elsewhere during the United States' colonial period, among them The Society of the Woman in the Wilderness and Ephrata. The ideal of the New World as a land of new hopes and new beginnings fed utopian longings. So, more tangibly, did the first amendment to the U.S. Constitution, passed by Congress in 1789 as part of the Bill of Rights: "Congress shall make no law respecting an establishment of religion, or prohibiting the free exercise thereof . . . "

The First Amendment promised religious freedom not only to U.S. citizens, but implicitly to foreigners who settled there. Since their separatist and counter-cultural character often made utopian communities in Europe the targets of persecution and suppression, many immigrated to the United States, particularly in the nineteenth century, seeking the First Amendment's protection of their religious beliefs and practices. The Shakers, after immigrating, composed a hymn that said in part, "Now free toleration to conscience is given/We're saved from the terror of tyrants and kings" (cited in Weisbrod 1980, 3). Similarly, the Harmony Society, in a petition to President Thomas Jefferson in 1804 seeking assistance in acquiring land on which to settle, referred to the persecutions they had experienced in Europe and their search "for a place, where is liberty of Conscience and where they may exercise unprevented the Religion of the Spirit of Jesus. Your Memorialists understanding by the History of the United States, America would be such a place. . ." (quoted in Arndt 1972, 84). Many other utopian communities formed within the United States during the nineteenth and twentieth centuries with the same expectations. Although First Amendment protections have generally been extended to these communities, there have been exceptions. The exceptions in the nineteenth century reveal the limits of governmental and public tolerance of divergent beliefs and practices.

The Meaning of Persecution

Intolerance and persecution are taken here to refer to hostile actions directed toward members of a utopian community, or hostile words intended to stimulate hostile action. Less flagrant acts, such as unwanted attention to or public criticism of a community, while harder to label persecution, nevertheless can make community members quite uncomfortable and should be considered in this context. According to common usage, groups rather than individuals enact intolerance and persecution. The group can be institutionalized, such as a government, church, or newspaper, or ad hoc, such as a mob or vigilante group.

The meaning of specifically religious persecution also needs to be considered, since the line is not always clear. For example, some neighbors of the Hutterites, a utopian group living in numerous colonies on the northern plains of North America, were hostile toward the group's practice of community of goods, which they saw as a form of communism. To these neighbors this was not a matter of religion but of economics, yet the Hutterites considered their communal order doctrinal and justified it in part on the grounds that it imitated the biblical description of the sharing of possessions among Christ's apostles. From the Hutterites' perspective, their neighbors' hostility was clearly religious persecution. In deciding whether an instance of persecution is religious, the views of the persecuted community must be considered. On the other hand, the interpretations made by outsiders should not be ignored. For instance, it might be thought that a nonreligious community would be immune from religious persecution. But the local press bitterly attacked the Valley Forge Community in the 1820s for its purported atheism, contributing to the community's dissolution. This, too, would have to be considered religious persecution.

Expressions of Intolerance in the Press

Since a free press is guaranteed by the same Constitutional amendment that protects freedom of religion, it is ironic that many U.S. newspapers and magazines in the nineteenth century published strong condemnations of particular intentional communities. Some negative accounts occurred in editorials and letters to the editor, but others were ostensibly neutral news stories. Broadsides, pamphlets, and entire books also appeared intending to expose the supposed evils of life in utopia.

The Shakers

Originating in England out of Quakerism, a handful of Shakers came to the United States in 1774 seeking converts to their beliefs, which included celibacy, confession of sins, and pacifism. Their leader, Ann Lee (1736–1784), viewed by her followers as a prophetess (and in the minds of some of them as the female incarnation of Christ), attracted much public attention, much of it negative. Three years after Lee's death the first Shaker community was established at New Lebanon, New York. Active proselytizing continued, first in New England and later in the Midwest, and by 1826 the Shakers had founded nineteen separate communities and had a total membership of more than two thousand.

The Shakers' success provoked criticism. Their practice of receiving children into their communities accompanied by only one parent, while the other parent remained in "the world," prompted claims that the group promoted spousal desertion and undermined the "natural bond" between parent and child. Although it was against Shaker statutes to receive children against the will of either parent or to admit anyone who by joining the Shakers was deserting a spouse, practice fell short of policy on occasion, providing grist for a muckraking press. In two famous nineteenth-century cases, Eunice Chapman and Mary Marshall Dyer enlisted the press in their strident battles to regain custody of children living among the Shakers with their fathers.

The press also targeted the Shakers' sacrifice of personal individuality for the sake of the community, and, especially in the eighteenth-century, their "wild and extravagant" worship services. An anti-Shaker Massachusetts newspaper, *The Western Star*, inveighed against the Shakers on a regular basis, causing them considerable trouble. The belief of some members in Ann Lee's divinity was ruthlessly attacked in the press and in broadsides, Mary Marshall Dyer claiming, for example, that far from being divine Ann Lee was nothing but a fortune-teller, a sadist, a hypocrite, and a drunkard.

The Oneida Community

The press responded similarly to rumors of the system of "free love" in the Oneida community in upstate New York in the 1840s. The community's founder, John Humphrey Noyes (1811–1886), interpreted the biblical statement that in heaven there was no marriage (on which the Shakers based their practice of celibacy) to mean only that the exclusive sexual relations implied by marriage were dispensed with there. Reasoning that through his doctrine of perfectionism the community was moving toward a condition of heaven on earth, Noyes instituted the system of "complex marriage," which abandoned conventional marriage but permitted sexual intimacy between pairs of consenting adults. Although Oneida's prosperity and orderliness had earned it a measure of public support, many newspapers attacked Noyes and the community early in the 1850s for promoting immorality, and one historian believes there is good evidence that in response Noyes discontinued complex marriage in the community for perhaps half a year. After the furor died down, complex marriage was resumed, and, curiously, the press remained silent on the issue for the next twenty-five years, until it again weighed in at the time the community itself terminated the practice in the late 1870s.

Physical Persecution

The ugliest forms of persecution faced by utopian communities have involved physical attacks against leaders, members, or property. These have occurred throughout U.S. history. Perhaps the most notorious example in the nineteenth century was the mob action against the Mormons at Nauvoo, Illinois, and the assassination of their jailed spiritual leader, Joseph Smith (1805–1844), by a mob. Motivated partly by the threat of Mormon political hegemony in Illinois, the action was extreme, yet it was not different in principle from violence against much smaller and less threatening groups.

The Shakers again provide numerous examples. Ruffians once abducted Ann Lee, intending to disrobe her, ostensibly to determine if she was in truth a woman, but several Shaker brothers managed to rescue her. Mob actions intended to break up church meetings or drive the Shakers from town occurred repeatedly in Shaker history. Union Village in Ohio, the first Shaker settlement outside New England, was attacked by mobs at least five times between 1810 and 1824. Here and elsewhere, vigilantes whipped, beat, and punched Shaker men (and sometimes women), threw Shakers off bridges, pulled them by the hair, force marched them, and expelled them from town or district with dire warnings against returning. Less often Shaker property was destroyed. Occasionally a mob might offer pretexts for its actions (the Shakers held individuals against their will, or were mistreating children), but more often the attacks seem motivated simply by intolerance of a different way of living or form of belief.

Historian Lawrence Foster has suggested that the intensity of persecution of the Shakers is explained less by the extent to which their beliefs clashed with those of the wider society than by the vigor and effectiveness of their proselytizing efforts. When the Shakers became more established in a particular region and sought converts less vigorously, they also encountered less hostility.

As with these examples, most physical persecution of utopian communities seems completely disproportional to the threat. In the 1890s, a rowdy mob attacked the leader of the Lord's Farm, a fifteen-member celibate community of vegetarians and pacifists in New Jersey; they cut off his hair and pulled out his whiskers. Among the mob's grievances were blasphemy, Sabbath-breaking, and rape. A subsequent court case exonerated the leader of all charges except blasphemy, for allowing himself "to be adored as a Son of God"(as quoted in Stockwell 1998, 127).

Cases of averted mob violence are also reported. On several occasions the Shakers were spared an attack because local ministers, courts, or influential citizens came to their defense at a tense moment. In response to perceived sexual improprieties at a community in Putney, Vermont, that was a forerunner to the Oneida community, townspeople joined together to rid their community of what they saw as unacceptable behavior of the future Oneidans, but neither Putney nor Oneida ever seem to have been actually attacked. During World War I, sentiment against the pacifist (and German-speaking) Amana Colonies ran high. A vigilante group formed in a neighboring town with the intention of burning down the colonies, but upon hearing that the town's sheriff was waiting with a posse to intercept them, the mob dispersed.

The Hutterites, on the other hand, were harassed terribly during World War I for their pacifism and German ancestry. Vigilante groups painted Hutterite churches yellow; at one colony they destroyed a dam that provided water power for the flour mill and burned down the mill; at another they put broken glass in the mill in order to accuse the Hutterites of sabotaging the war effort. They also forced individual Hutterites to kiss the U.S. flag, stole Hutterite wine and drank it, and stole Hutterite livestock, sold them, and used the money to buy war bonds (which out of principle the Hutterites had refused to buy). The hostility became so intense that many colonies relocated from the United States to Canada.

The U.S. government made no provisions at that time for conscientious objectors, except as uniformed noncombatants within the military. Hutterite leaders agreed that their men could register and report for military physical examinations, but should cooperate no further, either by wearing uniforms or taking orders. For their stance of conscience, Hutterite draftees were often brutally handled; they were beaten, bayoneted, thrown from windows, dragged along the ground by their hair and feet, chased across fields by guards on motorcycles, hung by their feet over tanks of water until they almost choked to death, and tortured with cold water "cures" for their "irrationality." Tragically, one notorious case of persecution resulted in death. The Army placed four uncooperative Hutterite draftees in a guardhouse at Camp Funston, Kansas, then sentenced each to thirty-seven years at Alcatraz. Still refusing to put on uniforms, they were put into solitary confinement, denied clothing, beaten with clubs, suspended from the ceiling by their arms, and given few rations. After four months of this treatment they were transferred to Ft. Leavenworth, Kansas, where they experienced further abuse. One of the four men managed to telegraph the wives of the two who had received the worst treatment. When a delegation of Hutterites finally arrived, they found the two near death, and by the next morning one had died. The man's wife had to plead with the commanding officer to be allowed to see her husband's body, and when permission was finally granted she found his corpse dressed in uniform. The other man died two days later.

The Hutterites had known great persecution in Europe. In fact, they made careful records of intolerance and actively kept the memory of it alive in their cultural heritage. The draftees' awareness of this tradition may well have helped sustain them through their torment. It may even be, as one scholar has claimed, that Hutterites are aware of the cohesion such intense persecution can produce; indeed, they have been remarkably successful in terms of community longevity and member retention. Undoubtedly, the success of utopian communities in recruiting members from the wider society tends to provoke persecution, but communitarians as well as scholars have also observed that persecution, when it does not destroy a community, can give it strength, as may have been the case with the Shakers and the Mormons.

Legal Persecution

Society's third way of expressing intolerance of utopian communities is legally, through the application of existing laws or the passage of new statutes. The former typically has involved federal or state efforts, while the latter has been used by state and local governments. Legal historian Carol Weisbrod makes two important points about the legal status of utopian communities in the nineteenth century that bear noting here. First, nineteenth-century legal theory viewed the First Amendment to the Constitution as a federal principle not automatically binding upon the states. Second, legal guarantees of freedom of association were not unqualified, but limited to associations that were not immoral or a threat to the body politic. These positions allowed state and local governments considerable latitude in dealing with utopian communities

Most of the legal pressure brought to bear on the Shakers revolved around mainstream society's perception of the family as a building block of society. That the Shakers were celibate and did not form family units, that they did not procreate but did rear children (either orphans or those brought into the community by converts), and that families were often divided by conversion to Shakerism raised legal questions about child support, spousal support, inheritance, and societal stability. For example, in 1811 the Ohio legislature concluded that Shakerism could cause husbands to abandon wives, sons and daughters to be taken from their mothers, and children to be raised in a way that discouraged the formation of conventional (which was to say, familial) social ties. Both the Ohio and Kentucky legislatures passed laws in the early nineteenth century prohibiting a man who had been married and then renounced his marriage in order to join a celibate sect from giving money to the sect if doing so deprived his wife or children of support. The efforts of Eunice Chapman led the New York legislature in 1818 to pass a bill that, in the words of Thomas Jefferson, one of the bill's many critics, declared Shakers "civilly dead, their marriages dissolved, and all of their children and property taken out of their hands" (quoted in Andrews 1963, 211), with no rights as citizens, on the disingenuous grounds that "it would do little more than carry into effect the principles they profess to believe" (quoted in Weisbrod 1980, 47). Shortly thereafter, the legislature revoked the Shaker's military exemption as well.

John Humphrey Noyes and Oneida community faced legal action on several occasions. Arrested on charges of adultery in 1847 while still at Putney, Vermont, Noyes was advised to leave the state with his followers. Not long after the Oneida community's founding that same year, charges were again brought concerning sexual practices. An intense trial followed in which members of the community were called on to provide detailed testimony about their personal lives. In the end the court concluded that Oneida was a closed society whose sexual practices were privately conducted among consenting members, and the charges were dismissed. In the 1870s, new crusades against the community's immorality again led to the threat of legal action, prompting Noyes to flee to Canada, after which the community abandoned complex marriage for good. In these examples, legal harassment clearly served as an instrument of persecution, the goal being either to force the offending community to cease its practices or to drive them out of the area.

Like attacks in the press and physical persecution, legal intolerance was directed at many utopian communities for a variety of reasons. Oneida ran afoul of the law in the 1870s when the Comstock Act (1873), which prohibited sending obscene materials through the mail, was invoked to prevent them from disseminating information about the technique of "male continence," the practice of *coitus reservatus* advocated by Noyes to prevent pregnancy in the system of complex marriage. Following the end of World War I, critics induced the South Dakota state's attorney to annul the Hutterites' status as a not-for-profit corporation on the grounds that their true purpose all along had been to make money, not to worship (the state's attorney wrongly claimed that Hutterite Colonies did not even have churches).

Whether declaring the Shakers "civilly dead," invoking the Comstock Act against Oneida, or forcing Hutterite conscientious objectors into military service—and ignoring cruel and unusual punishment of them—legal harassment of utopian communities was part of the U.S. history in the nineteenth and early twentieth centuries. Many utopian groups that hoped to find full acceptance of their religious beliefs and ways of life were disappointed. As the historian David Brion Davis has noted, Americans tend to distinguish groups and denominations that demand the individual's partial loyalty from those that demand unlimited allegiance, and to be more tolerant of the former. Many, though not all, utopian communities were of the latter kind, which helps to explain the intolerance they faced. The cost of the persecution to communitarians—financially, psychologically, and in terms of the weakening of ways of life that they had voluntarily embraced—has not been measured, but must have been substantial.

On the other hand, Carol Weisbrod reminds us of one fundamental point: that the communitarian enterprise itself was legal in the United States. The government prosecuted no utopian communities simply for existing. Only when specific laws or community norms were thought to be at stake did governments step in to curb communities, though not all decisions were enlightened. And although mobs and the press were even more judgmental, utopian communities enjoyed security from persecution more often than not in the United States in the nineteenth century.

Jonathan G. Andelson

See also Great Awakenings and the Antebellum Period; Millennialist Groups; Mormons

Further Reading

Andrews, E. D. (1963). *The people called Shakers.* New York: Dover Publications.

Arndt, K. J. R. (1972). *George Rapp's Harmony Society, 1785–1847.* Rutherford, NJ: Fairleigh Dickinson University Press.

Foster, L. (1981). *Religion and sexuality: Three American communal experiments of the nineteenth century.* New York: Oxford University Press.

Fogarty, R. S. (1980). *Dictionary of American communal and utopian history.* Westport, CT: Greenwood Press.

Hostetler, J. (1997). *Hutterite society.* Baltimore, MD: Johns Hopkins Press.

LeWarne, C. P. (1978). *Utopias on Puget Sound.* Seattle: University of Washington Press.

Lockridge, K. A. (1970). *A New England town: The first hundred years, Dedham, Massachusetts, 1636–1736.* New York: W. W. Norton.

Morse, F. (1980). *The Shakers and the world's people.* New York: Dodd, Mead and Company.

Oved, Y. (1988). *Two hundred years of American communes.* New Brunswick, NJ: Transaction Books.

Pitzer, D. E. (Ed.). (1997). *America's communal utopias.* Chapel Hill: The University of North Carolina Press.

Stein, S. J. (1992). *The Shaker experience in America: A history of the United Society of Believers.* New Haven, CT: Yale University Press.

Stockwell, F. (1998). *Encyclopedia of American communes, 1663–1963.* Jefferson, NC: McFarland and Company.

Weisbrod, C. (1980). *The boundaries of utopia.* New York: Pantheon Books.

O

Orthodox Christianity

Orthodox Christianity traces its origins to the largely Greek-speaking apostolic Christian communities found in the eastern Roman Empire. Today, Orthodoxy, which claims 250 million adherents worldwide, is the predominant form of Christianity in the eastern Mediterranean, southeastern Europe, and across the Eurasian landmass. Orthodoxy is organized into a federation of nationally based autocephalous (self-governing) churches in communion with each other that share a common confession of faith (as defined by the seven Ecumenical Councils which met from 325 CE to 787 CE). The Ecumenical Patriarch of Constantinople (today's Istanbul) is considered to be the "first among equals" within the hierarchy, while the Russian Orthodox Church is the single largest church within Orthodoxy.

Overview of Beliefs

As in other Christian denominations, Orthodoxy maintains that humanity, in misusing its free will, fell into sin, creating a rupture between God and mankind that could only be repaired by the death and resurrection of Jesus Christ. The Nicene Creed, finalized at the Second Ecumenical Council of Constantinople (381 CE), and as interpreted by the Fourth Ecumenical Council of Chalcedon (451 CE), sets forth the Orthodox understanding of a single God revealed in Three Persons (Father, Son, and Holy Spirit), and of Jesus Christ as fully divine and fully human (one person in two natures), who through his ministry and sacrifice paved the way for the redemption and transformation of human nature. The Seventh Ecumenical Council of Nicaea (787 CE) set apostolic tradition, of which the Bible forms a part, as the basis for Orthodoxy's beliefs and dogmas; this council also approved the use of icons (sacred pictures depicting Jesus Christ, other biblical figures, and the saints which decorate the interior of Orthodox churches) in worship and teaching.

Orthodoxy emphasizes collective worship (orthodoxy literally means "right glorification"); the services are often very ornate and are seen as a "glimpse" into the beauty of heaven. Through the liturgy and sacraments of the Church (especially baptism, confession, and the Eucharist), the individual believer is brought into a relationship with Jesus Christ within the context of the fellowship of all believers. Thus, the saints play a key role as "intercessors before the Lord" for their fellow Christians; an especially honored place is reserved for the Virgin Mary, the mother of Jesus, upheld as the most sublime example of what synergy between God and humanity can produce.

The Orthodox faithful are divided into two broad categories—clergy and laity. While all believers form "the royal priesthood," the clergy (deacons, priests, and bishops) lead the community in worship, administer the sacraments, and define administrative and pastoral duties within the Church. While all bishops share in the same ministry, titles such as "patriarch" or "metropolitan" designate bishops who have additional responsibilities for coordinating church affairs in a given area.

Divergences in ritual and church discipline, as well as disagreements over the role that the bishop of Rome (the Pope) should play within the Christian

RUSSIAN ORTHODOX CHURCH ACCEPTS NEW LAW ON RELIGIOUS FREEDOM

On 8–9 April 1998, The Holy Synod of the Russian Orthodox Church released the following press release, announcing that the Bishops of the Russian Orthodox Church accepted the new (1997) Russian policy on religious freedom.

Meeting of the Holy Synod met on 8–9 April 1998. It was chaired by *His Holiness* Patriarch Alexy II of Moscow and All Russia.

After a discussion on the new version of the Statute of the Parish of the Russian Orthodox Church, drafted to conform to the new Law of on the Freedom of Conscience and on Religious Association now in force, the Holy Synod adopted this Statute and resolved that it should be applied as universal to every parish of the Russian Orthodox Church.

Source: Jubilee Bishops' Council of the Russian Orthodox Church, August 13–16, 2000, Moscow. Retrieved 15 May 2002, from: http://www.russian-orthodox-church.org.ru/s2000e08.htm

Church, led to gradual estrangement between the Orthodox Churches and the Roman Catholic Church, culminating in the Great Schism of 1054. Orthodoxy is sometimes referred to as the "Eastern" Orthodox Church, based both on its geographic origins and its emphasis on mysticism and spirituality, in contrast to the "Western Church" (encompassing both Roman Catholicism and the Protestant denominations).

Orthodoxy and the State

Unlike Western Christian thinkers (beginning with Augustine of Hippo, 354–430 CE) who drew a distinction between the earthly "City of Man" and the divine "City of God," Orthodox thinkers maintained that it was possible (and even desirable) for the temporal order to emulate and imitate (the Greek term is *mimesis*), as far as is humanly possible, the divine order (*taxis*). Recognizing that the Kingdom of God could not be created on earth, some Orthodox theologians maintained that human society could nonetheless strive to model itself after divine principles. Thus, in an ideal society, Church and state could work together to realize shared goals.

The conversion of the Emperor Constantine in the early fourth century opened the possibility that the spiritual force of the Gospel could be joined with the temporal might of the Roman Empire. Bishop Eusebius of Caesarea (260–c. 339 CE), an influential churchman and advisor to Constantine, put forth the idea of a Christian commonwealth under the guidance of a Christian Emperor appointed by God as his agent to oversee both secular and spiritual matters. Eusebius' emphasis on the guiding role of the Emperor laid the basis for a vision of Church-state relations (*caesaropapism*) in which the secular ruler is viewed as the earthly head of the Church, and his views were, to some extent, later implemented in Imperial Russia.

Most Orthodox, however, rejected Eusebius' position in favor of a cooperative relationship between Church and state—one where the state enforced Orthodoxy as the norm for society in return for the Church's political loyalty. Two centuries later, the Emperor Justinian (527–565 CE) in his *Sixth Novella* (535 CE) put forth the idea of *symphonia* or harmony between Church and state as the basis for the Christian commonwealth. The ninth-century Byzantine law code (the *Epanagoge*), promulgated by Emperor Basil I (c. 813–886 CE), spelled out distinct areas of responsibility for the Emperor and the Patriarch. The delineation of specific areas of state and Church oversight for all aspects of public life was replicated by legislation in other Orthodox countries, such as the Church Statute promulgated by Grand Prince Vladimir of Kiev (c. 956–1015 CE) or the Serbian Law Code of Stefan Dushan (c. 1308–1355).

With few exceptions (such as the medieval Georgian kingdoms or the northern Russian city-state republics), *symphonia* proved difficult to realize since there was no mechanism to regulate conflicts between Church and state. Unlike medieval Roman Catholic Popes, Orthodox patriarchs never claimed the right to depose secular rulers from office. Between the fourth and ninth centuries, the Eastern Roman (or Byzantine) Empire was beset by disputes over theology and church practice. This was especially pronounced during the Iconoclast controversy (726–843 CE), when Emperors sought to ban the use of images in Church worship, and used this campaign in an effort to gain complete control over the internal life and administration of the Church. While Emperors sought to use their authority to impose unity on the Church, Church leaders struggled for the right to define Church teachings independent of state authority. Some Orthodox leaders, such as Athanasius, patriarch of Alexandria (298–373 CE), or John Chrysostom (347–407 CE), patriarch of Constantinople, fought to secure freedom for the Church to operate without state supervision and control, even at the cost of arrest, exile or death. Orthodox theologians during the Byzantine period, however, did not propagate the idea of separation of Church and state; tensions in Church-state relations were attributed to impious rulers seeking to usurp spiritual authority that was more properly the realm of the Church hierarchy.

The rise of Islam presented a major challenge to Orthodoxy; beginning in the seventh century, major portions of the Orthodox heartlands (in Syria and Egypt) fell under Muslim rule. By the fifteenth century, most traditionally Orthodox lands were controlled either by Muslim or Roman Catholic rulers, with the exception of northeastern Russia (the Grand Principality of Moscow) and the Ethiopian highlands. The Orthodox generally accepted rule by non-Orthodox governments, provided that freedom of worship was guaranteed. In Ottoman lands, governed under the *millet* system (by which people were grouped by religion rather than nationality), Orthodox bishops also served as *ethnarchs* (political leaders of their communities). Sustained persecution or harassment of Orthodox communities, however, did lead to rebellion, most notably the 1648 uprising in Ukraine against the Polish state for its aggressive promotion of Catholicism in the Orthodox lands it controlled.

The Russian Revolution (1917) brought to power a regime that was not simply indifferent but actively hostile to religion. Under such conditions, ideas about close cooperation between Church and state had no relevance. The spread of Communism in Eastern Europe after World War II (by 1980, some 85 percent of all Orthodox lived under Communist regimes) and the growing numbers of Orthodox living in the West led some modern Orthodox theologians, particularly those affiliated with the St. Sergius Academy in Paris, to conclude that Orthodoxy is in a post-Constantinian era, where the Church can no longer be affiliated with the state, but must exist as an autonomous actor in civil society. The collapse of the Soviet bloc (1989–1991) reinitiated an old debate among Orthodox Christians over whether to revive pre-Communist "symphonic" relations between the Church and governments in predominantly Orthodox areas.

Orthodoxy and Religious Freedom

The early Church's experience of three centuries of persecution under the Roman Empire has been seared into Orthodoxy's consciousness, joining with later periods of persecution and harassment of the Orthodox Church at the hands of Islamic, Roman Catholic, and Communist regimes. Drawing upon that legacy, early theologians like the lawyer Tertullian (b. 155? CE) proclaimed that freedom of worship was a natural right, a view codified by Emperor Constantine in the Edict of Milan (313 CE).

Many Orthodox hierarchs and teachers after the fourth century, however, maintained that "falsehood" had no place within a Christian commonwealth. Dissent (heresy) was a particularly vexing issue. If people were free to promulgate "errors" about the true faith, this could cause believers to stray from the proper path. More importantly, the unity of the local community would be shattered. The same Emperor Constantine who issued a proclamation of religious liberty also decreed that dissenters from Orthodoxy had no right to assemble, even privately, or propagate their beliefs. Such legislation was reconfirmed by succeeding emperors, who equated heresy with political treason and sought to use the coercive power of the state to enforce compliance with Orthodox teachings. Brutal persecutions were launched against groups deemed to be heretical, notably the Paulicians (in Asia Minor, ninth and tenth centuries) and the Bogomils (in the Balkans, tenth to fourteenth centuries), followers of a dualistic version of Christianity that, in particular, challenged the legitimacy of the Orthodox Church.

When Emperor Theodosius made Christianity the state religion of the Roman Empire (380/81 CE), pagan religions were banned outright, while Jews faced new restrictions on their civil rights. It soon became a crime for Orthodox Christians to change their religion or for non-Orthodox to proselytize among Orthodox.

A major problem developed, however, when Emperors tried to designate a particular dogma as "Orthodox," even over the objections of a large portion of the Church. For many of the great theologians of the Byzantine period, including Athanasius (c. 293–373 CE), Basil of Caesarea (c. 329–379 CE), John Chrysostom, John of Damascus (c. 675–c. 749 CE), and Maximus the Confessor (c. 580–662 CE), the experience of persecution at the hands of supposedly "Orthodox" rulers led many to question the efficacy of force as a means for coping with dissent.

This also became an issue in the medieval Russian Orthodox Church. On one side, the influential Abbot Joseph of Volokolamsk (1439–1515) urged harsh treatment of heretics and dissenters by the state, including imprisonment and death, on the grounds that heresy had no rights and could corrupt souls. Supporters of the hermit Nilus Sorskii (1433–1508), citing Chrysostom and other Church Fathers, denounced the use of civic penalties as a way of forcing compliance with Orthodox views on matters of faith and morality. After a major schism developed in the Russian Church during the seventeenth century (between the Orthodox and the Old Believers), state repression of the dissidents fueled several major rebellions against the Russian state.

In many parts of the Orthodox world there arose a notion of communal toleration, that particular ethnic groups who professed a religion other than Orthodoxy might enjoy freedom to practice their faith (even if not always enjoying full civic rights). This tolerance arose out of necessity, given the continuing existence of Jewish communities enjoying rights under Roman law. The major division in the Eastern Church after the Council of Chalcedon (451 CE) created large, mass-based Monophysite (or non-Chalcedonian, Oriental Orthodox) Churches in Egypt and Syria out of communion with the Imperial Church at Constantinople, and later, treaty arrangements with Muslim and Roman Catholic states regarding the fate of their coreligionists in Orthodox

lands. The Russian Empire also extended formal toleration to a variety of religions associated with ethnic groups who came under the protection of the Empire—Buddhist Kalmyks, Muslim Tatars, and Azeris or Protestant Germans and Finns—while making any attempt to convert Orthodox believers a crime under civil law.

Orthodox encounters with the West helped to develop concepts of freedom of conscience. The struggle of Orthodox populations living under Polish or Hapsburg rule for civil and political rights and the growing influence of the West in Russia, beginning with the rule of Peter the Great (1682–1725), acquainted Orthodox thinkers with Western European debates over religious freedom.

In 2000, the Bishops' Council of the Russian Orthodox Church gave a qualified endorsement to the principle of religious liberty, both as a reflection of the God-given free will of the individual, and more practically, as the best means for facilitating the Church's existence in modern, secular society (although the Church still maintains that the ideal situation would be a freely established Christian commonwealth). While most predominantly Orthodox countries have constitutional provisions enshrining freedom of conscience, there are still some difficulties that arise, especially in Russia and Greece, over legislation that places limits on the rights of minority religious communities to organize and proselytize.

Orthodoxy and Social Issues

Many Orthodox have maintained that the radical principles of social justice outlined in the New Testament (particularly equality between men and women, slave and free, rich and poor) could only be realized in the Second Coming. Nevertheless, a strong, philanthropic tradition developed within the Orthodox Church, stressing the obligation of the wealthy to use their largesse to fund hospitals, schools, and other charitable institutions. Orthodoxy, however, has traditionally shied away from any endorsement of radical, revolutionary methods as a means for securing justice; instead, there has been an emphasis on inducing change through stoic suffering of injustice, after the example of the crucified Christ.

From a modern perspective, women have had second-class status within Orthodoxy. In the early Church and during the Byzantine period, women served as deacons, performing a number of liturgical, educational, and charitable tasks for women believers, although never ordained to the priesthood or episcopacy. Alongside the Desert Fathers (monks who dispensed counsel and advice, especially in Egypt during the fourth through seventh centuries) were the Desert Mothers (women monastics who performed the same role). Nevertheless, concerns over maintaining social order and over the ritual purity of women (drawing in part upon regulations found in the Mosaic law) led to the defining of gender roles within Orthodoxy and the exclusion of women from many positions of leadership and authority within the Church. The Moscow Council (1917–1918), however, recognized "the usefulness of the active participation of women in serving the Church in all fields corresponding to their particular qualifications."

While Orthodox laypeople are encouraged to be active in social causes (for example, the Orthodox Peace Fellowship), the Church has eschewed any direct participation in secular politics and its clergymen are technically forbidden to seek office. However, the Orthodox Church, especially in Russia, Georgia, and Greece, works closely with the state in matters of health, education, and social welfare.

Nikolas K. Gvosdev

See also Balkans, East Europe, and Russia; Byzantine Empire; Turkey

Further Reading

Greenslade, S. L. (1983). *Church and state from Constantine to Theodosius*. Wesport, CT: Greenwood Press.

Gvosdev, N. K. (2001). *An examination of church-state relations in the Byzantine and Russian Empires with an emphasis on ideology and models of action*. Lewiston, NY: Edwin Mellen Press.

Hussey, J. M. (1986). *The Orthodox Church in the Byzantine empire*. Oxford, UK: Clarendon Press.

Magoulias, H. J. (1982). *Byzantine Christianity: Emperor, church, and the West*. Detroit, MI: Wayne University State Press.

Meyendorff, J. (1991). *Imperial unity and Christian divisions*. Crestwood, NY: St. Vladimir's Seminary Press.

Obolensky, D. (1994). *Byzantium and the Slavs*. Crestwood, NY: St. Vladimir's Seminary Press.

Runciman, S. (1968). *The great church in captivity*. Cambridge, UK: Cambridge University Press.

Ware, T. (1963). *The Orthodox Church*. London: Penguin.

Outsiderhood and American Protestantism

America has always embraced an astonishing level of religious diversity. Native inhabitants practiced and passed on their own diverse religious traditions; then European, and later African and Asian, migrants brought their vast range of beliefs and practices to American shores. Yet starting in the nineteenth century and continuing well into the twentieth, Protestantism—itself comprising a diverse group of related traditions—became a kind of public religion in the United States. As late as 1986, Laurence Moore remarked that "America's religious culture was and still is more Protestant than anything else, but the issue is complicated" (Moore 1986, vii). Indeed, America's Protestant culture, fast in decline, has always been easier to notice than define.

Most interpreters would agree that Protestantism is not a religion, but rather a principle. Its most obvious feature is a rejection of the presumed authority of the Roman papacy. Protestantism in America thus has a genealogy that traces back to the Reformation of the sixteenth century. Generally, however, many Protestants discern in their "protest" a rejection of any authority besides that of the Bible. Hence, in the nineteenth century, many Protestant splinter groups—claiming to speak for the "Bible alone"—rejected the main Protestant denominations as hierarchical and corrupt. A commitment to Scripture (*sola scriptura*) or a belief in justification by faith alone (*sola fides*) often constitutes a positive agenda for those claiming the mantle of Protestantism, but in practice most Protestants define themselves negatively.

Such flexible, negative definitions have proved immensely popular in the democratic atmosphere of the United States, and in the Second Great Awakening they ascended to the level of a confession of faith. "No creed but the Bible!" was the religious counterpart to the Revolution's violent overthrow of British governance. As Nathan Hatch and Mark Noll have shown, the early years of the United States witnessed an intermingling of Christian and republican themes. This produced a "Protestant Enlightenment" that at once brought the Protestant churches to the nation's service and warded off the perceived threats of French radicalism and Old-World hierarchicalism.

Historiography

Partly as a result of this republican–Protestant alliance, mid-nineteenth-century historians of American religion assumed that religious diversity would *decline* and that a Protestant middle ground would prevail. As Moore points out, the fact that Mormonism and Roman Catholicism grew numerically faster in the nineteenth century than Episcopalianism—or that sectarian groups generally do better in America than established churches—did not challenge the framework within which these historians worked. As late as 1888, after decades of exponential Roman Catholic growth, Daniel Dorchester wrote that the United States "is the biggest grave for popery ever dug on earth" (Moore 1986, 11). These conceptual frameworks were so compelling, in fact, that they persisted well into the twentieth century. While Herberg's influential *Protestant, Catholic, Jew* (1955) allowed two other enduring traditions to take their place along Protestantism, Herberg in fact argued that American culture tended to move people toward a faith held in common by all three traditions. Assimilation has been a popular American motif.

This understanding of American religious life is now under heavy assault, and for good reasons. While America has at times witnessed profound currents toward cultural and religious consensus, variety and irregularity have always characterized the "lived religion" of Americans. Historical scholarship on American evangelicalism has contributed to this new perspective. While Protestant evangelicalism was arguably the informal "establishment" of the nineteenth century, its appeals for a democratic Christianity gave rise to dozens of splinter groups, each challenging the status quo of the major denominations and, more than occasionally, of each other. Nathan Hatch's *Democratization of American Christianity* significantly included an analysis of the rise of Mormonism and African-American Christianity alongside his treatment of Methodists, Baptists, and the Disciples of Christ. Mormons, outsiders in American religious life, had much in common with the Methodists and Baptists and followed a similar, though slower, path to prominence. Whatever Mormonism's relationship to "mainstream" Protestantism is now, it has clearly flourished in American culture. Likewise black Christianity, long marginalized or even suppressed, thrived in the nineteenth century especially after emancipation and in doing so "ended forever the idea that Protestantism in America meant only white Protestants" (Noll 2002, 113). Social histories of immigration and ethnicity have also shifted the focus of religious historians toward groups, like the Lutherans, for which confessional

separatism encouraged a public invisibility only surmounted in the twentieth century. Indeed, even within the denominations that have been characterized as "American" and "mainstream," considerable opposition to the blurring of denominational distinctions has always existed. Confessional Presbyterians and Lutherans, Landmark Baptists, and High Church Episcopalians regularly resist the limitations they perceive in "mainstream Protestantism."

Outsiderhood *Is* Mainstream

If there ever was a "Protestant America" it was during the first two thirds of the nineteenth century. The Second Great Awakening and the concomitant proliferation of benevolent reform created an atmosphere in which white Protestant values permeated American life. Those who did not embrace these values—from slaves to Irish and German immigrants, from bowery girls in New York City to Indians on the Great Plains—were forced, one way or another, consciously to resist them.

Yet beginning in the 1830s this Protestant America came under attack, both from within and from without. Most of the major denominations were divided, with sizeable minorities beginning to question the tactics and consequences of the evangelical revival. Even defenders of revivalism, such as Charles Grandison Finney (1792–1875), grew disillusioned with revivalism's seemingly short-lived moral reform. The fragmentation of Protestantism, however, did most to undermine its cultural authority. The moral consensus of the early nineteenth century dissolved in a sea of *isms*—Millerism, Mormonism, Adventism, Scientism, to name a few of the most prominent. From without, increasing religious and cultural pluralism threatened the very numerical dominance that Protestantism had for so long maintained. Americanism and nativism notwithstanding, by the end of the nineteenth century the largest religious denomination in the United States was neither Methodism nor the Baptist groups, but Roman Catholicism.

Given the curious historiography that has so long emphasized the all-importance of Protestantism, and the actual challenges facing Protestantism in the last century and a half, it is remarkable that the idea of Protestantism has fared so well in the United States Laurence Moore, in a revisionist study titled *Religious Outsiders and the Making of Americans*, explains this by insisting that historians (and American Protestants more generally) are blinded by the same expectations that deceived nineteenth-century interpreters of American religion: they look for "usable pasts" that fit contemporary expectations. To dispel the myth of a Protestant past, Moore insists that "outsiderhood is a characteristic way of inventing one's Americanness" (Moore 1986, xi). Indeed, outsider status is what brought Protestants to power in the first place. Since "common myths do not have to be read in the same way," even the notion of a Protestant America was subject to divergent interpretations (Moore 1986, 202). Steven Nolt has demonstrated how German Lutherans and Reformed living in the early republic employed their unique ethnic and religious identity to make a bid for Americanness. Indeed if outsiderhood can serve as a bid for American, or in some cases Protestant, identity, then American identity itself needs to be understood as susceptible to multiple readings and applications.

Separation and Power

Despite the prevalence and proliferation of outsider groups and their resistance to the Protestant mainstream, the notion of a Christian (i.e., Protestant) America prevailed into the twentieth century—despite the supposed "separation of church and state" enshrined the United States Constitution. "Separation" itself, of course, is still a contested concept, since the Constitution only declared that "Congress shall make no law respecting an establishment of religion, or prohibiting the free exercise thereof," thereby stipulating merely that the federal government would not meddle with what were then local religious cultures. At that time, five of the nation's fourteen states provided tax support for ministers, and seven more had religious tests for local public office. As Mark Noll explains, "only Virginia and Rhode Island practiced the kind of separation of church and state that has since become common in America—where government provides no money for churches and poses no religious conditions for participation in public life" (Noll 2002, 72). Even these states did not object to discrimination against Roman Catholics in public life. Indeed, according to Philip Hamburger, the notion of "separation of church and state" was not popular until the mid-nineteenth century, when opponents of Roman Catholicism conveniently found it to be a "principle of government evident in most American constitutions, even if it was not guaranteed by those documents." Hamburger places the rise of "separation" firmly in "the nineteenth-century movement to impose an aggressively Protestant 'Americanism' on an 'un-American' Catholic minority" (Hamburger 2002, 10, 191). Thus, the separation of church and state initially served Protestant interests.

It should not be surprising that a sterner notion of separation should have emerged at roughly the same time as Roman Catholics began posing a political challenge to white Protestant values (for example, temperance). Yet in relinquishing the right of churches of any kind to act politically, Protestants turned to the use of other individual, voluntary channels to secure their dominance. As it turns out Protestants were quite adept at using these channels, and in this way, separation of church and state became a "Protestant and American ideal" (Hamburger 2002, 192).

The End of Protestant Dominance?

Perhaps it was this nineteenth-century transformation, and the accompanying "privatization" of religious belief, that ultimately undermined Protestant hegemony, for it had the effect of placing Protestant values squarely in a liberal context where they could be discarded or reinterpreted when expedient. Nineteenth-century Protestant liberals, of course, did not anticipate their own marginalization, since they saw virtue and hence (Protestant) religion as the necessary foundations of a liberal society. Without virtue, the argument ran, liberty would degenerate into license. In addition, the broader society had institutionalized so much Protestant culture that it obscured the degree to which liberal ideology undermined Protestant dominance. For example, the nation's universities and colleges were by and large Protestant institutions, with clergymen serving as presidents. The common schools were specifically designed to inculcate Protestant morality. Sundays regularly served as public holidays by law, and blasphemy statutes were not uncommon.

However difficult to see from the lofty spires of Protestant churches and the ivory towers of Protestant academia, America was never truly a Protestant country. The increasing religious diversity of the nation, moreover, has made it less and less possible to define America's public culture in Protestant terms. In the words of Eric Michael Mazur, "Political identity in 'American' culture, once closely tied to Protestantism (particularly evangelical

Protestantism), has now taken a form of its own and can no longer be assumed to parallel that one religious tradition" (Mazur 1999, xviii). And despite the strident claims of some religious conservatives that America was, or still is, a Christian nation, an increasing number of Christians are facing the fact of religious pluralism in America. But myths die slow deaths, and echoes of the nineteenth century will likely resonate into the twenty-first.

R. Bryan Bademan

See also Establishment, Separation of Church and State; Great Awakenings and the Antebellum Period

Further Reading

Chidester, D. (1988). *Patterns of power: Religion and politics in American culture.* Englewood Cliffs, NJ: Prentice Hall.

Conkin, P. K. (1997). *American originals: Homemade varieties of Christianity.* Chapel Hill, NC: University of North Carolina Press.

Hamburger, P. (2002). *Separation of church and state.* Cambridge, MA: Harvard University Press.

Handy, R. T. (1984). *A Christian America: Protestant hope and historical realities* (2nd ed.). New York: Oxford University Press.

Hatch, N. O. (1989). *The democratization of American Christianity.* New Haven, CT: Yale University Press.

Mazur, E. M. (1999). *The Americanization of religious minorities: confronting the constitutional order.* Baltimore: Johns Hopkins University Press.

Moore, R. L. (1986). *Religious outsiders and the making of Americans.* New York: Oxford University Press.

Noll, M. A., Hatch, N. O., & Marsden, G. M. (1983). *The search for Christian America.* Westchester, IL: Crossway Books.

Noll, M. A. (2002). *The old religion in a new world: The history of North American Christianity.* Grand Rapids, MI: Eerdmans.

Nolt, S. (2002). *Foreigners in their own land: Pennsylvania Germans in the early republic.* University Park, PA: Pennsylvania State University Press.

Ostling, R. N., & Ostling, J. K. (1999). *Mormon America: The power and the promise.* New York: Harper SanFrancisco.

Porterfield, A. (2001). *The transformation of American Religion: The story of a late twentieth-century awakening.* New York: Oxford University Press.

Pakistan

The Islamic Republic of Pakistan, with a population of about 150 million, is the second-most-populous Muslim nation in the world after Indonesia. With an approximately 97 percent Muslim population, its non-Muslim minorities include Christians, Hindus, Parsis, and Ahmadis (who regard themselves as Muslims). Among the Muslims, between 12 to 15 percent belong to the Shi'a sect and the rest are Sunnis.

Pakistan and Islam

Pakistan, which came into being as a result of the partition of British India in 1947, is unique among Muslim countries with regard to its relationship to Islam. It is the only Muslim country that was established in the name of Islam, and consequently its subsequent political experience is integrally related to its Islamic identity. The question of the new nation's ideological character has been a subject of continuous debate among Pakistani intellectuals and policy makers. Two distinct schools of thought have emerged on this issue: One contends that Pakistan was demanded and created in the name of Islam and therefore has to justify its existence only as an Islamic state; the other emphasizes that the country was created to safeguard the political, economic, and cultural interests of South Asian Muslims but was in no way intended to be a religiously based, ideological state.

There is ample evidence to show that Pakistan's founding fathers saw Pakistan as a progressive Muslim nation with democracy and pluralism as its foundational principles. Their vision of Pakistan as an Islamic state embodied Islamic ideals of justice, equality, and brotherhood rather than the specifics of *shari'a* (Islamic law). For them, as well as for the Muslim masses, building an Islamic state was thus synonymous with building a just and moral society. Hence, we see little, if any, reference to the introduction of specific Islamic laws in the speeches and statements of the founders of Pakistan. The majority of the leaders of the movement to create an independent Muslim state on the Indian subcontinent were Western educated, liberal-minded Muslim nationalists whose commitment to Islam was primarily defined by its spiritual and moral values, and by their own commitment to the economic, political, and cultural uplift of the Muslim community. Muhammad Ali Jinnah (1876–1948), the founder of Pakistan, addressing the first session of Pakistan's parliament, articulated this liberal vision of the new state by telling his countrymen "You are free; you are free to go to your temples, you are free to go to your mosques, or to any other places of worship in this state of Pakistan. You may belong to any religion or caste or creed—that has nothing to do with the business of the state. . . . We are starting with this fundamental principle that we are all equal citizens of the state" (Jinnah 1947). He went as far as to declare that "in course of time Hindus would cease to be Hindus and Muslims would cease to be Muslims, not in the religious sense, because that is the personal faith of each individual, but in the political sense as citizens of the state."

Islam and Politics in Pakistan

Although from the very beginning Pakistan faced critical problems of economic, political, and ethno-regional origins, the question that has generated the greatest number of political conflicts and caused the most social tension is that of the role of Islam in politics and the state. Debates over the nature of an Islamic political system and how it should be enshrined in the constitutional structure and socio-economic policies of the state often took the form of fierce confrontation, sometimes violent, between the state and organized religious groups and among the religious groups themselves.

The Islam-Pakistan relationship was first articulated in the Objectives Resolution, which was passed in the first Constituent Assembly of Pakistan in 1949 and which now forms a part of the 1973 constitution. While the Objectives Resolution promised that the state would enable Muslims to order their lives in the individual and collective spheres in accordance with the teachings of Islam, it also stated that the principles of democracy, freedom, equality, tolerance, social justice, and respect for minorities' rights would be fully observed. Notwithstanding its liberal proclamations, however, the Objectives Resolution laid the foundation for an enduring relationship between Islam and the state in Pakistan and thus encouraged religiously based political groups to press their demands for an increased role for Islam—and for themselves—in public affairs.

Pakistan has had three constitutions since its inception in 1947. In all three, Pakistan was named the "Islamic Republic of Pakistan," and Islam was declared the state religion. All three stated that existing laws should be brought into conformity with the injunctions of Islam and that no law should be enacted that is repugnant to Islam. All three constitutions required that the head of the state must be a Muslim.

Despite these Islamic provisions in the 1956, 1962, and 1973 constitutions, Pakistan remained a relatively liberal state in terms of religious freedom and the rights of religious minorities until the mid-1970s. Indeed, for seventeen years the chief justice of the Supreme Court of the Islamic Republic of Pakistan—who has final authority to interpret Islamic laws—was A. R. Cornelius, a Roman Catholic, the most respected name in the judicial history of Pakistan.

The qualitative change in Pakistan's religious politics came during the rule (as president, 1971–73; as prime minister, 1973–77) of Zulfikar Ali Bhutto (1928–1979). His rise to power parallels the rise of the political influence of religiously based political groups in Pakistan. He contributed to making political life more religiously oriented by giving in easily to almost all the demands of religiously based political groups in order to appease them. The ultimate incident was when the secular Bhutto agreed to amend the constitution to declare the Ahmadis to be non-Muslims, a demand that had been rejected in 1953 by a devout Muslim prime minister, Khwaja Nazimuddin (prime minister from 1951 to 1953).

Although the Islamic measures introduced by Bhutto were peripheral to the core of his socioeconomic policies, their impact on subsequent Islamic developments was quite significant and far-reaching. By incorporating extensive Islamic provisions into the 1973 constitution and by declaring the Ahmadis non-Muslims, Bhutto helped raise the expectations of the religious parties and prepared the ground for a full-grown Islamist movement during the regime (1978–88) of Muhammad Zia-ul-Haq (1924–1988).

The Rise of Islamists in Pakistan

Coming in the wake of worldwide Islamic resurgence, Zia's measures were much more substantive than the Islamic reforms introduced by earlier regimes. Working closely with the ulema (Muslim clergy) and organized religious groups, Zia created a network of state-sponsored legal and institutional structures to translate *shari'a* rules into public policies. The most important among them were penal laws with specific Islamic punishments, the law of evidence (which discriminated against minorities and women), and the laws severely restricting the religious, political, and civil rights of the Ahmadis. An ordinance issued in 1984 prescribes prison sentences and fines for any Ahmadi who used traditional Islamic terms to describe his or her religious practices. Moreover, Ahmadis who call themselves Muslims are subject to severe penalties. In order to vote, Ahmadis must register themselves as non-Muslims. Since the Ahmadi community has refused to accept their non-Muslim status, they have lost their voting rights as well.

All government employees are required to sign an oath declaring their faith. Similar oaths are also required to obtain passports and admission to government colleges and universities. Laws were also passed to disallow the testimony of a non-Muslim in criminal cases registered under the Islamic penal laws. The most frightening legislation was the blasphemy law, with its mandatory death penalty for making derogatory remarks against the Prophet Muhammad. Since the promulgation of the blasphemy law in the mid-1980s, allegations of blasphemy against members of minority communities, especially against Christians, have been made with alarming frequency. In several well-documented cases, the law was used against members of the Christian community as a weapon in political rivalries, property disputes, and competition for jobs. What was even more perilous from the point of view of religious freedom was the fact that the general sociopolitical and religious climate during the Zia regime created fertile ground for religious division, sectarianism, intolerance of religious dissent, and hostility toward minorities.

The introduction of *shari'a* laws brought to the surface old doctrinal and juristic differences between Shi'ite Muslims and Sunni Muslims. Thus, the question as to which interpretation of the Islamic laws should form the basis of public policy became a major source of conflict between the Shi'ite and Sunni ulama on the one hand and among different schools of Sunnis on the other. These controversies have caused frequent violent incidents and the assassination of dozens of prominent Shi'ite and Sunni leaders. Some extremist Sunni groups now demand that the Shi'ites be declared a non-Muslim minority. The same Sunni orthodox religious groups have also tried to advance legislation to declare the Zikris (a small sect concentrated primarily on the southern coast) to be non-Muslim.

The sectarian political legacy of the Zia period has also given rise to extremist religious groups who kill members of other religious groups even in places of worship and who recruit students from *madrasah*s (religious schools) to join military arms of these extremist groups. The Zia regime's mobilization of a broad spectrum of religious groups during the Afghan war of the 1980s further strengthened the political power and the material resource base of the religious groups, with funds and weapons being supplied to them from both domestic and external sources.

Coupled with this religious militancy and increasingly intolerant socioreligious climate, decades of military rule and misrule by civilian governments has left Pakistan political unstable, in a crisis of ungovernability, with state institutions near collapse and the nation suffering a general breakdown of law and order. All these factors have made the already fragile political system more vulnerable to pressures from extremist religious groups in the last years of the twentieth century and the first years of the twenty-first century.

Other Destabilizing Forces

International and regional developments have also contributed to religious and sectarian tensions and violence in Pakistan. Thus, the power struggle between Iran and Saudi Arabia in the region since the 1980s has enflamed the proxy war between Pakistani Shi'ites and Sunnis. (Iran is primarily Shi'ite; Saudia Arabia Sunni.) The rise of the Taliban in neighboring Afghanistan gave rise to Sunni militancy in Pakistan. In 1992, when right-wing Hindu fanatics demolished the historic Babri mosque in India, frenzied Muslim mobs went on a rampage in Karachi, Pakistan, targeting Hindu temples. In 1985, when U.S. president Ronald Reagan ordered the bombing of Libya, an angry mob of Muslim fanatics in Pakistani Punjab retaliated by burning the village of a poor Christian minority. In the wake of developments in Afghanistan following the 11 September 2001 terrorist attacks in New York City and Washington, D.C., some extremist Islamic groups in Pakistan began systematically targeting Christian churches, charitable institutions, hospitals, and educational institutions to express their anti-American and pro-Taliban sentiments.

Although the extremist groups that harass religious minorities remain marginal, their capacity to coerce the local authorities to concede to their demands by creating an emotionally explosive religious situation remains considerable. Much of what happens to religious minorities—from harassment to violence—is initiated by extremist elements who incite the local population (who are often poorly educated and therefore have no way to judge the merits of the extremists' arguments) to take law into their own hands in order to "defend Islam" against perceived blasphemies or acts of desecration. In most cases, the local enforcement agencies either willingly join the melee in support of the "defenders of Islam" or find themselves helpless before a religiously charged mob. In general, the state authorities at the level of central and provincial governments and the higher judiciary in Pakistan have been quite sensitive to the need to protect the life, liberty, and property of religious minorities. Thus, to date none of the punishments under the blasphemy law handed out by the lower courts has ever been upheld by the higher judiciary.

Prospects for the Future

As for the prospects for religious freedom under the present regime of General Pervez Musharraf and Prime Minister Zafarullah Khan Jamali, there is reason to believe that the situation will improve considerably. In terms of his religious orientation, Musharraf is probably Pakistan's most liberal leader since Ayub Khan (1907–1974; prime minister 1958–1969). However, Musharraf's regime must tread cautiously on Islamic grounds and must not allow Islam to become a political issue while it is seeking political stability. On the contrary, the new government will have to solicit political support from the religious groups as it faces the formidable challenge presented by opposition parties. It is, therefore, difficult to imagine that the new civil-military coalition, even if it wants to do so, will ever try to dismantle the legal and institutional structures seen as discriminatory by the minorities. Not legislating Islamic laws might be considered merely negligent, but abrogating those laws once they are legislated will provoke the wrath of the religious groups, which the new regime, already faced with a crisis of legitimacy, can hardly afford. What we can expect from Musharraf, however, is that he ignore the implementation of discriminatory laws or that he implement them in slow time. Given that the overall policy thrust of the new regime in Pakistan is liberal, progressive, nondiscriminatory, and nonsectarian, the situation with regard to religious freedom is likely to improve in the future.

Mumtaz Ahmad

See also Islam

Further Reading

Abbott, F. (1968). *Islam and Pakistan.* Ithaca, NY: Cornell University Press.

Ahmad, A. (1986). *Pakistan society.* Oxford, UK: Oxford University Press.

Binder, L. (1962). *Religion and politics in Pakistan.* Berkeley and Los Angeles: University of California Press.

Jinnah, Mohammad Ali. (1947). *Presidential Address to the Constituent Assembly of Pakistan.* Retrieved December 18, 2002, from http://pakistanspace.tripod.com/documents/jinnah11.htm

Mujahid, S. (2001). *Pakistan ideology.* Islamabad, Pakistan: Islamic Research Institute.

Nasr, S. V. R. (1994). *The vanguard of the Islamic revolution: The Jama'at-i-Islami of Pakistan.* Berkeley and Los Angeles: University of California Press.

Syed, A. H. (1982). *Pakistan: Islam, politics and national solidarity.* Westport, CT: Praeger.

Zulfiqar, G. H. (n.d.) *Pakistan as visualized by Iqbal and Jinnah.* Lahore, Pakistan: Bazm-i-Iqbal.

Peace Churches

The Mennonites, Society of Friends (Quakers), and Brethren are known as the historic peace churches. Although rooted in the same nonconformist tradition of Protestant sects, they differ from other religious traditions in their rejection of the moral acceptability of "just war." Most theological traditions hold that, under special limited circumstances, waging war to defend oneself or to protect others may be considered a just and moral action. The peace churches do not. To them, "turning the other cheek" is an absolute principle, and their pacifist tradition means that their adherents will neither engage nor have direct complicity in violent acts, even if for self-defense. From the time of their founding in the aftermath of the Protestant Reformation to today, the denominations have defined and redefined what is required under the peace tradition. This redefinition has affected and altered the relationship of the peace churches and the broader society.

The Mennonites

The Mennonites and their more conservative cousins, the Amish, first arose as a reaction against the violence of the radical elements of the Reformation (known as the Radical Reformation). As Anabaptism arose in Switzerland and Germany in the 1530s, its adherents refused to support violence in any form. For many, this meant not only a refusal to serve in the military, but to pay taxes or perform any act required by civil government. Menno Simons (1496–1561), a former priest, became the leader of a group of Swiss Anabaptists in 1536. The name Mennonites comes from his name, although he did not directly establish that particular sect. In addition

GEORGE WASHINGTON TO THE QUAKERS, 1789

To the Annual Meeting of Quakers

George Washington

September 1789

Government being, among other purposes, instituted to protect the persons and consciences of men from oppression, it certainly is the duty of rulers, not only to abstain from it themselves, but, according to their stations, to prevent it in others.

The liberty enjoyed by the people of these states of worshipping Almighty God agreeably to their consciences, is not only among the choicest of their *blessings*, but also of their *rights*. While men perform their social duties faithfully, they do all that society or the state can with propriety demand or expect; and remain responsible only to their Maker for their religion, or modes of faith, which they may prefer or profess.

Your principles and conduct are well known to me; and it is doing the people called Quakers no more than justice to say, that (except their declining to share with others the burden of the common defense) there is no denomination among us, who are more exemplary and useful citizens.

I assure you very explicitly, that in my opinion the conscientious scruples of all men should be treated with great delicacy and tenderness; and it is my wish and desire, that the laws may always be as extensively accommodated to them, as a due regard to the protection and essential interests of the nation may justify and permit.

W. B. Allen, ed.

Source: *George Washington, A Collection.*
(Indianapolis: Liberty Classics, 1989) p 533–534.

---

to a strict pacifism, the theology that Simons embraced included a belief in adult baptism by immersion, foot washing, the kiss of brotherhood, and a refusal to associate with those who have fallen from fellowship (shunning). As the Mennonite movement grew, it became more lenient. Jacob Amman (1644?–1730?) led a group of conservatives away from the main body of Mennonites in the 1690s to protest an increasing unwillingness to shun excommunicated members. The Amish, as they came to be known, immigrated to eastern Pennsylvania in the early eighteenth century, determined to remove themselves entirely from the corruption of "English" society.

The first Mennonites immigrated to Pennsylvania in 1683. William Penn granted 18,000 acres near Philadelphia to a group of settlers that probably included Dutch Quakers as well as Mennonites, and they settled in Germantown. Although the Mennonites initially participated in governmental affairs, they quickly withdrew, leaving those duties to the Friends in the area. As more and more German and Swiss "brethren" immigrated, Mennonites moved further west into Lancaster and Berks counties in Pennsylvania. This westward migration will eventually take Mennonite communities into the Midwest and the Southwest.

As long as the pacifist Quakers remained in firm control of Pennsylvania, the Mennonites could be assured that their right not to support military action in any way would be respected. The eighteenth century, however, proved to be more problematic. When the French and Indian War broke out in America in 1755, General William Braddock demanded, if not soldiers, then wagons. Although many Quakers refused on the grounds that to contribute any material used in war was to support the war itself, the Mennonites complied, provided that they not be asked to transport guns. As long as they were transporting food and medical supplies, they could claim a humanitarian and thus, nonviolent, mission.

The Revolutionary War, however, was much different. After hostilities broke out at Lexington and Concord in April of 1775, American patriots demanded laws requiring all able-bodied men to serve in the militia. The Mennonites refused, citing their religious principle of non-violence. The Mennonites' tenuous position was further compromised when the Pennsylvania Assembly began requiring loyalty oaths of all inhabitants. As non-English settlers, the Mennonites, through succeeding generations, had affirmed their loyalty to the British crown. This affirmation conveyed not merely political loyalty, but a sacred obligation. Many settlers lost not only their land but also their willingness to participate in civil government. Most Mennonites believed that voting, as long as it did not involve war appropriations, was consistent with their pacifistic principles. The American Revolution changed all that and thus began a withdrawal from public life that lasted into the twentieth century.

The Society of Friends

The Society of Friends or the Quakers arose in the seventeenth century as a reaction to Puritanism and the English Civil War. George Fox (1624–1691) reinterpreted the Puritan struggle against worldly evil to an individual battle within each human. The "Lamb's War" was to be won through simple worship, honesty, equality, nonresistance, and a focus on the "inner light." After the restoration in 1660, the Friends' quest for tolerance was ignored and thousands found themselves in jail. One of those jailed was William Penn, the future proprietor of Pennsylvania.

Although Quakers immigrated throughout the New World and faced persecution from Massachusetts to Virginia, most settled in the mid-Atlantic. In Pennsylvania and West Jersey, Quaker practice standardized in the early eighteenth century. After 1750, the commitment to peace became more complicated. William Penn had reconciled his paci-

fism with the reality of holding office by ensuring that a non-Quaker served as his deputy. The deputy, then, assumed responsibility for all military-related matters in the colony. Successive generations of Quakers, however, were not as easily convinced. Slavery became an issue of contention, and Quaker meetings excommunicated members who married outside the Meeting or who violated the dictate of pacifism. As a result, the Quaker dominance of Pennsylvania succumbed to political reality and economic growth.

During the nineteenth century, Quakers moved into the Midwest and the South, and their antislavery activity increased. Early on, the major conflicts were among Quakers themselves. Disputes over doctrine, dress, and the degree of cooperation with non-Quakers in abolitionist work, tended to absorb most Quaker energy until the Civil War. The years between the Civil War and the World Wars saw the fullest expression of the "peace testimony" as it came to be interpreted by modern-day Quakers.

The Church of the Brethren

Like the Mennonites, the Church of the Brethren (or simply, "Brethren") arose in the aftermath of the Protestant Reformation and was Anabaptist in doctrine. The Brethren believed firmly in the dictates of primitive Christianity, and accepted Scripture as divinely inspired. Their focus was to model the teachings of Jesus in their own lives. The church was separate from the world and individual members worked to deepen the faith of all within the community. The Brethren adopted a discipline that was neither Catholic nor Protestant. The church was the central authority, but that authority sprang from the collective membership and not from a structured hierarchy.

The Brethren first came to Pennsylvania in 1719. By 1790, the Brethren numbered fifteen hundred full members and lived throughout Pennsylvania as well as Maryland, Virginia, and the Carolinas. Known as Dunkers because of their outdoor baptisms, the first recorded baptisms occurred in 1723 in the Wissahickon Creek outside of Philadelphia.

During the Revolutionary War, the Brethren's devotion to pacifism subjected them to the same suspicions that plagued other nonresistant groups. Maryland Brethren faced large fines, harassment, and property vandalism and seizures. Some families were assessed damages to repay those who had been hurt by the war or were forced to provide supplies to the military. Peter Suman, a Dunker from Frederick, Maryland was convicted of treason and hanged on 6 July 1781. Local tradition, however, recounts a more grisly penalty. Sumam and two others were drawn and quartered and their body parts fed to dogs.

During the nineteenth century, the Brethren maintained a healthy respect for civil authority, albeit from a distance. A key element of Brethren doctrine concerned separation from the world in order to remain a part of the Kingdom of God. Part of that separation involved a commitment to nonresistance for themselves, but not necessarily for non-Brethren. As the century progressed, the requirements for membership became more precise. In 1804, members had to adopt "plain" dress. In 1837, they had to promise nonresistance. By 1848, the standard Brethren baptism included commitments to non-swearing, nonresistance, as well as nonconformity. Although some Civil War battles occurred around Brethren meetinghouses, the Brethren maintained a strict policy of nonresistance. Soldiers could only become Brethren if they promised to refrain from killing; in effect they had to leave the service.

The Peace Testimony in the Twentieth Century

For all the peace churches, the twentieth century marked significant changes. Although the Mennonites had adopted some "mainline" Protestant innovations, like Sunday Schools, their opposition to World War I brought a resurgence of charges of disloyalty. For both the Brethren and the Mennonites, World War I produced significant changes. Unable to demonstrate patriotism through military service, the Mennonites chose imprisonment. Fear of Americans of German descent placed the Mennonites and the Brethren in a more precarious position, having to prove their loyalty. On 15 May 1918, Congress passed the Sedition Act, which criminalized any refusal to buy war bonds or any antiwar statement. Anyone of German descent faced harassment, tarring and feathering, and in one case, lynching. By November, more than 6,000 Germans were imprisoned in internment camps.

When the United States entered World War I, the Mennonites held to their nonresistant witness. They would excommunicate any member who abandoned nonresistance, but they would support all those who suffered imprisonment because of their pacifist views. Although the Selective Service Act of 1917 provided for noncombatant service, it did not provide complete exemptions. Initially, the Mennonites believed that noncombatant service would be run by civilians but when it became clear that noncombatant service would still be run by the military, the Mennonites chose imprisonment.

Although "noncombatant" service was later defined, most Mennonites refused to do anything more than cook their meals and clean their quarters. That refusal carried serious consequences. Mennonite draftees reported being beaten, subjected to cold showers and being scrubbed raw with wire brushes. Some were imprisoned in Fort Leavenworth and Alcatraz until well after peace had been declared. Their more fortunate brethren, however, were furloughed into agricultural programs. Although there was some resistance, the program generally worked well and those in the furlough program were among the first men discharged in December 1918.

Post-World War I, the peace witness of the Mennonites took a more complex form than passive withdrawal from the world. Although the General Conference Mennonites dropped out of the ecumenical Federal Council of Churches, the founding of the Mennonite Central Committee in 1920 (MCC) brought Mennonites into more regular contact with the state. The need to reconstruct Europe in the aftermath of World War II was a catalyst in changing the peace testimony from one that focused only on the negativity of war to one that actively and positively promoted witness for peace.

The Church of the Brethren also changed with the times, but the change involved a broader definition of "just war" and more latitude for the decisions of individual members. In 1935, the Brethren endorsed the idea that war is sin and that it is sinful for any Christian to participate in any military activity. In 1939, however, although the Brethren remained opposed to war, they adopted a tolerant stance toward those who became soldiers. A soldier could be returned to full fellowship as long as he expressed desire to abide by Brethren doctrine. By 1948, that position had been fully explicated. Participation in military activities was a matter of personal conscience. The church would remain dedicated to peace and would champion the cause of nonresistance. Again, the focus switched from a negative position on war to a positive position on peace.

The Quakers maintained their commitment to peaceful social action throughout the Civil War and into the twentieth century. Historically, Quakers acted as mediators, attempting to avoid or end war-fare. As early as King Philip's War in 1675 up until the present day, Quaker diplomats have acted privately to end disputes. Public peace witness usually involves various relief activities. With the United States's entry into World War I in 1917, the American Friends Service Committee was created. Unlike the Mennonites who had isolated themselves from governmental activity and came under suspicion for their German ethnicity and ancestry, Quakers effectively continued their pacifism unhindered due to their presence at all levels of government and their access to power.

The American enthusiasm for the "war to end all wars" affected the Quaker organization. Some Quakers began to question the precise meaning of a "just war." If one massive conflict could prevent others, then would that war be just? Although all Quaker meetings (Orthodox, Hicksite, and Gurneyite) officially reaffirmed the witness to peace principles, more than two-thirds of Quaker men served in the military between 1918 and 1920. At Quaker colleges like Swathmore and Haverford, the peace position was subordinated to the necessity of fighting a just war.

The Quaker peace testimony has survived into the twentieth and the twenty-first century. After both World Wars and other troubles that have followed, the Friends Service Committee coordinated relief and reconstruction efforts in war-torn areas around the world. The Friends Service Committee also seeks to prevent the outbreak of hostilities through informal conferences bringing together mid-level diplomats, young leaders, and professionals who might be able to avert situations of potential conflict. Quakers also seek to prevent conflict by addressing the causes of injustice at home and abroad. The effectiveness of the British and the American Friends Service Committees was recognized in 1947, when they were awarded a Nobel Peace prize.

In the twentieth century and into the twenty-first, Mennonites have moved from a quietism to political engagement with the world. As a result of the World Wars, the Mennonites became actively involved in humanitarian service and relief efforts, premised in the Gospel mandate to care for others. The Mennonite Central Committee (MCC) in 1968 established offices in Washington, D.C., a move that facilitated yet another aspect of their humanitarian service: education. MCC workers just completing

their tours of duty stop in the Washington office in order to speak to federal staffers and legislators about the impact of United States' policies on the ordinary people of other countries. Their information has a direct impact because it comes from first-hand experience and is told accurately without ideological embellishments. In keeping with their pacifism, Mennonite testimony and lobbying efforts are nonconfrontational. One legislative aide noted the "gentleness and respect for others" (Miller 1998, 123) that Mennonite workers display. As the religious scholar Keith Graber Miller observes, "'Not doing violence,' whether through physical or verbal attacks, seems to be one of the guiding principles of MCC Washington's work. At the same time, Mennonites in Washington seek passionately to reduce the violences [sic] attributable, in part, to their government" (Miller 1998, 123).

Implications

Peace churches in America were historically persecuted for their pacifism, especially in times of armed conflict. The contributions that these small groups have had on American society continue to far exceed their actual membership numbers. Quakers in the nineteenth century, for example, were at the forefront of abolitionist and women's rights movements, and the Friends Service Committees received a Nobel Peace prize. Into the twentieth century, the Mennonites' experience and credibility as providers of humanitarian aid around the globe gives them influence, power, and an impact on foreign affairs.

Patricia Norred Derr and Catharine Cookson

See also Conscientious Objection and Pacifism

Further Reading

Barbour, H., & Frost, J.W. (1988). *The Quakers.* New York: Greenwood Press.

Bowman, C.F. (1995). *Brethren society: The cultural transformation of a peculiar people.* Baltimore, MD: Johns Hopkins University Press.

Miller, K.G. (1998). *Wise as serpents, innocent as doves: American Mennonites engage Washington.* Knoxville: University of Tennessee Press.

Williams, P.W. (2002). *America's religions: From their origins to the twenty-first century.* Champagne-Urbana: Illinois University.

Pennsylvania: Colonial to Early Republic

Traditionally, Pennsylvania is known as "Penn's Holy Experiment," and it has held a singular place in American religious history for its groundbreaking role in advancing freedom of conscience. This simple generality, however, obscures the more complicated reality. Based on the notion—radical for its time—that religious conformity was not necessary for civil peace, Pennsylvania was founded in 1682 when a small band of Quakers, led by William Penn (1644–1718), sailed up the Delaware River to an area north of already thriving Swedish settlements. Penn, a member of the Society of Friends or Quakers, received the land west of the Delaware River between New York and Maryland from Charles I of England in repayment for a debt. Penn was determined to establish a government, based not on conformity to narrow religious doctrine, but on morality and property ownership. Sectarian squabbles not only disturbed the peace but tended to limit political participation if otherwise qualified men were excluded based on their religious beliefs.

William Penn's Beliefs

Penn was a product of his age, and did not advocate complete religious freedom or tolerance. The right to dissent should belong only to Christians and then only to certain types of Christians whose beliefs would not pose a threat to the civil order. Like John Locke, Penn had great difficulty applying his standard of tolerance to Roman Catholics. While not directly opposing the settlement of Catholics, Penn feared the potential threat to English liberty that he believed Catholic immigrants would present. He was concerned that Catholics would owe their allegiance to a foreign authority, the pope. Regarding Roman Catholicism a tyrannical faith, Penn believed that "popery" represented the kind of blind allegiance to authority and forced uniformity of conviction that he specifically wanted to avoid. Penn was forced to admit, however, that violence and intolerance were not the sole provinces of Catholicism, and early colonial laws placed Roman Catholics in the same category as Protestants.

Early colonial laws further delimited "religious tolerance." Under *The Laws Agreed Upon in England* (1682), the earliest framework for Pennsylvania law,

tolerance was extended only to those who believed in God. Sunday was established as the official Sabbath, and colonial law forbid labor on this first day of the week. This practice impinged upon the religious liberty of Jews and anyone who did not observe Sunday as the Sabbath by making labor on Sunday a civil crime, punishable by a fine. Finally, the franchise was limited to those who professed the belief that Jesus Christ was the Messiah. By limiting the voting and office holding to Christians, Pennsylvania marginalized non-Christians.

In the early years of settlement, however, Penn's terms proved controversial for being too generous. In 1692, Governor Benjamin Fletcher limited the right to hold office to Protestants who believed in the Trinity. Pennsylvania's assembly objected only to the provision that assemblymen be required to swear to the provisions of the Toleration Act of 1689, rather than simply affirm their allegiance to it. Later, Pennsylvania's laws were stabilized to limit holding office in the legislative and executive branches generally to Christians, but anyone who believed in God would be free from government restraint.

Penn was as pragmatic as he was idealistic. Some historians have noted that laws trying to restrict religious freedom in Pennsylvania emerged during Penn's absences from the colonies. Most agree, however, that Penn's main concern was to insure the rights of Quakers to practice freely, as well as build his own fortune. He expected to sell large tracts of his grant to others, keeping large areas for his own use.

Ethnic and Religious Divergence

Pennsylvania grew rapidly with an estimated population of 30,000 in 1717 when large migrations from Ireland and Germany began. Originally attracted by ideals of religious tolerance and ethnic diversity, eighteenth-century settlers then separated themselves according to religious practice, language, and national origin. Even among English settlers, Penn's goal of shared power among religious groups met with some dissension. Some Quakers feared that they would be subject to the same discrimination they fled in England if they did not insure themselves firm control of the government. Practicing Anglicans objected to a government in which they were the minority and tried unsuccessfully to bring provincial law into greater agreement with English practice. Conversely, others warned that a completely Quaker-dominated province might alienate other groups and threaten the peace that Penn wanted to achieve. In 1710, the Philadelphia Yearly Meeting weighed in by advising Quakers to elect good, honest, God-fearing men to office who are more interested in the well-being of the province than in their own careers.

The beliefs that set Quakers apart and caused them to found their own colony where their religious freedom would be preserved also made governing such a colony difficult. Among these radical beliefs were a tendency to pacifism and a refusal to swear oaths. Quakers, along with many of the German settlers, were avowed pacifists, and the matter of colonial defense proved a constant struggle. Although Penn's charter provided for the creation of a militia, Penn delegated those duties to another. Getting the colonial assembly to appropriate money for defense was always a problem and nonpacifists resented being asked to pay and serve when their pacifist neighbors could opt out. Even substituting financial contributions for physical ones, as was attempted in the 1709 expedition against Canada, were unsuccessful. Appropriating money to hire mercenaries was just as sinful, the pacifists believed, as taking up arms themselves.

The refusal to swear oaths also created governing problems. At the time, swearing an oath was deemed to be required to protect against perjury or false testifying (because one who lied under oath courted eternal damnation). Thus, laws that protected Quakers by allowing the use of an affirmation (instead of an oath) also plunged the legal system into a crisis of credibility: non-Quakers would not trust the truth or accuracy of any testimony that was not sworn. English law prohibited the use of affirmations in certain cases. Pennsylvania law adopted a compromise that allowed individual magistrates to administer sworn oaths at their discretion and specified penalties for perjury. This act did not satisfy many Quakers, who believed that such sworn oaths would be injurious to the province as a whole. On the other hand, Anglicans believed that the use of affirmations provided insufficient guarantee of truthfulness in court and therefore threatened their civil and constitutional rights. To register their opposition, some Anglicans refused to serve on juries or function as magistrates, effectively shutting down the judicial system. Eventually, the presence of so many groups opposed to oath-taking and the practical consideration that a functioning court system was necessary resulted in the passage of a 1724 statute that recog-

nized different forms of assuring truthful testimony and punishing false assertions.

Although Pennsylvania rapidly became the most heterogeneous of all the English colonies, the earliest and greatest threat to the Quaker holy experiment came from a fellow Quaker. The so-called Keithian Controversy split the Society of Friends and ended with Keith being disowned in both England and America and standing convicted of defamation and sedition.

George Keith (1639–1716) arrived in Philadelphia in 1689 and at once set about trying to establish doctrinal standards that would significantly alter Quakerism. His attempts at reversing what he saw as errors only infuriated his fellow Quakers, particularly when he charged that Quaker participation in government was inconsistent with Quaker principles. Keith was also concerned that as the Quaker elite became more wedded to commercial activities, they were losing sight of the purpose of the "holy experiment." After forming a splinter group, the Christian Quakers and Friends, Keith eventually returned to England where he took orders in the Church of England and became one of the earliest missionaries for the Society for the Propagation of the Gospel in Foreign Parts (SPG). The Keithian Controversy highlighted the tension between a secular commonwealth and a holy experiment.

During the eighteenth century, England's wars for empire created problems for the Quaker elite. England, forced to protect colonists who settled the frontier areas (including western Pennsylvania) from Native Americans, sought payment for this expensive defense from the colonies. Pacifists objected to supporting war, yet Quakers who held governance positions had to do what was in the best interest of the colonists as well as comply with England's demands. Historian Margaret Hope Bacon notes that to appease the pacifists, Quakers in government developed more and more elaborate rationalizations for the taxes, but the protests grew. Finally, Quakers began to leave the government, which became dominated by the evangelical Protestant church members (Bacon 1995, 71).

The Revolutionary War in Pennsylvania caused a civil war as well. William Frost notes, "The Revolution marked the end of the Quaker or sectarian definition of religious liberty. The Quaker politicians who insisted that their continuance in office was necessary for the preservation of minority rights were correct. The revolutionary struggle, which began as an effort to preserve the rights of the majority on Pennsylvanians, resulted in the disenfranchisement of a substantial minority" (Frost 1990, 72). The new assembly, dominated by Presbyterians and Lutheran or Reformed Germans, enacted strict loyalty oaths that Frost describes as "clearly punitive, an act of political and religious persecution," targeting the sectarians of the colony.

While the onset of the Revolutionary War generally caused a crisis for pacifist religious groups, in Pennsylvania the crisis was most acute, for the non-resistant churches, including Mennonites and Dunkers, Schwenkfelders and Moravians, as well as Quakers, formed a significant minority (perhaps a quarter) of the population at the time. What the non-resistant sects could not under conscience do for the common cause was fight, make weapons, or pay military taxes. What in good conscience they could contribute to a war effort (as they had done in the French and Indian War), was to help refugees, contribute to poor relief, provide food and other such non-military supplies, provide horses and wagons and serve as teamsters to transport these supplies. Mennonites, for example, served in the wagon service during the Revolutionary War. Such items as "cattle, clothing, farm produce, and blankets" were also provided by the peace churches, both voluntarily and also by legal requisition (Macmaster 1979, 297–298, 345–349). Interestingly, Mennonite gunsmiths were renowned for their "Pennsylvania rifle" craftsmanship. Making rifles to kill deer for food was quite a different matter from filling an order for the military, however.

Nonresistors readily acknowledged their responsibility to pay general taxes. Instead, however, Pennsylvania developed a "tax on conscientious objectors as an equivalent to military service and intended for military purposes," a tax which was problematic for two reasons: (1) conscience was still violated because the money funded the war effort directly, and (2) the fine was severe and punitive, amounting to a confiscation. The tax was meant as a punishment, and was not of a realistic amount, but, rather, an amount meant to make up the entire difference between the small monies the colony had and the large amount needed to train, supply, and pay troops to fight the war. As indicated in a petition by conscientious objectors, the fine was "in such a Degree, whereby numbers of Families would be reduced to utter Ruin, and such Fines to be raised by distraint of their Goods, by military force" (Macmaster 1979, 256–257). By 1777, each colony

had in place a large-scale draft for men between the ages of 18 and 53. Conscientious objectors were to get substitutes or pay the confiscatory fine. When conscientious objectors could do neither, the pent-up frustration and fury of the populace over the war itself became directed against the nonresistant sects.

In 1790, after the end of the Revolutionary War, the Pennsylvania Constitution again underwent radical changes. With respect to religious matters, full civil rights were no longer predicated upon a belief in God, and while the religious test for holding office remained, it no longer required affirmation of the Christian Scriptures. The 1790 oath for office-holders simply required belief in God and in an afterlife with rewards and punishments. The convention, however, refused to repeal the tax on conscientious objectors. Indeed, as noted by Frost, "There was more freedom for a pacifist in Pennsylvania from 1680 until 1775 than there is today" (Frost 1990, 162).

Implications

While not perfecting government protection for religious freedom, the Quakers who governed William Penn's colony did succeed in establishing what Frost deemed "the most tolerant of all American colonies." Once the government passed out of the hands of the sectarians and into the hands of the churches in 1776, Pennsylvanians became less free. As Frost concludes (72–73), "The Revolution marked a transition from sectarian liberty to creating a Christian commonwealth."

Patricia Norred Derr and Catharine Cookson

See also Peace Churches; Roman Catholics, Colonial to Nineteenth Century

Further Reading

Ahlstrom, S.E. (1972). *A religious history of the American people.* New Haven, CT: Yale University Press.

Bacon, M.H. (1995). On the verge: The evolution of American Quakerism. In Miller, T. (Ed.). *America's alternative religions.* Albany: State University of New York Press, pp. 69–75.

Barbour, H., & Frost, J.W. (1988). *The Quakers.* New York: Greenwood Press.

Frost, J. W. (1990). *A perfect freedom: Religious liberty in Pennsylvania.* Cambridge, UK: Cambridge University Press.

Ireland, O.S. (1995). *Religion, ethnicity and politics: Ratifying the constitution in Pennsylvania.* University Park, PA: Penn State Press.

Macmaster, R.K. (1979). *Conscience in crisis: Mennonites and other peace churches in America, 1739–1789.* (Studies in Anabaptist and Mennonite History, No. 20). Scottsdale, PA: Herald Press.

Schwartz, S. (1987). *"A mixed multitude": The struggle for toleration in colonial Pennsylvania.* New York: New York University Press.

Pentecostalism

Pentecostalism is a fast-growing and vital global Christian movement that emerged in the late nineteenth century. Its incipient expressions were scattered globally among marginalized social groups. Its most storied center of beginnings was the Azusa Street Mission in Los Angeles, California, commencing in April 1906. Led by William Seymour, the son of former slaves, the grassroots religious awakening at the Azusa Mission reflected the restorationist and millenarian impulses so much a part of late-nineteenth- and early-twentieth-century North American Christianity. Humble beginnings notwithstanding, Pentecostalism has grown to embody the largest Protestant family of Christians, numbering well over 500 million participants globally.

Historic Roots of Pentecostalism

The growth of Pentecostalism during the twentieth century attracts a variety of explanations. When describing the impact of Pentecostalism, it is informative to note its five characteristic themes as a gestalt (an integrated structure). These historic themes include justification (God's forgiveness of sin), sanctification (freed of the power of sin), divine healing, the Second Coming of Christ, and the Baptism of the Holy Spirit. The last theme of the gestalt is characterized by the phenomenon of glossolalia or speaking in tongues. While the five themes of Pentecostalism are common to nineteenth-century North American Christianity, there has been a significant shift in Pentecostalism's understanding of how God accomplishes divine purposes in the lives of individuals and the larger society. This change in perspective sees a move of God's operation in earthly affairs from a historical continuity to transcendent and instantaneous operation beyond history. The dynamic of the Baptism of the Holy Spirit with accompanying glossolalia highlights this "beyond history" dimension that is a crucial aspect of understanding Pentecostalism's larger societal impact.

Interpreting Pentecostalism

Participants in the Pentecostal movement have historically described their existence with largely providential explanations, i.e., causation of the movement described as a divine work of God. Since the movement is seen as a spiritual End Times revival discontinuous with the previous 1900 years of Christianity, causal connections between Pentecostalism's emergence and sociopolitical realities contextually have not been the participants' favored explanations for their existence. However, a growing cadre of trained scholars, emerging from without and within Pentecostal ranks, is offering additional explanations for this movement's emergence as a significant influence religiously and socially. Included in these alternative explanations is the realization that Pentecostalism embodies a spiritual renewal movement in a long line of similar movements within 2000 years of Christian history. Such movements are most definitively understood in a broader evaluative context as religious realities that naturally intersect with social contexts. Such analysis has yielded, particularly when applied to non-Western (majority world) global realities, greater clarity on Pentecostalism's impact worldwide.

Pentecostalism as Compensation for Social Dislocation

The emergence of Pentecostalism has been viewed by some researchers as a response to the rapid industrialization and urbanization of North America. This view would not focus on the convergence of theological influences present in the late nineteenth and early twentieth centuries. Rather, the focus is centered on the socially outcast and psychologically maladjusted of the era who rejected secular solutions to their present dilemmas. This explanation of Pentecostalism sees the real source of the movement not in God's providential working, but the social and cultural realities of that period in history.

Many of the early adherents to Pentecostalism were poor farmers, recent immigrants, poverty-stricken city dwellers, and ethnic minorities. These disinherited persons were looking for an escape from

THREE INTERPRETATIONS OF PENTECOSTALISM

What began as a despised and ridiculed sect is quickly become both the preferred religion of the urban poor and the powerful bearer of a radically alternative vision of what the human world might one day become.

Harvey Cox

Source: Fire from Heaven: The Rise of Pentecostal Spirituality and the Re-shaping of Religion in the 21st Century. (Reading, MA: Addison Wesley Publishing Company, 1995), 83.

Pentecostals' distinctive understanding of the human encounter with the divine, which included both primitivist and pragmatic dimensions, enable them to capture lightning in a bottle and, more important, to keep it there, decade after decade, without stilling the ire or cracking the vessel. . . . The genius of the Pentecostal movement lay in its ability to hold (these) two seemingly incompatible impulses in productive tension.

Grant Wacker

Source: Heaven Below: Early Pentecostalism and American Culture. (Cambridge, MA: Harvard University Press, 2001), 10.

Pentecostalism extended among people already distant-either by choice or by change-from the cultural mainstream. Those who embraced Pentecostalism routinely explained their choice in theological terms: they saw it as restoration, as full gospel. . . . It also legitimated their reluctance and inability to address the overwhelming social evils of their own day by offering a simple explanation for social predicament. . . . But at face value, its primary significance lay in its ability to overwhelm human emotions, replacing despair with hope and uncertainty with assurance and an inner sense of peace.

Edith Blumhofer

Source: Restoring the Faith: The Assemblies of God, Pentecostalism and American Culture. (Urbana: University of Illinois Press, 1993), 72.

their present tragedies and thus the ecstatic religious experience and longing for the return of Jesus to "set the record straight" became an escape to a "safe refuge for the masses." When the harshness of immigration to a new country or the realities of rural disintegration and urban chaos became central to life, people who believed that religious experience was a matter of the heart and affirmed that the supernatural could overthrow the mundane gravitated enthusiastically and uncritically to Pentecostalism. In this view, the movement is most clearly seen as a substitute for the lack of material wealth and personal identity that was unattainable due to social disloca-tion. The ecstatic religious experiences inherent to Pentecostalism are viewed as the place where converts could escape to the otherworldly and therapeutic benefits of supernaturalistic religious experience.

Pentecostalism as a Functional Response to Deal with Social Dislocation

Pentecostalism's growth worldwide has arguably occurred most vigorously among the socially dislocated. While acknowledging the obvious influence of social history, some researchers have offered explanations of Pentecostalism that describe the movement as a creative resource to respond to adversity, as opposed to an escape from adversity. This view of Pentecostalism suggests that the movement has provided stability in the middle of social chaos. For example, an emphasis on the return of Jesus Christ and a better future can be used as a powerful response to an existence dominated by poverty in this present life.

The low socioeconomic status of many early Pentecostals yielded a natural defiance of certain restrictive social conventions of the day. The small groups of Pentecostals that formed into churches really became alternative communities where the ethos of their religious experience could find affirmation. No rational or empirical evaluative process could nullify the empowerment received as a Pentecostal participant. The common religious experience of Pentecostals created a natural egalitarianism that yielded a sturdy social cohesion. People with little human resource were transformed into individuals and groups of great boldness and confidence. This transformation became a ready antidote to the adversity present in all forms of social dislocation.

The political populism that heavily influenced the era of early Pentecostal growth created a context where a powerful form of social change occurred. Pentecostal groups functioned as all-inclusive social communities where the entirety of life was redefined in the light of a divine infusion of religious fervor and new social identity. The resultant human and social empowerment certainly gave the movement staying power. This capability to stand against social injustice as an alternative society has been evident throughout history. Governmental oppression of Pentecostals in the peasant revolts of the 1930s in El Salvador and the long civil strife in Guatemala from the 1950s onward demonstrate Pentecostal staying power in challenging political climates. Black Pentecostals, in the long struggle against apartheid in South Africa, maintained social identity despite oppressive conditions.

Pentecostalism as Protest against the Inevitability of Secularization

Social science literature documents the inevitability of religion losing its influence in a culture as people increasingly use secular rather than religious lenses to evaluate the world. In this scenario reason replaces religion in explaining natural and social realities. Researchers on new religious movements, including Pentecostalism, are increasingly discussing the anthropological protest against modernity resident in movements like Pentecostalism.

Modernity and secularization inevitably removes religion from the public arena, forcing it into the private sphere. The result of this shift in religious influence, however, may be negative. The secular substitutes become inadequate for providing a culture or individual with a system for integrating meaning. This "iron cage" that imprisons modern persons is challenged by religious movements like Pentecostalism that offer alternative explanations for meaning in this world. Thus, Pentecostalism bypasses the dominant societal explanations for what constitutes meaningful living in favor of explanations that rely much more upon affective rather than rational action.

The alternative explanations for what constitutes meaningful living are resident and legitimized in groups led by persons with charismatic authority. Weberian charismatic authority explains clearly the nature of leadership with "protest" groups like Pentecostals. These protest movements expect to receive transcendent guidance for personal and organizational concerns and consequentially reject the primacy of bureaucratic methods. Such a movement has a high percentage of its adherents actually participating in the phenomenological dimensions of the movement, hence a strong infrastructure of solidarity that rejects routinization.

Authority in such groups is viewed as residing outside the profane arena. Opposition to rational and/or institutional authority is obvious. Authority is legitimized by personal charisma of the leader of the protest movement. Simply put, the charismatic leader is seen to embody the "solution" to some dilemma or cultural status quo.

Pentecostalism, when seen as a protest movement, does not fit well into standard political or social definitions of such movements. The millenarian character of Pentecostalism does predispose it to future considerations with potential neglect for current societal issues. Historically apolitical, Pentecostal groups by their very nature have been cynical about humanly devised structures and institutions. Their lower socioeconomic status has predisposed them to avoid contact with political and governmental structures. Pentecostals distancing themselves from the usual social institutions creates obvious questions as to their long-term social impact. While such legitimate evaluation is necessary, Pentecostalism's greatest influence can only be observed when its alternative explanation for what constitutes empowerment and meaningful community life is given a fair hearing.

Pentecostalism as a Social Force in the Majority World

Pentecostalism's greatest growth continues to occur among lower socioeconomic groups in the (non-Western) majority world. While researchers have noted the negative impact of Pentecostalism's future orientation on current societal needs, alternative opinions are emerging. Acknowledging the millennial dimensions of Pentecostals, researchers have alternatively viewed these same dynamics as heightening the awareness of the Pentecostal group participant toward the present-time significance of God in their lives. The miraculous acts of God on behalf of oppressed people that are recorded in the Bible are seen as a promise to continue such divine initiative, thus producing hope rooted in the past and future, but operative in the present. The societally marginalized who are familiar with unnecessary death, illness, un/underemployment, prejudice, repressive war, and torture gravitate toward concrete religious experience as actualized in Pentecostal phenomena. The uncertainty of their status in life is countered by the personally actualized certainty of eternal life, and giving freedom to enrich one's present life. This dynamic present-tense experience is expressed in communities with common experience. Human dignity emerges in this kind of community of empowerment as nonpersons become "born again" with human identity and personhood. These communities subsequently are not waiting rooms for the "train to heaven," but grassroots social movements that demonstrate clear incentive and vision for substantially altering their present circumstances. A synthesis of this view of Pentecostals as a social force might say that Pentecostals do not have a social policy; they are a social policy.

Pentecostalism as Spiritual Force in the Public Arena

Pentecostalism does affirm that spiritual power is at hand to forge participants as communities of people. These communities have a deep sense of eternal purpose and expectantly and confidently view the substance of human experience with a sense of eternal destiny. At the heart of Pentecostalism as a spiritual force is what may be termed the restoration of "primal spirituality," which may be described as that largely unprocessed central fabric of humanity where an unending struggle for a sense of destiny and significance is ongoing. Pentecostals, as a spiritual force, may be viewed as a restoration of significance and purposefulness to masses of people whose daily experience is centered in despair, injustice, and hopelessness.

Pentecostalism as a restoration of primal spirituality may be expressed in three particular dimensions. First, primal speech may be described as ecstatic utterances (glossolalia). In a world where people feel as if their words don't count or where deconstructionist efforts have emptied words of all meaning, Pentecostals speak in a language of the heart that is understood by God alone.

Second, primal piety describes Pentecostals' affirmation of archetypal religious experiences including vision, healing, dream, and dance. These elemental forms of religious life, so marginalized by modern scholarship, enjoy a welcome place in Pentecostalism and a resurgence among persons hungry to recover this more universal spiritual framework.

Last, primal hope is Pentecostalism's insistence that a radically new world is about to dawn. This affirmation posits that what is visible is not the sum total of the reality that governs our lives.

Pentecostalism may be viewed as the reappearance not of an aberration but of a self-revealing explanation of the religious dimension of all humanity that secular explanations for life have failed to acknowledge. Pentecostalism clearly rejects the sacred-secular dichotomy that characterizes modernity and has replaced it with an affirmation of the immediate availability of God's power and presence in the public square to construct a reality that is powerfully experienced in the cultural fabric of any context.

Challenges to Pentecostalism's Continuing Influence in Global Societies

Redemption and lift is an observable phenomenon where participation in a religious movement actually lifts a person's social status. Pentecostalism has historically been the church of the poor and for the poor quite independent of Western power centers for continued effectiveness. However, as the redemption and lift phenomenon has occurred among Pentecostals in Western nations, there is the danger of the historic forgetfulness of people, as the Pentecostal participants are lifted beyond their cultural roots. Redemption and lift does challenge persons to remain connected to their former social status.

Globalization, and its insistence on reducing people to consumers impacted by the marketplace, is increasingly obvious in North America and Western Europe, where Pentecostals took root in the early twentieth century. As Pentecostalism grows exponentially in the majority world and their participants experience the social impact of the redemption-lift phenomenon, the challenge to be faced is whether Pentecostals will continue to have social influence on their cultural context. Will the Pentecostal movement rooted in those persons socially dislocated emerge as a new elite establishment? Grassroots social movements are not exempt from the inevitabilities of maturation neutralizing the initial impetus of the movement. Pentecostalism will face such global challenges in its second century of existence.

Continuing Multicultural Influences

The first decade of the twentieth century that paralleled Pentecostalism's initial emergence was a microcosm of ethnic realities. Against a background of Jim Crow laws, Pentecostals represented a new community of justice and equity. To participate in such communities was a truly liberating experience for immigrants and ethnic minority populations. For example, African-American Pentecostal historians would see the prophetic social consciousness rooted in slave religion actually preserved in black Pentecostalism.

A most unfortunate reality is that Pentecostalism, after that initial decade (1900–1910), sputtered in its attempts to reflect the incipient multiethnic character of its earliest communities. Pentecostalism has grown during the twentieth century, more often than not, along homogeneous lines. A continuing challenge to Pentecostals is to reflect the dynamics of liberation and empowerment that its early historical communities reflected. Against twenty-first-century ethnic realities, its full social impact among marginalized groups will be tested severely.

Political Challenges

Recent researchers on Pentecostalism have challenged the stereotypical portrayal of Pentecostals as passive and otherworldly. The emerging perspective is that Pentecostals have always been involved in here-and-now struggles. That involvement has been in grassroots movements of social transformation rather than political activism. While this historic grassroots involvement has been poorly documented, the stereotype of political nonparticipation is being critiqued by current research. A prime example of this is black Pentecostal participation in the U.S. civil rights movement. Among white Pentecostal groups in the United States, notable political figures

would be Attorney General John Ashcroft and Christian Coalition leader Pat Robertson.

With the civil strife in Latin America, the struggle against apartheid in South Africa, and totalitarian regimes on the Pacific Rim has come a new challenge. The sheer number of Pentecostals globally makes them a potential force for power in the politics of their respective regions. For example, national elections in Brazil, Peru, and Zambia have been swayed by the large numbers of Pentecostals in those nations. The relative isolation of Pentecostals, until recently, has left them disconnected from power centers that impact structural change. The continuing realities of economics and social change will yield a clashing of priorities that will bring pressure on Pentecostals for political involvement.

It is a huge leap from grassroots groups serving as "substitute societies" to effective political involvement. For example, two Guatemalan Pentecostals have served as presidents of that nation. Both Rios Montt and Jorge Serrano left office abruptly amidst political strife. This demonstrates that to date, social transition for Pentecostals has been problematic.

Byron D. Klaus

Further Readings

Anderson, R. M. (1979). *Vision of the disinherited: The making of American Pentecostalism.* New York: Oxford University Press.

Barrett, D., Kurian, G., & Johnson, T. M. (2001). *World Christian encyclopedia: A comparative study of churches and religions in the modern world* (Vols. 1–2, 2nd ed.). New York: Oxford University Press.

Blumhofer, E. (1993). *Restoring the faith: The Assemblies of God, Pentecostalism, and American culture.* Urbana: University of Illinois Press.

Blumhofer, E., Spittler, R., & Wacker, G. (Eds.). (1999). *Pentecostal currents in American Protestantism.* Urbana: University of Illinois Press.

Burgess, S., & van der Maas, E. (2002). *The new international dictionary of Pentecostal and charismatic movements.* Grand Rapids, MI: Zondervan.

Cleary, E. L., & Steward-Gambino, H. W. (Eds.). (1997). *Power, politics, and Pentecostals in Latin America.* Boulder, CO: Westview.

Clemmons, I. (1996). *Bishop C. H. Mason and the roots of the Church of God in Christ.* Bakersfield, CA: Pneuma Publishing.

Cox, H. (1995). *Fire from heaven: The rise of Pentecostal spirituality and the re-shaping of religion in the 21st cen-*

tury. Reading, MA: Addison Wesley Publishing Company.

Dayton, D. (1987). *Theological roots of Pentecostalism.* Grand Rapids, MI: Francis Asbury Press.

Dempster, M., Klaus, B., & Petersen, D. (Eds.). (1999). *The globalization of Pentecostalism: A religion made to travel.* Oxford, UK: Regnum Books.

Faupel, W. D. (1996). *The everlasting gospel.* Sheffield, UK: Sheffield Academic Press.

Hollenweger, W. (1997). *Pentecostalism.* Peabody, MA: Hendrickson Publishers.

Ma, W. S., & Menzies, R. (1997). *Pentecostalism in context.* Sheffield, UK: Sheffield Academic Press.

Martin, D. (1990). *Tongues of fire: The explosion of Protestantism in Latin America.* Oxford, UK: Basil Blackwell.

Moltmann, J., & Kuschell, K. J. (1996). *Concilium: Pentecostal movements as an ecumenical challenge.* Maryknoll, NY: Orbis Books.

Petersen, D. (1996). *Not by might nor by power: A Pentecostal theology of social concern.* Oxford, UK: Regnum Books.

Poewe, K. (Ed.). (1994). *Charismatic Christianity as a global culture.* Columbia: University of South Carolina Press.

Poloma, M. (1988). *The Assemblies of God at the crossroads: Charisma and institutional dilemmas.* Knoxville: University of Tennessee Press.

Shaull, R., & Cesar, W. (2000). *Pentecostalism and the future of Christian churches.* Grand Rapids, MI: Eerdmans Publishing.

Synan, V. (1997). *The Holiness-Pentecostal tradition: Charismatic movements in the 20th century.* Grand Rapids: Eerdmans.

Wacker, G. (2001). *Heaven below: Early Pentecostalism and American culture.* Cambridge, MA: Harvard University Press.

Pledge of Allegiance

In June 2002, the Ninth Circuit Court in San Francisco declared the Pledge of Allegiance unconstitutional insofar as it contains the words "under God." Yet the Pledge has been intertwined with religion and politics since it was written. The author of the original version was Francis Bellamy (1855–1931), a Baptist minister who was also a Socialist. He was the cousin of Edward Bellamy, author of the classic utopian novel, *Looking Backward* (1888). Francis shared Edward's dreams for a planned political economy. Forced out of his pulpit because of his socialist sermons, Bellamy took a position with the editor of *The Youth's Companion*, a popular magazine. The Pledge was published in the 8 September 1892 edition in time for public schools' four hundredth anniversary celebration of Columbus Day. By developing a common ritual around the flag, Bellamy hoped to heal the wounds caused by the Civil War and to teach children America's core values. His draft did not include the words "under God," but he did consider including the word "equality" before "liberty and justice for all." He realized, however, that this would be rejected by school superintendents who opposed encouraging any ideas of equality for women and African-Americans, and reluctantly left it out.

In the midst of post-World War II anticommunist fervor, the Catholic Knights of Columbus lobbied Congress to add the words "under God" after the words "one nation." President Eisenhower signed the bill in 1954. The Pledge is now recited daily during the school year by millions of children and at the meetings of countless social and fraternal clubs.

The Pledge has been modified twice and further attempts continue. In 1924, the American Legion and Daughters of the American Revolution changed Bellamy's original "my flag" to "the Flag of the United States of America." More recently, pro-life advocates have endeavored to include the words "born and unborn" after the words "with liberty and justice for all," while progressives have urged adding the word "equality" as Bellamy desired.

Although reciting the Pledge of Allegiance has been voluntary since the Supreme Court forbade compulsion in *West Virginia Board of Education v. Barnette* (1943), the lawsuit that led the Ninth Circuit Court to rule it unconstitutional was brought by Michael Newdow, an avowed atheist who argued that his school-age daughter's First Amendment rights were harmed because she was forced to "watch and listen as her state-employed teacher in her state-run school leads her classmates in a ritual proclaiming that there is a God, and that ours is 'One Nation under God'" (*New York Times*, 27 June 2002, A-1). In an aired interview with CNN, Newdow stated:

> I agree [that the United States] is the greatest nation and what has made it great is our Constitution. The framers were quite wise in recognizing what reli-

THE PLEDGE OF ALLEGIANCE

I pledge allegiance to the Flag of the United States of America, and to the Republic for which it stands: one Nation under God, indivisible, With Liberty and Justice for all.

gion can do and how it can cause hatred and how it can cause death. You don't have to go far in this world, outside of our nation, to see where that has happened. It is prevalent over the entire globe and the reason we don't have it here is because we have an establishment clause . . . If Mike there from Alabama [referring to a call-in listener] wouldn't mind saying "we are one nation under Buddha" every day, or "one nation under David Koresh" or "one nation" under some religious icon that he doesn't believe in . . . if he doesn't understand the difference then we have a problem. (CNN, 26 June 2002)

Newdow's estranged wife publicly stated that she and her daughter are regular church members and that the daughter is not at all troubled by reciting the Pledge of Allegiance.

Most legal scholars, while conceding that the Circuit Court's reasoning was solidly based on Supreme Court precedents, predicted that the decision would be overturned either because the "violation" was *de minimis* (too small to be considered constitutionally significant), or because the words "under God" were so embedded in a secular ritual as to have lost any sense of government endorsement of religion.

Paul Weber

Further Reading

Baer, J. W. (1992). *The pledge of allegiance: a centennial history, 1892–1992*. Annapolis, MD: Free State Press.

CNN (2002, June 26). Litigant explains why he brought Pledge suit. Retrieved November 13, 2002, from http://www.cnn.com/2002/LAW/06/26/Newdow.cnna/

The Great Pledge Debate. (2002, November/December). *Liberty Magazine* online. Retrieved November 13, 2002, from http://www.libertymagazine.org/article/articleview/311/1/2/

Nieves, E. (2002, June 27). Judges ban pledge of allegiance from schools, citing "under God." *The New York Times*, p. A1.

Miller, M. S. (1976). *Twenty-three words*. Portsmouth, VA: Printcraft Press.

Court Cases

Newdow v. U.S. Congress, Docket No. 00-16423, 9th Cir. (2002).

West Virginia State Board of Education v. Barnette, 319 U.S. 624 (1943).

Pluralism and Religious Identity in Lawmaking

Unrestricted religious freedom, like other liberties lacking in constraints, risks infringing upon the rights and freedom of others. More specifically, unfettered religious freedom exercised by religious lawmakers may infringe upon the constitutionally protected rights of other citizens, especially those of women and religious minorities. Since the moral identity and constitutionally protected free exercise rights of religious lawmakers are also at stake, problems posed by religious lawmaking cannot be resolved simply by expecting or demanding that such lawmakers not draw upon their religious convictions in making public policy decisions.

The term *lawmaking* refers broadly to the procedures by which the several types of public policy enactments and regulations are made legally binding and enforceable on citizens through the coercive power of the state. Lawmaking thus encompasses not only the formal enactments of a legislature, but also official executive rules and orders, policy enactments by other government officials, and judicial decisions. The terms *religion* and *religious* refer primarily to those religions that have established institutional bases in the United States—Christianity and Judaism—and to a far lesser extent, Islam, Buddhism, and Hinduism.

Religious lawmaking thus refers to the process of enacting, validating, interpreting, applying, or enforcing legally binding regulations (those backed by the coercive power of the state) on the basis of religious considerations. The determination of whether lawmaking is religious is an objective one. That is, there must be evidence that religious considerations played a significant part in the enactment of a law, one that results in discernible effects or consequences in order for it to be considered to be religiously based or influenced.

Lawmakers are government and public officials whose roles involve, in whole or part, the passage or enactment of laws. The category includes, most obviously, legislators, as well as executive branch officials such as presidents, governors, mayors, city and town council members, and also members of the judiciary. Lawmakers' roles generally distinguish them from other citizens in several respects, especially in terms of their responsibilities as public representatives, and their greater power and authority to use the law to coercively bind other citizens.

Religious lawmaking may conflict with fundamental rights of citizenship protected by the U.S. Constitution. The principle of equal citizenship mandates that all citizens have an equal right to participate in society, regardless of their race or gender or religion, as discussed in the works of Kenneth Karst (1989 and 1993). In addition to the constitutional guarantee of equal protection of the laws, citizenship rights include those constitutional rights that are most centrally impacted by religious lawmaking, including the rights to the free exercise of religion and to freedom from the establishment of religion protected by the First Amendment, which expressly states that "Congress shall make no law respecting an establishment of religion, or prohibiting the free exercise thereof."

Religious lawmaking also may raise establishment concerns, problems of alienation, exclusion, coercion, and political divisiveness that the Supreme Court has identified as relevant to its decision making under the First Amendment's establishment clause. The presence of establishment concerns in a particular case is an important consideration in analyzing the validity of religious lawmaking, even though they may not be sufficient, by themselves, to establish that citizenship rights have been violated.

What Makes Religious Lawmaking Problematic?

There are at least three components embedded in the question of what makes religious lawmaking problematic. The first has to do with the character of law. The second concerns the character of religion. And the third is an effect or consequence of the interaction of law and religion in a morally and religiously pluralistic polity.

The Character of Law

Because of the coercive character of the law itself, religious influences on lawmaking carry special risks of being coercive that are not evident in the context of religious influences on other aspects of public life. When religious rationales provide the basis for laws, the possibility that they will restrict individual freedoms, in violation of constitutional protections to substantive due process and equal protection, results because of the coercive character of law. This problem is not remedied by the theoretical freedom that members of all religious persuasions have to participate in establishing public laws since, realistically, the opportunities for members of less politically and socially powerful religious groups to influence lawmaking are more limited than for members of majoritarian religious faiths. Lawmakers still overwhelmingly are members of mainstream Christian religions, and do *not* reflect the diversity of religious traditions that is found in the larger society.

However, more than direct coercion of religiously influenced laws, it is the "publicly inaccessible" character of many religious beliefs that make religious lawmaking most problematic in a religiously pluralistic polity. "Publicly inaccessible" here means that religious beliefs tend to rely on premises that are either not publicly intelligible or not widely shared by non-members. For many religious adherents, the tenets of faith are authoritative: they are understood to be God's word or revelation, to be faithfully and rigidly adhered to, regardless of the consequences for others, even nonbelievers. Some religious adherents, for example, are more concerned about the *spiritual* consequences of their beliefs and actions than the temporal, this-worldly ones. Adherence to the teachings of their faith may take precedence over a commitment to democratic values, including a respect for religious pluralism or the constitutional rights of others.

In addition, the foundation of many religious beliefs in faith rather than reason or "fact" means that they may lack any basis likely to persuade nonbelievers of their validity. Although some nonreligious beliefs also lack publicly accessible reasons to support them, religious beliefs are based more frequently on faith, revelation, and emotion than upon reason, empirically demonstrable facts, or some other basis rooted in shareable human experience. Publicly inaccessible beliefs tend be exclusionary, alienating, and politically divisive (in other words, to raise establishment concerns). When laws are based on inaccessible religious premises that cannot be openly discussed and debated on terms available to nonbelievers in the way that laws based on secular rationales can, their coerciveness is increased.

The risk that such religious beliefs will violate the constitutional rights of others is enhanced when they are incorporated into public laws backed by the threat of coercive sanctions. The potential of religious lawmaking to coerce nonbelievers by compelling them, under penalty of punishment, to abide by the dictates of laws which are rooted in religious beliefs that conflict with their own personal convictions raises an additional concern. Such laws are inconsistent with democratic principles of free and open citizen participation in government. Such laws also may fail to gain widespread support or obedience, which may exacerbate problems of enforcement, since the effectiveness of law ultimately is dependent upon citizens' willingness to accept it.

Moral and Religious Pluralism

A second problem with religious lawmaking is highlighted in a religiously and morally pluralistic nation like the United States, which is one of the most religiously diverse nations in the world. At last count, according to *Newsweek* magazine (Woodward 1993), there were more than 1,500 different religious bodies and sects in the United States. The potential for religious lawmaking to be politically divisive is enhanced where there is such a wide range of radically different religious and moral beliefs.

These problems are exacerbated in the United States, where the vast majority of lawmakers belong to traditional Christian faiths, but many of their constituents do not. The disproportionate representation of certain dominant Christian faiths in government indicates that religious lawmaking is likely to infringe on the free exercise of religion and other citizenship rights and interests of citizens from other religious groups, particularly those from minority religious traditions who are more likely to be lacking

in political power—illustrated in the historical legal treatment of Mormon and Native American Indian religious beliefs in cases such as *Lyng v. Northwest Indian Cemetery Protective Association* (1988) and *Employment Division v. Smith* (1990). Thus, religious pluralism, in combination with disparities in political power among members of different religions, makes it more likely that lawmaking influenced by religion will result in the unjustified coercion of religious minorities, in violation of constitutional protections.

Since women have been excluded from participation in the formulation of religious beliefs and practices in most traditional and institutional religions, it is likely that laws based on beliefs and values rooted in religious traditions will fail to incorporate women's self-determined interests. In addition, the teachings of most world religions that women are divinely ordained to be child bearers and rearers help to perpetuate traditional essentialist ideologies that women *are* mothers, primarily if not exclusively, and thus not entitled to social, political, and economic equality. Thus, religious lawmaking is problematic for a number of reasons in a morally and religiously pluralistic society.

Religious Identity

At the same time that religious beliefs pose a potential problem for the protection of the constitutional rights of all citizens, especially religious minorities and women, religion is fundamental to the moral identity of many citizens. Moral identity means the basic assumptions underlying an individual's moral and ethical decisions. Daniel Conkle suggests that "religious beliefs, by their very nature, form a central part of a person's belief structure, his inner self. They define a person's very being—his sense of who he is, why he exists, and how he should relate to the world around him" (Conkle 1988, 1165).

According to these views, religion is so intertwined with a person's moral identity that it cannot be separated out. This means that the choices a person makes—whether they be personal or political—inevitably will be influenced by the person's religious convictions. Given this view of the relationship of religion to personal and moral identity, asking lawmakers to bracket their religious views in their public decision making unfairly requires them "to destroy a vital aspect of the self—in order to gain the right to participate in the dialogue alongside other citizens" (Carter 1993, 229). Given that many citizens consider religion to be fundamental, if not integral, to their moral identity, it seems unfair, if not unjust, to demand that they put aside their religious beliefs when acting in roles which include political decision making. In addition, like other citizens, lawmakers are also entitled to the free exercise of their religion under the First Amendment. Despite their special roles as public officials, lawmakers are similar to most other citizens in viewing themselves as religious persons. In fact, lawmakers may be even more religious as a body than citizens generally. Given the centrality that religion has to the moral identity of many believers, a demand that religious adherents set aside or bracket their religious convictions in the spheres of lawmaking may infringe upon, and even violate, their sense of identity as well as their free exercise rights. Herein lies the heart of the dilemma of religious lawmaking.

Resolving the Dilemma

As suggested by Peach (2002), the U.S. Constitution is a central consideration both in the analysis of religious lawmaking and in the fashioning of an adequate response to the dilemma it poses. As we have seen, although religious lawmaking potentially violates a number of important constitutional rights and interests of citizens, because the Constitution also protects the rights of religious lawmakers, it does not give us a clear method for addressing the dilemma. Scholars have proposed a number of solutions. These generally fall into two types of approaches, designated here as "liberal" and "communitarian."

On one side, liberal political theorists such as Kent Greenwalt, John Rawls, and Robert Audi have tended to address the issue principally as one involving moral pluralism in a religiously and culturally diverse society. Their theories have focused on the need to protect the free exercise of religion for all citizens—especially religious minorities—by prohibiting most religious influences on the political and lawmaking processes. On the other side, communitarian theorists, such as Michael Sandel and Charles Taylor, have largely fixed on the centrality that religion may have to moral identity and the positive role of religion in the formation of a strong moral community. They have conceptualized moral identity as inextricably linked to the values and ideas of the moral agent's community and tradition, including his or her religious community and tradition. Their position has emphasized the difficulties of separating religion from other aspects of moral identity and the

unfairness in making religious (but not other personal) bases for decision making illegitimate in the lawmaking arena.

There are significant limitations to both approaches to resolving the dilemma of religious lawmaking. Liberal theories tend to undervalue how fundamental religion may be to the moral identity of lawmakers. This unduly restricts the interests of religious lawmakers to rely on their religious convictions and undermines their constitutionally protected free exercise rights. In contrast, communitarian theories tend to ignore the capacity of moral selves for agency and judgment independent of community, including religious norms and values. Communitarian approaches tend to protect the religious identity of lawmakers as essential, while doing so at the expense of respect for religious pluralism.

An adequate approach to religious lawmaking must neither unduly limit the ability of public officials to rely on their religious convictions in their lawmaking nor sacrifice respect for religious pluralism. An approach to religious lawmaking based on the American pragmatist philosophy of George Herbert Mead suggests that lawmakers have a moral obligation to justify their political decisions on a secular rationale when relying on religious ones would harm the citizenship rights and interests of their constituents. An approach based on Mead's philosophy would recommend invalidating religiously influenced laws in a limited range of circumstances when establishment concerns are present and infringements upon citizenship rights cannot be fully justified by a secular rationale and/or by a compelling state interest. Such an approach would be one practical legal means of addressing the dilemma in a way that respects and protects interests on both sides of the dilemma of religious lawmaking.

Lucinda Joy Peach

See also Establishment, Equal Treatment; Establishment, Separation of Church and State

Further Readings

Audi, R. (1989). The separation of church and state and the obligations of citizenship. *Philosophy and Public Affairs, 18,* 259–308.

Audi, R. (1997). The church, the state, and the citizen. In P. Weithman (Ed.), *Religion and contemporary liberalism* (pp. 38–75). South Bend, IN: University of Notre Dame Press.

Carter, S. (1987). Evolutionism, creationism, and treating religion as a hobby. *Duke Law Journal, 6,* 977–996.

Carter, S. (1989). The religiously devout judge. *Notre Dame Law Review, 64,* 932–44.

Carter, S. (1993). *The culture of disbelief: How American law and politics trivialize religious devotion.* New York: Basic Books.

Conkle, D. (1993). Different religions, different politics: Evaluating the role of competing religious traditions in American politics and law. *Journal of Law and Religion, 10,* 1–32.

Conkle, D. (1988). Toward a general theory of the establishment clause. *Northwestern Law Review, 82,* 1113–1197.

Duke, J., & Johnson, B. (1992). Religious affiliation and Congressional representation. *Journal for the Scientific Study of Religion, 31,* 324–329.

Gaffney, E. (1990). Politics without brackets on religious convictions: Michael Perry and Bruce Ackerman on neutrality. *Tulane Law Review, 64,* 1143–1194.

Greenwalt, K. (1988). *Religious convictions and political choice.* New York: Oxford University Press.

Hertzke, A. (1988). *Representing God in Washington: The role of religious lobbies in the American polity.* Knoxville: University of Tennessee Press.

Karst, K. (1989). *Belonging to America: Equal citizenship and the constitution.* New Haven, CT: Yale University Press.

Karst, K. (1993). *Law's promise, law's expression: Visions of power in the politics of race, gender, and religion.* New Haven, CT: Yale University Press.

Peach, L. (2002). *Legislating morality: Pluralism and religious identity in lawmaking.* New York: Oxford University Press.

Perry, M. (1988). *Morality, politics, and law: A bicentennial essay.* New York: Oxford University Press.

Perry, M. (1991). *Love and power: The role of religion and morality in American politics.* New York: Oxford University Press.

Perry, M. (1997). *Religion in politics: Constitutional and moral perspectives.* New York: Oxford University Press.

Rawls, J. (1971). *A Theory of Justice.* Cambridge, MA: The Belknap Press of Harvard University Press.

Rawls, J. (1985). Justice as fairness: Political not metaphysical. *Philosophy and Public Affairs, 14,* 223–251.

Rawls, J. (1993). *Political liberalism.* New York: Columbia University Press.

Sandel, M. (1982). *Liberalism and the limits of justice.* Cambridge, UK: Cambridge University Press.

Schauer, F. (1986). May officials think religiously? *William and Mary Law Review Annual, 27,* 1075–1084.

Sorauf, F. (1976). *The wall of Separation: The constitutional politics of church and state.* Princeton, NJ: Princeton University Press.

Taylor, C. (1989). *Sources of the self: The making of modern identity.* Cambridge, MA: Harvard University Press.

Taylor, C. (1992). Religion in a free society. In J. D. Hunter & O. Guiness (Eds.), *Articles of faith, articles of peace: The religious liberty clauses and the American public philosophy* (pp. 93–113). Washington, DC: Brookings.

Wald, K. (1992). *Religion and politics in the United States.* Washington, DC: Congressional Quarterly Press.

Williamsburg Charter Foundation. (1988). *Survey on religion and American public life.* Washington, DC: Williamsburg Charter Foundation.

Wood, J. E. (1991). *The role of religion in the making of public policy.* Waco, TX: Baylor University Press.

Woodward, K. (1993, November 29). The rites of Americans. *Newsweek,* pp. 80–82.

Court Cases

Employment Division v. Smith, 494 U.S. 872 (1990).

Lyng v. Northwest Indian Cemetery Protective Association, 485 U.S. 439 (1988)

Political Attitudes and Religiosity

While religion is an institution and a belief system, what we measure in the behavior of individuals is religiosity, which is the adherence or the devotion to a particular belief system, any one of the ten thousand religions currently in existence. Religiosity is a continuous, rather than a discrete, variable. This means that we can describe in terms of intensity (from mild to extreme) as opposed to in terms of mere presence or absence. The expression of religious beliefs is the main measure of religiosity, which is then related to other beliefs, and to psychological and behavioral indicators. Researchers in political science, sociology, and social psychology have studied the relationship between religiosity on the one hand and social, civic, and political attitudes on the other.

Connecting Religiosity with Political Attitudes

The question before us is what is the general relationship between an individual's level of religiosity and that individual's beliefs and values related to social groups, social issues, civic ideals, and political ideologies. The first issue is whether there is a general relationship between religiosity writ large and a basic political stance. Discussing this particular relationship is hard because of historical and cultural variations. Can we assume a relationship that holds true for both British and Indian politics? Is there an inherent connection between higher levels of religiosity, or religious orthodoxy, and political conservatism? Is there an "issue consensus" within the "orthodox" or "liberal" religious communities? Are religious influences general or specific to explicit doctrinal issues?

One way of looking at the relationship between religious and political beliefs is to examine closely members of radical political groups. In 1965, two well-known groups in the United States were studied: the John Birch Society, a radical right-wing group, and Americans for Democratic Action (ADA), a left-wing group within the Democratic Party. There were clear-cut differences. Among the Birchers, 16 percent belonged to liberal Protestant groups or had no affiliation, while among ADA members 80 percent were in that category, or were Jewish. Among the John Birch Society members, 25 percent were Roman Catholic, while for the ADA, the corresponding figure was 5 percent. Radical students who were members of the students' Free Speech Movement at the University of California at Berkeley in 1964 (at the start of the 1960s upheavals on U.S. campuses) were more likely (compared with controls) to come from families that were identified as Jewish, agnostic, or atheist. Fifteen years later, they were likely to report the same affiliations.

In modern times, political movements tied to conservatism, tradition, family, and nationalism—that is, right-wing movements—have relied on the support of religious institutions. In surveys using representative samples of the U.S. population between 1973 and 1985, disaffiliation from religious denominations contributed to greater political and social liberalism. Numerous studies found correlations between orthodoxy, militarism, and nationalism.

Much research was done in the United States during the politically turbulent 1960s. In a 1966 sample of U.S. students at nine Midwestern private colleges, an inverse relationship was found between religiosity and support for the civil-rights movement active then. During the Vietnam War, studies in the United States showed that religious orthodoxy was tied to hawkish attitudes in support of U.S. involvement.

Among Christians in the United States, those who considered themselves more devout were found to be most militaristic. Researchers found in both 1952 and 1964, when the United States was involved in foreign wars, that Protestants were most supportive of strong military actions. Catholics were less supportive, and Jews were the least supportive. In both cases, those having no religious affiliations were most opposed to military measures. Among participants in demonstrations against the Vietnam War, 61 percent reported no religious affiliation, and among U.S. students in the 1960s, participation in protest demonstrations against the war was positively correlated with having no religious affiliation or coming from a Jewish family.

Since the 1940s, numerous studies in the United States have investigated attitudes to deviates of various kinds. The results have shown that the more religious are less tolerant; Jews and the irreligious are most tolerant. In surveys of representative samples of the U.S. population in 1974, 1977, and 1980, religious commitment was inversely related to political tolerance.

The least religious are also the most liberal in social and political attitudes. In surveys using representative samples of the U.S. population between 1973 and 1985, disaffiliation from churches contributed to greater political liberalism. Individuals raised as having no religious affiliation and who remained unaffiliated were more liberal in politics and morals than those who became religiously affiliated. Although most of the research reported here has been done in the English-speaking world, there is reason to believe that the findings hold true for the rest of the world. Extremism in politics seems to find support in various religious orthodoxies, whether in Japan, Egypt, Algeria, India, or Israel, to name just a few cases.

Early studies on religiosity and politics dealt mostly with support for political ideologies. In more recent research, political views are defined more broadly. Conceptions of contemporary politics include not just support for political parties and established ideologies, but also more generalized attitudes. Traditionally, political issues were defined in terms of political- or economic-justice debates, dealing with the distribution of wealth and power in society.

Today, political discourse has expanded the classical welfare debate and covers questions of individual and societal morals in new ways; for example, it includes concern about the environment. The meaning of equality and the rights of minorities, classical civil-rights issues, have come to the fore. Public disagreements have arisen around attitudes toward ethnic or racial minority groups, as well as toward such groups as the handicapped and the mentally ill, immigrants, refugees, homosexuals, and drug addicts. Do we support their rights to special consideration or equality? Do we support more or less public spending on welfare and unemployment insurance? Equal rights for women? Such questions frame the political debate in industrialized societies.

In the United States, members of mainstream Protestant denominations, which are more liberal in terms of religious beliefs, tend to be more liberal on several social or political issues, such as civil rights for minorities, women's rights, and sexual morality, when compared with members of more conservative Protestant denominations. In a 1988 representative sample of the U.S. population, fundamentalism correlated with support for the death penalty. In a 1994 public opinion survey in the United States, it was found that opposition to the death penalty was highest (34 percent) among those reporting no religious affiliation, and lowest (9 percent) among Mormons. The overall figure for opposition was 25 percent, and it was 26 percent among Jews, 27 percent among Protestants, and 25 percent among Catholics.

In a representative sample of the U.S. population in 1988 it was found that conservative Protestants supported corporal punishment of children, with belief in biblical literalism and a sinful human nature emerging as causal factors. Similarly, fundamentalism was found to correlate with support for punishment as an end in itself in dealing with convicted criminals.

What about environmental protection? In a representative sample of the U.S. population in 1988, it was found that moral rigidity (quest for certainties) and benign images of God were respectively correlated with environmental insensitivity and sensitivity in various denominations. Biblical literalism was inversely related to environmental concerns.

Authoritarianism

Authoritarianism is a belief complex that combines conformity, submission to authority, respect for tradition, and hostility toward out-groups. Studies since the 1950s have found that authoritarianism is on average greater for individuals with the most orthodox beliefs and is highest for Catholics and fundamentalists. The same was found to be true for Muslim fundamentalists in a study of students at Kuwait University, and for Muslim, Hindu, and Jewish fundamentalists in Canada.

Prejudice and Ethnocentrism

The term *prejudice* has been widely used in the social psychology literature to refer to unfavorable intergroup perceptions, judgments, or attitudes. *Ethnocentrism* is the technical name for the perception that one's own group is the center of everything, and that all others are scaled and rated with reference to it.

Many religions teach their followers to love others, most often members of the same faith. Christianity and a few other religions have emphasized love for everyone, including one's enemies, of all races and creeds. And yet, religion has been responsible for historical persecution, such as the Inquisition, and has been implicated in wars such as the Crusades and conflicts in India, Northern Ireland, and many other parts of the world. Psychologists have studied how far religion increases or decreases prejudice towards other groups. In one classical study of ethnocentrism and anti-Semitism, those respondents reporting no religious affiliation were found to have much lower levels of ethnocentrism than members of most religious groups. These findings have been confirmed many times since. In most studies there is a clear positive relation between ritual attendance, religious attitudes or orthodox beliefs, and racial prejudice. This positive relation between religiosity and prejudice has been found in the United States, Britain, Europe and Australia.

There have been a number of explanations for the connection between prejudice and religiosity. They can be classified according to whether they emphasize the content of the religious message, social factors, or personality factors. Religious hostility and competition, inspired by myth and doctrine, may be a factor in creating specific prejudices. Normal religious socialization then inculcates these ideas together with other teachings, creating religious chauvinism. This is especially so when groups compete over the idea of being the elect and claim the same historical tradition. Muslims, Christians, and Jews of all varieties have claimed to be the truly elect within the Biblical tradition. Shared mythologies may lead to an especially virulent prejudice, while a total lack of commonality in beliefs may create a more general hostility.

Conformity to social norms can produce both religious activity and prejudice if both are local norms. It has been suggested that conformity and membership in religious organizations are both related to authoritarianism. It has been noted that in many Western countries there is a gradual decline in prejudice, directly tied to secularization. This phenomenon again ties religiosity directly to prejudice.

Integration, Exclusion, and Tolerance

Religiosity is learned and maintained through solidarity and group membership. Religion helps legitimate a sense of group identity and individual self-esteem. Individuals value in-group overly highly, thereby enhancing their self-esteem; by the same token they systematically undervalue the out-group. Religion can provide a perfect outlet for in-group frictions and aggression because it redirects hostility and aggression toward out-groups and non-believers.

The special kind of group loyalty that religion creates may be the prototype of tribal and national loyalty. That religions encourage in-group altruism and support is a positive contribution, even if limited to one group. Guarding community and identity is a major effort, with both costs and gain for individuals. Being a member of a religious minority, just like being a member of any minority, may take its toll. One study in the United States in the late 1950s found that high school students who were members of local religious minorities showed lower self-esteem and more symptoms of anxiety and depression. Also on the negative side of the equation is the fact that prejudice found between different denominations can lead to conflicts and social exclusion.

We can conclude by stating that high levels of religiosity have been tied to social intolerance. As a consequence of intolerance, strong religious commitment may interfere with a commitment to religious freedom, and very often may lead to conflicts, as the concern of group members for their own rights will not necessarily extend to concern for the rights of other groups.

Benjamin Beit-Hallahmi

Further Reading

Argyle, M., & Beit-Hallahmi, B. (1975). *The social psychology of religion*. London and Boston: Routledge & Kegan Paul.

Beit-Hallahmi, B., & Argyle, M. (1997). *The psychology of religious behaviour, belief, and experience*. London: Routledge.

Wald, K. D. (1997). *Religion and politics in the United States*. Washington, DC: CQ Press.

Preservation of Faith Commitments

The concept of religious freedom has usually been understood implicitly and explicitly as the freedom to change one's religion. This understanding is implicit in the use of the word *freedom*, which means nothing if it does not mean freedom to choose among several options. This understanding is also reflected in the concept of religious freedom that gave rise to the creation of the United States Commission on International Religious Freedom (USCIRF), for example. The website for the Office of International Religious Freedom states:

> [The OIRF] has the mission of promoting religious freedom as a core objective of U.S. foreign policy. Headed by an Ambassador-at-Large for International Religious Freedom, its Office Director and staff monitor religious persecution and discrimination worldwide, recommend and implement policies in respective regions or countries, and develop programs to promote religious freedom. (U.S. Department of State n.d.)

The reports issued by the office focus upon religious persecution of all faiths. Yet, because the major political push for the establishment of such an office came from evangelical Christians, non-Christians (especially outside of the United States) perceive the office as equating "religious freedom" with the freedom allowed Christian missionaries to proselytize around the globe.

Only a little reflection is required to make one realize that religious freedom must also include the freedom to hold on to one's faith commitment. Yet the semantic aura around religious freedom barely allows for this sense to become clearly visible. As an example of this semantic asymmetry, one may allude to the fact that Article 18 of the Universal Declaration of Human Rights (UDHR), which is believed to enshrine religious freedom as a universal human right, does not explicitly refer to the right to retain one's religion, although it refers explicitly to one's right to change it (Stahnke 1998, 74).

FREEDOM TO CHOOSE IN THAILAND

The Central Thai of Thailand are a good example of a society where both freedom to choose and freedom to retain one's beliefs are both components of religious freedom.

In reality the Thai Buddhist people are quite tolerant toward other religions. Since Buddhism presses people with no dogma, people are free to choose their ways of life. In other words, while the ethical principles are laid out, people are not obligated under any external authority to follow them. They are completely responsible for their own actions. While they adopt the Buddhist faith, they are not submitted to a towering personality, they simply take Buddhism as a guiding light whereby they see things and then choose their own actions and consequences. Therefore, Buddhism and the Buddhist are not bound each to each by any absolute control; each exists with an independent entity. When the Christian missionaries come, most people still regard the Christian religion as another independent entity without an authority to overpower their existence.

Buddhism and the Buddhist Church can probably be compared to a free market. Goods are boundless and laid out with bands and labels for their qualities. People are allowed to try them, buy them, or leave them—all under their own choice and responsibility. The market is not owned by any authority or any individual. Thus, when a sense of ownership is not present, no one is affected by the other's exploitation. In other words, a feeling of loss and gain does not depend on the quantity or quality of other customers. It depends entirely on each individual, who either loses or gains from his own choice of ethical conduct.

When the Christian missionaries move into the neighborhood, people see them probably as sellers of some foreign products. They become part of the Buddhist open market.

Kingkeo Attagara

Source: *The Folk Religion of Ban Nai, a Hamlet in Central Thailand.*
(Ann Arbor, MI: University Microfilms, 1968), 229–230.

This right to retain one's religion as an element of religious freedom, however, should not be confused with the claim that one is not permitted by one's religion to change it, as for instance under classical Islamic law. According to *shari'a* the "punishment" for apostasy in Islam is death.

This was one of the reasons underlying Saudi Arabia's historic abstention when the UDHR came up for adoption before the United Nations on 10 December 1948. Such an absolutization of faith commitment represents an extreme end of the spectrum. The challenge posed by the preservation of one's faith commitment consistently with one's commitment to religious freedom has sometimes been met in a less radical fashion. Article 18 of the International Covenant on Civil and Political Rights (1966), for instance, substitutes the expression "freedom to change . . . religion or belief" of the UDHR with "freedom to have or adopt a religion or belief" (Stahnke 1998, 74), apparently to take into account Islamic sensitivities on this point.

Central to the further elucidation of the issue is the insight that the concept of religious freedom, and consequently the interpretation of what it means to preserve one's faith commitment, is intimately tied to the concept of religion itself. The blanket use of the term religion, the prototype of which is provided by Western religions of the Abrahamic tradition, to describe the faith commitments of people around the rest of the globe tends to obscure the fact that these other faith communities may possess a different conception of religion and therefore of religious freedom. The main point of contrast consists in the fact that while the Western conception of religion regards the various religions as mutually exclusive entities, such is not the case in India, China, or Japan or with the tribal or indigenous religions. It is a matter of common knowledge that modern Hinduism does not exclude Buddhism, Jainism, or Sikhism, the other three religions of Indian origin, from its scope. Similarly, it is well known that, in pre-Communist China, a Chinese person did not typically consider himself or herself exclusively as a follower of Confucianism or Taoism or Buddhism, but affiliated with them as and when appropriate. The case of Japan provides statistical support to these historical statements. According to the 1985 census, 95 percent of the population of Japan declared itself as followers of Shinto, and 76 percent of the same population also declared itself to be Buddhist (Reader 1991, 6). The fact that "conversion" is a virtually religious modality among the tribal and indigenous religions also allows them to be placed in this category and also brings into play the tension between "individual rights" as understood in modern rights discourse and the "group rights" of traditional society.

It is clear then that (1) the conception of religious freedom as understood in Western religions and Western culture presupposes a certain concept of religion; (2) a different concept of religion is associated with the religions of India and the Far East as well as the indigenous religions; and (3) the concept of religious freedom as involving the preservation of faith commitment rather than changing it acquires a greater salience in this second concept of religion.

Arvind Sharma

See also Universal Declaration of Human Rights

Further Reading

Arzt, D. E. (1996). The treatment of religious dissidents under classical and contemporary Islamic law. In J. Witte Jr. & J. D. Van Der Vyer (Eds.), *Religious human rights in global perspective: Religious perspectives*. The Hague, Netherlands: Martinus Nijhoff Publishers.

Ching, J. (2002). East Asian religions. In Oxtoby, W. G. (Ed.), *World religions: Eastern traditions* (2nd ed.). Toronto, Canada: Oxford University Press.

Glendon, M. A. (2001). *A world made new: Eleanor Roosevelt and the Universal Declaration of Human Rights*. New York: Random House.

Reader, I. (1991). *Religion in contemporary Japan*. London: Macmillan.

Stahnke, T., & Martin, J. P. (Eds.). (1998). *Religion and human rights: Basic documents*. New York: Center for the Study of Human Rights, Columbia University.

Tahzib, B. G. (1996). *Freedom of religion or belief: Ensuring effective international legal protection*. The Hague, Netherlands: Martinus Nijhoff Publishers.

U.S. Department of State. (n.d.). Office of International Religious Freedom website. Retrieved December 5, 2002, from http://www.state.gov/g/drl/irf/

Prisons

In the 1870s, San Francisco jailers cut off the queue—long braid of hair—of a prisoner from China. Though they justified this by emphasizing that the queue posed a security and hygiene risk, Ho Ah Kow successfully argued (*Ho Ah Kow v. Nunan*, 1879) that the queue symbolized his religious beliefs, that its absence disgraced him, and that the jailers' actions violated his free exercise rights.

There are many U.S. constitutional rights a prisoner cannot exercise, because they might endanger other inmates or interfere with security. The U.S. Bureau of Prisons has developed a "program statement" (PS) that lists religious practices "never authorized" in prison, including animal sacrifices, casting spells/curses, nudity, self-mutilation, and exclusion by race (PS 5360.08 Religious Beliefs and Practices, 25 May 2001). However, prisoners' religious rights are regarded as important in the United States, in part because religious instincts stand behind the development of the modern penitentiary's emphasis on rehabilitation.

A Brief History

In the Roman Empire, prisons primarily stored the incarcerated until they were either tried (when they would be freed, beaten, or executed) or were forgotten and died. The rise of Christianity led to the development of a fundamentally different penal institution: the penitentiary was developed as a place for penance, where confinement and reflection could still the mind and transform the individual. The first U.S. prisons had such a spiritual orientation, and prisons such as the Walnut Street Jail, founded by Quakers, or Philadelphia's Eastern State Penitentiary, built in 1820, encouraged contemplation and penance.

The United States locks up more of its citizens than any other nation—nearly two million inmates at the start of the third millennium, or almost a quarter of the world's prison population. Prisons have increasingly used Secure Housing Units, keeping inmates locked in them for twenty-three and a half hours per day. Because prison conditions in the United States are not oriented towards encouraging penance per se, issues relating to prisoners' religious freedom have become significant.

Establishment Clause Issues

Prisoner rights and state needs often clash, and the conflict is frequently settled by court interpretation of the First Amendment to the United States Constitution: "Congress shall make no law respecting an establishment of religion, or prohibiting the free exercise thereof . . . " This, the establishment clause, is applicable to areas where prisoners feel that the state has either promoted certain religions or tacitly or explicitly supported some more than others. The second clause, the free exercise clause, has been used by prisoners who feel that their religious rights have been denied because of prison regulations or policies. The tension between these clauses is obvious in prison, where inmates frequently must rely on the institution if they wish to practice their religion.

How can government funds be used to support prisoners' religious rights, when the state is not to engage in religious establishment? Although clergy serve all prisoners, there is the question as to which religions are to be represented by full-time, contracted, or volunteer clergy? Although prison religious spaces are shared by all religious groups (except for Native American sweat lodges), is the state tacitly engaging in establishment by providing chairs for Christians and Jews but not prayer mats for Muslims? Is the state justified when the prison chaplaincy provides bread and juice for Christian liturgical use but does not provide Muslims with the dates that are eaten when they break their daily Ramadan fast? Do atheists face discrimination when parole and sentence reductions may be related to participation in religious-based, prison-sponsored twelve-step programs, such as Alcoholics Anonymous? Because crosses and crucifixes had been used to indicate gang membership, the Wisconsin Department of Corrections ruled that such religious symbols were prohibited except when attached to rosaries. Although the state argued that it had compelling security concerns, in November 1999 the 7th U.S. Circuit Court of Appeals decided that such a policy both favored Catholicism and violated the rights of Protestant inmates (for whom the rosary had no liturgical meaning).

Free Exercise Clause Issues

How free exercise claims are to be adjudicated was articulated most thoroughly in the 1987 case, *Turner v. Safley*. The Supreme Court ruled that the reasonableness of a prisoner's challenge to a regulation depended upon four criteria: 1) the "valid, rational connection between the prison regulation and the legitimate governmental interest" which it served; 2) prisoner access to other means of exercising the right; 3) the impact that accommodating the prisoner would have on guards, inmates, and prison resources; and 4) possible other ways to satisfy the prisoner's religious needs.

The Religious Freedom Restoration Act (RFRA) of 1993 prohibited governments, both state and federal, from acting in a way that significantly burdened free exercise of religion, unless its action furthered a compelling state interest and was the least restrictive means of addressing that interest. This legislation led to an increase in free exercise test cases, but in June 1997 the Supreme Court ruled that the RFRA was unconstitutional as applied to the states. In direct response to the Supreme Court's action against RFRA, Congress passed the Religious Land Use and Institutionalized Persons Act of 2000 (Public Law No. 106-274, 114 Stat. 803-807). Section 3 of this provides: "No government shall impose a substantial burden on the religious exercise of a person residing in or confined to an institution . . . even if the burden results from a rule of general applicability, unless the government demonstrates that imposition of the burden on that person— 1) is in furtherance of a compelling governmental interest; and 2) is the least restrictive means of furthering that compelling governmental interest." As of 2002, the constitutionality of this statute was being tested, and in the May 2002 decision in Freedom Baptist Church of Delaware County v. Township of Middleton (No. 01-5345), the United States District Court for the Eastern District of Pennsylvania held RLUIPA to be constitutional.

Free exercise claims are still common. Inmates have asked to follow special religious diets (e.g., kosher, halal, vegetarian), to wear their hair or beards in ways consistent with religious requirements, to wear special clothing (e.g., kippah) or religious insignia (e.g., Santeria inmates won an injunction to wear Orshiba beads under their prison clothes). Inmates have asked for access to special clergy, for special religious literature or accouterments (e.g., wiccan inmates have requested tarot cards and bells, Native Americans have requested buffalo bones and eagle feathers), or to be called by religious names adopted in prison.

Future Issues

Courts will likely have to deal increasingly with issues relating to what constitutes a valid religion (an area constantly debated by academics, since "valid" religions need not be institutional) and what constitutes sincerity of belief. Because prisoner appeals need be based only on the sincerity of their beliefs, not the validity of those beliefs within any religious tradition, issues relating to religious freedom will continue to be significant in the American prison system.

Craig Wansink

See also Free Exercise Clause

Further Reading

Beckford, J. A., & Gilliat, S. (1998). *Religion in prison: Equal rites in a multi-faith society*. New York: Cambridge University Press.

Knight, B. (Autumn 1984). Religion in prison: Balancing the Free Exercise, No Establishment, and Equal Protection Clauses. *Journal of Church and State, 26*, 437–99.

Moore, K. (1991). Muslims in prison: Claims to constitutional protection of religious liberty. In Y. Y. Haddad (Ed.), *The Muslims of America*. New York: Oxford University Press.

Morris, N., & Rothman, D. J. (Eds.). (1995). *The Oxford history of the prison: The practice of punishment in Western society*. New York: Oxford University Press.

Mushlin, M., Kramer, D. T., & Gobert, J. J. (1993). *Rights of prisoners* (2nd ed.). Colorado Springs, CO: Shephards/McGraw Hill.

Religious Land Use and Institutionalized Persons Act of 2000 (42 U.S.C. Sections 2000cc-2000cc-5).

Richardson, J. (1995). *Religion behind bars: A report on the extent to which prisoners exercise their First Amendment right to freedom of religion*. Nashville, TN: The Freedom Forum First Amendment Center.

Schilder, D. M. (1999). *Inside the fence: A handbook for those in prison ministry*. Staten Island, NY: Alba House.

Court Cases

City of Boerne vs. Flores, 521 U.S. 507 (1997).

Freedom Baptist Church of Delaware County vs. Township of Middleton, Docket No. 01-5345 (E.D. PA)(Memorandum Opinion, Judge Dalzell, May 8, 2002).

Turner v. Safely, 482 U.S. 78 (1987).

Protestantism *See* Great Awakenings and the Antebellum Period; Baptist Dissenters in Virginia; British Empire; Christian Science; Church and State in Modern Europe; Civil Religion; Constitution, Founding Era of the; Creationism; English Civil War; Germany and Prussia; Leiden; Outsiderhood and American Protestantism; Pentecostalism; Reformation, Early Modern Europe; United Kingdom

Quakers *See* Conscientious Objection and
Pacifism; Peace Churches

Radical Religious Groups: African-American

A significant proportion of African-Americans who belong to what might be labeled radical religious groups by the cultural mainstream identify themselves as Muslims and/or practice a contextualized interpretation of Islam. Many of these African-American Muslims embraced Islam through the Moorish Science Temple of America (MSTA) and the original Nation of Islam (NOI) (as opposed to current movements that call themselves NOI). These radical religious movements were the seedbed for as many as seventeen varied and independent communities that continue to alter the religious, cultural, and social identities of black people in the United States. Moreover, their development also provides the backdrop for what has been referred to as African-American Islam. Although African-Americans also participate in radical Christian religious groups and occasionally in New Religious Movements (for example, as followers of Father Divine, who established "heavens" in the 1930s and 1940s), this article will focus on two radical Muslim religious movements.

The Moorish Science Temple of America

The MSTA, originally organized in New Jersey in 1913 as the Canaanite Temple, was the first Islamic mass movement targeting African-Americans in the twentieth century. Its founder, Timothy Drew (1886–1929), later added the surname Ali and the title "Noble" and adopted the practice of wearing a fez. His employment of the titles "Sheik" and "Sheikess" for the male and female spiritual leaders he appointed to oversee his temples, apparently was borrowed from the Shriners (officially, the Mystic Order of the Eternal Shrine), an organization established in the United States in the late-nineteenth century by Freemasons. Drew Ali's claims that he was divinely prepared with a prophetic message supported his use of the title "Prophet."

Before the abolition of slavery, pass laws forced African-Americans to carry passes or permits from their slave owners. Drew Ali made reference to this convention by issuing "Nationality and Identification" cards to his followers. Each card, with the Islamic symbol of the star and crescent, an image of clasped hands, and the numeral seven, identified the bearer as a "Moslem" and "citizen of the United States."

Drew Ali traced the genealogy of his followers back to Jesus and championed his orientation toward Islam, which he believed offered African-Americans an escape from racism. In both his oral and written teachings, Drew Ali told his followers that he was specially equipped with the five basic principles—Love, Truth, Peace, Freedom, and Justice—that were the keys to redemption. With regard to the treatment of women, Drew Ali considered his mission to include the work of guiding black people to have a mutual respect for the sexes, such as he said existed in early Islamic societies on the African continent.

Drew Ali formalized the structure of meetings and clarified the status and role of officials. Each temple, Drew Ali declared, would be led by a grand Sheik or Sheikess, a person with greater awareness of

MUSLIM CULT OF ISLAM

 . the Muslim Cult of Islam, which is also known as the Allah Temple of Islam, is a religious cult whose members

-3-

BS100-27649

regard Allah as their supreme being and claim to be the direct descendants of the original race on earth. The members fanatically follow the teachings of Allah as interpreted by ELIJAH MOHAMMED, the "true prophet of Allah" entitled titular head of the Muslim Clut of Islam in the United States and believe that any civil law which conflicts with the Muslim law should be disobeyed. The members disavow their allegiance to the United States and pledge their allegiance only to Allah and do not consider it their duty to register for Selective Service or to serve in the United States ArmedForces as they cannot serve two masters. According to the teachings of ELIJAH MOHAMMED and the cult's ministers, the members of a minority race in the United States are not citizens of this country but are merely slaves of this country and will continue to be slaves until they free themselves by destroying non-Muslims and Christianity in the war of "Armageddon."

the cult teaches that the Korean war is a futile effort by the United States to prevent the coming Asiatic conquest of the world and the defeat of the United States in Korea is a prelude to the "resurrection" when North America and Great Britain will be doomed and the original man, lead by Allah will reign supreme.

the following information taken from another letter of Subject which January 29, 1950:

"It is better to be jailed by the devil for serving Allah than it is to be allowed by the devil to walk free. The black man has been enslaved. The time is coming for the devils to be destroyed."

A page from the 17 February 1953 FBI Report on Malcolm K. Little (later known as Malcolm X). COURTESY OF THE FBI, HTTP://FOIA.FBI.GOV/ MALCOLMX.HTM his or her spiritual consciousness. With the approval of the Prophet, these temple leaders could designate other leaders to assist them in the work of spreading Drew Ali's teachings and establishing temples.

Today, as when Drew Ali founded the group, services take place on Friday, the day on which Muslims believe Allah created the human race. At each service, a member of the congregation reads and expounds on a portion of *The Holy Koran of the Moorish Science Temple of America,* their primary scripture, compiled by Drew Ali. The reading is followed by a more elaborate explanation delivered by the temple leader. Throughout the service, Moors sing congregational songs, randomly selected by any member who desires to start one. The inclusion of singing during congregational gatherings is peculiar to the MSTA; within most Muslim communities, weekly religious services generally concentrate on worship through prayer.

In a fashion similar to the rest of the Muslim world, Moors greet each other with "Islam," or peace. Their New Year is celebrated annually on January 15, seven days after the birthday of Ali. A Moor hyphenates or adds to his or her surname "Bey" or "El." The name change is liberating in at least two ways. Communally, it is a visible sign of the embracing of a new nationality that enables followers to cope with cultural and political oppression. Individually, it recognizes the individual's humanity—something that the dominant culture had denied.

In 1916, leadership squabbles among lower-ranking leaders led to visible discord among the followers of Drew Ali. One faction remained in New Jersey, calling themselves the Holy Moabite Temple of the World; the other eventually followed Drew Ali to the Midwest. Within fifteen years of the start of the movement, several business operations were flourishing, including the Moorish Cafeteria Service and the Moorish Manufacturing Corporation. These economic ventures reflected Dew Ali's desire that his followers be self-sufficient, linking together their material and spiritual uplift. By 1928, fifteen temples were operative to serve members in both the North and the South. That same year, Drew Ali made Chicago the new MSTA headquarters. It was in Chicago that the Moors became politically active. In fact, the staunch support of Drew Ali and Moorish residents of the first congressional district reportedly was instrumental in the election of Republican Oscar DePriest to the U.S. Congress, the first African-American to hold a seat in Congress during the twentieth century.

Throughout 1928, however, Drew Ali was forced to contend with internal opposition from rival disciples with competing agendas, many of whom he had personally appointed to key leadership positions. At least two followers were successful in forming rival movements, with branches in a number of cities, all of which continue to incorporate the MSTA in all or part of their name. Eventually, internal strife led to Drew Ali's being charged with the murder of one of his rival disciples. In an attempt to control his detractors, Drew Ali commissioned a new disciple, David Ford (1891–c. 1980s), to oversee the MSTA. From his jail cell, Drew Ali renamed him Ford-El and released the Chicago temple to him. In November, Ford-El moved to Detroit, where he assumed the names Wallace D. Fard and Wallace D. Fard Muhammad—the same aliases employed by the founder of the original NOI.

Drew Ali died at his South Side home on July 20, only weeks following his release from jail. The death certificate of the forty-three-year-old Drew Ali attributes the cause of death to tuberculosis. The negative publicity surrounding the murder for which he had been charged and the uncertainty following the death of Drew Ali threatened to further split the movement at a time when five disciples battled for the MSTA helm. In the end, Kirkman-Bey, who conducted the funeral ritual of his leader, won a straw vote in Chicago and was acknowledged as the successor. He directed the MSTA's activities for the next three decades. Thus, to most Moors, only Kirkman-Bey's successors, F. Nelson-Bey, J. Blakely-Bey, and R. (Robert) Love-El are recognized as leaders of the authentic MSTA.

Another distinguishing feature of the MSTA is the prominence of women among those Drew Ali commissioned for the ministry. As early as 1928, M. Whitehead-El, aunt of Ali's wife, Pearl Jones Drew Ali, was the Grand Sheikess of Temple Number 9, then located on Townsend Street in Chicago. She also was one of three officials who filed documents in August of the same year to incorporate the national body and permit it to assume its current name. In truth, Drew Ali's acceptance of female religious leadership may have exceeded that of his members, for only male candidates have yet emerged to succeed him.

Moors held worship services relatively free from government harassment. Unlike members of the original NOI, for example, Drew Ali's followers did not shun patriotism or political participation; rather, they actively engaged in election campaigns and fervently proclaimed their American citizenship. Moreover, Moors assimilated more easily into the larger culture and did not dress in a manner that drew public attention to their distinctive religious tradition.

The Original Nation of Islam

Wallace D. (W. D.) Fard, the founder of the original NOI, was born in New Zealand in 1891 to Zared and Beatrice Fard and sent to North America by his parents in the early 1900s. Fard employed any number of aliases, including Wallace Fard Muhammad and David Ford, the latter reflected the Anglicization of his surname to Ford. His ambiguous skin color, hair texture, and facial features, some scholars argue, allowed him to traverse African-American, Latin, Asian, and European communities. By the time he began peddling silk and other products in the poor neighborhoods of Detroit in the summer of 1930, Fard had fathered two children, served three years in San Quentin for drug possession, allegedly had become a Moor, and had attended services at the Chicago Ahmadiyya Mosque. When Drew Ali died, Fard announced that the spirit of the Prophet had entered him. The ensuing leadership battle compelled Fard to flee to Detroit. In time, news spread throughout the predominantly black section of Detroit called Paradise Valley about a man who gave his would-be customers a version of their history and identity that was both foreign and affirming. Some MSTA members from Newark followed Fard in the fall of 1930 to Detroit, becoming the core group of his new organization, the Allah Temple of Islam. Among his new listeners was Clara Evans Poole, a dignified Christian, whose husband was locked in the grips of despair.

Mother Clara Connects the Messenger to the Message

By 1931, Clara Evans Poole's husband, Elijah Poole (1897–1975), had lost his job and was drinking heavily, forcing his family to accept public assistance. A neighbor invited his wife, Clara, to a meeting at which Fard lectured on the history and future of black Americans. His messages represented a blending of Christianity, orthodox Islam, and black nationalistic ideology with other belief systems. Both Clara and Elijah were taken with the message, and soon after, Elijah discovered the energy to work two or three jobs each day while preaching Fard's message to anyone who would listen.

By 1932, Fard began to encourage his followers to withdraw their children from the public school system of the "white devils" and to instruct them at home. Elijah and Clara, also distrustful of the public school curriculum, which they felt propagated lies about the black man, complied. This practice of homeschooling eventually evolved into an educational system called the University of Islam.

Membership in the movement climbed toward the ten-thousand mark. Within months, however, a series of events, including the conviction of one member for murder as part of a "voodoo cult ritual," and a court order banning the group, compelled Fard to reorganize his movement as the Nation of Islam. By then his new Supreme Minister, Elijah, had also received a new surname, Karriem, and later, Muhammad. Fard reminded his followers that they were engaged in war, the War of Armageddon. In preparation, Fard organized the Fruit of Islam, a paramilitary training unit all male members were required to join, as well as a Muslim girls training class for women that prepared them for their roles at home and within the movement. Continued government harassment forced Fard to leave Detroit, providing a promotional opportunity for Muhammad.

Elijah Muhammad as Architect

When Muhammad assumed control, he needed a mechanism to solidify his authority. He conceived the idea of portraying Fard as Allah in human form, and characterized himself as the prophet and messenger of God. He continued the foundational beliefs Fard had espoused, but added a few others to strengthen his position. Primarily, Muhammad told his followers that:

- Black people are the original race
- All white people are devils by nature for they are the product of an evil experiment conducted by the mad scientist, Yacub
- Americans of African ancestry are not Negro or Colored but descendants of an African nation
- Women are the foundation of the Nation and must be protected

- Christianity is the white man's religion
- Islam is the natural religion of black people

Muhammad's message sounded heretical to some segments of the membership. In particular, they struggled with a theology that praised the divinity of their founder as well as strict dietary regulations. Consequently, a number of members left the organization. Some returned to the MSTA in New Jersey; others, such as Osman Sharrieff, left the Chicago temple, but remained in the area. Sharrieff himself formed a rival organization, the Moslem Brotherhood. Spurred by infighting and concerns for his own safety, Muhammad moved the headquarters of the NOI to Chicago. By the end of 1934, Muhammad was hard at work rebuilding his nation and fine-tuning his black separatist ideology.

In the formative stages of the reorganized movement, Fard had initiated the practice of choosing the surnames of his followers. Like Drew Ali, he distributed national identification cards, which listed each member's name in Arabic and stated that the bearers should be "law abiding, non-weapon-bearing people." When Muhammad became the leader, he required potential converts to correspond with him, detailing their desire to know their true selves and to obtain the name that would replace the slave name that had hitherto served as their surname. It became the practice for women to cover their hair and dress uniformly and for to men wear suits, white shirts, and bow ties. Weddings, officiated by a male leader, were conducted at the temple or in the homes of members. Most members, familiar with weekly attendance at their local church, had little difficulty attending the thrice-weekly meetings, whose teachings, they believed, enabled them to survive in the white man's world. In the process, Muhammad built a multimillion-dollar enterprise, fulfilling Fard's vision of a nation within a nation.

When the outbreak of World War II required many members of the NOI to respond to the draft, Muhammad (who was older than most draftees) and a number of his followers refused. As a result, they were convicted on draft evasion charges. Since early reports connected the original NOI to a "voodoo cult," Fard and his followers had been targeted by the Federal Bureau of Investigation and other law enforcement organizations. The organization was blacklisted by the U.S. attorney general by the early 1940s, and Elijah Muhammad's success at evading a trial date in the summer of 1942 drew the ire of FBI director J. Edgar Hoover. Not surprisingly, Muhammad was sentenced on 22 October 1942 to three years; he began serving his term at the Federal Corrections Institute in Milan, Michigan, on 23 July 1943. With the incarceration of her husband and movement leader, Clara quietly but authoritatively acted on her husband's behalf. Operating under the title Supreme Secretary, she served as the liaison between Elijah and his followers. At the age of forty-two, this mother of eight, whose formal education did not extend beyond primary school, assumed the leadership of a heretofore male-dominated structure and simultaneously more visibly defined and modeled emerging Black Muslim womanhood. By the time Elijah was released from prison in 1946, his message of hope and call to conversion and transformation had reached many who had been in prison with him. Soon, the NOI had an active and successful prison ministry that resulted in hundreds, perhaps thousands, of new recruits Today, leaders of various African-American Muslim groups conduct services within a growing number of prison systems. A few institutions, for example, have invited in Muslim chaplains to counsel and minister to inmates. Other institutions have set aside space for Muslims to hold weekly prayer services, adhere to a pork-free diet, and fast during the month of Ramadan.

The Movement after Elijah's Death

When Elijah died in 1975, his son, W. D. Mohammed (who preferred the spelling more closely associated with his pronunciation) was appointed his successor. Announcing that his father knew he would guide the movement into the mainstream Muslim fold, Mohammed deemphasized the hierarchical leadership, gave autonomy to local temples, lifted restrictions on communal dress, selected women to assume key positions, reinterpreted early NOI ideology that demonized whites and deified Fard, and instituted more traditions and practices commonly shared by the larger Muslim world. After a series of name changes, Mohammed settled in 2002 on American Society of Muslims. The ASM, successor to NOI, is headquartered in the Chicago area and has an estimated 2 million supporters around the globe. (A splinter movement, led by Louis Farrakhan, broke away from Mohammed's group in 1978. It preserves the name Nation of Islam.)

The Movement and Religious Freedom

In the twenty-first century, the ASM—successor to the original NOI—finds itself comfortably situated within the mainstream of the global Islamic community. Its leader, W. D. Mohammed, meets regularly with religious and political leaders around the world. He and his community are building bridges to other Muslim groups as well as non-Islamic organizations. The direction he has taken the ASM, Mohammed would argue, is consistent with the path his father and former leader, Elijah Muhammad, knew he would.

Debra Mubashshir

See also Islam

Further Reading

Clegg, III, C. A. (1997). *An original man: The life and times of Elijah Muhammad*. New York: St. Martin's Press.

Curtis, IV, E. E. (2002). *Islam in black America: Identity, liberation and difference in African-American Islamic thought*. Albany: State University of New York Press.

Dannin, R. (2002). *Black pilgrimage to Islam*. New York: Oxford University Press.

Davidson, B. (1991). *African civilization revisited*. Trenton, NJ: Africa World Press.

Evanzz, K. (1999). *The messenger: The rise and fall of Elijah Muhammad*. New York: Pantheon Books.

Jackson-Bey, S. C. (1995, September 30). The trials and tribulations of Prophet Noble Drew Ali. *Chicago Defender, 7*.

Lee, M. F. (1996). *The nation of Islam: An American millenarian movement*. Syracuse, NY: Syracuse University Press.

Lincoln, C. E. (1994). *The Black Muslims in America* (3rd ed.). Grand Rapids, MI: William B. Eerdmans Publishing Co.

Marsh, C. (2000). *The lost-found Nation of Islam*. Lanham, MD: The Scarecrow Press.

Mohammed, W. D. (1991). *Al-Islam: Unity & Leadership*. Chicago: The Sense Maker.

Muhammad, E. (1992). *Message to the black man in America*. Newport News, VA: United Brothers Communications Systems.

Turner, R. B. (1997). *Islam in the African-American Experience*. Bloomington: Indiana University Press.

Turner, R. B. (1986). *Islam in the United States in the 1920s: The Quest for a new vision in Afro-American Religion*. Princeton, NJ: Princeton University Press.

Warner-Bey, D. (1997). *Words of wisdom*. Lockport, IL: Author.

Radical Religious Groups: White

In the diverse religious climate of North America, religious freedom (if not always religious toleration) is a cherished principle, while in the United States it is a constitutional right guaranteed to all citizens. Similarly, in the increasingly cosmopolitan and multicultural societies of Western Europe, religious freedom is more and more accepted as a hallmark of contemporary civil society. On both sides of the Atlantic, waves of immigration—Catholic and Jewish from the late nineteenth century through the 1920s in the United States and Muslim immigrants in Western Europe since the 1960s—have presented challenges to the climate of religious freedom in these societies, but so far American constitutional freedoms and European civil society have managed to preserve the rights of religious minorities to practice their faiths. This should not be surprising inasmuch as each religious community offered in this example is accepted by all but the most biased observer as "legitimate"; that is, all have histories dating back more than a millennium, all have authoritative texts that have stood the test of time, and all have religious leaders who have undergone rigorous training in the laws, rites, and beliefs of their religious communities.

The challenges to religious freedom posed by white racist "radical religious" communities in the United States and, to a lesser degree, in Western Europe, need to be considered. These faiths do not enjoy the advantages of perceived legitimacy. They lack historical resonance, sacred texts, and a trained clergy. Indeed, they have yet to realize the success achieved by such other new religious communities as, for example, the Church of Jesus Christ of Latter-day Saints, which overcame legal proscription over the practice of polygamy and violent persecution to become today a pillar of the American establishment and a highly successful religious export to the rest of the world. Rather, white radical religions exist in the netherworld of racism and, on occasion, violence, which put their adherents beyond the pale of civil society on either side of the Atlantic. From the perspective of the dominant societies, it is the odious nature of the doctrines of these religious faiths that presents so stringent a challenge to religious freedom.

The religious belief systems appealing to a constituency of white racists are many and diverse, but they are reducible to three primary categories. First, there are those faiths that stem from what religious scholars might style "deviant hermeneutics," or unorthodox interpretations of biblical text. Second, over and against these Christian-based traditions are an array of belief systems that reject Christianity as in essence Jewish, and therefore anathema. Instead, these adherents look to strikingly modern adaptations of pre-Christian pagan traditions—particularly those drawn from the Norse/Germanic pantheons. Finally, there is a small class of anti-religions that reject both approaches, deifying the white race itself without regard to supernatural deities of any sort.

Descriptions of the Major Groups

The best known of the Christian-derived groups is Christian Identity. Identity beliefs evolved from British Israelism, a nineteenth-century school of biblical interpretation that made the eccentric claim that the Anglo-Saxon people are the descendants of the House of Israel to whom God gave for all time his covenant, making the English people God's chosen and giving a religious dimension to the British imperial project of the day. Imported to the United States, British Israelism was transmuted into the strongly racist and anti-Semitic Christian Identity faith, the chief tenet of which holds that Caucasians are not only the true descendants of Israel, but are in fact the only fully human members of God's creation. Jews are interpreted as the literal descendants of Satan, having emerged from the illicit coupling of Satan in the guise of a serpent and Eve in the Garden of Eden (Revelation 2:9, 3:9). Similarly, people of color (or "mud people" in Identity terms) are posited as less than human, a result of illicit mating of the "beasts of the field" (Genesis 1:25) with the Jews.

The transformation of Christian Identity into a racist and anti-Semitic belief system began in America in the late 1920s and was completed with the appearance of American Identity pastor Wesley Swift in the 1950s and such 1960s-era figures as Richard Butler, who went on to form the Aryan Nations, and John Potter Gale of the California Rangers and the Posse Comitatus. As this suggests, Christian Identity is not a young man's game, and the belief system has faded in importance as its adherents have aged and gradually passed from the scene. Identity itself, imported to the United States from Britain as British Israelism, has been reexported throughout the world, with active centers in England, Germany, Scandinavia, and southern Africa, although these redoubts remain even smaller and more isolated than those in the United States.

Younger and far more vital are the groups that seek either to reconstruct an idealized pagan tradition or to reject religion altogether, forming in effect an anti-religion that deifies the Caucasian race itself. Typical of the former is the highly diverse Odinist community. Odinists are followers of the Norse/Germanic pantheon of gods who take their name from the high god Odin. Odinists, who are strongly racist and anti-Semitic (beliefs that would have had no resonance whatever among the ancient Scandinavian and Germanic peoples), exist in uneasy proximity to followers of the Asatru tradition, who revere the same mythology, but who have no overtly racist or anti-Semitic beliefs.

Of the anti-religions, the most notable is the Church of the Creator (COTC), which was founded by Ben Klassen in the United States in the late 1970s. After Klassen's death in 1994, the COTC appeared to be moribund before being revived and reorganized as the World Church of the Creator (WCOTC) by Matt Hale in 1995. Together, these Christian-derived groups, pagan-derived groups, and idiosyncratic anti-religions constitute a transnational, oppositional, "radical religious" community whose very unpopularity and marginality present fascinating dilemmas for those concerned with religious freedom in Europe and in the United States. Each society has dealt very differently with the issues raised by these "radical religions," however.

White Radical Religious Groups and the Legal System

The First Amendment to the U.S. Constitution may reliably be posited as the primary source of these differences. In European states, laws proscribing racial or religious incitement serve to effectively check publication or media dissemination of what in the United States would be termed "hate speech," an odious but largely constitutionally protected form of communication that has worked to the considerable advantage of U.S.-based groups. To take one example, George Eric Hawthorn, an Odinist and former publisher of the skinhead music magazine *Resistance*, chose to locate his operation in Detroit rather than his native Canada in order to be afforded First

Amendment protections unavailable in either Canada or Europe. Indeed, the United States has since the 1970s been in the embarrassing position of being forced to rebuff German complaints that neo-Nazi materials appearing in Germany where they are stringently proscribed by law originated in the U.S., as well as the protests of France in the 1990s that racist Internet sites appearing in violation of French law similarly are of U.S. origin. Yet while First Amendment protections are formidable, they are hardly absolute, as the legal travails of radical white religious groups in recent years attest. The remainder of this entry will follow this history from the perspective of the United States, where efforts to legally suppress the activities (although not the existence) of these religious communities have of necessity been the most creative.

Ironically, due both to their relative paucity and to the stringency of laws already on the books dealing with racist violence, acts of violence have been of the least concern to American authorities. Violence is illegal without regard to First Amendment protections, and in recent years, sentencing enhancements have been enacted in both federal law and in many state and local jurisdictions when racial animus is found to be a motivating factor in a crime. Despite several particularly egregious cases in recent years, however, racist crime remains a rarity, and racist organizations—religious and secular—have learned to tread a fine line between protected speech and criminal culpability, and so have generally managed to avoid criminal prosecution when one of their members is involved in an act of violence.

A controversial way to effectively destroy organizations whose members were convicted of violent acts but who had no prior knowledge of such actions was pioneered by Morris Dees of the Southern Poverty Law Center (SPLC) in Montgomery, Alabama, with the innovative use of civil suits aimed at effectively shutting down these groups. Used for the first time in a case against a Ku Klux Klan group in the 1980s, the SCLC won a civil suit against the United Klans of America (UKA), which was deemed responsible for a killing by UKA members. Beulah May Donald, the murder victim's mother, was awarded control of the group's headquarters—essentially putting the UKA out of business. The tactic hit home with great effectiveness in a successful civil suit against Tom Metzger, one-time Identity minister and current leader of the White Aryan Resistance (WAR). Metzger was riding high in movement circles and was at the time considered with Richard Butler the face of American organized racism.

Metzger's star faded when he lost an expensive civil suit brought by Morris Dees and the SPLC in 1987, which found Metzger and WAR liable for the death of an Ethiopian immigrant at the hands of four Portland, Oregon, skinheads. The plaintiffs were awarded $10 million—$3 million more than they had requested. The judgment effectively crippled WAR, and the damage was compounded when it was belatedly discovered that as part of the settlement, a representative of the SPLC was allowed to monitor mail sent to the WAR in an effort to collect on the judgment.

The tactic proved so effective in the Metzger case that it was repeated with even more telling effect by the SPLC when two drunken guards at the Aryan Nations compound in Idaho accosted and beat a woman and her son who had taken a wrong turn on a dark night on the compound property. A civil suit later, the citizens of Coeur d'Alene had at last rid themselves of their troublesome and universally disliked neighbor, Richard Butler. Aryan Nations—the flagship center of Christian Identity theology in America since the 1970s—is no more and the property has been wrested from Butler's control. To many observers, the suits were salutary in that they impacted a widely unpopular belief system and—at their most effective—closed down religious or religiopolitical organizations deemed beyond the pale of their respective societies. But to many others, the wall protecting speech and religious liberty had suffered a breach that could, in the future, adversely affect other religious communities.

Finally, one other issue involving religious liberty and the white "radical religions" should be noted. American prisons are markedly dangerous places, and more vigilant enforcement and sentence enhancements have invariably increased the number of white racists behind bars. Conversely, American prisons are disproportionately composed of minorities, and race relations in American prisons are hostile to say the least. Yet prisoners have since the 1970s been seen as prime recruits for racist movements, and ideal converts for racist religions. Emulating the success of the Nation of Islam among African-American prisoners, a number of racist groups—including the Aryan Nations, the late pastor Robert Miles's Identity offshoot fancifully called Dualism,

Tom Metzger's White Aryan Resistance, the Church of the Creator and its World Church of the Creator successor, as well as a number of independent Odinists—have sought to tap this potential pool of angry and alienated white men. Indeed, the Aryan Nations' prison ministry appears to have been highly influential in the formation of the Aryan Brotherhood movement among white prisoners. The vexing question facing prison chaplains and prison administrators is how much—if any—recognition to afford Christian Identity or Odinist prisoners in particular, and what forms of communal worship and ritual content to allow in the prisons. For the white groups, the model for emulation remains the Nation of Islam and its hard-won place in prison culture, while to prison officials, it is often precisely this scenario that is to be avoided. Some local decisions have been made, although the pattern remains ambiguous. But it is certain that, for many years to come, religious freedom in the prisons will be a major test of a society's tolerance of religious dissent.

Jeffrey Kaplan

See also Radical Religious Groups: African-American

Further Reading

Aho, J. A. (1990). The politics of righteousness: Idaho Christian patriotism. Seattle: University of Washington Press.

Barkun, M. (1994). Religion and the racist right: The origins of the Christian Identity movement. Chapel Hill: University of North Carolina.

Dees, M., & Fiffer, S. (1993). Hate on trial. New York: Villard Books.

Dinnerstein, L. (1994). Antisemitism in America. New York: Oxford University Press.

Dumézil, G. (1973). Gods of the ancient northmen. Berkeley: University of California Press.

Flynn, K., & Gerhardt, G. (1990). The silent brotherhood. New York: Signet.

Kaplan, J. (1997). Radical religion in America. Syracuse, NY: Syracuse University Press.

Kaplan, J. (2000). Encyclopedia of white power: A sourcebook on the radical right. Walnut Creek, CA: AltaMira.

Landes, R. A. (2000). The encyclopedia of millennialism and millennial movements. New York: Routledge.

Ridgeway, J. (1990). Blood in the face. New York: Thunder's Mouth Press.

Rastifari and Religious Freedom

Rastafari, the modern social-religious movement of cultural resistance popularized by reggae music and associated with dreadlocks, exemplifies in many ways the struggle of modern religious groups to constitute themselves as entities with the right to free assembly and freedom of religion. Founded in Jamaica in 1930 as an African-consciousness movement of freedom from poverty and cultural and political domination, Rastifari holds that Haile Selassie (1892–1975), the former emperor of Ethiopia, is the messiah, that Marcus Garvey (a Jamaican-U.S. black nationalist, 1887–1940) is his prophet, and that blacks are the Israelites reincarnated, God's chosen people. Rastifari dictates a vegetarian diet, that men should not shave, cut, or comb their hair, and that ganja (cannabis, or marijuana) is sacred. Rastifari's adherents have fought for the right to be ideologically different and for the freedom to express their difference through their beliefs, their practices, and through their dress and lifestyle.

Negative Stereotyping of Rastas

From 1935 to 1966, Jamaicans had little tolerance for Rastas (as adherents are called) and, in waves of persecution, sought to rid the country of what most people regarded as a nuisance to society and threat to public safety. In response to persecution and constant harassment from the Jamaican police and anti-Rasta vigilantes in the 1940s and 1950s, many Rastas went dread (wore dreadlocks) and some shed their peaceful disposition for black militancy. In 1959 a small militant faction further tarnished Rastas' public image when it wrote Fidel Castro a letter inviting him to help them overthrow the Jamaican government.

In the 1960s, arresting of Rastas on charges of unlawful possession of ganja escalated until the Jamaican government amended the law to repeal the mandatory imprisonment clause, an action that substantially reduced the number of Rastas imprisoned on possession charges. In the 1970s, the international community condemned Rastas as ganja-smoking drug dealers. New York's growing Rastafari community was accused of violence, drug trafficking, criminal gunrunning, and homicide. The police and the British, Caribbean, and U.S media fed the public an overdose of Rasta stereotypes; major news media characterized Rastas as drug-crazed cultists, and Dan Rather, the anchor of the popular television new magazine *60 Minutes II* labeled Rastafari "a multinational drug-smuggling corporation that used religious beliefs to conceal its illicit narcotics-importing activity" (Murrell 1998, 202). These stereotypic images not only misrepresented the genuine Rastafarian ritual use of marijuana, but they fostered a climate of hostility that, in the 1980s and 1990s, forced Rastafarians to defend their religious freedom in court; the results of which have been mixed.

Court Cases

In the landmark case *Reed v. Faulkner* (1988), Homer Reed, a Rasta inmate in a state prison in Indiana, filed suit against prison authorities for infringing on his religious liberty under the constitution when they forced him to cut his shoulder-length dreadlocks to a specified length. Although prison officials allowed Native American inmates to retain their long hair, the judge ruled against Reed, claiming that his hair was a prison health hazard because it could harbor lice and other contagious diseases while posing a disciplinary problem for prison officials, who would be asked to make similar exceptions for other inmates. In a New York case, *People v. Lewis* (1986), the court upheld Rastas' right to wear dreadlocks. A convicted felon Rastafarian charged that a prison regulation requiring the head of all male inmates be shaved for reasons of health and sanitation infringed his First Amendment rights under the Federal Constitution, and the Court agreed.

In Zimbabwe, *Chikweche v. Zimbabwe* (1995) also was decided in the Rastas' favor. A presiding judge had refused to allow Enock Munyaradiz Chikweche, a devout Rastafarian who met all of the statutory requirements for admission to the High Court, to take the oath of office because, in the judge's estimation, the applicant was not properly dressed: He wore dreadlocks rather than the traditional court apparel. Counsel contended that for the court to refuse the applicant only on the grounds of his hairstyle infringed his rights to freedom of conscience and protection against discrimination under the Constitution of Zimbabwe, section 23 (1) (b). The Supreme Court carefully studied a wide range of evidence on the origin, history, practices, and major tenets of Rastafari; referenced several international cases in Canada, India, Britain, and the United States related to the contravention of Rastas' religious free-

dom with reference to the wearing of dreadlocks; and concluded that the ruling of the High Court judge was factually incorrect, since it was based on physical appearance rather than on statutory qualifications or personal character. The Supreme Court therefore directed the High Court to permit Chikweche to take the oaths of loyalty and office required in Schedule 1 of the constitution.

Rastas' battle in court to preserve their ritual use of marijuana, however, has not been successful. *U.S.A. v. Bauer* (1993) dealt with the claims of three defendants in a November 1992 grand jury indictment. The grand jury had indicted twenty-six defendants on many charges, including conspiracy to manufacture and traffic marijuana. Three defendants argued that at the time of the alleged offence they were practicing Rastafarians and that they used marijuana as a necessary religious ritual. Since the trial was under way in October 1993, when the U.S. Congress was proceeding with the Religious Freedom Restoration Act (RFRA), the defendants called attention to President Clinton's signing the bill and urged the court to withdraw its charges and preserve their First Amendment rights. The appellate court admitted that the illegality of marijuana burdened Rastafarian free exercise of their religion but, citing other court cases, claimed that the U.S. government has an overriding interest in regulating marijuana, and so ruled against Rastas' ritual use of it.

In the Jamaican case *Forsythe v. The Director of Public Prosecutions and the Attorney General* (1996), Dennis Forsythe, a barrister-at-law and distinguished scholar and professor, was charged with possession of less than a kilogram of cannabis and a chillum pipe. Forsythe's supporters saw his arrest and prosecution as government retaliation for his direct involvement in the campaign to legalize marijuana. Forsythe asked the Court to declare that section 21 of the Jamaican constitution was contravened in his case; he argued that his arrest under the Dangerous Drugs Act (DDA) on charges of possession of a tiny amount of marijuana and a chillum pipe for religious purposes infringed his fundamental right to freedom of religion. In denying Forsythe's challenge to the constitutionality of the DDA, the court held that his arrest was not unconstitutional. While the court recognized Forsythe's constitutional right to practice his Rastafari religion, it found him guilty of possessing "illegal marijuana" and fined him as a convicted felon.

It is left to be seen whether the recent landmark court decision on hoasca, a hallucinogenic substance used in religious ritual, will change the court's view on ritual marijuana. In August 2002, Judge James Parker of the U.S. District Court in New Mexico ruled that although in seizing hoasca used by a religious group in its ritual the government did not violate the group's free exercise rights under the First Amendment, the authorities seizing of a church's sacrament seems to violate RFRA and does not show that hoasca poses a serious health risk. Like their most well-known prophet of peace and king of reggae, Bob Marley, Rastas must continue their cry for freedom.

Nathaniel Murrell

See also Drugs and Religious Worship; Prisons

Further Reading

Barrett, Sr., L. (1977). *The Rastafarians*. Boston: Beacon Press.

Campbell, H. (1987). *Rasta and resistance, from Marcus Garvey to Walter Rodney*. Trenton, NJ: Africa World Press.

Chevannes, B. (1994). *Rastafari: Roots and ideology*. Syracuse, NY: Syracuse University Press.

Ford, D. R. (1997). *Marijuana: Not guilty as charged*. Sonoma, CA.: Good Press.

Jan van Dijk, F. (1993). *Jahmaica: Rastafari and Jamaican society*. Utrecht, Netherlands: ISOR.

Lewis, W. F. (1993). *Soul rebels: The Rastafari*. Prospect Heights, IL: Waveland Press.

Murrell, N. S., William, D, & McFarlane, A. A. (Eds.). (1998). *Chanting down Babylon: The Rastafari reader*. Philadelphia: Temple University Press.

Owens, J. (1976). *Dread: The Rastafarians of Jamaica*. Kingston, Jamaica: Sangster's Book Stores.

Roffman, R. A. (1982). *Marijuana as medicine*. Seattle, WA: Madrona Publishers.

Taylor, T. (1984). Soul Rebels: The Rastafarians and the free exercise clause. *Georgetown Law Review, 72*(June), 1605–1635.

Court Cases

People v. Lewis, 510 N.Y.S. 2d 73 (N.Y. Ct.App. 1986).

Reed v. Faulkner, 842 F.2d 960 (7th Cir. 1988).

USA v. Bauer, 84 F. 3d 1549 (9th Cir. 1996).

Chikweche v. Zimbabwe (4) SA 284 (ZC 1995).

Reformation, Early Modern Europe

The Reformation era is often dated from the German Benedictine monk Martin Luther's (1483–1546) nailing of the ninety-five theses to the Wittenberg Castle Church door in 1517, to the Peace of Westphalia that brought the Thirty-Years War to a close in 1648. In discussing the Reformation and its role in the development of religious liberty, three tendencies should be avoided. First, modern standards of religious freedom should not be applied to the sixteenth century in order to show how intolerant that era was. Second, one should not assume that western history was necessarily progressing toward modern notions of religious liberty and then ignore developments that do not seem pertinent to the modern story. Third, one should avoid the notion that the state of religious liberty was uniform across Europe during the period of the Reformation.

Reformation Background

The beginning of the Reformation is usually dated 1517, when Luther nailed his ninety-five theses to the door of the Wittenberg Castle Church. Luther's theses attacked the sacramental system of the medieval Roman Catholic Church. The heart of Luther's protest was that salvation came by faith alone in the saving work of Christ and not by faith combined with works performed by believers. In addition to his doctrinal concerns, Luther criticized abuses he and many others observed in the Church, but his chief concern was theological.

Eventually those who adopted the new views were called Protestants. Once Luther had taken his stand, two other major Protestant strands developed, Calvinism and the Anabaptist movement, each producing several distinct denominational groups. All Protestants agreed on two matters: salvation by faith alone (*sola fides* in the Latin of that day) and in the final authority of the Bible (*sola scriptura*). Beyond the doctrines *sola fides* and *sola scriptura*, Protestants disagreed on many matters, including how the church should relate to the state and to what degree people should enjoy religious freedom.

Church and State

Throughout the middle ages there was a broad consensus that a kingdom could not survive without religious unity. The primary problem created by the

EXTRACT FROM THE SCHLEITHEIM CONFESSION OF FAITH

6. The Sword

Sixth. We are agreed as follows concerning the sword: The sword is ordained of God outside the perfection of Christ. It punishes and puts to death the wicked, and guards and protects the good. In the Law the sword was ordained for the punishment of the wicked and for their death, and the same [sword] is [now] ordained to be used by the worldly magistrates.

In the perfection of Christ, however, only the ban is used for a warning and for the excommunication of the one who has sinned, without putting the flesh to death,—simply the warning and the command to sin no more.

Now it will be asked by many who do not recognize [this as] the will of Christ for us, whether a Christian may or should employ the sword against the wicked for the defence and protection of the good, or for the sake of love.

Our reply is unanimously as follows: Christ teaches and commands us to learn of Him, for He is meek and lowly in heart and so shall we find rest to our souls. Also Christ says to the heathenish woman who was taken in adultery, not that one should stone her according to the law of His Father (and yet He says, As the Father has commanded me, thus I do), but in mercy and forgiveness and warning, to sin no more. Such [an attitude] we also ought to take completely according to the rule of the ban.

Secondly, it will be asked concerning the sword, whether a Christian shall pass sentence in worldly disputes and strife such as unbelievers have with one another. This is our united answer: Christ did not wish to decide or pass judgment between brother and brother in the case of the inheritance, but refused to do so. Therefore we should do likewise.

Thirdly, it will be asked concerning the sword, Shall one be a magistrate if one should be chosen as such? The answer is as follows: They wished to make Christ king, but He fled and did not view it as the arrangement of His Father. Thus shall we do as He did, and follow Him, and so shall we not walk in darkness. For He Himself says, He who wishes to come after me, let him deny himself and take up his cross and follow me. Also, He Himself forbids the [employment of] the force of the sword saying, The worldly princes lord it over them, etc., but not so shall it be with you. Further, Paul says, Whom God did foreknow He also did predestinate to be conformed to the image of His Son, etc. Also Peter says, Christ has suffered (not ruled) and left us an example, that ye should follow His steps.

Finally it will be observed that it is not appropriate for a Christian to serve as a magistrate because of these points: The government magistracy is according to the flesh, but the Christians' is according to the Spirit; their houses and dwelling remain in this world, but the Christians' are in heaven; their citizenship is in this world, but the Christians' citizenship is in heaven; the weapons of their conflict and war are carnal and against the flesh only, but the Christians' weapons are spiritual, against the fortification of the devil. The worldlings are armed with steel and iron, but the Christians are armed with the armor of God, with truth, righteousness, peace, faith, salvation and the Word of God. In brief, as is the mind of Christ toward us, so shall the mind of the members of the body of Christ be through Him in all things, that there may be no schism in the body through which it would be destroyed. For every kingdom divided against itself will be destroyed. Now since Christ is as it is written of Him, His members must also be the same, that His body may remain complete and united to its own advancement and upbuilding.

Source: The Schleitheim Confession of Faith, translated by J. C. Wenger.
Retrieved 21 October 2002, from http://www.reformedreader.org/ccc/scf

Reformation, therefore, was religious disunity and the apparent threat it posed. Twentieth-century historian Roland Bainton identified three basic ways of dealing with the religious diversity created by the Reformation. The first was territorialism. In this scheme political unity was sacrificed to preserve the integrity of the faith. Following a series of Protestant-Catholic wars in the 1530s and 1540s, territorialism was tried in the Holy Roman Empire. In the Peace of Augsburg (1555), leaders adopted the formula *cujus regio, ejus religio*, (whose rule, his religion). This meant that if a particular state within the Empire was governed by a Catholic prince, that state would be Catholic, and if a state was governed by a Lutheran prince, that state would be Lutheran. The Empire would sacrifice its religious unity, as some states within it became Protestant while others remained Catholic. This form of territorialism broke down after about two generations, opening the way for the Thirty-Years War (1618–1648), the last major religious war in the history of the West.

In France there also developed a type of territorialism. After protracted religious civil wars from the 1560s to 1590s, King Henry IV (d. 1610) adopted a form of territorialism in his Edict of Nantes (1598), which tolerated French Protestants (known as Huguenots) in certain areas of the country. Many towns were designated Huguenot territory, while the majority remained Catholic. As in the Empire, France's territorialism also began to break down after about a generation, and the country reverted back to unified Catholicism.

The second way of dealing with the problem of religious division was comprehension. Adopted primarily in England, comprehension broadened the faith in an effort to comprehend or encompass the entire nation. Here the integrity of the faith was sacrificed, or diluted, to retain political unity. The Church of England (Anglican Church) did not satisfy all English citizens. Catholics on the right and radical Protestants on the left, continued to dissent, each believing that the Anglican Church was not pure

A Protestant Church in a small village in the Provence region of southern France in 2000. COURTESY OF DAVID LEVINSON.

The wall plaque provides a chronology of the Reformation in France. COURTESY OF DAVID LEVINSON.

enough, but the majority accepted the *via media* (middle way) that was designed by Queen Elizabeth and her administration. Comprehension, like territorialism, would eventually break down, and England would experience the English Civil War in the 1540s, which was led on the Parliamentarian side by dissenting Puritans.

The third way of dealing with the religious divisions brought on by the Reformation was religious liberty. The Anabaptists and a few other radicals advocated this, but few states tried it, and those that did, did so only briefly. France, for example, just before the Wars of Religion, issued an Edict of January (1562), which granted toleration to Huguenots, but the law was quickly swept aside when Protestant and Catholic armies went to war.

Luther's Views on Church and State

While the various states of Europe grappled politically with the problems brought on by the Reformation, the major Reformation thinkers attempted to write theologies of church and state, outlining what they believed was the proper relationship between the two entities and whether, or to what degree, there should be religious liberty for dissenters. Luther developed what was called his two regiments or two kingdoms theology. As no idea is ever completely cut off from the past, Luther's church-state ideas were related to the medieval, and even ancient, Christian view that on earth God had provided two forms of governance——two swords, as they came to be known. The medieval two-swords theory (first articulated by Pope Gelasius in 494) held that the sword wielded by the church was superior to that of the state. The church was under God and over the state, with the state receiving its authority from the church.

While Luther retained the basic idea of two entities, he wanted to separate these two kingdoms and understand them as both deriving their authority directly from God but for different purposes. This resulted in a kind of separation of church and state, but one that was different from the modern notion as it came to be expressed in the First Amendment to the United States Constitution.

In theory, Luther's two kingdoms functioned as follows: The spiritual regiment was in the hands of the ministers, not the state, and it dealt with the spiritual side of individuals. The church could discipline people, but only in spiritual matters. The second of the two kingdoms was the temporal regiment, or state, that deals with law and order; that is, external and not spiritual matters. The temporal regiment policed the outward behavior of men and women and generally kept the peace in society, but it was not to govern the spiritual lives of the people; that was left to the church. Of course, the spiritual regiment presupposed the need for the temporal as there must be an orderly society for the church to function properly. For Luther, the state was something of a necessary evil. Because of sin, society needed a government to keep order. If everyone were truly Christian in behavior as well as belief, there would be no such need.

However well Luther had worked out his two kingdoms in theory, it was much more difficult to implement in practice. This was especially so as an increasing number of Anabaptists and other radical sects began to develop in the German states of the Holy Roman Empire in the late 1520s and into the 1530s. Everyone in the middle ages feared the chaos that would ensue if a kingdom did not have fairly wide agreement in matters of theology, and Luther was no different. In the 1520s, when he first wrote on church-state matters, he believed that the magistrate had no authority over private belief. He did believe, however, that blasphemy (denying God's truths) was a public matter. The upshot of this was that later, when Anabaptists and other radicals preached doctrines very different from Luther's, he and the authorities regarded such teachings as blasphemous violations of public order and therefore subject to the magistrate's punishment.

In order to curb the development of ideas that Luther and other Protestant theologians believed dangerous, Luther adopted the idea that in a time of emergency the temporal rulers might have to step in and aid the church. As the radical reformers seemed to present just such an emergency, Luther advocated that the ruler protect the church. As a result, the magistrates were given a foot in the door of the church. As Roland Bainton has written, Luther left the door ajar for Caesaropapism, the phenomenon whereby the state came to rule over the church. Within a generation of Luther's death in 1546, there was a virtual state church in the northern German territories, and religious minorities, principally Anabaptists, suffered the consequences. The notion of religious liberty or even toleration for those who dissented from the official state-supported church was virtually nonexistent.

Calvinism

The Calvinist (also called Reformed) wing of the Protestant Reformation was shaped for the most part by John Calvin (1509–1564). He was a French classical humanist scholar who converted to Protestantism around 1531. After fleeing the Catholic University of Paris, Calvin went to Switzerland where he developed a reputation as a significant and influential theologian. Protestants in the city of Geneva invited him to their city in order to thoroughly reform it along Protestant lines. Calvin settled in Geneva in 1541, where he remained for the rest of his life. Although he never held political power, his influence was crucial over the city council that governed the city.

Like Luther, Calvin also believed there were two distinct institutions of church and state and that they were created by God for different purposes. Calvin, however, did not want the two kingdoms separated as much as Luther's theology stipulated. While distinct from one another in one sense, Calvin thought that church and state should cooperate closely with one another for the purpose of creating a godly society. For him, the state was not merely a necessary evil or a negative check on bad behavior, as was the case for Luther, but was truly an instrument created by God for positive good. While the church would cultivate inward spirituality, the state would enforce outward behavior in accordance with biblical morality, but neither institution was to rule over the other.

The situation in Geneva often looked something like this: The leaders of the church could not arrest people for violating biblical morality, but those leaders could persuade the city council to pass laws that would lead to the arrest of persons who acted immorally. On the other hand, the city council could not excommunicate someone from the church, but it could banish someone from the town of Geneva for teaching doctrines that were heretical. In instances of adultery, blasphemy, dancing, and other matters, the church elders, in the form of a consistory, would attempt to discipline church members within the church. If repeated remonstrations failed, such a person could be handed over to the authorities for civil punishment. Whereas in Luther's scheme church and state each did their jobs separately, Calvin advocated that they closely cooperate with each other and that each had the same end goal in mind, a godly society.

Understandably, there were a variety of statutes and ordinances outlawing things that people in con-temporary society believe are private matters, and many of the laws of the state and of the church were virtually indistinguishable from one another. This was not Caesaropapism, however, as the state did not rule over the church. Nor was it a pure theocracy, as the church did not rule over the state. Rather, God ruled through the elect (saved), some of them in the church and others in the state. Perhaps the greatest contribution of this scheme was the concept that the state's power was limited; it did not extend over the church. The influence of Calvin and Geneva can hardly be overstated. Much of the Netherlands, Scotland, and the New England colonies in America attempted to follow the Geneva model, with varying degrees of success.

Anabaptists

Anabaptists first appeared in 1521 in and around the city of Zurich, Switzerland. Three principal leaders who were already Protestant concluded from their study of the Bible that infant baptism was unbiblical. They baptized each other and a handful of followers and declared themselves a church. The word "Anabaptism" essentially means rebaptism. With no official recognition by the city of Zurich or any other political entity, the first Anabaptist congregation was considered illegal. Moreover, according to the ancient Justinian Code, rebaptism was considered a crime punishable by death. Because Anabaptists rejected the need for state recognition and uniform religious worship across a territory, they were considered a threat to the body politic and were persecuted severely virtually everywhere they went. They were arrested, their leaders often burned at the stake as heretics, while many others were given the "third baptism," drowning.

In a sense, whereas Calvin thought Luther had separated too widely the kingdoms of church and state, Anabaptists separated them even further. Where Luther taught that if Christians always acted as they should they would need no state to govern them, Anabaptists actually believed they could fashion a pure church of baptized believers who would live in complete separation from the state. They believed the state existed for unbelievers, so they would not participate, refusing to hold office, serve in the military, or even take oaths of allegiance. Just as the early church was completely disenfranchised by the Roman state, the Anabaptists attempted to restore the New Testament church of gathered, baptized believers who would live according to the kingdom of God and not the kingdom of man.

One of the key documents of the Anabaptist movement was the Schleiteim Articles. Authored principally by Michael Sattler (c. 1490–1527), the document outlined the relationship of church and state. Unlike the other Protestant reformers, the concept of the church was not one that encompassed a large territory and a significant number of people. Rather, the true church of baptized believers was small and completely set apart from the larger society. To the ancient question, "What does Rome have to do with Jerusalem?"—the Schleiteim Anabaptists answered, "nothing." The Schleiteim way came earliest to the Swiss Brethren who largely adopted the confession in the 1520s. It would take slightly longer for the Dutch and German Anabaptists to adopt such separation from society, but by the 1540s they too had come largely to this position.

The Anabaptist ideas of separation of church and state and complete religious liberty triumphed in no country during the Reformation era. Still, their witness against intolerance, often articulated from a burning stake, highlighted for a few sympathetic observers the folly of religious intolerance.

Implications

Perhaps the greatest contribution of the Reformation to religious liberty came not so much through the ideas articulated by Protestant theologians, nor through the political theories set forth by philosophers. Rather, the mere development of religious pluralism that necessarily accompanied the Reformation made religious conformity increasingly difficult to enforce and eventually untenable even to contemplate. The Reformation contribution to religious liberty, therefore, was more inadvertent and circumstantial than theoretical and principled.

Barry Hankins

See also Roman Catholicism; English Civil War

Further Reading

Bainton, R. H. (1952). *The reformation of the sixteenth century*. Boston: Beacon Press.
Bender, H. S. (1970). *The Anabaptists and religious liberty in the sixteenth century*. Philadelphia: Fortress Press.
Hancock, R. C. (1989). *Calvin and the foundations of modern politics*. Ithaca, NY: Cornell University Press.
Hopfl, H. (Ed. and Trans.). (1991). *Luther and Calvin on secular authority*. Cambridge, UK: Cambridge University Press.
Meuller, W. A. (1965). *Church and state in Luther and Calvin: A comparative study* (2d ed.). Garden City, MI: Doubleday.
Monter, E. W. (1975). *Calvin's Geneva*. New York: John Wiley and Sons; reprinted Huntington, NY: R. E. Krieger.
Thompson, W. C. (1984). *The political thought of Martin Luther*. Totowa, NJ: Barnes and Noble.
Weaver, J. D. (1987). *Becoming Anabaptist: The origin and significance of sixteenth-century Anabaptism*. Scottsdale, PA: Herald Press.

Religion and Nationalism

Nationalism is closely related to religion. The idea of the world ordered in terms of nations was first conceived by the German philosopher Georg Wilhelm Friedrich Hegel (1770–1831) as part of God's divine plan. From this concept of being part of a divine plan, nationalism drew much of its moral authority and found its way into metaphysical politics. A natural order (of nations) implied a natural assertion of national rights which, for nationalists provided a "why" to politics (for the nation) and a specific cosmic time and place. Nationalism then became a form of religion, witnessed in national churches where religion helps define national identity and provides a collective memory, symbols, and myths. Religious services are often central to national celebrations where God is invoked on behalf of the nation: for God and country.

Nationalism falls into two broad categories, unification and ethnic. Unification nations such as the United States and the United Kingdom are less metaphysical and associated with Enlightenment principles of rationalism and individuality where strong communal ties are disavowed for an association of individuals bound largely by legal-rational association and shared interest. Unification ideals were influenced by the Protestant theology of claims to the right of private conscience and judgement, freedom of worship and congregation, and the rational pursuit of truth. This evolved into what is known as civic nationalism and forms the basis for the secular state, which is also associated with modern industrial society.

Ethnic nationalism emphasises the primacy of the communal over the individual who was seen as a communally derived being. Ethnicity consequently stresses conformity to ethnic cultural norms over individual expression and has a strong metaphysical core, which stresses a mystical and metaphysical dimension to national being. Such nationalism is associated with rural, premodern societies of close-knit communities in which traditional religions, such as the Catholic Church in Ireland or the Orthodox Church in Yugoslavia, dominate.

Unification, rationalism, individualism, and Protestantism emphasize questions of "how" and form a continuity of values and beliefs in a cosmos that equates with the modern and a distant God. Ethnic, mystical, communal, and pre-Reformation religious forms equate with a premodern order and close God. This helps explain the bitterness of many nationalist disputes since they relate to higher questions of cosmic order and divine plan for activists. Nations are religious in that they become the modern religious community that can invoke the wrath of God.

Islamic Fundamentalism and Violence

Islamic fundamentalism refers to the use of violence invoked by Islamic radicals in reaction against the intrusion of modernist Western influences and disruption in highly traditional Islamic societies. Western political notions of democracy, nation, secular state, science, and economic markets are associated with Christian values, which are regarded as undermining Islamic values, identity, order, and community. This has become acute with globalization in which the dominant Western values are identified with loss of the sacred, i.e., the disruption of stable community and order. Such reaction is particularly strong where modernization has not produced hoped-for benefits, but only disruption of the old order wherein the world was known and interpreted through Islamic images and symbols. This has led to a violent backlash by adversely affected elements, as in Algeria.

Religion has always been a reference for decisions over life and death, the ultimate moral authority. It thus always plays a vital role in legitimating the use of violence, which, on behalf of God, can exceed the normal bounds laid down by humanity, particularly if God is regarded as under attack. Thus nations invoke religion in national wars just as Islamic fundamentalists do as part of a cosmic struggle. Terrorist groups such as the IRA (Irish Republican Army) and ETA (Euzkadi Ta Askatasuna, Basque separatists) are noted for their Catholic ethos, and most of the warring factions in the former Yugoslavia were identified largely by their religion. Violence has been central to religion and politics, with religion sanctifying acts of violence to mobilize forces to expel hostile elements from the community and to restore order. Consequently religion is often at the center of intercommunal violence as different communal orders—that is, communities ordered according to different religious precepts, principles, and morals—compete to establish their order at the expense of others.

James Dingley

Further Reading

Duffy, E. (1992). *The stripping of the altars*. New Haven, CT: Yale University Press.

Hastings, A. (1997). *The construction of nationhood*. Cambridge, UK: Cambridge University Press.

Haynes, J. (1998). *Religion in global politics*. London: Longman.

Hervieu-Leger, D. (2000). *Religion as a chain of memory*. New Brunswick, NJ: Rutgers University Press.

Inglehart, R., & Norris, P. (2002). *Church and state: Religion and world politics*.

Juergensmeyer, M. (2001). *Terror in the mind of God*. Berkeley: University of California Press.

Kedourie, E. (1993). *Nationalism*. Oxford, UK: Blackwell.

Porter, R. (2000). *Enlightenment*. New York: Palgrave.

van der Veer, P. & Lehmann, H. (1999). *Nation and Religion*. Princeton, NJ: Princeton University Press.

Religion and Politics

Religion and politics refers to the role that religion plays, or has ceased to play (secularization) in the ordering of human affairs and power relations. Modernist secular societies assume a separation between politics and religion and a privatization of religious belief or, simply, a decline in religious belief and its influence in politics. Here state, government, and politics are regarded as civil institutions concerned with material well-being and rational and technical competency in maintaining civil order and public good. Secularization has become regarded as the natural order of modernity, where rationalism and science replace traditional religion in guiding the political order. However, the late twentieth and early twenty-first centuries have seen the rise of a new religious activism in world politics, such as the "religious right" in the United States, the resurgence of the Orthodox Church in Russia, evangelical Christianity in Africa and Islamic fundamentalism. Additionally, in modern societies such as Britain (where church attendance is under 10 percent), religion is still able to influence politics, as indicated by the critiques of the Thatcher government's inner-city policies by the Church of England in the 1980s. The moral authority that religion provides can eclipse simple "number on pews." Further, in the nations where large immigrant populations now reside, such as Muslims and Jews in the United States, United Kingdom, or France, the immigrants' religion has become a focus for identity and political mobilization.

Continuities Between Religion and Politics

Both religion and politics are concerned with order. Religion refers to order in the cosmos within which men find a place, meaning and purpose in an otherwise chaotic and meaningless world; it answers questions of ultimate value—the "why" of life. In the modernist conception, politics is concerned with order in the present, in daily affairs and between the institutions men depend on for daily living, technical questions of "how" in the material world.

In premodern, preindustrial society, the religious and political were hardly separable. People engaged in a simple subsistence life, in which illiteracy was normal, fatalism was high, and an acceptance of dependence on natural forces inclined people to accept an early death in a natural order about which they could do little. The natural order (how things were arranged) was unquestioned since little could be done about it so questions concentrated on why they were on earth and what was life's purpose. Since order was accepted as God-given, religion inevitably played a significant role in legitimating existing political order. Religion functioned as an authority system and thus had a direct political role.

Also, as the only educated people and organized body of learning, religious bodies administered both dynastic states and parish affairs. They also played a central role in the economic system—for example, with the medieval guilds, as clerics often served as chairs and board members and dictated ethical codes

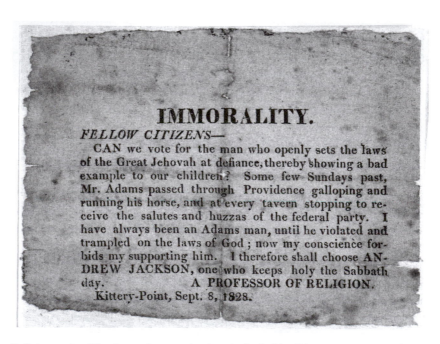

Religion and politics have always mixed, as indicated by this commentary on the upcoming presidential election, printed in Kittery-Point, Maine in 1828. COURTESY OF LIBRARY OF CONGRESS, RARE BOOK AND SPECIAL COLLECTIONS DIVISION.

of fair trade and competition—with religious institutions maintaining a moral, not market, economy. Religious organization at both parish and interparish level was often the only form of permanent sociopolitical organization existing in premodern societies. Politics and religion were heavily conflated and the idea of separating them out would have appeared unnatural, whatever the religious tradition. Illiterate premodern society was dependent on the literate and numerate skills of clerics who would act as arbiters and recorders for communities and interpret the world for them. Religious institutions were major providers of education, health, and welfare facilities and care for the poor, services now reserved for the state—and the substance of much modern politics. Religion also provided most of the imagery and symbols through which the world was imagined and perceived. Since religion was central to nearly all communities it provided the means for interpreting and understanding the world through its stories, metaphors, and signs thus also making the community religious: Both were the major ordering principle in people's lives. Politics was religious and vice versa.

Discontinuities in Religion and Politics

Modernity, heralded by the Reformation, the Enlightenment, and industrialization, radically altered man's world view as new knowledge enabled him to alter and affect his material condition; the "how'" of the present replaced "why'" as the dominant question along with increased specialization to tackle the problems of "how.'" Modernists separated religion from politics, and religion became relegated to a speciality, concerned with peripheral questions of "why." Total world views and ultimate values lost their relevance in a world concerned with the "how" of material improvement, and with technical rather than value questions. At the same time, politics also became a speciality, concerned with ordering the modernist (and man-made) complex industrial world: another "how" rather than "why." And since the modern order was man-made, questions pertaining to a natural order appeared redundant.

Modernity left the conceptualizations, imagery, and symbols of traditional religion void of relevance concerning the "how" of the world. Equally, the modern world needed an educated workforce with specialist skills (in science and technology) that religion could not supply, which further marginalized religious relevance. Only nontechnical questions of

ultimate values remained for religion in modern society, and even here it has had to compete with secular philosophy.

Secularization and Democracy

To the modernist, ultimate values and meaning (belief) have become private, individual concerns not to be brought into the public realm of politics. Individualism, itself a spin off of specialization, helped create a private world of subjectivity and experience that could not be shared and thus could not provide common answers. In premodern society men and women lived in small, close-knit communities and led a common life. Religion was able to provide a shared set of symbols and imaginings that could encompass the entire community. Modern society is a fragmented world of diverse experiences and imaginings making it difficult to provide a shared worldview. Thus religion has become personalized and private instead of collective and public; politics now takes on this latter role. As people became privatized in their religion so they claimed the same values in their politics, which helped generate the ideals of democracy and pluralism, particularly as the state became separated from religion in modern societies. This is particularly illustrated in the United States, where democratic ideals, enshrined in the U.S. Constitution, come straight out of Ulster-Scots Presbyterian theology. Freedom to find God in one's own way transcribed itself into freedom to order one's life, choose one's own community, and order one's own affairs in one's own way. This also matched the practical needs of larger and more anonymous populations in large urban centers.

Secularization, however, was never complete: because, first, religion still plays a public role in terms of informing the values behind political debates, and in terms of collective and individual memory in which religion acts as a link with the past. Also it links related religious populations and therefore still provides an overriding order and place in the cosmos which is still important in legitimating contemporary political authority by reference to the past. Next, humanity can never totally escape from ultimate values; the "how" eventually leads to "why." Collective memory is important to provide some explanation as to "why" in the cosmos; "how" is never a substitute for why and eventually people are forced to confront this question. Third, religious values were originally central to what is now regarded as secular processes; consequently people are often forced to refer back to these values both for explanation and legitimation. For example, many Enlightenment figures (such as Benjamin Franklin and Joseph Priestly) saw in the rational pursuit of technical knowledge (which inevitably led to science and individualism) the pursuit of God's laws whose discovery would help unravel God's purpose and meaning. Finally, because of the intimate connection between community, religion, and order, religious questions constantly reassert themselves as questions of meaning and purpose in life and a place in the collective order. There is consequently a question as to just how secular modern societies really are.

Modern Trends in Religion and Politics

Currently there is a resurgence of religious politics. Some modern societies have always had religious-based political parties, such as the Christian Democrats in Germany and Italy, and in the United Kingdom the Church of England was often described as the "Tory Party at prayer." However, such parties often felt compelled to play down any overt religiosity and function as broadly civic entities in a manner akin to the United States, where a formal distinction between church, state, and politics is enshrined (another product of Ulster-Scots Presbyterianism). Other states, such as Poland or the Irish Republic have an overt religious flavor (via their Roman Catholicism) where the church has been a strong source of collective memory, cultural and communal identity, and social cohesion. In these societies religion openly enters the political debate in areas such as education, welfare, health, and social teachings. Here communal solidarity and conformity with religious doctrine is emphasized at the expense of individuality, giving such states a more conservative image. This creates problems for pluralist political values where there are other religious identities likely to feel threatened by the dominance of majority religious values, such as the Protestants in Ireland, or the Christians in Muslim Sudan. Similar religious differences between Hindus, Muslims, and Sikhs in India and Pakistan or Buddhists and Hindus in Sri Lanka have been the cause of political strife in these nations. As a source of collective identity and communal belonging and a source of political legitimacy, religion poses serious problems in multi-faith societies for the problem of order.

Protestant societies are generally more secular since they emphasise a personal salvation and freedom of individual choice and action, which gives them a more liberal and progressive ethos closely aligned with modern ideas of democracy, pluralism, and a secular state. However, even here there is a tendency for acts of public worship and religious celebration at times of great public import, emphasising again the religious and collective origin of political values (the group has to agree to individualism for it to be accepted and gain legitimacy as a political value). But even in this regard there has been a resurgence of overtly religious politics in the "religious right" (such as in the United States). They are concerned with moral issues such as abortion and sexual mores and campaign against what they regard as excessive government interference in contemporary society. They particularly invoke Fundamentalist biblical interpretations and personal salvation, advocate direct action politics, and espouse economic individualism and minimal government interference (except for government prohibitions that support their moral issues).

The "religious right" can be contrasted with the left-wing "liberation theology" that was used in South America to oppose repressive, right-wing regimes. Liberation theology combined radical Catholic social teaching with Marxism to foment revolutionary opposition on the part of the poor and oppressed. And whereas religion is normally associated with conservatism, liberation theology invoked a radical tradition of Christianity to legitimate violent opposition to injustice. Religion, suitably interpreted, can be used to invoke both a conservative and a revolutionary tradition—Christ as a revolutionary—thus inducing change as well as conservatism.

Religion and Protest

Religious protests are practices by which members of a religion register discontent with social or political norms and customs. These largely public actions aim to expose and perhaps undo perceived injustices. Religious protest is not simply protest accompanied by religion; rather, it is conceived in religious terms, legitimated by religious ideals, and assumes specifically religious forms in practice.

THE PAWNEE GHOST DANCE AS PROTEST AND REVIVAL

This extract from an 1930s ethnographic account of the Pawnee of the American Plains indicates how the Ghost Dance ceremony served as a protest against the incursion of white culture and a means to revitalize some customs of traditional Pawnee culture.

Religion and ceremonialism in a primitive culture are maintained as oral tradition alone. There is always a gradual loss through cultural forgetting, and a somewhat compensatory gain through the development of new ramifications. The conditions of life of the Pawnee in the Nineteenth Century contributed to a rapid increase of the rate of cultural forgetting. This acceleration was in part due to the loss of function of the ceremonies and rituals, which made demonstrations more infrequent, and hence instruction rarer. At the same time, with loss of functional meaning there was lacking the incentive for the old men to teach and the young men to learn. But in addition, we must not overlook the increase of the death rate among the Pawnee. The learned died before their time; and those destined to carry on their teachings died at an early age. Death interfered abnormally with the traditional mode of handing on the knowledge of the ancients.

The traditional pattern of transmission involved the concept of private or personal ownership of ritual knowledge. What was lost through death was therefore lost beyond recovery. There was no sanction for carrying out any ritual, other than that the one who attempted it had learned about it from ritual predecessors.

The Ghost Dance doctrine supplemented by the Ghost Dance visions altered the general view. In a vision the subject would "see" some old way of life. He would "remember" it. His vision then became a command upon himself and others around him to carry out the old form.

Alexander Lesser

Source: *The Pawnee Ghost Dance Hand Game*, Columbia University Contributions to Anthropology, vol. 16. (New York: Columbia University Press, 1933), 108–109.

Historical and Theoretical Overview

Since no political order or cultural norm enjoys complete legitimacy, their authority is often challenged. Among the most contentious of such challenges are religious protests, which highlight the tensions between religions and other sources of authority.

While there have been religious protests throughout the ages and across the globe, their theorization is relatively recent. Disruptive activity has been regarded with mixed feelings in the modern West; U.S. president James Madison (1751–1836) feared the unruly potential of mass politics, but Marxism celebrates protest's liberating capacities. These political considerations of protest have often dismissed religion as excessively emotional or irrational, or at best as irrelevant to "real" politics. Yet political projects around the globe continue to be linked to the efforts of religious citizens to define themselves in political or public ways. Religious beliefs, practices, and affinities are often more deeply held than political ones, and hence they frequently may challenge the stability of the political realm. By seeing how religious protest is treated, one can learn something of the scope of a society's religious freedom and the extent of political authority.

Whenever practitioners have engaged in public criticism of established orders (political, religious, or otherwise), one may call the result religious protest. Indeed, many religions and political regimes themselves began as protest movements. Before the modern era established religions often went hand in hand with established political power, so that protest was rare and often tended to come from outside the dominant religion (examples include the prophets of ancient Israel, Christian martyrs who refused assimilation into the Roman empire, and peasant revolts such as that led in 1525 by the German Protestant Thomas Müntzer).

Religious protest has occurred with greater frequency in the modern era, when the expansion of sovereign political powers has often altered traditional practices and when the concept of religious freedom has become more accepted. The vast economic and political shifts of the nineteenth and twentieth centuries—particularly the expansion of political rights and proliferation of decolonization movements since the 1960s—have set the stage for an era of widespread protest.

Why Protest?

Religious protest is most common among people who believe they are suffering marginalization or oppression. The precipitating cause is generally the belief that an injustice has been committed or truth obscured. Both material conditions and symbolic concerns generate these beliefs. For protest to occur, practitioners must sense that the world is out of order and must be set right. When practitioners believe that the political laws, norms, and practices are consistent with their religious beliefs, they are less likely to protest; it is when practioners sense that these political elements are divergent from their religious traditions that protest becomes more likely. When practitioners become aware of themselves as having beliefs or practices distinct from those of an outside authority, opposition to that authority may develop around perceived infractions of religious norms. Allegiance to religion in such a situation is felt to require protest against social or political authority.

While not every protester insists that religious tradition always trumps "worldly" authority, there is nonetheless a presumption that religious language, practice, and identity are to be privileged when they conflict with other social or political goods. For example, an Orthodox Jewish antiabortion protester in the United States might judge that the value his or her tradition placed on the sanctity of life outweighs the temporal political good of freedom of choice and, further, that the defense of the former requires him or her to challenge the latter.

The existing culture of a religious community or tradition provides both ethical and practical resources for protest. Whether the actions occur in a highly visible manner or in a more subdued fashion (as with a decision to boycott certain products for religious reasons), what differentiates religious from nonreligious protest is the way religious emotions, convictions, and communities both motivate and sustain action. Backed by the fervor of faith and the community, practitioners believe that their voice and their concerns can break through to a public or political sphere that would otherwise ignore them.

What Happens in a Protest?

The style of and occasion for religious protest are partly dependent upon the protest's political context. In a democracy guaranteeing religious liberty, for example, religious protest may be less radical than in a regime outlawing some or all religious expression. Yet while religious protests assume multiple forms, there are common concerns among them.

Religious protest erupts at the intersection of culture, biography, politics, and material conditions. Practitioners both influence and are shaped by their historical moment. There are multiple ways in which this process is articulated. Spoken protest (for example, Muslim boxer Muhammad Ali's speech refusing conscription during the Vietnam era) is as common as more active forms. Protest may directly engage its object of criticism (for example, a demonstration at a governmental facility) or withdraw from it (as in the establishment of separatist communities). Some protesters seek to connect to common symbols or narratives to make their point, while others reject shared meanings in favor of their religious specificity. Finally, protest exists on a continuum of intensity from relatively passive civil disobedience to more disturbing, even violent acts.

Religious protests generally require a dramatic presentation and an audience. The tactics used are often quite innovative in their disruptive quality and in their demand to be noticed or to raise questions. The scale of religious protest is immensely variable, from a lone figure in a public square to an uprising involving thousands or an organizational entreaty to a legislature.

Rearranging Space

There are several more specific categories of protest that may be considered. Many protests focus on the rearrangement of space. For example, European neo-pagans have chained themselves to trees to protest deforestation of land held to be sacred.

African-American Christians have blocked the flow of pedestrian and automotive traffic to protest police brutality. They thereby rearranged the space of public discourse through words or acts that are out of place. Another example is the U.S. Reverend Fred Phelps's hoisting of a banner that read "God Hates Fags" in front of the Capitol building. In these instances, religions venture across social, political, or linguistic boundaries even as they insist on the inviolability of their own boundaries.

Embodying Protest in Individual Acts

Other protests involve working on the self through individual acts such as fasting and sacrifice, which practitioners feel embody the morality being threatened. The eighteenth-century American Quaker John Woolman refused to write a bill of sale for a slave because he considered slavery a religious abomination. The nineteenth-century Shawnee leader Tecumseh attempted to preserve his religious purity by refusing to wear wool made by white men or to eat food prepared by white men. Vietnamese Buddhist monks immolated themselves during the 1960s to protest the military conflict in their country.

Contesting Authority

Many of the most powerful religious protests have sought to challenge occupying regimes or to contest authority that practitioners deem illegitimate. Practitioners of the late-nineteenth-century Native American Ghost Dance ritual believed the spirits of their ancestors would help them combat the U.S. military. In the Chinese Taiping Rebellion (1851–64), rebels influenced by the unusual Christianity of their founder, who believed himself to be Christ's younger brother, attempted to supplant the extant regime with a state consistent with their beliefs. In the 1980s, Poland's Catholic-influenced Solidarity trade-union movement challenged Soviet Communism. The Nicaraguan and Salvadoran popular churches of the 1970s and 1980s led the faithful during those nations' civil wars. And in Nazi Germany, the Confessing Church of Dietrich Bonhoeffer (1906–1945) and others challenged Nazi power and helped 2,000 Jews escape to freedom.

Defending Threatened Beliefs

Many protests seek to defend a practice or belief they feel is being eroded by secular authority, governmental policy, or social convention. Examples include the seventeenth-century Baptist Roger Williams's rejec-tion of theocratic government in Massachusetts to declare and protect his belief in the integrity of religious tradition, free from the corruptions of political authority, the refusal by Jehovah's Witnesses to salute national flags on the grounds that it is a form of idolatry, or the spring 1999 assembly by neo-Buddhist meditation group Falun Gong in Beijing's Tiananmen Square to protest the Chinese government's outlawing of their practice. The Hindu leader Mohandas (Mahatma) Gandhi (1869–1948) challenged laws he regarded as unjust through nonviolent resistance, which he linked to the notion of *satyagraha* ("truth force"). This strategy influenced U.S. activists, including Christian pacifists in the 1930s and civil-rights leader Martin Luther King, Jr. His legacy is also evident in antiglobalization protests (for example, in those organized by the U.S. Wicca practitioner Starhawk). More violent challenges to policies include the extreme anti-abortion group Operation Rescue, active in the 1980s and infamous for its aggressive blockades of abortion clinics and challenges to patients in the United States.

Performing Symbolic Actions

One component of many religious protests is the performance of symbolic actions before that segment of the public that protesters feel are hostile to their beliefs. For example, the Women in Black movement around the Gaza strip has contemporary Palestinian women standing in silent vigil, mourning the innocents lost in combat and claiming that violence is unacceptable. The U.S. Baptist abolitionist William Lloyd Garrison ceremoniously burned the U.S. Constitution in 1854, claiming that if it did not protect African-Americans it was useless. The international Plowshares movement performs liturgical acts at military sites, often including the symbolic act of beating swords into plowshares by hammering on weapons.

Establishing Separate Communities

Finally, one might even regard the establishment of separate communities or worldviews as a form of protest against the world. Under this heading fall the self-styled Christian militias of the late-twentieth-century United States; communities in Latin America based on liberation theology, which fuse Marxist social analysis with Christian ethics; various forms of twentieth-century global fundamentalism; apocalyptic communities and worldviews; and the Melanesian cargo cults of the late nineteenth and twentieth centuries, which believed that European abundance would be redistributed to native peoples.

Issues and Implications

There is overlap between the categories listed above, and they are linked by the presumption that there is a fundamental distinction between human laws or conventions and sacred laws. In order to preserve the integrity of the sacred, religious protesters are willing to violate human laws in various ways: assembling without permits, trespassing, or provoking arrest. These risks are assumed in order to call attention to issues and demands felt by practitioners, to contrast one source of authority with another, and to give voice or power to those who feel they lack these things. Through the use of specifically religious symbolism, performance, and disruptive activity, religious protest distinguishes itself from conventional political modes of speech and action.

As a consequence, there are several implications for religious freedom and democracy. While religions are often regarded as private (at least in contemporary Western societies), protests are highly public by nature. Protest aims to generate an audience before which to dramatize practitioners' concerns. By contrasting morally robust religious action and speech with the purportedly neutral and secular character of public space, religious protest blurs the boundary between the public and private spheres characterizing many modern societies. This shows that religious protests are significant factors in ongoing conversations about the nature of the political order the boundaries by which order is defined, and the ways in which freedom is conceived, both of which are important topics of debate that have shaped and sustain democracy.

Though all religious protesters choose to participate—however briefly or tangentially—in public affairs, their goals vary widely, encompassing everything from recognition by the state to the restoration of religious purity through either separatism or conflict. Religious protests emphasize the coherence, authority, and meaning of the practices, traditions, and identities that shape them. Additionally, they call attention to the role that competing systems of moral allegiance play in shaping political thought and action. Religious protest is thus both an enduring feature of modern societies and a conceptual category that aids in the analysis of religious freedom, the

boundary between public and private, and the content of citizenship.

Jason C. Bivins

Further Reading

Fox, R. G., & Starn, O. (1997). *Between resistance and revolution: Cultural politics and social protest.* New Brunswick, NJ: Rutgers University Press.

Freeman, J., & Johnson, V. (Eds.). (1999). *Waves of protest: Social movements since the sixties.* New York: Rowman & Littlefield.

Hanagan, M. P., Moch, L. P., & Te Brake, W. (Eds.). (1998). *Challenging authority: The historical study of contentious politics.* Minneapolis: University of Minnesota Press.

Jasper, J. (1997). *The art of moral protest.* Chicago: University of Chicago Press.

Scott, J. (1990). *Domination and the arts of resistance: Public and hidden transcripts.* New Haven, CT: Yale University Press.

Smith, C. (Ed.). (1996). *Disruptive religion: The force of faith in social movement activism.* New York: Routledge.

Stephens, J. (1998). *Anti-disciplinary politics: Sixties radicalism and postmodernism.* Cambridge, UK: Cambridge University Press.

Religion and Public Education

No First Amendment issue in the United States has generated more controversy than religion and public education. In fact, public schools continue to be the battleground for many of society's so-called culture-war conflicts. Creationism, school prayer, religious holidays, and sex education are just a few of the issues vying for the spotlight. Part of the difficulty has arisen from the fact that for more than a century, Americans did not have a suitable model for the role of religion in the nation's common schools.

First, there was what some have called the *sacred public school*. The sacred public school was a place where the nation's Protestant leanings were reflected in daily prayers and devotions oftentimes led by the classroom teacher and occasionally by visiting clergy. As Catholic immigrants poured into the county, the sacred public school began showing signs of conflict. Even after Horace Mann's "great compromise" of simply reading the Bible without commentary, there arose the thorny question of which version of the

Bible would be read—the Protestant King James or the Catholic Douay? Fights broke out. In Cincinnati and Philadelphia, schools were picketed and convents burned. A growing Jewish population was also finding itself dissatisfied with an arrangement where their children were forced to excuse themselves from the classroom each morning while Christian prayers and Bible readings took place. Protestants also began questioning school-sponsored religious exercises, and one by one states began eliminating the centuries-old practice.

What was left of the sacred public school model came crashing down with the Supreme Court's prayer decisions of the early 1960s—*Engel v. Vitale* and *Abbington v. Schemmp*. In its place arose an equally flawed model—the so-called naked public school.

Fueled by a sincere yet misguided attempt to get their constitutional house in order, some schools, in the name of church-state separation, sought to create a "religion-free zone." The result was policies that infringed upon the First Amendment rights of students and a curriculum that was stripped of any teaching about religion. Schools routinely denied students the right to form religious clubs despite having a variety of extracurricular student groups, and textbooks largely ignored religion, thereby failing to teach accurate history. After decades of litigation, most school officials came to see that the naked public school, like its sacred counterpart of the past, was both unjust and, in some extreme cases, unconstitutional.

Before turning to the new consensus-based model that is rapidly replacing both the naked and sacred public school, a look at the underlying constitutional framework is in order.

The Constitutional Framework

During the first century of public education, there was little occasion for constitutional analysis due primarily to the fact that the First Amendment had not yet been applied to the states. By the middle of the twentieth century, however, the "liberty" portion of the Fourteenth Amendment ("No state shall deprive any person of life, liberty or property without due process of law . . . .") had been interpreted to include the liberties set forth in the First Amendment. Schools were now subject to the full impact of both the establishment clause and the free exercise clause.

The Establishment Clause

The establishment clause prohibits government policies and practices "respecting an establishment of religion." Its most famous explanation came from Justice Hugo Black in the landmark 1947 case of *Everson v. Board of Education*:

> The Establishment of Religion Clause means at least this: Neither a state nor the federal government may set up a church. Neither can pass laws that aid one religion, aid all religions, or prefer one religion over another. Neither can force a person to go to or to remain away from church against his will or force him to profess a belief or disbelief in any religion. . . . Neither a state nor the federal government may, openly or secretly, participate in the affairs of any religious organizations or groups and vice versa. In the words of Jefferson, the clause against establishment of religion was intended to erect "a wall of separation between church and state."

In 1971, the Supreme Court crafted a three-part test to assist courts in applying the establishment clause. The so-called Lemon Test (named after the case of *Lemon v. Kurtzman*, 1971) has been criticized by numerous Supreme Court justices but, in the absence of a replacement enjoying the support of a majority of the justices, continues to be the yardstick by which most lower courts decide cases. The test asks three questions. A positive answer to each question is required if the challenged government action is to pass muster under the establishment clause.

The first question is whether the challenged governmental action has a legitimate civic or secular purpose. Laws passed solely for religious purposes are not permitted under the Lemon Test.

Requiring a secular purpose does not mean that lawmakers can never be motivated by religion. To the contrary, a legislator's primary motivation for supporting a program for the homeless may be his or her religious convictions. Yet, the law would pass constitutional muster because it has a clear civic or secular purpose of attending to the welfare of the poor.

Similarly, Justice Sandra Day O'Connor has made clear that accommodating the religious beliefs and practices of students can also be a legitimate purpose. For example, schools may label pork products or permit students to pray voluntarily on school grounds without violating the establishment clause.

In fact, as discussed below, some accommodation of religion may even be required by the free exercise clause.

The second question under the Lemon Test is whether the challenged governmental action has a primary effect that neither advances nor inhibits religion. In other words, the primary effect must be *neutral*. It is not the business of government to either encourage or discourage religious faith. For example, while there might be a legitimate secular purpose for inviting a professional athlete to speak in a school assembly about the danger of drugs, the speaker would not be permitted to deliver a proselytizing religious message. Neither would it be appropriate for the school to provide a captive audience of students to a speaker who wished to discourage religious commitments. Neutrality, not hostility, is the standard under Lemon.

The third question is whether the challenged government action creates "excessive government entanglement" with religion. Although excessive entanglement rarely arise in the public school context, it could arise if schools began trying to monitor or exercise control over the religious activities of students. In most cases, if school policy has a neutral purpose and effect, it will pass muster under the establishment clause.

As mentioned, a number of Supreme Court justices have recommended alternatives to Lemon. Justice O'Connor, for example, likes to ask whether a particular government action has the purpose or effect of endorsing religion. According to O'Connor, a citizen's standing in a religious order should have no effect on his or her standing in the political order. State endorsements for or against religion are violative of this core establishment clause principle.

Similarly, Justice Anthony Kennedy has coined his own establishment clause test. For Kennedy, government actions do not violate the establishment clause unless they tend to coerce citizens in matters of faith. Although Kennedy's coercion test would appear less stringent than either Lemon or the endorsement test, he once used it to invalidate a Rhode Island graduation prayer that was only psychologically coercive.

With the possible exception of Chief Justice William Rehnquist, who has opined that the establishment clause was intended to prevent only the designation of a single national church, the remainder of the justices appear focused on the question of what is meant by governmental neutrality toward religion. Laws with a clear purpose and effect of advancing or inhibiting religion are likely to be struck down as unconstitutional for the foreseeable future.

Most of the current litigation under the establishment clause is focused on the rights of student speakers and when those rights might be subordinate to a captive audience's right to be left alone. Although lower courts are divided over where to draw the line, the Supreme Court has held that students do not have the right to offer prayers over the public address system at a high school football game.

The Free Exercise Clause

The First Amendment forbids any law prohibiting the free exercise of religion. While the protection sounds absolute, religious rights, like all First Amendment rights, have their limits. For example, a parent would not be allowed to offer his or her first-born child as a human sacrifice even if done in the name of religion. So, what are the limits?

Historically, courts used a four-part test to resolve cases arising under the free exercise clause.

The test, which was crafted in the 1963 Supreme Court case of *Sherbert v. Verner,* is often referred to as the Sherbert Test.

The first part of the test asks whether the person making the claim (usually a student or parent) has a *sincere* religious belief. There is no requirement that the belief be popular, sensible, or even rational—only sincere. The American arrangement does not allow judges or other government officials to decide whether or not a particular religious belief is worthwhile or legitimate.

The second question asks whether the government, or in this case the school, has imposed a "substantial burden" on the claimant's religion. Burdens arise when the government either forbids an activity required by one's faith or requires an activity forbidden by one's faith. If, for example, an Orthodox Jewish boy were told he could not attend public school with his yarmulke (i.e., skullcap), the burden on his faith would appear substantial. Similarly, attempts to keep a nondisruptive evangelical student from praying or reading his Bible would appear to be a substantial burden on his religious exercise. On the other hand, it would not be a substantial burden to impose reasonable time, place, and manner restrictions on a student's distribution of religious literature. More difficult questions arise when it comes to reading assignments that may be offensive to a student's faith. Although at least one federal judge has held that forcing students to read offensive passages may constitute a substantial burden on his religious exercise, the majority view seems to be that mere exposure to religiously offensive ideas without any attempt to force the student to ascribe to those ideas does not constitute a substantial burden on religious exercise.

Assuming the school has imposed a substantial burden on a student's sincerely held religious beliefs or practices, the Sherbert Test then asks two additional questions of the school. First, does the school have a "compelling" reason for imposing the restriction? And, second, is there a less restrictive means of accomplishing the school's compelling interest?

Schools have a number of compelling interests that spring to mind: safety, order and discipline, and teaching basic academic skills, for example. The Sherbert Test does not stop here, however. Even if the school has a compelling reason for its actions, Sherbert requires the school to exhaust all other possibilities before restricting a student's religious exercise.

For example, a school might have a compelling interest in teaching a student to read, but it might not have a compelling interest for forcing the student read a particular assignment. If the goal was mere reading comprehension, certainly an alternative reading assignment could accomplish the same goal. On the other hand, not every request for religious accommodation is feasible. If, for example, a parent requested an excusal for her child each time a religion other than her own were mentioned in class, a course in world history would become impossible. The student would be hopping up to leave on virtually a daily basis. In such cases, the parent's only option might be to withdraw her child from the public school altogether.

At bottom, the Sherbert Test was a balancing test that weighed the interest of the individual student against those of the school. In some cases, students won; in other cases, they lost; but in every case the government was required to provide significant justification for substantially burdening a student's sincere religious practices.

In 1990, the constitutional landscape changed. In *Employment Division v. Smith*, a sharply divided Supreme Court voted to restrict the Sherbert Test to unemployment compensation cases and to eliminate the decades-old requirement that the government satisfy the strictures of the compelling interest test. The test's application was limited to a handful of cases where a particular religious group or practice was singled out for discriminatory treatment. Neutral government actions (i.e., not aimed at a particular religion) that had an incidental effect of burdening religious exercise were no longer subject to challenge under the free exercise clause.

A great deal of confusion has arisen in the wake of the Supreme Court's *Smith* decision. First, the Court's opinion left open the possibility that the Sherbert Test might still apply if a person's free exercise claim could be linked to another constitutional claim such as freedom of speech or association. Lower courts have split over whether these so-called hybrid cases should be taken seriously. At the same time, nearly half of the fifty states have continued applying the Sherbert Test under either their own state constitutions or under separate civil rights legislation. Congress passed national legislation aimed at restoring the Sherbert Test to all cases arising under the free exercise clause, but it was struck down by the Supreme Court as an unconstitutional encroachment on states' rights. As a result, schools are left with a hodgepodge of state and federal law pertaining to free exercise claims. Local counsel should be consulted to determine which legal standards apply in a particular school district.

A New Consensus Emerges

Despite continuing litigation under the establishment clause and confusion under the free exercise clause, a new consensus-based model has arisen for resolving questions pertaining to religion in schools. Unlike the naked or sacred public schools of the past, this new model is based on a shared understanding of what constitutes government neutrality toward religion.

The new consensus is best captured by a joint statement of principles entitled *Religious Liberty, Public Education and the Future of American Democracy* and issued by twenty-three leading educational and religious organizations spanning America's ideological spectrum. The sponsoring organizations are American Association of School Administrators, American Center for Law and Justice, American Federation of Teachers, Anti-Defamation League, Association for Supervision and Curriculum Development, Carnegie Foundation for the Advancement of Teaching, Catholic League for

Religious and Civil Rights, Central Conference of American Rabbis, Christian Coalition, Christian Educators Association International, Christian Legal Society, Council on Islamic Education, The First Amendment Center, National Association of Elementary School Principals, National Association of Evangelicals, National Association of Secondary School Principals, National PTA, National Council of Churches, National School Boards Association, People for the American Way, Phi Delta Kappa, and the Union of American Hebrew Congregations. The statement reads in part:

> Religious liberty is an inalienable right of every person. As Americans, we all share the responsibility to guard that right for every citizen . . .
>
> Public schools may not inculcate nor inhibit religion. They must be places where religion and religious conviction are treated with fairness and respect. Public schools uphold the First Amendment when they protect the religious liberty rights of students of all faiths or none. Schools demonstrate fairness when they ensure that the curriculum includes study about religion, where appropriate, as an important part of a complete education . . . Parents are recognized as having the primary responsibility for the upbringing of their children, including education . . .
>
> (*Religious Liberty, Public Education and the Future of American Democracy* 1995, 11–12)

This statement of principles, along with the *Religion in the Public Schools: Joint Statement of Current Law* issued by the American Jewish Congress, American Jewish Committee, Baptist Joint Committee, and many of the organizations listed above, has become the framework for the *civil* public school model that is being implemented by school board policies in many of the nation's school districts.

Implications

For two centuries, Americans have struggled to define the proper role of religion in the nation's public schools. The failed models of the past included attempts to impose religion or to eliminate it from schools entirely.

Although the Supreme Court continues to wrestle with both its establishment clause and free exercise jurisprudence, many of the nation's leading religious and educational groups have seized upon a model that seems both constitutionally permissible and educationally sound. This new model affirms the religious liberty rights of believers and nonbelievers alike. It calls upon each citizen to take responsibility for the rights or others, and it tries to create schools that are fair, neutral, and respectful of all religions. In addition, study about religion is taken seriously in the curriculum as an important part of a child's education.

Most important, perhaps, is the acknowledgment that in a democratic society, differences of opinion on such a fundamental societal issue will remain. In the words of the joint statement of principles, *Religious Liberty, Public Education and the Future of American Democracy* (1995, 13):

> Civil debate, the cornerstone of a true democracy, is vital to the success of any effort to improve and reform America's public schools. Personal attacks, name-calling, ridicule and similar tactics destroy the fabric of our society and undermine the educational mission of our schools. Even when our differences are deep, all parties engaged in public disputes should treat one another with civility and respect, and should strive to be fair and accurate. Through constructive dialogue, we have much to learn from one another.

Oliver Thomas

See also Fourteenth Amendment; Free Exercise Clause

Further Reading

Haynes, C., & Thomas, O. (2002). *Finding common ground: A guide to religious liberty in public schools.* Arlington, VA: First Amendment Center.

Nord, W. (1995). *Religion and American education: Rethinking a national dilemma.* Chapel Hill: University of North Carolina Press.

Nord, W., & Haynes, C. (2000). *Taking religion seriously across the curriculum.* Arlington, VA: First Amendment Center.

Lynn, B., Stern, M., & Thomas, O. (1995). *The right to religious liberty: The basic ACLU guide to religious rights.* Carbondale: Southern Illinois University Press.

Miller, R. T., & Flowers, R. B. (1998). *Toward benevolent neutrality: Church, state, and the Supreme Court.* Waco, TX: Baylor University Press.

Noonan, J. T., & Gaffney, E. M. *Religious freedom: History, cases, and other materials on the interaction of religion and government.* Berkeley: University of California Press.

Religion in the public schools: Joint statement of current law. (1995, April). Retrieved 30 October 2002, from http://www.ed.gov/Speeches/04-1995/prayer.html

Religious liberty, public education and the future of American democracy. (1995). Retrieved 30 October 30, 2002, from http://www.freedomforum.org/publications/first/findingcommonground/B02.ReligiousLiberty.pdf

Court Cases

Abbington v. Schemmp, 374 U.S. 203 (1963).

Employment Division v. Smith, 494 U.S. 872 (1990).

Engel v. Vitale, 370 U.S. 421 (1962).

Everson v. Board of Education, 330 U.S. 1 (1947).

Lemon v. Kurtzman, 403 U.S. 602 (1971).

Sherbert v. Verner, 374 U.S. 398 (1963).

Religion in the Courtroom

Although popularly considered a secular setting, the U.S. courtroom has not escaped the trappings and influences of religion. Some are obvious, as when a witness puts his or her hand on a Bible and swears to tell the truth, "so help me God." Others are not at all obvious. Jurors and judges may make factual or legal decisions based in part on their religious faith; lawyers may attempt to persuade jurors by making claims of religious duty.

Religion and Actors in the Courtroom

Upon reaching the witness stand, witnesses are ordinarily required to swear an oath to tell the truth. Quakers refuse for religious reasons to swear, and courts in British colonial America accommodated their religious sensibilities by allowing Quakers to make an affirmation. This option of affirming rather than swearing was initially limited to religious believers; indeed, until the early 1800s, a witness who was not a religious believer was prohibited from testifying. A nonreligious witness was considered incompetent to testify because that witness did not believe in a future state of rewards and punishments (heaven and hell), and hence, it was thought, would have no incentive to tell the truth. By the 1830s courts rejected this testimonial prohibition, and the nonbeliever was allowed to testify in court. However, a party was permitted to ask questions about a witness's lack of religious belief and was allowed to argue to the jury that it should reject a witness's testimony if the witness was not a religious believer. This attack on a witness's credibility on the grounds of a lack of religious belief was largely prohibited by the end of the nineteenth century. Since the early twentieth century religious belief (or lack thereof) has been declared irrelevant to the credibility of a witness, and the rules of evidence in all states and in the federal court system prohibit any party from suggesting that a witness's religious beliefs have any connection to the truthfulness of his or her testimony.

This limitation has not solved the problem of bias or prejudice that can arise when the jury gains knowledge of the religious faith of a party, witness, or lawyer in the case. Many religiously devout persons wear identifiable religious garb (a yarmulke or a crucifix) in public as a sign of their faith, or as a religious duty, while others may bring religious books, such as the Bible or Qur'an, to the courtroom. Several judges have attempted to solve this problem by prohibiting persons appearing in court from wearing religiously identifiable clothing. Although this solution prevents the jury from learning the person's religious faith, it may infringe upon that person's religious liberty. The better practice is for the judge to instruct the jury that it must determine the facts based on the evidence, not on a person's religious beliefs, and to trust the jury to follow those instructions.

Juries are used in criminal and civil cases, which makes them extraordinarily powerful bodies in U.S. law. To constrain the exercise of this power, lawyers for the parties (in most state cases) and judges (in federal cases) are permitted to ask questions of prospective jurors to determine whether they are suited to jury service. Although there is no empirical data supporting this claim, some lawyers believe that a person's religious faith foreshadows how that person will judge a case and will attempt to learn about the faith of the prospective jurors. The trial judge has substantial authority to control what questions the lawyer asks, including questions about religious faith. However, some states ask jurors to include their religious faith on jury information forms, and sometimes even general questions may reveal information about a person's religious beliefs.

After questioning has ended, each side may exercise several peremptory challenges, excluding some persons from the jury. The U.S. Supreme Court has held that a peremptory challenge does not need to be supported by any reason, except when that challenge may be based on racial or gender-based discrimination. The Supreme Court has not yet decided whether a peremptory challenge based on the religion of the prospective juror violates the First Amendment of the Constitution. State courts addressing this issue based on state law have reached contradictory results: Several state courts have held that their state constitution permits peremptory challenges even when the reason for that challenge is the prospective juror's religion; other courts have held the opposite. The latter courts allow a party to exercise a peremptory challenge when a prospective juror's religious beliefs might affect his ability to follow the law.

Jury deliberations may turn on the religious beliefs of one or more members of the jury. In one dramatic case from the 1980s, a juror claimed that she had received a revelation from God that the defendant was guilty if his lawyer did not look the juror in the eye during closing argument. The lawyer failed to look her in the eye, the juror informed the rest of the jurors of her revelation during deliberations, and the defendant was found guilty. The defendant claimed that the juror had tainted the rest of the jury in deciding guilt based on a religious revelation. On appeal, the court held that the juror's declaration that she was voting to convict based on a revelation from God was not reversible error. Although it is impermissible to bring a Bible to jury deliberations for assistance in determining the verdict, members of the jury may pray, and courts will not reverse a jury's decision even when deliberations were affected by a general religious influence.

A judge is not required to forfeit his religious beliefs upon assuming judicial office, but may not base his decisions on his religious views. When announcing the reasons for a decision, a judge's use of religious metaphors or stories is permissible to illustrate the judge's proper exercise of judicial discretion. However, a judge may not use offense to her religion in determining an appropriate criminal punishment. A judge need not withdraw from a case merely because a party is the religious organization to which she belongs, or because a party attends the same house of worship.

Religious Claims in Court

Just as one may not be punished according to Biblical precepts, a person may not be convicted for violating religious law. Nevertheless, particularly in death penalty cases, where the stakes and emotions run high, both prosecutors and defense lawyers often invoke claims of religious duty or religious metaphors, particularly statements from the Bible, during closing argument. Some courts have barred any mention of religion in closing arguments; others have held that some, but not all, religiously based arguments are impermissible, and still others permit broad references to religion in death penalty cases. All three solutions are fraught with problems. Some religious stories have passed into the secular culture, partly because they resonate strongly in U.S. culture. Those stories are powerful not necessarily because they are religiously based but because they are timeless and universal. An absolute ban on religious references would deprive counsel of the use of those stories. On the other hand, allowing unbounded arguments based on religion may impermissibly imply to some jurors that they may follow religious law in deliberations. Finally, context-driven assessments of religiously based arguments are troublesome because the context cannot be replicated on appeal, which places an extraordinary burden on trial court judges.

Religious organizations are regularly parties to lawsuits. Most of these lawsuits are unexceptional and cause no constitutional concern. Determining whether a person was an employee of a religious institution, or ascertaining whether the religious organization is responsible for an injury suffered on property it owns or controls rarely is controversial. However, some lawsuits raise fundamental issues of religious liberty and therefore may not be decided in the civil-court system, even if the cases are couched in secular terms. For example, some religious organizations become bitterly divided on theological issues. Resolving those issues is clearly not within the province of civil courts. Those theological divisions, however, may cause two or more groups to claim ownership of the property of the organization. When such a disagreement reaches the civil courts, the courts are required, as a matter of constitutional law, to refrain from determining which faction is the true claimant to the property. Instead, the court is limited to using neutral principles of law, that is, principles of law unrelated to religious claims to the property, in determining the owner of the property of the religious organization. This prevents secular courts from interfering with the religious liberty of the organization. However, the fact that it forces religious organizations to organize their ownership and control principles according to secular law may itself affect the religious liberty of that organization.

Religious organizations also employ thousands of persons. In some circumstances, disaffected employees may sue for violation of contract, or may invoke the protections of labor or employment discrimination laws. When a law interferes with the religious liberty of the organization, an employee's efforts to use the protections of that law will fail because the organization is constitutionally permitted to arrange itself largely exclusive of state control. The difficult question is when this constitutional protection applies. As a constitutional matter, a court may not order a religious organization to install a person as a minister, priest, or rabbi, but it might be permitted to order the organization to rehire as a teacher someone who was fired for violating a tenet of the organization.

Courts rarely permit a criminal defendant to claim innocence because his actions were based on his religion. For example, parents may be held responsible for the death of their child if they relied solely on religious healing rather than taking the child to a medical doctor. Religious duties are superseded by legal duties as a matter of criminal law.

Evidence and Religion

In addition to the rules concerning witnesses noted above, there are two other evidentiary rules specifically directed to matters of religion.

In 1813, when most Americans were Protestant, a Roman Catholic priest was called to testify about a conversation he had with a parishioner concerning stolen goods. The priest asked that he be excused from testifying, on the ground that the conversation was made during the Catholic sacrament of confession. The trial court agreed, declaring that priest-penitent communications were protected from disclosure in court. The priest-penitent privilege, as it was known, was initially limited to communications between a Roman Catholic priest and a Roman Catholic penitent, for those communications were a sacrament of the Roman Catholic Church. Thus, communications between a Protestant minister and a member of his congregation were not protected from disclosure in court, because there was no sacrament of confession in Protestant ecclesiology. As the privilege became more accepted, several states expanded the privilege to protect confidential communications between ministers or rabbis and an individual when made for the purpose of communicating with the cleric as a spiritual adviser.

When the Federal Rules of Evidence were proposed in the early 1970s, a "Communications to Clergy" privilege was proposed. It defined a clergyman as "a minister, priest, rabbi, or other similar functionary" (*Rules of Evidence for United States Courts and Magistrates* 1973). Although Congress did not adopt this privilege, every federal court to address the matter of clergy-communicant privilege has held that it exists as a matter of common law, and that it extends beyond communications made during the sacrament of confession to a Roman Catholic priest. This broader-based privilege was acknowledged by about half of the states in 1900, and by 1960, most states recognized this privilege. All states accept some form or clergy-communicant privilege today.

The rules of evidence generally prohibit the use of hearsay evidence. One exception to this rule is the "dying declaration" exception, in which a person (the "declarant"), while conscious of dying, says something like, "Dave shot me." The justification for this hearsay exception is that a person aware he is about to die will not lie, a presumption that is traced to Christian beliefs about the afterlife. This exception applies to all declarants, however, regardless of their religious affiliation (or lack thereof).

Implications and Outlook

The United States is often described as an incorrigibly religious nation. As long as Americans remain religious, issues concerning the metes and bounds of the liberty of religious believers and the duty of the state to remain neutral regarding religion will arise. Even the courtroom, ordinarily perceived as a secular institution of the religiously neutral state, will remain a setting for such issues.

Michael Ariens

Further Reading

Ariens, M. (1992). Evidence of religion and the religion of evidence. *Buffalo Law Review, 40*(65), 65–111.

Ariens, M., & Destro, R. A. (2002). *Religious liberty in a pluralistic society* (2nd ed.). Durham, NC: Carolina Academic Press.

Collett, T. (2000). The king's good servant, but God's first: The role of religion in judicial decisionmaking. *South Texas Law Review, 41*(1277): 1277–1300.

Rules of Evidence for United States Courts and Magistrates (1973). Retrieved November 17, 2002, from http://

www.michaelariens.com/evidence/freandtre/fre-frame.htm#Rule 506

Yellin, J. C. (1983). The history and current status of the clergy-penitent privilege. *Santa Clara Law Review, 23*(95), 95–157.

Religious Displays on Public Property

Religious displays on public property are controversial in the United States insofar as the government (which by definition owns public property) is perceived as endorsing or "establishing" the religion or religions that the display is intended to celebrate or invoke. Examples of such displays include Christmas nativity scenes or Hanukkah menorahs erected in town squares during the winter holiday season, or Ten Commandments monuments installed outside state capitol buildings. In each instance a relationship—real or perceived—is created between government and religion; the controversy arises over the exact nature of that relationship, and whether or at what point the relationship violates constitutional principles of the separation of church and state. The U.S. Supreme Court has explicitly outlined the context in which religious holiday displays on public property can pass constitutional muster, and may soon revisit its rulings on Ten Commandments displays. Yet the law in this area is not completely settled, because recent establishment clause decisions embrace competing and sometimes contradictory

A religious sign on the highway between Columbus and Augusta, Georgia, in 1940. *Marion Post Wolcott,*
COURTESY OF LIBRARY OF CONGRESS, PRINTS AND PHOTOGRAPHS DIVISION, FSA-OWI COLLECTION.

legal theories, indicating that the full impact of the Court's ongoing shift toward a more accommodating stance (that is, a stance more tolerant of religious displays on public property) is not yet clear.

Religious Displays and the First Amendment

The U.S. Constitution protects religious freedom primarily through two pithy clauses in its First Amendment: "Congress shall make no law respecting an establishment of religion, or prohibiting the free exercise thereof . . ." With regard to religious displays on public property, the central legal issue is whether a particular display constitutes an establishment of religion as a consequence of the real or perceived connection that exists between church and state in that situation. (Free exercise and free speech rights enter the mix when a privately funded display is placed in a public forum.) To answer this question, state and federal courts rely upon precedent provided by several landmark Supreme Court decisions, most notably *Lemon v. Kurtzman* (1971). In the *Lemon* decision, the Court articulated a three-pronged test for assessing whether a government statute or practice violates the establishment clause. To be constitutional, the statute or practice must have "a secular legislative purpose," its "primary effect" must be neither the advancement nor inhibition of religion, and it must not foster "an excessive government entanglement with religion." The *Lemon* test, as it became known, has served as the starting point for establishment clause jurisprudence for over thirty years, notwithstanding several modifications and reformulations along the way. Several of the most conservative members of the present Court, led by Antonin Scalia, have argued that the *Lemon* test ought to be scrapped in favor of an approach that more fully accommodates religious expression, but for the present *Lemon* remains the key precedent.

Three kinds of religious displays on public property have generated the most legal controversies since 1980. First, there are government-sponsored celebrations or acknowledgements of religious holidays (such as Christmas or Hanukkah) with a public display of religious icons, symbols, or objects. Second are the displays of religious objects or symbols (such as a cross) by private citizens or groups in public places known as public forums (places of public assembly and debate). Third are the celebrations or acknowledgements of religion's influence on U.S. political and legal history with the installation of plaques or monuments inscribed with religious symbols or passages, especially the Ten Commandments. (There are of course many other ways in which religion is displayed on some sort of government property: religious language or symbols in government mottos, anthems, pledges, or seals; religious prayer or worship undertaken by individuals or groups on public property; and public activities undertaken by chaplains employed by legislatures or armed forces, to name a few. Each of these examples raise important constitutional questions, but they are not religious displays in the most common use of the phrase.) The next three sections take up each kind of display in turn.

Government-Sponsored Holiday Displays on Public Property

Federal, state, and local governments in the United States celebrate a wide range of holidays during the year, including some of religious origin, such as Christmas and Hanukkah. These winter holidays are often commemorated by the installation of festive displays in parks, capitol buildings, town halls or courthouses—public places of high visibility and unfettered access. In the 1980s a number of these public holiday displays were challenged in the courts as unconstitutional establishments of religion; two such cases were argued before the U.S. Supreme Court, which rendered landmark decisions that continue to serve as good law today.

In *Lynch v. Donnelly* (1984), the Court ruled five to four that the city of Pawtucket, Rhode Island, did not violate the establishment clause when it included a Christian nativity scene in its annual Christmas display in the city's central shopping district. Among other things, the display included a Christmas tree, a "Seasons Greetings" banner, and life-sized figures of Santa Claus and his mythical reindeer—all of which proved to be important as the Court evaluated the display's religious context. Applying the *Lemon* test, the Court majority determined that the nativity scene had a legitimate secular purpose (the depiction of the holiday's historical origins) and that, viewed in the context of the holiday season, it was not part of a government effort to convey a particular religious message.

In an important concurrence to *Lynch*, Justice Sandra Day O'Connor reformulated the *Lemon* test to ask whether a government action conveys a message of *endorsement* of religion. Government endorsement of religion is invalid, she wrote, because it "sends a message to nonadherents that they are outsiders, not full members of the political community, and an accompanying message to adherents that they are insiders, favored members of the political community. The key to assessing whether the government's use of an object with religious meaning has the effect of endorsing religion is to ask what viewers may fairly understand to be the purpose of the display. That inquiry, in turn, depends upon the context in which the contested object appears: hanging a religious painting in a museum, for example, would not neutralize the painting's religious content, but it would negate any message of government endorsement. By O'Connor's account, each government practice must be judged in its unique circumstances to determine whether it endorses religion.

Several Justices drew upon O'Connor's "endorsement test" in *Allegheny County v. Greater Pittsburgh ACLU* (1989) to clarify the permissible contexts for religious displays on public property. In *Allegheny*, the Court considered challenges to two separate holiday displays in Pittsburgh: a nativity scene, displayed alone on the grand staircase of the Allegheny County Courthouse; and a large Hanukkah menorah displayed alongside a Christmas tree and a sign promoting liberty on the grounds of the city-county building. Both displays had been donated to the city by religious groups and were maintained (at minimal cost) by government employees. The nine justices wrote five separate opinions in the case, with a five-member majority ruling that the nativity scene was unconstitutional and six members holding that the menorah display was constitutionally sound. Looking at the particular physical settings of each display, the Court found that the nativity scene (displayed without any nonreligious symbols such as Santa Claus, a sleigh, or reindeer) clearly conveyed an endorsement of Christianity, while the menorah (displayed alongside secular symbols) merely conveyed a recognition of cultural diversity.

Private Religious Displays in Public Forums

Lynch and *Allegheny* remain the controlling precedents for adjudicating challenges to government-sponsored religious displays on public property, and the Supreme Court has refused to hear additional cases on the topic since then. But six years after *Allegheny*, the Court did address the closely related issue of *private* religious displays on public property.

383

The fact that a religious display is located on public property is of course a critical aspect of this controversial issue. In most cases, religious displays on private property are protected as manifestations of free speech or the free exercise of religion, but the same displays on public property may violate the establishment clause. In the broadest sense, *public property* means the interior or exterior of any property owned by federal, state, or local governments; this includes public schools, city halls, courthouses, and capitol buildings, as well as parks, streets, sidewalks, town squares, plazas, and other public spaces. But the Supreme Court has recognized some of these places—those that have been devoted, by long tradition or government fiat, to public assembly and debate—as public forums, places in which the state's right to limit expressive activity is sharply circumscribed. When a place is considered a public forum, the courts are less likely to consider a religious display on the site to be an establishment or endorsement of religion.

During the 1993 winter holiday season, members of the Ku Klux Klan (KKK) sought a permit to construct an unattended cross on the plaza around the Ohio state house in Columbus. State law makes the plaza, known as Capitol Square, a forum for discussion of public questions and for public activities; its Advisory Board holds responsibility for regulating access to the square. The Advisory Board denied the KKK's application to erect the cross, arguing that the display would be construed as government endorsement of the organization's hateful and intolerant message. The Supreme Court rejected the Board's claim, ruling that the proposed display was private religious speech, fully protected under the First Amendment's free speech clause. Because Capitol Square is designated as a traditional public forum, where any group may express its views, the Court held that a reasonably informed observer would not see the KKK cross as the government's endorsement of its message. (In December 2002 the Supreme Court revisited this issue when it reviewed a Virginia law banning cross burning; in oral arguments, Justice Clarence Thomas appeared to reverse the stance he took for free speech protection of cross burning in *Pinette*, but the case has not yet been decided.)

Displays of the Ten Commandments on Public Property

An increasingly controversial kind of religious display on public property involves the Ten Commandments, or Decalogue, believed by Jews and Christians to be a fundamental theological, ethical and legal code given by God to Moses. The first four commandments, collectively known as the First Table, concern the relation between believers and God; the last six commandments, or Second Table, concern relations among believers. As one of the most ancient codes of conduct in the Western world, the Decalogue has deeply influenced Western conceptions of right and wrong, and thus it has also influenced, at least indirectly, the development of Western law. Despite recent historical studies that suggest otherwise, some advocates of Ten Commandments displays have also argued that U.S. laws were originally based on the Decalogue, and that such displays would therefore be merely historical, not religious, in nature. Others argue that the religious content is exactly what should be highlighted in public displays of the Ten Commandments.

In *Stone v. Graham* (1980), the U.S. Supreme Court did not explicitly deny that the Ten Commandments was a source of the U.S. legal code, but it nevertheless struck down a Kentucky law that required the state's public schools to post a copy of the Ten Commandments in every classroom. Mindful of the special concerns that arise when the religious consciences of schoolchildren are at stake, the Court ruled that posting a copy of the Decalogue (which it called "undeniably a sacred text") in every classroom was a form of religious coercion.

Since the early twentieth century, a number of civic, fraternal, and religious groups have donated dozens of stone monuments depicting the Ten Commandments to city and state governments across the United States. Many of these monuments were installed in courthouses, town squares, and state capitols, only to be removed by court order decades later when civil-rights groups challenged their presence as violations of the establishment clause. In response, legislatures, judges, and government executives have tried to find ways to secularize new and existing Ten Commandments displays in a fashion analogous to the secularizing force of a Santa Clause statue alongside a Christmas nativity scene. Most of these attempts have thus far failed. From 2000 to 2002 alone, high-profile cases in federal courts in Alabama, Indiana, and Kentucky led to the removal of existing Ten Commandments monuments or the cancellation of proposed monuments. A contrary ruling was handed down, however, in September 2002 when a federal judge in Austin, Texas, upheld the constitutionality of a monument on the state capitol grounds. If the Fifth Circuit upholds the Austin ruling, the Supreme Court may very well choose to adjudicate the differences.

Outlook for the Future

If the last twenty years are any indication, the near future will bring more establishment clause litigation over religious displays on public property of all kinds. The present Supreme Court has demonstrated a willingness to take dramatic steps away from older doctrines of separation—especially those concerning public education—and the *Lemon* test appears to be a target of the more conservative justices on the bench. Whether Justice O'Connor's endorsement test will eventually predominate over the approaches taken by Justices Kennedy and Scalia, for example, will have important implications for the future direction of the Court.

Erik C. Owens

See also Civil Religion; Establishment, Equal Treatment; Establishment, Separation of Church and State; Free Exercise Clause

Further Reading

Green, S. K. (2000). The fount of everything just and right? The Ten Commandments as a source of American law. *Journal of Law and Religion, 14*(2), 525–558.

Hamburger, P. (2002). *Separation of church and state.* Cambridge, MA: Harvard University Press.

Karst, K. (1992). The First Amendment, the politics of religion and the symbols of government. *Harvard Civil Rights–Civil Liberties Law Review, 27,* 503–530.

Perry, M. J. (1997). *Religion in politics: Constitutional and moral perspectives.* Oxford, UK: Oxford University Press.

Smith, S. D. (2001). *Getting over equality: A critical diagnosis of religious freedom in America.* New York: New York University Press.

Sullivan, W. F. (1994). *Paying the words extra: Religious discourse in the Supreme Court of the United States.* Cambridge, MA: Harvard University Center for the Study of World Religions.

Underwood, J. L. (2001). The proper role of religion in the public schools: Equal access instead of official indoctrination. *Villanova Law Review, 46,* 487–536.

Vicario, T. A. (2001). Religious monuments under attack: Undermining religion for the benefit of the irreligious in *Books v. City of Elkhart,* 235 F.3d (7th Cir. 2000). *Hamline Law Review, 25,* 151–191.

Witte, J., Jr. (2000). *Religion and the American constitutional experiment: Essential rights and liberties.* Boulder, CO: Westview Press.

Court Cases

Allegheny County v. Greater Pittsburgh ACLU, 492 U.S. 573 (1989).

Books v. City of Elkhart, 235 F.3d 292 (7th Cir. 2000), *cert. denied,* 532 U.S. 1058 (2001).

Capitol Square Review and Advisory Board v. Pinette, 515 U.S. 753 (1995).

Good News Club v. Milford Central School, U.S. 99-2036 (2001).

Indiana Civil Liberties Union v. O'Bannon, 259 F.3d 766 (7th Cir. 2001), *cert. denied,* 534 U.S. 1162 (2002).

Lemon v. Kurtzman, 403 U.S. 602 (1971).

Lynch v. Donnelly, 465 U.S. 668 (1984).

Marsh v. Chambers, 463 U.S. 783 (1983).

Perry Education v. Perry Local Educator's Association, 460 U.S. 37 (1983).

Stone v. Graham, 449 U.S. 39 (1980).

United States v. Grace, 461 U.S. 171 (1983).

Virginia v. Black, U.S. 01-1107 (2002).

Zelman v. Simmons-Harris, U.S. 00-1751 (2002).

Religious Nationalism

Religious nationalism exists where religion provides the ideology that gives legitimacy to the nation-state. It is a fact of contemporary international life; whether the issue is building, restructuring, or maintaining a nation, the process is, all over the world, deeply infused with religion. Religious nationalism connotes a deep and inherent connection between religious commitment and patriotism; it suggests a religious dimension to the national cause, whatever it might be.

Religious nationalism is a discourse that transforms preexistent forms of culture. In effect, it produces a national culture that can be described as "ethnoreligious"; this connotes a character that is grounded in both an ethnic or national nature and also in a religion. It has been associated both with loyalties to particular ethnic religious communities and also with commitments to certain political-religious ideologies.

PREAMBLE TO THE CONSTITUTION OF THE ISLAMIC REPUBLIC OF IRAN (ADOPTED ON: 24 OCT 1979)

The Preamble to the constitution of Iran is a good example of the ideology of religious nationalism in a contemporary nation.

The Constitution of the Islamic Republic of Iran advances the cultural, social, political, and economic institutions of Iranian society based on Islamic principles and norms, which represent an honest aspiration of the Islamic Ummah. This aspiration was exemplified by the nature of the great Islamic Revolution of Iran, and by the course of the Muslim people's struggle, from its beginning until victory, as reflected in the decisive and forceful calls raised by all segments of the populations. Now, at the threshold of this great victory, our nation, with all its beings, seeks its fulfillment.

The basic characteristic of this revolution, which distinguishes it from other movements that have taken place in Iran during the past hundred years, is its ideological and Islamic nature. After experiencing the anti-despotic constitutional movement and the anti-colonialist movement centered on the nationalization of the oil industry, the Muslim people of Iran learned from this costly experience that the obvious and fundamental reason for the failure of those movements was their lack of an ideological basis. Although the Islamic line of thought and the direction provided by militant religious leaders played an essential role in the recent movements, nonetheless, the struggles waged in the course of those movements quickly fell into stagnation due to departure from genuine Islamic positions. Thus it was that the awakened conscience of the nation, under the leadership of Imam Khumayni, came to perceive the necessity of pursuing a genuinely Islamic and ideological line in its struggles. And this time, the militant 'ulama' of the country, who had always been in the forefront of popular movements, together with the committed writers and intellectuals, found new impetus by following his leadership.

Source: International Court Networks. Retrieved 10 December 2002, from: http://www.oefre.unibe.ch/law/icl/ir00t_.html

The Notion of Religious Nationalism

Associating religion with a nationalistic or political agenda is a practice that extends back hundreds of years. For example, Christianity has been associated with political power since the time of Constantine (c. 280–337 CE), and has since had a history of clerical influence on political authority, with the result being a method of responding in a religious manner to a political situation. Religious nationalism is taken as a fact in many nations; some have even argued against the concept of separating the notions of religion and nation. Palestinian leader Sheik Ahmad Yassin noted that in some nations there is "no clear distinction between religion and politics; the distinction itself is a mark of Western ways of thinking"(Juergensmeyer 1993, 6).

Differences between Religious and Secular Nationalism

Modern secular nationalism emerged in the eighteenth century as a product of the European Enlightenment's political values; it adopted a distinctly anticlerical, if not antireligious, posture. As secular nationalism took hold, it had the effect of taking religion (at least church religion) out of public life. Secular nationalism differs from religious nationalism in that, for purely secular nationalism, the supreme loyalty of the individual is considered to be due to the nation-state. Individuals are linked to a political system in which the government attempts to remain unaffected by specific religious affiliations. Historically, secular nationalism has flourished especially in nations that were newly independent, and the main carriers of the banner of secular nationalism in these countries tended to be the urban educated elite. For many of these proponents, espousing a predominantly secular nationalism was a way of promoting the premise that religion and politics should be separated, thereby avoiding the obstacles that religious loyalties can create for a country's political goals. Political power based on religious values and traditional communities ceased to hold much authority, and secular nationalism thereby superseded traditional forms of faith.

Religious rejection of secular nationalism, however, emerged as a major motif in the latter decades of the twentieth century, especially in those geographical regions that had either been colonized or had come under the West's cultural and economic influence. The problem of asserting a secular nationalism was that nationalists had to have at least as much faith in a secular culture as they did in a religious one, but in many areas purely secular culture was associated with a breakdown in traditional societal patterns and values without any offsetting advantages. Socially, embracing an exclusively secular nationalism assumed that it could triumph over religion. Religious nationalism strongly dismisses secular nationalism for being fundamentally barren of moral or spiritual values.

Religious Nationalism as a Basis for Political Legitimacy

Religious nationalists have both religious and political concerns and interests. Though they reject secular ideas, they do not reject secular politics, but rather use religion as a basis to legitimize them: Religious nationalists respond in a religious way to a political situation. Religious nationalism is not concerned as much with the political structure of the nation-state as it is with the political ideology undergirding it. Therefore, religious nationalists have no problem affirming certain forms of political organization that have developed in the West, such as the democratic procedures of the nation-state, as long as they are legitimized not by the secular idea of social contract but by traditional principles of religion. Admittedly, in many countries political and religious ideas freely mix; however, to overlook religious motivations in favor of political ones is to fail to grasp the importance that religious nationalism plays in numerous countries.

It is not difficult to find religious justification for political aims. In fact, by the end of the twentieth century, virtually every religious tradition in the world had provided some justification for some form of religious nationalism. Further, since for many people there is an intense connection between loyalty to a nation and religion, it is only natural that politics should utilize this. Religious nationalism, in legitimizing politics, claims to be the guarantor of orderliness within society and to be the ultimate authority for the social order. In this respect, the issue of the use of force comes into play. Because religious nationalism is utilized to legitimize a political regime, it likewise serves to legitimize the use of force in order to compel obedience to its ways of thinking. As religious authority claims to be in possession of ultimate truth regarding right and wrong, it can invoke even the right to kill as a form of punishment without hesitation.

In the former Yugoslavia, Orthodox Serbs, Catholic Croats, and Muslim Bosnians engaged in violent ethnoreligious conflict. Their leaders could appeal to their people not merely on ethnic grounds, but also on religious ones, and for this reason commanded a greater degree of loyalty and more fervent support. In such a case, religious interests coalesce with national interests to displace purely political interests. As historian Donald Smith says, in most traditional religious societies, "Religion answers the question of political legitimacy" (Smith 1971, 11). Thus, religion typically sets the ultimate standards for the use of force and the conduct of political and legal affairs. Religion and nationalism, then, unite in establishing the basis for political legitimacy.

Even though religious nationalism is most common in strictly religious societies, it is not confined to them; even in secular Western nations religion may be drawn on to lend legitimacy to secular politics. This is especially apparent in the case of the United States, which claims to be a secular society but in which religion is a strong force politically.

Examples of Religious Nationalism

Examples of religious nationalism are numerous. Several significant cases can be identified. India provides an interesting showcase for the power of religious nationalism. From its beginnings in the nineteenth century, Indian nationalism has fed upon religious identifications. This is true for its two most important religious communities, Hindus and Muslims, as well as for less populous religious groups, such as the Sikhs. Indeed, at the time of

Indian independence in 1947, the region was partitioned into India and Pakistan (which at that time included present-day Bangladesh), with Pakistan specifically a homeland for Indian Muslims. Partition saw huge migrations across the newly established boundary, as Hindus in what had become Pakistan crossed into India, and Muslims in India moved to Pakistan. Even so, about 12 percent of the present-day Indian population remains Muslim. Although the Indian constitution established the state as a secular entity, the last two decades of the twentieth century saw the rise of Hindu nationalism, which viewed Muslims as not truly Indian. India's Muslims resent and oppose such actions by Hindu nationalists as the attempt to make Sanskrit (the language of the Hindu scriptures) a required course in all schools. The divide between India's Muslims and Hindus truly blends politics and religion, as both groups are guided politically and socially by their religious traditions. In this way, Indian society is partitioned by religion, and religious identity serves as the basis for communication between citizens. It should be noted, however, that although religious nationalism is a major issue for India, the nation faces many other problems that transcend questions of religious identity.

Bulgaria is an interesting case because of its Communist past. Since the resignation of its Communist leader in 1989 and the implementation of a new constitution in 1991, Bulgaria has experienced an outburst of nationalism, one that seems increasingly identified with Bulgarian Orthodoxy. Under the Communist regime, the Turkish Muslim minority was subject to enforced assimilation. This included the Bulgarizing of Turkish names, restrictions on the practice of Islam, and restrictions on the speaking of the Turkish language in public. When reformers came into power, they immediately extended the rights of cultural and religious freedom to the Turks; however, this policy of religious liberty provoked a passionate outcry on the part of the Christian Orthodox majority. Protestors have called for the protection of Bulgaria's heritage as one nation with one official language and religion guaranteed by the state constitution.

Judaism has also displayed nationalistic tendencies. Despite the fact that the original Zionists desired a secular state, the creation of Israel in 1948 remains the most striking and obvious example of Jewish nationalism. One of the chief rabbis of the new Israel, Z. Y. Kook, maintained that though Israel was a secular state, it was religiously useful, and its purification could help give rise to the coming of the Messiah. After the 1967 war in which Israel gained some land from adjacent Arab states, some Jewish nationalists thought that the time had come for the Jewish re-creation of the biblical nation of Israel. Jewish nationalist organizations have encouraged Jews to establish settlements on the West Bank of the Jordan River in order to recover from the Palestinians what they regarded as biblical lands. Palestinians have responded with their own nationalistic tendencies, claiming the lands on the West Bank as their own.

However, religious nationalism is not confined to any particular religious group. Religious nationalists exist among virtually every religious tradition, and most nations have experienced some kind of religious nationalism.

Implications for Religious Freedom

The immediate implications of religious nationalism for religious freedom are varied. In some nations the results are a subtle ostracizing of those who fall outside the majority; in others the results are bloody conflicts. However, it is safe to say that religious nationalism adversely affects religious freedom, even stifling it, as in the case of the Turks in Bulgaria. There is no monolithic solution to advancing the cause of religious liberty in nations in which religious nationalists are dominant. Religious liberty is dependent on many factors, including whether or not there is a state religion, the political power of religious nationalists, and the willingness of religious nationalists to use force or violence against those who do not conform.

In a few situations, religious nationalism can positively affect religious liberty. In the United States after the September 11 terrorist attacks in 2001, many Americans took the opportunity afforded by the increased religious fervor many were feeling to extend their faiths into other spheres of their lives. The outspokenness of key government officials regarding religious issues is an example of this, as are the occurrences of moments of silence and even prayer in schools and other public institutions.

It is important to recognize that, despite the increasing prevalence of religious nationalism, the fact that religion and nationalism sometimes go together does not mean that they must always go together. Religious traditions are nuanced, with varying themes and counterthemes. Many of these themes, such as peaceful, rather than violent persuasion, and love toward one's neighbor, directly oppose the violent ethnocentrism that is often associated with religious nationalism. Thus, it is impossible to speak of religions directly espousing or promoting religious nationalism.

It is also important to recognize that the international community often opposes many of the effects of religious nationalism. Several international documents enshrine principles that seek to guarantee freedom of religion and conscience. These include the Universal Declaration of Human Rights, the International Convention on Civil and Political Rights, and the United Nations Resolution on the Elimination of Intolerance Based on Religion or Belief. These human-rights documents undermine many of the assumptions of religious nationalism, largely by assuming that "the law of the spirit is not the same as the law of the sword" (Little 1994, 93). They posit an explicitly nonreligious basis for political authority and its exercise of force, sharply distinguishing a government's legitimacy from religious belief of any kind.

Jennifer Motwani Clary

See also Israel; Pakistan; Turkey

Further Reading

Catherwood, C. (1997). *Why the nations rage*. London: Hodder and Stoughton.

Coleman, J., & Tomka, M. (1995). *Religion and nationalism*. Maryknoll: Orbis Books.

Embree, A. T. (1990). *Utopias in conflict: Religion and nationalism in modern India*. Berkeley & Los Angeles: University of California Press.

Hastings, A. (1997). *The construction of nationhood: Ethnicity, religion, and nationalism*. Cambridge, UK: Cambridge University Press.

Juergensmeyer, M. (1993). *The new cold war? Religious nationalism confronts the secular state*. Berkeley & Los Angeles: University of California Press.

Kishwar, M. (1998). *Religion at the service of nationalism and other essays*. Oxford, UK: Oxford University Press.

Little, D. (1994). Religious nationalism and human rights. In G.F. Powers, D. Christiansen, & R. Hennemeyer (Eds.), *Peacemaking: Moral and policy challenges for a new world*. Washington, DC: U.S. Catholic Conference.

Marty, M. E., & Appleby, R. S. (Eds.), (1997). *Religion, ethnicity, and self-identity: Nations in turmoil*. Hanover, NH: University Press of New England.

O'Brien, C. C. (1988). *God land: Reflections on religion and nationalism*. Cambridge, MA: Harvard University Press.

Ruether, R. R., & Ruether, H. J. (2002). *The Wrath of Jonah: The Crisis of Religious Nationalism in the Israeli-Palestinian Conflict*. Minneapolis, MN: Fortress Press.

Smith, D.E. (Ed.). (1971). *Religion, politics, and social change in the Third World: A sourcebook*. New York: Free Press.

Smith, D. E. (Ed.). (1974). *Religion and political modernization*. New Haven, CT: Yale University Press.

Van der Veer, P. (1994). *Religious nationalism*. Berkeley & Los Angeles: University of California Press.

Religious Terrorist Groups

There has always existed a connection between heavenly aspirations and religiously motivated killing, rape, looting, and burning. And while all forms of religious violence are uniquely "terrifying" in their own right, it is important to distinguish between that carried out by soldiers who fight under the auspices of a state or a church (that is, an institution that has a monopoly over spiritual coercion in a territory), and religious violence that is not officially sanctioned, here defined as religious terrorism.

A classic example of the first type of religious violence were *peregrinatia* (pilgrims) *pro Christi* or Crusaders who flourished near the outset of the second millennium. Going by such titles as Hospitalers or Knights Templars, they were said to be ordained by an "eighth sacrament" of the Church and promised complete remission of sins by the pope if they fell in battle. As God's ministers of justice, their job was not to kill humans beings—after all, that would be homicide and thus unforgivable—but to kill evil (*malecide*), Muslims and Jews.

The alter ego of the soldier for Christ was the Muslim jihadist, whose violence was legally certified by a caliph, the supreme ruler of a Muslim state. The jihadist also struggled for righteousness (*aslama*)—a term cognate to the word *salaam* (*shalom*), peace—in the abode of the diabolic (*dar al-harb*). In his case, however, the diabolic were Christians and Jews. The jihadist who gave his life in battle was promised eternal life in a spring-fed, date-treed Eden, populated with perpetual virgins. Religiously motivated soldiering is by no means a historical relic. Witness the kamikaze suicide bomber, honored after the *kami*

THE HAMAS CHARTER

Hamas is a Palestinian organization that has been charged with and taken credit for some terrorist attacks against Israel. The Preamble to Hamas Charter provides some understanding of the motivation for the attacks.

Preamble: ". . . Israel will rise and will remain erect until Islam eliminates it as it had eliminated its predecessors." The Imam and Martyr Hasan al-Banna

Introduction: ". . . This is the Charter of the Islamic Resistance (Hamas) which will reveal its face, unveil its identity, state its position, clarify its purpose, discuss its hopes, call for support to its cause and reinforcement, and for joining its ranks. For our struggle against the Jews is extremely wide ranging and grave, so much so that it will need all the loyal efforts we can wield, to be followed by further steps and reinforced by successive battalions from the multifarious Arab and Islamic world, until the enemies are defeated and Allah's victory prevails. Thus we shall perceive them approaching in the horizon, and this will be known before long: "Allah has decreed: Lo! I very shall conquer, I and my messengers, lo! Allah is strong, almighty."

Sura 58 (Al-Mujadilah), verse 21.

Source: Raphael Israeli "Translation of the Hamas Charter," in *The 1988–1989 Annual on Terrorism.* (Dordrecht, Netherlands: Kinwer, 1990). Retrieved 15 May 2002, from http://www.cdn-friends-icej.ca/isreport/hamas.html

(sacred) *kaze* (wind) that was believed to have once saved Japan from the Mongol hordes. The Death Head units of the Nazi SS, to cite another example, reenacted a bowdlerized worship of the ancient Nordic god, Odin.

As states have secularized during the modern era, religiously based military organizations have generally disappeared. As a result, religiously inspired violence today is largely terroristic. This is not to say that religious terrorism is a new phenomenon. As early as 1420, Hussite and Taborite incendiaries wreaked havoc across the Czechoslovakian countryside.

Recounting a far earlier time, the Old Testament is replete with accounts of terrorism. Deborah and Barak defeat the Canaanites after the heroine Jael breaks the law of hospitality (a telling bedouin custom) and hammers a tent peg through the brain of their commanding general as he sleeps (Judges 4:17–22; cf. Judith's comparable act [Judith 13:1–20]). The Nazarites are another case. Disheveled-haired warrior ecstatics, "separated ones," they were conse-crated "from the womb" to advance Yahweh's cause by terror. The most illustrious among them, Samson, is reputed to have slain a thousand men armed with only the jawbone of an ass (Judges 15:9–17).

The titles of more than one ancient religious terrorist group have found their way into English as nouns standing for the crimes they were rumored to commit. Hindu adepts known as *thag*s gained notoriety by strangling their victims to death. Islam's Assassins were known both for silently killing their victims and for the hashish they presumably consumed (and after which they were named). Japan's *ninjas* hardened themselves with a simple diet, breathing exercises, and training in the arts of stealth and destruction. They were inspired by the meditative combat calisthentics (*ch'uan fu,* kung fu, or law of the fist), first taught at the Buddhist Shaolin monastery in China. Their practices would later become the basis of Zen, the style of Buddhism preferred by the samurai.

Financial support for terrorism is always haphazard at best; the soldier, in contrast, is paid a regular salary or in some other way supported by a state or

REJECTING TERRORISM

While the Right to Life movement in the United States has been associated with terrorism, including bombings of abortion clinics, attacks on women, and the murder of physicians, many pro-life organizations reject terrorism. This statement appears on the website of People for Life.

People for Life opposes all acts of violence. Violence directed against abortion facilities amounts to terrorism and deserves unequivocal condemnation. Such terrorism is not only an affront to the sanctity of human life; it is also an affront to the rule of law, without which we can never hope to achieve a just—or maintain a free—society.

Source: People For Life. Retrieved 15 May 2002,
from http://www.peopleforlife.org

church. Because of this the soldier's violence typically is regulated by a code of chivalry imposed upon them by their sponsors. For example, soon after Israelite king David's rule was secured (1030 BCE), Nazarite terrorism came to be seen as a liability. Like Samson, their locks were "shaved" (they were disempowered) and their place taken by soldiers who fought according to an elaborate Philistine military etiquette. Battle evolved from bloodthirsty chaos into a refined contest *(sahaq)* between pairs of knights, each holding the hair of his opponent with one hand while wielding a short sword with the other. Comparable examples of chivalric codes are the dharma (way) of the Hindu Kshatriya (warrior caste), the Bushido (warrior way) of the samurai, or to cite a more telling case, the Geneva conventions. These were agreed to by European states seeking to mitigate gratuitous harm during war. Among other things, they outlaw the use of poisonous gases, exploding bullets, and attacks on civilians, and they dictate humane treatment of prisoners.

Codes of honor and discipline are the source of a field army's strength. Yet they also explain its evident ineptitude when confronted by the more inventive and unpredictable tactics and weaponry utilized by terrorists. Terrorists are particularly fond of victimizing unarmed civilians in marketplaces, at night, with "unfair" weapons. Anciently, this meant crossbows and fire; today it means "dirty bombs," bacteriological agents, and "martyr attacks" or *istishadi* (Arabic, meaning "voluntary martyrdom"). To benefit from such assets while still maintaining a facade of civility, churches and states have been known to hire their own mercenary terrorists, surreptitiously. During the Thirty Years' War (1618–1648), Europe's first truly modern military conflagration, superbly disciplined Swedish troops used dagger-armed Finnish berserkers, Haapekelites, to do their dirty work. Around the same time, gentleman-like samurai were routinely employing *ninja* when chivalry failed to achieve desired results.

In the twenty-first century, the Iranian Ministry of Intelligence finances Hezbollah (the Party of God) in Lebanon, and through it Hamas and Islamic Jihad for their "martyr operations" in Israel. This is technically known as "state-sponsored" religious terrorism. In contrast, al-Qaeda (the Headquarters) receives most of its funding not from state coffers, but from "alms," private contributions (*zakat*) to ostensible religious charities such as the Holy Land Foundation. This is considered "church (mosque)-sponsored" religious terrorism.

When faced with superior (which is to say, military) force, terrorists retreat to jungle refuges and mountain redoubts. This is because being organized in elusively "leaderless" cells, while conveying certain advantages, is simultaneously the occasion of weakness. For all their bluff and swagger, in other words, terrorists are far less capable than standing armies of bringing force to bear on specific targets for sustained periods. It is neither rage nor even weapons that achieve strategic victory; it is discipline, the closed phalanx, "the lines of which," to quote Ibn Khaldun (1332–1406), "are orderly and evenly arranged like arrows or rows of worshipers at prayer."

391

The Motivations and Motives of Religious Terror

Besides the distinction between military violence and terrorism, a second concerns the motivations for terrorism versus its motives. The first refers to its supposed causes, the prior conditions historically associated with terrorist movements. The second encompasses the reasons terrorists give for their actions, how *they* understand what they do. Virtual libraries exist dealing with the matter of terrorism's causes. There are theories of relative deprivation and rising expectations, j-curve theories, and models of frustration and aggression. There are networking accounts of recruitment, community alienation narratives, and models of status insecurity. Some analysts explain the phenomenon by addressing how terrorists are "brainwashed" (socialized), while others stress the terrorists' lack of formal education. In short, regarding the matter of causality there is little agreement.

Just the opposite is true of terrorism's motives. Findings from in-depth interviews plus close readings of terrorist manifestos, handbills, sermons, correspondence, and (where available) pretrial clinical dossiers display a remarkable consensus. This, regardless of the specific faith of the terrorist in question or the terrorist's historical era. First of all, while they may be conspiratorial, xenophobic, narcissistic, and angry, few if any terrorists have been known to be certifiably insane. One of the least helpful ways to understand terrorism is to attribute it to lunacy or craziness. This does not mean that terrorists are "utility maximizers" in the microeconomic sense, who seek the greatest political "payoff," at least as this notion is ordinarily taken. Few religious terrorists labor for a "better world" of increased democratic rights for minorities, more comfortable housing arrangements, rapid transportation, a healthier diet, or a longer life expectancy. Instead, killing, raping, and looting are done "conscientiously," out of devotion to a higher (in this case, religious) cause, *regardless* of the costs or benefits to themselves or to others. For one terrorist group this cause may be *shar'ia* (Muslim sacred law); for another, it may encompass the *mitzvoth* (obligations) of Leviticus; for still another, God's presumed natural law.

Like contemporary American bombers of abortion clinics, porno shops, and gay bars, furthermore, few terrorists admit to acting out of "hate." On the contrary, they see themselves as "lovers," lovers of the higher cause. Indeed, given the recent notoriety of the term, they rarely accept the label "terrorist." Rather, they prefer self-descriptions like *mu'min* (Arabic, meaning "believer"), "Christian patriot," or "freedom fighter." The freedom they extol, however, has little to do with noncompulsion. Instead, freedom is seen as the condition of choosing to do what is "right"; choosing to obey God's higher law. For this kind of liberty, no cost is considered too great to bear. "Better dead than Red," proclaims the modern American Christian patriot. Better the earth in its entirety be destroyed, than righteousness be compromised. "Truly there is only one death," agrees his counterpart, the mujahideen (holy warrior). "Therefore let it be on the path of God" (as stated by Abdul Azis Rantisi, failed Hamas suicide bomber, quoted in Jurgensmeyer 2000, 71)

The religious terrorist pictures himself or herself as a hero. The religious terrorist fights alone, or at most with a tiny remnant, against those whose attachment to worldly things explains their presumed cowardice. The phrase "worldly things" naturally means different things in different times and places. To the ancient Nazarites it referred to the urbane Babylonian sophisticate; for the Hussite or Taborite terrorist two millennia later, it stood for the so-called whore of Babylon, the Roman Catholic Church. Today, it means modernism and its sundry "pathologies": secularism, humanism, democracy, and individualism. But there is immense irony here: In advertising his contempt for modernism (and love for the higher cause), the religious terrorist inevitably resorts to modern technology: to the personal computer and the Palm Pilot; to satellite communications and computerized logistics; and above all, to modern weaponry. This suggests that for all his prating about being devoted to "fundamentalism," the deeper, largely unconscious motive of the religious terrorist is not to stem the tide of modernity after all. Instead, it is to dramatize his personal magnificence in the cosmos. And what this implies to some who study religious terrorist groups (Jurgensmeyer 2000 and Aho 1990) is that terrorists do not fight merely because they have enemies; they manufacture enemies (and portray themselves as victims) so that they can fight.

Religious terrorism, that is to say, is nothing if not theater. And like all momentous drama, it utilizes the same scenarios and props: risk, agony, and, more than anything, blood. The targets are carefully selected less for tactical advantage than to maximize the effect on the audience: sports events, trade centers, cruise ships, passenger jets, shopping malls, public conveyances, government buildings, discos, schools, airport terminals, and the like. The attacks are staged on specially chosen days, such as holidays (holy days): Passover (as in the Seder meal attack staged by Hamas on Jewish devotees in April 2002); Ramadan (when Israeli fanatic Baruch Goldstein murdered Muslim worshipers at prayer in a mosque in 1994); or on arcane dates of "great significance," such as April 19 (the anniversary of the Branch Davidian conflagration, when the Oklahoma City federal building was destroyed) or April 20 (Hitler's birthday). And they are always played out with full awareness of the news cycle and the hovering presence of the videographer. Even the names of terrorist groups echo with performative symbolism. The title of the Palestinian al-Aqsa Brigades memoralizes the mosque near the Dome of the Rock (a major Muslim icon), at which Muslims were attacked by Israeli police. The military arm of Hamas, Iz al-Din al-Qassam, is named for a Muslim preacher and anti-British rebel killed in the 1930s, considered the "forefather" of modern terrorism and its "first martyr."

American Religious Terrorism

In the first years of the twenty-first century, reports of Muslim terrorism found themselves on front pages of American newspapers—which was both misleading and unfortunate. The fact is that every major world faith has its own terrorists: Sikhism, its Babbar Khalsa and Khalistan Commando Force; Japanese Buddhism, its Aum Shinrikyo (who released vials of poisonous sarin gas in a Tokyo subway killing commuters, hoping to initiate Armageddon). Hinduism has its Rashtriya Swayamesevak Sangh (National Patriotism Organization) whose most notable victim to date was Mohandas Gandhi. In the last two decades of the twentieth century alone in the United States, there were a so-called Army of God (whose favorite targets were abortion clinics and gay bars); a Phineas Priesthood (honoring the ancient Israelite who impaled a mixed-race couple with a spear); a Covenant, Sword, and Arm of the Lord (with the largest illegal arms cache ever discovered); a "secret [terrorist] brotherhood" (Bruders schweigen) of Identity Christians; a murderous Church of the Creator (with its own Montana *pontifex maximus* or "grand priest"); an armed Elohim City (literally, God Town, visited by Timothy McVeigh, the most deadly American terrorist); and renegade Mormon paramili-

tary secessionists called Freemen (after mythological Latter-day Saint heroes).

Indeed, religious terrorism in America can be traced to the very beginnings of its national history. The nation's most notable terrorist organization, the Ku Klux Klan, was anticipated during the pre–Civil War period by Know Nothings (who, under interrogation, were supposed to say that they "know nothing" about the group) and, after the war, by the anti-Catholic American Protection Association. With its mimicry of Catholic ritual and vestments, the Klan bragged of membership rolls of millions and of controlling state legislatures throughout the Deep South, as well as in Indiana and Oregon during the Roaring Twenties.

Several conclusions can be drawn about these and related movements.

1. Approximately every thirty years since 1800, there has been an outburst of religiously motivated terrorism in America. These outbursts are usually only the most disturbingly visible expressions of deeper upsurges of religious sentiment that temporarily seize large elements of the public imagination.

2. While the enemies of the movements naturally change over time—from the Illuminati and Freemasons to Jesuits, to the Hidden Hand, to Communists, to Jews, to Negroes, to satanists, witches, and homosexuals—the complaint issued against them essentially remains unaltered. First, they are accused of advocating an "evil agenda," consisting of secularism, humanism, tolerance of difference, and individual rights (for the nonpropertied, for ex-slaves, for women, for youth, for gays, and so on). Second, to advance this agenda they are locked in a secret cabal with Satan. Third, if Caucasian, Protestant, propertied male defenders of the Bible and the "organic" Constitution (that is, the original articles of the Constitution and the Bill of Rights) do not "stand tall" to this axis of evil, then the End Times will come.

3. There is no detectable connection between the thirty-year upsurges of American religious terrorism and economic booms and busts. The Klan activism of the 1920s and the anti-Communist hysteria of the 1950s occurred during times of unprecedented prosperity. The new Christian right of the 1980s, on the other hand, took place during a severe recession, as did the American Protection Association of the 1890s.

393

4. Instead, the outbursts seem generationally related. With enough notable exceptions to keep this from the status of a mechanical law of history, children of American Protection Association activists became Ku Klux Klan supporters when they came to political maturity three decades later. Their children in turn provided the vanguard of the anti-Communist brigades of the 1950s; and their grandchildren, the armies of the new Christian right.

5. As the American frontier has migrated west, the organizational centers of the movements have followed suit. At the end of the twentieth century, the Rocky Mountain and Pacific Coast regions were the hotbeds of religiously based terrorism.

6. Christian pastors always have played pivotal ideological and leadership roles in the movements: Jedidiah Morse, Billy Sunday, G. L. K. Smith, Billy James Hargis, Fred Schwarz, Carl McIntire, Wesley Swift.

7. Prototypical activists are demographically indistinguishable from their more moderate (Caucasian, Protestant, propertied, male) neighbors. They have comparable levels of formal education; are no more status-insecure, geographically transient, or occupationally isolated; and their marriages are just as stable.

8. Activists join the movement through their personal contacts with male family members (fathers, uncles, brothers), fellow workers, friends, and churchgoers already in it. In other words, they do not join because they first believe in movement doctrine; they alter their beliefs in order to nourish and sustain close relationships with movement participants whom they love and admire (Aho 1990).

It follows, then, that the most cost-effective way to deter American religious terrorism is not to subject its members to individual psychological counseling and sensitivity training. It is to destabilize in-group relationships between members of the group, while strengthening the defector's ties with those outside it.

James Aho

Further Reading

Aho, J. (1981). *Religious mythology and the art of war.* Westport, CT: Greenwood.

Aho, J. (1990). *The politics of righteousness.* Seattle: University of Washington Press.

Cohn, N. (1970). *The pursuit of the millennium.* London: Oxford University Press.

Davies, J. (1971). *When men revolt and why.* New York: Free Press.

Finch, P. (1983). *God, guts, and guns.* New York: Seaview/Putnam.

Juergensmeyer, M. (2000). *Terror in the Mind of God.* Berkeley: University of California Press.

Religious Test Oaths

One of the pernicious features of an establishment of religion (that is, a religion established or endorsed by the government) is the mistreatment of nonmembers of the established church. For example, the Church of England received financial support not only from freewill offerings of members, but also from public revenues collected from a coercive tax imposed on all, whether or not they were members of the established church. Similar arrangements prevailed in the American colonies. Nonmembers of the religion that was preferred or established in a particular colony (e.g., Baptists and Quakers in New England, where Congregationalism was established) led a tax revolt against coerced support for the Congregational church.

Establishment of religion thus has a negative impact on the free exercise of religion. Sometimes this has meant a direct prohibition of worship in a particular mode by nonmembers of the established religion. For example, recusant Catholics were forbidden by various penal laws from participating in the Mass.

In addition to such direct penalties of a specific form of prayer, Catholics and dissenting Protestants suffered penalties that deprived them of full membership in the civil or political community. For example, these groups and the small number of Jews, Muslims, and atheists in England could not vote or hold public office. The Act of Toleration of 1688 alleviated this situation for dissenting Protestants, but not for the other groups mentioned above.

The means used to enforce the exclusion of nonmembers of the established religion from full enjoyment of their civil and political liberties was a series of oaths designed to test whether a person could swear to a particular form of words about religious belief. Known as test oaths, these theological propositions derived from ecclesiastical inquisitions. The

ANTI-CATHOLIC RELIGIOUS TEST OATH IN COLONIAL PENNSYLVANIA

We and each of us do solemnly and sincerely profess and testify that in the Sacrament of the Lord's Supper there is no transubstantiation of the elements of bread and wine into the body and blood of Christ at or after the consecration thereof by any person whatsoever, and that the invocation or adoration of the Virgin Mary or any other Saint, and the sacrifice of the Mass, as they are now used in the Church of Rome, are superstitious and idolatrous.

And we and each of us for himself do solemnly profess, testify, and declare that we do make this declaration in the plain and ordinary sense of the words read to us, as they are commonly understood by English Protestants, without any evasion, equivocation, or mental reservation whatsoever, and without any dispensation already granted for this purpose by the Pope or any other authority whatsoever; and without any hope of any such dispensation from any such person or authority whatsoever, or thinking that we are or can be acquitted before God or man or absolved of this Declaration or any part thereof, although the Pope should dispense with or annul the same, or declare that it was null and void from the beginning.

And we the said subscribers, and each of us for himself, do solemnly and sincerely profess faith in God the Father, and in Jesus Christ his Eternal Son, the true God, and in the Holy Spirit, one God blessed for evermore. And we do acknowledge the Holy Scriptures to be given by Divine inspiration.

Source: "Religious Tests in Provincial Pennsylvania,"
Pennsylvania Magazine of History and Biography, (1885) 9: 391–392.

purpose of the oath in a church court was to differentiate between a true believer and an outsider to the faith. The effect of the oath in later civil law was to exclude the nonbeliever of the full benefits and burdens of citizenship. It was a classic illustration of the downside of governmental endorsement of religion: the excluded outsider was made to feel as a second-class citizen, or for all practical purposes was stripped of citizenship in any meaningful sense of the term.

History of Test Oaths

The American tradition of requiring religious oaths to test conformity of the subjects to a politically correct view is grounded in the English Reformation under Henry VIII (reigned 1509–1547). When the king desired a divorce from his queen, Catherine of Aragon, the Pope—who had final appellate jurisdiction over family law matters at the time—refused to grant a decree of nullity. This led to a break with Rome. When compliant bishops gave the king the divorce decree the Pope had withheld, Henry married Anne Boleyn. The new arrangements in church and state were enforced by means of an oath declaring Henry's marriage with Catherine null from the beginning, and declaring the king to be the "Supreme Head of the Church of England." All adults were meant to swear in conformity with this oath. The stakes for refusal to take the oath were high. The king's chancellor, Thomas More, and the Bishop of Rochester, John Fisher, declined to take the oath, and both were executed for treason. When Henry died in 1547, he had been married six times and was succeeded by his son by Anne Bolyn, Edward VI (reigned 1547–1553). Catherine of Aragon's daughter Mary Tudor (reigned 1553–1558) initiated a brief and fruitless effort to restore Roman Catholicism; her realm is remembered more for the brutality of the persecution of Anglicans than for anything else. Shortly after Elizabeth I (reigned 1558–1603) came to the throne, Parliament swiftly

TORCASO V. WATKINS, 1961

In *Torcaso v. Watkins*, a landmark case on religious oaths, U.S. Supreme Court Justice Hugo Black offered the following opinion:

> It was largely to escape religious test oaths and declarations that a great many of the early colonists left Europe and came here hoping to worship in their own way. It soon developed, however, that many of those who had fled to escape religious test oaths turned out to be perfectly willing, when they had the power to do so, to force dissenters from their faith to take test oaths in conformity with that faith. This brought on a host of laws in the new Colonies imposing burdens and disabilities of various kinds upon varied beliefs depending largely upon what group happened to be politically strong enough to legislate in favor of its own beliefs. The effect of all this was the formal or practical 'establishment' of particular religious faiths in most of the Colonies, with consequent burdens imposed on the free exercise of the faiths of nonfavored believers.

Source: *Torcaso v. Watkins*, 367 U.S. 488 (1961). Retrieved 10 December 2002, from http://religiousfreedom.lib.virginia.edu/court/torc_v_watk.html

passed the Act of Supremacy of 1558, which served as the prototype of a religious test act. Within a decade, all public officeholders—including members of the House of Commons—were required to swear their allegiance to the Queen in an oath replete with theological language.

Test oaths abounded in the American colonies. For example, in the Frame of Government of Pennsylvania, written in 1682, William Penn required "That all . . . Members elected to serve in the provincial Council and General Assembly, and all that have right to elect such Members, shall be such as possess faith in Jesus Christ . . . ." Jews, Muslims, and nonbelievers were thus excluded from public service. The more specific targets of laws of this sort were Roman Catholics, since the test oaths typically asked colonists to renounce Roman Catholic doctrine.

A decade before the American Revolution, William Blackstone noted in his summary of the common law that no one could hold office in the military of the government or even become a naturalized citizen of England without acknowledging under oath the King as the head of the church.

Prohibition of Test Oaths in the U.S. Constitution

The original text of the U.S. Constitution proposed by James Madison did not contain a prohibition against test oaths for federal offices. Other members of the Constitutional Convention offered their own opinions on test oaths. Charles Pinckney proposed such a provision on the view that "the prevention of Religious Tests, as qualifications to Offices of Trust or Emolument . . . [is] a provision the world will expect from you, in the establishment of a System founded on Republican Principles, and in an age so liberal and enlightened as the present" (Elliot 1836, Vol. 1, 145). Roger Sherman stated that the provision was unnecessary, given the "prevailing liberality." Governeur Morris and Charles Cotesworth Pinckney spoke in favor of the proposal, which was adopted without dissent.

In his report to the Maryland legislature, Luther Martin noted that the Pinckney amendment was adopted "without much debate," adding that "there were some members so unfashionable as to think, that a belief of the existence of a Deity, and of a state of future rewards and punishments would be some security for the good conduct of our rulers, and that, in a Christian country, it would be at least decent to hold out some distinction between the professors of Christianity and downright infidelity or paganism" (Elliot 1836, Vol. 1, 344ff).

In the debates in the state ratifying conventions, some expressed chagrin at the ban on religious test oaths for federal offices. For example, Major Rusk of Massachusetts "shuddered at the idea that Romans

Catholics, Papists and Pagans might be introduced into office and that Popery and the Inquisition may be established in America." Another delegate to the Massachusetts convention, Colonel Jones, added that even if test oaths might have been abused in England, leaders in America should believe in God or Christ. These views were rebutted by a Congregationalist minister, Daniel Shute, who characterized test oaths as a "privation on part of [the] civil rights . . . of individuals . . . who, in every other respect, are qualified to fill some important post in government. . . ." The famous Baptist preacher, Isaac Backus, also endorsed the ban on religious tests, in a speech: "Let the history of all nations be searched from that day [of the Roman emperor Constantine (reigned 306–337 CE)] to this, and it will appear that the imposing of religious oaths had been the greatest engine of imposing tyranny in the world. And I rejoice to see so many gentlemen, who are now giving in their rights of conscience in this great important matter" (Elliott 1836, Vol. 2, 248–249).

Although all of the thirteen original states maintained some kind of religious qualifications for public office, no state convention objected to the prohibition on religious tests for federal offices. Article VI of the Constitution of the United States provides: "no religious Test shall ever be required as a Qualification to any Office or public Trust under the United States."

The Supreme Court had no cause to construe this provision until the late nineteenth century. In 1882 Congress enacted the Edmonds Act, which allowed a federal prosecutor to strike from the jury anyone "who believes it right for a man to have more than one living and undivorced wife at the same time." The United States Attorney sought an indictment against Rudger Clawson from a grand jury from which anyone was excluded if he stated that he believed in the doctrines and tenets of the Mormon Church, or specifically in the Mormon doctrine of plural marriage. In *Clawson v. United* States, (1885), the Court sustained a criminal conviction for polygamy, and Clawson served four years in federal prison. The legislature of the federal territory of Idaho went further than Congress, enacting a requirement that all jurors and voters take the following oath: ""I am not a bigamist or polygamist. . . . I am not a member of any . . . organization . . . which practices bigamy or polygamy. . . I do not . . . in any manner whatever, teach, advise, counsel, or encourage any person to commit the crime of bigamy or polygamy. . . ." Another prominent

Mormon, Samuel Davis, took this oath, and was convicted for taking it falsely. In *Davis v. Beason*, (1890) the Court unanimously sustained the conviction, which had been challenged as a violation both of the ban on religious tests in Article VI and of the religion clause of the First Amendment.

In *Girouard v. United States*, (1946) Justice William O. Douglas wrote: "The test oath is abhorrent to our tradition." Douglas would have been more accurate if he had simply stated that the U.S. Constitution prohibited the practice, and that the Court ignored the ban in the only cases brought before it where the ban mattered.

Survival of Test Oaths in State Customs and Practices

As noted above, several states used test oaths to keep Jews, Catholics, Muslims, and atheists from service in public office. Thus Justice Hugo Black was not historically accurate when he wrote in *Torcaso v. Watkins*, (1961): "When our Constitution was adopted, [there was a] desire to put the people 'securely beyond the reach' of religious test oaths. . . ." Indeed, *Torcaso* was the case in which the Court finally sounded the death-knell of this odious practice by the states.

Like all of the other twelve original states, Maryland had discriminated against Jews, Catholics, and Muslims in its qualifications for public service. By the time Torcaso was appointed to serve as a notary public, the sole remaining religious disqualification was a requirement of belief in the existence of God. As an atheist, Torcaso could not declare a belief in God and was refused his commission. Citing the colonial history of religious test oaths, the Court ruled that the Maryland religious test for public office unconstitutionally invades freedom of belief and religion and therefore cannot be enforced against an atheist.

Edward Gaffney, Jr.

Further Reading

Elliott, J. (Ed.). (1836). *The Debates in the Several State Conventions on the Adoption of the Federal Constitution* (Vol. 1–5). Retrieved January 7, 2003, from http://memory.loc.gov/ammem/amlaw/lwed.html

Penn, W. (1682, April 25). *Frame of Government of Pennsylvania*. Retrieved January 7, 2003, from http://www.libertystory.net/LSDOCPENN1682FRAMEGOVERNMENT.htm

Court Cases

Clawson v. United States, 114 U.S. 477 (1885).
Davis v. Beason, 133 U.S. 333 (1890).
Girouard v. United States, 328 U.S. 61, 69 (1946).
Torcaso v. Watkins, 367 U.S. 488 (1961).

Religious Tolerance

Freedom of belief is the oldest human right, predating every other right. It is the one right with which the international community has the longest experience. Freedom of belief is such a basic human right that without it other fundamental rights are less secure. Free belief is the first hallmark of a free society.

Freedom of belief has given us freedom of religion. Freedom of religion has in turn given us religious human rights. Religious human rights are the right of every person to "thought, conscience and religion" and include most importantly the "freedom to change his religion or belief and freedom either alone or in community" and "to manifest his religion or belief, in worship, teaching, practice and observance" (Universal Declaration of Human Rights 1948, Article 18). This right has such normative force that it is universally recognized as a valid principle of law. Religious tolerance goes with religious freedom. All religions are equal before the law. But this also means that all beliefs, whether religious or nonreligious, are equal. It requires true tolerance of all and everyone. (It should be noted that the use of the term "tolerance" in this article to mean personal tolerance for other religions by adherents of other religions differs from how the term "tolerance" is often used in the United States. In the United States, tolerance means something less than full religious freedom for people of different religions and the distinction between tolerance and freedom has been an important one since colonial times.)

Tolerance in Religion and Secularism

Yet, throughout history, religion has been a chief source of human conflict. More wars have been waged in the name of religion than in the name of any other cause. This was because for much of history, religious liberty came to define communities in conflict. Whether it was Israelites and Canaanites, Christians and Jews, Jews and Muslims, Catholics and Protestants, or Hindus and Sikhs, religion was

An itinerant preacher spreading "religion" to farmers outside warehouse while tobacco auction sales are going on in Durham, North Carolina. Depending on the laws of the nation, permitting such preaching to occur could be interpreted as a sign of religious tolerance or freedom. *Marion Post Wolcott,* COURTESY OF LIBRARY OF CONGRESS, PRINTS AND PHOTOGRAPHS DIVISION, FSA-OWI COLLECTION.

corrupted to imply the right of "the One" against "the Other" and to sow the seeds of division and distrust. Tragically, religion remains central to most political conflicts of the world today—from Northern Ireland's sectarian divide, to Osama Bin Laden's cult status in Nigeria as an Islamic hero, to the threat of nuclear war posed by India and Pakistan. Religion has become synonymous with strife, conflict, and intolerance.

However, secularism too has had its share of intolerance. The level of human suffering caused by the big secular ideas of the twentieth century was unprecedented, with that century becoming the bloodiest in human history. Stalin's Communism, Hitler's fascism, and Pol Pot's anarchism were such perversions of ideology that mankind was again forced by its end to seek solace in religious thought. Religion still had an enduring role. But the disenchantment with secular ideology by the end of the twentieth century also paved the way for an identity politics, creating its own perversions of religious righteousness and intolerance and setting the scene for a new conflict in the twenty-first century.

Religionists would say that religion helps to set the moral norms by which society can live. Secularists would say you do not need religion to do that. Religion may be a good way to coordinate a struggle by giving it structure. But secular society can equally set the standards for good and bad behavior. Religionists would say that the failure of modernity has been precisely the failure of systems of liberalism or social democracy to provide good articulation of an effective bounded moral system. Instead, secularism has led to a moral deskilling of society. At least in religious thought, there has been a very well-developed moral system about how people might find happiness, how to redeem oneself with good deeds, and how to morally skill oneself with the idea of virtues as a set of ethical values. On the other hand, say religionists, secular society has failed to give us a successful system of secular morality.

But secularists would say that one must first agree on a system of moral values before deciding whether it has been successfully implemented or not. Without universal agreement on moral values, secularists would say that even religion cannot be described as moral. There must first be a moral determination as to what goodness is before it can be said that religion has a higher claim to virtuous living. Secularists may, in turn, point to the treatment of women or of nonbelievers in certain religious practices to demonstrate

that religious thought does not have a claim to moral superiority over secular thinking in all cases.

It is in this regard that religious human rights have an indispensable role to play in the practice of religion. Religious liberty exists because human conscience exists. The intrinsic sanctity and moral worth of all individual beings—whether secular or religious—are rooted in the inviolability of the human conscience because it is this that constitutes the sacredness of the human person. It is the right to conscience that provides the principle of voluntarism in religious belief and it is the principle of voluntarism that is the foundation of all human rights law. No one should be compelled to do that which he does not want to do. It is the right to conscience that forms the rational, intellectual, and philosophical basis of a commitment to religious human rights. This is challenging for all religionists. Any religious practice that violates the right to conscience is indefensible. In fact, all religious practices need to be conceptualized in terms of the right to conscience. This is what the international instruments on religious human rights have sought to do. The historical particularity of religion that provided the justification for caricatures of intolerance and for iniquitous human rights abuses then becomes unsustainable.

Religionists need to search historically for a tradition of tolerance in their respective faiths, for all great religions of the world have this tradition. It may have been forgotten. It may have been suppressed. It may even have been lost. But it is there provided it is searched for. Historically all great religions had to begin with a plea for religious toleration and respect. They were once religious minorities and dissenters. They were once the religiously disenfranchised and persecuted. Their teachings, when they made those pleas, should remind them now of the full glories of their past. These glories come not from narrow-minded religious coercion, condemnation, or disrespect of others, but from interfaith relations, mutual respect, goodwill, and dialogue. In secular society, any legal and constitutional protection for religious human rights will only be practicable in the future, under national or international law, if it meets this test. Religious human rights will otherwise retain their precarious and fragile status to date, and deservedly so.

Tolerance in Western Religions

The tradition of religious tolerance exists in the religions of the West as well as those of the East. The

Judeo-Christian tradition, which predominates in the West, has been criticized for its intolerant past, but it contains shining examples of toleration. Judaism recognizes the infinite worth of every person. Divergent faiths are shown respect in the Talmud. The tradition of Judaism unhesitatingly affirmed religious rights of others. God's covenant with Israel was emphatic that "All the families of the earth are to be blessed" (Genesis 12:3). In the Tosefta, Rabbi Joshua declares that "There are righteous men among the nations who have a share in the world to come" (Tosefta Sanhedrin 13:2). The Mishnah accordingly states that "Therefore, was a single person [first] created to teach thee that if anyone destroys a single soul . . . Scripture charges him as though he had destroyed a whole world, and whosoever rescues a single soul . . . Scripture credits him as though he had saved a whole world" (Mishnah Sanhedrin 4:5). Even as recently as the twentieth century, Rabbi Abraham Heschel, one of the most respected of modern Jewish scholars, had said that "God's voice speaks in many languages" (God in Search of Man: 142). In Christianity, the whole of humanity is created in the image of God. Christian Scripture speaks of "the true Light, which lighteth every man that cometh into the world" (John 1:9). All human beings are treated equally. Peter, who was a leader of early Christianity and one of Jesus' disciples, is one of the most eloquent in this respect, stating, "Truly, I perceive that God shows no partiality, but in every nation anyone who fears and does what is right is acceptable to him" (Acts 10:34–35). Matthew wrote of the principle of voluntarism with the words "whosoever will" and "if you want to," making it clear that there was no compulsion in Christianity (Matthew 19:21–22). The Book of Revelation similarly tolerates the right of the nonbeliever when it records, "Behold I stand at the door and knock; if any person hears my voice and opens the door, I will come into his house and eat with him, and he will eat with me" (Revelation 3:20).

In Islam, the Qur'an is clear that "there shall be no compulsion in religion" (Sura 2:256). It too is unequivocally emphatic in upholding the principle of voluntarism: "Proclaim, O Prophet, This is the truth from your Lord; then let him who will, believe, and let who will, disbelieve" (Sura 18:29). In the Qur'an, the injunction to tolerate other faiths is quite explicit: "Revile not those deities whom the unbelievers call upon and worship" (Sura 6:108). The unbelievers that must be respected are not just those from Judaism and Christianity but from other faiths not mentioned in the holy book (Sura 35:24; 40:78; 22:67). To compel these nonbelievers to accept Islam is to destroy the majesty and diversity of faith: "If it had been the Lord's will, all the people on the earth would have come to believe, one and all. Will you compel mankind against their will, to believe?" (Sura 10:99–100).

Tolerance in Eastern Religions

In the traditions of the East, toleration of others is a distinctive feature of all religious practice. Unlike in the West, Eastern religions do not have a tradition of proselytism. One of the earliest religions is Buddhism, founded by Siddhartha Gautama (c. 563–c. 483 BCE), which was among the first religions to become international. It directed that "To be attached to a certain view and to look down upon other views as inferior is considered wrong by wise men" (Sutta Nipata 798). The Buddha even forbade his disciples to attack those that criticized him: "If anyone were to speak ill of me or of my doctrine or my Order, do not bear ill-will towards him" (Digha Nikaya 1.3). In fact, Buddhism cautions against the foolishness of monopolized truth. A man may say, "This is my faith," but he cannot say, "This alone is Truth, and everything else is false" (Majjhima Nikaya 2.176).

The Jain faith, founded as early as six centuries before the birth of Christ, also celebrates the diversity of religious faith by enjoining believers to "comprehend one philosophical view through comprehensive study of another one" (Acarangasutra 5.113). Jain scriptures make religious bigotry, and religious war, impossible by recording that "Those who praise their own doctrines and disparage the doctrines of others do not solve any problem" (Surakritanga 11.50). In the I Ching, a classic text of Confucianism, it is observed that "In the world there are many different roads but the destination is the same. There are a hundred deliberations but the result is one" (I Ching 2.5).

Similarly, Hinduism condemns the castigation of the beliefs of others. Fundamental to the Hindu belief is the Vedic idea that "Truth is One, but Sages call it by different names" (Rig Veda 1; Hymn 164.46). Like Jainism, it too records that "Ignorant is he who says, 'That I say and know is true; others are wrong.' It is this attitude that causes dispute among men" (Srimad Bhagavatam 11.3). The tradition of tolerance is unmistakably clear in Hinduism when it is declared that "The wise man accepts the essence of different scriptures and sees only good in all religions" (Srimad Bhagavatam 11.3).

In the same way, Sikhism, one of the world's youngest and most progressive religions, proclaims the moral validity of all just faiths. Its founder, Guru Nanak, observed that "Some read the Vedas, some read the semitic scriptures. Some wear blue robes, some wear white robes. Some call themselves Muslims, some call themselves Hindus. Some aspire to *bahishat* [Muslim heaven], some to *swarga* [Hindu heaven]. Nanak says, Whoever realises the will of the Lord will find the way to the Lord" (Adi Granth, Rag Ramkali, p. 885). This statement is all the more remarkable when it is realized that the Sikhs' own holy scriptures, in the Adi Granth, are all-important to them.

The claims of religious believers to moral superiority over secularists is diminished if they fail to preach the message of tolerance and mutual respect. Historically, this has not been religion's greatest strength. It will have to be now. Religion must claim back its tolerant traditions.

Satvinder S. Juss

See also Human Rights; Secularism and Modernity

Further Reading

Emerich, J., & Dalberg-Acton, E. (1967). *The history of freedom and other essays*. New York: Books for Libraries Press.

European convention on human rights. (1970). Retrieved December 19, 2002, from http://www.echr.coe.int/Eng/BasicTexts.htm

Heschel, A. J. (1997). God in Search of Man. (Reprint ed.). New York: Noonday Press.

Humphrey, J. P. (1985). Political and related rights. In T. Meron (Ed.), *Human rights in international law*. Oxford, UK: Clarendon Press.

Juss, S. (1997). Freedom of conscience rights: Lessons for Great Britain. *Journal of Church & State, 39*.

Sieghart, P. (1983). *The international law of human rights*. New York: Oxford University Press.

United Nations. (1948). *Universal declaration of human rights*. Retrieved December 17, 2002, from http://www.un.org/rights/HRToday/

Roman Catholicism

Catholicism is the oldest and largest branch of Christianity. The term "Catholic" (universal) was first used to refer to the Christian church by Ignatius, the Bishop of Antioch (d. c. 107). After Western and Eastern Christianity split in 1054, "Catholic" referred to the Western Church and "Orthodox" to the Eastern. After the sixteenth-century Protestant Reformation, "Roman Catholic" was employed to distinguish the churches that remained loyal to the pope (the Bishop of Rome) from the Protestants. Despite the Roman name, Roman Catholicism also includes Eastern-rite (or "Uniate") Catholics who are in communion with Rome but retain their particular rites. The Roman Catholic Church was "the last of the great Christian denominations to embrace wholeheartedly the principle of religious freedom" (Tierney 1996, 30) with the 1965 promulgation of the *Declaration on Religious Freedom* at the Second Vatican Council.

From Persecution to Power

The early Christians were subject to religious persecution in the Roman Empire, and the apostles Peter and Paul died martyrs' deaths in Rome, the city that became the leading city in Western Christianity and gave its name to Roman Catholicism. Christians believed that they were obligated to worship the one true God, but within the empire, their "refusal to participate in the state cult and to think as the state does was a crime against the state" (Küng 2001, 24). The severity of persecution varied, Christians enjoying more freedom under some emperors than others. During the first three centuries of Christianity, the reigns of Emperors Nero, Diocletian, Decius, and Valerian were especially harsh and many Christians were executed by the state.

The situation changed dramatically in the fourth century, when Emperor Constantine (306–337) converted to Christianity. With the Edict of Milan in 313, Constantine granted freedom of religion to Christian as well as non-Christian religion; his successors, however, persecuted non-Christians while protecting Christianity. By the end of the fourth century, Emperor Theodosius had banned paganism and established Christianity as the state religion. Non-Christians could now be executed for not following the state religion. Twentieth-century Catholic theologian Hans Küng has commented: "What a revolution! In less than a century the persecuted church had become a persecuting church" (Küng 2001, 38).

Although early Christians had sought religious freedom within the empire, once in power they used state resources against unorthodox or hereti-

PROPOSITIONS CONDEMNED AS ERRONEOUS BY POPE PIUS IX IN THE *SYLLABUS OF ERRORS* (8 DECEMBER 1864)

15. Every man is free to embrace and profess that religion which, guided by the light of reason, he shall consider true.

16. Man may, in the observance of any religion whatever, find the way of eternal salvation, and arrive at eternal salvation.

17. Good hope at least is to be entertained of the eternal salvation of all those who are not at all in the true Church of Christ.

77. In the present day it is no longer expedient that the Catholic religion should be held as the only religion of the State, to the exclusion of all other forms of worship.

78. Hence it has been wisely decided by law, in some Catholic countries, that persons coming to reside therein shall enjoy the public exercise of their own kind of worship.

Philippe Levillain, ed.

Source: "Syllabus of Errors," in *The Papacy: An Encyclopedia,*
vol. III. (New York: Routledge, 2002).

cal Christians. The influential theologian Bishop Augustine of Hippo (354–430) provided a persuasive theological rationale for using coercion against heretics. The Donatists, for example, were North-African Christians who challenged orthodox Catholics beliefs. Augustine decided that the state could use force to repress the Donatists and other heretics. His argument depended upon the biblical expression *compelle intrare*, i.e, "compel them to come in" (Luke 14:23). In the New Testament's Gospel of Luke, when the guests refused the invitation to the banquet, the servant was told to go out and "compel them to come in." According to Augustine, so too could the state employ coercion to promote the salvation of heretics by forcing their return to the Church. In Western Christianity, Augustine's argument provided a rationale for the repression of heretics that endured for many centuries.

Two There Are

After the fall of the Roman Empire in the fifth century, the Catholic Church assumed many secular powers. The papacy grew in prominence as it acquired more political and temporal clout. Pope Gelasius (492–496) recognized that "two there are": church and state. From the fifth to nineteenth centuries, the Church's role fluctuated: its power waxed and waned depending on its relations and balance of power with the state.

The pre-eminence of the Church led to a number of paradoxes in the history of religious freedom. Now there were two powers. A strong church could protect religious freedom against the encroachments of the state. Yet an alliance of spiritual and temporal institutions could crush individual freedom. For example, when Pope Leo III crowned Charlemagne the Holy Roman Emperor on Christmas Day 800, the "line between church and state" was "practically erased" (McBrien 1987, 432). From then on, the "two swords" battled for primacy with the Church, arguing that the temporal ruler must yield to the spiritual. The centuries-long struggle of popes and kings did not always promote individual freedom, as Professor Brian Tierney has acknowledged:

The *libertas ecclesiae* that medieval popes demanded was not freedom of religion for each individual person but the freedom of the church as an institution to direct its own affairs. It left open the possibility,

SELECTION FROM DECLARATION ON RELIGIOUS FREEDOM (DIGNITATIS HUMANAE)

Proclaimed by His Holiness Pope Paul VI on 7 December 1965.

15. The fact is that men of the present day want to be able freely to profess their religion in private and in public. Indeed, religious freedom has already been declared to be a civil right in most constitutions, and it is solemnly recognized in international documents. [38] The further fact is that forms of government still exist under which, even though freedom of religious worship receives constitutional recognition, the powers of government are engaged in the effort to deter citizens from the profession of religion and to make life very difficult and dangerous for religious communities.

This council greets with joy the first of these two facts as among the signs of the times. With sorrow, however, it denounces the other fact, as only to be deplored. The council exhorts Catholics, and it directs a plea to all men, most carefully to consider how greatly necessary religious freedom is, especially in the present condition of the human family. All nations are coming into even closer unity. Men of different cultures and religions are being brought together in closer relationships. There is a growing consciousness of the personal responsibility that every man has. All this is evident. Consequently, in order that relationships of peace and harmony be established and maintained within the whole of mankind, it is necessary that religious freedom be everywhere provided with an effective constitutional guarantee and that respect be shown for the high duty and right of man freely to lead his religious life in society.

May the God and Father of all grant that the human family, through careful observance of the principle of religious freedom in society, may be brought by the grace of Christ and the power of the Holy Spirit to the sublime and unending and "glorious freedom of the sons of God" (Rom. 8:21).

Source: Christus Rex et Redemptor Mundi.
Retrieved 12 November 2002, from" http://www.christusrex.org

---

all too fully realized from the twelfth century onward, that the church might organize the persecution of its own dissident members. And, when the interests of church and state happened to coincide, as they often did in dealing with heresy, there was room for a savage suppression of religious dissent (Tierney 1996, 36).

Thomas Aquinas (1225–1274), the pre-eminent medieval theologian, followed Augustine in encouraging the state to use force to enforce Christian orthodoxy. Thomas distinguished between non-Christians, such as Jews or pagans, and heretical or apostate Christians. He taught, as did the medieval Church, that a non-Christian could not be compelled to faith, which must arise from an act of free will. Heretical or apostate Christians, however, could be punished because they had betrayed the promise of their baptism. Baptism was the key: Even an individual who was unwillingly baptized could be compelled to practice the Christian faith.

Inquisitions

The crusades to wrest control of the Holy Land from the Muslims occurred in the eleventh through thirteenth centuries. In the late twelfth century, the Church developed the investigative tribunals to detect and punish heresy that are remembered as the "Inquisition." In 1215, the Fourth Lateran Council asked secular authorities to "exterminate all heretics pointed out by the church" (Tierney 1996, 31). The tribunals used torture to identify and assess the guilt of the heretics. Some received a public penance or imprisonment; unrepentant heretics were put to death. During the thirteenth century, the Inquisitors vigorously pursued the dissident Albigensians in Southern France.

King Ferdinand and Queen Isabella directed the Spanish Inquisition in the fifteenth century. In Spain the focus was on converted Jews or Muslims who secretly practiced their former religion. Because they had been baptized, often by force, they were thus heretical Christians and subject to punishment. When the heretics fled Spain the Portuguese Inquisition ensued.

In response to the Protestant Reformation, Pope Paul III established the Roman Inquisition in 1542 to stamp out the heresy of fellow Christians. Although the Spanish and Portuguese Inquisitions had declined by the late eighteenth or early nineteenth centuries, the Roman Inquisition, under the name of the Roman Congregation of the Holy Office, continued to protect Catholic orthodoxy by condemning theological works and practices that endangered the faith.

In sixteenth and seventeenth century Europe both Catholics and Protestants engaged in fierce and debilitating Wars of Religion. Neither party truly advocated religious freedom: each propounded its own "truth" while seeking to repress the other. Exhaustion eventually forced both sides into a wary peace based upon religious *toleration* but not freedom, and Catholic and Protestant states emerged as the fighting stopped. In the post-Reformation world, the Catholic Church accepted that church and state could not coerce the individual to believe. During that time, the "principle was gradually established that even the absolutist prince may not compel a man to act against his conscience or punish him for reasons of conscience" (Murray 1965, 40).

Error Has No Rights

In 1870 the Italian army conquered the Papal States, ending the era of the Roman Catholic Church's temporal power. Pope Pius IX (1846–1878) opposed liberal reformers who challenged Catholic rule throughout Europe, leaving him "prisoner in the Vatican" in the new Italian state. In the *Syllabus of Errors* (1864), he condemned both religious freedom and the separation of church and state.

From then on, the dominant account of Catholic teaching on church and state and religious freedom became the so-called thesis/hypothesis distinction. Its premise was that Catholicism is the one true religion and thus should be the established religion of every state. The Church, however, could not always attain this goal. The thesis stated the ideal: Catholicism should be the established religion of the state. A non-Catholic state was the "hypothesis" that had to be tolerated as an evil. Catholics could tolerate non-establishment when they could do no better, but should change the hypothesis to thesis when they could do so.

The slogan connected to the thesis/hypothesis distinction was that "error has no rights." The implications of this were most severe in the realm of public worship. Catholics in the minority have the right, as their religion is true. But error has no right to public worship, so minority non-Catholics should have no right to public worship. This teaching demonstrated the limitations of the post-Reformation principle of tolerance: Although the state could not compel the individual to believe, in Catholic thought it could restrain the public *practice* of erroneous belief.

Catholic opposition to religious freedom and to the separation of church and state directly conflicted with the First Amendment of the United States Constitution. John Fitzgerald Kennedy confronted questions about this conflict throughout his successful campaign to become the first Catholic president of the United States in 1960. The Jesuit John Courtney Murray (assisted by Pietro Pavan, a priest and professor of social economy at the Lateran in Rome), an American theologian, later defeated the thesis/hypothesis proponents at the Second Vatican Council.

An Ecumenical Pope and Council

On 25 January 1959, three months after his election to the papacy, Pope John XXIII (1958–1963) announced the convocation of the Second Vatican Council, the first in the Roman Church since Vatican I was disrupted in 1870 by the invasion of the Italian army. Vatican II met in Rome from October 1962 to December 1965.

Early in his career, Pope John had been the Apostolic Delegate to Bulgaria, Turkey, and Greece, and he retained a life-long commitment to ecumenism. By the 1960s, "error has no rights" was a formidable barrier to Catholic participation in the Christian ecumenical movement. The World Council of Churches urged Roman Catholics to reconsider religious freedom at the Council. In his opening conciliar remarks about religious freedom in November 1963, Belgian Bishop Emile de Smedt explained why ecumenists suspected Catholics of "a kind of Machiavellism": "we seem to them to demand the free exercise of religion when Catholics are in a minority in any nation and at the same time refuse and deny the same religious liberty when Catholics are in the majority" (de Smedt 1964, 237–238).

The subject of religious freedom originally formed one chapter of a proposed document on ecumenism; instead, by December 1965 religious freedom had its own declaration. Throughout the three years of preparation for the meeting, Pope John supported the advocates of religious freedom and ecumenism against traditionalists who opposed any change in Church teaching.

Before the Council Fathers debated religious freedom, Pope John issued his noteworthy encyclical letter, *Pacem in Terris*, in April 1963. It was the first official Catholic document to recognize a right to religious freedom, i.e., "of being able to worship God in accordance with the right dictates of his own conscience" (no. 14). The encyclical's reference to religious freedom was brief, however, and the "right dictates" language suggested that error might still have no rights. A fuller analysis of religious freedom was left to Murray, Pavan, and the Council, a task that they completed after Pope John's death in June 1963.

The Dignity of the Human Person

From November 1963 until December 1965, there were 6 "schemata" (drafts), 3 public debates, 120 speeches, 600 written interventions, numerous oral and written critiques of the schemata, consultations with Council observers, and over 2000 *modi* (suggested corrections) concerning a proposed declaration on religious freedom (Murray 1966, 672).

The *Declaration on Religious Freedom* (*Dignitatis Humanae*) was the last and most controversial text promulgated by the Council. After the bishops passed it by a final vote of 2308:70, Pope Paul VI (1963–1978) signed the document on 7 December 1965. The only conciliar document to address the whole world, it held that every human possessed the right to religious freedom, which must be protected as a civil right by the constitutional state. The foundation of the right is the dignity of the human person, not the truth of his beliefs. Moreover, the right provides twofold immunity, from coercion and from restraint. The government may not coerce the individual conscience into belief, nor may it restrain her from the practice of religion (within due limits). Although the first immunity had been recognized post-Reformation, the second immunity was "the new thing" in Catholic thought (Abbott 1966, 678). After 1965, even erroneous belief had the right to public worship.

The *Declaration* marked a dramatic change in Catholic teaching about religious liberty. Even its drafter Murray, however, insisted that "[i]t can hardly be maintained that the Declaration [was] a milestone in human history—moral, political, or intellectual" (Murray 1966, 673). The United Nations and numerous constitutions had long recognized this right. Murray conceded that the "Church [was] late in acknowledging the validity of the principle" of religious liberty (Murray 1966, 673).

After the Council ended, both Murray and Pavan noted that the *Declaration* had not addressed the difficult issue of freedom within the Church. The *Declaration* presented only a limited political and legal argument that religious freedom is a *civil* right of all humans (women and men, Catholic and non-Catholic) that must be protected by every *state*. The Roman Catholic Church has not recognized a comparable right to religious freedom within the Church, where there are no civil rights because the Church is not a democracy. Thus women's participation in the governance of the Church may be limited because there is no right to priestly ordination. Moreover, a Holy Office—renamed the Congregation for the Doctrine of the Faith in 1965, the year of the *Declaration*'s passage—continues to monitor the orthodoxy of Catholic theologians through secret investigation of their work. Although the Church may not coerce the act of faith, which must be freely undertaken, unlike the state it retains its power to restrain by means of excommunication, investigation, silencing, or dismissal of unorthodox individuals from Catholic institutions.

Leslie Griffin

See also Church and State in Modern Europe; Crusades; English Test Oaths and Toleration Act; French Colonies in North America; Germany and Prussia; Inquisition; Reformation, Early Modern Europe; Roman Catholics, Colonial Nineteenth Century; Spanish Colonies in North America; Spanish Empire; State Churches; Vatican II

Further Reading

Bates, M. S. (1945). *Religious liberty: An inquiry.* New York: International Missionary Council.

Borromeo, A. (2002). Inquisition: Modern era. In P. Levillain (Ed.), *The papacy: An encyclopedia* (Vol.2, pp. 815–820). New York: Routledge.

Abbott, W. M. (Ed.). (1966). Declaration on religious freedom. In *The documents of Vatican II* (pp. 675–700). New York: Guild Press.

de Smedt, E. J. (1964). Religious liberty. In H. Küng, Y. Congar, & D. O'Hanlon (Eds.), *Council speeches of Vatican II* (pp. 237–253). Glen Rock, NJ: Paulist Press.

Küng, H. (2001). *The Catholic Church: A short history* (J. Bowden, Trans.). New York: Modern Library.

McBrien, R. P. (1987). Roman Catholicism. In M. Eliade (Ed.), *The encyclopedia of religion* (Vol. 12, pp. 429–445). New York: Macmillan.

McBrien, R. P. (Ed.). *(1995). The HarperCollins encyclopedia of Catholicism.* San Francisco: HarperCollins.

Murray, J. C. (1965, January 9). This matter of religious freedom. *America, 112,* 40–43.

Murray, J. C. (1966). Religious freedom. In W. M. Abbott (Ed.), *The documents of Vatican II* (pp. 672–674). New York: Guild Press.

Pavan, P. (1969). Declaration on religious freedom. In H. Vorgrimler (Ed.), *Commentary on the documents of Vatican II* (Vol. 4, pp. 49–65). New York: Herder & Herder.

Reid Jr., C. J. (1999). The Fundamental freedom: Judge John T. Noonan, Jr.'s historiography of religious liberty. *Marquette Law Review, 83,* 367–433.

Tierney, B. (1996). Religious rights: A historical perspective. In N. B. Reynolds & W. C. Durham, Jr. (Eds.), *Religious liberty in Western thought* (pp. 29–57). Atlanta: Scholars Press.

Roman Catholics, Colonial to Nineteenth Century

Catholicism arrived in the Americas with the voyages of Christopher Columbus a generation before the Protestant Reformation. In the great colonial American empires of Spain and France, the Catholic Church was established by governmental intent if not always by specific legislation; but in the English colonies Catholics were frequently persecuted as religious dissenters, living under the shadow of the established Church of England in the southern colonies or the gathered churches of Puritan New England. As these colonies evolved into the United States, Catholics remained a minority in a predominantly Protestant nation and were subject to periodic persecution from those who contended that Catholic teachings were inimical to democratic values. Despite this tradition of anti-Catholic bias, or perhaps because of it, some American Catholics emerged as strong proponents of religious liberty.

The Spanish and French Colonies

Sailing under the flag of a state that had recently been unified under the rule of the "Catholic Monarchs" Ferdinand of Aragon and Isabella of Castile, Christopher Columbus brought Spanish Catholic dominion to the American continents. Spain justified its conquest of land and native peoples, in part, by appeals to Catholic expansion and evangelization. Armed with a series of papal concessions known collectively as the *patronato real* ("royal patronage"), the Spanish crown utilized its authority over ecclesiastical appointments and control of finances to make the church and its mission system engines of colonization. Competing religions had no place in the Spanish empire. Native traditions were often ruthlessly suppressed by the religious orders that staffed the missions, and the practice of Christian traditions other than Catholicism was forbidden. The first permanent European settlement in what would later become the United States, St. Augustine in Florida, was established in 1565 when a Spanish garrison destroyed a nearby colony of French Protestants that presented a religious as well as a political challenge to Spanish claims.

Although Spain and France shared the same Catholic faith, their political rivalry made them religious competitors as well, and both nations raced to create a Catholic administrative infrastructure and win the alliance of native groups in North America. When René-Robert Cavelier de La Salle (1643–1687) founded a colony at Matagorda Bay in 1685, the Spanish not only fortified Pensacola but rushed garrisons and missionaries to east Texas to counter the French advance. As with Spain, France employed its clergy and religion to extend imperial aims, but was never quite as successful at integrating Catholicism with colonialism. Under the provisions of the Edict of Nantes, Protestantism had been tolerated in France since 1598 although Catholicism remained the officially established religion. This toleration was ini-

SELECTIONS FROM THE PAPAL ENCYCLICAL CONCERNING NEW OPINIONS, VIRTUE, NATURE AND GRACE, WITH REGARD TO AMERICANISM

Pope Leo XIII

Encyclical promulgated on January 22, 1899.

To Our Beloved Son, James Cardinal Gibbons,

Cardinal Priest of the Title Sancta Maria, Beyond the Tiber, Archbishop of Baltimore:

Beloved Son, Health and Apostolic Blessing:

We send to you by this letter a renewed expression of that good will which we have not failed during the course of our pontificate to manifest frequently to you and to your colleagues in the episcopate and to the whole American people, availing ourselves of every opportunity offered us by the progress of your church or whatever you have done for safeguarding and promoting Catholic interests. Moreover, we have often considered and admired the noble gifts of your nation which enable the American people to be alive to every good work which promotes the good of humanity and the splendor of civilization. Although this letter is not intended, as preceding ones, to repeat the words of praise so often spoken, but rather to call attention to some things to be avoided and corrected; still because it is conceived in that same spirit of apostolic charity which has inspired all our letters, we shall expect that you will take it as another proof of our love; the more so because it is intended to suppress certain contentions which have arisen lately among you to the detriment of the peace of many souls.

[. . .]

The underlying principle of these new opinions is that, in order to more easily attract those who differ from her, the Church should shape her teachings more in accord with the spirit of the age and relax some of her ancient severity and make some concessions to new opinions. Many think that these concessions should be made not only in regard to ways of living, but even in regard to doctrines which belong to the deposit of the faith. [. . .]

But in regard to ways of living she has been accustomed to so yield that, the divine principle of morals being kept intact, she has never neglected to accommodate herself to the character and genius of the nations which she embraces.

[. . .]

But, beloved son, in this present matter of which we are speaking, there is even a greater danger and a more manifest opposition to Catholic doctrine and discipline in that opinion of the lovers of novelty, according to which they hold such liberty should be allowed in the Church, that her supervision and watchfulness being in some sense lessened, allowance be granted the faithful, each one to follow out more freely the leading of his own mind and the trend of his own proper activity. They are of opinion that such liberty has its counterpart in the newly given civil freedom which is now the right and the foundation of almost every secular state.

[. . .]

cont.

SELECTIONS FROM THE PAPAL ENCYCLICAL CONCERNING NEW OPINIONS, VIRTUE, NATURE AND GRACE, WITH REGARD TO AMERICANISM

These dangers, viz., the confounding of license with liberty, the passion for discussing and pouring contempt upon any possible subject, the assumed right to hold whatever opinions one pleases upon any subject and to set them forth in print to the world, have so wrapped minds in darkness that there is now a greater need of the Church's teaching office than ever before, lest people become unmindful both of conscience and of duty.

[. . .]

Those who so bind themselves by the vows of religion, far from having suffered a loss of liberty, enjoy that fuller and freer kind, that liberty, namely, by which Christ hath made us free. . . .

From the foregoing it is manifest, beloved son, that we are not able to give approval to those views which, in their collective sense, are called by some "Americanism." But if by this name are to be understood certain endowments of mind which belong to the American people, just as other characteristics belong to various other nations, and if, moreover, by it is designated your political condition and the laws and customs by which you are governed, there is no reason to take exception to the name. But if this is to be so understood that the doctrines which have been adverted to above are not only indicated, but exalted, there can be no manner of doubt that our venerable brethren, the bishops of America, would be the first to repudiate and condemn it as being most injurious to themselves and to their country. For it would give rise to the suspicion that there are among you some who conceive and would have the Church in America to be different from what it is in the rest of the world.

[. . .]

Source: Eternal Word Television Network. Retrieved 4 September 2002, from http://www.ewtn.com/library/PAPALDOC/L13TESTE.HTM

tially extended to France's American colonies, but eventually Catholicism was established throughout French America and non-Catholic religions were proscribed. In 1627, the Company of New France banned non-Catholics, first in Quebec and then in Acadia. The Catholic Church was established in the French Caribbean through the provisions of the Code Noir (1685), and the charter for the Company of the Indies (1717) charged its directors to permit only the practice of the Catholic faith in French Louisiana and to finance the erection of churches and the maintenance of priests.

A lack of colonists meant that many of these restrictions against religious freedom were sporadically enforced. Despite the mandates of its charter, the Company of the Indies settled Protestants upriver from New Orleans, and even during the period of Spanish control in Louisiana (1763–1803), non-Catholics were allowed for a time to settle in the colony, although they were required to practice their religion in private. For the most part, however, religious liberty was never an enduring feature of Spanish or French colonial rule.

The English Colonies

The religious situation was reversed in the English colonies. In England, Catholics represented not only a minority religious tradition in an officially Protestant nation, but they were subject to political suspicions and a long history of anti-Catholicism and penal laws. By the middle of the seventeenth century, many English Catholics had come to accept their minority status as permanent and so had begun to see the value of religious toleration for themselves as well as other dissenting groups.

One such Catholic was George Calvert (1580?–1632), who secured a charter for the colony of Maryland in 1632. Although the historical documentation is ambiguous, it is likely that Calvert planned that Maryland would be a haven for English Catholics, free from the constraints of the penal laws. The only way to assure such freedom, however, would be by a general toleration of religious differences. Although Calvert died before the enterprise was actually launched, his son and heir Cecilius Calvert (1605–1675) recruited colonists and instructed them not to dispute religious issues either en route or once settled. Since Catholics constituted only a small percentage of the company, they were especially exhorted to practice their faith in private out of consideration for the Protestant majority. In spite of Calvert's intentions, however, religion became a contentious political issue in the colony. In 1649, at Calvert's request, the Assembly passed the Act Concerning Religion as a means to pacify dissension by legally tolerating all Christians who professed belief in the Trinity and the deity of Christ. Despite this limitation, this act was one of the earliest attempts to legislate some form of religious toleration in the English colonies. Unfortunately, it was repealed by a subsequent Protestant-dominated Assembly and replaced by anti-Catholic penal laws.

Catholics fared far worse in other colonies, although their numbers were insignificant. In 1642, Virginia passed its own penal laws; Massachusetts Bay followed five years later. Similar anti-Catholic legislation continued to be passed for the next century, even as religious toleration was extended to other dissenting groups. In 1732, when Georgia was founded as the last of the "original thirteen" colonies, religious liberty was guaranteed to all except Catholics. Only in Pennsylvania, a colony founded by William Penn to be a refuge for religious dissenters, did Catholics remain free from penal legislation.

Outside of Maryland, Catholics themselves also contributed to the development of religious toleration in the colony of New York. The proprietor of this colony was James (1633–1701), the Duke of York, who was the brother of King Charles II (1630–1685), a future king himself (James II), and a practicing Catholic. In 1682, James appointed an Irish Catholic named Thomas Dongan (1634–1715) to the post of governor. The following year, Dongan prodded the legislature to pass a set of laws known as the Charter of Liberties and Privileges, which, among other things, secured religious toleration for all Christians in the colony. Although this allowed Dongan himself the freedom to open a Catholic chapel and school, to support Jesuit missions to the Iroquois, and to import English Jesuits to serve as priests and missionaries, he was careful to recognize equal liberties for Anglicans, the Dutch Reformed (who remained from the original Dutch colonization of the region), and other Protestants. Dongan's policies, however, were not continued by his successor Richard Coote (1637–1701), the Earl of Bellamont, who introduced penal legislation into the colony and threatened priests with life imprisonment if they performed any Catholic ceremonies.

The penal period drew to a close with the coming of the Revolution. Although the Continental Congress vehemently protested the Quebec Act of 1774, in which England granted religious freedom to the Catholics living there after eleven years of British rule, the desire to encourage the Canadian colonies to enter the conflict on the American side led to a sudden cessation of anti-Catholic hostility. George Washington (1732–1799) banned the celebration of "Pope Day" (during which an effigy of the pope was burned in celebration of the discovery of the Gunpowder Plot of 1605) by the Continental Army in 1775, and the following year an official congressional delegation that included Benjamin Franklin (1706–1790) and two Maryland Catholics—cousins Charles Carroll (1737–1832) and John Carroll (1735–1815)—traveled to Canada to seek an alliance. Although the Canadian mission failed, subsequent alliances with France and Spain helped to create an era of religious concord and contributed to the passage of various bills for disestablishment and religious liberty by the first state legislatures.

The Early National and Antebellum Periods

In keeping with the Maryland Catholic tradition of religious toleration, John Carroll emerged as an outspoken advocate of religious liberty during the early national period. Carroll had been ordained a priest in 1761, and ten years later took his final vows to join the Society of Jesus (Jesuits), in which he served as a college professor in Bruges, Belgium. When the society was suppressed by Pope Clement XIV less than two years later, Carroll returned to America and became the de facto leader of the former Jesuits in Maryland. His leadership abilities were recognized by the pope in 1784 when he was appointed Superior of the American Mission, and again in 1789 when he was appointed to the newly created Diocese of Baltimore as the first bishop in the United States.

Carroll realized that support of religious liberty was the only way that Catholics could guarantee themselves such freedom, and he enthusiastically supported this religious "revolution" as "more extraordinary than our political one" (Hanley 1976, 1:80). Carroll's vision of a American Catholic Church conformed to republican ideals was perhaps too radical for his time, but his embrace of religious liberty would be repeated by many subsequent American Catholic bishops and clergy.

Carroll's vision was also clouded by the changing fortunes of the church in the United States. When Carroll became bishop, the Catholic population of the United States was small and concentrated in and around Baltimore. Increasing immigration, especially from Ireland and the Catholic regions of the German states, not only caused a sharp spike in numbers but shifted the Catholic population to the port cities of the north, especially New York. Anti-Catholic prejudices returned, coupled with a nativist fear of excessive immigration. Nativist riots erupted in many cities, including Charlestown, Massachusetts, where an Ursuline convent and school were burned to the ground in August 1834. In 1844, two Catholic churches were likewise destroyed in riots in Philadelphia. A new genre of anti-Catholic literature appeared filled with stories of lecherous priests and imprisoned nuns. Within the church itself, controversies over the extent of authority held by boards of lay trustees made Catholicism appear antidemocratic and thus anti-American to many non-Catholics. Nor was the situation helped by papal denunciations of religious liberty and other democratic ideals. Anti-Catholic nativism gained the height of its cultural power in the 1850s with the formation of the "Know Nothing" political parties, named after the response that members were supposed to give to any inquiries about their activities. Fortunately for the Catholics persecuted by Know-Nothing legislation, the movement quickly collapsed because of political incompetence and the growing sectionalism that diverted the nation's attention to the approaching Civil War.

The Americanist Crisis

In 1865, Catholicism became the largest denomination in the United States, although Catholics were still outnumbered by the various Protestant denominations by a three to one ratio. In the aftermath of the war, anti-Catholicism and nativism had all but disappeared, but the increasing Catholic population—soon to be supplemented by a new surge of immigration—and the aversion of Rome to support democratic reforms in revolutionary Europe eventually resurrected these prejudices. Pope Pius IX's (1792–1878) *Syllabus of Errors* (1864) condemned both religious liberty and the separation of church and state as "errors" that should not be held by Catholics; nevertheless, bishops such as James Cardinal Gibbons of Baltimore (1834–1921) and John Ireland of St. Paul, Minnesota (1838–1918) worked to convince non-Catholic Americans that the church remained amenable to democratic values and tried, at the same time, to persuade Rome that such ideals carried positive benefits for the church in the United States.

Under pressure from Rome, a council of bishops meeting in Baltimore in 1884 mandated that a system of parochial schools be created. Since most Americans regarded the public school system as the nursery for democracy, this decision led to increased anti-Catholic activities, including the founding of the nativist American Protective Association in 1887. Gibbons and Ireland sought a compromise solution, arguing that public schools helped to assimilate the immigrants more rapidly into American culture, but Rome was unconvinced. When liberal Catholics in France began to view the church in the United States as a model of accommodation to democratic values such as religious liberty, Pope Leo XIII responded with the apostolic letter *Testem benevolentiae* (1899), which condemned certain propositions as constituting the heresy of "Americanism." Although no American Catholic was ever indicted as a proponent of this "phantom heresy," the effect of *Testem benevolentiae* was to chill further the relations of the church with the larger culture and underscore the non-Catholic claim that the church was hostile to religious liberty. Not until the 1960s, with the election of John F. Kennedy as the nation's first Catholic president and the promulgation of the "Declaration on Religious Liberty" by the Second Vatican Council, did American Catholics emerge from the shadow of Americanism.

Rodger Payne

See also French Colonies in North America; Roman Catholicism; Spanish Colonies in North America

Further Reading

Billington, R. A. (1938). *The Protestant crusade.* New York: Macmillan.

Cross, R. D. (1958). *The emergence of liberal Catholicism in America.* Cambridge, MA: Harvard University Press.

Ellis, J. T. (1965). *Catholics in colonial America.* Baltimore: Helicon.

Ellis, J. T. (1987). *Documents of American Catholic history* (Vols. 1–3). Wilmington, DE: Michael Glazier.

Hanley, T. O. (Ed.). (1976). *The John Carroll papers* (Vols. 1–3). Notre Dame, IN: University of Notre Dame Press.

Hennesey, J. J. (1981). *American Catholics: A history of the Roman Catholic community in the United States.* New York: Oxford University Press.

Ray, M. A. (1936). *American opinion of Roman Catholicism in the eighteenth century.* New York: Columbia University Press.

Roman Empire

In the late Roman Republic, Cicero offered a typical Roman perspective on religion when he looked with pride on the strong link between the administration of religious institutions and the rule of the state: "Gentlemen of the pontifical college: Among the many divinely-inspired expedients of government established by our ancestors, there is none more striking than that whereby they expressed their intention that the worship of the gods and the vital interests of the state should be entrusted to the direction of the same individuals, to the end that citizens of the highest distinction and the brightest fame might achieve the welfare of religion by a wise administration of the state, and of the state by a sage interpretation of religion" (Cicero, 133). Because the Romans believed that their fortune and destiny depended on the proper worship of the state gods, political officials were custodians not only of the state but also of the piety of the people. As the Roman Republic was replaced by the empire (during the reign of Augustus, 27 BCE–14 CE), religious life increasingly was shaped by the emperor himself.

Religion and the Roman Empire

The religion of the Roman Empire was characterized by divine notions of time; by divine landscape, like temples, altars, sacred precincts, and groves; by household shrines and ancestor worship; and by rituals involving processions, prayers, even theatrical performances and chariot racing. It was characterized by many types of religious officials, by religious images on coins, by inscriptions revealing names of gods. It was characterized by animal sacrifices and offerings of wine and incense.

What characterized Roman religion throughout the Empire—both chronologically and geographically—was its corporate and legal nature. Religion was understood neither as a private matter for the individual, nor as a focus of belief, but as a civic duty, based in the community and characterized primarily by participation in centuries-old rituals. The piety of the Romans was demonstrated by their public worship and their sacrifices, in return for which the gods provided peace and prosperity to the Empire.

Although Roman deities such as Jupiter, Vesta, and Neptune were recognized in the state pantheon, they represented only some of the religious influences in the Empire. Gods of the countryside or gods who protected crafts and trades also were important, if not empire-wide then on local levels. Other "oriental" deities were worshiped among particular nationalities, such as Egyptians who followed Isis, or among particular professions, such as Roman soldiers who engaged in Mithras worship. Rome could be accommodating toward other religions, the results of which can be seen in the taunting of the fourth-century Christian Arnobius who claimed, against the pagans, "Your theologians, then, and authors on unknown antiquity, say that in the universe there are three Joves . . . five Suns and five Mercuries" (Roberts, et al., 14).

Rome had been receptive to religious innovation in the early and middle Republic, but not during the Principate: No new gods were admitted into the state religion until the early third century, when Caracalla incorporated Isis and Serapis into the pantheon. During the time of the Empire, the government was wary of new religions and was suspicious of mystery religions, particularly of any *superstitio* that had the potential to threaten the state. As a result, the Romans were primarily concerned with the origins of each religion, the behavior patterns of the adher-

THE *CODEX THEODOSIANUS* ON RELIGION, FOURTH CENTURY CE

In 429, Theodosius II formed a committee of eight people to establish a unified code of laws for the Roman Empire. This code was completed and became the law in both the Eastern and Western Empires in 438. The following extracts concern the practice of religion.

C. Th. XVI.v.1: It is necessary that the privileges which are bestowed for the cultivation of religion should be given only to followers of the Catholic faith. We desire that heretics and schismatics be not only kept from these privileges, but be subjected to various fines. Constantine Augustus.

C. Th. XVI.x.4: It is decreed that in all places and all cities the temples should be closed at once, and after a general warning, the opportunity of sinning be taken from the wicked. We decree also that we shall cease from making sacrifices. And if anyone has committed such a crime, let him be stricken with the avenging sword. And we decree that the property of the one executed shall be claimed by the city, and that rulers of the provinces be punished in the same way, if they neglect to punish such crimes. Constantine and Constans Augusti.

C. Th. XVI.vii.1: The ability and right of making wills shall be taken from those who turn from Christians to pagans, and the testament of such an one, if he made any, shall be abrogated after his death. Gratian, Valentinian, and Valens Augusti.

C. Th. XI.vii.13: Let the course of all law suits and all business cease on Sunday, which our fathers have rightly called the Lord's day, and let no one try to collect either a public or a private debt; and let there be no hearing of disputes by any judges either those required to serve by law or those voluntarily chosen by disputants. And he is to be held not only infamous but sacrilegious who has turned away from the service and observance of holy religion on that day. Gratian, Valentinian and Theodosius Augusti.

C. Th. XV.v.1: On the Lord's day, which is the first day of the week, on Christmas, and on the days of Epiphany, Easter, and Pentecost, inasmuch as then the [white] garments [of Christians] symbolizing the light of heavenly cleansing bear witness to the new light of holy baptism, at the time also of the suffering of the apostles, the example for all Christians, the pleasures of the theaters and games are to be kept from the people in all cities, and all the thoughts of Christians and believers are to be occupied with the worship of God. And if any are kept from that worship through the madness of Jewish impiety or the error and insanity of foolish paganism, let them know that there is one time for prayer and another for pleasure. And lest anyone should think he is compelled by the honor due to our person, as if by the greater necessity of his imperial office, or that unless he attempted to hold the games in contempt of the religious prohibition, he might offend our serenity in showing less than the usual devotion toward us; let no one doubt that our clemency is revered in the highest degree by humankind when the worship of the whole world is paid to the might and goodness of God. Theodosius Augustus and Caesar Valentinian.

C. Th.XVI.i.2: We desire that all the people under the rule of our clemency should live by that religion which divine Peter the apostle is said to have given to the Romans, and which it is evident that Pope Damasus and Peter, bishop of Alexandria, a man of apostolic sanctity, followed; that is that we should believe in the one deity of Father, Son, and Holy Spirit with equal majesty and in the Holy Trinity according to the apostolic teaching and the authority of the gospel. Gratian, Valentinian and Theodosius Augusti.

C. Th. XVI.v.iii: Whenever there is found a meeting of a mob of Manichaeans, let the leaders be punished with a heavy fine and let those who attended be known as infamous and dishonored, and be shut out from association with men, and let the house and the dwellings where the profane doctrine was taught be seized by the officers of the city. Valentinian and Valens Augusti.

Oliver J. Thatcher, ed.

Source: *The Early Medieval World*, The Library of Original Sources, vol. IV. (Milwaukee, WI: University Research Extension Co. 907), 69–71.

ents, and the way devotees' duties as citizens might be affected. The official policy of the early Empire was generally one of passive acceptance of other religions unless there was suspicion of sedition (as with the Druids, who were seen as Gallic nationalists), or of immorality (as with the Magna Mater, which could involve frenzied castration). Although it did not disallow new religions, sometimes the state responded passively, simply allowing the religions to exist without official approval.

Among the wide number of gods and religious traditions in the Roman Empire, one unifying aspect of worship was the emperor cult, a natural extension of traditional state religion. The fundamental claim was that emperors, their families, or their predecessors were associated with the gods or seen as divine. Thus, Julius Caesar and Augustus were seen as divine after they died. Each subsequent emperor negotiated his divine/human status in a way peculiar to himself, but emperors like Caligula and Domitian, who demanded to be worshiped as divine even while they were still alive, frequently were seen as assuming the divine prerogative, because they desired to engage in less than divine (i.e., immoral) activities. This cult was readily accepted throughout the Empire; it kept subjects loyal to the emperor, and it promoted imperial ideology and loyalty.

The Distinct Role of Judaism

Many Jews both refused to take part in the state religion of the Empire and distanced themselves from civic and social practices. Jews were withdrawn from Roman society because of endogamy (their marrying only Jews), their practice of circumcision (which Romans saw as self-mutilation), and their commensal restrictions (kosher law, for instance, kept Jews from eating pork, the most widely consumed meat in Rome). However controversial Jews were, within the Empire Judaism had a privileged status. Jews were allowed to practice their own religion without interference; they were exempted from worshiping the deities of the Roman state. Furthermore, they were allowed to use their religious law in structuring life within their own community and, occasionally, Roman magistrates allowed them exemptions from working on the Sabbath or engaging in military service. Why? Judaism was venerable, because it was an ancient religion. In addition, Jews had a history of being independent allies of Rome. In the first century CE, Tiberius and Claudius had granted rights to the Jews, much as Julius Caesar had, and these rights had created a powerful precedent for the state to follow.

At the same time, Romans were willing to grant exemptions, in part because Jews were willing to accommodate Rome by sacrificing daily, on behalf of the reigning emperor, to their God in the Jewish Temple. What this meant, however, was that in the year 66 CE, at the beginning of the Jewish War with Rome, the Jews' refusal to offer this sacrifice was then seen as tantamount to a declaration of war. Even after the revolt, when the Temple was destroyed, Jews themselves were not forced to worship Roman deities. As a reminder of their impudence, however, they were forced to pay a tax that supported the worship of a pagan deity. Some fifty years later, the emperor Trajan banned circumcision in response to a subsequent Jewish revolt against Rome (115–117 CE). After yet another Jewish revolt (132–136 CE), Jews were forbidden to enter Jerusalem. Although ethnic Jews eventually were allowed to engage in circumcision, converts to Judaism were still forbidden to do so. Jews were allowed to practice their religion, but they were forced to adapt to the dictates of the Empire. As Rabbi Meir said in the Talmud, "When in Rome do as the Romans do" (Genesis Rabbah 48).

Imperial Responses to the First Christians

Initially, the Roman authorities did not distinguish between Christianity and Judaism, so Christianity shared in the legal protection and special privileges received by the Jews. Christian scripture, such as Acts 18:12–17, illustrates how Romans saw conflicts between Jews and Christians as intrafamily squabbles.

In 64 CE, the emperor Nero was the first Roman to persecute Christians as Christians. Seen by Nero as lacking the antiquity of the Jewish religion and the support of the Roman people, Christians were blamed for starting the city of Rome on fire. After Nero dressed them in animal skins and allowed wild dogs to tear them up, after he illuminated the night skies with the flames coming from their burning bodies, it became clear both that Christians would no longer be seen as Jews and that they could be persecuted simply because of their faith.

This is seen in a particularly significant letter from 112 CE. Pliny, the first governor in Pontus/Bithynia (in Asia Minor, just south of the Black Sea), had never participated in the trials of Christians. Although he was convinced that being Christian constituted a capital crime, he wrote the emperor Trajan to ask him if Christians should be persecuted for simply identifying themselves as Christians or, rather, for specific illegal acts. He asked if he should pardon and release Christians who renounced their faith. Pliny then told Trajan how he had proceeded with those trials which he had overseen. Pliny had tested the individuals, to see if they truly were Christians, by requiring them to (1) call on the gods, (2) sacrifice to the emperor's image, and (3) curse Christ. Those Christians who were Roman citizens were sent to Rome. The others were given three opportunities to renounce their faith. If they then chose not to do so, Pliny mentioned that he "ordered them to be exe-

cuted. For whatever the nature of their creed might be, I could at least feel no doubt that contumacy and inflexible obstinacy deserved chastisement" (Pliny 1909–1914, 10.96).

Typical of the pragmatism of Roman policy, Trajan responded by acknowledging that Pliny had acted appropriately. He also wrote, however, that Christians were not to be actively prosecuted by the Roman authorities or hunted down. Rather, judicial action was to be taken against them only when others had brought official accusations against them; anonymous charges were seen as unacceptable and undignified. Trajan's response ended up being normative for Rome's treatment of Christians.

The Threat of Christianity

Why Christianity was a capital offense is not discussed in the Pliny/Trajan correspondence; it is assumed. A number of reasonable explanations, however, stand out. Christians came to be persecuted when they were seen as distinct from Jews. Without antiquity on their side, they were seen as a novelty or a curious superstition at best. At worst, they were a threat to public order and morality. They threatened public order, because they not only worshiped a criminal who had been executed by the government, but also refused to sacrifice to the gods of the state. Frequently called "atheists," because they did not worship the Roman gods, Christians also displayed to other peoples' gods an uncompromising intolerance that was uncharacteristic of the age. Furthermore, according to Pliny, at least some of these Christians were simply disrespectful to the Roman authorities. Christianity threatened public order, because—unlike the mystery religions and so many Eastern cults—this religion had a strong central organization that represented a potential challenge to the government.

Christians also threatened public morality. They met illegally at night, they referred to each other as "brother" and "sister," they engaged in a ritual known as "the holy kiss," they spoke of eating the flesh and drinking the blood of "the son." Since much of this language was cryptic to non-Christians, Christians found themselves accused of taking part in incestuous orgies, of engaging in cannibalism, and of practicing infanticide. It is not surprising that such accusations would circulate. Because of the Christian faith, temples were deserted and, consequently, the temple meat trade suffered and commercial interests were threatened.

The best explanation why Romans did not accept the presence of Christianity as a legitimate religion is that it endangered the *pax deorum* ("peace of the gods"). Christians did not worship the state gods and so they upset that relationship between the gods and the Roman empire, which kept the Romans in the gods' favor. In short, Christians were accused of subversion on a cosmic level.

In an effort to revitalize paganism, Decius issued an edict (in 249 or 250 CE) that required sacrifice to the gods. Decius targeted Christian clergy, hundreds were martyred empirewide, and Christianity was weakened. Though the persecutions stopped, Diocletian (284–305) later initiated the Great Persecution, an empirewide hunting down of Christians. Edicts were issued that demanded the destruction of all churches and Christian scripture, the elimination of class privileges for Christians, the imprisonment of all clergy, and the death or forced labor of all Christians who did not sacrifice to the gods of the state. Only after recognizing that Roman religion would not be restored by these measures did Galerius, in the year 311 CE, issue the Edict of Toleration, which allowed Christians the freedom to worship as they pleased.

Constantine and His Legacy

Constantine (312–337 CE), who had increasingly come to identify with Christianity, offered a comparable edict in 313. In that year, he and his co-emperor, Licinius, issued the Edict of Milan, through which the state granted both complete toleration to anyone who was Christian and the return of church property. Christians were no longer persecuted, but were free to worship. And they faced a very different world. Through Constantine, Roman laws and political structures developed in support of Christian ideals and social interests. Laws were developed to combat the abandonment of infants, the branding of slaves' faces, and gladiatorial shows. If marriage laws hurt Christian celibates or widows who did not remarry, the laws were abandoned. Constantine closed the courts on Sundays and discouraged Sunday labor in general. Furthermore, he gave the church grants from the state, resulting in the financing of clergy, church buildings, and Bibles. Clergy were even given exemptions from compulsory civic duties, with Constantine emphasizing the importance of their dedication to worship. As he noted, "for when they render supreme service to the Deity, it seems they confer incalculable benefit on the affairs of the States" (Eusebius, *Ecclesiastical History* X.7.2). By making this claim, Constantine started the process by which traditional state religion would no longer be seen as the only vehicle for ensuring the success and security of the Empire.

Constantine also made Christianity more attractive when he encouraged and rewarded cities to abandon pagan cults. He had some pagan statues destroyed, closed some pagan shrines, and dismantled others. In his role as emperor, he allowed the state religion to continue, but he referred to paganism as an "error" and saw sacrifice as "false pollution."

Finishing the process that Constantine seemed to have started, Theodosius I made Christianity the state religion. Although Judaism was a legal religion, Jews were at the fringe of society and had been banned from a number of public offices. In 380 CE, Theodosius I—the last emperor of the undivided Roman Empire—delivered an edict against heresy, ensuring that "religious freedom" would not be a reality for those who did not follow acceptable forms of Christianity. In 388, public discussions of religion were prohibited, and by 392 Theodosius prohibited paganism and the polytheism that had so characterized the Roman state. By 435, there was even a law threatening death for those who continued to practice those religious traditions.

Religious Freedom at the End of the Roman Empire

By the end of the fourth century, Constantine and Licinius's words from the Edict of Milan were only a distant memory: "We should grant both to Christians and to all people freedom to follow whatever *religio* each one wished, whereby whatever divinity exists in the celestial abode can be placated and propitious to us and all who are placed under our power. Accordingly, we thought than on sensible and most proper grounds this plans should be adopted, that we should not deny this right to anyone, whether he has devoted himself to the Christians' observance or to any *religio* which he considers most suitable for himself, so that the supreme divinity, whose *religio* we obey with free minds, can provide for us in every matter his accustomed favour and benevolence" (Beard et al. 1998, 283). These words, which had given Christians their essential religious freedom, came to be muffled by the edicts of Theodosius I and by the state's demand for order. At the close of the Empire, like at the close of the Republic, most Romans would have agreed that proper religious practice and maintenance belonged in the hands of the rulers of the state. At the close of the Roman Empire, Christianity had shifted from the persecuted to the privileged position and had largely become identified with the Roman state. Some three and a half centuries earlier, Jesus had said, "Render to Caesar the things that are Caesar's, and to God the things that are God's" (Mark 12:17, RSV). At the close of the Empire the line between the two had clearly become blurred.

Craig Wansink

Further Reading

Arnobius (1994). Against the heathen. In A. Roberts and J. Donaldson (Eds.), *Ante-Nicene Fathers, vol. 6* (pp. 403–540). Peabody, MA: Hendrickson Publishers.

Beard, M., North, J., & Price, S. (1998). *Religions of Rome* (Vols. 1–2). New York: Cambridge University Press.

Benko, S. (1984). *Pagan Rome and the early Christians.* Bloomington: Indiana University Press.

Cicero, M. T. (1925). De Doma Sua. In *Cicero* (pp. 131–311). Cambridge, MA: Harvard University Press.

Cohn-Sherbok, D., & Court, J. M. (2001). *Religious diversity in the Graeco-Roman world: A survey of recent scholarship.* Sheffield, UK: Sheffield Academic Press.

Eusebius. (1932). *The ecclesiastical history* (Vol. 2). (J. E. L. Oulton, Trans.). Cambridge, MA: Harvard University Press.

Ferguson, J. (1970). *The religions of the Roman Empire.* Ithaca, NY: Cornell University Press.

Fox, R. L. (1986). *Pagans and Christians.* San Francisco: Harper & Row.

Guterman, S. L. (1951). *Religious toleration and persecution in ancient Rome.* London: Aiglon Press.

MacMullen, R. (1981). *Paganism in the Roman Empire.* New Haven, CT: Yale University Press.

Pliny. (1909–1914). *Letters* (Vol. 2). (W. Melmoth, Trans.). New York: P. F. Collier & Son.

S

Sabbatarians

Sabbatarianism generally denotes the strict observance of a weekly day of rest from secular work and pleasure from sunset to sunset for the purpose of worshiping God. This article focuses on the contributions of "seventh-day" or Saturday Sabbatarianism to religious liberty.

The oldest existing Sabbatarians, Seventh Day Baptists, originated after the English Civil War when Puritans sought religious, political, and social reforms. Sabbatarianism in the United States began with the establishment of the first Seventh Day Baptist church in 1671 in Newport, Rhode Island. Baptist Sabbatarians have steadily declined in North America since 1900. The church joined the Baptist Joint Committee on Public Affairs in 1963 as its official channel for addressing religious liberty concerns.

Adventist Sabbatarianism arose after the collapse of the Millerite movement in the mid-1840s. A Baptist lay preacher, William Miller (1782–1849), preached that Christ would literally return to the earth in 1843–1844, later revised to 22 October 1844. One of the fragmented groups evolved into the Seventh-day Adventist Church (hereafter Adventist), formally organizing in 1863. Adventists incorporated into their doctrines the seventh-day Sabbath learned from a non-Millerite Seventh Day Baptist woman. Since the 1880s, Adventists began a trend of continuous membership growth and institution building that has exceeded all other Sabbatarian groups. From the Adventist church came the Church of God strand: Church of God (Seventh Day, 1866), from which Herbert W. Armstrong's (1982–1985) Worldwide Church of God withdrew (1937), from which his son Ted started the Church of God International (late 1970s), followed by further fragmentation after Herbert's death in 1986 when his successors repudiated his main teachings, including the literal Sabbath concept. The much smaller Davidian strand originated in the 1930s with Victor Houteff's (1885–1950) Shepherd's Rod that later splintered into several Davidian groups out of which came David Koresh's (born Vernon Howell [1959–1993]) Branch Davidians, known for its 1993 standoff with the U.S. government at a compound twenty miles outside Waco, Texas. Sabbatarians, exclusive of Adventists, currently have an estimated worldwide membership of fewer than 500,000 in contrast to Adventists numbering 13 million by 2003, including one million members in the United States and Canada.

Religious Liberty Developments

Seventh Day Baptists, apart from the Sabbath issue, have more in common with mainstream Christianity resulting in less conflict with social policies, in contrast to the apocalypticism of other Sabbatarians with the emphasis on separating from the world.

Adventist advocacy for religious liberty developed in the last decade of the nineteenth century. The publication, *The American Sentinel*, was founded in 1883, renamed *Liberty* in 1906; the National Religious Liberty Association was founded in 1889, later renamed the International Religious Liberty Association. The former continues to promote religious liberty in North America among "thought leaders," such as politicians, judges, lawyers, and

ELLEN WHITE'S VISION

For Seventh-day Adventists, the vision reported below by Ellen G. White (1827–1915) became a key source of their beliefs and practices regarding the Sabbath. White was a prophet, teacher, preacher, and prolific author, and one of the founders of the Adventist church in the United States.

We felt an unusual spirit of prayer. And as we prayed the Holy Ghost fell upon us. We were very happy. Soon I was lost to earthly things and was wrapped in a vision of God's glory. I saw an angel flying swiftly to me. He quickly carried me from the earth to the Holy City. In the city I saw a temple, which I entered. I passed through a door before I came to the first veil. This veil was raised, and I passed into the holy place. Here I saw the altar of incense, the candlestick with seven lamps, and the table on which was the shewbread. After viewing the glory of the holy, Jesus raised the second veil and I passed into the holy of holies.

In the holiest I saw an ark; on the top and sides of it was purest gold. On each end of the ark was a lovely cherub, with its wings spread out over it. Their faces were turned toward each other, and they looked downward. Between the angels was a golden censer. Above the ark, where the angels stood, was an exceeding bright glory, that appeared like a throne where God dwelt. Jesus stood by the ark, and as the saints' prayers came up to Him, the incense in the censer would smoke, and He would offer up their prayers with the smoke of the incense to His Father. In the ark was the golden pot of manna, Aaron's rod that budded, and the tables of stone which folded together like a book. Jesus opened them, and I saw the ten commandments written on them with the finger of God. On one table were four, and on the other six. The four on the first table shone brighter than the other six. But the fourth, the Sabbath commandment, shone above them all; for the Sabbath was set apart to be kept in honor of God's holy name. The holy Sabbath looked glorious—a halo of glory was all around it. I saw that the Sabbath commandment was not nailed to the cross. If it was, the other nine commandments were; and we are at liberty to break them all, as well as to break the fourth. I saw that God had not changed the Sabbath, for He never changes. But the pope had changed it from the seventh to the first day of the week; for he was to change times and laws

I saw that the holy Sabbath is, and will be, the separating wall between the true Israel of God and unbelievers; and that the Sabbath is the great question to unite the hearts of God's dear, waiting saints.

Ellen G. White

Source: *Early Writings of Mrs. White.* (Washington DC: Review and Herald Publishing Association, 1907), 32–33.

educators, while the latter holds world congresses for international religious and governmental leaders. From these beginnings, Adventists steadily became the primary advocates of religious liberty among Sabbatarians in the twentieth century. Additionally, legal departments were initiated by Adventists in the late 1930s and by the Worldwide Church of God in the early 1960s to more readily address their historical tensions with society regarding military service, Sunday legislation, and other church-state concerns.

Military Service and Bearing of Arms

Seventh Day Baptists generally entered military service as combatants in American wars while others, including German Seventh Day Baptists and Church of God Sabbatarians, were strict pacifists that suffered fines and imprisonment until conscientious objector exemptions were granted after World War I. Recently, the Worldwide Church of God dropped its strict pacifist stance in conjunction with the general repudiation of its founder's teachings. During the Civil War, the newly formed Adventist church initially took a pacifist stand. By the time of World War I, Adventists shifted to a strict noncombatancy policy; the rapid extension of Adventists in the early twentieth century, however, created difficulties in applying the policy uniformly in other countries. During the two world wars, Adventists in Argentina, Germany, and Russia officially cooperated with authoritarian governments in order to thwart state reprisals. The American-based General Conference headquarters recognized only the official German and Russian Adventist churches despite the fact that disfellowshipped underground Adventist groups had supported the non-combatancy policy.

Adventists in North America during World War II cooperated with the respective militaries in supplying chaplains and in developing medical cadet training programs on college campuses. Trained by military personnel, these programs enabled both Adventists and non-Adventists to support the war without violating religious convictions, with Adventists comprising the largest segment (12,000) of non-combatants. Similar arrangements continued during the Korean and Vietnam Wars; however, one hundred South Korean Adventists were beaten and imprisoned because noncombatancy accommodation was not an option.

The Adventist church in practice established two patterns of international military service: noncombatancy in most of Western Europe and English-speaking democracies, and bearing arms to avoid severe penalties in communist Eastern Europe, Franco's Spain, Latin America, and Asia. The denomination replaced its historical noncombatancy policy in 1972 with a policy that allowed the issue of military service to be a matter of individual conscience in choosing to serve as a combatant, noncombatant, or conscientious objector with the full support of the church. Related to military service was the Immigration Service's refusal from 1931 to 1945 of several Sabbatarian immigrant applications for citizenship. Some of these went to court with mixed results. In *Giroud v. United States* (1946), however, the first Supreme Court case involving an Adventist, the Court ruled that the promise to bear arms was not intended by Congress when making the law and that citizenship should not be denied because of an applicant's religious convictions.

Sunday Legislation and Sabbath Observance in the Workplace

Sabbatarians have traditionally opposed the theological rationales and practical enforcement of Sunday legislation as a burden to the conscience and to economic well-being. These "blue laws", which derives its name form the color of the colonial paper upon which they were printed, existed in many states, some dating to colonial times. Seventh Day Baptists, and later Adventists, lobbied for exemptions from these laws as a claim for the granting of religious liberty. When the National Reform Association in 1888 pressed for a federal Sunday law to buttress state blue laws, Adventists changed course and opposed exemptions on the basis of rights embodied in the Bill of Rights. Adventist apocalypticism formed the conceptual basis for opposition to Sunday laws, infusing Sunday bills with a prophetic significance not shared by the Seventh Day Baptists. This emphasis infused Sunday bills with a prophetic significance not shared by the Seventh Day Baptists.

Sabbatarians lobbied against 150 Congressional Sunday bills from the late 1880s until the 1930s, when interest in Sunday legislation waned. Sabbatarians made little headway in the states due to lack of legal expertise and because the Supreme Court held that the federal Constitution permitted states to establish a church and religious principles, for example, Sunday laws. The Court reversed course in the 1930s when it began to incorporate or apply First Amendment rights as binding to the states through the "due process" clause of the Fourteenth Amendment. Thus states could no longer deny basic rights without providing due process of the law. The First Amendment's free exercise of religion clause was incorporated in *Cantwell v. Connecticut* (1940), and the establishment clause was incorporated in *Everson v. Board of Education* (1947). The shift in Supreme Court doctrine opened the way for Sabbatarians and others to challenge religion-based laws in the states. Sabbatarians, mostly Jews and members of the Worldwide Church of God, as well as secular businesses, successfully challenged the religious nature of many state blue laws. Meanwhile, Sunday closing advocates shifted from religion-based to science-based rationales for justifying blue laws so that the Supreme Court in 1961 ruled in four related Sunday cases that

Sunday laws had become secular in nature and were thus constitutional.

For Adventists and members of the Worldwide Church of God, the development of the doctrine of incorporation encouraged the use of the courts in addressing the ongoing dilemma of employment lost for refusing to work on the Sabbath. One case in particular, *Sherbert v. Verner* (1963), reached the Supreme Court and resulted in a landmark decision. When fired for refusing to work on the Sabbath, an Adventist employee was denied state unemployment benefits. The Court upheld the employee's right to the benefits, stating that being forced to choose between job and religious convictions placed a burden on the free exercise of religion. To alleviate the burden, the Court established the first precedent of free exercise clause jurisprudence by requiring states to demonstrate a compelling state interest in order to withstand Court scrutiny. This case guaranteed unemployment benefits for persons with religious convictions in the workplace.

Sabbatarians, however, still faced the lack of employer accommodation. Partial remedy came through the efforts of Senator Jennings Randolph (1753–1813), a Seventh Day Baptist, who also authored the twenty-sixth amendment to the U.S. Constitution, which lowered the voting age to eighteen. His efforts in 1972 succeeded in amending section 701(j) of Title VII of the Civil Rights Act of 1964 to require employers to accommodate employees' religious principles unless it imposed an "undue hardship" on the employer. Undue hardship was further defined in *Trans World Airlines v. Hardison* (1977). A member of the Worldwide Church of God proceeded with a suit contrary to the counsel of the church's legal department. The Court upheld "reasonable" employer accommodation but defined undue hardship on the basis of minimum costs incurred. The decision made it more difficult for Sabbatarians to win cases. The gains acquired by Sabbatarians from *Sherbert* suffered yet another setback in *Employment Division v. Smith* (1990), which ruled that a generally applicable law that burdened religious practice was to stand if the burden was an incidental effect and not the object of the law. *Smith* effectively limited the compelling state interest test in *Sherbert* and essentially limited litigation to Title VII precedents. The net effect of the various Sabbatarian legal efforts and the outcome of *Smith* accomplished conflicting results in protecting Sabbath convictions in the workplace.

Conscientious Objection to Union Membership

Adventists asserted conscientious objection to union membership because unions resort to the use of strikes and violence. The church lobbied for over thirty years with limited success for laws and amendments granting "escape" clauses. Litigation of a number of cases was initiated in the 1970s by denominational lawyers, culminating in three cases that brought resolution: *Nottelson v. Smith* (1981), *Tooley v. Martin-Marietta Corporation* (1981), and *International Association of Machinists and Aerospace Workers v. Boeing* (1987). These cases established reasonable accommodation standards without creating undue hardship for unions and employers, thus protecting the religious convictions of all individuals from unacceptable burdens imposed by union membership.

Institutional Church-State Issues

An unusual case involved the intervention of the State of California in the affairs of the Worldwide Church of God over charges of mishandling finances that was alleged by dissident members. The State placed all Church property under receivership in 1979, based on the unprecedented rationale that churches were charitable trusts owned by the state. The church was unsuccessful in the courts, but was helped by the state legislature due to the intervention of the state's religious community resulting in withdraw of the case.

In the two most important gender discrimination cases pitting Adventist employees against church institutions, *Equal Employment Opportunity Commission and Silver v. Pacific Press Publishing Association* (1976) and *Equal Employment Opportunity Commission v. Pacific Press* (1982), the Supreme Court ruled in favor of employees not classified as ministers in religious organizations and prohibited discrimination against such employees regarding wages, promotions, and job dismissals. The cases established firm precedents for the rights of non-ministerial employees of all religious organizations in the years since the rulings.

Political Involvement and Government Relations

Sabbatarianism has had a varied pattern regarding involvement in politics. Seventh Day Baptists have served in political office producing a U.S. senator, Jennings Randolph, and a governor, George H. Utter (1854–1912). Sabbatarian Church of God and Davidian groups continue to adhere to apolitical attitudes, with the exception of recent changes in the Worldwide Church of God, which rejected founder William Armstrong's teachings on antitrinitarianism, British/American Israelitism, Old Testament-based dietry and Sabbath laws, and apoliticism, to name a few. Adventists, since the late nineteenth century, have engaged social issues related to public health and church-state relations while eschewing party politics. Adventism has increasingly moved toward accommodating particular societies, illustrated by the church's changing stance on military service and the bearing of arms, use of the courts to resolve workplace conflicts, and in seeking government accreditation and funding of medical and higher educational institutions in the United States and overseas. Adventists also revamped humanitarian work into the Adventist Development and Relief Agency (ADRA) in order to take advantage of U.S. foreign aid funding. In recent decades, Adventists have had success in gaining political office in Uganda, in Micronesian Palau, in Jamaica, and in the South Pacific islands, all regions where Adventists have a large presence.

Sabbatarians often must negotiate with governments on a variety of issues, including, exemptions from mandatory school attendance on Saturdays, legal incorporation of the church, and grants-in-aid for schools. To avoid antagonizing authorities into retributive action harming the church's mission, the Adventist church has typically been silent about human rights' violations in countries where they have a presence. Adventists historically have followed a course of practicality to better preserve the mission and institutions of the church.

Matthew F. McMearty

Further Reading

Blaich, R. (1993). Religion under national socialism: The case of the German Adventist church. *Central European History, 26,* 255–280.

Bull, M., & Lockart, K. (1989). *Seeking a sanctuary: Seventh-day Adventism and the American dream.* San Francisco: Harper and Row.

Butler, J. M. (1974). Adventism and the American experience. In E. S. Gaustad (Ed.), *The rise of Adventism: Religion and society in mid-nineteenth-century America.* New York: Harper and Row.

Dudley, R. L., & Hernandez, E. I. (1992). *Citizens of two worlds: Religion and politics among American Seventh-day Adventists.* Berrien Springs, MI: Andrews University Press.

Heinz, D. (1993). *Church, state, and religious dissent: A history of Seventh-day Adventists in Austria, 1890–1975.* New York: Peter Lang.

Lawson, R. (1998). Seventh-day Adventists and the U.S. courts: Road signs along the route of a denominationalizing sect. *Journal of Church and State, 40,* 553–588.

Lawson, R. (1996). Church and state at home and abroad: The evolution of Seventh-day Adventist relations with governments. *Journal of the American Academy of Religion, 64,* 279–311.

Lawson, R. (1996). Onward Christian soldiers? Seventh-day Adventists and the issue of military service. *Review of Religious Research, 37,* 97–122.

Lawson, R. (1995). Sect-state relations: Accounting for the differing trajectories of Seventh-day Adventists and Jehovah's Witnesses. *Sociology of Religion, 56,* 351–377.

Morgan, D. (2001). *Adventism and the American republic.* Knoxville: University of Tennessee Press.

Plantak, Z. (1998). *The silent church: Human rights and Adventist social ethics.* New York: St. Martin's Press.

Sanford, D. A. (1992). *A choosing people: The history of Seventh Day Baptists.* Nashville: Broadman Press.

Sapiets, M. (1990). *True witness: The story of Seventh-day Adventists in the Soviet Union.* Keston, England: Keston College.

Syme, E. (1973). *A history of SDA church-state relations in the United States.* Mountain View, CA: Pacific Press.

Court Cases

Cantwell v. Connecticut, 310 U.S. 296 (1940).

Equal Employment Opportunity Commission v. Pacific Press Publishing Association, 676 F.2d 1272 (1982).

Equal Employment Opportunity Commission and Silver v. Pacific Press, 535 F.2d 1182 (1976).

Everson v. Board of Education, 330 U.S. 1 (1947).

Giroud v. United States, 328 U.S. 61 (1946).

Nottelson v. Smith, 643 F.2d 445 (1981).

Sherbert v. Verner, 374 U.S. 398 (1963).

Tooley v. Martin-Marietta Corporation, 648 F.2d 1239 (1981).

Trans World Airlines, Inc. v. Hardison, 432 U.S. 63 (1977).

Sacred Space and Conflict

Conflicts over sacred space are a pervasive and global phenomenon. They have triggered ethnic and international conflict and have appeared as symptoms or as by-products of existing conflicts. Disputes have erupted over the ownership of sacred sites, the desecration or destruction of tombs, temples, churches, mosques, and shrines, or over demands for free exercise of controversial rituals on pilgrim routes or burial grounds. Appealing to religious absolutes, conflicts at sacred sites mobilize tribal, nationalist, and ethnic sentiments, leading to violence that spreads rapidly beyond the boundaries of the sacred place. Because sacred space is perceived as indivisible, disputes over sacred space can impede the peaceful resolution of longstanding disputes. Employing the powerful symbolism of the sacred space, radical elements will use disputes over sites as justification for their efforts to spoil accommodation between parties to negotiations.

In regions such as South Asia, the Balkans, and the Middle East, where political and religious boundaries often coincide, disputes over sacred sites have sparked interethnic riots and armed confrontations that have exasperated preexisting conflicts. A dispute in 1852 between Christian denominations over rights in the churches of the Holy Land led to French and Russian intervention on behalf of the Catholic and Orthodox communities in Jerusalem and triggered the Crimean War. In 1964, deadly Hindu-Muslim riots in response to the theft of a relic from the Hazratbal Mosque in Srinagar, Kashmir, propelled the mass exodus of 700,000 refugees into India and contributed to the outbreak of the second Indo-Pakistani war. Over six hundred mosques were destroyed by Serbs during the ethnic war in Bosnia in the 1990s. In September 2000, a provocative visit by then Israeli opposition leader Ariel Sharon to the Temple Mount in Jerusalem, a site revered by Jews and Muslims, sparked an unprecedented wave of violence in the Middle East. Osama bin Laden listed the proximity of U.S. troops stationed in Saudi Arabia to the shrines in Mecca and Medina as one justification for his attacks against the United States.

The costs of mismanaging disputes over sacred space in the twenty-first century will be substantial, and measured in human lives. Resolving disputes over sacred space poses challenges unlike any encountered in disputes over secular territory, but also unique opportunities for cooperating with religious actors that can influence the definition of the disputed space.

Sacred Space Defined

Sacred spaces are religious centers at which the heavenly and earthly meet; they connect the human and the divine world. Three functions are characteristic of sacred places: They are places of communication with divinity through prayer, movement, or visual contact with an image of the divine; they are places of divine presence, often promising healing, success, or salvation; and they provide meaning to the faithful by metaphorically reflecting the underlying order of the world. Sacred places are replete with forms, actions, and objects that convey religious meaning.

Sacred spaces appear in an infinite variety of shape, location, importance, and purpose. Their prevalence has suggested to some students of religion that sacred space is an essential, perhaps the most essential component in all great religious traditions. Mircea Eliade (1907–86), the foremost scholar of sacred space, described sacred places as historical, spiritual, and cosmological centers, axes connecting heaven and earth around which the world revolves. Often, they are recognized as the locus of creation or the end of time. Pilgrims who journey to sacred places travel towards the center, seeking in the sacred space a microcosm of the universe and of the specific religion it represents. Sacred space may encompass an entire land, a sanctified structure, such as a temple or shrine, or a natural site interpreted as sacred, such as a mountain, river, forest or lake. The sanctity of some sites is communicated by the gods through a special sign. Other sites are recognized as sacred because a religiously significant event took place there or because of the presence of relics.

The sociologist Émile Durkheim (1858–1917) argued that the clear distinction between the sacred and the profane is the basis of all religious practice. To maintain this distinction, access to sacred space and behavior within it must be strictly delimited. Gestures of approach are often necessary before entering the circumscribed site. Religious codes may regulate dress and prohibit a narrow range of activities within the sanctuary or forbid all but a narrow range of behaviors. Access to many sacred places is limited to members of the religion, members of a specific gender or caste, or single chosen individuals.

THE DIVERSITY OF SACRED PLACES AROUND THE WORLD

Across cultures there are thousands of types of places that are defined as sacred and millions of actual sacred places. As these examples below show, many of the places are part of the natural world.

The Lapps of northern Europe

In the parish of Gallivare the saivo-lakes were everywhere real lakes of sacrifice and at every lake there was a place of offerings which was frequently associated with a seidi stone. There also existed the rule in regard to every real place of offerings (passepaike) that women should not on any account enter such a place nor pass the lake in a boat. If they did so they would certainly die.

As to the spirits of the springs, these were evidently, like the lakes, worshipped in connection with the spiritual beings inhabiting the under-world, and it is by no means necessary to assume a Scandinavian or Finnish origin of this cult. The clear-water, uninterruptedly welling forth from the earth, awoke the wonder of the pagan Lapp and easily suggested to him the idea of a supernatural origin of this phenomenon.

Rafael Karsten

Source: *The Religion of the Samek: Ancient Beliefs and Cults of the Scandinavian and Finnish Lapps.* (Leiden, Netherlands: E. J. Brill, 1955), 18.

Aranda Aboriginals in Australia

Among the Wik-munkan the pulwaiya (ancestor) has a sacred place of origin, its auwa, where it resides and whence it issues forth. These auwa, or totem centers, are sometimes the nests and breeding places of the birds, animals, and plants concerned and are always situated on the hunting grounds of the clan to which they belong, where the totemic species is abundant. Each auwa has its own peculiar characteristics. Trees, bushes, rocks, naturally or artificially arranged, ant beds or holes in the ground in the vicinity of the auwa, are sacred to the totems. There is always water nearby in the shape of river, creek, lagoon, waterhole or swamp, or well, at the bottom of which the pulwaiya resides and into which the dead of the clan are believed to go. They are said to play about the vicinity of the auwa in the form of their totem. This is perhaps why plants or animals are protected near the auwa of their representative totem and why the killing of an animal or the injuring of a plant near its auwa is not only strictly forbidden but believed to be attended by grave consequences.

Geza Roheim

Source: *The Eternal Ones of the Dream: A Psychoanalytic Interpretation of Australian Myth and Ritual.* (New York: International Universities Press, 1945), 152.

cont.

THE DIVERSITY OF SACRED PLACES AROUND THE WORLD cont.

Lau of Fiji

The chief priest on Mothe belonged to the Kamali clan. The foundation of the principal god house, located on the old Kamali hamlet site in west Mothe, may still be seen. It is surrounded by sweet smelling plants. It is still regarded as a sacred place, and as they approach it the Mothe people become silent and remove their turbans and ornaments. The god of Kamali was incarnated in the scaled shark (nggio thave), the vivili, and the matamila fish which were tabu to Kamali. Members of the clan think that the kaisevou bird, which is common on Mothe, used to be tabu also. The principal fore-father of Kamali is not known but the clan genealogy is traced seven generations back to the priest Mirakilangi. Other priests in the clan pedigree are Malanamailangi, Wanggathiri, Ndolosambau, and Mbatchimalungu.

Laura Thompson

Source: *Southern Lau, Fiji: An Ethnography.*
(Honolulu, HI: Bernice P. Bishop Museum, Bulletin 162, 1940), 111.

Saramaka of Suriname

As we made a tour of the village, we discussed all this with the chief and his bassia, and with the other men who accompanied us. When we reached the open place sacred to the great gods, we stopped. The shrine was a fenced-in space, perhaps eight or nine feet long and almost as wide. Inside was a slender pole, with a head carved on its top, and a cotton tunic about its middle, and this was the wife of the Great God, the chief said. The ladder with the platform on it, on which stood a bottle, was the shrine of the great Sky God. At the base of the image with the tunic were several bottles, some white clay, and a few empty glasses, and everywhere were sticks with cloth on them, many with the cloth in tatters. Where the cotton had altogether rotted away, the stick alone remained.

Melville J. Herskovits

Source: *Rebel Destiny: Among the Bush Negroes of Dutch Guiana.* (New York: McGraw-Hill, 1934), 161.

Causes of Conflict over Sacred Space

Sacred space is an earth-bound, material facet of religion. In it, the sacred becomes tangible and can be owned, built upon, dug in, fought over. Where conflict over sacred space breaks out it is often linked to ethnic or sectarian conflict, and has the potential to aggravate existing regional and international disputes. Disputes over sacred space erupt either as result of competition between religious actors or as a result of clashes between secular and religious forces. Four broad types of disputes over sacred space can be identified.

Sectarian Rivalry

When religious traditions split into rival branches, they create competition over a common sacred space. Disputes over tombs in the West Bank, such as the Tomb of Rachel in Bethlehem or the tombs of Abraham, Isaac, Rebecca, Jacob, and Leah in Hebron, stem from the shared reverence of Jews and Muslims for their common patriarchs. Greek Orthodox, Latin, Armenian, Coptic, Syrian, and Ethiopian Christians compete over control of the Church of the Holy Sepulcher in Jerusalem as well as over the Church of the Nativity in Bethlehem. In the United States two churches that seceded from the Church of Jesus Christ of Latter-day Saints (the Mormon church) have vied over the site of the future Temple of Christ in Independence, Missouri. By staking claim to a sacred site that once united the religious movement, each rival asserts its claim as inheritor of the true faith.

Conquest and Religious Syncretism

Disputes also erupt when successive conquests and religious syncretism lead to the layering of sacred spaces one on top of another. The outcome is a series of competing claims to strata along the sacred axis, demanding different and often conflicting rites from members of opposed religious affiliation. These disputes are common in the Middle East, Europe, Asia Minor, and the Indian subcontinent, where conquerors have sought to integrate sacred sites into their traditions in a simultaneous attempt to displace the local tradition and utilize the convenience of a ready-made focal point to introduce their own religious practices. The dispute over the Temple Mount in Jerusalem as well as the Hindu-Muslim dispute over the Babri Masjid in Ayodhya are examples of this type of dispute.

Conflicts with Secular Forces

In a third category of disputes, worshippers clash with secular forces who want to use the land for development, exploration, or tourism. This is the most common type of dispute over sacred space in the United States: Native Americans have protested the desecration of sacred hunting and gathering grounds, ceremonial grounds, secluded sites dedicated to vision quests and purification ceremonies, sacred mountains, rivers, lakes, or burial grounds. At times the disputes involve developers who want to utilize the sacred land as a resource, as in the litigation by the Inupiat against oil companies seeking to drill in their sacred fishing grounds or the legal battles between the Lakota and Tsistsistas tribes, on one hand, and mountain climbers, hikers, and park facilities developers, on the other, over Devil's Tower, Wyoming. Other disputes have involved scientific institutions such as museums and universities that have staked claim to burial grounds and their contents. The 1990 Native American Grave Protection and Repatriation Act assigned full ownership and control of relevant cultural items, human remains, and associated funerary objects to Native Americans.

The Sacred Site as a Tool for Political Control

A fourth and final type of conflict over sacred space occurs when political actors seek control over a site in order to exert control over a community. These actors exploit the spiritual and political centrality of that space in the daily life of the community to achieve their purpose. Rulers have barred access, desecrated and destroyed sites, or funded the construction and restoration of sacred sites as means for penalizing or rewarding their subjects. Control over shrines is most crucial when these shrines attract mass pilgrimages, as evidenced by the clashes between Shi'ite Muslim pilgrims and Sunni Muslim governments in Mecca, Saudi Arabia or in Najaf and Karbala, Iraq. Pilgrimage offers the host regime opportunities for punishing rival regimes or demonstrating exceptional generosity and hospitality. To rival regimes and religious minorities these mass events offer a forum for organized protest and subversive activities.

Barriers to Resolving Conflicts over Sacred Space

The attributes of sacred space complicate the resolution of conflicts. The clearly defined boundaries of sacred space make it hard to compromise on a site's precise size and location; the uniqueness of the sacred impedes the search for substitutes; the centrality of the sacred axis prohibits the division of disputed sacred space. These three attributes create a situation unlike any arising in secular territorial disputes: The disputed location is indivisible. The parties to such a dispute can accept no partition or concession over the site. The more central the space in the religious landscape of the community, the greater the divine power vested in the place and the greater the obligation of the community to defend its sanctity. This obligation is owed, not only to all members of the community, but to future generations, deceased ancestors, and the gods themselves, leaving the community with no ability or desire to bargain over the space with rivals. The more access to the sacred space and behavior within it are circumscribed, monitored, and sanctioned, the greater the risk that foreign presence or conduct will be interpreted as an offensive act.

Only rarely will change in the status of a sacred place succeed without the cooperation of religious actors. Decision makers have often chosen to apply standard political tools to resolve these conflicts rather than deal with their religious complexities. In

Israel and India, for example, governments have attempted to impose shared use of disputed Jewish-Muslim or Hindu-Muslim shrines only to discover that resolutions by fiat tend to be highly unstable, routinely violent, and exceedingly short-lived. The destruction of sacred places is equally unfeasible, since sacred shrines are merely markers for a sacred place. As the continued Jewish reverence towards the Temple Mount in Jerusalem exemplifies, destruction of this marker can aggravate a dispute by enhancing the attachment of the group to its defiled site

Resolution by means of force can only succeed if religious leaders and their followers are too weak to penalize political leaders. This was the case in the course of English and French iconoclastic revolutions or during the Communist revolutions in China and the Soviet Union. Where this is not the case, the costs of unilateral action can be prohibitive to both the leader and the community. In 1984 Indira Gandhi attempted to oust an insurgent from the Sikh shrine in Amritsar by means of a military force without consulting the High Priests of the shrine. The attack destroyed the shrine, provoked months of deadly riots across India, and prompted the assassination of Gandhi by her Sikh bodyguard. An equally destructive 1989 military operation to end a hostage crisis in the Great Mosque in Mecca might have had similar consequences for the Saudi royal family, had it not requested and received a religious ruling supporting the undertaking from Saudi Arabia's religious elite.

Sacred places cannot be partitioned by leaders according to political priorities. They may, for considerable segments of the population, be irreplaceable and indivisible. The odds of resolving these intricate disputes can be improved by cautiously incorporating religious actors into the conflict resolution process. Left out of the process, charismatic religious actors can exasperate a dispute by enhancing the centrality and exclusivity of a site in the eyes of their followers. Brought in, religious leaders may be induced to issue rulings that favor compromise over sacred space or at the very least disclose crucial information about the meaning, importance, and boundaries of a disputed site.

Ron E. Hassner

Further Reading

Brereton, Joel P. (1987). Sacred Space. In M. Eliade (Ed.), *The encyclopedia of religion* (Vol. 12, pp. 526–535). New York: Macmillan.

Chidester, D., & Linenthal, E. T. (Eds.). (1995). *American sacred space*. Bloomington: Indiana University Press.

Durkheim, É. (1976). *The elementary forms of the religious life* (J. W. Swain, Trans.). London: Allen and Unwin.

Echo-Hawk, R. C., & Echo-Hawk, W. R. (1994). *Battlefields and burial grounds: The Indian struggle to protect ancestral graves in the United States*. Minneapolis, MN: Lerner Publications Company.

Eliade, M. (1963). *Patterns in comparative religion* (R. Sheed, Trans.). New York: World.

Friedland, R., & Hecht, R. (1998). The bodies of nations: A comparative study of religious violence in Jerusalem and Ayodhya. *History of Religions, 38*(2), 101.

Hassner, R. E. (in press). Sacred space and Native American sacred grounds. In P. A. Djupe & L. R. Olson (Eds.), *Encyclopedia of American religion and politics*. New York: Facts on File.

Holm, J., & Bowker, J. (1994). *Sacred place*. London and New York: Pinter Publishers.

Mending the circle: A Native American repatriation guide: Understanding and implementing NAGPRA and the official Smithsonian and other repatriation policies. (1996). New York: American Indian Ritual Object Repatriation Fund.

van der Leeuw, G. (1967). *Religion in essence and manifestation*. Gloucester, MA: Peter Smith.

School Prayer and Discrimination

When considering public school prayer the tendency is to focus on the U.S. Constitution. Yet many school districts ignore relevant constitutional mandates, with problematic results for religious minorities and dissenters (those opposing public school prayer where it still occurs). From the Philadelphia Bible Riots of 1844 to modern cases, school prayer and bible reading have sometimes served as a flashpoint for conflict, violence, and harassment.

Public school prayer as discussed in this essay is public prayer at public school events or on school property during school-sponsored activities. This article focuses on how such prayer can occasion discrimination against and harassment of religious minorities and those opposing public school religious exercises.

The discrimination perceived by religious individuals as arising from the secularization of public schools is not a focus, nor are incidents where overzealous school officials deny students the right to pray privately at school, although these concerns will be discussed. The United States Supreme Court acknowledges that children have a right to pray privately during the school day. When school officials violate this right they are acting unconstitutionally, even if they do so in the name of the establishment clause of the First Amendment. The violence and harassment discussed in this article, however, is not generally associated with overzealous enforcement of the establishment clause. Rather it tends to occur when school officials ignore their duties under the establishment clause or when they seek, or are asked to support, methods aimed at circumventing Supreme Court school prayer decisions.

Organized Public School Prayer and Discrimination Against Religious Minorities and Dissenters

Virtually all the legal discourse concerning school prayer has focused on the Constitution. Yet the Constitution itself has often proven ineffective in protecting the rights of religious minorities and those who object to religious exercises in public schools. Many school districts simply ignore constitutional mandates, mandates which themselves are not always clear.

U.S. history is replete with examples of public school religious exercises intentionally or unintentionally facilitating discrimination against and intolerance of religious minorities and dissenters. From the earliest days, such religious exercises have called attention to difference by singling out students, families, or groups who do not hold the dominant faith or support public school religious exercises.

Despite the Supreme Court prohibition against organized school prayer, some school districts still conduct such prayer while others work within the parameters the court has laid down. The latter may still hold religious exercises, usually through moments of silence sanctioned by state legislation or attempts to facilitate organized "voluntary, student initiated" prayer at school events. The Supreme Court, however, found the latter practice unconstitutional in 2000, but some groups and schools are trying to circumvent this. When such religious exercises have been conducted, discrimination aimed at religious minorities and dissenters sometimes results.

While school prayer and similar activities do not automatically facilitate discrimination every time they occur, the number of documented cases clearly illustrates the link. Such discrimination is pre-

dictable, since religious exercises call attention to differences that are frequently perceived negatively and tend to create in- and out-groups.

The following case description exemplifies the trauma sometimes facilitated by public school religious exercises. There are many other such documented cases, but many who experience the type of discrimination described below do not file lawsuits for fear of even worse discrimination. Moreover, few lawsuits progress to the issuance of a written opinion, and many published cases dealing with school prayer issues do not address the discrimination involved because of a lack of applicable legal doctrines.

The Herdahl family moved from Wisconsin to Mississippi in 1993 for work-related reasons. The Herdahl children were baptized Lutheran and attended a Pentecostal church, while the area to which they moved was predominantly Southern Baptist. Mrs. Herdahl was shocked to learn that the local K-12 public school in her new home in Ecru, Mississippi, conducted public prayer over the public address system and bible study thirty years after the Supreme Court had prohibited such practices. These activities, moreover, had a decidedly Southern Baptist bent. Her children were harassed by both students and teachers because they did not share the majority faith and were referred to as devil worshipers and atheists. Friends of the children stopped playing with them for fear of being beaten up. One child tried avoiding school. Another asked whether their persecutors were Christian; when his mother answered yes, the child said he did not want to be Christian because he did not want to be like them.

When the practices did not stop, Mrs. Herdahl filed a lawsuit and the harassment only worsened, her family even receiving bomb and death threats. Though the Herdahls ultimately won their lawsuit and obtained an order prohibiting the religious exercises, Mrs. Herdahl stated that others who felt the way she did, even in her own school district, were afraid to say so publicly.

Fear to oppose practices that facilitate discrimination against one's family or which are offensive to one's beliefs is common. Even harsher response often results when one opposes such practices. The Herdahl's case is far from isolated and is not even the worst example of zealous school districts that ignore Constitutional requirements pertaining to religious exercises.

Some well-known Supreme Court cases dealing with religion in public schools included allegations of discrimination aimed at religious minorities or those opposing the practices in question. These allegations were not addressed in the Supreme Court opinions, likely because they are not generally actionable or relevant to the constitutional claims that were the focus. Significantly, much of this discrimination stemmed from the victims' challenging the offending religious exercises.

In response to their complaint in *Illinois ex rel. McCollum v. Board of Education* (1948), in which James Terry McCollum challenged a Christian release time program (a program that relseases students from a public school on the condition that they attend religious classes), the McCollum family was subjected to vitriolic harassment. While the suit was pending the family received thousands of hostile letters containing expressions such as "you slimy bastard," and "[y]our filthy rotten body produced three children so that you can pilot them all safely to hell." The McCollum's child was regularly beaten up and called a "godless communist." While the now famous *Lee v. Weisman* (1992) case was pending, the Weismans received hate mail and death threats. In a rare example of judicial recognition of this problem, Justice Blackmun acknowledged the divisiveness, violence, and strife that can be facilitated by government-sanctioned religious activity in public schools in his concurring opinion in *Lee v. Weisman*.

A highly organized and well-funded campaign currently aims to return prayer and other religious exercises to public schools. This will increase the likelihood of discriminatory incidents and the potential for religious divisiveness in public schools and their surrounding communities. Unfortunately, no consistent legal mechanism is currently available that directly and effectively addresses such discrimination and harassment.

Discrimination Against Religious Individuals

There is a flip side to the above dynamic. Many religious individuals, especially those calling themselves conservative Christians, perceive the secularization of public schools and society as a form of discrimination. This is especially evident where school officials deny religious students or student groups access to facilities based on the erroneous view that the establishment clause requires that all religion be excluded from public schools. Significantly, the U.S. Supreme Court has never held that religious students should

be prevented from privately engaging in religious activities or that religious student groups must be denied equal access to facilities open to all student groups. In fact, the Court has repeatedly recognized the right of students to pray privately and non-disruptively during the school day, most recently in *Santa Fe Independent School District v. Doe* (2000), and the right of religious students and student groups to access facilities at public schools, most recently in *Good News Club v. Milford Central School* (2001). Unfortunately, school officials do sometimes interfere with the rights of religious students, usually in the name of compliance with the establishment clause.

This, along with the secularization of American public life, can be perceived as "discrimination," or at least hostility, against religion. In his book, *The Rhetoric of Church and State: A Critical Analysis of Religion Clause Jurisprudence* (1995), Frederick Mark Gedicks characterizes these feelings as follows: ". . . all too often, religious organizations and individuals experience the Supreme Court's religion clause jurisprudence as oppressive and alienating at the same time that others sincerely believe it to be neutral" (27).

Though many no doubt view secularization as discrimination against religion, and experience it as oppressive and alienating, such "discrimination" is unlike the vitriolic and often violent conduct previously discussed. This is more a case of losing some battles, and winning others, in what James Davison Hunter referred to as the "culture war" between secular society and religious believers, a war that sometimes plays out in the courts. Where overzealous school officials discriminate against religious students, for example, by denying them equal access to school facilities, the dynamic can be closer to the conduct that is the focus of this essay, especially if the officials insult or belittle the religious individual. Yet, vitriolic or violent harassment as described earlier is rare in such cases. Students subjected to such discrimination have valid constitutional claims and the Federal Equal Access Act and state Religious Freedom Restoration Acts often provide legal recourse. The discrimination that is the focus of this essay is harder to deal with legally, because even though public school religious exercises facilitate the discrimination, it is frequently private actors who carry it out; when victims raise constitutional challenges the underlying harassment and discrimination often worsens.

The Social Dynamics of the Problem

No legal mechanism is currently available directly addressing discrimination and harassment perpetrated by non-governmental parties, such as students or parents, in the school prayer context, even when such conduct is facilitated by public school religious exercises. Since discrimination is not directly relevant to the constitutional issues generally raised in school prayer cases, the incidents of discrimination that are reported in court proceedings represent only the tip of the iceberg. However, the anecdotal nature of much of the evidence, and the apparent paradox that increased religion in an environment sparks increased intolerance and prejudice, make it difficult to measure the likelihood of religious exercises in public schools facilitating broader prejudice and discrimination. Existing social science research helps in answering this question, though more needs to be done.

The existence and perpetuation of discrimination are complex phenomena, and research suggests a connection between certain religious personality types and the discrimination that occurs in connection with school prayer. Some of this research is documented and discussed in *School Prayer and Discrimination: The Civil Rights of Religious Minorities and Dissenters*.

Of course, this research does not support absolute connections between religious exercises, religious orientation, and discrimination, and much of it does not focus on public school religious exercises. Still, it does suggest that discrimination is predictable when public school religious exercises occur in areas with particular social dynamics, and that even in other areas there is a significant chance such exercises will facilitate discrimination given the right circumstances.

Current Laws Do Not Address the Problem

The Constitution is the primary means for vindicating legal rights concerning public school religious exercises and any resulting discrimination or harassment. Yet the remedies it offers and the conduct that it can achieve, differ greatly from those available under civil rights law (which would seem better tailored to addressing the situation). Injunctions and declaratory relief are available under both the Constitution and civil rights law, but under the Constitution the conduct that may be enjoined or declared in violation of the law excludes much relevant discrimination. Moreover, the availability of damages for constitu-

tional violations in public schools is based on Federal Statute 42 U.S.C. 1983, which also excludes much discriminatory conduct in these cases.

The remedies available for *constitutional* violations naturally aim at the conduct of *government*-sector actors and the constitutional rights government action may infringe upon. In the current context, that would generally exclude the actions of students, non-policy-making employees (although it could include teachers), or others such as parents or community members. In the school prayer context it is frequently such actors' conduct that is overtly discriminatory—not that of policy-making school officials—even if school policies did foster an environment where discrimination was more likely. More importantly, even if the school could somehow be held liable for the discriminatory acts of these individuals, such acts are not the basis for the constitutional violation in these cases. The school district's policy or practice which violates the establishment clause is the constitutional violation, not the third party discrimination it fosters.

No federal law directly addresses discrimination facilitated by public school prayer, and the Constitution provides no remedy for such discrimination and harassment itself. Federal or state criminal laws could address some of the conduct in these cases, but those laws are hard to enforce in these situations. Few, aside from the victims, would be willing to testify truthfully if subpoenaed in these cases, either because of animosity toward the victims or sympathy with the dominant group, including those engaged in the discrimination. Some state constitutions or civil rights laws could offer recourse, but there are no reported cases where state laws have been used to provide direct remedy for such discrimination and harassment. Moreover, the state laws and constitutions best tailored to these situations are generally found in the states that least need them, i.e., states that are more religiously diverse or have a low incidence of school prayer-related discrimination.

Discrimination and the Broader School Prayer Debate

Discrimination has received little attention in the debate over school prayer, which has focused mainly on constitutional issues. School prayer supporters have no interest in focusing on this issue because it could provide another reason to oppose school prayer. Some of those opposing school prayer do acknowledge the discrimination issue, although they rarely address it as a discrete issue, generally regarding it as a byproduct of constitutional violations. Academics such as the author and Robert Alley have written specifically about this phenomenon, and others have referenced it, but it remains to be seen whether this work and the issues it raises will move discrimination more directly into the mainstream of the school prayer debate.

Frank S. Ravitch

See also Religion and Public Education

Further Reading

Alley, R. S. (1996). *Without a prayer: Religious expression in public schools.* Amherst, NY: Prometheus Books.

Carter, S. L. (1993). *The culture of disbelief: How American law and politics trivialize religious devotion.* New York: Anchor Books.

Epstein, S. B. (1996). Rethinking the Constitutionality of Ceremonial Deism. *Columbia Law Review, 96,* 2083.

Gedicks, F. M. (1995). *The rhetoric of church and state: A critical analysis of religion clause jurisprudence.* Durham, NC: Duke University Press.

Hewitt, D. (Executive Producer). (1966, June 16). *60 Minutes* (segment on Lisa Herdahl v. Pontotoc County).

Hunsberger, B. (1995). Religion and prejudice: The role of religious fundamentalism, quest, and right-wing authoritarianism. *Journal of Social Issues, 51,* 113.

Hunter, J. D. (1991). *Culture wars: The struggle to define America.* New York: Basic Books.

McCollum, V. C. (1961). *One woman's fight* (Rev. ed.). Madison, WI: Freedom From Religion Foundation.

McFarland, S. G. (1989). Religious orientations and the targets of discrimination. *Journal for the Scientific Study of Religion, 28,* 324.

Peters, W. (1987). *A class divided then and now.* New Haven, CT: Yale University Press.

Pullium, R. M. (1989). *Cognitive styles or hypocracy? An explanation of the religiousness-intolerance relationship.* In W. Garrett (Ed.), *Social consequences of religious belief* (pp. 80–90)). St. Paul, MN: Paragon House.

Ravitch, F. S. (1999). *School prayer and discrimination: The civil rights of religious minorities and dissenters.* Boston: Northeastern University Press.

Ravitch, F. S. (2000). A crack in the wall: Pluralism, prayer and pain in the public schools. In S. M. Feldman (Ed.), *Law & Religion: A critical anthology* (pp. 296–314). New York: New York University Press.

Strossen, N. (1995). How much God in the schools? A discussion of religion's role in the classroom. *William and Mary Bill of Rights Journal, 4,* 607.

Court Cases

Good News Club v. Milford Central School, 533 U.S. 98, 121 S.Ct. 2093 (2001).

Illinois *ex Rel.* McCollum v. Board of Education, 333 U.S. 203 (1948).

Lee v. Weisman, 505 U.S. 577 (1992).

Lee v. Weisman, 505 U.S. 577 (1992) (Blackmun, J., concurring).

Santa Fe Independent School District v. Doe, 530 U.S. 290, 120 S.Ct. 2266 (2000).

Scientology

A constant presence in debates over religious freedom in the last half of the twentieth century, the Church of Scientology has been continually forced to defend its very status as a religious community since its founding in 1954. The Church grew out of the thought of L. Ron Hubbard (1911–1986), a writer and former naval officer, who in the years after World War II began systematically to present his thoughts on human well-being and humanity's place in the cosmos. His approach was initially formulated as Dianetics, a program for actualizing mental health. Following the publication of the basic textbook on Dianetics in 1950, a popular movement utilizing Hubbard's techniques and insights emerged.

During the early 1950s, Hubbard continued to develop his approach, and his research led him into areas that many of his colleagues considered too metaphysical. For example, Hubbard spoke of people living multiple lives (the doctrine of reincarnation). He also switched his focus from the mind, the central concern of Dianetics, to the spirit, which he termed the thetan. This move to a more metaphysical emphasis underlay the founding of the Church of Scientology in Los Angeles in 1954.

The Basics of Dianetics

Dianetics postulated the existence of a bifurcated human mind. One aspect, the analytical mind, receives data, reasons, remembers, and decides. The second aspect, the reactive mind, which comes into operation in times of distress, pain, or unconsciousness, simply records in great detail pictures of traumatic moments. Lodged in one's memory banks, these emotionally charged pictures, called engrams, can unconsciously operate to cause irrational aberrant behavior in the present. Through Dianetics, one can locate the engrams and remove the emotional charge they carry, thus eliminating their ability to negatively effect the present.

The main tool for dealing with the engrams is auditing, a form of counseling developed by Hubbard. Auditors listen while observing the individual's reactions on what is termed an e-meter. The e-meter records changes in a minute electrical current passing through the body, and its changes are believed by Scientologists to indicate differing internal states. One major step in one's life as a Scientologist is reaching the state of "clear," which happens when one has removed all the engrams. As one moves toward and beyond clear, one also become more concerned with the spirit, or thetan, with the goal of rehabilitating it and freeing it to operate fully in this life. While Hubbard outlined most of the material concerning the origin, history, and present predicament of the thetan in lectures in the 1950s and 1960s, instructions on how specifically to produce a fully operating thetan are contained in confidential materials available only to those Church members who have attained the state of clear and participated in the programs through which that material is released—the OT (for "operating thetan") Levels. By 2002, eight (of a projected fifteen) OT Levels had been released to members.

Church Organization

The Church of Scientology is organized similarly to the Church of Christ, Scientist (often referred to as Christian Science), with the Church of Scientology International based in Los Angeles operating as a mother church for autonomous local churches and missions around the world. Missions provide basic services, and local churches assist members to the state of clear. Additional advanced church facilities found in the United States, the United Kingdom, Denmark, and Australia have been established to provide the training for OT Levels. OT8, currently the highest level, is available only on the *Freewinds*, a ship that operates from the Caribbean island of Curaçao.

Beginning in the 1960s, national and international leadership in the Church was passed in stages to the Sea Organization, an ordered community of dedicated adherents originally formed to support Hubbard's research. The Sea Organization was assigned the task of releasing the OT levels to qualified adherents. The name of the organization recalls its formation at a time when Hubbard was residing on an oceangoing vessel, the *Apollo*. In the 1970s, that organization was transferred to Clearwater, Florida, to what is now termed the Flag Land Base. Most full-time workers for the Church and all people in a policy-making position are members of the Sea Organization.

As in other ordered and quasi-monastic communities, Sea Org members make a lifetime commitment, which because of their belief in past lives is worded as a billion-year commitment, and adopt a subsistence lifestyle. They are allowed to marry, but their spouse must also be a Sea Org member.

Unique to the Church's organization is the Religious Technology Center in Los Angeles, California. Its task is to ensure that the processes developed by Hubbard (Scientology technology) are applied uniformly and precisely. It exercises authority through the many copyrights, trademarks, and licenses that grant Scientology churches the rights to operate as churches of Scientology, offer auditing and other services to members, and display its symbols. Deviation from proper technology and misuse of trademarks and copyrights are grounds for the revocation of a church's licenses.

The Church also has nurtured organizations that attempt to bring its insights and teachings to nonchurch members. ABLE (Association for Better Living) promotes a drug-free life, literacy, and uplift of the moral level of society. Social reform is pursued through the Citizen's Commission on Human Rights and the National Commission on Law Enforcement and Social Justice. The International Association of Scientologists was formed in 1984 to work on religious-freedom issues, especially those that directly impinge upon the Church.

Challenges to Religious Freedom

Beginning very soon after its founding, the Church found itself in a position of continually defending its right to exist and practice its faith. The challenge to the Church's status as a religion began in 1963 when the Pure Food and Drugs Administration raided the Founding Church of Scientology church in Washington, D.C. and seized e-meters and a number of texts. The agency essentially charged the Church with practicing medicine without a license and labeled the e-meter an illegitimate medical device. Ten years of litigation led to a ruling in the Church's favor. However, the initial action of the FDA encouraged Scientology critics elsewhere, the most serious arising in Australia. In 1965, a government-commissioned report by Kevin V. Anderson led to the state of Victoria's passing the Psychological Practices Act in 1965. That act prohibited the practice of Scientology, the use of its name, and the dissemination of its teachings. The passing of subsequent similar legislation in South Australia and Western Australia forced the Australian Church of Scientology to reorganize as the Church of the New Faith in 1969. In the decades that followed, the Church was granted recognition (1973) and then full tax exemption (1983) in Australia.

One consequence of the attacks was that the Church created the Guardian's Office, a semiautonomous structure designed to defend the Church both in the courts and the media. In the 1970s, when a number of books that they felt libeled Scientology and its founder appeared, they took each to court in an attempt to have them withdrawn. Their actions against authors earned them a reputation for litigiousness that continues to the present. While the Church has sued the majority of its critics, it has filed cases against publications based on what are believed to be factual errors. Most recently, the Church sued *Time* magazine (unsuccessfully) following the publication of a lengthy article in 1991.

During the 1970s, the Guardian's Office overstepped its mandate and undertook activities such as break-ins of U.S. government offices to copy or steal documents. (Scientologists maintain that "dupes" infiltrated the Guardian's Office.) Then, in 1979, U.S. government authorities conducted a massive raid of Church facilities, which led to the trial of various Church officials, including Hubbard's wife, charged with the infiltration and theft of documents from a spectrum of government agencies, including the FBI. The period following the raid saw an intense power struggle within the Church, the eventual dissolution of the Guardian's Office, and the restructuring of the Church into its present form. Most of the responsibilities formerly handled by the Guardian's Office were reallocated to the new Office of Special Affairs within the Church of Scientology International.

Complaints against the Church

Most of the charges against the Church of Scientology that have substance derive from the era and actions of the Guardian's Office. Its actions negatively affected the Church's reputation worldwide, and the offenses of the 1970s remain prominent on the laundry list of charges still presented by those opposed to legal recognition of the Church. A large number of critical former members were among those fired from their positions or excommunicated from the Church as a result of the Church's own internal investigation of the Guardian's Office.

Since the close of the Guardian's Office, the number of new complaints against the Church has significantly dropped. However, in the 1990s several former members of the Church's elite Sea Organization began to raise issues about the demands placed upon members. While many allegations were similar in nature to those made by former members of other ordered communities, a set centered upon the Sea Organization's internal disciplinary program, the Rehabilitation Projects Force (RPF).

The Church of Scientology has its own code of ethics. When members of the Sea Organization violate that code in a significant manner, they have the choice of leaving the Organization or going through a program in which they work on their ethical life in an intense manner. The program includes physical labor and a period of mutual counseling with another program participant for several hours each day. After completing the program, which may take from one to three years, members return to their Sea Organization position. Accusations that the program abused participants led to a number of studies of the RPF that have tended to allay fears concerning it.

The various criticisms of the Church of Scientology have followed it as it has expanded internationally (it had a presence in more than seventy countries by 2000). While it has been recognized as a church in many countries, some, such as Greece, Germany, and France, have withheld recognition, and hence the Church still lives in contested space in many locales—including, for many years, the United States, which only in October 1993 finally granted the Church and all its corporate entities full tax-exempt status as a religion.

Some of Scientology's problems have resulted from its esoteric organization. The Church is designed to encounter people at a very personal level with a program of help. The more metaphysical and religious teachings are most clearly presented in the upper levels in material available only to more advanced members. The Church does not p resent outsiders with a clear theological alternative to established religions, and to many people its basic activity appears to be little more than another self-help program.

The Church's stance concerning reciprocity in finances also alienates outsiders. In the majority of transactions between the Church and its members, both give and both receive. The Church gives its knowledge and access to spiritual reality; the members give of their resources—time, service, or money (or some combination thereof). This is interpreted by some as the Church charging for its services and in the process accumulating significant wealth. Only when the Internal Revenue Service was convinced that income was not flowing into the pockets of the leadership did it grant the Church tax-exempt status.

While the Church of Scientology has won most of the battles to exist and propagate its beliefs, it still has some challenges before it, as different countries continue to evaluate its place on the larger religious landscape.

J. Gordon Melton

Further Reading

Melton, J. G. (1998). *Scientology: Theology and practice of a contemporary sect*. Los Angeles: Bridge Publications.

Melton, J. G. (1998). *What is Scientology*? Los Angeles: Bridge Publications.

Melton, J. G. (2001). *The Church of Scientology*. Salt Lake City, UT: Signature Books.

Whitehead, H. (1987). *Renunciation and reformulation: A study of conversion in an American sect*. Ithaca, NY: Cornell University Press.

Secularism and Modernity

Secularism derives, possibly through French, from the Late Latin *saecularis* (temporal) and Latin *saeculum* (generation, age). In political discourse it refers primarily to the structure of the state, the separation of the state from religious institutions like the church, and the religious neutrality of the state.

Modernity derives, through the French *moderne*, from the Latin *modo* (just now). In its popular sense it is used in various contexts as reflecting the contemporary, the advanced, or the improved. However, it has distinct connotations in politics and social organization.

The Vision Widens

Modernity in politics and social organization and also the secular ideal are both immediately derived from and related to the rise and growth of liberal ideas in the nineteenth century and after. This development was itself made possible by the humanist movement, with man as the measure of all things, and the sociopolitical trend of the Enlightenment in the seventeenth and eighteenth centuries. With Huigh de Groot (Hugo Grotius) (1583–1645), law began "to extricate itself from the perilous embrace of theology" (Cassirer 1951, 238). This brought about an intellectual independence and, in defining the domain of law, limits also began to be set on state absolutism. What Bingham claims for the Scottish Enlightenment is true of the movement as a whole: "Those who contributed to it subjected everything which was accepted through habit or hallowed by tradition—religion, law, government, the social order, the laws of nature—to question, and to reasoned examination" (Bingham 1983, 166). "Sapere Aude" or "dare to know" became, as it were, the motto of the Enlightenment (Cassirer 1951, 163).

The Enlightenment had a pervasive impact and the basic constructs of the modern world as we know it began to be formed. Baruch Spinoza (1632–1677), the Dutch philosopher, related the purpose of religion not to the explanation of things but to the introduction of moral principles. He exalted the freedom of thought that he wished to see protected from encroachments by the state and by religion. Voltaire (1694–1778) emphasized the historical evolution of man autonomously from the church and monarchy, Marquis de Condorcet (1743–1794) charted the meaning and implications of man's progress, and Jean-Jacques Rousseau (1712–1778) produced the political theory that displaced the sovereign monarch with the people themselves. What Grotius had earlier done for the autonomy of law, Immanuel Kant (1724–1804), who was also influenced by Rousseau and the Scottish philosopher David Hume (1711–1776), did for morality. Kant's *Critique of Pure Reason* (1781) sought to define right and wrong in terms of individual conscience, without reference to revealed religion. The categorical imperative thus arrived at is formulated thus: "So act, that the rule on which you act admits of being adopted as a law by all rational beings" (Schapiro 1958, 19).

The ferment in which such views arose contained also the intellectual sources on which the U.S. Declaration of Independence (1776) drew, and the French Revolution (1789) occurred in that same ferment. From here onward the progress of political modernity took different trajectories in Europe

An Amish farmer driving a horse-drawn carriage in Honey Brook, Pennsylvania. Within the United States, the Amish are the group probably most-often associated with a way of life based on an adherence to traditional religious beliefs and resistance to the influence of secularism and modernity. COURTESY OF LIBRARY OF CONGRESS, PRINTS AND PHOTOGRAPHS DIVISION.

and in the United States of America. In Europe the convulsions immediately following the French Revolution delayed further significant developments by about four decades. In England, there was a gradual widening of franchise, and the Catholic Emancipation took place in 1829. Marriage laws, tied to the Anglican Church, began to be liberalized. Oxford and Cambridge students were freed in 1871 from having to sign the thirty-nine articles of the Anglican creed in order to graduate. Parliamentary legislation in 1902 brought church schools under the control of local authorities. The Church Act of 1869 sponsored by the British statesman William Ewart Gladstone (1809–1898) disestablished the Anglican Church of Ireland and so far as the law in Ireland was concerned "all religious denominations were placed on a footing of equality" (Moody & Martin 1967, 281). The position of women began to be liberalized. In 1865 girls were allowed, in England, to sit for the Cambridge local examination. Laws against child labor and for compulsory education came to be passed. Going further than traditional liberal opinion, trade union rights came to be protected, factory legislation was passed, and working hours were controlled. Later, after suffragette agitations in the

early twentieth century, women also won the right to vote.

All this combined with great advances in science and technology and much flowering of artistic and literary sensibilities contributed to what we know today as modernity. The extent of the change is reflected in a passage from the U.S. jurist Learned Hand written as far back as 1930, referring to the developments that had occurred between the time of Jefferson and his own: Rural life as Jefferson understood it is now impossible, he said, because "[t]he motor, the airplane, the telephone, and telegraph, the radio, the Linotype, the modern newspaper, the 'movie'—and most horrible, the 'talkie'—have finally destroyed it" (Dilliard 1954, 70). With scientific advance, as the space occupied by the "unknown" gradually came to be reduced, so correspondingly did the space available to God and religion get constricted. Julian Huxley noted that "Natural science has pushed God into an even greater remoteness, until his function as ruler and dictator disappears and he becomes a mere first cause or vague general principle" (Huxley 1948, 132). Huxley, however, made a biologist's distinction and noted that while science had so far revealed much of the external world, it had not been as successful in unraveling humanity's "internal environment" and prophesied that religion would continue to occupy the psychological space this created until science made substantive progress in this direction. This incidentally since the time of Huxley it has considerably done. It would seem therefore that we may expect considerable further changes in the manner religion is viewed. Huxley had admitted though that the lack of sufficient scientific progress applied likewise to matters relating to the "structure of society which provides the social environment for the individual and the race" (Huxley 1948, 134).

New forms grew also in art. Impressionism shifted the focus from the country to the urban landscape and reflected "the overstrained nerves of modern technical man. It is an urban style because it describes the changeability, the nervous rhythm, the sudden, sharp but always ephemeral impressions of city life. And precisely as such, it implies an enormous expansion of sensual perception, a new sharpening of sensibility, a new irritability" (Hauser 1951, 168). Literature came to express social concerns.

There is one more vital ingredient that went into the making of the modern world. Panikkar (1962, 68) makes the perceptive observation that "the period of liberal predominance witnessed the growth of an international conscience." For all its selective and often cynical nature, the coming into being of international opinion as an important factor in the modern world must be admitted. International organizations also came to be formed throughout the twentieth century encompassing several issues relating to, but not limited to, war, peace, trade, development and, finally, the environment.

Toward Secularism

Liberal ideas, for all their weaknesses, limitations, and biases on economic issues relating especially to property and trade, had entailed greater tolerance for dissenters. This in turn strengthened what became the secular doctrine—that is, separation of church and state and political equality or state neutrality toward religious belief. This fascinating process is still ongoing and incomplete.

The Edict of Nantes (1598) was issued by Henry IV (who had earlier been himself a Protestant and in fact a leader of the Huguenots but had later became a Catholic). The edict assured tolerance for the Protestant Huguenots by Catholic France on certain conditions. It was denounced by the pope as an unacceptable concession. The edict was revoked by Louis XIV in 1685. Debates in Europe at this time relate largely to the extent of toleration to be permitted. Even John Locke (1632–1704) in his *Letter Concerning Toleration* (1689) is reluctant to extend toleration to Catholics and atheists (Schapiro 1958, 105–6). In Europe it is Voltaire, in his *Treatise on Tolerance,* who makes that leap, subject to the need for maintaining public order (Schapiro 1958, 107–8).

Thomas Paine (1737–1809) moves on to critique even the idea of toleration as inadequate. In *Rights of Man* (1791), Paine wrote:

> The French Constitution has abolished or renounced *toleration,* and *intolerance* also, and has established *universal right of conscience.* Toleration is not the *opposite* of intoleration, but is the *counterfeit* of it. Both are despotisms. The one assumes to itself the right of withholding liberty of conscience, and the other of granting it. The one is the Pope armed with fire and faggot, and the other is the Pope selling or granting indulgences. The former is church and state, and the latter is church and traffic. (Adkins 1953, 92)

Paine ridiculed the idea even further, saying it was an attempt to interpose between God and man. He declared provocatively: "Were a bill brought into Parliament entitled, 'An *act* to tolerate or grant liberty to the Almighty to receive the worship of a Jew or a Turk' or to 'prohibit the Almighty from receiving it,' all men would startle and call it blasphemy"(Adkins 1953, 92). Paine was burnt in effigy throughout England after the publication of his works there.

In the English colony of Rhode Island, however, the English-born Roger Williams (1603?–1683) had preached religious pluralism and freedom of conscience, saying that enforced religious uniformity is not required by God. He spoke out against persecution of Jews, Turks, and pagans in Christ's name and spoke of citizenship and modern government, many of his publications having been made in the course of visits to England. Civil and religious matters should not, according to him, be unduly mixed. He had an abiding influence in the United States. The Quaker William Penn (1644–1718) had pleaded for liberty of conscience in *The Great Case of Liberty of Conscience* (1670). Persecution and faith cannot go together he argued, because involuntary religion is invalid. Even in the late eighteenth century, however, the debate

435

centers often on a limited degree of toleration and there are ambiguities and qualifications in the works of many of the writers on toleration. It is in the nineteenth century that the thread is taken forward again and the term secularism begins to be used, initially by George Jacob Holyoake (1817–1906) and Charles Bradlaugh (1833–1891). Initially the idea was to coin a term that would not have negative connotations like atheism. Bradlaugh, however, was more emphatic in his stress on atheism. These writers and publicists stood at the head of the tradition critiquing religious and racial persecution. Bradlaugh's "Humanity's Gain from Unbelief" (1889) was a relentless attack on the involvement of Christians in the slave trade and in religious persecution and other social evils. He gave no quarter to religion, even where this may have been due. So we find him commenting: "It is said that William Wilberforce, the abolitionist, was a Christian. But at any rate his Christianity was strongly diluted with unbelief" (Bradlaugh 1933, 146).

In political discourse, strictly speaking, secularism refers to the nature of the state and how it stands in relation to religion, although it seems that Holyoake and Bradlaugh did not so limit its usage. Even in relation to the state, there are some noteworthy nuances to this concept. In some contexts and countries, emphasis has been placed on the separation of the church and the state, while in others the main emphasis has been on the religious neutrality of the state. In many European countries like England, for example, the stress is on the church-state separation, without necessarily doing away with an official religion. In post-1947 India, on the other hand, the stress is on equal treatment of religions with the cultural and educational rights of linguistic and religious minorities additionally protected by special provisions in the constitution itself. The church-state separation does not, in these terms, figure prominently because Asian religions often do not have church-like institutions.

In the United States, both nuances have tended to coexist. In June 1776 Virginia adopted a Declaration of Rights guaranteeing the freedom of religion. Ten years later, in 1786, the Virginia legislature enacted the Law for Establishing Religious Freedom, drafted by James Madison (1751–1836) and Thomas Jefferson (1743–1826). According to this act "all men shall be free to profess, and by argument to maintain, their opinions in matters of religion, and that the same shall in no wise diminish, enlarge, or affect their civil

capacities" (Koch & Peden 1944, 313). Two years before this, in 1784, Madison wrote a memorandum against a legislative proposal in Virginia to impose a tax in support of churches. As a result of the efforts of Jefferson and Madison the proposal was defeated. Five years later, the first ten amendments to the U.S. Constitution, forming the Bill of Rights, were proposed and subsequently enacted into law. The First Amendment lays down, among other things, that Congress shall not make any law establishing a religion or prohibiting the free exercise of religion. Even at the time of this amendment some states in the United States had official religions that were actively and preferentially promoted. The Fourteenth Amendment (1868), however, made this difficult, if not impossible, as the rights granted by the U.S. Constitution became entrenched, with the states barred from making any law that could abridge the privileges or immunities of U.S. citizens. Some states, like New York in 1842, had legislated to provide that a school in which a sectarian religious doctrine is taught would not receive state educational funds.

Largest Secular Democracy

With the breakup of the Ottoman Empire, Turkey adopted in 1924 a secular constitution after the declaration of a Turkish republic by Mustafa Kemal Ataturk (1881–1938) in 1923. On the emergence of a multiracial South Africa in the last decade of the twentieth century, it too adopted a secular form of government with the constitution recognizing no state religion.

Considering its population of around one billion, India is the largest secular democracy in the world. Its secular democratic constitution, adopted in 1949, has now been in force in this multireligious country for more than half a century. Secularism was part of the political vocabulary of the Indian National Congress, which Bradlaugh had addressed in Bombay in December 1889. The party led the country to freedom, which it achieved on 15 August 1947. M. K. Gandhi (Mahatma Gandhi) (1869–1948), Jawaharlal Nehru (1889–1964), and Maulana Abul Kalam Azad (1888–1958), the prominent leaders of the independence movement, had a commitment to secularism and protection of the rights of national minorities. This was made clear, for example, in the resolution of the Indian National Congress at Karachi (then part of undivided India) in March 1931. It was reiterated again after independence on 16 August

1947 by Gandhi when he expressed the opinion that "the state should undoubtedly be secular" (Gandhi 1983, 51) and on 22 August 1947, when he called on government officials and members of the public to work "wholeheartedly for the creation of a secular state" (Gandhi 1983, 79). His assassination on 30 January 1948 by a Hindu fanatic once again deepened the national resolve to resist religious sectarianism. The secular constitution, framed by a drafting committee headed by B. R. Ambedkar (1893 1956) and adopted by the Constituent Assembly of India on 26 November 1949, came fully into force on 26 January 1950. Indian opinion relates secularism, in its aspect of equal respect for or treatment of all religions, also to traditional Indian sources, such as the Twelfth Rock Edict of Asoka (d. 238 or 232 BC) (Nikam & McKeon 1962, 49–50), the religious tolerance of the sixteenth-century Mughal emperor Akbar (1542–1605), and the religious eclecticism of many poet saints and the seventeenth-century Mughal prince regent Dara Shikoh (1615–1659), apart from the traditions associated with the Indian freedom movement, especially in the first half of the twentieth century. In recent years, almost simultaneously with the rise of Islamist forces in Iran and elsewhere in the late 1970s, there has been in India an upsurge of Hindu sectarian groups, especially since 1987. These groups are however facing considerable resistance from the secular-oriented political parties.

Implications

Neither the struggle for secularism nor the full implications of modernity have completely played themselves out. In many societies, these ideas and their ramifications are still politically, socially, and culturally radical. Even in societies such as England, older forms of organization, like an official state religion and church, persist—howsoever multicultural the society itself may have become. The resultant tension between secularism and opposing worldviews, as also between modernity and traditional forms of social organization, underlies several international and domestic convulsions and conflicts even of the late twentieth century and the early years of the twenty-first century. The place of religion in the century that has now opened seems both ambiguous and ubiquitous. Many recent conflicts, such as in Afghanistan, and persistent conflicts, such as in Palestine, appear increasingly and overtly to have an ethnoreligious character. Clearly, the development of

science and technology and the political ideals of secularism have not been enough to shrink the space still available to religious strife, howsoever restricted the space available to God himself may have become.

Nauriya

Further Reading

Adkins, N. F. (Ed.). (1953). *Thomas Paine: Common sense and other political writings*. New York: The Liberal Arts Press.

Berlin, I. (Selector and Compiler). (1956). *The age of enlightenment: The 18th-century philosophers*. New York: The New American Library of World Literature.

Bingham, C. (1983). *Land of the Scots: A short history*. Glasgow, UK: Fontana Paperbacks.

Bradlaugh, C. (1933). *Champion of liberty*. London: C. A. Watts & Co. Ltd. and The Pioneer Press.

Cassirer, E. (1951). *The philosophy of the enlightenment*, (F. C. A. Koelln & J. P. Pettegrove, Trans.). Princeton, NJ: Princeton University Press.

Derrett, J. D. M. (1968). *Religion, law, and the state in India*. London: Faber and Faber.

Dilliard, I. (Compiler). (1954). *The spirit of liberty: Papers and addresses of Learned Hand*. New York: Alfred A. Knopf.

Douglas, William O. (1954). *An almanac of liberty*. London: Collins.

Edwards, C. S. (1981). *Hugo Grotius: The miracle of Holland: A study in political and legal thought*. Chicago: Nelson-Hall.

Gandhi, M. K. (1983). *Collected works of Mahatma Gandhi* (Vol. 89). New Delhi, India: Publications Division, Ministry of Information and Broadcasting, Government of India.

Gupta, N. L. (Ed.). (1965). *Nehru on communalism*. New Delhi, India: Sampradayikta Virodhi Committee.

Hauser, A. (1951). *The social history of art* (Vol. 4). New York: Vintage Books.

Hearnshaw, F. J. C. (Ed.). (1967). *The social and political ideas of some great thinkers of the Renaissance and the Reformation*. London: Dawsons of Pall Mall.

Hobhouse, L. T. (1911). *Liberalism*. London: Oxford University Press.

Husain, S. A. (1969). *Gandhiji and communal unity*. Bombay, India: Orient Longmans.

Huxley, J. (1948). *Man in the modern world*. New York: The New American Library of World Literature.

Koch, A., & Peden, W. (Eds.). (1944). *The life and selected writings of Thomas Jefferson*. New York: Random House.

Limaye, M. (1989). *Mahatma Gandhi and Jawaharlal Nehru: A historic partnership 1916–1948* (Vol 2 [1932–1942]). Delhi, India: B. R. Publishing Corporation.

Magill, F. N. (1973). *Great events from history: Modern European series* (Vol. 1). Englewood Cliffs, NJ: Salem Press.

Malezieux, R., & Rousseau, J. J. (1950). *The Constitution of the Fourth Republic* (R. C. Ghosh, Trans.). Calcutta, India: Das Gupta & Co.

Moody, T. W., & Martin, F. X. (1967). *The course of Irish history*. Cork, Ireland: The Mercier Press.

Nehru, J. (1936). *India and the world*. London: George Allen & Unwin.

Nehru, J. (1981). *The discovery of India*. New Delhi, India: Jawaharlal Nehru Memorial Fund.

Nikam, N. A., & McKeon, R. (1962). *The edicts of Asoka*. Bombay, India: Asia Publishing House.

Panikkar, K. M. (1962). *In defence of liberalism*. Bombay, India: Asia Publishing House.

Sastri, V. S. S. (1925). *The rights and duties of the Indian citizen*. Calcutta, India: Calcutta University.

Schapiro, J. S. (1958). *Liberalism: Its meaning and history*. Princeton, NJ: D. Van Nostrand Company.

Sharma, G. S. (Ed.). (1966). *Secularism: Its implications for law and life in India*. Bombay, India: N. M. Tripathi Private Ltd.

Spinoza, B. de. (1955). *The chief works of Benedict de Spinoza* (R. H. M. Elwes, Trans.). New York: Dover Publications.

Tribe, L. H. (1985). *Constitutional choices*. Cambridge, MA: Harvard University Press.

Shintoism

At first glance, the religious tradition known as Shinto appears an ideal candidate for inclusion in an encyclopedia dedicated to religious freedom. It stands in dramatic contrast to conventional Western notions of religion because Shinto (practiced primarily in Japan) has no centralized dogma, no charismatic founders, no weekly worship services attended by a congregation, and no sacred texts. These characteristics have served to promote an autonomy and freedom at the local level leading to widely diverse practices and beliefs. At Shinto institutions closer to the centers of political power, however, the tradition has been and remains a viable means for legitimating regimes, ensuring social and political stability, and making sacred by means of ritual everything from the coming harvest to the nation's wars.

Overview

The tradition called Shinto emphasizes rituals that try to control and revitalize a community's relationship with powerful deities (*kami*) beneficial to society, as well as exorcising harmful forces and defilements of every sort. Many *kami* acquired names and specific powers from the third to the sixth centuries CE that imbued them with personality traits not unlike those of human beings. *Kami* could be coarse and violent, causing earthquakes, typhoons or surprise attacks, but they could be benevolent and nurturing as well. A bumper rice harvest, good health, many children, political stability—all were evidence of a harmonious relationship with the *kami*. Certain ritual strategies were thought efficacious in controlling the temperament and influence of *kami* and through which a tenuous though reciprocal balance between human, phenomenal, and transcendental worlds was maintained.

Shinto's system of rituals are intended to positively influence a person's livelihood, family, and surroundings; thus, sanctuaries for the *kami* (*jinja* or shrines) were integrated within or adjacent to communities. There was probably very little disagreement about whether or not to participate in honoring and venerating one's local *kami*—it was a practice fully informed by an individual's daily activities. Prior to the late nineteenth century, there had been no central authority dictating how individual men and women were to behave regarding the deities, although an attitude of sincerity and a physical cleanliness enhanced by rituals of purification since earliest times had been fundamental to the act of worship. There are said to be around 80,000 Shinto shrines in Japan in the early 2000s, although before a 1906 government policy of modernization that attempted to merge existing shrines so as to have only one shrine per village, there were over 190,000.

As a religious tradition, Shinto predates the early sixth-century arrival of Buddhism in Japan, with some features (such as ritual intervention) extending back into the stone age (28,000–10,500 BCE). Once Buddhism arrived in 538 CE, a term was needed to distinguish rituals for the "way of the *kami*" (*shinto*) from those of the buddhas. Shinto, however, is a problematic term when used in the singular. Some scholars believe that this usage implies the ideological stance of shrine priests and administrators that is rooted in reverence for the imperial institution of the emperor. For most Japanese, however, the tradition is

SELECTION FROM THE SHINTO DIRECTIVE OF 1945

In order to free the Japanese people from direct or indirect compulsion to believe or profess to believe in a religion or cult officially designated by the state, and in order to prevent a recurrence of the perversion of Shinto theory and beliefs into militaristic and ultranationalistic propaganda designed to delude the Japanese people and lead them into wars of aggression. . .It is hereby dictated that. . .(a.) the sponsorship, perpetuation, control and dissemination of Shinto by the Japanese national, prefectural, and local governments, or by public officials, subordinates, and employees acting in their official capacity are prohibited and will cease immediately. (h.) The dissemination of Shinto doctrines in any form and by any means in any educational institution supported wholly or in part by public funds is prohibited and will cease immediately. (k.) God-shelves (*kamidana*) and all other physical symbols of State Shinto in any office, school, institution, organization, or structure supported wholly or in part by public funds are prohibited and will be removed immediately. (m.) No official of the national, prefectural, or local government, acting in his public capacity, will visit any shrine to report his assumption of office, to report on conditions of government or to participate as a representative of government in any ceremony or observance.

Source: H. Hardacre *Shinto and the State: 1868–1988*. (Princeton, NJ: Princeton University Press, 1989), 168.

represented not by this specialized term but through practices such as visiting shrines at certain times of year or at critical stages of the life cycle, participating in periodic festivals, or turning to the deities in times of trouble. For the purposes of this discussion, the term Shinto is used as a generic, collective noun for a wide range of practices, histories, and ideologies.

Much of the sociocultural identity of the Japanese people is broadly shaped by Shinto. Examples could be drawn from its obvious impact on national holidays, community festivals, and familial rites of passage, to less obvious areas such as national self-sufficiency in foodstuffs (especially the role of rice agriculture) and the influence of Shinto views of nature on Japanese behavior in the global environment. A cross-cultural parallel would be trying to understand contemporary India without a knowledge of Hinduism, or Italy without a knowledge of Catholicism. The people of other cultures draw upon and implement aspects of religious traditions to varying degrees. Worldviews thus are shaped in part by the symbolic logic of a particular religious tradition, the rhetoric and rituals of legitimization, and the subtle integration into the fabric of social and cultural life.

The importance of a renewed appreciation of Shinto's broader significance is recognized in the context of discussions of postmodernism, the global rise of religio-political fundamentalism, increasing debates regarding a coming "clash of civilizations," and the use of ethnic symbols in the process of what might be called willful nostalgia. In short, Shinto-oriented perspectives continue to have relevance within a much wider range of Japanese behavior, extending from everyday personal interaction to national behavior in the global economic and political spheres. As an orientation to the world that recognizes the potential for natural phenomena to become deities, that deifies and venerates ancestors or leaders of exceptional merit, and that has influenced through its rituals everything from rice planting to the construction of buildings to the maintenance of hearth fires for cooking, its historical influence upon the development of Japanese society is powerful and enduring.

Shinto and Religious Freedom

One of Shinto's many contributions to Japanese society and culture includes a powerful political influence shaped by elite priests at large shrines. Numerous institutions (such as Izumo, Iwashimizu Hachimangu, Suwa, Kamo, and Kasuga) have played key roles in the administration of imperial and feudal regimes, authenticating and even making sacred the political rulers of the time. In fact, for much of Japanese political history, the symbiotic nature of the state and those ritual functions connected with the veneration of Shino deities was encompassed by a single concept: *saisei-itchi*, the union of ritual and rule. This is not to diminish the importance of Buddhist temples and sects within Japanese political history, since they also contributed to and frequently helped to shape the political order. To regard Buddhism and Shinto as separate, rather than syncretic and complementary institutions, would be misleading. And yet, there are no recorded instances of a shrine being converted to a Buddhist temple or vice versa.

The relevance of Shinto has been intertwined with various ways of making a living, especially those traditional pursuits of rice agriculture, forestry, and fishing. These endeavors all have specialized deities and are economic activities instrumental to the stability of the state. Thus, for fifteen centuries, the highest priest within Shinto has been the male head of one family line thought to have descended from the original *kami*, the emperor. The sanctity and power of the high priest increased during the mid-nineteenth-century reinvention of Shinto as a tool for the modernizing state. Debates regularly arise concerning the use of taxpayer funds to support the imperial family, the political role of the emperor, the legal status of shrines like Yasukuni (where the spirits of the military dead are enshrined), and the tutelary shrines for the imperial family at Ise. Although the Japanese postwar Constitution is clear that no collusion can exist between religion and the state, the status of Shinto has been ambiguous. Several postwar Supreme Court decisions, mirroring edicts by the Ministry of the Interior before the war, have deemed it to be beyond mere religion and a matter of social protocol. Only in 1997 did the Japanese Supreme Court rule that Shinto was indeed a religion.

Changing Dynamics Among the Individual, State, and Shinto

In premodern Japan, one of the defining characteristics of Shinto was a lack of centralized authority and doctrine that enabled a broad-based participation and great freedom of choice and interpretation in the ways people interacted with their local deities. Individuals and groups in Japan have rarely been exclusive in their religious affiliations, pursuing instead a variety of options so as to ensure maximum efficacy for their prayers and petitions. What mattered was not so much whether one patronized a Pure Land Buddhist temple or a Shinto shrine dedicated to a *kami* of lightning and thunder, but simply having faith in particular *kami* or buddhas. In fact, there was no word to denote a category of life as "religious," or to think of religion as a "general phenomenon, of which there would be variants like Christianity, Buddhism, and Shinto" (Hardacre 1989, 18). For example, if the problem at hand is a couple unable to have children, they may call upon the deity of a local shrine noted for increasing fertility. But they may also pray before the Buddhist bodhisattva of compassion, Kannon, who is noted for her powers of intervention. Similarly, if a business is having financial difficulty, its owner may go first to an Inari shrine known for bringing financial prosperity, then walk a few meters to a Buddhist temple housing a famous sculpture of a fierce-looking guardian (*Fudo*), venerated for quelling misfortune and evil while protecting that which is precious.

In 1868, the government issued a dramatic order to separate Buddhism from Shinto, causing the former to suffer through a brief, violent, and unauthorized persecution, often at the hands of overzealous Shinto priests. Thus began a decades-long process of experimentation and innovation within the diverse tradition of *kami* veneration, now revived as "Shinto." With governmental sponsorship and policies, local priests and educators in Japan's schools promoted Shinto's ancient mythology associated with the *kami* as the origins of the imperial regime (and, by extension, the Japanese race). The government also required every individual to be registered as a parishioner of his or her local, government-approved shrine. These rulings fostered a relationship between Shinto priests and political rule that, although altered dramatically by Japan's defeat in 1945, is still seen by many as ensuring political stability by promoting the spiritual unity of the Japanese people.

Despite the guarantee of religious freedom in the 1889 Meiji Constitution, the law seemed to apply only to the extent that a citizen's duty to the state was not compromised by his or her religious affiliations. During one of the peaks of what is known as state–Shinto, professional educators and politicians risked imprisonment if they challenged any part of the officially sanctioned doctrine. In fact, Shinto was seen by many during the Meiji period (1868–1912), as well as in the late twentieth century, as being *above* religion. But this did not create an atmosphere of religious freedom. On the contrary, individuals could be obligated to participate in shrine rituals as Japanese subjects, yet this was thought not to impinge on one's religious freedom. Leaders from rapidly growing new religious sects in the 1930s (such as Omotokyo and Soka Gakkai) were harassed and imprisoned, and their institutions dismantled by force.

After Japan's defeat in World War II, government-sponsored Shinto was prohibited by the Occupation authorities in the Shinto Directive of 1945. This act led to a new era of religious freedom and tolerance for the Japanese people. Women in particular benefited in religious as well as social, political, and cultural ways. Early in the Meiji period, women serving in Shinto shrines as spirit mediums or performers of sacred dance had been dismissed by a government directive aimed at reorganizing the shrine system. Many male priests who were turned out by this edict later were able to gain recertification; women were not recertified. After the war, not only were women's human rights guaranteed by the postwar Constitution, but, as in the premodern period, so was their freedom to affiliate with any and all religious traditions they found beneficial. In the early 2000s, about 7 percent of all priests are women.

Freedom of Expression in Contemporary Shinto

In 2002, around 83 percent of the Japanese population visited a Shinto shrine (or Buddhist temple, or both) on New Year's Eve. As at other times of year, visitors exemplify a wide range of religious behavior that is in no way controlled by the shrine's priests. Because shrine offices are generally a short distance from the primary ritual center, and because priests are engaged in clerical work for most of the day in those offices, their authoritative presence as specialists is largely absent from the shrine grounds. Consequently, there is little to interfere with the highly subjective ways in which people interact with the site. A casual visitor to a shrine may have no idea what deity is venerated, despite explanatory signs posted on the premises. As with the signs, a visitor may also bypass the water basin used for purifying one's actions (hands) and words (mouth) before approaching the inner sanctuary. At the gate, through which the general public may not pass (unless accompanied by one of the shrine's priests for a formal ritual within), visitors may enact the clapping of hands and bowing gestures (*kashiwade*) typical of ritual protocol for acknowledging and petitioning the deities. But they may also simply peek inside and continue their meandering tour of the shrine's lovely grounds. At all points in this process, visitors are completely on their own. And yet, like a roadmap, the "layout of a shrine is a technology of power leading people into behavioral practices often unexpected and unanticipated but which have the potential to give expression to inner mental or emotional states" (Nelson 2000, 25). A visitor professing no religious affiliation or belief may assess the behavior of those around him or her and join in accordingly at each stage described above.

This public freedom of expression is inherent to the structural longevity and future of shrine Shinto, especially in the first decades of the twenty-first century. The ancestors of rural people had little choice but to acknowledge those deities thought responsible for ensuring rice cultivation or seas full of fish. Japanese living in more densely populated areas may also have petitioned regularly local *kami* for protection from fire, success in business, school, marriage, or to maintain good health. While many of these practices and beliefs continue, creating substantial income via rituals and amulets for shrines nationwide, a Japanese person's religious freedom may also be exercised by their conscious choice *not* to participate in local shrine affairs. However, as the steady number of visitors to major shrines indicates, the tradition of Shinto probably has at least another fifteen hundred years of history.

John K. Nelson

See also Japan

Further Reading

Breen, J., & Teeuwen, M. (2001). *Shinto in history: Ways of the kami.* Honolulu: University of Hawai'i Press.

Grapard, A. (1992). *Protocol of the gods: A Study of the Kasuga cult in Japanese history.* Berkeley: University of California Press.

Hardacre, H. (1989). *Shinto and the state: 1868–1988.* Princeton, NJ: Princeton University Press.

Kuroda, T. (1981). Shinto in the history of Japanese religion. *Journal of Japanese Studies, 7*(1), 1–21.

Matsumae, T. (1993). Early kami worship. In D. Brown (Ed.), *The Cambridge history of Japan* (Vol. 1, pp.

217–358). Cambridge, UK: Cambridge University Press.

Nelson, J. (1996). *A year in the life of a Shinto shrine.* Seattle: University of Washington Press.

Nelson, J. (2000). *Enduring identities: The guise of Shinto in contemporary Japan.* Honolulu: University of Hawai'i Press.

Schnell, S. (1999). *The rousing drum.* Honolulu: University of Hawai'i Press.

Smyers, K. (1999). *The fox and the jewel.* Honolulu: University of Hawai'i Press.

Sonoda, M. (1988). Festival and sacred transgression. In I. Nobutaka (Ed.), *Matsuri: Festival and rite in Japanese life* (pp. 33–77). Tokyo: Institute for Japanese Culture and Classics.

Sikhism

The Sikh faith, the most recent of the world's great religious movements, was founded by Guru Nanak (1469–1539?), who set out to modernize and reform the practice of religious faith. A man ahead of his time, he advocated remarriage for women and allowed them to become priests, thereby foreseeing the emancipation of women by five hundred years before the arrival of universal suffrage in the West. The word *Sikh* means a disciple or student and is a corollary of the word *Guru*, which means Teacher. Today, there are nearly 20 million Sikhs worldwide, one-third of whom live outside India in countries as diverse as Canada, the United States, Malaysia, Great Britain, Kenya, and Tanzania.

Guru Nanak and the Bhakti Movement

Guru Nanak belonged to the bhakti movement, a tradition based on the expression of the loving adoration of God. The bhakti movement reacted to the rigidity and unfairness of medieval Hinduism, denouncing its emphasis on caste and idolatry. Hinduism at the time was already under challenge from the egalitarian faiths of Buddhism, Jainism, and Islam (Banerjee 1983, 1). The bhakti movement rose to this challenge by its insistence on the unity of God and the relaxation of the caste system. The idea of the loving adoration of God itself, however, came from ancient Hinduism. In Hinduism, the devotion to the gods of Indra and Varuna in the Rig-Veda (the sacred text of the Hindus) is expressed through a longing desire (Radhakrishnan:, 704). Indeed, the word *bhakti* appears for the first time in Svetasvatara Upanishad (Radhakrishnan, 108), composed in the post-Buddha period.

The bhakti movement was also influenced by the Sufis. The Sufis derive their name from their garments of coarse wool (Arabic, *suf*), which they wore as an emblem of poverty (Arabic, *faqr*). Sufis advocated mystical doctrines of union with God, achieved through love of God. They were secretive and aloof and lived in seclusion. The tomb of Iman Nasiruddin at Jalandhar, in the Punjab in northern India, dated 945 CE, shows their early presence in India long before the arrival of Muslim rule in the fourteenth century. The Sufis founded three main orders in India: Chisti, based around Delhi and Doab, and among whose members figured the historian Barani (1285–after 1357) and the legendary poet Amir Khosrow (1253–1325); Suhrawardi, based in the Sindh; and Firdausi, based in the Bihar. All three orders of Sufis dissociated themselves from the established centers of orthodoxy because they believed that the ulema, the Muslim priesthood, was misinterpreting the Qur'an. They believed that the ulema was combining religion and political policy and deviating from the original democratic and egalitarian principles of Islam. Given their isolation from the society that they opposed, the impact of the Sufis was, however, less direct and enduring in India than it otherwise might have been. On the other hand, the bhakti movement had more impact. Its leaders, who traced their lineage to the devotional cults of India and shared common ground with the Sufis, did not believe in Sufi mysticism. They were not aloof or isolated from the people. They wanted to make their teaching comprehensible to the ordinary person on the street. They attacked caste, institutionalized religion, priesthood, and the worship of icons. They taught in the local vernacular and encouraged women to join their gatherings (Juss 1995, 496). The leaders of the bhakti movement were known as *sant*s (or saints). To be a *sant* was a method of spiritual liberation was well as a form of social protest. *Sant*s laid an unqualified emphasis on the interior nature of spiritual understanding and scorned those who claimed to exercise authority as purveyors of religious merit or as mediators of divine grace (McLeod 1997, 91). Accordingly, the bhakti saints came from a variety of nonorthodox backgrounds, such as Kabir the weaver, Ravidas the leather worker, and Namdev the haberdasher.

Guru Nanak himself came from a rural background. He was a son of a Hindu village accountant, but educated through the generosity of a Muslim friend. He first joined the Sufis, as a Muslim reform movement, but later left in 1500 to travel for twenty-two years across the length and breath of the Indian subcontinent and the Middle East, to develop a new path to God, a path based on equality, justice, and the fellowship of humanity. Guru Nanak set out to simplify and democratize religion. He taught that God was personally knowable to every man, woman, and child. All that was needed was personal devotion to a personal God. To communicate this message, he spoke in the ordinary language of the day and he rejected the select priesthood, rituals and sacrifices, and the ritual recital of a sacred text in Sanskrit (the ancient Indian classical language).

Guru Nanak's idea of a personal devotion to a personal god was expressed through meditation (bhakti), the utterance of the name of God (Nam), and the singing of hymns (shabads). Guru Nanak advocated that any person, irrespective of sex, status, or creed, could read the sacred text of the Sikhs and officiate as a priest in Sikh congregations. Guru Nanak was followed by nine other gurus or prophets of the Sikh faith: Guru Angad (1504–1552); Guru Amar Das (1479–1574); Guru Ram Das (1534–1581); Guru Arjun (1563–1606); Guru Hargobind (1595–1644); Guru Har Rai (1630–1661); Guru Harkrishan (1656–1664); Guru Tegh Bahadur (1621?–1675); and Guru Gobind Singh (1666–1708).

The scriptures of the Sikhs, the Shri Guru Granth Sahib were compiled by the first five gurus. The Granth is written in the Punjabi language, which is the spoken language of the Sikhs. It contains 5,894 verses in 1,430 pages. These scriptures, completed in 1604 by the fifth guru, Guru Arjun, paint Sikhism as an egalitarian religion setting out to emancipate all. For men there are no requirements of priestly celibacy. For women there are no taboos about menstruation and fertility. Indeed, the third prophet, Guru Amar Das, condemned purdah (required wearing of the veil), female infanticide, and sati (the burning of a widow on her husband's funeral pyre). Guru Amar Das's teachings inspired charity and communal responsibility. Today in Sikhism women and men worship in the same congregation, eat side by side on the floor of the communal kitchen (guru-ka-langar), and undergo the same rites at birth, marriage, and death.

The Khalsa Panth

Unsurprisingly, Sikhism flourished rapidly by the sixteenth and seventeenth centuries. In the eighteenth century Sikhism was formalized by the tenth guru, Guru Gobind Singh, who, upon discovering that it is often necessary for new faiths to fight for their beliefs, baptized his followers in 1699 into the Khalsa Panth ("The Order of the Pure"), with strict rules of personal discipline by combining the spiritual and martial sides of human nature and enshrining the duality of the sant/shupa (saint/soldier). The closest analogy in the West is the Knights Templars of Medieval Europe, who also fought for the survival of their faith. The creation of the Khalsa is the defining moment in Sikh history. It is justly regarded as Guru Gobind Singh's greatest achievement. It is also controversial. The question that has most perplexed observers of Sikhism is how a religion that started off as a system of interior devotion in the sixteenth century became by the end of the eighteenth century associated with a martial tradition. They have thought there to be a conflict between these two ideas. As all serious studies of Sikhism show, there is no conflict. To understand this, it is necessary to understand both how and why the Khalsa Panth was set up.

The martyrdom of two of the ten Sikh gurus under Moghul rule are two of the most cataclysmic events in Sikh religious history. On both occasions, the Sikhs were driven to take arms against their oppressors. First, in the seventeenth century, as the egalitarian ideals of the Sikh faith began to question the social and political structure of the Punjab, the Moghul emperors in Delhi saw this as a threat to their authority. Emperor Jahangir (1569–1627) ceremonially burned alive Guru Arjun in 1606 when he refused to convert to Islam. The religious historian Karen Armstrong explains that unlike Emperor Akbar (1542–1605), "who made bigotry impossible" (Armstrong 1993, 303), had a Hindu vizier, and was one of the greatest and most enlightened rulers that the world has ever seen, his son Jahangir was intent on forcibly converting Hindus to Islam. After the martyrdom of Guru Arjun, Guru Hargobind took up arms to defend the Sikhs against the Moghuls. However, he did not set up an order of spiritual and military discipline. When Guru Tegh Bahadur was publicly beheaded in 1675 in Delhi by Emperor Alamgir (also known as Aurangzeb; 1618–1707), Guru Gobind Singh felt the need to create an order. He realized that his Sikhs were so demoralized that none had dared to step forward and claim the body of their fallen guru. "Sikh tradition reaches a climax in the execution of Guru Tegh Bahadur" (McLeod 1997, 47). The creation of the Khalsa Panth has to be understood in the changed circumstances of the eighteenth century, when Mughal rule embarked on a policy of particularly virulent religious persecution under Aurangzeb, whose intolerance of other faiths was so pronounced that even his own sister, Jahanara, together with many liberal Muslim fakirs, was in full sympathy with Guru Gobind's plan of bringing Hindus and Muslims together (H. Banerjee 1990, 119). It seems that "the Moghul Empire never recovered from the destructive bigotry he had unleashed and sanctified in the name of God" (Armstrong 1993, 304), and it was not long before the Khalsa Panth defeated the Moghul Empire, leading to its rapid disintegration thereafter. However, it is the way in which Guru Gobind inaugurated the Khalsa Panth that is most instructive and revealing.

Guru Nanak had taught that initiating novices into the faith was not the exclusive province of the priest. Guru Gobind went one step further and established that it was not the province of the guru either. Everyone was born with the same rights. Uniquely in the world of religion, therefore, Guru Gobind insisted that he take the baptismal water (*amrit*) from his first five disciples just as they had taken it from him, so that he might become a "Singh" (lion) through their baptism. In recognizing the collective body of disciples as guru, Guru Gobind abolished personal guruship, merged himself with the Khalsa, and invested the whole Panth (Order) with the dignity of gurudom. The abolition of the caste system had been a cardinal principle of the Sikh religion since its birth. Guru Gobind now logically insisted on the remodelling of Sikh society according to that principle. To that end, the traditional surname (which signified caste) would be abolished for all religious purposes and replaced with the common surname "Singh" to denote a uniform religious status. Contrary to any suggestion that he had deviated from the path of early Sikhism by establishing the Khalsa, Guru Gobind Singh brought to a climax the teachings of Guru Nanak by taking them to their ultimate and logical conclusion and establishing the principle that the guru (teacher) and the disciple (student) were equals in matters of personal and spiritual worth.

Views of Guru Gobind Singh

Sikhs see in Guru Gobind Singh the standards by which all human beings should live. These are the standards that secular society recognized later for the first time in 1789 as liberty, equality, fraternity, and the rights of man. They remember that this was the guru who at start of his life, at the tender age of nine in 1675, had asked his father, Guru Tegh Bahadur, to help five hundred Kashmiri Brahmins who were being denied the right to practice their faith, and as a result of that attempt Guru Tegh Bahadur was beheaded. This was the guru who in the final years of his life, while still staunchly standing up for religious freedom and the human rights of others, saw two of his sons, Ajit and Jujahar, die at the Battle of Chamkaur in 1704 and the other two, Fateh Singh and Zorawar Singh, bricked up alive at Sirhind for refusing to give up their faith. Sikhs fought for their own faith as well as for the faiths of others.

Such is the contribution of Guru Gobind Singh to the modern era that the best accounts of his life are given not by the Sikhs but by others, including Western writers such as Max Arthur Macauliffe, J. D. Cunningham, and W. H. McLeod. Perhaps the most insightful have been those by Bengali writers, in the early years of the twentieth century, at a time of a growing upsurge of militant nationalist opposition to foreign rule in India. To many of these writers, who were searching for a new Indian identity, Guru Gobind's Khalsa was in the best Indian traditions of fighting against tyranny, foreign invasion, and exploitation of the poor by a ruling class. For them, the birth of Sikhism, the rise of the Khalsa, the martyrdom of the gurus, the resistance to the Mughals and Afghans, the remarkable success of Maharajah Ranjit Singh (1780–1839) in building up a powerful Sikh monarchy when other Indian rulers were meekly submitting to foreign rule, and finally the bravery of the Sikh army in the Anglo-Sikh wars epitomized the strength of Sikhism.

The finest pieces of Bengali creative writing on Guru Gobind Singh were written by the Nobel laureate Rabindranath Tagore (1861–1941) over a period of nearly twenty-five years (1885–1909). Tagore wrote about Guru Gobind's moments of joy and sorrow, his triumphs and anguish, and his deep commitment to the cause of Sikh cultural heritage. In *Bir Guru,* his first work, written in his twenties, Tagore wrote that the guru fought for "oppressed humanity" and laid down his life for bringing an end to Mughal authority in the Punjab. Later, when Tagore was disillusioned with what he called the "degrading mendicancy policy" of the Indian National Congress of the 1880s, he wrote *Guru Gobinda,* where he made no secret of his admiration for Guru Gobind Singh, who had spent twenty years of his life in obscurity before agreeing to lead his community at the age of thirty-five. During those years of self-exile, Tagore wrote, the guru devoted himself to the study of sacred literature along with self-analysis and introspection that was hardly paralleled in contemporary politics. Tagore visualized that his ideal leader, like Guru Gobind Singh, would pay very little attention to any short-term gain, fame, and self-publicity. Instead he would devote himself to the service of the community. In this work, Tagore recounts how when the guru was requested by his closest disciples to come out of obscurity and take up the leadership of the Panth, he promptly turned them down. For the right leadership, he still had much to learn. Until completion of his learning, he told them, he would remain in obscurity developing himself and gaining inspiration before serving the community. In *Nishpal Upahar,* Tagore notes the guru's contempt for wealth and projects him as his ideal Indian leader.

Indeed, the Bengali literary world was so enthralled by the spirit of martyrdom and self-sacrifice of the Sikhs that Bengali monographs like *Sikher Balidan* (1904), *Sikh-Ithias* (1907), and *Sikher Jagaran* (1929) not only highlighted this tradition but provided an added stimulus to India's fight for freedom. A few of them made a direct appeal to militant nationalists of Bengal to bring an end to the Raj following the path of the Sikh martyrs. Consequently, this led to the imposition of a ban on many of them. *Sikher Athmauti,* for example, was so effectively proscribed by the colonial government that not even a single copy of it can be found in any leading library of India.

Others, like Jadunath, a noted sociologist and historian of the twentieth century, have argued that the transformation of Sikhism in the seventeenth century was dictated by the pressing needs of contemporary society that faced widespread religious persecution at the hands of India's Mughal rulers at the time. In the changed conditions of that society something more

was needed than what had originally been preached by Guru Nanak. The Khalsa symbolized this change. Thus, we could say that Guru Nanak's teachings had not been negated by Guru Gobind Singh but upheld in the face of overwhelming odds. Another writer, Kartikchandra Mitra explained in *Sikh Guru* that the "radicalisation" of Sikh politics provided a new lease of life for the Panth. The Mughal persecution would have crushed the Sikhs had there been no Khalsa. The Khalsa, in fact, saved the Sikhs during the critical years of their jeopardy by offering them a symbol of unity without which they would have been vanquished by Mughal persecution (H. Banerjee 1990, 119–32). The Khalsa was inevitable in Sikhism. Today, it remains necessary for the survival of Sikhism.

Satvinder S. Juss

See also Hinduism

Further Reading

Alam, M. (1986). *The crisis of empire in Mughal north India, Awadh, and the Punjab 1707–1748.* Oxford: Oxford University Press.

Armstrong, K. (1993). *A history of God.* London: Mandarin.

Banerjee, H. (1990). Bengali perceptions of the Sikhs: The nineteenth and twentieth centuries. In J.T. O'Connell, M. Israel, & W.G. Oxtoby (Eds.). *Sikh history and religion in the twentieth century.* New Delhi, India: Manohar Publications Daryaganj.

Juss, S. (1995). The constitution and Sikhs in Britain. *Brigham Young University Law Review.*

McLeod, W. H. (1997). *Sikhism.* London: Penguin Books.

Slavery

Slave religion in the New World is unique because—unlike Egyptian, Greek, or Roman slaves in antiquity who often held common religious beliefs with their masters—New World slaves created a separate, secret reality. New World masters may have introduced their slaves to Christian beliefs and practices, but New World slaves rarely shared their secret (African) reality with their masters.

In *Freedom in the Making of Western Culture,* a comprehensive study of slavery and Western thought, Jamaican-born sociologist Orlando Patterson makes a

DESCRIPTION OF THE HUSH HARBOR FROM A SLAVE NARRATIVE

Not being allowed to hold meetings on the plantation, the slaves assemble in the swamps, out of reach of the patrols. They have an understanding among themselves as to the time and place of getting together. This is often done by the first one arriving breaking boughs form the trees, and bending them in the direction of the selected spot. Arrangements are then made for conducting the exercises. They first ask each other how they feel, the state of their minds, etc. The male members then select a certain space, in separate groups, for their division of the meeting. Preaching in order, by the brethren; then praying and singing all round, until they generally feel quite happy. The speaker usually commences by calling himself unworthy, and talks very slowly, until, feeling the spirit, he grows excited, and in a short time, there fall to the ground twenty or thirty men and women under its influence. Enlightened people call it excitement; but I wish the same was felt by everybody, so far as they are sincere.

The slave forgets all his sufferings, except to remind others of the trials during the past week, exclaiming: "Thank God, I shall not live here always!" Then they pass from one to another, shaking hands, and bidding each other farewell, promising, should they meet no more on earth, to strive and meet in heaven, where all is joy, happiness and liberty. As they separate, they sing a parting hymn of praise.

Peter Randolph

Source: *From Slave Cabin to the Pulpit, The Autobiography of Rev. Peter Randolph: The Southern Question Illustrated and Sketches of Slave Life.* (Boston: James H. Earle, 1893), 202–203.

---

strong case that the ideas concerning freedom shared by America's founding fathers were greatly influenced by the presence of slaves in the New World. Patterson effectively argues that Americans "came to value freedom, to construct it as a powerful shared vision of life, as a result of their experience of, and in response to, slavery" (1991, xiii). Many signers of the Declaration of Independence were themselves slaveholders, and concepts like "freedom of religion" appear in stark contrast to the lack of religious freedom afforded slaves. Ultimately, Patterson concluded that American ideals concerning "religious freedom" were informed by observing degrees of freedom that were denied to the slave community.

Religious freedom can be examined from the perspectives of (1) freedom of belief and practice and (2) freedom of assembly. From both perspectives, slave religion in the Americas was highly restricted. Nevertheless—as in other historical contexts—slave owners found it easier to restrict religious assembly than to control the religious beliefs and practices of their slaves. For example, slaves preserved African tribal traditions by blending elements taken from African religions with Christian elements, and a number of African beliefs were taken "underground." African-style ceremonial spirit possession and conjure both survived and sometimes thrived within the hostile environment of New World slavery.

It must be recognized that Christianity was not the only option for slaves. Slaves from Muslim parts of Africa were also enslaved in the Americas. While Muslim slaves left few narratives of their experiences, a number of narratives—written in Arabic—survive. Islam was not widespread among slaves in the American South, but nevertheless eighteenth-century Christian missionaries noted that Muslim slaves in Georgia and South Carolina blended Christianity and Islam by identifying God with Allah and Jesus with Muhammad. Some aspects of Islamic ritual were also maintained; for example, missionaries noted that Muslim slaves prayed five times a day facing Mecca. In addition, slaves who had been

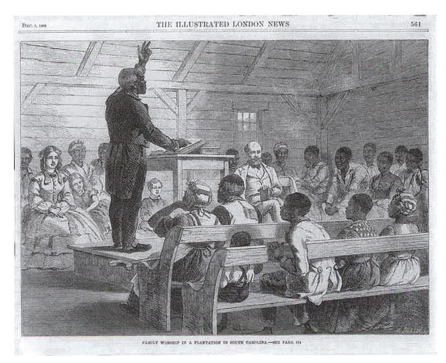

A highly romanticized illustration of slaves worshipping on a South Carolina plantation, published in the *Illustrated London News*, 5 December 1863. COURTESY OF WWW.GWU.EDU/~FOLKLIFE/BIGHOUSE/IMAGES

Muslims in Africa were familiar with the Qur'an and—like African-American slaves who converted to Christianity—evidenced a great respect for literacy and the written word.

Freedom of Belief and Practice

Slave religion in the Americas followed three paths, according to historian Charles Joyner: (1) a merging of African religions and Christianity; (2) underground alternative non-Christian religions usually involving ceremonial spirit possession; and (3) a belief in magic and witchcraft. All three paths have been discerned throughout the Americas, but the first path is best documented for the United States, while the second (ceremonial spirit possession) is best documented in Latin America and the Caribbean. Archaeologist Laurie A. Wilkie indicates that conjure is more difficult to investigate than the others, but select aspects of conjure have been identified almost everywhere in the New World where slavery existed.

In terms of belief, slaves were afforded their greatest freedom while professing Christianity and considerably less freedom in terms of ceremonial spirit possession and conjure. During the early years of slavery, plantation owners in the American South were ambivalent concerning the religious lives of their slaves. Prior to 1700, many Southern slaves were discouraged from practicing religion of any kind. According to Albert J. Raboteau, serious, concerted efforts to convert slaves to Christianity did not begin until the eighteenth century and even those attempts were not particularly effective prior to 1740. Once Christianity took hold, however, slaves converted in great numbers; and by 1770, African-American preachers in the South had established numerous independent churches.

Mechal Sobel points out that American slaves were not converted to Christianity all at once. Slave in the Americas embraced Christianity selectively, and they squeezed and shaped Christianity to fit their immediate needs. They also squeezed and shaped African religions to fit their immediate needs. Slaveholders deliberately separated African tribal and language groups, and in many cases tribal deities and rituals were lost in the passage to the New World. A common explanation for this loss is that African religious specialists were rarely enslaved. Most slaves were young males (under twenty-five years of age), and since African tribal religions are revealed over time, those who were carried into slavery had but a limited knowledge of their respective tribal religions.

Forms of Slave Worship

Spirit possession and trance occupied a predominant place in slave religion. But spirit possession in the New World was not as public as it had been in Africa and often took the form of possession by the Holy Ghost rather than possession by African deities. A major focus became a personal seeking after God. Among slaves in the American South, the process of conversion was seen as a spiritual journey. It was understood as a way of becoming "free."

The most common form of spiritual journey was contained within rituals known as "mourning" or "tarrying." Similar rituals have been noted throughout the Americas. In modified form, these same rituals are still practiced on the Sea Islands of South Carolina and in the English-speaking Caribbean, according to Glazier. Mourning or tarrying is part of a lengthy, complex ceremony involving fasting, lying on a dirt floor, and other physical deprivations. Raboteau shows that its major components are derived from West African initiation rites. For participants, mourning symbolized death and rebirth. A major goal of these rites is to be a constant reminder of human frailty and imperfection in the midst of life. Traditionally, mourning ceremonies were carried out over a period of weeks and took place during "slow times" on the plantation. Sometimes, slaves who desired to participate in these rituals feigned illness. But if they were caught, they were severely punished.

Despite the inherent risks, many New World slaves managed to carry on African-style ceremonial spirit possession. Such rituals seem to have been more common in the Caribbean than in the United States. The "ring shout" or "shout"—a formally structured hitching dance movement and chant designed to induce spirit possession—was widely practiced according to R. Simpson. In a ring shout, dancers moved in counterclockwise circles, shuffling to dirge-like music. Ring shouts continued for many hours, becoming increasingly energetic as each member in turn "caught the spirit."

As Janet D. Cornelius notes, there was a close association between conversion to Christianity and slaves' quest for literacy. In the Americas, slaveholders both encouraged and discouraged their slaves from learning to read and write. There was considerable debate among slaveholders as to whether slaves who converted to Christianity would become better slaves or become more difficult to manage. Some masters punished their slaves for learning to read, but they considered it more acceptable to learn to read in a Christian context.

Literacy was highly prized within the slave community itself, and a major goal of missionary organizations like the Society for the Propagation of the Bible in Foreign Parts was to teach slaves to read and write English. Through the work of the SPBFP, the King James Version of the Bible became the dominant language of the African-American church and played a vital role in merging African traditional religions and Christianity.

Reading lessons were interspersed with Bible study. Almost immediately, slaves began to recognize that Biblical teachings concerning slavery were contradictory; for example, 1 Peter 2:18 states: "Servants, be submissive to your masters with all respect, not only to the kind and gentle, but also to the overbearing." But in Galatians 5:1, Paul argues: "For freedom Christ has set us free; stand fast therefore, and do not submit again to a yoke of slavery." Ultimately, many slaves ended up identifying strongly with passages taken from the Old Testament, especially from the book of Exodus. Passages from the book of Exodus continue to occupy an important place in contemporary black preaching. As in other aspects of slave religion, slaves appropriated biblical imagery selectively. They began to identify themselves with the tribes of Israel. Abraham became their symbolic father, while Moses became their symbolic liberator. Over time, the Old Testament was transformed into a common African-American "sacred history."

L. Ramey emphasizes that slave worship was highly lyrical and dramatic. Its language, movement, and rhythms were intended to "move" their audiences. Preachers infused everyday happenings with a deep spiritual significance and used modes of expression that were common in West Africa (i.e., chanted sermons, call-and-response, repetition of the last word of an utterance as the first word of the next, falsetto shrieks, and high, forced tones). They were also adept at relating biblical symbolism to daily life. In contrast to white forms of worship,

African-American sermons were highly participatory with enthusiastic exclamations from the congregation.

Like slave sermons, slave prayers also evidenced creative use of King James English. Prayers paraphrased Biblical verses, borrowing especially from the book of Job. African-American prayers were characterized by their rhythmic quality, biblical allusions, and high sense of emotional urgency.

Above all, slave worship services were loud and enthusiastic, and while slaves readily adopted European hymns and harmonies, they added African-style rhythm. Music in Africa—especially drumming—was believed to provide a pathway to the gods. But drumming was illegal on the plantation and slaves substituted spoons, tin buckets, hoes, oars, sticks, and hand clapping, foot stomping, or body slapping to induce rhythm. Slaves altered tunes to conform to West African musical patterns. Two of the most common features of slave hymnody were repeated chorus or refrain and a call-and-response pattern.

Conjure and Divination

In the societies of West and Central Africa, religion was never seen as distinct from the rest of activity. It was a way of life, which grounded all social structures, institutions, and relationships. Yvonne Chireau correctly notes that many magical and occult beliefs in the New World were derived mainly from African tribal religions.

African-American occultism, referred to as conjure, encompasses spells, healing, and the use of supernatural objects, according to Wilke. Slaveholders generally regarded conjure as a form of paganism, and if caught conjurers were severely punished. It was one of a few offenses for which a slave might be executed.

But not all conjurers saw themselves as pagans. Christians—slaves and free African-Americans—also acted as conjurers, and many Christian rituals and symbols were readily incorporated into conjure rites. According to Chireau, conjure gave slaves a greater sense of personal control as it "spoke directly to the slaves' sense of powerlessness and danger by providing alternative—but largely symbolic—means for addressing suffering" (1997, 240).

Conjurers possessed multiple skills and talent as diviners, soothsayers, and clairvoyants. Most notable among these skills were the interpretation of dreams and visions, the reading of signs, and astrology. Some conjurers were believed to be able to tell the future by looking into a flame or water. They also offered their clients protection through the use of portable talismans, charms, or *grisgris* (the French Creole word for what is known as gregory bags in English).

In the British West Indies, conjurers were also known as obeahmen and were recognized as major spiritual authorities. In the North American setting, however, conjure was largely private, noncollective, and noninstitutionalized. Sometimes, the religious authority of Christian leaders and conjurers overlapped. Often, North American conjurers were able to avoid detection and punishment by blending elements of Christianity with African practices. During the 1700s, it became increasingly common for North American conjurers to profess strong Christian commitment. Some may have professed Christianity to avoid punishment, but in the view of Chireau it is clear that many conjurers were also devout Christians.

Freedom of Assembly

As noted, slaveholders were most effective in curtailing religious assembly than curtailing either religious belief or religious practice. Slave worship took place in a variety of settings under various degrees of white supervision. Four major ritual settings for slave worship were hush harbors, praise houses, plantation chapels, and town churches.

A "hush harbor" is an area slaves created for themselves outside the slave quarters. They were located mostly in wooded areas. Slaves constructed these informal worship sites out of poles and brush. The locations of hush harbors were often secret—not only to plantation owners but to other slaves on the plantation as well.

Hush harbors were located in remote areas because slave worship was often noisy. Services generally began with slow renditions of regular European-style hymns. This was followed by lengthy prayers. While anyone could offer prayers, only preachers—who were chosen by the slave community—were allowed to give the lesson and sermon. Hush harbor services built gradually; becoming noisier and noisier as the tempo increased. Services culminated in ritual spirit possession.

White reactions to ring shouts and spirit possession were mixed. In a majority of cases, these activities were successfully hidden from masters. Some masters forbade hush harbor activities altogether and punished participants if caught. Other masters were aware of but ignored these activities. Surprisingly, some white masters observed hush harbor rituals, and many of the best descriptions of hush harbor services are based on observations by white missionaries.

Some masters allowed their slaves to worship publicly in formally designated religious buildings on the plantation called "praise houses." These buildings were usually small and were used on Sundays and for other gatherings during the week. Cornelius contends that slaves identified very strongly with their praise houses—so much so that they replicated them away from plantation land after Emancipation. She notes that many of these reconstructed praise houses are still in existence.

In addition, public Christian worship was encouraged in plantation "chapels," which were constructed by the slave owners. But these were not as readily accepted by slaves. Chapels were often simple, windowless buildings, but a number of chapels were quite elaborate. A fine plantation chapel served to demonstrate the piety and prestige of plantation owners. Other places that were utilized for slave worship included barns, carriage houses, and cotton gin houses.

On some occasions, slaves were permitted to attend Christian services off the plantation and worship alongside whites in mixed (black and white) town churches. In such cases, slaves were restricted to particular locations within the church (back rows, standing in the rear, or the balcony). While African-Americans could be admitted into church membership, they received communion separately from whites, could not preach, and were not allowed to initiate public prayer. Even when slaves were allowed to attend white churches in town, they usually supplemented church attendance with secret hush harbor meetings.

The Aftermath of Slavery

During the first generations of slavery, African-American religious leaders provided a valuable link to the African past. But their presence was seldom acknowledged by whites. Some slave leaders embraced Christianity, while others operated entirely outside of it. Chireau convincingly argues that conjurers were a vital bridge between old and new traditions. During the late 1700s and early 1800s

many enslaved and free blacks embraced Methodism. Others became Baptists. The flexibility of Baptist organizations made it possible for both slaves and free blacks to begin their own worship groups. By the 1800s, some black churches operated independently from white churches, while other African-American churches shared resources with whites. In addition, Presbyterians, Methodists, Baptists, and Episcopalians sponsored missionaries to travel to plantations in order to provide religious education to slaves. Episcopal missionaries formally appointed plantation slaves as prayer leaders, while Methodist and Baptist missionaries encouraged slave leaders to conduct prayer meetings during the week.

During the antebellum period, African-American preaching and assembly were outlawed in most Southern states, but independent city churches continued to meet the needs of slaves and free blacks. African-Americans owned many of these church buildings and hired their own preachers; for example, large all-black churches were established in Kentucky, Alabama, Missouri, and Maryland.

Slave religion represents an important chapter in the African-American struggle for religious freedom. As Raboteau has argued, slave religion was very much an "invisible institution" in the Americas, but it is an institution that has profoundly shaped the religious lives of contemporary African-Americans.

Stephen D. Glazier

See also Code Noir; Great Awakenings and the Antebellum Period

Further Reading

Chireau, Y. (1997). Conjure and Christianity in the nineteenth century: Religious elements in African-American magic. *Religion and American culture, 7,* 225–247.

Cornelius, J. D. (1999). *Slave missions and the black church in the antebellum south.* Columbia: University of South Carolina Press.

Glazier, S. D. (1983). Mourning in the Afro-Baptist tradition: A comparative study of religion in the American south and in Trinidad. *Southern quarterly, 23, 3,* 141–156.

Joyner, C. (1984). *Down by the riverside: A South Carolina community.* Urbana: University of Illinois Press.

Patterson, O. (1991). *Freedom in the making of Western culture.* New York: Basic Books.

Pitts, W. F., Jr. (1993). *Old ship of Zion: The Afro-Baptist ritual in the African diaspora.* New York: Oxford University Press.

Raboteau, A. J. (1978). *Slave religion: The "invisible institution" in the antebellum South.* New York: Oxford University Press.

Simpson, R. (1983). The shout and shouting in slave religion of the United States. *Southern quarterly, 23,* 3, 34–48.

Sobel, M. (1979). *Trabelin' on: The slave journey to an Afro-Baptist faith.* Westport, CT: Greenwood Press.

Ramey, L. (2002). The theology of the lyric tradition in African American spirituals. *Journal of the American Academy of Religion, 70,* 347–364.

Wilkie, L. A. (1997). Secret and sacred: Contextualizing the artifacts of African-American magic and religion. *Historical archaeology, 31,* 81–107.

South Africa

Religious freedom is a fundamental human right enshrined in the Republic of South Africa's Bill of Rights. It guarantees freedom of conscience, religion, thought, belief, and opinion. Historically, conflicts in Europe and European political and economic interests in other parts of the world shaped the South African religious landscape. Restrictions on Catholic and Islamic public forms of worship in the Cape during the early period of Dutch settlement in the mid-seventeenth century was due to Catholic-Protestant conflict in Europe and the Dutch East India Company's need to suppress Islamic resistance in Indonesia. In South Africa's history the struggle for religious freedom has been inextricably linked to the struggle for liberation from colonialism and apartheid, as religion was used to exclude black people from political processes.

Absence of Religious Freedom

From the time of Dutch colonization, there was no religious freedom for people who were not Christian, although the nation has a rich diversity of religious traditions. The denial of religious freedom to those who practiced indigenous religions, Islam, and other Asian religions was coupled with political and cultural oppression in the form of colonialism and apartheid. Christianity was elevated over other religions, and it was used to define what was normative in terms of morality and ethics.

Prior to the twentieth century, Christian missionaries experienced very few conversions. There was dialogue between the missionaries and African religious practitioners. In this dialogue each group defined what it meant to be human in terms of resources at its disposal. The African worldview was more open to other interpretations of the world; the missionaries for their part believed themselves in possession of absolute truth. Initially white settlers denied that Africans even had a religion; that view was based on the idea that Africans had no idea of a Supreme Being. For the Europeans of that time, such an assertion implied that Africans were at the same level as animals and therefore had no human rights, which justified the seizure of African land and oppression of Africans in general. Later there was recognition of the fact that Africans had their own religions, but European opinion was that those religions were mere superstitions and decidedly inferior.

Some missionaries saw the independence of African polities as a stumbling block to African conversion; they went as far as to encourage the subjugation of African polities as a step toward the conversion of local populations to Christianity. The period after the fall of African polities (various conquests, by both the Dutch and the British, occurred throughout the nineteenth century; the British conquest of Zululand in 1887 was the last) was marked by an increase in the numbers of people converting to Christianity. The majority of those who converted did so in order to have access to resources such as food and education that were available at the mission stations.

Victory of the National Party

In 1948 the National Party came to power and adopted as its state religion a brand of Calvinist Protestantism that justified the exclusion of Africans, Coloreds (people of mixed white and nonwhite heritage), and Asians from the political process in the country, thus supporting the National Party's policy of apartheid. The Dutch Reformed Church theologians drew support and legitimacy for the apartheid ideology from the Bible. Apartheid did not mean only separation of racial groups but also white supremacy. In 1961 South Africa became a republic and declared itself a Christian state, a move that privileged Christianity over other religions.

Religious education was a euphemism for Christian education, as learners were given instruction in various aspects of the Bible. The approach adopted was not geared toward an "open, plural, intercultural and interdisciplinary study of religion" (Chidester 1994, 1) but was intended to indoctrinate learners. South Africa is one of the few countries in the world in which biblical studies is a subject in the secondary school curriculum. The syllabus was designed to foster a certain Protestant understanding of Christianity.

New South Africa

Following the ending of apartheid in 1990–1991, a new constitution, promulgated in 1993, ushered in a dispensation of racial inclusiveness and human rights. Freedom of religion was one of the rights introduced. The writers of the constitution attempted to avoid privileging one religion over others: The constitution recognized that South Africa was a religiously plural society and aimed to protect people's rights to belong to any religion without any fear of being discriminated against or persecuted. Religious freedom was also extended to those who held no religious beliefs. This protection of religious freedom was part of a larger effort to cultivate tolerance in what has been a deeply divided society.

The 1996 constitution (which followed the 1993 constitution and an interim constitution of 1994) subordinates religion to the authority of the state. Although Section 15 (1) of the Bill of Rights says that "Everyone has the right to freedom of conscience, religion, thought, belief and opinion," Ebrahim Moosa, a scholar of religion, believes that the South African constitution has a dualistic view of religion that distinguishes religion in the abstract from religion in practice. The translation of belief into practice is severely limited by the constitution.

The constitution individualizes religion and confines it to a private space. If religion appears in public spaces it must be regulated in such a way that it does not interfere with the norms and values of the secular state. Individuals can hold beliefs and put them in practice as long as they do not violate the constitution or the law. For example, Muslims, African traditionalists, and Hindus can believe in polygamy, but the law will not recognize polygamous unions. Similarly, Rastafarians can believe in the spiritual power of cannabis, but it remains illegal to possess or smoke it.

The Future

Recognizing that religion has the ability to mold people, the 1996 constitution restrains it within the parameters of state authority. The future should see state morality being challenged by religious morality, as in the constitutional court challenge brought by the attorney Gareth Prince, a Rastafarian, who petitioned for the legalization of cannabis after the law society of the Western Cape refused to admit him because he had two convictions for possession of cannabis. Prince's loss by a single vote (four to five) indicates how divided the South African courts remain on matters of religious freedom.

Sibusiso Masondo

Further Reading

Chidester, D. (1992). *Religions of South Africa.* London and New York: Routledge.

Chidester, D. (1994). *Authentic forgery or forging authenticity: Comparative religion in South Africa.* (Inaugural Lecture No. 186). Cape Town, South Africa: University of Cape Town.

Chidester, D. (1996). *Savage systems: Colonialism and comparative religion in Southern Africa.* Charlottesville and London: University Press of Virginia.

Du Plessis, L. (1994). The genesis of South Africa's first Bill of Rights. *Journal of Theology for Southern Africa, 86,* 52–66.

Du Plessis, L. M. (2001). Freedom *of* or freedom *from* religion? An overview of issues pertinent to the constitutional protection or religious rights and freedom in "the new South Africa." *Brigham Young University Law Review, 2,* 439–466.

Du Plessis, L., & Corder, H. (1994). *Understanding South Africa's transitional Bill of Rights.* Cape Town, South Africa: Juta and Co.

Etherington, N. (1987). Missionary doctors and African healers in mid-Victorian South Africa. *South African Historical Journal, 19,* 77–91.

Kiernan, J. (1995). The impact of white settlement on African traditional religions. In M. Prozensky & J. de Gruchy (Eds.), *Living faiths in South Africa* (pp. 72–82). Cape Town, South Africa: David Philip.

Kunnie, J. (1992). Religion and the state in contemporary South Africa. In A. M. Ahanotu (Ed.), *Religion, state, and society in contemporary Africa: Nigeria, Sudan, South Africa, Zaire and Mozambique* (pp. 153–186). New York: Peter Lang.

Moosa, E. (2000). Tensions in legal and religious values

in the 1996 South African constitution. In M. Mamdani (Ed.), *Beyond rights talk and cultural talk* (pp. 121–135). Cape Town, South Africa: David Philip.

Opoku, K.A. (1993). African traditional religion: An enduring heritage. In J. Olupona & S. Nyang (Eds.), *Religious plurality in Africa: Essays in honour of John S Mbiti* (pp. 67–82). New York: Mouton de Gruyter.

Prozensky, M., & de Gruchy, J. (Eds.). (1995). *Living faiths in South Africa*. Cape Town, South Africa: David Philip.

Sachs, A. (1992). *Religion, education, and constitutional law*. Institute for Comparative Religion in Southern Africa, Second Annual Lecture.

Tahzib, B. G. (1996). *Freedom of religion or belief: Ensuring effective international legal protection*. The Hague, Netherlands: Martinus Nijhoff Publishers.

van der Vyver, J. D., & Witte, J., Jr. (Eds.). (1996). *Religious human rights in global perspective*. The Hague, Netherlands: Martinus Nijhoff Publishers.

van der Vyver, J. D. (1998, October 4–6). Constitutional perspective of church-state in South Africa. *Conference on religious liberty: International perspectives during the 50th anniversary of the Universal Declaration of Human Rights*. Brigham Young University, Provo, UT.

South America

South America is a geographical designation and not a historical marker or entity. From the standpoint of the history of religious freedom, South America is an inadequate marker to designate at the very least five hundred years of religious encounter, conflict, and evolution. The limited used of the geographical marker "South America" is exacerbated when one attempts to determine where the boundaries between the South and the North lie. If one is in North America, one may say that South America begins south of the United States' borders with Mexico. But if one stands in Chile, or Argentina, South America ends at the border between Colombia and Panama. For a South American, Central America is a subcontinent between North and South America. For some Mexicans, twentieth-century Mexico is part of North America. Alternatively, one may opt to use the designator *Latin America,* but this one is also highly polemical as it is charged with ideology. Latin America is a term that was coined during the 1840s in order to

distinguished the United States, a former British colony, and the countries that had been colonies of Spain and Portugal. Latin America thus also obfuscates the way in which former British, Spanish, and Portuguese colonies underwent extremely similar processes of discovery, colonization, revolution, independence, modernization, and democratization. Socially, culturally, racially, and religiously, the Americas have undergone the same dynamic process spanning five hundred years. Nonetheless there are fundamental differences that cannot be erased and that make it worthwhile to study each subregion within the American continent separately.

To understand the history of religious freedom in the Americas in general, and South and Central America in particular, it is necessary that we be minimally acquainted with the pre-Colombian past, that is, the times before the arrival of Christopher Columbus to the Caribbean Islands in 1492. Before the Spaniards arrived, the American continent could be divided into three major regions in accordance with the type of social organization and groupings that inhabited them: high Indian cultures, semi-sedentary peoples, and nomadic hunting and gatherings tribes. The high Indian cultures were found in contemporary Central America and the Andean altiplano on the Pacific coast of South America. The Aztecs and the Incas were among these high Indian cultures. The semisedentary peoples were to be found in the jungles and savannas of South America and in parts of North America. The nomadic hunting and gathering tribes were also to be found in the extreme parts of North and South America, especially in the Amazonian jungles of contemporary Brazil. The differences between these three regions and their respective inhabitants are important when trying to understand the evolution of religious ideas, practices, and freedom in the Americas. While the semisedentary peoples and nomadic tribes possessed religions that are called shamanistic, animistic, and totemistic, the high civilizations had religions that were highly formalized, were integral to theocratic systems, and had elaborate theogonies and cosmologies that resulted in highly sophisticated beliefs systems. Furthermore, the high Indian civilizations of Central America and the Andean altiplano had developed sophisticated social hierarchies, cities with fortifications, temples, schools, and systems of highways and irrigation. This level in social and cultural development determined the nature of the encounter between Europeans and Amerindians.

453

THE EFFECT OF MISSIONS ON THE TUCANO

The following extract of ethnographic text provides some insight into both the methods used by missionaries to gain converts among native peoples of South America and also the effects of missionary activity.

Since the arrival of the religious Missionary and the rubber worker in the region, two important phenomena have occurred. The most significant and most noticeable one is the rapid incorporation and diffusion of occidental material culture. The aluminum pix has replaced the pottery bowl, trousers have replaced the loincloth, the cotton dress has taken the place of the tree-bark skirt, hunting is no longer done with bow and arrow, but with a shotgun, and fishing is more often done with the fishhook than with the trap.

In the field of spiritual culture the influence of occidental culture has been more subtle and not so rapidly accepted. It is certain that the system of social organization is suffering a process of disintegration; the Indian who wishes to have a woman must be willing to settle in a mission, because the Missionaries have shrewdly gathered together all the women of marriageable age and have taken them to the Missions; the kinship terms no longer correspond to the present system; very few Indians still practice polyandry; but in spite of all this evidence. An adult Tukano Indian of today has not stopped thinking according to the typical Tukano mental processes. For example, Manuel Sierra, our interpreter, in spite of having lived for four consecutive years with his wife in the Departamento del Tolima, in Central Colombia, and in spite of having left the Vaupes at 17 years of age, still has the conviction that having eaten fish after the birth of his son without a Tukano shaman's having "blown" the food beforehand was the cause of the appearance of ulcers on his legs.

Marcos Fulop

Source: "Aspectos de la cultura Tucana: Cosmogonia"
[Aspects of the Tucano culture: Cosmogony].
Revista Colombiana de Antropologia (1954) 3: 7.
Translated from the Spanish for the HRAF by Mary Louise Bravo.

Sword and Cross

While Europeans arrived in what they termed the New World in 1492, their conquest of the Americas only began in 1521, when Hernán Cortés (1485–1547) finally conquered Tenochtitlán, the capital of the Aztec empire. Francisco Pizarro (c. 1475–1578) did not conquer the lands of the Inca empire until almost two decades later in 1531–33; civil wars among the conquerors then ensued. With the European sword came the cross and the Bible. The conquest of the New World was an imperial project, but one that was justified with religious reasons. In 1493, Pope Alexander VI promulgated a papal bull that entrusted the Catholic monarchs of Spain with the mission of bringing the Gospel to the heathen and establishing the Church in the New World. This papal bull also divided the New World between Spain and Portugal along a line that was later pushed west by the Treaty of Tordesillas (1494). In effect, the Spanish crown was granted royal patronage over the newly discovered lands, a patronage that extended the royal patronage Rome had granted to the Spanish monarchy in Granada in 1486 for the purpose of expelling the (Muslim) Moors from the Iberian Peninsula. The conquest of the New World was an extension of the battle against Islam in the Old World. With the patronage came economic and religious power (the power to inspect papal dispatches to the New World), but also scrutiny and the duty to fulfill a religious mission in accordance with a proper understanding of Christianity. This dual aspect of the patronage was embodied in two institutions that affected the evolution of religious freedom in the New World: the *encomienda* and the missions. The former was a grant to the Spanish conquistadors or colonists that consisted of monies, lands, goods, and tributes or taxes, but also the labor of the Amerindians captured during the conquest. The colonists or conquistadors, in turn, were obliged to evangelize and educate the Amerindians entrusted (hence the word *encomienda*, to give someone in trust) to them. Another term that is sometimes used synonymously with *encomienda* is *repartimiento* (distribution), which referred to the assignation of lands and claims over Amerindians in return for the services performed on behalf of the church and crown. The *encomiendas* or *repartimientos* in effect were labor camps, the equivalent of the United States' antebellum slave plantations. But since they were organized under a religious imperative and justification, critics of these institutions could hold their most violent, dehumanizing, and devastating aspects in check. The missions, on the other hand, reflected the religious devotion and missionary zeal of the different orders that came to the New World to carry out their evangelizing work. There were in fact two crosses: the cross of the conquistador and the colonists, and the cross of the missionaries. From their first appearance in the New World, these two groups were in permanent struggle, until the eventual disappearance of the *encomienda*. Their conflict formed the ground on which religious liberty unfolded, and continues to unfold, in Central and South America.

The Missions and the Religions of the Amerindians

After conquest was accomplished and conquered territories were renamed New Spain and New Granada, conquest gave way to evangelization. This evangelization was undertaken by mendicant orders (orders whose members take a vow of poverty), predominantly the Dominicans and the Franciscans, although the Jesuits played also played a key role, especially in the seventeenth century, before their expulsion from America and Spain in 1767. From the fifteenth through the nineteenth century, the Franciscans, Jesuits, and Dominicans, accounted for

almost 90 percent of all the missionaries in the New World (other orders included the Capuchins, Mercedarians, Augustinians, and Carmelites), with Franciscans accounting for a full 55.9 percent.

The history of the missions in the New World can also be told in terms of three major periods: the sixteenth century, when the Dominicans led missionary activity, mostly in New Spain; the seventeenth century, when Jesuits were the most active, mostly in the outer boundaries of the Spanish colonies, in the jungles, pampas, and llanos of South America (contemporary Paraguay, Uruguay, Chile, and southwestern Brazil); and the nineteenth century, when the Franciscans took the lead. The fact that mendicant orders undertook the evangelization of the Amerindians is profoundly significant for the evolution of religious freedom and indeed for the Church itself in the Americas. In the seventeenth and eighteenth centuries in New Spain—what in essence was Mexico—the Dominicans carried out one of the most significant programs of missionary work in the history of the encounter of religions and faiths. They founded missions, universities, language schools, wrote what are arguably the first ethnographic and anthropological works, inaugurated New World literature, wrote grammars of indigenous languages, and preserved (though they also destroyed) the cultural knowledge of the high Indian civilizations. One of the most notable examples of the missionaries' approach was the establishment of the college of Tlatelolco, where children of the Aztec nobility were schooled in Latin and Nahuatl (a native tongue), and were taught rhetoric, logic, theology, philosophy, and what was certainly a novelty at the time—native medicine.

Just War and Religious Freedom

The crucial role the mendicant orders played in the evolution of religious freedom in the New World is epitomized by the 1550 debate between Fray Bartolomé de las Casas, who was one of the most important of the early missionaries, and Juan Ginés de Sepúlveda, a cleric and historian for the Spanish crown. The debate concerned whether the Spaniards were justified in waging war against the Amerindians to force their submission to Spanish rule. Sepúlveda appealed to Aristotle to justify the validity of a just war in this instance. De las Casas, expressing the general belief of the Church and even the Spanish crown, argued that under no circumstance were the Spaniards allowed to wage war against the Indians, and certainly not in the name of the cross. The gospel of Christ required respect for the integral dignity of all human beings. The only way to the true faith was by persuasion and appeal to reason.

The position argued by de las Casas summarized the position that had been articulated by the Spanish crown at least since the proclamation of the Laws of Burgos in 1512, as well as the rulings of Pope Paul III in *Sublimis Deus* in 1537, which affirmed the humanity of the Indians, and the duty to impart to them the faith. It is against this background of papal bulls, encyclicals, and royal edicts that the relatively malignant effects of the Inquisition in the New World must be gauged. For the New World heathen were viewed on a different theological register from the Old World Jews and Moors. They were not contenders, defectors, detractors, or apostates of the "true faith." The violence, intolerance, and devastation of their conquest were at least nominally constrained by the religious and theological imperative to carry out the task of evangelizing in accordance with Christian principles and values. All of this, however, was never a mere theological or missionary issue. The violence and injustice of the conquest, and the attempt to constrain it and humanize it, as oxymoronic as that attempt may sound, affected the development of international law as well as the idea of human rights, the idea of the general will, and the right to rebel against unjust monarchs. It is not hyperbole to suggest that the New World debates about just war, about how to conduct the colonization of the New World, and about how to deal with the religious beliefs of newly encountered cultures were as important to Europe and Western identity as were the European religious wars of the sixteenth and seventeenth centuries. Religion freedom is not only freedom of confession, of conscience, that is, freedom to believe in the Christian message in accordance with one's calling and conviction; it is also freedom to believe differently, to believe in an entirely different faith and confession. That is what Fray Bartolomé de las Casas expressed in his debate with Juan Ginés de Sepúlveda and all who believed that their faith granted them the power and authority to subjugate others to their will and religion.

Democracy and Political Justice

The conflict between naked power and legitimate authority has always assumed religious dimensions in Central and South America. The wars of independence in the early part of the nineteenth century therefore were marked by an ambiguous stance toward the Church, which had become emblematic of the power of the Crown and thus of the power to be overthrown. For this reason, liberals were highly anticlerical, although not antireligious. In fact, many of the arguments on behalf of independence appealed to the theological doctrine of natural rights, the jurisprudence developed by the Salamanca school, and the political philosophy of the *comuneros* (citizens who opposed arbitrary government infringement of their rights) of New Granada, who believed that taxation without representation was despotic. These same ideas and institutions led to the abolition of slavery in most former Spanish colonies around 1830. As the historian Robin Blackburn wrote, " British and French Abolitionists were to be encouraged by reports from independent Spanish America. Unlike the United States, the South American Republics had put slavery on the road to extinction throughout their national territory" (Blackburn 1988, 375). This, again, relates to the fact that evangelization in Central and South America was mostly carried out by mendicant orders, and later by the Jesuits, whose spirit of tolerance, respect, compassion, and beneficence guided the way the religious beliefs of other cultures were approached. It is for this reason that in contrast to the United States, where the colonists tried to exterminate indigenous populations, in Central and South America, the practice of religion has been marked by syncretism (the combination of several beliefs). Just as the Spaniards and the Portuguese mixed with the indigenous peoples, giving birth to a mestizo population, Christians mixed with non-Christians.

Syncretism and the Third Millennium

In Latin America, religious freedom has also been freedom to mix one's religion. Just as denominations proliferated in North America, in South America different forms of religions emerged from the mixing of Christianity, indigenous, and African religions. As Protestantism fragmented and subdivided, Catholicism itself divided into different forms in accordance to whether it was practiced in the metropolises of the former viceroyalties, with their half-century of history, or in the towns of the republics formed in the nineteenth century with the influx of European immigrants from western and central Europe.

In the last decade of the twentieth century and at the dawn of the twenty-first, indigenous peoples in what is today called Latin America have been undergoing demographic growth. In tandem, their religions, or what remains of them in mutated and mixed forms, have been undergoing a renaissance. What is significant is that the conflicts that Christians faced in the fifteenth and sixteenth centuries when they confronted the New World peoples are conflicts that continue to face Christianity in the new millennium. In the second half of the twentieth century, Catholicism was said to have undergone a second reformation. The Christian base communities, small groups established by committed priests and other religious leaders that combined scriptural study with social activism, became the launching pad for this reformation. In Central and South America, liberation theology became the theological and philosophical expression of the beliefs of these humble and popular religious communities. The Christian base communities of the poor, mestizo, and Indians peoples throughout Latin America confronted the genocidal violence of regional dictatorships in the 1960s, 1970s, and 1980s. The Catholic Church underwent major and irreversible transformations in Latin America due to the Second Vatican Council (1962–1965), the second general conference of the Latin American Bishops in Medellín, Colombia (1968), and three pivotal papal encyclicals: *Mater et Magistra* (Mother and Teacher, 1961), *Pacem in Terris* (Peace on Earth, 1963), and particularly *Popularum Progressio* (On the Development of Peoples, 1967). For two decades it looked as though the Vatican had aligned itself on the side of the popular church, on the side of the oppressed, the beleaguered, the persecuted, the mestizo and indigenous. In the eighties, however, as the Cold War heated up throughout the continent due to the insurgent struggles in Nicaragua, Guatemala, El Salvador, Ecuador and Peru, the United States' politics of containment took a violent turn in Latin America. The wars of containment turned into religious wars, wars against the missionaries, and once again, into wars against the indigenous populations (as was clearly the case in Guatemala, El Salvador, and southern Mexico, in the state of Chiapas). Perhaps the most famous act of violence against the activist Church was the killing of six Jesuits at the Central American University José Simeón Cañas in El Salvador on 16 November 1989.

The history of the Americas is the history of a utopian dream. Integral to this dream of America as the land of justice, has been the idea of religious freedom. This dream tempered the actions of the missionaries as they sought the conversion of indigenous peoples in the jungles of South America and the deserts of what is now the southwestern United States. It guided the dreams of civil-rights activists in the twentieth century, and it now guides the indigenous movements of the twenty-first century and the ecumenical struggles for political, cultural, and ecological justice.

Eduardo Mendieta

Further Reading

Alberro, S. (1988). *Inquisición y Sociedad en México, 1571–1700*. Mexico City, Mexico: Fondo de Cultura Económica.

Arciniegas, G. (1975). *Latin America: A cultural history*. New York: Alfred A. Knopf.

Ardao, A. (1993). *América Latina y la latinidad*. Mexico City, Mexico: Universidad Nacional Autónoma de México.

Bakewell, P. (1997). *A history of Latin America: Empires and sequels, 1450–1930*. Malden, MA: Blackwell Publishers.

Blackburn, R. (1988). *The overthrow of colonial slavery*. London: Verso.

Cleary, E. L., & Stewart-Gambino, H. (Eds.). (1997). *Power, politics and Pentecostals in Latin America*. Boulder, CO: Westview Press.

Crow, J. A. (1971). *The epic of Latin America* (Rev. ed.). Garden City, NY: Doubleday.

Dussel, E. (1981). *A history of the Church in Latin America: Colonialism to liberation*. Grand Rapids, MI: William B. Eerdmans Publishing Company.

Dussel, E. (Ed.). (1992). *The Church in Latin America: 1492–1992*. Maryknoll, NY: Orbis Books.

Ellacuria, I., & Sobrino, J. (Eds.). (1993). *Mysterium liberationis: Fundamental concepts of liberation theology*. Maryknoll, NY: Orbis Books.

Elliott, J. H. (1989). *Spain and its world 1500–1700*. New Haven and London: Yale University Press.

Fernández Herrero, B. (1992). *La Utopía de América. Teoría, Leyes, Experimentos*. Barcelona, Spain: Anthropos.

Hanke, L. (1949). *The Spanish struggle for justice in the conquest of America*. Philadelphia: University of Pennsylvania Press.

Hanke, L. (1974). *All mankind is one: A study of the disputation between Bartolomé de las Casas and Juan Ginés de Sepúlveda in 1550 on the Intellectual and Religious Capacity of the American Indians*. DeKalb: Northern Illinois University Press.

Irarrázaval, D. (2000). *Inculturation: New dawn of the church in Latin America.* Maryknoll, NY: Orbis Books.

León-Portilla, M. (1990). *Endangered cultures.* Dallas, TX: Southern Methodist University Press.

Lewin, B. (1962). *La inquisición en Hispanoamérica: Judios, Protestantes, y Patriotas.* Buenos Aires, Argentina: Editorial Proyección.

Luño, A. E. P. (1992). *La polémica sobre el Nuevo Mundo: Los clásicos españoles de la Filosofía del Derecho.* Madrid, Spain: Trotta.

Mignolo, W. (1995). *The darker side of the Renaissance: Literacy, territoriality and colonization.* Ann Arbor: The University of Michigan Press.

Noll, M. A. (2002). *The old religion in a new world: The history of North American Christianity.* Grand Rapids, MI: William B. Eerdmans Publishing Company.

Pagden, A. (1993). *European encounters with the New World.* New Haven, CT, and London: Yale University Press.

Pagden, A. (1995). *Lords of all the world: Ideologies of empire in Spain, Britain and France, c. 1500–1800.* New Haven, CT, and London: Yale University Press.

Ricard, R. (1966). *The spiritual conquest of Mexico: An essay on the apostolate and the evangelizing methods of the mendicant orders in New Spain, 1523–1572.* Berkeley and Los Angeles: University of California Press.

Richard, P. (1987). *Death of Christendoms, birth of the Church: Historical analysis and theological interpretation of the church in Latin America.* Maryknoll, NY: Orbis Books.

Sahagún, B. (1981). *El Mexico Antiguo.* Caracas, Venezuela: Biblioteca Ayacucho.

Sanderlin, G. (Ed.). (1992). *Witness: Writings of Bartolomé de las Casas.* Maryknoll, NY: Orbis Books.

Subirats, E. (1994). *El Continente Vacio.* Mexico City, Mexico: Siglo XXI Editores.

Todorov, T. (1984). *The conquest of America: The question of the other.* New York: HarperCollins.

Urbano, F. C. (1992). *El pensamiento de Francisco de Vitoria. Filosofía politica e Indio Americano.* Barcelona: Anthropos.

Ureña, P. E. (1978). *La Utopia de America.* Caracas, Venezuela: Biblioteca Ayacucho.

Williamson, E. (1992). *The Penguin history of Latin America.* London: Penguin Books.

South, U.S.: Colonial to Early Republic

Despite its apparent geographic precision, "the South" is not an easily defined region. Most contemporary definitions take as a point of departure the eleven states of the Confederacy, but for the colonial period these later boundaries have no relevance. Louisiana was alternately governed by France and Spain until the Purchase of 1803; Florida was part of the Spanish Empire until 1821; and Kentucky, Tennessee, Alabama, and Mississippi were largely frontier territories until the early nineteenth century. Maryland, a border state during the Civil War, was an integral part of colonial Chesapeake culture. For the purposes of this article, "the South" refers only to the British colonies of Virginia, Maryland, the Carolinas, and Georgia.

The Anglican Establishment

One of the distinguishing features of the colonial South was the religion of the region. At one time or another, the Church of England was by law established in each of these five colonies. The first permanent British colony in North America was that of Virginia, founded in 1607 with the settlement of Jamestown. Although there was a religious motive at work in the establishment of the colony, it was based on the challenge that a Protestant colony would pose for Spanish claims on the land, rather than in the intention of founding a religious enterprise in the sense of the later Puritan colonies of Plymouth and Massachusetts Bay. The initial charter to the Virginia Company (1606) slighted religious concerns other than to justify colonization as a basis for the propagation of Christianity; but a second charter issued three years later restricted settlement to Protestants by prescribing the anti-Catholic Oath of Supremacy. Not until the arrival of Governor Thomas Dale in 1611, however, was there specific legislation regarding religious life. Dale's Laws, as this code came to be known, imposed a severe religious discipline for every aspect of colonial life and enforced a rigorous sabbatarianism with required attendance at all religious services. These laws were repealed in 1619, but the assembly that met that year maintained many of the religious provisions. The actual establishment of the Church of England in the colony developed through such piecemeal legislation, which was designed to address specific problems rather than to define a Holy Commonwealth.

In 1663, King Charles II (1600–1685) issued a royal charter to eight Lords Proprietors for the colony of Carolina. Although the charter assumed an establishment of the Church of England, it urged that conformity not be forced so long as public order was maintained. In their own subsequent Declaration and Proposals, the Proprietors promised colonists "freedom and liberty of conscience in all religious or spiritual things" (Thorpe 1909, 5:2755); in 1669, they proposed the Fundamental Constitutions for Carolina, which was authored in part by John Locke (1632–1704), the great theorist of religious liberty. Although this document excluded atheists from the colony and established the Church of England (against Locke's objections), it otherwise permitted freedom of worship to "Jews, heathens, and other dissenters from the purity of the Christian religion" (Thorpe 1909, 5:2783–84). The Constitutions, however, were never fully enacted and were ultimately rescinded in 1693. By that time, Carolina was effectively being administered as two separate colonies, both of which sought to strengthen the Anglican Establishment through further legislation. In North Carolina, the 1701 Vestry Act created for the first time an Anglican infrastructure of parishes, vestries, and a tax-supported ministry; a similar act was passed in South Carolina in 1706. During the remainder of the colonial period, South Carolina created a moderately successful establishment, but the heterogeneous religious population of North Carolina kept the establishment there very weak, even after the colony was placed under the control of the crown in 1729.

A completely different situation developed in Maryland. An English Catholic, George Calvert (c. 1580–1632), obtained in 1632 a royal grant for colony north of the Potomac River. There is little doubt that Calvert intended that his colony would provide a sanctuary for English Catholics persecuted under English penal laws, although Catholics never formed more than a small minority of the settlers in the colony. They did, however, represent the core of its economic elite and were granted religious toleration by the Assembly as early as 1639. Outraged Puritans from Virginia succeeded in overthrowing the proprietary government and introducing penal legislation, but the Calvert family regained control in 1648 and pushed the Assembly to pass the *Act Concerning Religion* the following year, which granted religious toleration to all Trinitarian Christians. Continued friction between Catholic and Protestant elements, however, kept the political situation in turmoil and led eventually to the revocation of the charter and the erection of Maryland as a royal colony with an established Anglican Church in the early eighteenth century.

The last of the original thirteen colonies was founded in 1732, when King George II (1683–1760) granted a charter to twenty-one trustees who proposed to found a colony for debtors between Carolina and Florida. The trustees, led by James Oglethorpe (1696–1785), had been inspired by the vision of the Reverend Thomas Bray (1656–1730), founder of the Society for the Propagation of the Gospel in Foreign Parts, to evangelize Native Americans and African slaves. The colony remained for the most part a philanthropic project for pious Anglicans such as Charles (1707–1788) and John Wesley (1703–1791), the founders of Methodism, and the evangelist George Whitefield (1714–1770). The trustees appointed Anglican chaplains to minister to the colonists, but the charter granted "liberty of conscience . . . in the worship of God" and the "free exercise" of religion to all except Catholics (Thorpe 1909, 2:773). The lure of religious freedom led Jews as well as various Protestant groups to settle there. The trustees surrendered their charter in 1752 and Georgia became a royal colony, with the Church of England officially established four years later. Thus, on the eve of the American Revolution, Anglicanism had been established in each of the southern colonies, but the strength of this establishment differed widely.

Dissent

The very existence of an established church meant that all competing religions were subject to legal restrictions and even persecution at the hands of the government. Nevertheless, diversity and dissent appeared early during the colonial period and eventually, in the form of Protestant evangelicalism, became the predominant religion in the region.

Conformity to the Church of England was not necessarily easy to define. The Thirty-Nine Articles and the *Book of Common Prayer*, the two distinguishing features of the Church of England, left room for some latitude in belief and practice. The imposition of Test Oaths clearly set boundaries that most Catholics would not transgress, but their intent was to define religious authority rather than belief. When the English colonial enterprise began in earnest at Jamestown, the religion of the Virginia colonists ranged from devout Puritanism to crypto-Catholicism, from pious Christianity to avowed skepticism. As the British government itself reconsidered and recast its limits of tolerance during the turbulence of the Stuart monarchy, the Civil Wars, the Restoration, and the Glorious Revolution, so too did the colonial governments where dissent was more widespread and the machinery of ecclesiastical control much weaker.

The first organized challenge to the Establishment came in the middle of the seventeenth century when itinerants from the Society of Friends (Quakers) arrived on the eastern shore of the Chesapeake. They soon won numerous converts and spread quickly to the western coast of the Bay and southward into Carolina where they were numerically sufficient enough to entice George Fox (1624–1691), the founder of the movement, to tour the area in 1672. The legislatures of Virginia and Maryland attempted to prevent Quakers from serving in public office by imposing Test Oaths (which, out of principle, the Quakers refused to take), but the persistence of Quaker objections to such restrictive legislation often led to its modification or repeal.

During the latter half of the seventeenth century, Quaker émigrés from Pennsylvania made their way into Virginia and Carolina through the Shenandoah Valley, which also served as an important conduit for German Protestants (Lutheran and Reformed) and Scotch-Irish Presbyterians. These immigrants often served as catalysts for local dissenters to challenge the Anglican Establishment in favor of greater toleration and religious liberty.

In 1738, the Anglican priest and associate of the Wesley brothers, George Whitefield (1714–1770), arrived in Savannah and began an evangelistic tour of the British colonies. Whitefield's dramatic style and preaching eloquence soon drew together many dissenting groups and individuals into networks of activity. In Hanover County, Virginia, disaffected laity from the Established Church gathered to read from Whitefield's published sermons and other works of evangelical piety. When their leaders were summoned before the governor and asked to explain their behavior, they admitted that they were not members of any legally tolerated sect, but suggested that they might be Lutherans since they had read from Martin Luther's works. A visiting minister brought them into conformity with New Light Presbyterianism, and the dissenters petitioned the Presbytery of New Castle to supply their ministerial needs. In 1748, the Presbytery appointed Samuel Davies (1723–1761). Davies brought immediate stability to the movement by obtaining a license under the provisions of the English Act of Toleration of 1689, and he continued to use the Act to win further liberties for Protestant dissent.

The dissent in Hanover was the first significant episode in what has been labeled the "Great Awakening" in the South. As in other parts of British North America in the mid-eighteenth century, Whitefield's travels helped to create a new, militant form of Protestantism (evangelicalism) that eroded the popular support of the established churches from the Anglican South to Puritan New England. In the 1750s, Separate Baptists from New England, led by former Congregationalist Shubal Stearns (1706–1771), settled in North Carolina and southern Virginia. Unlike the Presbyterians, the Separates refused to conform to the toleration laws and their acerbic attacks on the morals and manners of the established ministry (as well as other dissenters) led to significant persecution at the hands of the authorities. The Baptists soon became the most vocal proponents of disestablishment and full religious liberty, based on their theological conviction that all stood spiritually equal before God and should be allowed to worship according to the dictates of conscience. As the initial enthusiasm of the Baptists began to wane in the 1760s, the first Methodist itinerant, Robert Strawbridge (?–1781), appeared in Maryland and introduced a new form of evangelicalism to the region. The Methodist phase of the revival lasted well into the 1770s and further increased opposition to the Establishment in the years just prior to the Revolution.

Evangelicalism provided a means of religious and social challenge for other groups as well. In 1619, a Dutch man-of-war had sold its cargo of African slaves to the Virginia colonists, and the labor-intensive agriculture of the southern colonies soon made slavery a feature of southern life. The colonists generally disregarded the traditional religions of the Africans, and although both ecclesiastical and civil legislation encouraged slave owners to teach their slaves the rudiments of Christianity, not until laws were passed disallowing manumission on the basis of baptism did any real effort begin to convert the Africans. The Society for the Propagation of the Gospel emerged as the most successful Anglican missionary society to the slaves, but still conversions were few. The spirited worship and theological egalitarianism of early evangelicalism, however, had great appeal, and ministers such as Davies reported significant numbers of conversions in the mid- to late-eighteenth century. Still, as white evangelicals themselves gained political power, African-American religious practices continued to be subject to legal constraints as means of social control.

Rational Religion

Another challenge to the Establishment came in the form of the rational religious thought that was a part of the American Enlightenment. Following theorists such as John Locke, the rationalists argued against the government support of any religion and in favor of religious liberty. Although the rationalists were often deist in their religious beliefs (typically rejecting Christian doctrines such as the Trinity and the deity of Christ) they made common cause with the evangelicals against what James Madison (1751–1836) termed "That diabolical hell-conceived principle of persecution" (Hunt 1900, 1:21). As political leaders, the rationalists were in a position to effect change, and their most significant contribution came with the Bill for Establishing Religious Freedom in Virginia, which was drafted by Thomas Jefferson (1743–1826) in 1779 and guided to passage in the legislature by Madison in 1786. The Virginia bill, which disestablished the Anglican Church and guaranteed that no person would be molested by the government for their beliefs or lack thereof, was the most radical religious settlement of the new southern states. The constitutions of North Carolina and South Carolina still limited public office to professing Protestants; Georgia dropped a similar restriction only in 1789. Maryland opened public office to all Christians, but considered supporting churches in the state with tax revenues. By the early years of the nineteenth century, however, most restrictions and attempts at quasi-establishment had been repealed, and the Virginia model extended throughout the region.

Rodger Payne

See also Sabbatarians; Virginia Statute of Religious Freedom

Further Reading

Brinsfield, J. W. (1983). *Religion and politics in colonial South Carolina.* Easley, SC: Southern Historical Press.

Buckley, T. E. (1977). *Church and state in revolutionary Virginia, 1776–1787.* Charlottesville: University of Virginia Press.

Gewehr, W. M. (1930). *The great awakening in Virginia, 1740–1790.* Durham, NC: Duke University Press.

Hanley, T. O. (1959). *Their rights and liberties: The beginnings of religious and political freedom in Maryland.* Westminster, MD: Newman Press.

Heyrman, C. R. (1997). *Southern Cross: the Beginnings of the Bible Belt.* New York: Knopf.

Hill, S. S. (Ed.). (1983). *Religion in the southern states: A historical survey.* Macon, GA: Mercer University Press.

Hunt, G. (Ed.). (1900–10). *The writings of James Madison.* 9 vols. New York: G. P. Putnam's Sons.

Isaac, R. (1982). *The transformation of Virginia, 1740–1790.* Chapel Hill: University of North Carolina Press.

May, H. F. (1976). *The enlightenment in America.* New York: Oxford University Press.

Monroe, H. (1962). Religious toleration and politics in early North Carolina. *North Carolina Historical Review, 29,* 267–283.

Pilcher, G. W. (1971). *Samuel Davies: Apostle of dissent in colonial Virginia.* Knoxville: University of Tennessee Press.

Schmidt, L. E. (1986). Church-state issues in the colonial South. In J. F. Wilson (Ed.), *Church and state in America: A bibliographic guide. The colonial and early national periods* (pp. 75–114). New York: Greenwood Press.

Thorpe, F. N. (Ed.). (1909). *The federal and state constitutions, colonial charters, and other organic laws of the states, territories, and colonies now or heretofore forming the United States of America.* 7 vols. Washington, DC: Government Printing Office.

Woodmason, C. (1953). *The Carolina backcountry on the eve of the Revolution; the journal and other writings of Charles Woodmason, Anglican itinerant.* Chapel Hill: University of North Carolina Press.

Woolverton, J. F. (1984). *Colonial Anglicanism in North America.* Detroit, MI: Wayne State University Press.

Spanish Colonies in North America

On 2 April 1513, Juan Ponce de Léon (1460–1521) landed on the southern end of North America's East Coast. Ponce de Léon named the new land *Pascua de Florida* (Feast of Flowers)—*La Florida.* He left a small settlement that did not last. On a subsequent voyage in 1521, the explorer sustained a fatal wound in a skirmish with Calusas Indians and was again unable to institute a permanent settlement. While there would be more unsuccessful settlement attempts in North America in the sixteenth century,

SPANISH CONTROL WEAKENS

Spanish colonization of the indigenous peoples of North America went through several phases. In Mexico, the period from about 1720 to 1850 saw a weakening of control and greater autonomy for indigenous peoples. The following is a letter sent by Bishop Polanco to the Royal Court of Justice of Guatemala in 1781 warning them of the deterioration of Spanish control.

It is wondrous that in the town of Chamula, contiguous to Ciudad Real. Indians have need of interpreter to defend themselves or to beg for what they desire. So that the are as they were twenty years after their conquest, in such a state of blindness and ignorance they find themselves In the town of San Andres, next to Chamula, there are many saints, old and indecent, whom I thought of burying: I did not do it because those evil souls say that they make them see clearly and alleviate their needs. I suspected a riot without having assistance.

Oh my Lord their audacity and shamelessness are such that they even come to command in the church, without respect for the priest. They hold to the idea that the third person of the Holy Trinity is the Sun, because, they say it was thus taught to them by the old fathers.

The mistakes, lack of attention and pretensions of the Indians in regard to the Christian doctrine, who they say they know, and the ones instructed best in them, say as many heretic words as Christian, is consequence or necessary sequel of the lack of care in the secular and ecclesiastical government.

Source: Alfonso Villa Rojas "The Tzeltal," in *Handbook of Middle American Indians*, vol. 7. (Austin, TX: University of Texas Press, 1969), 198.

these initial explorations set a foundation for Spain's later widespread colonization of North America's South, Southeast, Southwest, Midwest, and Pacific Coast.

Cabeza de Vaca

In 1528, Pánfilo de Narváez (c. 1478–1528) journeyed to Florida's present day Tampa Bay area. Upon reaching his destination, Narváez ventured by land to the northwestern region of Florida in search of affluent cities. Not only did Narváez and his crew not find gold, they also lost contact with the ship. In September of 1528, realizing that they would not last long in the wilderness, Narváez and the remaining 242 men attempted to sail across the gulf to New Spain. The trip was a disaster, and three of the five shoddy horsehide barges sank. On 6 November 1528, fifteen survivors landed off the Texas shore (present-day Galveston Island, Texas).

Alvar Núñez Cabeza de Vaca (c. 1490–1557), a treasurer, was one of the fifteen survivors. In the six years that followed Cabeza de Vaca and three of his fellow surviving shipmates ventured throughout the Southwest. Cabeza de Vaca gained a reputation as a healer and was thus revered by the natives he met. In 1536, he made his way to San Miguel de Culiacan in New Spain (present-day Sinoloa, Mexico). In 1542, Cabeza de Vaca's narrative account, *Los Naufragios* (The Shipwrecks), became widely known and tremendously popular throughout New Spain. Cabeza de Vaca's impact on Spain's future colonization of the southwest cannot be underestimated. Pragmatically, he brought back linguistic and cultural knowledge that would facilitate future dealings with Indians. But his story, while compelling for its own sake, gave credence to the rumors of Cíbola—a mythical set of seven golden cities that was purportedly north of New Spain. Cabeza de Vaca's contact with the Indians also excited the con-

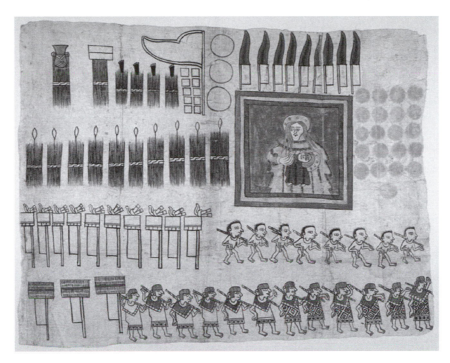

The Huexotzinco Codex, and eight sheet pictorial document used as testimony when Cortes' administrators forced Nahua natives to pay excessive taxes in 1529–1530 Mexico. The Nahua were successful in the litigation. COURTESY LIBRARY OF CONGRESS.

version-minded missionaries who were looking for new challenges.

The Search for Golden Cities and the Strait of Anián

Encouraged by Cabeza de Vaca's description of Cíbola, Francisco Vásquez de Coronado (1500–1553) led an expedition to the Southwest on 25 February 1540. Coronado reached Cíbola in July only to find an austere Zuni village with no golden structures. Undaunted, Coronado continued to search the southwest for gold. In 1541, Coronado's soldiers met an Indian who told elaborate tales of Quivira, a wealthy city to the north. The Spaniards called the Indian El Turco (The Turk). Coronado took a segment of his troops northward with El Turco as their guide. Over time, they ventured through present-day Texas, Oklahoma, Nebraska, and Kansas, but failed to find the promised riches. In April of 1542, Coronado left New Mexico and returned to New Spain.

From 1527 to 1539 Hernán Cortéz (1485–1547) sponsored numerous expeditions to California's Pacific Coast. He hoped to find the mythical Strait of Anián, a waterway that connected the Atlantic and Pacific oceans that would offer an expedient passage to the Orient. In 1542, Juan Rodriguez Cabrillo (c. 1498–1543) journeyed to the San Diego bay and Santa Barbara channel. Cabrillo met his death on January 1543 and Bartolomé Ferrer assumed command. Ferrer sailed north, perhaps as far as Oregon. Unable to locate the strait, he returned to New Spain on 14 April 1543.

Missions in North America

Mandates from the Spanish mainland would profoundly shape how Spanish life was brought to North America. Specifically, the Comprehensive Orders for New Discoveries of 1573 dictated that Indians could no longer be militarily forced into conversion. It was missionaries, not conquistadors, that would become the agents for exploration and pacification in North America. Unlike the brutal campaigns of Mexico (1519–1522) and Peru (1531–1533), Spain would enter North America under the auspice of the cross.

In North America, missions were established in every Spanish territory. Missions spread throughout present-day Florida, Georgia, South Carolina, Alabama, Texas, Arizona, Louisiana, and California. These missions were primarily established by the Franciscans, although the Jesuits had limited influence in Florida (1566–1572) and Arizona (1700–1767).

Missions, ideally, were temporary institutions. Once the local Indians were duly converted, missions would become secularized or absorbed by a parish. Getting Indians to come to the missions was a challenge in itself. Some natives came freely. In other cases, missionaries were known to offer novelty items such as beads or colored cloth to Indians as a brand of religious bribery. Doing their part, the soldiers would sometimes forcibly take natives from nearby villages.

There was little religious freedom extended to the mission Indians. The friars considered Indian culture and religion to be evil and proceeded to Hispanicize the Indians. While natives learned the Catechism, they also learned Spanish agriculture, language, dress, and technology. Indians who did convert were required to stay on the mission. Troops posted at the missions would often retrieve those who ran away.

Florida Missions

North America's missions had their beginnings in Florida. In 1562, French Huguenots led by Jean Ribault (1520–1565) established a small settlement on the mouth of the Saint John's River. This settlement was a mainstay for the French pirates who were raiding Spain's gold-heavy eastward-bound ships. Reacting to this, King Philip II (1527–1598) sent Pedro Menéndez de Avilés (1519–1574) and three hundred troops to remove the French. In late 1565, Menéndez established the settlement of Saint Augustine (North America's first permanent settlement) and decimated the French Protestants.

In 1566, Spanish Jesuits came to Florida with the intention of instituting missions. Fledgling missions were housed in some of Menendez's strongholds such as Saint Augustine, San Felipe (Parris Island, South Carolina), and Santa Elena (Tybee Island, Georgia). Indian hostility forced the Jesuits to abandon their missions in 1572. In 1573, Franciscans resumed missionary work in Florida. By 1615, Franciscans had established approximately twenty missions. By 1655, seventy Franciscans worked thirty-eight missions that served mostly Timucuans, but also Calusas, Tocobagas, and Apalachicolas. The missions spread north to the Georgia and South Carolina coasts and west into Alabama. In 1655, Franciscans claimed to be serving 26,000 *cristianos* or Indian converts.

Mission activity in Florida began to decline in the eighteenth century. By 1746, most of Florida's missions had diocesan clergy. Spain ceded Florida to England in 1763, thus abandoning the missions. In 1783 Spain

regained Florida, but the mission era had long since past. Spain ceded Florida to the United States in 1821.

New Mexico Missions

In the spring of 1598, Juan de Oñate (c. 1550–1624) left Mexico with eighty-three wagons and two hundred men for New Mexico's Rio Grande Valley. Upon finding a suitable destination, Oñate established San Juan de los Caballeros (thirty miles north of Santa Fe) as his base in New Mexico. Tensions with the local Indians quickly became an issue. Soon after Oñate arrived, Indians from the Acoma pueblo killed eleven of Oñate's men. Oñate reacted by slaughtering, maiming, and enslaving the Indians. Similar abuses occurred as Oñate roamed the Midwest looking for the legendary riches in Quivira. Oñate was recalled to Mexico in 1606 and charged with cruelty, immorality, and mismanagement.

Although Franciscan missionaries had to face a resentful Indian population, by 1626 they nevertheless had built twenty-seven missions in New Mexico. That same year, they claimed to have converted approximately 34,000 Indians. By 1630, fifty friars in twenty-five missions served an estimated 60,000 Zuni, Acoma, and Hopi Indians. By the late 1700s, however, many natives were displeased with the Spanish presence. In 1675, Governor Juan Francisco Treviño ordered public floggings for forty-three Indian religious leaders. Additionally, Indians were being forced to work while epidemics and raids from Apaches and Navajos depopulated their villages. On 10 August 1680, the Pueblo communities led by an Indian named Po'pay launched a statewide revolt. As a result, Spain vacated New Mexico for twelve years. In the mid-1690s, Diego de Vargas led a campaign that reclaimed New Mexico. After Vargas' campaign, the missions returned to nearly full capacity. As the eighteenth century progressed, however, diocesan clergy took control of the missions. Mission activity came to a definite end when Mexico ceded the territory to the United States in 1848.

Texas Missions

In 1685, Frenchman René Robert Cavelier de La Salle (1643–1687) established a colony near the Matagorda Bay in Texas named Fort Saint Louis. Illness and Indian attacks compelled the French to abandon the colony in 1687. Word of La Salle's presence reached New Spain. In 1689, Governor Alonzo de León led an expedition to remove the French, and León reached the vacant French settlement later that year. Even though his expedition was a lark, León's journey through Texas provided useful reconnaissance that helped to establish future Spanish settlements.

From 1690 to 1719, Spain founded six missions and one fort in East Texas. These institutions evangelized to the natives and also guarded against any potential French advances from Louisiana. In 1718, mission San Antonio de Valero (in present-day San Antonio) was established as a midway stop for missionaries, troops, and colonists coming from New Spain. East Texas missions began to relocate when disease and Indian hostility became too great. In 1720, Father Antonio Margil de Jesus (1657–1726) moved the east Texas mission of San José to San Antonio. In 1731, three more east Texas missions (San Juan, Concepcion, and Espada) relocated to San Antonio.

By 1731, San Antonio was the center of missionary activity in Texas. These missions made some financial headway; baptisms, however, were not as prodigious as in Florida and New Mexico and the San Antonio missions rarely had more than three hundred Indians in residence. Franciscans established thirty-seven missions in present-day Texas and one, Mission San Miguel de Linares de los Adaes (1717–1763), near present-day Robeline, Louisiana. In 1791, the missions were secularized. The republic of Texas (established 16 March 1836) was ceded to the United States in 1845.

California Missions

California missions spread northward from the Baja Peninsula. In 1769, José de Gálvez (1720–1787) led an expedition from New Spain to San Diego and Monterey. He intended to establish missions and presidios along the coast. Franciscan Junípero Serra (1713–1784) was a resident friar on this journey. Assigned to a land party, Serra ambled northward to present-day San Diego. Here, he established California's first mission on 16 July 1769. Serra eventually established nine more missions along the California coast that stretched as far north as Sonoma. As president-father of the California missions, he maintained headquarters at mission San Carlos Borromeo in Carmel until his death on 28 August 1784.

In 1769, there were an estimated 300,000 Indians within the borders of present-day California. Conversion opportunities were plentiful. The early missions, however, had a difficult time getting Indians to convert. In his initial years at San Diego, Serra did not baptize any natives. By 1784, there were 4,650 Indians in Serra's nine missions. Steadily these numbers rose, and by 1821 California had twenty missions with approximately 21,000 Indian inhabitants.

To protect the missions, four presidios were tactically located along the coast. In the mid-1770s, New Spain began offering land grants and tax exemptions to lure settlers willing to supply soldiers at the presidios with living necessities. Three settlements were established for these colonists: Santa José (San Jose, 1777) Nuestra Señora la Reina de Los Angeles del Rio de Porciuncula (Los Angeles, 1781), and Villa de Branciforte (Santa Cruz, 1797). By the early nineteenth century these colonists began to covet the fertile lands occupied by the missions. With Mexican independence declared in 1821, a call came for the secularization of missions. In 1834, Governor Jose Figueroa officially proclaimed the missions secularized. California was ceded to the United States on 4 July 1848.

Arthur J. Remillard

Further Reading

Gutiérrez, R. A. (1991). *When Jesus came, the corn mothers went away: Marriage, sexuality, and power in New Mexico, 1500–1846.* Stanford, CA: Stanford University Press.

Haring, C. H. (1947). *The Spanish empire in America.* New York: Oxford University Press.

McGrath, J. T. (2000). *The French in early Florida: In the eye of the hurricane.* Gainesville: University of Florida Press.

Rabasa, J. (2000). *Writing violence on the northern frontier: The historiography of sixteenth-century New Mexico and Florida and the legacy of conquest.* Durham, NC: Duke University Press.

Steele, I. K. (1994). *Warpaths: Invasions of North America.* New York: Oxford University Press.

Weber, D. J. (1992). *The Spanish frontier in North America.* New Haven, CT: Yale University Press.

Wellman, P. I. (1954). *God, glory and gold: A narrative history.* Garden City, NY: Doubleday & Company, Inc.

Spanish Empire

In the sixteenth century, the Spanish empire maintained an almost ubiquitous presence in both the

ROMAN CATHOLICISM AMONG NATIVE SOUTH AMERICAS

One effect of Spanish colonization in the Americas was the conversion of many native peoples to Roman Catholicism. However, the conversion process produced new, unique forms of religion combining elements from Catholicism with elements from the indigenous religions. The extract that follows describes a religion of this type practiced by the Aymara people of the Andes region of South America.

In keeping with other contemporary Indian cultures from Mexico to Bolivia, the religion of the Aymara is neither wholly native nor entirely orthodox Catholic, but rather an intricate blending of these two traditions. . . .

During this early period the Indians were nominally converted to Catholicism and, in the course of four centuries, elements of Catholic doctrine and practice became grafted onto the substructure of native belief. The contemporary Indians, of course, do not dissect their religion into its Aymara and Spanish components; to them it is a unified, if somewhat inconsistent, whole. For this reason, therefore, it is as important to describe their beliefs about God as their conceptualization of the mountain spirits. While it would be inaccurate to say that all supernaturals are equally important, it is valid to state that there is no feeling that some are "true" and therefore all-powerful while others are "pagan" and therefore false; rather, each supernatural tends to have his proper place in the scheme and must be considered within the proper context of situation.

It is likewise unprofitable to attempt to draw inflexible distinctions between "religion," "magic," "divination," "sorcery," and "curing," since all of these arbitrary categories are merely aspects of one central problem: the ways in which the Aymara conceptualize and deal with supernatural beings. . . . It follows, as is discussed in more detail in a later section (pp. 219–225), that it is equally futile to attempt to formulate rigid distinctions between the several specialized manipulators of the supernatural. Just as the roles of the supernaturals themselves overlap, so the abilities to cure disease, to divine the future, and to employ magical techniques are shared by several classes of practitioners.

Harry Tschopik, Jr.

Source: *The Aymara of Chucuito, Peru.* (New York: Anthropological Papers of the American Museum of Natural History, vol. 44, 1951), 188.

European continent and New World. The marriage in 1467 of King Ferdinand (1452–1516) and Queen Isabella (1451–1504) united the two Iberian kingdoms of Aragón (one million inhabitants) and Castile (five to six million inhabitants). While these kingdoms shared common policies, they remained as separate domains until the Bourbon reforms of the seventeenth century. Nevertheless, by the dawn of the sixteenth century, Spain was becoming the dominant European empire due in large part to a prosperous campaign of westward expansion.

Religious Purity in Spain

The reign of Ferdinand and Isabella was, in part, a quest for religious purity. Jews residing in Spain were targets, and from 1391 to 1415, many Spanish Jews reacted to Christian hostility by converting en masse to Catholicism. It was believed, however, that the *Conversos* (Jewish Converts) were surreptitiously practicing and possibly propagating Judaism. In 1478, Isabella revived the draconian Inquisition as a device for authenticating the *Conversos'* commit-

A SELECTION FROM THE *REQUERIMIENTO*

The excerpt below details the punishments to be inflicted on Indians who refuse to convert.

[If] you do not [convert], and maliciously make delay in it, I certify to you that, with the help of God, we shall powerfully enter into your country, and shall make war against you in all ways and manners that we can, and shall subject you to the yoke and obedience of the Church and of their highnesses; we shall take you, and your wives, and your children, and shall make slaves of them, and as such shall sell and dispose of them as their highnesses may command; and we shall take away your goods, and shall do you all the mischief and damage that we can, as to vassals who do not obey, and refuse to receive their lord, and resist and contradict him; and we protest that the deaths and losses which shall accrue from this are your fault, and not that of their highnesses, or ours, nor of these cavaliers who come with us.

W. Washburn, ed.,

Source: *The Spanish Requirement. The Indian and The White Man.* (New York: New York University Press, 1964), 308.

---

ment to Christianity. Later, the Inquisition was instituted in the West Indies (1517), New Spain (1570), and New Mexico (1626) to confirm Indian conversions in the same manner.

War was also used to protect Spain's Catholic faith. On 2 January 1492, Spain definitively defeated, and thereafter expelled, the Moors living in the southern province of Granada. Known as the *Reconquista* (Reconquest), this military campaign had been waging in some form since 711. The victory ignited a nationalistic zealousness within Spain that demanded religious purity, or *limpieza de sangre* (cleansing of blood). Following the *Reconquista*, both Muslims and Jews were faced with two options—conversion or expulsion.

Overseas Exploration

By the late fifteenth century Spain looked to expand its overseas financial empire. Spain's only notable colony prior to 1492, however, was the Canary Islands. Pope Alexander VI (papacy, 1492–1503) granted Portugal control of Africa and India. Thus, the proposal by Christopher Columbus (1451–1506) to find a western trade route to the Orient was a welcome proposition to Isabella. On 12 October 1492, Columbus reached an island in the Caribbean. He named this discovery San Salvador. Columbus falsely believed that he had reached the Orient;

instead, he had initiated what was to become sustained European contact with the New World.

The issue of land was of central importance from the outset. On 4 May 1493, Pope Alexander VI issued the *Inter Caetera Divinae,* which gave Spain dominion over all newly discovered lands. The Treaty of Tordesillas (7 June 1494) would slightly revise Pope Alexander's longitudinal demarcation by granting Portugal lands in Brazil, Africa, and India. Spain retained the remainder of the Americas. Early Spanish settlements began on the islands of Hispaniola (1494), Puerto Rico (1508), and Cuba (1511).

Governance in the New World was an unprecedented challenge, as the New World was 3,000 miles from the Iberian peninsula. By 1504, governmental, judicial, and religious authorities were established in Santo Domingo. Such structures would spread throughout the West Indies and the Americas. Additionally, a special domestic council was created by King Charles V (1500–1558) on 1 August 1524, the *Real y Supremo Consejo de las Indian* (the Council of the Indies), which replaced the Council of Castile as the continental center of overseas affairs.

Requerimiento

Spain's new territory, as granted by Pope Alexander VI, came with the condition that the Indians be converted to Catholicism. In demanding conversion,

467

Nineteenth century painting of Bartolome de Las Casas. COURTESY HUMANITIES-INTERACTIVE.ORG.

Pope Alexander invoked a precedent set late in the Crusades (1096–1291) by Pope Innocent IV (papacy, 1243–1254). Innocent had maintained that, by virtue of his divine authority, he was responsible for the souls of all peoples, not just Europeans. Thus, conversion was his divine obligation that could be militantly thrust upon any reluctant population. Written by Juan Lopez de Palacios Rubios of the Council of Castile in 1510 and issued by Ferdinand in 1513, the *Requerimiento* (the Requirement) first informed Indians of their holy duty to convert and then listed the gruesome consequences that Indians would face if they did not, including torture enslavement, and impoverishment. After hearing the *Requerimiento*, however, few Indians converted. It is possible that the document presenting the *Requerimiento* was not clearly translated; however, even with a clear translation, it is unlikely that the natives could have comprehended the nature of the document. In most cases

the *Requerimiento* was offered in a rather perfunctory manner. Conquistadores, hungry for glory and gold, were probably not concerned with the religious well-being of the Indians.

Indeed, the spirit of the *Reconquista* had moved to the New World, and the Indians' land and labor were the new objectives. From 1519 to 1522, the Aztecs, an Indian nation in Mexico, were obliterated by the conquistador Hernán Cortéz (1485–1547). From 1531 to 1533, Francisco Pizarro (c. 1476–1541) decimated the Incas in Peru. In both cases, disease was the Spaniards' greatest weapon. Some historians estimate that smallpox reduced the Aztec population by 90 percent and the Incan by 50 percent.

Surviving Indians were often forced into slave labor on *encomiendas,* sizable tracks of land granted by Royal authority to worthy Spanish colonists. Indians occupying *encomiendas* were considered part of the property. The exploitation of the Indian population became an issue of contention in the early- and mid-sixteenth century. The Dominican priest, Bartolomé de Las Casas (c. 1490–1558), had once owned an *encomienda* in Cuba. Upon seeing the horrific treatment of Indians, however, he renounced his land in 1514. In *Tears of Indians*, de Las Casas described the cruelties endured by Indians living on *encomiendas* in Hispaniola, Cuba, and Jamaica. He was dismayed that such cruelty could be performed under the auspice of Christianity. De Las Casas maintained that, by virtue of the Christian faith, a conversion should be persuaded through gentleness and kindness, not brute force.

De Las Casas' sentiments received notice in Rome. *Sublimis Deus*, issued by Pope Paul III (papacy, 1534–1549) in 1537, declared that Indians did indeed have souls. This, then, meant that enslaving them was not permissible. Also as a result of de Las Casas' influence, the Crown passed the *Nuevas Leyes* (New Laws) in 1542 that effectively banned Indian slave labor. De Las Casas returned to Guatemala in 1545 as the Bishop of Chiapas with the aim of enforcing the New Laws. His efforts, however, were met with noticeable resistance from a Spanish population unwilling to acquiesce.

Expansion into North America and the Pacific

The expansion of the Spanish Empire first came to North American in 1513 when Juan Ponce de Léon (1460–1521) claimed *La Florida* for the Crown. Neither this settlement nor the approximately six attempts that followed were successful. By the mid-sixteenth century, Spain was prepared to abandon any further settlement attempts in *La Florida*. From the years 1556 to 1560, however, Spain's gold shipments from the New World was reduced by half, mostly because of French pirates in the Atlantic. In 1562, a French Huguenot settlement near the mouth of the Saint Johns River supported these pirates. Thus, in 1565, Pedro Menéndez de Avilés (1519–1574) was sent by the Crown to eradicate this French presence. Before taking military action, Menéndez established Saint Augustine (8 September 1565), which would become North America's first permanent settlement. Later that year, Menéndez destroyed the French settlement and secured the Atlantic Coast for Spain.

Despite the efforts of de Las Casas and others, the treatment of North American Indians remained oppressive. Indians were forced to provide the manual labor needed to build missions. They were also forced to farm the missions' fields. Moreover, Spanish missionaries considered Indian religion and culture to be inherently evil. For Indians to be Christian, then, they had to be expunged of their Indian heritage. Some embittered Indians revolted. In 1597, the Guale Indians of Santa Catalina in Georgia burned the mission to the ground and murdered five Franciscans.

Revolts notwithstanding, by the end of the sixteenth century, mission efforts along the Atlantic coast took the Spanish presence through present-day Florida, South Carolina, and Georgia. The Spanish Empire also extended far into the Pacific. In 1565, Miguel de Legazpi (c. 1510–1572) claimed both Guam and the Philippines for Spain.

The Decline of an Empire

Spain was at the forefront of the Counter Reformation. For the already overextended Spanish Empire, however, battling Protestantism produced great financial strain. King Philip II (1527–1598), although preferring diplomacy over warfare, wanted a Catholic Europe even if it meant conflict. In 1567, following a Protestant revolt in the Netherlands, Philip sent permanent troops to quell any further uprisings. In response, Dutch Protestants receiving aid in 1585 from England's Queen Elizabeth I (1533–1603), tried to expel the Spanish. The campaign in the Netherlands was financially burdensome for Spain.

England became Spain's chief adversary in the late-sixteenth century. Reacting in large part to Elizabeth's support of the Dutch, Philip invaded England in 1588. The execution of Mary Queen of Scots (1542–1587) on 8 February 1587 may have further provoked the invasion. Mary was a potential Catholic heir to the English throne, and as such, she could have brought England back to Catholicism. Mary, however, also had familial ties to the French. Some historians maintain that, due to Philip's profound distrust of the French, Mary's execution was inconsequential in the decision to invade England. The invasion did not go well for Spain. In September of 1588, inadequate leadership, brutal weather, and an underestimated English Navy all led to the Spanish Armada's defeat. Spain was unable to recover. The Treaty of London (1604) marked the end of the Anglo-Spanish War. The English victory signified both the decline of Spanish prominence and the rise of English eminence.

The battle to preserve Catholicism led to crippling financial strain for Spain. Neither domestic industry, nor the annexation of Portugal in 1580, nor overseas gold shipments could support the vast Spanish Empire. Philip also inherited war debts from Charles V. Consequently, in both 1557 and 1575 Philip was forced to declare bankruptcy. Spain's financial woes continued as pirates raided bullion shipments coming from the New World. Taxation offered a temporary solution, but the burden compelled many to emigrate. Also, from 1599–1600 an epidemic took approximately 500,000 Castilian lives leaving even fewer people to tax. Attempts to regain prominence in the mid-sixteenth century were countered by internal strife and the inept leadership of Philip IV (1605–1665). Indeed, the Spanish empire grew beyond its means and this very vastness led to its decline.

Arthur J. Remillard

See also Convivencia; Spanish Colonies in North America

Further Reading

Bakewell, P. (1997). *A History of Latin America: Empires and Sequels 1450–1930*. Oxford and Malden, MA: Blackwell Publishers.

Blacker, I. R. (Ed.). (1963). *Prescott's histories: The rise and decline of the Spanish empire*. New York: The Viking Press.

Bodmer, B. (1992). *Armature of conquest: Spanish accounts of the Discovery of America, 1492–1589*. (L.Longstreth, Trans.). Stanford, CA: Stanford University Press.

Hanke, L. (1951). *Bartolomé de Las Casas: An interpretation of his life and writings*. The Hague, Netherlands: Martinus Nijhoff.

Haring, C. H. (1947). *The Spanish empire in America*. New York: Oxford University Press.

Pierson, P. (1999). *The history of Spain*. Westport, CT: Greenwood Press.

Schwaller, J. F. (2000). *The Church in Colonial Latin America*. Wilmington, DE: Scholarly Resources.

Washburn, Whilcomb E. (Ed.) (1964). The Indian and the white man. New York: New York University Press.

Spiritual Healing

Spiritual healing, or faith healing, refers broadly to efforts aimed at curing or ameliorating physical or psychological ailments through religious belief, prayer, or ritual. So defined, the practice of spiritual healing need not, and normally does not, pose an issue of religious freedom. In many instances, a patient's understanding of spiritual healing is limited to prayer or devotional activities that complement rather than supplant conventional medical treatment. Consequently, there is rarely a conflict between the practice of spiritual healing and the delivery of conventional health care. Moreover, the medical community largely understands that one's spiritual health may affect, and be affected by, one's physical and mental health, and modern research has generally confirmed the therapeutic efficacy of prayer and faith.

Spiritual healing can become a matter of religious freedom, however, when its exercise conflicts with interests that the government, through the legal system, either embodies or protects. In particular, when the government advances or recognizes these interests in a way that makes spiritual healing more difficult or costly, its practitioners or patients may perceive that the government is effectively, even if unintentionally, restricting their religious practice. Of course, insofar as all conduct is subject to limitation at some point, the ultimate question is whether, under the First Amendment to the U.S. Constitution or a comparable guarantee, the practice of spiritual healing has been *impermissibly* abridged by the government.

To answer that question, it is helpful to examine specific aspects of spiritual healing and the law. There are, for example, substantial differences among religious traditions concerning the nature, methods, and significance of spiritual healing, and these differences may affect how a particular legal claim is assessed. Likewise, there are many and often divergent legal interests at stake in spiritual healing controversies. Religious freedom is only one of several interests at play, and courts must find the constitutionally acceptable balance among them. Lastly, courts and litigants must ascertain and apply the correct legal framework, which in the spiritual healing context consists presumptively, though not exclusively, of the doctrines and principles of the First Amendment.

An Overview

The notion of spiritual healing can be traced to the dawn of humanity. The very idea of healing, in fact, appears to be a universal facet of the human religious impulse, and many contemporary religions, and hence many religious adherents, continue to believe in the value of spiritual healing. At the same time, it

SPIRITUAL HEALING

Spiritual healing is a significant function of religion around the world. These extracts of ethnographic text about African-Brazilians in Bahia, Brazil, make clear both the importance of spiritual healing and the various forms it may take.

The mau olhado, or "evil eye," a magical power presumed in many parts of the world, including Europe, to be possessed, often unwittingly, by certain individuals, is thought at Bahia to bring death to plants, birds, and even small children whom the person has coveted or, perhaps, merely admired. More natural forces are the ar do vento, or "air of the wind," a cold draught said to result in indigestion, deformity, insanity, or death; the espinhela caida, or "fallen breastbone," which presumably brings on an emaciated condition of the body; and sangue nova, or "new blood," thought to be responsible for the breaking-out of a rash. Dew must not be allowed to fall on the head. Certain diseases, like syphilis and leprosy, are considered defects common to all men. However, the persistent efforts of agencies like the Rockefeller Foundation have widely disseminated the idea that malaria results from the bite of a mosquito. . . .

The treatment or prevention of disease is the logical counterpart of a magical theory of causation. Thus, members of this section of the Bahian population attempt to control personal destiny through the use of charms or other magical means or through the direct intervention of a deity, whose favor is sought by the offering of gifts or the performance of prescribed rituals. Thus, to counteract the influence of the "cvil eye," charms are worn, or pieces of the Guine, Arruda, or Vassourinha Doce plants are passed, to the accompaniment of magical words, over and about the affected person's head. . . .

The wearing of paluas, or written prayers, is presumed to "close the body" (fechar o corpo) against disease or accident. The nut known as chapeu de Napoleao ("Napoleon's hat"), if worn on a string about the neck, similarly is reputed to possess magical power. A cord of deerskin passed over the affected area is presumed to cure erysipelas; a string of white beads worn about the neck of a mother is thought to increase the flow of her milk; a cord tied tightly about the waist of a pregnant woman will, it is believed, "keep the baby from going to the head"; and a stone in the hair is thought to retard delivery. Considered particularly efficacious in all cases of illness is the "ita of Xango" [stone of Xango]. "Prayers," or the use of magical words or phrases over an affected part of the body, are also extensively employed. A common belief is that the pae de santo can in this way cure snakebite . . .

The direct intervention of a deity may be invoked as when presents are made to the maes d'agua (female deities who are presumed to inhabit bodies of water) to remove illness or misfortune or to assure future success. Thus, fishermen, anxious for a good year's catch, or individuals wishing to be rid of some illness, to obtain employment, or to secure a satisfactory resolution of unrequited love, will purchase foods, wearing apparel, toilet articles, jewelry, and other gifts pleasing to a lady and place them with appropriate ceremonies in a body of water presumed to be inhabited by one of the maes d'agua.

Donald Pierson

Source: *Negroes in Brazil: A Study Of Race Contact at Bahia*.
(Carbondale and Edwardsville: Southern Illinois University Press, 1967), 252–255.

Crutches and icons left behind by pilgrims to El Santuario de Chimayo in Chimayo, New Mexico, in 1993. The church draws some 300,000 visitors a year, many who come seeking cures from El Posito, the sand pit in the floor of the sanctuary that continuously fills with sand. COURTESY OF JO ANN CALLEGARI AND DAVID LEVINSON.

is important to recognize that the methods and conceptualization of spiritual healing are as wide-ranging as American religious pluralism. Within several traditions, for example, spiritual healing is undertaken in conjunction with conventional medical treatment. Within others, such as Christian Science and certain Native American religions, it may be undertaken in lieu of conventional treatment, even for serious medical conditions. Religions also differ with regard to who may practice spiritual healing. While most do not restrict laity from engaging in general practices such as prayer, more specific healing practices or rituals may in some traditions be confined either to clerics, for example, a priest or shaman, or to church-authorized practitioners.

The nature of the patient's participation in the spiritual healing process can also vary among and within religious faiths. For example, it may be practiced without the physical presence or even the awareness of the patient, a technique that in certain circles is called remote, absent, or distant healing. Prayers of healing said by congregations or distant acquaintances might also be considered efforts at remote healing, although

they are often viewed as being intercessory, as opposed to unmediated, in nature. Alternatively, spiritual healing practices may involve the patient directly, such as by touching (or the laying on of hands), by praying or reciting scripture or stories with the patient, by the patient's repentance or atonement, by the use of objects such as beads or crystals, by the administration of oils or water, by fasting or dietary restrictions, or, in some Christian traditions, by receipt of communion bread and wine.

Finally, there are important differences among faith traditions concerning how the processes and consequences of spiritual healing are conceptualized. To some, spiritual healing methods are believed to invite divine intervention or to harness supernatural entities or energies, which in turn may effect a cure or amelioration of the patient's ailment. To others, the path of spiritual healing serves largely as an expression of devotion and obedience to divine will, the fruits of which may not be realized in the material, temporal realm. To others still, especially those who reject divine intervention, there may simply be an expectation that the use of prayer will yield psychic benefits to the patient and the participating religious community.

The Clash of Legal Interests

Once engendered, conflicts between spiritual healing and the law can be especially difficult to resolve because of the quantity, gravity, and alignment of the interests and values at stake. Resolution can be further complicated by the multiplicity of sources from which these interests and values emanate, including not only the patient and the government, but also the patient's relatives, the medical community, and potentially liable third parties such as insurers or civil litigants. In addition, many of these entities are not monolithic and their constituents may have different interests and hold different perspectives.

Of these interests, the patient's are perhaps the easiest to delineate. The most obvious is the patient's interest in religious freedom, which may be protected by the First Amendment, by an analogous state constitutional provision, or by federal or state statute. Accompanying and potentially strengthening the patient's interest in religious freedom is most likely an interest in autonomous medical decision making, especially if framed as a right to refuse conventional medical treatment. American courts have widely recognized such a right, and recent U.S. Supreme Court decisions indicate that it may be embraced by the Constitution's due process472 clauses. Alternatively, to the extent that the spiritual healing is chosen by a parent on behalf of a child, an interest in parental or familial decision making, which is already recognized as a due process right, may be implicated as well.

A second body of interests are those of the government representing the public. Traditionally, these have been embodied in the police power, which is the government's authority to enact regulatory or criminal laws to secure the health, safety, welfare, as well as the morals of the community. To the extent that spiritual healing displaces or undermines conventional treatment and causes preventable harm, these public interests become jeopardized. Moreover, where a child's welfare is involved, the government's *parens patriae* authority, which specifically empowers it to protect minors in place of, and sometimes against the wishes of, their parents is implicated as well. In the first instance, this authority can be used to impose a duty on parents to provide medical care to their children, one that may conflict with an exclu-sive regimen of spiritual treatment. If this duty is violated, it may then allow the government to assume temporary custody of a child for the administration of medical care, notwithstanding parental religious beliefs.

A final grouping of interests includes all other private (nongovernmental) rights and liabilities that spiritual healing scenarios may affect. For example, the patient's relatives, especially a spouse, may either support or oppose the patient's use of spiritual healing in place of conventional treatment and by law may be able to interpose that position with some effect. Furthermore, should the patient be harmed by the attendant exclusion of conventional care, the spouse or relative may then be able to recover monetary damages for the cost of the injury. Also affected by spiritual healing may be the interests of the medical community. Doctors and hospitals, for example, might well be caught between a parent's choice of spiritual rather than conventional medical treatment for a child and the prospect of professional discipline and legal liability if conventional care is not provided. Lastly, to the extent that spiritual healing, when undertaken in lieu of conventional treatment, exacerbates a patient's condition, insurers may question their contractual obligation to provide coverage, while persons otherwise responsible for compensating the patient (for example, one who negligently causes the patient's original injury) may question the extent of their liability.

Legal Framework

Many of these interests, though not intrinsically related to religious freedom, can significantly guide a court's effort to define the socially, economically, and morally feasible scope of that freedom. Broadly speaking, the law discernibly interacts with spiritual healing either by restricting it or by protecting it. Ordinarily, the restrictions it imposes are functional, not formal. That is, they do not take the form of outright prohibitions as such, but rather comprise the deterrent or punitive effect resulting from the enforcement of generally applicable legal rules. These include both criminal and regulatory statutes, which are enacted by legislatures, as well as the law of tort and possibly contract, which may be either legislatively codified or judicially fashioned. State criminal and civil laws, for example, may subject parents (and potentially practitioners) to liability for resulting harm to children, including the associated failure to use conventional treatment. Likewise, compensation for injury by a private third party may be reduced by the share of harm caused by using spiritual treatment in place of, or in addition to, conventional care.

Conversely, many states also have separate legal provisions that may actually protect spiritual healing. The religious freedom provisions of some state constitutions, for example, may provide protection to practitioners of spiritual healing, although the degree to which they do is, at present, largely undefined. In addition, many state laws explicitly allow spiritual healing in place of conventional medical treatment, especially by parents for their children, without fear of legal consequence such as a finding of child neglect or abuse. These exemptions are not boundless, however. Often they are limited to cases of nonserious harm. By legal presumption, moreover, their relevance is confined to the specific statute in which they are located and, therefore, they may not shield a parent from liability under some other law. Also, such exceptions, if not carefully crafted, may violate the First Amendment establishment clause, which prohibits the government from making any law respecting the establishment of religion. This may occur if an exception is too denominationally specific, if it explicitly incorporates religious doctrine or terminology, or if it vests governmental authority with a religious entity such as a church or cleric.

Finally, spiritual healing may present an issue under the First Amendment free exercise clause, which bars federal, state, and local governments from prohibiting the free exercise of religion. This clause, like most domestic religious freedom guarantees, operates by judicial balancing. Courts weigh the respective interests of the religious claimant (whether the church, the spiritual healer, or the patient) against those of the government or private third parties, which is why the earlier recitation of these interests is so critical to the analysis and resolution of spiritual healing claims.

The Free Exercise Clause

To state a free exercise claim, one must normally demonstrate that the government, by law or official action, has substantially burdened the practice of one's religion. In the spiritual healing context, a substantial burden can arise from the enforcement of one or more of the legal interests noted earlier. To hold parents criminally or civilly liable for harm to their children resulting from spiritual treatment, particularly to the exclusion of conventional care, is effectively to punish, and thus substantially burden, the practice of their religion. (The same could hold true for the spiritual healer or sanctioning religious organization.) Likewise, to reduce the amount of compensation that an injured person can recover, if the injury is aggravated or prolonged by a religious treatment decision, is effectively to impose a monetary penalty, and thus a substantial burden, on that person's religious practice.

Demonstrating a substantial burden is, however, only the first stage of the analysis. Once such a burden has been shown, the court must decide how rigorously the law being challenged should be scrutinized. There are two possibilities. If the claimant can also demonstrate that the law is not neutral or generally applicable (that is, if the law is not truly evenhanded with regard to religion) or that the law burdens certain constitutional liberties in addition to religious freedom, then the court may apply what is called strict scrutiny and will invalidate the law unless the government can demonstrate that its action is the only means to achieve a compelling interest. If, by comparison, the claimant cannot make this additional showing, then the court will apply what is called rational basis scrutiny and will uphold the law unless the claimant can further demonstrate that the government's action does not rationally advance a legitimate interest. This last demonstration is quite difficult to make, and thus most claimants attempt in earnest to persuade the court that strict scrutiny should be applied.

Employing this framework, courts have ruled that parents may not subject their unemancipated children to spiritual treatment, particularly when conventional care is excluded, if doing so would pose a demonstrable danger to life or health. Because the government has a compelling interest in children's welfare, and where it appears that the only means to achieve that interest is by forced medical care, there is ultimately no free exercise violation. As the Supreme Court has stated, "[p]arents may be free to become martyrs themselves. But it does not follow that they are free, in identical circumstances, to make martyrs of their children . . ." (Prince 1944, 170). Thus, parental decisions to that effect may be judicially overridden, and, absent a statutory exemption, parents and possibly practitioners may be held civilly and criminally responsible for the harm that results. Only where the conventional care is itself comparably dangerous and risky does it appear that courts might be willing to defer to parental decision making, essentially because the use of conventional care is no longer demonstrably necessary to preserve the child's health.

By contrast, competent adults may choose for themselves to forego conventional medical treatment and pursue spiritual healing, even if it exacerbates their condition or hastens their death. The government can likely require that the spiritual healing does not independently cause serious harm, and where additional harm does result the courts have generally held that it does not violate religious freedom to reduce proportionately the patient's monetary compensation. As one court stated, "[t]he freedom to act upon one's religious convictions does not encompass the privilege of imposing tort liability on another for injuries resulting, not from another's tortious conduct, but rather from the voluntary practice of one's religious convictions" (Corlett 1990, 262).

It is important to note that these holdings are not immutable; they merely represent the judiciary's collective judgment regarding the appropriate balance of interests among religious claimants, the government, the medical community, and various other private parties. With time, as the respective importance and attainability of these interests change, so also may the scope of protection for spiritual healing. Nevertheless, spiritual healing cases, especially those involving children with serious medical conditions, will continue to pose difficult issues for the law.

Scott C. Idleman

See also Free Exercise Clause

Further Reading

Abraham, H. J. (1993). Abraham, Isaac and the state: Faith-healing and legal intervention. *Richmond Law Review, 27*(5), 951–987.

DesAutels, P., Battin, M. P., & May, L. (1999). *Praying for a cure: When medical and religious practices conflict.* Lanham, MD: Rowman & Littlefield.

Fuller, R. C. (1989). *Alternative medicine and American religious life.* New York: Oxford University Press.

Ingram, J. D. (1998). State interference with religiously motivated decisions on medical treatment. *Dickinson Law Review, 93*(1), 41–66.

Koenig, H. G., McCullough, M. E., & Larson, D. B. (2000). *Handbook of religion and health.* New York: Oxford University Press.

Marty, M. E., & Vaux, K. L. (1982). *Health/Medicine and the faith traditions: An inquiry into religion and medicine* (multivolume series). Philadelphia: Fortress Press.

Monopoli, P. A. (1991). Allocating the costs of parental free exercise: Striking a new balance between sincere religious belief and a child's right to medical treatment. *Pepperdine Law Review, 18*(2), 319–352.

Nobel, B. (1993). Religious healing in the courts: The liberties and liabilities of patients, parents, and healers. *University of Puget Sound Law Review, 16*(2), 599–710.

State Churches

For centuries before the rise of the Roman Empire, structures of governance in the early states of Egypt, Mesopotamia, Africa, Central and South America, and other parts of the world exhibited a near seamless integration of religious and political authority. Kings were understood to be the high priests of their societies, receiving divine wisdom directly from the gods for their exercise of both civic and sacral duties. As human culture became more differentiated and religious and political institutions became more distinct, the concept of the state church emerged as a model of religious-political integration among social orders. A state church is a religious institution that is sanctioned as "the" official church for a given political entity by its ruling authority. The seminal act in the development of the state church in Western civilization was an edict of the Roman emperor Theodosius I (347–395 CE) in 380 CE that declared that Christianity should be practiced by all peoples as the official religion of the Roman Empire. Although the dissolution of the Roman Empire in the centuries that followed meant the coequal loss of the Roman Catholic Church's official status, the idea of the state church was revived during the Protestant Reformation and the rise of nation-states in the sixteenth century. Today state churches most commonly are observed in several European countries as remnants of their Reformation heritages.

State churches, also called official, or established, churches, are granted unique privileges and responsibilities by virtue of their special relationships with the governments of the countries in which they exist. In countries with a state church, the government generally provides funding of certain church functions, offers unique political and legal advantages to the state church that are not available to other churches,

SELECTION FROM HENRY VIII'S *ACT OF SUPREMACY* (1534)

Be it enacted by authority of this present Parliament, that the king our sovereign lord, his heirs and successors, kings of this realm, shall be taken, accepted, and reputed the only supreme head in earth of the Church of England, called *Anglicana Ecclesia*, and shall have and enjoy, annexed and united to the imperial crown of this realm, as well the title and style thereof, as all honours, dignities, pre-eminences, jurisdictions, privileges, authorities, immunities, profits, and commodities to the said dignity of supreme head of the same Church belonging and appertaining; and that our said sovereign lord, his heirs and successors, kings of this realm, shall have full power and authority from time to time to visit, repress, redress, reform, order, correct, restrain, and amend all such errors, heresies, abuses, offences, contempts, and enormities, whatsoever they be, which by any manner spiritual authority or jurisdiction ought or may lawfully be reformed, repressed, ordered, redressed, corrected, restrained, or amended, most to the pleasure of Almighty God, the increase of virtue in Christ's religion, and for the conservation of the peace, unity, and tranquillity of this realm; any usage, custom, foreign law, foreign authority, prescription, or any other thing or things to the contrary hereof notwithstanding.

Source: Ecclesiastical Law Society of America. *Act of Supremacy 1534 (26 Henry VIII, c. 1).* Retrieved 24 June 2002, from http://www.canonlaw.anglican.org/act.sup.henry8.htm

and, in many cases, actively partners with the official church in the provision of social services and other activities. State churches are typically structured such that ecclesiastical responsibilities are performed by individuals or groups within the national government, who often hold religious titles in addition to their official governmental positions. Countries with a state church often designate it as the official religion of the state within their respective constitutions.

The Church of England

One of the most commonly referenced examples of a state church is the Church of England, both for its clear delineation as *the* official church within the British social order and for its history, which marked the most distinctive formation of an established state church in Western civilization after the dissolution of the Roman Empire. The well-known split between England and the Roman Catholic Church was occasioned by the desire of King Henry VIII (1491–1547) to divorce Catherine of Aragon (1485–1536) in his passion to secure a male heir to the English throne. Pope Clement VII (1478–1534), himself embroiled in various conflicts with the powerful Holy Roman Emperor Charles V (1500–1558; Catherine's nephew),

was in no position to grant Henry a divorce. Henry therefore undertook certain steps to distance his nation from Rome. In 1529 he called together what has come to be known as the Reformation Parliament, which undertook reforms in both political and religious life that were unprecedented for any previous legislative assembly. The measures that Henry VIII enacted to separate England from papal authority culminated in his issuance of the Act of Supremacy in 1534. That act signaled not only the birth of the Church of England but, more importantly, the usurpation of the Pope's authority through the installment of the English monarch as head of the Church of England.

The fundamental state church structure established by the Act of Supremacy remains in place in England today. Kings and Queens who ascend to the English throne must pledge to protect and maintain the Anglican faith as the established church of England. The authority for appointing Anglican bishops remains with the monarch, who receives recommendations for appointments from the British prime minister. The British monarch, as titular head of the Church of England, is also responsible for selecting the church's spiritual leader, the Archbishop of Canterbury. Other close ties exist between the

British government and the Church of England, including the requirement that the British Parliament approve "legislation" passed by the Anglican Church's General Synod. In addition, twenty-six seats in the House of Lords are reserved for the most senior bishops of the Anglican Church, who represent "the episcopate" in Great Britain's legislative assembly.

Secular Appointment of Religious Officials: Investiture and Its Consequences

The process by which governments became involved in the appointment of bishops and other religious leaders described in the context of the Anglican Church above had been the philosophical basis for a rift within the Roman Catholic Church of medieval Christendom. The practice of investiture, originating during a period of weakness in the Church between the eighth and eleventh centuries, opened the door to greater state involvement in the day-to-day operations of the Church. Investiture was the means by which monarchs, princes, and other secular rulers granted the official titles and material benefits associated with religious offices (principally those of bishops and abbots). Investiture not only had the practical effect of denying the Church's monopolistic power over religious affairs, but its ability to enrich or to impoverish individual religious officials or entire religious orders also meant that the state continued to grow in cultural influence vis-à-vis the Church. Furthermore, the fact that investiture involved the actual granting of religious titles by secular rulers undoubtedly had the effect of the elevating political over religious authority in the minds of people in those countries (most notably Germany) where it occurred.

In the eleventh century, the investiture controversy precipitated one of the greatest schisms in the history of the Roman Catholic Church. Recognition of the abuses spawned by this system and of the need for more general reform of the Church's institutions resulted in a serious rift between Pope Gregory VII (c. 1020–1085) and Holy Roman Emperor Henry IV (1050–1106), and it precipitated a movement to reclaim for the Church the authority of religious appointments. Pope Gregory formally prohibited the practice of lay investiture—so-called because monarchs and princes, regardless of their worldly power, were laymen—in 1075. Yet, conflict over the investiture practice continued beyond Gregory's death in 1085 as power vacillated between church and state, often conditioned by the effectiveness of leadership of various popes and emperors. At the Concordat of Worms (1122), Pope Calixtus II (d. 1124) and Holy Roman Emperor Henry V (1081–1125) reached a settlement in which it was agreed that the power to invest bishops, abbots, and other religious officials with ecclesial authority would reside within the Church, while kings and princes would retain jurisdiction over the granting of secular forms of authority.

The practice of investiture laid the groundwork for the formation of state churches in Europe by breaking down a significant barrier that traditionally had separated religious and political authority: the control of religious appointments. Although the Concordat of Worms restored much religious autonomy to the Church, controversies continued between the two realms of politics and religion in the centuries leading up to the Protestant Reformation. Significantly, in countries where the religious and political forces unleashed by the Reformation ultimately overwhelmed the Catholic Church (as in England and the Scandinavian countries), investiture became institutionalized as a principal component of the partnership between church and state.

The *Explicatio* of Thomas Erastus

The European wars of religion in the sixteenth and seventeenth centuries only deepened the growing entrenchment of religious authority in the secular realm. Both the Peace of Augsburg (1555) and the Peace of Westphalia (1648) reinforced the image of the state as the controlling force in the religious affairs of nations through their implementation of the principle of *cuius regio, eius religio* (commonly translated "whose region, his religion"), which enabled princes to choose the religion for all who resided within their territory. This unmistakable growth in the state's power over religion in sixteenth- and seventeenth-century European society also came to be associated philosophically with the thought of a particular historical figure, the Swiss theologian Thomas Erastus (1524–1583). Erastus wrote his famous *Explicatio* in 1568, though it was not published until three decades later. In this work Erastus presented his argument that civil rather than religious authorities should be principally responsible for punishment even of sins such as heresy, and Erastus insisted that the state rather than the church should have the authority and exercise the power of excommunication. Thus the term *Erastian* has come to define relationships between church and state in which the church is subordinate to the state in virtually all civil matters and often defers to the state even in what traditionally have been viewed as religious affairs.

The Scandinavian State Churches

In the modern period, several countries of Europe in addition to England have state churches. Formally established churches are found in Sweden, Norway, and Denmark (all Lutheran state churches), and in Scotland (Presbyterian Church of Scotland). In the Scandinavian countries the Lutheran state churches enjoy several privileges by virtue of their special relationships with their respective states. For example, the salaries and pensions of Lutheran priests are subsidized by the state in those countries. Also, as in England, the authority for the appointment of bishops resides with the state in the three Scandinavian countries; however, the state churches are permitted to nominate candidates, although their respective governments need not heed those recommendations.

However, the Lutheran Church of Sweden suffered a significant reduction in its status as a state church when the government and the Church severed most of their legal ties on 1 January 2000. And it appears that other European countries may be on the verge of similarly separating church and state due to changes in their religious demographics. The state-established Lutheran Church of Norway, for example, has formed a committee to assess its status as a state church and to make a recommendation as to whether or not such a designation is appropriate to its mission. The state churches of Europe simply no longer represent the vast majority of the populations in their respective countries as they once did, and recognition of the changing religious demographics of European society is precipitating a significant reassessment of the role and relevance of state churches in those countries.

Germany: Multiple Official Churches

Germany offers an example of a modern country with multiple "official" churches but no single state religion. The German constitution specifies that there is no state church and further that religious communities have the right to organize and practice their beliefs within the boundaries of law. However, the process by which religious groups attain the legal status of "religion in public law" grants certain privileges to what are effectively the official religions of Germany. The German government has established certain requirements for membership, organizational structure, and other perceived measures of stability and longevity that enable a particular church to become a religion in public law. The Roman Catholic, Lutheran, and Evangelical Reformed churches enjoy "automatic" public law status. Beyond these three officially sanctioned state religions, the national constitution is constructed such that individual German states have considerable flexibility in assigning public-law status. Thus, the number and exact composition of official churches within the various German states vary significantly.

Greece and Eastern Orthodoxy

Greece, a nation where the Greek Orthodox Church traditionally has received considerable advantages as the country's official religion, has altered its constitution and expanded individual religious rights, although certain restrictions still apply to minority churches that limit religious freedom. Even after revisions to the Greek constitution in 1975 and 1986, the Greek Orthodox Church is still considered by many to be the state church of Greece, retaining, for example, authority over the granting of construction permits to minority religions for church building. However, the revised Greek constitution did remove the restriction that the president of Greece must be an Orthodox Christian, and it classifies the Greek Orthodox Church only as the prevailing national religion rather than the state church. Thus it has served to reduce the identification of Orthodox Christianity with the Greek government. The existing constitution also recognizes the rights of minority religious groups to practice their religions, but it continues to prohibit proselytism by those groups. Moreover, the Greek government continues to pay the salaries of the Orthodox clergy and Orthodoxy still enjoys certain privileges that most often are associated with state religions.

Similarly, the Serbian Orthodox and Russian Orthodox churches enjoy many of the privileges of state religions in their respective countries without holding that specific designation. While the United States State Department has accepted the contention of the Serbian government that there is "no state religion" in Serbia, the reality is that Serbian Orthodoxy carries great weight within the government and often uses its leverage to pressure religious minority groups. The recent transition in Serbian political power has not diminished this relationship; in fact, in certain ways, the strength of association between the Orthodox Church and the state has increased. Protestant Christian minority groups especially have been critical of the preferential treatment that the Serbian Orthodox Church has received in the government's new religious education program in the public schools and in the assignment of chaplains at military bases and other government institutions.

Human rights groups have accused the Russian Orthodox Church and the Russian government of similar forms of collusion in repressing the rights of religious minorities in that country. Russian Orthodoxy is granted a preferred position and receives special privileges from the government in exchange for its support of state policies and actual involvement in carrying out many of those policies. Minority groups such as the Jehovah's Witnesses, Unification Church, Church of Scientology, and several Pentecostal groups have insisted that officials from the Russian Orthodox Church aid or even inspire the government to take measures that repress their activities and even harass their members. Thus, while most Eastern European countries where some form of Orthodoxy is predominant do not profess an actual state church, it is obvious that Orthodox Christianity does enjoy a preferential position vis-à-vis other religious groups and often uses that status to secure its dominant position among those nations' religions.

Non-Christian State Churches

Outside the West the identification of state church structures in social orders is more difficult, especially among the nations of the Islamic world. Some Islamic states are fully integrated religious-political systems founded on strict interpretations of Islamic law and thus qualify as church states rather than as nations with state churches. However, Malaysia is an example of an Islamic nation whose church-state relationship approaches that of the state church structures of modern Europe. The Malaysian constitution designates Islam as the religion of the Malaysian Federation yet concurrently grants toleration to other religions. Although there are legal restrictions on proselytizing by non-Muslim religious groups, the constitution avoids any reference to the establishment of an Islamic state or the application of the *shari'a* (Islamic law) to all citizens.

The Outlook for State Churches

The prominence of the state church as a unique institution for the promotion of religious and political integration in the structure of nations appears to be waning. The rise of religious pluralism in modern, liberal states undoubtedly has contributed to its lessening prominence and influence. Yet some countries, such as England, continue to point to the state church as a symbol of national pride and a cornerstone of national tradition. The confluence of various social forces, including the restructuring of nation-states and changes in the religious demographics of modern countries, will determine whether the state church remains a viable institution in the religious and political structure of nations in the future.

Charles McDaniel

Further Reading

Boyle, K. and Sheen, J. (1997). *Freedom of religion and belief: A world report*. London: Routledge.

Centre for Citizenship. (1998–1999). *Church and state in Britain: The church of privilege.* Retrieved October 8, 2002, from http://www.centreforcitizenship.org/church1.html

Church of England to remain state church. (1994). *Christian Century, 111*(22), 717–718.

Halsall, P. (Ed.). (1996). *Internet medieval sourcebook.* Retrieved October 8, 2002, from http://www.fordham.edu/halsall/sbook.html

McGrath, A. E. (1993). *Reformation thought: An introduction* (2d ed.). Cambridge, UK: Blackwell Publishers.

Monsma, S. V., & Soper, J. C. (1997). *The challenge of pluralism: Church and state in five democracies*. New York: Rowman & Littlefield Publishers.

Robbins, T., & Robertson, R. (1987). *Church-state relations: Tensions and transitions*. New Brunswick, NJ: Transaction Books.

United States Department of State (1999). *Annual Report on International Religious Freedom for 1999: Serbia-Montenegro*. Washington, DC: Bureau for Democracy, Human Rights, and Labor. Retrieved November 14, 2002, from: http://www.state.gov/wwww/global/human_rights/irf/irf_rpt/1999/irf_serbiamo99.html

Wood, J. E., Thompson, E. B., & Miller, R. T. (1958). *Church and state: In scripture, history and constitutional law*. Waco, TX: Baylor University Press.

T

Taoism *See* Daoism

Tibet

Since the invasion and annexation of Tibet by the People's Republic of China (PRC) in the 1950s, the region has been a source of concern for human rights groups. China's human rights record in Tibet has been condemned in numerous resolutions by the United Nations, the United States Congress, and several parliaments in other countries, including Denmark and the Netherlands. The Tibetan government-in-exile, headquartered in Dharamsala, India, regularly issues reports detailing Chinese atrocities, and in the past several decades a number of Tibet support groups have formed around the world to bring attention to the human rights situation in Tibet and to pressure the PRC government to adhere to international norms.

Despite this pressure, the PRC consistently maintains that negative assessments of its treatment of Tibetans are the result of ignorance or anti-Chinese racism. Tibet is regularly described in Chinese government publications as the "Socialist Paradise on the Roof of the World," a region whose people are prospering. The PRC further claims that the vast majority of Tibetans are happy and content under Chinese rule, and that aside from a few malcontents and counterrevolutionaries, Tibetans recognize that they have greater freedom and prosperity than at any time in the past.

Chinese Invasion

When China initially sent troops from the People's Liberation Army (PLA) into Tibet, the ostensible reason was to liberate the region from foreign imperialists. According to official Chinese policy, Tibet had been an integral part of China since at least the thirteenth century, but had drifted away from the motherland due to the sinister machinations of foreigners. China ignored the fact that when the troops arrived there were only five foreigners in the whole Tibetan plateau (and that none had any influence with the Tibetan government).

Initially, PLA troops avoided antagonizing the populace. They were polite and paid for everything they needed, and they promised that they were only in Tibet to help the people. Moreover, they claimed that they would leave as soon as the work of liberation was done and that Tibetans would then be entirely in charge of their own affairs. Tibetan culture would be unharmed, and Tibet's religion would be fully protected. Despite these promises, the Chinese began to make increasingly significant changes in Tibet, and in March 1959 the Tibetan populace rose in revolt, hoping to force China to leave their country. The rebellion was brutally suppressed, and the Dalai Lama—the religious and temporal leader of Tibet—fled into exile in India. He was aided by Tibetan resistance fighters who were waging a guerilla war against the invaders. He was granted asylum by Jawaharlal Nehru, the Indian prime minister, and subsequently established his government-in-exile.

Following the revolt, Chinese officials initiated a program of increasing oppression and destruction of

UNITED NATIONS GENERAL ASSEMBLY—RESOLUTION 2079 (XX)

New York, 1965

The General Assembly

Bearing in mind the principles relating to human rights and fundamental freedoms set forth in the Charter of the United Nations and proclaimed in the Universal Declaration of Human Rights,

Reaffirming its resolutions 1353 (XIV) of 21 October 1959 and 1723 (XVI) of 20 December 1961 on the question of Tibet,

Gravely concerned at the continued violation of the fundamental rights and freedoms of the people of Tibet and the continued suppression of their distinctive cultural and religious life, as evidenced by the exodus of refugees to the neighboring countries,

1) *Deplores* the continued violation of the fundamental rights and freedoms of the people of Tibet;

2) *Reaffirms* that respect for the principles of the Charter of the United Nations and of the Universal Declaration of Human Rights is essential for the evolution of a peaceful world order based on the rule of law;

3) *Declares* its conviction that the violation of human rights and fundamental freedoms in Tibet and the suppression of the distinctive cultural and religious life of its people increase international tension and embitter relations between peoples;

4) *Solemnly* renews its call for the cessation of all practices which deprive the Tibetan people of the human rights and fundamental freedoms which they have always enjoyed;

5) *Appeals* to all States to use their best endeavors to achieve the purposes of the present resolution.

Source: The Government of Tibet in Exile.
Retrieved 12 July 2002,
from http://www.tibet.com/Resolution/un65.html

Tibetan culture and religion, which reached its peak during the Cultural Revolution of the 1960s and 1970s. During this period, Communist cadres attempted to destroy vestiges of China's feudal past in order to facilitate the implementation of Communism. In Tibet the persecution was especially severe: Thousands of monasteries and temples were destroyed, monks and nuns were killed or forced to return to lay life, and religious practice was labeled "feudal superstition." Any overt attachment to religion was viewed by the Chinese as a sign of reactionary tendencies and severely punished.

Reliable figures of the destruction are impossible to obtain because Tibet's human rights situation has become highly politicized. The government-in-exile claims that from the beginning of China's invasion until the end of the Cultural Revolution over 1.2 million people were killed, either directly by Chinese troops or as a result of Chinese-caused famines. The PRC angrily rejects these claims and asserts that only a small number of people perished. While China now admits that mistakes were made during the Cultural Revolution, it claims that this was a difficult time for all of China and that it is offset by Tibet's current situation of prosperity and respect for human rights.

Contrary to China's assessment of the situation in Tibet, groups like Human Rights Watch Asia and Amnesty International regularly issue reports documenting repression of religion and other violations of human rights. At present hundreds of monks and nuns are political prisoners in Tibet. According to human rights groups, over 90 percent of Tibetan prisoners are subjected to physical torture, and many die as a result. A major blow to China's denials of torture was struck when Palden Gyatso, an elderly Tibetan monk who had been incarcerated in Chinese prisons for more than twenty years, managed to escape to India in 1991 and to smuggle a bag of Chinese torture instruments that had been used on him during his confinement. His biography became an international best-seller, and he has spoken before government bodies all over the world, including the United Nations, vividly describing his experiences as a political prisoner in Tibet. Human rights groups assert that his story is typical of thousands of other Tibetan monks and nuns and that, contrary to Chinese claims, the repression continues.

A recent example of China's continuing repression of religious freedom in Tibet is the destruction of Serthar Monastery. The monastery was founded in the 1980s by Khenpo Jikphun, a charismatic religious scholar, who together with a small group of students established a center for study and meditation in a remote, uninhabited Tibetan valley about 700 miles by dirt road from the nearest city. During the past several decades, increasing numbers of people have moved there in order to study Buddhism, and by 2001, there were over ten thousand monks and nuns in residence. While this small group of religious practitioners posed no conceivable threat to the government of China, the authorities were particularly concerned that several hundred ethnic Han Chinese had become monks or nuns at the center, and in July 2001, they sent armed troops to destroy the buildings and force the residents to leave. Khenpo Jikphun was placed in detention, and, despite never having been formally charged, remains a prisoner in the early 2000s.

Implications

Similar examples of Chinese repression of religious freedom in Tibet are regularly detailed in human rights publications and on the websites of Tibet support groups as well as the international media. Perhaps the most graphic illustration of the nature of Chinese rule in Tibet is the ongoing migration of Tibetans into exile. An average of four thousand Tibetans flee every year, and monks and nuns are strongly represented among the exiles. They tell stories of intolerable religious repression and of their inability to practice their religion in the land of its origin. While the situation is certainly better than during the Cultural Revolution, it seems clear that in the early 2000s there is no real religious freedom in Tibet.

John Powers

See also Buddhism; China, Communist

Further Reading

Gyatso, P. (1997). *Fire under the snow: Testimony of a Tibetan prisoner*. London: The Harvill Press.

Patt, D. (1992). *A strange liberation: Tibetan lives in Chinese hands*. Ithaca, NY: Snow Lion.

Powers, J. (2000). The free Tibet movement: A selective narrative. In C. S. Queen (Ed.), *Engaged Buddhism in the West* (pp. 218–244). Boston: Wisdom Publications.

Tibet information network and human rights watch Asia. (1996). *Cutting off the serpent's head: Tightening control in Tibet, 1994–1995*. New York: Human Rights Watch.

Tibetan Centre for Human Rights and Democracy. Retrieved November 14, 2002, from http://www.tchrd.org

Turkey

Turkey, a secular Muslim country, offers a unique example of the compatibility of Islam and democracy. Its location on the Bosphorus, straddling Europe and Asia, is emblematic of the tension throughout Turkey's history between Eastern and Western cultural influences.

Ataturk and the Foundation of the Republic

The Ottoman empire (1453–1922), which ruled the area that is now Turkey prior to the establishment of the Turkish republic, essentially functioned as a theocratic state. During World War I, Mustafa Kemal (1881–1938, from 1934 called Ataturk) led a successful nationalist revolution and established modern Turkey. He instituted a republican government and a series of reforms that secularized and Westernized Turkish society. Six principles—the Six Arrows of Kemalism—guided these reforms: republicanism, nationalism, populism, reformism, etatism, and secularism. The first five refer to the establishment of an elected legislative assembly and president (but only one political party), nationalistic sentiment, Western cultural traits, and state involvement in economic

THE CONSTITUTION OF THE REPUBLIC OF TURKEY ON RELIGION

VI. Freedom of Religion and Conscience

ARTICLE 24. Everyone has the right to freedom of conscience, religious belief and conviction.

Acts of worship, religious services, and ceremonies shall be conducted freely, provided that they do not violate the provisions of Article 14.

No one shall be compelled to worship, or to participate in religious ceremonies and rites, to reveal religious beliefs and convictions, or be blamed or accused because of his religious beliefs and convictions.

Education and instruction in religion and ethics shall be conducted under state supervision and control. Instruction in religious culture and moral education shall be compulsory in the curricula of primary and secondary schools. Other religious education and instruction shall be subject to the individual's own desire, and in the case of minors, to the request of their legal representatives.

No one shall be allowed to exploit or abuse religion or religious feelings, or things held sacred by religion, in any manner whatsoever, for the purpose of personal or political influence, or for even partially basing the fundamental, social, economic, political, and legal order of the state on religious tenets.

Source: Turkish Embassy at Washington, D.C.
Retrieved 8 March 2002,
from: http://www.turkey.org/politics/p_consti.htm

policy. Secularism, perhaps the most important, removed the body politic from religious control by relegating religion to a department of state. Specific reforms, such as deposing the caliph (the ruler of the Ottoman empire; he was also the nominal spiritual head of the Islamic world) and abolishing Islamic law in favor of a civil code, neutralized Islam's political influence. Significantly for the state's political development, Ataturk outlawed the formation of societies based on religion and prohibited political parties from engaging in religious activity or disseminating religious propaganda.

After Ataturk's death, his ideas remained entrenched in the minds of the educated elites and of the armed forces. Because of Ataturk's military prowess, the generals felt a particular loyalty to his theories of government and have acted as the self-appointed guardians of secularism since his death. From 1946 to the present, Turkey has had a multiparty system, and on three occasions the generals have expelled the elected government from office (by force or persuasion) in the name of restoring civil order and ensuring that these secular principles remained intact.

Multiparty Politics and Military Intervention (1950–1983)

From the 1950s to the 1980s, restraints on religion were liberalized. During that period, many believed that an increased presence of religion in the public square and in education would combat Communism, inculcate moral values, and maintain a link with tradition in the midst of Westernization. Unfortunately, easing the restrictions on religion resulted in violent controversies between the secularists and Islamists. The military intervened in 1960–61, in 1971, and in 1980 to restore order before returning power to the democratic process.

In the 12 September 1980 intervention, the military, led by General Kenan Evren, suspended all political parties and trade associations and set up a National Security Council with military commanders replacing the regular government personnel. In 1982 this regime promulgated the constitution that governs Turkey today. It guarantees the right to freedom of belief and worship, subject to limitations in times of war or martial law. It also requires state-designed compulsory educational courses in the elementary and secondary schools and sets up state control over instruction in religion and ethics. Perhaps most importantly for this discussion, the constitution prohibits the exploitation of religion for personal or political influence, or any attempt to base the fundamental order of the state on religious tenets.

The Rise of Islamist Parties (1983–present)

In 1983, the military regime disbanded and allowed democratic elections, leaving Evren in office as president. The Motherland Party, headed by Turgut Ozal (1927–1993), supported the reinterpretation of secularism to allow more religious expression. Ozal demonstrated his own religious commitment by completing the hajj (the pilgrimage to Mecca that Muslims should perform if possible at least once in their lifetime) while in office—the first Turkish prime minister ever to do so. Ozal's government allowed the Islamists a significant amount of influence and respectability, facilitating the emergence of a new group of Islamist intellectuals.

Islamist parties had slowly gained popularity since the 1970s. Necmettin Erbakan (b. 1926) established a series of political parties that attempted to avoid the prohibitions against religious parties through the careful use of semantics. His National Order Party, later reorganized as the National Salvation Party, participated in coalition governments during the 1970s. Erbakan resurrected the group in 1983 as the Welfare Party. His platform advocated industrialization and technological development combined with social justice, closer ties with the East, and the reformation of laws that inhibited religious exercise.

In the 1995 elections, the Welfare Party captured the largest number of seats in the Assembly, due to its efficient party machinery and public dissatisfaction with the policies and corruption of the center-right and center-left parties. Erbakan became the nation's first Islamist prime minister in a coalition government. His very presence in the position, although legitimately obtained through democratic means, posed a challenge to the secular system. Liberal women feared an Islamist government would abridge their rights. Although skeptics questioned Erbakan's loyalty to the secular constitution if he obtained enough power to change it, others believed that because changing the basic structure of the secular system had little popular support, the democratic process itself offered sufficient protection. Erbakan resigned in June 1997 under pressure from the military, and the constitutional court officially banned the party for activities incompatible with secularism and attempting to introduce Islamic law the following year. Prominent politicians criticized the ban, and some Turkish intellectuals feared that shutting down the party would only galvanize support for it.

Members of the Welfare Party had anticipated the ban and had founded a successor Virtue Party in advance of the closing. This party reflected a more moderate view than its predecessor—it integrated more of the secular state into its platform so as to build a broader base of support. As the new moderate face of Islam gained popularity, the government began rigorously enforcing a law against Islamic dress (such items as headscarves for women or long beards for men) in public places. A female Virtue Party deputy was expelled from the Assembly for wearing a headscarf in parliament. Secularists see such actions as the wearing of a headscarf in parliament as "political Islam," not as expressions of religious liberty. The Turkish Constitutional Court shut down the Virtue Party in June 2001 for engaging in antisecular activity.

After Virtue's closure, the Islamist movement split into two even more moderate groups, both of which accepted the secular state. The traditionalist wing formed the Felicity Party. The reformist wing evolved into the Justice and Development Party, which aimed to turn the Islamist movement into a mainstream center-right party. The Justice and Development Party won a landslide victory in the 3 November 2002 elections, capturing 363 of the 550 seats in parliament. Although the popular party leader Recip Tayyip Erdogan was banned from participating in politics for three years for reciting a poem at a rally (a court held incited hatred along religious lines), deputy leader Abdullah Gul will serve as prime minister in the country's first single-party government in fifteen years. While the party has Islamist roots, it has secularized itself to such an extent that its charismatic leadership and voter frustration with other parties may have contributed as much or more to its success than its position on religion. If Turkish politics has finally produced an Islamist party that sufficiently allays the fears of secularists, Turkey may have indeed harmonized Islam and democracy.

Susanna Dokupil

Further Reading

Ahmad, F. (1977). *The Turkish experiment in democracy, 1950–1975.* Boulder, CO: Westview Press.

Ahmad, F. (1993). *The making of modern Turkey.* New York: Routledge.

Berkes, N. (1964). *The development of secularism in Turkey.* Montreal, Canada: McGill University Press.

Geyikdagi, M.Y. (1984). *Political parties in Turkey: The role of Islam.* New York: Praeger.

Heper, M., Oncu, A., & Kramer, H. (Eds.). (1993). *Turkey and the West: Changing political and cultural identities.* New York: I. B. Tauris.

Kinross, L. P. (1964). *Ataturk: A biography of Mustafa Kemal, father of modern Turkey.* New York: William Morrow.

Lewis, B. (1996, March). The Middle East: Westernized despite itself. *Middle East Quarterly, 13,* 53–61.

Mango, A. (1994). *The Washington Papers: Vol. 163. Turkey: The challenge of a new role.* Westport, CT: Praeger.

Pittman, Paul M., III, (Ed.). (1988). *Turkey: A country study* (4th ed.). Washington, DC: Federal Research Division, Library of Congress.

Sayari, S. (1996, September). Turkey's Islamist challenge. *Middle East Quarterly, 3,* 35–43.

U.N. Declaration on Discrimination

The 1981 U.N. Declaration on the Elimination of All Forms of Intolerance and of Discrimination Based on Religion or Belief constitutes the United Nations' preeminent specification and endorsement of the right to freedom of religion or belief. Adopted by consensus after almost twenty years of controversy, compromise, and delay, the 1981 Declaration is a landmark in the development of international human-rights standards.

While a U.N. declaration is not legally binding, strong arguments can be made that all eight articles of the 1981 Declaration have acquired legally binding status. Article 1 tracks the already binding language of the first three paragraphs of Article 18 of the International Covenant on Civil and Political Rights (ICCPR). That is, it specifies the scope of freedom of religion or belief, proscribes coercion in matters of choice of religion, and specifies the narrow circumstances under which manifestations of religion can be limited. The only significant alteration is that explicit mention that freedom of religion includes the right to change religion was dropped out of deference to Muslim sensitivities about conversion from Islam. However, this compromise language is offset by the "saving clause" in Article 8, which makes it clear that nothing in the Declaration should be construed as "restricting or derogating from" earlier, more explicit instruments.

Articles 2 through 4 restate the obligation not to discriminate on the basis of religion, an obligation that is recognized in a variety of other legally binding international instruments. Article 5 specifies the rights of parents to raise their children in accordance with their beliefs. While there are arguably some respects in which Article 5 strikes the balance among the interests of parents, children, and the state more strongly in favor of the parents than does the Convention on the Rights of the Child (CRC), Article 5 is fundamentally a more detailed articulation of the parental rights specified in Article 18 (4) of the ICCPR. Article 7 boils down to an assurance that the ideals of the Declaration will be given operative legal effect in national legal systems.

That leaves only Article 6, which contains a nonexclusive and uncontroversial list of concrete examples of what freedom of religion protects: the right to worship or assemble in connection with belief; to establish and maintain charitable institutions; to make, acquire, and use religious articles; to write and disseminate religious publications; to teach religion in suitable places; to receive voluntary financial contributions; to choose religious leaders; to observe days of rest and religious holidays; and to maintain religious communications among religious individuals and communities.

In short, the 1981 Declaration enunciates principles that are generally regarded as deriving from other widely accepted legally binding instruments or, in the case of Article 6, that constitute clear instances of these principles. Not surprisingly, the argument has been made that even if the Declaration does not rise to the level of a binding treaty, it articulates widely recognized and accepted principles that are (at least for the most part) widely accepted and already part of customary international law.

The United Nations seems no longer to be actively seeking to adopt a convention on the topic of the 1981 Declaration. Among other things, there are considerable fears that the compromises necessary to secure a convention might result in watering down principles already recognized in the Declaration. Beginning in 1986, the United Nations has adopted the more practical expedient of commissioning a Special Rapporteur on Freedom of Religion or Belief (previously, the Special Rapporteur on Religious Intolerance). The special rapporteur monitors governmental action inconsistent with the 1981 Declaration, submits annual reports, and recommends remedial measures.

W. Cole Durham, Jr.

Further Reading

Dickson, B. (1995). The United Nations and Freedom of Religion. *International and Comparative Law Quarterly, 44*, 327–357.

Office of the High Commissioner for Human Rights. (1981). *Declaration on the Elimination of All Forms of Intolerance and of Discrimination Based on Religion or Belief.* Retrieved December 31, 2002, from http://193.194.138.190/html/menu3/b/d_intole.htm

Sullivan, D. J. (1988). Advancing the freedom of religion or belief through the U.N. Declaration on the Elimination of Religious Intolerance and Discrimination. *American Journal of International Law, 82*, 487–520.

Tahzib, B. G. (1996). *Freedom of religion or belief: Ensuring effective international legal protection.* The Hague, Netherlands: Kluwer Law International.

van Boven, T. C. (1991). Advances and obstacles in building understanding and respect between people of diverse religions and beliefs. *Human Rights Quarterly, 13*, 437–449.

van der Vyver, J. D., & Witte, J., Jr. (Eds.). (1996). *Religious human rights in global perspective: Legal perspectives.* The Hague, Boston, and London: Martinus Nijhoff Publishers.

Unification Church

The Unification Church (UC; established 1954) is a new religious movement that became prominent throughout the world during the 1970s. It was founded in South Korea by the Reverend Sun Myung Moon (b. 1920). The church is best known for its mass weddings or "International Marriage Blessings" involving many thousands of participants in high-profile venues such as Seoul Olympic Stadium and Madison Square Garden. The movement sparked controversy due to its messianic claims; aggressive proselytizing; interlocking networks of industrial, media, commercial, and educational enterprises; and alleged ties to the South Korean government. Opponents labeled the church a "cult" and engaged in strenuous efforts to block its activities. This embroiled the church in a succession of religious freedom disputes in the United States and other countries.

The Struggle for Recognition

The most serious and sustained religious freedom issues faced by the church have been those of establishing itself as a bona fide religion and securing basic protections for its members including the right to practice their faith. In Korea, though founded in 1954, the church was not able to obtain legal standing until 1963. In the United States, where the church has been active since 1959, a number of adherents were subject to deportation proceedings until *Unification Church, Nikkuni, et al. v. INS* (1982) vindicated the right of foreign members of the UC to enter the country as missionaries on the same basis as members of other churches. That same year, after a five-year struggle, the New York Court of Appeals, in *HSA-UWC v. Tax Commission of New York City* (1978), held that the UC was a legitimate religious organization entitled to the same tax exemption privileges granted to all religious groups. In a number of European countries and the former Soviet Union, there continues to be resistance against recognizing the UC and other new religious movements as bona fide faiths.

Within the context of broad-based opposition and the lack of recognition by civil authorities, the church at times was unable to secure legal protection for its members. The most egregious offenses were vigilante-style "deprogrammings" that included forceful abductions, confinement, and pressure on adherents to give up their church involvement. Self-styled "deprogrammers" and the UC members' parents who hired them operated under the premise that UC adherents were subject to coercive persuasion or "brainwashing" and, in effect, were programmed zombies who needed to be physically removed from UC control. The first deprogramming of an American church member occurred in 1973. Despite

Reverend Moon with his family, circa 1969. COURTESY WWW.TPARENTS.ORG.

jailing of some of the most notorious deprogrammers and public outcries against it, the practice continued for nearly a decade with some three hundred adherents subjected to deprogramming. In *Ward v. Conner* (1981), the U.S. Supreme Court upheld on appeal a lower court decision allowing a church member to bring suit against thirty-one people, including family members and others hired to break his faith. This decision established a precedent, holding that UC members were entitled to the same civil rights protections the law grants to racial minorities.

Religious deprogramming of UC members virtually ended in the United States in the mid-1980s. However, it greatly proliferated in Japan, where coercive methods of abduction, confinement, and counterindoctrination persisted. The Unification Church of Japan (UCJ) reported to Japanese courts and international human rights organizations that its members were subjected to 150–300 deprogrammings a year during the 1990s. There, unlike in the United States, Christian ministers from the United Church of Christ in Japan (UCCJ) and several evangelical denominations took the lead in deprogramming, establishing interdenominational networks and committees for "rescue and consultation." Although sev-

eral cases were working their way through the Japanese court system, there have been no precedent-setting decisions and the practice continued into the new millennium.

An additional problem faced by the church in the United States was the banning of its fund-raising by numerous municipalities throughout the nation. In some instances, local governments rewrote solicitation and licensing statutes to bar church members. However, few if any of these restrictions held up against legal challenges as the UC won hundreds of solicitation cases. In *Larson v. Valenti* (1982), the U.S. Supreme Court struck down a Minnesota law that resulted in an unacceptable "denominational preference," targeting "for stricter state scrutiny those religious groups which solicited funds in airports, parks or shopping centers, as opposed to those which received most of their funds from Sunday morning collection plates." The "larger lesson" was that "governments may not pass laws that enable them to inflict greater surveillance and regulation on controversial religious groups."

Bans against Rev. Moon's travel and the consequent lack of access to their spiritual leader has been a significant barrier to church members' freedom to

DEPROGRAMMING IN JAPAN

The following account was provided by a Japanese Unification Church member at the Conference on Religious Freedom and the New Millennium in Washington, D.C., in April 1998.

Deprogramming in Japan is going on today. I prefer that a Japanese fellow Unificationist explain the situation. This is Shunsuke Uotani.

Mr. Uotani: I would like to give a brief report about the kidnapping and deprogramming of Japanese Unification Church members. Even now, 200 to 300 members annually are kidnapped, confined, and deprogrammed. It is a very big problem. Though they are basically kidnapped by their parents, behind their parents are Christian ministers and professional deprogrammers and psychologists who are educating the parents on how to kidnap and how to deprogram. This is a book written by a medical doctor who was kidnapped and confined for two years. He finally escaped and returned to the church. The name of the book is *Escape from a Kidnapper.* At this time, I would like to mention just one case of deprogramming, specifically concerning the administrative agency's unfair attitude in dealing with this problem. There are many cases in which Japanese administrative agencies, including police and the Ministry of Justice, deal with the incidents relative to religious organizations and their believers' faith quite unfairly from the viewpoint of religious freedom and fundamental human rights.

From August 22 to November 8, 1997, a 25-year-old female believer was confined by her parents and relatives in an apartment house from which she could not escape, only because of her faith in the Unification Church. She took advantage of an unguarded moment and escaped to the room next door, from which she called the police. The police rushed to the apartment house and heard her explanation of the matter in detail. After bringing her to the police station, they realized she was not a psychiatric patient or incompetent but lived a normal life as a member of society. She explained that she was confined in the apartment house against her will and that there was a terrible infringement on her bodily freedom and religious freedom. She appealed to the police for liberation from her parents and return to the church. However, the police who heard her explanation instead helped her parents move her to another confinement place. They put her in an official police car and drove her to a highway interchange where her parents were waiting for her. At the interchange she was put into her parent's car and driven for two hours to a place in a mountain village where she was confined and pressed for apostasy for more than a week. Although the female believer explained to the police that her religious freedom was being infringed on and asked for liberation, her request was not accepted. When she asked the policeman, "Where are you going to take me?" He said, "I will take you to a church of my acquaintance."

Eventually this believer was able to escape and revealed the fact. She protested against this unfair treatment but the police ignored her will and one-sidedly supported the explanation of those who confined her. Through an attorney she requested an apology from the police station and the policeman on the grounds of abuse of authority and infringement of religious freedom, but there was no apology, no explanation. This was an obviously illegal act by the policeman. This kind of case happens frequently in Japan. Police basically regard this as a parent-child problem and refuse to intervene. So we are not protected legally.

Source: Jesus Gonzalez Lesorda, *Unification Church.*
Paper delivered at the International Coalition for Religious Freedom Conference on Religious Freedom and the New Millennium. Washington, D.C., 17–19 April 1998. Retrieved 17 July 2002, from http://www.religiousfreedom.com

THE UNIFICATION CHURCH IN COURT

Nearly all of the Unification Church's history has been marked by court cases filed by the Church to end discrimination by governments and harassment by private citizens. This press release from the German Federal Administrative Court on 10 July 2001 indicates the legal complexity of these cases and the difficulties they pose for the Church and its leaders and members.

Entry Ban for Mr. and Mrs. Moon

The Federal Administrative Court has decided today that the legal action of the Unification Church of Germany (Vereinigungskirche e.V.), which belongs to the so-called Moon-Movement, against the entry ban for Mr. and Mrs. Moon in effect since 1995, is valid.

Mr. Moon—he and his wife being citizens of the Republic of Korea with legal residence status in the USA—is the founder and leader of the Unification Church with its world wide activities. In November 1995 while on a speaking tour in Europe, he was invited by the Unification Church to deliver a speech on the theme "True Family and I" in Frankfurt/Main. To prevent this, the Frontier Protection Headquarters (Grenzschutzdirektion) in Koblenz listed Mr. and Mrs. Moon in the information system of the Schengen Convention, refusing permission to enter. This was based on the assumption of the Federal Government that the Moon Movement counts among the so-called youth sects and psycho groups which may possibly hold dangers for young people. Based on this listing Mr. and Mrs. Moon were denied entry into the territories of the states belonging to the Schengen Convention upon their arrival at Paris airport by the French authorities. The entry ban was extended for a further 3 years, against which Mr. and Mrs. Moon have not taken legal action.

With its legal action the Unification Church seeks to establish that the listing is unlawful. It considers it a violation of its right of free religious practice according to Art. 4 para. 1 and 2 of the German Constitution. The Administrative Court of Koblenz has dismissed the case on the grounds that this basic law doesn't grant a religious organisation the right of entry of its foreign spiritual leader. On the other hand, the Higher Administrative Court in Koblenz has affirmed the right of action in a preliminary judgement.

The Federal Administrative Court has affirmed the decision of the Higher Administrative Court. It has stated as follows: The action is based on the assessment that the continuation of the entry ban against Mr. and Mrs. Moon is violating proper rights of the Unification Church. With this request the action is permissible. For the admission of an action it is sufficient according to the practice of law, that the asserted infringement of the law seems to be possible. This has to be answered in the affirmative here. According to the assessment of the Higher Administrative Court the Unification Church is to be regarded as a religious association and therefore entitled to the fundamental right of religious freedom. The interest of the Unification Church in the entry of its religious leader can be protected by Article 4 par. 1 and 2 of the Basic Law, especially if the presence of its leader is of significant meaning for the religious practice of its community. Whether this is the case and whether these interests will possibly prevail against the view of the authorities asserting public interests for the entry ban, will have to be considered by the Higher Administrative Court in the context of justifying the action.

Source: International Coalition for Religious Freedom.
Retrieved 17 July 2002, from http://www.religiousfreedom.com

practice their faith in Japan and most Western European countries. The major legal justification for banning Rev. Moon from Japan stemmed from his 1982 felony conviction and thirteen-month imprisonment in the United States on criminal tax evasion charges. Tax convictions have been a time-honored way of rooting out undesirables and Rev. Moon was not without his supporters. More than forty organizations, including nearly all of the country's mainline religious bodies, filed amicus curiae briefs against the conviction. Most of them maintained that in holding funds for the church in his name, Rev. Moon had no tax liability and exercised an accepted and widely practiced trustee role known as "corporation sole."

Prospects

The indictment, prosecution, conviction and imprisonment of Rev. Moon should not overshadow gains the church made, particularly in the United States. Though embroiled in near-constant litigation, the church won gradual recognition as a bona fide religion with tax exemption privileges, public solicitation rights, and access to missionary visas. The UC also has been able to extend constitutional protections to its members and press for action against deprogrammers. While there is still suspicion and negativity expressed toward Rev. Moon, attempts to restrict the movement's activities or treat it in any way differently than other religious groups have been met by broad-based public outcries. During the late 1990s, this was evident in highly publicized opposition to an attempt by the Maryland State Legislature to study the effects of "cults" on college and university campuses. In the United States there have been no restrictions on Rev. or Mrs. Moon's speaking and, in some instances, media outlets have apologized for use of the term "Moonie."

Worldwide, the church still faces significant challenges, notably continuing religious deprogramming in Japan, registration problems in some European and former Soviet nations, and bans placed against Rev. Moon's entry to Japan, England, and most of the Schengen Treaty nations of Europe (most western European nations). These hindrances against church members' freedom to practice their faith are being contested in international courts, thus far to no effect.

Elsewhere, church members have endured riots in Brazil, imprisonment and torture in Iran and other Islamic nations, bombings in France, and arrests of leadership in Thailand. These situations, of course, are not inconsistent with the global experience of numerous religious groups including the world's major faiths.

Dan Fefferman and Michael Mickler

See also Brainwashing

Further Reading

Biermans, J. (1986). *The odyssey of new religious movements, persecution, struggle, legitimation: A case study of the Unification Church.* Lewiston, NY: Edwin Mellen.

Chryssides, G. (1991). *The advent of Sun Myung Moon.* New York: St. Martin's Press.

Galanter, M., Buckley, P., Deutsch A., Rabkin R., & Rabkin J. (1979). The Moonies: A psychological study of conversion and membership in a contemporary religious sect. *American Journal of Psychiatry, 136,* 165–170.

Mickler, M. (2000). *Forty years in America: An intimate history of the Unification movement, 1959–1999.* New York: HSA Publications.

Richardson, H. (Ed.). (1984). *Constitutional issues in the case of Rev. Moon: Amicus briefs submitted to the U.S. Supreme Court.* New York: Edwin Mellen.

Sciarrino, A. (1984). United States v. Sun Myung Moon: Precendent for tax fraud prosecution of local pastors? *Southern Illinois University Law Journal, 2,* 237–281.

Sherwood, C. (1991). *Inquisition: The persecution and prosecution of Reverend Moon.* Washington, DC: Regnery Gateway.

Sontag, F. (1977). *Sun Myung Moon and the Unification Church.* Nashville, TN: Abingdon.

Shupe, A., & Bromley, D. (1979). The Moonies and anti-cultists: Movement and counter-movement in conflict. *Sociological Analysis, 40,* 325–334.

Court Cases

HSA-UWC v. Tax Commission of New York City, 59 N.Y. 2d 512, 435 N. E. 2d 662, 450 N. Y. S2d 292 (1978).

Larson v. Valenti, 102 S. Ct. 1673 (1982).

Unification Church, Nikkuni, et al. v. INS, 547 F. Supp. 623 (1982).

Ward v. Conner, 657 F. 2d 45 (1981).

United Kingdom

The United Kingdom is unusual among industrialized Western societies in that it does not have separation of church and state; there is an officially sanctioned, established faith of the state. This is the Church of England. Historically, faith and state have been inseparable. In the seventeenth century, when the Stuart kings asserted the right to rule based on the divine right of kings, Parliament opposed them, with the result being the English Civil Wars (1642–1651). On the side of Parliament were the Puritans, religious reformers led by Oliver Cromwell (1599–1658) who were called Puritans because they wanted to purify the Church of England. Purification of the Church was to be achieved through a belief in the power of individual faith, a simple prayer book, the removal of bishops from Parliament, and the denial of the divine right of kings. The seventeenth-century conflict was thus as much religious as political, and the Parliamentarians won.

The Establishment of Religion

After the restoration of the monarchy in 1660, a series of constitutional statutes were passed to establish the Church. Under the Coronation Oath Act (1688), the monarch is duty-bound to "maintain the laws of God the true profession of the Gospell and the Protestant reformed religion established by law" (Section 3). The Bill of Rights (1689) declared that Roman Catholics "shall be excluded and be forever incapable to inherit possess or enjoy the crowne and government of this realme" (Section 1, paragraph 36) and the Act of Settlement (1700) completed the process of unification between Church and Crown in decreeing "that every King and Queen of this realm who shall come to and succeed in the imperiall Crown . . . shall have the Coronation Oath administred to him her or them" (Section 2).

A number of quite unpalatable consequences flow from the requirement that the sovereign belong to the Church of England. This requirement limits the liberty of those who may succeed to the throne. It also has the implication that the sovereign should be a Christian and represent a particular ideal. The requirement may offend religious minorities who are not Christian. The requirement may also offend Christians who do not aspire to a state-sanctioned Christian ideal. The sovereign must by law take an interest in the advancement of the established faith, but there is no legal requirement that the sovereign take an interest in the welfare of other faiths. The sovereign must personally approve the appointment to the upper legislature, the House of Lords, of twenty-one of the most senior bishops in the Church of England. No other faith has the legal right to have its senior clergy appointed to Parliament through the Crown. Church of England state schools are funded through the taxation of Christians and non-Christians alike. Muslim and Sikh schools have found it much harder to acquire state funding.

Religious Minorities in the United Kingdom

Minority religions in the United Kingdom are likely to become increasingly impatient with institutionalized religious discrimination. The United Kingdom has an ethnic minority population of some 3 million people; ethnic minorities make up 5.6 percent of Britain's total population. This is likely to double to 6 million in the next forty years, according to the latest census report. Politically, their influence is also growing. In elections in 1997, in thirty-six constituencies the Asian vote was larger than the majority obtained by the sitting member of Parliament. In twelve of the top sixty seats that the prime minister, Tony Blair, needed to win power, Asian voters determined the outcome. Government is likely to come under increasing pressure to address minority voter concerns.

Disestablishment and Repeal of the Act of Settlement

Minority concerns about religious and cultural discrimination may make continued institutional discrimination hard to sustain. This could add to the pressure for disestablishment. Disestablishment of the Church has happened in one part of the United Kingdom already: In 1920 the Anglican Church in Wales was disestablished when, thanks to the sheer strength and influence of other Protestant churches, the Welsh Church Act of 1914 was finally passed.

The real catalyst for change, however, is more likely to come from the repeal of the Act of Settlement, given the practical implications of this Act. Currently, if a natural heir to the throne wishes to marry a Catholic (more than just a hypothetical scenario, as the current crown prince, Charles, is linked romantically to Mrs. Camilla Parker-Bowles, a Catholic), he would become ineligible to ascend to the throne. The Act is simply unworkable in these circumstances, because the United Kingdom now has a political system that makes such religious discrimination by the state unacceptable. The incorporation of the European Convention of Human Rights (1950) into British domestic law by the Human Rights Act of 1998, which protects the right to freedom of conscience and religion, makes enforcement of the Act of Settlement even more untenable.

Cases of Religious Discrimination

Yet it has been a struggle to prove cases of religious discrimination in the United Kingdom, whether they have been tried under domestic or Convention law. This is seen from the decided cases. These have encompassed cases dealing with conscientious objection, traditional rights to pray, and New Age religious groups. In all cases the state has been victorious. Thus, Pat Arrowsmith, an undisputed pacifist, was famously convicted in 1974 under the rarely enforced Incitement to Disaffection Act (1934) for having distributed antimilitary leaflets to the British troops about to be posted to Northern Ireland. When she appealed to the European Commission of Human Rights, that body held in 1981 that Arrowsmith's pacifism was within the parameters of freedom of thought and conscience, but then declared that not every act motivated by religious belief is covered by the Convention. It was not even considered to what extent Arrowsmith's actions were based on her sincerely held beliefs.

In another case, a Muslim teacher at a state school in Britain resigned his position on religious grounds. He had asked for a forty-five minute extension to his lunch break on Fridays to attend prayers, but his school would not allow him to attend. He brought a case of unfair dismissal to every court in Britain and lost them all; in 1982 the Commission heard the application. Without even considering whether or not the school could reasonably accommodate the teacher's request, the Commission held that the fact that the teacher had willingly accepted his employment and that he was free to resign if he wanted provided him with enough of a guarantee of his religious freedom.

In yet another case, the British government prohibited Druids from worshiping at the prehistoric

archaeological site of Stonehenge in southwestern England. Yet, Stonehenge had been granted to the government by deed by a Druid on condition that Druids be allowed to worship there and that the site be open to the public. Following disturbances at the site—for which the Druids were not responsible—the government banned Druids from holding midsummer solstice ceremonies there. The Commission heard the application in 1987 and upheld the ban without requiring the British government to show that there was no reasonable alternative to prohibiting the Druids' worship.

It can be argued that these cases show that religious liberty is better protected under a system of the separation of church and state. Whether one is looking at British domestic law or at the application of international human-rights law, it appears from these cases that without separation of church and state, it is free expression of religion that is hindered when the state interferes.

Satvinder S. Juss

See also British Empire; England, Early Modern; England, Victorian; English Civil War; English Test Oaths and Toleration Act

Further Reading

Act of Settlement 1700 (n.d.). Retrieved December 19, 2002, from http://www.geocities.com/CapitolHill/Senate/2295/aost.html

Addison, W. G. (1944). *Religious equality in modern England, 1714–1914.* London: SPCK.

Avalon Project (n.d.). *English Bill of Rights 1689.* Retrieved December 19, 2002, from http://www.yale.edu/lawweb/avalon/england.htm

Colley, L. (1994). *Britons.* London: Verso.

Coronation Oath Act 1688 (n.d.). Retrieved December 19, 2002, from http://www.geocities.com/CapitolHill/Senate/2295/coat.html

Lawrence, J. (2001). *The rise and fall of the British empire.* London: Abacus.

Court Cases

Ahmad v. UK, App. No. 8160/78, 4 Eur. H.R. Rep. 126 (1981).

Arrowsmith v. UK, App. No. 7050/75 19 Eur. Comm. H.R. Dec. & Rep. 5 (1980).

Chappell v. UK. App. No. 12587/86, 53 Eur. Comm. H.R. Dec. & Rep. 241 (1987).

United States, History *See* Great Awakenings and the Antebellum Period; Confederate Constitution and Religion; Constitution, Founding Era of the; Fourteenth Amendment; French Colonies in North America; Immigration; Jews in the United States; Maryland: Colonial to Early Republic; New England: Colonial to Early Republic; New York: Colonial to Early Republic; Nineteenth-Century U.S. Utopian Communities; Pennsylvania: Colonial to Early Republic; Pledge of Allegiance; Roman Catholics, Colonial to Nineteenth Century; Slavery; South, U.S.: Colonial to Early Republic; Spanish Colonies in North America; Virginia Declaration of Rights; Virginia Statute for Religious Freedom.

Universal Declaration of Human Rights

On 10 December 1948, the General Assembly of the United Nations adopted and proclaimed the Universal Declaration of Human Rights (UDHR), regarded as a landmark achievement in world history for two main reasons. First, drafted in the wake of World War II, it marked the first occasion in which individual human rights had been set forth in such detail. Second, it was the first international recognition that human rights and fundamental freedoms are applicable to every person, everywhere.

Historical Background

Shortly after World War II, representatives from forty-six nations met in San Francisco to negotiate the terms of the United Nations Charter. This legally binding founding document for the United Nations defines four purposes of the U.N., including the promotion of respect for human rights and fundamental freedoms for all without distinction as to race, sex, language, or religion. The Universal Declaration of Human Rights was negotiated under the auspices of the United Nations and on 10 December 1948 was adopted (without dissent) by the U.N.'s General Assembly.

Eleanor Roosevelt was the most prominent figure involved with the drafting of the UDHR. Mrs. Roosevelt became a member of the U.N. Human Rights Commission and was elected its chairwoman in 1947, a year after she was appointed a United Nations delegate. Her drafting skills, diplomacy, and perseverance were largely responsible for the success of the Commission in issuing the Universal Declaration, as the members of the Commission represented a wide diversity of personalities and nationalistic loyalties that were frequently in opposition with one another. Mrs. Roosevelt presented the final version to the Commission and then finally to the General Assembly. The text took two years to draft, beginning in January 1947, when the Commission on Human Rights first met to prepare an International Bill of Human Rights.

The General Assembly scrutinized the draft Declaration in depth. There were many debates, and the fifty-eight member states voted on practically every word and every clause of the text. Some Islamic states objected to the articles on equal marriage rights and on the right to change religious belief, while several Western countries criticized the inclusion of economic, social, and cultural rights.

The resulting document outlines basic human rights and responsibilities. Mrs. Roosevelt considered the UDHR to be a flawed success. She had hoped for a short and simple document that could be easily memorized by people everywhere; the document ultimately contained thirty articles and was several pages long. In addition, Mrs. Roosevelt had sought unanimous approval; in the final voting, however, several countries abstained, including the Communist bloc. Nonetheless, the fact that there were no negative votes in the final count was considered an enormous tribute to Mrs. Roosevelt's diligent work.

As a Declaration, the UDHR was never intended to have legally binding force, but to provide a preamble to the U.N. Charter. In addition, it established the foundation for a covenant that would require a commitment from member nations to enforce the designated human rights. Because of political disagreements during the drafting process, however, the envisioned covenant became two documents: the International Covenant on Civil and Political Rights (ICCPR) and the International Covenant on Economic, Social and Cultural Rights (ICESCR). Both covenants were signed in 1966 and ratified in 1976. (The United States has ratified the International Covenant on Civil and Political Rights and signed but not ratified the International Covenant on Economic, Social and Cultural Rights.)

Provisions Relevant to Religion

The first cluster of articles in the UDHR, sets forth civil and political rights to which everyone is entitled. The right to life, liberty, and personal security, recognized in Article 3, establishes the base for other political rights and civil liberties, including freedom from slavery, torture, and arbitrary arrest, as well as the rights to a fair trial, free speech, freedom of movement, and privacy. The second cluster of articles sets forth the economic, social, and cultural rights to which all human beings are entitled. The third and final cluster of articles provides a larger protective framework in which all human rights are to be universally enjoyed.

Recognizing how fundamental the right of religious belief is to basic human freedom, the committee that drafted the UDHR explicitly provided for the right to freedom of religion, along with freedom of thought and conscience. Several provisions in the UDHR pertain to religious human rights, the most pertinent being Article 18, which states, "Everyone has the right to freedom of thought, conscience and religion; this right includes freedom to change his religion or belief, and freedom, either alone or in community with others and in public or private, to manifest his religion or belief in teaching, practice, worship and observance." Article 2 prohibits distinctions, including religious ones, in the enjoyment of the rights and freedoms specified in the document. And Article 26, which relates to education, specifies that education "shall promote understanding, tolerance and friendship among all nations, racial or religious groups." These provisions provide the basis for the protection of religious human rights embodied in the ICCPR and later in the Declaration on the Elimination of All Forms of Intolerance and Discrimination Based on Religion or Belief (U.N. 1981).

Controversies

Being a declaration rather than a binding treaty, no enforcement mechanisms for protecting the religious (and other) rights specified in the UDHR existed until 1976, when the ICCPR and ICESCR were ratified. Many have found several provisions in the Document to be so vague or idealistic as to be unenforceable. In addition, a major controversy concerns the assumption of the universality of human rights. The universal nature of human rights is also written into the title of the Declaration, as well as the Preamble, which states that the Declaration is a "common standard of achievement for all peoples and all nations." The first two articles declare that human beings are equal because of their shared

essence of human dignity; human rights are universal, not because of any state or international organization, but because they belong to all of humanity.

Those holding the view of legal positivism or cultural relativism dispute the accuracy of this perspective. They consider human rights to be the product of particular cultures and legal systems, rather than existing innately or naturally in human beings. The controversy over the universality of human rights continues, especially in view of the U.N.'s renewed commitment to the universal view in the Vienna Declaration adopted by the United Nations World Conference on Human Rights in Austria in 1993, which states that "All human rights are universal, indivisible and interdependent and interrelated."

Despite these problems, the UDHR has been widely accepted. It has been translated into nearly 250 languages and is the best known and most often cited human rights document in the world. It is the foundation for more than sixty international human rights laws, which together constitute a comprehensive system of legally binding treaties for the promotion and protection of human rights, and it has been incorporated in the constitutions and laws of many nations.

Lucinda Joy Peach

Further Reading

Ayton-Shenker, D. (2002). United Nations background note: The challenge of human rights and cultural diversity. Retrieved August 7, 2002, from http://www.un.org/rights/dpi1627e.htm

Glendon, M. (2001). *A world made new: Eleanor Roosevelt and the universal declaration of human rights.* New York: Random House.

United Nations. (1948). *Universal declaration of human rights.* Retrieved August 7, 2002, from http://www.un.org/rights/HRToday/

United Nations. (1966). *International covenant on civil and political rights.* Retrieved August 7, 2002, from http://www.un.org/rights/HRToday

United Nations. (1966). *International covenant on economic, social and cultural rights.* Retrieved August 7, 2002, from http://www.un.org/rights/HRToday/

United Nations. (1981). *Declaration on the elimination of all forms of intolerance and of discrimination based on religion or belief.* Retrieved August 7, 2002, from http://www.un.org/rights/HRToday/

United Nations. (1993). *Vienna declaration and programme of action.* New York: United Nations.

United Nations. (2002). Universal declaration of human rights, U.N. human rights today. Retrieved August 7, 2002, from http://www.un.org/rights/HRToday

Utilitarianism and J.S. Mill

The British social and political theorist Jeremy Bentham (1748–1832) is commonly credited with founding the philosophy known as utilitarianism, although both earlier and later thinkers contributed notable ideas, including the British philosophers Thomas Hobbes (1588–1679) and David Hume (1711–1776), and the Italian reformer Cesare Beccaria (1738–1794). All utilitarians shared a commitment to the principle of utility, which holds that the ethical value of anything is determined by the principle of the greatest good for the greatest number of people. Beyond commitment to this principle, utilitarians entertained varying opinions concerning the manner of its application in particular cases. They also had more profound differences of opinion, for example regarding the roles of the government and the individual in a society organized along utilitarian lines.

The success of the utilitarian school owed much to the activities of the philosopher and economist James Mill (1773–1836), who for a long time served as Bentham's primary disciple and interpreter. James was the father of an even more famous son, John Stuart Mill (1806–1873), the last of the major utilitarian philosophers. The younger Mill is known for the extraordinary education he received from his father, as well as for his contributions to philosophy.

The Concept of Utility

The classical formulation of the principle of utility is found in Bentham's *Fragment on Government* (1776), in which he articulated as an axiom that "it is the greatest happiness of the greatest number that is the measure of right and wrong." The phrase "the greatest good of the greatest number" had been used previously by Beccaria and before him, by the Scottish philosopher Francis Hutcheson (1694–1746). This principle is also referred to by Bentham and John Stuart Mill as the "Greatest Happiness Principle." In his *Introduction to the Principles of Morals and Legislation* (1789), Bentham provided a more elaborate definition: "By the principle of utility is meant that principle which approves or disapproves of every

action whatsoever, according to the tendency which it appears to have to augment or diminish the happiness of the party whose interest is in question." He then proceeded to specify that a true supporter of utility has in view the interest of the community, which is only "the sum of the interests of the several members who compose it." Thus the two formulations coincide.

By utility and happiness, the utilitarians meant a great many things, as revealed in the synonyms they commonly used for these terms, including profit, gain, advantage, and, most common of all, pleasure. Utility consisted of the maximization of pleasure and the minimization of pain, considered quantifiable in the same way as economic value. Bentham was committed to the possibility of a scientific calculus of pleasure or utility modeled on the natural sciences as well as on the new science of economics.

Bentham's Reform of the Common Law

As a lawyer, Bentham's primary mission was to reform the English common law. His first major work, the *Fragment*, launched an attack on *Commentaries on the Laws of England* (1765), by the British jurist William Blackstone (1723–80). Bentham dismissed Blackstone as an "expositor," one who merely states what the law is, as opposed to a "censor," one who declares what it ought to be. The general willingness of the utilitarians to overturn all established authority, rewrite the laws, and reorganize the political institutions of society led the French historian Elie Halevy (1870–1937) to call them "philosophic radicals."

Throughout his career, Bentham proposed an enormous number of schemes for reform, including plans for a circular prison called the Panopticon, in which the prisoners in their individual cells could be clandestinely observed by a centrally located guard. The majority of Bentham's writings, however, concentrated on reform of the law through codification, meaning the reduction of the law to a logically organized set of explicit written injunctions based on utilitarian principles.

One of the first areas of laws Bentham treated was the penal law. He sought to introduce a rational and ideal association between a crime and its punishment by increasing the certainty and adjusting the duration of the punishment, along with its proportionality, "characteristicalness" (resemblance), and propinquity (proximity) to the crime. In this way, the pleasure or profit to be gained by the crime would be offset by the pain of the punishment, deterring the would-be criminal. Note that two different calculations of utility are involved here: The first determines whether the net result of an action produces more pain than pleasure for the aggregate of individuals, in which case it constitutes a wrong and, potentially, one that ought to be proscribed as a crime; the second determines the quantity and other attributes of punishment necessary to offset the prospective advantages of a crime for the individual criminal.

Utilitarian Attitudes toward Religion

In theory, the principle of utility was compatible with a range of different religious beliefs. The British theologian William Paley (1743–1805) had argued for a Christian form of utilitarianism even before Bentham published his *Introduction*, and many others found no contradiction between utility and Christianity. However, most utilitarians, like other British philosophers before them, tried to establish a scientific morality through appeal to reason and human experience alone, and in this endeavor rejected any appeal to religion due to its supernaturalism and traditionalism. Consequently, many did tend toward agnosticism, if not atheism. Bentham, the most virulently partisan utilitarian, argued in his *Introduction* that the principle of utility is opposed both to the principle of asceticism, which is always against pleasure and utility, and to the principle of sympathy and antipathy, which bases moral judgments on irrational individual preferences and is only sometimes against utility. Bentham felt that although both these principles fail to produce judgments founded on a reasoned examination of human experience, it is the principle of asceticism, associated with religion, that is more consistently and perversely opposed to utility. It is no surprise that Bentham was a free-thinker or an atheist, or that he wrote essays critical of traditional religion, especially the pseudonymously published *Analysis of the Influence of the Natural Religion on the Temporal Happiness of Mankind* (1822). It was this essay that John Stuart Mill took as precedent for his own essay, *Utility of Religion* (1874).

Utility, Authority, and Liberty

Despite the fame of John Stuart Mill's essay *On Liberty* (1859), utilitarianism was, at least initially, more concerned with the justified exercise of author-ity than with the problems that may arise from authority that opposes liberty. Hobbes, who had earlier argued for a powerful sovereign in the context of a social contract between the government and the governed, had been more afraid of anarchy than of oppression. Bentham replaced the fiction of a social contract with the principle of utility as the justification of government. His requirement that the government attend to the greatest happiness of the greatest number of individuals did approach a form of egalitarianism. However, Bentham specifically rejected the idea of natural rights, which he termed an "anarchistical fallacy." He came only slowly and under the influence of James Mill to be a supporter of more radical democratic reforms, which would, the two men hoped, overcome the division of interests between the government and the governed.

The new science of economics described a market in which, as if by an invisible hand (to use the famous simile of the eighteenth-century British economist Adam Smith) and without governmental interference, there was a natural identity of interests. Of course, not all of society could operate as the market did, and in other areas, such as that defined by criminal law, the government was needed to impose an artificial identification of interests by adding a political or legal sanction. The utilitarians were in agreement on this point, but less certain where to draw the limit on governmental interference with the individual. Many, including Bentham, appear to have believed that a government in accordance with utilitarian principles would naturally establish the proper balance of interests. However, in *On Liberty*, John Stuart Mill described the dangers posed to individual liberty by an excess of governmental authority, and attempted to define the appropriate limits of interference in individual interests. Although he believed he had reconciled liberty with utilitarianism, his analysis exposed the dangers to liberty presented even by a utilitarian democracy in which the interests of the majority differ from those of the minority, and the calculus of interests can therefore lead to a tyranny by the majority.

John Stuart Mill on Freedom and Religion

John Stuart Mill broadened utilitarianism beyond Bentham's narrow calculus of pleasure and pain in several ways. In response to criticisms that utilitarianism was only a crass hedonism that leveled all morality to the pursuit of gross pleasure, Mill affirmed the importance of qualitatively different and higher levels of pleasures. In response to theories of natural rights, he affirmed, in *On Liberty*, that the end of a good society is the development of the higher capacities of the individual, and that the best manner of guaranteeing this development is to limit governmental interference with individual thought and expression and even, to some degree, with individual behavior.

The difficulty, of course, is in where to draw the line. Mill argued that "the sole end for which mankind are warranted, individually or collectively, in interfering with the liberty of action of any of their number, is self-protection . . . The only part of the conduct of any one, for which he is amenable to society, is that which concerns others" (Mill 1961, 263). Although this principle is clear, its application beyond the sphere of ideas and expressions to that of actions remains very difficult. Mill's own attempts to apply the principle were, in retrospect, anything but clear-cut. A rigorous and consistent application of the principle of utility would seem to allow many of the encroachments on individual liberty that he abhorred, including prohibiting the use of intoxicants, which can be profoundly harmful to the individual even in the absence of harm to society. Mill's depiction of an atomistic society in which the behavior of the individual may be considered apart from its social consequences has, to some extent, been superceded by the very different conditions of the modern welfare state in which the government increasingly assumes the consequences of individual behavior.

In Mill's discussion of freedom, religion played a crucial role, and an ambivalent one. One of the freedoms he affirmed to be most important was the freedom of religious belief, including the right to believe or disbelieve in God. Mill argued that the chief threat to religious freedom is religious bigotry. His paradigm cases of persecution were those of Socrates and Jesus, both of which he characterized as cases of religious persecution. For Mill, religious freedom meant freedom from religion at least as much as freedom of religion. He condemned especially the tyranny of opinion that can obtain even in the absence of legal and political sanctions, and named religion as one of the most powerful forces contributing to this more subtle encroachment on liberty.

In common with Bentham, Mill took a largely negative view of the utility of religion, its supernaturalism, traditionalism, and asceticism. However, Mill's more expansive ideas of utility and liberty allowed more scope to religious sentiments. In his *Utility of Religion*, Mill argued that a religion devoid of superstition and advocating utilitarian principles, which he called the Religion of Humanity, can play a positive role in society. Elsewhere, however, Mill warned of the dangers even a rationalized substitute for religion may pose to individual liberty.

The Continuing Significance of Utilitarianism

Although utilitarianism has receded in importance as an independent school, its leading principles continue to make an important contribution to political, legal, and social debate. It is in large part due to the triumph of the concept of utility as a guide for policy in the modern state that the conflict between utility and liberty has become more apparent to us than it was to John Stuart Mill, whose efforts to reconcile the two principles, despite or because of his lack of complete success, are more relevant than ever.

Robert A. Yelle

Further Reading

Bentham, J. (1843). *The works of Jeremy Bentham*. (J. Bowring, Ed.). Edinburgh, UK: William Tait.

Crimmins, J. B. (Ed.). (1990). *Religion, secularization and political thought: Thomas Hobbes to J. S. Mill*. London: Routledge.

Halevy, E. (1972). *The growth of philosophic radicalism*. (M. Morris, Trans.). London: Faber and Faber.

Long, D. G. (1977). *Bentham on liberty: Jeremy Bentham's idea of liberty in relation to his Utilitarianism*. Toronto, Canada: University of Toronto Press.

Lyons, D. (1994). *Rights, welfare, and Mill's moral theory*. New York: Oxford University Press.

Mill, J. S. (1961). *Essential works of John Stuart Mill*. (M. Lerner, Ed.). New York: Bantam.

Plamenatz, J. (1958). *The English Utilitarians* (2nd rev. ed.). Oxford, UK: Basil Blackwell.

Postema, G. J. (1986). *Bentham and the common law tradition*. Oxford, UK: Oxford University Press.

Vatican II

Vatican II refers to the meeting of the worldwide Catholic bishops in communion with the Roman Catholic Church for the purpose of addressing concerns of the world-wide community. The Second Vatican Council, twenty-first ecumenical council of the Catholic Church, began in Vatican City on 11 October 1962 and continued each subsequent fall through 1965. It was initiated by John XXIII (papacy, 1958–1963) and continued by his successor Paul VI (papacy, 1963–1978). The Council is significant not only because representatives from other Christian denominations attended but also because it marked the beginning of Catholicism's dialogue with modernity. (Catholicism, as used in this article, refers to the Roman Catholic Church, which is in communion with seven non-Roman churches that use other rites. The term "catholic" can apply to all Christian denominations who use the creed: "One, holy, catholic and apostolic.")

The Second Vatican Council issued sixteen documents with three different authoritative valences. The documents with the highest authoritative voice are The Dogmatic Constitution on the Church, *Lumen gentium*; The Dogmatic Constitution on Divine Revelation, *Dei verbum*; The Constitution on the Sacred Liturgy, *Sacrosanctum concilium*; and The Pastoral Constitution on the Church in the Modern World, *Gaudium et spes*. The Latin name, by convention, is taken from the opening words of the text: *Lumen gentium*, "light of the nations"; *Dei verbum*, "word of God"; *Sacrosanctum concilium*, "this sacred Council"; and *Gaudium et spes*, "joys and hopes."

Each of these texts includes developments toward greater freedom in Catholic teaching.

During Pius IX's pontificate (1846–1878) the "thesis/hypothesis" codified negative reaction to the rise of the nation-state. This teaching had its roots in the principle *cuius region, eius religion*, which means "the religion of the prince is the religion of the place." The "thesis" required the state to protect Catholics when they were in the minority, but to privilege them when in the majority. The "hypothesis" claimed that no other religious traditions compelled protection from the state because error has no rights. The Second Vatican Council formulated new thinking with regard to the church-state relationship, as well as the relationship among all Christian denominations, the relationship to the other faith traditions, the relationship to atheism, and the relationship between the centuries-old Catholic Church and the rest of modern thought. It also confronted the issue of the nature and mission of the Church itself. The Council is significant with regard to religious freedom because of its Declaration on Religious Freedom (*Dignitatis humanae*), often called the "American document" because of the influence of an American Jesuit, John Courtney Murray (1904–1967), who found constitutional church-state separation efficacious in protecting religious practice through its emphasis upon human rights and duties. Murray's ideas where condemned in 1954 by the Holy Office of the Roman Curia, headed by Cardinal Ottaviani (1890–1979). These same ideas emerged in 1965 as the official teaching of the Church. The declaration denies any sacred function to government, relinquishes any favored legal status for the Catholic

Church (thus rejecting thesis/hypothesis), retrieves freedom of the conscience from the centuries-old tradition in Catholic moral and sacramental theology, and calls for the autonomy of religious bodies except when they interfere with the common good or other civil rights and laws.

Sally M. Vance-Trembath

See also Roman Catholicism

Further Reading

Ferguson, T. P. (1993). *Catholic and American: The political theology of John Courtney Murray.* Kansas City, CO: Sheed & Ward.

Hastings, A. (Ed.). (1991). *Modern Catholicism: Vatican II and after.* New York: Oxford University Press.

Hopper, J. L. (Ed.). (1994). *Bridging the sacred and the secular: Selected writings of John Courtney Murray.* Washington, DC: Georgetown University Press.

Karl, R. (1986). Basic theological interpretation of the Second Vatican Council. In *Concern for the Church* (pp. 77–89). New York: Crossroad.

McBrien, R. P. (Ed.). (1995). *HarperCollins encyclopedia of Catholicism.* San Francisco: Harper.

McElroy, R. W. (1989). *The search for an American public theology: The contribution of John Courtney Murray.* New York: Paulist Press.

Miller, J. H. (Ed.). (1966). *Vatican II: An interfaith appraisal.* Notre Dame, IN: University of Notre Dame Press.

Murray, J. C. (Ed.). (1966). *Religious liberty: An end and a beginning. The declaration on religious freedom, an ecumenical discussion.* New York: Macmillan.

Rynne, X. (1999). *Vatican Council II.* Maryknoll, NY: Orbis.

Virginia Declaration of Rights

On Monday, 6 May 1776, the General Convention of Virginia Delegates assembled at the capitol in Williamsburg and declared the Virginia Colony independent of England. Of first concern in that Williamsburg gathering was the matter of a "Declaration of Rights." The convention voted in their first day of meeting for a committee to "prepare a Declaration of Rights, and . . . a plan of government." George Mason was the force behind this declaration, as well as the architect of the plan of government for the Commonwealth of Virginia. However, he did not arrive in the capital until 18 May. It was only then that the delegates began their task in earnest. After taking his seat Mason was quickly named to chair the committee to devise the Declaration of Rights. Twenty-eight men joined Mason in the task. However, historians are of one mind in attributing the major work on the Declaration to Mr. Mason. In ringing words the document affirmed that all governmental power was "derived from the People" (Article 2). Agreement was forthcoming to affirm a free press, trial by jury, separation of powers, and free elections. The committee's first recorded act was the adoption of "A Declaration of Rights" on 12 June 1776, "which rights do pertain to them (the good people of Virginia.), and their posterity, as the basis and foundation of Government."

A very young James Madison had been added to the Rights Committee on 16 May, two days prior to Mason's arrival. Mason proposed, as the first article, the following words concerning religious freedom: "That as Religion, or the Duty which we owe to our divine and omnipotent Creator, and the Manner of discharging it, can be governed only by Reason and Conviction, not by Force or Violence; and therefore that all Men shou'd enjoy the fullest Toleration in the Exercise of Religion, according to the Dictates of Conscience, unpunished and unrestrained by the Magistrate, unless, under Colour of Religion, any Man disturb the Peace, the Happiness, or safety of Society, or Individuals. And that it is the mutual Duty of all, to practice Christian Forbearance, Love and Charity towards Each other."

Madison responded to the Mason draft of that article, finding a serious problem with the wording. He saw a clear danger in the use of the term "toleration." In the give and take of political activity in Orange and Culpeper Counties beginning in 1772, Madison had come face-to-face with religious persecution. In January 1774 he wrote the following sentiments to his Princeton classmate, William Bradford:

> That diabolical Hell conceived principle of persecution rages among some and to their eternal infamy the Clergy can furnish their quota of Imps for such business. This vexes me the worst of anything whatever. There are at this time in the adjacent County not less than 5 or 6 well meaning men in close Goal [jail] for publishing their religious

Sentiments, which in the main are very orthodox. I have neither patience to hear talk or think any thing relative to this matter, for I have squabbled and scolded abused and ridiculed so long about it, [to] so little purpose that I am without common patience. So I leave you to pity me and pray for Liberty of Conscience [to revive among us].

Better than any of his colleagues, the young scholar Madison, through personal experience, had fixed in his mind the clear difference between freedom and toleration. He had witnessed "toleration" at work up close and recognized that, as Tom Paine asserted, toleration is the counterfeit of freedom. In 1776, faced with a concept he rejected, Madison found the words that matched his vision: "all men are equally entitled to the free exercise of religion, according to the dictates of conscience." After some debate the Virginia Declaration of Rights was passed with Madison's words replacing "toleration." In its new form the sixteenth article of the Declaration was passed along with the other fifteen. It read:

> That religion, or the duty which we owe to our Creator, and the manner of discharging it, can be directed only by reason and conviction, not by force or violence; and therefore, that all men are equally entitled to the free exercise of religion according to the dictates of conscience, and that it is the mutual duty of all to practice Christian forbearance, love, and charity, towards each other.

Final approval came on 12 June 1776.

As the nation took shape Madison became the primary voice in the new Virginia House of Delegates on the subjects of religious freedom and establishment. In 1785 he penned his most thorough analysis of church-state relations. This time the focus was upon establishment. Faced with a bill to assess all citizens for support of religious education, Madison circulated his classic statement—*A Memorial and Remonstrance*—which served, along with petitions by Baptists, Presbyterians, and Methodists, to defeat the assessment. Within weeks he succeeded in gaining passage of Jefferson's "Act for Establishing Religious Freedom" in 1786.

The final chapter in this saga occurred in 1789 when Madison proposed to the newly elected United States Congress that it adopt what are now known as the First Amendment religion clauses. Mason's Virginia Declaration of Rights, Article 16, amended by Madison, had launched a debate that culminated, thirteen years later, in a new light of freedom for the infant nation.

Robert S. Alley

Further Reading

Hening, W. (1821). *The statutes at large: Being a collection of all the laws of Virginia* (Vol. 9). Commonwealth of Virginia: Richmond, VA.

Hutchinson, W., & Rachal, W. (1962). *The papers of James Madison* (Vols. 1 & 8). Chicago: University of Chicago Press.

Madison, James. (1774, January 24). *James Madison to William Bradford*. Retrieved April 16, 2003. http://press-pubs.uchicago.edu/founders/documents/amendI_religions16.html

Miller, W. L. (1986). *The first liberty: Religion and the American republic*. New York: Alfred A. Knopf.

Smith, J. M. (Ed.). (1994). *The republic of letters: The correspondence of letters between Jefferson and Madison* (Vols. 1–3). New York: W. W. Norton.

Virginia Declaration of Human Rights. (First Draft, c. May 20–26, 1776). Retrieved December 20, 2002, from http://gunstonhall.org/documents/vdr-draft.html

Virginia Declaration of Human Rights. (Final Draft, June 12, 1776). Retrieved December 20, 2002, from http://gunstonhall.org/documents/vdr.html

Virginia Statute for Religious Freedom

The significance of the Virginia Statute for Religious Freedom, drafted by Thomas Jefferson (1743–1826) in 1777, extends far beyond the practice of any faith by advancing the principle of restraining government from intrusions into the private lives of citizens. It declared that the exercise of religion is a natural and inalienable right bestowed by God and hence outside the authority of legislatures or courts. The Statute was part of a comprehensive package of proposals by Jefferson to revise and perfect Virginia law between 1776 and 1786. He predicted that the normal course of human complacency would inevitably lead to corrupt rulers and careless citizens. Jefferson explained in *Notes on Virginia* (1787) that it was crucial to consider revisions to the law while the country was young, unified, and receptive. The intent of these proposed revisions was to lay a foundation for a republican government and eradicate the aristocratic tradition that the Anglican Church had helped to perpetuate.

History and Passage of the Statute

While drafted by Jefferson in 1777, the Virginia Statute for Religious Freedom was not enacted into law until 1786, while Jefferson himself was out of the country. Its passage is owed to the skills of James Madison and the momentum brought about by a confluence of enlightenment and religious dissenter-based opposition to a bill offered by Patrick Henry to fund religious teachers through tax monies. Henry's rationale for such a measure was a fear that a separation of church and state would lead to a downfall in the morals of citizens and thus harm the state. Despite the freedom of choice the Bill provided, it was roundly defeated through political action in the form of remonstrances and petitions that overwhelmingly opposed the Bill.

The most famous and enduring of the oppositions is James Madison's "Memorial and Remonstrance." Madison declared the assessment bill in support of Christianity to be "a dangerous abuse of power" (Madison 1785, para. 1). Among the reasons given for opposing such a bill was that, as a matter of logic and precedent, there is no *de minimis* exception to encroachment on inalienable rights—either the civil state has the jurisdictional authority to usurp such rights, or it doesn't. The most basic of the objections was that very lack of jurisdiction over religion and religious duties, which are matters for the individual conscience, inalienable and hence non-delegable to the assembly. The bill, which called for the establishment and support of the "Christian Religion," improperly favored one religion, Christianity. This raised an issue of inequality because "all men are to be considered as entering into Society on equal conditions; as relinquishing no more, and therefore retaining no less, one than another, of their natural rights. Above all are they to be considered as retaining an 'equal title to the free exercise of Religion according to the dictates of Conscience'" (Madison 1785, para. 5).

When Patrick Henry's bill was withdrawn, Madison seized the moment and introduced Jefferson's 1777 Bill for Establishing Religious Freedom, which was enacted in 1786 by the overwhelming vote of 74 to 20. Jefferson's statute read, "Be it enacted by the General Assembly, That no man shall be compelled to frequent or support any religious worship, place, or ministry whatsoever, nor shall be enforced, restrained, molested, or burthened in his body or goods, nor shall otherwise suffer on account of his religious opinions or belief; but that all men shall be free to profess, and by argument to maintain, their opinion in matters of religion and that the same shall in no wise diminish, enlarge, or affect their civil capacities" (Jefferson 1777, para. 2).

The Cultural Context of the American Revolution

Jefferson and the Founding Fathers were faced with the task of educating colonial Americans, rooted in English monarchical traditions, to an unknown system of republican democracy where people could live and grow according to their natural moral state. The English monarch was regarded as God's anointed sovereign supported by a powerful church. Jefferson blamed the Anglican Church for spreading the seeds of oppression and tyranny in the New World. One of Jefferson's complaints was that "the theological invention of sin led man to regard himself as outcast from his Creator, so that he lost his sense for true religion" (Sanford 1984, 64). The English sovereignty was characterized by an aristocracy that held all power of property and wealth, sustained by the labor of the lower classes.

Thomas Jefferson was troubled by the threat that uneducated minds presented to the life of American liberty. Without education to free thought and free religion, the models of religion and class system that had been created by English sovereignty were the only models Americans could refer to in their social and political interactions. The basic assumptions were clarified in a letter to William Green Munford dated 18 June 1799, in which Jefferson wrote: "I join you therefore in branding as cowardly the idea that the human mind is incapable of further advances. This is precisely the doctrine present despots of the earth are inculcating, & their friends here re-echoing; and applying especially to religion & politics; 'that it is not probable that anything better will be discovered than what was known to our fathers.' We are to look backwards then & not forwards for the improvement of science, & to find it amidst feudal barbarisms and the fires of Spital-fields. But thank heaven the American mind is already too much opened, to listen to these impostures; and while the art of printing is left to us, science can never be retrograde; what is once acquired of real knowledge can never be lost" (Peterson 1984, 1065).

Social, economic, educational, and spiritual themes that championed freedom instead of servitude were imperative if independence was to survive. Jefferson recognized that conscience was an attribute common among men, from the ploughman to the scholar, and he aimed to cultivate it by employing universal metaphors of spirituality, which he believed to be morality and reason. As a practical matter, the purpose in liberating religion from state control was to make it more generally influential in society. Jefferson made it clear that imposing Anglican dogma would have negative consequences as long as the aristocracy continued to derive its livelihood from the ignorant and oppressed underclass.

The Role of God

Jefferson's vision of a truly republican state was one in which the natural rights that comprised freedom and equality for all men were considered to be divinely bestowed; therefore, they were inviolable by government or other men. In his original draft of the Declaration of Independence, Jefferson maintained that the "sacred & undeniable" truth was that men had equally been created with "rights inherent & inalienable, among which are the preservation of life, & liberty & the pursuit of happiness" (Mayer 1995, 69).

The Jeffersonian concept of self-government was unique in that concepts of civil equality and liberty were wedded to the ideals of natural society. Stemming from the Aristotelian idea that government should promote the common good, Jefferson built new relationships between virtue, religion, and state by setting men free to be human beings to develop to their fullest potential in more creative and informed ways, according their own individual consciences. Strongly influenced by Enlightenment ideals, Jefferson maintained that the sole purpose of government was to secure the natural rights of men by addressing only those threats that necessitated a collective response. He believed in the inherent goodness of men and their natural inclination to form society and to exercise charity. The most effective way to enhance those natural proclivities was to set them free.

Separation of Church and State

As an additional safeguard against tyranny by the state, Jefferson believed there should be a statutory wall between the public domain of government and the private domain of individual citizens. His core conviction was that "God created the mind free" and "the opinions of men are not the object of civil government, nor under its jurisdiction" (Mayer 1995, 159). Although those words were stricken from the final draft of the Statue for Religious Freedom by the Virginia legislature, Jefferson considered the boundary between the role of government in the public sector and the prerogatives of the individual in the private life to be a basic principle of the bill (Mayer 1995, 69). Because the Statute for Religious Freedom was based upon the principle that men's private lives are not the domain of the state, Jefferson's success in separating church and state was a pivotal aspect in facilitating the spread of religious freedom in American.

Leri M. Thomas

Further Reading

Estep, W. R. (1990). *Revolution within the revolution: the First Amendment in historical context, 1612–1789.* Grand Rapids, MI: William B. Eerdmans.

Gilbert, C. (Ed.). (1926). *The commonplace book of Thomas Jefferson.* Baltimore: Johns Hopkins Press.

Ketcham, R. (1993). *Framed for posterity: The enduring philosophy of the Constitution.* Lawrence: University of Kansas Press.

Jefferson, T. (1777). Statute of religious freedom. Retrieved November 15, 2002, from http://www.pbs.org/jefferson/archives/documents/ih195802.htm

Madison, J. (1785). Memorial and remonstrance against religious assessments. Retrieved November 15, 2002, from http://religiousfreedom.lib.virginia.edu/sacred/madison_m&r_1785.html

Malone, D. (1948–1981). *Jefferson and his time* (6 vols.). Boston: Little Brown.

Mayer, D. N. (1995). *The constitutional thought of Thomas Jefferson.* Charlottesville: University Press of Virginia.

Miller, W. L. (1986). *The first liberty: Religion and the American Republic.* New York: Alfred A. Knopf.

Peterson, M. D. (Ed.). (1984). *Thomas Jefferson, writings.* New York: Library of America.

Peterson, M.D., & R.C. Vaughan (1988). *The Virginia Statute for Religious Freedom: Its evolution and consequences in American history.* New York: Cambridge University Press.

Sanford, C. B. (1984). *The religious life of Thomas Jefferson.* Charlottesville: University Press of Virginia.

Wood, G. S. (1991). *The radicalism of the American Revolution.* New York: Random House.

Waldensians

Of the popular heresies of the Middle Ages, Waldensianism had likely the largest number of adherents and the widest geographical distribution. It was also the longest-lived of these heresies, as its history extends into the present age. The Waldensian movement commenced in Lyon, France, around 1173 with the conversion of the Lyonese citizen Valdes (d. before 1218) from an affluent merchant to an itinerant preacher who exhorted his fellow men and women to embrace apostolic simplicity and poverty. From Lyon, the Waldensian movement spread to the heartlands of western Christendom: the industrial centers of northern Italy, the politically fragmented areas of southern France, and the German empire's trade routes and eastern territories. Against the background of expanding market economies, political autonomization in the cities, the aftermath of ecclesiastical changes instigated by the Gregorian reforms, and advances in lay literacy in the twelfth century, the leaders of the Waldensians saw themselves as members of a reform movement within the Catholic church. Waldensians advocated a simple way of life prescribed in the Gospels and the austere morals of the early Christian communities. Key Waldensian tenets were preaching, voluntary poverty, and abstention from killing, swearing, and lying. The early Waldensians placed a concomitant emphasis on itinerancy, manual labor, and good works.

The ecclesiastical reaction was swift but not decisive at first. By the early 1180s the Waldensians were faced with restrictions on their preaching, which was to be authorized by their local (Catholic) priests.

Pope Lucius III then generally excommunicated them as schismatics for defying proper ecclesiastical authority in 1184, but despite the formal inquisition of heresy in his decretal *Ad abolendam*, the persecution of heresy proved ineffective because it rested with local bishops. Around 1205, the Waldensian movement split into two main factions, the Poor Leonists and the Poor Lombards, who disagreed over the value of manual labor, organizational issues, and their position vis-à-vis Catholic clergy. These conflicts were not resolved; furthermore, some Waldensians groups were reconciled with orthodoxy in the years that followed.

It took until the 1230s in France and until the 1250s in Italy before decrees and laws against heretics were fully and effectively implemented in persecutions. In Germany, there were a series of large-scale inquisitions that continued into the fifteenth century. Once the Waldensians faced mendicant inquisitors, they were quickly swept underground and forced to live clandestinely. This led to what the Italian historian Grado Merlo has called "Waldensianisms," that is, the existence of marginalized but locally influential Waldensian groups with their own individual localized beliefs and customs.

In the wake of the Reformation, the Waldensians adopted Protestant views and practices, but persecutions continued and led some Waldensians to set up new settlements, as was the case with Henri Arnaud (1641–1721), who led a large group from Savoy to Switzerland and Germany. By the nineteenth century, the Waldensians had been given full civil and religious rights in many European countries. Emigrant groups settled first in Uruguay and then the United States. In

Italy, the Waldensians merged with the Methodist church and have their headquarters in Torre Pellice (Piedmont). Today, the Waldensian churches are a member of the World Council of Churches.

Lutz Kaelber

Further Reading

Biller, P. (2001). *The Waldensians, 1170–1530: Between a religious order and a church.* Aldershot, UK: Ashgate.

Cameron, E. (2000). *Waldenses: Rejections of holy church in medieval Europe.* Oxford, UK: Blackwell.

Lambert, M. (1992). *Medieval heresy: Popular movements from the Gregorian reform to the Reformation.* Oxford, UK: Blackwell.

Merlo, G. (1984). *Valdesi e valdismi medievali: Itinerari e proposte di ricerca* (The Waldensians and medieval Waldensian groups: Directions and suggestions for research). Turin, Italy: Claudiana.

Tourn, G. (1999). *Les vaudois: L'étonnante aventure d'un peuple-église, 1170–1999* (The Waldensians: The astonishing adventure of a popular church, 1170–1999). Turin, Italy: Claudiana.

Williamsburg Charter

Published 25 June 1988 to mark the 200th anniversary of Virginia's call for the Bill of Rights and of the U.S. Constitution, the Williamsburg Charter reaffirmed the First Amendment religious liberty clauses of the Constitution. Encouraged by Chief Justice Warren Burger, Os Guinness—an Englishman and visiting Brookings Institution scholar—proposed the Charter. It was drafted over two years by Protestant, Catholic, Jewish, and secularist scholars, who consulted with religious figures from all traditions. The drafters included Os Guinness, Nat Hentoff of the *Village Voice*, Dean Kelley of the National Council of Churches, Father Richard John Neuhaus, and George Weigel, the biographer of Pope John Paul II.

The Charter is neither a legal document nor a statement of ecumenical agreement: As stated in the introduction to the Charter:"We readily acknowledge our continuing differences. Signing this Charter implies no pretense . . . that our differences over policy proposals, legal interpretations and philosophical groundings do not ultimately matter." Rather it is "a renewed national compact . . . on how we view the place of religion in American public life and how we should contend with each other's deepest differences in the public sphere."

Part One sets out the genius of the religious liberty clauses as the "true remedy" (James Madison) for the problems of religion and public life, arguing that religious liberty is more than liberty for the religious, but is foundational to a free society. Part Two reviews contemporary "culture-warring" over religion and public life, critiquing four widespread errors that have exacerbated the controversies. Part Three rejects two extreme views of public life—the "naked public square" and the "sacred public square"—calling for a new engagement of citizens in a "civil public square," and spelling out guidelines for such a vision.

Named for Williamsburg, Virginia, the cradle of American religious liberty, the Charter was formally presented at the Hall of the House of Burgesses. Among the distinguished signers were former presidents Gerald Ford and Jimmy Carter, Chief Justice William Rehnquist, congressmen, and leaders from all walks of life.

In hindsight, the Charter can be seen as a substantive success, though it did not achieve its highest political goals. As the boldest statement on U.S. religious liberty in the twentieth century, it inspired constructive later initiatives such as the Common Ground movement led by Dr. Charles Haynes. However, opposition by the religious right blocked President Ronald Reagan from signing, meaning that the Charter did not fulfill its drafters' ultimate goals: providing a new vision of "living with our deepest differences," resolving the culture wars, and restoring the relationship of faith and freedom to its foundational place in the American republic.

Os Guinness

Further Reading

Hunter, J. D., & Guinness, O. (Eds.). (1990). *Articles of faith, articles of peace: The religious liberty clauses and the American public philosophy.* Washington, DC: The Brookings Institution.

Guinness, O. (1993). *The American hour: A time of reckoning and the once and future role of faith.* New York: Free Press.

Miller, W. L. (1986). *The first liberty.* New York: Alfred Knopf.

Williamsburg Charter (1988). Retrieved October 31, 2002, from religiousfreedom.lib.virginia.edu/const/Willburg.html

Witch-Hunts

Witch-hunts were campaigns conducted by European and colonial American authorities to identify, accuse, and prosecute individuals for practicing witchcraft between 1450 and 1750. The crime of witchcraft, as it was defined during these years, consisted of two main components. The first was the alleged practice of harmful magic, which was the use of some kind of supernatural, preternatural, or mysterious power to bring misfortune upon one's neighbors. These misfortunes often involved the infliction of disease, injury, or death on human beings or their livestock. Witches were also accused of making men sexually impotent. Misfortunes inflicted on the entire community, such as the destruction of crops by hailstorms or the burning of towns, were also occasionally attributed to witchcraft. Christian theologians claimed that the power to perform these maleficent magical deeds came from the Devil.

The second component of the witches' crime was the worship of the Devil. Witches were accused of having made an explicit, face-to-face pact with the Devil, by which they allegedly promised to serve him as their god in return for the power to inflict magical harm. In many countries it was also believed that witches would gather in remote locations to worship the Devil collectively. At these assemblies, often referred to as sabbats, witches would allegedly kiss the Devil's buttocks, trample on the cross, and have themselves rebaptized in the religion of their new demonic master. In Roman Catholic countries the witches were often accused of making a mockery of the Mass, with the priest saying the Mass backwards while standing on his head and consecrating a black host. At the sabbat witches allegedly reversed all the moral norms of society. In particular, they were accused of dancing naked and engaging in promiscuous sexual relations with the other witches and the numerous demons in attendance. They allegedly sacrificed young unbaptized children to the Devil and then ate them. In some countries it was believed that witches flew to these assemblies, sometimes on broomsticks or on the backs of animals. There is no reliable evidence that any of these charges of collective Devil worship had a basis in reality. Most of the confessions of witches were coerced and therefore provide a better indication of what judges wanted defendants to say than what the accused witches had actually done. Confessions given voluntarily reflected either the dreams or fantasies of witches, the suggestions of confessors, or the confused statements of those who were senile or mentally ill.

Witch Trials

During the fifteenth century European judicial authorities became alarmed that they were faced with a vast conspiracy of witches who had rejected their Christian religion and were assisting the Devil in his work of physical destruction. Inquisitors appointed by the papacy, clerical judges of episcopal courts, and lay judges of municipal courts took steps to identify witches and prosecute them. Most of the witch trials before 1500 took place in Switzerland, southeastern France, northern Italy, and western Germany. In order to secure the conviction of these witches, it was usually necessary to obtain their confessions. In so doing judicial authorities often subjected the accused to physical torture. Accused witches would have their thumbs screwed tight in iron vises, their legs crushed until the bones were reduced to pulp, and their bodies hung by their wrists from the ceiling in order to make them confess to harmful magic and the worship of the Devil. In most circumstances, especially when the torture was extreme, the accused witches confessed to the crimes that their inquisitors were convinced they had perpetrated. Then, in order to extract the names of their alleged confederates, they were asked, once again under torture, to identify other witches who had joined them at the sabbat.

The Old Witch House, Salem, Massachusetts, c. 1906.
COURTESY OF LIBRARY OF CONGRESS, PRINTS AND PHOTOGRAPHS DIVISION, DETROIT PUBLISHING COMPANY.

HUNTING WITCHES IN EARLY MODERN EUROPE

The extract of text below—from a widely used witch-hunting handbook—provides practical advice on how to identity a witch.

To sum up our distinction on this matter, it is to be said that, following the above distinctions, those who are suspected of the heresy of witchcraft are separated into three categories, since some are lightly, some strongly, and some gravely suspected. And they are lightly suspected who act in such a way as to give rise to a small or light suspicion against them of this heresy. And although it has been said, a person who is found to be suspected in this way is not to be branded as a heretic, yet he must undergo a canonical purgation, or he must be caused to pronounce a solemn abjuration as in the vase of one convicted of a slight heresy. . . .

And note that, in the purgation imposed upon them, whether or not they consent to it, and whether or not they fail in it, they are throughout to be judged as reputed heretics in whom a canonical purgation is to be imposed.

And that a person under this light suspicion can and should be caused to pronounce a solemn abjuration is shown in chapter *Accusatus*, where it says: A person accused or suspected of heresy, against whom there is a strong suspicion of this crime, if he abjures the heresy before the Judge and afterwards commits it, then, by a sort of legal fiction he shall be judged to have relapsed into heresy, although the heresy was not proved against him before is abjuration. But if the suspicion was in the first place a small or light one, although such a relapse renders the accused liable to sever punishment of those who relapse into heresy.

But those who are strongly suspected, that is, those who have acted in such a way as to engender a great and strong suspicion; even these are not necessarily heretics or to be condemned of so great a crime by reason of a strong suspicion. And it says:

Therefore we order that, when the accused is only under suspicion, even if it be a strong one, we do not wish him to be condemned of so grave a crime; but such a one so strongly suspected must be commanded to abjure all heresy in general and in particular that of which he is strongly suspected. . . .

From these words it is clear that there are three cases in which a person under strong suspicion of heresy shall, after his abjuration, be punished as a backslider. The first is when he falls back into the same heresy of which he was strongly suspected. The second is when he has abjured hall heresy in general, and yet lapses into another heresy. The third is when he receives and shows favor to heretics. And this last comprises and embraces many cases. . . .

There are others again who are violently or gravely suspected, whose actions give rise to a violent suspicion against them; and such a one is to be considered as a heretic, and throughout he is to be treated as if he were taken in heresy, in accordance with the Canon Law. For these either confess their crime or not; and if they do, and wish to return to the faith and abjure their heresy, they are to be received back into penitence. But if they refuse to abjure, they are to be handed over to the secular court for punishment.

But if he does not confess his crime after he has been convicted, and does not consent to abjure his heresy, he is to be condemned as an impenitent heretic. For a violent suspicion is sufficient to warrant a conviction, and admits no proof to the contrary.

Source: *The Malleus Maleficarum of Heinrich Kramer and James Sprenger*.
Translated by Montague Summers. (New York: Dover Publications, [c. 1486] 1971), 238.

It was this last procedure, the naming of accomplices, that explains why a single witch-hunt could take such a high toll in human life. Most of the large witch-hunts occurred in the late sixteenth and seventeenth centuries, which was the most intense period of executions throughout Europe. Some hunts, such as those in the diocese of Trier between 1587 and 1593, and the city of Würzburg between 1627 and 1629, claimed hundreds of victims. Within the lands of the Prince Bishop of Eichstätt, 274 persons were executed for witchcraft in 1629. On the lands of the convent of Quedlinberg in Germany in 1589, 133 witches were executed *in one day*. A witch-hunt in 1585 left two German villages with only one female inhabitant each.

Many of the most severe hunts took place in German territories, especially those where torture was administered with few restraints. Prosecutions in some of the Swiss cantons were just as severe as in German lands. Other locations of intense witch-hunting were Scotland, Hungary, Poland, the Spanish Netherlands, and the French-speaking territories on the eastern border of France. There were fewer executions in Scandinavian countries, England, Ireland, Spain, Portugal, and the Italian territories. The intensity of prosecutions in various localities was determined by the strength of the belief in the sabbat, the degree to which judicial authorities were willing to allow the use of excessive torture, and the severity of social and economic conditions that might lead villagers to accuse their neighbors.

Almost all European countries experienced at least one large witch-hunt. In England, where torture was forbidden except by command of the Privy Council, the notorious witch-finder Matthew Hopkins secured the conviction and execution of more than one hundred witches during the years 1645–1647. Many of these witches confessed after Hopkins had kept them awake for up to seventy-two hours. This tactic was justified as an effort to make the witches' imps (personal demonic spirits) appear; but for all intents and purposes, it was a form of torture. In Sweden, where torture could be administered only under special circumstances, a large witch-hunt took place between 1668 and 1676, claiming the lives of more than two hundred persons. The hunt began when several children accused parents, neighbors, and other children of taking them to the sabbat. At Salem, Massachusetts, thirty witches were convicted and nineteen executed in 1692 after a group of teenage girls who manifested the signs of demonic possession accused individuals of causing their afflictions by means of witchcraft.

Altogether about 100,000 persons, the great majority of them women, were tried for the crime of witchcraft. Of these, approximately forty-five thousand were executed, very often by burning at the stake. Even these grim figures do not indicate the extent to which the suspicion and accusations of witchcraft disrupted early modern villages and towns. The fear of being harmed by witchcraft was part of the everyday life of small, close-knit communities. In some cases local communities took illegal action against suspected witches by lynching them. During the large hunts, the fear of witchcraft occasionally led people to suspect and accuse members of their own families. As the naming of alleged accomplices grew, villagers and townspeople became more frightened that they too might be identified as witches. Friedrich Spee, a Jesuit critic of the trials, wrote in 1631 that if the trials continued, no one would be safe from the accusations.

Most witch-hunts began when villagers accused their neighbors of harming them by magical means. About 80 percent of those accused were women, although that percentage varied considerably from country to country. In Estonia and Russia most witches were men. Many women accused of witchcraft actually were healers who were the main source of health care in rural areas. When their cures failed, these women became vulnerable to the charges that they had caused their patients' death by magical means. In a few instances witches were midwives, who could also be easily suspected of deliberately causing the death the infants they helped to deliver. Other women accused of witchcraft were those who came into the household after the birth of baby and assisted the mother with childcare. It was only natural that the mother, resenting this intrusion by other women into their homes, would suspect these persons of causing any harm that might befall her child. Witches were often described as bad or cruel mothers, who instead of nurturing young children, caused their illness or death.

The villagers who made the original accusations of witchcraft were almost exclusively concerned with the magical, as opposed to the diabolical, aspects of the witch's crime. They were aggrieved because their neighbors had harmed them, not because they had made a pact with the Devil or attended the sabbat. Charges of Devil worship were usually introduced by judges who had studied at the universities or who had read some of the many witchcraft treatises that were published during these years. The most famous of these treatises was the *Malleus maleficarum* (The hammer of witches), which was written by two Dominican inquisitors, Heinrich Kramer and Jacob Sprenger, in 1486. The authors of these treatises had their own explanation why most witches were women. Most of them emphasized the weakness of women and their greater vulnerability to demonic temptation. The *Malleus* claimed that women were also the more carnal of the species and more eager therefore to have sexual relations with the Devil.

Witchcraft and Religion

Witch-hunters were often inspired by religious zeal. Claiming to be doing God's work, they set out to rid their communities of the Devil's confederates and thereby create a godly state. The biblical condemnation of witchcraft, "Thou shalt not suffer a witch to live" (Exodus 22:18, KJV) strengthened the determination of both ecclesiastical and secular judges to bring witches to justice. Protestant and Catholic reformers, inspired by a heightened fear of the Devil, were among the most zealous witch-hunters, although the persons they identified as witches were usually nominal members of their own religious faith. Individuals suspected of various forms of moral deviance or of not attending religious services were particularly vulnerable to charges of witchcraft.

Since witches were believed to be apostates and heretics, they were victims of the same intolerance that other religious minorities experienced during this period. The end of witch-hunting, which was achieved in many countries by legislation in the eighteenth century declaring witchcraft no longer to be a crime, coincided with the growth of greater religious tolerance and a decline in the ideal of the godly state. The end of witch-hunting did not, however, contribute to the growth of religious freedom. Despite the claims of inquisitors and other witch-hunters, witchcraft was not a religion or cult. The argument made by anthropologist Margaret Murray that those persons accused of witchcraft during the period of witch-hunting belonged to a pagan fertility cult that the church was determined to wipe out is not supported by any reliable evidence. Unlike many modern witches, who practice a pagan religion known as Wicca, the persons accused of witchcraft in the sixteenth and seventeenth centuries were usually innocent scapegoats for the misfortunes of their neighbors. A few of them might have practiced forms of magic that had pagan origins, but they did not belong to any kind of organized pagan religion. Witch-hunts were manifestations of religious intolerance, but unlike the persecution of heretics during the Middle Ages, they did not actually deny individuals the right to practice their religion freely.

The term *witch-hunt*, coined in the twentieth century, has been used to describe the investigation of any unpopular group, especially those of a political nature, such as communists in the United States during the 1940s and 1950s. Witch-hunts are characterized by a determination to incriminate people who subscribe to a certain set of beliefs or behave in a certain way. Just like the prosecution of witches in early modern Europe, contemporary witch-hunts involve a presumption of guilt and a violation of individual rights.

Brian P. Levack

Further Reading

Ankarloo, B., & Henningsen, G. (Eds.). (1990). *Early modern European witchcraft: Centres and peripheries*. Oxford, UK: Clarendon Press.

Briggs, R. (1996). *Witches and neighbors: The social and cultural context of European witchcraft*. New York: Viking Penguin.

Clark, S. (1997). *Thinking with demons: The idea of witchcraft in early modern Europe*. Oxford, UK: Clarendon Press.

Ginzburg, C. (1983). *The night battles: Witchcraft and agrarian cults in the sixteenth and seventeenth centuries*. Baltimore: Johns Hopkins University Press.

Godbeer, R. (1992). *Satan's dominion: Magic and religion in early New England*. Cambridge, UK: Cambridge University Press.

Goodare, J. (Ed.). (2002). *The Scottish witch-hunt in context*. Manchester, UK: Manchester University Press.

Levack, B. P. (1995). *The witch-hunt in early modern Europe* (2d ed.). London: Longman.

Midelfort, H. C. E. (1974). *Witch hunting in southwestern Germany, 1562–1684: The social and intellectual foundations*. Stanford, CA: Stanford University Press.

Thomas, K. (1971). *Religion and the decline of magic*. New York: Charles Scribner's Sons.

Women, Religious Freedom, and Human Rights

Is freedom of religion compatible with the recognition of human rights for women? Both U.S. law and international law (as embodied in treaties and other documents of the United Nations) prohibit discrimination based on religion as well as sex and provide affirmative protections for both religious freedom and gender equality. These documents reflect an assumption that governments both can and should protect women's human rights and religious freedom to engage in traditional religious and cultural practices. But how valid is this assumption?

Upon examination, it is evident that tensions exist between these two spheres of rights. This tension is especially prominent with respect to the religious freedom of lawmakers to legislate their religious beliefs, on the one hand, and women's human rights to reproductive freedom, on the other.

In the United States, lawmakers, like other citizens, are entitled to the free exercise of their religion under the First Amendment to the U.S. Constitution, which states that "Congress shall make no law respecting an establishment of religion, or prohibiting the free exercise thereof." Despite their special roles as public officials, lawmakers are similar to most other citizens in viewing themselves as religious persons. In fact, lawmakers may be even more religious as a body than citizens generally. Given the centrality that religion has to the moral identity of many believers, a demand that religious adherents set aside or bracket their religious convictions in the spheres of lawmaking may infringe upon, and even violate, their sense of identity as well as their free-exercise rights.

The Platform for Action ("Platform") drafted at the United Nations Fourth World Conference on Women held in Beijing, China, in 1995 frames women's rights "as indivisible, universal, and inalienable human rights" (United Nations 1995, para. 213). The linkage of reproductive rights and women's human rights has been consistently endorsed in United Nations' sponsored reports, conferences, agreements, and conventions. The Platform also states: "The human rights of women include their right to have control over and decide freely and responsibly on matters related to their sexuality, including sexual and reproductive health, free of coercion, discrimination and violence"

(United Nations 1995, para. 96), that "the right of all women to control all aspects of their health, in particular their own fertility, is basic to their empowerment" (para. 92) and "forms an important basis for the enjoyment of other rights" (para. 97). Given how fundamental reproductive rights are to women's other rights, when religious lawmakers use their religious freedom to restrict reproductive rights, it serves to weaken, if not completely undermine, the goals of establishing women's rights as human rights.

Within the international sphere, women's human rights have often been given lower priority than the protection of religious freedom. Within the United States as well, the Supreme Court has dealt with the tension between religious freedom and women's rights in ways that have given priority to religious freedom. In both arenas, further consideration needs to be given to protecting religious-freedom rights of both men and women in ways that do not undermine women's human rights.

International Law

From the founding of the United Nations, its agreements have prohibited discrimination based on religion as well as sex. The principle of protecting human rights for all, regardless of religion, is contained in almost all major U.N. human-rights documents, including the *United Nations Charter* (1945), the Universal Declaration of Human Rights (1948), the UN International Covenant on Civil and Political Rights, or ICCPR (1966), and several subsequent treaties and other documents. In addition, the right to the free exercise of religion is explicitly protected.

With respect to gender, although framing women's rights as human rights is fairly recent, the U.N. has prohibited discrimination based on sex since the U.N. Charter was ratified, and this prohibition has been repeated in the Universal Declaration of Human Rights and several human-rights treaties. Despite these clear pronouncements, international law itself facilitates religious restrictions on women's human rights around the world by failing to establish clear limitations on the extent to which religiously motivated laws and practices will be permitted to restrict women's rights, especially in the sphere of reproduction.

The teachings of most world religions that women are divinely ordained to be child bearers and rearers help to perpetuate traditional essentialist ide-

513

MISSION STATEMENT OF THE PLATFORM OF ACTION OF THE FOURTH WORLD CONFERENCE ON WOMEN (BEIJING, SEPTEMBER 1995)

1. The Platform for Action is an agenda for women's empowerment. It aims at accelerating the implementation of the Nairobi Forward-looking Strategies for the Advancement of Women and at removing all the obstacles to women's active participation in all spheres of public and private life through a full and equal share in economic, social, cultural and political decision-making. This means that the principle of shared power and responsibility should be established between women and men at home, in the workplace and in the wider national and international communities. Equality between women and men is a matter of human rights and a condition for social justice and is also a necessary and fundamental prerequisite for equality, development and peace. A transformed partnership based on equality between women and men is a condition for people-centered sustainable development. A sustained and long-term commitment is essential, so that women and men can work together for themselves, for their children and for society to meet the challenges of the twenty-first century.

2. The Platform for Action reaffirms the fundamental principle set forth in the Vienna Declaration and Programme of Action, adopted by the World Conference on Human Rights, that the human rights of women and of the girl child are an inalienable, integral and indivisible part of universal human rights. As an agenda for action, the Platform seeks to promote and protect the full enjoyment of all human rights and the fundamental freedoms of all women throughout their life cycle.

3. The Platform for Action emphasizes that women share common concerns that can be addressed only by working together and in partnership with men towards the common goal of gender* equality around the world. It respects and values the full diversity of women's situations and conditions and recognizes that some women face particular barriers to their empowerment.

4. The Platform for Action requires immediate and concerted action by all to create a peaceful, just and humane world based on human rights and fundamental freedoms, including the principle of equality for all people of all ages and from all walks of life, and to this end, recognizes that broad- based and sustained economic growth in the context of sustainable development is necessary to sustain social development and social justice.

5. The success of the Platform for Action will require a strong commitment on the part of Governments, international organizations and institutions at all levels. It will also require adequate mobilization of resources at the national and international levels as well as new and additional resources to the developing countries from all available funding mechanisms, including multilateral, bilateral and private sources for the advancement of women; financial resources to strengthen the capacity of national, sub-regional, regional and international institutions; a commitment to equal rights, equal responsibilities and equal opportunities and to the equal participation of women and men in all national, regional and international bodies and policy-making processes; and the establishment or strengthening of mechanisms at all levels for accountability to the world's women.

Source: Fourth World Conference on Women Follow-up.
Retrieved 2 December 2002,
from http://www.un.org/womenwatch/daw/beijing/platform

ologies that women are mothers, primarily if not exclusively, and thus not entitled to social, political, and economic equality. The influence of such religious teachings is enhanced when they are given official state sanction, backed by the coercive power of law to deny women access to the means to control their reproduction. Yet the U.N. endorses this result by according sovereignty to governments to determine how to implement the relevant U.N. treaties in accordance with their local cultural and religious traditions and norms. These pronouncements are seemingly oblivious to the potential for conflict between protecting women's human rights and giving full respect to religious values when those values deny reproductive rights to women.

Although the official teachings of many world religions support the principle of human rights generally, their positions on women's human rights, especially reproductive rights, are frequently contrary to that of the United Nations. During the United Nations International Conference on Population and Development, held in Cairo, Egypt in September 1994, for example, members of the Vatican Delegation and Islamic fundamentalists were allied in opposing family planning, contraception, sex education for adolescents, and homosexuality. Vatican representatives lobbied fundamentalist Muslim groups to join them in opposing a draft program on the basis that it could be interpreted to endorse abortion, and attempted to eliminate all references to abortion in all Conference documents.

The influence of religion in limiting women's human rights is also evident in the many reservations and interpretive statements filed by a number of member nations in connection with the Platform for Action in order to limit their full adoption of the principles of reproductive rights enunciated in that document. Several of these nations, virtually all predominantly Catholic or Muslim countries or constituencies, expressly cite religion as the reason for restricting their adoption of the Platform's protections for reproductive rights. These include the officially or predominantly Islamic countries of Egypt, Iraq, and Libya and the Catholic nations of Guatemala and Honduras. Other member nations reject abortion as part of the right to control one's sexuality or as part of reproductive rights.

Although such reservations and limitations on women's reproductive rights may strike liberal Western opinion as inconsistent with protection for the rights and ethical values of all persons, regardless of gender, the protection U.N. documents accords to the religious and cultural values of individuals and communities enables governments to make these contentious restrictions.

United States

In the United States, the separation of church and state is guaranteed by the religion clauses of the First Amendment to the U.S. Constitution. That separation has been extended to the states via Supreme Court interpretations incorporating the guarantees of other constitutional provisions into the Fourteenth Amendment. (The Court incorporated the establishment clause in 1947 in *Everson v. Board of Education* and the free exercise clause in 1940 in *Cantwell v. Connecticut*.) In a religiously pluralistic society such as the United States, such guarantees are essential to protecting the liberty of all citizens. However, lack of clarity about the extent to which the Constitution restricts religious freedom when that freedom directly influences lawmaking has resulted in women's rights being restricted in a number of areas.

In early judicial decision making, religious rationales were expressly used to validate laws that discriminated against women. For example, a Hawaii state court explained the difference between the sexes as divinely ordained, "as we are told in Holy Writ, when God created man, 'male and female created he them'" (*Territory v. Armstrong* [1924]). Laws upheld on religious grounds have included the denial of women's right to vote until 1920 on the ground that God's will was that women be in the home bearing and raising children. The history of restrictive abortion laws illustrates that they were premised on religious views of women as solely child rearers.

Religion also has obstructed women's rights in spheres of U.S. law relating to property ownership, employment, marital rights, and violence against women, as well as sexuality and reproduction, sex discrimination, and abortion. Religious influences also contributed to the derailment of the Equal Rights Amendment, which would have outlawed discrimination against women.

Unfortunately, religious influences on lawmaking that result in adverse consequences for women have not ended. Despite the formal legal equality of women in most spheres of U.S. society, vestiges of such traditional religious beliefs continue to influence religious lawmakers' attitudes about women's proper roles and appropriate status. Since women have been excluded from participation in the formulation of religious beliefs and practices in most traditional and institutional religions, it is likely that laws based on beliefs and values rooted in religious traditions will fail to incorporate women's self-determined interests.

The priority given to religious freedom over women's human rights in United States law has enabled religious groups to succeed in restricting access to reproductive rights for many women. Although the discussion here will focus on abortion, it is important to remember that many forms of birth control and family planning also have been legally opposed on the basis of religious beliefs.

Immediately following the Supreme Court's landmark 1973 decision in *Roe v. Wade* declaring that the right to an abortion was a constitutionally protected right of privacy, several religiously affiliated groups, many of them associated with the Roman Catholic Church, mobilized their ranks in a highly developed, well-organized, and generously funded campaign to reverse the effect of the Court's decision. The Church, often in conjunction with other pro-life groups, has been integral to many of the efforts to pass a Human Life Amendment to the Constitution that would reverse the effect of *Roe*.

Another flurry of religiously motivated activity to restrict state abortion laws followed the Supreme Court's 1989 decision in *Webster v. Reproductive Health Services,* which said that states have an interest in protecting potential life throughout a woman's pregnancy, not only after the point of viability, as the Court had stated in *Roe*. The Catholic Church was very influential in the passage of the restrictive Pennsylvania abortion statute upheld by the Supreme Court's 1992 decision in *Planned Parenthood v. Casey*, which upheld the constitutionality of all restrictions in the Pennsylvania abortion law, including parental consent requirement and extensive reporting and filing provisions, and only found that a requirement of spousal consent constituted an undue burden. Other religious groups have been influential in the passage of restrictive abortion laws in a number of other states.

In addition, religious groups have influenced the passing of a number of federal restrictions on abortion, including the Hyde Amendment (prohibiting the use of public funds for abortion), which was first passed in 1976, and various restrictions on the ability

of doctors and other federally funded health care providers to counsel pregnant women about abortion. The religious right has also limited the access of women in developing countries to abortions by persuading Congress to pass the Helms Amendment (2000) to the Foreign Assistance Act. The Helms Amendment prohibits the direct use of foreign-aid funds for abortion services in recipient nations.

U.S. courts have seldom recognized the implications of unrestricted religious freedom for women's human rights. One exception was the federal district court in the 1980 *McRae v. Califano* case, which invalidated the constitutionality of the Hyde Amendment under the free exercise clause, finding that it prevented some women from making abortion decisions in accordance with their religious beliefs or conscience. In the 1980 *Harris v. McRae* case, the Supreme Court reversed the federal district court's decision, ruling that a pregnant woman must be able to show "that she sought an abortion under compulsion of religious belief" while pregnant and eligible to receive Medicaid in order to be eligible to claim that her free exercise rights had been violated by state restrictions on Medicaid funding for abortions. The Supreme Court held that religious influences on the Hyde Amendment were irrelevant since the Church lacked a monopoly on influencing passage of the law.

The Future of Women's Rights in the Context of Religious Freedom

Even though a separation of church and state theoretically exists in the United States, unrestricted religious freedom, especially of those having the authority to influence law and public policy, has succeeded in significantly limiting women's rights, especially their reproductive rights. While both international and domestic law recognize that reproductive rights are especially integral to the fulfillment of women's rights as human rights, simultaneous protection of the religious freedom of lawmakers undermines the actual protection accorded to women's human rights. In many nations, according priority to religious freedom in cases of conflict with women's rights has seriously restricted women's human rights, despite explicit protections for women's human rights in international law. This result undermines the validity of the United Nations' assumptions that religious freedom is perfectly compatible with women's human rights.

It is clear, then, that human rights of women are especially vulnerable to being overridden by the institutionalization of religious values in law and social practice. Therefore, religious freedoms cannot remain completely protected from regulation when they result in curbing women's human rights if the international community is to realize the goal of recognizing and protecting women's rights.

Lucinda Joy Peach

See also Fourteenth Amendment; Universal Declaration of Human Rights

Further Reading

Blanchard, D. (1994). *The anti-abortion movement and the rise of the religious right: From polite to fiery protest.* New York: Twayne Publishers.

Byrnes, T. (1991). *Catholic bishops in American politics.* Princeton, NJ: Princeton University Press.

Byrnes, T., & Segers, M. (Eds.). (1992). *The Catholic Church and the politics of abortion: A View from the states.* Boulder, CO: Westview Press.

Cook, R. (1991). International protection of women's reproductive rights. *New York University Journal of International Law and Politics, 24*(3), 645–727.

Cook, R. (1994). *Women's health and human rights: The promotion and protection of women's health through international human rights law.* Geneva, Switzerland: World Health Organization.

Karst, K. (1989). *Belonging to America: Equal citizenship and the constitution.* New Haven, CT: Yale University Press.

Karst, K. (1991). Religion, sex, and politics: cultural counterrevolution in constitutional perspective. *University of California at Davis Law Review, 24*(3), 677–734.

Karst, K. (1993). *Law's promise, law's expression: Visions of power in the politics of race, gender, and religion.* New Haven, CT: Yale University Press.

Mansbridge, J. (1986). *Why we lost the ERA.* Chicago: University of Chicago Press.

Melton, J. G. (Ed.). (1989). *The churches speak on: Abortion.* Detroit, MI: Gale Research.

Mews, S. (Ed.). (1989). *Religion in politics: A world guide.* Chicago: St. James Press.

Peach, L. (1993–1994). From religious description to legal prescription: The status of women as fetal containers in the law. *Journal of Law and Religion, 10*(1), 199–247.

Peach, L. (2002). Human rights law, religion, and the gendered moral order. In M. Barnhart (Ed.), *Varieties of ethical reflection* (pp. 203–233) Lanham, MD: Lexington Books.

Petchesky, R. (1990). *Abortion and woman's choice: The state, sexuality, and reproductive freedom.* Boston: Northeastern University Press.

Pizzarello, A. (1990). *Abortion, religion, and the state legislator after Webster.* Chicago: The Park Ridge Center.

Sachdev, P. (Ed.). (1988). *International handbook on abortion.* New York: Greenwood Press.

Sacred Congregation for the Doctrine of the Faith (1987). *Instruction on respect for human life in its origin and on the dignity of procreation.* London: Catholic Truth Society.

United Nations. (1948). *Universal declaration of human rights.* New York: author.

United Nations. (1966). *International covenant on civil and political rights.* New York: author.

United Nations. (1979). *Convention on the elimination of all forms of discrimination against women.* New York: author.

United Nations. (1993). *Vienna Declaration and Programme of Action.* New York: author.

United Nations. (1994). *Programme of action of the United Nations international conference on population and development.* New York: author.

United Nations. (1995). *Beijing declaration and draft platform for action.* New York: author.

Court Cases

Harris v. McRae, 448 U.S. 297 (1980).

Territory v. Armstrong, 28 Haw. 88, 96 (1924).

Zoning

Land use regulations such as zoning and historic-preservation ordinances frequently interfere with the exercise of religion. Restrictions on building churches, synagogues, or mosques, or on converting existing buildings for religious use, give rise to some of the most common conflicts between law and religious practice in the United States.

The conflict stems from sharply different understandings of church buildings. From the religious community's standpoint, adequate physical space is crucial to the free exercise of religion, and especially to its communal aspects, including worship, education, and social and outreach activities. From this point of view, constructing and altering church buildings is a core First Amendment right, subject to regulation for important public reasons, but protected from nonessential regulation.

From the standpoint of most neighborhood groups and regulators, religious land uses are troublesome and require careful government control. Residential neighbors object that churches create noise or traffic. Such objections can reflect real problems, as when too large a church is in too congested a place, but sometimes reflect hypersensitivity or even intolerance. In commercial zones—often the only areas where large lots are available for big churches and where inexpensive storefronts are available for small churches—the most common objection is that religious land uses are tax-exempt. This otherwise legitimate concern for keeping property on the tax rolls generates regulatory hostility to all religious uses, despite their special protection in the First Amendment.

Whatever the reason for regulation, the *process* of land use regulation often gives rise to discrimination against religion in general or against particular faiths. There is both anecdotal and statistical evidence that minority faiths are more heavily regulated: One study showed that small religious groups representing 9 percent of the population accounted for 50 percent of the reported court decisions involving disputes between religious groups and zoning authorities. Under historic-preservation laws, which prevent an owner from changing a building's appearance, churches are likely to be designated as landmarks because they are viewed as interesting or distinctive. One study found that churches were designated as landmarks at 42 times the rate of other structures. Many of the governing legal standards are necessarily open ended. Regulators are asked to decide a proposed "special use" would affect a city's "general welfare," or whether landmark designation deprives the owner of too much of the property's value. Consequently, zoning decisions are made on a highly individualized, parcel-by-parcel basis. All these factors make it possible for regulators to discriminate covertly or even unconsciously. Even when zoning rules are expressed more categorically, churches are often excluded from areas where other places of public assembly, such as theaters, lodge halls, or recreation centers, are permitted.

It is also clear that many church buildings are approved without difficulty, and some states partially exempt churches from local land use regulation. Hostile and discriminatory regulation of church land use is widespread, but no one has good data on the proportion of church building projects that are affected.

Free Exercise Law

The First Amendment clause barring laws that prohibit the free exercise of religion would appear to allow religious organizations to challenge unduly restrictive land use decisions. In the early 1990s, however, two judicial developments limited challenges under the free exercise clause.

First, the U.S. Supreme Court ruled in *Employment Division v. Smith* (1990) that free exercise rarely requires exemption from a "neutral law of general applicability." The meaning of "neutral" and "generally applicable" remains disputed. Governments argue that nearly all laws are generally applicable, and that the Court requires special justification only for laws that single out religion for uniquely hostile regulation. Some language in Supreme Court opinions supports that interpretation. But *Smith* also said that when the challenged law includes "a system of individualized exceptions" from the generally applicable standard, the government must have compelling reasons for refusing to extend the exceptions to "cases of religious hardship." The Supreme Court made clear in *Church of the Lukumi Babalu Aye v. City of Hialeah* (1993) that the government may not treat religion less favorably than comparable secular activities. Some lower court decisions, most notably *Fraternal Order of Police v. City of Newark* (1999), hold that any secular exception to a law must also extend to comparable religious activity.

This dispute over the meaning of "generally applicable'" is especially important in land use cases. Cities say that land use laws apply to the whole city and thus are generally applicable. But many land use laws have special provisions for churches, and nearly all have highly individualized procedures for "variances," or for regulating "special uses," a category that often includes churches. From this perspective, land use is a prime example of regulation that is *not* generally applicable. Lower courts remain divided on the meaning of "generally applicable."

The other setback to religious land use claims came from narrow interpretations of what is a sufficient "burden" on religious exercise to require justification. In decisions such as *Rector of St. Bartholomew's Church v. City of New York* (1990), lower courts held that land use restrictions do not impose significant burdens, because they interfere with the *secular* act of building rather than the *religious* act of worship, because they merely increase churches' costs, or because churches have no religious mandate to worship at a particular place.

The Religious Land Use and Institutionalized Persons Act (RLUIPA)

Congress, believing that the *Smith* conception of free exercise was far too narrow, passed the Religious Freedom Restoration Act of 1993 (RFRA), which required that federal or state laws imposing a "substantial burden" on religious exercise must serve a "compelling governmental interest" and use the "least restrictive means" to achieve that interest. However, in *City of Boerne v. Flores* (1997), a case involving landmark restrictions on a church building, the Supreme Court invalidated RFRA as applied to state and local laws—which include nearly all land use regulations. *Boerne* held that RFRA exceeded Congress's power to enforce constitutional rights.

Congress considered a new statute protecting religious liberty to the fullest extent possible under its power to regulate the spending of federal funds, its power to regulate interstate commerce, and, in the land use context, its power to enforce constitutional rights as interpreted in *Smith* and *Boerne*. The broad bill failed to pass. But in the land use area, the political opponents were quiet, and the record supporting Congress's power to legislate was especially strong. Building churches affects interstate commerce, and land use regulations are often individualized or discriminatory, and thus may violate constitutional rights even as free exercise was interpreted in *Smith*. Thus in September 2000, Congress passed the Religious Land Use and Institutionalized Persons Act (RLUIPA), which covers religious claims against land use laws and prison regulations.

RLUIPA recognizes the religious understanding of religious buildings; it provides that building or converting real property for religious use is an exercise of religion. It then provides for two kinds of challenges to zoning and historic-preservation laws. First, RLUIPA applies the "compelling interest" standard where the burden on religious exercise affects interstate commerce, or where the land use law permits the government to make "individualized assessments of the proposed uses for the property involved." The compelling-interest standard invalidates substantial burdens on religious exercise unless the government shows that they are the least restrictive means to a compelling government interest.

Second, RLUIPA prohibits various forms of discrimination. Local governments may not enforce a land use regulation that treats a religious assembly or institution "on less than equal terms" with a secular one, that "discriminates against any assembly or institution on the basis of religion or religious denomination," that "totally excludes religious assemblies from a jurisdiction," or that "unreasonably limits religious assemblies, institutions, or structures within a jurisdiction."

By the time of writing (late 2002), there were few reported court decisions under RLUIPA. Whether the statute proves effective will depend in part on whether courts accept the statutory provision that building a church is an exercise of religion, and recognize that imposing substantial additional costs can be a "substantial burden" on religion. Once that hurdle is passed, courts are almost certain to find that preventing safety hazards, serious traffic congestion, and disruptive noise problems are compelling interests. The key will be whether even in these cases the courts hold the authorities to the least restrictive method of regulation, and whether they recognize that less tangible rationales for land use restrictions—the general welfare, conforming to a city plan, or preserving the architectural style of a neighborhood—ought not to count as compelling in the first place.

The Constitutionality of RLUIPA

RLUIPA and other protections for religious land uses have been attacked as unconstitutional. First, opponents of RLUIPA claim that the statute's various provisions exceed Congress's legislative powers. The sections that rely on congressional power to regulate interstate commerce may be challenged on the grounds that religion is not an economic activity per seand churches seem like local projects. But the sections that rely on the commerce power apply only when an economic transaction—for example, the construction, sale, or rental of a building—affects interstate commerce, and only when the aggregate effect of all similar transactions will be substantial. A more serious claim is that the sections based on the commerce power regulate state government, and thus infringe on state rights. But RLUIPA may fairly be characterized not as regulating states, but as

deregulating churches by preempting certain state regulation of churches, as Congress did earlier with the railroad, trucking, and airline industries.

The provisions based on Congress's power to enforce the Constitution are valid, under *Boerne*, if they are "proportional and congruent" with the Court's understanding of constitutional rights as set forth in *Employment Division v. Smith* (1990) and other cases. These sections of the statute all use language from the Court decisions, and are also based on the relevant congressional committees finding a substantial history of discriminatory regulation of church land use. Federal trial courts have so far upheld RLUIPA, but the issue will not be finally resolved until several courts of appeals agree, or until the Supreme Court speaks.

Cities also argue that some of RLUIPA's provisions violate the First Amendment's establishment clause by favoring religion—that is, by exempting religion from land use laws while not exempting secular activities or institutions. This argument has been raised in several recent cases challenging specific statutory exemptions from land use laws. In each case, the federal Court of Appeals or a state supreme court rejected the challenge and upheld the exemption. These decisions emphasized several themes: that exempting religious land use does not promote religion but merely leaves it alone, that exemption actually reduces the church–state entanglement that is a central concern of the establishment clause, and that exemption from general laws serves the First Amendment goal of protecting minority faiths. But in each case there was dissent, showing that the arguments against exemption are also attractive to many judges.

Supreme Court decisions from other regulatory contexts indicate that a statutory exemption for religious activity should be upheld if it removes a significant state-imposed burden from religious conduct and does not impose a disproportionate burden on other persons. Proponents of RLUIPA argue that it meets this test because it is triggered only by a "substantial burden" on religion, and because the "compelling interest" standard allows the government to restrict religious land uses when they would cause significant safety hazards or noise or traffic nuisances to others.

The Underlying Conflict

Religious liberty advocates regard it as absurd that creating a place of worship should require a discretionary permit from a governmental official. But zoning bodies feel it is absurd that anyone should be able to erect a building without careful government review. The two sides often mistrust each other, and tend to view any protection for the other side's interests as excessive and likely to be abused. RLUIPA attempts to split the difference, permitting regulation for substantial reasons but not for insubstantial ones. For RLUIPA to work, courts must take an active role in these cases and sort out the importance of the many different reasons offered for land use regulations.

Thomas C. Berg and Douglas Laycock

Further Reading

Becket Fund for Religious Liberty. (2000 and continuing). *RLUIPA—Religious land use and institutionalized persons act: An internet resource*. Retrieved December 12, 2002, from http://www.rluipa.org

Carmella, A. C. (1991). Houses of worship and religious liberty: Constitutional limits to landmark preservation and architectural review. *Villanova Law Review*, *36*, 401–515.

Keetch, V. G., & Richardson, M. K. (1999). The need for legislation to enshrine free exercise in the land use context. *U. C. Davis Law Review*, *32*, 725–53.

Laycock, D. (1999). State RFRAs and land use regulation. *U. C. Davis Law Review*, *32*, 755–84.

L'Heureux, N. J. (1986). Ministry v. Mortar: A landmark conflict. In D. M. Kelley (Ed.), *Government Intervention in Religious Affairs 2* (pp. 164–180). New York: Pilgrim Press.

Nelson, L. S. (1999). Remove not the ancient landmark: Legal protection for historic religious properties in an age of religious freedom legislation. *Cardozo Law Review*, *21*, 721–780.

Parnas, S. M. (1999). The religious liberty protection act: The national league of cities perspective. *Cardozo Law Review*, *21*, 781–793.

Storzer, R. P., & Picarello, A. R. (2001). The religious land use and institutionalized persons act of 2000: A constitutional response to unconstitutional zoning practices. *George Mason Law Review*, *9*, 929–1000.

Tuttle, R. W. (2000). How firm a foundation? Protecting religious land uses after *Boerne*. *George Washington Law Review*, *68*, 861–924.

Court Cases

Boyajian v. Gatzunis, 212 F.3d 1 (1st Cir. 2000).

Church of the Lukumi Babalu Aye, Inc. v. City of Hialeah, 508 U.S. 520 (1993).

City of Boerne v. Flores, 521 U.S. 507 (1997).

Corporation of the Presiding Bishop v. Amos, 483 U.S. 327 (1987).

East Bay Asian Local Development Corp. v. State, 13 P.3d 1122 (Cal. 2000).

Ehlers-Renzi v. Connelly School of the Holy Child, Inc., 224 F.3d 283 (4th Cir. 2000).

Employment Division v. Smith, 494 U.S. 872 (1990).

Fraternal Order of Police v. City of Newark, 170 F.3d 359 (3d Cir. 1999).

Rector of St. Bartholomew's Church v. City of New York, 914 F.2d 348 (2d Cir. 1990).

Texas Monthly, Inc. v. Bullock, 489 U.S. 1 (1989).

List of Contributors

Ahmad, Mumtaz
Hampton University
Pakistan

Aho, James
Idaho State University
Religious Terrorist Groups

Alley, Robert
University of Richmond
Government Funding of Religious Organizations
Virginia Declaration of Rights

Andelson, Jonathan G.
Grinnell College
Nineteenth-Century U.S. Utopian Communities

Anderson, Fred
University of Richmond
Baptist Dissenters in Virginia

Ariens, Michael
St. Mary's University School of Law
Religion in the Courtroom

Badawi, Zakir
Muslim College, London
Islam

Bademan, R. Bryan
University of Notre Dame
Outsiderhood and U.S. Protestantism

Beck, Albert R.
Baylor University
New England: Colonial to Early Republic

Beit-Hallahmi, Benjamin
University of Haifa
Political Attitudes and Religiosity

Berg, Thomas
University of St. Thomas, Minneapolis
Zoning

Berthrong, John
Boston University
Confucianism

Besier, Gerhard
University of Heidelberg
Germany and Prussia

Bivins, Jason C.
North Carolina State University
Religion and Protest

Bromley, David G.
Virginia Commonwealth University
Brainwashing
Family, The

Burgdoff, Craig
Capital University
Falun Gong

Chu, Jolene
Watch Tower Society
Jehovah's Witnesses, Global

Conkle, Dan
Indiana University School of Law
Free Exercise Clause

Cookson, Catharine
Virginia Wesleyan College
Children and Freedom in the United States
Christian Science
Law, Disorder, and Religious Freedom
Peace Churches
Pennsylvania: Colonial to Early Republic

Crowther, Edward
Adams State College
Confederate Constitution and Religion

Davis, Derek
Baylor University
Constitution, Founding Era of the
Fourteenth Amendment

Derr, Patricia Norred
Kutztown University
Peace Churches
Pennsylvania: Colonial to Early Republic

Dingley, James
University of Ulster–Jordanstown Campus
British Empire
Religion and Politics

Dixon, Sandy
University of Denver
Augustine on Religious Coercion

Dokupil, Susanna
Houston, TX
Turkey

Drees, Clay
Virginia Wesleyan College
Inquisition

Durham, Cole
Bringham Young University
CSCE Vienna Document
U.N. Declaration on Discrimination

Epps, Garrett
University of Oregon
Native American Church

Fefferman, Dan
International Coalition for Religious Freedom
Unification Church

Feldman, Stephen
University of Wyoming
Jews in the United States

Foster, James C.
Oregon State University
Establishment, Separation of Church and State

Foy, Geoff
Graduate Theological Union
Daoism

Gaffney, Jr., Edward
Pepperdine University
Religious Test Oaths

Gallagher, Eugene V.
Connecticut College
Law Enforcement and Religious Groups
Millennialist Groups

Glazier, Stephen D.
University of Nebraska–Lincoln
Creationism
Slavery

Griffin, Leslie
Emory University
Roman Catholicism

Guinness, Os
The Trinity Forum
Williamsburg Charter

Gutierrez, Cathy
Sweet Briar College
Great Awakenings and the Antebellum Period

Gvosdev, Nikolas K.
Baylor University
Balkans, East Europe, and Russia
Orthodox Christianity

Hankins, Barry
Baylor University
English Civil War
Reformation–Early Modern Europe

Hassner, Ron E.
Stanford University
Sacred Space and Conflict

Hernandez-Muzquiz, Rowena
Old Dominion University
Convivencia

Horton, John
Keele University
Letter on Toleration

Hutchinson, Dawn L.
Florida State University
Coptic Christians

Idleman, Scott
Marquette University
Spiritual Healing

Juss, Satvinder Singh
King's College, London
European Convention on Human Rights
Jainism
Religious Tolerance
Sikhism
United Kingdom

Kaelber, Lutz
University of Vermont
Waldensians

Kaplan, Jeffrey
University of Wisconsin, Oshkosh
Radical Religious Groups: White

Kim, Rebecca
University of California–Los Angeles
Immigration: United States

Klaus, Bryon D.
Assemblies of God Theological Seminary
Pentecostalism

Konvitz, Milton R.
Cornell University
Judaism

Kooi, Christine
Louisiana State University
Leiden

Kyriazopoulos, Kyriakos
Aristotle University of Thesaloniki
Church and State in Modern Europe

Larsen, Timothy
Wheaton College
England, Victorian

Laycock, Douglas
University of Texas
Zoning

Levack, Brian P.
University of Texas, Austin
Witch-Hunts

Levinson, David
Berkshire Publishing Group LLC
Hinduism

Long, Jerry M.
Baylor University
Jihad

Lorion, Amy E.
University of North Carolina
New York: Colonial to Early Republic

Masondo, Sibusio
University of Cape Town
South Africa

Mazur, Eric
Bucknell University
Freedom of Conscience

McDaniel, Charles
Baylor University
State Churches

McGuckin, John A.
Union Theological Seminary
Byzantine Empire

McMearty, Matthew F.
Baylor University
Sabbatarians

McNeil, J.E.
Center on Conscience & War
Conscientious Objection and Pacifism

Melton, J. Gordon
Institutes for the Study of American Religion
Scientology

Mendieta, Eduardo
State University of New York, Stony Brook
South America

Mickler, Michael L.
Unification Theological Seminary
Unification Church

Miskimin, Patricia Behre
Fairfield University
French Revolution

Monsma, Stephen V.
Pepperdine University
Establishment, Equal Treatment

Moore, Jonathan
University of Chicago
Civil Religion

Moosa, Ebrahim
Duke University
Islamic Empire, Medieval

Motwani Clary, Jennifer
Waco, TX
Religious Nationalism

Mubashshir, Debra
Beloit College
Radical Religious Groups:
African-American

Murrell, Nathaniel S.
University of North Carolina at Wilmington
Rastifari and Religious Freedom

Nadeau, Kathleen
California State University
Buddhism

Nauriya, Anil
New Delhi, India
Secularism and Modernity

Nederman, Cary
Texas A&M University
Heresy

Nelson, John K.
University of San Francisco
Shintoism

Obayashi, Hiroshi
Rutgers University
Japan

O'Neil, Robert
University of Virginia
Free Speech Clause

Owens, Erik
University of Chicago Divinity School
Religious Displays on Public Property

Panitz, Michael
Temple Israel
Jews in Europe

Patterson, Sara Mya
Baylor University
Drugs in Religious Worship

Payne, Rodger
Louisiana State University, Baton Rouge
Code Noir
English Test Oaths and Toleration Acts
French Colonies in North America
Maryland: Colonial to Early Republic
Roman Catholics, Colonial to Ninetenth Century
South, U.S.: Colonial to Early Republic

Peach, Lucinda Joy
American University
Human Rights
Pluralism and Religious Identity in Lawmaking
Universal Declaration of Human Rights
Women, Religious Freedom, and Human Rights

Pegg, Mark Gregory
Washington University
Cathars

Peters, Shawn
Madison, WI
Jehovah's Witnesses: United States

Powers, John
Australian National University
Tibet

Rahne Kidwell, Erin
Georgetown University Law Center
England, Early Modern

Ravitch, Frank S.
Michigan State University
School Prayer and Discrimination

Redd, Hamish
St. Kilda, Australia
Canada, Australia, New Zealand

Remillard, Arthur
Florida State University
Spanish Colonies in North America
Spanish Empire

Richardson, James T.
University of Nevada–Reno
New Religious Movements

Salamone, Frank A.
Iona College
Africa

Schwartz, Nathan
University of Louisville
Israel

Schweitz, Martha Leach
Baha'i National Center
Baha'i

Sewell, Elizabeth
Brigham Young University
Mormons

Sharma, Arvind
McGill University
Preservation of Faith Commitments

Tay, Alice
The University of Sydney
Canada, Australia, New Zealand

Thomas, Leri M.
Wolftown, VA
Virginia Statute for Religious Freedom

Thomas, Oliver
Tusculum College
Religion and Public Education

Townsend, Joan B.
University of Manitoba
Individualist Religions

Vance-Trembath, Sally M.
University of San Francisco
Vatican II

Wansink, Craig
Virginia Wesleyan College
Prisons
Roman Empire

Weber, Paul J.
University of Louisville
Chaplains - Military and Legislative
Natural Law
Pledge of Allegiance

Wiktorowicz, Quintan
Rhodes College
Middle East

Williams, Daniel K.
Brown University
Fundamentalist Politics and Religious
Freedom

Yelle, Robert A.
University of Chicago
Utilitarianism and J.S. Mill

Zhou, Jinghao
Hobart and William Smith Colleges
China, Communist
China, Imperial

INDEX